Handbook of

Software Engineering & Knowledge Engineering

Vol. 2
Emerging Technologies

Also Published by World Scientific

Handbook of Software Engineering & Knowledge Engineering, Vol. 1
Fundamentals
ISBN 981-02-4973-X

Handbook of

Software Engineering & Knowledge Engineering

Vol. 2
Emerging Technologies

Editor

S K Chang

University of Pittsburgh, USA
and
Knowledge Systems Institute, USA

Published by

World Scientific Publishing Co. Pte. Ltd.

P O Box 128, Farrer Road, Singapore 912805

USA office: Suite 1B, 1060 Main Street, River Edge, NJ 07661

UK office: 57 Shelton Street, Covent Garden, London WC2H 9HE

British Library Cataloguing-in-Publication Data
A catalogue record for this book is available from the British Library.

HANDBOOK OF SOFTWARE ENGINEERING & KNOWLEDGE ENGINEERING, Vol. 2
Emerging Technologies

ISBN 981-02-4974-8
ISBN 981-02-4514-9 (Set)

Printed in Singapore by Mainland Press

PREFACE

The *Handbook of Software Engineering and Knowledge Engineering* is the first comprehensive handbook covering these two important areas that have become interwoven in recent years. Many international experts contribute to this Handbook. Each article is written in a way that a practitioner of software engineering and knowledge engineering can easily understand and obtain useful information. Each article covers one topic and can be read independently of other articles, providing both a general survey of the topic and an in-depth exposition of the state of the art. Practitioners will find this Handbook useful when looking for solutions to practical problems in software engineering and knowledge engineering. Researchers in turn can use the Handbook to quickly obtain background information, current trends and the most important references on a certain topic.

The Handbook consists of two volumes. Volume One covers the basic principles and applications of software engineering and knowledge engineering. Volume Two expands the coverage of basic principles and also contains many articles that specifically addresses visual and multimedia software engineering, and emerging topics in software engineering and knowledge engineering such as software patterns, data mining for software knowledge, etc. The two volumes form a complete set, but can be used separately for different purposes.

Turning Knowledge into Software

There is a growing awareness that the central issue in software engineering and knowledge engineering is how to turn knowledge into software. Traditionally software engineering is concerned with the specification, design, coding, testing and maintenance of software. It also implicitly deals with the issues of transforming knowledge into software in the sense that the gathering of knowledge about the problem domain is incorporated into the requirements analysis phase of the software life cycle. Often, informal techniques of knowledge acquisition are used. Thus in the past, the role of knowledge engineering in the software process is an implicit one.

However it has long been recognized by many people that knowledge engineering plays an increasingly important role in software design. Indeed it is because of this conviction that the international conference series on Software Engineering and Knowledge Engineering (SEKE) was founded in 1988, followed by the publication of the *International Journal of Software Engineering and Knowledge Engineering* (*IJSEKE*) three years later. For both the SEKE conference series and the IJSEKE journal, the basic viewpoint is that the interdisciplinary area of software engineering and knowledge engineering is concerned with the interplay between software engineering and knowledge engineering — how software engineering can be applied to knowledge engineering, and how knowledge engineering can be applied to software engineering.

This viewpoint should now be modified and expanded because, both in theory and in practice, more and more software engineers and knowledge engineers are explicitly incorporating knowledge into the software process. In editing this two-volume handbook, this expanded viewpoint — that software engineering is concerned with the transformation of knowledge into software — has been carefully taken into consideration to conceptually organize the recent progresses in software engineering and knowledge engineering.

Software Patterns

Let us start with two distinct, yet complementary, viewpoints on software engineering. The two viewpoints may seem completely different, but they are but different ways of viewing the "elephant" that is software engineering.

The first viewpoint, as stated above, is that software engineering is concerned with the transformation of knowledge into software. The second viewpoint is somewhat more technical. It says that software engineering is concerned with the specification, design, transformation, verification and validation of patterns.

Software is nothing but patterns. A program is constructed from some basic patterns, and the construction rules can in turn be expressed as other types of patterns. With grammars, formal languages and automata, there are many approaches to describe the basic patterns and how they are composed into programs.

Specifications are composed of patterns that are the basic building blocks of formal, informal or visual specifications. The specification, in the ideal case, can then be automatically transformed into programs, and verified and validated in the transformational process.

As mentioned above, knowledge used to be described informally, but now there are formal techniques and more precise ways of dealing with knowledge. With advances in object oriented methods, one comes to the inevitable conclusion that knowledge is also composed of patterns. Knowledge is first acquired, then transformed into formal/informal/visual specification, design and finally program.

Therefore, software engineering can now be viewed as the transformation of knowledge into software through the transformation of patterns. The central issue of software engineering is how to turn knowledge into software by means of the creation, composition and transformation of various types of patterns. A key question that can be asked repeatedly for any topic or sub-topic is the following: how to turn what-kind-of knowledge patterns into what-kind-of software patterns?

Overview of Volume One

As mentioned above, the *Handbook of Software Engineering and Knowledge Engineering* is a comprehensive handbook providing readers with both useful overviews and detailed explanations of the methodologies, techniques and current research issues in software engineering and knowledge engineering. Volume One deals with the fundamentals of software engineering and knowledge engineering. Topics relevant to the traditional software life cycle are covered. Current research in software engineering and knowledge engineering are also surveyed.

The first group of articles deal with the basics in software engineering, including such topics as requirements engineering, domain engineering, object technology, software architecture, computer languages, program slicing techniques, incremental software development, technical reviews, formal verification, software maintenance, software reliability engineering, management of inconsistencies in software engineering, software configuration management, reengineering, software measurement, software metrics for identifying critical components in software projects, software engineering standards, engineering access control, usability issues in the software life cycle, software processes in software engineering and knowledge engineering, and message sequence charts in the software engineering process.

The second group of articles deal with the basics in knowledge engineering, including such topics as: conceptual modeling, case based reasoning, logical abduction in software engineering, knowledge-level models of knowledge systems, knowledge discovery and data mining, knowledge based Information access, machine learning for software engineering, and neural networks.

The third group of articles deal with the interplay of software engineering and knowledge engineering, including such topics as: pattern based software reengineering, agent-oriented software engineering, ontologies in software design, rationale management in software engineering, learning software organization, software engineering and learning theory, task models for interactive software systems, software engineering and knowledge engineering issues for web based education systems, and software engineering and knowledge engineering issues in bio-informatics.

Overview of Volume Two

Volume Two expands the coverage of the basic principles of software engineering. However, this volume also addresses many current topics in software engineering and knowledge engineering such as visual patterns, multimedia software engineering, etc.

A central issue is how to turn knowledge patterns into visual software patterns and visual specifications such as UML. Techniques for knowledge acquisition, software visualization and knowledge visualization, are also of great interest.

The first group of articles deal with software engineering, including such topics as: formal description techniques, software specification and design, software inspections, component-based software engineering, versions of program integration, software reuse, assessing different testing strategies for software engineering and knowledge engineering, automated knowledge-based selection of suitable unit testing techniques, verification and validation, software cost estimation, data model metrics, uncertainty management, software project management, and reverse engineering,

The second group of articles deal with visual and multimedia software engineering, including such topics as: multimedia software engineering, web engineering, object-oriented modeling of multimedia applications, visual languages in software engineering, software engineering for visual programming languages, assessing visual programming languages, visual parallel programming, software visualization, and visualization of knowledge structures.

The third group of articles deal with emerging topics in software engineering and knowledge engineering, including such topics as: software patterns, supporting software processes using knowledge management, methods for knowledge elicitation, knowledge elicitation from software code, nonmonotonic reasoning and consistency management in software engineering, agent-oriented software construction with UML, improving UML designs using automatic design pattern detection, application of knowledge-based systems for supervision and control of machining processes, system-level design notations for embedded systems, situated computing for mobile users, and the synchronization of interactive web documents.

In a rapidly expanding area such as software engineering and knowledge engineering, no handbook can claim to cover all the subjects of interest. However it is hoped that this Handbook is comprehensive enough to serve as a useful and handy guide to both practitioners and researchers for a number of years to come.

Shi-Kuo Chang
University of Pittsburgh and
Knowledge Systems Institute

CONTENTS

MULTIMEDIA SOFTWARE ENGINEERING

SHI-KUO CHANG

Department of Computer Science, University of Pittsburgh,
Pittsburgh, PA 15260 USA
E-mail: chang@cs.pitt.edu

TIMOTHY K. SHIH

Department of Computer Science and
Information Engineering, Tamkang University, Tamsui,
Taiwan 25137, R.O.C.
E-mail: tshih@cs.tku.edu.tw

Multimedia software engineering is an emerging area combining software engineering, multimedia computing, visual languages and visualization. We can view multimedia software engineering from two different, yet complementary, perspectives: (1) to apply multimedia computing, visual languages and visualization to the practice of software engineering; and (2) to apply software engineering principles to the development of multimedia applications and systems. This chapter surveys some of the approaches and recent advances in multimedia software engineering.

Keywords: Software engineering, multimedia, visual languages, visualization, WWW, software life cycle, multimedia documents.

1. Introduction

Multimedia software engineering is an emerging area combining software engineering, multimedia computing, visual languages and visualization [8]. Software engineering provides methodologies, procedures and techniques to transform knowledge into well-engineered software products of guaranteed quality. Multimedia computing supports the use of graphics, sound, animation and video in many applications. Visual languages and visualization techniques are increasingly used in software engineering for product development, and in multimedia computing for human-computer interaction. We can view multimedia software engineering from two different, yet complementary, perspectives: (1) to apply multimedia technology to the practice of software engineering, or (2) to apply software engineering principles to the design of multimedia systems.

Multimedia has two fundamental characteristics that can be expressed by the following formula: *Multimedia = Multiple Media + Hypermedia.*

Advantages of multiple media are: (1) full utilization of all senses (eye, ear, etc), (2) dynamic presentations, and (3) better understanding by the user. The disadvantages include: (1) greater demands on storage, bandwidth and computing resources, (2) cognitive overload, and (3) system complexity.

Hypermedia is a style of building systems for information representation and management around a network of multimedia nodes connected together by typed links [15]. The advantages of hypermedia include: (1) ease of documentation, (2) ease of conceptualization and/or visualization, and (3) dynamic expansion of information hyperspace. The disadvantages are also well recognized: (1) disorientation due to "lost in hyperspace" phenomenon, (2) cognitive overload, and (3) system complexity.

In this chapter, we will give a focussed survey of current research in MSE to apply multimedia technology to the practice of software engineering, or to apply software engineering principles to the design of multimedia systems. Since multimedia is basically multimedia objects plus links, in the following survey the concept of *links and association* will come up time and again as the central theme. The survey is by no means exhaustive, but the topics presented in this survey are a fair representation of the current research issues in multimedia software engineering.

2. Project Management Using Multimedia Tools

One successful application of multimedia technology to software engineering is in project management using hypermedia CASE tools [26]. Since the traditional project management tools lack the ability to capture a multitude of decisions and do not provide document control, a new Decision Based Systems Development paradigm (DBSD) was developed [25]. In decision based systems development, usually the following steps are to be taken:

- Identification and articulation of the problem.
- Identify alternative solutions.
- Choose decision criteria.
- Justify alternatives.
- Evaluate conditional decisions.
- Put the decision into context.
- Build decision view.

Multimedia technology allows the decision makers to use text for problem description, graphs and diagrams for representing problem space, and different colors and symbols for denoting status and the latest information. Moreover, hypermedia allows the linking of documents and people in a variety of ways.

In the Decision-based Hyper-multimedia CASE (DHC) tool, objects in an extended document base are linked by five types of links: (1) *Reference to problems/decisions in problem space* or SEE links, (2) *Reference to a single on-line document* or REFER on-line links, (3) *Reference to a Decision View of a document set* or VIEW links, (4) *Timed reference to a contact person* or CONTACT links, and (5) *References to off-line documents* or REFER off-line links.

Some link types may be motivated by unix/DOS system commands. For example REFER is similar to *xloadimage* for bit-mapped pictures in DOCS.

This DHC tool was applied to Low-Visibility Landing and Surface Operations (LVLASO) project at NASA Langley Research Center. The impact on LVLASO is that the DHC tool is applicable to early stages in systems development. Also, brainstorming was easily documented and not lost. It encourages people to be more goal-oriented so that tasks that did not clearly fit in were immediately dropped. Finally, it keeps people up to date with decisions. Future additions may include a CONTACT hyperlink, group Decisions by functional areas, and better GUI. The importance of this project is that it indicates the desirability of having many different types of links for information/people association.

3. Software Documentation

Another successful area of application of multimedia technology is in software documentation. By exploiting the nature of hypermedia, powerful multimedia-based program documentation systems can be developed.

3.1. *RST documentation model*

Reliable Software Technologies Documentation Model uses standard C comments with the addition of design documents on the WWW [4]. Standard C Comments are added to program lines whose purpose is not clear, to the beginning of each function or procedure to explain its purpose and the Pre and Post conditions, and to the header function to describe its purpose.

The following information is also maintained:

- CVS revision history.
- Requirements document.
- Relevant research.
- Architecture diagram.
- UML diagrams.

RST documentation web page includes the following information:

- Welcome to the new program web page.
- Short description of the project goals and the specific problem to solve.
- Related links.
- Project design document.
- Project specifications document.
- Architecture document.
- Research Links: Linkl, Link2, Link3.

3.2. *Linux HQ kernel documentation*

Linux HQ Kernel Documentation provides the following:

- Hypertext transformation of the code.
- Links to function definitions.
- Function search engine.

Similar to CVS file hierarchy with links to associated files, Linux documentation maintains alphabetic listing of file names. It supports a function search engine. Function calls are linked to function definition, and there are links to include header files. However, it still relies on the reader to understand the comments. More information can be found at: *http://www.linuxhq.com.*

3.3. *Variorum*

The American Heritage Dictionary (1998) defines "variorum" as follows: "contains notes or comments by many scholars or critics". The creators of Variorum define it as a "multimedia tool that aids in the documentation of programs. ... The integration of WWW capabilities is a key aspect of variorum's usefulness".

Variorum [10] allows programmers to record the process of "walking through" codes using multimedia technology. Variorum supports hypertext transformation of code and the addition of programmer/author walkthroughs as voice annotations. Variorum modifies the source code to include annotation links. However, its effectiveness depends critically on individual authors' annotation style. The amount of voice storage can also become excessive. However, in the future audio/visual software documentation systems may overcome the deficiencies of today's Variorum.

4. Design of Multimedia Applications Using Object-Oriented Tools

From the above survey, it can be concluded that multimedia is useful in software documentation, but whole-hearted incorporation of multimedia in software engineering has not yet happened [16]. There is an ongoing paradigm shift — from business orientation to entertainment orientation [16]. New software process models and paradigms, in particular the object-oriented approach, are needed in multimedia systems design. This section surveys several object-oriented approaches in multimedia systems design.

In what follows, we will discuss:

- DAMSEL — Dynamic Multimedia Specification Language.
- MET++ — Multimedia Application Framework.
- MME — Object-Oriented Multimedia Toolkit.
- PREMO — Presentation Environment for Multimedia Standard.

4.1. *DAMSEL*

DAMSEL is developed at the University of Minnesota. It includes the design and implementation of advanced multimedia constructs such as object-oriented extensible and temporal data model. It supports an execution environment based upon JAVA/CORBA. The temporal model describes along three axes: the temporal relations, delays and exec-based behavior. The representation using OO supports complex object definition and queries.

The temporal model of DAMSEL is very flexible. It supports user, system, application-generated events and therefore enables very interactive dynamic application creation. In the execution architecture, specifications are written to define the environment behavior and run time execution is determined by various events. DAMSEL specifications can be embedded with C++ or JAVA.

Data flow model assists in analyzing and modifying multimedia data. Data is modeled as stream flowing from a media source to a sink. It allows the insertion of additional stream objects as the data flows. It also enables modification and analysis of data. The presentation model provides higher level abstraction for dealing with and controlling presentations. Data flow is connected to a presentation server that interacts with the application.

The heart of DAMSEL is a distributed client-server run-time event manager, which is a multi-user, interactive, internet-wide execution environment implemented using CORBA and JAVA.

More information about DAMSEL can be found at its web site: *http://www-users.cs.umn.edu/~pazandak/damsel.html*

4.2. *MET++*

MET++ is an object-oriented application framework developed at the University of Zurich. It supports the development of multimedia applications using reusable objects for 2D, 3D graphics, audio, video, etc. The framework consists of a set of interconnected objects that provide the basic functionality of a working application, which can be easily specialized into individual application. Through subclassing and inheritance, it supports the reuse of code as a class library and the reuse of design structures. Similar dependencies between object are pre-implemented through predefined object composition, event dispatching and message flow.

Time synchronization [1, 19] is an important part of a multimedia presentation. In MET++, this is specified in a hierarchical composition. As illustrated by Fig. 1, implicit information is made visually explicit due to the hierarchy.

Example applications done using MET++ and more information about MET++ can be found at its web site: *http://www.ifi.unizh.ch/groups/mml/projects/met++*

4.3. *MME*

The MME Multimedia Extension is a project by Computer Graphics Center (Fraunhofer), Germany. The software package features a class hierarchy and

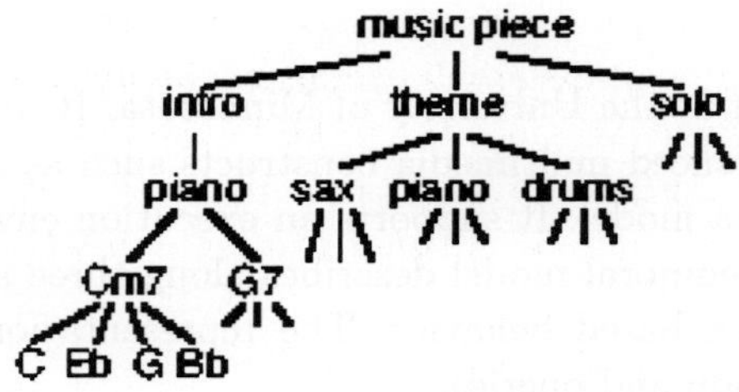

Fig. 1. Temporal composition.

development tools for composing multimedia applications. The goals of MME are:

- OO modeling of various media.
- Encapsulation of distributed media access and control.
- Modeling of time as a precondition to define arbitrary temporal relations.
- Relations between media objects designed at a higher abstraction level and its realization at run time.

MME objects have the following characteristics:

- Application (AO), Multimedia (MO).
- Media objects handle the transfer of media data from a set of ports (source) to another.
- Set of ports (sinks).
- Ports (devices like VCR, windows, files or sockets).
- Complex media objects handle the definition and maintenance of relations (temporal and spatial) objects.

MME is realized by executing:

- Instantiation of media objects out of predefined multimedia classes.
- Instantiation of complex media objects to define spatial/temporal relations.
- Definition of new media classes as subclasses of predefined objects and classes.

User interaction such as starting, stopping and cueing are supported in real time (interactive multimedia). MME is implemented in C++ on top of UNIX, Xwindows system with Xvideo extension, with about 4500 lines of code. The OO benefits include reuse, encapsulation, and less time to develop (about one man-year). More information about MME can be found at its web site: *http://zgdv.igd.fhg.de/www/zgdv-uig/software/MME*

4.4. *PREMO*

PREMO (Presentation Environment for Multimedia Objects) is a new standard under development by ISO. The goals of PREMO are:

- To provide a general framework and a reference model for the creation and programming of distributed multimedia applications.
- To allow existing media devices to be interfaced to an application.
- OO programming infrastructure to support the development.
- To recognize the evolution of multimedia system technologies for research tools to mature.
- To certify products that meets QoS and fundamental requirements.

PREMO is being developed at the CWI-Computer Center, Netherlands, and more information about PREMO can be found at its web site: *http://dbs.cwi.nl/cwwwi/owa/*

5. Specification and Design of Multimedia Software Systems

Specification and design of multimedia applications pose new challenge to authoring systems due to temporal and spatial relations. Common design of hierarchical composition of objects needs to be found, thus leading to object-oriented tools. For the specification of multimedia software systems, a new paradigm is espoused: software engineers will do evolutionary design of complex systems through: (1) architecture specification, (2) design rationale capture, (3) architecture V&V, and (4) architecture transformation, using an object-oriented architecture description language [24]. Another recent approach is to extend UML, the Universal Modeling Language, for the modeling of multimedia applications [22]. In what follows, we survey two more formal approaches in specification and design.

5.1. *An actor based approach to multimedia software specification*

Dattolo [11] applies the actor model for modeling software as collections of distributed, cooperative entities, as illustrated in Fig. 2. It is felt that the classical notion of object is too vague to support large-scale concurrency. On the other hand, actors combine object-oriented and functional programming in order to make the management of concurrency easier for the user. An actor reacts to the external environment by executing its procedure skills (scripts). An example for TeleoActor class definition based upon the ESAL (Extended Simple Actor Language) is as follows:

```
(Def TeleoActor
{Actor}
(stor info
hypServices image
inSuggestion brSuggestion cnSuggestion)
[(apply-filter), (visualize), (tree-brws), (grph-brws),]).
```

The Dexter model for hypermedia is used, which is essentially a two-layer model — runtime layer and storage layer — for hypermedia. The architecture was

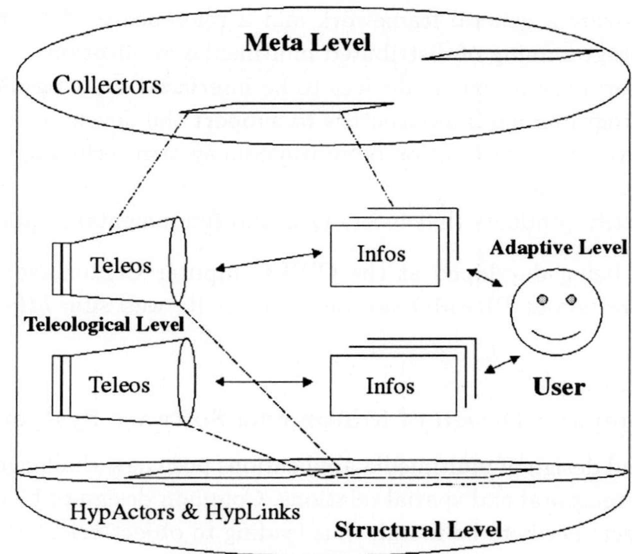

Fig. 2. Hypermedia information system based upon the actor model.

applied in the development of a hypermedia system named DiBlue, which is a distributed version of Blue, a traditional OPLA hypermedia programming environment. It supports an object-oriented logic programming system in OPLA, a hybrid language originated from the marriage between Prolog and CLOS.

5.2. *Teleaction objects for multimedia software specification and prototyping*

Multimedia systems incorporating hyperlinks and user interaction can be prototyped using TAOML, an extension of HTML. TAOML is used to define a Teleaction Object (TAO) which is a multimedia object with associated hypergraph structure and knowledge structure. The user can create and modify the private knowledge of a TAO so that the TAO will react automatically to certain events. The knowledge structure of a TAO is an active index [5], which consists of a collection of index cells (ICs) with behavior similar to that of agents. The hypergraph structure supports the effective presentation and efficient communication of multimedia information. The static aspects of the hypergraph structure are described by a Multimedia Static Specification (MSS). TAOs are valuable since they improve the selective access and presentation of relevant multimedia information [6].

The structure of the multimedia application development system is shown in Fig. 3 below. It mainly consists of two tools. The Formal Specification Tool allows a specification of the MSS to be created. The specification may be either visual or text-based. The specification is then validated using a Symbol Relation (SR)

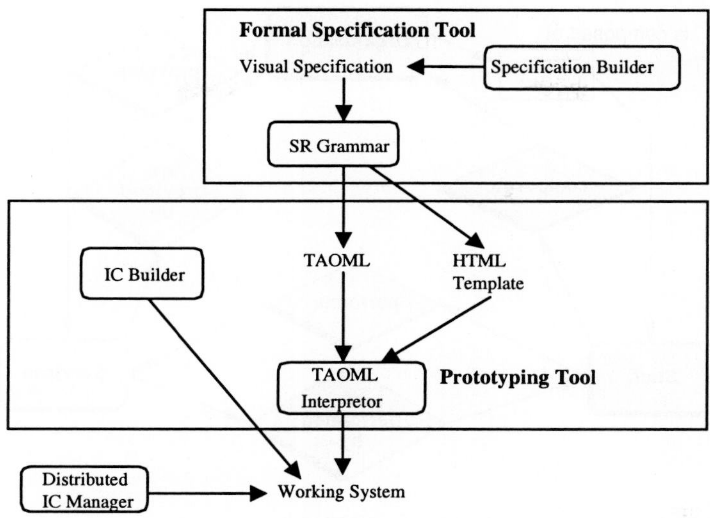

Fig. 3. The structure of the multimedia application development environment.

grammar [2, 3, 13]. Such a multidimensional grammar is particularly attractive for multimedia applications since it can describe the spatial and temporal aspects of an application [7]. If the specification is valid, the tool generates TAOML and an HTML template for the specified system.

The Prototyping Tool includes an IC Builder to create the index cells comprising the knowledge structure of the TAOs. A TAOML interpreter generates HTML code from the TAOML and HTML template from the information produced by the IC builder. The application generated can then be executed from any web browser working with the distributed IC Manager that controls the active knowledge structure built out of active index cells. Multimedia applications in many domains were developed using these tools, mostly notably e-learning [9].

The above described tools provide a way to formally specify the TAOs comprising the application, verify and validate the specification, and rapidly prototype the application. TAOs provide one of the first unified approaches for multimedia software engineering.

6. Model-and Pattern-Based Design Approaches

6.1. *A model-based approach to hypermedia design*

In the model-based approach to hypermedia design, the key concept is to provide a comprehensive model for software specification and design. For instance, the Relationship Management Methodology (RMM) comprises (1) Entity-Relationship design, (2) Application diagram design, (3) M-slice (aggregate) design, (4) Navigational design, (5) User interface design, (6) Protocol conversion design, (7) Run-time behavior, and (8) Construction and testing [18].

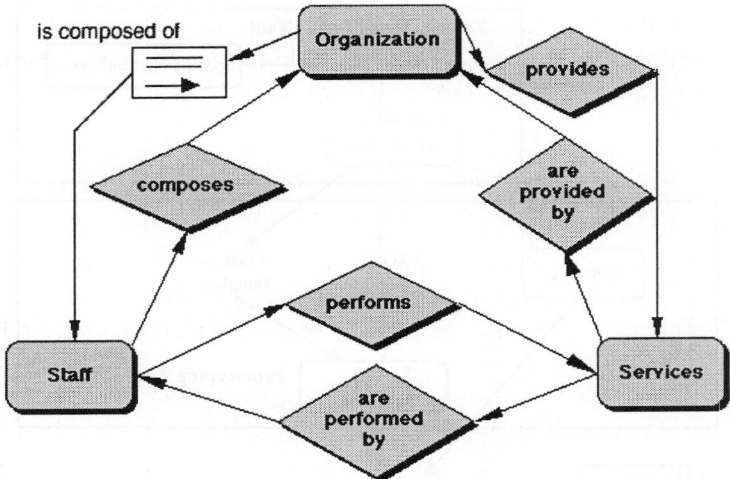

Fig. 4. An RMDM diagram.

The Relationship Management Data Model (RMDM) is the cornerstone of the RMM methodology. It includes elements for representing information domain concepts such as entities and relationships, along with navigation elements such as links. As illustrated in Fig. 4, an application design is described via an RMDM diagram.

During the E-R Design, a study of the relevant entities and relationships of the application domain is conducted. These elements form the basis of the hypermedia application and show up as nodes or links. During the navigational design, relevant relationships are identified and made available for navigation. Since information units can have a very large number of attributes, the RMM groups the attributes into slices called M-Slices.

The way navigation is applied in the application by RMM is through the Access Primitives. The RMM Access Primitives include: (1) Unidirectional link, (2) Bidirectional link, (3) Grouping, (4) Conditional index, (5) Conditional guided tour, and (6) Conditional indexed guided tour.

Regarding links, navigation establishes an association between an original data component and destination data components. The associative link, or simply link, is what effectively allows navigation through data components, and represents the main characteristic of hypertext and hypermedia. The consideration of link types by definition establishes semantic information that allows hypermedia systems to efficiently manage data or data modeling, preventing this task to be the sole responsibility of designers or users. Link types can be used through almost every step of model-based approaches to hypermedia design.

What presently are found in most of the hypermedia systems are static, persistent and explicit links, defined over content. In RMM, there are links that can initiate a process such as email, a video exhibition, an audio exhibition, or a file download. Finally, *destination influence* establishes what of the operational services is going to be supported by the link. Links types are further broken down into two categories:

- Historical category (related to performed navigation).
- Speculative category (related to possible navigation).

A category that supports the retrieval service allows the presentation of the meaning associated to the description when it exists. *Destination influence* can provoke the definition of new links that were not initially related to infological modeling.

In conclusion, a framework is presented to categorize link types, which allows the design and construction of richer hypermedia applications. Link design, which is the kernel of model-based approaches to hypermedia design, is one of the areas that can benefit from the use of link types. Both information and operational elements influence link creation, so these issues should be considered during link design efforts. Information influence is related to conceptual relationships from the domain of interest, while operational influence is related to data manipulation services. It is also proposed that service and destination influences should be considered during link design. Links types and categories can also be identified and considered both with model based approaches and with authoring tools to hypermedia design.

6.2. *A pattern-based approach to design*

In the pattern-based approach to design, the idea is to identify important and relevant design patterns, so that complex design can be constructed from these design patterns [20]. This approach can be applied to hypermedia applications [14]. The patterns for hypermedia applications mainly deal with navigational structure and interface organization. The navigational contexts may include: class-derived context, link-derived context, composite-derived context, and arbitrary context. Two important navigational structures are *News* for new information and *Landmarks* for subsystems. In what follows, one such pattern will be discussed.

News is motivated by the following problem: "Given a large and dynamic web site, how do you tell users that there is new information or updates somewhere inside the site?" In huge web sites, it is not a good solution to compromise structure in order to make updates easy available. The solution is to structure the home page in such a way that a space is devoted to the newest additions:

- Presenting descriptive "headlines" regarding them.
- Using those headlines as anchors to link them with their related pages.

In summary, a software engineering strategy for developing hypermedia applications is proposed, emphasizing the use of an object-oriented design method, the use of design patterns, and the partitioning of the development life cycle in a set

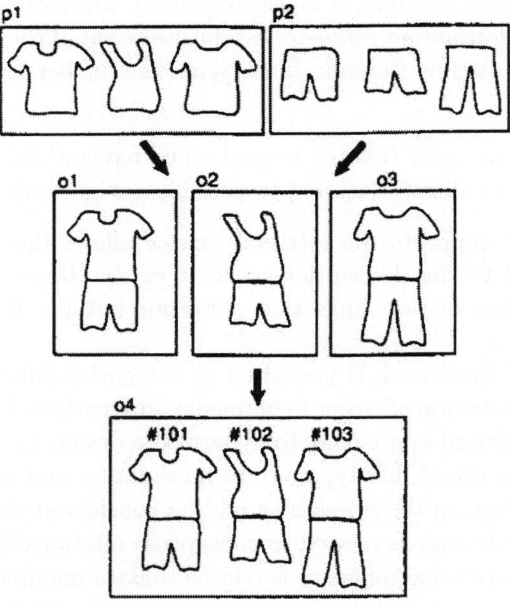

Fig. 5. Virtual multimedia objects.

of activities addressing different design concerns. The design patterns may help to capture and reuse experience and to provide more comfortable and understandable navigation space.

6.3. *The virtual multimedia object*

Links can be explicit or virtual. For example, queries can be considered as virtual links. Multimedia objects can also be real or virtual. An example of virtual multimedia objects is illustrated in Fig. 5.

The Virtual Multimedia Object (VMO) [17] is virtually created based upon other multimedia objects. A pointing entry (a kind of virtual link) represents the mapping between a VMO and its original data. It can be implemented as user-defined deriving procedures.

A prototype system has been constructed under Solaris 2.5.1 in C++. The system has two layers: Virtual Object layer and Storage layer. Virtual Object Layer manages VMO and their types. Storage layer has the responsibility for storing objects. The technique can be applied to any media type.

7. The Life Cycle for Multimedia Web Document Development

Web documents are programs that contain both data and methods (such as Java applets). Therefore, developing Web documents is similar to developing software programs. However, Web documents are different because they focus on different criteria:

- Web documents focus on information delivery while software programs focus on problem solving. Although Web documents may embed programs to be downloaded by clients, these programs have less complicated computation logic, as compared to those for scientific calculation.
- Since Web documents contain information to be accessed by human users, human factors are more important in Web documents, as compared to scientific calculation programs.
- A Web document is a collection of HTML files, with uniform resource locators (URLs) linking these files. The size of a Web document and its linked references cannot be predicted, because references can be changed due to network configurations or updates of the referenced content. On the other hand, a program usually has a fixed size of executable code.
- Due to the use of inter-station hyperlinks, Web documents are always evolving. A hyperlink is valid only within a certain period of time. Similarly, the update of an embedded program may introduce new bugs. A developing Web document is not robust because invalid hyperlinks and changing environment may affect what can be accessed. In contrast, software programs, in general, are relatively stable after several cycles of testing.

Traditional software development paradigms such as the Waterfall model and object-oriented paradigm have their advantages in building complex software systems. However, due to the differences mentioned above, these paradigms are not quite suitable for the development of Web documents.

Since a Web document is evolving constantly, sufficient testing will be difficult. Instead, testing and maintenance of a Web document should be the same activity while the document is delivered. A Web document, or its supporting environment, should have the ability to correctly update inter-station hyperlinks (including adding new links). Moreover, since Web documents are meant to deliver information, the content should be updated periodically. Either through the use of dynamic home page or manually changed by a designer, the Web document should always keep the most current information. Thus, the assessment of documentation usability should be an umbrella activity covering all the tasks in the development paradigm.

The development of Web document contains three parts: (a) document script development, (b) document implementation, (c) and document testing. The script portion of a Web document can be a text file with references, to describe the requirements of the document. The implementation of a Web document usually contains some HTML, XML or TAOML (see Sec. 4.2) files, with embedded multimedia information and control programs (e.g. Java Applets). Different portions of a Web document implementation are connected by URLs within a station, as well as the references of the document linked to files located in remote stations. A Web document implementation may have one or more entry URLs. Starting from these URLs, testing records of the Web document can be constructed either automatically or manually.

Web document development should focus on the following issues:

- Stepwise refinement.
- Information consistency.
- Layered Web document scope.
- Automatic document testing.
- Content assessment.

To design a Web document, the designer may start from a draft document and refine the document towards a final version. Different portions of a document can be stored in a repository for future references. Since Web documents evolve, we need a facility to maintain the changes of such an evolving process. We also want to maintain the consistency of information in the process. From a sketch outline, to the implementation of the Web home page, to the testing records of such a home page, information should be consistent. From the perspective of implementation, a Web document can be divided into two parts: (a) the intra-station document and (b) the inter-station document. The former refers to the documentation files stored within a single workstation. These files are further divided according to two types of links: intra-directory hyperlinks and inter-directory hyperlinks. The latter (i.e., inter-station document) are files, which can be retrieved via local area networks or the Internet. This layered definition defines the testing scope of the specific home page implementation. Web documents should be automatically tested using tools. The layered definition is also used in maintenance. The testing tools should be able to check the validity of links from time to time in order to maintain a Web page. With a supporting environment, the Web document designers should be able to assess the development status of documents with respect to Web document script, implementation, and testing.

A Web document script is similar to the specification of the software. However, the script may include the process of collecting digital multimedia resources, such as scanning a picture or recording an MPEG video file. A Web document script can be specified in natural language or in formal specifications. The script should be realized as HTML, XML or TAOML programs, which can also be generated by commercial Web document design software (such as the FrontPage software by Microsoft). Testing and maintenance of these programs should be carefully conducted, and incomplete implementation or erroneous connections should be detected and reported.

A Web document development paradigm [23] was proposed based on the spiral model for software development. The traditional spiral model for software development has four phases: (a) analysis of requirements and specification, (b) design and implementation, (c) testing and releasing, and (d) risk analysis. The first two phases of this proposed paradigm are similar to the spiral model, except that Web documents have different focuses as discussed earlier. Since Web documents are to deliver information, the content is more important than the feasibility analysis of a system, as it is in a software system. We also incorporate testing in the process of maintenance, since Web documents should be tested for obsolete URLs and missing tag objects in its maintenance. Instead of using risk analysis after testing, Web document assessment should be used in each and every cycle of the spiral model. The result of content assessment and testing decides whether the Web document designer should deliver a version of the document, or continue to go through another iteration in the spiral model.

The development activities in the three phases (i.e., script, implementation, and testing/maintenance) as well as Web document assessment are based on the status of a document repository. With a centralized repository, this paradigm enforces the consistent changes in each step of the development cycle. Starting from a requirement, the developer designs a Web script. This script can be a text description of the requirement of a home page, with optional multimedia resources (e.g. picture, sound, or video) as on-line references. Alternatively, the script can be presented in a spoken language and recorded as audio records. Whether the script is recorded in text or voice, the implementation of the Web script is produced either automatically or semi-automatically. The physical testing can be conducted afterwards. The Web document will be delivered after a number of iterations in the spiral model. If the content of this Web document is suitable, a version of this document is delivered. However, the document should be constantly tested, retested and updated. The development life cycle of a Web document can be considered at three different levels: intra-directory level, intra-station level, and inter-station level. Documents at each phase are designed depending on the range of references or URLs. For instance, a document script may refer to a multimedia resource file within the local station, or another Web page in a remote site. The implementation will use different ranges of URLs with respect to the script. The testing scope of the URLs can thus be decided afterwards.

This Web document development paradigm is yet another example of applying software engineering methods to the development of multimedia systems.

8. Multimedia Software Project Effort Measurement

In Sec. 1 of this chapter, we discussed how multimedia technology is utilized in software engineering project management. In this section, we discuss how to apply software engineering technology in multimedia project management, and address the issue of multimedia software project effort measurement.

Why multimedia software project effort measurement is an issue? Can't multimedia projects be treated in the same way as other types of software projects? To answer this question, we note that there have been substantial efforts in measuring traditional transaction processing and process control systems, but relatively little effort in determining and evaluating multimedia effort measurements. In fact multimedia software is unique in its emphasis on contents and the need for storyboarding early in the development cycle. Because of that, we not only need tools and techniques specific to multimedia, but also should emphasize different aspects in software project management. For one, managers from diverse background are needed for such projects, to form cross-disciplinary teams. For another, due to the inherently different nature of multimedia systems, the direct application of existing models and measures may not meet multimedia project management needs.

A preliminary empirical study to develop an algorithmic mapping to "effort" using product characteristics appropriate to multimedia software systems other than LOC (Line of Codes) or external files is reported in [12]. The development effort is regarded as a function of (1) building the system content — each media form might have a different impact on development effort — including file name, media type, creation effort, digitizing effort, editing effort, and (2) authoring the system — a screen that incorporates a greater number of objects and events would take proportionally greater effort to develop. The empirical study on projects developed by senior-level students and delivered in two stages: prototype and final delivery. The students are information science students focussed on programming and design students concentrated on content and interface development. Forty-five observations were recorded in media component development, but no correlation between development effort and either of the component variables — media type and media status. Since data sets were small, generalizations are not possible from this study.

There is a lack of industry driven determination of important attributes. Moreover, data collection needs to be exploratory and student projects are not representative of industry developments. Thus, there is a need to develop an industry-based metrics framework in order to determine system and component characteristics considered influential in multimedia software system development efforts. The Goal/Question/Metric (GQM) model shown in Fig. 6 is one such framework.

The key issues considered to reflect industry perspective include:

- Development Tools: Authoring tools and other more complex tools offering visually based high productivity development languages or high level scripting languages.
- Delivery Platform: Platform dictates media format and optimization considerations, for example, CD-I must conform to PAL or NTSC.
- Content Development: Media content development is labor intensive, but difficult to quantify. It depends on media mix, the number of components, and complexity of each component. Artistic considerations also play a role in satisfactory completion of project.
- Organizational Capability: Indirect effects such as size, personnel mix, etc.
- Personnel: Wide variety of skills is required in successful multimedia software development. The core members are a producer, programmer(s), and graphic artist(s).

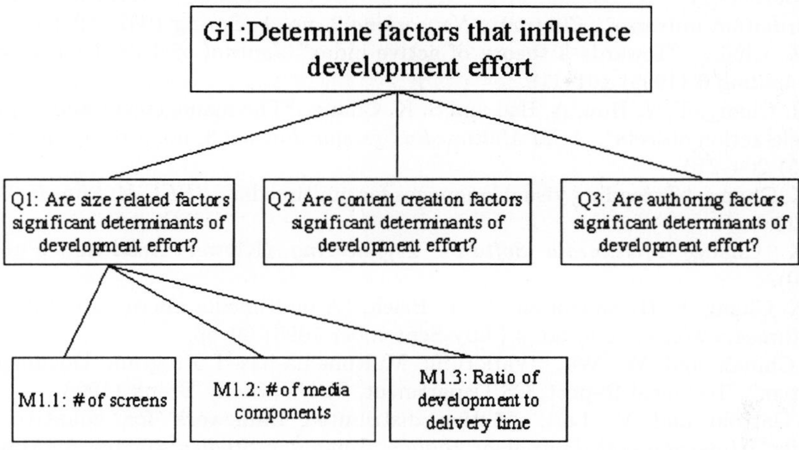

Fig. 6. The goal/question/metric model (a small portion is shown for illustrative purpose).

To perform preliminary verification of the above framework, a pilot study was conducted [21]. Structured interviews were conducted with three multimedia development organizations. Results suggest the type of project almost entirely determines development environment and workload. Results of pilot study were combined with components of GQM framework to develop a postal survey. The focus is to determine factors that influence development efforts. It was found that 50% of respondents use no formal methodology. None of the traditional software metrics is used. Rather, experience from previous projects is used. Project tracking is performed at very high level, indicating immature project management. Staff experience and project size are obviously important factors.

To summarize, (1) traditional software metrics such as COCOMO and FPA are usually not utilized in multimedia software development; (2) pilot study and questionnaire reinforce the non-formal approach to multimedia software development; (3) although there are attempts to formalize the approach to software development, there is uncertainty on how to achieve this. In other words, multimedia software engineering as a scientific discipline is still evolving, making it an exciting research area to explore.

References

1. J. F. Allen, "Time and time again: The many ways to represent time", *International Journal of Intelligent Systems* **9**, no. 3 (June 1991) 413–428.
2. T. Arndt, A. Cafiero and A. Guercio, "Multimedia languages for teleaction objects", *Proceedings of 1997 IEEE Symposium on Visual Languages* (September 1997) 318–327.

3. T. Arndt, A. Cafiero and A. Guercio, "Symbol relation grammars for teleaction objects", Technical Report, Dipartimento di Informatica ed Applicazioni, University of Salerno (1997).
4. T. Berners-Lee, R. Calliau, J. F. Groff and B. Pollermann, "World-wide web: The information universe", *Electronic Networking* **2**, no. 1 (Spring 1992) 52–58.
5. S. K. Chang, "Towards a theory of active index" *Journal of Visual Languages and Computing* **6** (1995) 101–118.
6. H. J. Chang, T. Y. Hou, A. Hsu and S. K. Chang, "The management and application of tele-action objects", *ACM Multimedia Systems Journal* **3**, no. 5–6 (Springer Verlag, 1995) 204–216.
7. S. K. Chang, "Extending visual languages for multimedia", *IEEE Multimedia* **3** (1996) 18–26.
8. S.-K. Chang, *Multimedia Software Engineering* (Kluwer Academic Publishers, 2000).
9. S. K. Chang, E. Hassanein and C. Y. Hsieh, "A multimedia micro-university", *IEEE Multimedia Magazine* **5**, no. 3 (July-September 1998) 60–68.
10. T. Chiueh and W. Wu, "Variorum: Multimedia-based Program Documentation System", Technical Report, CS Department, SUNY, Stony Brook (1998).
11. A. Dattolo and V. Lois, "Active distributed framework for adaptive hypermedia", *International Journal of Human Computer Studies* **46**, no. 5 (May 1997) 605–626.
12. T. Fletcher, S. G. MacDonell and W. B. L. Wong, "Early experiences in measuring multimedia systems development effort" (1998).
13. F. Ferrucci, G. Pacini, G. Satta, M. I. Sessa, G. Tortora, M. Tucci and G. Vitiello, "Symbol relation grammars: A formalism for graphical languages", *Information and Computation* **131**, no. 1 (1996) 1–46.
14. A. Garrido, G. Rossi and D. Schwabe, "Pattern systems for hypermedia", *Proceedings of the PloP'97* (1997).
15. F. Halasz, "Reflections on notecards: Seven issues for the next generation of hypermedia systems", *CACM* **31**, no. 7 (1995) 836–855.
16. M. Hirakawa, "Do software engineers like multimedia?" ICMCS'99, Firenze, Italy (June 1999).
17. T. Hochin, M. Harada, M. Nakata and T. Tsuji, "Virtual multimedia objects as the platform of customizing of multimedia data", *Proceedings the International Workshop on Multimedia Software Engineering*, Kyoto, Japan (April 1998) 20–27.
18. T. Isakowitz, E. A. Stohr and P. Balasubramanian, "RMM: A methodology for structured hypermedia design", *CACM* **38**, no. 8 (August 1995) 34–44.
19. T. D. C. Little and A. Ghafoor, "Interval-based temporal models for time-dependent multimedia data", *IEEE Transactions on Data and Knowledge Engineering* **5**, no. 4 (1993) 551–563.
20. D. Lyardet, G. Rossi and D. Schwabe, "Using design patterns in educational multimedia applications", *Proceedings of the ED-MEDIA'98*, Friburg (June 1998).
21. S. G. MacDonell and T. Fletcher, "Industry practices in project management", *Proceedings of the Metric'98* (IEEE CS Press).
22. S. Sauer and G. Engels, "Extending UML for modelling of multimedia applications", *Proceedings of IEEE Symposium on Visual Languages* (Tokyo, 1999) 80–87.
23. T. K. Shih, S.-K. Chang and P. Shih, "A web document development paradigm and its supporting environment", *Proceedings of the Sixth International Conference on Distributed Multimedia Systems* (*DMS'99*), University of Aizu, Japan (July, 1999) 26–30.

24. J. P. Tsai, "Knowledge-based software architecture", *IEEE Transactions on Knowledge and Data Engineering* **11**, no. 1 (January 1999).
25. J. C. Wild, K. Maly and L. F. Liu, "Decision-based software development", *Journal of Software Maintenance* **3**, no. 1 (1991).
26. J. C. Wild *et al.*, "Project management using hypermedia CASE tools", Technical Report, Department of Computer Science, Old Dominion University (1998).

OBJECT-ORIENTED MODELING OF MULTIMEDIA APPLICATIONS

GREGOR ENGELS and STEFAN SAUER*
University of Paderborn, Mathematics and Computer Science Department, D–33095 Paderborn, Germany
E-mail: {engels,sauer}@upb.de

The field of multimedia software engineering is still in an inmature state. Significant research and development has been dedicated towards multimedia services and systems technology such as networking or database systems. Multimedia document formats have been standardized. But when it comes to multimedia application development, the development process is truncated to an implement-and-test method. Either specialized multimedia authoring systems or multimedia frameworks or libraries complementing programming languages or system software are directly used for implementation. No preceding modeling phases for requirements specification, analysis, or design of the system to build are enforced. The development of sophisticated multimedia process models and established, usable graphical notations tailored to the specification of multimedia systems is still underway.

In order to fill this gap, it is the purpose of this chapter to show current achievements in object-oriented modeling of multimedia applications. Based on an analysis of the state of the art in multimedia application development, we shortly present approaches to object-oriented hypermedia modeling and extensions of the Unified Modeling Language (UML) for hypermedia and interactive systems. The main part of the chapter is dedicated towards a recent approach to the Object-oriented Modeling of MultiMedia Applications (OMMMA).

Keywords: Multimedia software engineering, object-oriented modeling, integrated modeling, Unified Modeling Language.

1. Introduction

Multimedia applications can be defined as interactive software systems combining and presenting a set of independent media objects of diverse types that have spatio-temporal relationships and synchronization dependencies, may be organized in structured composition hierarchies, and can be coupled with an event-based action model for interaction and navigation. Media objects contribute essentially to presentation and interaction via the user interface. Two major categories of media types can be distinguished:

- *static media types*: time-independent media that do not show any temporal expansion and whose presentation is invariant over time, e.g. text, image, and graphics; and

*Corresponding author.

- *temporal media types*: time-dependent media that possess time-dynamic behavior and whose presentation varies over time, e.g. animation, video, and audio.

Interactive multimedia applications are becoming a widely-used kind of software systems. By integrating multimedia elements, application programs can be made more comprehensible. For instance, it is better to provide auditive examples of musical pieces within an encyclopedia of classical composers or to show a video on the deployment and functioning of a computer tomograph than to simply provide this information textually or with single pictures. Therefore, multimedia is especially useful if the information to present is itself inherently multimedia. Additionally, multimedia can also make user interaction more intuitive by reproducing natural forms of interaction, e.g. with simulated laboratory instruments like rotary switches or analogue indicators, or by speech and gestures [9]. We expect that typical multimedia application domains will not be restricted to purely presentational objectives, like web pages, educational courseware, interactive entertainment, or multimedia catalogues, but conventional business, technical, and information systems will be extended with multimedia features.

State of the art in multimedia software development is that multimedia applications are directly built either by deploying multimedia authoring systems or by coding them using multimedia frameworks or toolkits adding multimedia features to (object-oriented) programming languages or system software. In both cases, no preceding modeling phase as part of a sophisticated software engineering process is carried out prior to implementation. But the importance of such an activity in the course of multimedia software development has been advocated (see, e.g. [3] or [8]).

From a software engineering perspective, the problem with the current state of multimedia application development is not only the absence of *sophisticated, yet practical multimedia software development process models*, but also the lack of *usable (visual) notations to enable an integrated specification* of the system on different *levels of abstraction* and from different *perspectives.* Such languages must be understandable by the different people and stakeholders involved in the multimedia development process.

While support by authoring systems, multimedia technologies, services, and standard formats eases the implementation and exchange of multimedia software, they must be complemented by more abstract, yet precise modeling or specification methods for these systems. What is especially missing is the integrated specification of the multiple aspects of multimedia systems like real-time behavior, user interaction, and application logic. This becomes a key issue when multimedia applications continue to evolve towards higher complexity, and multimedia features become prominent in almost any application domain in order to make information more conceivable as well as user interaction more sophisticated and lively. Effective management and maintenance of such applications requires testing and quality assurance, adaption and reuse of its parts, as well as readable and structured documentation. These requirements are supported by a modeling activity within the development process. Precise specification techniques add to this the capability of validation other than testing by model analysis. Instead of authoring systems supporting the instance-level assembling of interactive multimedia presentations, multimedia CASE tools are needed to support an integrated development process. The implement-and-test paradigm used during multimedia authoring resembles the state of software development before leading to the software crisis of the 1980s.

From this observation, we claim that the development process of multimedia applications should include a *modeling* activity, predominantly on analysis and design level, like they are essentials in conventional software engineering methods. Especially the design phase is required to achieve a clearly structured and error-free implementation. Concepts, languages, methods, and tools must be developed that take the specific requirements of multimedia systems into account and support a methodical multimedia software process. As regards software specification prior to implementation, we consider an *integrated visual modeling language* with capabilities to describe all relevant aspects of the system in an interrelated fashion as the most promising approach. Since the object paradigm has proven many intrinsic properties to support software product and development process quality — like encapsulation, modularity, extensibility, adaptability, portability, integrated specification of structure and behavior, or seamless integration by using a uniform paradigm throughout the process — we regard an *object-oriented modeling language for multimedia* that enables an integrated specification as being well-suited for this task. Object-oriented modeling eases the transition to the implementation of a multimedia application since implementation technologies as well as multimedia databases are mostly based on the object paradigm, too.

A number of models have been proposed for multimedia applications. One striking disadvantage of most models is that they only support partial models for individual aspects of the system, but not a holistic model for the integration of these modeling dimensions. Primarily, they focus on modeling of temporal relations and synchronization of multimedia presentations (e.g. [41, 61]; consult [6] for a general classification). Some more elaborated models also account for interactivity (e.g. [31]). Others concentrate on logical structure and navigational concepts for hypermedia (e.g. [33, 51]). Another problem with many of these models is that they are not intended to be directly used by a multimedia software engineer during a development project. Instead, they form the conceptual basis of (proprietary) authoring systems. Thus, they are not suited for directly supporting modeling activities in a multimedia software development process.

In traditional software engineering, the Unified Modeling Language (UML [47, 11]) has become the *de facto* standard notation for software development from the early stages of requirements specification up to detailed design. It has been adopted as the standard modeling language by the Object Management Group (OMG) and has been submitted for standardization to the International Standardization Organization (ISO).

UML is a family of visual, diagrammatic modeling languages that facilitate the specification of both software systems and process models for their development. The diverse language elements of its constituent sub-languages enable modeling of all relevant aspects of a software system, and methods and pragmatics can be defined how these aspects can be consistently integrated.

Unfortunately, UML does not support all aspects of multimedia applications in an adequate and intuitive manner (see Sec. 4.1). Especially, language features for modeling time, synchronization, and user interface aspects are not explicitly provided. Other concepts of UML are not mature enough or less vivid and thus aggravate multimedia modeling unnecessarily.

But UML comes with built-in extension mechanisms and a so-called profiling mechanism [47] in order to adapt and extend the general-purpose modeling language for specific development processes and application domains.

These fundamental concepts of the UML form the basis for the object-oriented modeling approach for multimedia applications that is presented as the main content of this chapter. Based on the characteristics of multimedia applications, we have developed extensions of the UML to specify all relevant aspects of multimedia applications in a single and coherent model.

The aim of this contribution is therefore to give an overview of existing approaches to object-oriented multimedia software modeling and, in particular, to introduce the UML-based, visual multimedia modeling language OMMMA-L (**O**bject-oriented **M**odeling of **M**ulti**M**edia **A**pplications — the **L**anguage). In this intention, we first identify the characteristic dimensions of multimedia software engineering and their relevance for an object-oriented modeling approach for multimedia applications in Sec. 2. We then give an overview of the state of the art in (object-oriented) multimedia software development. The UML-based modeling approach OMMMA is presented in Sec. 4 where we point out the essential elements of OMMMA-L for the specification of the different aspects of multimedia applications. Section 5 sketches some future directions of research and practice in the area of multimedia software engineering influenced by object-oriented modeling, and Sec. 6 concludes this chapter by summarizing the current achievements.

2. Dimensions of Multimedia Software Engineering

Software engineering can be approached from both the process and the system perspective. Within these perspectives, a wide range of dimensions exist that need to be considered. Each dimension captures a particular aspect of software engineering. But these dimensions do not exist in isolation. They have interdependecies with each other. Dimensions can be represented by partial models of software engineering that must be integrated. A formal, graph-based model for integrated software engineering has been presented in the GRIDS approach by Zamperoni (see [63]). The instantiation of this generic (meta-) model is exemplified by a three-dimensional model of software engineering 3D-M. This model identifies software processes, architectures, and views of the system as the three fundamental dimensions of software engineering and addresses the integration of the corresponding partial models.

The *process* dimension distinguishes different development phases (or activities) such as requirements specification, analysis, design, implementation, and testing. Modeling and implementation phases generally correlate to different levels of abstraction. Coordinates of the *architecture* dimension are different system components, e.g. interfaces with the user or external systems, control, processes, or a repository, whereas the *views* on the system can be distinguished in e.g. structure, function, dynamic behavior, etc. Each view captures specific aspects of the system. (Note that architecture can also be regarded as a high-level internal view of the system to be built.) Software development can thus be understood as a (multi-) path through the multi-dimensional space of this integrated software engineering model, where the trajectory is defined by a process model, and suited software engineering technologies on the levels of concepts, languages, methods, and tools are applied.

If we look at the characteristics of multimedia applications and their development processes, we easily observe the necessity to tailor and extend these general dimensions. Multimedia specific aspects introduce new process activities, new requirements regarding the architectural structure, and new views on the system.

The *process* dimension must be extended to account for specific life-cycles of multimedia applications (see e.g. [52]) and to include activities of content and media production. Traditional development activities must be adapted, e.g. through new kinds of testing.

The *architecture* dimension needs to be refined for multimedia systems. *Multimedia systems* require complex architectures combining a multitude of hardware and software components. Thus, architectural design resembles software hardware co-design of embedded systems. Architectural extensions are needed to account for different notions of media that co-exist in a multimedia system such as perception, presentation, representation, storage, and transport media (see [36]), or for media-related processors like filter, converter, and renderer components. Software components of multimedia systems can be categorized into system, service, and application components. *Multimedia applications* are interactive and have a strong emphasis on a multimedia user interface. Thus, software architectures from the field of interactive system modeling, e.g. Model-View-Controller (MVC [39]) or Presentation-Abstraction-Control (PAC [16]) can be considered as a basis for the architecture of multimedia applications. (A similar approach was followed in the development of the MET++ framework [1].) Since multimedia applications in general allow for multimodal interaction, architectures for interactive systems have to be specialized by adapting the control component to incorporate support for modes of interaction.

Views need to be added or reconsidered: the structure view has to account not only for domain objects, but also for media objects of static and temporal media types. Multimedia-specific application frameworks and patterns may be deployed. A presentation view, i.e., the design of the user interface with respect to spatial (and temporal) relations of its constituents becomes fundamental — more than in traditional interactive systems. Although space and time are mainly perceivable at the user interface, other system entities, such as media or domain entities, are subject to spatial and temporal relations (or constraints), too. In fact, the most important new aspect of multimedia systems is that of space and time, i.e., whether parts of the system have a temporal expansion relative to some time axis or a spatial within some two or three-dimensional coordinate space. Thus, a temporal and a spatial view or an integrated spatio-temporal view are mandatory. Temporal behavior must also account for real-time features and synchronization. Behavior can be predefined (algorithmic) or interactive, i.e., non-deterministic at specification time, because the system has to react to (run-time) events that are unpredictable in time. Multimedia-specific events, e.g. regarding the processing of temporal media data or specific media system services, need to be incorporated.

As has been stated above, the dimensions for architecture and views on the system are interrelated with each other. The relations between different views are partly influenced by architectural structures of the system and, vice versa, views on particular application aspects influence the architectural separation of concerns. For example, the interactive behavior view has to account for degree and modes of interaction (encapsulated in user interface components). Due to multimodal inputs resulting in the same applications events, the coupling of interactive control behavior and system function needs to be revised. The coupling of these views can, for example, be accomplished by the architectural separation of physical user actions in user interface components — wrapping input devices — from application behavior in process components, mediated by different levels of technical and logical events exchanged and handled by the respective architectural components.

In case of hypermedia systems, navigation views can be understood as a further refinement of both the structure and the function views. Other characteristics that can be represented by dedicated views are security, media presentation adaption, quality of service (QoS), or presentation environment (compare [55]).

Since the primary focus of this contribution is not on the multimedia software process dimension, but on the multi-dimensional modeling of multimedia applications, the dimensions of the system perspective, i.e., architecture and views, are mainly relevant in the following. What remains as a requirement for a modeling language from the process dimension is the necessity to support models with different levels of abstraction. From the aforementioned views, the following can be identified as being fundamental (see [50] for a discussion):

- media and application *structure*,
- spatio-temporal *presentation*,
- *temporal behavior* (function),
- interactive *control*.

Together with the architecture dimension, these views will be used in the remainder to characterize the different presented approaches.

3. State of the Art in Multimedia Software Development

Researchers and practitioners agree that multimedia systems pose new requirements on software engineering (see e.g. [12] or [45] for an overview of topics).

Research and development projects in the multimedia field have been mainly focused on either multimedia enabling system technologies and services, e.g. networking or multimedia database systems, or the use of of scripting-based authoring systems as well as XML-based or object-oriented programming technologies for the implementation of multimedia applications. Multimedia software engineering in the sense of specialized multimedia software development process models and usable multimedia specification languages and methods has only drawn minor attention.

In recent time, three different kinds of approaching multimedia software programming have become dominant.

- Most multimedia applications and documents are nowadays developed using multimedia authoring systems. Multimedia authoring systems are visual, interactive programming tools for the development of multimedia applications that can be used by developers with different degrees of expertise.
- With the advent of more complex multimedia software that needs to be integrated with other sophisticated application features, frameworks and application programming interfaces complementing standard object-oriented programming languages or system software were introduced.
- With the growing importance of web-based multimedia applications that are portable between multiple platforms, XML-based approaches to multimedia document authoring like the Synchronized Multimedia Integration Language (SMIL [62]; see [32]) — uptaking the SGML-based HyTime approach — are being implemented aside from proprietary web-enabled formats like Flash (by Macromedia) or Apple's Quicktime.

Since the focus of this chapter is on object-oriented modeling of multimedia applications, we refer to these implementation technologies only in their relations to object-orientation and/or modeling in the following. In particular, authoring systems are discussed in the perspective of integration with modeling, and object-oriented frameworks are presented that show fundamental concepts based on which object-oriented modeling can be easier understood. Nevertheless, we stress that implementation of object-oriented models of multimedia applications can be done with any implementation technology, regardless of its degree of object-orientation. The architecture and views of object-oriented models can, for example, be easily mapped to the main concepts of most authoring systems. Technology-specific decisions would only influence the modeling on the level of detailed architecture and design.

3.1. *Multimedia authoring systems and modeling*

Authoring systems are (partly) visual programming environments that support *ad hoc* implementation and rapid prototyping of multimedia applications based on direct-manipulative graphical user interfaces and intuitive media production and processing metaphors. They are in general supplemented by a scripting language containing simple language constructs to program extended functionality by hand. Pre-existing media and user interface objects are coupled with built-in mechanisms for dynamic execution, e.g. event handling. Extensibility of this functionality is rather limited.

Architecturally, authoring systems integrate four main functional components: media object tools, composition and structure tools, interpreters, and generators. Multimedia authoring systems can be classified according to the media metaphors they deploy as their main abstractions for design and content provision:

- *Screen or card-based* authoring systems, e.g. HyperCard [2] or ToolBook [13], place media objects on cards, slides, or pages, and navigational interaction allows users to switch between these cards.
- In *icon or flowchart-based* systems like Authorware [42], media objects have iconic representations that are used as nodes in a navigational flow graph.
- Macromedia Director [43] is an example for a *timeline-based* authoring system where media objects are positioned along a time axis and navigational interactions lead to jumps on this axis.

Regarding behavior, both card- and timeline-based categories rely in general on scripting-based event handlers that are associated with user interface elements, while dialogues in flowchart-based system can be graphically specified.

Authoring systems are object-based rather than object-oriented, i.e., developers work with objects and component instances instead of classes and component types. Reuse in the form of composition of existing artifacts is possible only on the level of instances and scripts specifying object behavior. Inheritance is, if at all supported, restricted to the instance level.

Other disadvantages of most authoring systems are scripting languages built from primitive programming constructs; weak support for structuring, modularization, and reuse, especially in timeline-based systems; unsufficient support for team development; lack of user-defined types; limited documentation generation; and limited semantic foundation for analysis, test design, and maintenance. A striking disadvantage of most authoring systems is that they do not offer open and standardized interfaces for individual extensions or adaptions. Furthermore, the authored applications generally are not platform-independent because they use proprietary formats and languages.

The wide use of authoring systems and the lack of sophisticated and practically approved multimedia software process technology are responsible for a multimedia development practice that is *de facto* truncated to implementation and testing phases. This leads to problems well-known in traditional software engineering like missing conceptualization and documentation. Although the multimedia software engineering process is not the topic of this chapter, we will shortly reference two approaches for an integration of UML-based modeling and tool-supported authoring. We hereby intend to show how the current practice of development can be maintained and extended by modeling activities.

Boles *et al.* deploy UML for modeling and Director [43] for implementing a virtual genetics lab (see [10]). They use class, sequence, and statechart diagrams of UML to specify the application structure and behavior, i.e., possible user interactions as well as internal course of control, of simulated lab experiments. The Model-View-Controller (MVC [39]) paradigm is used as a pattern for implementation, it is not explicitly represented in the model. To transform the model to an executable application, they propose a translation approach into Lingo, the scripting language of Director, bypassing the visual programming capabilities of the authoring system. Events that trigger transistions in statechart diagrams are implemented as methods of the corresponding classes. Afterwards, view and controller classes for the direct-manipulative user interface are added. In this case, modeling is restricted to the application internals, user interface aspects are instantly coded.

To overcome the limitations regarding software engineering principles, we have proposed a process model for improving the development of multimedia applications from a software engineering perspective in [17]. It combines object-oriented modeling in analysis and design phases with an implementation based on a commercial authoring system, exemplified with Director [43]. The main idea is to transform a framework-based analysis model of the application, that is independent of the technology used for implementation, into a program. Key feature of this transformation is a conceptual programming model of the authoring system that bridges the gap between analysis model and implementation. This authoring system model is used during design to map an object model instantiating the analysis-level class model to an object model instantiating the authoring system model. The resulting design-level instance model can then be implemented in a straightforward manner. This approach has so far only covered the structural aspects of the multimedia application. It has not yet integrated a behavioral or dynamic view.

Depending on their main metaphors, authoring systems more or less explicitly support the different views on an application identified in Sec. 2. While the presentation view is generally well supported, complex application structures and behavior require sophisticated programming. The underlying architecture is transparent to the developer. Since authoring systems are visual programming environments, different levels of abstraction are not supported. From the above discussion we conclude that both multimedia authoring and object-oriented modeling can benefit from each other when they are used as complementary techniques within a multimedia software development process. Which role object-orientation plays in the current practice of multimedia software development will be presented in the next sections.

3.2. *Object-orientation in the development of multimedia applications*

The important role of object-orientation for multimedia has been stated by many research contributions proposing object-oriented models as a conceptual basis for multimedia. Also, standardization efforts in the multimedia domain have discovered the advantages of object models. The family of MHEG standards [36] for the specification of interoperable interactive multimedia documents (see [19] for an overview of MHEG-5 and its complementary parts) is based on an object-oriented model with abstractions for applications and scenes as well as links, streams, and other basic elements (so-called ingredients). Its focus is on coding and exchange of hypermedia documents. PREMO (Presentation Environment for Multimedia Objects [34]) is directed towards a standardization of the presentation aspects of multimedia applications. It incorporates temporal and event-based synchronization objects (see e.g. [29, 30, 28]). Its object model originates from the OMG object model for distributed objects. PREMO contains an abstract component for modeling, presentation, and interaction that combines media control with aspects of modeling and geometry. For the definition of the MPEG-4 [35] standard, objects have been discovered as a potential source for compression of video data instead of data reduction based on image properties.

But object-orientation is also promoted by the existence of object-oriented class libraries, toolkits, and frameworks that support the programming of multimedia applications. In the following, we summarize some characteristics of the latter since some of these approaches are accompanied by graphic authoring systems that enable visual programming based on an object-oriented conceptual model.

3.3. *Object-oriented multimedia frameworks*

Besides authoring systems, several object-oriented toolkits and frameworks have been proposed to support a programming-based development of multimedia applications. They reify architectural structures and fundamental abstractions of multimedia systems based either on extensions to object-oriented programming languages or on conceptual object-oriented languages that abstract from concrete programming environments. An important characteristic feature of object-oriented multimedia frameworks is their open and extensible architecture. It supports portability and adaptability, e.g. in the advent of new media types that can be integrated. Some developments in this field are, beyond others, the Media Editor Toolkit

(MET++ [1]), MultiMedia Extensions (MME [18]), the Berkeley Continuous Media Toolkit (CMT [54]), and Nsync [4]. A recent development is the Java Media API [57] consisting of several components such as the Java 2D and 3D APIs or the Java Media Framework (JMF [58]; see e.g. [25]) for continuous media. Microsoft's DirectX [44] is a multimedia extension on the operating system level.

The main objective of object-oriented multimedia frameworks is to supply a multimedia developer with a software abstraction for multimedia programming. The framework should comply with the fundamental object types and operations that appear in multimedia applications. Conceptually, a framework consists of interrelated abstract classes that have to be implemented by concrete classes for different multimedia platforms. Therefore, one can distinguish at least two layers within such a framework. On the higher level, the abstract framework classes build an application programming interface that can be used by a multimedia developer independently of the target platform when implementing a multimedia application. On the lower level, concrete classes realize a platform-dependent implementation of the abstract concepts on the higher level. To achieve such an implementation, the framework classes make use of a system programming interface. The framework classes are organized in a generalization hierarchy where the abstract superclasses specify interfaces that are realized by their specialized, concrete subclasses.

Requirements for a multimedia framework are openess, robustness, ability to be queried, scalability, support for architectural structuring, availability of general, high-level concepts and interfaces for spatio-temporal media composition and synchronization, hardware control, database integration, and concurrency.

We shortly refer to some representative frameworks in the following.

Framework by Gibbs and Tsichritzis. A prototypical object-oriented multimedia framework has been presented by Gibbs and Tsichritzis [24]. It specifies an abstract application programming interface (API) that serves as a homogeneous interface to heterogeneous platforms. It combines two fundamental concepts, a media hierarchy that encapsulates media values and a hierarchy of components. Transform and format class hierarchies are used as supporting concepts.

IMD. Another prominent approach that has been widely recognized is the modeling method for interactive multimedia documents (IMD) by Vazirgiannis [59]. It integrates the temporal and the spatial domain of multimedia documents in a common event-based framework. It comprises an object-oriented event model where elementary events of different, hierarchically specialized event types are combined by algebraic and spatio-temporal operators. Events are conceived as representatives of actions that generate these events, e.g. start or end of an action, parameterized by their subject (triggering object) and object (reactive object) and a spatio-temporal signature. Composite objects are combined from basic media objects by temporal and spatial operators. Based on these concepts, an authoring system is provided that allows developers to specify scenarios as a set of autonomous functions, so-called scenario tuples, to which start and end events, action lists and synchronization events, raised at the begin or end of the tuple, can be assigned.

MET++. MET++ [1] is an application framework in that multimedia presentations are modeled as hierarchical compositions of temporal objects. The modeled compositions are automatically transformed in temporal layout mechanisms and propagated. Real-time behavior and user interaction are integrated in the controller part of an extended MVC model. The MET++ class hierarchy includes compositional time-layout objects providing synchronization behavior for temporal relations and time-dependent media objects. Dynamic behavior of temporal media objects is specified by time-related functions that are themselves specializations of complex temporal objects.

Java Media API. The Java Media API [57] contains classes for the integration of animation, imaging, two and three-dimensional graphics, speech, and telephony. The Java Media Framework (JMF [58]), which is part of the Java Media API, offers an interface for accessing and controlling continuous media objects. It does not come with a general time concept that would enable the integrated synchronization of temporal and static media, only synchronization of the former is supported. Furthermore, no sophisticated mechanism for temporal composition is built in.

The presented frameworks and their inherent structring can be used as sources for the architectural structuring of multimedia systems and applications, and partly for modeling language design. Additionally, their implementations are promising technologies for the implementation of object-oriented models of multimedia applications, especially for complex applications. But all the different views on multimedia applications must be mapped to basic object-oriented programming principles such as objects, messages, and events. Only in cases where the frameworks are themselves accompanied by graphical development (authoring) tools, like MET++, different views are explicitly supported on a higher (visual) level of abstraction.

We now step from object-oriented implementation technologies to modeling techniques. We first direct our attention to object-oriented modeling approaches for hypermedia and interactive systems that can contribute to a holistic multimedia modeling, before we return to the object-oriented modeling of multimedia applications in Sec. 4.

3.4. *Hypermedia modeling*

Hypermedia software development has been addressed by different modeling approaches. Because these models focus mainly on *hyperlinked* media, emphasis is put on the design of navigational structures. Conceptual models of the hypermedia application are accompanied by some form of navigation model and sometimes by an abstract user interface model. Other aspects of multimedia, especially temporal behavior of continuous media and synchronization, are underrepresented.

The Object-Oriented Hypermedia Design Model (OOHDM [51]) starts modeling with a conceptual model of the semantics for the application domain that is complemented by a navigational model in a second step. This part of the model is based on an extended Entity-Relationship model. As a third activity, abstract user interface design completes the model. The browsing semantics of OOHDM is based on the static navigation structure specified in the navigational model. OOHDM is an object-oriented extension of HDM [23] and comprises the same basic modeling activities.

The Relationship Management Methodology (RMM [33]) is a method for design and implementation of hypermedia systems. In contrast to OOHDM, navigational structures are modeled within the domain model. Furthermore, RMM enables the generation of HTML documents or code for authoring systems from the model.

HyDev [48] is another proposal for decomposing hypermedia application models in different partial models. The domain model is accompanied by an instance model whose objects are instances of the domain model. The instance model is regarded important since the behavior of multimedia applications often relies on the characteristics of individual objects, and thus multimedia software development has to deal with both type and instance level views. Relevant features of object presentation and navigation between objects are captured in a so-called representation model that abstracts from media formats and concrete media objects.

HyperProp [55] comprises a conceptual model that represents authoring requirements by spatio-temporal constraints, and a formatting algorithm for run-time presentation adaption in reaction to occurrences of specified events. HyperProp is based on a logical document model for the composition of hypermedia artifacts. Architecturally, it distinguishes three layers for representation objects, data objects, and storage objects, respectively. The authoring system prototype contains a graphical editor for constraint specification.

From the perspective of modeling multimedia applications by extensions of the Unified Modeling Language, the work by Baumeister, Hennicker, Koch, and Mandel is of particular interest. In [5], they propose extensions of the UML to specify hypermedia based on the concepts of OOHDM. In [27], these extensions are used for a further underpinning of the process associated with their language extensions. There, they give a set of guidelines how to (semi-) automatically derive information for a model view from previous models. They start with a conceptual model of the application domain from which they derive a navigation space model for the hypermedia application based on views on conceptual classes and additional navigation associations. From the navigation space model, they build a navigational structure model by incorporating navigational elements such as index, guided tour, query, and menu. Finally, they use the navigational structure model to construct an abstract presentation model focussing on the structural organization of the presentation rather than on the physical presentation on the user interface. The disadvantage of this approach is that interaction is restricted to the navigation via predefined links within the application.

In summary, the main shortcoming of hypermedia approaches is their limited capability of modeling behavior that is in most cases restricted to hyperlink navigation. Other forms of user-initiated control and temporal behavior are only partly considered. Additionally, application structure is often restricted to trees with hyperlinked nodes. Because multimedia applications are highly user-interactive, we look at user interface modeling next.

3.5. *User interface modeling based on UML*

In the UML field, there have also been some research contributions on how to extend the general purpose modeling language UML towards a better representation of user interface modeling dimensions. These are important for multimedia modeling since we have identified the multimedia user interface presentation and interaction as key views of multimedia systems in Sec. 2. Human-computer interaction has to deal with representations of user roles; of user behavior when performing tasks; of abstract conceptual and concrete physical user interfaces. To capture user roles and user requirements, use case diagrams of UML can be deployed. This approach is described in detail by Constantine and Lockwood [15]. In [60], so-called user interaction diagrams (UID) are introduced to detail use cases for requirements specification. For the modeling of behavior from the user's perspective, Kovacevic [38] proposes a UML extension for task analysis.

From a software analysis and design perspective, the UML profile for interaction design suggested by Nunes and Cunha [46] is of importance. Here, analysis and design models for the specification of user interfaces are presented. The analysis classes from the UML built-in profile for software development processes [47] are further refined to architecturally distinguish between interfaces to external systems and for user interaction. On the design level, a dialogue model for structuring dialogues and a presentation model for capturing navigation between different interaction spaces (contexts) are introduced.

The problem with all these models is that they are either on a high level of abstraction such as use cases or other requirement gathering approaches or they mostly focus on the architectural dimension or structural rather than behavioral aspects (views). An exception is the UML-based approach described in [53] that addresses dynamics of abstract user interfaces. Extended UML activity diagrams are employed to detail the interaction for realizing a use case. But since activity diagrams are still rather high-level behavior descriptions, they are not well-suited to describe detailed behavior of a concrete user interface.

None of the presented approaches of user interface modeling based on UML accounts for specific characteristics of multimedia applications and their implications on user interface modeling or the integration of multimedia applications with the proposed user interface models. Multimedia-specific architectures or system views beyond interaction are hardly supported. In the following section, we show how the OMMMA approach attempts to integratedly specifiy the different aspect of multimedia applications that have been identified in Sec. 2.

4. OMMMA — Object-oriented Modeling of Multimedia Applications

In this section, we introduce the modeling language OMMMA-L [50]. We show how this language extends the standard object-oriented modeling language UML appropriately and allows all aspects of a multimedia application to be modeled in an integral and coherent form.

4.1. *UML and its extensibility towards multimedia*

The Unified Modeling Language (UML [47], see [11, 49] for an introduction, [21] for an overview) consists of a family of diagrammatic languages which are tailored to modeling diverse aspects of a system. Those are grouped into four categories: use case diagrams, structural diagrams, behavioral diagrams, and implementation diagrams. While use case diagrams are intended for capturing functional requirements of a system, implementation diagrams are used to describe physical system structures and runtime entities. Structural aspects are modeled in class and object diagrams. Behavioral aspects can be described using sequence, collaboration, statechart, and activity diagrams. For the modeling of multimedia applications, we have to analyze how well these diagram types are suited for modeling the architecture of multimedia applications and the four fundamental system views identified in Sec. 2: media and application structure, spatio-temporal presentation, temporal behavior (function), and interactive control.

Use case diagrams and implementation diagrams can be used to model requirements and architectural structure and components, respectively. In the following, we will focus on the fundamental system views within analysis and design models. Thus we only discuss the structural and behavioral diagrams regarding their appropriateness. As it turns out, the structure of an application can be adequately modeled in UML class (and object) diagrams, interactive control can be modeled in statechart diagrams, accompanied by a tailored dialogue signal hierarchy in class diagrams (although some specific abstractions for dialogue and user interaction specification as they are discussed is Sec. 3.5 may be desirable), and parts of (predefined) temporal behavior can be adequately modeled with UML sequence diagrams. But the analysis of UML's features reveals that specialized and more advanced language constructs are needed to describe the temporal assembling of different objects. Additionally, UML does not offer an explicit notation for spatial modeling in order to specify e.g. the presentation view of user interface layouts intuitively. Finally, UML lacks appropriate pragmatic guidelines on how to deploy the different diagram types cooperatively to model complex multimedia applications. Such guidelines relate to both which diagram types to use for a particular view on the system and how to deploy a particular diagram on a specific level of abstraction, and how the different views and levels of abstraction relate to each other. (Note that we concentrate on a single level of abstraction herein.) These shortcomings have led to the development of an extension of UML towards multimedia entitled OMMMA-L (**O**bject-oriented **M**odeling of **M**ulti**M**edia **A**pplications — the **L**anguage) that captures the application characteristics represented in the different views and to deriving pragmatics on how to model multimedia applications with an object-oriented language based on UML.

The extensions of OMMMA-L can be integrated with UML by deploying UML's built-in extension mechanisms allowing existing model elements to be specialized by stereotypes, constraints, and tagged values (see [47]). These light-weight extensions do not influence the syntax and semantics of the UML itself, but semantics can be specialized for domain-specific extensions. The extensions can then be used to build profiles for specific application domains or kinds of applications.

OMMMA-L is presented in the next subsections, starting by introducing an example application to be modeled.

4.2. *OMMMA-L modeling example: Automotive information system*

The UML-based modeling language OMMMA-L has been designed to model a wide range of aspects of interactive multimedia applications. We illustrate its capabilities by showing extracts from a model of a simulation application of an automotive information system.

Car cockpits nowadays evolve towards being highly-integrated multimedia information interfaces that interact with many embedded components as well as with external and distributed information systems and services. Diverse applications have to be integrated, like car audio, navigation and communication systems, travel or tourist information, and automotive system monitoring and control.

Regarding interactivity with a human user, several levels of abstraction can be distinguished: on a low level of interaction, a user has to interact with hardware input and output devices (presentation media) that are visual, haptic, or voice-enabled. Input devices produce signals that need to be transformed to semantic events on application level. For example, clicking the right mouse button on a specific point on the screen has a specific semantics for the application when it is in a particular state. Pressing a specific button in a multi-functional automotive control panel also shows a context-dependent behavior.

We return to the appropriate aspects of this application in the following subsections in order to illustrate the language concepts of OMMMA-L. The four fundamental views identified in Sec. 2 each relate to a particular diagram type in the OMMMA approach:

- media and application structure are modeled in the class diagram;

- the spatial aspect of the presentation is modeled in OMMMA-L presentation diagrams (that are related to OMMMA-L sequence diagrams for the spatio-temporal integration);
- temporal behavior (function) is modeled in OMMMA-L sequence diagrams; and
- interactive control is modeled in statechart diagrams.

Architectural considerations also appear on these diagrams, although they are not explicity modeled within these OMMMA-L diagram types. The individual diagrams are presented in the succeeding sections, before we explain the integration of these diagrams in Sec. 4.7.

4.3. *Class diagram*

Class diagrams are the core of an object-oriented application model and are used to model the static structure of the multimedia application. Essentially, they consist of class and association definitions which describe the structure of objects and their possible structural interrelations. As UML's language features for defining a class diagram are expressive enough, they have been incorporated unchanged into OMMMA-L. But in order to express the two structural model aspects of application semantics and media types, each OMMMA-L class diagram consists of (at least) two closely interrelated parts:

- an *hierarchy of media type definitions*, which comprises classes for all (representation) media types; and
- the logical model of an application, which comprises classes and associations to describe application domain objects and their interrelations.

The two aspects are linked by associations which interrelate application objects with corresponding media objects. For the specification of interaction, these class hierarchies must be accompanied by a *signal hierarchy* as a basis for event-based interaction. *Presentation classes* may be deployed (possibly in a different package) in addition to model the possible composition of user interfaces as a basis for the presentation diagrams introduced in Sec. 4.5. Figure 2 shows a part of the class diagram for the sample application of a simulated automotive information system shown in Fig. 1. The lower part of the diagram depicts the media type hierarchy and the upper part the structure of the logical model. It shows that the automotive information system simulation is a complex composition of five subsystems: an automotive status system and systems for navigation, communication, information services, and entertainment. The status and navigation systems are more detailed. The status system comprises a speedometer, a mileage counter, a revolution counter, and a set of status monitors. The navigation system contains multiple maps that can be associated with an unrestricted number of routes. In turn, routes can be related to multiple maps. For each route, there is a start and a destination location. A route relates to a set of directions that are qualified from the perspective of a route by

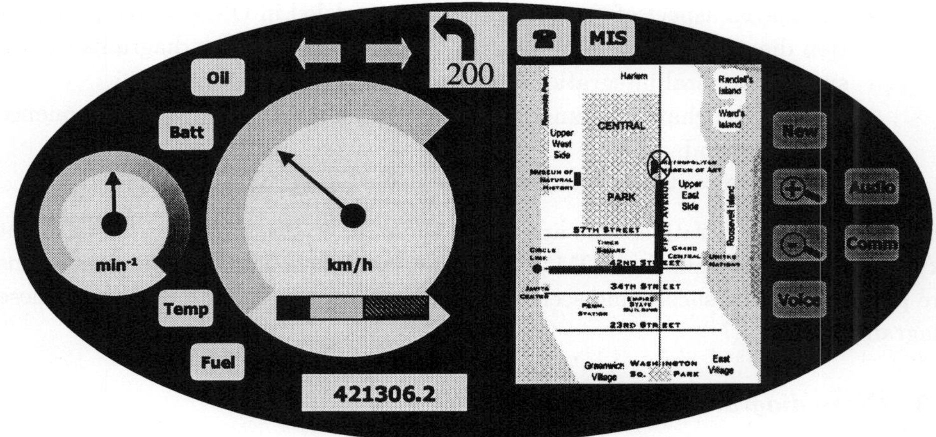

Fig. 1. Display of an automotive information system.

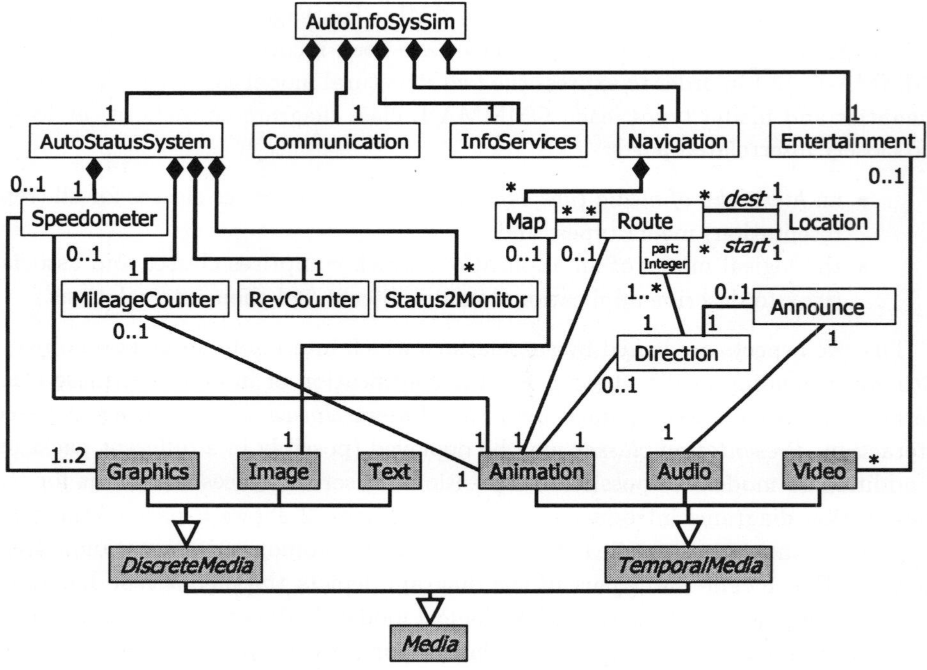

Fig. 2. OMMMA-L class diagram.

a part number defining their position in the sequence of directions. Additionally, a direction may be accompanied by a spoken announcement of the way to drive. For some of these application classes, the associations to elements of the media class hierarchy are shown. The speedometer, for instance, is related to one or two graphics and an animation, e.g. to enable a day and night design of the background and a moving indicator for presentation of the actual speed. Also, routes shown on the map (which is related to an image) and the directions are realized as animations. An announcement is related to an audio object whereas the (simplified) entertainment system relates to multiple video objects.

OMMMA explicitly distinguishes between application objects as regards content and media objects to allow an application to present one application entity by different (representation) media, e.g. accounting for distinct presentation media, such as screens, or resource availability. Thus, media objects are not specializations of application objects or vice versa. The dimension of media types is based on a generalization hierarchy of static and temporal media types as it can be found in several multimedia standards, e.g. MHEG [36], and frameworks, e.g. the framework by Gibbs and Tsichritzis [24] or MET++ [1].

4.4. *Extended sequence diagram*

UML offers various diagram types to model behavioral aspects of an application. Due to their emphasis on modeling temporal sequences (of messages), sequence diagrams are deployed in OMMMA-L to model the (predefined) *temporal behavior* of a multimedia application. But, in order to be able to model specific characteristics of a multimedia application more directly and thus more intuitively, standard UML sequence diagrams are extended by a series of features, especially regarding timing and time constraints. These are for example:

- *Refinement of the time dimension* by defining local time axes for objects supporting a notion of local time. Local time can be related to global (real) time (represented by the actor's timeline) to specify *intra-object* synchronization or to the time of other objects to specify *inter-object* synchronization. Durations and points in time can be specified by different forms of fixed, bounded or unbounded time intervals restricting their possible temporal positions. Time intervals are represented by their start and end points. (Syntactically, these timing requirements can be written as constraints using (in-)equalities or in an interval notation.)
- *Sychronization bars* (bold lines) instead of message arrows between object activations to specify the continuous inter-object synchronization between temporal media presentations that may abstract from a message direction.
- *Activation and deactivation delays* of media objects in order to model tolerated variations of synchronization relations for media objects (compare maximum start and end times in [31]).
- A notion of shallow and deep *History* on a sequence diagram that UML only provides for statechart diagrams. It allows the designer to specify whether a specified scenario can be interrupted and later returned to at the same point of virtual time where it had been interrupted. Deep history (H*) denotes that this temporal reconstruction is possible even on nested

invocation levels with the semantics of pause and resume for the possibly complex presentation, whilst shallow history (H) restricts returning to the situation on the top level with the semantics that the sequence diagram can be restarted from the interruption time, but already started presentations of objects cannot be cued to their last presentation state.

- *Parallely composed activation* of media objects in order to model the simultaneous presentation of an application object across different presentation channels (or media) and/or by different media objects.
- *Sequentially composed activations* resulting in an *automatic triggering* of subsequent activations (segments), e.g. to present an animated object that is sequentially presented via different channels and/or by different media objects.
- Activations of application objects can be annotated with presentation objects, either abstractions from hardware devices (presentation media) or software user interface objects — depending on the level of use — such as audio channels or graphical objects on a screen, and/or media objects designated to represent an application object during an activation or activation segment. Associated media objects, that must conform to the types specified in the class diagram, are enclosed in ⟨⟩. The identifiers of presentation objects appear as pure strings (as they are used on presentation diagrams, cf. Sec. 4.5).
- Activations of objects may be overlayed by *media filters*, which describe time functions, e.g. the incremental increase of an audio level over time.

Each OMMMA-L sequence diagram models the temporal behavior of a predefined *scenario* of the multimedia application. The scenario specified by the sequence diagram is represented by the (initial) message sent from an actor symbol (or some user interface component) to an object within the sequence diagram that acts as the scenario controller. The message can be parameterized, e.g. by time stamps for start and end of execution of a sequence diagram, in order to support its re-use, or by parameters that may be used in guard expressions or nested message calls.

All objects in one diagram relate to the same (global) timeline to which they can be synchronized if required. The projection of a single continuous media object on the corresponding (global) timeline specifies intra-object synchronization. Concurrent scenarios with an independent timeline need to be modeled by different sequence diagrams related to parallel substates within an *and*-superstate of the corresponding statechart diagram (see Sec. 4.6), i.e., they do not have a common notion of time. Different message types between objects enable specification of synchronous or asynchronous messaging. A propagation mechanism has to ensure consistency of temporal specifications or the mapping of a local time axis to its relative temporal coordinate system.

Figure 3 gives an example of an OMMMA-L sequence diagram. It describes the execution of showRoute(Location A, Location B) which is an operation of the

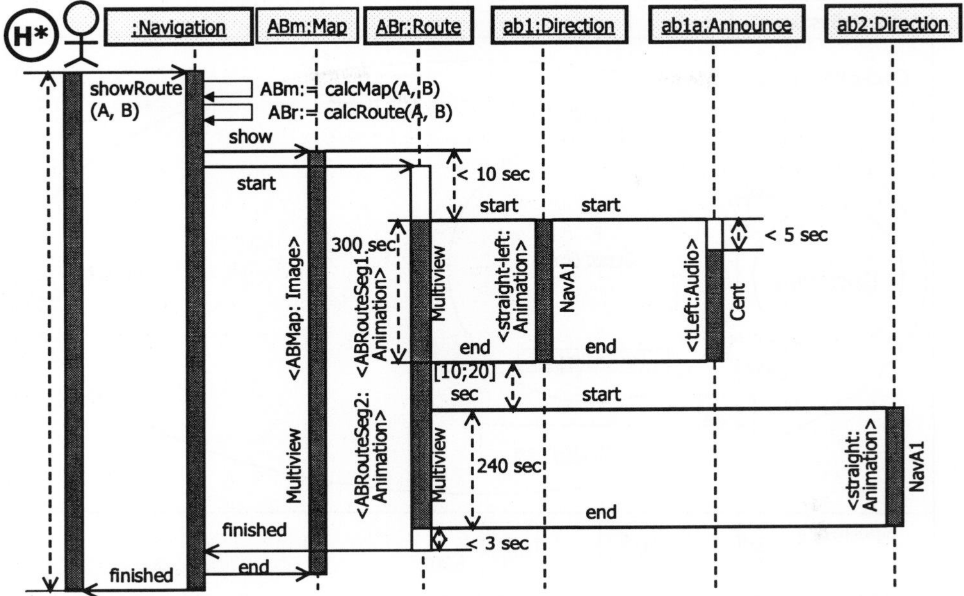

Fig. 3. OMMMA-L sequence diagram.

navigation system. All objects shown in the horizontal object dimension are semantic, i.e., application objects. Based on the parameters for start and destination (A respectively B), the Navigation object determines a route object ABr and a map object ABm that is then called to be shown. After a maximum activation delay of ten seconds relative to the start of the presentation of the map, an animation of the route from location A to B has to be presented. This animation consists of two parts of which the first one is associated with the media object ABRouteSeg1:Animation that is shown for 300 seconds and the second one is associated with the media object ABRouteSeg2:Animation that is shown for 250 up to 260 seconds. (These presentation time intervals do not necessarily coincide with the duration of the animation objects themselves.) Both animations are presented via a screen object referenced as Multiview (see Fig. 5). Parallel to the first part of the route animation, direction ab1:Direction is presented at NavA1. It is accompanied by a spoken annoucement that must be started at most five seconds after the invocation by the direction object ab1, and whose end is synchronized with the ends of both the first part of the route animation and the corresponding direction ab1. The annoucement is to be output via a center speaker denoted by Cent as specified in Fig. 4. The synchronization bars at the start and the end of these activations specify that a continuous inter-object synchronization is intended and has to be ensured by the renderer at presentation time. The end of the first part of the route animation directly triggers the execution of the second part. After a delay that is between 10 and 20 seconds, another direction animation ab2 is started. It (synchronously) co-ends

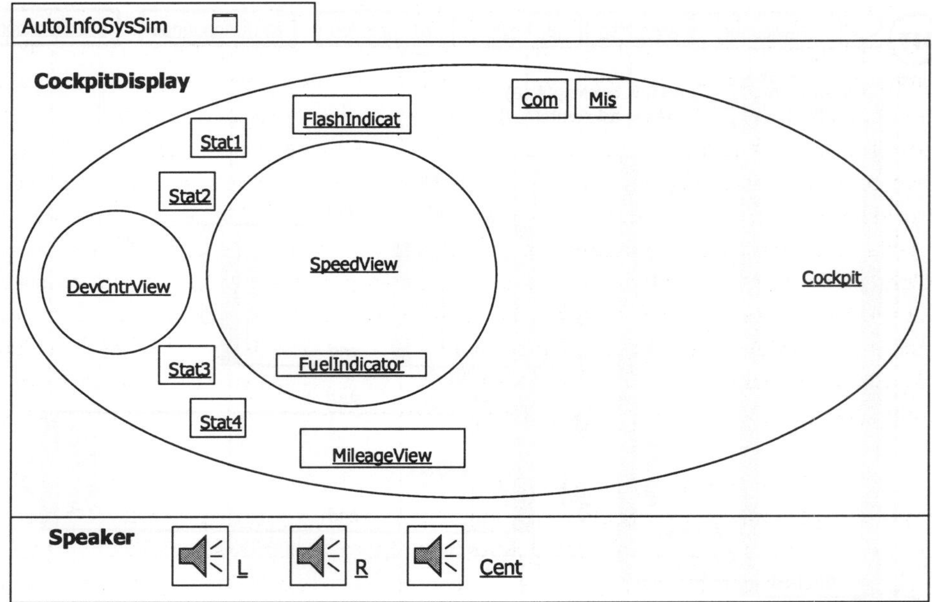

Fig. 4. Application-level OMMMA-L presentation diagram.

with the presentation end of the second part of the route animation. After finishing its presentation, the route object has to signal to the navigation component within 3 seconds that presentation is finished.

For the specification of activation and deactivation delays, we use the UML presentation option to distinguish periods of actual computing by shading the activation segments from periods where objects are activated, but do not own the focus of control of the associated thread, by plain activation segments [47].

4.5. *Presentation diagram*

Class diagrams are used to model the media and application structure view in OMMMA-L, OMMMA-L sequence diagrams model the temporal behavior (function) view. Before we continue with interactive control in the next subsection, we first explain how the spatial structure of the presentation (view) is modeled in OMMMA-L.

Due to the fact that UML does not offer a diagram type which is well-suited and appropriate for modeling this view, the new *presentation diagram* type is added to OMMMA-L. Presentation diagrams support an intuitive description of the layout, i.e., the spatial arrangement of *presentation objects* at the user interface. Spatial relationships (and constraints) can thus be graphically depicted. In addition, by incorporating the user interface design into the modeling language, consistency relations to other diagram types can be formulated and checked.

The presentation diagrams of OMMMA-L follow the idea of structuring the presentation area of the user interface by bounding boxes for presentation objects (more precisely, these can be roles as in UML collaboration diagrams that can be substituted by conforming objects) that are to be presented. Bounding boxes show geometry and size characteristics and are positioned on a virtual area relative to some specified coordinate system. Presentation objects are distinguished into visualization objects and interaction objects. *Visualization objects* are passive objects that are used to present e.g. text, pictures, video, or animation objects. *Interaction objects* enable user interactions and may raise events in the running system. Examples are scroll or menu bars, buttons, input fields or a hypertext containing links. Bounding boxes for interaction objects are indicated by bold borders (like active objects are marked in UML). The visual layout specification is accompanied by an iconic representation of audio channels beside the visual presentation area.

We use the notation of a stereotyped UML package to depict a presentation diagram. The presentation diagram can be further divided into different compartments representing hardware output devices such as different screens or audio channels. In Fig. 4, the presentation diagram is divided in two compartments, one for a dashboard cockpit display and one for the left, right, and center speakers as channels of an audio system (in the same way, local areas for input devices can be described).

Since, in our example, there is no direct interaction with the presentation objects like in direct-manipulative graphical user interfaces, but interaction is via specific input devices such as knobs, all bounding areas are marked as visualization objects (an area for input elements has been omitted).

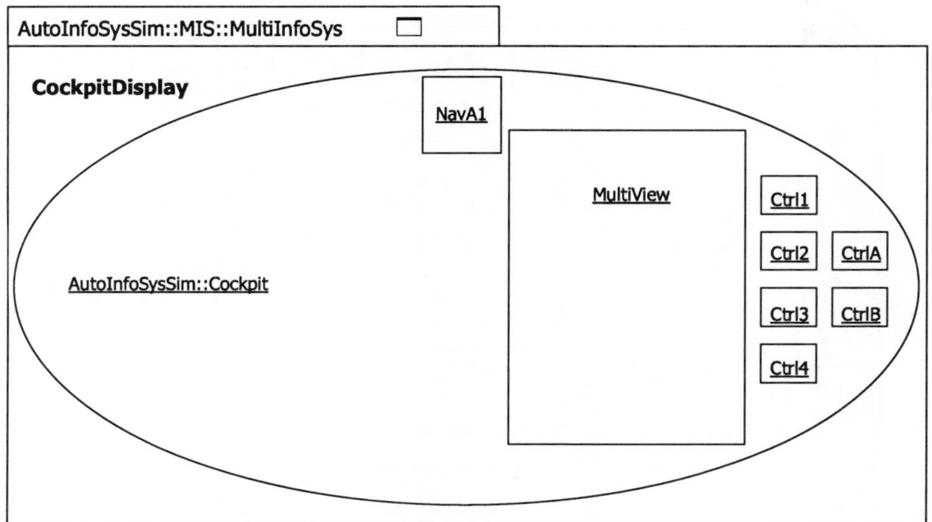

Fig. 5. Lower-level OMMMA-L presentation diagram.

The complete presentation of a certain application unit may be described by several presentation diagrams that may be composed by a layered placement on the virtual area (e.g. Figs. 4 and 5). Positioning of presentation elements is by convention relative to the directly surrounding element unless otherwise specified, e.g. by a separate hierarchical composition of presentation elements. For instance in Fig. 5, MultiView is positioned relative to Cockpit from the presentation diagram AutoInfoSysSim, given by the path expression on the diagram.

Following this description of spatial modeling of the presentation view, now the interactive control view, modeling system reaction to (user) inputs and other events, is shown.

4.6. *Statechart diagram*

In UML, statecharts are assigned to classes to specify the behavior of their instances. They can be used on different levels of granularity. On a high level, they can specify the behavior of an application or substantial parts thereof. On a low level, they can be used to specify the behavior of simple classes, such as user interface element classes, to model e.g. the behavior of a button or the control state of a media object or its associated media player. The high-level statecharts are used to specify the control behavior within the context of the application since it must be specified which event regarding which particular element of the application triggers a transition from a state of the application. Examples of high-level statecharts that are partly schematic for simplification of presentation can be seen in Figs. 6 and 7. They are used on an application-semantic rather than a user interface level.

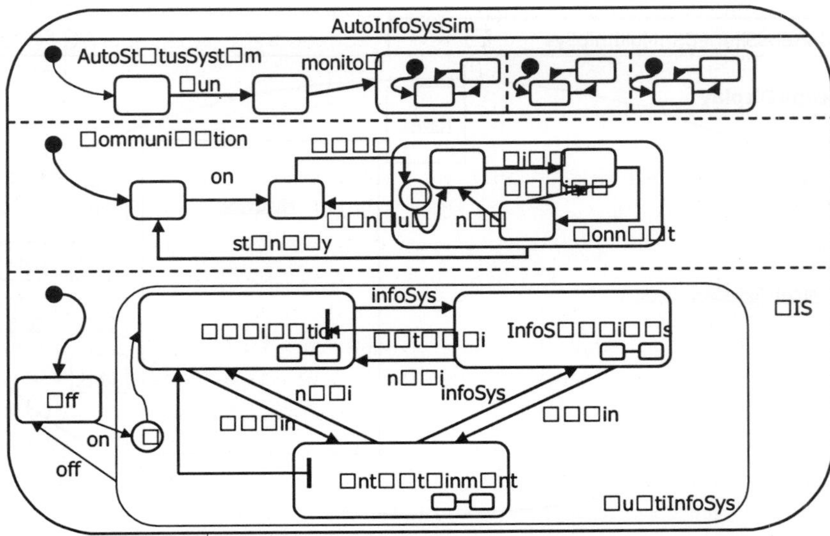

Fig. 6. OMMMA-L statechart diagram for the automotive information system application.

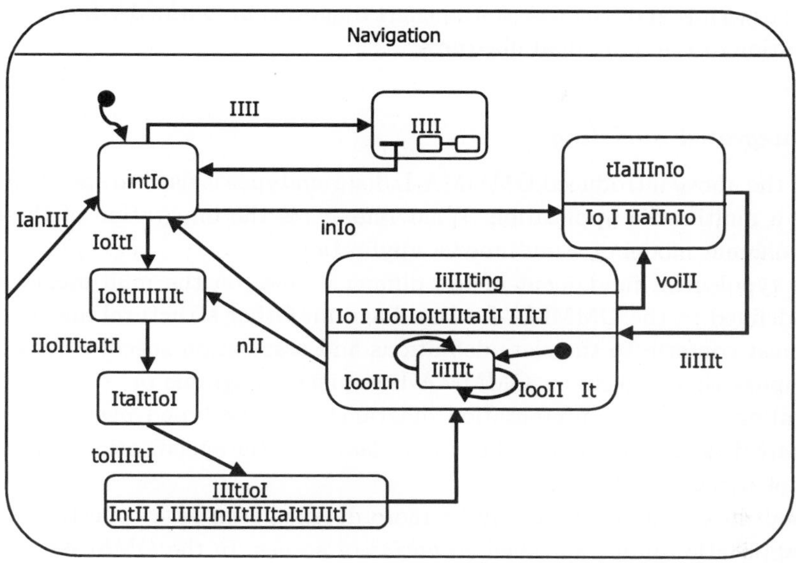

Fig. 7. OMMMA-L statechart diagram for the navigation subsystem.

While OMMMA-L sequence diagrams are used to specify the (predefined) temporal behavior of a multimedia application, statechart diagrams are used to specify the system states as well as state transitions triggered by user interactions or other system events, i.e., the *interactive control* or dynamic behavior. OMMMA-L statechart diagrams are syntactically and semantically equal to UML statechart diagrams. This means that e.g. they may be structured by *and*- and *or*-superstates or refined by embedded statechart diagrams. An action appearing on an OMMMA-L statechart may represent a multimedia scenario (see Sec. 4.4). For example, internal entry- and exit-actions, or do-activities of states may be labeled with names of actions or action expressions.

To enable dialogue specification on an adequate level of abstraction, e.g. the selection of navigational alternatives or the control of media playout, the OMMMA-L application model needs to be accompanied by an appropriate signal hierarchy (see [47], cf. Sec. 4.3). This must be based on a spatio-temporal event model for user interactions on the control interface. It should, in perspective, also account for modal parameters of event instances. Events on statechart diagrams relate to such signals. Signals may be categorized according to user interaction events, application events, system events, and timer events. The event model that can be used within OMMMA-L statecharts is not restricted. It is therefore possible to integrate event algebras as they have been specified in the area of active database management systems, that have also been used as a basis for the spatio-temporal event model in [59]. Events can then be composed by algebraic and temporal operators such as and, or, or seq.

This description of the use of statechart diagrams in OMMMA-L concludes the presentation of the individual diagrams.

4.7. *Integrated modeling*

Each of the above introduced OMMMA-L diagram types is used to specify a certain view of a multimedia application. What remains is the integration of these views into a coherent model of a multimedia application.

The typological fundament of the different views on the multimedia application is defined in the OMMMA-L class diagram. Other structural and behavioral views must conform to the class definitions and association specifications therein. This implies that objects on OMMMA-L sequence diagrams or — if intended — presentation objects on presentation diagrams must be typed over these classes. Statechart diagrams are assigned to these classes for the specification of interactive control or dynamic behavior.

A multimedia application may be more detailed seen as a collection of multimedia application units, so-called *scenarios* or scenes. In the OMMMA approach, each scenario corresponds to a statechart within an high-level statechart diagram which is associated to the class of the overall application or some class encapsulating a substantial part thereof. Furthermore, each scenario is via its associated state related to a presentation, possibly composed of different presentation diagrams.

A state associated to a scenario may be refined by a nested statechart diagram or nested states (as depicted for state directing in Fig. 7) which describe the possible interactive behavior during this scenario. (Thus, scenarios can be hierarchically composed.) For example, state directing is not left when zooming, implying the semantics that the temporal behavior of the scenario related to *showRoute* is not influenced by zoom operations.

In order to couple the interactive control with the predefined functional behavior views of a multimedia application, actions on a statechart diagrams can be associated with OMMMA-L sequence diagrams that specify the scenarios, more precisely, the predefined, timed pieces of functional behavior within a scenario, corresponding to such actions or action expressions. An entry-action or do-activity means that the behavior specified by the sequence diagram is automatically triggered whenever the corresponding state is entered, exit-actions are executed before the state is left. The semantics of the (concurrently executed) do-activity is thereby to be interruptible by events triggering a transition from that particular state, whilst entry-actions and exit-actions are non-interruptible as specified by the UML run-to-completion semantics (see [47]). Figure 7 gives examples for an entry-action in state destpos and for two do-activities in states traffInfo and directing. The latter do-activity is specified by a sequence diagram with a (deep) history indicator denoting that the assigned scenario can be completely resumed after interruption. This construction is semantically feasible since do-activities on statechart diagrams are executed concurrently.

Based on this coupling of function and control views, mutually exclusive substates of an *or*-superstate enable the specification of alternative presentation flows triggered by events on incoming transitions comparable to the timeline-tree model in [31].

A presentation diagram is associated to a state of the interactive control view in order to couple presentation and control views. Therefore, its name coincides with the name of the state to which it is assigned. Semantically, this presentation diagram will be part of the user interface presentation as long as the application or the respective part thereof is in that specific state. In Fig. 4, the presentation diagram is labeled with the name of the top-level state AutoInfoSysSim, meaning that these objects are addressable for presentation as long as the application is running.

The composition of a complete presentation of a certain application unit (or state) is based on the hierarchical composition of states to which the constituent presentation diagrams are assigned. Figure 5 shows a presentation diagram that is assigned to state MultiInfoSys which is a nested substate of AutoInfoSysSim (via state MIS) as can be seen from the path expression in the name compartment in the upper left. When the application is in state AutoInfoSysSim::MIS::MultiInfoSys or a substate thereof, the complete presentation is composed of (at least the given) two presentation diagrams, i.e., the general diagram for all application states and the diagram for the multi-information system being active (compare Fig. 6).

In OMMMA-L sequence diagrams, an activation of an application object can reference a media object that is being presented during this activation as well as a presentation object that may be used on a reachable presentation diagram in order to specify the spatio-temporal constraints of the presentation to the user. Reachable presentation diagrams are defined by the coupling statechart diagram. They either relate to the same state to which the action belongs that is specified by the sequence diagram — either an internal action of that state or an action on a transition within that state in case of a complex state — or to a superstate of that state.

Figure 8 gives a simplified example of the interrelations between diagrams in such a complete specification where small parts of each diagram type are depicted. Diagrams are interrelated by using the same identifier names in different diagrams. Examples are the name of a specified scenario (initial message) in a sequence diagram used as the action expression of an internal action within a state of the state diagram, or the name of a state used as the identifier of a presentation diagram, or the name of a (visual) presentation object or audio channel on a presentation diagram used within a sequence diagram in association to an activation box. Other relations (consistency constraints) between diagrams are depicted by overlayed arrows in Fig. 8. These constraints are precisely specified in a UML profile for multimedia applications that extends standard capabilities of UML for the modeling of multimedia applications according to the OMMMA approach.

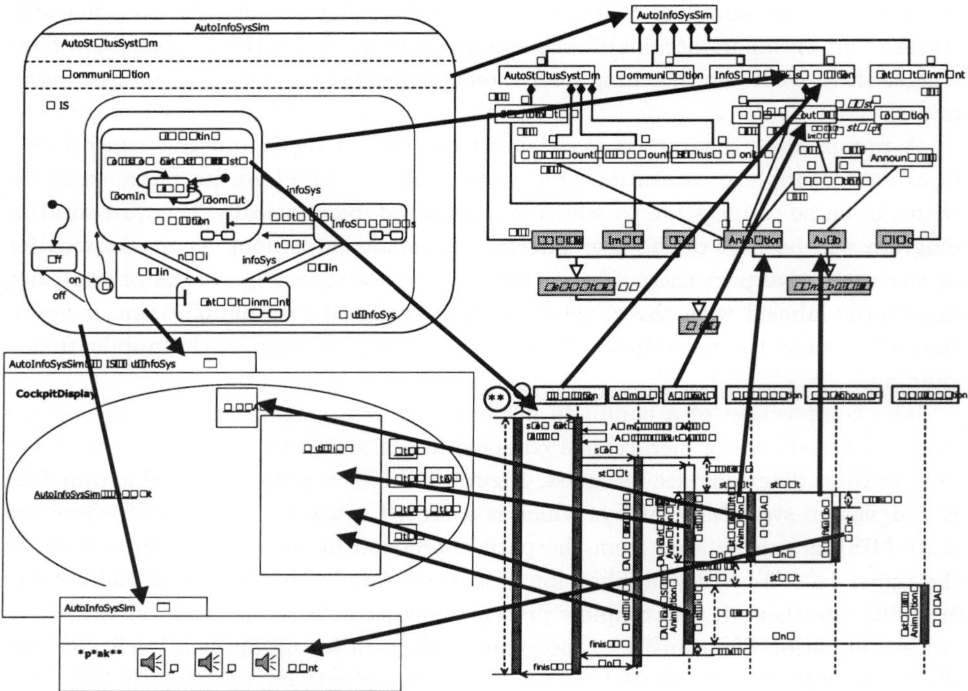

Fig. 8. An integrated OMMMA-L specification.

5. Future Directions

The modeling approaches presented herein still have to show their feasibility in real-world applications and complex application settings. Case studies are necessary to underpin their real achievements in practice.

The extension of UML by profiles for specific application domains has been widely recognized as indicated by a diverse range of (prototypical) custom profiles, e.g. for architectures of web applications [14], and several requests for proposals issued by the OMG in order to standardize profiles for several domains, like embedded real-time applications and CORBA. A major drawback still is the absence of generally accepted, formal and precise specifications of UML semantics, and, therefore, also for most proposed extensions of UML. But with the forthcoming appearance of diverse profiles, the issues of consistency between and semantically sound integration of profiles need to be analyzed in detail. Orthogonal aspects should be placed in isolated profiles that could then more easily be combined. For the profiles presented herein, the integration of user interface, hypermedia, and multimedia modeling extensions is an interesting challenge.

A recent trend in the specification of multimedia applications is the use of constraint-based approaches more flexibly describe the requirements and properties of multimedia presentations (see e.g. [40, 7, 56, 26]). Some contraints can be graphically expressed in the current OMMMA-L notation, other constraints can be integrated into a model by UML's built-in constraint language OCL [47] or by using other textual or diagrammatic (for instance, constraint diagrams [37]) constraint languages.

Some interesting challenges exist regarding the integration of the proposed object-oriented modeling approach into general multimedia software development processes. Especially the transformation between the model and an implementation, based on either object-oriented frameworks or authoring systems, that does account for both structure and behavior, is an obvious task at hand to prove the feasibility of the concept.

6. Conclusion

In this chapter, we presented approaches for the object-oriented modeling of interactive, hypermedia, and multimedia applications. We also examined the current state of application development based on multimedia authoring systems and object-oriented programming. By doing this, we illuminated some important aspects of the multi-dimensional task of multimedia software engineering.

In our presentation, we focused on OMMMA-L, a visual, object-oriented modeling language for multimedia applications. OMMMA-L is based on the standard modeling language UML. New language features have been incorporated into OMMMA-L in order to support integrated modeling of all aspects of a multimedia application. Particularly, a presentation diagram type and appropriate extensions to sequence diagrams have been introduced.

The modeling language is accompanied by a method description on how to deploy the language elements in a multimedia software development process and a prototype implementation. Furthermore, the language extensions are being formalized by a precise semantics specification based on graphical operational semantics (cf. [20]). As a refined conceptual basis, we intend to define a formal model for the composition within and between the different behavioral diagrams.

References

1. P. Ackermann, *Developing Object-Oriented Multimedia Software — Based on MET++ Application Framework* (dpunkt, Heidelberg, 1996).
2. Apple, Hypercard, *http://www.apple.com/hypercard/*
3. T. Arndt, "The evolving role of software engineering in the production of multimedia applications", *Proceedings of the IEEE International Conference on Multimedia Computing and Systems (ICMCS'99)* **I** (1999) 79–84.
4. B. Bailey, J. A. Konstan, R. Cooley and M. Dejong, "Nsync — A toolkit for building interactive multimedia presentations", *Proceedings of the 6th ACM International Conference on Multimedia'98* (ACM Press, 1998) 257–266.
5. H. Baumeister, N. Koch and L. Mandel, "Towards a UML extension for hypermedia design", eds., R. France and B. Rumpe, *Proceedings of the ≪UML≫'99 — The*

Unified Modeling Language, Beyond the Standard, 2nd International Conference, Lecture Notes in Computer Science 1723 (Springer, 1999) 614–629.
6. E. Bertino and E. Ferrari, "Temporal synchronization models for multimedia data", *TKDE* **10**, no. 4 (1998) 612–631.
7. E. Bertino, E. Ferrari and M. Stolf, "MPGS: An interactive tool for the specification and generation of multimedia presentations", *TKDE* **12**, no. 1 (2000) 102–125.
8. A. Bianchi, P. Bottoni and P. Mussio, "Issues in design and implementation of multimedia software systems", *Proceedings of the IEEE International Conference on Multimedia Computing and Systems (ICMCS'99)* **I** (1999) 91–96.
9. M. M. Blattner and E. P. Glinert, "Multimodal integration", *IEEE MultiMedia* **3**, no. 4 (1996) 14–24.
10. D. Boles, P. Dawabi, M. Schlattmann, E. Boles, C. Trunk and F. Wigger, "Objektorientierte Multimedia-Softwareentwicklung: Vom UML-Modell zur Director-Anwendung am Beispiel virtueller naturwissenschaftlich-technischer Labore", *Proceedings of the Workshop Multimedia-Systeme, 28th Annual Conference of the German Computer Science Association (GI)* (1998) 33–51 (in German).
11. G. Booch, J. Rumbaugh and I. Jacobsen, *The Unified Modeling Language User Guide* (Addison-Wesley, Reading, MA, 1998).
12. S.-K. Chang, *Multimedia Software Engineering* (Kluwer, Boston, MA, USA, 1999).
13. Click2Learn, Toolbook II. *http://home.click2learn.com/*
14. J. Conallen, *Building Web-Applications with UML* (Addison-Wesley, Reading, MA, 2000).
15. L. L. Constantine and L. A. D. Lockwood, *Software for Use: A Practical Guide to the Models and Methods of Usage-Centered Design* (ACM Press, New York, NY, 1999).
16. J. Coutaz, "PAC-ing the architecture of your user interface", eds. M. D. Harrison and J. C. Torres, *Design, Specification and Verification of Interactive Systems, Proceedings of the 4th Eurographics Workshop '97* (Springer, 1997) 13–27.
17. R. Depke, G. Engels, K. Mehner, S. Sauer and A. Wagner, Ein Vorgehensmodell für die Multimedia-Entwicklung mit Autorensystemen, *Informatik: Forschung und Entwicklung* **14** (1999) 83–94 (in German).
18. D. Dingeldein, "Modeling multimedia objects with MME", *Proceedings of the EUROGRAPHICS Workshop on Object-Oriented Graphics (EOOG'94)*, 1994.
19. M. Echiffre, C. Marchisio, P. Marchisio, P. Panicciari and S. Del Rossi, "MHEG-5 — Aims, concepts, and implementation issues", *IEEE MultiMedia* **5**, no. 1 (1998) 84–91.
20. G. Engels, J. H. Hausmann, R. Heckel and S. Sauer, "Dynamic meta modeling: A graphical approach to the operational semantics of behavioral diagrams in UML", in [22], pp. 323–337.
21. G. Engels, R. Heckel and S. Sauer, "UML — A universal modeling language?" eds. M. Nielsen and D. Simpson, *Proceedings of the 21st International Conference on Application and Theory of Petri Nets (ICATPN 2000), Lecture Notes in Computer Science 1825* (Springer, 2000) 24–38.
22. A. Evans, S. Kent and B. Selic, *Proceedings of the ≪UML≫ 2000 — The Unified Modeling Language, Advancing the Standard, 3rd International Conference, Lecture Notes in Computer Science 1939* (Springer, 2000).
23. F. Garzotto, P. Paolini and D. Schwabe, "HDM — A model-based approach to hypertext application design", *TOIS* **11**, no. 1 (1993) 1–26.
24. S. J. Gibbs and D. C. Tsichritzis, *Multimedia Programming: Objects, Environments and Frameworks* (Addison-Wesley, Wokingham, 1995).
25. R. Gordon and S. Talley, *Essential JMF: Java Media Framework* (Prentice-Hall, Englewood Cliffs, NJ, 1999).

26. V. Hakkoymaz, J. Kraft and G. Özsoyoglu, "Constraint-based automation of multimedia presentation assembly", *Multimedia Systems* **7**, no. 6 (1999) 500–518.
27. R. Hennicker and N. Koch, "A UML-based methodology for hypermedia design", in [22], pp. 410–424.
28. I. Herman, N. Correia, D. A. Duce, D. J. Duke, G. J. Reynolds and J. van Loo, "A standard model for multimedia synchronization: PREMO synchronization objects", *Multimedia Systems* **6**, no. 2 (1998) 88–101.
29. I. Herman, G. J. Reynolds and J. van Loo, PREMO: An emerging standard for multimedia presentation — Part I: Overview and framework", *IEEE MultiMedia* **3**, no. 3 (1996) 83–89.
30. I. Herman, G. J. Reynolds and J. van Loo, "PREMO: An emerging standard for multimedia presentation — Part II: Specification and applications", *IEEE Multimedia* **3**, no. 4 (1996) 72–75.
31. N. Hirzalla, B. Falchuk and A. Karmouch, "A temporal model for interactive multimedia scenarios", *IEEE MultiMedia* **2**, no. 3 (1995) 24–31.
32. P. Hoschka, "An introduction to the synchronized multimedia integration language", *IEEE MultiMedia* **5**, no. 4 (1998) 84–88.
33. T. Isakowitz, E. Stohr and P. Balasubramanian, "RMM: A methodology for structured hypermedia design", *CACM* **38**, no. 8 (1995) 34–44.
34. ISO/IEC JTC1/SC24/WG6 — Multimedia Presentation and Interchange, PREMO (ISO/IEC 14478), *http://www.iso.ch.*
35. ISO/IEC JTC1/SC29/WG11 — Moving Picture Experts Group (MPEG), MPEG-4 (ISO/IEC 14496), *http://www.iso.ch, http://www.cselt.it/mpeg/.*
36. ISO/IEC JTC1/SC29/WG11 — Multimedia and Hypermedia Expert Group, MHEG (ISO/IEC 13522), *http://www.iso.ch.*
37. S. Kent, "Constraint diagrams: Visualising invariants in OO modelling", *Proceedings of the OOPSLA'97* (ACM Press, 1997) 327–341.
38. S. Kovacevic, "UML and user interface modeling", eds. J. Bézivin and P.-A. Muller, *Proceedings of the ≪UML≫'98 — The Unified Modeling Language, Beyond the Notation, 1st International Workshop, Lecture Notes in Computer Science 1618* (Springer, 1998) 253–266.
39. G. E. Krasner and S. T. Pope, "A cookbook for using the model-view-controller user interface paradigm in Smalltalk-80", *Journal of Object-Oriented Programming* **1**, no. 3 (August/September 1988) 26–49.
40. Y.-M. Kwon, E. Ferrari and E. Bertino, "Modeling spatio-temporal constraints for multimedia objects", *Data and Knowledge Engineering* **30**, no. 3 (1999) 217–238.
41. T. D. C. Little and A. Ghafoor, "Synchronisation and storage models for multimedia objects", *IEEE Journal on Selected Areas in Communications* **8**, no. 3 (April 1990) 413–427.
42. Macromedia, Authorware, *http://www.macromedia.com/software/authorware/*
43. Macromedia, Director, *http://www.macromedia.com/software/director/*
44. Microsoft, DirectX, *http://www.microsoft.com/directx/*
45. M. Mühlhäuser, "Issues in multimedia software development", *Proceedings of the Internatonal Workshop on Multimedia Software Development* (IEEE Computer Society, 1996) 2–9.
46. N. J. Nunes and J. F. e Cunha, "Towards a UML profile for interaction design: The Wisdom approach", in [22], pp. 101–116.
47. Object Management Group, *OMG Unified Modeling Language Specification*, version 1.3, June 1999, *http://www.omg.org*

48. P. Pauen, V. Voss and H.-W. Six, "Modelling hypermedia applications with HyDev", eds. A. A. Sutcliffe, J. Ziegler and P. Johnson, *Designing Effective and Usable Multimedia Systems, Proceedings of the IFIP 13.2 Working Conference* (Kluwer, 1998).
49. J. Rumbaugh, I. Jacobson and G. Booch, *The Unified Modeling Language Reference Manual*, Object Technology Series (Addison-Wesley, Reading, MA, 1999).
50. S. Sauer and G. Engels, "Extending UML for modeling of multimedia applications", eds. M. Hirakawa and P. Mussio, *Proceedings of the IEEE Symposium on Visual Languages (VL'99)* (IEEE Computer Society, 1999) 80–87.
51. D. Schwabe and G. Rossi, "An object oriented approach to web-based applications design", *Theory and Practice of Object Systems* **4**, no. 4 (1998) 207–225.
52. T. K. Shih, S.-K. Chang and P. Shih, "A web document development paradigm and its supporting environment", *Proceedings of the 6th International Conference Distributed Multimedia Systems (DMS'99)*, 1999.
53. P. P. da Silva and N. W. Paton, "UMLi: The Unified Modeling Language for interactive applications", in [22], pp. 117–132.
54. B. C. Smith, L. A. Rowe, J. A. Konstan and K. D. Patel, "The Berkeley Continuous Media Toolkit", *Proceedings of the 4th ACM International Conference on Multimedia'96*, (ACM Press, 1996) 451–452.
55. L. F. G. Soares, R. F. Rodrigues and D. C. Muchaluat Saade, "Modeling, authoring and formatting hypermedia documents in the HyperProp system", *Multimedia Systems* **8**, no. 2 (2000) 118–134.
56. J. Song, G. Ramalingam, R. E. Miller and B.-K. Yi, "Interactive authoring of multimedia documents in a constraint-based authoring system", *Multimedia Systems* **7**, no. 5 (1999) 424–437.
57. Sun Microsystems, Java Media API, *http://java.sun.com/products/java-media/*
58. Sun Microsystems, Java Media Framework, *http://java.sun.com/products/java-media/jmf/*
59. M. Vazirgiannis, *Interactive Multimedia Documents — Modeling, Authoring and Implementation Experiences, Lecture Notes in Computer Science 1564* (Springer, Berlin, 1999).
60. P. Vilain, D. Schwabe and C. S. de Souza, "A diagrammatic tool for representing user interaction in UML", in [22], pp. 133–147.
61. T. Wahl and K. Rothermel, "Representing time in multimedia systems", *Proceedings of the IEEE 1st International Conference on Multimedia Computing and Systems (ICMCS'94)* (IEEE Computer Society, 1994) 538–543.
62. World Wide Web Consortium (W3C), Synchronized Multimedia Integration Language (SMIL), *http://www.w3.org/AudioVideo/*
63. A. Zamperoni, "GRIDS — Graph-based integrated development of software: Integrating different perspectives of software engineering", *Proceedings of the 18th International Conference on Software Engineering (ICSE)* (IEEE Computer Society, 1996) 48–59.

EXPLOITING VISUAL LANGUAGES IN SOFTWARE ENGINEERING

FILOMENA FERRUCCI, GENOVEFFA TORTOTA and GIULIANA VITIELLO
Dipartimento di Matematica ed Informatica, Università di Salerno, 84081 Baronissi (SA) Italy
E-mail: {fferrucci,gvitiello,tortora}@unisa.it

In the present chapter, we illustrate some methodologies and assessed results achieved in the area of visual languages that can be profitably exploited in the field of software engineering. The discussion will start with an overview of the most common graphical notations used to support software engineering activities, and with the description of some popular visual environments. Then, we will illustrate some tools for the automatic generation of visual languages, based on formalisms for the specification of visual languages. A discussion on some relevant applications of the described tools will conclude the chapter.

Keywords: Visual Languages, visual programming environments, graphical user interfaces, models.

1. Introduction

Graphical and diagrammatic representations play a central role in the field of software engineering. They are widely employed to support many activities of the software development process, such as specification, analysis and design (e.g. Petri nets, FSAs, Statecharts, and Dataflow diagrams). Indeed, graphical notations are recognized as powerful aids for the description and understanding of complex systems for which traditional textual descriptions are inadequate. They are able to provide abstract models and different views of complex systems, which allow software designers to devise solutions and design systems.

In the last decades much efforts have been devoted to the field of visual languages. The development of such research area was motivated by the observation that the human visual system is more inclined in processing graphical information than textual one, making visual information easily understood by people regardless of the individual cultures [56]. Thus, the primary goal of the visual language community has been to exploit icons and graphical notations to effectively convey information and to allow for multimodal communication and interaction between humans and computers. Several studies have been performed aimed to formalize the human-computer interface by providing methodologies for high-level specification of the syntax and the semantics of the set of graphical configurations and of the interactive language which allows the user to exploit the interface.

The field of visual languages has been nourished by including all types of visual notations which may occur in specific application domains, such as spatial databases, education, and software engineering. In particular, the widespread use of computers as communication medium of people connected by the World Wide Web has made the design of visual languages which allow for an effective human-to-human communication an emergent and timely issue. The rapid progress of this research area has caused the need to structure the literature on visual languages, resulting in some useful organized bibliographies, which are available on-line [6, 9, 30].

In the present chapter, we illustrate the well-settled methodologies and the assessed results achieved in the area of visual languages that can be profitably exploited in the field software engineering. The discussion will start with an overview of the most common graphical notations used to support software engineering activities. Then, in Sec. 3, the concept of visual programming languages is introduced and some popular visual environments are described. Section 4 is concerned with the formal specification of visual languages. The use of such formalisms for the construction of automatic generators of visual languages is described in Sec. 5, and some interesting applications of such tools are shown in Sec. 6.

2. Graphical Formalisms for Software Engineering

A typical approach for problem solving is the construction of a kind of problem representation, which gives insight into the structure of the problem, and allows one to find a possible solution. Spatial diagrammatic representations such as trees, tables, and graphs, are important tools for reasoning both in everyday situations and in formal domains. The level of abstraction which characterizes them allows us to identify structural similarities among problems apparently very different. As an example, a tree can be used to represent a taxonomy of animal species, a tennis tournament or a genealogical tree. Thus, a hierarchical structure can be associated to quite different situations. As a consequence, a solution scheme defined in a context can be transferred to others quite straightforwardly.

In the field of software engineering, designers often use graphical notations and structured information to provide abstract models and different views of complex systems. Focusing only on the relevant information, such models can be profitably used to achieve a deep understanding of the systems, to devise solutions and design systems. The strength of such visual representations also derives from their ability to construct documents which are easily understood by different individuals allowing for an effective exchange of information among people, which is crucial for collaborative work during both software development and software maintenance. In fact, software comprehension is a major issue in important activities of software development (e.g. reuse and quality control) and software maintenance [58]. It is also one of the most expensive tasks in the process of software reengineering. As a consequence, several visual formalisms, program visualization tools and graphical debuggers have been developed, which aim at supporting people to build a comprehensive model of software systems. In particular, most of the proposed tools for software reengineering are based on a static analysis of the source code meant to provide different views of it in terms of graphical representations, such as dataflows, call graphs, and control flows. In the sequel, we recall the main features of some visual formalisms, which are widely used in software engineering.

2.1. *Dataflow diagrams*

Dataflow diagrams represent a simple and intuitive graphical notation used in analysis and design to show how data are processed by a system and how the output is derived from the input through a sequence of functional transformations [19]. An example of Dataflow diagram is shown in Fig. 1. Dataflow models are an integral part of several structured analysis and design methods (see, e.g. [5]).

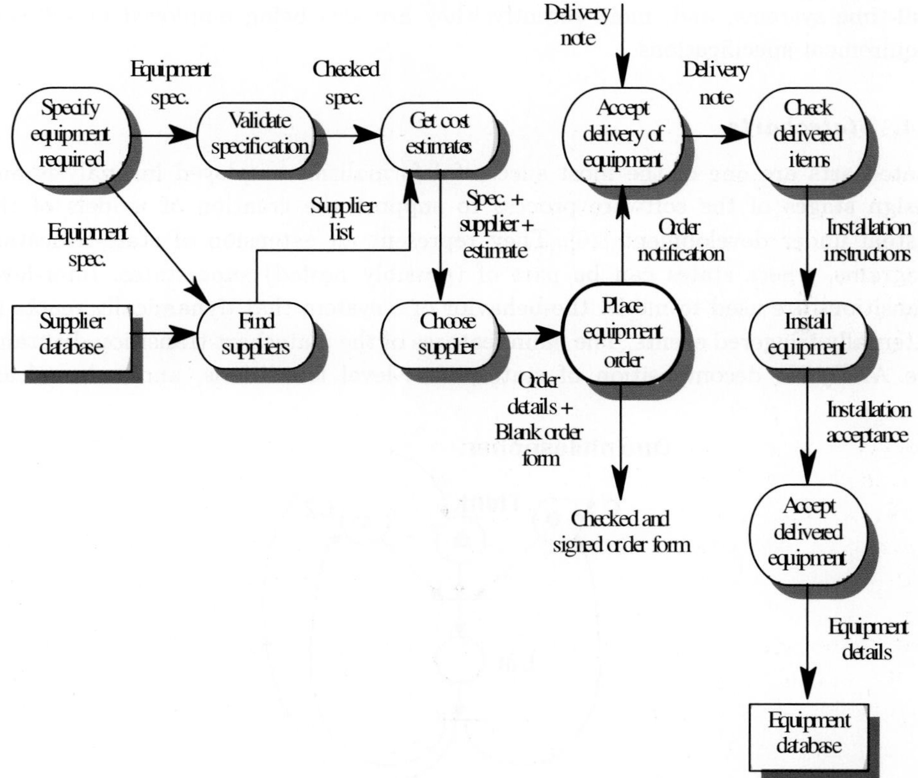

Fig. 1. A dataflow diagram which illustrates the process of procuring and installing an item of equipment [58].

2.2. *Flow graphs*

Flow graphs provide a skeletal model of all the independent paths through a program. Each node in a flow graph represents a condition, while edges show flow of control. They support several activities. In particular, they allow us to identify the test cases needed for the program structural testing. They are employed during program restructuring, allowing for the application of simplification and transformation techniques without affecting program semantics. They also play a central role in the reverse engineering process to support program comprehension.

2.3. *Petri nets*

Petri nets are a popular graphical formalism especially suitable for modeling systems with concurrency. They represent an extension of finite state machines (see Fig. 2). Petri nets have been widely used to model systems of events in which it is possible for some events to occur concurrently but there are constraints on the concurrence, precedence or frequency of these occurrences. Thus, their major use has been the specification of synchronous processes during the design of hard real-time systems, and, more recently, they are also being employed in software requirement specifications.

2.4. *Statecharts*

Statecharts are one of the most successful formalisms employed in analysis and design stages of the software process to support the creation of models of the system under development [26]. They represent an extension of state-transition diagrams, where states can be part of (possibly nested) superstates. Inter-level transitions are used to model the behavior of a system that dynamically reacts to externally triggered events. The main features of the statechart transition diagrams are AND/OR decomposition of states, inter-level transitions, and a broadcast

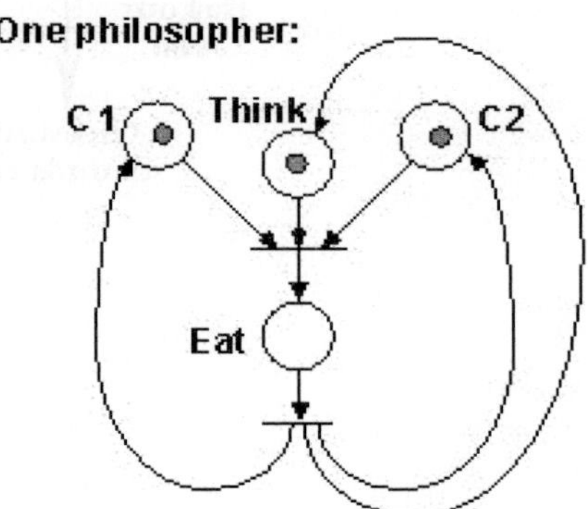

Fig. 2. A Petri net for the dining philosophers problem (http://www.cs.cmu.edu/afs/cs.cmu.edu/academic/class/15671-f97/www/index.html).

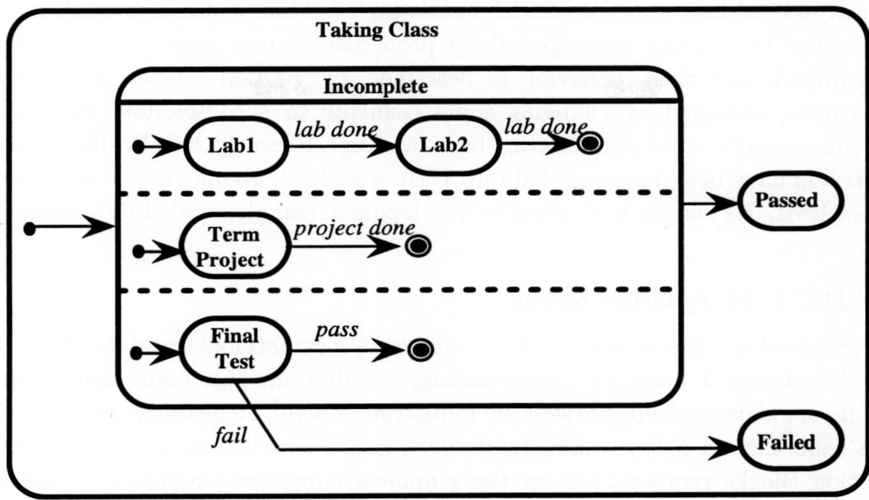

Fig. 3. An expansion of a state into concurrent substates is shown by tiling the graphic region of the state using dashed lines to divide it into subregions. Each subregion is a concurrent substate. Each subregion may have an optional name and must contain a nested state diagram with disjoint states. The text compartments of the entire state are separated from the concurrent substates by a solid line. (http://models.distance.cmu.edu/shared/lectures/14StateCharts/).

mechanism for communication between concurrent components (see Fig. 3). Some variations of the original formalism have also been proposed to take into account time requirements in real-time systems and to describe multimedia applications (see, e.g. [45, 53]). The statechart formalism is widely recognized as a powerful aid for describing complex systems and plays a central role in the Unified Modeling Language (UML), where a statechart is associated with each class to specify the behavior of the objects in the class.

2.5. *UML*

UML is presently considered a standard modeling language for specifying, visualizing, constructing, and documenting object-oriented systems [3]. It is a set of visual, diagrammatic languages which are tailored to model distinguished aspects of a system and simplify the complex process of software design and the specification of business processes. This allows for a uniform treatment of applications and the process models for their development. The employed visual languages can be grouped in four categories, namely, use case, structural, behavioral, and implementation diagrams.

2.6. *ROOM*

ROOM is another powerful visual language, which was especially conceived for modeling real-time object-oriented systems [54]. For all phases of the development process ROOM uses a unique model, consisting of actors which communicate with each other by sending messages along protocols. Actors may be hierarchically decomposed and their behavior is described by ROOM charts, a variant of statecharts, obtained by changing some elements to accommodate modeling of real-time aspects (e.g. by eliminating broadcasting). Recently, ROOM-like modeling constructs have been incorporated into UML standard, giving rise to an extension named UML/RT, which is directed to developers of complex real-time systems [55].

2.7. *IEC* 1131 *function blocks*

The International Electrotechnical Commission's international standard IEC 1131-3 provides standard tools for programming, installation, and maintenance phases of software development projects in industrial control in order to generate software code that is better understandable, reusable, verifiable, and maintainable. Function Blocks represent one of the graphical languages proposed by the standard. Function Blocks are equivalent to integrated circuits in the sense that program elements appear as blocks connected. Each block is a graphical object that performs a specific control function (see Fig. 4). Function Block language exploits

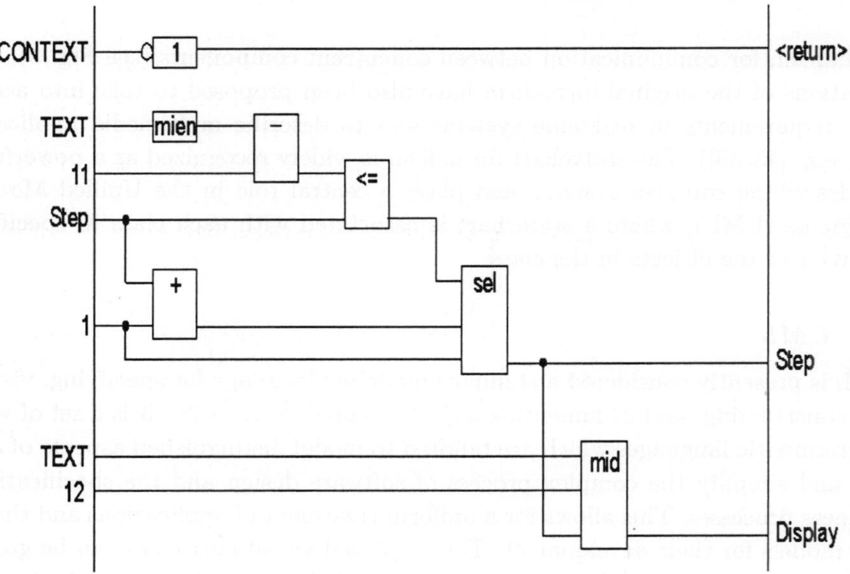

Fig. 4. The lines in FBD denote Signal Flow and represent data types. In the figure, CONTEXT has been defined as a BOOLEAN input, TEXT is a Message (character string) Input, Step is an Integer, and Display is a Message Output. This program fragment selects characters from the TEXT variable and places them into the Display variable in accordance with the value of the Step input variable, if and only if the CONTEXT input variable is TRUE. Signal Flow lines may branch when it is required to transport a value to several places. (http://www.nrc.gov/NRC/NUREGS/CR6463/appa.htm#A.5 Function Block Diagram).

a structured approach to access and visualize data, which is useful in applications that involve a large flow of information between control components.

Several graphical notations are also used during software management in order to illustrate the project schedule. In particular, bar charts are employed to indicate the responsible(s) for each activity and the scheduled period. An activity network shows the interdependencies among the activities composing a project, and allows us to estimate the minimum time required to complete it by considering the longest path on the network.

3. Visual Programming Languages

The widespread use of personal computers in diverse domains and the different typologies of users have motivated the investigation of kinds of interactions able to make simple and intuitive the approach with a computer. The widely recognized value of icons, diagrams and other graphical notations in human-computer interaction and human-to-human communication, and the decreasing cost of hardware technologies and graphics software have caused the development of a novel approach named *visual programming*. Visual programming covers a wide variety of activities that make an extensive use of icons and diagrams to convey information and to allow for multimodal communication and interaction between humans and computers. Indeed, in spite of the terminology adopted, "visual programming" does not denote merely the specification of graphical programs but it is rather referred to the ability of using graphics as a communication means in any activity which involves human-computer interaction.

As a consequence, notable efforts are devoted to the field of visual programming languages, where a language is usually conceived as a collection of sentences given by pictorial components which are suitably arranged in two or more dimensions [10, 56]. Visual programming languages allow a user to communicate with the system by spatially arranging visual objects on the screen, thus forming a so-called "visual sentence". From the user's point of view, a visual sentence is able to intuitively evoke the meaning that the system assigns to it. Thus, several benefits come from the use of visual programming languages thanks to a more effective modeling of the human thought processes. These include direct manipulation, immediate visual feedback, explicit depiction of relationships, and the need to learn fewer programming concepts.

The theoretical research on visual languages aims at providing a basis to understand the communication process realized by means of visual languages. In particular, two main research issues can be identified. The first is concerned with providing methods which allow us to specify how the elements of the language are structured to form a legal sentence (the syntax) and to infer the meaning conveyed by legal sentences (the semantics). In Sec. 4, we will give an overview of the formal methods proposed for the specification of visual languages. The second issue involves also aspects of cognitive science and requires the investigation of properties that make visual languages effective and usable so as to identify some general guidelines for their development. This requires the comprehension of what makes a visual language better than another for communicating a particular message in a specific application domain, and when a visual notation is more effective than purely textual notation. In the last years several empirical studies have been carried out and some cognitive models of how humans comprehend and reason with visual notations have been developed [25, 62]. Nevertheless, much work has to be done on this topic.

A well-experimented subclass of visual programming languages is represented by *iconic* languages. An iconic sentence is a spatial arrangement of icons, which are pictorial representations of conceptual entities and operations [10, 60]. Each icon is an object with the dual representation of a logical part (the meaning) and a physical part (the image). The effectiveness of iconic languages strongly depends on the capability of icons to resemble their meaning through the physical representation. Thus, an important issue in the visual language research is the construction of tools able to generate customized visual languages and to enhance the consistency between users intention and machine interpretation. Another peculiar aspect of iconic sentences is that their meaning is determined also by the positions of the pictures in the sentence (see Fig. 5).

Another important class of visual languages consists of the so-called *diagrammatic* languages. A diagrammatic language is a set of diagrams, each one composed of graphical objects, which are related in two or more dimensions. Diagrammatic languages have traditionally been adopted in a variety of application domains, such as architectural design, software system design, software process engineering, telecommunication services, chemical studies, and so forth. As empirical studies have also shown, the success of those languages derives from their ability to provide abstract models and different views of complex systems which are easily understood by different people, thus representing an excellent medium for human-to-human communication [34]. The use of diagrammatic notations in visual programming

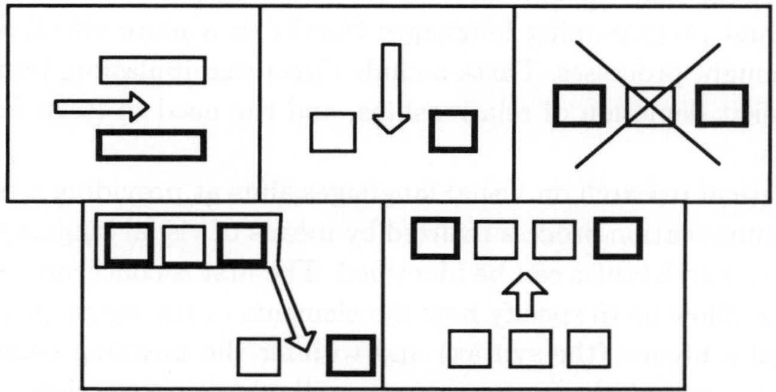

Fig. 5. The semantics of the above iconic sentences is: insert line, insert a string, delete a string, move a string to a new place, and replace a string (Chang *et al* 1989).

languages allows the programmer to directly map the diagram representing the conceptual solution of the problem into the syntax of the program. Thus, it is no longer necessary to transform the solution so that it fits the syntax of the textual programming language through the use of abstract symbols and variables to represent subproblems and their dependencies.

Initially, most of the general-purpose visual programming languages were developed by simply embedding into a visual environment traditional programming languages, such as Pascal, C, and Lisp. However, those environments often limited the potentiality of the underlying language, and at the same time resulted in little help for people unfamiliar with programming. Later, a solution came from the introduction of new paradigms, specific to visual programming, which allow for the development of advanced general-purpose visual programming languages. Examples of such paradigms are *rule-based*, *dataflow*, *controlflow*, *form-based*, and *program-by-demonstration*. The controlflow approach is the closest one to textual programming languages. Indeed, conventional control flow constructs are expressed by using visual representations. Dataflow languages represent one of the main successful subclasses of visual programming languages. They exploit dataflow diagrams to visually depict dependencies between data and processes [28]. One of the key success of such languages is represented by their declarativeness due to the absence of control aspects in pure dataflow languages. The declarativeness is a feature characterizing also form-based visual languages. Indeed, also those languages focus on relationships between data without considering their evaluation sequencing. In rule-based languages a system has some state and a set of rules that change its current state into another state. Finally, the idea of the program-by-demonstration approach is to exploit sequences of user's actions to infer a more general program.

3.1. *Visual programming environments*

It is widely recognized that a visual language can be effectively used only if it is supported by a powerful integrated visual environment. This is mainly due to two specific issues of visual programming languages. First, for any visual programming language a specialized editor is needed, which assists the user in the specification of visual programs, by providing him/her with a set of graphical symbols and relationships. Indeed, the use of general-purpose drawing editors would force programmers to the unacceptable task of drawing the (possibly) complex shapes representing symbols and relationship of the language, in fact much limiting the benefits of visual programming. The second issue is related to the lack of a standard representation for visual input expressions, analogous to the ASCII format for textual languages. As a result, any parser is based on the specific input representation which is used by the associated editor. Thus, any visual programming language requires its own environment where the editor and the compiler components must be integrated. For that reason, in the sequel, we will not distinguish between a visual programming language and the corresponding environment, and we will refer to either of them indiscriminately.

At present, a wide variety of visual programming environments is available. The visual programming environments *HI-VISUAL* [29], and *Show and Tell* [37] provide an iconic framework to program by composing icons in a two-dimensional display screen according to pre-defined rules. Such systems, as *Pecan* [46] and *PegaSys* [39], are instead diagrammatic systems designed to provide a programming environment where all steps of software life cycle are supported by graphical interaction languages. More recently, the visual programming language *PROGRES* has been developed, as an executable specification language [52]. It is a rule-oriented visual programming language based on graph rewriting systems [2]. It tightly integrates textual and graphical elements consisting of EER-like and UML-like class diagrams. The language has been successfully applied for specifying and rapidly prototyping several interactive systems with graphical user interfaces, such as reengineering, process modeling, and distributed system analysis tools and for other different purposes such as defining the syntax of visual languages, generating visual language parsers and editors, manipulating knowledge representations.

Another rule-based visual programming language is *Agentsheet* [47, 49]. It combines visual and tactile programming as an extension to object-oriented programming. Agentsheets was designed for allowing people with no programming experience to build simple simulations. The *KidSim* environment and its subsequent versions *Cocoa* and Stugecast Creator have been introduced with similar purpose [57, 57b]. Indeed, they are especially conceived for allowing children to create their own simulations and video games, with no need to learn a conventional programming language, but rather using a program-by-demonstration approach.

Forms/3 represents a declarative general purpose object-oriented visual programming language [7]. It is a form-based language which uses the cells and formulas of spreadsheets to represent data and computations. Forms/3 emphasizes data abstraction by providing the capability of organizing cells into a group called form. It exploits techniques such as direct manipulation and continuous visual feedback in order to enhance the programming process.

VIPR is a controlflow general-purpose object-oriented visual programming language which uses nested series of concentric rings to visualize programs [14]. VIPR exhibits all aspects of object-oriented programs including objects, classes, inheritance, polymorphism, and dynamic dispatch. The semantics of a VIPR program can be entirely described by simple graphical rules. It is possible to visualize program execution as walking down a network of pipes which branches off in different directions while changing the state based on actions written on the inside of the pipes [14]. As an example, see the picture given in Fig. 6.

Cube represents the first three dimensional visual programming language aimed towards a virtual-reality-based programming environment [42]. The language uses a dataflow approach for program construction and is based on Show and Tell main ideas.

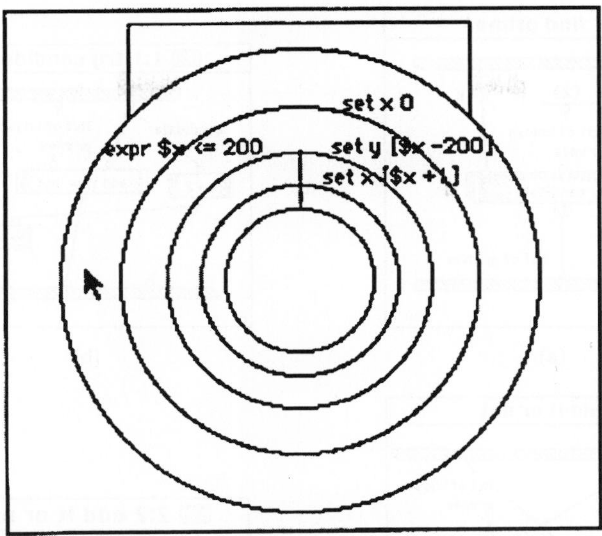

Fig. 6. The picture expresses a VIPR while loop which is executed until $x > 200$. The statement on the left of a loop is the guard. If it is true, then the statement on the right of the loop is executed and execution continues by going to the loop nested within the current loop. When the arrow is reached, execution returns to the loop the arrow points to.

Prograph and *LabVIEW* represent widely experimented visual programming languages designed for commercial use. Prograph is a general-purpose visual object-oriented language whose more recent release (Prograph/CPX) has been developed by Pictorius, Inc. [59]. It integrates the concepts of classes and objects, represented as icons, with visual dataflow techniques used for graphically specifying the internal methods of a class (see Fig. 7).

Prograph can be seen both as a sophisticated application builder and as a visual programming language, supported by a powerful program development environment. The integrated editors, interpreter and interactive debugger allow the developer to inspect and to edit both code and data as the program executes thus accelerating the development process. A wide variety of applications have been developed in Prograph, such as web-based business applications, neural networks, tools for designing layered protocols user interfaces, and so forth.

LabVIEW is a visual dataflow language commercialized by National Instruments Corp. [33]. In LabVIEW, the usual box-and-line structure of dataflow diagrams is enriched with icons representing constructs for conditionals, loops, and sequences (see Fig. 8). It provides operators which are an excellent medium to construct a virtual electronic instrument operating in real time. As a matter of fact, the accompanying visual programming environment is specialized for data acquisition and analysis but is considerably less suitable for other application domains.

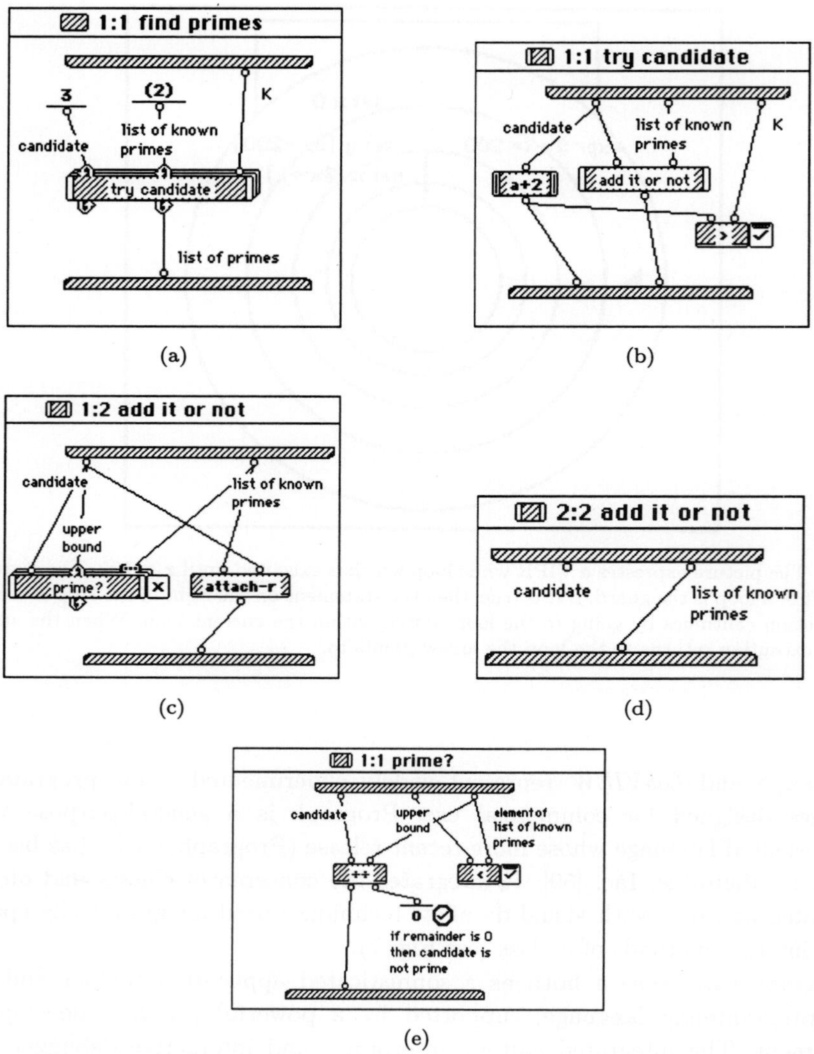

(a) (b) (c) (d) (e)

Fig. 7. Some rules in Prograph for the primes problem. In pane (a), "try candidate" has three inputs, the second of which is a list. The call on "try candidate" in the first pane shows that it is iterated, with the left output being supplied as the left input and the list recycling in the middle (b). The comparison of candidate+2 with K determines when to terminate the loop. The call on "add it or not" determines whether to add the candidate to the list. This function is implemented with the panes (c) and (d). The first of these iterates through the list of known primes with predicate "prime?" calling it once for each element of the list as indicated by "...". When the list is exhausted, the case attaches the candidate to the list of known primes. If the predicate fails, the x in the square — called a "next case control" — terminates the first case and initiates the second, which discards the candidate. The "prime?" block (e) determines whether the candidate is divisible by a known prime. The check in the square terminates the graph — succeeding — if the current list element exceeds the upper bound. The octagon terminates with failure if the division produces a remainder of zero. (The 1994 Visual Languages Comparison, http://www-cgi.cs.cmu.edu/~wjh/papers/bakeoff.html.)

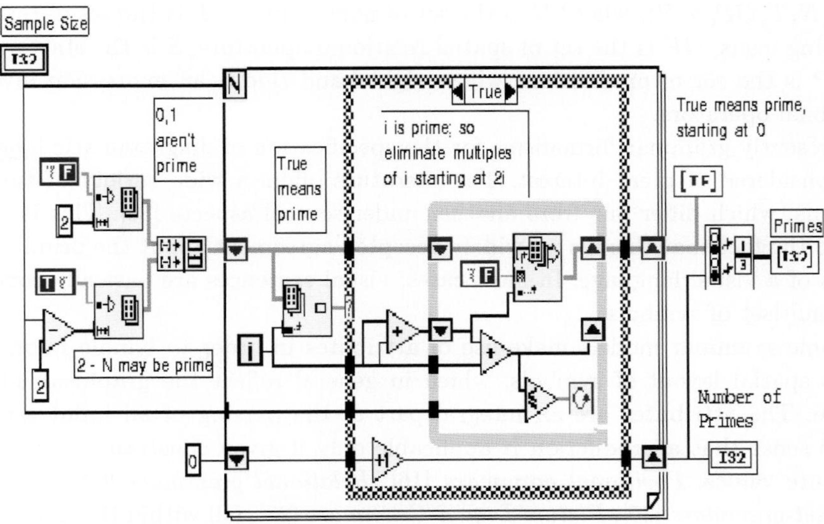

Fig. 8. The block diagram corresponding to the prime numbers problem stretches from input of SampleSize on the left to output of Primes and NumberOfPrimes on the right. The left side of the diagram initializes a Boolean array to contain two false values (for 0 and 1) and SampleSize-minus-2 true values. Then a FOR loop is executed N times with SampleSize supplied as the value for N; if the ith element is false, the number isn't prime and the box with the dark grey border is not executed. If the ith element is true, it is prime; so all multiples of i, starting at twice i, are set to false by the computation within the innermost box. (The 1994 Visual Languages Comparison, http://www-cgi.cs.cmu.edu/~wjh/papers/bakeoff.html.)

4. Formal Specifications of Visual Languages

The research on visual language syntax specification has been heavily influenced by the work in formal language theory. The main motivation of this is the aim of exploiting the well-established theoretical background and techniques developed for string languages in the setting of multidimensional visual languages. As a result, most of the methods proposed for visual language specification are grammar-based, although, in the last years other different approaches have been proposed and investigated, such as logic-based [27] and algebraic approaches [61].

One of the most appealing features of the class of iconic visual languages is the fact that it has a well-established theoretical background, derived from the deep investigation following Chang's early work [10]. In agreement with such formalization, two kinds of icons are considered, namely process icons and object icons. The former express computations; the latter can be further subdivided into elementary object icons and composite object icons. Elementary object icons identify primitive objects in the language, whereas composite object icons identify objects formed by combining on the screen elementary object icons using spatial operators, such as *hor* (for horizontal composition), *ver* (for vertical composition), *ovl* (for overlay), and *con* (for connect). An iconic visual language can be specified using a grammar

$G = (N, T, OP, S, P)$, where N is the set of nonterminals, T is the set of terminals denoting icons, OP is the set of spatial relational operators, S is the start symbol, and P is the set of productions whose right hand side is an expression involving relational operators.

Presently grammar formalisms for the specification of diagrammatic languages are considered of great interest. The literature offers a wide variety of such formalisms, which differ one from another under several aspects [36]. This is mainly due to the fact that there is no widely accepted agreement about the primitive elements of a visual language. In most cases, visual sentences are basically conceived as a multiset of symbols.

Some grammar models make use of attributes in order to handle information about spatial layout of symbols, which in general reflect the graphical interface nature. The attributes are an integral part of the parsing of an input sentence, in the sense that a production is applicable only if given constraints hold among attribute values. *Positional grammars* [16], *Relational grammars* [63], *Constraint Multiset-grammars* [35], *Picture Layout Grammars* [23], fall within this class. Other grammar formalisms do not use attributes. They specify the relationships among the symbols in the multisets at a higher level of abstraction, which is less dependent on the underlying implementation of a graphical interface. *Symbol-Relation grammars* [20] and several graph grammar models, such as *edNLC grammars* [31], *Hypergraph grammars* [38] and *Layered graph grammars* [48] belong to this class.

In general, grammar formalisms for diagrammatic language specification extend traditional string grammars in that they rewrite sets or multisets of symbols rather than sequences, and specify several relationships between objects rather than the concatenation relationship only. As a consequence, the analysis of visual programming languages is much harder, due to the high cost of parsing. Indeed while strings naturally drive a sequential scanning of the symbols, no precise scanning order is implicit in multi-dimensional structures. However, the effective use of grammars for specifying visual language syntax requires efficient parsing techniques. The parsing issue for visual languages has been widely investigated in the literature and several methods have been proposed which impose some restrictions to the form of the grammars balancing the ability to express visual languages and the efficiency of parsing techniques [36].

Close to grammar-based approaches, are the formal specification methods based on rewriting systems [4, 43]. In particular, it is worth mentioning the *Visual Attributed Rewriting* systems which were especially conceived to specify the pictorial and computational aspects of visual languages in order to automatically generate control mechanisms of the interaction [4].

Although most commercially available visual languages, such as ProGraph and LabView, have not a complete formal specification, several benefits can be derived from providing a formal specification of a visual language. In particular, the use of (context-free style) grammar formalisms can simplify the development of complex visual languages since they can support an incremental approach. Customization and modifications due to user's preferences and needs can be easily performed as well as the maintenance and the debug of the language. Code and report generation can be effectively realized by defining an attribute grammar. Then a syntax-directed translation can be carried out based on the parse tree, which is the output of the syntactic analysis process. Finally, powerful visual environment generators can be constructed which generate a visual environment specific for a language starting from a syntax and semantic specification of the language itself.

5. Visual Programming Environment Generators

The widespread use of visual programming environments and the observation that the development of language specific environments is a cumbersome and time-consuming activity, have motivated the need for general environments offering the opportunity to the programmer of defining a visual language which best fits the particular application. In fact, in recent years much effort has been devoted to the development of tools that assist the designer in the specification and implementation of visual environments. Special focus has been put on the implementation of systems that generate visual environments starting from formal specifications of visual languages.

The *SIL* (*Syntactic*, *Interactive*, *Learning*) system has been the first visual programming environment supporting the definition of a visual language for user interaction based on a formal visual grammar model [12]. It includes a general icon interpreter performing the syntactic and semantic analysis according to each specific visual grammar. The visual language customization issue has been addressed with the *VLG* (*Visual Language Generator*) system, which exploits grammatical inference techniques in the design of adaptive visual languages [18]. The system is a powerful tool for specifying, designing, and interpreting customized iconic languages for different applications. A more general visual grammar model, the Picture Layout Grammar, is considered in *VPW* (*Visual Programmer's Workbench*), which is a system to synthesize and customize visual programming environments not restricted to iconic languages [50].

During the last years much effort has been spent in the implementation of integrated environments supporting the designer in both the specification and the analysis of diagrammatic languages. On the basis of the supplied specification, such systems generate an integrated environment consisting of a graphical editor that supports the user in the composition of a diagrammatic sentence and a syntax and semantic analyzer which interprets the sentence in agreement with the specified language. The capabilities of each system mainly depend on the characteristics of its underlying syntactic framework. Some systems are based on grammar models which make use of attributes in order to handle information about spatial layout of symbols (see, e.g. [13, 15]). Others exploit grammar formalisms which do not use attributes, but specify the relationships among the symbols in a sentence at a higher level of abstraction [21]. Finally, graph grammar principles, with the corresponding rewriting approaches, have also been taken as a basis for visual environment generation [1, 38].

The Visual Language Compiler-Compiler (VLCC) is a graphical system for the automatic generation of visual programming environments, which is based on the Positional grammar model [15]. The most appealing feature of VLCC is that it inherits and extends to the visual field concepts and techniques of traditional compiler generation tools like YACC. This is due to the characteristics of the Positional Grammar model which represents a natural extension of the context-free grammars. This has allowed for an efficient LR-like parser for Positional grammars based on a syntax-directed scanning of the input [16]. Despite the efficiency of the parsing algorithm, the expressive power of positional grammars is still sufficient to describe real-world complex visual languages. As a matter of fact, the notion of hybrid and hierarchical types specific of VLCC makes such system a useful tool to model complex languages such as Statecharts and UML visual notations [17]. In Fig. 9, it is shown an example of visual environment generated by using VLCC.

In VLCC, the generated editor does not control the syntactic correctness of the sentence drawn by the user. Such a control is committed to the generated language compiler. In other system proposals, a formalism is used to generate a syntax-directed editor which drives the language users in their editing actions [24]. However, the consideration about the strict editing rules imposed by those editors and the consequent limitations in the manipulation of visual sentences has led to the introduction of the metaphor of *intelligent editing.* This metaphor is used by the *Penguin* system, which has the Constraint Multiset Grammars as underlying formalism [13]. The approach is based on the application of an incremental parsing technique to the sentence under construction, allowing for incorrect intermediate visual sentences, providing feedback of the recognized parts, and supporting object manipulation.

The same approach is also adopted by the *DiaGen* system that allows for the rapid development of powerful diagram editors [38]. The generated editors combine free-hand editing with syntax-directed editing. Indeed, an analysis module, which is based on hypergraph transformations and grammars, verifies the structure and the syntactic correctness of diagrams on-line during the editing process. The results of structural analysis are used to provide syntactic highlighting and an interactive automatic layout facility. The layout mechanism is based on flexible geometric constraints and relies on an external constraint-solving engine.

The visual language programming environment generator VLPEG benefits from the appealing features of the underlying Symbol-Relation grammar formalism which allows for a high level of abstraction during the language specification. This is possible also due to a lexical analyzer able to interpret the physical layout of the input visual sentence and to identify the relevant relationships between the graphical symbols composing the sentence [21, 22]. The system provides further support in the rapid prototyping process, offering the capability of automatically generating the syntax of the language by using an inference module. Such a module extends

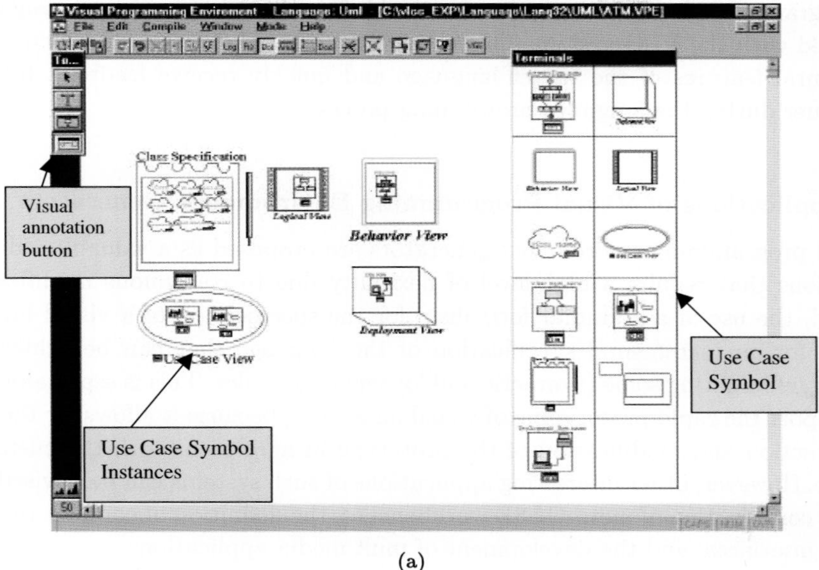

(a)

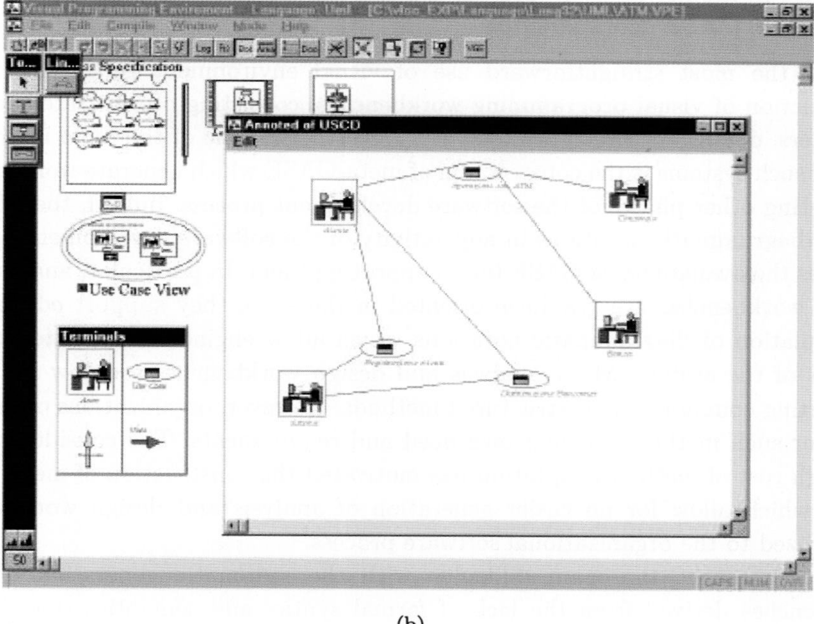

(b)

Fig. 9. VLCC allows us to generate a visual environment for the hierarchical visual notations of UML. As an example, the *Class* object of the *Class Diagram* language can be visually annotated with the *State Diagram* language. Figure (a) shows the generated visual programming environment. The user can click on the annotation button highlighted in the figure and then on the Class object that he/she needs to annotate. As an effect, the user can draw a class diagram and possibly zoom in a class to define or modify its state diagram (b).

to diagrammatic languages the grammatical inference techniques previously experimented with the VLG system. This capability allows the designer to focus on the structural features of the target language and quickly receive feedback from the customer during the language prototyping process.

6. Applications of Visual Programming Environment Generators

Visual programming environment generators are proposed as a valuable aid in applications that require a high-level of flexibility due to continuous modifications. Indeed, the use of a grammar formalism for the specification of a visual language allows for an incremental specification of the language that can be achieved by adding/eliminating some (syntactic and/or semantic) rules. This is especially useful to support the rapid prototyping of visual languages, because it allows for the rapid construction and modification of the prototype in agreement with the customer's advice. However, other interesting applications of such systems can be devised, such as the construction of meta-CASE workbenches, the definition of complex diagrammatic interfaces, and the development of multimedia applications.

6.1. *Meta-CASE workbenches*

One of the most straightforward use of visual environment generators is the construction of visual programming workbenches, consisting of integrated editors, compilers, debuggers, prettyprinters, etc. Nevertheless, one of the most interesting uses of such systems is the construction of meta-CASE which generate workbenches supporting other phases of the software development process. Indeed, the effective use of diagrammatic notations in any activity of the software development process requires the availability of CASE tools supporting them. In particular, analysis and design workbenches are graphical oriented in the sense they support editing and manipulation of diagrammatic notations which allow engineers to create suitable models of the system. Many analysis and design workbenches are now available, supporting commonly used structured methods. However, organizations often wish to tailor such methods to their own need and requirements. The consideration of the high cost of method adaptation has motivated the construction of meta-CASE tools, which allow for an easier generation of analysis and design workbenches customized to the organizational software process.

Until recently, the main difficulty with the automatic generation of such workbenches derived from the lack of formal syntax and semantics specification of diagrammatic notations used as part of analysis and design methods. The formal specification methods proposed in the visual language research area can be profitably used to this aim. In particular, visual language generation tools can represent the core part of meta-CASE tools, and several research efforts are presently being put on this topic.

6.2. *Graphical user interfaces*

The advent of graphical user interfaces as a means of human-computer interaction has greatly contributed to the usability of computer systems. Such an interface presents the user with visual objects representing elements of their information space that they can directly manipulate without having to describe the action to be executed. However, the creation of GUIs represents a difficult and expensive task. The development of these modern interfaces often requires the major part of software project resources due to the costs for their design, implementation, debug and modification.

In recent years much effort has been devoted to make the development of interactive graphical applications more effective, so that they better address users' needs. The effectiveness of a graphical user interface is related to the capability of satisfying user preferences, tasks and problems and is determined by the consistency between user's intention and machine interpretation. It is well-known that one of the main difficulties in the development of graphical user interfaces lies in the achievement of a clear and unambiguous comprehension of the customer's needs [58]. For that reason the user must take part in the interface design process, giving rise to a user-centered approach. In that sense, the prototyping approach represents the most appropriate development methodology to generate customized GUIs. The success of such an approach is strongly affected by a rapid construction and modification of the prototype in agreement with the customer's requirements.

To this aim, several User Interface Management Systems (UIMS) have been developed, which use special purpose languages or other formalisms such as state transition networks in order to describe the interfaces and make the user interface development easier. However, these systems have two major faults. First, the semantic meaning of interactions with the user interface can only be described via conventional programming techniques. Second, there is a limited, fixed set of behaviors allowable, which are generally insufficient to the tasks required. Indeed, most UIMS do not integrate into the interface the application representation domain. Thus, the generated interfaces are not actually graphical, but are rather based on the use of standard widgets. As pointed out in [44], the effective monitoring and maintenance of complex systems, such as electric power plants, the life support systems of space stations, systems for fault diagnosis in orbiting satellites, require sophisticated graphical interfaces able to organize and present relational information. For that purpose, such interfaces need to rely on diagrammatic languages, which are suitable for graphically representing the relationships among involved objects. The result is that such application building tools provide a starting point for building applications, but they are generally inadequate to complete the job.

In the last years, the observation that graphical user interfaces for direct manipulation may be seen as visual languages for human-computer interaction has suggested to use visual languages methodologies and techniques as a basis for the construction of tools able to generate visual interaction systems from formal specification of visual syntax and semantics. Such tools are meant to both generalize and provide facilities to support building applications with richer user interface designs than are currently possible via existing tools. In fact, grammar-based visual environment generators allow the designer to define the target graphical interface by providing the syntactic and semantic specification of the visual language, disregarding the visual environment creation which is automatically performed by the system.

6.3. *Multimedia applications*

A multimedia application is formed by a collection of multimedia objects. Many multimedia applications are mainly based on visual objects. Thus, the techniques and methodologies developed in the field of visual languages can be profitably used in the development of multimedia systems. As a matter of fact, in the last years increasing attention has been put on visual languages with customization capabilities, which allow users to introduce new icons, and edit iconic sentences with different meanings and with dynamic and interactive aspects. Such languages can support dynamic access of media, by letting users customize icons for accommodating multimedia objects [11].

On the other hand, the use of visual environment generators could simplify not only the development, but also the generation of control mechanisms for multimedia presentations. Although there is no standard methodology yet for specifying multimedia applications, most current methods for multimedia development employ graphical notations, like hypergraphs, Petri nets, extensions of UML [51]. These graphical notations could be effectively realized through visual environment generators. Moreover, the parsing of visual notations used in multimedia development could provide means to control the associated multimedia presentations.

7. Conclusions

Many important issues in the area of visual programming languages can be pointed out, whose investigation may strongly impact the field of software engineering. Among them, the *scaling–up* problem should be addressed, in order to make visual programming languages more suitable for handling large real world applications. Several visual programming languages, such as LabVIEW, provide visual abstraction mechanisms that have turned out to be effective for an efficient complexity management in the development of large applications. Other languages tackle the scaling–up issue adopting an object-oriented approach where the inheritance allows for a sort of refinement in the system modeling. This is the case for Prograph, where an object subclass may modify the inherited methods of its superclass arbitrarily. Thus, we might expect that a solution to the scaling–up issue will derive from the exploitation of those successful approaches.

Another relevant issue is concerned with the design and characterization of cognitively effective visual languages. Several efforts have been put on this matter, but much work has to be done to provide methodologies for the empirical and systematic evaluation of visual languages.

Finally, the advances in hardware technologies and software graphics will provide further challenges to the visual language research community. In particular, dramatic new capabilities for human-computer interaction will derive from the extension of visual languages to 3D interaction languages.

References

1. R. Bardohl, "GENGED — A generic graphical editor for visual languages based on algebraic graph grammars", *Proceedings of the IEEE Symposium on Visual Languages* (1998) 48–55.
2. R. Bardohl, M. Minas, A. Schürr and G. Taentzer, "Application of graph transformation to visual languages", *Handbook on Graph Grammars: Applications*, ed. G. Rozenberg, Vol. 2 (World Scientific, 1998) 105–180.
3. G. Booch, J. Rumbaugh and I. Jacobson, *The Unified Modeling Language User Guide* (Addison-Wesley, 1998).
4. P. Bottoni, M. F. Costabile, S. Levialdi and P. Mussio, "Specifying dialogue control in visual interactive systems," *Journal of Visual Languages and Computing* **9** (1998) 553–564.
5. D. Budgen, *Software Design* (Addison-Wesley, 1993).
6. M. M. Burnett, *http://www.cs.orst.edu/~burnett/vpl.html.*
7. M. M. Burnett and A. L. Ambler, "Interactive visual data abstraction in a declarative visual programming language", *Journal of Visual Languages and Computing* **5** (1994) 29–60.
8. M. M. Burnett and M. J. Baker, "A classification system for visual programming languages", *Journal of Visual Languages and Computing* **4** (September 1994) 287–300.
9. S. K. Chang, *http://VisualLanguages.ksi.edu.*
10. S. K. Chang, (ed.), *Visual Languages and Visual Programming* (Plenum Publishing Corporation, New York, 1990).
11. S. K. Chang, *Multimedia Software Engineering* (Kluwer, 2000).
12. S. K. Chang, M. J. Tauber, B. Yu and J. S. Yu, "A visual language compiler," *IEEE Transactions on Software Engineering* **15** (1989) 506–525.
13. S. S. Chok and K. Marriott, "Automatic construction of intelligent diagram editors", *Proceedings of the UIST'98*, San Francisco, California (1998) 185–194.
14. W. Citrin, R. Hall and B. Zorn, "Programming with visual expressions", *Proceedings of the IEEE Symposium on Visual Languages* (1995) 249–301.
15. G. Costagliola, A. De Lucia, S. Orefice and G. Tortora, "Automatic generation of visual programming environments", *IEEE Computer* **28** (1995) 56–66.
16. G. Costagliola, A. De Lucia, S. Orefice and G. Tortora, "A parsing methodology for the implementation of visual systems", *IEEE Transactions on Software Engineering* **23** (1997) 777–799.
17. G. Costagliola, F. Ferrucci, G. Polese and G. Vitiello, "Supporting hybrid and hierarchical visual language definition", *Proceedings of the IEEE Symposium on Visual Languages* (1999) 236–243.
18. C. Crimi, A. Guercio , G. Pacini, G. Tortora and M. Tucci, "Automating visual language generation", *IEEE Transactions on Software Engineering* **16** (1990) 1122–1135.

19. T. DeMarco, *Structured Analysis and System Specification* (Yourdon Press, New York, 1978).
20. F. Ferrucci, G. Pacini, G. Satta, M. Sessa, G. Tortora, M. Tucci and G. Vitiello, "Symbol-relation grammars: A formalism for graphical languages", *Information and Computation* **131** (1996) 1–46.
21. F. Ferrucci, F. Napolitano, G. Tortora, M. Tucci and G. Vitiello, "A predictive parser for visual languages specified by relation grammars", *Proceedings of the IEEE Symposium on Visual Languages* (1997) 292–299.
22. F. Ferrucci, G. Tortora, M. Tucci and G. Vitiello, "VLPEG: A system for rapid prototyping of visual language environments", Technical Report, *Dip. Di Matematica e informatica*, University of Salerno (2000).
23. E. J. Golin and S. P. Reiss, "The specification of visual language syntax", *Proceedings of the IEEE Workshop on Visual Languages*, Rome, Italy (October 1989) 105–110.
24. C. A. M. Grant, "Visual language editing using a grammar-based visual structure editor", *Journal of Visual Languages and Computing* **9** (1998) 351–374.
25. T. R. G. Green and M. Petre, "Usability analysis of visual programming environments: A 'Cognitive Dimensions' Framework'", *Journal of Visual Languages and Computing* **7** (1996) 131–174.
26. D. Harel, "StateCharts: A visual formalism for complex systems", *Science of Computer Programming* **8** (1987) 231–274.
27. R. Helm and K. Marriott, "Declarative specification of visual languages", *Proceedings of the IEEE Workshop on Visual Languages*, Skokie, Illinois (1990) 98–103.
28. D. D. Hils, "Visual languages and computing survey: Data flow visual programming languages", *Journal of Visual Languages and Computing* **3** (1992) 69–101.
29. M. Hirakawa, M. Tanaka and T. Ichikawa, "An iconic programming system, HI-VISUAL", *IEEE Transations on Software Engineering* **16** (1990) 1178–1184.
30. B. Ibrahim, *http://cuisung.unige.ch/Visual/VP.TechRep.html.*
31. D. Janssens and G. Rozenberg, "On the structure of node-label controlled graph languages", *Information Sciences* **20** (1980) 191–216.
32. T. D. Kimura, J. W. Choi and J. M. Mack, "Show and tell: A visual programming language", *Visual Programming Environmments*, ed. E. P. Glinert (IEEE Computer Science Press) 397–404.
33. LabVIEW, *http://www.ni.com/labview/default.htm.*
34. J. H. Larkin and H. A. Simon, "Why a diagram is (sometimes) worth ten thousand words", *Cognitive Science* **11** (1987) 65–99.
35. K. Marriott, "Constraint multiset grammars", *Proceedings of the IEEE Symposium on Visual Languages* (1994) 118–125.
36. K. Marriott and B. Meyer (ed.), *Visual Language Theory* (Springer-Verlag, 1998).
37. P. McLain and T. D. Kimura, "Show and Tell user's manual", Washington University Technical Reporta WUCS-86-4 (March 1986).
38. M. Minas, "Diagram editing with hypergraph parser support", *Proceedings of the 13th IEEE Symposium on Visual Languages*, Capri, Italy (1997) 226–233.
39. M. Moriconi and D. F. Hare, "Visualizing program design through PegaSys", *IEEE Computer* **18** (1985).
40. B. A. Myers, "Taxonomies of visual programming and program visualization", *Journal of Visual Languages and Computing* **1** (1990) 97–123.
41. B. A. Myers, *Peridot: Creating User Interfaces by Demonstration* (MIT Press, Cambridge, MA, 1993).
42. M. A. Najork and S. M. Kaplan, "The cube language", *Proceedings of the IEEE Workshop on Visual Languages*, Kobe, Japan (1991) 218–224.

43. M. A. Najork and S. M. Kaplan, "Specifying visual languages with conditional set rewrite systems", *Proceedings of the IEEE Workshop on Visual Languages* (1993) 12–18.
44. B. A. Nardi and C. L. Zarmer, "Beyond models and metaphors: Visual formalisms in user interface design", *Journal of Visual Languages and Computing* **4** (1993) 5–33.
45. F. B. Paulo, P. C. Masiero and M. C. Ferreira de Oliveira, "Hypercharts: Extended statecharts to support hypermedia specification", *IEEE Transactions on Software Engineering* **25**, no. 1 (1999).
46. S. R. Reiss, "Graphical program development with PECAN program development system", *Sigplan Notices* **19** (1984) 30–41.
47. C. Rader, G. Cherry, C. Brand and A. Repenning, "Principles to scaffold mixed textual and iconic end-user programming languages", *Proceedings of the IEEE Symposium of Visual Languages*, Nova Scotia, Canada (1998) 187–194.
48. J. Rekers and A. Schürr, "Defining and parsing visual languages with layered graph grammars", *Journal of Visual Languages and Computing* **8** (1997) 27–55.
49. A. Repenning and W. Citrin, "Agentsheets: Applying grid-based spatial reasoning to human-computer interaction", *Proceedings of the IEEE Workshop on Visual Languages*, Bergen, Norway (1993) 77–82.
50. R. V. Rubin, J. Walker II and E. J. Golin, "Early experience with the visual programmer's workBench", *IEEE Transactions on Software Engineering* **16** (1990) 1107–11221.
51. S. Sauer and G. Engels, "Extending UML for modeling multimedia applications", *Proceedings of the IEEE Symposium on Visual Languages* (1999) 80–87.
52. A. Schürr, A. Winter and A. Zündorf, "Visual programming with graph rewriting systems", *Proceedings of the IEEE Symposium on Visual Languages* (1995) 326–335.
53. B. Selic, "An efficient object-oriented variation of the statecharts formalism for distributed real-time systems", *CHDL'93: IFIP Conference on Hardware Description Languages and Their Applications*, Ottawa, Canada (1993).
54. B. Selic, G. Gullekson and P. Ward, *Real-Time Object-Oriented Modeling* (John Wiley & Sons, New York, 1994).
55. B. Selic and J. Rumbaugh, "Using UML for modeling complex real-time systems", *http://www.objectime.com/otl/technical/umlrt.html* (1998).
56. N. C. Shu, "Visual programming languages: A perspective and a dimensional analysis", *Visual Languages*, eds. S. K. Chang, T. Ichikawa and P. A. Ligomenides (Plenum Publishing Corporation, New York, 1986) 11–34.
57. D. C. Smith, A. Cypher and J. Spohrer, "Kidsim: Programming agents without a programming language", *Communication of the ACM* **37** (1994) 55–67.
57b. D. C. Smith, A. Cypher and L. Tesler, "Novice Programming Comes of Age", *Communications of the ACM* **43**, no. 3 (2000) 75–81.
58. I. Sommerville, *Software Engineering* (Addison Wesley, 1995).
59. S. Steinman and K. Carver, *Visual Programming with Prograph CPX* (Manning Publications/Prentice-Hall, Englewood Cliffs, 1995).
60. G. Tortora "Structure and interpretation of visual languages", *Visual Languages and Visual Programming*, ed. S.-K. Chang (Plenum Press, New York, 1990) 3–30.
61. S. M. Uskudarli and T. B. Dinesh, "Towards a visual programming environment generator for algebraic specifications", *Proceedings of the IEEE Symposium on Visual Languages*, Darmstadt, Germany (1995) 234–241.
62. K. N. Whitley, "Visual programming languages and the empirical evidence for and against", *Journal of Visual Languages and Computing* **8** (1997) 109–142.

63. K. Wittenburg and L. Weitzman, "Relational grammars: Theory and practice in a visual language interface for process Modeling", *Visual Language Theory* (Springer-Verlag, 1998) 193–217.

SOFTWARE ENGINEERING FOR VISUAL PROGRAMMING LANGUAGES

MARGARET BURNETT

Department of Computer Science,
Oregon State University, Corvallis, OR 97331
E-mail: burnett@cs.orst.edu

This article describes emerging research into how visual programming languages may lead to and even require the development of new software engineering support paradigms.

Keywords: Visual programming languages, software engineering, end-user programming, end-user software engineering, Forms/3.

1. Introduction

Visual programming languages (VPLs) are becoming increasingly common in several domains. For example, visual programming languages or sublanguages are becoming the most common way to do some kinds of GUI programming, are becoming the most common way of specifying visualization graphics depicting scientific data, and are also starting to appear as macro generators for end-user applications. However, despite the increase in the use of VPLs for these and other programming tasks, there has been almost no attention to software engineering support mechanisms when working in these languages.

Visual programming is programming in which more than one dimension is used to convey semantics [3]. Examples of such additional dimensions are the use of multidimensional objects, the use of spatial relationships, or the use of the time dimension to specify "before-after" semantic relationships. Each such potentially significant object or relationship is a token (just as in traditional textual programming languages each word is a token) and the collection of one or more such tokens is a *visual expression.* Examples of visual expressions used in visual programming include diagrams, free-hand sketches, icons, or demonstrations of actions performed by graphical objects. When a programming language's (semantically significant) syntax includes visual expressions, the programming language is a *visual programming language.*

VPLs often include text in a multidimensional way. Traditional textual programming languages sometimes also incorporate a little two-dimensional syntax for text, but only in very limited forms.[a] Thus, multidimensionality is the essential difference between VPLs and strictly textual languages.

This point — that the difference between programming languages that are VPLs and those that are not comes down simply to multidimensionality — seems to predict that software engineering methodologies and devices developed for software written in non-visual programming languages should serve for software written in VPLs as well. However, multidimensionality has led VPLs researchers into new programming frontiers, and there have so far been only the beginnings of accompanying software engineering research into these frontiers. This article surveys several such beginnings using as an example VPL the research visual spreadsheet language Forms/3 [5].

We begin with a discussion of software engineering issues particular to VPLs, and then survey how these issues affect the following subareas of software engineering for VPLs: supporting program comprehension in visual programs, testing visual programs, debugging visual programs, and reusing visual code.

2. Software Engineering Issues Particular to VPLs

Three features alluded to above have particular implications to software engineering in VPLs. The first is diversity of audience: while some users of VPLs are professional programmers, some are end users with no training in professional software engineering notions and methods.

The second is how to develop software engineering approaches that are fully compatible with the non-traditional paradigms and mechanisms used in VPLs. For example, specifying program semantics by directly manipulating objects or demonstrating with concrete examples is not the way programming is done in traditional languages, and there is as yet little research into suitable software engineering support mechanisms for these non-traditional language features.

The third is more an opportunity than a problem: many of the language features made possible by multidimensionality and pioneered in VPLs have inherent elements of software engineering support. The most common of these features are *concreteness*, *directness*, *explicitness*, and *immediate visual feedback*.

Concreteness means expressing some aspect of a program using particular instances, such as specifying some aspect of semantics by specifying desired behavior using a specific object or value. A software engineering implication of concreteness is that, because testing is also done in terms of concrete values, concreteness during program development automatically performs incremental testing on at least one test value.

[a]For example, in traditional languages the x-dimension connects a linear string in the language, but the y-dimension may allow optional line spacing as a documentation device or for limited semantics (such as "continued from previous line"). Here only one of these dimensions truly conveys semantics, and the second dimension has been limited to a teletype notion of spatial relationships so as to be expressible in a one-dimensional string grammar.

Directness in the context of direct manipulation is usually described as "the feeling that one is directly manipulating the object" [18]. From a cognitive perspective, directness in computing means a small distance between a goal and the actions required to achieve the goal [7, 8, 10]. In VPLs, both of these definitions are relevant. As Green and Petre point out in their distillation of psychology-of-programming literature for VPL designers, since "programming requires mapping between a problem world and a program world, the closer the programming world is to the problem world, the easier the problem solving out to be" [7]. An example of directness in a VPL would be manipulating an object to specify its change in location — that is, using movement to specify movement, rather than using functions on numbers (x and y screen coordinates) to specify it.

Some aspect of semantics is *explicit* in the environment if it is directly stated (textually or visually), without the requirement that the programmer infer it. An example of explicitness in a VPL would be explicit depiction of dataflow relationships via edges among related program objects. Such drawings are common software engineering support devices for traditional languages, but only as separate tools that must be invoked in some step separated from the editing or debugging process. In VPLs, such drawings can be part of the language syntax or an automatic side effect maintained by the environment.

In the context of visual programming, *immediate visual feedback* refers to automatic display of effects of program edits. Tanimoto has coined the term *liveness*, which categorizes the immediacy of semantic feedback that is automatically provided during the process of editing a program [21]. An example of a high degree of liveness is the automatic recalculation feature of spreadsheets. This feature provides some of the functionality of traditional debuggers, but is much more incremental.

Given VPLs' unique features, the challenge is to develop software engineering approaches that are compatible with these features and take advantage of the opportunities they offer, yet have the power and rigor of traditional approaches.

3. Dynamic Documentation and Program Comprehension

Program comprehension is critical in the debugging and maintenance phases of the software lifecycle. The combination of concrete values with visual feedback leads naturally to the idea of software animation, and many VPLs include various forms of this. Software animation can be thought of as a dynamically computed documentation mechanism for supporting program comprehension. However, a difference between software animation and separately prepared documentation is that, since the documentation-oriented code is tied to the logic-oriented code, software animations do not become out of date as the source code evolves.

Several empirical studies have been done on VPLs' effects on program comprehension. See Whitley [24] for a survey of this work. The results of these studies have been mixed, reporting findings for some kinds of programs or audiences in which VPLs and/or visual notations are linked with greater comprehension, and others in which strictly textual languages and/or notations have been linked with greater comprehension. Unfortunately, almost all of these studies have investigated only static diagrammatic notations, omitting the dynamic graphics, concreteness, and feedback mechanisms found in many VPLs. However, the use of dynamic

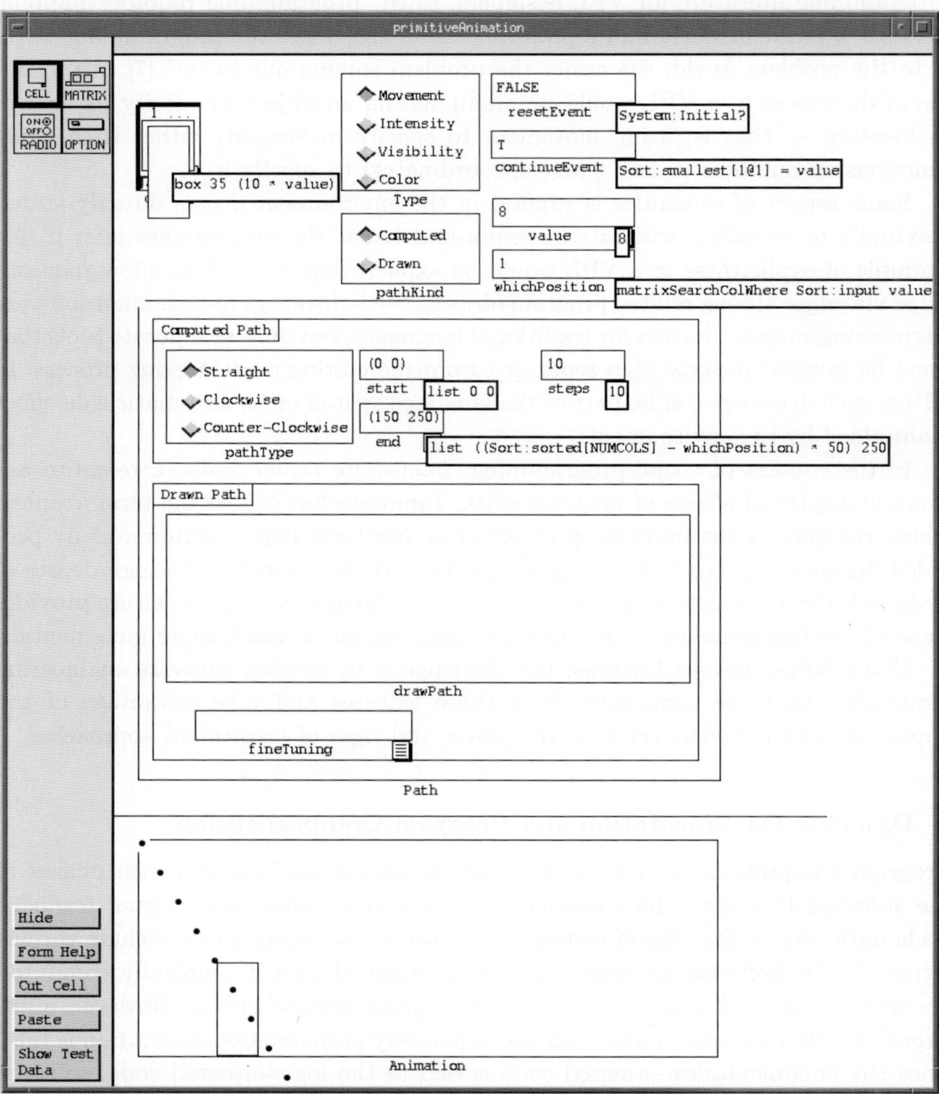

Fig. 1. An animation form for one element of the selection sort animation. The parameters are established in cell formulas at the top and middle (through a flexible combination of text and/or drawing), and the result is at the bottom. Automatic generalization of the formula that references this form causes, on a lazy basis, a copy of this form to be created to animate whichever element is actively being sorted.

graphics of concrete values as a program comprehension mechanism was specifically investigated in two studies regarding software animation's effects on people's ability to comprehend and work with previously existing programs [9, 20]. The results were that animations helped the participants with program comprehension if the participants were actively involved in working with the animations.

The type of animation investigated in these two studies was graphical animation of textual programs, but, as pointed out above, VPLs often include similar capabilities simply as by-products. In Forms/3, animation follows naturally from the combination of support for graphical types, evolving data values, and incremental visual feedback as computations evolve and program edits are made [5]. For example, to provide animated documentation of a selection sort, a programmer may wish to emphasize the "move" portion of the algorithm, having each element glide down the screen to its new location. To specify such an animation, the programmer gives formulas for the intermediate positions through which a graphical depiction of an element should travel, either by specifying straight/clockwise/counter-clockwise and the start, end, and number of steps, or by directly drawing the path (middle of Fig. 1). When the user provides formulas in this form to create an animation of one element of a matrix being sorted, the system automatically generalizes it for the remaining elements of the matrix [6]. After this generalization of Fig. 1, the result is as shown in Fig. 2. For animation effects other than spatial movement, the programmer

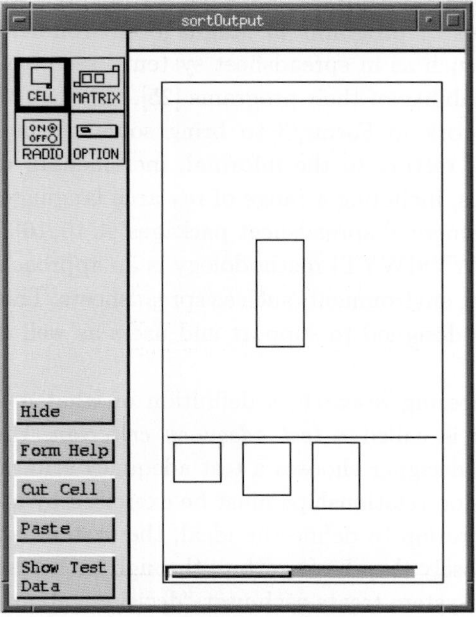

Fig. 2. A sort animation shows the elements of the unsorted group at the top being moved one at a time to the sorted group at the bottom. The final element is moving from the top left corner to the bottom right at this point in the animation.

can select options on the animation form to specify paths through "visibility space" (for fade-in/fade-out sequences), through "color space" (for gradual color transitions), or through "intensity space" (for brightening/dimming transitions).

4. Testing

The high degrees of concreteness and immediate visual feedback present in some VPLs have been motivated in part by a kind of "instant testing" goal, with the idea that if the user immediately sees the result of a program edit, he or she will spot programming bugs as quickly as they are made, and hence will be able to eradicate them right away. This motivation has been especially prevalent in end-user VPLs, but is also found in VPLs for professional programmers.

However, spreadsheet systems provide evidence that concreteness and immediate visual feedback have not been enough for finding and removing most of the bugs in a spreadsheet's formulas: there is a substantial body of research showing that spreadsheets often contain bugs. For example, field audits of real-world spreadsheets have found that 20–40% of these contain bugs, and that between 1% and 4% of all cells contain bugs [22]. Also, in an early empirical study of experienced spreadsheet users, 44% of the spreadsheets created by those users were found to contain user-generated bugs [2]. Results of several later studies have been similar: between 10% and 90% of the spreadsheets examined have been found to contain bugs. (See Panko and Halverson [11] for a survey of these studies.) Compounding this problem, creators of programs in language environments featuring immediate visual feedback, such as in spreadsheet systems, seem to express unwarranted confidence in the reliability of their programs [25].

There is recent work in Forms/3 to bring some of the benefits of applying formalized notions of testing to the informal, incremental, development world of spreadsheet-like VPLs, including a range of research languages in this paradigm as well as standard commercial spreadsheet packages [4, 15, 16]. The "What You See Is What You Test" (WYSIWYT) methodology is an approach to testing for highly visual problem-solving environments such as spreadsheets. The methodology is completely visual, and is designed to support end users as well as more sophisticated programmers.

In software engineering research, a definition of what it means for a program to be tested enough is called a *test adequacy criterion.* Under the WYSIWYT approach, the VPL's designer chooses a test adequacy criterion, such as that each pairing of subexpression relationships must be exercised by at least one test. Using the test adequacy criterion to define the ideal, the system continuously communicates to users how closely they have gotten, through their testing activities, to this ideal. To do this, the system treats each user "decision" about correctness as a test, and the user communicates those decisions to the system by checking off a value whenever he or she notices that it is correct. The system tracks these tests and their implications, and also keeps track of what previous tests need to be redone as a result of formula edits. This approach provides feedback about testing adequacy at all stages of spreadsheet development, with the intent of helping users detect bugs in their spreadsheets.

The methodology has been prototyped in Forms/3, but to best illustrate how an end user might use it, the following scenario illustrates instead how the WYSIWYT methodology might appear if integrated into widely used commercial spreadsheet packages.

Suppose an end user has a printout of a tax form such as in Fig. 3 in front of her, and she wants to use a spreadsheet to figure out the answers. To do this, she has created a spreadsheet such as the one in Fig. 4.

Although this spreadsheet is simple, there are several ways the user could end up reporting the wrong answer. Like many taxpayers, she may be struggling to gather

Form
1040EZ

Department of the Treasury - Internal Revenue Service
Income Tax Return for
Single Filers With No Dependents **1991**

Name & Address

Use the IRS label (see page 10). If you don't have one, please print.

Your social security number

Please see instructions on the back. Also, see the Form 1040EZ booklet.

Presidential Election Campaign (see page 11)
Do you want $1 to go to this fund?

Yes No

Report your income

Attach Copy B of Form(s) W-2 here. Attach tax payment on top of Form(s) W-2.

Note: *You must check Yes or No.*

1 Total wages, salaries, and tips. This should be shown in Box 10 of your W-2 form(s). (Attach your W-2 form(s).)

2 Taxable interest income of $400 or less. If the total is more than $400, you cannot use Form 1040EZ.

3 Add line 1 and line 2. This is your **adjusted gross income**.

4 Can your parents (or someone else) claim you on their return?
☐ **Yes**. Enter amount from line E here.
☐ **No**. Enter 5,550.00. This is the total of your standard deduction and personal exemption.

5 Subtract line 4 from line 3. If line 4 is larger than line 3, enter 0. This is your **taxable income**.

Fig. 3. A portion of a tax form.

1040EZ calculations:				
Presidential election?	yes			
1. Total wages	$5,132			
2. Taxable interest	$297			
3. Adjusted gross	$5,429			
4. Parents?	$1,500		Line E	$1,500
5. Taxable income	$3,929			

Fig. 4. The user's spreadsheet to figure out the taxes. The first few cells are simply data values. Line 3's formula is line 1 + line 2, line 4's formula is a reference to line E, and line 5's formula is line 3–line 4.

up all the required data, and may change her mind about the right data values to enter. If she has been taking shortcuts with the formulas, basing them upon the conditions present in her first version of the data (such as not bothering to use a *max* operator in line 5 to prevent negatives), the formulas are probably not very general, and may cause problems if her data changes. For example, if she entered "line 4–line 3" as the formula for line 5, but later changes line 4 to 5500 because her parents tell her they did not claim her this year after all, then the formula for line 5 will not give the correct answer. Similar problems could arise if she discovers that she entered data from the wrong box of her W-2, and so on.

Even in this simple case, the WYSIWYT methodology can provide benefits. Figure 5 shows a mock-up of how it might be incorporated into a popular spreadsheet package. All cells containing formulas (as opposed to data values) are initially red-bordered with checkboxes, as in Fig. 5(a). The first time the user sees a red border, she moves her mouse over it and the tool tips inform her that "red borders mean untested and blue borders mean tested. You can check cells off when you approve of their values". The user checks off a value that she is sure is correct, and a checkmark ($\surd$) appears in the cell the user checked off, as in Fig. 5(b). Checkmarks are used to show where the user has *explicitly* checked off a value. The wider *implications* of this checkmark are reflected by border colors. Thus, the border of this explicitly approved cell and of cells contributing to it become blue. If she then changed some data, any affected checkmarks would be replaced with question marks (?). This would remind her to check again the cells whose values she thought were important enough to check off before.

Now suppose that, instead of replacing a data value, the user makes the formula change in line 4 alluded to above, changing the previous formula to the constant 5500 instead of the former reference to line E. Since the change she made involved a formula (the one she just changed to a data value), the affected cells' borders revert to red and downstream $\surd$s and ?s disappear, indicating that these cells are now completely untested again. See Fig. 5(c). The maintenance of the "testedness" status of each cell throughout the editing process, as illustrated in Fig. 5(c), is an important benefit of the approach. Without this feature, the user may not realize that the testing she did before became irrelevant with her formula change and now needs to be redone.

1040EZ calculations:				
Presidential election?	yes			
1. Total wages	$5,132			
2. Taxable interest	$297			
3. Adjusted gross	☐ $5,429			
4. Parents?	☐ $1,500		Line E	$1,500
5. Taxable income	☐ $3,929			

(a)

1040EZ calculations:				
Presidential election?	yes			
1. Total wages	$5,132			
2. Taxable interest	$297			
3. Adjusted gross	☐ $5,429			
4. Parents?	☐ $1,500		Line E	$1,500
5. Taxable income	☑ $3,929			

(b)

1040EZ calculations:				
Presidential election?	yes			
1. Total wages	$5,132			
2. Taxable interest	$297			
3. Adjusted gross	☐ $5,429			
4. Parents?	$5,500		Line E	$1,500
5. Taxable income	☐ -$71			

(c)

Fig. 5. A mock-up of a popular spreadsheet package if enhanced by the WYSIWYT technology. In this black-and-white shot, red shows as dark gray and blue shows as lighter gray. (a): All cells containing formulas are initially red, meaning untested. (b): Whenever the user makes a decision that some data value is correct, she checks it off. The checkmark appears in the cell she explicitly validated. Further, all the borders of cells contributing to that correct value become more tested (closer to pure blue). This example has such simple formulas, all the cells at this point are pure blue, meaning fully tested. (c): The user changes the formula in line 4 to a constant. This change causes the affected cell in the bottom row to be considered untested again; hence it is now pure red.

A primary goal of this approach is to reduce overconfidence about the correctness of spreadsheet formulas. In an empirical study, the methodology significantly reduced overconfidence about how tested spreadsheets were, as well as improving effectiveness and efficiency of testing [17].

The next year, the user may want to improve the spreadsheet so that she can use it year after year without having to redesign each formula in the context of the current year's data values. For example, she adds the yes/no box from the tax form's line 4 to her spreadsheet's line 4 and uses the *if* operator in the formula for line 4.

1040EZ calculations:					
Presidential election?		yes			
1. Total wages		5132			
2. Taxable interest		297			
3. Adjusted gross		=C4+C5	☐		
4. Parents?	yes	=IF(B7="yes",F7,5550)	☐	Line E	1500
5. Taxable income		=C6-C7	☑		

Fig. 6. Some cells require more than one test value to become completely tested, as this formula view with purple cell borders and red and blue arrows between subexpressions shows. The adjusted gross value is blue-bordered, the two below it are purple, the arrow from F7 is blue, and the arrow from 5550 is red.

Because of this *if*, she will need to try at least two test cases for line 4's cell to be considered tested: one that exercises the "*yes*" case and one that exercises the "*no*" case. (See Rothermel *et al* [15, 16] for descriptions of the coverage criteria currently in use as well as other possible criteria that can alternatively be employed.)

Because of this, when the user checks off one data value as in Fig. 6, the border for lines 4 and 5 turn purple (50% blue and 50% red). To figure out how to make the purple cells turn blue, the user selects one of them and hits a "show details" button. The system then draws arrows pertaining to the subexpression relationships, with colors depicting which cases still need to be tested. The arrow from the last subexpression is red, pointing out that the "no" case still needs to be tried.

5. Debugging

We pointed out earlier that the concreteness and immediate visual feedback features present in a number of VPLs provide some of the functionality needed for debugging. However, the prevalence of formula errors in spreadsheets shows that this functionality, valuable though it is, is not enough to either keep the errors out in the first place, or to get the errors out once they get in.

In order to begin debugging, a user must first know that something is wrong. The animations (dynamic documentation) described in Sec. 3 are one potential way VPLs can use to help the user spot incorrect behavior. Another possibility is that, during the testing interactions described in Sec. 4, the user comes across a value that is not correct.

After the user has detected the presence of an error, debugging is classically said to have three stages: locating the error, fixing it, and then verifying that the fixed portion is now correct. To provide support for locating the error, the WYSIWYT methodology has been extended as follows. In addition to marking values correct with a checkmark, a user can mark a value incorrect by X'ing it out. The dataflow path contributing to the X'd out value is the portion of the spreadsheet in which the fault exists, and this is highlighted to the user; see Fig. 7. The technique used to decide which cells to highlight is a set of heuristics based on ideas from research in slicing and dicing [12].

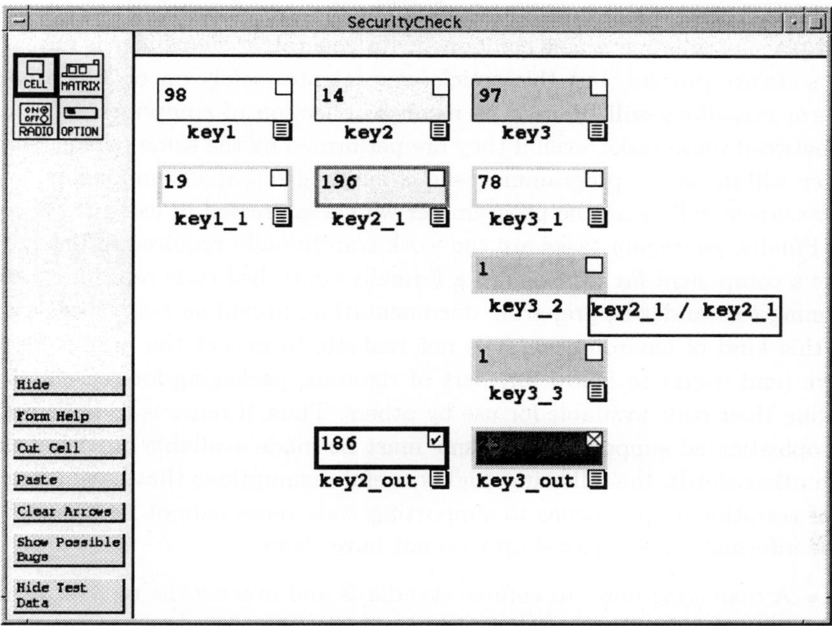

Fig. 7. An incorrect value is present in cell key3_out, indicated by an X in the checkbox, placed by the user. The system can display the sub-slice in which the fault lies (highlighted cells). Each cell's likelihood of containing the fault is communicated by the darkness of its background.

Forms/3 does not explicitly support the fixing stage, other than to follow the VPL common practice of allowing formulas to be edited incrementally without requiring separate tools for editing, compiling, etc. However, the verify stage is the same idea as regression testing, which is supported by the WYSIWYT methodology. In Forms/3, if a cell is edited, downstream cell colors, border colors, checkmarks, and question marks are reset, making explicit to the user which cells need to be re-examined at this point.

6. Code Reuse

Although the idea of reusing code is very appealing, effective reuse has long been acknowledged as a problem. To help address the difficulties, many advocate a strong management commitment to code reuse, leading to the treatment of code as an asset to be carefully managed in a well organized repository. However, the advent of the web may bring a change to this outlook, encouraging informal, loosely organized code repositories. This may be particularly true for the VPLs that are aimed at end users, whose software creations are not usually managed by anyone other than themselves. In fact, some recent commercial end-user VPLs such as AgentSheets [13] and Stagecast (previously known by the names Cocoa and KidSim) [19] already provide just such repositories.

This discussion of reuse will be confined to the use of an existing code component in place of creating a new component. In general, a *component* is any artifact of the software process, but this article concentrates solely on code components. The term *repository* will be used to mean a collection of components. To distinguish between reuse tasks, even if they are performed by the same person, the term *producer* will mean the programmer who is building reusable components, and the term *consumer* will mean the programmer who is interested in using these components. Finally, *packaging* tasks are the work traditionally required of producers to prepare a component for inclusion in a formally controlled code repository, such as conforming to standards, preparing documentation, providing test suites, etc.

In this kind of environment, it is not realistic to expect the producers of the software (end users) to follow any sort of rigorous, packaging-for-reuse standards in making their code available for use by others. Thus, if reuse is to be supported, more sophisticated support mechanisms must be made available on the consumer side. In other words, the following, highly useful assumptions that have formed the basis of traditional approaches to supporting code reuse cannot be assumed here because informal repositories simply do not have them:

- A managing body to enforce standards and oversee the repository.
- A set repository structure such as a hierarchy of component categories or collections.
- Component producers who meticulously provide component packaging to aid the consumer.

Biggerstaff and Richter [1] identify four fundamental reuse problems a successful reusability system must address: finding components, understanding components, modifying components, and composing components. But given a constantly evolving repository with no requirement for classification or packaging by the code producer, how can a VPL support these needs?

Finding components has been the area best supported by traditional software engineering support mechanisms, namely query facilities allowing consumers to search by keyword, author, comment contents, etc. Some VPLs have employed these mechanisms as well, and in fact have easily taken them a step forward: by depicting their availability explicitly in the programming environment, a VPL can provide a continual reminder that reuse opportunities exist. For example, the environment of Forms/3 automatically provides a display and query facility for code components available for incorporation and/or specialization into an evolving program [23], as shown in Fig. 8.

Having found a possibly reusable component, a consumer's next step will be to understand enough about its behavior to determine whether to consider making use of it. This is an area of opportunity for VPLs, because if a VPL includes aids to program comprehension, and if the VPL also features tightly integrated encouragement for reuse, then the two can work together to form a "whole bigger than the sum of its parts". For example, in Forms/3, if the consumer is interested

(a)

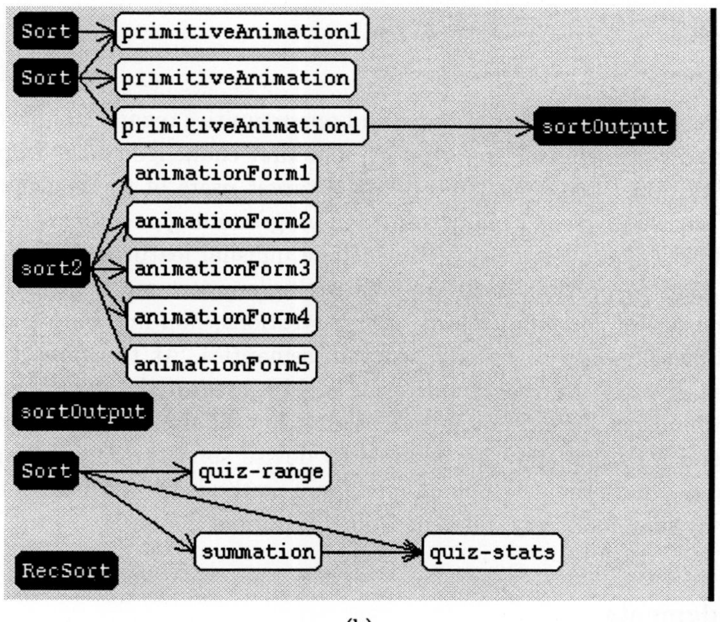

(b)

Fig. 8. (a): Forms/3 has a query facility to help users find potentially useful code components. (b): Interrelationships with other components are shown. Arrows leading out of a node give examples of how other components have used this component.

in a sorting component, he or she can search for it using the query facility in Fig. 8 and, upon clicking on the animation nodes, can watch the dynamic documentation of the sort described in Sec. 3.

Modifying and composing components are the ways consumers actually make use of components they have selected. A recent study of professional Smalltalk users [14] observed that consumers make extensive use of previous usage contexts when figuring out how to use unfamiliar components. The bottom of Fig. 8 shows how the two-dimensional repository display with explicit depiction of relationships with other components helps to facilitate finding examples of how to use it. As with the top of the figure, touching the quiz-stats node brings into view the executable source code of quiz-stats and its supporting nodes, where the user can watch its execution, provide different sample values and try again, and modify or copy portions of quiz-stats as needed for their own purposes. Once a user begins making such changes to incorporate the new component, the testing and debugging features discussed earlier can support this effort.

This ability to browse, retrieve and experiment with usage contexts seems critical to allowing consumers to successfully reuse even code that has not been specially packaged by its producers. This ability permits an alternative to the documentation and standardization procedures traditionally required of producers, which is important in informal repositories and in cooperative repositories not "owned" by any organization.

7. Conclusion

Three features of VPLs raise challenges and opportunities regarding how to provide appropriate software engineering support. The first challenge comes from the fact that non-traditional audiences are often the target users of these languages, and these users are usually not formally trained in programming or software engineering. The second arises because many VPLs include unusual features that do not seem to directly map to previous software engineering support mechanisms. Such features include use of concrete objects, demonstrations, non-imperative paradigms, and multidimensionality to specify program semantics. At the same time, these features also give rise to opportunities for highly integrated software engineering support mechanisms. By attending to the significant differences between traditional languages and VPLs, it may be possible to devise software engineering support methods that achieve the desirable properties of methods for traditional languages, although they may look very different from traditional methods.

Acknowledgments

This work was supported in part by the National Science Foundation under CCR-9806821 and NYI Award CCR-9457473 and by Hewlett-Packard. The material on software animation in Forms/3 summarizes collaborative work by the author with

Paul Carlson and J. J. Cadiz. The material on code reuse in Forms/3 summarizes collaborative work by the author with Rebecca Walpole Djang, Martin Griss, and Gregson Siu. The material on the WYSIWYT methodology summarizes collaborative work by the author with Gregg Rothermel, Lixin Li, James Reichwein, Andrei Sheretov, Curtis Cook, Thomas Green, and Karen Rothermel, with assistance and contributions from several graduate students in the Oregon State University Visual Programming Research Group; patents pending.

References

1. T. Biggerstaff and C. Richter, "Reusability framework, assessment, and directions", eds. T. J. Biggerstaff and A. J. Perlis, *Software Reusability: Concepts and Models*, Vol. 1 (Addison-Wesley, Reading, MA, 1989).
2. P. Brown and J. Gould, "Experimental study of people creating spreadsheets", *ACM Transactions on Office Information Systems* **5** (1987) 258–272.
3. M. Burnett, "Visual programming", ed. J. Webster, *Encyclopedia of Electrical and Electronics Engineering* (John Wiley & Sons, 1999).
4. M. Burnett, A. Sheretov and G. Rothermel, "Scaling up a 'What You See Is What You Test' methodology to testing spreadsheet grids", *1999 IEEE Symposium on Visual Languages* (September 13–16, 1999) 30–37.
5. M. Burnett, J. Atwood, R. Djang, H. Gottfried, J. Reichwein and S. Yang, "Forms/3: A first-order visual language to explore the boundaries of the spreadsheet paradigm", *Journal of Functional Programming* **11**, no. 2 (March 2001) 155–206.
6. P. Carlson, M. Burnett and J. Cadiz, "A seamless integration of algorithm animation into a visual programming language", *ACM Proceedings of AVI'96, International Workshop on Advanced Visual Interfaces* (May 1996) 194–202.
7. T. Green and M. Petre, "Usability analysis of visual programming environments: A 'cognitive dimensions' framework", *Journal of Visual Languages and Computing* **7**, no. 2 (June 1996) 131–174.
8. E. Hutchins, J. Hollan and D. Norman, "Direct manipulation interfaces", eds. D. Norman and S. Draper, *User Centered System Design: New Perspectives on Human-Computer Interaction* (Lawrence Erlbaum Assoc., Hillsdale, NJ, 1986) 87–124.
9. A. Lawrence, A. Badre and J. Stasko, "Empirically evaluating the use of animations to teach algorithms", *1994 IEEE Symposium on Visual Languages* (October 4–7, 1994) 48–54.
10. B. Nardi, *A Small Matter of Programming: Perspectives on End User Computing* (MIT Press, Cambridge, MA, 1993).
11. R. Panko and R. Halverson, "Spreadsheets on trial: A survey of research on spreadsheet risks", *Hawaii International Conference on System Sciences* (January 2–5, 1996).
12. J. Reichwein, G. Rothermel and M. Burnett, "Slicing spreadsheets: An integrated methodology for spreadsheet testing and debugging", *Conference on Domain Specific Languages (DSL'99)* (October 3–5, 1999) 25–38.
13. A. Repenning and J. Ambach, "Tactile programming: A unified manipulation paradigm supporting program comprehension, composition and sharing", *IEEE Symposium on Visual Languages* (September 1996) 102–109.
14. M. Rosson and J. Carroll, "The reuse of uses in smalltalk programming", *ACM Transactions on Computer-Human Interaction* **3**, no. 3 (September 1996) 219–253.

15. G. Rothermel, L. Li, C. DuPuis and M. Burnett, "'What You See Is What You Test': A methodology for testing form-based visual programs", *International Conference on Software Engineering* (April 1998) 198–207.
16. G. Rothermel, M. Burnett, L. Li, C. DuPuis and A. Sheretov, "A methodology for testing spreadsheets", *ACM Transactions on Software Engineering and Methodology* (January 2001) 110–147.
17. K. Rothermel, C. Cook, M. Burnett, J. Schonfeld, T. Green and G. Rothermel, "WYSIWYT testing in the spreadsheet paradigm: An empirical evaluation", *International Conference on Software Engineering* (June 2000) 230–239.
18. B. Shneiderman, "Direct manipulation: A step beyond programming languages", *Computer* **16**, no. 8 (August 1983) 57–69.
19. D. Smith, A. Cypher and J. Spohrer, "Kidsim: Programming agents without a programming language", *Communications of the ACM* **37**, no. 7 (July 1994) 54–67.
20. J. Stasko, A. Badre and C. Lewis, "Do algorithm animations assist learning? An empirical study and analysis", *INTERCHI '93* (April 24–29, 1993) 61–66.
21. S. Tanimoto, "VIVA: A visual language for image processing", *Journal of Visual Languages Computing* **2**, no. 2 (June 1990) 127–139.
22. T. Teo and M. Tan, "Quantitative and qualitative errors in spreadsheet development", *Hawaii International Conference on System Sciences* (January 1997) 149–155.
23. R. Walpole and M. Burnett, "Supporting reuse of evolving visual code", *1997 IEEE Symposium on Visual Languages* (September 23–26, 1997) 68–75.
24. K. Whitley, "Visual programming languages and the empirical evidence for and against", *Journal of Visual Languages and Computing* **8**, no. 1 (February 1997) 109–142.
25. E. Wilcox, J. Atwood, M. Burnett, J. J. Cadiz and C. Cook, "Does continuous visual feedback aid debugging in direct-manipulation programming systems?" *ACM Conference on Human Factors in Computing Systems* (*CHI'97*) (March 22–27, 1997) 258–265.

EVALUATION ISSUES FOR VISUAL PROGRAMMING LANGUAGES

TIM MENZIES

Department of Electrical & Computer Engineering, University of British Columbia, 2356 Main Mall, Vancouver, B.C., Canada V6T 1Z4
E-mail: tim@menzies.com

Many claims are made regarding the benefits of visual frameworks. The case that pictures assist in explaining complicated knowledge seems intuitively obvious. But is it correct? Pre-experimental intuitions must be verified, no matter how compelling they may seem. This article takes a critical look at the available evidence on the efficacy of visual programming (VP) systems. With the available experimental evidence, we find numerous contradictory results regarding the super value of visual over textual languages.

Keywords: Visual languages, evaluation.

1. Introduction

Many systems used in software engineering and knowledge engineering use some sort of visual presentation. Many researchers claim numerous benefits for visual frameworks. For example:

> *When we use visual expressions as a means of communication, there is no need to learn computer-specific concepts beforehand, resulting in a friendly computing environment which enables immediate access to computers even for computer non-specialists who pursue application* [8].

This case that pictures assist in explaining complicated knowledge seems intuitively obvious. But is it correct? Other widely held intuitively obvious beliefs have been found to be incorrect, and sometimes even spectacularly so:

- Galen's incorrect descriptions of human physiology were treated as virtual gospel for 1300 years until one up-start surgeon had the gall (pun intended) to pick up a scalpel and perform dissections for himself (see Versalius' *De Humani Corporis Fabrica*, 1543).
- It took six decades before empirical studies [15] demolished the traditional picture of managers as systematic planners. Those studies found that, in the usual case, managers lacked the time to be systematic. For example, that study found:
  - — Foremen who performed one new task every 48 seconds during their entire shifts.

— Managers who worked for half an hour or more without interruption only once every two days.

Clearly, pre-experimental intuitions must be verified, no matter how compelling they may seem. This article takes a critical look at the available evidence on the efficacy of visual programming (VP) systems. After an introduction to VP, we will review theoretical studies and small scale experimental studies suggest an inherent utility in visual expressions. However, when we explore the available experimental evidence, we find numerous contradictory results.

2. A (Brief) Introduction to Visual Programming

As a rough rule-of-thumb, a visual programming system is a computer system whose execution can be specified *without scripting* except for entering unstructured strings such as *Monash University Banking Society* or simple expressions such as *X above* 7. Visual representations have been used for many years (e.g. Venn diagrams) and even centuries (e.g. maps). Executable visual representations, however, have only arisen with the advent of the computer. With falling hardware costs, it has become feasible to build and interactively manipulate intricate visual expressions on the screen.

More precisely, a non-visual language is a one-dimensional stream of characters while a VP system uses at least two dimensions to represent its constructs [3]. We distinguish between a *pure VP* system and a *visually supported* system:

Pure VP systems: These must satisfy two criteria.

(1) *Rule* 1: The system must execute. That is, it is more than just a drawing tool for software or screen designs.
(2) *Rule* 2: The specification of the program must be modifiable within the system's visual environment. In order to satisfy this second criteria, the specification of the executing program must be configurable. This modification must be more than just (e.g.) merely setting numeric threshold parameters.

Visually supported: Most commercial VP systems such as VISUAL BASIC do not satisfy rules one and two, yet offer some graphical support such as a tree description of the class hierarchy. We call these systems *visually supported*, not *pure VP.*

3. Arguments for the Advantages of VP

Many authors argue that VP systems are a better method for users to interact with a program. Green *et al* [7] and Moher *et al* [16] summarize claims such the above quote from [8] as *the superlativist position*; i.e., graphical representations are inherently superior to textual representations. Both the Green and Moher groups argued that this claim is not supported by the available experimental evidence.

Further, they argue against claims that visual expressions offer a higher *information accessibility*; for example:

> *Pictures are superior to texts in a sense that they are abstract, instantly comprehensible, and universal* [8].

My own experience with students using visual systems is that the visual environment is very motivating to students. Others have had the same experience:

> *The authors report on the first in a series of experiments designed to test the effectiveness of visual programming for instruction in subject-matter concepts. Their general approach is to have the students construct models using icons and then execute these models. In this case, they used a series of visual labs for computer architecture. The test subjects were undergraduate computer science majors. The experimental group performed the visual labs; the control group did not. The experimental group showed a positive increase in attitude toward instructional labs and a positive correlation between attitude towards labs and test performance* [24].

For another example of first year students being motivated by a VP language, see [5] (pp. 18–19). However, merely motivating the students is only half the task of an educator. Apart from motivating the students, educators also need to train students in the general concepts that can be applied in different circumstances. The crucial case for evaluating VP systems is that VP systems improve or simplify the task of comprehending some conceptual aspect of a program. If we extend the concept of VP systems to diagrammatic reasoning in general, then we can make a case that VP has some such benefits. Larkin and Simon [12] distinguish between:

- *Sentential representations* whose contents are stored in a fixed sequence; e.g. propositions in a text.
- *Diagrammatic representations* whose contents are indexed by their position on a 2-D plane.

While these two representations may contain the same information, their computational efficiency may be different. Larkin and Simon present a range of problems modeled in a diagrammatic and sentential representation using production rules. Several effects were noted:

- *Perceptual ease*: Certain features are more easily extracted from diagrams than from sentential representations. For example, adjacent triangles are easy to find visually, but require a potentially elaborate search through a sentential representation.
- *Locality aids search*: Diagrams can group together related concepts. Diagrammatic inference can use the information in the near area of the current focus to solve current problems. Sentential representations may

store related items in separate areas, thus requiring extensive search to link concepts.

A common internal representation for a VP systems is one that preserves physical spatial relationships. For example, Narayanan *et al* [17] use Glasgow's array representation [4] to reason about device behaviors. In an array representation, physical objects are mapped into a 2-D grid. Adjacency and containment of objects can be inferred directly from such a representation. Inference engines can then be augmented with diagrammatic reasoning operators which execute over the array (e.g. boundary following, rotation).

Other authors have argued that diagrams are useful for more than just spatial reasoning. Koedinger [11] argued that diagrams can support and optimize reasoning since they can model whole-part relations. Kindfield [10] studied how diagram used changes with expertise level. According to Kindfield, diagrams are like a temporary swap space which we can use to store concepts that:

- Don't fit into our head right now and ....
- Can be swapped in rapidly; i.e., with a single glance.

Goel [6] studied the use of ill-structured diagrams at various phases of the process of design. In a well-structured diagram (e.g. a picture of a chess board), each visual element clearly denotes one thing of one class only. In a ill-structured diagram (e.g. an impressionistic charcoal sketch), the denotation and type of each visual element is ambiguous. In the Goel study, subjects explored

- preliminary design,
- design refinement, and
- design detailing.

using a well-structured diagramming tool (MacDraw) and a ill-structured diagramming tool (freehand sketches using pencil and paper). Free-hand sketches would generate many variants. However, the well-structured tool seemed to inhibit new ideas rather than help organize them. Once something was recorded in MacDraw, that was the end of the evolution of that idea.

> *One gets the feeling that all the work is being done internally and recorded after the fact, presumably because the external symbol system (MacDraw) cannot support such operations* [6].

Goel found that ill-structured tools generated more design variants (i.e., more drawings, more ideas, more use of old ideas) than well-structured tools. We make two conclusions from Goel's work. Firstly, at least for the preliminary design, ill-structured tools are better. Secondly, after the brain-storming process is over, well-structured tools can be used to finalize the design.

4. Evaluating the Arguments for VP

It is not clear which of the above advantages apply to general software or knowledge engineering. Many software engineering or knowledge engineering problems are not naturally two-dimensional. For example, consider a commonly used visual representation — the entity-relationship diagram used in database design. Such diagrams, by definition, show the relationships between entities *but the positions of the entities in 2-D space do not effect the inferences drawn from that diagram.*

In terms of the ill-structured/well-structured division, the VP tools I have seen in the SE/KE field are all well-structured tools. That is, they are less suited to brain-storming than producing the final product.

Jarvenpaa and Dickson (hereafter, JD) report an interesting pattern in the VP literature [9]. In their literature review on the use of graphics for supporting decision making, they find that most of the proponents of graphics have never tested their claims. Further, when those tests are performed, the results are contradictory and inconclusive. For example:

- JD cite 11 publications arguing for the superiority of graphics over tables for the purposes of elementary data operations (e.g. showing deviations, summarizing data). None of these publications tested their claims. Such tests were performed by 13 other publications which concluded that graphics were better than tables (37.5 percent), the same as tables (25 percent), or worse than tables (37.5 percent).
- JD cite 11 publications arguing for the superiority of graphics over tables for the purposes of decision making (e.g. forecasting, planning, problem finding). None of these publications tested their claims. Such tests were performed by 14 other papers which concluded that graphs were better than tables (27 percent), the same as tables (46 percent), or worse than tables (27 percent).

Similar contradictory results can be found in the study of control-flow and data-flow systems.

- The utility of flowcharts for improving program comprehension, debugging, and extensibility was studied by Shneiderman [21]. Shneiderman found no difference in the performance of the subjects using/not using control-flow diagrams.
- On the other hand, recent results have been more positive [20].
- Studies have reported that Petri nets are comparatively worse as specification languages when compared to pseudo-code [1] or E-R diagrams [22].
- On the other hand, another study suggests that Petri nets are better than E-R diagrams for the maintenance of large expert systems [22].

Given these conflicting results, all that can conclude at this time is that the utility of control-flow or data-flow visual expressions are an open issue.

In other studies, the Green group explored two issues: superlativism and information accessibility (defined above). Subjects attempted some comprehension task using both visual expressions and textual expressions of a language. The Green group rejected the superlativism hypothesis when they found that tasks took longer using the graphical expressions than the textual expressions. The Green group also rejected the information accessibility hypothesis when they found that novices had more trouble reading the information in their visual expressions than experts. That is, the information in a diagram not *instantly comprehensible and universal.* Rather, such information can only be accessed after a training process.

The Moher group performed a similar study to the Green group. In part, the Moher study used the same stimulus programs and question text as the Green group. Whereas the Green group used the LABVIEW data-flow system, the Moher group used Petri nets. The results of the Moher group echoed the results of the Green group. Subjects were shown three variants on a basic Petri net formalism. In no instance did these graphical languages outperform their textual counterparts.

The Moher group caution against making an alternative superlativism claim for text; i.e., text is better than graphics. Both the Moher and Green groups distinguished between sequential programming expressions such as a decision true and circumstantial programming expressions such as a backward-chaining production rule. Both sequential and circumstantial programs can be expressed textually and graphically. The Moher group comments that:

> *Not only is no single representation best for all kinds of programs, no single representation is ... best for all tasks involving the same program* [16].

Sequential programs are useful for reasoning forwards to perform tasks such as prediction. Circumstantial programs are output-indexed; i.e., the thing you want to achieve is accessible separately to the method of achieving it. Hence, they are best used for hypothesis-driven tasks such as debugging.

5. VP as Explanation

The core of the case for VP is something like VP lets us *explain* the inner workings of a system at a glance. This section explores the issue of VP and explanation using the BALSA system.

In the BALSA animator system [2], students can (e.g.) contrast the various sorting algorithms by watching them in action. Note that animation is more than just tracing the execution of a program. Animators aim to explain the inner workings of a program. Extra explanatory constructs may be needed on top of the programming primitives of that system. For example, when BALSA animates different sorting routines, special visualizations are offered for arrays of numbers and the relative sizes of adjacent entries.

Animators like BALSA may or may not be pure VP systems. BALSA does not allow the user to modify the specification of the animation. To do so requires extensive textual authoring by the developer. BALSA therefore does not satisfy the Rule 2 of pure VP system (defined above). Nevertheless, BALSA is an important case study in the use of diagrams to explain a system.

One drawback with the BALSA system is that its explanations must be handcrafted for each task. General principles for explanation systems are widely discussed in AI. Wick and Thompson [23] report that the current view of *explanation* is more elaborate than merely *print the rules that fired* or the *how* and *why* queries of traditional rule-based expert systems. Explanation is now viewed as an inference procedure in its own right rather than a pretty-print of some filtered trace of the proof tree. In the current view, explanations should be customized to the user and the task at hand. For example:

- Paris [18] describes an explanation algorithm that switches from process-based explanations to parts-based explanations whenever the explanation procedure enters a region which the user is familiar with.
- Leake [13] selects what to show the user using eight runtime algorithms. For example, when the goal of the explanation is to minimize undesirable effects, the selected structures are any pre-conditions to anomalous situations. Leake's explanation algorithms require both a cache of prior explanations and (like Paris) an active user model.

Summarizing the work of Wick and Thompson, Leake, and Paris, I diagnosed the reason for the lack of generality in BALSA's explanation system as follows. BALSA's explanation systems were hard to maintain since BALSA lacked:

(1) The ability to generate multiple possible explanations.
(2) An explicit user model.
(3) A library of prior explanations.
(4) A mechanism for using (2) and (3) to selectively filter (1) according to who is viewing the system.

6. Summary

On the positive side, we have seen that:

- Visual systems are more motivating for beginners than textual systems.
- In the case of spatial reasoning problems, a picture may indeed be worth 10,000 words [12]. Given some 2-D representation of a problem (e.g. an array representation), spatial reasoning can make certain inferences very cheaply.
- Also, ill-structured diagramming tools are a very useful tool for brainstorming ideas.

On the negative side, beyond the above three specific claims, the general superlativist case for VP improving SE and KE tasks is not very strong:

- Many software engineering and knowledge engineering problems are not inherently spatial.
- Most of the VP systems I am aware of do not support Goel's ill-structured approach to brainstorming.
- The JD research suggests that claims of the efficacy of VP systems have been poorly documented.
- The Moher and Green groups argue that VP evaluations cannot be made in isolation to the task of the system being studied.
- Lastly, a diagram may not necessarily support information accessibility for knowledge. A good explanation device requires far more than impressive graphics (recall the BALSA case study).

Rigorous methods exist for separately assessing textual systems (e.g. [14]) and visual systems (e.g. [19]). The conclusion from this paper is that it is time to comparatively assess the merits of textual vs visual representations for programming.

References

1. D. A. Boehm-Davis and A. M. Fregly, "Documentation of concurrent programs", *Human Factors* **27** (1985) 423–432.
2. M. B. Brown and R. Sedgewick, "Techniques for algorithm animation", *IEEE Software* (January 1985) 28–39.
3. T. B. Brown and T. D. Kimura, "Completeness of a visual computation model", *Software-Concepts and Tools* (1994) 34–48.
4. J. Glasgow, H. Narayanan and B. Chandrasekaran (eds.), *Diagrammatic Reasoning: Cognitive and Computational Perspectives* (MIT Press, 1995).
5. E. P. Glinert and S. T. Tanimoto, "Pict: An interactive graphical programming environment", *IEEE Computer* (November 1984) 7–25.
6. V. Goel, "'Ill-structured diagrams' for ill-structured problems", *Proceedings of the AAAI Symposium on Diagrammatic Reasoning Stanford University*, March 25–27 (1992) 66–71.
7. T.R.G. Green, M. Petre and R.K.E. Bellamy, "Comprehensibility of visual and textual programs: The test of superlativism against the 'match-mismatch' conjecture", *Empirical Studies of Programmers: Fourth Workshop* (1991) 121–146.
8. M. Hirakawa and T. Ichikawa, "Visual language studies — A perspective", *Software-Concepts and Tools* (1994) 61–67.
9. S. L. Jarvenpaa and G. W. Dickson, "Graphics and managerial decision making: Research based guidelines", *Communications of the ACM* **31**, no. 6 (June 1988) 764–774.
10. A.C.H. Kindfield, "Expert diagrammatic reasoning in biology", *Proceedings of the AAAI Symposium on Diagrammatic Reasoning Stanford University*, March 25–27 (1992) 41–46.
11. K. R. Koedinger, "Emergent properties and structural constraints: Advantages of diagrammatic representations for reasoning and learning", *Proceedings of the AAAI Symposium on Diagrammatic Reasoning Stanford University*, March 25–27 (1992) 154–159.

12. J. H. Larkin and H. A. Simon, "Why a diagram is (sometimes) worth ten thousand words", *Cognitive Science* (1987) 65–99.
13. D. B. Leake, "Focusing construction and selection of abductive hypotheses", *IJCAI'93* (1993) 24–29.
14. T. J. Menzies and B. Cukic, "How many tests are enough?" ed. S. K. Chung, *Handbook of Software Engineering and Knowledge Engineering, Vol. II*, (World Scientific, 2002). Available from *http://tim.menzies.com/pdf/00ntests.pdf*
15. H. Mintzberg, "The manager's job: Folklore and fact", *Harvard Business Review* (July–August 1975) 29–61.
16. T. G. Moher, D. C. Mak, B. Blumenthal and L. M. Leventhal, "Comparing the comprehensibility of textual and graphical programs: The case of petri nets", *Empirical Studies of Programmers: Fifth Workshop* (1993) 137–161.
17. N. H. Narayanan, M. Suwa and H. Motoda, "Behaviour hypothesis from schematic diagrams", eds. J. Glasgow, B. Chandrasekaran and N. H. Narayanan, *Diagrammatic Reasoning* (The AAAI Press, 1995) 501–534.
18. C. L. Paris, "The use of explicit user models in a generation system for tailoring answers to the user's level of expertise", eds. A. Kobsa and W. Wahlster, *User Models in Dialog Systems* (Springer-Verlag, 1989) 200–232.
19. G. Rothermel, L. Lixin, C. DuPuis and M. Burnett, "What you see is what you test: A methodology for testing form-based visual programs", *International Conference on Software Engineering*, Kyoto, Japan (1998) 198–207.
20. D. A. Scanlan, "Structured flowcharts outperform psuedocode: An experimental comparison", *IEEE Computer* **6**, no. 5 (1989) 28–36.
21. B. Shneiderman, "Direct manipulation: A step beyond programming languages" *Computer* (August 1983) 57–69.
22. K. M. Swigger and R. P. Brazile, "Experimental comparisons of design/documentation formats for expert systems", *International Journal of Man-Machine Studies* **31** (1989) 47–60.
23. M. R. Wick and W. B. Thompson, "Reconstructive expert system explanation", *Artificial Intelligence* **54** (1992) 33–70.
24. M. G. Williams, W. A. Ledder, J. N. Buehler and J. T. Canning, "An empirical study of visual labs", *Proceedings 1993 IEEE Symposium on Visual Languages* (IEEE Computer Society Press, 1993) 371–373.

VISUAL PARALLEL PROGRAMMING

KANG ZHANG

Department of Computer Science, The University of Texas at Dallas, Richardson, TX 75083-0688, USA

WENTONG CAI

School of Computer Engineering, Nanyang Technological University, Singapore 639798

NENAD STANKOVIC and MEHMET A. ORGUN

Department of Computing, Macquarie University, Sydney, NSW 2109, Australia

Visualization has been recognized as a powerful means in conveying structural and design information and has been widely used in software development processes. The use of visual programming techniques to design and construct parallel programs has received much attention in recent years due to a great demand for rapid and effective development of parallel programs for high performance computing platforms. This paper reviews the usefulness and challenging issues in visual parallel programming. It demonstrates the visual semantics of several visual parallel programming environments and systems and illustrates, through several examples, how parallel programs could be intuitively constructed.

Keywords: Visual programming, visual languages, parallel programming.

1. Introduction

Programming can be viewed as a conversion process: a programmer transforms an abstract algorithm into a form which can be interpreted by a computer. In general, it is more difficult to perform the transformation when a parallel computer is the target. This is due to the two gaps between programmers and parallel programming languages:

- the desire of programmers to describe their algorithms with manageable abstraction versus the detailed descriptions of parallel constructs required by most parallel programming languages; and
- the programmers' mental conception of a solution versus the realization of a parallel program that actually solves it.

When developing a parallel program, we find that there are four main stages: problem partitioning, program construction, debugging, and performance tuning

[30]. To bridge aforementioned gaps, a variety of visual programming environments have emerged for parallel processing, in which graphics have been used to assist parallel programming according to a pre-defined notation. Such an environment facilitates primarily the first half of the software engineering cycle, i.e., the construction of a parallel program and mapping it onto a multiprocessor system. Various visual notations have been used in different environments and systems. For example, CODE [29], HeNCE [1] and Phred [2] are based on the notion of *dependence graphs*, VPE [5] is based on *BLOX diagrams* [14], and PCG [25] is based on *space-time diagrams* [20]. Graphical visualization techniques have been used in parallel program debugging and performance tuning, i.e., the activities involved in the second half of the software engineering cycle. There have been several reviews [17, 18, 30] on parallel program visualization for debugging and performance tuning. The focus of this paper is on the first half of the software engineering cycle, i.e. visual parallel program design and construction.

In parallel applications, we assume many processors running in parallel. Each processor can run one or more processes. When programming, these processes may be identified individually or grouped together into a structure that closely resembles the aggregation required by algorithms. The interaction between processes is either through the use of shared memory or by message-passing.

Environments like VPE, PCG, and HeNCE are designed for message-passing based systems. In a message-passing environment, a message can be communicated selectively from one process to another or amongst a group of processes. The involved processes may have to be synchronized, or may perform their functions asynchronously. CODE and Phred are designed for both shared memory and distributed memory multiprocessor systems. Whatever the possible solution, a visual programming tool must be scalable and easy to use, providing the programmer with a hardware independent graphical representation of a solution to the problem.

The next section identifies some desired features of a visual parallel programming environment. Section 3 introduces the visual semantics used in several typical systems. A visual program is usually represented by a graph (or a diagram) of interrelated visual symbols. A symbol in a visual programming language, for example, a circle, a line or a box, usually consists of two components: the logical semantics and the physical image. The logical semantics gives the actions to be taken when the program is executed; and the physical image gives the physical appearance of the symbol. The physical image of a symbol should correspond to its logical semantics. Different systems use different visual semantics.

After introducing the semantics of visual symbols in Sec. 3, Sec. 4 focusses on some examples to demonstrate the ways in which VPE and PCG can be used in solving various problems, followed by a comparison of VPE and PCG in Sec. 5. Finally, Sec. 6 concludes the paper with a summary and a recommendation on further readings.

2. Design Factors

Miller [21] outlined several criteria for good visualization techniques, which are also applicable in some aspects when designing visual parallel programming languages. Often, a visual language designer finds it useful to study existing visualization tools or even documentations relating to a particular language before he/she embarks on the design process.

In visualization problems, we first have to come up with a model for describing the behavior of the system under study, and then decide on a graphical or textual representation that will best demonstrate and present its behavior. Visualization tools can be evaluated by observing how close the model is conceptually to the system and how well the representation illustrates the model. In visual programming, we are aiming at providing a set of graphical and/or textual notations for programmers to describe the systems' behavior. Therefore, the same criteria used for evaluating visualization techniques can also be used to evaluate visual languages for parallel programming:

Guidance: A good visual language should "guide" the programmers through the use of intuitive pictorial notations.

Suitability: The visual representations should be easily understandable by the programmer and closely correspond to the underlying parallel computational model; pictorial notations should be simple and easy to work with.

Scalability: It is important for the language to be able to accommodate the development of large and complex parallel programs; multiple levels of hierarchy and abstraction would be necessary in program development.

Interactivity: Interactive feedbacks would be very helpful in increasing the user's program productivity.

Abstraction: Low-level details should be hidden as much as possible so that programmers can concentrate on essential issues.

Ease of use: A good visual language should allow a less steep learning curve than text-based languages so that even a novice programmer can easily master and use it.

Expressiveness: A good visual language for parallel programming should be more expressive than a textual counterpart. It should express parallel computations in a straighforward and intuitive fashion, and should be easily used to solve various complex computational problems.

Environment support: It is more critical for a visual parallel programming system to have an integrated programming environment that consists of a visual editor, compiler, debugger, visualization and performance tuning tools than for a conventional textual parallel programming system.

Some of the above criteria are, in fact, inter-related. For example, a well-understood visual representation can usually give users a good indication as to how it can be used in parallel program construction. Scalability requires that the system supports hierarchical program construction.

In constructing a parallel program, we also need to consider partitioning, communication and synchronization. So, a good parallel visual language should also provide mechanisms to help the programmer to specify these additional programming requirements. In some languages, for example, CODE [29] and HeNCE [1], communication and synchronization can be specified implicitly. VPE and PCG assume that a parallel program consists of a number of processes that interact with each other by passing messages, and express communication and synchronization explicitly. However, as can be seen in the next section, the specification of communication and synchronization in VPE and PCG is straightforward.

Using a visual parallel programming system, a programmer needs to create a conceptual model of his/her problem first, according to message-passing or shared memory parallel programming paradigm. A process (or a group of processes) can then be built using visual notations provided. Finally, processes will be connected graphically to represent either data dependencies or message-passing communications.

3. Visual Semantics

To make a visual language easy to use, first of all, the semantics (or the meaning) of a visual symbol must be easily understood from its appearance (i.e., the image). To make this association straightforward, different levels of visual abstraction are usually adopted in visual language designs.

3.1. *Levels of visual abstraction*

In each of the visual parallel programming systems discussed in this section, the visual language is structured as a three-tiered system. The three layers of visual abstraction are closely related to the way in which a parallel program can be constructed visually (see Sec. 4.1). At the top layer, the visual representation of a process or a group of processes is addressed. A set of visual symbols is provided in the middle layer to allow further construction of a process, such as the specification of message-passing communication in BLOX diagrams and space-time diagrams [20], and dataflow and control-flow in dependence graphs [12]. Finally, at the bottom layer, a visual symbol can be complemented by textual information that is used to either annotate the visual symbol or specify its sequential behaviour.

Programming in those languages is not visual in every aspect, but rather exploits visual mechanisms wherever data flow or parallel controls are found. Sequential code fragments and declarations are formulated in the actual programming language like C or FORTRAN, and as such do not represent visual components of the language. Hence, in this way, for example, the graphical symbols and textual information from the three layers work together to express various message-passing, flow of data and control, and parallel constructs. The languages expressed in VPE, PCG, CODE, HeNCE, and Phred are synthetic, since primitive and composite language components are combined together into real-life constructs. They do not force the programmer to be familiar with every aspect of the message-passing or shared memory paradigm, but rather provide an incremental approach to program construction, since each language itself hides the complexity of the paradigm.

For all the systems to be discussed, the visual semantics of the bottom and the top layers are quite obvious. The major difference between them is the way in which a process is constructed and the way in which the communication or flow of data and control is specified. Therefore, in Secs. 3.2, 3.3 and 3.4, we concentrate on the middle layer of the systems.

3.2. *BLOX Diagram and VPE*

In VPE, at the top layer, a process is represented by a VPE diagram. To allow programmers to visually construct a VPE diagram, a set of visual symbols, representing various constructs in a program, is provided as the middle layer of visual abstraction. The VPE notation is designed based on the BLOX diagram which was first introduced by Glinert [14]. Glinert designed a set of notations for use in a visual programming environment based on strict-spatial representations/metaphors. In a BLOX diagram, for example, the "lock and key" metaphors can facilitate the construction of programs. Some target objects can be constructed using building blocks that look very much like pieces in a "jigsaw puzzle" (see Fig. 1). In this way, the visual appearance of blocks can give hints on interlocking objects, whereby *knobs* are "plugged" into *sockets.*

In a BLOX diagram, the "lock and key" metaphors also present the computation as well as data flow of the program in an easily visible and understood form. Therefore, the complex transformation from abstract algorithm to a computer-understandable form can then be achieved without much effort if metaphors specified by the application domain are properly defined.

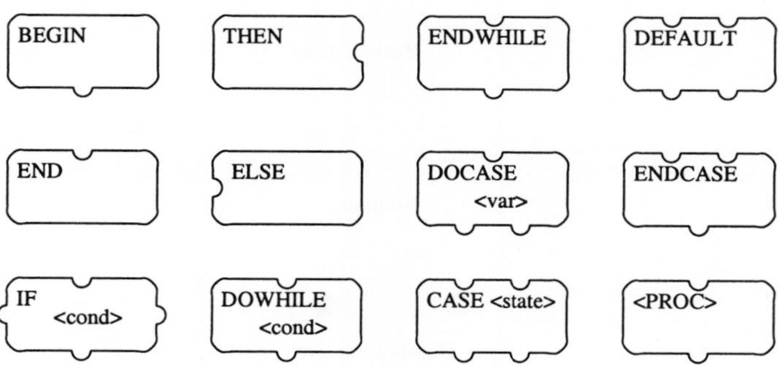

Fig. 1. Primitive building blocks in VPE.

At the bottom layer of visual abstraction, each block has a textual association which corresponds to a C programming language construct. This gives a logical implication of the corresponding physical visual symbol. Figure 1 shows the primitive blocks in VPE. The basic blocks are: `BEGIN`, `END`, `IF`, `THEN`, `ELSE`, `DOWHILE`, `ENDWHILE`, `DOCASE`, `CASE`, `DEFAULT`, `ENDCASE`, `<PROC>`.

The semi-circled *connectors* in each block are used to denote control flow from one block to another. Variables, declared only at a `BEGIN` block, flow along such connectors from block to block. The scope of variables can then be clearly specified as from a `BEGIN` block to the corresponding `END` block. Other basic blocks are self-explanatory according to their names.

Each primitive block is associated with two attributes: *Variable Set* and *Statement Code*. The first attribute allows users to attach variables to a block and the second is for binding a segment of code from a specific programming language to a block.

Some primitive blocks can be used to create hierarchy of diagrams. A composite symbol embedded in the lower right corner of a block, such as the one shown in (Fig. 2), signifies that a lower level diagram is "contained" in the block. We have defined the `THEN`, `ELSE`, `CASE`, `DEFAULT` and `<PROC>` blocks to have this property.

The primitive parallel constructs are: `RECV`, `SEND`, `BARRIER`, `OP`, *adaptors* and *communicators* (see Fig. 3). The adaptors are named as (from left to right in

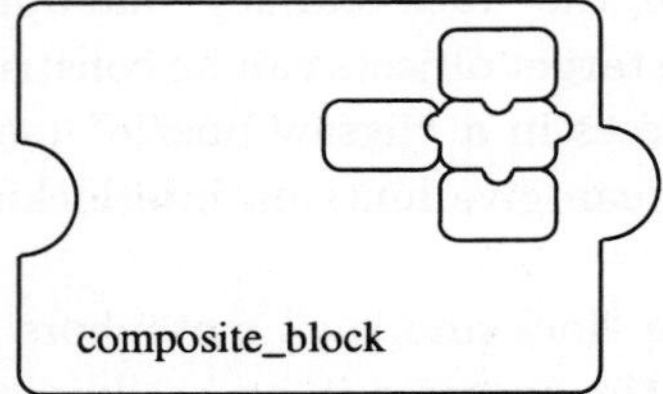

Fig. 2. A composite block in VPE.

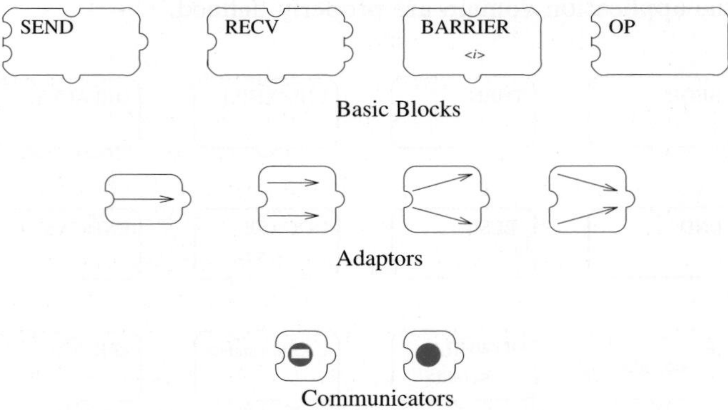

Fig. 3. Primitive blocks for parallel constructs in VPE.

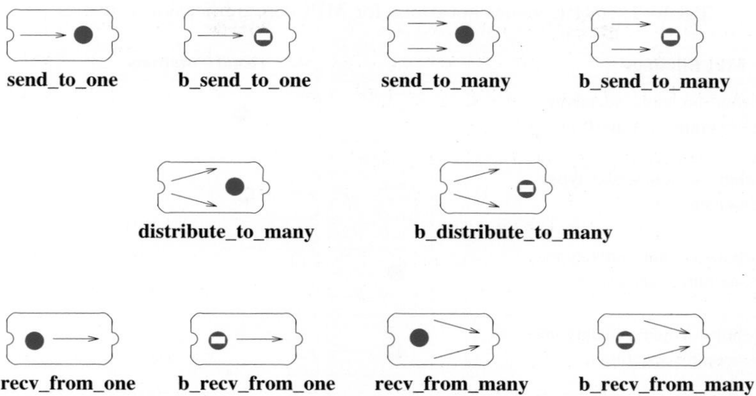

Fig. 4. Communication blocks in VPE.

Fig. 3): `one-to-one`, `one-to-many`, `one-distribute-many` and `many-to-one`. The first indicates a point-to-point communication; the second, a one-to-many communication with the same data set; the third, a one-to-many communication with data scattered over a data set; and the last, a many-to-one communication with data gathered into a single data set. Communicators are differentiated as `blocking` and `non-blocking`, representing synchronous and asynchronous communication respectively.

Using adaptors and communicators, we can create communication blocks that represent different communication patterns in parallel programming. For example, a one-to-one adaptor followed by a blocking communicator can be transformed to a blocking-send communication block: `b_send_to_one`. The communicator selects the mode of communication, while the adaptor causes replications of the communication. The set of communication blocks is shown in Fig. 4.

Communication blocks can be treated as modifiers to the `SEND` and `RECV` blocks. Combination of these blocks will create a rich repertoire of communication routines: different combinations will result in different communication calls. Some examples using MPI [22, 23] are presented in Table 1.

As mentioned earlier, the programming paradigm in VPE is based on message-passing. Both MPMD (Multiple Program Multiple Data) and SPMD (Single Program Multiple Data) style programs can be constructed. In VPE, each top level diagram corresponds to a program, and each execution instance of a program corresponds to a process. Depending on the programming style, a parallel program may consist of a number of top level VPE diagrams. Communication between programs can be specified using the drag-and-drop metaphor from one communication block to another. This operation will make the communicators of the corresponding communication blocks appear in the same colour. Colour coding, instead of a directed line, is used to represent a communication between two processes so that the situations where lines may cross over diagrams are avoided.

Table 1. VPE visual notations for MPI communication routines.

MPI Bindings	Visual Notations
MPI_Isend(<buf>,<count>,<datatype>, <dest>,<tag>,<comm>,<request>);	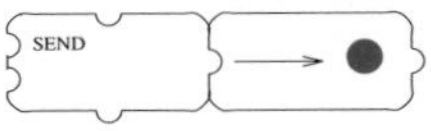 SEND
MPI_Send(<buf>,<count>,<datatype> <dest>,<tag>,<comm>);	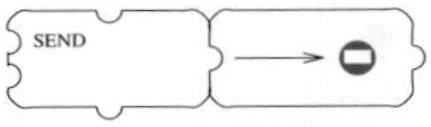 SEND
MPI_Irecv(<buf>,<count>,<datatype>, <src>,<tag>,<comm>,<request>);	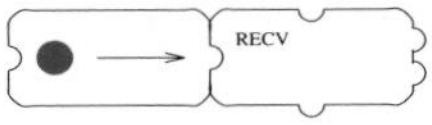 RECV
MPI_Recv(<buf>,<count>,<datatype> <src>,<tag>,<comm>,<status>);	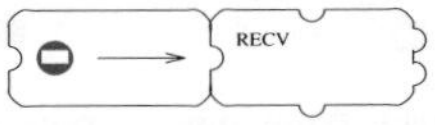 RECV
MPI_Scatter(<sendbuf>,<sendcount>, <sendtype>,<recvbuf>,<recvcount>, <recvtype>,<root>,<comm>);	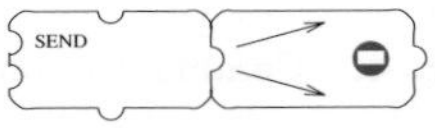 SEND
MPI_Bcast(<buf>,<count>,<datatype>, <root>,<comm>);	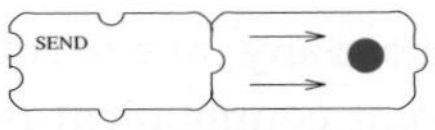 SEND
MPI_Gather(<sendbuf>,<sendcount>, <sendtype>,<recvbuf>,<recvcount>, <recvtype>,<root>,<comm>);	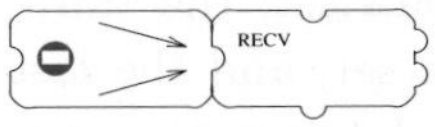 RECV
MPI_Reduce(<sendbuf>,<recvbuf>, <count>,<datatype>,<op>, <root>,<comm>);	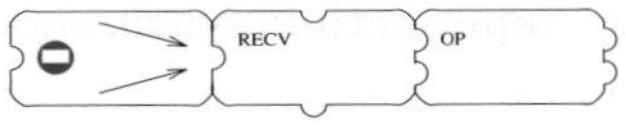 RECV OP
MPI_Allgather(<sendbuf>,<sendcount>, <sendtype>,<recvbuf>,<recvcount>, <recvtype,<comm>);	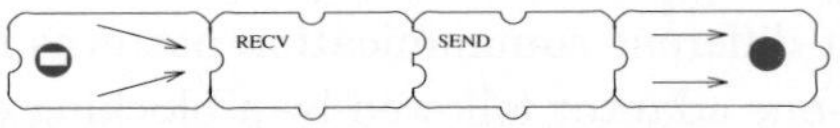 RECV SEND

A simple example of VPE can be found in Fig. 5, in which *program1* reads in a string of characters and passes it to *program2* that converts all the lower-case characters in the string into upper-case. After processing the string, *program2* then passes the result back to *program1*. In the diagram, the numbers besides communicators indicate the linkage of the communication, which in fact represents colour coding in the implementation. There is only a single instance for both *program1* and *program2* in this example.

3.3. *Space-time diagram and PCG*

Space-time diagrams, first proposed by Lamport [20], overcome the disadvantage of animation that does not clearly show patterns of behaviour occurring across time. A space-time diagram presents the execution of a parallel program in a two-dimensional display with time along one direction (vertical or horizontal) and individual processes along the other. It provides a compact view of the event history by showing the temporal relationships and even race conditions among processes.

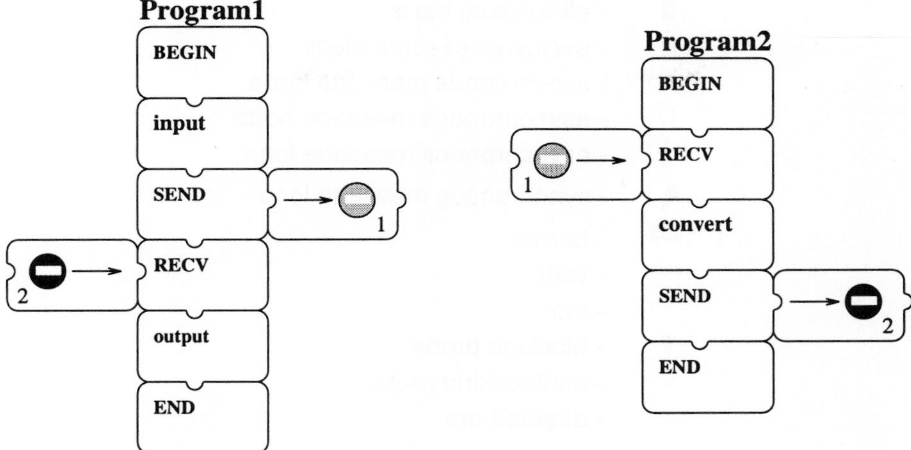

Fig. 5. Example: Point-to-point communication in VPE.

Space-time diagrams have been used for debugging and tuning of parallel and distributed programs, but not for program construction.

Process communication graph (i.e., PCG) [25, 26] originates from the concurrency map [27] and the space-time diagram [20]. It adopts a radical solution to extend the concept of these diagrams into the program construction phase, by redefining the time axis as a control flow axis and adding to the process axis the concept of groups.

Vertical lines in PCG are the top layer of visual abstraction, representing processes and group of processes. We refer to them as *resource lines*. Individual processes are represented by thin lines. There are two types of groups in PCG. A thick solid line represents an unbounded group. It is used when the actual number of processes is not known at design time. A hollow thick line represents a bounded group, where the individual processes that belong to the group are known at design time.

Each resource line has a unique *name* associated with it. The name can also define that process P belongs to group G: $P(G)$, or that group G_1 is a child of group G: $G_1(G)$. A process or a group that has no parent group name associated with it belongs to a default group, the *world*.

At the middle layer of visual abstraction in PCG, graphical symbols are used to describe control sequence, as well as parallel constructs like synchronization and message-passing routines provided in the environment. In the graph language of PCG, annotations can be thought of as attributes, and graphical symbols shown in Fig. 6 as predicates. We refer to predicates as *control symbols* or just *controls*, for short.

Execute blocks are used to add sequential code to the graph. An *all-execute block* designates the code that is executed by all resources in the system. Consequently,

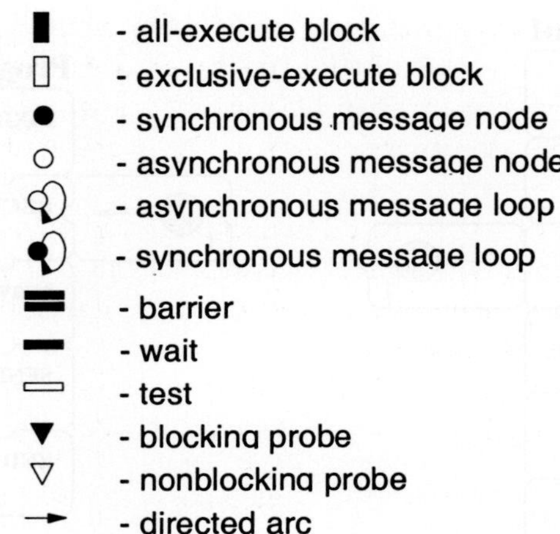

Fig. 6. Control symbols in PCG.

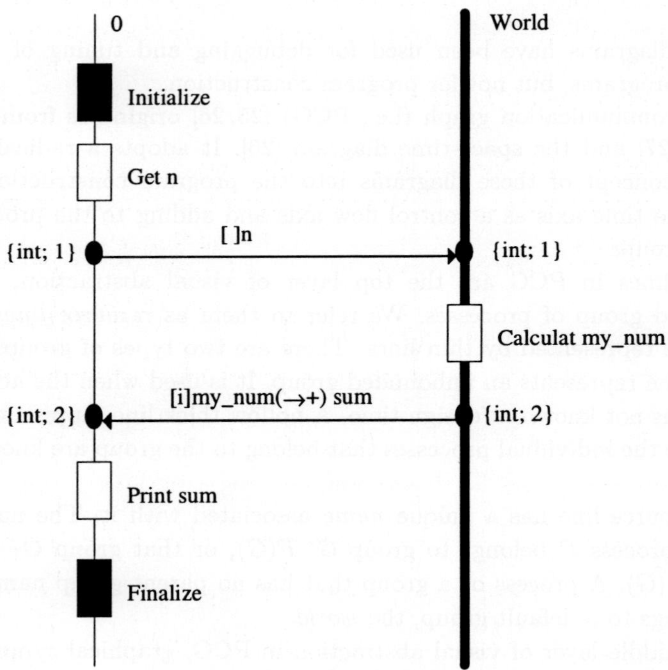

Fig. 7. Example: Communication in PCG.

the resource it is attached to in the graph does not modify its scope. Each main PCG must begin and end with an all-execute block. We refer to them as *Initialize* and *Finalize* blocks, respectively (see example in Fig. 7). An *exclusive-execute block* designates the code that is bounded to the resource it belongs to.

Synchronous and asynchronous *message nodes* describe point-to-point messages and one-to-many or many-to-one collective messages. A *directed arc* that designates direction of the data flow connects them. *Message loops* are used to represent many-to-many collective messages. Other controls in Fig. 6 are used for various types of synchronization.

At the bottom layer of visual abstraction, the annotation in PCG represents the textual information added to a control that follows the graph annotation syntax. Its purpose is to describe modalities of message-passing routines. It is classified in four stanzas: *copy*, *type*, *wait* and *probe*.

Copy stanza, in a most general form, defines the data buffers local to each end of a communication channel and the processes involved in a communication event:

[pR]`sendBuffer`[`bI`]−> [pR]`receiveBuffer`[`bI`]

where `pR` is the processor rank and `bI` is the buffer index. Its syntax is similar to the arc topology specification found in CODE [29], but it does not require dots to be used before the buffer names, because in PCG resource names are used to resolve the ownership. In PCG, copy stanza can be used to annotate communication to represent various collective communication routines. Table 2 shows visual representations of some MPI collective routines.

Table 2. PCG visual notations for MPI communication routines.

MPI Routines	Visual Notations
MPI_Scatter	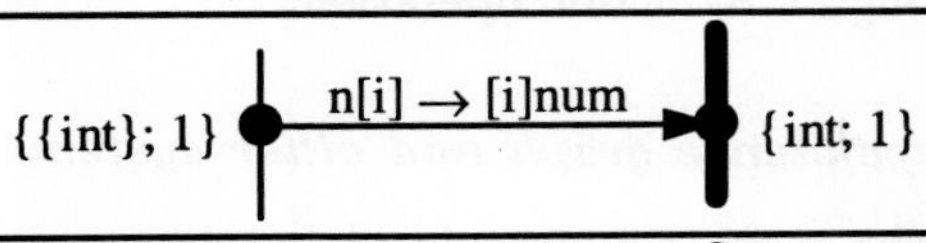 {{int}; 1} n[i] → [i]num {int; 1}
MPI_Bcast	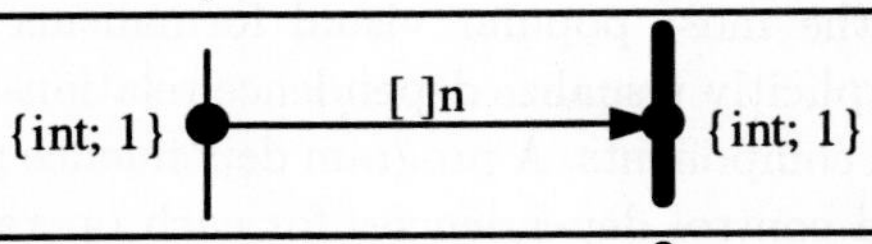 {int; 1} [ ]n {int; 1}
MPI_Gather	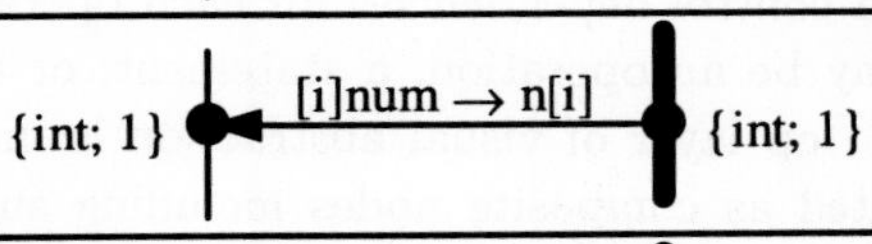 {int; 1} [i]num → n[i] {int; 1}
MPI_Reduce	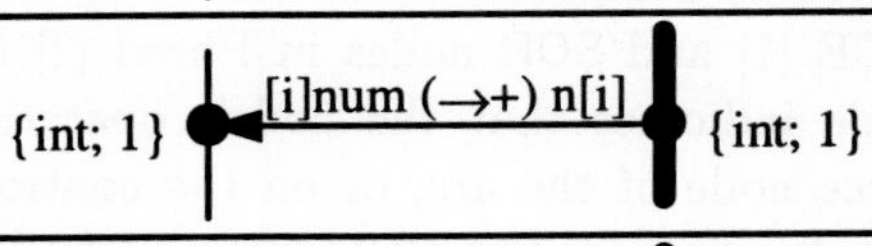 {int; 1} [i]num (→+) n[i] {int; 1}
MPI_Allgather	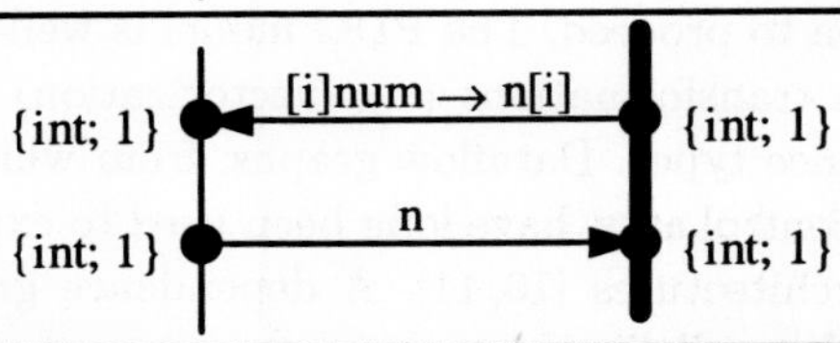 {int; 1} [i]num → n[i] {int; 1} {int; 1} n {int; 1}

Type stanza is used to define the type of the data in a buffer and message protocol (i.e., tag). Therefore, it takes two attributes: a type and a tag and the syntax is:

$$\{\texttt{type; tag}\}$$

Some examples of type stanza can also be found in Table 2.

Wait and probe stanzas are used with corresponding controls to define their properties like the number of messages to monitor or the source of the message. A wait stanza takes two arguments: a request that represents the variable name with the posted requests and a count that defines the monitoring mode like: all, some or any of the posted requests, and the syntax is:

$$\{\texttt{request; count}\}$$

Probe stanza is similar except that the first attribute it takes defines the source of the message to test for, and the syntax is:

$$\{\texttt{source; count}\}$$

An example of a PCG program is given in Fig. 7. As can be seen in the figure, each main PCG begins and ends with an all-execute block. The blocks `Get n` and `Print sum` will only be executed by process 0; and similarly the block `Calculate my_num` will only be executed by all the processes in the `World`. Process 0 will broadcast a number, n, to all processes. After receiving the number, each process will carry out some calculation and produce a result stored in *my_num*. Finally, process 0 will collect the results from all other processes and add them together in *sum* through a reduction operation.

3.4. *Dependence graph and other systems*

One of the most popular visual formalisms is the so-called *dependence graphs*, which explicitly visualize dependence relationships (control, data, or hybrid) among program components. A program dependence graph (PDG) makes explicit both the data and control dependencies for each operation in a program [12]. A node in a PDG may be an operation, a statement, or a sub-PDG with higher level grouping. The top layer of visual abstraction is implicit in a PDG since processes are represented as composite nodes including sub-PDGs, such as "subgraph" nodes in HeNCE [1] and SOR nodes in Phred [2] as discussed below. An arc pointing to a node indicates that the node's operation depends on an input data from the source node of the arc, or on the control condition for the execution of the operation to proceed. The PDG model is well-suited for program optimization and program transformations (e.g. vectorization) that require interaction of different dependence types. Dataflow graphs, from which the PDG notation is extended by adding control arcs, have long been used to exploit parallelism independent of computer architectures [10, 11]. A dependence graph, like a dataflow graph, exposes potential parallelism.

A Visual Program Dependence Graph (VPDG) [8], an extension of a program dependence graph (PDG), supports both code transformations when parallelizing programs and mapping when visualizing the code. In an object-oriented version of PDG, known as the Object-Flow Graph [28], nodes and arcs carry similar visual semantics as in other program dependence graphs. However, the entities that flow along the arcs are the handles to computation objects, rather than the objects themselves or simple data items. Common features of all dependence graphs include high scalability, direct correspondence with programs, and semantic support for parallelism.

The dependence graph in HeNCE (Heterogeneous Network Computing Environment) [1] is read from the bottom up, as the arrows on the arcs indicate. To designate a replication in HeNCE, a pair of triangle icons called *fan icons* are used. Circles are used to designate nodes and tasks that represent computations. CODE (Computationally-Oriented Display Environment) [29] uses dataflow graphs where nodes represent sequential computations and arcs represent the flow of data between the nodes. With a small number of visual notations, CODE relies on a complex set of textual annotations.

Graph nodes in PDGs may be specialized for some specific purposes when they are used for program construction. For example, HeNCE has different notations for conditional, loop, pipe, and fan-in/out nodes, apart from normal nodes which are drawn as circles representing user-supplied subroutines. In CODE, normal computation nodes (represented as circles) obey the dataflow firing rule, i.e., a node is executed once data is present on all inputs to the node. These nodes, known as SUC nodes, can also be encapsulated into "subgraph" nodes (as boxes). The switch nodes in CODE are similar to the conditional nodes in HeNCE. CODE introduces an additional type of arcs, "hyperarcs", to annotate shared data among computation nodes while having a semantics for preventing race conditions when accessing the data. A similar system, known as Phred [2], supports a graph model based on control-flow and data-flow graphs. A major feature of Phred is its capability of analyzing the deterministic behaviour of a parallel program through the Phred graph grammar.

Phred is developed in an environment where the user can construct a Phred program expressed in dependence graphs. A Phred dataflow graph represents data sharing among procedures, while a control flow graph shows the sequential flow of control, alternation, parallelism, and synchronization. Figure 8 illustrates an example Phred program graph adapted from [2], which computes the values for the vector x in Ax=b where A is a matrix and b is a vector. The example program uses the successive overelaxation technique. The two triangle nodes in the graph represent the start and end of the program, and square nodes are data repositories that contain shared variables. Access to the repositories is indicated by arcs connected to them and the connections form the dataflow graph. Textual annotations are used at the bottom layer of abstraction to further identify graphical notations. For example, the filled circles marked "input" are the diverging conjunctive

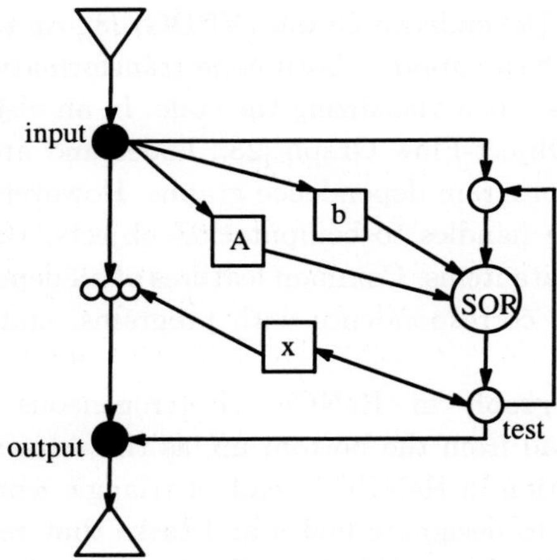

Fig. 8. A Phred program graph which computes the vector x values in Ax=b.

nodes and those marked "output" are converging conjunctive nodes. The disjunctive construct is similarly represented by a pair of nodes which are unfilled. The ellipsis node (the one with three circles) in the conjunctive construct indicates replications of the construct body. The large circle embedded with SOR is a task node, which reads the A, b, and x repositories and computes a new value for each element of the x vector. The part of the graph containing SOR is replicated multiple times, controlled by the test node. The replicated copies can be run in parallel.

Parallelism is implicitly represented in this example. But in general, different branches of a common conjunctive node may be run in parallel. Therefore, Phred graphs can also visualize parallelism explicitly. A converging conjunctive node following a parallel computation will execute only after all the conjunctive branches terminate. It therefore plays a role of barrier synchronization. Apart from visualizing parallelism, Phred defines a formal way of finding parallelism through a straightforward marking scheme. Phred's static analyzer is able to parse the graphs to determine whether they are syntactically correct, and to analyze syntactically correct graphs for determinacy.

Apart from the graph nodes shown in Fig. 8, there are also nodes annotating pipelined processes. Determinacy is checked by analyzing parallel writes and reads to the shared repositories. Phred graphs are scalable because they allow task nodes to be further defined as conjunctive, disjunctive, pipe, or loop constructs.

4. Program Construction Examples

The layers of visual abstraction introduced in Sec. 3.1 naturally create levels of hierarchies in program construction. In the next subsection, hierarchical program construction will be described. In Sec. 4.2, a VPE example is given for a *block triangular solver problem.* In Sec. 4.3, a PCG example is given for the problem of *calculating the value of* π. Finally, in Sec. 4.4, we demonstrate the capabilities of both VPE and PCG in solving the *matrix multiplication problem*.

4.1. *Hierarchical program construction*

One problem in the visual construction of parallel programs is that the diagram representing a program can grow to be very large, particularly in the case of massive parallelism, where there are many processes. To solve this scalability problem, in VPE and PCG, hierarchical construction strategies are employed: programs can be constructed at four levels of abstraction (see Fig. 9), from the top level where separate groups of processes are mapped to run in parallel on a network of processors (*network level*), down to the lowest level where individual blocks are described (*code level*). This abstraction scheme makes the task of program construction easy and manageable. It also provides a convenient way to navigate a large parallel application.

At the central level of abstraction (*block level*), which corresponds to the middle layer of visual abstraction introduced in Sec. 3.1, there is a framework for constructing parallel programs based on either VPE or PCG diagrams. To keep the complexity of the process of building the diagrams under control, a hierarchical decomposition technique is used by defining *composite blocks*. A composite block contains a lower level diagram and represents a "compressed" form of the contained diagram. Therefore, at the block level, a visual program for example, a top level

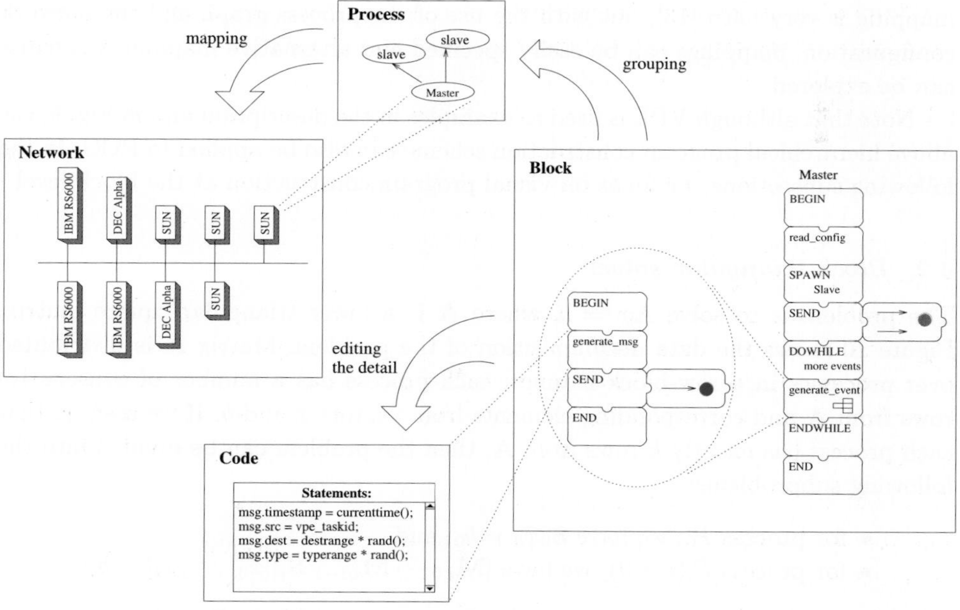

Fig. 9. Hierarchical visual program construction.

VPE diagram, can be expressed as a hierarchy of diagrams, and a whole picture of the program can be obtained by expanding all composite blocks (see Fig. 9).

At the *code level*, which corresponds to the bottom layer of visual abstraction introduced in Sec. 3.1, a text editor can be used to enter program code of a particular block. This function is necessary, since the visual symbols need to be complemented using textual representations to a certain extent. Using composite blocks, a visual program can be decomposed into smaller and smaller diagrams. When a block becomes sufficiently simple, then it can be easily described using the textual programming language.

A grouping mechanism will transform a parallel program at the block level to the *process level* that corresponds to the top layer of visual abstraction introduced in Sec. 3.1. At the process level, the program is represented as a directed graph (*process graph*) with nodes representing processes and arcs representing communication. The process graph allows programmers to have a clearer view of the communication patterns in the application. Each process in this graph is actually an execution instance of a top level diagram, and the communication between diagrams can be extracted. Thus, the grouping can be performed automatically.

At the *network level*, the configuration of the processor network is shown for the programmer to map processes to processors. Dependencies between processes should be considered together with the network configuration in the mapping operation. In VPE or PCG, the mapping can be performed manually with the help of the process graph displayed at the process level and the network configuration at the network level. In general, the problem of obtaining an optimal process-processor mapping is very hard [13], but with the use of the process graph and the network configuration, mappings can be easily specified and alternative mapping strategies can be explored.

Note that although VPE is used as examples in the description and in Fig. 9, the above hierarchical program construction scheme can also be applied to PCG. In the following subsections, we focus on visual program construction at the block level.

4.2. *Block triangular solver*

The problem is to solve $\mathbf{A}x = b$, where $\mathbf{A}$ is a lower triangular square matrix. Figure 10 shows the data decomposition of the problem. Matrix $\mathbf{A}$ is distributed over processes in a row-block manner: each process has a number of consecutive rows from $\mathbf{A}$ and corresponding elements from vectors x and b. If we assume that each process has exactly k rows from $\mathbf{A}$, then the problem can be divided into the following subproblems:

- for process P_0, we have $\mathbf{S}_0 x_0 = b_0$; and
- for process $P_i (i > 0)$, we have $[\mathbf{M}_{i,0} \cdots \mathbf{M}_{i,i-1}\ \mathbf{S}_i][x_0, \ldots, x_i] = b_i$;

where $\mathbf{S}_i (i \geq 0)$ is a $k \times k$ lower triangular matrix, and $\mathbf{M}_{i,j} (0 \leq j \leq i-1)$ is a $k \times k$ square matrix. x_i and b_i are k-element vectors.

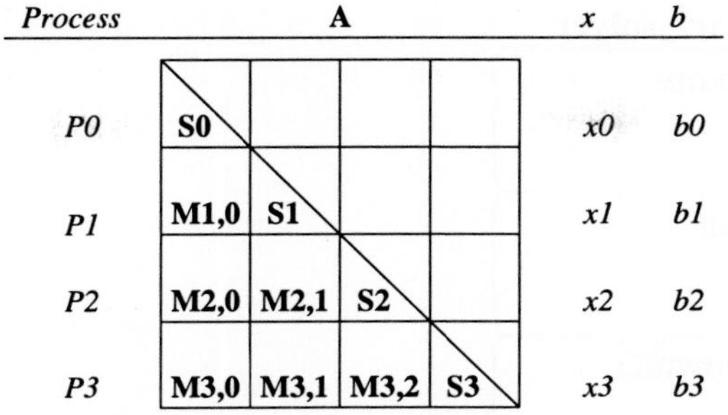

Process	A				*x*	*b*
P0	S0				*x0*	*b0*
P1	M1,0	S1			*x1*	*b1*
P2	M2,0	M2,1	S2		*x2*	*b2*
P3	M3,0	M3,1	M3,2	S3	*x3*	*b3*

Fig. 10. Data decomposition: Block triangular solver.

The parallel algorithm for this problem can then be described as follows: for each process P_i, the following steps are executed (assuming that data have been distributed accordingly)

$m = 0$;
WHILE $m < i$ **DO**
  receive x_m from process P_m;
  calculate new b_i: $b_i = b_i - \mathbf{M}_{i,m} x_m$;
  update m: $m = m + 1$;
ENDWHILE
solve $\mathbf{S}_i x_i = b_i$;
broadcast x_i to processes $P_j (j > i)$.

According to the abstract algorithm, the corresponding VPE diagram can be constructed in a straightforward fashion, as shown in Fig. 11. This is an SPMD program: all processes execute exactly the same program. So, there are multiple execution instances of the diagram.

If the task of a block is sufficiently simple, it can be described using a conventional programming language. For example, Fig. 11 also shows the code level of block `calculate_b`, where matrix $\mathbf{M}[m]$ corresponds to the matrix $\mathbf{M}_{i,m}$ in the abstract algorithm. For simplicity, the code levels of other abstract blocks are not shown. However, the tasks of these blocks can be easily derived from their names.

4.3. *Calculation of π*

Figure 12 shows a main PCG drawn by the programmer to calculate the value of π by the Monte Carlo method of integration. Figure 15 depicts the subgraph for the *Calculate XY* module that performs the calculation. The method uses a circle with the radius equal to one, and a square around it with the surface equal to 4. Therefore, the ratio r of the area of the circle to the area of the square is $\pi/4$. The ratio is computed by generating random points (x, y) in the square and counting how many of them are in the circle. The user must provide the required precision in the calculation.

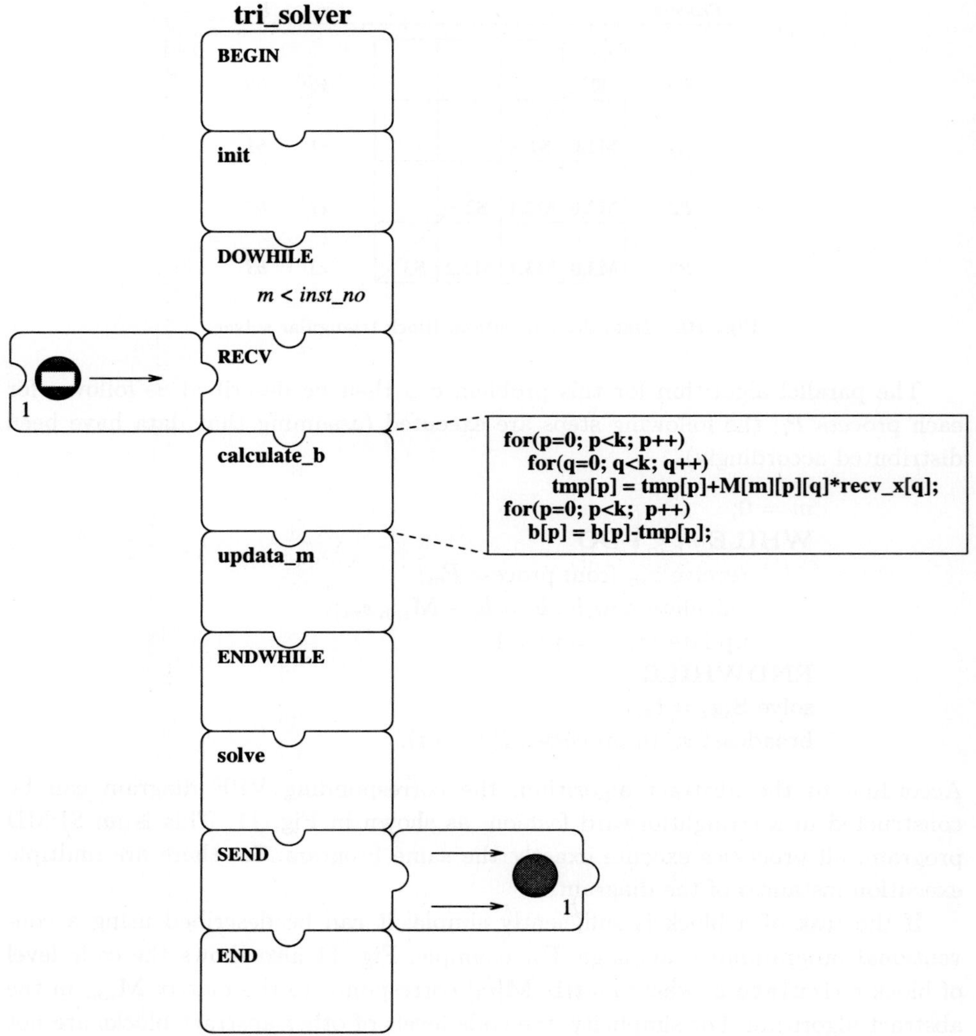

Fig. 11. VPE diagram: Block triangular solver.

The resources used by the program consist of two groups (`World` and `Workers`), and two processes (0 and `random`). The program first sets the communication environment up and creates a group of processes called `Workers`. The group comprises all processes within the `World` except for the `random`. Since all processes in the `World` must perform these operations, we use all-execute blocks. The program then enters the *Main Loop* that dispatches work to the processes (see Fig. 13). The pair of horizontal lines in Fig. 13 represent repeated program tasks, i.e., a loop.

The *Main Loop* allows the user to test different values of precision without restarting the program. In Fig. 14, process 0 prompts the user to enter the required

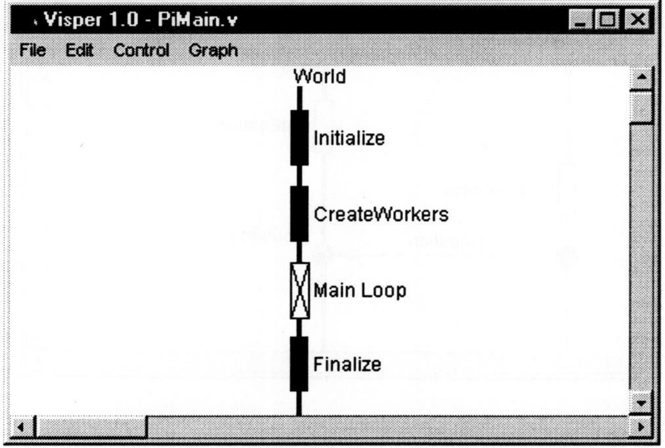

Fig. 12. Main PCG: π calculation.

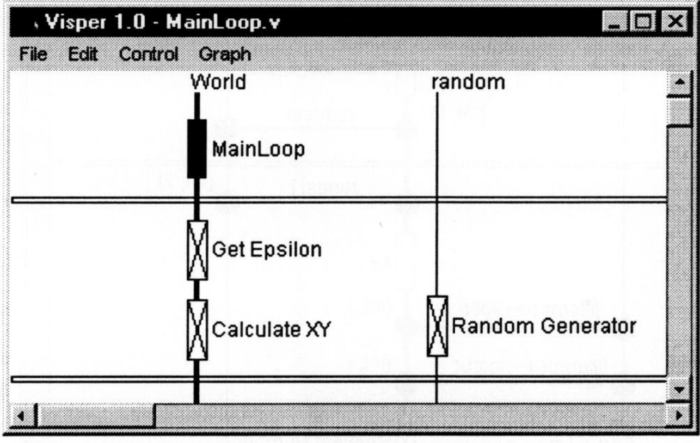

Fig. 13. PCG main loop subgraph: π calculation.

precision of the computation epsilon, the value of which is broadcast to all processes in the `World`. In Fig. 15, each process in the `Workers` sends a request to the `random` for a new random number *rands*. Since a point-to-point call is used to make the request, the receiver uses a wildcard as the tag. The server sends back an array of random numbers: *rands*[]. A pair of empty brackets indicates that the server sends an array. Based on the *rands*, x and y coordinates are calculated and the result is sent to process 0 by two MPI_Reduce calls. The syntax for the call is:

```
[i]temp(->+)totin
```

We use an `(->+)` to describe the summation performed by the calls. Finally, if the required accuracy is met, process 0 prints out the result, or else the whole process is repeated.

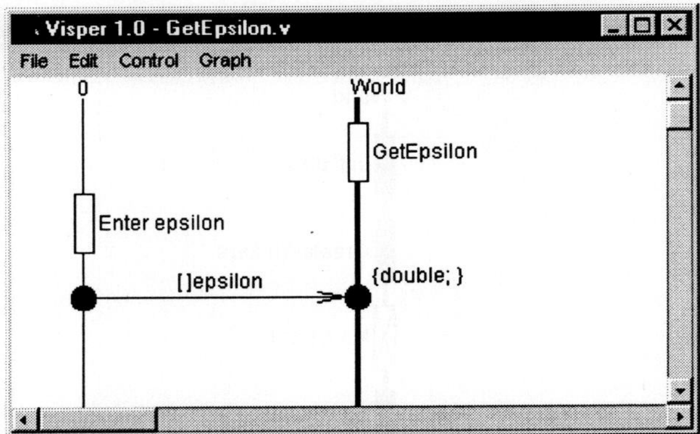

Fig. 14. PCG **Get Epsilon** subgraph: π calculation.

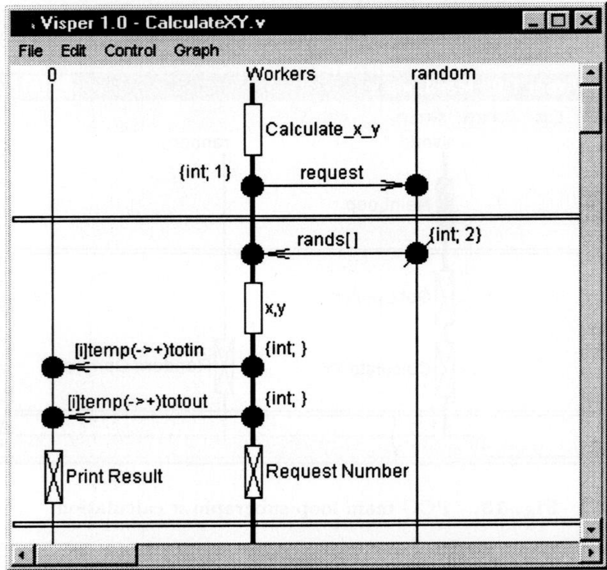

Fig. 15. PCG **Calculate XY** subgraph: π calculation.

4.4. *Matrix multiplication*

We now consider the multiplication of two $m \times m$ matrices: $C = A \times B$. Each matrix is decomposed as $p \times p$ sub-matrices each of dimension $n \times n$, where $n = \frac{m}{p}$

$$\begin{pmatrix} \hat{C}_{(0,0)} & \hat{C}_{(0,1)} & \cdots & \hat{C}_{(0,p)} \\ \hat{C}_{(1,0)} & \hat{C}_{(1,1)} & \cdots & \hat{C}_{(1,p)} \\ \vdots & & & \vdots \\ \hat{C}_{(p,0)} & \hat{C}_{(p,1)} & \cdots & \hat{C}_{(p,p)} \end{pmatrix} = \begin{pmatrix} \hat{A}_{(0,0)} & \hat{A}_{(0,1)} & \cdots & \hat{A}_{(0,p)} \\ \hat{A}_{(1,0)} & \hat{A}_{(1,1)} & \cdots & \hat{A}_{(1,p)} \\ \vdots & & & \vdots \\ \hat{A}_{(p,0)} & \hat{A}_{(p,1)} & \cdots & \hat{A}_{(p,p)} \end{pmatrix} \cdot \begin{pmatrix} \hat{B}_{(0,0)} & \hat{B}_{(0,1)} & \cdots & \hat{B}_{(0,p)} \\ \hat{B}_{(1,0)} & \hat{B}_{(1,1)} & \cdots & \hat{B}_{(1,p)} \\ \vdots & & & \vdots \\ \hat{B}_{(p,0)} & \hat{B}_{(p,1)} & \cdots & \hat{B}_{(p,p)} \end{pmatrix}.$$

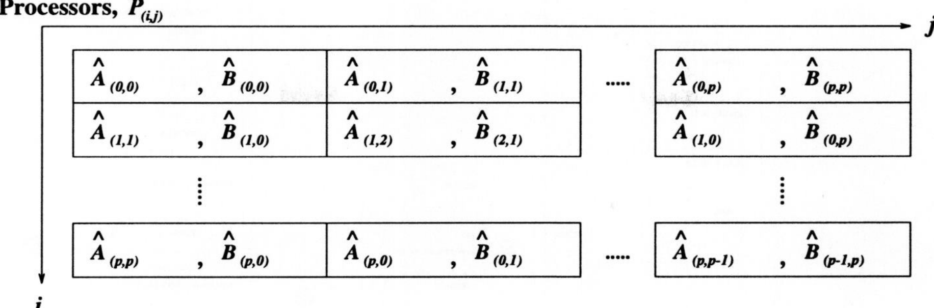

Fig. 16. Initial data distribution for matrix multiplication problem.

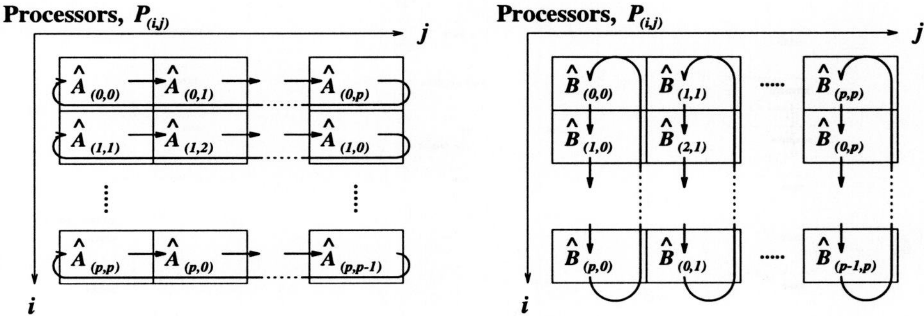

Fig. 17. Data redistribution for matrix multiplication problem.

The algorithm is implemented using $p \times p$ processes. Initially, all the $\hat{C}_{(i,j)}$ will be set to zero matrices and sub-matrices of A and B are distributed to the processes, $P_{(i,j)}$, as shown in Fig. 16. Each row of the A matrix will be shifted to the left by r columns, where r is the row number starting from 0; and each column of the B matrix is shifted upwards by c rows, where c is the column number starting from 0. All processes, $P_{(i,j)}$ performs the sub-matrices multiplication: $\hat{C}_{(i,j)} = \hat{A}_{(i,k)} \times \hat{B}_{(k,j)}$, in parallel. After each multiplication, the sub-matrices of A and B will be re-distributed as shown in Fig. 17.

The algorithm for process, $P_{(i,j)}$, to solve the problem in parallel is given as follows:

> *count* = 0;
> **WHILE** *count* $< p$ **DO**
> compute sub-matrix multiplication, $\hat{C} = \hat{A} \times \hat{B}$;
> send sub-matrix $\hat{A}$ to process $P_{(i,(j+1) \bmod p)}$
> receive new sub-matrix $\hat{A}$ from process $P_{(i,(j+p-1) \bmod p)}$
> send sub-matrix $\hat{B}$ to process $P_{((i+1) \bmod p,j)}$
> receive new sub-matrix $\hat{B}$ from process $P_{((i+p-1) \bmod p,j)}$
> increment *count*
> **ENDWHILE**

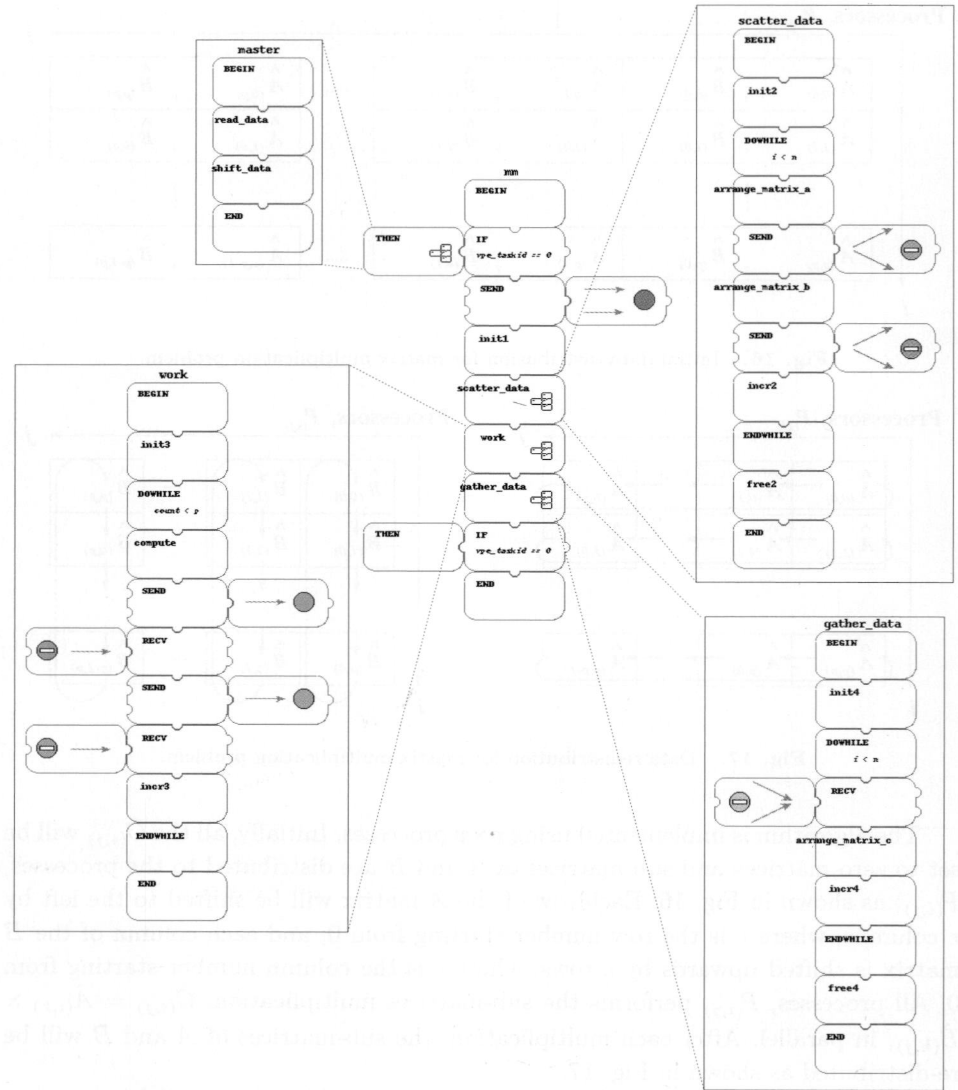

Fig. 18. VPE diagram: Matrix multiplication.

Figure 18 depicts the VPE diagram constructed for the problem. There are $p \times p$ instances of diagram mm. The **read_data** block reads in matrices A and B from a file while the **shift_data** block will setup the matrices according to the initial distribution as shown in Fig. 16. The value of m is broadcast to all processes. The **scatter_data** diagram distributes the sub-matrices $\hat{A}$ and $\hat{B}$ to each mm. The **work** diagram implements the above algorithm and matrices $\hat{C}$'s are combined into the resultant matrix C by the **gather_data** diagram.

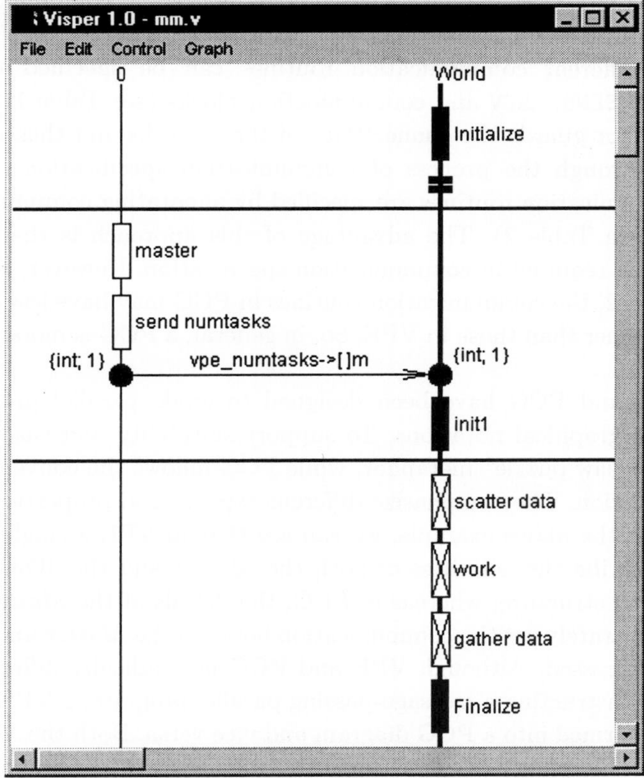

Fig. 19. Main PCG: Matrix multiplication.

Figure 19 shows the main PCG for the matrix multiplication problem. Similar to the VPE diagram shown in Fig. 18, the *master*, i.e., process 0 in the diagram, will initialize the matrices and broadcast the number of tasks to the *workers* (i.e., all the other processes in the `World`). The operations *Scatter Data*, *Work* and *Gather Data* will perform similar functions as these shown in the VPE diagram. As shown in the figure, each of these functions is depicted as a composite block, hence needs to be further defined using a PCG diagram.

5. Comparison of VPE and PCG

Having introduced VPE and PCG in Sec. 3 and illustrated programming examples in Sec. 4, we now summarize the major differences and similarities of the two formalisms in terms of their visual expressions and design properties.

From Figs. 5 and 7, we can see that VPE and PCG diagrams are very different. A VPE diagram closely resembles its textual counterpart. It allows the visual construction of a process at the programming construct level. However, a PCG diagram focuses more on inter-process communication and coordination. The basic building blocks of a process are sequential code blocks and communication control symbols. Visual programming level in PCG is, therefore, higher than that of VPE.

In VPE, different communication routines can be specified using various combination of `SEND`, `RECV` and communication blocks (see Table 1). The "jigsaw puzzle" metaphor guards the connectivity of these blocks and thus can guide the programmer through the process of communication specification. As for PCG, different communication routines are specified by annotating communication using copy stanza (see Table 2). The advantage of this approach is that fewer visual symbols may be required in communication specification. However, as can be seen in Tables 1 and 2, the communication routines in PCG may have less visual impact to the programmer than those in VPE. So, in general, a PCG is more abstract than a VPE diagram.

Both VPE and PCG have been designed to guide parallel programmers by using intuitive graphical notations. To support suitability and ease of use, VPE inherits the "jigsaw puzzle" metaphor, while PCG follows the convention of space-time representation. They emphasize different aspects and properties of a parallel program. From the above example, we can see that in VPE a single diagram can be used to describe the activities of both the *Master* and the *Workers* and thus show the overall structure; whereas in PCG, the details of the *Master* process are represented separately yet the communication between the *Master* and the *Workers* is explicitly expressed. Although VPE and PCG use radically different graphical notations for constructing a message-passing parallel program, a VPE diagram can be easily transformed into a PCG diagram and vice versa. Both the VPE and PCG visual formalisms support scalability and can explicitly express parallelism as shown in the example. In fact, both VPE and PCG diagrams can eventually generate an SPMD parallel program on the target platform.

6. Summary

Research in the area of visual programming languages started in the 80's (see the edited volumes of collected papers [7, 15, 16]), and has become very active in the 90's. Early attempts to formalize the concept of visual programming languages were made by Shu [24], in which visual languages are grouped based on the pictorial supports in the various aspects of the languages, such as, scope, level and data representation. Another work on taxonomies for classifying visual languages was done by Chang [6]. A more recent classification scheme was presented by Burnett *et al* [3], which categorizes visual languages based on different programming paradigms. The up-to-date version of this classification has been published on the Web [4], which is a very comprehensive coverage of the current research in visual programming and visual languages.

However, most of the works reported in the literature, as mentioned above, are about sequential visual programming languages and systems. Zhang *et al* [30] surveyed graph models used for visual parallel program construction and visualization assistance in other stages of parallel program development. In this paper, the visual semantics and visual syntax of several visual parallel programming languages, that is, VPE based on the BLOX diagrams, PCG based on Space-Time diagrams, and CODE, HeNCE and Phred based on dependence graphs, have been discussed. From the discussion in this paper, it can be seen that visual parallel programming systems for different programming paradigms use very different visual formalisms. Even though both VPE and PCG diagrams support message-passing parallel programming, their visual notations are quite different. They stand out as two contrasting representatives of parallel visual programming approaches. Therefore, the further discussions on how they are used to construct parallel programs through examples provided useful insights into the important issues in the design of a parallel visual programming system.

This paper has also discussed the concepts of layers of visual abstraction and hierarchical program construction. Many visual parallel programming systems support three layers of visual abstraction, i.e.,

- visual representation of processes and groups of processes;
- visualized communication and process construction patterns; and
- textual annotations and sequential program code.

Parallel programs can be constructed hierarchically from the code level to the network level. The association between the layers of abstraction and the hierarchical program construction makes such systems scalable and easily understandable.

In summary, this paper has demonstrated the usefulness and feasibility of visual programming technologies in parallel programming. Through the use of visual parallel programming tools and environments, we believe, the productivity of programmers and the quality of the software developed on high performance computing platforms can be greatly improved.

Acknowledgments

We would like to thank Hung Khoon Tan for his implementation of VPE. The work of Mehmet A. Orgun has been supported in part by a small Australian Research Council (ARC) Grant. We are also grateful to the anonymous reviewers for their constructive comments that have helped us to improve the final presentation.

References

1. A. Beguelin *et al*, "HeNCE: Graphical development tools for network-based concurrent computing", *Proceedings of Scalable High Performance Computing Conference*, Williamsburg, Virginia (IEEE CS Press, April 1992) 129–136.
2. A. Beguelin and G. Nutt, "Visual parallel programming and determinacy: A language specification", *Journal of Parallel and Distributed Computing* **22**, no. 4 (1994) 235–250.
3. M. M. Burnett and M. J. Baker, "A classification system for visual programming languages", *Journal of Visual Languages and Computing* **4** (September 1994) 287–300.

4. M. M. Burnett, Visual language research bibliography. *http://www.cs.orst.edu/~burnett/vpl.html*, up to date.
5. W. Cai, H. K. Tan and S. J. Turner, "Visual programming for parallel processing", *Software Visualisation*, eds. P. Eades and K. Zhang, Vol. 7 of *Software Engineering and Knowledge Engineering* (World Scientific, 1996) 119–140.
6. S.-K. Chang, "Introduction: visual languages and iconic languages", *Visual Languages*, eds. S.-K. Chang, T. Ichikawa and P. A. Ligomenides (Plenum Press, 1989) 1–7.
7. S. K. Chang, (ed.), *Visual Languages and Visual Programming* (Plenum Press, 1990).
8. S. K. Chang, C. R. Dow and M. L. Soffa, "A visualization system for parallelizing programs", *Proceeding of the Supercomputing'92*, Minneapolis, USA (November 1992) 194–203.
9. G. Costagliola, G. Tortora, S. Orefice and A. de Lucia, "Automatic generation of visual programming environments", *IEEE Computer* (March 1995) 56–66.
10. A. L. Davis and R. M. Keller, "Data flow program graphs", *IEEE Computers* **15**, no. 2 (February 1982) 26–41.
11. J. B. Dennis, "First version of a data flow procedure language", *Revised Computer Structure Group Memo 93, MIT Lecture Notes in Computer Science* (May 1975).
12. J. Ferrante, K. J. Ottenstein and J. D. Warren, "The program dependence graph and its use in optimization", *ACM Transaction of Programming Languages System* **9**, no. 3 (July 1987) 319–349.
13. A. Gerasoulis and T. Yang, "Scheduling program task graphs on MIMD architectures", *Parallel Algorithm Derivation and Program Transformation*, eds. R. Paige, J. Reif and Ralph Wachter, Chap. 5 (Kluwer Academic Publishers, Boston/Dordrecht/London, 1993) 153–186.
14. E. P. Glinert, "Towards 'second generation' interactive, graphical programming environments", *Proceedings of 1986 IEEE Workshop on Visual Languages*, Dallas (1986) 61–70.
15. E. P. Glinert, (ed.), *Visual Programming Environments: Applications & Issues* (IEEE CS Press, Los Alamitos, 1990).
16. E. P. Glinert, (ed.), *Visual Programming Environments: Paradigms & Systems* (IEEE CS Press, Los Alamitos, 1990).
17. M. T. Heath, A. D. Malony and D. T. Rover, "Parallel performance visualisation: From practice to theory", *IEEE Parallel and Distributed Technology* (Winter 1995) 44–60.
18. M. T. Heath, A. D. Malony and D. T. Rover, "The visual display of parallel performance data", *IEEE Computer* (November 1995) 21–28.
19. P. Kacsuk, "Performance visualization in the grade parallel programming environment", *The Fourth International Conference/Exhibition on High Performance Computing in Asia-Pacific Region*, Beijing China (IEEE Computer Society Press, May 2000) 446–450.
20. L. Lamport, "Time, clocks and the ordering of events in a distributed system", *Communications of the ACM* **21**, no. 7 (July 1978) 558–565.
21. B. P. Miller, "What to draw? When to draw? An essay on parallel program visualization", *Journal of Parallel and Distributed Computing* **18**, no. 2 (June 1993).
22. Message Passing Interface Forum, MPI: A message-passing interface standard, Technical Report, University of Tennessee, Knoxville, Tennessee (May 1994).
23. Message Passing Interface Forum, MPI-2: Extensions to the Message-Passing Interface, *http://www.mcs.anl.gov/mpi* (July 1997).
24. N. C. Shu, *Visual Programming* (Van Nostrand Reinhold Company, New York, 1988).

25. N. Stankovic and K. Zhang, "Towards visual development of message-passing programs", *Proceedings of 1997 IEEE Symposium on Visual Languages*, Capri, Italy (IEEE Computer Society Press, 1997) 144–151.
26. N. Stankovic and K. Zhang, "Visual programming for message-passing systems", *International Journal of Software Engineering and Knowledge Engineering* **9**, no. 4 (1999) 397–423.
27. J. M. Stone, "Debugging concurrent processes: A case study", *Proceedings of SIGPLAN 1988 Conference on Programming Language Design and Implementation* (June 1988) 145–153.
28. J. Webber and P. A. Lee, "Visual, object-oriented development of parallel applications", *Proceedings of IEEE VL Workshop on Visual Methods on Parallel and Distributed Programming*, Seattle, USA (September 2000) 49–58.
29. J. Werth *et al*, "The integration of the formal and the practical in parallel programming environment development: Code", *Languages and Compilers for Parallel Computing*, ed. U. Banerjee *et al* (Springer-Verlag, 1991) 35–49.
30. K. Zhang, T. Hintz and X. W. Ma, "The role of graphics in parallel program development", *Journal of Visual Languages and Computing* **10**, no. 3 (1999) 215–243.

SYSTEM AND SOFTWARE VISUALISATION

CLAIRE KNIGHT
Visualisation Research Group, Department of Computer Science,
University of Durham, Durham, DH1 3LE, UK
E-mail: C.R.Knight@durham.ac.uk

The progress of software visualisation, beyond that of nodes and arcs in various forms, has lagged behind the developments made in such fields as information visualisation. That is now starting to change and recent innovations are reviewed, based on a historical view of software visualisation, and followed by some of the many outstanding research issues. The use of three-dimensions is almost as new as the more recent research directions and the focus is on the newer visualisations that make use of the extra dimension for the display of information. Whilst this leaves many unanswered questions and unsolved areas, it is a field where much fruitful work has been done and is ripe for further research.

Keywords: Software visualisation, system visualisation, intelligence amplification, program comprehension, software maintenance.

1. Introduction

If the entire of what many consider to be the software visualisation field is reviewed, then this article would be much larger in size and also consist mainly of variations on the nodes and arcs theme. Because the use of the third dimension for system and software visualisation is emerging as a viable alternative for the representation of complex artefacts then it was considered much better to focus on this form of software visualisation. The previous techniques had various identified shortcomings and the space and freedom afforded by the extra dimension has the potential to be usefully employed to overcome some of these problems.

Software visualisation can be seen as a specialised subset of information visualisation. This is because information visualisation is the process of creating a graphical representation of abstract, generally non-numerical, data. This is exactly what is required when trying to visualise software. The term software visualisation has many meanings depending on the author. For the purposes of this thesis software visualisation can be taken to mean any form of program visualisation that is used after the software has been written as an aid to understanding (i.e., it does not mean visual programming). More formally software visualisation can be defined as [1]:

> "*Software visualisation is a discipline that makes use of various forms of imagery to provide insight and understanding and to* <u>*reduce complexity*</u> *of the existing software system under consideration.*"

The goal of software visualisation is included in the above definition. To create a visualisation for no real purpose would be a pointless exercise. It has long been known that understanding software is a complex and hard task because of the complexity of the software itself. Therefore techniques that aid the programmer in his comprehension of an existing software system deserve research focus. Software visualisation aims to aid the programmer by providing insight and understanding through the graphical displays and views, and to reduce the perceived complexity through the use of suitable abstractions and metaphors.

In presenting spatially arranged and located information, i.e., visually, there is the benefit that the human perception skills can be used for part of the comprehension. This moves some of the comprehension load away from the conscious cognitive processing. The double navigation and orientation load of virtual reality visualisations could be seen as a burden but it can be useful. The two mapping processes, that of virtual space movement and of the data comprehension, can feed each other and help to build up a solid mental representation of both. Using three dimensions for visualisation adds an element of familiarity and realism into systems. The world is a three-dimensional experience and by making the visualisation more like that world means there is less cognitive strain on the user. This in turn makes the system easier and more comfortable to use because of all the experience and knowledge the user has built up elsewhere. In using three dimensions the depth cues that make the world, and the visualisation, appear three-dimensional can be used as part of the visualisation. This means that the aim of the visualisation to aid the comprehension of complex phenomena can be achieved without adding unnecessary complications because of the visualisation used.

One of the main problems for software visualisation (and other forms of information visualisation) is of trying to create a tangible representation of something that has no inherent form. Therefore the aim is to visualise the intangible in an effective and useful way. Effective and useful here refer to the visualisation being able to increase the understanding of the user whilst reducing the perceived complexity. Whilst this article does not focus particularly on providing complete overviews of the preceding tools and techniques used for program comprehension and more recently that of information visualisation it does present some of these as the background for later work. It is also useful to provide a yardstick to see where improvements have been made; or even where newer representations have not lived up to expectation. As with much emerging research, when it relies on certain popular technologies it tends to become part of the wider hype. This has, unfortunately, been the case with much of the visualisations in three-dimensions because of their reliance on technologies such as Virtual Reality (VR) for implementation.

2. Historical Perspective

This section traces the origins of software visualisation through program comprehension, features identified as important for program comprehension tools and techniques (such as visualisation), taxonomies, and then finally the nodes and arcs usually associated with the term software visualisation.

2.1. *Program comprehension*

Program comprehension is an important part of not only software maintenance, but also the entire software engineering process. It is required for many tasks that are carried out under these broad headings but all the aim is the same. Program comprehension is carried out with the aim of understanding an existing piece of code. It is a gradual process of building up the necessary understanding by examining sections of the source code. Using the knowledge gained from the source code explanations and understanding can be built and refined. According to Biggerstaff *et al* [2], this process of discovery and refinement is known as the *Concept Assignment Problem*, whilst several other program comprehension strategies have different terms or processes to describe the same activities (such as bottom up comprehension). An overview of many types of program comprehension can be found in Robson *et al* [3] and Von Mayrhauser and Vans [4]. Many authors have documented the ways in which studies have shown that programmers understand code such as Corbi [5], Oman and Cook [6] and Chan and Munro [7]. These documents provide brief overviews of the strategies.

Program comprehension is very much a gradual process where the maintainer gathers information through studying various aspects of the code at different times, and possibly by returning to previously examined pieces of code. Wiedenbeck [8] supports this view of program comprehension. This process is true regardless of the strategy employed to examine the various pieces of code that constitute the system. Despite the importance of program comprehension to such a diverse and wide range of other software maintenance activities there still remains much work to be done to improve the tools and refine the techniques that exist today. Software continues to increase in size and complexity and whilst the program comprehension theories may support this growth, the tools and techniques developed for helping maintainers do not keep up with the speed, and size of change.

2.2. *Features of program comprehension tools*

Storey *et al* [9] identified a hierarchy of cognitive issues that are important when considering what facilities a program comprehension tool should include. They identify the fact that software exploration tools can be likened to hypermedia document browsers. Because of this a hierarchy of hypermedia cognitive issues has been adapted to form program comprehension guidelines. Also identified is the lack of support in existing systems for the integrated and top-down models of comprehension and the inability to switch between different mental model information. Navigation and orientation cues were also identified as an area for future research.

The work done by Chan and Munro [7] identifies the need to provide different viewpoints for maintainers. This allows them to choose the most appropriate view for the current task, and also to be able to switch between views to gain a higher or lower level understanding of some piece of information.

As long ago as 1987, authors had realised the benefit of cross-referencing information but few tools have actually implemented such functionality. Munro and Robson [10] implemented an interactive cross-reference tool that solved a problem at the time of cross referencers, only producing large listings of textual information. Foster and Munro [11] produced a cross-reference tool that allowed maintainers to cross-reference the source code, and included documentation. Fletton and Munro's [12] work is also related to this cross-referencing idea. An alternative view is that of Landis *et al* [13], who identified the use of cross-referencing but suggested it is only useful for variable information and determining where to make changes of that nature. In terms of dataflow it was considered to be of less use, and a criticism of the method was that variables with the same names in different scopes could be listed and confused the programmer. Von Mayrhauser *et al* [14] suggested that cross-referencing of related areas of code would make identification of areas where changes need to be made easier. These cross-reference links should be, where possible, hypertext and also link to algorithm and/or domain information. They also identify the need to provide orientation cues in the documentation and propose the use of some form of browser history with on-line sticky notes to make this effective. They also think that documentation of the system (which could be included in any tool that was used to aid comprehension) should have a high-level *road map of the system structure.*

2.3. *Visualisation taxonomies*

Early work often contained animation, or was thought to have to contain animation. This is reflected in the detail of the various classification and evaluation taxonomies developed in the early 90's. Whilst such detail is beyond the scope of this article it is worth reviewing the major points of the three main taxonomies. Myers [15] identifies one of the first program visualisation taxonomies. In this taxonomy he makes the distinction that all the included systems use graphics to illustrate some part of the program after it has been written. This distinction is important because it makes clear that the taxonomy covers only program visualisation and not visual programming. Other authors are not so clear and even confuse the two terms.

Other authors have produced taxonomies of program visualisation and classified things in a different way to Myers [15]. Price *et al* [16] produced a taxonomy of software visualisation systems that is based on six categories. In creating such a taxonomy the authors aimed to create a "road map" of the research to the point when the taxonomy was created. The taxonomy created by Price is more detailed than that of Myers' and can be arranged into a hierarchical structure. This structuring was a deliberate move by the authors to allow for the taxonomy to be extended and revised as software visualisation (the term they use instead of program visualisation) systems evolved and matured. Another taxonomy is the one defined by Roman and Cox [17] which is derived from their earlier work [18]. This is closer to the taxonomy of Price *et al* [16] than the one of Myers [15] and some parallels can be drawn between the two.

2.4. *Early representations; nodes and arcs*

For many years, basic visualisation, based around simple boxes and lines, has been done in an attempt to be able to ease some of the cognitive overload caused by program comprehension. The problems with such visualisations is that they can very easily become incomprehensible by trying to force large amounts of information into a small space, relying solely on two-dimensions for the representations. Baker and Eick [19] acknowledge the problems of such approaches:

> "*When applied to production-sized systems, routines for producing flow charts, function call graphs and structure diagrams often break because the diagram is too complicated. Or they produce displays that contain too much information and are completely illegible.*"

Much effort has been spent on visualising programs in two-dimensions, with graph structures such as call-graphs being prominent. It is acknowledged that these forms of visualisation suffer when the number of, and relationships between, information is complex. The representations themselves can even become more complicated than the code itself. An example of this can be seen in Fig. 1. If this is the only thing that can be used to aid the comprehension of a well maintained medium sized commercial system, then it is obvious that something more is needed.

In attempts to address the obvious problems with the existing representations several systems and layout algorithms have been developed. The following sections provide more detailed information on a representative sample of these. Another technique that has been applied, with little success due to the same problems still

Fig. 1. Call graph of a medium sized system.

being prevalent, is the representation of node and arc structures such as call graphs in three-dimensions [43, 44, 30]. Much of this work was done without thought or design being applied to the virtual space in which the graphics were located which destroyed the possible usefulness of such an environment.

3. Examples

The examples in the following four sections are representative of the advances made in software visualisation in the last ten years. The first three are refinements and enhancements of node and arc technology with improved browsing and node management, and the final one is one of the early software visualisations to move away from total reliance on nodes and arcs. Whilst these four tools show slightly different aspects of the program code, they are all intended for the tasks of program comprehension and software maintenance, hence their inclusion.

3.1. *SHriMP*

SHriMP (Simple Hierarchical Multi-Perspective) [20] is a visualisation that combines the nodes and arcs representation so cherished by software visualisers with the fisheye filtering technique. As the name implies, the fisheye technique emulates the behaviour of a fisheye lens. The information at the centre of the view is magnified, whilst that at the periphery is reduced in size. SHriMP also incorporates the use of nested graphs for the display of software structures. The use of these two techniques provides, according to the authors, the ability to create multiple views at different levels of abstraction and perspective. To be able to interact with the data in this way is a powerful way of dealing with large amounts of information as selective filtering and viewing can take place. Such extensions are a step towards being better able to deal with the large and complex software that is so pervasive today, but the user of two-dimensions and the standard representation as the basis may limit the applicability and use of such tools.

3.2. *VIFOR*

VIFOR stands for Visual Interactive FORtran and is a software tool that is geared towards maintaining Fortran 77 code [21]. This system works by using a database of code detail from the Fortran code and then allowing it to be viewed and queried in either the textual form of the code or a graph layout based visualisation. This layout mechanism was developed for the VIFOR tool and attempts to merge the standard call graph and data dependency graphs that are more commonly used.

Early work on a C maintenance and understanding tool is also documented in this paper; VIC. An extension of this work was the development of VIFOR 2 [22]. This improved the browsing system to allow the integration of incremental recording and retrieval of documentation.

3.3. *CARE*

CARE (Computer Aided Re-Engineering) is an understanding tool that works with C source code [23]. This understanding tool makes use of two-dimensional visualisations in windows and browsers (as with the previous tools) to show graphs of some of the code relations. As with VIFOR, CARE displays the data flow and call structure of the program using an extension of the VIFOR layout algorithm. In order to do this, a repository of the structural and functional dependencies in the code is generated, and the presentation part of the tool uses this information when displaying the visualisations. The tool also supports the creation and use of both graphical and textual slices through the information.

As with VIFOR, an extension of the tool was developed to deal with other languages. OO!CARE [24] is an extension of CARE that deals with C++ code, hence the Object Oriented addition to the name. It is also able to deal with C code because of the syntactical similarities of the language notwithstanding the object oriented part of C++.

3.4. *SeeSys and SeeSoft*

In an attempt to address some of the shortcomings of relying solely on nodes and arcs for data representation, the tools SeeSys [19] and SeeSoft [25] were developed. These tools are part of a research effort that produced similar displays for several underlying data types. The visualisation technique used by these systems is based on the idea of decomposition of the information to be visualised into its component form. Colour and interaction are incorporated into the systems, and the displays make much use of colour scales to visualise extra information about the underlying data. The system also uses the overlay of additional information onto the display to provide yet more facts for the user.

SeeSys is a visualisation system for software metrics whilst SeeSoft visualises the program code and the constituent files. These visualisations are based on three principles:

(1) The individual components can be assembled to form the whole. This allows the user to easily see the relationships between them.
(2) Pairs of components can be compared to understand how they differ.
(3) The components can be disassembled into smaller components. This important feature of the components allows the structure of the display to reflect the structure of the software.

The individual components are visible whilst maintaining a view of the whole system. This sort of technique has also been applied in the Information Mural visualisations of Jerding and Stasko [26], whilst the concept of encoding wear as a coloured property of source code was originally documented by Hill and Hollan [27].

3.5. *Summary*

In his paper *No Silver Bullet* [28], Brooks wrote

> "*Software is invisible and unvisualizable.*
>
> ...
>
> ... *software is very difficult to visualize. Whether one diagrams control flow, variable-scope nesting, variable cross-references, dataflow, hierarchical data structures, or whatever, one feels only one dimension of the intricately interlocked software elephant. If one superimposes all the diagrams generated by the many relevant views, it is difficult to extract any global overview.*"

At the time Brooks wrote this, visualising software meant displaying some information about (or some aspect of) the software in a graph structure. From what can be seen in Fig. 1, he has a point. This need not now be the case with the advances in computer hardware and graphics technology.

Two-dimensional techniques have shortcomings, but this is not to trivialise the issues that still remain with the nodes and arcs techniques. Layout, for example, is a hard problem and one that is not appreciated by many [50]. The systems presented in the previous sections provide a representative sample of the sorts of program comprehension tools that have been developed to aid understanding and are early attempts at visualisation. The last of these sections shows that the reliance on nodes and arcs and solely investigating layout algorithms and clustering is not necessarily the only way forward, even with two-dimensions. This work is a stepping stone to moving onto three-dimensional, coloured, and non-arc reliant representations.

4. Recent Research

Despite the identified problems with the traditional forms of software visualisation, it is not simply enough to throw the techniques of information visualisation at the source code and expect useful and usable visualisations to emerge. Information visualisation influences have produced many hierarchical and tree oriented visualisations, and some information landscape style visualisations [45–49] and these could have application for software visualisation. Indeed, Hendley and Drew [43, 44] produced springs layout algorithms for nodes and arcs in three-dimensions, which bears a similarity to such research.

Notwithstanding these advances, there are general unsolved problems with three dimensional visualisations, such as scalability and evolution, which are important to all visualisations but paramount to software visualisation due to the complexity and changeability of the underlying data; the source code. There may also be issues that are pertinent to software visualisations that do not have much effect on information visualisations; database visualisation is a subset of information visualisation because of the nature of the data source being visualised. For a more complete review of information visualisation in three-dimensions, the interested reader is referred to the comprehensive survey by Young [29].

Recently more attempts at utilising three dimensions for software visualisation have been carried out by Feijs and De Jong [30] where they visualised node and arc structures using variously coloured lego blocks for the nodes. These visualisations showed architectural structures and relationships present in the code and used various colours to indicate different pieces of information about that structure to the viewer. Whilst this paper acknowledged that they have more research to do the work does not seem to address many of the issues and limitations of the use of three dimensions. The creation of their visualisations relies again on nodes and arcs but using an extra dimension. This does provide a greater degree of flexibility than the two-dimensional form of such structures but again does not scale or evolve well; two very important issues.

In an attempt to move away from the obvious connectivity displayed in software visualisations Young and Munro [31] and Young [32] produced visualisations based around abstract three-dimensional geometrical shapes. The first, known as *CallStax*, showed the visualisation of the calling structure of *C* code (essentially the same information as a call graph) with coloured stacks of blocks showing the routes through the graph. The second, *FileVis*, showed a view of the software system with the code files represented individually as floating platforms around a central point which represented the connectivity of the source code files. A view of these visualisations can be seen in Fig. 2. This visualisation combines both in order to show two aspects of the *C* code at the same time.

Further advancing the three-dimensional space aspect of the visualisations, work by Knight and Munro [1, 33, 34] moved to consider the use of virtual reality environments for software visualisation. *Software World* was created to show that three-dimensions (in this case also showing the viability of real world metaphors)

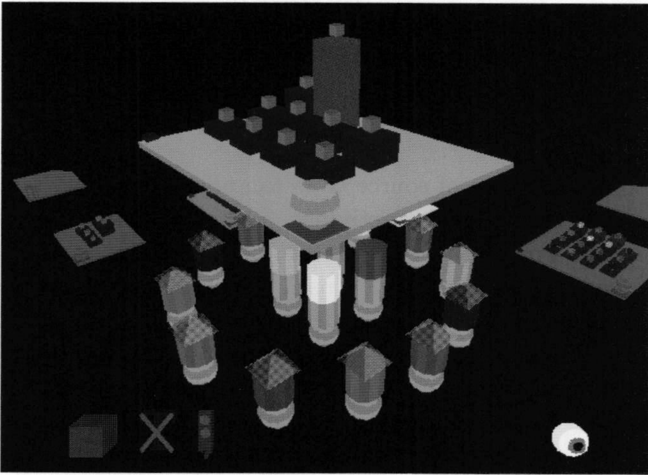

Fig. 2. CallStax visualisation underneath part of a FileVis display.

Fig. 3. View over a software district showing many, possibly complex, methods.

could be used to create automatable and scalable software visualisations. Buildings, cities, and also at the highest level atlas views, were used to represent Java source code. An example view of this visualisation can be seen in Fig. 3.

In order to show some of the method level views that can be created with this visualisation over 17,000 lines of Java code (which together composed a package) written by others was parsed, and district visualisations automatically generated. The code was split across 70 classes, which provided different district views. Two of the images that came out of this can be seen in Figs. 3 and 4.

The use of environments allowed extensions of this work to consider the benefits and challenges of creating virtually inhabitable spaces where the visualisation provides a view of the data under consideration and facilitates communication and collaboration within that data by those working on the same tasks or having similar knowledge. Some of these further issues can be found in [35].

4.1. *Example of use: impression*

The condition of any piece of source code can affect the effort required for future comprehension and maintenance activities. There are many measures that can be utilised to provide a prediction of the condition of many aspects of the source code in numerical form and these may be used to justify a preventative maintenance process taking place. It is also useful in these situations, especially if the numbers that come out of the measured analysis of the code are averaged, to be able to "see" possible problem areas of the code and to know where to direct efforts.

Such a process can be achieved through the use of the visualisation tools for browsing and a more exploratory form of comprehension. These overviews immediately make obvious anything that is extreme and can draw the user to that area. It may be that these apparently anomalous areas of the code are fine considering

Fig. 4. A district representing a class containing only very small methods.

the use to which that piece of code is put; i.e., if the task is complex the code to achieve it may well be unavoidably complex.

In order to find this information using *Software World*, the following stages are necessary:

- Use the world and country views to gain an overview of the split and top-down structure of the system and packages.
- Query to locate class (for each class) which is highlighted from the country view down. If the package is not specified then several could be highlighted. This is done from the user's office in the visualisation environment.
- The class of interest is selected and the district that represents this class is then made the focus of the virtual environment. This district is shown in the context of the file in which the class is located so that the file information and any related classes can be seen.
- The district can then be explored, the heights of buildings surveyed and the colours of buildings used to provide an indication of the accessibility of the code. Differing visual examples of this can be seen in Figs. 3 and 4.

Once methods of interest have been identified then they can be explored in more detail by entering the appropriate building. Source code (actual text) and also other extracted information can be viewed and analysed from this point in the visualisation. This will then lead any further exploration considered necessary for this method and/or class.

These recent research initiatives have shown that such software visualisations are viable, and have the potential to become powerful additions for aiding understanding and providing a forum in which knowledge about the data is also managed, viewed, and interpreted.

5. Moving Forward

Unfortunately it is not simple a case of following a recipe book set of simple steps when creating visualisations because of the very purpose of visualisation data sources. The underlying data can be sizeable, and it can be complex. These facts alone preclude the use in many situations of what could be traditionally termed "off-the-shelf" visualisations, but there are a wider range of issues as to why this is not necessarily the best way of visualising software and systems.

One of the main problems for software visualisation (and other forms of information visualisation) is of trying to create a tangible representation of something that has no inherent form. Therefore the aim is to visualise the intangible in an effective and useful way. Effective and useful here refers to the visualisation being able to increase the understanding of the user whilst reducing the perceived complexity. Many authors have identified the intangible nature of software including Walker [36], Ball and Eick [37] and Chapin and Lau [38].

5.1. *Intelligence amplification*

Intelligence amplification (IA) is the use of computers to aid and enhance human intelligence rather than the artificial intelligence (AI) aim of trying to substitute humans with computers. Intelligence amplification builds on the skills that humans already have, and tries to augment the areas that are lacking in some way. Frederick Brooks (documented in by Rheingold [39]) describes his beliefs about intelligence amplification in the following way:

> "*I believe the use of computer systems for intelligence amplification is much more powerful today, and will be at any given point in the future, than the use of computers for artificial intelligence (AI). In the AI community, the objective is to replace the human mind by the machine and its program and its data base. In the IA community, the objective is to build systems that amplify the human mind by providing it with computer-based auxiliaries that do the things that the mind has trouble doing.*"

Brooks identifies three areas in which humans are more skilled than computers. The first is *pattern recognition* (aural or visual). The second is in performing *evaluations*, and the third is the *overall sense of context* that allows previously unrelated pieces of information to become related and useful in a new situation.

Walker [36] also touches on the subject of intelligence amplification in his discussion on the challenges of visualisation.

> "*A natural and intuitive visual interface can retain the critical contribution from human perceptual skills, ensuring that opportunities for lateral thinking or perhaps an unexpected leap of imagination are not lost. Programming a computer to 'look for something interesting' in a database is*

> *a major undertaking, but given appropriate tools, it is a task for which humans are well equipped.*"

The first sentence can be seen to the similar to the third skill identified by Brooks, that of a sense of context. The second sentence by Walker is essentially talking about the pattern recognition skill specified by Brooks in [39].

Intelligence amplification is of importance to software visualisation (and any other form of visualisation) because in representing large and complex data sets graphically the aim is to help the user to get a better understanding of content of the data sets. By aiding the user in this way visualisation tools are acting also as intelligence amplification tools. Reading through many thousands of pieces of information and then summarising them in a finite graphical space would be an immense, complex and possibly tedious task. For a computer with the right "instructions", it is a simple data processing exercise.

Hubbold *et al* [40] make a similar connection with the field of VR (and therefore visualisations that make use of VR as an enabling technology). They also identify the pattern recognition and contextual abilities of humans.

> "*In our everyday existence we cope with, and filter out, tremendous amounts of information almost effortlessly and with very little conscious thought. Indeed, if the same information, in all its detail, were to be presented in a form that we had to think about consciously, then we would be overwhelmed quite easily. Spatial awareness, pattern recognition, information filtering, coordination of multiple information streams are things we take for granted. Rather than look for a solution in AI, part of the VR thesis is that information presented in a suitable way can be processed far more effectively and directly by people.*"

The role of a visualisation system as an intelligence amplification tool rather than as a system that tries to second guess the information the user requires is emphasised by Crossley *et al* [41]:

> "*... the role of the system is not to select documents similar to a user-supplied query but to organise and display information about many documents in such a way as to assist users to select useful documents on their own.*"

This shows that the important challenges and research issues for visualisations are to be able to handle such tasks well and provide the necessary support as transparently as possible. Changing the query mechanism in order to improve performance (for example in the situation above) is not going to help in another situation or be widely applicable to other visualisations.

5.2. *Important factors*

There are many factors that are important for visualisation. The main ones in the context of software visualisation [42], and indeed for all information visualisation, are:

- Scalability.
- Evolution.
- Automation.
- Navigation, Interaction, and Orientation.

Navigation, interaction, and orientation are presented together because they are often highly interconnected. Orientation features are also very often useful for navigation and vice-versa. Interaction mechanisms are also affected by the navigation available to users. The final three bullet points cover issues that should be considered vital for all visualisations, including those that create virtual environments. Obviously there may have to be trade-offs for a particular system with respect to some of these features but striving to achieve all of these goes some way towards creating reliable useful and usable visualisations.

The first of these points is to do with the scalability of the visualisation. It is all very well for a visualisation system to work with a small source code sample but unless it works with large systems, with little human intervention then it is of no use to programmers and maintainers. The visualisation needs to scale well, and because of this the metaphors and abstractions used should be carefully considered. There is also a need for automation. If each facet of the visualisation needs to be created by hand there is little point in using the visualisation with real systems. Some human intervention can be considered to be acceptable, but on the whole the visualisation needs to be created with as little as possible. Navigation and orientation are the final points to consider. It does not matter how well drawn the graphics of a visualisation are, or how suitable the mapping and metaphor chosen, if the resulting visualisation cannot be navigated adequately. It is important to be able to explore the information presented and to be able to locate the desired pieces of information. It is also vital, especially when considering three-dimensional displays, that the visualisation itself is navigable and able to be comprehended in some way by users. Without either of these two then the visualisation is immediately unusable and the effort on representations etc. wasted.

5.3. *Summary*

Much research still needs to be done in many areas both in and around software visualisation and this section has identified some of the more pressing concerns, and presented a rationale for the use of visualisation techniques. It should not be considered a failing of the field to have not answered all such questions at this moment in time; it provides a rich forum in which further research can be done to make the necessary future advances. It also provides a basis on which the technique of visualisation for understanding can start to be applied to larger projects and data sets and usefully used by those outside of research.

6. Conclusion

This article has introduced and discussed many facets of the three-dimensional research agenda and provided rationale for the creation of software visualisations that exploit the extra dimension. Software visualisation is still a hard problem and purely by using the extra dimension the field cannot hope to solve the identified deficiencies of the two dimensional representations. What this information has tried to show is that there is a way forward from nodes and arcs, and that the complex software of today is capable of being (and should be) visualised. As Myers [15] concludes so succinctly:

> "*The success of spreadsheets demonstrates that if we find the appropriate paradigms, graphical techniques can revolutionize the way people interact with computers.*"

Visualisation for the sake of it may well produce pretty pictures but the visualisations developed for program and system comprehension should have two aims; to reduce the complexity of the perceived view of the software and to increase the user's understanding of the software.

Acknowledgements

Much of this work has been financed by an EPSRC ROPA grant: VVSRE; Visualising Software in Virtual Reality Environments.

References

1. C. Knight and M. Munro, "Comprehension with[in] virtual environment visualisations", *Proceedings of the IEEE 7th International Workshop on Program Comprehension* (May 5–7, 1999) 4–11.
2. T. J. Biggerstaff, B. G. Mitbander and D. E. Webster, "Program understanding and the concept assignment problem", *Communications of the ACM* **37**, no. 5 (May 1994) 72–82.
3. D. J. Robson, K. H. Bennett, B. J. Cornelius and M. Munro, "Approaches to program comprehension", *Journal of Systems and Software* **14** (1991) 79–84.
4. A. Von Mayrhauser and A. M. Vans, "Program comprehension during software maintenance and evolution", *IEEE Computer* (August 1995) 44–55.
5. T. A. Corbi, "Program understanding: Challenge for the 1990s", *IBM Systems Journal* **28**, no. 2 (1989) 294–306.
6. P. W. Oman and C. R. Cook, "Typographic style is more than cosmetic", *Communications of the ACM* **33**, no. 5 (May 1990) 506–520.
7. P. S. Chan and M. Munro, "PUI: A tool to support program understanding", *Proceedings of the IEEE 5th International Workshop on Program Comprehension* (May 28–30, 1997) 192–198.

8. S. Wiedenbeck, "The initial stage of program comprehension", *International Journal of Man-Machine Studies* **35** (1991) 517–540.
9. M.-A. D. Storey, F. D. Fracchia and H. A. Müller, "Cognitive design elements to support the construction of a mental model during software visualization", *Proceedings of the 5th IEEE International Workshop on Program Comprehension* (May 28–30, 1997) 17–28.
10. M. Munro and D. J. Robson, "An interactive cross reference tool for use in software maintenance", *Proceedings of the 20th Annual Hawaii International Conference on System Sciences* (1987) 64–70.
11. J. R. Foster and M. Munro, "A documentation method based on cross-referencing", *Proceedings of the IEEE Conference on Software Maintenance* (1987) 181–185.
12. N. T. Fletton and M. Munro, "Redocumenting software systems using hypertext technology", *IEEE Conference on Software Maintenance* (1988) 54–59.
13. L. D. Landis, P. M. Hyland, A. L. Gilbert and A. J. Fine, "Documentation in a software maintenance environment", *Proceedings of the IEEE Conference on Software Maintenance* (1988) 66–73.
14. A. Von Mayrhauser, A. M. Vans and A. E. Howe, "Program understanding behaviour during enhancement of large-scale software", *Journal of Software Maintenance: Research and Practice* **9** (1997) 299–327.
15. B. A. Myers, "Taxonomies of visual programming and program visualization", *Journal of Visual Languages and Computing* **1** (1990) 97–123.
16. B. A. Price, R. M. Baecker and I. S. Small, "A principled taxonomy of software visualization", *Journal of Visual Languages and Computing* **4**, no. 3 (1992) 211–266.
17. G. C. Roman and K. C. Cox, "A taxonomy of program visualization systems", *IEEE Computer* (December 1993) 11–24.
18. G.-C. Roman and K. C. Cox, "Program visualization: The art of mapping programs to pictures", *Proceedings of the 14th International Conference on Software Engineering* (May 1992) 412–420.
19. M. J. Baker and S. G. Eick, "Space filling software visualization", *Journal of Visual Languages and Computing* **6** (1995) 119–133.
20. M.-A. D. Storey and H. A. Müller, "Manipulating and documenting software structures using SHriMP views", *Proceedings of ICSM '95* (October 17–20, 1995) 119–133.
21. V. Rajlich, N. Damaskinos and P. Linos, "VIFOR: A tool for software maintenance", *Software Practice and Experience* **20**, no. 1 (January 1990) 67–77.
22. V. Rajlich and S. R. Adnapally, "VIFOR 2: A tool for browsing and documentation", *IEEE International Conference of Software Maintenance* (1996) 296–300.
23. P. Linos, P. Aubet, . Dumas, Y. Helleboid, P. Lejeune and P. Tulula, "Facilitating the comprehension of C programs: An experimental study", *Proceedings of the 2nd IEEE Workshop on Program Comprehension* (July 8–9, 1993) 55–63.
24. P. K. Linos and V. Courtois, "A tool for understanding object-oriented program dependencies", *Proceedings of the 3rd IEEE Workshop on Program Comprehension* (November 14–15, 1994) 20–27.
25. S. G. Eick, "Engineering perceptually effective visualizations for abstract data", *Scientific Visualization Overviews, Methodologies and Techniques* (IEEE Computer Science Press) (February 1997) 191–210.
26. D. F. Jerding and J. T. Stasko, "Using information murals in visualization applications", *Proceedings of UIST '95 (ACM)* (November 14–17, 1995).
27. W. C. Hill and J. D. Hollan, "History-enriched source code", Computer Graphics and Interactive Media Research Group, Bell Communications Research (submitted to ACM UIST '93, 1993).

28. F. P. Brooks, "No silver bullet", *IEEE Computer* (April 1987) 10–19.
29. P. Young, "Three dimensional information visualisation", University of Durham, Computer Science Technical Report 12/96 (1996).
30. L. Feijs and R. de Jong, "3D visualization of software architectures", *Communications of the ACM* **41**, no. 12 (December 1998) 72–78.
31. P. Young and M. Munro, "Visualising software in virtual reality", *Proceedings of the IEEE 6th International Workshop on Program Comprehension* (June 24–26, 1998) 19–26.
32. P. Young, "Visualising software in cyberspace", PhD Thesis, University of Durham (October 1999).
33. C. Knight and M. Munro, "Visualising software — A key research area", *Proceedings of the IEEE International Conference on Software Maintenance* (August 30 — September 3, 1999) short paper.
34. C. Knight and M. Munro, "Virtual but visible software", *Proceedings of the IEEE International Conference on Information Visualisation* (July 2000) (in publication).
35. C. Knight and M. Munro, "Should users inhabit visualisations?" (to appear in the post proceedings of *Knowledge Media Networking workshop of IEEE WETICE*, June 2000).
36. G. Walker, "Challenges in information visualisation", *British Telecommunications Engineering Journal* **14** (April 1995) 17–25.
37. T. Ball and S. G. Eick, "Software visualization in the large", *IEEE Computer* (April 1996) 33–43.
38. N. Chapin and T. S. Lau, "Effective size: An example of use from legacy systems", *Journal of Software Maintenance: Research and Practice* **8** (1996) 101–116.
39. H. Rheingold, "Virtual reality", *Mandarin Science* (1992).
40. R. Hubbold, A. Murta, A. West and T. Howard, "Design issues for virtual reality systems" Presented at the First Eurographics Workshop on Virtual Environments (September 7, 1993).
41. M. Crossley, N. J. Davies, R. J. Taylor-Hendry and A. J. McGrath, "Three-dimensional Internet developments", *BT Technology Journal* **15**, no. 2 (April 1997) 179–193.
42. C. Knight, "Virtual software in reality", PhD Thesis, University of Durham (June 2000).
43. B. Hendley and N. Drew, "Visualisation of complex systems", University of Birmingham (UK) School of Computer Science (1995).
44. R. J. Hendley, N. S. Drew, A. M. Wood and R. Beale, "Narcissus: Visualising information", University of Birmingham, Advanced Interaction Group Technical Report (1995).
45. J. D. Mackinlay, S. Card and G. G. Robertson, "Perspective wall: Detail and context smoothly integrated", *Proceedings of the ACM SIGCHI '91 Conference on Human Factors in Computing Systems* (April 1991) 173–179.
46. G. G. Robertson, J. D. Mackinlay and S. Card, "Cone trees: Animated 3D visualizations of hierarchical information", *Proceedings of the ACM SIGCHI '91 Conference on Human Factors in Computing Systems* (April 1991) 189–194.
47. K. M. Fairchild, "Information management using virtual reality-based visualizations", *Virtual Reality: Applications and Explorations*, ed. A. Wexelblat (Academic Press Professional, Cambridge, MA, 1993) 45–74.
48. M. Hemmje, "A 3D based user interface for information retrieval systems", *Proceedings of IEEE Visualization '93, Workshop on Database Issues for Data Visualization* (October 25–29, 1993).

49. M. Hemmje, C. Kunkel and A. Willet, "LyberWorld — A visualization user interface supporting fulltext retrieval", *Proceedings of ACM SIGIR '94* (July 3–6, 1994).
50. R. Tamassia, G. D. Battista and C. Battini, "Automatic graph drawing and readability of diagrams", *IEEE Transactions on Systems, Man, and Cybernetics* **18**, no. 1 (January/February 1988) 61–79.

SITUATED COMPUTING: A PARADIGM TO ENHANCE THE MOBILE USER'S INTERACTION

K. PRIYANTHA HEWAGAMAGE and MASAHITO HIRAKAWA

Database Systems Lab, Graduate School of Information Engineering,
Faculty of Engineering, Hiroshima University,
1-4-1 Kagamiyama, Higashi-Hiroshima, 739-8527, Japan
E-mail: {hewa,hirakawa}@isl.hiroshima-u.ac.jp

When people interact with computers, they have to pay attention for things that are not related to the situation of their problems because the interfaces are not contextualized to their working environment. Hence, it is sometimes hard to integrate computers as embedded tools, which facilitate users to accomplish their objectives easily in the working life. Situated computing is a new paradigm for mobile computer users based on their physical context and activities carried out in the workspace. It defines the infrastructure how the situated interaction can be provided using applications. In this chapter, we first describe a model called situation metaphor to design interaction between the user and mobile computers as the basis for the situated computing. Thereafter, a framework called Situated Information Filing and Filtering (SIFF) is presented as the foundation for situated application development. In general, a three-stages schema is given considering the top stage for situated applications. Four applications based on the SIFF are also presented to demonstrate the enhancement of mobile user's interaction that can be achieved.

Keywords: Situated interaction, metaphors, personal information management, context-aware applications.

1. Introduction

Computers have become the vehicle for an increasing range of everyday human activities. A decade ago, computers were used for a specific set of secretariat types of works, but now the acquisition of information, communication, management and even social interactions are becoming more and more computer-mediated interactive activities. Despite recent technological breakthroughs like personal computers and Internet, many people still find it difficult to interact with computers while maintaining their normal flow of work in the real world. The key reason for this dissatisfaction arises since applications have no knowledge about the user's real world situation and they are conventionally developed to provide explicit functionalities.

Situated computing is an activity-centered paradigm to enhance the user's interaction in a mobile environment through applications that can understand the user's context and activities. It goes beyond the conventional user-interaction provided through the fixed-location desktop metaphor based computing. When the desktop metaphor was presented, the computer was treated to be a tool for specific tasks such as writing a document, drawing an image and calculating budgets. With the technological development, the computing now can be easily carried out in a mobile environment. At the same time, the objects in the environment can be powered by integrating computing and communicating capabilities to further enhance the mobile computing (referred to ubiquitous computing). The changing context and user's activities are analyzed to understand the user's situation in a centralized manner independent of applications. Then this information is passed to applications to enhance interaction with them or to provide new functionalities based on the user's current situation.

In this chapter, we are presenting a new paradigm called situated computing and how it can be achieved through developing situated applications with respect to a mobile user and his/her information management. The main objective in situated computing is to enhance the human-computer interaction through simplified interfacing based on the user's real world situations. Hence, we first present a user-model called *Situation Metaphor*, which is proposed as the foundation for achieving the personal situated computing. It is not only an interactive metaphor for visual and non-visual interaction but also a design metaphor that influences on the functional and algorithmic design of applications.

We explain in this chapter the situation metaphor from the design to its realization, to strength its stability as well as to demonstrate its functional effectiveness. In a pilot project, the development was carried out on three stages. The first stage corresponds to the design of the model and the formal description of situation metaphor. The SIFF, Situated Information Filing and Filtering framework is developed on the second stage to provide the software abstraction as the core foundation for all services/applications in situated computing. At the third stage, tools and applications are implemented based on the SIFF framework. In the chapter, four such applications are presented.

The rest of the chapter is organized as follows. First, in Sec. 2, we describe the necessity of considering user-situations to enhance human-computer interaction. In Sec. 3, we review a selected set of studies that have been contributed to the development of situated computing. Section 4 gives the formal description of the situation metaphor and its components. The SIFF framework is described in Sec. 5. The Situation-dependent Browser, which is an application developed for the personal information space based on the SIFF framework, is given in Sec. 6. In Sec. 7, we present another application for personal photographing called Augmented Album. The Pattern Browser in Sec. 8 is developed for the interactive information visualization in situation metaphor. The Situation-dependent Chat Room application, given in Sec. 9, is a collaborative tool developed for a community in the same situation. Finally, we conclude the chapter in Sec. 10.

2. Situated Interaction

Computers have been treated as a kind of machinery tools that can be used to enhance human capabilities specially in information processing. In general, we can classify the tools into two categories, physical and psychological. The physical tools such as shovel, saw and pen extend our physical abilities while psychological tools such as language, mathematics, and symbolic systems enhance our mental capabilities. The computers have peculiarities of both physical and physiological tools, and they are the most powerful tools that could enhance both the physical and psychological human capabilities in seamless ways. However, this diversity of computers makes the human-computer interaction not so simple like one with many other tools.

In order to reduce the complexities in human-computer interaction, interfaces of computer systems are presented based on real world metaphors. The purpose here is to gradually educate users how to use systems functions while hiding internal architecture. The desktop metaphor based interface is the most popular approach generally adopted in computer systems. Although it was successful in the early stages of personal computing, but eventually it failed to support new interaction requirements in mobile environments where computers are brought out from the desktop. In such environments, tasks are heterogeneous and the system behavior should be personalized according to physical and personal circumstances. Simply, the interaction should be combined with the user's situation to enhance the usage of computers.

Suppose, for example, a salesperson who brings his/her mobile computer and visits customers for different business purposes. S/he may carry out different activities at those places while accessing and creating information. Those information as well as any services provided by the system should be associated with the physical location and the type of work rather than the monolithic file/directory found in the desktop. Otherwise, it is hard to maintain effective usage of the computers without disturbing the user's workflow.

The integration of human-computer interaction and the user's situation in a particular working context in a mobile environment is identified as the *situated interaction*. This combination defines that the interaction is not only a function of device but also strongly dependent on the user's activities and context in which the device is used. The necessity of situated interaction has been emphasized in both the situation action theory [1] and the Russian developed activity theory [2, 3] in cognitive science. At the same time, the situated interaction initiates a new paradigm of computing by extending the conventional applications and also by creating a new set of applications.

The general applications can be further developed to provide the enhanced interaction if they are aware of the user's current situational information, although such information is not a main input for their functionality. For example, if a web browser obtains the user's situational information such as the location, type of work and status in his/her vicinity, then it can personalize its graphical interface and other facilities to provide him/her a situational use. On the other hand, the new set of applications, which we define as *obligatory situated applications*, take the user's situation as a compulsory input for their functionality. The output or service of these applications completely relied on the extent to which they can obtain the user's situational information. If a location-dependent mobile assistance, for instance, cannot receive the location information and/or the user's current requirements, it fails to communicate the useful information to the user.

In this chapter, we are presenting a possible approach the authors have used in developing situated applications and a mechanism to integrate the user's situation with his/her interaction [4]. The primary objective in the situated computing paradigm is to embed computers by allowing the people to interact with them as naturally as they do with many personal appliances in the real world. Before moving into details, we briefly describe in the next section, a selected set of interesting studies that have contributed to situated computing paradigm.

3. Related Work

The inspiration and motivation for the situated computing came from many sources. In cognitive science studies, we could identify three information processing theories namely cognitive psychology, situated action theory and activity theory. They describe frameworks that could be used to enhance situated interaction.

The cognitive psychology analyses the human mental processes with the aim of understanding human behavior. Humans are sometimes viewed as "active process of information eternally striving to sum up and interpret the incoming data, and to interpret and reproduce the information stored in its memory through variety of algorithms and strategies" [5]. In other words, cognitive psychology attempts to represent mental constructs such as goals or plans, and then stipulate the procedures by which associated actions take the place of a lively, moment-by-moment assessment of action. This view tries to equate the rigid model of intent and plans in the head with actions in the real world. However, this mechanism falls short of its expectations [6] in a complex reality around human being. There is no sense of model that is divorced from the task contexts in which it finds itself in the real world.

In Situated Action Theory [1], actions are described as something that is solely dependent upon people and their surroundings, not abstract, formal models in the head. Human activity cannot be described sufficiently beforehand and computers need these plans since they cannot properly interact. In situated action theory, a plan is another resource that a person can draw upon; however, it is one that does not strongly determine the outcome of events. Unlike the rigid plans in cognitive psychology, most plans for human activity remains fairly rough and tacit level. In her theory, Suchman explains in details that actions are to a great extent linked to a specific situation at hand and therefore hard to predict by using generic rules. Actions as well as learning, understanding and remembering are situated.

Russian developed activity theory [2, 3] which proposes the view that tools mediate thought, presents an alternative framework for human-computer interaction research and design based on the shortcomings of situated action theory and cognitive psychology. It provides more complete analysis of human nature while providing a paradigm for the description and understanding of the way humans interact with computers and within the context of their environment. The activity theory consists of five basic principles of the hierarchical structure of activity, object-orientedness, internalization/externalization, mediation and development.

According to Nardi [2], the major difference between activity theory and situated action theory is the way in which the structuring of an activity is determined. In activity theory, it is determined by human intentionally before the unfolding in a particular situation, whereas in the situated action theory an activity can be known only as it plays out in a situation. The goals and plans are determined after activities have taken place and then they become "constructed rationalizations" that can be applied to particular situations. By contrast in activity theory, "object-goal" is determined upon prior to analysis. An object is said to proceed and motivate an activity, and it is partially determinative of the activity. Whereas in situated action theory, each activity is created by particular factors that converge to form a situation. Thus situated action theory rejects the notion that an object engages activity. Furthermore, in situated action theory, goals and plans are *post hoc* artifacts of reasoning about action after the action has taken place.

In software engineering viewpoint, the motivation for situated computing raises from context-aware information systems [7], in which physical contextual information is used to retrieve information by assisting people to specify queries in office environments. The situated computing is regarded as an appropriate paradigm that would enhance the power of mobile, wearable, ubiquitous and augmented computing than the traditional stationary desktop computing. Although in many studies including ours, it has been considered that the user's situation is highly relevant to the physical location, it is also possible to model the user's situations independently of such parameters, for example, to augment his/her memory [8, 9]. Generally, the situation is defined going beyond the contextual factors of the user considering his/her activities, personal status and requirements. In some other studies, the core concepts in situated computing are further being extended by including human characteristics in affective computing [10] and social behaviors in pervasive computing [11]. In the rest of this section, we briefly describe some of the studies related to situated computing.

The situated information space [12] is a kind of augmented reality applications, which uses a hand-held display rather than head-up display. It is one of early presentations to demonstrate how the information overload could be overcome by segmenting information and attaching them to physical objects in a space. The idea is that a user equipped with a track-sensitive palm-top computer will receive the information based upon their proximity to objects within the real world. For example, a user may browse the space near a fax machine. By approaching to an in-tray, the information about received faxes will be displayed on the palm-top computer. The system could be used in a library too, where electronic information would guide users to the written publication they require. The tracking unit used is a 6D device giving x, y, and z positional coordinates plus the pitch yaw and roll orientation of the palm-top device. This device can only work within one-meter cube, thereby severely limiting its applications.

Brown [13] proposed a framework called Stick-e Documents for creating context-aware applications and it highlighted the importance of contextual awareness in mobile computing. The stick-e document framework is composed of a set of stick-e notes, each of them resembles a page of HTML. Each stick-e note consists of the contents and relevant contextual information to be triggered. When a mobile user is carrying a PDA equipped with location sensing software, s/he can place a stick-e note at a physical point of interest. Once the user returns to that location in the future, the stick-e note will be triggered and s/he is informed by the PDA that the associated note exists. A stick-e note can be considered as an electronic form of Post-it notes which people place in their working places not to forget or inform different things to be done. Some other examples of context that could trigger a stick-e note are the adjacency of a person to physical objects and the temperature above/below a certain level. The stick-e note approach offers a useful general mechanism for the creation of context-aware applications and it became a basis for many other researches. However, further work would be required on system aspects, such as the management of location information and the delivery of contextual information to applications.

The virtual reality techniques can also be used to augment the user's conventional view with additional contextual information while the user is moving around the real world. Starner [14] describes wearable computers, which use a head-up display to overlay graphics, text and sound onto the wearer's normal view of the physical world. In one example, the emacs editor is projected using the head-up display so that the image overlaps the user's view of the real world. Pull-down menu options are displayed as usual along the top. By mounting a video-camera on the user's head which transmits its output by radio for remote processing, the user's finger is recognized and its position is interpreted in the same way as the position of a mouse pointer on a conventional display. The user can therefore select menu options and carry out other mouse-oriented activities.

The feasibility of situated computing was directly discussed in [15]. Hull [15] describes comprehensively the issues associated with the development and deployment of situated applications. He has illustrated the design requirements of sensing technologies and the importance of interpreting the sensor data, which is hard without representing different forms of knowledge such as social issues. The Situated Computing Service (SitComp) is a single server that encapsulates context acquisition and abstraction, and provides both an event-driven and query interface to applications.

The necessity of situated computing has been addressed and illustrated in the work at CSTaR Institute [16] through a set of situated applications. The gap that exists when people find it difficult to interact with the electronic media while maintaining the flow of normal activities is described as the discontinuity between the electronic and physical world. In order to demonstrate the fact that situated computing is about providing people necessary means to make right decisions and take actions, a number of applications is discussed in [17–20].

In order to reduce the complexity and cumbersome of developing context-aware applications, a toolkit for handling context information has been introduced in [21]. In this impressive work that has some similar objectives close to ours, a new concept called context widgets have been introduced. They mediate between environment and applications in the same way graphical widgets given in GUI toolkits mediate between the user and the application. The widget library facilitates the application developers to high level programming by reusing and integrating those widgets in context-aware applications.

In addition to the above mentioned and some other works that directly discuses the requirement of situated computing, few other studies, Time-Machine Computing [22] and Lifestreams [23] indirectly address some vital issues giving a useful feedback for the success of situated computing.

The research study presented in this chapter addresses the perspective of situated computing from viewpoint of human-computer interaction while proposing a software engineering approach that could facilitate the development of situated applications. We went beyond simply discussing how to achieve the software abstraction through an interface to developers. An analysis was carried out in order to integrate the situated computing not only at the application level but also as a system that could assist its users in an activity-centered approach. Although we didn't adopt all principles in activity theory, it was heavily influenced on us drafting a possible solution, which will be discussed in the next section as the basic model for situated computing. We introduced the situatedness as a property at the system level by allowing the user to visualize, imagine and treat computing with his/her situations in a working space. Based on this model, we developed a framework for the application development.

4. Situation Metaphor

Metaphors have long been recognized to play an important role in the user interface design. They can serve as a means of making an unknown complexity into an understandable format. Simply metaphors provide intuition of how things work using the world knowledge. The best example is desktop metaphor. Recently, there has been an increased recognition of metaphor's larger role in the design process of, for example, the language [24, 25], program functionality [26, 27], system architecture [28], knowledge-representation [29], and scientific discovery [30, 31].

When it is necessary to introduce the user's situations with his/her computing, authors strongly believe that such integration should begin at the system level allowing users to imagine and treat computers as tools that could be used to improve their interaction and decision-making in a particular context. The conventional desktop metaphor based model could hardly support this requirement [32] since it was employed to guide users using features of graphical user interfaces. Hence, any new proposal for modeling the personal computing should support the property of situatedness. One of related proposals is "Personal Assistant (PA)" [33], in which human-human interaction is tried to impose for the situational use of computers. PA is expected to provide interfaces according to the user's anticipations through voice dialogs. In other words, it depicts having a mobile consultant who speaks like the user's digital secretary.

Our proposed model, situation metaphor, differs from conventional metaphors since it corresponds to an intangible thing. It refers to a particular circumstance how the user will react in order to achieve a particular target. People continuously learn through their experiences and utilize those knowledge whenever they want to carry out some tasks. Simply, human interaction in a particular situation depends on the knowledge gained through their past experiences. Although computers are electronic devices, we enforce the situation metaphor on the interface of system behavior to integrate gradually the user's real world activities and interaction with mobile devices. The resulted model depicts neither an intelligent consultant at once nor a static picture but learns through the user to provide him a personalized interface.

In metaphoric approaches [34], metaphors are presented in the form of "A is B", where B is said to be the source metaphor and A is the target. Generally, the source metaphor is determined based on the common knowledge in the real world and the target is the complex entity that should be represented. In Black's interaction theory of metaphor [24], the metaphor is not simply a process of transferring properties from the source to the target, but a complex interaction between them in which our knowledge of the target is equally capable of changing our understanding of the source. Simply, metaphor includes complex shifts of meaning across the target and the source. In situation metaphor, the source corresponds to "the user's reactions in a particular situation based on the personal history" and the target to "the model that defines a suitable interface for his/her interaction in mobile environment".

4.1. *Interaction model*

The basic concept given by the source and target in the situation metaphor was then extended to form an interaction model based on the significant properties of the source, which influence the user's interaction in mobile environment. This process refines the vague idea in the basic concept into an initial design specification [24]. Figure 1 shows the interaction model in the situation metaphor. In this model, the mobile computer/device is a mediated tool between the user and his/her goal

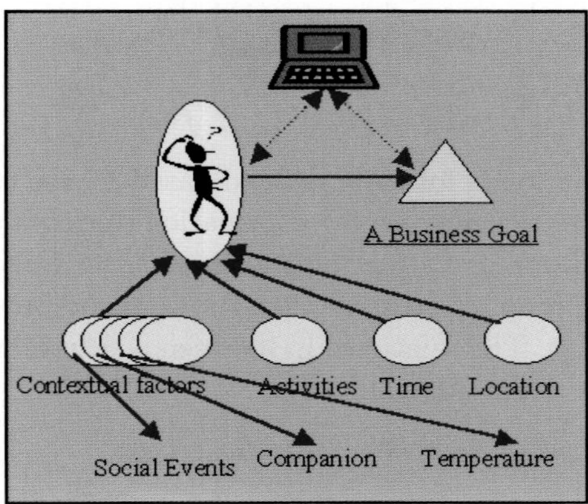

Fig. 1. Interaction model in the situation metaphor.

in the workspace. Then the user's interaction is interpreted based on the physical location, time period, his/her activities and contextual factors in the vicinity.

The physical location is given the highest priority in a mobile environment since the user is supposed to move among different places as part of his/her working style. This pivotal factor, physical location, could significantly influence the user's interaction and hence classifies his/her interaction space. Time is a universal factor of human behavior and it shows the path of everyday life. In the situation metaphor, the time is identified as a period and visualized as a segment on the timeline with begin and end points. When a situation is interpreted, links are established with previous corresponding periods on the user's timeline. A particular business goal is supposed to be consist of one or more activities. An activity is identified as a particular engagement of user [2] whether it is mediated or unmediated through a mobile device. The contextual factors are identified depending on their influence on the user's activities and their vicinity with respect to his/her physical location. Generally, it is a set that consists of social events, objects or environmental variables that would be useful for the interpretation of the user's situation.

With respect to the interaction model in the situation metaphor, we formally define a particular situation (Si) below using those four attributes that influence the user's interaction. The purpose of this definition is to precisely state about the situation in this user-model and facilitates the description of other concepts in the situation metaphor.

$$Si = S(Li, Ti, Ai, Fi)$$

- Li gives the physical location coordinates (latitude and longitude) values.
- Ti is a continuous period of time with start and end time points.
- Ai is a set of activity points with respect to all activities engaged in the workspace and an activity is described as a sequence of (action, object) pairs.

- F_i describes the set of contextual factors that directly affect the interaction.

$$Fi = \{f1, f2, \ldots, fm\}$$

Importantly, a situation is formally defined based on the context and activities. On the other hand, the user may access information during a specified situation. A logical piece of information in a situation is defined as an *Entity*, which is identified based on some specific properties rather than its storage representation (details will be discussed in Sec. 5.2). The relationship between a situation and the relevant set of Entities is given by a function called ID.

$$ID(Si) = \{e1, e2, \ldots, eq\}$$

This formal notation is used to declare and describe the theoretical foundation of the situation metaphor, which is based on the concept called *Situation Space.*

4.2. *Situation space*

In situation metaphor, the Situation Space is the user's interaction space in which s/he may have used the mobile computer/device as an embedded tool to achieve his/her business objectives. Both the computer mediated activities and non-mediated activities are included in the Situation Space. The main objective of Situation Space is to describe all identified past user-situations in a meaningful way that could be utilized to provide appropriate system behaviors and functionalities of applications. At the same time, it integrates the physical context, user activities and information entities by providing a single interface based on the user's business goals. Although the interaction history is an underline source for the Situation Space, the semantic relations among all possible past situations make it a meaningful multi-dimensional space.

Situation Space is regarded as an *n-dimensional* space as there could be variable number of forces affecting user's interaction in a mobile computing environment. The location, which is the most significant one, has two dimensions (latitude and longitude) to precisely define it. Time is one-dimensional but has logical attributes like day of week, month of year, etc. User activities as well as contextual factors are varying from a situation to another and their dimensions depend on a particular case. The Situation Space SS is defined as follows.

SS is a set of elements Si on which following properties should exist. Let two distinct situations Si and Sj such that Si, $Sj \in SS$ and operator Δ indicates the concatenation between two situations.

(1) $Si = Sj$ *iff* $(Li = Lj \wedge Ti = Tj \wedge Ai = Aj \wedge Fi = Fj)$.
(2) If $Si \Delta Sj \in SS$ then $\|Li - Lj\| < \varepsilon$ for a given $\varepsilon > 0$ and $Ti + Tj$ is a continuous period. $\|Li - Lj\|$ gives the geographical distance between two locations Li and Lj. $Ti + Tj$ is a single segment on the Timeline. If $Si \Delta Sj \in SS$ then we can call Sj is $Si + 1$.

(3) If $ID(Si) = \phi$ then Si is defined as a *null situation* in the Situation Space.

(4) Relatedness ($\mathfrak{R}$) is a property that exists between any two non-null situations in SS.

$$\mathfrak{R}(Si, Sj) = |ID(Si) \cap ID(Sj)| + k$$

k is a value calculated based on the content analysis of Entities in the two sets.

(5) If $\mathfrak{R}(Si, Sj) > h$ for a given threshold value h, then Si and Sj are said to be strongly-*related* situations.

(6) If $\mathfrak{R}(Si, Sj) > h$ and $\mathfrak{R}(Sj, Sk) > h$ but $\mathfrak{R}(Si, Sk) < h$ then $\mathfrak{R}(Si, Sj)$ is said to be *weakly-related* situations for a given threshold value h.

Based on the declaration of SS, the navigation is given using following function.

$$F(Si, d) \rightarrow \{Sdi, Sd2, \ldots, Sdn | \forall k = di, \ldots, dn, Sk \in SS \wedge \mathfrak{R}(Sk, Si) > h\}$$

d is a parameter that describes the expansion of Si along a specified dimension.

The Situation Space is not a plain history of the user's interaction in a mobile environment and it facilitates to understand the user's anticipated behavior in a particular situation. The formal declaration of SS provides the guidelines to establish a proper organization for the Situation Space. By applying the principal of "object-orientedness" in the activity theory [2] on the user's goals, we first declared three categories of user-situations, namely *Abstract Situation*, *Instance Situation* and *Basic Situation*. Abstract situations are like classes in the object-oriented framework. Instance situations are comparable to composite objects that may consist of one or more primitive objects. Basic situations are considered as such primitive objects. Then the relatedness property in the SS is used to identify those situations and a hierarchical organization is built based on their composition as shown in Fig. 2. This hierarchy is the basis to provide the pragmatic interpretation of the user's current situation and visualization in the situation metaphor. The details of its construction will be given in Sec. 8.1.

4.3. *Functional development*

The interpretation of a metaphor [35] is referred to as a process of discovering how the functions of the source metaphor can be used to understand the target. We call such functions as the functional features in the situation metaphor and they impose a structure on the enormous problem space found in the target area. The list of functional features given below is our current identification and their effectiveness has been demonstrated through implementation of several tools which will be explained later in this chapter. These significant functions are the positive components [24] that are needed to be highlighted in presenting the situation metaphor.

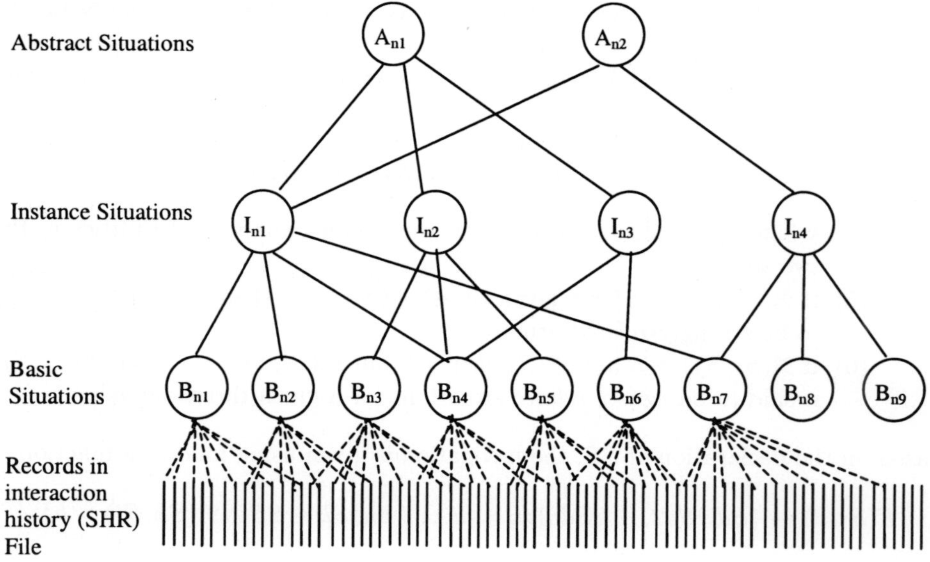

Fig. 2. Hierarchical organization in situation space.

(1) Spatial identity
Real world situations in mobile environment are naturally tagged with a location name found in the user's personal vocabulary. People's behavior is significantly correlated to these locations. In the situation metaphor, the functionality of the system is strictly related to the location information. Hence, the spatial identity is used to augment the access to information, and the functionality of both system services and applications.

(2) Temporal identity
Although the time is linear in abstract, its relationship with human behavior is periodical. Generally, many of user's situations in real life have some periodical relationships with each other. At the same time, a particular behavior varies with respect to time of day and its relationship to individual/social factors (for example, lunch time in a working day and a holiday). Hence, the period of time of a situation is analyzed with respect to the individual and social information and made it available for system services and applications. Temporal identity consists of those derived information as well as exact time intervals. In addition, the user can navigate on the system status based on the time (referred as time-machine computing in [22]) and personalize the functionality of both system services and applications.

(3) Activity identity
In many real world user-situations, when people recall past situations [7], they sometimes remember only events or special activities rather than

locations or time. In situation metaphor, users can retrieve information based on real world activities and they can also personalize the system behavior based on possible future activities.

(4) Filing information
Generally a real life situation consists of some information and people hardly refer them using explicit naming structure. In the situation metaphor, the filing of information doesn't depend on the storage structure in the device or on a particular naming convention. The users can identify them by describing the situations partially or fully, in which they were created or modified. The user can include logically related set of information in an Entity as their container.

(5) Linking and navigation
People organize gathered information in a particular structure that would simplify them to locate information. In the desktop metaphor, an interface is provided using files/directories to maintain the user's digital information collection and it is also presented as the user's storage structure. The user can explicitly create links among Entities in the situation metaphor and the system builds an implicit links structure based on the situations in which those Entities are created or modified. Hence, the navigation can be presented just like recalling memory in the past situations.

(6) Filtering information
Information should be presented to users not only based on their identified interests but also current working context. Therefore, the system maintains the necessary indexes based on the structure in Situation Space to support the situation dependent filtering.

(7) Visualization
When a person analyzes "how a particular thing has happened", s/he uses visual thinking [36] on a subset of corresponding events as the starting pattern before moving into statistical or textual evaluations. In the situation metaphor, Basic Situations or Instance Situations are considered as sequence of events with respect to their parent situations when the Situation Space is visualized.

4.4. *Development schema*

The situation metaphor is proposed as a model to integrate the user's situations in mobile working environment at the system level. One of the main expectations is to separate the capturing, processing and management of the user's situation information from applications and communicate such situational information to applications whenever it is necessary. Hence, it is possible to simplify the development of context-aware applications if the underline system is based on the situation metaphor.

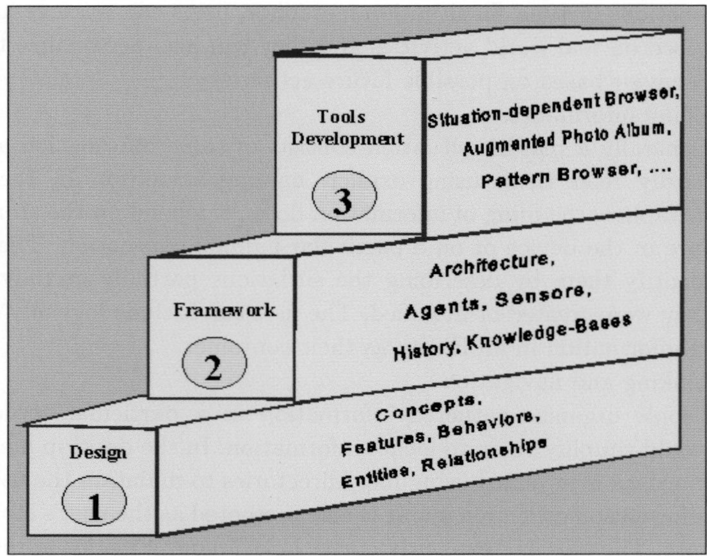

Fig. 3. The development stages in situation metaphor.

The development of situation metaphor is a complex project since it is not a straightforward to determine the software development of internal functionalities and how the communication between the system and applications is properly maintained. At the same time there are many challenges in capturing, interpreting and managing the user's situations. In addition, the functional features described in the previous section are our anticipation in the first stage. The set of functional features should be refined by developing prototype applications. Then it would lead to remove any negative components and include new positive components that would become apparent in the evaluation. Having these objectives, authors started a pilot project to study the feasibility as well as to demonstrate proposed approach of integrating situated interaction with applications.

The schema that we followed in developing the pilot project of situation metaphor consists of three stages as shown in Fig. 3, namely design, framework and tools development.

The design stage corresponds to the theoretical development of situation metaphor including the refinement of functional features. Simply, everything stated about the situation metaphor in this section defines the first stage in the development. In the second stage, we tried to realize what is specified in the situation metaphor as software components. The Situated Information Filing and Filtering (SIFF) framework, given in the next section, has been developing as a common middleware to centralize the processing and management of the user's situational information. Then SIFF framework became the basis to include the situated interaction in the prototype applications on the third stage. Those applications would be able to utilize the functional features as well as other information about the user's situations in order to include the situated interaction. In fact some of the applications are system tools of the situation metaphor. Four prototype applications that have been developed based on SIFF framework are discussed in details later in the chapter.

5. SIFF Framework

The SIFF, *Situated Information Filing* and *Filtering*, framework is a generic architecture that provides structure and behavior of software components in the situation metaphor. Generally, it works like a virtual machine that tries to hard code user-situations while making abstractions open-ended by designing specific plug-ins that are reusable and extendable. Hence, SIFF is not an application but a middleware that would communicate about the user's situations with applications based on the SIFF framework.

In the pilot project, the SIFF framework was developed as a lightweight component on top of the desktop metaphor based file system. According to the model of situation metaphor, we identified that following requirements should be supported in a software design for the SIFF framework.

(1) Capture the physical context of the user when s/he is persuading on a business goal.
(2) Collect meta data about Entities accessed in a particular situation.
(3) Gather information about non-mediated activities occurred in the vicinity of user.
(4) Interpret the situational information that could be able to identify from the user's point of view.
(5) Integrate and maintain the situational information with relevant information Entities.
(6) Maintain the interaction history and its high level derivations (i.e., Basic, Instance and Abstract situations).
(7) Communicate situational information to applications and tools.

The development work that are needed to cover requirements given in above steps is very challenging since it is required to integrate different engineering approaches collectively. Authors initiated this pilot project two years ago and it is now in the beginning of the second stage. Number of research students has contributed for its development. Although we were able to achieve many goals, specially capturing and interpreting situational information, some works are pending before starting its evaluation and usability at the time of writing this chapter. For the rest of this section, we will describe the system architecture and data organization in SIFF framework.

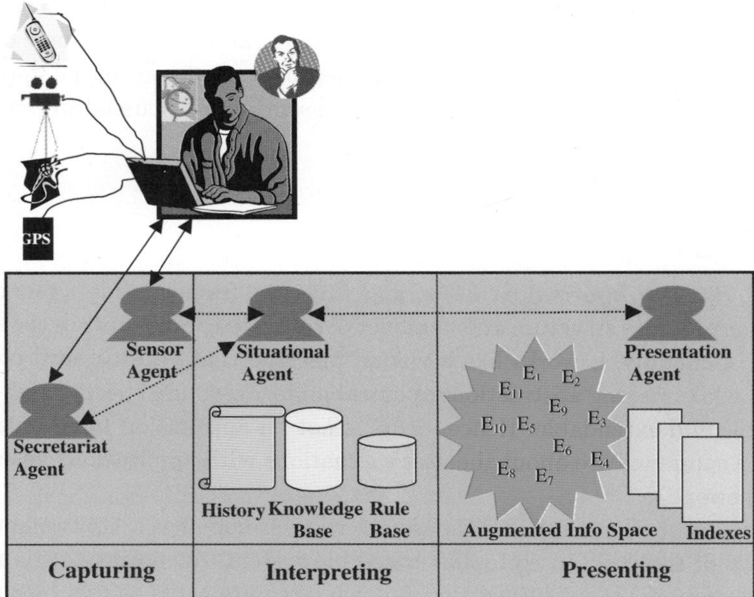

Fig. 4. The system architecture of SIFF.

5.1. *System architecture*

We adopted *multi-agent based system architecture*, as it is more suitable to provide solutions for robotism and interoperable problems. It is also deemed that the architecture should be opened and extendable for making the future possible expansions whenever new sensors and peripherals are added. The user-interaction has to be carefully monitored continuously with respect to activities, time and location. Therefore, the system should be able to sense directly the user's vicinity and also to obtain any useful information from applications. If adequate contextual information cannot be gathered, it will notify the user requesting to describe the relevant details.

The system architecture of the SIFF framework as shown in Fig. 4 is partitioned into three divisions based on its functionality. The first part concentrates on capturing the user's context and activities carried out when s/he is persuading goals in the workspace. There are two agents called *Secretariat Agent* (*SEC*) and *Sensor Agent* (*SEN*) developed as interface and reactive agents, respectively. The middle part works to interpret the data captured from the first part and it consists of a collaborative agent named *Situational Agent* (*SIT*), a rule base and a knowledge base. The third part, presentation, provides the interface for external applications as well as tools developed on top of the SIFF framework. It consists of an agent named *Presentation Agent* (*PEN*), three index files and the augmented information space.

5.2. Data organization

The organization of data in the personal information space plays an important role to achieve functional features in the situation metaphor. In SIFF, the information space is reorganized by integrating situational data as meta data and this new organization, augmented information space, is maintained on its third division.

In the conventional systems, the data are organized and managed by the file system and presented as the interface of the storage structure. The primary element in the personal information space corresponds to a file in the conventional file system. Although a file is defined as a logical collection of information, it represents only a set of information stored together. No relationships are described with respect to external context in which the content of a file is generated or accessed. Simply the conventional file system forces the user to maintain filenames and directories.

A file in the conventional system consists of a header and a body. In the header, there are very few meta data such as a time stamp and the file system doesn't provide any facility to integrate any meta data into an application in a customizable way. At the same time, the organization of files is static and it gives a single hierarchical view of the information. Hence, the conventional data/file organization is not adequate to provide an augmented interface for the information space, which is a fundamental requirement in the situation metaphor. Thus, it is extended both conceptually and technically.

In the situation metaphor, an information entity (Entity) is identified as a logical collection of multimedia data sources with respect to an initial situation. Both the user and system (precisely agents in SIFF) can create Entities. They are completely independent from storage structure and restrictions like filenames. The structure of an Entity contains two parts; extendable interface and data segment as shown in Fig. 5. The interface contains a set of attributes to record contextual information and it provides the identification to the Entity. Some attributes may take multiple values and multiple hierarchies are identified using these values.

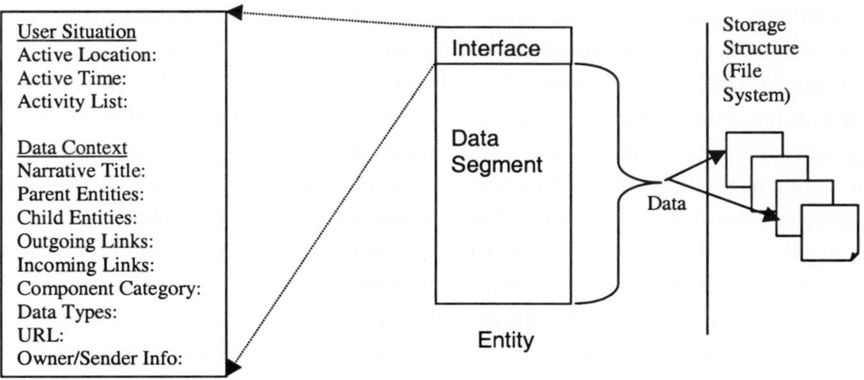

Fig. 5. The structure of an entity.

The body of an Entity, data segment, may contain one or more objects just like a compound document. It is noted that the actual data are not replicated in a data segment.

6. Situation-dependent Browser for the Personal Information Space

In the situation metaphor, the information and the relevant user-situations are identified as their contextual relationship. (In the desktop metaphor, the information and the relevant files are identified as their storage location in the directory hierarchy.) Hence, the navigation in the information space is carried out based on this contextual relationship.

Situation-dependent Browser (SD Browser) [37] is a tool developed on top of the SIFF framework to demonstrate the situation-dependent navigation in the Situation Space according to its formal navigation function. In addition, it uses the functional features in the situation metaphor allowing the user to specify his/her past situations on a graphical user interface. The browser provides the feedback about the availability of information on the graphical interface whenever the querying is done. It facilitates the user to express the query conditions in navigation. Before discussing the interface of SD Browser, we first illustrate some details about the Information Roll in situation-dependent browsing.

6.1. *Information roll*

An Information Roll is a logical representation technique defined in the situation metaphor and it is ideally a one-dimensional roll of information sheets to describe a set of information entities at a particular situation with a navigation mechanism. It is capable of folding up and unfolding the information sheet to hide and control displayed area (see Fig. 6). This design could be applied to present a large number of sets within a small displayed area with an easy interaction technique of rotating a small roll such as in Microsoft Intelli mouse.

At the highest abstract level, the Information Roll presents all entities linearly ordered in accordance with respect to specific features in the Situation Space. Since the linear ordering is not apparent in some features like physical location, it is determined according to information in the personal preference registry. During the situation-dependent browsing, the user may specify a particular situation, which may be associated with a set of Entities that are not consecutive in the Information Roll as shown in Fig. 6. Then a compressed view is created by placing those Entities together. The user can define different views on the Information Roll by specifying different situations. These views are considered dynamic virtual directories [38] in the situation metaphor. The user can click boundaries on the view to expand and show all Entities in the abstract Information Roll, when it is necessary.

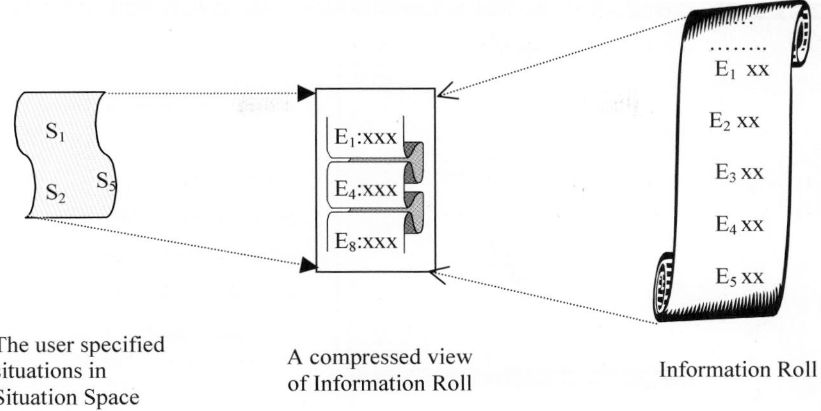

Fig. 6. A view of the information roll.

6.2. *User interface*

The user interface of the SD Browser is organized by three components — Map component, Time Frame component and User Activity component, as in Fig. 7.

The Map component uses a geographical map as its interface with zoom-in/out facilities. On the map, a small (file) icon appears if there is an entity associated with its location. It is allowed for the user to choose certain icons by clicking them or selecting an area on the map, in which icons are included.

Time Frame component takes a spreadsheet like interface [39] to specify the time intervals of a situation. The user can interactively change the scale of both the column and row to analyze the data and then s/he can select rows, columns or some isolated cells to describe specific time intervals of a target situation. The possible scales for rows are hours of a day $(1, 2, \ldots, 24)$, days of a week (Mon, ..., Sun), weeks of a month (First, Second, Third and Fourth), dates of a month $(1, \ldots, 31)$ and months of a year (January, ..., December). By dragging on the row headings, the user can change the scale from one to another. Columns of Time Frame component are used to represent the regular timeline. Hence, the basic representation is that one column corresponds to one day. By dragging on the column headings, the user can change the period into a week, a month, a quarter of year, a semester of year, and a year.

In addition, the user can change the coordinates of columns using *combining* and *hiding* functions. For example, suppose the user combines any seven consecutive days into one column using *combining* function, then the system will monitor the action and perform the same action for all other columns. Thereafter, each column represents a week instead of a day. In a similar way, the user can change coordinates of columns into different combinations such as months, semesters, and years. By using the hiding function, the user can have more interesting coordinates for columns. For example, when a column represents months, and suppose the user

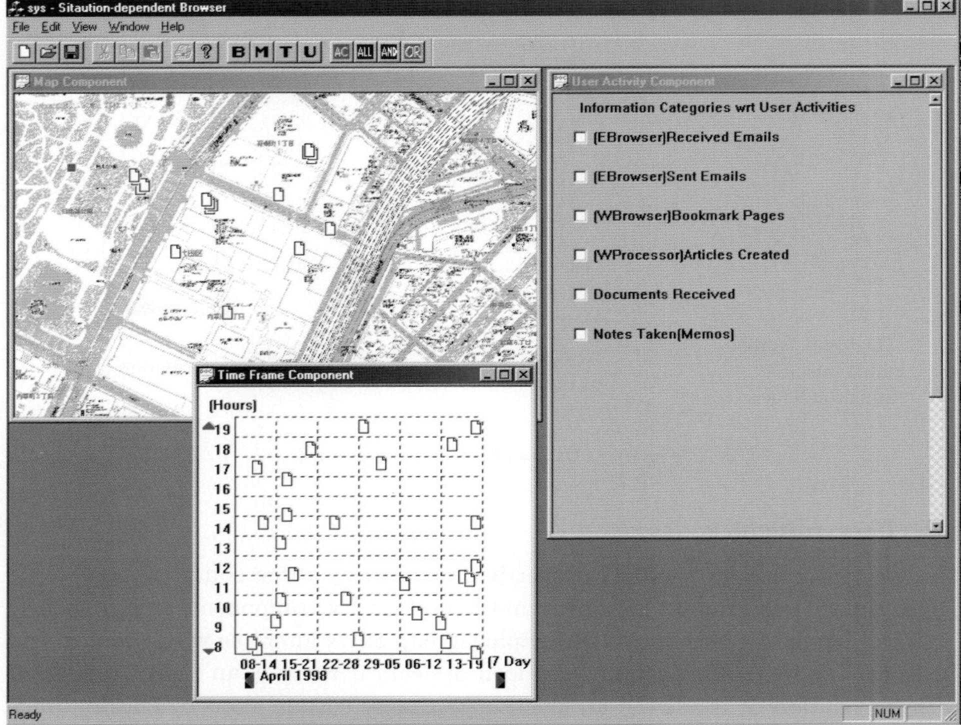

Fig. 7. Situation-dependent browser with three components.

hides columns from February to December in a certain year. Then the system will hide all columns of February to December for each year and then Time Frame component will have only the January column of each year. Hence, the user may find some interesting rules like a periodicity of some activities through the different visualization with respect to the time of the activities.

User Activity component in Fig. 7 displays possible information categories with respect to user activities associated with the specified period of time shown in the Time Frame component and the locations/areas in the Map component. The user can mark one or more activities and then relevant icons are selected for browsing.

Those three components are synchronized each other. When the user specifies certain conditions using three components of map, time and activities, s/he can combine them using AND and OR operators in the tool bar. In response to user's description of the situation, the SD Browser presents a list of Entities in a scrolling window (See Fig. 8). This list is a compressed view of the Information Roll as described earlier. By double clicking on an Entity, the user can open it for both reading and writing. The user can expand the list to navigate to Entities that are not displayed by clicking on the edge between Entities.

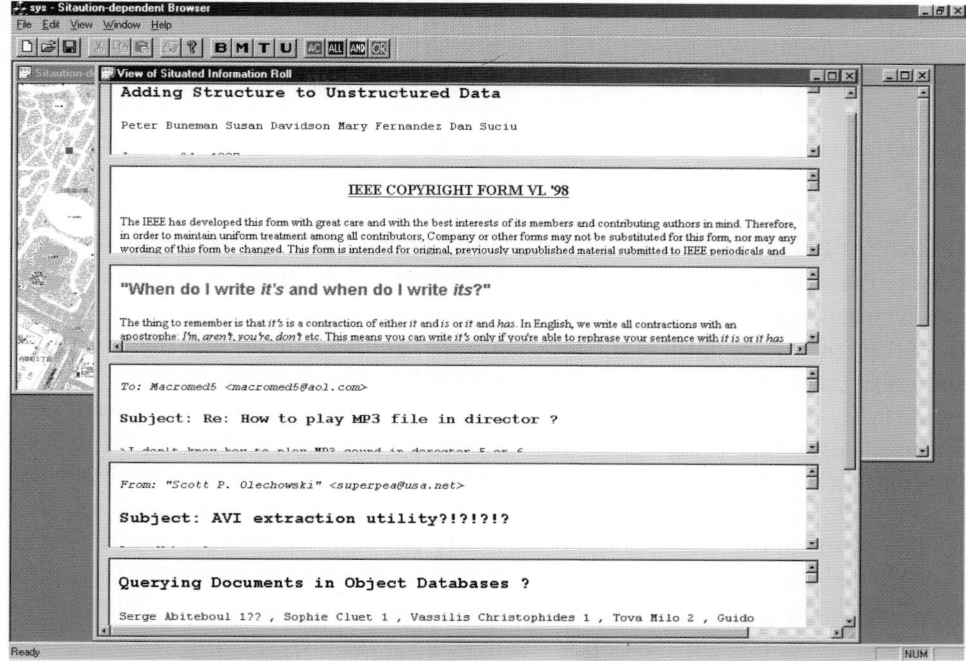

Fig. 8. A view of information roll for a specified situation.

7. Augmented Album for the Personal Photography

Two decades ago, the personal photographing was described as taking still images to print on special papers. Today, it covers taking both the still images and moving pictures (video clips) as a major part of documenting the real life situations. Recent advances in digital technology have made the digital photographing inexpensive as well as popular in a large user community.

The benefit of digital photographing includes the ability to take, process, and display images and video clips using computers in seamless ways. However when pictures are taken, we never think about filenames and folders for those images/video clips. The storage location, file names and directory structure are the unwanted overheads that the desktop computer users have been forced to consider in their filing.

Augmented Album [40] is an application developed to demonstrate how the user-situations based on the situation metaphor can be used to provide an easy-to-use system with easy-to-remember interface for the management and retrieval of digital image/video clips. It is developed on top of the SIFF framework. In this system, the contextual information such as the location, time, and user's social events, are captured when a picture is taken. It represents the meaning of the picture as well as its content information to some extent and, thus, benefits us to retrieve images/video clips. For example, consider a query "Find pictures of X'mas party last year at my uncle's house". This type of query can be processed by context-based framework very easily, but the content-based retrieval mechanisms in multimedia database are limited in handing such queries. Finding uncle's face or house is not so easy and such operations take considerable amount of resources to execute the query.

The prototype application has been implemented on a laptop computer with a Hitachi MPEG/JPEG portable digital video camera. In the camera, each video clip is stored as a file on a PC-card type hard-disk drive with timing information. In addition, whenever a digital photograph is taken (identified as unmediated activity), the SIFF framework gathers the location, time, and any contextual information of the user. Later, when the camera is connected to the mobile computer, the SIT agent in the SIFF activates to associates video/image files with the relevant contextual information using timing information of data files. If there is not enough information about the clips, the SEC agent in SIFF inform the user to obtain additional information about the clip such as social events. At that time, the user is allowed to specify any narration, keywords and other contextual factors for the clip. Though the computer is not directly connected with the camera in the prototype, we would say that the implementation doesn't lose any practicability of the system.

7.1. *Browsing interface*

The user interacts with the system by three components as in the Situation-dependent Browser: Map Component, Time Frame Component and Events Component (see Fig. 9). These three components could function together or independently to select images/video clips relevant to a specified past user-situation. The functionality of Map and Time Frame components is the same with that in the Situation-dependent Browser.

Events Component, as shown in Fig. 9 is used to show the event categories that exist according to the current view in the Map Component and the Time Frame Component. Event categories are used to group images/video clips as a way to show the contextual relevancy of those icons (e.g. birthday parties, events in schools, and exhibitions). When the user selects a particular event category, icons appeared in the Map and Time Frame Components are restricted to be the ones in that category. Hence, the Events Component displays a contextual classification of the pictures and allows the user to refine the focus of user-situations.

By selecting all or a subset of icons in Map or Time Frame component, the user can open the corresponding pictures as a compressed view of the Information Roll (See Fig. 9). It contains the first frame view for all pictures according to the visual display size. These views give visual clues of the content and the user can open those images and video clips by clicking corresponding one on the screen.

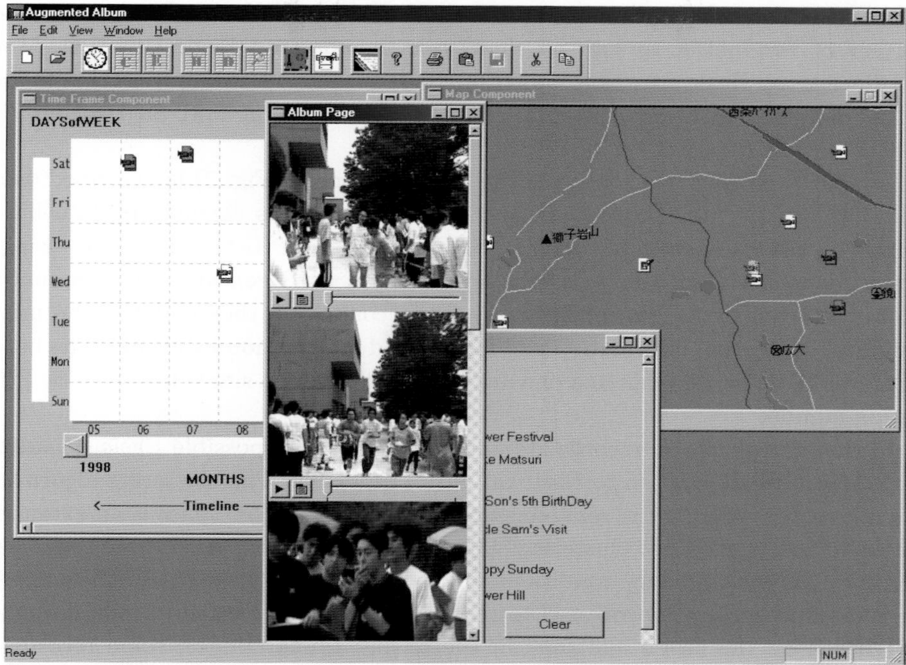

Fig. 9. Browsing interface of augmented album.

8. Pattern Browser to Visualize Personal Workflow

8.1. *Hierarchical organization*

In previous tools, we demonstrated how the user can retrieve/filter information based on their contextual relations that are identified within the Situation Space. In such circumstances, the user precisely specifies a particular situation. However, in some cases, the user prefers to analyze different situations with respect to semantic organization in the Situation Space. The Pattern Browser [41, 42] is an interactive visualization tool and aims at helping a user to find valuable *spatiotemporal patterns* in Situation Space.

In the visualization of situation metaphor, the semantic organization is the hierarchical structure defined using Abstract, Instance and Basic situations as described in Sec. 4.2. The Abstract situation which is a top level situation describes a particular category of the user's goals and is not necessary to refer to a particular location or time intervals. "Sales of Product A" and "Customer inquiries of Product A" are two possible examples of the Abstract situation for a traveling salesman. Instance situations are occurrences of Abstract situations with actual attribute values. For example, "Sale of Product A to Lawson shops (widespread chain stores)" would be an instance of the Abstract situation "Sales of Product A". Basic situations represent actual occurrences (stages) of Instances situations in the real world. They thus have actual values of location, time and activities. In the above example, each delivery of Product A to Lawson shops corresponds to a Basic situation. More specifically, the Basic situation indicates the fact that, for example, "the Product A was delivered to Lawson shop on Hirodai-mae street at 9:21 on December 1, 1999".

The hierarchical organization in the Situation Space (Fig. 2) is described using index files in the SIFF framework and its construction is carried out as a batch process on the interaction history file (SHR — Situation History Registry) using a clustering algorithm of the data mining technique. SHR contains huge amount of records inserted by SIT agent for every five seconds and they describe the user's activities, contextual information and interpreted information by agents. The batch of records that corresponds to a one day is maintained in a single file given by SHR version number.

In the first phase, all records are analyzed to identify possible Basic situations and the results are written to Basic Situation Index file. The clustering algorithm, which used to represent the relatedness property in Situation Space is an extension of hierarchical single-lined clustering [43]. All records are processed three times considering different boundary conditions. In the first round, the spatial and temporal variances in records are processed to recognize clusters. These clusters are further split based on the user's idle time in the second round. Hence, some records in SHR are discarded without linking to Basic situations. In the third round, other information in each record of a cluster is matched to identify possible sub-clusters. Using a weighting schema, the similarity among records in a cluster is measured based on the Euclidean distance formula [44]. The records in a final cluster are used to determine the corresponding Basic situation and its information.

In the second phase, the links between Basic and Instance situations are established updating both Basic Situation Index and Instance Situation Index files. (A record in an index file uniquely describes a corresponding situation). The similarity distance between a Basic situation and an Instance situation is calculated using Euclidean distance formula with different weighting schema. Basic Situations, which fail to link existing Instance Situations, are matched with one another to determine possible new Instance situations. In the pilot project, the user is requested to verify the results before committing them to index files once in a day. At this time, the user can delete/insert links between Basic and Instance situations, and create new Instance situations manually.

Linking Instance and Abstract situations is similar to one between Basic and Instance situations but weighting schema and threshold values are different.

8.2. *Visualization*

Pattern Browser has mainly two components allowing the user to specify conditions for the visualization and also to observe patterns from different angles. One is called the map window and the other is the spiral window.

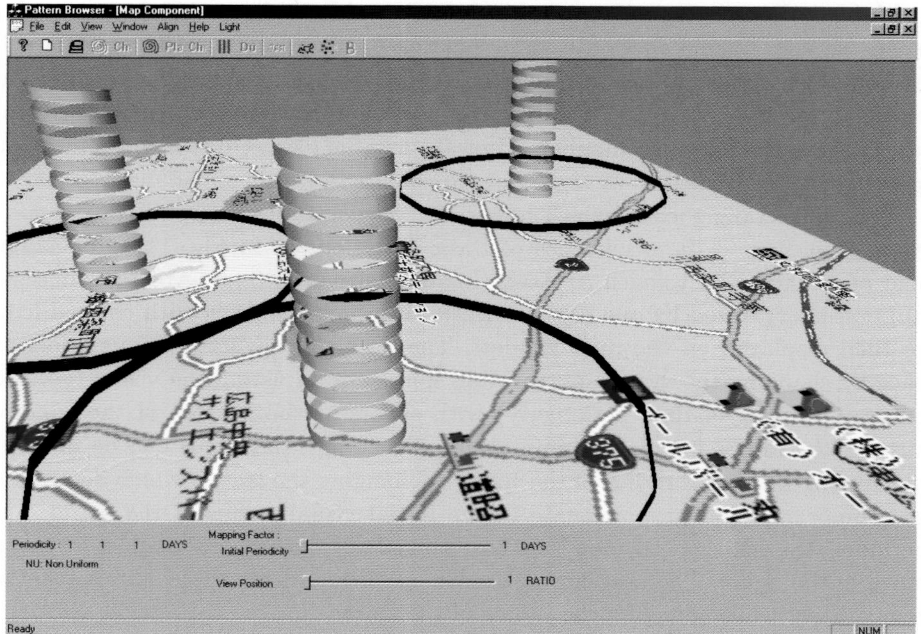

Fig. 10. Map window — spatial viewpoints defined on the geographical map.

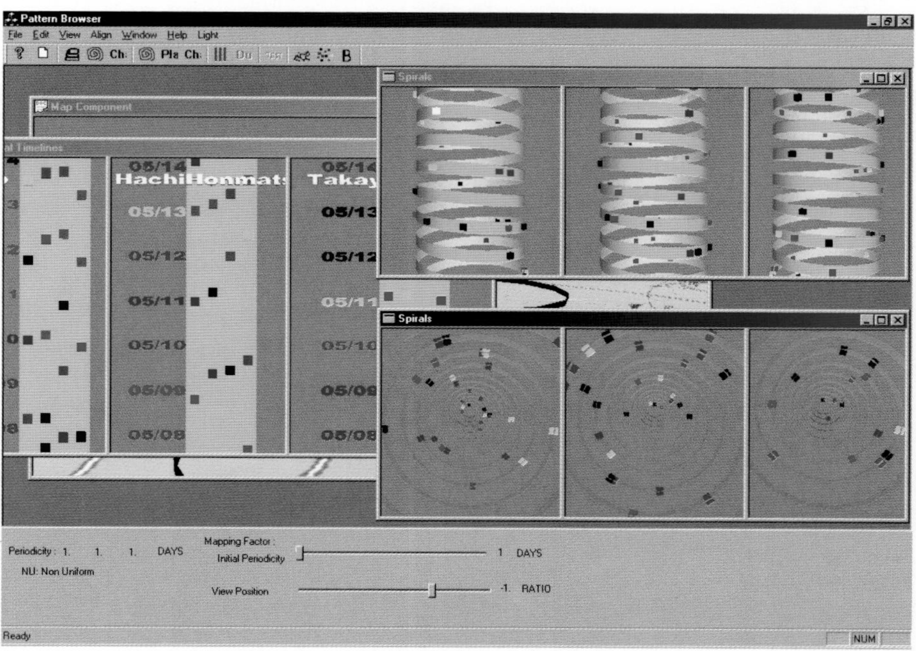

Fig. 11. Planar view and linear view of timelines defined for three spatial viewpoints.

Map window displays a geographical map in a three dimensional visual space. When the user double clicks a certain location on the map, a spiral appears with the boundary indicating the geographical area it covers, as shown in Fig. 10. This spiral can be moved and its boundary can also be adjusted by dragging it. In this way, the user specifies any number of spirals, as s/he likes. Of course, zoom-in/out operations are provided so as to be able to change the scale of the map.

Colored rectangle icons, which represent Basic situations, appear on the spiral bands according to the occurrence of Basic situations as in Fig. 11, after assignment of certain color to each Abstract/Instance situation (each Abstract/Instance situation is organized by one or more Basic situations). Spirals with colored icons are then displayed on the map window. The user can navigate through this 3D space by changing the viewpoint, rotating spirals, or adjusting the visual radius of spirals (i.e., scale of time periodicity) with sliders at the bottom of the window. Initially, the radius of spirals proportionate to a single day. This can be modified by changing the visual radius of the spiral or changing the factor, which determines the temporal period proportionate to the initial visual radius of the spiral. Furthermore, the helix spiral view can be changed to planar view or linear view as shown in the figure. The user can also move up/down, rotate these spirals together or separately while changing the radius of the spiral.

It is noted that the visualization mechanism of the Pattern Browser is based on the interactive visual language STVL for spatiotemporal patterns [45]. Using one of the interactive functions of STVL visual language, a set of Basic situations

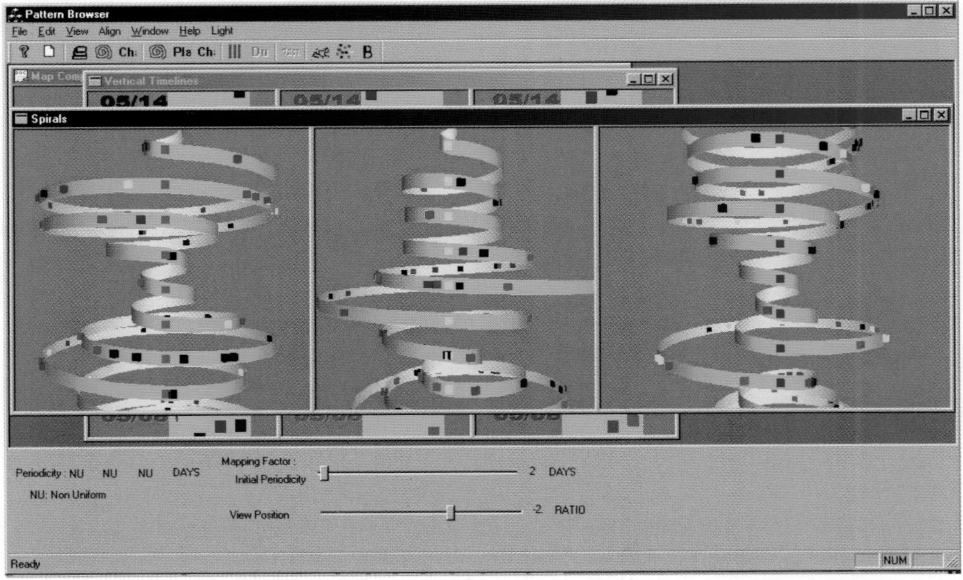

Fig. 12. Spatiotemporal patterns of the instance situation "Sales of product A to Lawson shops".

associated with a particular Abstract/Instance situation (i.e., specified using different colors) are aligned vertically by forming a non-uniform spiral. Figure 12 shows an example, which visualizes sales distribution at three locations by application of the alignment operation to the Instance situation "sale of the product A to Lawson shops". They are the three visual statements given in STVL describing spatiotemporal patterns of the Instance situation specified.

These patterns can be read in two different ways. First each individual pattern is read from top to bottom analyzing its shape and icons. The user does the horizontal reading while comparing three patterns together. The first pattern says that the sale of product A increases and then decreases repeatedly. On the other hand, the second pattern shows a rather uniform sale of the product A but sometimes a sudden decrease. The third pattern is similar to the first one. In addition, it would be said that the sale decreases at almost the same time with the first pattern. To get more details about each pattern, the user can open a window having the corresponding view of Information Roll for the pattern, in the same way as Situation-dependent Browser and Augmented Album.

9. Situation-dependent Chat Room

Situation-dependent Chat Room is a different application which demonstrates how the situated communication can be initiated and are useful in specific social environments [46]. It allows people in a particular social context to collaborate each other through situated computing without exposing their personal identities. For example, a place like amusements park such as the Disneyland, is a social environment in which people who have same objective/willingness gather in a specific area (the place for Mickey Mouse Dance, the place for Play House, etc). In such a social environment, people like to communicate with others but they are naturally shy and afraid of exposing their personal identities to strangers. We identify such a group of people who are persuading a particular social requirement within a specific area as *a community having the same situation.* The situation-dependent chat room provides facilities to establish communication using their mobile computers while protecting each one's individual identity. This application is applicable to many other application domains such as railroad stations, airports, stadiums and museums.

9.1. *System design*

The system is designed by integrating the SIFF framework with the wireless network architecture for a social institute concerned. A single local area network is maintained with a number of infrared wireless transceivers spread within the physical space to easily establish the connection with mobile computers' users. According to the gathering places in the institute, the physical space is logically partitioned into a number of physical segments to identify groups. A chat room is allocated to each physical segment in which people in the group can talk to each other

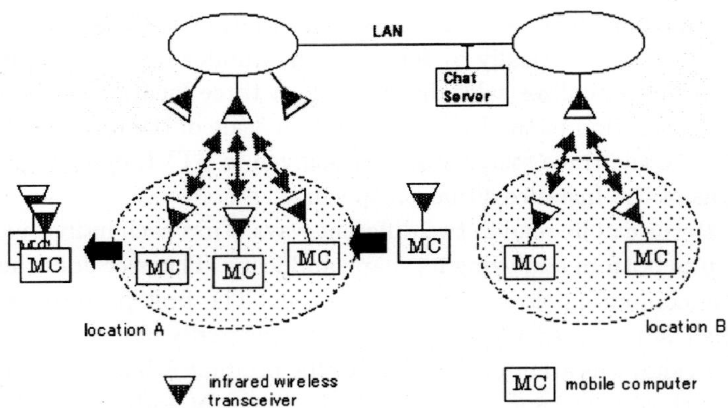

Fig. 13. The prototype system: Architecture.

through their portable terminals. A server called Chat Server maintains all these chat rooms. Generally, physical segments are not overlapping but chat rooms can be created while integrating number of physical spaces. The PEN agent in SIFF passes the user's relevant situational information at short periods to the client component, which directly establishes connection with the chat server using the wireless network.

Figure 13 shows the network architecture of the prototype system that has been developed to evaluate the system functionality. In the current system, the active range of a transceiver is approximately seven meters. Locations A and B indicate two separate physical segments. When a user moves into an active area (a physical segment), the system automatically connects him into the relevant chat room. The connection disappears when the user moves out from the area.

9.2. *User interface*

Figure 14 shows two chat windows and a map pad. As seen in the chat window, when a user enters into a physical segment, the chat server allocates a character icon for his/her identification. A user can draw figures and mark locations using the map pad and then can share it with other users in the room. It is maintained to include other than text-based conversations among members in the room. A message is usually sent to all members in the room but if necessary the sender can restrict it to a specific person. Such private messages are sent after clicking corresponding character icon of the target user and they are distinguished by changing the background color as shown in the sixth message in the figure.

In addition, the system also provides a facility called a steady link that allows two members to identify each other whenever they meet again in other physical segments. When one user asks for the steady link, the server requests to other user whether s/he accepts it. When they share a same situation later again, the system assists them to start a cheerful conversation.

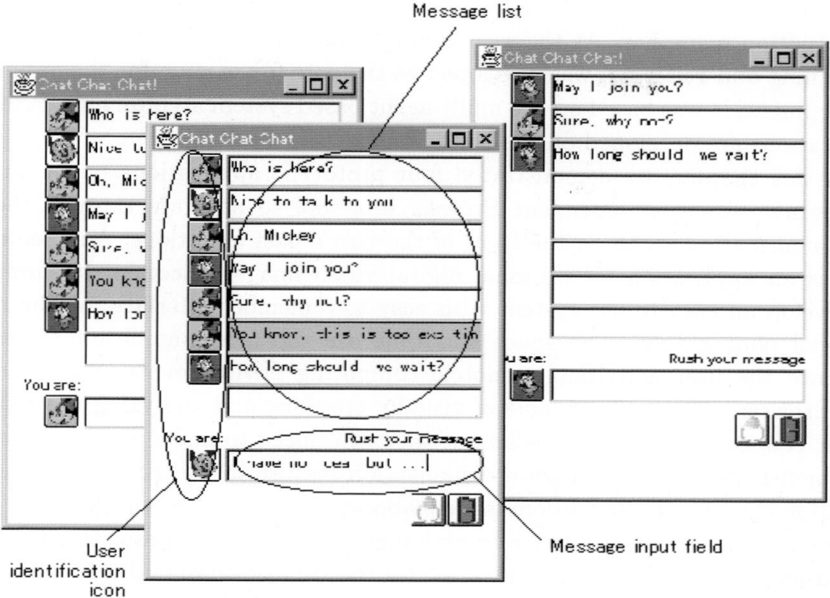

Fig. 14. Chat windows and map pad.

10. Conclusion

The authors presented in this chapter a new computing paradigm for mobile computing environments by considering the situation in which the user is placed. This work was motivated by the fact that the recent advances in technology have made the mobile computers small enough to possess in many occasions and powerful enough to automatically identify the current physical location. However, such mobile computers still adopt the desktop metaphor based interaction without any serious consideration. Hence, a new interaction scheme to fully utilize those technological benefits to provide better interaction with mobile computers is an imminent requirement. To make this successful, we presented an interactive model called the *Situation Metaphor* that is capable of representing the user's changing context and his/her activities. It provides facilities allowing users to interact with computers as naturally as they do with many other tools in the real world.

In the situation metaphor, user-situation in mobile computing is modeled as an *active context* that consists of both his/her physical context in the environment and the activities performed in persuading goals in his/her workspace. The functional features of the situation metaphor were determined according to the possible requirements that should be supported in the use of computer as an embedded tool. They have been refined incrementally in the development cycle. Moreover the situation metaphor influences the system architecture and design of applications. We presented a three-stages development methodology for implementing the situation metaphor. The first stage gave the design and theoretical foundation for the situation metaphor. At the second stage, SIFF framework, Situated Information Filing and Filtering, was developed as the core foundation for the application development. It was based on the multi-agent based system architecture. Prototype applications are developed on the third stage.

In this chapter, we demonstrated four prototype applications based on SIFF framework. Situation-dependent Browser is a tool to navigate through the personal information space on the basis of the user's past situations. Augmented Album is an application for personal digital video/image collection. It shows how to develop an easy-to-use system with easy-to-remember interface for the mobile personal photography. The space and time are the most significant forces that influence the user activities in mobile computing environments. With the Pattern Browser, the user is capable of visually browsing and analyzing the Situation Space. A spiral visualization technique was introduced to make patterns of events. It demonstrated the information visualization feature in the situation metaphor. Situation-dependent Chat Room is a collaborative application, which allows a user community in the same situation to exchange messages while protecting their individual identities. SIFF framework provides the user's situational information and the chat server maintains rooms with respect to specified physical areas.

Finally, the work discussed in this chapter summarizes the first stage of our research project "Situation Metaphor for Mobile Computing" [47]. The authors followed a software engineering approach to achieve the expectations in situated computing. Situation metaphor integrates the property of situatedness to enhance the human-computer interaction with mobile computers. The SIFF framework shows how to achieve the functional features of situation metaphor and is the foundation to develop the situated applications. They provide a new paradigm to interact based on the user's situation with multimedia information sources.

Acknowledgement

This work is supported by JSPS (Japan Society for the Promotion of Science) Research Fellowship to the first author. The authors would also like to thank Professor Tadao Ichikawa for his guidance and assistance.

References

1. L. A. Suchman, *Plans and Situated Actions: The Problem of Human-Machine Communication* (Cambridge University Press, 1987).
2. B. Nardi (ed.), *Context and Consciousness: Activity Theory and Human-Computer Interaction* (MIT Press, 1996).
3. A. N. Leontjev, *Activity, Consciousness, Personality* (Prentice-Hall, 1978).
4. K. P. Hewagamage, M. Hirakawa and T. Ichikawa, "Situation-dependent metaphor for personal multimedia information", *International Journal of Software Engineering and Knowledge Engineering* **6**, no. 9 (December 1999) 725–743.
5. O. K. Tikhomirov, *The Psychology of Thinking* (Progress Publishers, 1988).

6. T. K. Landauer, "Relations between cognitive psychology and computer system design", *Interfacing Thought*, ed. J. M. Carroll (MIT Press, 1987).
7. M. G. Lamming and W. M. Newman, "Activity-based information retrieval: Technology in support of personal memory", *Proceedings of 12th World Computer Conference* (1992).
8. M. Lamming, P. Brown, K. Carter, M. Eldridge, M. Flynn, G. Louie, P. Robinson and A Sellen, "The design of a human memory prosthesis", *The Computer Journal* **37**, no. 3 (1994).
9. B. J. Rhodes, "The wearable remembrance agent: A system for augmented memory", *Proceedings of the First International Symposium of Wearable Computers* (October 1997) 123–129.
10. R. W. Picard, *Affective Computing* (MIT Press, 1997).
11. W. S. Ark and T. Selker, "A look at human interaction with pervasive computers", *IBM Systems Journal* **38**, no. 9 (1999) 504–507.
12. P. J. Brown, "The stick-e document: A framework for creating context-aware applications", *Electronic Publishing* **9**, no. 1 (September 1996).
13. G. W. Fitzmaurice, "Situated information spaces and spatially aware palmtop computers", *Communication of the ACM* **36**, no. 7 (July 1993) 38–49.
14. T. Starner, S. Mann, B. Rhodes and J. Levine, "Augmented reality through wearable computing", Technical Report 397, MIT Media Laboratory (Cambridge, 1997).
15. R. Hull, O. Neaves and J. Bedford-Roberts, "Towards situated computing", *Proceedings of the First International Symposium on Wearable Computing* (*ISWC'97*) (Cambridge, 1997).
16. A. V. Gershman, J. F. McCarthy and A. E. Fano, "Situated computing: Bridging the gap between intention and action", *Proceedings of the Third International Symposium on Wearable Computing* (*ISWC'99*) (October 1999).
17. D. Wan, "Magic home: Exploiting the duality between the physical and the virtual worlds", *Proceedings of ACM Conference of Human Factors in Computing Systems* (*CHI 2000*) (April 2000).
18. A. B. Brody and E. J. Gottsman, "Pocket bargainfinder: A handheld device for augmented commerce" *Proceedings of First International Symposium on Handheld and Ubiquitous Computing* (*HUC'99*) (September 1999).
19. A. E. Fano, "Shopper's eye: Using location-based filtering for a shopping agent in the physical world", *Proceedings of Second International Conference on Autonomous Agents* (May 1999).
20. D. Wan, "Magic medicine cabinet: A situated portal for consumer healthcare", *Proceedings of First International Symposium on Handheld and Ubiquitous Computing* (*HUC '99*) (September 1999).
21. D. Salber, A. K. Dey and G. D. Abowd, "The context toolkit: Aiding the development of context-enabled applications", *Proceedings of the ACM Conference on Human Factors in Computing Systems* (*CHI '99*) (May 1999).
22. J. Rekimoto, "Time-machine computing: A time-centeric approach for the information environment", *Proceedings of ACM UIST'99* (1999).
23. E. Freeman and D. Gelernter, "Lifestreams: A storage model for personal data", *ACM SIGMOD Bulletein* (March 1996).
24. M. Black, *Models and Metaphors* (Cornell University Press, 1972).
25. R. W. J. Gibbs, *The Poetics of Mind* (Cambridge University of Press, 1994).
26. J. Carroll, R. Mack and W. Kellogg, "Interface metaphors and user interface design", *Handbook of Human-Computer Interaction*, ed. Hellander (Elsevier, 1988).
27. T. Erickson, "Working with interface metaphors", *The Art of Human-Computer Interface Design*, ed. B. Laurel (Addison-Wesley, 1990).

28. K. H. Madsen, "A guide to metaphorical design", *Communication of ACM* **37**, no. 12 (1994) 57–62.
29. R. Coyne, *Designing Information Technology in the Postmodern Age: From Method to Metaphor* (MIT Press, 1995).
30. D. Gentner, "Flowing water or teaming crowds: Mental model in electricity" *Mental Models*, eds. D. Gentner and A. L. Stevens (Elbaum Associates, 1983).
31. W. A. Stubblefield, *Source Selection for Analogical Reasoning: An Interactionist Approach*, University of New Mexico (1995).
32. B. Rhodes, "WIMP interface considered fatal", *Proceedings of VRAIS'98* (1998).
33. A. F. Clark, "What do we want from a wearable user interface?" *Proceedings of Workshop on Software Engineering for Wearable and Pervasive Computing* (June 2000).
34. W. A. Stubblefield, "Patterns of change in design metaphor", *Proceedings of ACM CHI'98* (1998) 73–80.
35. D. Gentner, "Structure mapping: A theoretical framework for analogy", *Cognitive Science* **7** (1983) 155–170.
36. A. Rudolf, *Visual Thinking* (University of California Press, 1969).
37. M. Hirakawa, K. P. Hewagamage and T. Ichikawa, "Situation-dependent browser to explore the information space", *Proceedings of IEEE Symposium on Visual Languages* (September 1998) 108–115.
38. D. K. Gifford, P. Jouvelot, M. Sheldom and J. O'Toole, "The semantic file system", *Proceedings of 13th ACM Symposium on Operating Systems Principles* (October 1991).
39. E. H. Chi, J. Konstan, P. Barry and J. Riedl, "A spreadsheet approach to information visualization", *Proceedings of ACM User Interface System Technologies* (October 1997) 79–80.
40. K. P. Hewagamage and M. Hirakawa, "Augmented album: Situation-dependent system for a personal digital video/image collection", *Proceedings of IEEE International Conference of Multimedia and Expo* (July 2000).
41. K. P. Hewagamage and M. Hirakawa, "Pattern browser: Spiral-based interactive visualization using timeline on a geographical map", *IEICE Transactions on Information Systems* **E83-D**, no. 8 (August 2000) 1679–1686.
42. K. P. Hewagamage, M. Hirakawa and T. Ichikawa, "Interactive visualization of spatiotemporal patterns using spirals on a geographical map", *Proceedings of IEEE Symposium on Visual Languages* (September 1999) 296–303.
43. A. K. Jain and R. C. Dubes, *Algorithms for Clustering Data* (Prentice-Hall, Inc., 1988).
44. A. K. Jain and J. Mao, "Artificial neural networks: A tutorial", *IEEE Computer* **29** (March 1996) 31–44.
45. K. P. Hewagamage and M. Hirakawa, "An interactive visual language for spatiotemporal patterns", *International Journal of Visual Languages and Computing* **12**, no. 3 (2001) (to appear).
46. M. Hirakawa and A. Yoshitaka, "Support of accidental communication among users sharing a common physical space", *Interactive Systems and Software*, eds. M. Yasamura (Kindai-Kagakusha Publishing, 1998) 17–22 (in Japanese).
47. K. P. Hewagamage, "A study on situation-dependent human-computer interaction in mobile computing environment", PhD Dissertation, Graduate School of Information Engineering, Hiroshima University (September 2000).

WEB ENGINEERING: MODELS AND METHODOLOGIES FOR THE DESIGN OF HYPERMEDIA APPLICATIONS

GENNARO COSTAGLIOLA, FILOMENA FERRUCCI and RITA FRANCESE

Dipartimento di Matematica e Informatica — Università di Salerno Via S. Allende, 84081 Baronissi (SA), Italy

E-mail: {gencos,filfer,francese}@unisa.it

The development of Web applications requires a variety of tasks, some of them involving aesthetic and cognitive aspects. As a consequence, there is a need for appropriate models and methodologies which allow the heterogeneus members of hypermedia projects to effectively communicate and guide them during the development process. In this chapter, we describe some hypermedia models and methodologies proposed for the development of hypermedia applications.

Keywords: Hypermedia, hypertext, World Wide Web, model, methodology, structured design.

1. Introduction

Hypermedia applications are often advocated as the most powerful tool for an effective presentation and delivery of information. Indeed, on one hand the combination of a variety of media, such as text, sound, video and image, allows us to have multiple different representations of concepts and gives our senses new possibilities of enjoying information. On the other hand, the use of links allows for a natural and flexible access of information according to the associative nature of the human mind. As a matter of fact, the main goal of hypermedia applications derives from the Bush's idea to supplement human memory in order to provide an effective access and management of the growing knowledge and information [7].

Presently, an enormous number of hypermedia applications have been developed and the technological evolution of the last decades has made the World Wide Web the primary support for their delivery. Indeed, organizations, industries, commercial activities, and people are putting an enormous amount of information on the Web. Nevertheless, such applications often fail to achieve their primary goal. As a matter of fact, the dimension of the navigation space and the high complexity of information can determine disorientation and cognitive overhead that may discourage the user. Moreover, such applications generally result in very poor quality products, with a "spaghetti-like" structure, which makes them hard to maintain and reuse [27].

The main reason of these problems is that the development of hypermedia and web applications is usually *ad hoc*, without the support of appropriate methodologies able to manage the high complexity of information. On the other hand, it is worth pointing out that traditional software engineering methodologies turn out to be inadequate for the development of such applications, because they generally do not address aesthetic and cognitive aspects that are especially relevant for an effective hypermedia design [28].

As a result, it is now widely recognized for a need to develop a *Web/hypermedia engineering* meant to provide a systematic and disciplined approach for developing, documenting and maintaining Web/hypermedia applications. The problem is especially felt for large-scale applications with a long lifespan, such as digital libraries, software documentation, informative kiosks, archives, etc for which maintenance and reuse are especially important issues.

As a consequence, Web/hypermedia engineering represents an active research area, as also proved by the growing interest of journals and symposia for this topic [32, 29]. In particular, in the last years, several models and methodologies have been proposed for supporting the development of hypermedia applications [11, 14, 17, 18, 22, 27]. The main goal of such models is to help designers to reason in a structured way on aspects that are specific of hypermedia, such as links, structure, navigation, etc. Moreover, they should enhance the communication among the heterogeneous members of a hypermedia project, such as programmers, system analysts, software managers, and users, as well as content-authors, librarians, musicians and graphic designers [20]. On the other hand, the methodologies should help engineers to manage the overall complexity of Web/hypermedia development which requires a variety of activities, such as organizing the structure, choosing the contents and the presentation modality, some of them involving aesthetic and cognitive aspects. So, methodologies usually provide guidelines for performing such activities and suitable models for expressing the results of such operations.

In the present chapter, we will focus on the models and the methodologies that have been proposed for the development of hypermedia applications. The discussion starts with a brief introduction of the main issues concerning with the design of hypermedia applications. Next, in Secs. 3 and 4, the main features of the most representative models and methodologies are described. Finally, in Sec. 5, we conclude by comparing the models and the methodologies illustrated in the chapter.

2. Basic Concepts and Cognitive Design Issues

Before introducing the main issues and principles concerning the design of hypermedia applications, we give a brief overview of the characteristics of hypertext, multimedia and hypermedia [5, 34].

A *hypertext* is modeled as a network of nodes that are connected through a set of links. A node usually represents a concept and a link connects related concepts.

A *multimedia* presentation is characterized by a combination of multiple media, such as text, sound, and/or motion video. Multimedia presentations differ from the usual motion pictures or movies because of the user interaction.

A *hypermedia* is a combination of hypertext and multimedia, having each component of the hypertext a self contained multimedia presentation. Links can be defined among any set of multimedia objects, including sound, motion video, and virtual reality.

In the literature, the terms of hypertext and hypermedia are often used interchangeably and we will make the same assumption in the sequel.

The design of hypermedia applications involves specific cognitive aspects since it is necessary to make the document readable and the information effectively accessible. The readability of a given document can be measured taking into account the time the reader spends for constructing his/her mental model, where for mental model we intend the conceptual and operational representation that readers develop while interacting with a complex system. Mental models are formed by objects and by their semantic relationships [22].

To improve the document readability, the designer must facilitate the reader in the construction of his/her mental model by enforcing document coherence. Moreover, he/she should avoid exposing him/her to excessive cognitive overhead, due to the additional effort required for deciding what links it is worth following. Indeed, it is worth considering that the presence of a large complex hypermedia network provides the user with more degrees of freedom but at the same time increases his/her overhead and can make the reader disoriented with the feeling to be "lost in the hyperspace". For avoiding this sensation and allowing the reader to find the expected information, it is necessary to provide suitable context and orientation functions able to give the user the clear perception of his/her position in the "information space". Guided tours, history lists, breadcrumbs, bookmarks, and maps can be used to allow the reader to know his/her position in the overall *navigational structure*; how he/she has reached the actual position; how he/she can leave it. The navigational structure should also be carefully designed by providing the user with comfortable navigation spaces. They can be organized in different ways, such as linear, network, hierarchical, matrix and/or combination of them, depending on the information nature and user typologies.

Moreover, it is worth pointing out that the development of complex hypermedia applications requires that the nodes can be reached in different ways. For example, we can reach "William Shakespeare", display his book list and then choose "Macbeth". This author could also be reached by exploring the "Tragedies". To this aim it is necessary to provide different indexes or links to present the same information depending on the *context*. In this way the hypermedia structure is formed not only by nodes and links, but also by a set of contexts used to access the nodes [19].

The previous considerations are summarized in the Thuring Framework by eight cognitive design issues and principles that should be taken into account during the hypermedia design process [22].

P1. Typed link tables should represent semantic relation, indicating the meaning of the connection between the content of two nodes.

P2. Equivalencies should be indicated, i.e., the reader has to understand that the information associated to the same node is separated in several windows.
P3. The context of a node should be preserved; it should display the actual node together with the neighboring nodes.
P4. Information Units with a higher-order should be used to collect information in composite components and to structure the document.
P5. The document structure should be visualized in order to obtain a global view and to identify the relationship among topics.
P6. The presentation should show cues describing the position of the reader into the structure.
P7. The presentation should provide the appropriate facilities for direction — a reader can go forward and backward. If the document structure is complex and is organized in composite nodes, two additional movement types should be added: up and down, to move, respectively, to the higher layers and to the lower layers of the presentation.
P8. The presentation should have a stable screen layout.

To determine the appropriate process model for developing hypermedia applications it is important to point out that such applications often present unclear requirements that cannot be individuated without progressing in the advanced phases of the development process. Thus, the traditional "waterfall" software lifecycle is inappropriate [8]. As a matter of fact, this model does not admit any feedback between the various phases and any iteration, but it assumes that the process goes ahead from the beginning to the end, limiting the interaction with the user to the earlier developing phases and providing a system software too late for verifying whether or not it meets users needs. In these circumstances, to go back to the early phases and apply the appropriate modifications can be very hard and expensive. Indeed, process models that better support the requirement comprehension, such as incremental, prototyping and Spiral ones, turn out to be more suitable.

The essence of the incremental development is to implement the final product as a series of successive increments, where each increment is a subsystem of the system we are implementing. An increment is developed by following the lifecycle phases, such as analysis, design, coding, testing, and integration and it is preceded by an exploratory phase, where it is possible to take in account the experience matured during the previous increments [13]. Another approach particularly appropriate when the initial requirements are not well defined is the prototyping. It is in developing a software system prototype to validate the requirements at the beginning of the project. The spiral development life cycle methodology is used to develop projects with a high degree of uncertainty for both the requirements comprehension and the nature of the technology that changes rapidly. Hypermedia development projects have these characteristics and are particularly risky. Thus, such a spiral approach can be used for incrementally growing the application while

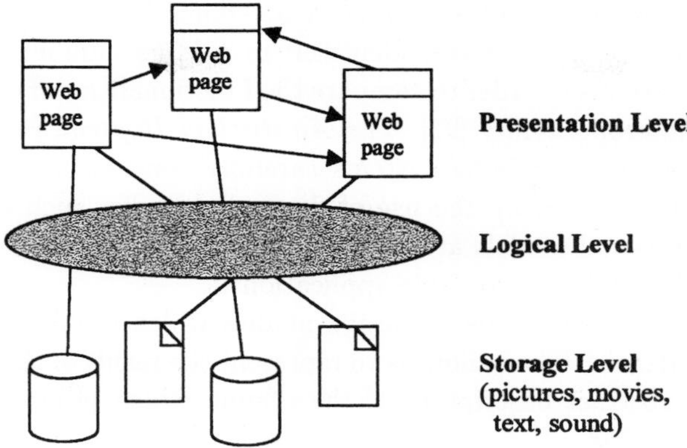

Fig. 1. A typical three layers modeling.

decreasing the risks, using appropriate risk management activities offered by this development method.

Finally, we recall other some basic issues concerning the design of Web/ hypermedia applications, such as independence between data and presentation, independence between data and application, and independence between application and presentation. The independence between data and presentation requires that the logical description of data is independent from the way the data are presented to the user. This permits, for example, to change the presentation format and the navigation structure without altering the database schema and to use existing database schema for putting an application on the Web. Moreover, it enhances the independence between data and application. Such independence favors the reuse of data that can be employed by different applications and gives the possibility to have different views of the information depending on the user profile. The independence between application and presentation allows us to generate applications on different platforms and to enhance portability.

To realize such independences, it is suitable to model such applications on three levels as shown in Fig. 1 [25]:

- a presentation level, describing how the information should be displayed;
- a storage level, describing the physical representation of data; and
- a logical level, creating the correspondences between data stored in databases or files and the information accessible to the user.

3. Models

With regards to hypermedia applications, two kinds of models can be considered, namely the *representational models* and the *design models*. The representational models provide a mechanism to model the underlying structure of documents in order to facilitate the interchange of documents between different authoring tools.

For example, the aim of the *Dexter Hypertext Reference Model* is to unambiguously define some important abstractions identified in a large number of existing and future hypertext systems in order to compare the functionalities of different systems and to enhance interoperability [23]. The *Amsterdam Hypermedia Model* extends the Dexter model to hypermedia systems carefully considering the synchronization problem which derives by the use of dynamics media, such as video, sound etc [5]. Representational models are useful for developing authoring environments generating portable and interoperable applications.

In this chapter, we will focus on design models which are not system-oriented but application-oriented. They allow us to represent the result of the design activity by providing an abstract description of the system which points out some most meaningful features [30].

In general, the role of a design model is to allow for a deeply understanding of how an object has to be realized [29]. In the database area, for example, the popular Entity-Relationship model is used for both developing new applications and documenting existing ones. Hypermedia design models should answer to the need of formalizing the design of hypermedia applications and helping to reason in a structured way on the aspects that are specific of hypermedia such as links, structure, navigation, etc.

They eliminate the natural language ambiguity, and enhance the communications among people involved in the project helping them to identify structural inconsistencies and errors and to compare alternative designs [27]. Moreover, they improve the reusability, as the designed structure is available for developing similar applications. Finally, such models can be adopted as a basis to implement tools for the design of hypermedia applications.

It is worth pointing out that hypermedia design models concern two aspects, such as *authoring-in-the-large* and *authoring-in-the-small*. In the first case the model refers to the specification and design of global and structural point of views of hypermedia applications and collects characteristics that are common to several applications of a given domain [21]. On the contrary, authoring-in-the-small refers to details about the specific application's organization and behavior, and depends on the implementation tools [20]. In the following two subsections, we recall the main features of two models for authoring-in-the-large, namely the *Trellis Hypertext Reference Model* and *Hypertext Design Model*. Other models will be described in the next section where methodologies for hypermedia development will be illustrated.

3.1. *The Trellis Hypertext Reference Model*

The *Trellis Hypertext Reference Model* is based on a Petri net representation of the structure of a document [1, 14, 15]. This model can be considered a "behavioral" model for hypertext [20]. In fact, the timed colored place/transition nets describe in an appropriate way the hypertextual interaction. Since a Petri net is a direct graph, the Trellis model can be employed for specifying the hypertext structure and the synchronization aspects.

Petri net based hypermedia structure is an excellent way to represent parallel activities. Using this formalism, the designer can describe the contents that should be simultaneously shown in different windows on the screen; he/she can specify two or more sequences of contents that are displayed at the same time. In the latter case, the author can define the interaction between the parallel paths and establish that be synchronized at a given time.

Moreover, this formalism allows us to restrict the user access, to realize different versions of the same document and several browsing semantics that describe how information has to be visited.

3.2. *The Hypertext Design Model*

The *Hypertext Design Model* (*HDM*) is based on the entity-relationship model that is extended with a hierarchical organization [21]. HDM allows the designer to identify not only the atomic components of a hypermedia, but also the criteria for assembling the structures. Indeed, HDM is concerned with the aspects of authoring-in-the-large, and describes only the structure of hypertext, without considering specific implementation issues. Such a structure is represented through *primitives* and consists of information structures called *entities*, which represent physical or conceptual objects of the domain. An entity is the smallest independent piece of information which can be added or deleted from an application. For example, a Musical Opera (say Verdi's "La Traviata"), a Painter (say "Piero della Francesca") a lex (lex 8/11/2000) are entities.

Entities are grouped in *entity types*; for example, the entity "la Traviata" and "L'Aida" belong to the entity type "Musical Opera". These entity types differ from the ones of the entity-relationship modeling because they have an internal structure. Indeed, they are formed by hierarchies of *components*. As examples, let us consider the "Ouverture" component of "La Traviata" and "Le Baptism of Crist", painting component of the entity "Piero della Francesca". Components are not autonomous and exist only as a part of an entity. Components are in turn made by units. Each *unit* shows the content of a component under a particular *perspective*. A perspective is a different presentation of the same content. For example, in multilanguage applications the same argument must be described with different languages (i.e., Italian and English).

A *unit* is characterized by a *name* and a *body*. Filling the contents into the appropriate bodies corresponds to authoring-in-the small. For example, "Piero della Francesca/Italian-life" is the unit describing in Italian the life of the painter Piero della Francesca.

All the entities belonging to a given type have the same set of possible perspectives on their components. For example, if the entity has four perspectives, all the components associated to it must have four perspectives too. In Table 1, each

Table 1. An example of the entity composition.

ENTITY		"Vivaldi's Four Season"		
COMPONENTS:	SPRING		SUMMER (ETC)	
PERSPECTIVES	Digital Recording	Musical score	Textual Comments/English	Textual Comments/I1 alian
	UNIT	UNIT	UNIT	UNIT

component "musical piece" contains a digital recording, a musical score, a textual comments exposed in English and a textual comment exposed in Italian [3].

One of the most appealing features of HDM is the introduction of different categories of links that take into account the different relationships existing among information elements, such as the relation among entities (i.e., capturing domain relations) and the navigational rules (how the user can move on the hypermedia structure). In particular, *perspective links* allow us to associate its units to a component, for example "Le Baptism of Crist/Italian-text" and "Le Baptism of Crist/Italian-picture" are associated to the component "Le Baptism of Crist". They associate homogeneous elements under the same perspective and regarding to the same subject.

Extending the definition used in the database field, an HDM *schema* is a set of entity and link type definitions, whilst a schema's *instance* is a set of actual entities and links, obeying the constraints which have been defined in the schema. A hypertext application is composed by a hyperbase, formed by entities, components, units and links, and a set of access structures, said *outlines*. An outline is a part of the hypertext containing navigational information, such as guides, maps and tours. Outlines allow the author to organize a set of links in the hyperbase and are not specified in the schema, but can be added in the application in order to give an entry point to the user.

HDM and its descendent HDM2 let the designer describe the schema, but provide little information on the procedure to be used in hypermedia design and development [26]. It naturally favors a top-down development approach, even if this methodology is only induced by HDM, but not explicitly described in the model. Nevertheless, such a model has a notable relevance because the Relationship Management Methodology (RMM) and the Object-Oriented Hypermedia Design Model (OOHDM), two important methodologies described in the following, are based on it.

3.3. *The UML extensions to Model Hypermedia Applications*

In recent years, many object-oriented modeling languages have been developed for software engineering. The Unified Modeling Language (UML) is the synthesis of many of such notations and it is considered a standard for the industrial development software. It is a modeling language, *not* a methodology, for object-oriented design and analysis.

In [11], UML has been extended to support the temporal synchronization of multimedia objects and to describe the spatial presentation, while in [16], UML has been extended on the base of OOHDM methodology, described in the following. Navigational modeling features have been added to UML, such as a new diagram type for describing the object to visit, their access modality and the corresponding contexts.

4. Methodologies

A *methodology* is a comprehensive, multiple-step approach to system development that guides the development process and influences the quality of the final product. It consists in detailing both the activities to be carried out and the deliverables that should be provided at the end of each activity. Indeed, it gives a full set of concepts and models which are internally self-consistent and a collection of rules and guidelines.

It is obvious that does not exist the best methodology, but only the most appropriate for the product we are developing. Moreover, different methodologies can be employed in different phases of the development process, because each one better solves a specific problem. In the sequel, we recall the main features of some notable methodologies which have been proposed for the development of Web/hypermedia applications. Some approaches based on visual and multidimensional languages are summarized elsewhere in this book.

4.1. *The Relationship Management Methodology*

The *Relationship Management Methodology* (*RMM*) is a *methodology* for structured design of hypermedia systems aiming to facilitate the design of WWW sites, and their seamless integration with databases and enterprise-wide information systems [24, 26]. Indeed, as a notable feature it allows us to obtain separation of data, structure and user-interface.

RMM is focused on the design phase and employs the *Relationship Management Data Model* (*RMDM*), which represents an integration of E-R and HDM models. RMDM provides a language for describing information objects and navigation modality in hypermedia applications. The language primitives are illustrated in Fig. 2 while the example of application's design specified by an RMDM diagram is shown in Fig. 3 [26].

The RMDM primitives can be divided into E-R primitives, m-Slice domain primitives, and access primitives.

E-R primitives are taken from the Entity-Relationship modeling, and describe how information is structured in the application domain. Entities and

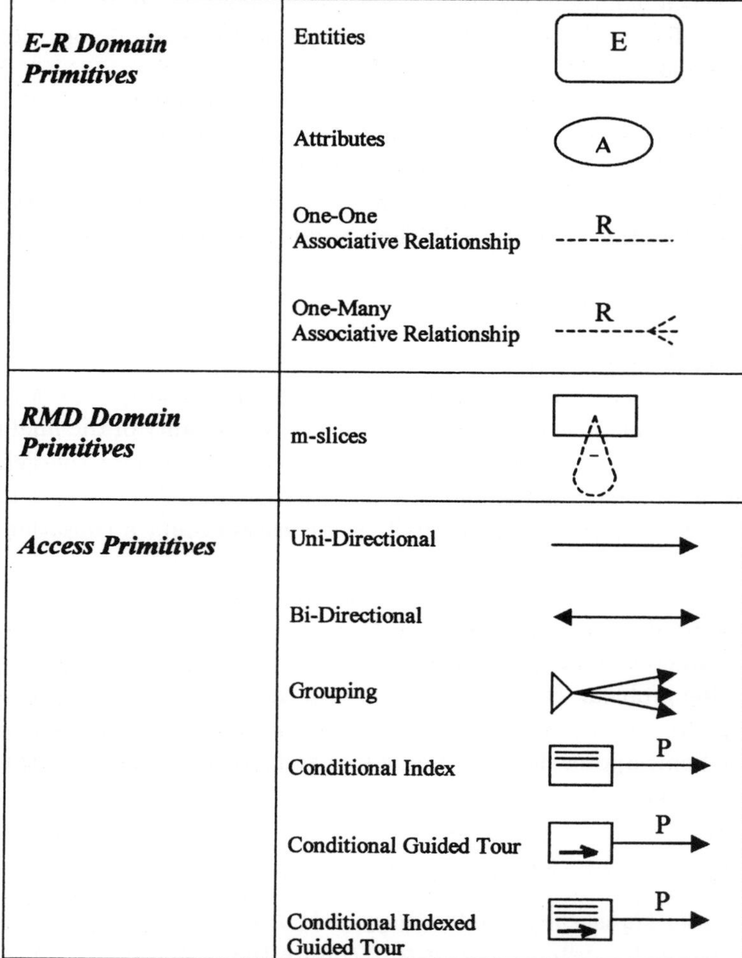

Fig. 2. The relationship management data model primitives.

their attributes represent abstract or concrete objects and the relationship between entities are modeled by 1-1 or 1-n associative relationships.

m-*Slices* are used to model small information units of a presentation. Indeed, m-Slices are defined by grouping attributes of a given entity of the E-R diagram or by grouping other m-Slices. The "m" refers to Russian Matrjeska dolls, because m-Slices are nested in other m-Slices until the presentation unit is defined. This approach let the design of user interface be more modular and support reuse, because m-Slices can be employed several times in the presentation.

access primitives allow us to model and to support navigation across different entities. An RMDM diagram describes how users will navigate across a hypermedia application. In Fig. 2, the access primitives are classified into *unidirectional links*; *bidirectional links*; *grouping*, *conditional guided tour*, *conditional index*, and *conditional indexed guided tour*. A guided tour is a linear path through a collection of elements allowing the user to move either forward or backward on the path. An index is a table of content to a list of entity instances, providing the access direct to all the elements of the list. A grouping is a mechanism serving as an access point to other parts of the hypermedia document. For example, the initial screen of many applications contains a menu or a set of buttons that provide access to different functions or classes of information. It is also possible to combine index and guided tour to have the *indexed guided tour*. A predicated is associated to the links of the access primitives to indicate which instances of an entity are accessible through that primitive. For example, the predicate "(rank = "associate")" indicates that only the entities whose rank is associate are involved in the guided tour, obtaining a *conditional guided tour*.

RMM describes completely the software development cycle, but focuses on the critical design phases. It does not address early and late lifecycle activities, such as project management, feasibility studies, requirement analyses, planning, evaluation and maintenance. The methodology foresees an iterative approach to the development since it encourages feedback between the various development steps.

Let us give a brief description of the eight steps forming RMM, some of which can be conducted in parallel.

During the *Entity-Relationship design*, the designer models the information domain and its relationship via an E-R diagram. This model is familiar to the designers, well documented and can be used for modeling the information dependencies in a variety of application domains. This kind of analysis helps to determine a view of the application domain independent from the presentation and to identify relationships across which navigation can be supported. Moreover, if the target application is a Web interface for an existing database, its E-R diagram can be reused.

The next step, the *application diagrams design*, consists in modeling the information at presentation level and focuses only on the presentation structure. Application diagrams show the content of each web page and the connections among them.

During the *m-Slice design* (*E-R+ diagram*), the attributes of one or more entities that should be displayed simultaneously on the screen are modeled and details are hidden, such as elements of the user interface or details nested in other *m*-Slices. The methodology suggests how to create this kind of diagrams in detail.

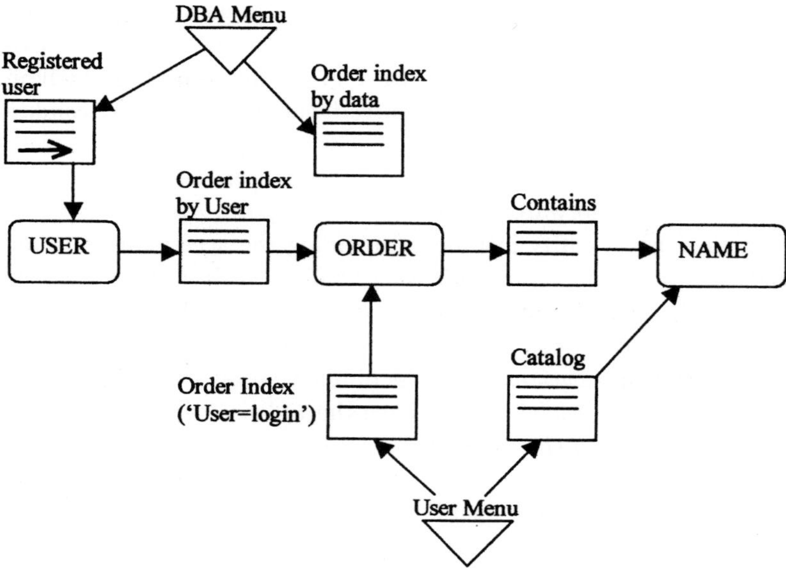

Fig. 3. An RMDM diagram.

Navigational design: this phase allows the designer to establish both how users will access to information and the paths for the hypermedia navigation. To this aim, designers specify menu-like structures using indices and guided tours. The lower level structure can be collected in higher level structure, obtaining a hierarchical access based on menu. At the end of this step all the access structures will be described by a RMDM diagram, as shown in Fig. 3.

The remaining steps are not characteristics of this methodology and are briefly illustrated in the following.

In the *conversion protocol design* phase, the designer describes how abstract constructs have to be transformed into physical-level constructs; for example, it is possible to define how a slice is converted into an HTML Web page, or an index can be implemented by using an HTML form.

The *User-Interface Design and Construction* step considers how the information structured in the previous phases has to be presented to the final user. For example, index aspect, button layout, etc. In this phase, it is important to take into account that for many WWW applications it is crucial to exhibit a common look and feel.

Run-time behavior design describes the functionality to be realized at run-time; for example, possible inclusion of search engines, dynamic generation of pages, backtracking that allows the user to go back to previously visited nodes; history lists, maintaining an ordered list of each visited node, etc.

The methodology allow the designer to use both top-down and bottom-up approach. The development process is flexible and iterative and the quality of the final product is improved because it turns out to be structured, extensible, maintainable and reusable.

Another appealing feature of the RMM methodology is the availability of a software tool, named RM-Case, supporting RMM design and development and producing the diagrams associated [10].

4.2. *The Object-Oriented Hypermedia Design Model*

The *Object-Oriented Hypermedia Design Model* (*OOHDM*) is an object-oriented hypermedia design *methodology*, based on HDM [31]. It allows us to build large hypermedia applications using a mix of incremental and prototype-based process model. OOHDM supports the most part of development process, except the early phases of the lifecycle. It consists of four steps, namely *conceptual design*, *navigational design*, *abstract interface design* and *implementation*. Each step allows us to build an object-oriented model focused on a design aspect. These steps can be accomplished separately, obtaining a reusable and modular design.

Conceptual Design

An object model is used to provide a conceptual model of the application domain. This model refers to the usual object-oriented modeling principles, extended by concepts derived from HDM and similar to perspectives.

Navigational Design

During this phase the information described in the conceptual model is structured to define different views, a view for each user profile. To this aim, OOHDM defines a navigational model that takes into account the different user types and the actions they can perform. Navigational design is accomplished through the definition of two schemas: the *navigational class schema*, and the *navigation context schema*.

The *navigation class schema* let the designer define classes having similarity with the conceptual classes, but with several differences. For example, in a fly-company Website, a node class "Fly" for a travel agent does not contain several attributes of the "Fly" conceptual class; e.g. crew name, etc... as they represent information which would not be visible in the travel agent view.

The *navigation context schema* allows the designer to define which information is reachable in a given node in a particular context. Thus, a navigational context is a set of nodes, links, context classes and other (nested) navigational contexts.

Abstract Interface Design

The application interface is defined through the *abstract interface model*. It is built by defining interface classes, i.e., objects visible to the user (e.g. a picture, a city map, etc). They are an aggregation of primitive classes, for example buttons and text fields, and recursively of interface classes. In this phase, the designer establishes how to activate the navigation and to realize the synchronization among multimedia interface objects. Here, the association between interface objects and navigational objects is created. Interface behavior is declared by specifying how to handle external and user-generated events and how the communication takes place between interface and navigational objects.

Implementation

This phase consists mapping the interface objects into implementation objects, related to the implementation environment that can involve different platforms, such as, Hypercard, Toolbook, Director, HTML.

The OOHDM methodology improves maintainability and reusability, thanks to both the separation of the design phases and the abstraction capabilities which are characteristics of the object-oriented design.

OOHDM extends the model HDM by including special purpose modeling primitives for both navigational and interface design. Moreover, it introduces the navigational contexts and offers a great relevance to the interface design. In fact, it models the man-machine interaction and considers the effect of each event generated by the user both on the interface and the navigational aspects. In conclusion, it is one of the best available methodologies and is supported by the design patterns described below.

4.3. *Design patterns*

Several design patterns have been proposed to support a hypermedia design methodology [19]. These patterns favor the reuse of the navigation, interaction and interface structure of hypermedia applications and help the designer in creating a navigation structure without cognitive overhead and a more comfortable navigation through the hyperspace. In the sequel, we report some relevant patterns.

The *navigational design patterns* suggest to the designer how to organize navigation in a clear and understandable way for the reader. To this aim, a node should be considered as a self-contained unit of information, focused on a given argument. It should not be fragmented on a large number of pages, neither containing information on too many topics. In creating a node, static node creation can be employed whether the information is rarely updated; otherwise, as in the case of data obtained from a database, a node should be created dynamically. Similarly, links are created statically if the application is static and the nodes are created statically too. Otherwise, dynamic links are preferred.

The interface patterns are thought as guidelines for GUI designers. Let us consider, for example, information on demand. This aspect regards how to present information that cannot be integrally displayed on the screen. It is advisable to display only a subset of the information on the screen and let the reader ask for the remaining information by using active interface objects, such as buttons.

The *Information-interaction decoupling pattern* allows the designer to differentiate controls and contents in the interface. The solution consists in grouping separately input and output communication channels. Another pattern suggests to group the different kinds of controls in different parts of the screen. For example, we can decide to use three different areas, one for global navigation controls (index, back, menu, etc), another for information on demand and another for context controls.

Behavior anticipation pattern: let the reader have a way to understand the result of the activation of an object. To this aim, the designer provides a differentiated feed-back for each interface object. For example, an interface similar to the "tool tips" of Windows can show a brief explanation of the target node when this is selected. Process feedback consists in informing the user about the status of the interaction. This aspect is important whether the operation to be executed is non-atomic, takes a long time or may fail. In these circumstances, the user can become impatient and he/she can select more times the same option or other ones with unpredictable results. To avoid these troubles, it is advisable to give the reader the appropriate feed-backs describing the status of the operation in course, such as "host contacted", "transferring", "done".

News patterns regard the need of communicating to the user if there is new information on the Web site. To this aim, the site homepage has to show an area dedicated to the news which presents the descriptive "headlines" regarding them and that are linked to the associated pages.

4.4. *The Entity-Relationship Modeling of Information Artifacts*

The *Entity-Relationship Modeling of Information Artifacts* (*ERMIA*) is a high-level design method [18]. Information artifacts store, retrieve and elaborate information. They are modeled through an enriched version of the Entity-Relationship modeling, called Entity-Relationship Modeling of Information Artifacts.

As a notable aspect, ERMIA provides a support for cost analysis. In particular, it concentrates on metrics for measuring the effort needed to search or to modify a structure. To this aim, the model takes into account the internal structures of entities, making the modeling process independent from the implementation details. Each internal structure has its requirements of memory and time. Five types of internal structures are proposed: pile, chain, sorted list, hashed, unsearchable. The first four structures have the usual meaning, the fifth means that data can only be accessed through a catalog, i.e., it is not providing any particular access mechanism.

This model allows the designer to distinguish between the conceptual information and its representation by defining *viewports*, which represent relations between entities and displays. A conceptual information can have different viewports.

ERMIA is applicable in the early phases of the lifecycle where it encourages reasoning on the different design strategies and allows us to evaluate the interfaces (cost of search, working memory load, etc), compare different mental models (designers'/users', across different users), and reflect about both the conceptual description and the perceptual aspects of a system.

5. Conclusions

The increasing demand of services and information on the WWW requires the development of high-level quality presentations. The challenge is to support this technological evolution with appropriate Web/hypermedia engineering approaches, appearing very different from the traditional software engineering ones.

Such applications, for their nature, present unclear requirements that cannot be individuated without progressing in the advanced phases of the development process. Thus, it is widely recognized that the traditional "waterfall" software lifecycle is inappropriate for hypermedia applications [8]. Process models that better support the requirement comprehension, such as incremental, prototyping and Spiral ones, turn out to be more suitable.

Besides process models we have to consider appropriate methodologies for guiding the development of such applications. Hypermedia development processes and methodologies influence the quality of the final product and the general management style, improving the organization. In this chapter, we have overviewed several methodologies and models that have been proposed for an effective development of Web/hypermedia applications. Table 2 summarizes the comparison among the approaches to hypermedia application design we have described and, in particular, underlines the following salient aspects:

- *methodology*: the considered approach provides models and guidelines;
- *completeness*: the most part of the lifecycle is deeply treated;
- *model*: the approach gives some models;

Table 2. Models and Methodologies comparison.

	RMM	HDM	OOHDM	ERMIA	TRELLIS	UML ext.
Methodology	X		X			
Completeness			X			X
Model	X	X	X	X	X	X
Perspective/Context		X	X			
Tool Case	X				X	
Cognitive Aspects			X	X		
Cost metrics				X		
Synchronization			X		X	X

- *perspective/context*: the approach presents the information by using different indexes or links depending on the context;
- *tool CASE*: there exists a tool CASE supporting the considered approach;
- *cognitive aspects*: the approach gives guidelines to improve the document readability;
- *cost metrics*: the approach supports cost analysis; and
- *synchronization*: the approach allows the designer to describe temporal relationships between different media.

Each one of the models and the methodologies focuses on specific issues. In particular, the Hypertext Design Model is based on an extension of the Entity-Relationship data model and allows us to describe the global structure of the application (authoring-in-the-large). HDM is the root of the Object-Oriented Hypermedia Design Model, a methodology for the construction of large hypermedia application through an incremental, prototype-based development approach. The Relationship Management Methodology carries a structural construction of Web sites, emphasizing navigation aspects, and integrates Web sites and enterprise database. A notable aspect of the Trellis model is the possibility to specify the hypertext structure and the synchronization aspects, whilst ERMIA is a high-level design method providing a support for cost analysis. Finally, UML extensions integrate UML with navigational modeling features. Thus, it is worth noting that neither the "best methodology" nor the "best model" exists, but only the most appropriate for the product we are developing.

References

1. V. Balasubramanian, "State of art review on hypermedia issues and applications", *http://members.tripod.lycos.nl/Lollie*
2. V. Balasubramanian, M. Bieber and T. Isakowitz, "Systematic hypermedia design", *Information Systems* (1998).
3. M. Bernstei, F. Garzotto, P. Paolini and D. Shwabe, "Tools for designing hyperdocuments", *Hypertext/Hypermedia Handbook, Software Engineering Series* (McGraw Hill, 1991) 179–207.
4. G. Booch, J. Rumbaugh and I. Jacobson, *The Unified Modeling Language User Guide* (Addison-Wesley, Reading, MA, 1998).
5. D. Bulterman, L. Hardman and G. Van Rossum, "The Amsterdam hypermedia model", *Communication of the ACM* **37**, no. 2 (February 1994).
6. D. C. A. Bulterman, J. Jansen, K. S. Mullender and G. van Rossum, "CMIFed: A presentation environment for portable hypermedia documents", *ACM Multimedia* (August 1993) 183–188.
7. V. Bush, "As we may think", *Atlantic Monthly* (July 1945).
8. H. J. Chang, T. Y. Hou, A. Hsu and S .K. Chang, "The management and application of tele-action objects", *ACM Multimedia Systems Journal* **3**, no. 5–6 (Springer-Verlag, 1995) 204–216.
9. S. K. Chang, *Multimedia Software Engineering* (Kluwer Academic Publishers, 2000).

10. A. Diaz, T. Isakowitz, V. Maiorana and G. Gilabert, "RMCase: A tool to design WWW application", *World Wide Web Journal* **1**, no. 1 (1995).
11. G. Engels and S. Sauer, "Extending UML for modeling of multimedia applications", *Proceedings of the 1999 IEEE Symposium on Visual Languages*, Tokyo, Japan (1999) 80–87.
12. M. Farooq and W. Dominick, "A survey of formal tools and models for developing user interfaces", *International Journal of Man-Machine Studies* **29** (1988) 479–496.
13. Martin Fowler, *http://www.aw.com/cseng/titles/0-201-89542-0/techniques/evolution.htm*
14. R. Furuta and D. Stotts, "Petri net based hypertext: Document structure with browsing semantics", *http://www.cs.unc.edu/~stotts/pds/cv.html*
15. R. Furuta and D. Stotts, "The Trellis project", *http://www.cs.unc.edu/stotts/Trellis/*
16. A. Garrido, A. Helmerich, N. Koch, L. Mandel, L. Mandel, L. Mandel, G. Rossi, L. Olsina, G. Rossi and M. Wirsing, "Hyper-UML: Specification and modeling of multimedia and hypermedia applications in distributed systems", *Second Workshop on the German-Argentinian Bilateral Programme for Scientific and Technological Cooperation, Königswinter*, Germany (March 1999).
17. A. Ginige, D. Lowe and J. Robertson, "Hypermedia authoring", *IEEE Multimedia* **2**, no. 4 (1995).
18. T. Green and D. Benyon, "The skull beneath the skin: Entity-Relationship models of information artifacts", *International Journal of Human-Computer Studies* **6**, no. 44 (1996) 801–828.
19. A. Garrido, G. Rossi and D. Schwabe, "Pattern systems for hypermedia", *Proceeding Plop* (1997).
20. F. Garzotto, L. Mainetti and P. Paolini, "Hypermedia design, analysis and evaluation issues", *Communication of the ACM* **38**, no. 8 (August 1995).
21. F. Garzotto and P. Paolini, "HDM — A model-based approach to hypertext application design", *ACM Transaction on Information Systems* **11**, no. 1 (January 1993) 1–26.
22. J. Haake, J. Hannemann and M. Thuring, "Hypermedia and cognition: Designing for comprehension", *Communication of the ACM* **38**, no. 8 (August 1995).
23. F. Halasz and M. Schwartz, "The Dexter hypertext", *Communication of the ACM* **37**, no. 2 (February 1994).
24. T. Isakowitz, "What is RMM?", *http://www.stern.nyu.edu/~tisakowi/rmm/What_is_RMM.html*
25. T. Isakowitz, A. Kamis and M. Kuofaris, "Extending the capability of RMM: Russian dolls and hypertext", *Proceedings of the Thirtieth Annual Hawaii International Conference on System Sciences*, Hawaii, USA (1996).
26. T. Isakowitz, E. A. Sthor and P. Balasubramanian, "RMM: A methodology for structured hypermedia design", *Communication of the ACM* **38**, no. 8 (August 1995).
27. D. Lowe and W. Hall, "Hypermedia and the web", *Worldwide Series in Computer Science* (John Wiley & Sons, 1999).
28. J. Nanard and M. Nanard, "Hypertext design environments and the hypertext design process", *Communication of the ACM* **38**, no. 1 (1995) 49–56.
29. R. Pressman, *Software Engineering: A Practitioner's Approach*, 5th ed. (The McGraw-Hill Companies, June 1, 2000).
30. I. Sommerville, *Software Engineering*, 5th ed. (Addison-Wesley, 1995).
31. D. Schwabe and G. Rossi, "Developing hypermedia applications using OOHDM", *Workshop on Hypermedia Development Processes, Methods and Models, Hypertext'98*, Pittsburgh, USA (1998).

32. Special Issue "Web engineering", *IEEE Multimedia*, guest editor, A. Ginige and S. Murugesan (January–Mar 2001).
33. B. White, "Web document engineering", *http://www5conf.inria.fr/fich_html/slides/tutorials/T14/overview.htm*
34. *http://whatis.techtarget.com/*

VISUALIZATION OF KNOWLEDGE STRUCTURES

CHAOMEI CHEN
The VIVID Research Centre,
Department of Information Systems and Computing,
Brunel University, Uxbridge UB8 3PH, UK
E-mail: chaomei.chen@brunel.ac.uk

Tracking the growth of scientific knowledge has become increasingly challenging even in one's own specialized field due to the vast amount of new scientific publications becoming available. As a rapidly advancing and expanding field of computing and information technology, information visualization has focused on the discovery of interrelationships among various scientific publications. However, visualizing intrinsic structures among documents in scientific literatures can only capture some aspects of scientific knowledge. For example, the number of citations received by a scientific work is a widely accepted hallmark of its significance. This chapter describes approaches to the visualization of knowledge structures with emphasis on the role of citation-based methods. Instead of relying upon occurrence patterns of content-bearing words, visualization of knowledge structures aims to capture perceived intellectual structures of a particular knowledge domain. An ultimate goal for the visualization of knowledge structures is to provide scientists with a tool that can detect the existence of a scientific paradigm and movements of such paradigms. This chapter also includes a summary of the history of tracking the growth of scientific knowledge. The state of the art is presented to highlight the trend of future research.

Keywords: Knowledge visualization, intellectual structures, domain analysis.

1. Introduction

Dictionaries explain *knowledge* at two levels: (1) understanding, the facts, information, and skills that one has gained, and (2) what is collectively known to the human being. To philosophers, this is to ask "What is the nature of knowledge?" Epistemology, a branch of philosophy, studies the nature of knowledge. An understanding of the nature of knowledge has a profound connection to an understanding of the nature of science. Philosophy of science aims to find an answer to this question. Approaches to the visualization of knowledge structures aim to reveal insightful patterns of intellectual structures shared by scientists in a subject domain. In order to visualize and interpret structures of knowledge, we must have a clear understanding of contemporary views on the nature of knowledge in a broader context.

1.1. *What is knowledge?*

Thomas Kuhn's landmark work *Structure of Scientific Revolutions* was published in 1962 [18]. He used the term *paradigm* to refer to the conceptual frameworks and worldviews of various scientific communities. In a nutshell, a paradigm represents a prevalent way of thinking. Science constitutes periods alternate between normal science, crisis, and revolution. During periods of normal science, the way of thinking is relatively stable, but in revolutionary periods a traditional way of thinking may be replaced by a new way of thinking, which could be radically different from its predecessor. This movement from one paradigm to another is widely known as a *paradigm shift.*

Widely known paradigm-shift examples in the past include Copernicus's revolutionary theory in contrast to Aristotle's model of the world and Einstein's general relativity theory in contrast to Newtonian physics. Before the Copernican revolution, it was believed that the earth was at the center of the solar system and the Sun was orbiting the earth, and that each planet has a perfect circular orbit. Much of these also appeared to be consistent with one's own observation. It was through several generations that the Copernican revolution started to change ones' beliefs to what we know today: the earth and other planets circle around the Sun in elliptical orbits. According to Kuhn, the two competing paradigms are incommensurable, nor are the concepts that can be used to understand and explain basic facts and beliefs. The two groups live in different worlds.

Despite critics of the notion of paradigm shifts, Kuhn's work has had enormous influence outside of the history of science. The profound and far-reaching significance of Kuhn's insight is akin to what Darwin's natural selection to evolutionary biology.

Kuhn emphasized that the paradigm determines the kinds of experiments that scientists perform, the types of questions they ask, and the problems they consider important. A shift in the paradigm alters the fundamental concepts underlying research and inspires new standards of evidence, new research techniques, and new pathways of theory and experiment that are radically incommensurate with the old ones.

Kuhn's structure of scientific revolution provides a far-reaching framework for visualizing knowledge structures. In this chapter, we will explain how knowledge structures can be visualized and interpreted in the notion of paradigm and paradigm shift.

1.2. *What is knowledge visualization?*

Information visualization has become a truly wide-ranging and interdisciplinary field of research and a vibrant global industry. There is a rapid growth in the literature of information visualization [2,3]. Knowledge visualization shares some intrinsic characteristics with cartography — an art of making maps. The evolution of the geographic map of the world is a good starting point for us to illustrate what we might need to produce a map of knowledge structure and what we may expect given our knowledge of the nature of science. We will first look at the Greek astronomer Ptolemy's map of the world in nearly 2000 years ago, and then look at a cybermap — a map of the Internet. The evolutionary history of these maps provides us an interesting yardstick to measure where we are regarding the status of visualizing knowledge structures.

1.2.1. *Mapping the real world*

The British Library has a collection of famous old world maps.[a] One of the widely known world maps is the one generated by the Greek astronomer Ptolemy in about 150 AD. Unfortunately, none of his maps survived and his work was lost to the West until the Renaissance. Scholars in the 15th century recreated Ptolemy's map following the instructions in his work *Geography*, which explain how to project a sphere onto a flat piece of paper using a system of gridlines — longitude and latitude.

Ptolemy's map only shows the world known to him, and as he worked in Alexandria the map is most detailed round the Mediterranean. The map shows only three continents: Europe, Asia and Africa. The two red lines are the Tropics of Cancer and Capricorn; the sea is light brown, the rivers are in blue and the mountains in dark brown. The surrounding heads represent the major winds.

1.2.2. *Cybermaps*

The ever-growing Internet has flourished cybermaps. The idea of making a map of Internet has certainly been very popular. A wide variety of cybermaps have been produced. The following map is generated by the peacockmaps company on the millennium. The inset shows a close-up view of a region in the global map. Blue stars and lines represent *.net* nodes and backbones, which are typically non-profitable organizations, two green stars are large European nodes, and dark red lines throughout the map show North American hosts.

From the old world maps to the latest image of the Internet, human mind has been searching something profoundly in common — a big picture of an environment in which we live and work. For the same reason, a big picture of science has always been the most intuitive pursuit of a fascinating dream. Visually representing the structure of knowledge is thus a very attractive idea.

One fundamental aspect of information visualization in general, and knowledge visualization in particular, is how to identify and group various knowledge-bearing units according to certain criteria. Clustering and classification algorithms form a substantial amount of the resources of knowledge visualization. The following section summarizes some of the major theories and methodologies in measuring the relevancy of textual documents and in extracting the most significant elements from the source.

[a] *http://portico.bl.uk/exhibitions/maps/*

2. A Historical Summary

A number of existing information visualization systems are particularly worth mentioning since they address common issues concerning knowledge visualization, for example, selecting appropriate similarity metrics and displaying high-dimensional structures. In the 80's, SemNet produces three-dimensional graphic representations of large knowledge bases to help users grasp complex relationships involved [9]. The design of SemNet focuses on the graphical representations of three types of components: identification of individual elements in a large knowledge base, the relative position of an element within a network context, and explicit relationships between elements. SemNet represents elements of a knowledge base of Prolog rules, a logic programming language, as labeled rectangles connected by lines or color-coded arcs. A Prolog module, a set of rules, is represented as a rectangle labeled by the module's name. In SemNet, the closeness between two rectangles indicates the strength of the connection between two modules. The designers of SemNet experimented various techniques such as multidimensional scaling (MDS), simulated annealing, fisheye views, and even a sprite traveling down arcs between rectangles to show the process of the knowledge base in action. In this section, we include a number of useful techniques for detecting and extracting salient elements from unstructured text. Interrelationships between these salient elements will form the basis for the visualization of knowledge structures.

2.1. *Information retrieval models*

The vector-space model [27] originally developed for information retrieval, is a widely used framework for indexing documents based on term frequencies. In this model, each document d is represented by a vector V of terms t's. Terms are weighted to indicate how important they are in representing the document. The distance between two documents can be determined by the distance between vectors in a high-dimensional space, or the angle between the two vectors. A large collection of documents can be split into a number of smaller clusters such that documents within a cluster are more similar than documents in different clusters.

The discriminative power of a term is determined by the well-known $tf \times idf$ model, term frequency (tf) and inverse document frequency (idf). Each document can be represented by an array of terms T and each term is associated with a weight determined by the above $tf \times idf$ model. In general, the weight of term T_k in document D_i, is estimated as follows:

$$w_{ik} = \frac{tf_{ik} \times \log\left(\frac{N}{n_k}\right)}{\sqrt{\sum_{j=1}^{T}(tf_{ij})^2 \times \log\left(\frac{N}{n_j}\right)^2}} \tag{1}$$

where tf_{ik} is the occurrences of term T_k in D_i, N is the number of documents in a given collection, and n_k represents the number of documents containing term T_k.

The document similarity is computed as follows based on corresponding vectors $V(D_i) = (w_{i1}, w_{i2}, \ldots, w_{iT})$ and $V(D_j) = (w_{j1}, w_{j2}, \ldots, w_{jT})$:

$$\text{sim}_{ij}^{\text{content}} = \sum_{k=1}^{T} w_{ik} \times w_{jk} \,. \tag{2}$$

2.2. *Bayesian theory*

Thomas Bayes' work on mathematical probability focused on the probabilistic relationship between multiple variables and determining the impact of one variable on another. Bayesian theorem has become a central part of modern statistical probability modeling.

A good introduction to Bayesian modeling and neural networks can be found in a book entitled *Bayesian Learning for Neural Networks* [22]. The author of the book, Radford Neal, has made software described in this book available on the Internet,[b] in particular, on Bayesian regression and classification models based on neural networks and Gaussian processes, and Bayesian mixture models. The software is written in ANSI C for Unix and Linux systems. The website also includes software that supports a variety of Markov chain sampling methods, which may be applied to distributions specified by simple formulas, including simple Bayesian models defined by formulas for the prior and likelihood.

Bayesian theory can be used to judge how relevant a document is to a given query based on what we already know. More formally, $p(d|q)$ denotes the relevancy of a document d to a given query q. We may be able to work out $p(d)$ and $p(q|d)$ based on, for example, users' previous records and their profiles. We can then estimate this relevance as follows

$$p(d|q) = \frac{p(q|d) \cdot p(d)}{\sum_{d' \in \{d\}} p(d|d') \cdot p(d')} \,. \tag{3}$$

Extensions of the theory go further than relevance information for a given query against a text. Adaptive probabilistic concept modeling analyzes correlation between features found in documents relevant to an agent profile, finding new concepts and documents. Concepts important to sets of documents can be determined, allowing new documents to be accurately classified.

2.3. *Shannon's information theory*

Information Theory is the mathematical foundation for all digital communications systems. Claude Shannon's innovation was described in his "Mathematical Theory of Communication" published in 1949, which shows that "information" could be treated as a quantifiable value in communications.

[b] *http://www.cs.toronto.edu/~radford/fbm.software.html*

Consider the basic case where the units of communication (for example, words or phrases) are independent of each other. If p_i is the probability of the ith unit of communication, the average quantity of information conveyed by a unit, the degree of uncertainty can be measured by Shannon's *entropy*, which is defined as:

$$H = -\sum_i p_i \cdot \log_2(p_i)\,. \tag{4}$$

This formula reaches its maximum when the probabilities are all equal; in this case, the resulting text would be random. See Sec. 2.4 for a measure of the occurrences of content-bearing words based on the singularity among randomness. If this is not the case the information conveyed by the text will be less than this maximum; in other words there is some redundancy. This result is then extended, by more sophisticated mathematical arguments, to when units are related.

Natural languages contain a high degree of redundancy. A conversation in a noisy room can be understood even when some of the words cannot be heard; the essence of a news article can be obtained by skimming over the text. Information theory provides a framework for extracting the concepts from the redundancy.

2.4. *Condensation clustering value*

Information retrieval systems typically distinguish between content-bearing words and terms on a stop list. But "content-bearing" is relative to a collection. For optimal retrieval efficiency, it is desirable to have automated methods for custom building a stop list. Bookstein *et al* [1] developed the method for serial clustering of words in text and use such clustering as an indicator of a word bearing content.

The idea is that occurrences of a term sensitive to content are more likely to cluster, or occur in the same textual neighborhood than those of non-content-bearing terms. However, it is not easy to determine by intuitive means which objects tend to cluster. A person may see clusters forming even among objects that are randomly distributed. Therefore, formal tests of clustering are needed. There are several possible ways to measure the strength of clustering. Condensation Clustering Value (CCV) is one of them.

If text is fed into the system as a stream, one word at a time, one would expect that occurrences of a given content-bearing word will tend to occur in clumps (just like London buses). This is an indication of the content of a textual neighborhood. If we now analyze the text in segments, i.e., strings of words, some segments should contain more of these words than expected by chance. This is in fact a serial-clustering mechanism, known as *condensation clustering* [1]. In general, consider the context of words as a container. A sentence is a container and a paragraph is a container. Containers should attract some words more effectively than others. Since non-content-bearing words are likely to appear at random across such containers, i.e., text segments, if the occurrences of a word are different from such random distributions, then the word is likely to be significant to the topic in question.

If terms are distributed at random over a number of textual units, several may land in a single unit. Thus, we expect the number of units containing at least one occurrence of the term to be less than the total number of occurrences of the term. But if the terms tend to cluster, in the condensation sense, then we expect even fewer units will contain a term. A simple measure of condensation clustering is the ratio of the actual number of units that have at least one occurrence of the term to the expected number of units having at least a single occurrence, assuming random distribution. The statistical properties of this measure can be derived using basic combinatorial arguments.

Suppose that our document is divided into D textual units. (We are currently developing effective methods for accomplishing this division. For the moment, any arbitrary segmentation method — for example, taking successive groups of five sentences, or accepting existing paragraphs — are possibilities.) Consider then the distribution of the occurrences of a term over these units.

For that term, we know:

N: the number of units containing the term; and

T: the total number of occurrences of the term.

Then $p(n,T)$, the probability of exactly n units containing a term can be shown to be given by

$$p(n,T) = \frac{n! \left\{ \begin{matrix} D \\ n \end{matrix} \right\} \left\{ \begin{matrix} T \\ n \end{matrix} \right\}}{D^T} . \tag{5}$$

The expected number of textual units containing the term, $E_1 = \Sigma_n n \times p(n,T)$, can be shown to satisfy

$$E_1 = D \left[1 - \left(1 - \frac{1}{D} \right)^T \right] . \tag{6}$$

If N units actually contain the term, N/E_1 is a measure of condensation strength. If the terms do cluster within textual units, then we expect that fewer units will contain the term than predicted by the independence model — that is, that the observed N will be small compared to the value expected on the basis of the independence assumption.

As a test of statistical significance, we can compute the probability $P(N,T)$ that N or fewer units contain the term, given the independence assumption. This value should be unreasonably small for most content-bearing terms. This observation forms the basis of Test 1 of the hypothesis that the terms are randomly distributed. This probability y is given by:

$$P(N,T) = \sum_{n=1}^{N} p(n,T) . \tag{7}$$

In this manner we can assign to each term both a measure of condensation strength and the statistical significance of that value: the probability that it will occur in no more units than it actually does occur in. These quantities measure the tendency of a single term to condense into a few textual-units.

The value of Condensation Clustering Value (CCV) has been demonstrated later on by researchers at PNL in SPIRE, a suite of visualization and spatial exploration tools for information retrieval [37]. In SPIRE, topical words are extracted using the following procedure:

- remove stopwords;
- stem remaining words;
- band pass to remove both high- and low-frequency words so that remaining words appear $3 \sim 5$ times in a document;
- compute condensation clustering value of each word remained; and
- select words whose CCV values are less than 1 (these are topical words).

This procedure can be easily extended to select sentences that would summarize an abstract. In the following example, we develop a light-weight algorithm based on this procedure to produce a one-liner summary for each abstract. The example is based on a keyword search in the Web of Science on "visualiz* knowledge". The Web of Science will automatically expand the wildcard* in the query to match visualization, visualizing, and visualized. The abstracts of the top 300 articles returned by Web of Science form the test data. Two additional steps are added to the topic-word-selection procedure as follows:

- compute the content-bearing level of every sentence in each abstract;
- select the sentence with the least value as the summary sentence.

If T is the set of all the selected topic words, t is a word in this set, and s is a sentence for all the sentences S from a given abstract, then the inverted condensation level of the sentence $\xi(s)$ can be measured as follows:

$$\xi(s) = \prod_{t \in T \cap s} ccv(t) \,. \tag{8}$$

The more topical words a sentence contains, the more likely that the sentence summarizes the abstract. Therefore, the best summary sentence is the sentence that has the least inverted condensation level

$$\lambda(\{s_\alpha\}) = \min_{s \in \{s_\alpha\}} \xi(s) \,. \tag{9}$$

For example, the following paragraph is the abstract of a real article:

> Sex-differences in route-learning past literature on map-learning tasks has generally inferred that males tend to use a geometric strategy, and females tend to use a landmark strategy to learn a map. However, none of the studies have controlled for possible effects of extra-map superior visual

> memory in females on their memory for landmarks, and few have probed the actual relation between accuracy of performance and geometric or landmark knowledge. This study investigated sex differences in strategies for route-learning, controlling for visual-item memory. All subjects (48 female, 49 male) were required to learn a route to criterion through a novel map. As expected, males made fewer errors and took fewer trials to reach criterion. Females remembered more landmarks both on and off the route than males, and superior memory for landmarks was not accounted for by a superior visual-item memory. Males outperformed females in knowledge of the Euclidean properties of the map. However, despite the pronounced sex differences in knowledge retained from the maps, both males' and females' performance was related to spatial ability rather than to landmark recall.

Using the CCV algorithm, a number of content-bearing, or thematic words can be extracted. The lower the CCV value of a word, the stronger this indicates a thematic word. Selected thematic words are listed in the following table.

Table 1. Content-bearing words in the abstract.

Content-Bearing Words	CCV
Knowledge	0.012
Map	0.148
Superior	0.181
Memory	0.187
Landmarks	0.338
Males	0.632
Females	0.721

Table 2. Sentences in the abstract and the ccv of each sentence.

Sentences in the original sequence	$\xi(s)$
Sex-differences in route-learning past literature on map-learning tasks has generally inferred that males tend to use a geometric strategy, and females tend to use a landmark strategy to learn a map.	0.067439
However, none of the studies have controlled for possible effects of extra-map superior visual memory in females on their memory for landmarks, and few have probed the actual relation between accuracy of performance and geometric or landmark knowledge.	0.000009
This study investigated sex differences in strategies for route-learning, controlling for visual-item memory.	0.187000
All subjects (48 female, 49 male) were required to learn a route to criterion through a novel map.	0.148000

Table 2. (*Continued*)

Sentences in the original sequence	$\xi(s)$
As expected, males made fewer errors and took fewer trials to reach criterion.	0.632000
Females remembered more landmarks both on and off the route than males, and superior memory for landmarks was not accounted for by a superior visual-item memory.	0.005213
Males outperformed females in knowledge of the euclidean properties of the map.	0.000809
However, despite the pronounced sex differences in knowledge retained from the maps, both males' and females' performance was related to spatial ability rather than to landmark recall.	0.000809

Figure 1 shows the results of the simple summarization algorithm. It is currently a challenging task assessing to what extent the automatically generated summaries match the ones that human experts would choose.

2.5. *Self-organized feature maps*

Self-organized feature maps are generated based on artificial neural network techniques. It is essentially a classification process through a neural network. Xia Lin is the first to use self-organized maps to visual information retrieval [19]. ET-Map[c] is another example of site maps on the Web. ET-Map is a prototype Internet homepage categorization system developed at the University of Arizona [7]. ET-Map aims to demonstrate a scalable, automatic, and concept-based approach to Internet homepage categorization and search.

WEBSOM[d] uses self-organized maps to organize textual documents for exploration and search. WEBSOM has been used to map discussion groups. A click in any area on the map will lead to a zoomed view. Color denotes the density or the clustering tendency of the documents. Lighter areas are clusters and darker areas are empty space between the clusters. The most specific discussions are mostly found in the clearest "clusters", i.e., light regions surrounded by darker color. Near the edges of the map you typically find the most "different" documents represented on the map. In the central areas, the discussions are more "typical", or they may concern many different topics found on the map. Viscovery SOMine is a recently launched commercial product.[e] It can generate self-organized maps. The standard version costs $289, but can only deal with 50 variables. The enterprise version is $1990.00, which can handle a lot more variables.

[c] *http://ai2.BPA.Arizona.EDU/ent/*
[d] *http://websom.hut.fi/websom/*
[e] *http://www.unisoftwareplus.com/products/somine.html*

Doc 100

A structured visual language for a knowledge-based front-end to statistical-analysis systems in biomedical-research within the last few years, several knowledge-based systems for statistical analysis systems have been proposed (0.012000). Most of these systems provide so-called 'natural-language' interfaces for acquisition and application of meta-data.(1.000000). Since graphics have been very efficient in displaying results (e.(1.000000). G.(1.000000). , as scatter, qq and residual plots), some attempts have been made (cf.(1.000000). Refs.(1.000000). 5,6) to use graphics also to display knowledge of the statistical strategy.(0.012000). In the present paper i will concentrate on the visualization of knowledge of the experimental design and its impacts on the design of a structured visual syntax language for acquisition and application of this knowledge in the field of biomedical research.(0.012000).

Doc 101

Structural basis of t cell recognition exciting breakthroughs in the last two years have begun to elucidate the structural basis of cellular immune recognition.(0.206000). Crystal structures have been determined for full-length and truncated forms of alpha beta t cell receptor (tcr) heterodimers, both alone and in complex with their peptide-mhc (pmhc) ligands or with anti-tcr antibodies.(0.004416). In addition, a truncated cd8 coreceptor has been visualized with a pmhc.(1.000000). **Aided in large part by the substantial body of knowledge accumulated over the last 25 years on antibody structure, a number of general conclusions about tcr structure and its recognition of antigen can already be derived from the relatively few tcr structures that have been determined.(0.000910).** Small, but important, variations between tcr and antibody structures bear on their functional differences as well as on their specific antigen recognition requirements.(0.000910). As observed in antibodies, canonical cdr loop structures are already emerging for some of the tcr cdr loops.(0.004416). Highly similar docking orientations of the tcr v alpha domains in the tcr/pmhc complex appear to play a primary role in dictating orientation, but the v beta positions diverge widely.(1.000000). Similar tcr contact positions, but whose exact amino acid content can vary, coupled with relatively poor interface shape complementarity, may explain the flexibility and short half-lives of many tcr interactions with pmhc.(1.000000). Here we summarize the current state of this field, and suggest that the knowledge gap between the three-dimensional structure and the signaling function of the tcr can be bridged through a synthesis of molecular biological and biophysical techniques.(0.048000).

Doc 102

Mesenteric duplex scanning a blinded prospective-study purpose: based on retrospective comparisons of duplex scanning with arteriography of the celiac (ca) and superior mesenteric (sma) arteries in 34 patients, we previously suggested that an sma peak systolic velocity of 275 cm/sec or greater or no flow signal and a ca psv of 200 cm/sec or greater or no flow signal were reliable indicators of a 700r greater angiographic stenosis of the sma and ca, respectively.(0.036000). We now report the results of a blinded, prospective study in a larger patient group designed to determine the ability of mesenteric duplex scanning to visualize the ca and sma and to validate our proposed duplex criteria

Fig. 1. Summary lines extracted from abstracts.

2.6. *Citation indexing*

Today's widely available of citation index databases was originated in the 50's. Indexing in the 50's was inconsistent and uncoordinated. There was widespread dissatisfaction with the array of traditional discipline-oriented indexing and abstracting services. In 1955, Eugene Garfield published his pioneering paper in *Science* [10], aiming to improve the retrieval of science information.

Garfield presented a history on the sociological and historical uses of citation data in 1975.[f] He acknowledged that the most important paper on sociometric analysis with citation data was the one by Sher and Garfield on patterns for Nobel Prize winners [30]. The following historical account of citation indexing is drawn from his description.

One of the pioneering science mapping based on citation data is the creation of the historical map of research in DNA, which was done manually more than 30 years ago in the early 60's [12]. The same data was soon used by Derek Price in his classic work of mapping scientific networks [23].

Mapping of science is also known as scientography [11]. Because in maps of science interrelationships between research fronts are spatialized, users can navigate the scientific literature according to the depicted spatial relationships.

One of the most central objectives of science mapping is to identify trend associated with a field of study. As the maps of science cover the literature year by year, the map created through citation analysis provides a series of historical views. Traditionally, from a global viewpoint, these maps show latent semantic connections among fields or disciplines. The maps reveal which realms of scholarship are being investigated today and the individuals, publications, institutions, regions, or nations currently eminent in these areas. This is echoed in the more recent work of Hjorland [16].

Longitudinal mapping is another concept discussed by Garfield [11]. By using a series of chronologically sequential maps, one can easily see how knowledge advances. By observing changes from year to year, one can detect trends. In this way, these maps become forecasting tools. Since some co-citation maps include core works, even a novice can instantly identify those articles and books used most often by members of the "invisible college", or specialties. Citation-based mapping evolves into a distinct discipline known as scientometrics, which applies bibliometrics to scientific literature. Scientometrics is the quantitative study of scientific communications. The "father of scientometrics" was Derek Price (1922–1983), as regarded by Robert Merton and Eugene Garfield in their foreword[g] to the second edition of Price's landmark work *Little Science, Big Science, and Beyond* [24]. Price's most important contribution to information science is his another seminal work *Networks of Scientific Papers*, published in science [25].

[f] *http://www.garfield.library.upenn.edu/papers/retrospectivey1975.html*
[g] *http://www.garfield.library.upenn.edu/lilscibi.html*

In 1981, Institute for Science Information (ISI) published the *Atlas of Science* in biochemistry and molecular biology. The Atlas was constructed based on co-citation index associated with publications in the field over a limited period of one year. 102 distinct clusters of articles were identified, which were called research front specialties, in order to give researchers a snapshot of significant research activities in biochemistry and molecular biology.

More than 100 people were involved in the project for several months. In the Atlas, journal articles were clustered according to associated co-citation index. The atlas provides a clear, distinct snapshot of the scientific network and how it was structured. More recently, ISI developed Sci-Map software for users to navigate the citation network. Garfield and Small [13] explained how they visualized the changing frontiers of science based on citation relationships.

Henry Small described ISI's SCI-Map in a case study of mapping AIDS research in [31]. SCI-Map creates maps of individual research areas specified by the user. Given an author, paper, or keyword as a starting point, one can seed a map and then grow the map by specifying various desired connections at different thresholds of co-citation strength or distance. The network of connected nodes is formed by a series of iterations of clustering, including additional core papers with each successive node. The nodes are selected according to the strength of their links, and positioning is determined by the *geometric triangulation method.* A map of AIDS research by SCI-Map (Small, 1994) is available at *http://www.isinet.com/isi/hot/essays/*.

In 1977, Henry Small published his longitudinal study of co-citation linkages [32]. He identified the most important advances in collagen research over a period of five years. The results were validated by questionnaires. In 1998, the American Society for Information Science (ASIS) awarded him the ASIS Award of Merit[h] for his outstanding contributions to the field of information science and for his groundbreaking work on co-citation as a dynamic measure of the scientific literature.

In his most recent work, Small explored the notion of a passage through science [33, 34]. Passages linking the literature of different disciplines are likely to import or export a method established in one discipline into another. This has been known as cross-disciplinary fertilization. As Small has noted, this reaching out or stretching can import or export methods, ideas, models, or empirical results from the author's field to the other field. This requires scientists to have not only a broad awareness of literature, but also the creative imagination to foresee how the outside information fits with the problem at hand. He developed algorithms to blaze a magnificent trail of more than 300 articles across the literatures of different scientific disciplines. This is a pioneering development that brings Bush's concept of associated information trails to life.

The latest idea of mapping the tracks of science is explained by Garfield in [11]. The aim of such work is to identify research fronts in science. We use a simple timeline to highlight the development of science mapping.

[h] *http://www.asis.org/Bulletin/Jan-99/small.html*

2.7. *Author co-citation analysis*

Author co-citation analysis (ACA) aims to find out how scientists in a particular subject domain are intellectually interrelated as perceived by authors in their scientific publications. White and Griffith are the first to introduce author co-citation analysis (ACA) in 1981 as a literature measure of intellectual structure [35]. McCain [20] produced a comprehensive technical review of mapping authors in intellectual spaces. In 1998, White and McCain applied ACA on information science in their award-winning paper — the best JASIS paper award of the year [36]. In ACA, the unit of analysis is authors and their intellectual relationships as reflected through scientific literatures.

Typically, the process of an ACA starts with sampling representative publications from a literature of a given field of study. Science Citation Index (SCI) and Social Science Citation Index (SSCI) are among the most widely used sources of citation data — both from Institute for Scientific Information (ISI). An intellectual structure of prominent authors in the field provides a good candidate for knowledge visualization. Normally the predominance of an author is determined by citations he or she has received or by other criteria, such as the membership of a scholarly institution. Author co-citation frequencies among these selected authors are then calculated. If a pair of authors X and Y are cited by the same scientific publication, the author co-citation counts of the pair will increase by one. ACA traditionally relies on a range of data analysis methods in order to identify emergent patterns in the co-citation data. Commonly used methods include cluster analysis, factor analysis, and multidimensional scaling (MDS).

2.7.1. *Factor analysis*

Factor analysis has been a very powerful step in author co-citation analysis. Factor analysis, notably Principal Component Analysis (PCA), has been used to identify the latent dimensionality of given co-citation data. It has been routinely used to identify specialties of a subject domain.

In addition to cluster authors into mutual exclusive groups, or specialties, the use of factor analysis allows a multiple-specialty membership for each author. For example, White and McCain demonstrated in their recent author co-citation analysis of the information science field that some authors indeed belong to several specialties simultaneously.

Factor analysis can be conducted on standard statistical packages such as SPSS. For large datasets, the size of the corresponding author co-citation matrix can be very big and the analysis becomes computationally expensive. Following [36], first, the raw co-citation counts should be transformed into Pearson's correlation coefficients using the factor analysis. These correlation coefficients measure the proximity between authors' co-citation profiles. Self-citation counts should be replaced with the mean co-citation counts for the same author. In factor analysis, principal component analysis (PCA) with varimax rotation is a recommended option to extract

Table 3. Procedure of citation analysis.

Step	Operation
1	Draw citation data from bibliographic databases
2	Select bibliographic records corresponding to the range of citation analysis
3	Clean up data
4	Compute co-citation index
5	Convert co-citation index to Pearson correlation coefficients
6	Identify specialties using factor analysis
7	Generate overall co-citation maps
8	Add specialty information into co-citation maps
9	Add citation history into co-citation maps
10	Repeat above steps for longitudinal mapping
11	Interpret the results
12	Repeat above steps for longitudinal mapping

factors. The default criterion, eigenvalues greater than one, is normally chosen to determine the number of factors extracted. Missing data should also be replaced by mean co-citation counts for corresponding authors.

The following SPSS script illustrates how to conduct factor analysis in SPSS. This example is based on our author co-citation of ACM Hypertext data. The input file is "hypertext.dat", which represents the lower triangle of author co-citation matrix. Elements on the diagonal positions will be ignored because they will be regarded as missing values and to be replaced by the mean for corresponding authors. 367 authors identified in the matrix as author1, author2, ..., author367. The factor extraction uses principal component analysis with varimax rotation.

```
MATRIX DATA /VARIABLES author1 to author367 /FILE'hypertext.dat'
  /CONTENTS N_MATRIX /FORMAT LIST
LOWER NODIAGONAL.
SET LISTING 'hypertext' RESULTS LISTING.
FACTOR /VARIABLES author1 to author367 /MISSING MEANSUB
  /PRINT EXTRACTION /EXTRACTION PC /ROTATION VARIMAX.
```

The following SPSS script can be used to generate factor loading data, which can be used subsequently to enhance the visualization. Factor loading indicates the strength that an author belongs to a particular specialty. There are many possible ways that domain visualization can utilize this information.

```
FACTOR /VARIABLES author1 to author367 /MISSING MEANSUB
  /PRINT FSCORE /EXTRACTION PC /ROTATION VARIMAX.
```

Pearson's correlation coefficient r can be used as a measure of similarity between pairs of authors. According to [36], it registers the likeness in shape of their co-citation count profiles over all other authors in the set.

2.7.2. *Multidimensional scaling*

Multidimensional scaling (MDS) is a multivariate statistical technique, which is often used to map high-dimensional numerical data onto a spatial structure in lower dimensions. A classic MDS algorithm was given by Kruskal [17], known as KYST. KYST places N points in a space of dimension LDIM so as to minimize STRESS, which measures the "badness-of-fit" between the configuration of points and the data. If it finds the minimizing configuration by starting with some configuration perhaps found by the classical scaling procedure and moving all the points a bit to decrease the stress, then this procedure will be iterated over and over again until the stopping criteria are reached. KYST uses the iterative numerical method of gradients, the method of steepest descent, with a step-size procedure based primarily on the angles between successive gradients.

The most common measure of the stress is used to evaluate how well a particular configuration reproduces the observed distance matrix. The raw stress value ϕ of a configuration is defined by:

$$\phi = (d_{ij} - \delta_{ij})^2 . \tag{10}$$

In this formula, d_{ij} stands for the reproduced distances, given the respective number of dimensions, and δ_{ij} stands for the observed distances. The expression $f(\delta_{ij})$ indicates a non-metric, monotone transformation of the observed distances. There are several measures that are commonly used, including the sum of squared deviations of observed distances from the reproduced distances. The smaller the stress value, the better is the fit of the reproduced distance matrix to the observed distance matrix. The greater the stress, the greater the distortion.

Interpreting the essence of a MDS map focuses on clusters and dimensions. Clusters are groups of items that are closer to each other than to other items. Within a cluster, one should bear in mind not over interpret local patterns because such patterns within a tight cluster are not reliable. Dimensions may exist if items appear to be placed in the MDS map along a continuum. The underlying dimensions provide the basis to explain the perceived similarity between items.

The most common complaint about MDS maps is probably about the ambiguity in the nature of each dimension involved. The interpretation of MDS solutions has been mainly subjective in nature. Figure 2 shows a 2D MDS map of a network of top 100 most cited authors derived from their co-citation relationships in ACM Hypertext proceedings [5].

2.7.3. *Minimum spanning trees*

Although MDS has been a widely used method in many disciplines, interpreting MDS maps is often subject to one's experience and the familiarity with the data.

Fig. 2. Top 100 authors in the field of hypertext in a 2D MDS map [5].

There is a need for an alternative representation that has more accurate local details and more explicit interpretation of dimensionality.

A wide range of real-world problems can be transformed into a network problem in one way or another. A network representation is generally a good candidate for capturing the essence of a structure. From a graph-theoretical perspective, a large number of widely available graph-handling algorithms have been a great gold mine.

In a complete graph, there exists a link between each pair of vertices. So for a given graph of N vertices, there could be as many as $N \times (N - 1)$ edges. It is often desirable to reduce the number of edges while the most significant ones can be preserved. Minimum spanning trees (MSTs) are widely used solutions, which include all the vertices from the original graph, but only consist of $N - 1$ edges at most. MST algorithms are widely available. Many visualization systems rely on MSTs to represent complex structures, such as the well-known cone trees [26] and hyperbolic views [21].

Figure 3 shows a minimum spanning tree (MST) solution of the same author co-citation network derived from the ACM Hypertext conference proceedings [4]. This is a network of 367 prominent scientists in the field of hypertext. The

Fig. 3. A MST solution to the same author co-citation network of 367 prominent scientists in the field of hypertext (Nodes = 367, Links = 366).

interconnection between a pair of authors is determined according to the co-citation frequencies between the two authors. The original network consists of 61,175 links among these authors. As a graph, the maximum number of possible links in a fully connected graph would be

$$\frac{N(N-1)}{2} = \frac{367 \times 366}{2} = 67161\,. \tag{11}$$

In this case, 91% of the maximum possible co-citations are observed. The number of links in an MST is $N-1$, i.e., 366 in our example, which is only 0.6% of the actual observed co-citation links. It leads to a much simplified picture of the patterns.

Hierarchical structures are one of the most commonly used data structures in many application domains. Since MST solutions can simplify a complex network into a hierarchical structure, MST is regarded as a standard method to deal with the visualization of complex structures. A relatively recent visualization technique for displaying a large hierarchical structure is called hyperbolic views. Hyperbolic views are originally developed at Xerox PARC. It is now available from its spin-off company *Inxight.* Hyperbolic visualization is also licensed to Microsoft's SiteMap. Much of the work in hyperbolic views is motivated to balance both the focus and its context in each screen display.

A hyperbolic view is specified by a mathematical model, especially suitable to display a large, unbalanced hierarchy. The greatest advantage of a hyperbolic display is that nodes higher up in the hierarchy are initially displayed in the center of the view, while nodes further down in the hierarchy are displayed with an increasingly reduced screen estate. Inxight is a spin-off company from Xerox. It commercializes a tree visualization interface based on hyperbolic views.

The explicit display of edges in a network representation has an advantage over spatial-proximity designs such as multidimensional scaling (MDS), where

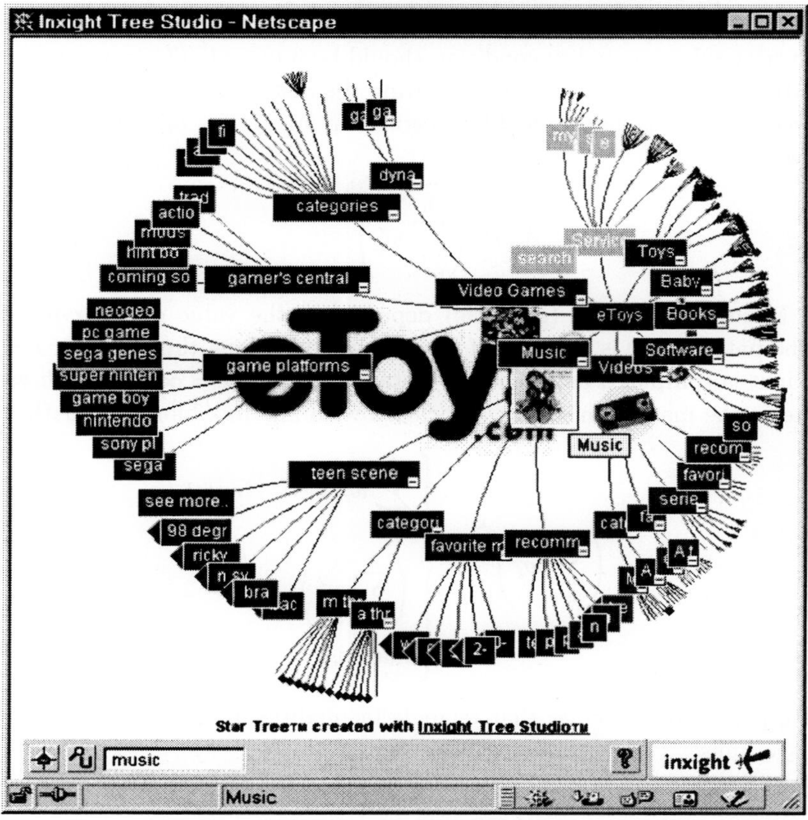

Fig. 4. A hyperbolic visualization from Inxight.

interrelationships are implicitly conveyed by spatial arrangements of objects. Explicit links tell a more detailed story about the latent structure. Pathfinder network scaling is a method that can select salient relationships from proximity data and maintain the semantic integrity over the entire graph.

2.7.4. *Pathfinder network scaling*

Pathfinder network scaling is a method originally developed by cognitive psychologists for structuring modeling [29]. Pathfinder network scaling relies on a criterion known as the triangle inequality condition to select the most salient relations from proximity data. Results of Pathfinder network scaling are called Pathfinder networks, consisting of all the vertices from the original graph. The number of edges in a Pathfinder network, however, is determined by the intrinsic structure of semantics. On the one hand, a Pathfinder network with the least number of edges is identical to an MST. On the other hand, additional edges in a Pathfinder network indicate salient relationships that might have been missed from an MST solution.

The topology of a PFNET is determined by two parameters q and r and the corresponding network is denoted as PFNET(r, q). The q-parameter controls the scope that the triangular inequality condition should be imposed. The r-parameter refers to the Minkowski metric used for computing the distance of a path. The weight of a path with k links is determined by weights $w_1, w_2, \ldots, w_k$ of each individual link as follows:

$$W(P) \left(\sum_{i=1}^{k} w_i^r \right)^{\frac{1}{r}} . \tag{12}$$

The Minowski distance (geodetic) depends on the value of the r-metric. For $r = 1$, the path weight is the sum of the link weights along the path; for $r = 2$, the path weight is computed as Euclidean distance; and for $r = \infty$, the path weight is the same as the maximum weight associated with any link along the path.

$$W(P) = \left(\sum_{i=1}^{k} w_i^r \right)^{\frac{1}{r}} = \begin{cases} \sum_{i=1}^{k} w_i & r = 1 \\ \left(\sum_{i=1}^{k} w_i^2 \right)^{\frac{1}{2}} & r = 2 \\ \max_i w_i & r = \infty . \end{cases} \tag{13}$$

The q-parameter specifies that triangle inequalities must be satisfied for paths with $k \leq q$ links:

$$w_{n_i n_i + 1} = \left(\sum_{i=1}^{k-1} w_{n_i n_i + 1}^r \right)^{\frac{1}{r}} \quad \forall k \leq q . \tag{14}$$

When a PFNET satisfies the following three conditions, the distance of a path is the same as the weight of the path:

(1) The distance from a document to itself is zero.
(2) The proximity matrix for the documents is symmetric; thus the distance is independent of direction.
(3) The triangle inequality is satisfied for all paths with up to q links.

If q is set to the total number of nodes less one, then the triangle inequality is universally satisfied over the entire network. The number of links in a network can be reduced by increasing the value of parameter r or q. The geodesic distance between two nodes in a network is the length of the minimum-cost path connecting the nodes. A minimum-cost network (MCN), PFNET($r = \infty, q = n - 1$), has the least number of links. See [3, 28] for further details.

Figure 5 is a Pathfinder network solution of the author co-citation matrix described earlier in our MST example. Red circles highlight the additional links with reference to the MST solution. A total of 398 links are included in the network — the pathfinder network contains additional 32 links compared with the MST solution, and these links are semantically non-trivial.

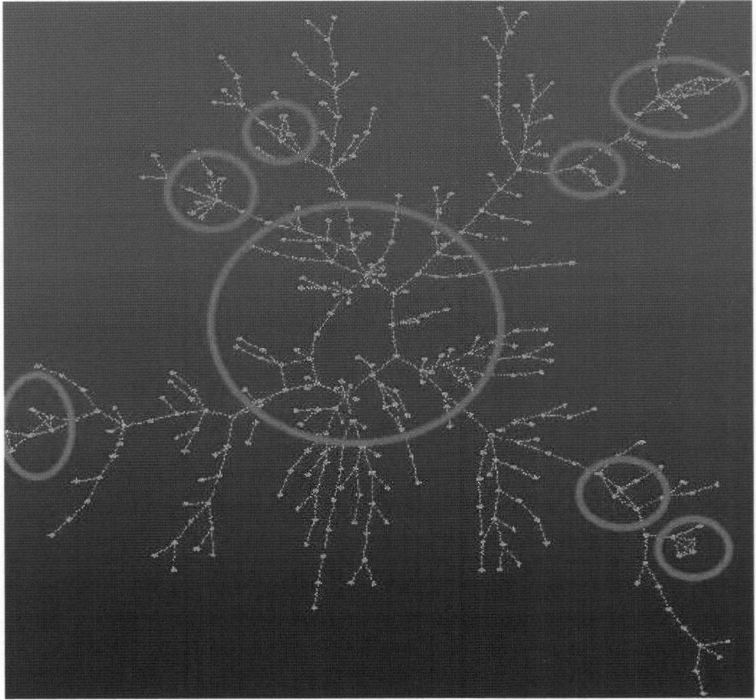

Fig. 5. A Pathfinder network of the Hypertext author co-citation network, consisting of the same 367 predominant scientists as in the MST, but a total of 398 links.

Table 4. Relevant techniques for knowledge extraction.

Company	Software	Further Information
Autonomy	Portal-in-the-Box	http://www.autonomy.com/
Cartia	Themescape	http://www.cartia.com/
Excalibur	RetrievalWare	http://www.excalibur.com/
Inxight	TableLense	http://www.inxight.com/
Institute for Scientific Information	SCI-Map	http://www.isi.net/
Pacific National Laboratories	ThemeView	http://www.pnl.gov/
Sandia National Laboratories	VxInsight	http://www.sandia.gov/
TextWise	DR-LINK	http://www.textwise.com/

3. Practical Approaches

This section collects several examples of practical approaches to knowledge extraction from unstructured documents. These examples highlight the state of the art in areas relevant to the visualization of knowledge structures. Our focus in this section is on how the key techniques discussed earlier in this chapter have been commercialized in various companies.

3.1. *Autonomy*

Autonomy is a company specialized in knowledge management. It was founded in 1996. Autonomy's software is based on a combination of Bayesian inference and Shannon's Information theory to automatically extract the key concepts from unstructured information.

As explained earlier in this chapter, Bayesian inference is a mathematical technique for modeling the significance of ideas based on how they occur in conjunction with other ideas. Shannon's information theory provides the heuristics of extracting the most meaningful ideas in these documents.

Autonomy takes one step further from traditional search engines by actively matching information to user's interest. Furthermore, the interest of a user is constantly monitored and updated by observing and analyzing actions of the user. The user's topical interests and expertise are modeled by key concepts extracted from the articles the user reads online. The system updates the user profile by replacing concepts that are no longer important with newly emerged concepts. For example, UK experienced a petrol crisis in September 2000. The word *petrol* may be best characterized by the user's interest at the time. When the crisis was over, petrol is no longer an issue. The word *petrol* will disappear from the user's more recent reading and writing habits. Therefore, it will also disappear from the updated user profile. There is no need for users to update their profiles explicitly.

Autonomy's software supports not only individual users, but also a group of users. For example, one can borrow someone else' profile. This could be useful, if

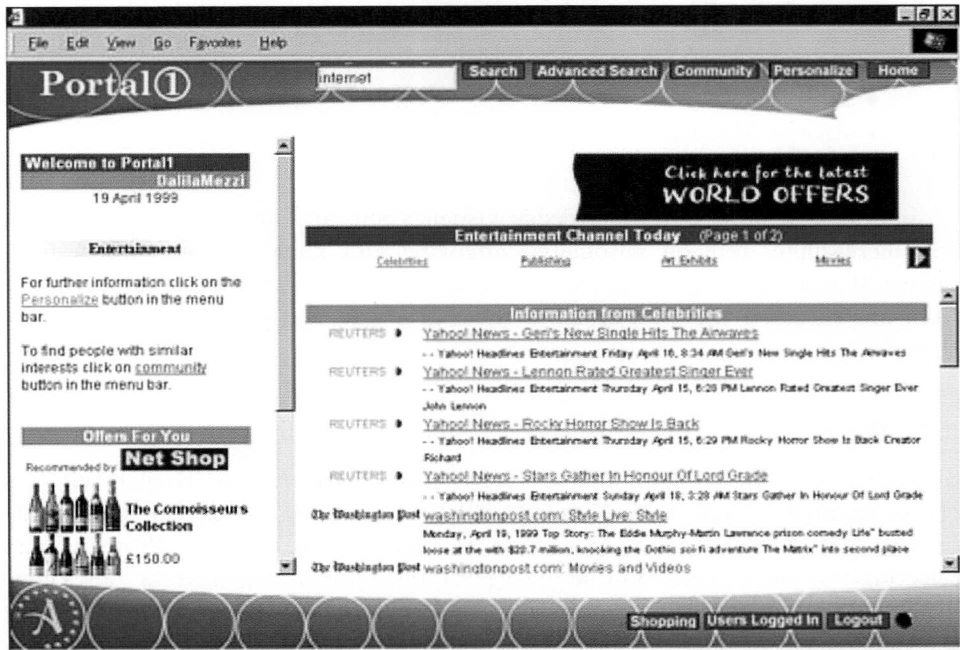

Fig. 6. Autonomy's portal interface.

one needs to find information outside one's own expertise, but has access to the profile of an expert in that area.

3.2. *TextWise*

KNOW-IT is a commercial product from TextWise. It generates a rich conceptual representation of textual content and provides a suite of tools for mining the information content of the material. KNOW-IT supports information exploration and knowledge discovery by exploiting in-depth semantic analysis of textual information. KNOW-IT has been developed with funds from DARPA and the US Air Force's Rome Lab. Manning & Napier Information Services (MNIS) is a company established to commercialize information retrieval and text processing products (*http://www.mnis.com*). MNIS-TextWise Labs was founded in 1993 at Syracuse University as a wholly owned subsidiary of MNIS.

The system can take raw text, such as newspaper articles, as input and create a knowledge base of concepts and relations automatically. These concepts and relations can then be used to help users locate desired information. Users can formulate questions in ordinary English, for example, "What is the effect of the prolonged US presidential election on economics?" Visually presented answers allow users to explore documents of interest. KNOW-IT is in fact an integrated suite of four different knowledge discovery tools:

- Topic Miner,
- Link Miner,
- Answer Miner,
- Information Extractor.

Information processing, knowledge visualization, and knowledge management will increasingly rely on automated archiving and knowledge extraction techniques. It is a rapidly growing market for tools that can extract relevant segments from unstructured text and organize them in a way that one can easily retrieve them.

3.3. *ThemeView*

SPIRE™, the Spatial Paradigm for Information Retrieval and Exploration is a classic example of information visualization developed by Pacific Northwest Laboratory [38]. SPIRE in fact is a suite of visualization tools for browsing and selecting text documents from large corpora, including a visualization view called Themescapes, which is later known as ThemeView. The SPIRE project is funded by the Department of Energy and the US intelligence agencies. ThemeView provide a fine example of information landscapes, which have become one of the most widely known metaphors in information visualization. Wise provided a detailed description of the procedure they used to generate the relief map in his recent paper published in the *Journal of the American Society for Information Science* [37].

ThemeView forms abstract, three-dimensional landscapes of information that are constructed from a large set of documents, also known as a document collection, or corpus. A thematic terrain simultaneously communicates both the primary themes of the underlying document collection and a measure of their relative prevalence in the collection. Thematic peaks and valleys in ThemeView produce a simplified representation of the complex content of a document corpus.

The SPIRE used the classic vector space model [27]. The greatest advantage of the ThemeView approach over the use of traditional high-dimensional vector spaces is that the user is able to establish connections easily between the construction and the final visualization. In particular, their procedure usually results in $300 \sim 500$ nouns to be visualized, which represent a significant improvement on the readability of the final result.

In a nutshell, the Galaxies visualization is based on clustering documents and projecting them into a two-dimensional plane. ThemeView extends this document space into a three-dimensional landscape visualization. The third dimension is used to convey the probability of finding a particular word in the document underneath. In terms of the thematic landscape, there are peaks and valleys of thematic terms.

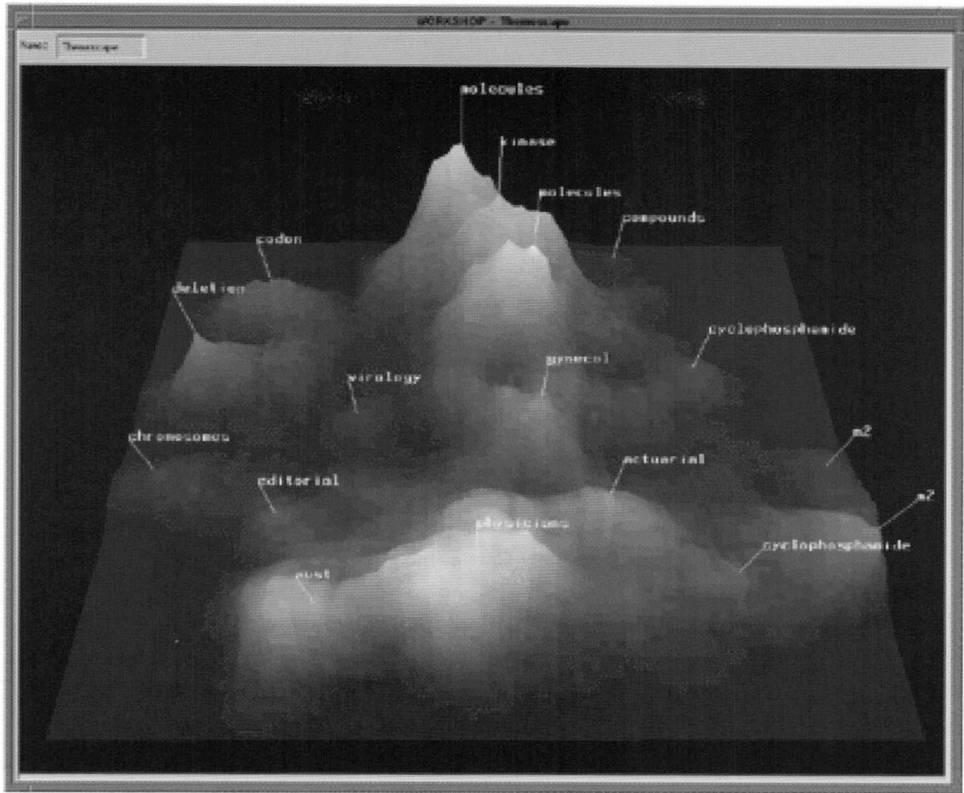

Fig. 7. Valleys and peaks in ThemeView. (©Pacific Northwest National Laboratory).

3.4. *Themescape of Cartia*

Cartia recently launched a commercial product for visualization. The product is called ThemeScape. Cartia's ThemeScape has stirred up a great deal of enthusiasms in knowledge extraction. It represents a new generation of visualization software, which is now regarded not only as a text visualization tool, but also as a knowledge extraction tool.

The predecessor of ThemeScape is called Spyr, which is an experimental visualization technology developed at Batelle Memorial Institute for the CIA. US intelligence agents used Spyr to analyze patterns in Iraqi message traffic in order to determine that Saddam Hussein's threat to re-enter Kuwait after the Gulf War was a hoax.[i] Spyr eventually evolved into ThemeScape as a commercial product launched by Cartia.

[i] *http://www.topsecretnet.com/knowmag.htm*

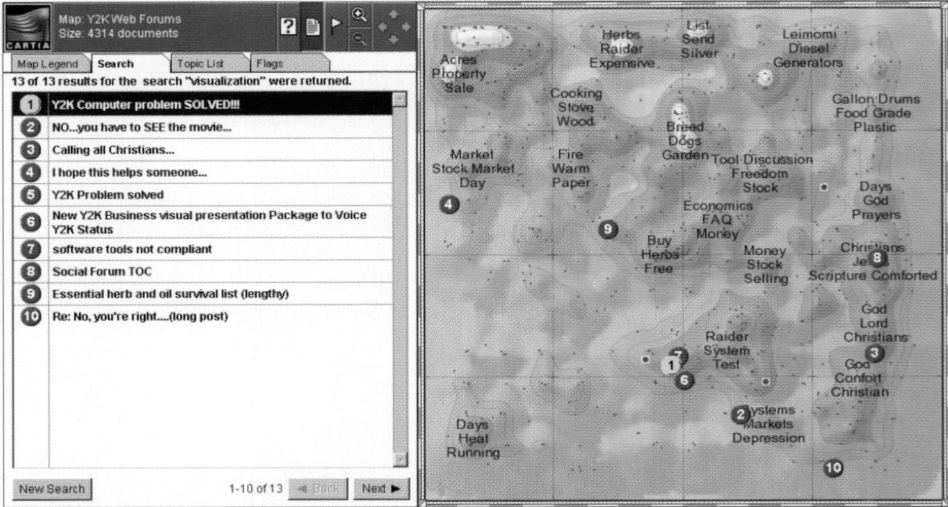

Fig. 8. Themescape (©1999 Cartia, Inc.) *http://www.cartia.com/*

The user model of ThemeScape is to look at information from 30,000 feet. One can instantly recognize important patterns and relationships without ever opening a document. ThemeScape creates a visual landscape of information — a topographical map — that shows what's inside large collections of documents and web pages. With a quick scan of the landscape, one can locate the major topics within thousands of documents, and how different topics relate to one another.

As with any map, ThemeScape shows points of interest and the distance between them. The concept is simple: the greater the similarity between any two documents, the closer together they appear on the map. Concentrations of documents about a similar topic literally "pile up" to form peaks — points of interest — and the distance between peaks shows how closely the topics are related. For example, a map about the Millenium Bug problem, also known as the Y2K problem, is shown in Fig. 8. Prices for a ThemeScape publishing system vary depending on configuration, beginning at about $20,000 in 2000.

3.5. *VxInsight*

VxInsight [8] is another example that uses an information landscape metaphor. It is a knowledge visualization tool developed by Sandia National Laboratories. In VxInsight, data elements from very large datasets are grouped by similarity. VxInsight uses the height of a mountain in a three-dimensional virtual landscape to portrait the density of data elements distributed underneath. One application of VxInsight is the visualization of nuclear physics based on a subset of the Science Citation Index (SCI), a citation database from the Institute for Scientific Information (ISI). The similarity between two documents is proportional to the extent that the two

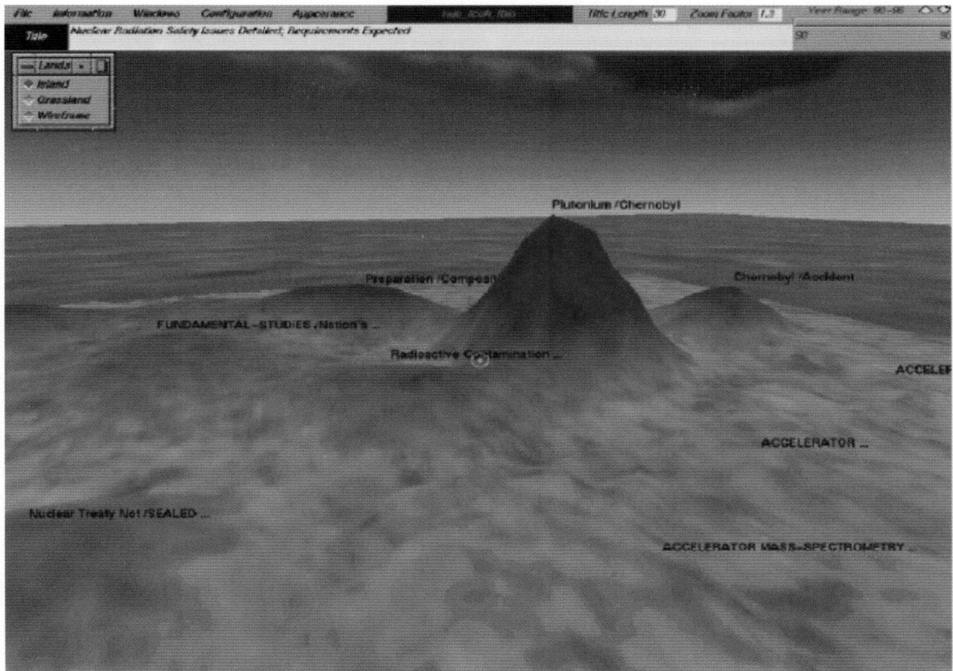

Fig. 9. The mountain terrain of nuclear physics (©Sandia National Lab).

documents have common citation links. VxInsight generates visualizations using a combination of eigenvector-based and force-directed placement solutions.

3.6. *Visualizing knowledge structures*

Figure 10 illustrates the four-step procedure of our approach [6]. First, select authors who have received citations above a threshold. Intellectual groupings of these authors represent snapshots of the underlying knowledge domain. Co-citation frequencies between these authors are computed from a citation database, such as ISI's SCI and SSCI. ACA uses a matrix of co-citation frequencies to compute a correlation matrix of Pearson correlation coefficients. According to [36], such correlation coefficients best capture the citation profile of an author.

Second, apply Pathfinder network scaling to the network defined by the correlation matrix. Factor analysis is a standard practice in ACA. However, in traditional ACA, MDS and factor analysis rarely appear in the same graphical representations. In order to make knowledge visualizations clear and easy to interpret, we overlay the intellectual groupings identified by factor analysis and the interconnectivity structure modeled by the Pathfinder network scaling. Authors with similar colors essentially belong to the same specialty and they should appear as a closely connected group in the Pathfinder network. Therefore, one can expect to see the two

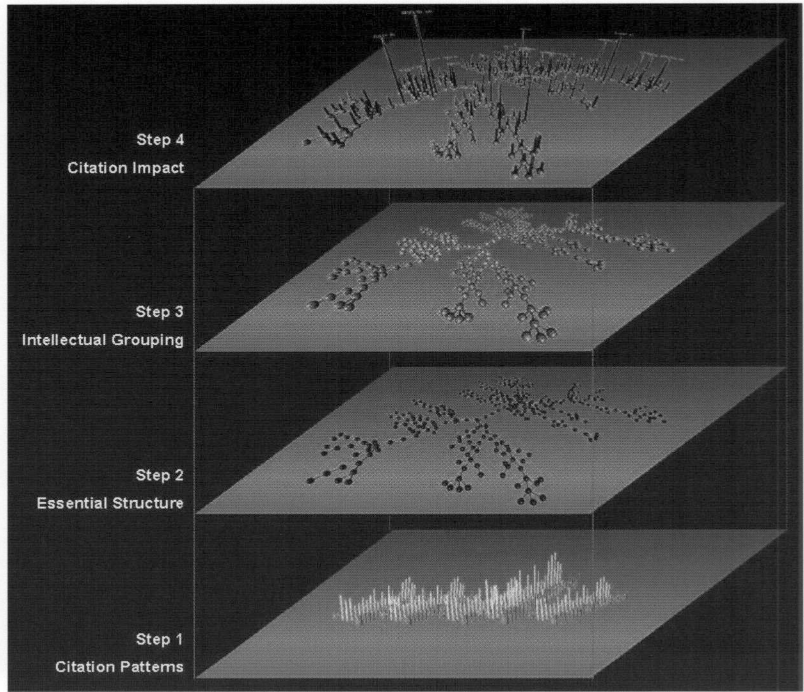

Fig. 10. The procedure for visualizing intellectual structures [6].

perspectives converge in the visualization. This is the third step. Finally, display the citation impact of each author on top of the intellectual groupings. The magnitude of the impact is represented by the height of a citation bar, which in turn consists of a stack of color-coded annual citation sections.

3.6.1. *Intellectual maps*

In order to incorporate multiple aspects of author co-citation networks, we have developed the following design. An author co-citation network is represented as a Pathfinder network, the specialty membership of an author is denoted by color coding based on corresponding factor loading for the author, and the citation history of the author is depicted by a stacked bar.

Figure 11 shows an author co-citation map rendered by this method. The author co-citation map is derived from all the citations appeared in the 1998 ACM Hypertext conference proceedings. A factor analysis on the data found 39 factors, which correspond to 39 specialties in the field of hypertext. In the map, nodes, i.e., authors, are colored by the first three of the 39 factors. The strongest specialty is in red. The next two strongest ones are in green and blue. The strongest specialty branches out from the top of the ring structure, whereas the second strongest specialty appears to

Fig. 11. The author co-citation map of hypertext in 1998.

Fig. 12. The author co-citation map in 1998 with citation indices displayed as stacked bars to provide additional cues for understanding the implications of the structure. (©1999 IEEE, reproduced with permission).

concentrate around the lower left-hand corner of the ring. The color map provides additional information on the context of a particular author's specialty.

Figure 12 shows an author co-citation map based on author co-citation patterns derived from the proceedings of 1998. It contains 259 authors. Citation indices over three periods are displayed as stacked bars to provide additional cues for

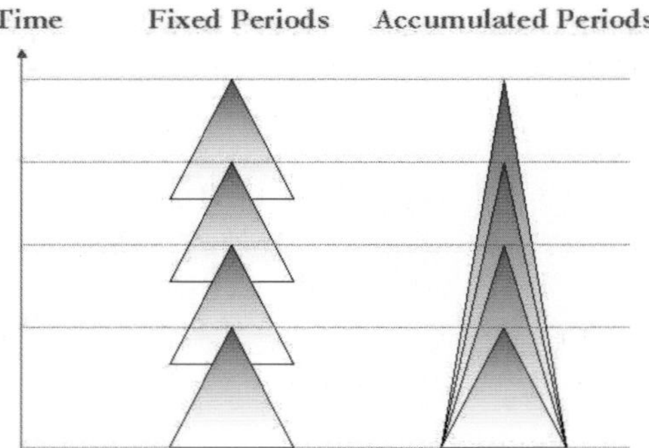

Fig. 13. Examples of two different types of periodical snapshots.

understanding the implications of the overall structure. The higher the stacked bar, the more frequently the author has been cited in this sample of the literature. We used the factor loading of the first three of the 18 factors extracted from the co-citation patterns to color the network. The first three factors together explain 42.2% of the variance. Color-coded nodes and links allow users to identify and distinguish authors from different specialties, or invisible colleges.

We have learned a lot of how to interpret the resultant Pathfinder networks by using different ways of triangulation. It is clear that when it is adapted to the visualization of semantic spaces, there are two types of documents in terms of their distribution in a Pathfinder network: those tend to appear in the center or a relatively fully connected area, and those tend to appear towards the tips of the Pathfinder network. The more central the location, the more likely that the document is of a generic nature. The more peripheral the location, the more likely that the document is about a rather specified topic or a perspective.

3.6.1.1. Longitudinal maps

A single snapshot of a scientific discipline reveals the structure of the domain at a particular time point. A series of periodical snapshots have the advantage of uncovering the dynamics and trends in the changing structure over a long period of time. Henry Small refers the generation of such periodical snapshots as longitudinal mapping.

If S denotes the set of years of publication corresponding to the source domain of citations to be analyzed and T denotes the set of years of publication for the target domain of corresponding citations, one can think of a variety of ways to arrange a series of periodical snapshots. For example, one can choose to fix the length of each period to 3 years or 5 years to have a moving window of 3 or 5 years across the timeline of the literature. Alternatively, one can choose to accumulate periods one over another so that an increasingly enlarged window of citations will be analyzed. A moving, fixed-size window is more appropriate for revealing the contemporary views at each time point when snapshots are taken, whereas an accumulating, comprehensive window is more suitable to produce a combined big picture.

The following example is based on all the papers appeared in nine ACM Hypertext conferences over a period of ten years (1989–1998). In order to discover significant advances and trends in the history of the field, the series of nine conferences are divided into 3 sub-periods: 1989–1991, 1992–1994, and 1996–1998. Author co-citation analysis was conducted on each of the three individual detests. The domain snapshot in the first period includes 196 authors, the second period reveals 195 authors, and the third period identifies 195 authors.

Figure 14 includes three author co-citation maps: the left-hand side map (L) for (1989–1991), the middle map (M) for (1992–1994), and the right-hand side map (R) for (1996–1998). The names of specialties are annotated by hand in these maps. The map L includes 196 authors who have five or more citations during the first period. We followed the links from the map to detailed citation information and found that authors were clearly grouped with reference to papers describing hypertext systems, which are all well-known today, including NoteCards, Intermedia, KMS, and Microcosm. Information retrieval has a much longer history as a field of research. A sub-field in hypertext is rooted in information retrieval. And this specialty of information retrieval was already in place in the first period.

The second period, 1992–1994, was predominated by SEPIA, a famous collaborative hypermedia system developed at GMD, Germany. Six members of GMD occupied the central area of the map M. In this map, Pearl became the branching node for the Microcosm group, and Leggett and the Pearl's branch appeared on the

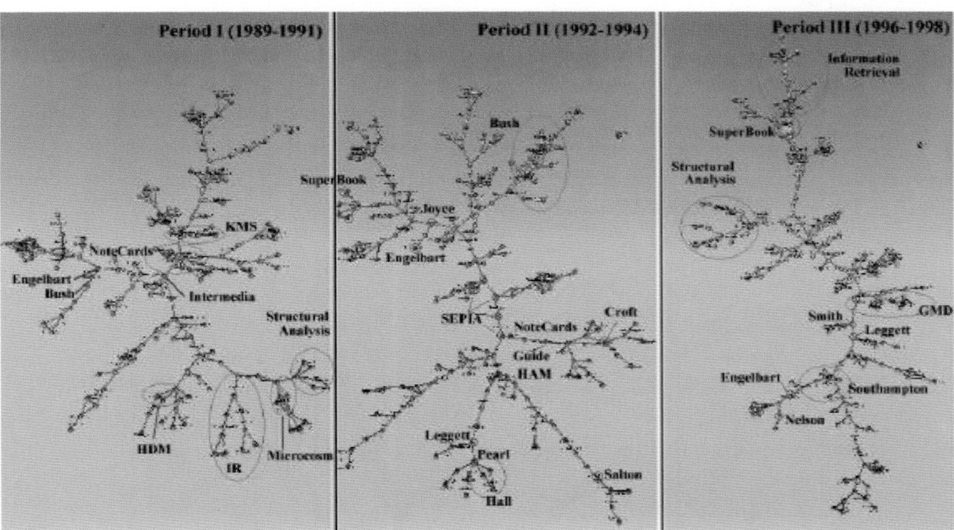

Fig. 14. Three snapshots of the evolution of the hypertext literature (1989–1991, 1992–1994, 1996–1998). (©1999 Springer-Verlag London).

same major branch. We have identified an open hypermedia specialty in the overall author co-citation map. This movement indicated the emergent open hypermedia specialty. Remarkably, Salton and Croft are not in the same major branch in this map. Although we need to check more detailed citation information regarding both Salton's and Croft's work in this period, this example shows that author co-citation maps can be used to highlight the impact of particular aspects of one's work.

The latest period ranges from 1996 through 1998. We expected to identify a specialty of the World Wide Web in map L, given the apparent influence of the rapid advances of the Web and the growth of the WWW as a research field. However, this is not clear from the map. We need to examine the citation details more thoroughly. The information retrieval specialty is located towards the North of the map. The structural analysis specialty is located to the West of the map.

3.6.2. *Towards the visualization of a paradigm*

Kuhn's work on the structure of scientific revolution has influenced a wide range of scientific disciplines. However, the existence of a paradigm and paradigm shifts in the past have never been shown in an empirical approach. If we can transform the visualization of intellectual structures into a tool that represents a paradigm visually, then such tools will enable scientists to identify more detailed information they need within this context. Furthermore, it will then be possible to visualize the co-existence of two competing paradigms and a paradigm shift. We are currently investigating this approach. Here we provide a few examples to illustrate our ideas.

In 1988, Halasz addressed seven issues for new generations of hypermedia systems [15]. It was this article that had been the most cited article throughout the ACM Hypertext conferences. In 1997, a spatial hypertext reached the top of the most cited article list. For the first time, the top cited paper was written

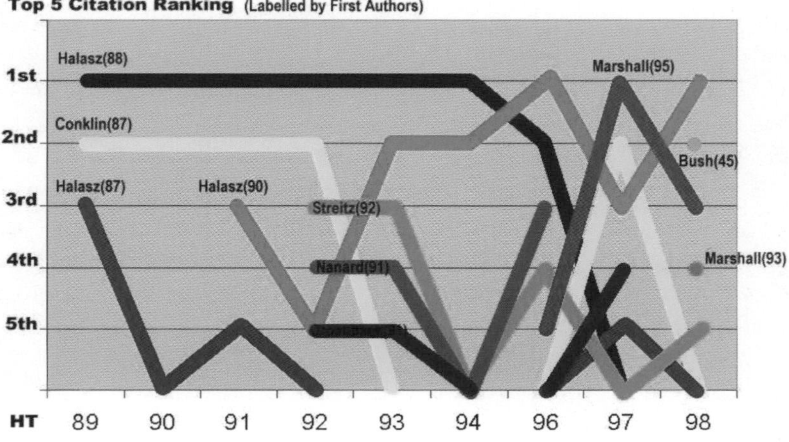

Fig. 15. Do we see a paradigm shift?

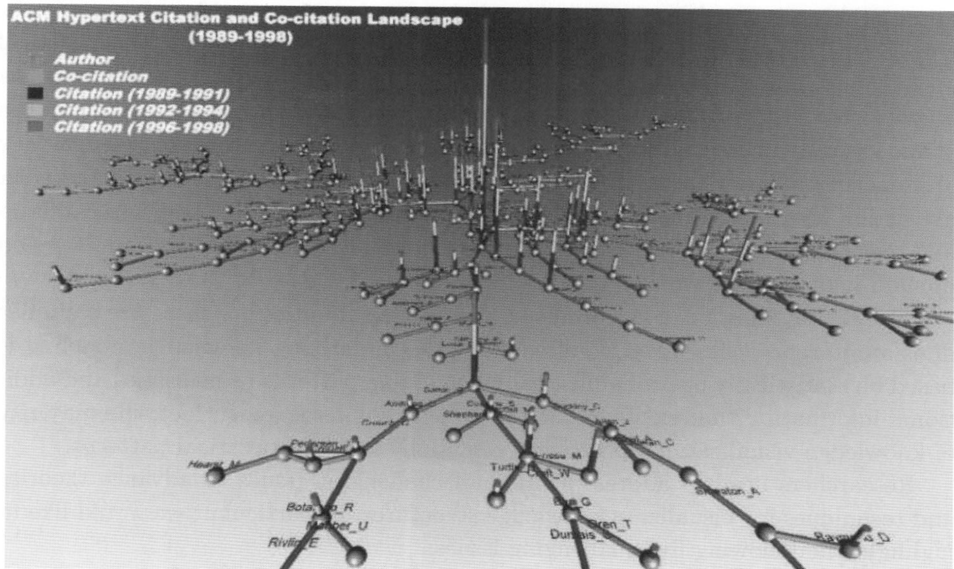

Fig. 16. A citation and co-citation landscape of the field of hypertext. Does the single peak in the center indicate the existence of the paradigm since the beginning of this field? Can we track its movement so as to detect a paradigm shift in the future?

by researchers other than Halasz, although in 1996 and 1998, another article written by Halasz in 1990 regained the first position.

Figure 16 is a citation and co-citation landscape of the field of hypertext. The landscape was derived from an author co-citation analysis of the ACM Hypertext conference proceedings between 1989 and 1998. The highest peak at the center of the landscape represents the impact of Halasz's work on this community. According to Kuhn's paradigm theory, once a paradigm is established, scientists working within the paradigm do not challenge the assumptions and principles. Does the single peak in the landscape indicate the existence of a paradigm in the field of hypertext? If so, is the paradigm defined by Halasz's articles that have influenced so many researchers in this field? How can we visualize a paradigm in a discipline in general? Is it possible to visualize a paradigm shift with this visualization framework?

If there are several areas that contain authors with very high citation rates, will the paradigm view still be applicable to this domain? If there appear to be several smaller paradigms, does the paradigm view still make sense? In a long run, our ultimate goal is to provide scientists with visualizations that can clearly show the existence of a paradigm or the co-existence of two or more competing paradigms.

4. Challenging Issues

Visualizing knowledge structures is a very promising field of research and its commercial potential is great. Habn and Mani recently identified approaches to automatic text summarization into knowledge-poor and knowledge-rich approaches [14]. Knowledge-poor approaches refer to those essentially relying on statistical and probabilistically methods to solve problems in text summarization, whereas knowledge-rich approaches make use of external sources of rules and heuristics in the summarization process. In their opinion, at least for the short term, knowledge-poor approaches are likely to dominate applications, particularly when augmented with extraction learning mechanisms. Knowledge-rich approaches will begin to catch up and eventually replace extraction when we have reasonably sized grammars and domain knowledge sources.

Visualizing knowledge structures is in a similar situation — there are a similar division of approaches in terms of whether the underlying knowledge modeling is based on statistically or probabilistically detectable patterns or heuristics and additional information that exists outside the scientific literature. In fact, the majority of knowledge visualization approaches essentially rely on statistical patterns.

Researchers need to address a range of challenging issues to advance theories and techniques for visualizing knowledge structures. In particular, we would like to highlight the following five challenging issues:

(1) What is the best way to detect new and significant developments in knowledge?
(2) What measures a new paradigm?
(3) Can we detect a paradigm shift of science solely based on the reflection of scientific literature?
(4) What is the best way to track the growth of knowledge: a landscape of documents or an intellectual network of people?
(5) How do we match the visualized intellectual structure to what scientists have in their mind?

Author co-citation analysis (ACA) provides a promising basis for modeling and visualizing knowledge structures reflected in scientific literatures. The greatest advantage of ACA-based approaches is that the strengths associated with particular intellectual bonds between scientists are measured by an integral part of scientific practice. On the other hand, this practice is likely to hinder the process for analysts to obtain the necessary data timely. A more fundamental challenge is rooted in the fact that we are extracting patterns from the scientific literature. A new and potentially significant piece of work might not be captured and recognized in this way, at least very unlikely in knowledge-poor approaches.

Is it possible to track the rise and fall of a scientific paradigm as defined by Thomas Kuhn in his philosophy of science [18]? White and McCain [36] have done a splendid job in their award-winning article to demonstrate how this could be achieved. They have identified information retrieval and citation analysis as two intellectual camps in information science. In order to track the development of science, the ultimate challenge is to detect and predict the shift of a paradigm as it occurs.

Judging the extent to which a visualized knowledge structure matches or mismatches to what leading scientists have in their mind is yet another fundamental challenge. To meet this challenge, we must equip ourselves with a deeper understanding of the nature of knowledge and cognition. This is likely to be an interdisciplinary endeavor, involving disciplines such as epistemology, sociology of knowledge, and philosophy of science.

5. Conclusions

In this chapter, we have highlighted the history and the state of the art of visualizations of knowledge structures. We have emphasized the central idea of painting the big picture of science and its profound connections to philosophy of science, especially Kuhn's structure of scientific revolution. Some of the most influential theories and methods of analysis, modeling, and visualization have been included. Challenging issues to be resolved in the future are discussed.

In conclusion, visualizing knowledge structures is a challenging but ultimately rewarding route to capture the essence of a scientific paradigm. Potential applications will be valuable to multiple domains. These are tough challenges, but the potential benefits are tremendous and profound.

References

1. A. Bookstein, S. T. Klein and T. Raita, "Detecting content-bearing words by serial clustering", *SIGIR '95* (ACM Press, Seattle, WA, 1995) 319–327.
2. S. Card, J. Mackinlay and B. Shneiderman (eds.), *Readings in Information Visualization: Using Vision to Think* (Morgan Kaufmann, 1999).
3. C. Chen, *Information Visualisation and Virtual Environments* (Springer-Verlag, London, 1999).
4. C. Chen, "Visualising semantic spaces and author co-citation networks in digital libraries", *Information Processing and Management* **35**, no. 2, 401–420.
5. C. Chen and L. Carr, "Visualizing the evolution of a subject domain: A case study", *IEEE Visualization '99* (San Francisco, CA, 1999).
6. C. Chen and R. J. Paul, "Visualizing a knowledge domain's intellectual structure", *Computer* **34**, no. 3, 65–71.
7. H. Chen, A. L. Houston, R. R. Sewell and B. R. Schatz, "Internet browsing and searching: User evaluations of category map and concept space techniques", *Journal of the American Society for Information Science* **49**, no. 7, 582–608.
8. G. S. Davidson, B. Hendrickson, D. K. Johnson, C. E. Meyers and B. N. Wylie, "Knowledge mining with VxInsight: Discovery through interaction", *Journal of Intelligent Information Systems* **11**, no. 3, 259–285.
9. K. Fairchild, S. Poltrock and G. Furnas, "SemNet: Three-dimensional graphic representations of large knowledge bases", ed. R. Guidon, *Cognitive Science and its Applications for Human-Computer Interaction* (Lawrence Erlbaum Associates, 1988) 201–233.
10. E. Garfield, "Citation indexes for science: A new dimension in documentation through association of ideas", *Science* **122**, 108–111.
11. E. Garfield, "Scientography: Mapping the tracks of science", *Current Contents: Social and Behavioural Sciences* **7**, no. 45, 5–10.

12. E. Garfield, I. H. Sher and R. J. Torpie, "The use of citation data in writing the history of science", Institute for Scientific Information, Philadelphia (1964).
13. E. Garfield and H. Small, *Identifying the Changing Frontiers of Science* (The S. Neaman Press, 1989).
14. U. Habn and I. Mani, "The challenges of automatic summarization", *IEEE Computer* **33**, no. 11, 29–36.
15. F. Halasz, "Reflections on NoteCards: Seven issues for the next generation of hypermedia systems", *Communications of the ACM* **31**, no. 7, 836–852.
16. B. Hjorland, *Information Seeking and Subject Representation: An Activity-Theoretical Approach to Information Science* (Greenwood Press, Westport, 1997).
17. J. B. Kruskal, "Multidimensional scaling by optimizing goodness of fit to a nonmetric hypothesis", *Psychometrika* **29**, 1–27.
18. T. S. Kuhn, *The Structure of Scientific Revolutions* (University of Chicago Press, Chicago, 1962).
19. X. Lin, D. Soergel and G. Marchionini, "A self-organizing semantic map for information retrieval", *SIGIR '91* (ACM Press, Chicago, IL, 1991) 262–269.
20. K. W. McCain, "Mapping authors in intellectual space: A technical overview", *Journal of the American Society for Information Science* **41**, no. 6, 433–443.
21. T. Munzner, "H3: Laying out large directed graphs in 3D hyperbolic space", *IEEE Symposium on Information Visualization, 1997* (IEEE, Phoenix, AZ, 1997) 2–10.
22. R. Neal, *Bayesian Learning for Neural Networks* (Springer-Verlag, New York, 1996).
23. D. Price, "Networks of scientific papers", *Science* **149**, 510–515.
24. D. D. Price, *Little Science, Big Science and Beyond* (Columbia University Press, New York, 1986).
25. D. D. Price, "Networks of scientific papers", *Science* **149**, 510–515.
26. G. G. Robertson, J. D. Mackinlay and S. K. Card, "Cone trees: Animated 3D visualizations of hierarchical information", *CHI '91* (New Orleans, LA, 1991) 189–194.
27. G. Salton, "Developments in automatic text retrieval", *Science* **253**, 974–980.
28. R. W. Schvaneveldt, ed., *Pathfinder Associative Networks: Studies in Knowledge Organization* (Ablex Publishing Corporations, Norwood, NJ, 1990).
29. R. W. Schvaneveldt, F. T. Durso and D. W. Dearholt, "Network structures in proximity data", ed. G. Bower, *The Psychology of Learning and Motivation* **24** (Academic Press, 1989) 249–284.
30. I. Sher and E. Garfield, "New tools for improving and evaluating the effectiveness of research", *Research Program Effectiveness* (Gordon and Breach, Washington, D.C, 1966) 135–146.
31. H. Small, "Co-citation in scientific literature: A new measure of the relationship between publications", *Journal of the American Society for Information Science* **24**, 265–269.
32. H. Small, "A co-citation model of a scientific specialty: A longitudinal study of collagen research", *Social Studies of Science* **7**, 139–166.
33. H. Small, "A passage through science: Crossing disciplinary boundaries", *Library Trends* **48**, no. 1, 72–108.
34. H. Small, "Visualizing science by citation mapping", *Journal of the American Society for Information Science* **50**, no. 9, 799–813.
35. H. D. White and B. C. Griffith, "Author co-citation: A literature measure of intellectual structure", *Journal of the American Society for Information Science* **32**, 163–172.
36. H. D. White and K. W. McCain, "Visualizing a discipline: An author co-citation analysis of information science", *Journal of the American Society for Information Science* **49**, no. 4 (1972–1995) 327–356.

37. J. A. Wise, "The ecological approach to text visualization", *Journal of the American Society for Information Science* **50**, no. 13, 1224–1233.
38. J. A. Wise, J. J. Thomas, K. Pennock, D. Lantrip, M. Pottier, A. Schur and V. Crow, "Visualizing the non-visual: Spatial analysis and interaction with information from text documents", *IEEE Symposium on Information Visualization '95* (IEEE Computer Society Press, Atlanta, Georgia, USA, 1995).

FORMAL DESCRIPTION TECHNIQUES

MOTOSHI SAEKI

Department of Computer Science, Tokyo Institute of Technology, Ookayama 2-12-1, Meguro-Ku, Tokyo 152-8552, Japan

This article surveys the state of the art in formal description techniques (FDTs), i.e., formal languages to describe the specifications of software-intensive systems. In the first part, we provide the brief introduction of the typical FDTs together with a simple example; Z based on set theory and predicate logic, an algebraic language for abstract data types and LOTOS. Furthermore, we illustrate software development processes using FDTs and discuss the future directions of FDTs.

Keywords: Formal Method, Z, algebraic specification language, LOTOS, proof obligation, method integration, lightweight approach.

1. Introduction

Generally, formal methods are the techniques for developing software-intensive systems using mathematics such as set theory, algebra, and mathematical logic. Especially formal description techniques (FDTs) mean formal languages, whose semantics is based on mathematics, in order to specify software systems. It has been said that one of the major benefits of FDTs is the possibility of mathematical verifications of various kind of properties of software systems based on the FDT's axiomatic or deductive systems, and the verifications could improve the reliability of the produced software. The FDT researches in the first stage focused on:

(1) Constructing a formal specification of a software system,
(2) Deducing or inferring from the formal specification the properties that the system being developed must have,
(3) Synthesizing or deriving an executable program from the formal specification like [25],
(4) Proving the correctness of the program, i.e., proving that the program satisfies its formal specification.

Until the last decade, many researchers studied the techniques for program synthesis and for proving the correctness of programs. However these techniques were applied to small problems, so called toy problems, and it was still difficult to apply them to practical systems. Practical systems were much larger and more complicated than the researchers expected, and great efforts for synthesizing a program or proving the correctness were necessary. Note that many researches on developing automatic-verification techniques like theorem provers and model checkers go on still and notable advances are appearing. The cost of practitioners' writing formal specifications was beyond the budget of the development project, because the practitioners should be well-trained and be made expert for the FDTs before starting the project. In addition, writing formal specifications took much more time than using natural language because the developers should rigorously and completely specify the details of the systems. As a result, the practitioners neither tried to write formal specifications in actual development projects, nor performed the synthesis and the correctness verification of the practical systems. The lack of practical experiences prevented the researchers from advancing the FDT techniques, especially verification techniques.

However, recently the success stories of applying FDTs to actual projects have been increasing. In addition, some techniques such as LOTOS, Estelle, SDL, Z and VDM have been or being standardized by ISO or CCITT [55–58]. This surveys the state of the art on FDTs and their future directions. Roughly speaking, it consists of two parts; the first part offers basic and minimum knowledge to understand FDTs, by using standardized FDTs as simple examples, while the second part summarizes the current status of FDT researches and experiences that can lead to future directions. The first part is for newcomers to FDTs.

2. What are FDTs?

2.1. *Model-oriented languages and property-oriented languages*

Various kinds of FDTs, i.e., formal specification languages have been developed especially by academic researchers. Generally, they can be categorized into the following [94];

(1) Model-oriented language
The languages belonging to this category are used for constructing an abstract model of the system by using mathematical concepts, e.g. set, function, Cartesian product etc. The examples are VDM [62], Z [81], B Language [66], CSP [52], CCS [74] and Petri-net [80].

(2) Property-oriented language
The languages specify not a model of the system but properties that the system should have. The languages based on mathematical logic are for describing the properties as axioms, while the other types of the languages based on algebra are for describing the properties with equations. Larch [44] and temporal logic based languages are the former examples and the latter ones are algebraic specification languages for abstract data types [45], e.g. OBJ3 [42], Clear [19], Act one [55] and CafeObj [39].

There are some languages that have both of the characteristics of these categories. For example, LOTOS (Language of Temporal Ordering Specification) [55], which was standardized by ISO in 1988, results from the amalgamation of the model-oriented language CCS and the property-oriented language Act one.

LOTOS is frequently used to specify communication systems with OSI architecture. In LOTOS, the behavior of the system is specified with behavior expressions semantically based on Process Algebra [6], while data and the manipulations on them are specified as abstract data types by using the algebraic specification language Act one. In the subsequent sub-sections, we will focus on three typical languages; Z [91] as an example of model-oriented languages, Act one as a property-oriented language and LOTOS as a mixture. To clarify the remarkable differences between a model-oriented language and a property-oriented one, we use a traditional example Stack to introduce Z and Act one.

Note that this categorization of FDTs is not exclusive. Although Z is suitable for specifying an abstract model of the system and for modeling system behavior with a state transition machine, we can write the properties of the system by using predicate logic part of Z. The categorization is based on the easiness of writing an abstract model or properties.

2.2. *Z*

Z (pronounced Zed) is semantically based on set theory and predicate logic. We model a system as mathematical and abstract objects like sets, maps, functions, sequences and so on. To specify system behavior with Z, we define the internal states that the system can have, the operations allowable to the system, the state transitions when the operations are applied, and the invariants that should hold whenever any state change occurs. The following example is the specification of *Stack*, and the operations *Push*, *Pop* and *Top* on a stack.

We model a stack (precisely speaking, the internal state of a stack) as a sequence of *ITEM* and the sequence is the data that are stored in the stack. *ITEM* denotes

$[ITEM]$ (Declaration of Basic Type)

Stack
$elements : \mathrm{seq}\ ITEM$

Stack$_{init}$
Stack

$elements = \langle\, \rangle$

Push
$\Delta Stack$
$i? : ITEM$

$elements' = \langle i? \rangle \frown elements$

Pop

$$\Delta Stack$$

$$elements \neq \langle\,\rangle$$
$$\exists\, i : ITEM \bullet elements = \langle i \rangle \frown elements'$$

Top

$$\Xi Stack$$
$$i! : ITEM$$

$$elements \neq \langle\,\rangle$$
$$\exists\, e : \mathrm{seq}\, ITEM \bullet elements = \langle i! \rangle \frown e$$

the type of the elements that can be stored in the stack. The description style of *Stack*, $Stack_{init}$, *Push*, *Pop* and *Top* is called Z schema. The Z schema defines variables and constraints on them with predicate logical formulas. The schema *Stack* has the variable *elements* whose allowable value is the sequence of ITEM. It defines the current state of a stack and denotes the contents of the stack. $Stack_{init}$ represents that the initial state of a stack is empty (the value "*elements*" is an empty sequence $\langle\,\rangle$), i.e., it has no data when it is created.

The additional schemas *Push*, *Pop* and *Top* define the allowable operations to the *Stack*, and specify the value-change on its variables in the form of pre- and post-conditions. The variables used in these schemas have several notational conventions. The Δ notation in the signature part (variable declaration part: the upper part of the Z schema) declares the variables whose values may be updated by the operation. The variables with the prime ($'$) decoration represent the values after the operation is executed, while the variables that are not decorated represent the values before the operation. For example, the operation schema *Push*, which is the specification of the push operation, says that the contents of the stack (the value of *elements*) is changed to "$\langle i? \rangle \frown elements$", which expresses the result of adding the value $i?$ to the head of the sequence *elements*. On the other hand, although Ξ provides the same effect as Δ on declaring the variables decorated with the prime in the schema, it additionally presents that any variables are unchanged by the operation. In the case of *Top*, the variable $elements'$ is declared implicitly and $elements' = elements$ holds. The variables decorated with "?" and "!" stand for inputs to the schema and outputs from the schema respectively.

2.3. *Algebraic specification language : Act one*

Act one is a specification language for abstract data types, semantically based on many-sorted algebra. The idea of abstract data types is that data can be modeled not as their concrete structure or their implementations, but only as the operations that are allowable on them. In algebraic specification languages, data corresponds to the elements of the sorts that the underlying algebra has, and the operations are for manipulating the elements of the sorts [11]. The effect of applying the operations are defined with the equations that specify the relationships among them. We can have the following Act one description for the stack example.

```
type Stack is Boolean
    formalsorts ITEM
    sorts stack, Bool
    opns
        Push : ITEM, stack ⟶ stack
        Pop : stack ⟶ stack
        Bottom : ⟶ stack
        Top : stack → ITEM
        IsEmpty : stack → Bool
    eqns    for all i : ITEM, s : stack
        ofsorts stack
            Pop(Push(i, s)) = s ;
        ofsorts ITEM
            Top(Push(i, s)) = i ;
        ofsorts Bool
            IsEmpty(Bottom()) = true ;
            IsEmpty(Push(i, s)) = false ;
endtype
```

Mathematically, an algebra is a set with operations on the elements of the set. When the set is divided into several subsets, we call this algebra many-sorted algebra and each of the subsets is a sort. A *signature* declares the name of sorts and the operation symbols appearing in the algebra. The sections **formalsorts**, **sorts** and **opns** in the stack description correspond to the signature of the algebra that provides the formal semantics. The algebra for the stack data type has the sorts "ITEM" and "stack". Note that the sort "ITEM" is a formal parameter and we should replace it with the actual sort name, e.g. integer, string etc, when we use this description. The operation "Bottom" is a term denoting an empty stack and the predicate "IsEmpty" is used for identifying an empty stack. The equations on the terms, appearing in the **eqns** section, such as Pop(Push(i,s))=s specify the effects of the application of the operations, while from algebraic view, they define the congruence relation = on the terms in this algebra. For example, we can get the congruence relation $Pop(Push(i, Bottom(\ ))) = Bottom(\ )$ by applying the first equation of the stack example.

We can recognize the meaning of the equation $Pop(Push(i, Bottom(\ ))) = Bottom(\ )$ not only as the congruence relation on the two terms, but also as the process of executing combined applications of the "Push" and "Pop" operations. When we apply the "Push" operation to the "Bottom" stack (where no data are stored), then do the "Pop", and finally we can get the "Bottom" stack as a final result. In this interpretation, we capture the equations as term rewriting rules. And a rewriting process to get a terminating term (the term to which no rewriting rules are applicable) can be considered as an execution of the specification. The major feature of a family of algebraic languages is executability. The execution by a term rewriting system includes some crucial issues; uniqueness (if we can have more than one applicable rewriting rules and we actually apply any of them, we can always get a unique terminating term) and termination of rewriting processes (any rewriting processes are finite, i.e., we can eventually get a terminating term). Some techniques such as Church-Rosser theorem and a well-founded set method to check whether a term rewriting system has the uniqueness property and the termination property have been studied. As for a family of algebraic languages of abstract data types, there are some problems, e.g. the selection of constructors can frequently result in over- and under-specification as pointed in [5].

2.4. *LOTOS*

The descriptions written in LOTOS consist of behavior specifications and data specifications. The formal semantics of LOTOS is based on CCS (Calculus of Communicating Systems) for behavior specifications and on algebra of abstract data types for data specifications. The behavior specifications define the observable behavior, i.e., interaction sequences of the system to be specified. The system is captured as a set of *processes* interacting with each other at their *gates*. These *processes* may be hierarchically decomposed into several *sub-processes*. The atomic unit of the interaction is an *event*, and it is also an unit of synchronized interaction. The *process description* contains the *behavior expression* defining the observable behavior of the process. LOTOS has several operators for constructing behavior expressions, e.g. ";" (*action prefix*) and "$\gg$" (*enabling operator*) for sequential composition, "[]" (*choice operator*) for selection, and "$|[a_1, \ldots, a_n]|$" (*general parallel operator*) for parallel composition with synchronous *events* $a_1, \ldots, a_n$. The basic constructors for behavior expressions are listed in Table 1.

Intuitively speaking, the *event* "g ?x:Nat", where g is a *gate name*, represents the input of a natural number through the *gate* g and the assignment of the input data to the variable x. "Nat" denotes the sort of natural number. The *event* "g !a" stands for an output of the value "a" through the *gate* g. Abstract data type definitions express what values are handled. Let's consider the following LOTOS behavior expression.

```
(in ?x:Nat ; middle !x ; stop)
|[middle]|
 (middle ?y:Nat[not(y=0)] ; out !y ; stop)
```

This behavior expression represents that the two *event* sequences may be executed in parallel. They communicate and synchronize with each other through the *gate* "middle". The behavior expression in the left side expression of "$|[middle]|$"

Table 1. Basic constructor of behavior expressions.

Operators	Naming	Intuitive Meaning
$a;\ B$	Action Prefix	The event a occurs, and after that B
$B_1 \gg B_2$	Enabling Operator	B_1 first and then B_2
$B_1[\,]B_2$	Choice	Either B_1 or B_2 is executed
$[G_1] \rightarrow B_1$ $[\,][G_2] \rightarrow B_2$	Choice with Guard Conditions	If G_i $(i = 1, 2)$ then, B_i is executed
$B_1[> B_2$	Disabling Operator	During B_1, B_1 is discarded and B_2 is executed
$B_1 \mid \mid B_2$	Interleaving Operator	B_1 and B_2 are independently, i.e., asynchronously executed in parallel
$B_1 \mid B_2$	Synchronizing Operator	B_1 and B_2 are executed in parallel and synchronously with all events.
$B_1 \mid [a_1, \ldots, a_n] \mid B_2$	General Parallel Operator	B_1 and B_2 are executed in parallel and synchronously with $a_1, \ldots, a_n$

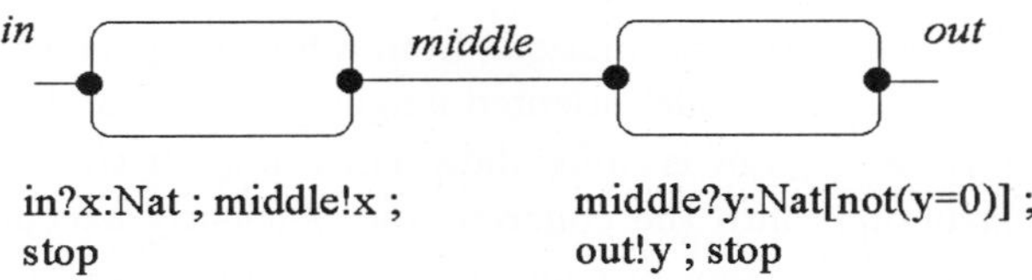

Fig. 1. Interaction of the behavioral expression.

sends synchronously the natural number x, which is an input through the *gate* "in", to the right side through the gate "middle". The right-hand side expression can receive the value only if the value is not 0 because of the guard condition "[not(y=0)]". After the right-hand side expression receives the value, it outputs the received value through the *gate* "out". Figure 1 depicts the interaction between the above two behavior expressions. In the figure, the black circles stand for the gates included in the behavior expressions and the solid lines connecting with the circles represent which gates are synchronized.

2.5. *Software development process based on FDT*

Consider the ideal software development processes by using FDTs, as shown in Fig. 2. Since a formal specification is semantically based on a mathematical deductive system, we can transform it to another description without changing the semantic properties by applying the deductive rules. If an artifact finally obtained by the series of these transformations is a source code, this transformation process finishes. If each transformation can preserve the semantic properties between the

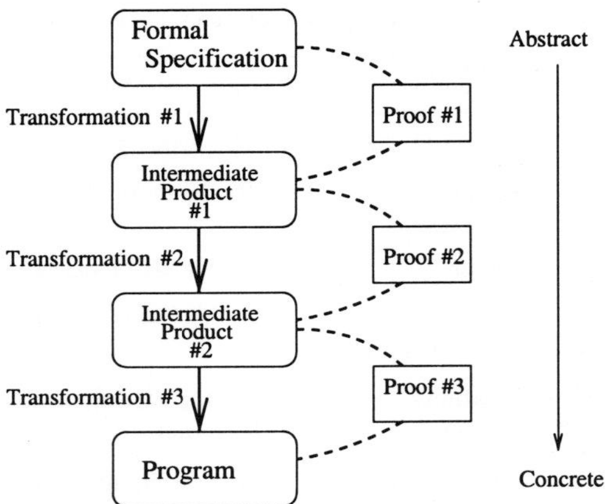

Fig. 2. Software development based on FDTs.

two artifacts before and after the transformation, it can be guaranteed that the source code satisfies the specification. Needless to say, fully automatic transformations are impossible and the developers should assist in them. We can find several studies about this transformation-based development and its supporting tools, i.e., techniques for incremental transformations from a formal specification to a source code by using the rules. The model-oriented languages VDM and Z have two types of transformation rules [13]; one is called data reification, for transforming abstract models of data structures into the concrete and efficiently executable structures that real programming languages provide, e.g. array and record types, and another is operation refinement for implementing the operations with the programming languages. Note that we should verify that some properties hold after each of the transformations in order to prove the correctness of the final artifacts. We call this duty proof obligation.

Balzer *et al* proposed the combination of the prototype technique. In this approach, the developers describe the specification with an executable specification language as a prototype (should be executable), and to make the specification more complete, i.e., more satisfactory for users and/or customers (stakeholders), they show their stakeholders the execution processes of the prototype and obtain some feedback [7]. Based on this feedback, they make the prototype more complete in the sense that the stakeholders can accept the prototype. After repeating this specification and examination cycles, the developers get a formal specification and incrementally transform it into a source code in the same manner as in Fig. 2.

2.6. *Proof obligation: example*

Let's consider proofs and proof obligations, mentioned before, more concretely, by using the stack example. First of all, we will show a more concrete specification of Stack. While a stack was represented with a sequence in an abstract specification, its concrete specification uses the concept of array, which usual procedural programming languages provide.

$$
\begin{array}{l}
\textit{Stack\_c} \\
\hline
\textit{elements\_c} : \mathbb{N} \ffun \textit{ITEM} \\
\textit{index} : \mathbb{N} \\
\hline
\textit{elements\_c} = \varnothing \\
\quad \Rightarrow \textit{index} = 0 \\
\textit{elements\_c} \neq \varnothing \\
\quad \Rightarrow (\textit{index} > 0 \land \\
\qquad\qquad \forall i : \mathbb{N} \cdot (i \geq 0 \land i < \textit{index} \Rightarrow i \in \operatorname{dom} \textit{elements\_c})) \\
\hline
\end{array}
$$

$$
\begin{array}{l}
\textit{Stack\_c}_{init} \\
\hline
\textit{Stack\_c} \\
\hline
\textit{elements\_c} = \varnothing \\
\textit{index} = 0 \\
\hline
\end{array}
$$

$$
\begin{array}{l}
\textit{Push\_c} \\
\hline
\Delta \textit{Stack\_c} \\
i? : \textit{ITEM} \\
\hline
\textit{elements\_c}' = \textit{elements\_c} \oplus \{\textit{index} \mapsto i?\} \\
\textit{index}' = \textit{index} + 1 \\
\hline
\end{array}
$$

$$
\begin{array}{l}
\textit{Pop\_c} \\
\hline
\Delta \textit{Stack\_c} \\
\hline
\textit{elements\_c} \neq \varnothing \\
\textit{index}' = \textit{index} - 1 \\
\textit{elements\_c}' = \{\textit{index}'\} \lhd \textit{elements\_c} \\
\hline
\end{array}
$$

$$
\begin{array}{l}
\textit{Top\_c} \\
\hline
\Xi \textit{Stack\_c} \\
i! : \textit{ITEM} \\
\hline
\textit{elements} \neq \varnothing \\
i! = \textit{elements\_c}(\textit{index} - 1) \\
\hline
\end{array}
$$

The state of a stack, i.e., data stored in the stack are represented with a finite map from natural numbers to ITEM, and this map is a mathematical representation of an array structure. This transformation is one of data reification, which transforms data types appearing in an abstract specification into the types that a computer can handle easily and efficiently. Some new operators occur in the concrete specification. The operator "dom" means the domain of the map and "$A \oplus \{x \mapsto a\}$" generates a new map that is the same as A except $A(x) = a$. The operator "$\lhd$" is called domain restriction and the expression "$\{a\} \lhd A$" is the map that is the same as A except that a is removed from the domain of A.

The aim of proof obligations is to provide the logical formulas that should be mathematically proved in order to guarantee that the concrete specification satisfy the abstract specification. At the first step of constructing proof obligations, we establish the relationship between the states represented with the concrete specification and those of the abstract specification. Let the set of the states of the concrete specification and the states of the abstract one be $State\_c$ and $State\_a$ respectively. We define the function called *retrieve function* for corresponding the states of the concrete specification to those of the abstract one, i.e.,

$$retrieve : State\_c \mapsto State\_a$$

In the stack example, we can have the following retrieve function.

$$\begin{aligned}
&retrieve : ((\mathbb{N} \twoheadrightarrow ITEM) \times \mathbb{N}) \mapsto \text{seq}\, ITEM \quad \text{(declaration of the signature)}\\
&retrieve\ (elements_c, 0) = \langle\ \rangle\\
&retrieve\ (elements_c, index + 1)\\
&\qquad = \langle elements_c\ (index)\rangle ^\frown retrieve\ (elements_c, index)
\end{aligned}$$

The proof obligations imposed on this data reification transformation are as follows:

(1) **Correspondence of the initial states:**
An initial state defined in the concrete specification $(init\_S_c(State\_c))$ should correspond to the initial state in the abstract one $(init\_S_a(State\_a))$.

$$\frac{\begin{array}{l} State\_a = retrieve\ (State\_c) \\ init\_S_c\ (State\_c) \end{array}}{init\_S_a\ (State\_a)}$$

(2) **Suitability of the retrieve function:**
The retrieve function should be suitable. More concretely, for each state of the abstract specification there exists the states of the concrete specification that can represent it.

$$\frac{}{\exists\, State\_c \cdot (retrieve(State\_c) = State\_a)}$$

On account of simplicity, we omit the descriptions about the domains of the variables appearing in the rules.

These proof obligations are described in schematic form and we can instantiate them for the stack example as follows:

(1) **Correspondence of the initial states:**

$$\frac{\begin{array}{l} sa : seq\ ITEM \\ f : \mathbb{N} \twoheadrightarrow ITEM \\ i : \mathbb{N} \\ f = \phi \\ i = 0 \\ sa = retrieve(f, i) \end{array}}{sa = \langle\ \rangle}$$

(2) **Suitability of the retrieve function:**

$$\frac{sa : seq\ ITEM \quad \text{(the domain expression about variable } sa)}{\exists\, i : \mathbb{N}\ f : (\mathbb{N} \twoheadrightarrow ITEM) \cdot (retrieve(f, i) = sa)}$$

To show the correctness of this transformation, i.e., that data of sequence type are implemented with array type (rigorously, map type), we should prove the above two proof obligations. We can use the axioms and inference rules specific to data types, like structural induction, in addition to a usual axiomatic system of predicate logic. We introduce a brief proof of the example proof obligation.

(1) **Correspondence of the initial states**
In the hypothesis of the proof obligation, we can get $retrieve(\phi, 0)$ by $f = \phi$ and $i = 0$. And furthermore we can rewrite the term $retrieve(\phi, 0)$ by using the definition of *retrieve*, and get $\langle\ \rangle$ as its result immediately. Thus $sa = retrieve(\phi, 0) = \langle\ \rangle$.

(2) **Suitability of the retrieve function**
We use the structural induction of sequence type. That is, we prove that the obligation holds in the case of $sa = \langle\,\rangle$ first. And then we prove the obligation in the case of $sa = \langle j \rangle ^\frown sa'$ for any $j : ITEM$, under the assumption that it holds in the case of $sa = sa'$, i.e., under the assumption $\exists\, f', i' \cdot (sa' = retrieve(f', i'))$.

   (a) (Case 1) Assume $sa = \langle\ \rangle$. We have $retrieve(\phi, 0) = \langle\ \rangle$. By this, we can show the existence of f, i by supposing $f = \phi$ and $i = 0$.

   (b) (Case 2) Assume that there is a f', i' such that $sa' = retrieve(f', i')$.

$$\begin{array}{l} retrieve(f' \oplus \{i' \mapsto j\}, i' + 1) \\ \quad = \langle (f'^\frown \{i' \mapsto j\})(i') \rangle ^\frown retrieve(f', i') \\ \qquad \text{by the definition of } retrieve \\ \quad = \langle j \rangle ^\frown sa' \\ \qquad \text{by the definition of } \oplus \end{array}$$

   By supposing $f = f' \oplus \{i' \mapsto j\}$ and $i = i' + 1$, we can show the existence of f and i in the case of $sa = \langle j \rangle ^\frown sa'$ for any $j : ITEM$.

The proof has been done rigorously and precisely in the same way as a proof in mathematical logic.

In addition, we have proof obligations for operation refinement, another type of transformation, and the readers can find the complete descriptions of these rules in [13] and [81], and proof examples in [12].

3. What Do FDTs Bring Us?

What do we get and what do we lose when we use FDTs in software development projects? According to many case studies and assessments of FDTs through the experiences in applying FDTs to practical projects have been done up to now, the merits and the demerits of the current FDTs are being clearer. In this section, based on many reports of the case studies, we summarize them and discuss the merits and the demerits of FDTs. The readers can find more experience reports in [1], the investigation of the industry experiences in [27], and the debate on FDTs in [15].

3.1. *Positive side*

Verification and Validation:

A number of success stories in applying FDTs to real and practical development projects have been reported, and in particular, in many projects, to verify or to validate the correctness of source codes and/or the consistency of specifications, FDTs were applied and the artifacts of higher quality were produced. One of the famous success stories could be found in the application to a metro train control system in Paris. The first trial of applying the B method [66], based on Hoare Logic technique, to the metro train control system was presented in [21]. A development team tried mathematical proofs to show the partial correctness of the source code fragments to its specification. These kinds of efforts have been continued and been applied to the metro line that was recently constructed in Paris [8]. The development team used the B method to develop an automatic pilot and signaling system for metro trains, which was safety-critical software. From natural-language documents, the team constructed an abstracted model using the B language and the abstract model consisted of 11,600 lines of the B statements. The team refined it to a concrete model together with proving proof obligations, and finally has got an Ada program with 86,000 lines. The lemmas that had to be proved was 27,800 and 81% of them could be automatically produced by means of the proof obligation rules. In another project in related to train control systems, RAISE (Rigorous Approach to Industrial Software Engineering) [43] was successfully applied in order to specify and to verify the algorithm for keeping safety in a German distributed railway control system [48]. In addition to the above work, we can find many experience reports of applying FDTs to safety-critical systems, e.g. air traffic control for avoiding collisions [49], and to nuclear generation control. The other successful application domains of FDT are telecommunication systems, embedded systems

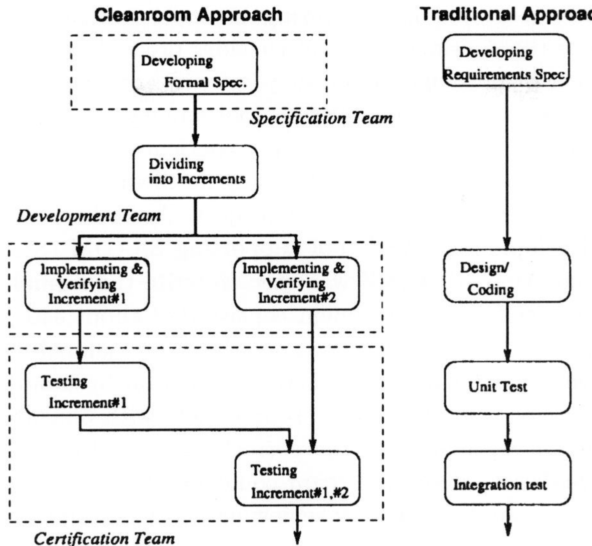

Fig. 3. Cleanroom approach.

such as control modules of oscilloscopes [30], information systems including data base systems[47], power plant controls, monitoring systems, user interface systems, banking systems [17] and so on [22, 51].

In Cleanroom approach [68] of IBM, the specification of a system is modeled based on Stimulus-Response model and formally described by a specific team called specification team. After describing the specification, it is divided into smaller segments called increments, and for each increment a development team designs and codes it. Furthermore the team verifies whether the code of the increment is satisfied with its specification or not. Another team called certification team performs the integration test of the developed codes with statistical techniques and incrementally integrate them toward a final artifact. The flow of Cleanroom approach is illustrated in Fig. 3. Linger investigated the 15 development projects that used Cleanroom approach, and found that there were, on average, only 3.3 errors/KLOC included in the artifacts in the testing stage of the development processes. The artifacts that were developed with conventional approaches included from 30 to 50 errors/KLOC in the testing stage, and the comparison of these numerical data suggested that Cleanroom approach played a significant role of producing artifacts of high quality [67].

Review:

Besides the mathematical verification or validation of specifications and/or codes, the documents written in FDTs are useful to find errors by hand through review and walkthrough-check processes. FDTs have much effect on finding ambiguous points in a customers' requirements and on recognizing misunderstanding of the specification developers, because the developers should consider precisely and seriously the details of the system to be developed when they write its specification. And FDTs can be used as an unambiguous communication tool among various kind of engineers in the development project. We introduce an experience of the project in which a FDT was used but the developers did not do any mathematical proofs for verifying the consistency of the specification in the project. According to [46], the CASE project was for developing a CASE tool supporting SSADM (Structured System Analysis and Design Method) and Z was used to write the formal specification in the project. The Z specification document consisted of about 340 pages (including comments) and included about 280 operations that were defined with about 550 Z schemas. The development team constructed a program by hand from this specification and finally got the Objective C source code with 58,000 lines. Although neither mathematical verification of the correctness of the code nor mathematical program synthesis was done, the team could find many errors resulting from misunderstanding the requirements, by reviewing the Z descriptions.

Cost Benefits:

The development costs in a specification stage is sometimes increasing when FDTs are used, because extra costs such as the cost for training engineers should be spent. According to [46], however we can reduce the total costs of software development processes, because we can avoid the repetition of debugging, modifying and rewriting specification documents. A notable case study on cost benefit of FDTs has been reported in [63]. The case study was on developing a system for aiding the landing and taking-off operations of helicopters on ships, and the developers wrote the Z specifications and used a subset of Ada for its implementation. They carried out about 150 proofs on the Z specifications and verified approximately 9000 conditions on the codes. Its comparative analysis with the conventional testing showed that these proofs were more efficient in detecting faults as early as possible rather than testing.

3.2. *Negative side*

Difficulty in understanding and writing formal specification:

Although it is simpler to understand and to write formal specifications than programs because the formal specifications are written in more abstract level than the programs [46], it is difficult to write complete and correct specifications. Some experience works reported that the existing formal specifications included errors or were of low quality [2, 77], and that even for experienced persons it was difficult to read formal specifications [37]. Mathematical proofs by hand are also difficult, and readers can find through the presented reports that the developers have made mistakes on their proofs and/or on the formulas that they set up as goals to be proved

[46]. Insufficient technology-transfer from research results to industries brings to the practitioners the difficulty in understanding formal specification [53].

Non-functional specification:

In spite of wider variety of the problem domains to which FDTs have been applied, FDTs define the functional aspects of the system only, but it is difficult to specify non-functional aspects such as reliability, portability, usability, maintainability, etc. Although some of FDTs like timed Petri net techniques can specify the system performance as timing constraints and offer its validation techniques such as simulation, specifying various kinds of non-functional aspects still remain one of the big problems.

Tool Support:

For automated or semi-automated supports of verification and validation, efficient algorithms of model checking, simulation and reasoning have been developed. However, they are not necessarily sufficient to be applied to large-scale and complicated systems in practical projects. The tools based on these techniques can partially assist in the developers' activities, but the developers should still have a great deal of labor, e.g. producing lemmas, thinking out the strategies of mathematical proofs, etc. Although complete automation would be impossible, the tools should provide the developers with the suitable guidance suggesting how to go on with the verification processes. Many FDT tools are independent on and isolated from the tools for the other steps of software development processes. Combining and integrating the FDT tools with the other tools are very important to get the seamless support of the whole of software development processes.

4. Where Will FDTs Go?

Extension of FDTs:

To extend the application domains, some syntactic constructs have been added to the existing FDTs. The typical extension is adding the constructs for describing timing parameters in order to specify real-time systems, e.g. Timed CSP [29], Timed LOTOS [14] etc. Some researchers have extended the time structure on temporal logic from discrete linear time [72] to branching time [35], time interval [3] and real-time [76]. Mobile systems become a new application domain of FDTs. π calculus is an extended version of CCS with parameterized communication channels for specifying behavior of mobile systems [75]. To model the mobile systems, the concepts of mobile units and their locations are significant and the FDTs that can specify them easily have been developed, such as Mobile UNITY [85].

The concepts of development methods or methodologies such as object-oriented methods are amalgamated to FDTs so that the writeability of FDTs could be improved. Object-oriented extension of FDTs, e.g. Object Z [33], VDM++ [65], CafeOBJ [39] (an object-oriented extension of the algebraic specification language OBJ with modularization constructs) and object-oriented Petri net like CO-OPN2 [18] are the examples. Computational reflection on a program is a mechanism to access and to modify its execution state which the interpreter has, and we can describe meta-level control of the execution in the same level of the source code. To specify exception handling in a communication system and the meta-level control of processes in an operating system comprehensively, the reflection mechanism was embedded into FDTs, e.g. RLOTOS [89].

Multi-paradigm Specification Techniques:

To specify both of system behavior and data, LOTOS has taken an approach of combining process algebra and many-sorted algebra. As the systems to be developed are more complicated, the FDTs that can express multiple aspects of the systems, i.e., multi-paradigm languages are much more necessary. Blending or combining the existing and resultful FDTs together is one of the easiest way to get a powerful multi-paradigm FDT. There are many researches on blending together the FDTs for describing static properties like constraints and data types and the FDTs for behavioral specifications, e.g. Z+ CSP [98], B+ CSP [20], Object Z+ Timed CSP [71], VDM+ process algebra [65], State Transition Machine + Attribute Grammar [32]. Note that if the combined descriptions have a certain overlap, inconsistency problems [78] appear, and these problems may also occur in the method integration technique which will be discussed later.

Integrating FDTs with Methods:

From technical view, the lack of methods or methodologies for FDTs is also one of serious disadvantages. One of the solutions to this disadvantage is integrating the existing methods like structured methods [31, 96] and object-oriented methods [86, 61] into FDTs and this is called method integration. And almost all of the methods produce diagrams as specifications that are easy for the developers to understand. We can find several work related to method integration [9, 64, 90] e.g. the integration of Object-Oriented Analysis and Z. And the work related to CASE tools supporting to these methods is also expected as the improvement of the current supporting environment of FDTs.

The artifacts like class diagrams of object-oriented methods express the static structure of the system and FDTs can specify the details of the system, even the dynamical aspect of the system. Thus developers construct a class diagram first, and then following the class diagram they refine the details by using a formal description technique such as Z. To achieve this kind of method integration, a transformational approach is applied, e.g. a class diagram is automatically transformed into the structure of Z schema [87] and the developers fill the slots of the generated *Z* schema to complete the formal specification.

The readers can find another type of integration in Fusion [24] and Syntropy [26]. In usual object-oriented methods, the operations that objects have are defined with natural language and their signatures are declared in a class diagram only. To describe the contents of the operations formally, VDM-like notation, i.e., pre- and post-conditions described with predicate logic, is blended instead of natural language in the above methods.

Debugging Formal Specifications and Prototyping:

Program slicing techniques [93] are to systematically extract the fragments that have high dependency to each other in a source code, and are used to identify which parts in the code include the bugs. To find the bugs included in formal specifications, the slicing techniques can be adapted to them. One of these adaptation examples is for Z descriptions [79]. Consistency checkers and visualizing tools as debuggers and simulators are also useful to write the consistent and correct formal specifications [50, 92].

Specification Patterns: Applying Software Reuse Techniques:

Reusing past good experiences is one of the promising approaches to construct an artifact of high quality. Conventional reuse techniques focus on reusable and modularized artifacts only, e.g. libraries of modules. Software patterns are a new technique for reusing not only reusable modules but also the combinations of modules, and various levels of patterns have been discovered and catalogued to Analysis Pattern [38], Design Pattern [40] etc. Requirements Apprentice was the first trial to elicit and to construct requirements specifications by using the pattern technique [84]. Recent work on the patterns related to FDTs involves the reuse from the viewpoint of proofs and verification activities; more concretely, one is the patterns of reusable proof strategies [28] and the other is the reusable specification patterns whose consistency has been already and successfully verified [34]. One of the dangerous points in reuse is that a developer can use the components even if they include the mismatches to the context [41].

Retrieving the components from a library and adapting them are one of the crucial topics of reuse technology. Signature matching techniques support the automated retrieval of reusable components [97]. In component-based development, it is necessary to check whether the selected components consistently fit to a software pattern or a framework and the readers can find some researches on formally modeling and defining design patterns and frameworks [88].

Informal, Semi-formal, vs Formal: Lightweight FDTs:

In [73], Meyer listed the shortcomings of specification documents written in natural language as the seven sins. In addition to ambiguity, lacking of descriptions, over-specifications and redundant descriptions sometimes appear in natural language specifications. He also argued that the usage of FDTs is effective to avoid these shortcomings. Furthermore, to improve the understandability of the formal descriptions, it is preferable that we should translate them into natural language descriptions, i.e., we use both of FDTs and natural language simultaneously.

Although formal descriptions have no ambiguity of their meaning, much more training and expertise are required for practitioners to read and to write them. As FDTs are more extended so as to have many complicated concepts, deeper knowledge is necessary to master them. The usage of diagrammatic languages such as UML [83] is one of the techniques to improve the readability and the writeability of the descriptions. However these languages are semi-formal in the sense that we cannot precisely describe the details of the system only with them. A lightweight approach is to restrict the application of FDTs and to formalize the specifications partially according to the application, while the existing FDTs emphasize their powerful expressive power and full formalization of the descriptions. In this sense, lightweight FDTs can be semi-formal. By making the FDTs lightweight, the cost of training practitioners and of automatically analyzing the specifications can be reduced [36]. Alloy [60] is a lightweight formal language to describe the structural properties of the system from an object-oriented view. It is based on Z and the complicated concepts of Z have been excluded to make it easier to use. As a result, it has very small syntax and the Alloy descriptions can be automatically analyzed with less efforts.

Software Architecture:

Recently many researchers, even practitioners, have applied FDTs to the descriptions of software architectures and architecture styles. Z was used for describing the static combinations of components and connectors [4], while π-calculus [70], chemical abstract machine [54] and Petri net [95] were applied to the behavioral specifications of the architectures. Formal architectural descriptions can provide the basis on assessing the performance of the architectures [16, 59] and the basis on conforming their quality [23]. These approaches can suggest how to deal with non-functional properties by using FDTs.

Specification-based Testing:

Roughly speaking, software testing can be divided into two categories; white box testing and black box testing. In white box testing, source codes are abstracted to the representations from control-dependency and/or data-dependency viewpoints, such as control graphs. Test cases for the codes are generated from the control graphs so that they cover the nodes, the edges and the paths of the graphs as many as possible. On the other hand, in black box testing, the developers analyze not source codes but specifications to generate the test cases. In some of FDTs, a formal specification can be transformed into a representation that abstractly expresses all of the system behavior like a finite state transition machine, a labeled transition system and a reachability tree. By tracking and analyzing this representation in the similar way to control graphs in white box testing approach, the test cases of high coverage can be generated [10, 69]. Boundary values analysis and equivalence partitioning technique on input and output data domains [82] are applicable for the specifications written in logical formulas or in mathematical functions.

Standardization

Since LOTOS was internationally standardized by ISO in 1989, other languages have been standardized or being standardized. The typical examples are Z and VDM. The standardization focuses not only on specifying the syntax of the languages, but also on defining their formal semantics and on preparing guidelines and textbooks to help in applying them into practical projects. Advancing standardization spurs on the usage of FDTs. In particular, we can expect that customers often request to include the usage of FDTs in their contracts of software development, in order to get the products of high quality.

References

1. Special Section on Formal Methods in Software Practice, *IEEE Transactions on Software Engineering* **24**, no. 1 (1998).
2. H. Alexander, "Comments on formal specification of user interfaces: A comparison and evaluation of four axiomatic approaches", *IEEE Transactions on Software Engineering* **14** (1988) 438–439.
3. J. Allen, "Maintaining knowledge about temporal intervals", *Communications of the ACM* **26**, no. 11 (1983) 832–843.
4. R. Allen and D. Garlan, "A formal basis for architectural connection", *ACM Transactions on Software Engineering and Methodology* **6**, no. 3 (1997) 213–249.
5. S. Antoy, "Systematic design of algebraic specifications", *Proceedings of 5th International Workshop on Software Specification and Design* (1989) 278–280.
6. J. C. Baeten and W. P. Weijland (eds.), *Process Algebra* (Cambridge, 1990).
7. R. Balzer, T. Cheatham and K. Green, "Software technology in the 1990's : Using a new paradigm", *Computer* **16**, no. 11 (1983) 39–45.
8. B. Behm, P. Benoit, A. Faivre and J.-M. Meynadier, "A successful application of B in a large project", *Lecture Notes in Computer Science* (*FM'99 — Formal methods*) ***1708*** (1999) 369–387.
9. D. Berry and M. Weber, "A pragmatic, rigorous integration of structural and behavioral modeling notations", *Proceedings of 1st International Conference on Formal Engineering Methods* (1997) 38–48.
10. A. Bertolino, F. Corradini, P. Inverardi and H. Muccini, "Deriving test plans from architectural descriptions", *Proceedings of the 22th International Conference on Software Engineering* (2000) 220–229.
11. A. Berztiss and S. Thatte, "Specification and implementation of abstract data types", *Advances in Computers* **22** (1983) 295–353.
12. J. C. Bicarregui (ed.), *Proof in VDM: Case Studies* (Springer-Verlag, 1997).
13. J. C. Bicarregui, J. S. Fitzgerald, P. A. Lindsay, R. Moore and B. Ritcchie, *Proof in VDM: A Practitioner's Guide* (Springer-Verlag, 1994).
14. T. Bolognesi, F. Lucidi and S. Trigila, "From timed petri nets to timed LOTOS", *Protocol Specification, Testing, and Verification* **X** (1990) 395–408.

15. J. Bowen, R. Butler, D. Dill, R. Glass, D. Gries, A. Hall, M. Hinchey, C. Holloway, D. Jackson, C. Jones, M. Lutz, D. Parnas, J. Rushby, J. Wing and P. Zave, "An invitation to formal methods", *Computer* **29**, no. 4 (1996) 16–30.
16. G. Bricconi, E. Di Nitto and E. Tracanella, "Issues in analyzing the behavior of event dispatching systems", *Proceedings of the 10th International Workshop on Software Specification and Design* (2000) 95–104.
17. M. Buchi, "The B bank : A complete case study", *Proceedings of the Second IEEE International Conference on Formal Engineering Methods* (1998).
18. D. Buchs and N. Guelfi, "A formal specification framework for object-oriented distributed systems", *IEEE Transactions on Software Engineering* **26**, no. 7 (2000) 635–652.
19. R. M. Burstall and J. A. Goguen, "An informal introduction to specifications using CLEAR", eds. R. S. Boyer and J. S. Moore, *The Correctness Problem in Computer Science* (Academic Press, 1981) 185–213.
20. B Butler, "csp2B: A practical approach to combining CSP and B", *Lecture Notes in Computer Science (FM'99 – Formal methods)* ***1708*** (1999) 490–508.
21. M. Carnot, C. DaSilva, B. Dehbonei and F. Meija, "Error-free software development for critical systems using the B-methodology", *Proceedings of 3rd International Symposium on Software Reliability Engineering* (1992).
22. E. Clarke and J. Wing, "Formal methods: State of the art and future directions", *ACM Computing Surveys* **28**, no. 4 (1996) 626–643.
23. P. Clements, L. Bass, R. Kazman and G. Abowd, "Predicting software quality by architecture-level evaluation", *Proceedings of the 5th International Conference on Software Quality* (1995).
24. D. Coleman, P. Arnold, S. Bodoff, C. Dollion, H. Gilchrist, F. Hayes and P. Jeremaes, *Object-Oriented Development: The Fusion Method* (Prentice-Hall, 1994).
25. R. L. Constable *et al*, *Implementing Mathematics with the Nuprl Proof Development System* (Prentice-Hall, 1986).
26. S. Cook and J. Daniels, *Designing Object Systems: Object-Oriented Modeling with Syntropy* (Prentice-Hall, 1994).
27. D. Craigen, S. Gerhart and T. Ralston, "Formal methods reality check: Industrial usage", *IEEE Transactions on Software Engineering* **21**, no. 2 (1995) 90–98.
28. R. Darimont and A. van Lamsweerde, "Formal refinement patterns for goal-driven requirements elaboration", *Proceedings of the 4th ACM SIGSOFT Symposium on Foundation of Software Engineering* (1996) 179–190.
29. J. Davies, *Specification and Proof in Real-Time CSP* (Cambridge University Press, 1993).
30. N. Delisle and D. Garlan, "A formal specification of an oscilloscope", *IEEE Software* **27**, no. 5 (1990) 29–36.
31. T. DeMarco, *Structured Analysis and System Specification* (Yourdon Press, 1978).
32. S. Ding and T. Katayama, "Specifying reactive systems with attributed finite state machines", *Proceedings of the 7th International Workshop on Software Specification and Design* (1993) 90–99.
33. R. Duke, P. King, R. Rose and G. Smith, "The Object-Z specification language", Technical Report 91-1, Software Verification Center, University of Queensland (1991).
34. M. Dwyer, G. Avrunin and J. Corbett, "Patterns in property specifications for finite-state verification", *Proceedings of 21th International Conference on Software Engineering* (1999) 411–420.
35. E. Emerson and J. Halpern, "Sometime and not never revisited: On branching versus linear time temporal logic", *Journal of the ACM* **33**, no. 1 (1986) 151–178.

36. M. Feather, "Rapid application of lightweight formal methods for consistency analyses", *IEEE Transactions on Software Engineering* **24**, no. 11 (1998) 949–959.
37. K. Finney, "Mathematical notation in formal specification: Too difficult for the Masses?", *IEEE Transactions on Software Engineering* **22**, no. 2 (1996) 158–159.
38. M. Fowler, *Analysis Patterns: Reusable Object Models* (Addison-Wesley, 1997).
39. K. Futatsugi and A. Nakagawa, "An overview of CAFE specification environment: An approach for creating, verifying and maintaining formal specification over networks", *Proceedings of the 1st IEEE International Conference on Formal Engineering Methods* (1997) 170–181.
40. E. Gamma, R. Helm, R. Johnson and J. Vlissides, *Design Patterns: Elements of Reusable OO Software* (Addison-Wesley, 1995).
41. D. Garlan, R. Allen and J. Ockerbloom, "Architectural mismatch: Why reuse is so hard?", *IEEE Software* **12**, no. 6 (1995) 17-26.
42. J. A. Goguen "Parameterized programming", *IEEE Transactions on Software Engineering* **10**, no. 5 (1984) 528–543.
43. The RAISE Method Group, *The RAISE Development Method* (Prentice-Hall, 1995).
44. J. V. Guttag and J. J. Horning, *Larch: Languages and Tools for Formal Specification* (Springer-Verlag, 1993).
45. J. V. Guttag, E. Horowitz and D. R. Musser, "Abstract data types and software validation", *Communication of the ACM* **21**, no. 12 (1978) 1048–1064.
46. A. Hall, "Seven myths of formal methods", *IEEE Software* **7**, no. 5 (1990) 11–19.
47. A. Hall, "Using formal methods to develop an ATC information system", *IEEE Software* **12**, no. 6 (1996) 66–76.
48. A. Haxthausen and J. Peleska, "Formal development and verification of a distributed railway control system", *IEEE Transactions on Software Engineering* **26**, no. 8 (2000) 687–701.
49. M. Heimdahl and N. Leveson, "Completeness and consistency in hierarchical state-based requirements", *IEEE Transactions on Software Engineering* **22**, no. 6 (1996) 363–377.
50. C. Heitmeyer, R. Jeffords and B. Labaw, "Automated consistency checking of requirements specifications", *ACM Transactions on Software Engineering and Methodology* **5**, no. 3 (1996) 231–261.
51. M. Hinchey and J. Bowen (eds.), *Applications of Formal Methods* (Prentice-Hall, 1995).
52. C. A. R. Hoare, *Communicating Sequential Processes* (Prentice-Hall, 1985).
53. C. A. R. Hoare, "The role of formal techniques: Past, current and future or how did software get so reliable without proof?", *Proceedings of the 18th International Conference on Software Engineering* (1996) 233–234.
54. P. Inverardi and A. Wolf, "Formal specification and analysis of software architectures using the chemical abstract machine model", *IEEE Transactions on Software Engineering* **21**, no. 4 (1995) 373–386.
55. ISO 8807, "Information processing systems — Open systems interconnection — LOTOS — A formal description technique based on the temporal ordering of obsevational behaviour" (1989).
56. ISO 9074, "Information processing systems — Open systems interconnection — Estelle — A formal description technique based on an extended state transition model" (1989).
57. ISO/IEC JTC1/SC22 N1982, "Information technology — Programming languages, their environments and system software interfaces", Z Notation (1995).

58. ISO/ITC DIS 13817, "Information technology — Programming languages, their environments and system software interfaces", Vienna Development Method (1995).
59. P. Inverardi, C. Mangano, F. Rosso and S. Balsamo, "Performance evaluation of a software architecture: Case study", *Proceedings of Ninth International Workshop on Software Specification and Design* (1998) 116–125.
60. D. Jackson, "Alloy: A lightweight object modelling notation", Technical Report, MIT Laboratory for Computer Science (2000).
61. I. Jacobson, G. Booch and J. Rumbaugh, *The Unified Software Development Process* (Addison Wesley, 1999).
62. C. B. Jones, *Systematic Software Development Using VDM* (Prentice-Hall, 1986).
63. S. King, J. Hammond, R. Chapman and A. Pryor, "Is proof more cost-effective than testing?", *IEEE Transactions on Software Engineering* **26**, no. 8 (2000) 675–686.
64. K. Kronlöf (ed.), *Method Integration — Concepts and Case Studies* (Wiley, 1993).
65. K. Lano, *Formal Object-Oriented Development* (Springer-Verlag, 1995).
66. K. Lano, *The B Language and Method: A Guide to Parctical Formal Development* (Springer, 1996).
67. R. C. Linger "Cleanroom software engineering for zero-defect software", *Proceedings of 15th International Conference on Software Engineering* (1993) 2–13.
68. R. C. Linger, "Cleanroom process model", *IEEE Software* **11**, no. 2 (1994) 50–58.
69. I. MacColl, L. Murray, P. Strooper and D. Carrington, "Specification-based class testing: A case study", *Proceedings of the Second IEEE International Conference on Formal Engineering Methods* (1998).
70. J. Magee, J. Kramer and D. Giannakopoulou, "Software architecture directed behaviour analysis", *Proceedings of Ninth International Workshop on Software Specification and Design* (1998) 144–145.
71. B. Mahony and J. Dong, "Timed Communicating Object Z", *IEEE Transactions on Software Engineering* **26**, no. 2 (2000) 150–177.
72. Z. Manna and A. Pnueli, *The Temporal Logic of Reactive and Concurrent Systems* (Springer-Verlag, 1992).
73. B. Meyer, "On formalism in specifications", *IEEE Software* **2**, no. 1 (1985) 6–26.
74. R. Milner, *Communication and Concurrency* (Prentice-Hall, 1989).
75. R. Milner, *Communicating and Mobile Systems: The pi-Calculus* (Cambridge University Press, 1999).
76. A. Morzenti, D. Mandrioli and C. Ghezzi, "A model parametric real-time logic", *ACM Transactions on Programming Languages and Systems* **14**, no. 4 (1992) 521–573.
77. M. Neil, G. Ostrolenk, M. Tobin and M. Southworth, "Lessons from using Z to specify a software tool", *IEEE Transactions Software Engineering* **24**, no. 1 (1998) 15–23.
78. B. Nuseibeh, J. Kramer and A. Finkelstein "A framework for expressing the relationship between multiple views in requirements specifications", *IEEE Transactions on Software Engineering* **20**, no. 10 (1994) 760–773.
79. T. Oda and K. Araki, "Specification slicing in formal methods of software development", *Proceedings of 17th International Computer Software and Applications Conference* (1993) 313–319.
80. J. L. Peterson, *Petri Net Theory and the Modeling of Systems* (Prentice-Hall, 1981).
81. B. Potter, J. Sinclair and D. Till, *An Introduction to Formal Specification and Z* (Prentice-Hall, 1996).
82. R. S. Pressman, *Software Engineering: A Practitioner's Approach*, 3rd ed. (McGraw-Hill, 1992).
83. Rational, *Unified Modeling Language 1.01* (1997).

84. R. Reubenstein and R. Waters, "The requirements apprentice: Automated assistance for requirements acquisition", *IEEE Transaction on Software Engineering* **17**, no. 3 (1991) 226–240.
85. G.-C. Roman, P. McCann and J. Plun, "Mobile UNITY: Reasoning and specification in mobile computing", *ACM Transactions on Software Engineering and Methodology* **6**, no. 3 (1997) 250–282.
86. J. Rumbaugh, M. Blaha, W. Premerlani, F. Eddy and W. Lonrensen, *Object-Oriented Modeling and Design* (Prentice-Hall, 1991).
87. S. Saeeiab and M. Saeki, "Method integration with formal description techniques", *IEICE Transactions on Information and Systems* **E83-D**, no. 4 (2000) 616–626.
88. M. Saeki, "Behavioral specification of GOF design patterns with LOTOS", *Proceedings of 7th Asia-Pacific Software Engineering Conference* (2000) 408–415.
89. M. Saeki, T. Hiroi and T. Ugai, "Reflective Specification: Applying a reflective language to formal specification", *Proceedings of the 7th International Workshop on Software Specification and Design* (1993) 204–213.
90. D. Scholz and C. Petersohn, "Towards a formal semantics for an integrated SA/RT & Z specification language", *Proceedings of 1st International Conference on Formal Engineering Methods* (1997) 28–37.
91. J. M. Spivey, *The Z Notation — A Reference Manual* (Prentice-Hall, 1987).
92. J. Thompson, M. Heimdahl and S. Miller, "Specification-based prototyping for embedded systems", *Lecture Notes in Computer Science (Proceedings of ESEC/FSE'99)* ***1687*** (1999) 163–179.
93. M. Weiser, "Program slicing", *Proceedings of 5th International Conference on Software Engineering* (1981) 439–449.
94. J. M. Wing, "A specifier's introduction to formal methods", *Computer* **23**, no. 9 (1990) 8–24.
95. W. Wu and M. Saeki, "Specifying software architectures based on coloured petri nets", *IEICE Transactions on Information and Systems* **E83-D**, no. 4 (2000) 701–712.
96. E. Yourdon and L. L Constantine, *Structured Design: Fundamentals of a Discipline of Computer Program and Systems Design* (Prentice-Hall, 1979).
97. A. Zaremski and J. Wing, "Signature matching: A tool for using software libraries", *ACM Transactions on Software Engineering and Methodology* **4**, no. 2 (1995) 146–170.
98. P. Zave and M. Jackson, "Where do operations come from? Multiparadigm specification technique", *IEEE Transactions on Software Engineering* **22**, no. 7 (1996) 508–528.

SOFTWARE SPECIFICATION & DESIGN METHODS AND METHOD ENGINEERING

MOTOSHI SAEKI

Department of Computer Science, Tokyo Institute of Technology, Ookayama 2-12-1, Meguro-Ku, Tokyo 152-8552, Japan

This article summarizes the state of the art in software specification & design methods, which assist developers in constructing the models of the problem domain and of the system and in writing requirements and design specifications. The typical methods such as structured methods and object-oriented methods are summarized. The new discipline called "Method Engineering", engineering for constructing methods, is briefly presented.

Keywords: Specification, structured methods, object-oriented method, UML, method engineering.

1. Introduction

Software development can be considered as activities for composing various kinds of documents, e.g. requirements specifications, design specifications, source codes, test documents, reference manuals and so on, and we have many kinds of description notations and formats for these documents, e.g. natural language, structured natural language, tables, diagrams, and formal languages having rigorous syntax rules and semantics. As software-intensive systems being developed are larger and more complicated, how to write these documents of high quality becomes one of the most crucial problems. In particular, the techniques to abstract and model the essential information of the systems and their environments are the most significant in order to write the documents. Methods or methodologies (we simply use the term "methods" from now on) offer the guides for modeling the systems and environments, more concretely guiding the developers in what kind of artifacts or documents they should produce and in what activities they should perform in what order. It is frequently said that the meaning of the term "methods" is very similar to the recipes of cooking or cooking books. Recipes specify the procedures of cooking and the foods. For example, one of them says "you boil spaghetti of 200 g, and then you put the boiled and mashed tomato on it, ... you can get spaghetti with tomato sauce". The recipes guide what food you produce from what materials and how you do that. Methods can be considered as some version of recipes for software development. Although we have methods for each stage of development processes, in this article, we will survey the methods for requirements analysis and design stages. The reason is that these two stages have much effect on development costs and on the quality of the products. In addition, we will introduce a new engineering discipline called "Method Engineering" and it can be considered as a significant future research direction on specification & design methods.

Note the usage of the word "Methodology". It has two meanings; one is "a collection of methods" and the other one is a discipline related to methods [7]. In this article, to avoid this ambiguity, the word "methodology" is not used except for the trade names of the specific methods. Instead, we write "methods", "a collection of methods", "a family of methods" if we intend to express "a set of methods" instead of Methodology.

2. What are Methods?

2.1. *An example of methods*

Several methods for constructing requirements and design specifications have been developed and put into practice in the past twenty years. These methods, so called software specification and design methods provide the developers with the guidelines in modeling the problem domains and the systems and in documenting the models as specifications. Let's illustrate a simple example of a method. Following Coad & Yourdon's Object-Oriented Analysis Method (OOA) [12], the method for requirements analysis phase, we perform a sequence of activities shown in Table 1 and produce a set of intermediate artifacts. The artifact that we can get finally is called class diagram and its example is depicted in Fig. 1.

Similar to a cooking recipe, the readers can find that the technical terms such as "Class", "Attribute", and "Aggregation" appear in the description of the OOA method. In the example of Fig. 1, "Lift" and "position" are a class and the attribute of the lifts respectively, and "Motor" has an aggregation relationship to "Lift". Unless we know the meaning of these method-specific terms, we cannot use the method effectively or correctly.

We can classify the methods that have been proposed until the last five years, as shown in Table 2. Note that the table includes conventional methods only. The recent methods such as Unified Process will be discussed separately in Sec. 4

Table 1. An Example of a method : Coad & Yourdon's OOA.

	Activities	Artifacts
1	Identify the objects and classes in problem domain	List of the identified objects and classes
2	Identify the structure of the problem domain by using the identified objects and classes	Diagram depicting the relationships among the classes (a part of a class diagram)
3	Grouping the classes from a certain view into a subject	Diagram depicting groups of the classes
4	Define the attributes of the objects	a class diagram including the attributes
5	Define the services (operations) on the objects	a class diagram including the services (complete class diagram)

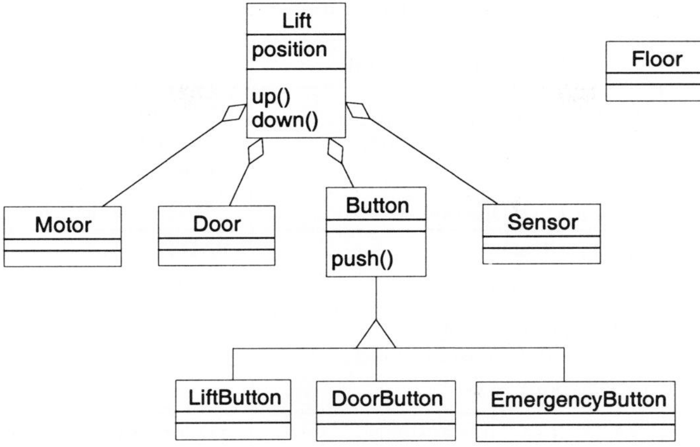

Fig. 1. Class diagram: UML notation.

because they have been derived from the conventional ones and can be considered as their integrated and evolved ones. In structured methods of the table, we focus on the function of the system to be developed, while in data oriented methods we mainly clarify what data the system manipulates. Most of methods adopt diagrammatic notation because of its high understandability and Fig. 2 summarizes the diagrams that are used in these methods.

2.2. *History of method evolution*

The history of methods begin with tackling the problem of how to write complicated programs. In the beginning of the 70's, structured programming [15] and the idea of modularization based on information hiding [45] were proposed. In the later 70's, many interests were on the methods for constructing specifications. The family of structured methods such as ISDOS [64], SREM [4] and SADT [50] were developed at that time, and they supported the construction of specification documents only, especially for business systems. In the 80's, the methods have evolved into ones so that they could support the whole of software development processes, i.e., the phases from requirements analysis to implementation. The typical example was Jackson Systems Development method (JSD) [32], which partially included the concept of object-orientation as mentioned later. The methods appeared in the 90's have two conspicuous features. The first one is that they took the concepts of object-orientation in, and the second is that they were the results of integrating the existing older methods. For example, Shlaer & Mellor's Object-Oriented Analysis, which was the first generation of object-oriented methods, can be considered as an integration of extended Entity Relation Diagram (Class Diagram), State Transition Diagram and Data Flow Diagram. Note that the readers can find the detailed descriptions of the conventional methods and their history from another perspective in [35].

Table 2. Classification of methods.

	Requirements Analysis	Design
Structured Method (Function & Behavior)	Structured Analysis (SA) (DeMarco, Gane & Sarson, Yourdon etc) : Data Flow Diagram	Structured Design (SD) (Yourdon & Constantine, Myers etc) : Module Structure Diagram
	SADT (Ross) : SADT Diagram	SADT : SADT Diagram
	ISDOS/PSL (Teichroew) : Entity Relationship Model (Diagram)	
	SA for Real-Time Systems (Hatley, Ward & Mellor, Harel etc) : Data Flow Diagram, Control Flow Diagram : State Transition Diagram (incl. State Chart)	SD for Real-Time Systems (Gomaa, Edwards etc) : Task Structure Diagram (Task Communication Diagram) : Module Structure Diagram
	SREM (Alford *et al*) : Extended Flow Chart (R_net)	
Object-Oriented (Object)	Object-Oriented Analysis (Shlaer & Mellor, Coad & Yourdon, Rumbaugh etc) : Class Diagram, Object Diagram : Data Flow Diagram, State Transition Diagram etc.	Object-Oriented Design (Booch, Coad & Yourdon, Rumbaugh, Wirfs-Brock etc) : Object Communication Diagram Class Diagram etc.
	Jackson System Development (JSD)(Jackson & Cameron)	
	: Entity Structure Diagram	: System Specification Diagram (Process Communication Diagram)
Data-Oriented (information)	Entity Relationship Model (Chen) : Entity Relationship Diagram	
	Information Modeling (Martin etc)	
	: Enterprise Model : Entity Relationship Model, Data Flow Diagram etc.	: Data Structure Diagram, Process Structure Diagram : Data Flow Diagram, Flow Chart (Action Diagram) etc.
	Data Structure Oriented Method (Warnier Method, Jackson Structured Programming)(Warnier, Jackson) : Data Structure Diagram (Jackson Tree)	

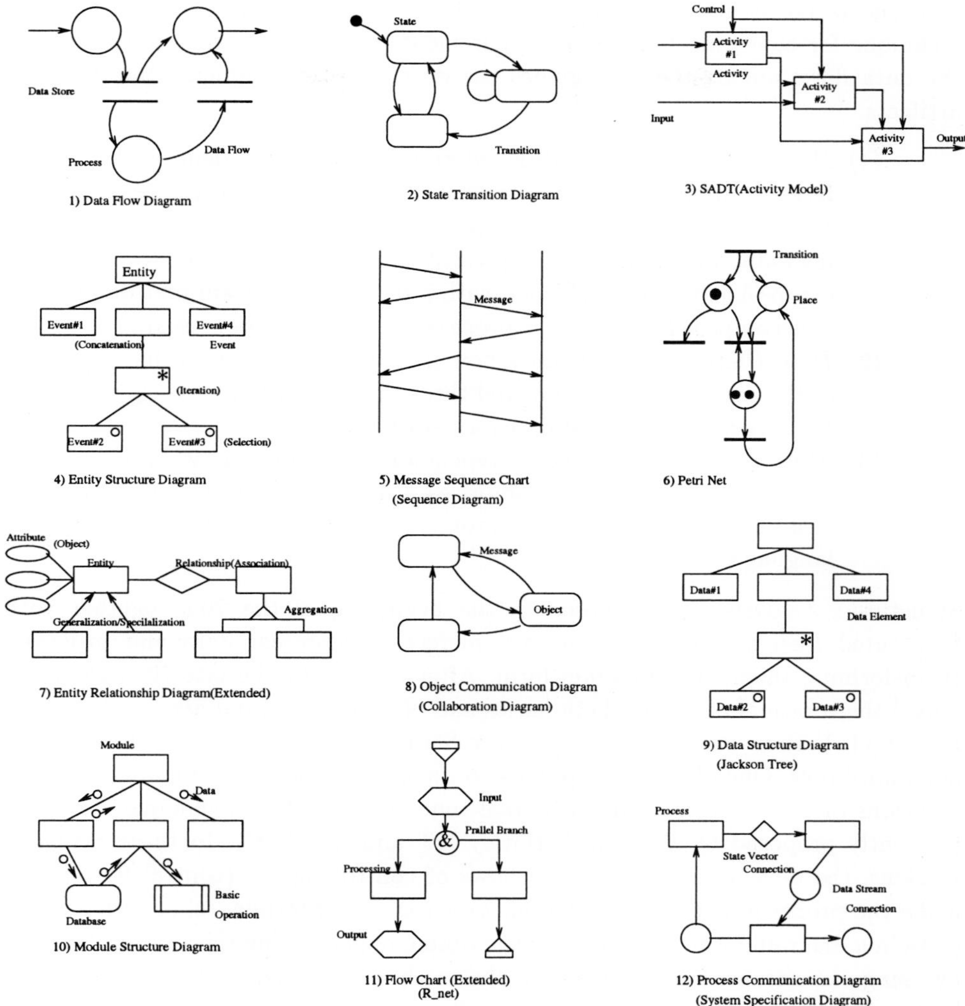

Fig. 2. Diagrams in methods.

In the subsequent sections, we select the typical and popular methods and discuss them. Although some of which we have selected may be outdated, they are frequently still used by practitioners or include significant idea that are adopted by modern methods such as Unified Process and Catalysis.

3. Conventional Methods

3.1. *Structured methods*

The typical examples of structured methods are the well known Structure Analysis and Design. Structured Analysis (SA) [14, 67] supports the phase of requirements analysis, while Structured Design is for design phase. Structured Analysis is a technique for capturing the system requirements with the system's functions and the data flows among them. It guides the developers in producing the following artifacts:

(1) *Data Flow Diagram*: A directed graph whose nodes denote either interfaces from/to external environments (called external entities, or source & sinks), the functions (called processes or bubbles), or data stores holding data, and whose edges represent data flows between nodes. A process can be hierarchically defined with a data flow diagram and its function is decomposed into smaller processes (called sub-processes).
(2) *Data Dictionary*: Each data flow in a data flow diagram has the name of the data which are conveyed through it. A data dictionary represents the structure of the data, i.e., a data type.
(3) *Mini-spec*: As a process is repeatedly decomposed, we can get sub-processes each of which comprises atomic operations only. Mini-specs describe the contents of an atomic operation with structured natural language.

Structured Analysis was proposed in the beginning of the 70's together with Structured Design. Its initial aim was merely to represent data and processes (transforming them) in a diagram form. After that, until the late 70's, DeMarco added the concepts of a data dictionaries and of mini-specs, and arranged them as a method. Various extensions to this basic Structured Analysis method have been done until now. One of the most popular ones is the embedding of state transition diagrams or state charts to describe real-time systems. This technique was independently proposed by Ward [65], Hatley [29] and Harel [25]. In these extended versions, the developers describe the flows of control signals (control flows) that make the processes activate (start their execution) and terminate, as well as data flows in a diagram form. They specify the timing of generating these control signals by using state transition diagrams. In the method proposed by Ward and Mellor [40], control flows are described in a data flow diagram, while in Hatley's method control flows are specified separately from the data flow diagram, i.e., in another diagram.

One of the most serious problems in describing the behavior of a complicated system with state transition diagrams is the explosion of states. Harel proposed a state chart, which has hierarchical decomposition mechanisms of states called AND/OR decomposition [23]. State charts can be used together with the specific diagrams called module charts and activity charts that represent the flows of data and control signals. However, although the technique of state charts has the powerful hierarchical decomposition mechanisms, it is not a method but a kind of language. Several methods adopted the state chart technique to specify the behavior of the system, e.g. OMT [52]. Some extensions to these state-transition based diagrams or nets, e.g. object-oriented extension like Object Chart [13] and O-Chart [24] for state charts, and like G-net [10] for Petri-nets also appeared. In a family of Structured Analysis, other formalisms that theoretically have more expressive power like Petri-nets can be used instead of state transition diagrams in order to define the behavioral aspects of the system such as true concurrency and hard real-time [47].

Structured Design (SD) [42, 68] is a top down design method for systematically mapping processes in a data flow diagram to program modules, and its aim is to offer the design with high modularity. Modularity means functional independence among the modules and we have two types of the measure of modularity; one is "cohesion" for measuring the intra-relation of the constituents in a module, and another is "coupling" for measuring the interrelation among modules.

Structured Design method contains transform analysis method and transaction analysis method. After structured design, we can get module structure charts that express a set of program modules, caller-callee relationships among the modules and the interfaces (input data and output data) of the modules.

In transform analysis, we divide the flow paths from data inputs to outputs into the following three categories:

(1) The part where the system transforms input data to internal representation.
(2) The essential part of the data transformation (called "transformation center").
(3) The part where the system transform the internal representation of the data to output formats.

Based on this classification, we group the processes into a module.

Some processes in a data flow diagram route and pass incoming data flows into one of many outgoing data flows. In transaction analysis, we focus on these "routing" processes and modularize the other processes so that they are called by the "routing" processes. The routing process is called "transaction center" and outgoing data flows are called "active paths". For each active path, we group into a module the processes on the path, and make the structure in which the module corresponding to the transaction center calls the module.

Gomaa *et al* extended Structured Design method to the method suitable for real-time systems DARTS (Design Methods for Real Time Systems) [22]. In the first step of DART, based on the data flow diagram, we divide the system into tasks and the tasks are units being executed concurrently. That is to say, we should consider which processes can be concurrently executed and which processes are sequentially executed, and should group the processes based on this consideration to the tasks. The second step is to design interfaces among the tasks. Next, for each of the identified tasks, we modularize the processes (which are executed sequentially) included in it, by using usual Structured Design method. The criteria and guidelines assisting in identifying tasks and in deciding task interfaces are included in DARTS. The reader can find another Structured Design method for real-time systems in [18] and in the method, entity relationship diagrams are used to design the structure of the information that is manipulated by the system. Recently, several methods for modeling and designing real-time systems based on object-orientation have been developed, such as ROOM [57].

3.2. *Jackson Systems Development (JSD)*

Jackson Systems Development (JSD) [32, 62] supports seamlessly the processes from requirements analysis to implementation phase. The idea of seamless support of the whole of software development processes is taken to the recent object-oriented methods. JSD consists of three phases to construct the systems which are solid to specification changes. In the first phase, we model the problem domain of the real world. The second phase is for adding functions to the constructed model, and we implement it according to the real execution environment in the third phase. These three phases are called Modeling phase, Network phase and Implementation phase respectively. In Modeling phase, we extract entities and events (actions) on the entities from the real world, and describe the event sequences on each entity with event sequence diagrams, which is shown in Fig. 2. This diagram is called Entity Structure Diagram. The concept of "Entity" in JSD is the same as "Object" in the family of object-oriented methods, except for super-subclass hierarchy. And after extracting the entities, the subsequent development activities are preformed based on the entities. For this reason, it was categorized into a family of object-oriented methods.

In Network phase, we consider the identified entities as the processes communicating concurrently with each other, called entity processes. We model both of the real world and the system and in this model, the entity processes of the real world concurrently interact with the processes denoting the system functions. Data passing between the processes is described with a kind of data flow diagram called System Specification Diagram. A system specification diagram has two types of data passing mechanisms based on control of data passing, i.e., whether a sender process or a receiver takes the initiative in controlling data passing; state vector connection and data stream connection. Through the several assessments of the user groups, JSD was extended to the method where the phase for making a plan is embedded and where the decomposition of processes into tasks is emphasized [38].

3.3. *Data-oriented methods*

In the family of data-oriented methods, we begin with the activity for capturing a problem domain with data and modeling the data. Information Modeling and Data Modeling methods, which are for database applications, model the data with entity relationship model [11]. The difference from object-oriented methods is that they model with entities the only objects that we can consider as data.

In some methods, we model the data structure with three data constructors; concatenation, selection and iteration at their first step. These methods are called data structure oriented methods and are for designing program modules from the specification of the data structure in a systematic way. In Jackson Structure Programming (JSP) [31], one of the typical examples of the data structure oriented methods, we analyze and model the structures of input data and output data with the constructors concatenation, selection and iteration, and describe them in the form of data structure diagram (called Jackson tree) shown in Fig. 2. After completing the two trees, one is for input data structure and the other one is for output data, we explore the relationship on the nodes between the two trees which should satisfy some constraints. The case that we cannot find the relationship is called Structure Crash, and if this case occurs, JSP provides several techniques, e.g. introducing an intermediate file, to solve structure crash.

Information Modeling proposed by Martin [39] is for developing the information system that all of the organizations in a business enterprise use. In this method, we plan what information is necessary in each organization and which techniques are applicable to solve the current problem in the enterprise, and construct an enterprise model. This first phase is called Information Strategy Planning. This enterprise model contains the organizational structure, the functions of the organizations, the information that the organizations use and the relationships among them (e.g. which functions use which information, and which organization manipulate the information). The model is represented with entity relationship diagrams. Based on the enterprise model, we construct data models and extract business processes. This second phase is called Business Area Analysis. The data model and the business processes are described with entity relationship diagrams and data flow diagrams respectively. The relationships among the business processes are frequently depicted with work flow diagrams, a kind of data and control flow diagrams. In the third phase, called System Design, we design the information system by refining these data models and business processes.

4. Object-Oriented Methods

4.1. *Overview*

The methods where we start capturing the problem domain or solution domain with "objects" are object-oriented methods. What is an object? Rumbaugh *et al* discussed that objects have three features: (1) Class concept, (2) Polymorphism, and (3) Inheritance [52]. Object-oriented methods make effective use of the above features to develop software-intensive systems. Many object-oriented analysis and design methods have been proposed and they have wide varieties of intermediate artifacts and of the activities for producing the artifacts. As will be mentioned later in Sec. 4.2, the notations of the artifacts that are produced in object-oriented methods are being standardized to Unified Modeling Language (UML).

In almost all of object-oriented methods, we begin with the activity for identifying objects in the problem domain or solution domain. The identified objects that have the same properties are abstracted to a class, and we represent the classes and their relationships (called association) with a class diagram. Although a class diagram can be considered as the extended version of an entity relationship diagram, some notations use specific symbols to express generalization-specialization relationship (is-a relationship, or super-subclass hierarchy) and aggregation relationship (has-a relationship), which are specific to object-oriented methods. The readers can find the comparison with various object-oriented methods, including the notation of class diagrams in [41].

After identifying objects and classes, the attributes of the objects, operations (services) on the objects, associations among the classes, and the behavior of the objects are identified and modeled. Some of them are added to the class diagram, while the others are defined with other diagrams, e.g. state transition diagrams (state charts or state diagrams in UML), data flow diagrams, activity flow charts (activity diagrams), message sequence charts (sequence diagrams), object communication diagrams (collaboration diagrams) and so on. For example, the behavior of the objects belonging to a class can be represented with a state transition diagram or a state chart.

4.2. *Unified Modeling Language* (*UML*)

There are wide varieties on how to write the diagrams and on what notation is used in the existing object-oriented methods. To aim at the standardization of the notation of artifacts, Rumbaugh's OMT [52], Booch's method [6] and Jacobson's OOSE [34] have been unified into UML (Unified Modeling Language) by these method creators themselves [49, 53]. UML has nine diagrams as shown in Table 3. Note that it is not a method but just a language where the concepts of the three methods, notation and its semantics are unified. It does not provide the guides to construct the UML artifacts, or does not suggest how to use and combine nine UML diagrams in development projects. As will be mentioned in Sec. 4.3, some methods based on UML have been developed and some textbooks [19] on the usage of UML diagrams have been published. At the first stage of their unification task, Rumbaugh, Booch and Jacobson of Rational had tried to unify their three methods. Although they could unify the notations of their diagrams, they gave up standardizing the other aspects such as procedures of constructing the diagrams. The readers can find the difficulty of the standardization of all aspects of methods including development procedures at this point. What kind of method is suitable for your project greatly depends on your development situation including development organizations and on your application domains, and it is very difficult to decide a unique and standard method that is suitable for any situation and domain. This fact motivates a new engineering discipline called Method Engineering, which will be introduced as a future direction in Sec. 5.

A use case diagram expresses what functions the system should have when we observe it from the external environments, and depicts use cases, actors and their relationships. A use case is an unit of a function, while an actor participates in the

Table 3. UML diagrams.

Static Structure	
Class Diagram	Identified classes and their static structure
Object Diagram	The objects existing at a moment and their relationships
Behavior and Function	
Use Case Diagram	Interactions between external components (actors) and the functions of the system
Sequence Diagram	Message sequences among the objects
Collaboration Diagram	Interactions and their sequences for the collaboration among the objects
State Diagram	The states and the state transitions that are allowable in the objects
Activity Diagram	Activity sequences in an interaction. Control flows in an interaction
Implementation	
Component Diagram	Physical components and their relationships in the system
Deployment Diagram	Allocation of executable components into resource parts of the system (computation nodes, memories, devices and so on).

use case, e.g. it invokes the use case and it passes and/or receives the data to/from the use case. Figure 3 illustrates the use case diagram of banking business. In the diagram, the occurrences of the symbol of "stick man" stand for actors, while the ovals are use cases. Note that an actor need not be a person alone. For example, we can take as an actor a hardware equipment such as a sensor and a disk system. Since a use case and an actor can be considered as a class, we can have some associations between them such as generalization-specialization. The figure expresses that bank staffs can be customers of the bank, i.e., the actor "bank clerk" is a subclass of "customer". The association "uses" means the usage of the description of another use case to define the use case. The description of a use case comprises its allowable activity sequences written in natural language, as shown in Fig. 4, and they present the behavior of the use case to the system and/or the actors.

Sequence diagrams and collaboration diagrams are used for the interaction among objects from behavioral view and Fig. 5 illustrates these examples. These diagrams represent which messages the objects pass to the others in what order. Sequence diagrams and collaboration diagrams are essentially the same as message sequence charts and object communication diagrams of Fig. 2 respectively. The

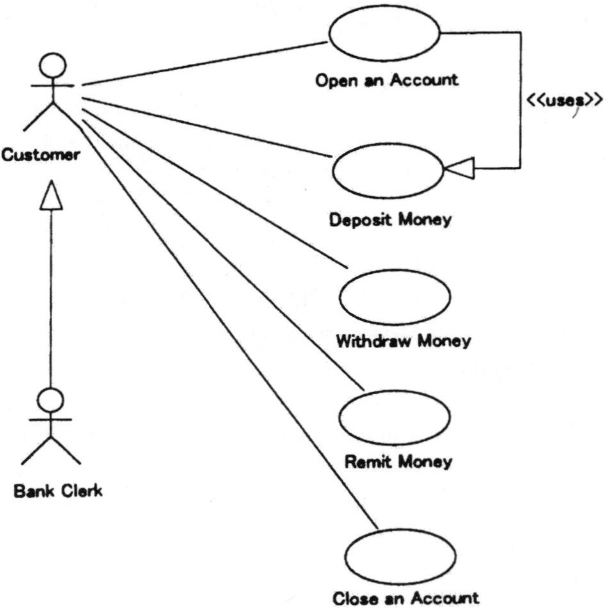

Fig. 3. Use case diagram.

Use Case Name: Open an Account
Actor: Customer (Person who will open an account)
Objective: Open an account and deposit money
Pre Condition: An actor should really exist.
Normal Sequence:

1. An actor fills an application form and hands in it with his seal.
2. The system checks whether the actor is the person himself.
3. The system makes a new bankbook for the actor.
4. The actor deposits money.
5. The system returns the seal and the bankbook to the actor.

Post Condition: The seal and the bankbook are in the actor's hand.
Alternate Sequence:

1. If the system cannot check or fail the check in the normal sequence 2, the system informs the actor that his bank account cannot be open, and finishes the activity.

Fig. 4. Use case description.

order of message passing can be specified with the numbers prefixed to the message names even in collaboration diagrams. Note that a sequence diagram or a collaboration diagram specifies a typical instance of behavior, i.e., a scenario, and the diagram does not define all of the allowable behavior of the system. If a developer likes to specify all of the behavior, he or she should use state diagrams (state charts) and/or activity diagrams. Activity diagrams are an extended version of flow charts so as to represent non-determinism and parallelism,

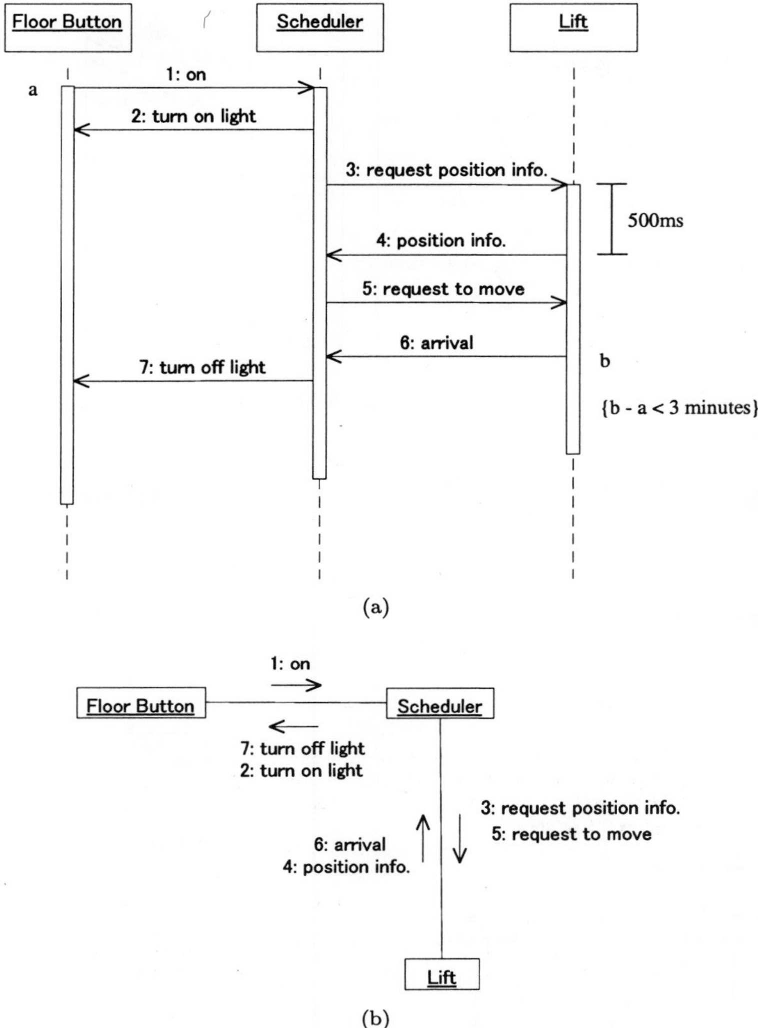

Fig. 5. Sequence diagram and collaboration diagram. (a) Sequence diagram and (b) Collaboration diagram.

and are very similar to R-nets in Fig. 2. They specify the execution order of the activities that are performed by the system. The constructs of activity diagrams include not only conditional branch but also parallel branch (for branching several activities that are performed in parallel) and guarded expressions (for selecting which activities can be performed next). State diagrams and/or activity diagrams can specify the behavior of an object or the total behavior of the system. In order to define the behavior of an object, we write a state diagram or an activity diagram for each object. Figures 6 and 7 illustrate the self-explanatory examples

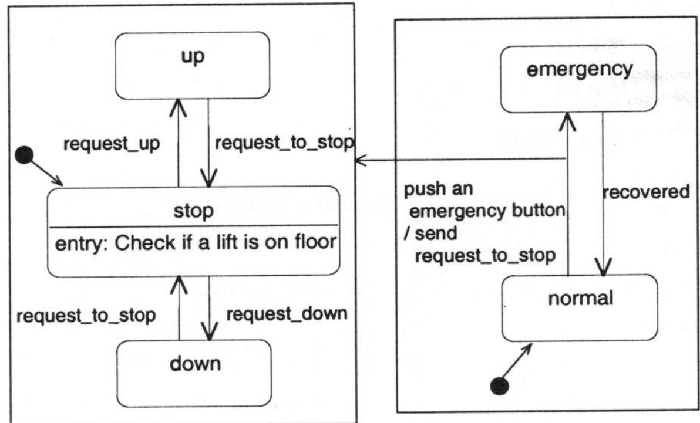

Fig. 6. State diagram.

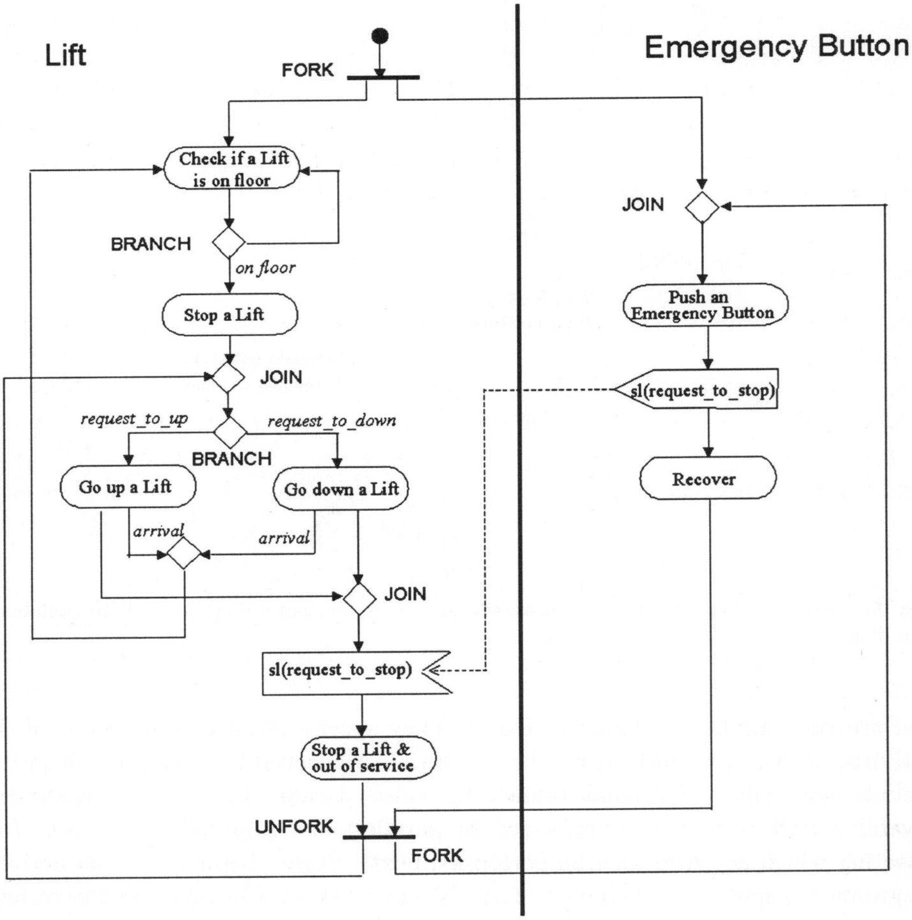

Fig. 7. Activity diagram.

and they specify the behavior of a lift object. The example of Fig. 6 consists of two state diagrams, which are decomposed with AND decomposition technique. In Fig. 7, the diagram is divided with two lanes, "Lift" and "Emergency Button", each of which specifies the object that is responsible for the execution of the activities in it.

Note that the original version of UML, version 0.8 and 1.0 [49] has been extended so that it has some syntactic constructs for describing real-time systems. Return back to the sequence diagram in Fig. 5. The readers can find that some timing constraints appear in the sequence diagram. For example, the timing constraint "$b - a < 3\ minutes$" presents that a lift must arrive within 3 minutes after the floor button is pushed, i.e., after a passenger requests a lift at the floor. The version of UML having these syntactic constructs for defining timing constraints was called Real-Time UML [16] and these constructs have been adopted in the recent version of UML, UML 1.3 [44] and upcoming UML 2.0. ROOM Language (Real-Time Object-Oriented Modeling Language) [57] can also be considered as an extension of UML, in the sense that the modeling concepts for real-time systems are added to a UML based language. In particular, it has the concepts "protocol", "port" and "connector" to explicitly represent the collaboration among the objects that are concurrently executed. Note that UML has met several criticisms, e.g. the weakness of UML use case model, and the readers can find them in [21].

4.3. *Methods based on UML*

As mentioned before, UML is just a language but not a method. Rational developed a method called Unified Process (the previous name is Objectory) [33], where UML is used. The features of Unified Process include (1) use case driven, (2) architecture centric, and (3) incremental and iterative development. A cycle of a development process consists of the four phases: (1) Inception (understanding customers' requirements and deciding the scope of the development), (2) Elaboration (developing a prototype of the executable architecture), (3) Construction (designing and implementing the system), and (4) Transition (fixing bugs and improving the quality). In each phase, the development activities are iterated and the artifact of the phase is incrementally made more complete. Each phase consists of nine common sequences of development activities, which are called process workflows. Which process workflows are mainly iterated depends on the phase. For example, in the early stage of Elaboration phase, business modeling, requirements definition, analysis, and design workflows are mainly iterated, while the iteration of these workflows decreases and the workflows for implementing a prototype is being increasingly performed as the phase progresses. Customers' requirements are described with use case diagrams and these use case descriptions are used in all phases. In addition, as Unified Process is called "Process Framework", it does not specify a method but recommends that it should be customized and adapted to actual development projects. Although Unified Process recommends the construction of a use case model (a use case diagram plus use case descriptions) and its usage at the subsequent phases for validating the products, in fact it is a quite difficult question which diagrams of UML should be constructed first. In some cases, to extract use cases and their activity sequences, a developer writes sequence diagrams before a use case diagram, and in the other cases, he or she constructs a set of sequence diagrams after constructing a use case diagram just to validate it. Developers, including project managers, should adapt the usage of UML diagrams to their development projects.

Catalysis [17] is also the method based on UML and it has syntactic constructs expressing reusable components such as frameworks and template packages in a diagram form. It also supports the activities for breaking down the developed object models into reusable components and for composing the reusable components into the model of the system.

4.4. *Assessment of object-oriented methods*

Many case studies in applying object-oriented methods to real development projects have been reported. Let's introduce one of the reports, which was done by Aksit *et al* [3]. They focused on twelve projects developing various kinds of systems, e.g. network database system, chemical process control, intelligent tutor system, distributed office system, programming environments for an object-oriented language, distributed operating system and so on, and analyzed the obstacles that have not been solved by the existing object-oriented methods. They classified the extracted obstacles into three categories: (1) obstacles when we capture the real world by objects, (2) obstacles on relationships among objects such as aggregation, generalization-specialization, etc and (3) obstacles on interactions among objects. One of the obstacles belonging to the first category is the difficulty in extracting a reusable structure from a problem domain. Recently, to tackle this problem, several results on cataloguing design patterns are appearing [20]. The mechanism of inheriting the attributes and the operations of a super class to its subclasses including overriding mechanism was too weak, and this shortcoming belongs to the second category of obstacles. The obstacles belonging to the third category were frequently detected in the analyzed case studies. The obstacles of the category were listed as follows. (1) Objects cannot be modeled from multiple views.[a] The concept of stereo type of UML is the suggestion to solve this obstacle. (2) The methods have no mechanisms to explicitly describe integrity constraints, transactions and inquiries that database systems have. As for describing constraints, UML has a specific language called OCL (Object Constraint Language) which is a kind of predicate logic, and it is used together with class diagrams. (3) The interaction mechanism

[a]For example, consider a teacher class and a student class. It is possible that an instance of the teacher class takes a lecture of another teacher. In this case, it is natural that the instance is considered as an instance of the student class. This example suggests that we need capture an instance as both a teacher view and a student view, i.e., from multiple views.

is message passing between two objects only, and the methods cannot define the abstract interactions in higher level. In particular, the problem of lacking the abstraction mechanism of object interactions were detected in six projects, half of the analyzed projects.

Almost all of methods belonging to a family of object-oriented methods use multiple diagrams. In particular, the static structure of the system is described with a class diagram completely separated from the behavioral aspects. OPM (Object Process Methodology) uses a single diagram that can depict the classes, the processes and the activities included in the system. According to the assessment, it seems to be comprehensive and effective for beginners such as students to develop small-sized real-time systems [46].

On account of space, we could introduce very few analytic results in applying the object-oriented methods to practical projects, but the readers can find the other analysis results in [1].

5. Method Engineering

5.1. *Overview*

Until now, many textbooks and instruction manuals of methods have been published, and their supporting tools, so called CASE tools have been commercially developed. In information technology industries, methods and supporting tools are putting into practice in actual development activities. However as the systems to be developed are larger and more complex, we spend much time and effort on applying the methods effectively in these development projects. One of the reasons is that the methods which are introduced in textbooks and manuals include some parts unsuitable for actual projects. Some methods work well in a specific problem domain, while they do not work well in other domains. For instance, it is pointed out that data flow diagrams are not suitable for developing real-time systems because they cannot represent system behavior. As mentioned in Structured Analysis for real-time systems, incorporating state transition diagrams is one of the solutions to this problem. In particular, considering software development for Internet and Web, we require the methods different from the conventional methods [30]. In this situation, the following question arises. Can we have a universal method that is suitable for every problem domain? The answer may be "No". The best and feasible solution of the above problem is that developers construct suitable methods for their problem domains and development environments. Method engineering is a discipline where the target of Engineering are methods themselves, e.g. to explore engineering techniques how to construct methods [37]. According to Brinkkemper [8], method engineering is "engineering discipline to design, construct and adapt methods, technique and tools for the development of information systems".

One of the simplest ways to construct methods is an approach based on "reuse". Meaningful constituents or parts of methods, called method fragments, are stored in a database called "method base". Special engineers called method engineers

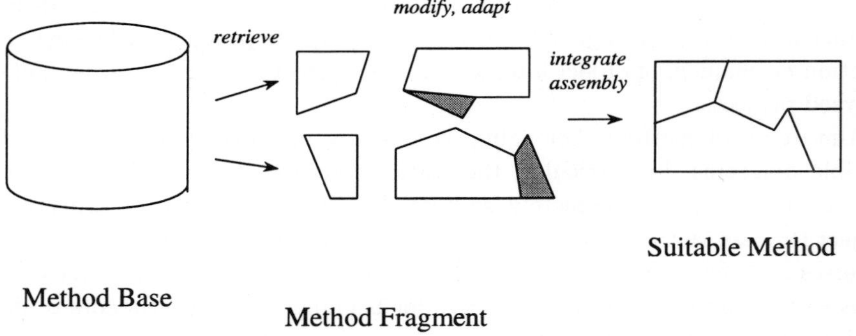

Fig. 8. Method construction process using method base.

retrieve the suitable method fragments, adapt them, and integrate them into a new method. For instance, we can get Rumbaugh's OMT by integrating four method fragments: Class Diagram, Sequence Diagram, State Transition Diagram (State chart) and Data Flow Diagram. The method engineers have enough knowledge and skills to the methods so that they can construct the methods. Figure 8 illustrates this process to construct a new method by using reuse and integration technique.

The current techniques of method engineering can be listed up as follows:

(1) Meta-modeling technique
It is necessary to model and to represent method fragments and methods (simply, methods) formally in order to store them in a method base. A model and a description of a method are called meta model.

(2) Techniques for method adaptation and method integration
How to adapt and to integrate the retrieved methods is one of the significant techniques [9]. Especially, several researchers investigate the techniques to resolve inconsistency that appears in method integration [43]. The computer support to construct methods is called Computer Aided Method Engineering (CAME) and a couple of CAME tools have been developed [27]. Several method-base systems have been also implemented by using Meta-CASE and by PCTE (Portable Common Tool Environment) [56], and are being assessed.

(3) Relationship between actual development projects and methods
What kind of methods is suitable for actual development projects? The approach to answer this question is case studies like [59]. We apply the methods to the real projects, observe the project processes, and analyze the observation results. Analysing methods themselves is also a useful approach. In addition to the case study that was mentioned in Sec. 4.4, several case studies of software development processes following the methods have also been reported [5, 66].

(4) Generation of CASE tools
CASE tools supporting a new method are necessary to put it into practice. Meta-CASE technology allows us to efficiently construct or to automatically generate CASE tools.

5.2. *Meta-modeling*

Many researchers have studied meta-modeling techniques to model and represent methods, and they have proposed various techniques and languages. Entity relationship model including its extended versions such as object model and object-property-role model (OPR model) has been widely used to describe the product parts of methods. In Fig. 9, a part of class diagrams is specified in the form of entity relationship diagram. Rectangular boxes and arrows appearing in the diagram express entities and their relationships respectively. This approach is very simple and easy to implement in conventional CASE tools [61]. MOF (Meta Object Facility) is a standard of meta-modeling and the notation of meta models, which has been worked out by OMG (Object Management Group), and is based on class diagram of UML [69]. However entity relationship model and MOF can only represent the structure of the products to be developed in the projects, but cannot represent procedural parts of the methods or constraints on the products. To describe the constraints, predicate logic was embedded into entity relationship model in [7]. The major aim of methods is the guides of human activities to develop a system. The methods suggest to the developers what products such as documents they should construct in a development process, and what activities and in what order they should perform. Thus we should consider two types of information to

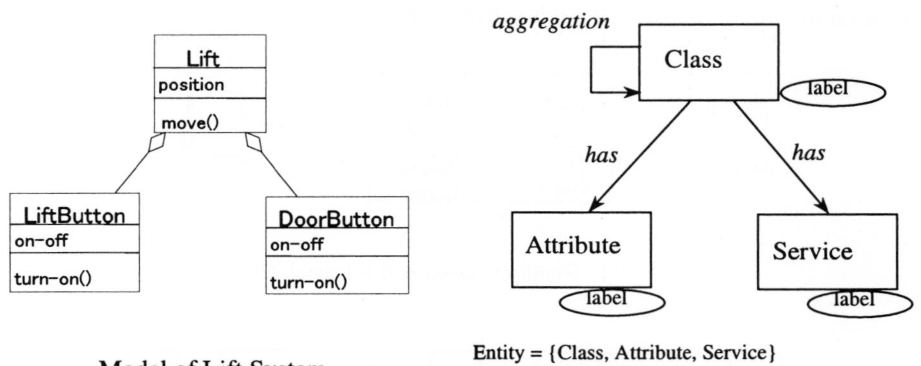

Fig. 9. Modeling class diagram.

develop a meta model; the structure of products and the procedures to produce the products. Very few approaches to describe the procedural parts of methods are being studied. They used formal grammars [58] such as regular grammars and attribute grammars [60], programming languages [63], and formal specification languages like Object Z [55], in order to describe the procedures and their execution order. Several meta-modeling techniques and their comparative studies can be found in [28].

Meta models play an important role in analyzing the features of the methods. Rossi and Brinkkemper considered that the difficulties in applying and learning the methods resulted from the complexity of the concepts that the methods themselves have [51]. They defined the complexity of methods, i.e., method metrics, with the number of their concepts on their meta models. More concretely, they represented a meta model of a method with entity relationship model and calculated the number of the entities, of the relationships, and the average numbers of the attributes per entity and of the relationships per entity. In the example shown in Fig. 9, the number of the entities (the number of the concepts that the method has) is 3, and the average numbers of the attributes and the relationships per entity are 1 and 2 respectively. They calculated the method metrics of 23 object-oriented methods and compared with their complexity. Although this type of method metrics is absolute, we can also consider the method metrics that vary from the situation such as application domain and development organization, i.e., relative metrics.

5.3. *Method integration*

As shown in Fig. 10, there are two types of method integration; one is product-oriented and the other one is process-oriented integration. In product-oriented integration, we integrate several types of products and the integrated products play a complementary role to each other. For instance, in Fig. 10(a), we integrate

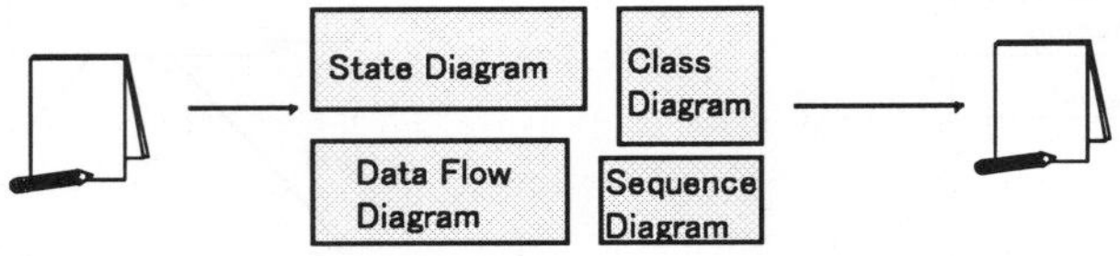

1. Product-Oriented Integration

2. Process-Oriented Integration

Fig. 10. Method integration.

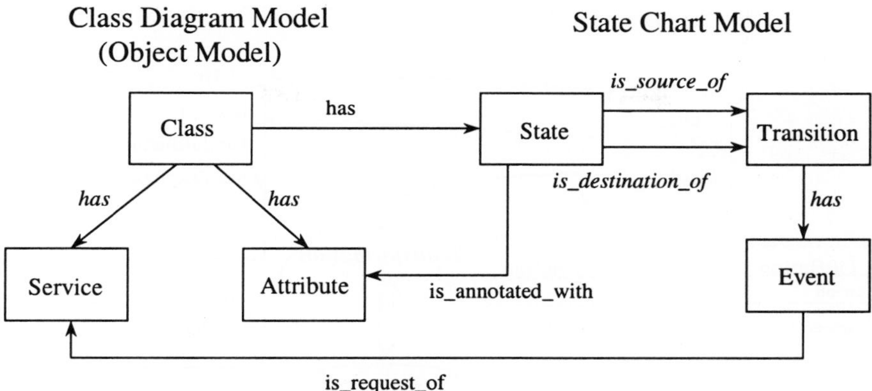

Fig. 11. Method integration example.

four diagrams: class diagrams (Object Model), sequence diagrams, state charts (Dynamic Model) and data flow diagrams (Function Model) following some rules, and can get Object Modeling Technique (OMT) [52]. This type of integration can be done on meta models, as shown in Fig. 11. This example partially illustrates the integration of meta models of class diagrams and of state charts, which are written in entity relationship diagram, into object charts [13] by the following constructions: (1) a Class has a State chart, which specifies its behavior, (2) Attributes of a Class may be annotated to States in its State chart and this indicates which attribute values are meaningful or visible in a specific state, and (3) an Event issued during a Transition is a request of a Service to the other Object. These constructions allow us to introduce new relationships "has" between Class and State, "is_annotated_with" between Attribute and State, and "is_requested_of" between Service and Event. Although the manipulations that we applied here are the addition of a new relationship only, we have the other manipulations on meta models such as the addition of a new entity and the addition of a new attribute.

The second example of Fig. 10 is called process-oriented integration and we integrate methods that are used in the different steps. The developers construct a class diagram and then refine the details by using a formal method such as Z, because a class diagram cannot specify the details of the services of the class but can just declare the signatures of the services. The transformation techniques are used to define this type of method integration, and by applying the transformation rules, we can get the structure of a formal description from the class diagram [54]. Figure 12 sketches the process-oriented integration based on transformation rules, and in the figure, the developers can automatically get the structure of Z schema from a class diagram by applying the pre-defined set of transformation rules.

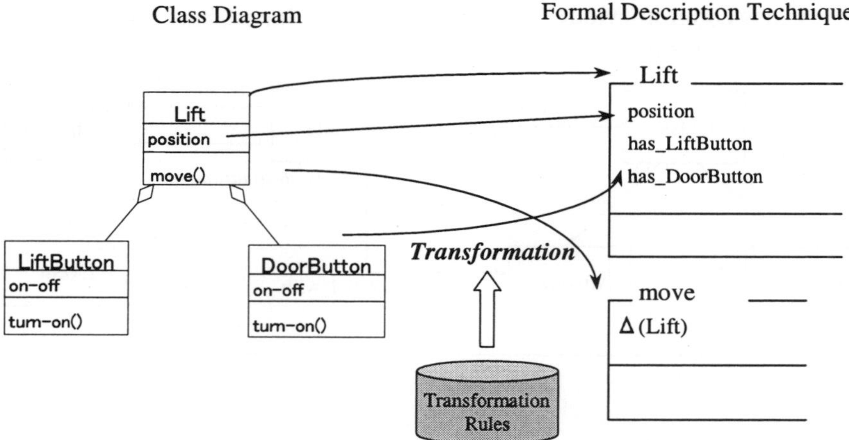

Fig. 12. Method integration based on transformation.

5.4. *Computer Aided Method Engineering: CAME*

In this section, we show several CAME systems that have been developed or are being studied now. Decamerone [26] has been developed by F. Harmsen and S. Brinkkemper in the group of University of Twente, and it adopted meta-CASE technology for generating CASE tools. Using meta-CASE technology seems to be one of the simplest way to implement a CAME. The novel aspect of Decamerone is to have a specific language called MEL (Method Engineering Language) [26] to describe not only methods but also the manipulations on methods. MEL can define the way to adapt and integrate methods stored in a method base. It is based on entity relationship model for describing the product part of a method and on procedural languages for defining the procedures part. We can write the manipulations of methods, including the retrieval of methods from a method base, with SQL-like description style. The method integration example of Fig. 11 can be defined with MEL as follows:

Join Class Diagram **With** State Chart
Through State is_annotated_with Attribute,
Event is_requested_of Service
Into Object Chart.

The manipulation descriptions with MEL seem to apply to the version control of methods and method integration processes. Figure 13 depicts the architecture of Decamerone. Method engineers can manipulate the methods in a method base by inputting MEL descriptions as commands. Decamerone produces a schema for a repository of a CASE tool from the method and the actual CASE tool is generated by the commercial Meta-CASE.

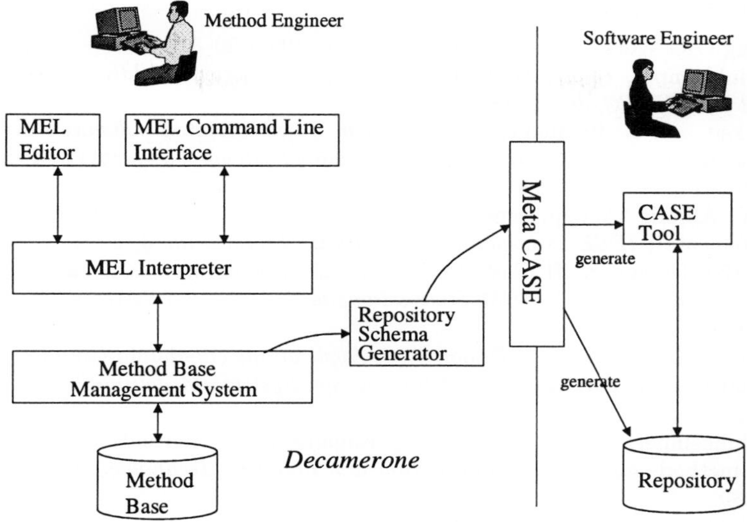

Fig. 13. Decamerone.

In a sense, Mentor [58], which was developed by C. Rolland *et al*, the project of University of Paris, focuses on the procedural aspect of methods. They call the constituents of methods "method chunks", and each chunk consists of "context" and "situation". "Context" can correspond to procedure parts of methods. Mentor provides a kind of patterns for method engineers to easily design the "context" of method chunks. The way to design and specify methods is one of the crucial problems for the method engineers and the method patterns in Mentor may provide them with a suggestion of its solution. Furthermore in the newer version of Mentor, the research group tried to describe a part of method chunks with SGML, and to combine meta-modeling with scenario based analysis in order to support the enhancement of the existing methods [48].

MetaEdit or MetaEdit+ is based on entity relationship model for meta-modeling technique and meta-CASE [36], and it has several tools for CAME. It also focuses on the usage of generated CASE tools for multi-users. This direction, i.e., how to support group work in method engineering technology is one of the most significant ones for the application of CAME.

MethodBase [56] was developed by Saeki, *et al* of Tokyo Institute of Technology and offered a common meta model for the product part of method integration. However the varieties of method integration on the tool is limited to the product parts of methods only, not including procedure parts.

Method Engineering Encyclopedia [2] is a kind of dictionary of methods on WWW. Although its aim does not include method integration support or sufficient CAME functions, it is very useful to construct standardized Web pages of methods in order to share with method knowledge in distributed development environment.

References

1. Making O-O Work, *IEEE Software* **10**, no. 1 (1993) 20–87.
2. S. Brinkkemper, *et al*, "Method engineering encyclopedia", *http://panoramix.univ-paris1.fr/CRINFO/dmrg/MEE* (1996).
3. M. Aksit and L. Bergmans, "Obstacles in object-oriented software development", *Proceedings of 7th Object-oriented Programming Systems, Languages and Applications* (1992) 341–358.
4. M. W. Alford, "A requirements engineering methodology for real-time processing requirements", *IEEE Transactions on Software Engineering* **3**, no. 1 (1977) 60–69.
5. J. P. Bansler and K. Bödker, "A reappraisal of structured analysis : Design in an organizational context", *ACM Transactions on Information Systems* **11**, no. 2 (1993) 165–193.
6. G. Booch, *Object Oriented Design With Applications* (Benjamin Cummings, 1991).
7. S. Brinkkemper, *Formalisation of Information Systems Modelling* (Thesis Publisher, 1990).
8. S. Brinkkemper, "Method engineering: Engineering of information systems development methods and tools", *Information and Software Technology* **37**, no. 11 (1995) 275–280.
9. S. Brinkkemper, M. Saeki and F. Harmsen, "Meta-modelling based assembly techniques for situational method engineering", *Information Systems* **24**, no. 3 (1999) 209–228.
10. S. Chang, A. Perkusich, J. de Figuerideo, B. Yu and M. Ehrenberger, "The design of real-time distributed information systems with object-oriented and fault-tolerant charcteristics", *Proceedings of 5th International Conference on Software Engineering and Knowledge Engineering* (1993) 36–53.
11. P. Chen, "Entity-relationship model: Towards a unified view of data", *ACM. Transactions on Database Systems* **1**, no. 1 (1976) 9–36.
12. P. Coad and E. Yourdon, *Object-Oriented Analysis* (Prentice Hall, 1990).
13. D. Coleman, F. Hayes and S. Bear, "Introducing objectcharts or how to use statecharts in object-oriented design", *IEEE Transactions on Software Engineering* **18**, no. 1 (1992) 9–18.
14. T. DeMarco, *Structured Analysis and System Specification* (Yourdon Press, 1978).
15. E. Dijkstra, "Structured programming", *Software Engineering, Concepts and Techniques* (Van Nostrand Reinhold, 1976).
16. B. Douglass, *Real-Time UML* (Addison Wesley, 1998).
17. D. D'Souza and A. Wills, *Object, Components, and Framework with UML* (Addison Wesley, 1998).
18. K. Edwards, *Real-Time Structured Methods* (John & Wiley, 1993).
19. M. Folwer and K. Scott, *UML Distilled: Applying the Standard Object Modeling Language* (Addison Wesley, 1997).
20. E. Gamma, R. Helm, R. Johnson and J. Vlissides, *Design Patterns : Elements of Reusable OO Software* (Addison-Wesley, 1995).
21. M. Glinz, "Problems and deficiencies of UML as a requirements specification language", *Proceedings of 10th International Workshop on Software Specification and Design* (2000) 11–22.
22. H. Gomaa, *Software Design Methods for Concurrent and Real-Time Systems* (Addison Wesley, 1993).
23. D. Harel, "STATECHARTS: A visual formalism for complex systems", *Science of Computer Programming* **8** (1987) 231–274.

24. D. Harel and E. Gery, "Executable object modeling with statecharts", *Proceedings of 18th International Conference on Software Engineering* (1996) 246–257.
25. D. Harel, H. Lachover, A. Naamad, A. Pnueli, M. Politi, R. Sherman and A. Shtul-Trauring, "STATEMATE: A working environment for the development of complex reactive systems", *IEEE Transactions Software Engineering* **16** (1990) 403–414.
26. F. Harmsen, *Situational Method Engineering* (Moret Ernst & Young Management Consultants, 1997).
27. F. Harmsen, S. Brinkkemper and H. Oei, "Situational method engineering for information system project approaches", *Methods and Associated Tools for the Information Systems Life Cycle* (North-Holland, 1994) 169–194.
28. F. Harmsen and M. Saeki, "Comparison of four method engineering languages", eds. S. Brinkkemper, K. Lyytinen and R. Welke, *Method Engineering: Principles of Method Construction and Tool Support* (Chapman & Hall, 1996) 209–231.
29. D. Hatley and I. Pirbhai, *Strategies for Real-Time System Specification* (Dorset House Publishing, 1987).
30. T. Isakowitz, E. Stohr and Balasubramanian, "RMM: A methodology for structured hypermedia design", *CACM* **38**, no. 8 (1995) 34–43.
31. M. A. Jackson, *Principles of Program Design* (Academic Press, 1975).
32. M. A. Jackson, *System Development* (Prentice-Hall, 1983).
33. I. Jacobson, G. Booch and J. Rumbaugh, *The Unified Software Development Process* (Addison Wesley, 1999).
34. I. Jacobson, M. Christerson, P. Jonsson and G. Overgaard, *Object-Oriented Software Engineering: A Use Case Driven Approach* (Addison Wesley, 1992).
35. A. K. Jordan and A. M. Davis, "Requirements engineering metamodel : An integrated view of requirements", *Proceedings of 15th International Computer Software and Applications Conference* (1991) 472–478.
36. S. Kelly, K. Lyytinen and M. Rossi, "MetaEdit+: A fully configurable multi-user and multi-tool CASE and CAME environment", *Lecture Notes in Computer Science (CAiSE'96)* **1080** (1996) 1–21.
37. K. Kumar and R. Welke, "Methodology engineering: A proposal for situation-specific methodology construction", *Challenges and Strategies for Research in Systems Development* (John Wiley & Sons, 1992) 258–269.
38. LBMS, *LBMS Jackson System Development — Method Manual* (Wiley, 1992).
39. J. Martin, *Information Engineering I, II, III* (Prentice-Hall, 1990).
40. S. J. Mellor and P. T. Ward, *Structured Development for Real-Time Systems I, II, III* (Yourdon Press, 1986).
41. D. E. Monarchi and G. I. Puhr, "A research typology for object-oriented analysis and design", *CACM* **35**, no. 9 (1992) 35–47.
42. G. J. Myers, *Composite/Structured Design* (Van Nostrand, 1978).
43. B. Nuseibeh, J. Kramer and F. Finkelstein, "Expressing the relationships between multiple views in requirements specification", *Proceedings of the 15th International Conference on Software Engineering* (1993) 187–196.
44. Object Management Group, "OMG unified modeling language specification", *ftp://ftp.omg.org/pub/docs/ad/99-06-08.pdf* (1999).
45. D. L. Parnas, "On criteria to be used in decomposing systems into modules", *CACM* **14**, no. 1 (1972) 221–227.
46. M. Peleg and D. Dori, "The model multiplicity problem: Experimenting with real-time specification methods", *IEEE Transactions on Software Engineering* **26**, no. 8 (2000) 742–759.

47. L. Peters, *Advanced Structured Analysis and Design* (Prentice Hall, 1988).
48. J. Ralyte, C. Rolland and V. Plihon, "Method enhancement with scenario based techniques", *Lecture Notes in Comupter Science (CAiSE'99)* **1626** (1998) 103–118.
49. Rational, *Unified Modeling Language 1.01* (1997).
50. D. T. Ross and K. E. Schoman Jr, "Structured analysis for requirements definition", *IEEE Transactions on Software Engineering* **3**, no. 1 (1977) 6–15.
51. M. Rossi and S. Brinkkemper, "Complexity metrics for system development methods and techniques", *Information Systems* **21** (1996) 209–227.
52. J. Rumbaugh, M. Blaha, W. Premerlani, F. Eddy and W. Lonrensen, *Object-Oriented Modeling and Design* (Prentice-Hall, 1991).
53. J. Rumbaugh, I. Jacobson and G. Booch, *The Unified Modeling Language Reference Manual* (Addison Wesley, 1999).
54. S. Saeeiab and M. Saeki, "Method integration with formal description techniques", *IEICE Transactions on Information and Systems* **E83-D**, no. 4 (2000) 616–626.
55. M. Saeki, "Object-oriented meta-modelling", *Lecture Notes in Computer Science (Proceedings OO-ER'95)* **1021** (1995) 250–259.
56. M. Saeki, "A meta-model for method integration", *Information and Software Technology* **39** (1998) 925–932.
57. B. Seric, G. Gullekson and P. Ward, *Real-Time Object-Oriented Modeling* (John & Wiley, 1994).
58. S. Si-Said, C. Rolland and G. Grosz, "MENTOR: A computer aided requirements engineering environment", *Lecture Notes in Comupter Science (CAiSE'96)* **1080** (1996) 22–43.
59. K. Slooten and B. Hodes, "Characterizing IS development projects", eds. S. Brinkkemper, K. Lyytinen and R. Welke, *Method Engineering: Principles of Method Construction and Tool Support* (Chapman & Hall, 1996) 29–44.
60. X. Song and L. J. Osterweil, "Experience with an approach to comparing software design methodologies", *IEEE Transaction on Software Engineering* **20**, no. 5 (1994) 364–384.
61. P. Sorenson, J. Tremblay and A. McAllister, "The metaview system for many specification environments", *IEEE Software* **2**, no. 5 (1988) 30–38.
62. A. Sutcliffe, *Jackson System Development* (Prentice Hall, 1988).
63. S. Sutton Jr and L. Osterweil, "PDP: Programming a programable design process", *Proceedings of the 8th International Workshop on Software Specification and Design* (1996) 186–190.
64. D. Teichroew and E. A. Hershey III, "PSL/PSA: A computer-aided technique for structured documentation and analysis of information processing systems", *IEEE Transactions on Software Engineering* **1**, no. 3 (1977) 6–15.
65. P. Ward, "The transformation schema: An extension of the data flow diagram to represent control and timing", *IEEE Transactions on Software Engineering* **2**, no. 12 (1986) 198–210.
66. J. M Wing, "A study of 12 specifications of the library problem", *IEEE Software* **5**, no. 4 (1988) 66–76.
67. E. Yourdon, *Modern Structured Analysis* (Yourdon Press, 1989).
68. E. Yourdon and L. L Constantine, *Structured Design: Fundamentals of a Discipline of Computer Program and Systems Design* (Prentice-Hall, 1979).
69. Object Management Group, "Meta object facility (MOF) specification", *ftp://ftp.omg.org/pub/docs/formal/00-04-03.pdf* (2000).

COMPONENT-BASED SOFTWARE ENGINEERING

WILHELM HASSELBRING
Software Engineering Group,
Computer Science Department, University of Oldenburg,
PO Box 2503, D-26111 Oldenburg, Germany

With component-based software engineering, it is expected that software systems can be created and maintained at lower costs and with increased stability through reuse of approved components in flexible software architectures. We survey the state-of-the-art of this approach, hereby discussing issues such as reuse, architecture, various forms of component integration, component middleware, and impact on the development process.

Keywords: Software components, software reuse, software architecture, component integration.

1. Introduction

A software component can be defined as an executable unit of code that provides a set of services through specified interfaces:

> "A software component is a unit of composition with contractually specified interfaces and explicit context dependencies only. A software component can be deployed independently and is subject to third-party composition". [1]

The kind of "unit" is important: As a technical goal, minimal coupling with the outside world and maximal cohesion inside the unit is desirable. However, component-based software engineering has impact from both a managerial and a technical perspective.

1.1. *Managerial goals for component-based software engineering*

The managerial goals of component-based software engineering can be identified as follows:

Cost reduction: One important goal of any development process is to be cost-effective in developing the software system.

Ease of assembly: Components need to be designed in a manner that facilitates the subsequent assembly process when components are assembled together to develop software systems.

Reusability: This addresses the component's potential for reuse in multiple applications. In component-based software engineering, reusability is the extent to which a component is (re)used during the assembly process in developing software systems.

Customization and flexibility: In component-based software engineering, when a set of components are made available to the application developers, they can customize their systems by assembling components according to their specific requirements.

Maintainability: Maintainability is the ease with which software features can be added, removed, or modified in a component; according to new and emerging requirements.

1.2. *Technical features of component-based systems*

The technical features of component-based systems can be summarized as follows:

Coupling (inter-relatedness among components):
In component-based software engineering, coupling for a component is defined as the extent to which that component is coupled with other components. Low coupling is desired.

Cohesion (strength of association among elements within a component):
Cohesion refers to the strength of association of elements within a system. In component-based software development, cohesion of a component is the extent to which its contained elements are inter-related. High cohesion is desired.

Granularity (number of components in a system, complexity):
In component-based software engineering, the number of components used to realize a particular system is an important design parameter. The trade-off between many small components and a few large components must be considered in component and system design.

1.3. *Chapter overview*

The chapter starts with a look back at object-oriented development as one basis for components. A major part then discusses software reuse and software architectures. Various forms of component integration, such as integrating legacy systems and enterprise/office application integration are discussed subsequently. Component middleware, the impact on the development process, and questions of finding the right components are discussed before we summarize the chapter.

2. Object-Oriented Development as a Basis for Components

The basic idea of object-oriented development is that a software system consists of a set of interacting objects [2]. A class describes the structure and behavior of

Table 1. Basic similarities and differences between objects and components.

Objects	Components
An object is a unit of instantiation; it has a unique identity.	A component is a unit of independent deployment.
An object has state; this state can be persistent state.	A component has no persistent state.
An object encapsulates its state and behavior.	A component is a unit of third-party composition.

objects. Objects encapsulate information (information hiding). This capability is highly relevant for component-based systems: client components are not interested in the internals of server components, only the services that are specified in their interfaces should be required for using those components. Therefore, objects are good candidates for components, provided their granularity is sufficient.

Object-oriented *analysis* aims at understanding the application domain and identifying requirements. Object-oriented *design* and *implementation* aim at achieving the identified requirements in a particular environment. Table 1 illustrates the basic similarities and differences between objects and components (based on [1]). As objects get instantiated, there needs to be a "template" for their creation, which is their class. The creation mechanism can be regarded as an *object factory* that produces individual objects with own identity and (persistent) state. Opposed to that, components are deployed at some sites. Several objects could be managed by deployed components. Granularity (size of components) is an important issue within this context.

Object-oriented programming languages usually do not support explicit "uses" relationships as they are available with module definition languages [3] and module interconnection languages [4, 5]. This restriction has good reasons: "uses" defines implementation rather than abstraction in object-oriented programming. However, for composing components, "uses" relationships are relevant. Similar to using a class in object-oriented programming, with component-based software engineering it is relevant what a component offers, not how it realizes offered services. Anyway, it is possible to realize components without employing object techniques. A well-organized library of functions in a procedural setting is a good basis for component-based development, too.

It is important to note that inheritance is problematic for component composition, because it breaks encapsulation. Inheritance is an "open" relation among classes: the inheriting class usually has full access to the internals of the base class. This allows for extensibility and incremental construction of classes. Conversely, uses relationships among classes are "closed" relations: only the public interfaces are shared, the internal implementations is encapsulated to decouple the classes.

This distinction is also called the open/closed principle [2]. With inheritance, the fragile base class problem may emerge: the question whether a base class can evolve without breaking independently developed subclasses. This problem may cause unacceptable dependencies (coupling) among components. As discussed earlier, in component-based software engineering, low coupling and high cohesion are desired. For a more detailed discussion of the fragile base class problem refer to [1, Sec. 7.4].

3. Reuse of Components and Software Architectures

We can distinguish two classes of concerns based on whether components are used as a design philosophy independent from any concern for reusing existing components, or seen as off-the-shelf building blocks used to design and implement a component-based system.

Reuse on the design level plays an important role in component-based software engineering. On the programming level, reuse is usually accomplished by means of high-level programming language constructs, function libraries, or object-oriented class frameworks. For well-understood domains, generators [6] may be used for assembling applications by automatically composing pre-written components. On the design level, design patterns and established software architectures are essential. However, the borderline between design and programming cannot always be pinpointed precisely.

3.1. *Domain engineering*

The inability of software developers to achieve low costs, high productivity, and consistent quality has often been attributed to a lack of software reuse. Re-creating similar systems without capturing components for future development wastes time, money, and human resources. While a universal software reuse solution may prove ineffective, significant improvements can be realized by focusing on well-understood domains. Architectures support domain-specific reuse by serving as frameworks for understanding families of systems, which may be called *product lines* [7–10].

Domain engineering [11] is an activity for building reusable components, whereby the systematic creation of domain models and architectures is addressed. Domain engineering aims at supporting *application engineering* which uses the domain models and architectures to build concrete systems. The emphasis is on reuse and product lines. The Domain-Specific Software Architecture (DSSA) engineering process was introduced to promote a clear distinction between domain and application requirements [12]. A Domain-Specific Software Architecture consists of a domain model and a reference architecture, and guides in reusing components as modeled in Fig. 1. Appropriate management of component libraries is essential for successful reuse. The DSSA process consists of domain analysis, architecture modeling, design and implementation stages as illustrated in Fig. 2.

Domain models represent the set of requirements that are common to systems within a specific domain. Usually, those systems can be grouped into product lines,

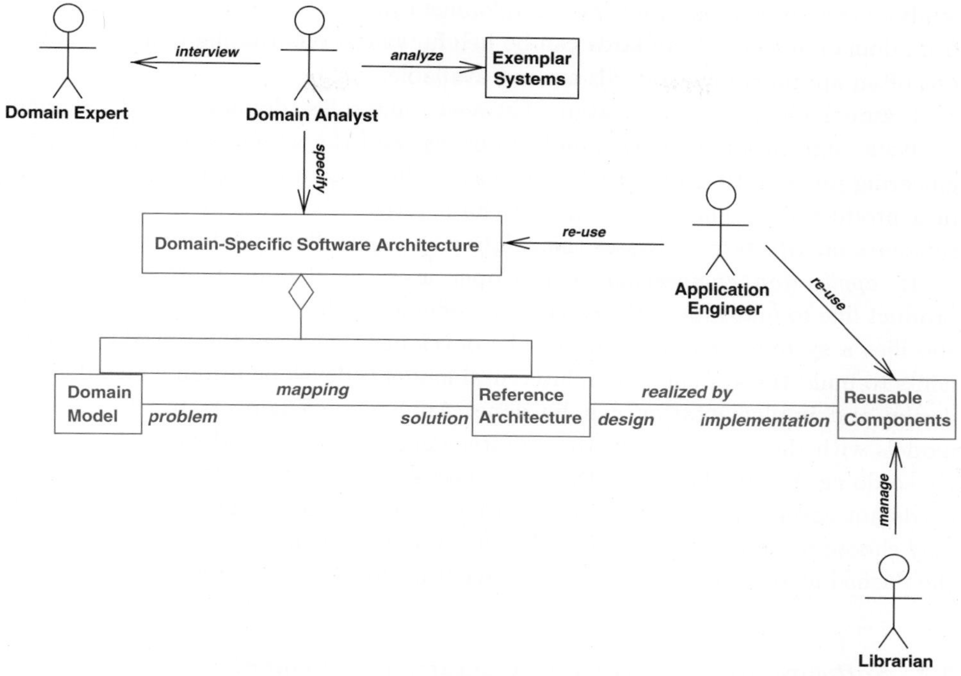

Fig. 1. Relations between some roles and artifacts in the DSSA engineering process. Hollow diamonds indicate part-of relations. We use the UML notation for actors to model the roles [13].

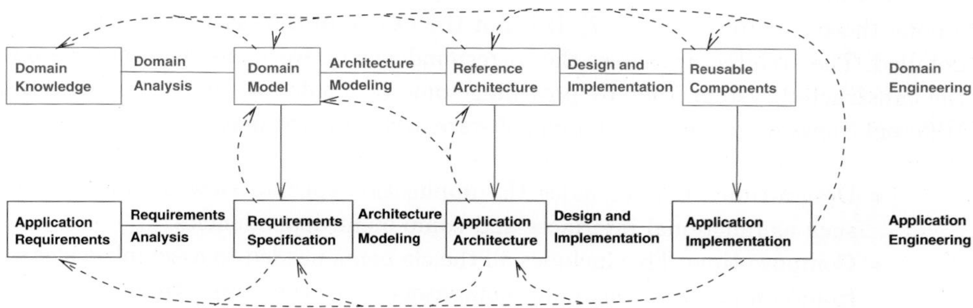

Fig. 2. The DSSA engineering process. In application engineering, software systems are developed from reusable components created by a domain engineering process. As indicated by the backward arrows, various forms of feedback are possible. This figure does not address time dependencies. Typically, the two tracks are not done in parallel, but concurrently.

for instance for the insurance or banking domain. Product lines cover both commonality and variance for a family of systems. There may be many domains, or areas of expertise, represented in a single product line and a single domain may span multiple product lines. *Domain analysis* is the process of identifying, collecting, organizing, and representing the relevant information in a domain, based upon the study of existing systems and their development histories, and knowledge captured from domain experts. Standards can be helpful when constructing domain models, but often appropriate standards are not available.

Figure 1 illustrates the relations between some roles (domain experts, domain analysts, application engineers, and librarians) and the artifacts in the DSSA engineering process. Reference architectures are the structures used to build systems in a product line. The domain model characterizes the *problem space*, while the *reference architecture* addresses the *solution space*, as illustrated in Fig. 1.

In *application engineering*, a developer uses the domain models within the product line to understand the capabilities offered by the reference architecture and specifies a system for development. The developer then uses the reusable components to build the system. An architectural model is developed from which detailed design and implementation can be done. Application engineers use the domain models with the users to elicit the requirements for the planned software systems. By so doing, the models cover the user's needs in terms of existing models. Those needs not covered by a domain model are new requirements. The domain analysts may choose to update a domain model with the new requirements. As indicated by the dashed arrows in Fig. 2, various forms of feedback are possible.

3.2. *Software architectures for structuring components*

For large, complex software systems the design of the overall system structure (the software architecture) is a central problem. The *architecture* of a software system defines that system in terms of components and interactions/connections among those components [14–17]. It is not the *design* of that system which is more detailed. The architecture shows the correspondence between the requirements and the constructed system, thereby providing some rationale for the design decisions. Different views on component-based software architectures may be distinguished:

- Design-time: This includes the application-specific view of components, such as functional interfaces and component dependencies.
- Compose-time: This includes all the elements needed to assemble a system from components, including generators and other build-time services; a component framework may provide some of these services.
- Runtime: This includes frameworks and models that provide runtime services for component-based systems.

These characteristics suggest that components are complex design-level entities, that is, both abstractions and implementations. Some authors, additionally, consider all artifacts that are produced during the different phases of the development process as components (for instance, parts of design specifications) [18]. However, in this chapter we restrict ourselves to software components. Anyway, specifications should be structured in modular ways, too.

Architectures can themselves be reusable assets, but they also support the reuse of design and code components by standardizing interfaces, protocols, and the packaging of functionality at a high level of abstraction, to be further refined at more detailed levels. Standardization facilitates smooth integration of both off-the-shelf and custom components during initial development and subsequent maintenance phases.

3.3. *Object-oriented application frameworks and design patterns*

Object-oriented application frameworks are class hierarchies plus models of interactions which can be turned into complete applications through various kinds of inheritance and usage associations [19, 20]. An object-oriented framework defines a class structure as well as an interaction model for cooperating objects involved. Thus, besides a generic architecture, also controls for specific applications are offered; the places where specific functionality has to be added are predefined. Design patterns often guide the construction and documentation of frameworks [21]. Frameworks can offer reusable components in the domain engineering process.

Design patterns [22] are "micro-architectures" while software architectures are more coarse-grained designs. A design pattern describes a family of solutions to a recurring problem. Patterns form larger wholes like pattern languages, systems or handbooks when woven together so as to provide guidance for solving complex problem sets. Patterns express the understanding gained from practice in software design and construction. Design patterns are descriptions of communicating objects and classes that are customized to solve a general design problem in a particular context. The patterns community catalogs useful design fragments and the context that guides their use. They do not make special distinctions between architectural patterns and patterns for code. An organized collection of related patterns for a particular application domain can be called a *pattern language*.

All aspects of software systems, their development and their deployment are suitable topics of individual patterns or comprehensive pattern languages. Patterns might be so specific as to name particular objects, their responsibilities, and interaction. A well-known pattern of this kind is, for example, the Observer pattern from [22]. It supports keeping co-operating components consistent, with help of a change propagation mechanism.

The run-time architecture of a framework is characterized by an inversion of control: event handler objects of the specific application are invoked via the framework's reactive dispatching mechanism. In general, event-based interaction is very important for component-based systems. With traditional imperative and functional programming, the control flow is usually organized within a hierarchical call graph. With event-based interaction, the control flow is not restricted to hierarchies allowing for a loose coupling among (autonomous) components. For instance, the CORBA event services [23] may be used to provide synchronous or asynchronous transfer of objects using event channels to decouple the communication between

Fig. 3. Decoupled push and pull communication with CORBA event services.

distributed objects. Consumer objects can either receive notification of events that concern them (*push* model) or can connect to the event channel to wait for their events (*pull* model). Figure 3 illustrates both mechanisms, where suppliers deposit information at the event channel and consumers fetch them in different ways. The event service can be implemented as a specialized CORBA object which means that it can be used by multiple suppliers and consumers simultaneously. In effect, this means that multiple suppliers can pass information to multiple consumers using the same event channel without any supplier or consumer having direct knowledge of each other. Suppliers and consumers may register and unregister with an event channel with no consequences to either other suppliers who could be providing events or consumers who may be listening for events. Event channels provide a decoupling of the consumer and producer components.

4. Component Integration

Components need to be integrated to constitute usable software systems. Various forms of component integration, such as integrating legacy systems and enterprise/office application integration are discussed in the following subsections.

4.1. *Integrating legacy systems into component-based systems*

There is often no time and justification to replace existing legacy systems. New functionality must be integrated with other components, existing applications and data sources. Component-based software engineering aims at building applications that are adaptable to business and technology changes, while retaining legacy applications and legacy technology as far as possible and reasonable. The speed of business and technology change does not allow time for total replacement, therefore, evolution and migration of legacy and new application systems is required [24]. Migration and evolution aim at protecting existing investments and enabling rapid response to the changing user requirements.

When the legacy components are information systems, an often occurring requirement is that the systems to be integrated are to remain autonomous [25]. Preexisting applications (legacy systems) must still be able to use their local data without modification. In this way (financial) investment can be preserved and a smooth migration towards modern systems can take place. A federated database system is an integration of such autonomous database systems, where both local applications and global applications accessing multiple database systems are supported [26]. The notion of "federation" is originally a political term: several states join together and constitute a federal system in which each state retains its autonomy up to a certain degree. This idea of federation can be transferred to the integration of preexisting information systems which could have been developed independently (autonomously) within different departments of an enterprise.

On the technical level, wrappers [27] that provide unified interfaces are an established technique for accessing legacy systems in a component-based setting. Here, the question arises, how to freeze interfaces and let the components evolve without further interaction. For enabling such an evolution, a modular design [28] of the overall system is required. The interfaces between the independent components form *contracts* among the involved parties. Those contracts have to be fulfilled. With advanced interface definition languages that define, for instance, pre- and post-conditions for services, a middleware system could check the compliance with the contract. As an example, the Eiffel language supports the *design by contract* principle, where such conditions are checked by the runtime system [2].

4.2. *Enterprise application integration*

With Enterprise Application Integration the goal is to integrate independent Enterprise Resource Planning (ERP) systems. This is usually achieved by means of some kind of messaging services. Even the SAP R/3 approach, which basically aims at enterprise integration via one single database (no borders between enterprise units), meanwhile acknowledges the fact that specific services are required for integrating autonomous ERP systems, both within and across enterprises [29]. TSI Software's Mercator product, for instance, specializes on pre-built application adapters, data transformations, and messaging services for the ERP systems SAP R/3 and PeopleSoft.

The deployment of ERP systems often requires the business processes to reengineer to align with the ERP system. However, it is usually unacceptable to require the business to change to the applications functionality; instead the information architecture should align with the business organization. Component-based software engineering aims at supporting the business processes with flexible component architectures that are readily adaptable to changing requirements.

For Enterprise Application Integration, applications need to *understand* the data provided by other applications, for instance a common understanding is required of what a person's bank account is. Standardization of message formats and message contents plays an important role in that context [30]. Meanwhile, XML [31] emerges as the standard for defining the syntax of data structures to be transferred over the Internet. In order to provide interoperability across implementations, the concrete syntax *and* the semantics of standardized messages must be defined. Traditional EDI (Electronic Data Interchange) is often being re-examined to define the *meaning* of the transferred data, and XML is employed as the practical foundation in which to structure this information [32].

A technical and organizational question is where to store and manage schemas and Document Type Definitions (DTDs) for XML messages. XML.org, for instance, aims at being an independent industry portal for the standardization of XML applications in electronic commerce, whereby it serves as a reference for XML DTDs. BizTalk.org is a competing industry initiative started by Microsoft, and mySAP.com is SAP's approach. These initiatives are highly relevant for integrating enterprise applications of dissimilar organizations.

4.3. *Office application integration of COTS tools*

With Enterprise Application Integration, mainly the "backoffice" part of software systems is addressed. Another domain is to integrate software systems on the personal desktop computer. For instance, [33] report on the development of a dynamic fault-tree analysis tool, which is an assemblage of commercial off-the-shelf tools (COTS). The composed tool integrates Visio Corporation's drawing application Visio Technical, Microsoft's Word, and Microsoft's Internet Explorer into one user interface. Technically, Microsoft's OLE is used to drive the components through their application programming interfaces and Microsoft's Active Document Standard is used to integrate the individual user interfaces. A consistency maintenance engine has been built to keep the graphical (Visio) and textual (Word) tools consistent.

In general, such Office Application Integration works well with a small number of (coarse-grained) components. If those components are from one vendor, the integration task is manageable (meanwhile, Visio has been acquired by Microsoft). Anyway, the approach has serious limitations:

- It is usually limited to the integration on personal computers. Heterogeneous environments are not supported.
- It is limited to a small number of components. These components are usually already complex software systems.
- New versions of the components may require re-building the composed application.

However, if it works, powerful applications may be constructed with limited effort.

5. Middleware for Component-based Software Engineering

Primarily, component-based software engineering is a fundamental approach for structuring systems in a modular way. To support the actual construction of component-based systems, middleware for connecting components provides a technical foundation. Currently, the three major middleware approaches for component-based software engineering are:

- The Common Object Request Broker Architecture (CORBA) of the Object Management Group (OMG) [34].
- Sun's Java Beans and Enterprise Java Beans [35].
- Microsoft's Component Object Model (COM+) [36].

In addition, XML can be combined with such object-oriented middleware, whereby data is encoded in XML and transferred via the middleware system. An example is the Tigra architecture which combines XML with CORBA [37].

When employing such middleware, the following architectural concepts are relevant:

- Components that are the building blocks.
- Connectors that provide the "glue" among the components.
- Containers that deliver some non-functional quality services to contained components. Examples are persistence, transactions, and security.

Using such middleware, programmers are expected to be able to get their applications running quicker. In addition, these technologies often provide graphical development tools to drag and drop any component into their applications, where (in the most optimistic situation) they are included in a plug-and-play way. As a result, programmers are allowed to focus their efforts on their particular application problems.

To allow third-party composition of components, standards for the technical infrastructure are important. Basically, tow approaches to standardization are followed:

- Implementation follows standardization (the OMG way).
- Standardization follows implementation (the Microsoft way).

The first approach puts emphasis on well-defined interfaces, while the second puts emphasis on available implementations.

Middleware Integration addresses the syntactical level ("plumbing" and "wiring") while Enterprise Application Integration also addresses a semantical level. The borderline between Enterprise Application and Middleware Integration cannot always be pinpointed precisely. For instance, the Object Management Architecture of the OMG defines the Object Request Broker, which can be deployed for middleware integration, and also high-level services (e.g. business objects) that address Enterprise Application Integration.

6. Impact on the Development Process

Component-based software engineering changes the focus of software engineering from one of traditional system specification and construction to one requiring simultaneous consideration of

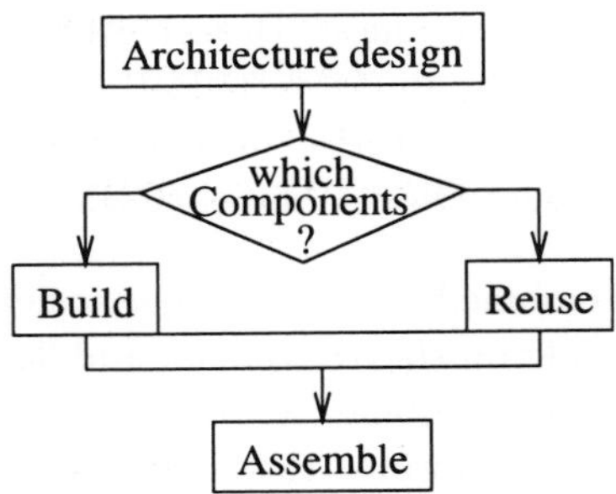

Fig. 4. The selection process for components.

- the system context (system characteristics such as requirements, cost, schedule, operating and support environments); and
- also the capabilities of legacy systems and products in the marketplace for components. Figure 4 illustrates that selection process for components.

Essentially, the development process changes from a top-down partitioning of the problem towards a bottom-up assembly of available components. In a comprehensive development process both basic approaches should be combined [38].

The impact of this fundamental change is profound. Not only must engineering activities such as requirements specification change to support simultaneous consideration of system requirements and the marketplace, but so must acquisition processes and contracting strategies. For example, integration contractors and commercial product vendors must be treated as partners and rewarded for identifying the best value to be achieved through the (re-)use of (third-party) component products.

The design, development, and maintenance of component-based systems, and the migration of legacy systems towards components are complex. New products and technologies constantly emerge into the marketplace. The vendors of existing products work to differentiate their products from those of competitors. This leads to a marketplace characterized by a vast array of products and product claims, extreme quality and capability differences between products, and many product incompatibilities, even when they adhere to the same middleware standards.

7. Finding Components

For organizations designing and implementing a component-based system, or upgrading a legacy system with of-the-shelf components, the current market state presents a number of challenges. It is difficult to discover the actual technical capabilities of a product or set of competing products, since there is no objective forum for product evaluation. Once individual products are selected, it is difficult to identify and resolve mismatches between products, and to avoid becoming dependent on the products of a single vendor or set of vendors. Equally difficult but necessary is the ability to forecast what technologies and products will be relevant over the life of the system. Professional library management is a prerequisite for finding the right components. As illustrated earlier in Fig. 1, a separate role — the librarian — is responsible for managing the reusable components in a way that the application engineers are able to effectively and efficiently reuse those (high quality) components.

The question arises, how domains and components can be described for retrieval. Important in this context are classification techniques. Classification aims at grouping "things" into classes with common characteristics. Basically, two approaches to classifying classes exist:

- hierarchical enumeration of classes; and
- grouping on the basis of features (facets).

Faceted classification assigns attributes to software components [39]. These facets are then used for retrieving components with required features.

When organizing a library of components (in a hierarchy or by facets), it is important to use appropriate terms for the components and their attributes. The term "ontology" has been used in many ways and across different communities. In general, each person has her individual view on the world and the things she has to deal with every day. However, there is a common basis of understanding in terms of the language we use to communicate with each other. Terms from natural language can therefore be assumed to be a shared vocabulary relying on a (mostly) common understanding of certain concepts with only little variety. This common understanding relies on the idea of how the world is organized. We often call this idea a "conceptualization" of the world. Such conceptualizations provide a terminology that can be used for communication.

The main problem with the use of a shared terminology according to a specific conceptualization of the world is that much information remains implicit. When a mathematician talks about a binomial he has much more in mind than just the formula itself. He will also think about its interpretation (the number of subsets of a certain size) and its potential uses (e.g. estimating the chance of winning in a lottery). Ontologies have set out to overcome the problem of implicit and hidden knowledge by making the conceptualization of a domain (e.g. mathematics) explicit. Ontologies are explicit specifications of conceptualizations [40].

An ontology is used to make assumptions about the meaning of a term available. It can also be seen as an explication of the context a term is normally used in. There are many different ways in which an ontology may explicate a conceptualization and the corresponding context knowledge. The possibilities range from a purely informal natural language description of a term corresponding to a glossary up to strictly formal approaches with the expressive power of full first order predicate logic or even beyond.

Standardized terminologies and ontologies could be helpful, but so far no generally accepted standards exist. The standardization of domain-specific CORBA facilities, for instance, is an initiative in the right direction. Within the standardization efforts of the Object Management Group Domain-Specific Task Forces, several Business Object Facilities are standardized. The scope of the OMG's Financial Domain Task Force (CORBAfinancials Task Force), for instance, comprises financial services and accounting. The Insurance Working Group is part of the OMG's Financial Domain Task Force. The Insurance Working Group aims at developing domain-specific interfaces to enable insurance companies and other financial institutions to leverage purchased componentry and integrate their data. Another area is addressed by the Manufacturing Domain Task Force whose goals are interoperable manufacturing domain software components through CORBA technology. More information is available at: *http://www.omg.org/* Such standards are also useful for semantic interoperability of information system components [30].

8. Summary

Despite the fact, that the discussion on component-based software development started some decades ago [41], we seem today not even have realized the full potential of this software construction approach; not only for technological reasons. In the beginning, there was an emphasis on compositional reuse, with libraries of components which were supposed to be interconnected. During the early 90's, the reuse community found out that this did not lead to much, i.e., the cost of finding, adapting and integrating small components did not pay off [42]. Meanwhile the focus is very much on product lines, component frameworks, and software architectures.

Beside the various technological deficiencies accompanied with many decisions to take such as:

- Which component architecture to take?
- Which components are most appropriate?
- Which infrastructure/middleware is needed to develop, deploy, and maintain component-based software systems?
- How to develop components, if no reusable components are available?
- How to test components and component-based systems?
- How can component mismatches [43] be rectified in a system?
- How can we engineer system attributes such as reliability, security, and performance in spite of decreasing control over individual system components?
- How do we integrate component products with the legacy code that continues to provide the core of many systems?

Beside that, organizational issues need to be taken into account, for instance:

- The right granularity of the components for successful marketing.
- Searching for components and finding the right ones.
- Describing the functionality of components (semantics).
- Versioning and configuration management for components.

- Buying components, not building them yourself. The "not-invented-here" syndrome comes into play: programmers often do not trust the code of others.

Many problems to be solved are non-technical! Thus, in designing and constructing a component-based system, or in modifying a legacy system to take advantage of component architectures, an organization should find answers to those questions. It is also important to realize that only in the long run, investments in reusable components will generate profits.

Anyway, component-based software is a promising technology for increasing developer productivity and software quality. Unfortunately, many available components do not meet the users' expectations, even when they are based on popular component middleware, such as JavaBeans, COM+, or the CORBA Component Model. The reason is simple: middleware component models only provide the infrastructure that forms the basic building blocks for large-scale systems. The internal design of components, particularly the aspects related to component evolution, component configuration, distribution, concurrency, and scalability, are not addressed by most conventional component models. Handling these issues effectively remains the responsibility of component developers and assemblers.

The promises of component-based software engineering are cost reduction and increased quality through reuse of proven components, as well as better maintainability through flexible software architectures. Possible pitfalls for establishing component-based software engineering are performance issues (modular systems are often less resource efficient than monolithic systems), security, safety, trust in third-party components, and configuration management of complex componentized systems.

References

1. C. Szyperski, *Component Software* (Addison-Wesley, Harlow, England, 1998).
2. B. Meyer, *Object-Oriented Software Construction*, 2nd ed. (Prentice Hall, Englewood Cliffs, NJ, 1997).
3. C. Ghezzi, M. Jazayeri and D. Mandrioli, *Fundamentals of Software Engineering* (Prentice-Hall, Englewood Cliffs, NJ, 1991).
4. R. Prieto-Diaz and J. M. Neighbors, "Module interconnection languages", *Journal of Systems and Software* **6**, no. 4 (November 1986) 307–334.
5. M. D. Rice and S. B. Seidmann, "A formal model for module interconnection languages", *IEEE Transactions on Software Engineering* **20**, no. 1 (January 1994) 88–101.
6. D. Batory, G. Chen, E. Robertson and T. Wang, "Design wizards and visual programming environments for GenVoca generators", *IEEE Transactions on Software Engineering* **26**, no. 5 (May 2000).
7. R. Macala, L. Stuckey and D. Gross, "Managing domain-specific, product-line development", *IEEE Software* (May 1996) 57–66.
8. D. Dikel, D. Kane, S. Ornburn, W. Loftus and J. Wilson, "Applying software product-line architecture", *Communications of the ACM* **30**, no. 8 (August 1997) 49–55.

9. D. M. Weiss and C.T.R. Lai, *Software Product Line Engineering* (Addison-Wesley, Reading, MA, 1999).
10. J. Bosch, *Design and Use of Software Architectures: Adopting and Evolving a Product-line Approach* (Addison-Wesley, Harlow, England, 2000).
11. J. L. Diaz-Herrera, "Domain engineering", *Handbook of Software Engineering and Knowledge Engineering*, Vol. I (World Scientific Publishing, 2001).
12. R. N. Taylor, W. J. Tracz and L. Coglianese, "Software development using domain-specific software architectures", *ACM SIGSOFT Software Engineering Notes* **20**, no. 5 (December 1995) 27–38.
13. G. Booch, J. Rumbaugh and I. Jacobson, *Unified Modeling Language User Guide*, Object Technology Series (Addison-Wesley, Reading, MA, 1999).
14. R. Kazman, "Software architecture", *Handbook of Software Engineering and Knowledge Engineering*, Vol. I (World Scientific Publishing, 2001).
15. L. Bass, P. Clements and R. Kazman, *Software Architecture in Practice* (Addison-Wesley, Reading, MA, 1998).
16. M. Shaw and D. Garlan, *Software Architecture: Perspectives on an Emerging Discipline* (Prentice Hall, 1996).
17. L. Barroca, J. Hall and P. Hall (eds.), *Software Architectures: Advances and Applications* (Springer-Verlag, London, 2000).
18. S. Yacoub, H. Ammar and A. Mili, "Characterizing a software component", *Proceedings of the Second International Workshop on Component-Based Software Engineering*, Los Angeles, CA, Available at *http://www.sei.cmu.edu/cbs/icse99/* (May 1999).
19. W. Pree, *Design Patterns for Object-Oriented Software Development* (Addison-Wesley, Wokingham, England, 1995).
20. M. E. Fayad and D. C. Schmidt, "Object-oriented application frameworks", *Communications of the ACM* **40**, no. 10 (October 1997) 32–38.
21. S. Srinivasan, "Design patterns in object-oriented frameworks", *IEEE Computer* **32**, no. 2 (February 1999) 24–32.
22. E. Gamma, R. Helm, R. Johnson and J. Vlissides, *Design Patterns — Elements of Reusable Object-Oriented Software* (Addison Wesley, Reading, MA, 1995).
23. T. J. Mowbray and R. Zahavi, *The Essential CORBA: Systems Integration Using Distributed Objects* (Wiley, New York, 1995).
24. M. L. Brodie and M. Stonebraker, *Migrating Legacy Systems: Gateways, Interfaces and the Incremental Approach* (Morgan Kaufmann, San Francisco, CA, 1995).
25. W. Hasselbring, "Information system integration", *Communications of the ACM* **43**, no. 6 (June 2000) 32–38.
26. A. Sheth and J. Larson, "Federated database systems for managing distributed, heterogeneous, and autonomous databases", *ACM Computing Surveys* **22**, no. 3 (1990) 183–236.
27. M. T. Roth and P. M. Schwarz, "Don't scrap it, wrap it! A wrapper architecture for legacy data sources", *Proceedings of the 23rd International Conference on Very Large Data Bases (VLDB'97)* (Morgan Kaufmann, 1997) 266–275.
28. D. Parnas, "On the criteria to be used in decomposing systems into modules", *Communications of the ACM* **15**, no. 12 (December 1972) 1053–1058.
29. R. Munz, "Usage scenarios of DBMS", Keynote Address at *VLDB'99*, Available at *http://www.dcs.napier.ac.uk/~vldb99/IndustrialSpeakerSlides/* (September 1999).
30. W. Hasselbring, "The role of standards for interoperating information systems", ed. K. Jakobs, *Information Technology Standards and Standardization: A Global Perspective* (Idea Group Publishing, 2000) 116–130.

31. S. McGrath, *XML by Example: Building e-commerce Applications* (Prentice Hall, Upper Saddle River, NJ, 1998).
32. W. Hasselbring and H. Weigand, "Languages for electronic business communication: State of the art", *Industrial Management and Data Systems* **101**, no. 5 (2001) 217–227.
33. D. Coppit and K. J. Sullivan, "Multiple mass-market applications as components", *Proceedings of the 22th International Conference on Software Engineering* (IEEE Computer Society Press, Limerick, Ireland, June 2000) 273–282,
34. K. Seetharaman, "The CORBA connection", *Communications of the ACM* **41**, no. 10 (October 1998) 34–36.
35. R. Monson-Haefel, *Enterprise JavaBeans*, 2nd ed. (O'Reilly, 2000).
36. G. Eddon, "COM+: The evolution of component services", *IEEE Computer* **32**, no. 7 (July 1999) 104–106.
37. W. Emmerich, E. Ellmer and H. Fieglein, "Tigra — An architectural style for enterprise application integration", *Proceedings of the 23th International Conference on Software Engineering* (IEEE Computer Society Press, Toronto, Canada, May 2001).
38. W. Hasselbring, "Top-down vs bottom-up engineering of federated information systems", *Engineering Federated Information Systems* (*Proceedings of EFIS'99*) (Infix-Verlag, 1999) 131–138.
39. R. Prieto-Diaz, "Implementing faceted classification for software reuse", *Communications of the ACM* **34**, no. 5 (1991) 88–97.
40. B. Chandrasekaran, J. R. Josephson and V. R. Benjamins, "What are ontologies, and why do we need them?", *IEEE Intelligent Systems* **14**, no. 1 (1999) 20–26.
41. M. D. McIlroy, "Mass produced software components", eds. P. Naur and B. Randell, *Proceedings of the NATO Conference on Software Engineering*, Garmisch, Germany, (October 1968) 88–98.
42. E.-A. Karlsson (ed.), *Software Reuse: A Holistic Approach* (John Wiley & Sons, 1995).
43. D. Garlan, R. Allen and L. Ockerbloom, "Architectural mismatch: Why reuse is so hard", *IEEE Software* (November 1995).

SOFTWARE COST ESTIMATION

HARETON LEUNG and ZHANG FAN
Department of Computing, The Hong Kong Polytechnic University,
Hung Hom, Kowloon, Hong Kong
E-mail: {cshleung,csfzhang}@comp.polyu.edu.hk

Software cost estimation is the process of predicting the effort required to develop a software system. Many estimation models have been proposed over the last 30 years. This paper provides a general overview of software cost estimation methods including the recent advances in the field. As a number of these models rely on a software size estimate as input, we first provide an overview of common size metrics. We then highlight the cost estimation models that have been proposed and used successfully. Models may be classified into 2 major categories: algorithmic and non-algorithmic. Each has its own strengths and weaknesses. A key factor in selecting a cost estimation model is the accuracy of its estimates. Unfortunately, despite the large body of experience with estimation models, the accuracy of these models is not satisfactory. The paper includes comment on the performance of the estimation models and description of several newer approaches to cost estimation.

Keywords: Project estimation, effort estimation, cost models.

1. Introduction

In recent years, software has become the most expensive component of computer system projects. The bulk of the cost of software development is due to the human effort, and most cost estimation methods focus on this aspect and give estimates in terms of person-months.

Accurate software cost estimates are critical to both developers and customers. They can be used for generating request for proposals, contract negotiations, scheduling, monitoring and control. Underestimating the costs may result in management approving proposed systems that then exceed their budgets, with underdeveloped functions and poor quality, and failure to complete on time. Overestimating may result in too many resources committed to the project, or, during contract bidding, result in not winning the contract, which can lead to loss of jobs.

Accurate cost estimation is important because:

- It can help to classify and prioritize development projects with respect to an overall business plan.
- It can be used to determine what resources to commit to the project and how well these resources will be used.
- It can be used to assess the impact of changes and support replanning.

- Projects can be easier to manage and control when resources are better matched to real needs.
- Customers expect actual development costs to be in line with estimated costs.

Software cost estimation involves the determination of one or more of the following estimates:

- effort (usually in person-months);
- project duration (in calendar time); and
- cost (in dollars).

Most cost estimation models attempt to generate an effort estimate, which can then be converted into the project duration and cost. Although effort and cost are closely related, they are not necessarily related by a simple transformation function. Effort is often measured in person-months of the programmers, analysts and project managers. This effort estimate can be converted into a dollar cost figure by calculating an average salary per unit time of the staff involved, and then multiplying this by the estimated effort required.

Practitioners have struggled with three fundamental issues:

- Which software cost estimation model to use?
- Which software size measurement to use — lines of code (LOC), function points (FP), or feature point?
- What is a good estimate?

The widely practiced cost estimation method is expert judgment. For many years, project managers have relied on experience and the prevailing industry norms as a basis to develop cost estimate. However, basing estimates on expert judgment is problematic:

- This approach is not repeatable and the means of deriving an estimate are not explicit.
- It is difficult to find highly experienced estimators for every new project.
- The relationship between cost and system size is not linear. Cost tends to increase exponentially with size. The expert judgment method is appropriate only when the sizes of the current project and past projects are similar.
- Budget manipulations by management aimed at avoiding overrun make experience and data from previous projects questionable.

In the last three decades, many quantitative software cost estimation models have been developed. They range from empirical models such as Boehm's COCOMO models [5] to *analytical* models such as those in [8, 29, 30]. An *empirical model* uses data from previous projects to evaluate the current project and derives the basic formulae from analysis of the particular database available. An *analytical model*, on the other hand, uses formulae based on global assumptions, such as the rate at which developer solve problems and the number of problems available.

Most cost models are based on the size measure, such as LOC and FP, obtained from size estimation. The accuracy of size estimation directly impacts the accuracy of cost estimation. Although common size measurements have their own drawbacks, an organization can make good use of any one, as long as a consistent counting method is used.

A good software cost estimate should have the following attributes [31]:

- It is conceived and supported by the project manager and the development team.
- It is accepted by all stakeholders as realizable.
- It is based on a well-defined software cost model with a credible basis.
- It is based on a database of relevant project experience (similar processes, similar technologies, similar environments, similar people and similar requirements).
- It is defined in enough detail so that its key risk areas are understood and the probability of success is objectively assessed.

Software cost estimation historically has been a major difficulty in software development. Several reasons for the difficulty have been identified:

- Lack of a historical database of cost measurement.
- Software development involving many interrelated factors, which affect development effort and productivity, and whose relationships are not well understood.
- Lack of trained estimators and estimators with the necessary expertise.
- Little penalty is often associated with a poor estimate.

2. Process of Estimation

Cost estimation is an important part of the planning process. For example, in the top-down planning approach, the cost estimate is used to derive the project plan:

(1) The project manager develops a characterization of the overall functionality, size, process, environment, people, and quality required for the project.
(2) A macro-level estimate of the total effort and schedule is developed using a software cost estimation model.
(3) The project manager partitions the effort estimate into a top-level work breakdown structure. He also partitions the schedule into major milestone dates and determines a staffing profile, which together forms a project plan.

The actual cost estimation process involves seven steps [5]:

(1) Establish cost-estimating objectives.
(2) Generate a project plan for required data and resources.

(3) Pin down software requirements.
(4) Work out as much detail about the software system as feasible.
(5) Use several independent cost estimation techniques to capitalize on their combined strengths.
(6) Compare different estimates and iterate the estimation process.
(7) After the project has started, monitor its actual cost and progress, and feedback results to project management.

No matter which estimation model is selected, users must pay attention to the following to get best results:

- coverage of the estimate (some models generate effort for the full life-cycle, while others do not include effort for the requirement stage);
- calibration and assumptions of the model;
- sensitivity of the estimates to the different model parameters; and
- deviation of the estimate with respect to the actual cost.

3. Software Sizing

The software size is the most important factor that affects the software cost. This section describes five software size metrics used in practice. The line of code and function point are the most popular metrics among the five metrics.

Line of Code: This is the number of lines of the *delivered source code* of the software, excluding comments and blank lines and is commonly known as *LOC* [10]. Although LOC is programming language dependent, it is the most widely used software size metric. Most models relate this measurement to the software cost. However, exact LOC can only be obtained after the project has completed. Estimating the code size of a program before it is actually built is almost as hard as estimating the cost of the program.

A typical method for estimating the code size is to use experts' judgement together with a technique called *PERT* [3]. It involves experts' judgment of three possible code-sizes: S_l, the lowest possible size; S_h the highest possible size; and S_m, the most likely size. The estimate of the code-size S is computed as:

$$S = \frac{S_l + S_h + 4S_m}{6}.$$

PERT can also be used for individual components to obtain an estimate of the software system by summing up the estimates of all the components.

Software science: Halstead proposed the *code length* and *volume* metrics [13]. Code length is used to measure the source code program length and is defined as:

$$N = N1 + N2$$

where $N1$ is the total number of operator occurrences, and $N2$ is the total number of operand occurrences.

Volume corresponds to the amount of required storage space and is defined as:

$$V = N \log(n1 + n2)$$

where $n1$ is the number of distinct operators, and $n2$ is the number of distinct operands that appear in a program.

There have been some disagreements over the underlying theory that supports the software science approach [14, 32]. This measurement has received decreasing support in recent years.

Function points: This is a measurement based on the functionality of the program and was first introduced by Albrecht [1]. The total number of function points depends on the counts of distinct (in terms of format or processing logic) types in the following five classes:

(1) *User-input types*: data or control user-input types.
(2) *User-output types*: output data types to the user that leaves the system.
(3) *Inquiry types*: interactive inputs requiring a response.
(4) *Internal file types*: files (logical groups of information) that are used and shared inside the system.
(5) *External file types*: files that are passed or shared between the system and other systems.

Each of these types is individually assigned one of three *complexity levels* of {1 = simple, 2 = medium, 3 = complex} and given a weighting value that varies from 3 (for simple input) to 15 (for complex internal files).

The *unadjusted function-point counts* (*UFC*) is given as

$$UFC = \sum_{i=1}^{5} \sum_{j=1}^{3} N_{ij} W_{ij}$$

where N_{ij} and W_{ij} are respectively the number and weight of types of class i with complexity j.

For example, if the raw function-point counts of a project are 2 simple inputs ($W_{ij} = 3$), 2 complex outputs ($W_{ij} = 7$) and 1 complex internal file ($W_{ij} = 15$). Then $UFC = 2 * 3 + 2 * 7 + 1 * 15 = 35$.

This initial function-point count is either directly used for cost estimation or is further modified by factors whose values depend on the overall complexity of the project. This will take into account the degree of distributed processing, the amount of reuse, the performance requirement, etc. The final function-point count is the product of the UFC and these project *complexity factors.* The advantage of the function-point measurement is that it can be obtained based on the system requirement specification in the early stage of software development.

The UFC is also used for code-size estimation using the following linear formula:

$$LOC = a * UFC + b\,.$$

The parameters a, b can be obtained using linear regression and previously completed project data. The latest *Function Point Counting Practices Manual* is maintained by the IFPUG (International Function Point Users Group) in ***http://www.ifpug.org/***

Extensions of function point: ***Feature point*** extends the function point to include algorithms as a new class [21]. An *algorithm* is defined as the set of rules which must be completely expressed to solve a significant computational problem. For example, a square root routine can be considered as an algorithm. Each algorithm used is given a weight ranging from 1 (*elementary*) to 10 (*sophisticated algorithms*) and the feature point is the weighted sum of the algorithms plus the function points. This measurement is especially useful for systems with few input/output and high algorithmic complexity, such as mathematical software, discrete simulations, and military applications.

Another extension of function points is ***full function point*** (**FFP**) for measuring real-time applications, by also taking into consideration the control aspect of such applications. FFP introduces two new control data function types and four new control transactional function types. A detailed description of this new measurement and counting procedure can be found in [35].

Object points: While feature point and FFP extend the function point, the object point measures the size from a different dimension. This measurement is based on the number and complexity of the following objects: screens, reports and 3GL components. Each of these objects is counted and given a weight ranging from 1 (*simple screen*) to 10 (*3GL component*) and the object point is the weighted sum of all these objects. This is a relatively new measurement and it has not been very popular. But because it is easy to use at the early phase of the development cycle and also measures software size reasonably well, this measurement has been used in major estimation models such as COCOMO II for cost estimation [6]..

4. Cost Estimation

There are two major types of cost estimation methods: *algorithmic* and *non-algorithmic*. Algorithmic models vary widely in mathematical sophistication. Some are based on simple arithmetic formulas using such summary statistics as means and standard deviations [9]. Others are based on regression models [38] and differential equations [30]. To improve the accuracy of algorithmic models, there is a need to adjust or calibrate the model to local circumstances. These models cannot be used *off-the-shelf*. Even with calibration the accuracy can be quite mixed.

We first give an overview of non-algorithmic methods.

4.1. *Non-algorithmic methods*

Analogy costing: This method requires one or more completed projects that are similar to the new project and derives the estimation through reasoning by analogy using the actual costs of previous projects. Estimation by analogy can be done either at the total project level or at subsystem level. The total project level has the advantage that all cost components of the system will be considered while the subsystem level has the advantage of providing a more detailed assessment of the similarities and differences between the new project and the completed projects. The strength of this method is that the estimate is based on actual project experience. However, it is not clear to what extend the previous project is actually representative of the constraints, environment and functions to be performed by the new system. Positive results and a definition of project similarity in term of features were reported in [33].

Expert judgment: This method involves consulting one or more experts. The experts provide estimates using their own methods and experience. Expert-consensus mechanisms such as Delphi technique or PERT will be used to resolve the inconsistencies in the estimates. The **Delphi technique** works as follows:

(1) The coordinator presents each expert with a specification and a form to record estimates.
(2) Each expert fills in the form individually (without discussing with others) and is allowed to ask the coordinator questions.
(3) The coordinator prepares a summary of all estimates from the experts (including mean or median) on a form requesting another iteration of the experts' estimates and the rationale for the estimates.
(4) Repeat steps (2)–(3) as many rounds as appropriate.

A modification of the Delphi technique proposed by Boehm and Fahquhar [5] seems to be more effective: before the estimation, a group meeting involving the coordinator and experts is arranged to discuss the estimation issues. In step (3), the experts do not need to give any rationale for the estimates. Instead, after each round of estimation, the coordinator calls a meeting to have experts discussing those points where their estimates varied widely.

Parkinson: Using Parkinson's principle "work expands to fill the available volume" [28], the cost is determined (not estimated) by the available resources rather than based on an objective assessment. If the software has to be delivered in 12 months and 5 people are available, the effort is estimated to be 60 person-months. Although it sometimes gives good estimation, this method is not recommended as it may provide very unrealistic estimates. Also, this method does not promote good software engineering practice.

Price-to-win: The software cost is estimated to be the best price to win the project. The estimation is based on the customer's budget instead of the software functionality. For example, if a reasonable estimation for a project costs 100 person-months but the customer can only afford 60 person-months, it is common that the estimator is asked to modify the estimation to fit 60 person-months' effort in order to win the project. This is again not a good practice since it is very likely to cause a bad delay of delivery or force the development team to work overtime.

Bottom-up: In this approach, each component of the software system is separately estimated and the results aggregated to produce an estimate for the overall system. The requirement for this approach is that an initial design must be in place that indicates how the system is decomposed into different components.

Top-down: This approach is the opposite of the bottom-up method. An overall cost estimate for the system is derived from global properties, using either algorithmic or non-algorithmic methods. The total cost can then be split up among the various components. This approach is more suitable for cost estimation at the early stage.

4.2. *Algorithmic methods*

The algorithmic methods are based on mathematical models that produce cost estimate as a function of a number of variables, which are considered to be the major cost factors. Any algorithmic model has the form:

$$\text{Effort} = f(x_1, x_2, \ldots, x_n)$$

where $\{x_1, x_2, \ldots, x_n\}$ denote the cost factors. The existing algorithmic methods differ in two aspects: the selection of cost factors, and the form of the function f. We will first discuss the cost factors used in these models, then characterize the models according to the form of the functions and whether the models are analytical or empirical.

4.2.1. *Cost factors*

Besides the software size, there are many other cost factors. The most comprehensive set of cost factors are proposed and used by Boehm *et al* in the COCOMO II model [6]. These cost factors can be divided into four types:

Product factors: Required reliability; product complexity; database size used; required reusability; documentation match to life-cycle needs.

Computer factors: Execution time constraint; main storage constraint; computer turnaround constraints; platform volatility.

Personnel factors: Analyst capability; application experience; programming capability; platform experience; language and tool experience; personnel continuity.

Project factors: Multisite development; use of software tool; required development schedule.

The above factors are not necessarily independent, and most of them are hard to quantify. In many models, some of the factors appear in combined form and some are simply ignored. Also, some factors take discrete values, resulting in an estimation function with a piece-wise form.

4.2.2. *Linear models*

Linear models have the form:

$$\text{Effort} = \alpha_0 + \sum_{i=1}^{n} a_i x_i$$

where the coefficients $a_1, \ldots, a_n$ are chosen to best fit the completed project data. The work of Nelson belongs to this type of models [26]. We agree with Boehm's comment that "there are too many nonlinear interactions in software development for a linear model to work well" [5].

4.2.3. *Multiplicative models*

Multiplicative models have the form:

$$\text{Effort} = a_0 \prod_{i=1}^{n} a_i^{x_i} .$$

Again the coefficients $a_1, \ldots, a_n$ are chosen to best fit the completed project data. Walston-Felix [38] used this type of model with each x_i taking on only three possible values: -1, 0, $+1$. Doty model [16] also belongs to this class with each x_i taking on only two possible values: 0, $+1$. These two models seem to be too restrictive on the cost factor values.

4.2.4. *Power function models*

Power function models have the general form:

$$\text{Effort} = a \times S^b$$

where S is the code-size, and a, b are (usually simple) functions of other cost factors. This class contains two of the most popular algorithmic models in use, as follows:

COCOMO (Constructive Cost Model) models

This family of models was proposed by Boehm [4, 5]. The models have been widely accepted in practice. In the COCOMOs, the code-size S is given in thousand LOC (KLOC) and Effort is in person-month.

(A) *Basic COCOMO.* This model uses three sets of $\{a, b\}$ depending on the complexity of the software only:

(1) for simple, well-understood applications, $a = 2.4$, $b = 1.05$;
(2) for more complex systems, $a = 3.0$, $b = 1.15$; and
(3) for embedded systems, $a = 3.6$, $b = 1.20$.

The basic COCOMO model is simple and easy to use. As many cost factors are not considered, it can only be used as a rough estimate.

(B) *Intermediate COCOMO* and *Detailed COCOMO*. In the intermediate COCOMO, a nominal effort estimation is obtained using the power function with three sets of $\{a, b\}$, with coefficient a being slightly different from that of the basic COCOMO:

(1) for simple, well-understood applications, $a = 3.2$, $b = 1.05$;
(2) for more complex systems, $a = 3.0$, $b = 1.15$; and
(3) for embedded systems, $a = 2.8$, $b = 1.20$.

Then, fifteen cost factors with values ranging from 0.7 to 1.66 (see Table 1) are determined [5]. The overall *impact factor* M is obtained as the product of all individual factors, and the estimate is obtained by multiplying M to the nominal estimate.

Table 1. The cost factors and their weights in COCOMO II.

Cost Factors	Description	Rating				
		Very low	Low	Nominal	High	Very high
	Product					
RELY	required software reliability	0.75	0.88	1.00	1.15	1.40
DATA	database size	—	0.94	1.00	1.08	1.16
CPLX	product complexity	0.70	0.85	1.00	1.15	1.30
	Computer					
TIME	execution time constraint	—	—	1.00	1.11	1.30
STOR	main storage constraint	—	—	1.00	1.06	1.21
VIRT	virtual machine volatility	—	0.87	1.00	1.15	1.30
TURN	computer turnaround time	—	0.87	1.00	1.07	1.15
	Personnel					
ACAP	analyst capability	1.46	1.19	1.00	0.86	0.71
AEXP	application experience	1.29	1.13	1.00	0.91	0.82
PCAP	programmer capability	1.42	1.17	1.00	0.86	0.70
VEXP	virtual machine experience	1.21	1.10	1.00	0.90	—
LEXP	language experience	1.14	1.07	1.00	0.95	—
	Project					
MODP	modern programming practice	1.24	1.10	1.00	0.91	0.82
TOOL	software tools	1.24	1.10	1.00	0.91	0.83
SCED	development schedule	1.23	1.08	1.00	1.04	1.10

While both basic and intermediate COCOMOs estimate the software cost at the system level, the detailed COCOMO works on each sub-system separately and has an obvious advantage for large systems that contain non-homogeneous subsystems.

(C) COCOMO II. Perhaps the most significant difference from the early COCOMO models is that the exponent b changes according to the following cost factors: precedentedness, development flexibility, architecture or risk resolution, team cohesion, and process maturity. Other differences include newly added cost factors and models for solidifying software architecture and reducing risk.

Putnam's model and SLIM

Putnam derives his model based on Norden/Rayleigh manpower distribution and his finding in analyzing many completed projects [30]. The central part of Putnam's model is called *software equation* as follows:

$$S = E \times (\text{Effort})^{1/3} t_d^{4/3}$$

where t_d is the software delivery time; E is the *environment factor* that reflects the development capability, which can be derived from historical data using the software equation. The size S is in LOC and the Effort is in person-year. Another important relation found by Putnam is

$$\text{Effort} = D_0 \times t_d^3$$

where D_0 is a parameter called *manpower build-up* which ranges from 8 (entirely new software with many interfaces) to 27 (rebuilt software). Combining the above equation with the software equation, we obtain the power function form:

$$\text{Effort} = (D_0^{4/7} \times E^{-9/7}) \times S^{9/7} \quad \text{and}$$

$$t_d = (D_0^{-1/7} \times E^{-3/7}) \times S^{3/7} .$$

Putnam's model is also widely used in practice and SLIM is a software tool based on this model for cost estimation and manpower scheduling.

4.2.5. *Model calibration using linear regression*

A direct application of the above models does not take local circumstances into consideration. However, one can adjust the cost factors using the local data and linear regression method. We illustrate this model calibration using the general power function model: Effort $= a \times S^b$.

Take logarithm of both sides and let $Y = \log(\text{Effort})$, $A = \log(a)$ and $X = \log(S)$. The formula is transformed into a linear equation:

$$Y = A + b \times X .$$

Applying the standard least square method to a set of previous project data $\{Y_i, X_i : i = 1, \ldots, k\}$, we obtain the required parameters b and A (and thus a) for the power function.

4.2.6. *Discrete models*

Discrete models have a tabular form, which usually relates the effort, duration, difficulty and other cost factors. This class of models contains Aron model [3], Wolverton model [39], and Boeing model [4]. These models gained some popularity in the early days of cost estimation, as they were easy to use.

4.2.7. *Other models*

Many other models exist and the following have been used quite successfully in practice.

Price-S is proprietary software cost estimation model developed and maintained by RCA, New Jersey [27]. Starting from an estimate of project size, type and difficulty, the model computes project cost and schedule.

SoftCost relates size, effort and duration to address risk using a form of the Rayleigh probability distribution [36]. It contains heuristics to guide the estimators in dealing with new technology and complex relations among the parameters involved.

The algorithmic models can be grouped as shown in Table 2.
Table 3 compares the strengths and weaknesses of different methods. From the comparison, we can conclude that

- No one method is the best for all projects.
- Parkinson and Price-to-win methods are not suitable for organizations which aim to win more business.
- Using a combination of techniques may provide the best estimation. For example, combining top-down estimation with expert judgement and analogy methods may provide a superior result.

Table 2. Classification of algorithmic models.

Algorithmic Models					
	Linear	Multiplicative	Power Function	Discrete	Others
Empirical	Nelson	Walston-Felix Herd *et al*	COCOMOS	Aron Boeing Wolverton	Price-S
Analytical			Putnam		SoftCost

Table 3. Summary of strengths and weaknesses of different methods.

Methods	Strengths	Weaknesses
Non-algorithmic		
Expert Judgment	Expert with the relevant experience can provide good estimation; Fast estimation	Dependent on the "expert"; May be bias; Suffer from incomplete recall
Analogy	Based on actual project data and past experience	Similar projects may not exist; Historical data may not be accurate
Parkinson Price-to-win	Often win the contract	Poor practice; May have large overruns
Top-down	System level focus; Faster and easier than bottom-up method; Require minimal project detail	Provide little detail for justifying estimates; Less accurate than other methods
Bottom-up	Based on detailed analysis; Support project tracking better than other method, as its estimates address low level tasks	May overlook system level cost factors; Require more estimation effort compared to Top-down; Difficult to perform the estimate early in the lifecycle
Algorithmic	Objective, repeatable results; Gain a better understanding of the estimation method	Subjective inputs; Calibrated to past projects and may not reflect the current environment; Algorithms may be company specific and not be suitable for software development in general

4.3. *Measurement of model performance*

Various researchers have used different error measurements. The most popular error measure is *Mean Absolute Relative Error* (*MARE*):

$$MARE = \sum_{i=1}^{n} (\,|\,(\text{estimate}_i - \text{actual}_i)/\text{actual}_i\,|\,)/n$$

where estimate_i is the estimated effort from the model, actual_i is the actual effort, and n is the number of projects.

To establish whether models are biased, the *Mean Relative Error* (*MRE*) can be used:

$$MRE = \sum_{i=1}^{n}((\text{estimate}_i - \text{actual}_i)/\text{actual}_i)/n\,.$$

A large positive MRE would suggest that the model generally overestimates the effort, while a large negative value would indicate the reverse.

The following criteria can be used for evaluating cost estimation models [5]:

(1) *Definition* — Has the model clearly defined the costs it is estimating, and the costs it is excluding?
(2) *Fidelity* — Are the estimates close to the actual costs expended on the projects?
(3) *Objectivity* — Does the model avoid allocating most of the software cost variance to poorly calibrated subjective factors (such as complexity)? Is it hard to adjust the model to obtain any result the user wants?
(4) *Constructiveness* — Can a user tell why the model gives the estimates it does? Does it help the user understand the software job to be done?
(5) *Detail* — Does the model easily accommodate the estimation of a software system consisting of a number of subsystems and units? Does it give accurate phase and activity breakdowns?
(6) *Stability* — Do small differences in inputs produce small differences in output cost estimates?
(7) *Scope* — Does the model cover the class of software projects whose costs the user need to estimate?
(8) *Ease of Use* — Are the model inputs and options easy to understand and specify?
(9) *Prospectiveness* — Does the model avoid the use of information that will not be well known until the project is complete?
(10) *Parsimony* — Does the model avoid the use of highly redundant factors, or factors which make no appreciable contribution to the results?

5. Performance of Estimation Models

Many studies have attempted to evaluate the cost estimation models. Unfortunately, the results are not encouraging, as many of them were found to be not very accurate. Kemerer performed an empirical validation of four algorithmic models (SLIM, COCOMO, Estimacs, and FPA) [22]. No recalibration of models was performed on the project data, which was different from that used for model development. Most models showed a strong over estimation bias and large estimation errors, ranging from a MARE of 57% to 800%.

Vicinanza, Mukhopadhyay and Prietula used experts to estimate the project effort using Kemerer's data set without formal algorithmic techniques and found the results outperformed the models in the original study [37]. However, the MARE ranges from 32 to 1107%.

Ferens and Gurner evaluated three models (SPANS, Checkpoint, and COSTAR) using 22 projects from Albrecht's database and 14 projects from Kemerer's data set [11]. The estimation error is also large, with MARE ranging from 46% for the Checkpoint model to 105% for the COSTAR model.

Another study on COCOMO also found high error rates, averaging 166% [23].

Jeffery and Low investigated the need for model calibration at both the industry and organization levels [19]. Without model calibration, the estimation error was large, with MARE ranging from 43% to 105%.

Jeffery, Low and Barnes later compared the SPQR/20 model to FPA using data from 64 projects from a single organization [20]. The models were recalibrated to the local environment to remove estimation biases. Improvement in the estimate was observed with a MARE of 12%, reflecting the benefits of model calibration.

There were also studies based on the use of analogy. With the use of a program called ANGEL that was based on the minimization of Euclidean distance in n-dimensional space, Shepperd and Schofield found that estimating by analogy outperformed estimation based on statistically derived algorithms [33].

Heemstra surveyed 364 organizations and found that only 51 used models to estimate effort and that the model users made no better estimate than the non-model users [15]. Also, use of estimation models was no better than expert judgment.

A survey of software development within JPL found that only 7% of estimators use algorithmic models as a primary approach of estimation [17].

6. New Approaches

Cost estimation remains a complex problem, which continues to attract considerable research attention. Researchers have attempted different approaches. Recently, models based on artificial intelligence techniques have been developed. For example, Finnie and Wittig applied artificial neural networks (ANN) and case-based reasoning (CBR) to estimation of effort [12]. Using a data set from the Australian Software Metrics Association, ANN was able to estimate development effort within 25% of the actual effort in more than 75% of the projects, and with a MARE of less than 25%. However, the results from CBR were less encouraging. In 73% of the cases, the estimates were within 50% of the actual effort, and for 53% of the cases, the estimates were within 25% of the actual.

In a separate study, Mukhopadhyay, Vicinanza and Prietula found that an expert system based on analogical reasoning outperformed other methods [24].

Srinivasan and Fisher used machine learning approaches based on regression trees and neural networks to estimate costs [34]. The learning approaches were found to be competitive with SLIM, COCOMO, and function points, compared to the previous study by Kemerer [22]. A primary advantage of learning systems is that they are adaptable and nonparametric.

Briand, El Eman, and Bomarius proposed a hybrid cost modeling method, COBRA: Cost estimation, Benchmarking and Risk Analysis [7]. This method was based on expert knowledge and quantitative project data from a small number of projects. Encouraging results were reported on a small data set.

7. Conclusion

Today, almost no model can estimate the cost of software with a high degree of accuracy. This state of the practice is created because

(1) there are a large number of interrelated factors that influence the software development process of a given development team and a large number of project attributes, such as number of user screens, volatility of system requirements and the use of reusable software components;
(2) the development environment is evolving continuously; and
(3) the lack of measurement that truly reflects the complexity of a software system.

To produce a better estimate, we must improve our understanding of these project attributes and their causal relationships, model the impact of evolving environment, and develop effective ways of measuring software complexity.

At the initial stage of a project, there is high uncertainty about these project attributes. The estimate produced at this stage is inevitably inaccurate, as the accuracy depends highly on the amount of reliable information available to the estimator. As we learn more about the project during analysis and later design stages, the uncertainties are reduced and more accurate estimates can be made. Most models produce exact results without regard to this uncertainty. They need to be enhanced to produce a range of estimates and their probabilities.

To improve the algorithmic models, there is a great need for the industry to collect project data on a wider scale. The recent effort of ISBSG is a step in the right direction [18]. They have established a repository of over 790 projects, which will likely be a valuable source for *builders* of cost estimation model.

With new types of applications, new development paradigms and new development tools, cost estimators are facing great challenges in applying known estimation models in the new millenium. Historical data may prove to be irrelevant for future projects. The search for reliable, accurate and low cost estimation methods must continue. Several areas are in need of immediate attention. For example, we need models for development based on formal methods, or iterative software process. Also, more studies are needed to improve the accuracy of cost estimate for maintenance projects.

References

1. A. J. Albrecht and J. E. Gaffney, "Software function, source lines of codes, and development effort prediction: A software science validation", *IEEE Transactions on Software Engineering* **SE-9** (1983) 639–648.

2. US Army, *Working Schedule Handbook*, Pamphlet No. 5-4-6 (January 1974).
3. J. D. Aron, *Estimating Resource for Large Programming Systems*, NATO Science Committee, Rome, Italy (October 1969).
4. R.K.D. Black, R. P. Curnow, R. Katz and M. D. Gray, *BCS Software Production Data*, Final Technical Report, RADC-TR-77-116, Boeing Computer Services, Inc. (March 1977).
5. B. W. Boehm, Software Engineering Economics (Englewood Cliffs, NJ, Prentice-Hall, 1981).
6. B. W. Boehm *et al*, "The COCOMO 2.0 software cost estimation model", *American Programmer* (July 1996) 2–17.
7. L. C. Briand, K. El Eman and F. Bomarius, "COBRA: A hybrid method for software cost estimation, benchmarking, and risk assessment", *International Conference on Software Engineering* (1998) 390–399.
8. G. Cantone, A. Cimitile and U. De Carlini, "A comparison of models for software cost estimation and management of software projects", *Computer Systems: Performance and Simulation* (Elisevier Science Publishers B.V., 1986).
9. W. S. Donelson, "Project planning and control", *Datamation* (June 1976) 73–80.
10. N. E. Fenton and S. L. Pfleeger, *Software Metrics: A Rigorous and Practical Approach* (PWS Publishing Company, 1997).
11. D. V. Ferens and R. B. Gumer, "An evaluation of three function point models of estimation of software effort", *IEEE National Aerospace and Electronics Conference* **2** (1992) 625–642.
12. G. R. Finnie and G. E. Wittig, "AI tools for software development effort estimation", *Software Engineering and Education and Practice Conference* (IEEE Computer Society Press, 1996) 346–353.
13. M. H. Halstead, *Elements of Software Science* (Elsevier, New York, 1977).
14. P. G. Hamer and G. D. Frewin, "M. H. Halstead's software science — A critical examination", *Proceedings of the 6th International Conference on Software Engineering* (September 13–16, 1982) 197–206.
15. F. J. Heemstra, "Software cost estimation", *Information and Software Technology* **34**, no. 10 (1992) 627–639.
16. J. R. Herd, J. N. Postak, W. E. Russell and K. R. Steward, "Software cost estimation study — Study results", Final Technical Report, RADC-TR77-220, Vol. **I** (Doty Associates, Inc., Rockville, MD, 1977).
17. J. Hihn and H. Habib-Agahi, "Cost estimation of software intensive projects: A survey of current practices", *International Conference on Software Engineering* (1991) 276–287.
18. ISBSG, International software benchmarking standards group, *http://www.isbsg.org/au*
19. D. R. Jeffery and G. C. Low, "Calibrating estimation tools for software development", *Software Engineering Journal* (July 1990) 215–221.
20. D. R. Jeffery, G. C. Low and M. Barnes, "A comparison of function point counting techniques", *IEEE Transactions on Software Engineering* **19**, no. 5 (1993) 529–532.
21. C. Jones, *Applied Software Measurement, Assuring Productivity and Quality* (McGraw-Hill, 1997).
22. C. F. Kemerer, "An empirical validation of software cost estimation models", *Communications of the ACM* **30**, no. 5 (May 1987) 416–429.
23. Y. Miyazaki and K. Mori, "COCOMO evaluation and tailoring", *Eighth International Conference on Software Engineering* (1985) 292–299.

24. T. Mukhopadhyay, S. S. Vicinanza and M. J. Prietula, "Examining the feasibility of a case-based reasoning model for software effort estimation", *MIS Quarterly* **16**, no. 2 (June 1992) 155–172.
25. G. Myers, "Estimating the costs of a programming system development project", Systems Development Division, Poughkeepsie Laboratory, IBM (May 1972).
26. R. Nelson, *Management HandBook for the Estimation of Computer Programming Costs*, AD-A648750 (Systems Development Corporation, 1966).
27. R. E. Park, "PRICE S: The calculation within and why", *Proceedings of ISPA Tenth Annual Conference*, Brighton, England (July 1988).
28. G. N. Parkinson, *Parkinson's Law and Other Studies in Administration* (Houghton-Miffin, Boston, 1957).
29. N. A. Parr, "An alternative to the Raleigh curve model for software development effort", *IEEE Transactions on Software Engineering* (May 1980).
30. L. H. Putnam, "A general empirical solution to the macro software sizing and estimating problem", *IEEE Transactions on Software Engineering* (July 1978) 345–361.
31. W. Royce, *Software Project Management: A Unified Framework* (Addison Wesley, 1998).
32. V. Y. Shen, S. D. Conte and H. E. Dunsmore, "Software science revisited: A critical analysis of the theory and its empirical support", *IEEE Transactions on Software Engineering* **9**, no. 2 (1983) 155–165.
33. M. Shepperd and C. Schofield, "Estimating software project effort using analogy", *IEEE Transactions on Software Engineering* **SE-23**, no. 12 (1997) 736–743.
34. K. Srinivasan and D. Fisher, "Machine learning approaches to estimating software development effort", *IEEE Transactions on Software Engineering* **21**, no. 2 (February 1995) 126–137.
35. D. St-Pierre, M. Maya, A. Abran, J. Desharnais and P. Bourque, *Full Function Points: Counting Practice Manual*, Technical Report 1997-04, University of Quebec at Montreal (1997).
36. R. Tausworthe, *Deep Space Network Software Cost Estimation Model* (Jet Propulsion Laboratory Publication 81-7, 1981).
37. S. S. Vicinanza, T. Mukhopadhyay and M. J. Prietula, "Software-effort estimation: An exploratory study of expert performance", *Information Systems Research* **2**, no. 4 (December 1991) 243–262.
38. C. E. Walston and C. P. Felix, "A method of programming measurement and estimation", *IBM Systems Journal* **16**, no. 1 (1977) 54–73.
39. R. W. Wolverton, "The cost of developing large-scale software", *IEEE Transactions on Computer* (June 1974) 615–636.

DATA MODEL METRICS

MARIO PIATTINI, MARCELA GENERO and CORAL CALERO
Grupo ALARCOS, University of Castilla-La Mancha, Ronda de Calatrava, 5, 13071, Ciudad Real (Spain)
E-mail: {mpiattin,mgenero,ccalero}@inf-cr.uclm.es

Due to the central role that conceptual data models play in the design of databases, it is crucial to assure their quality since the early phases of database life cycle. For assessing (and if it is necessary improving) conceptual data model quality it is necessary to dispose of quantitative and objective measures in order to avoid bias in the quality evaluation process. It is in this context that software measurement can help IS designers to make better decision during design activities. The main interest of this article is to provide a state-of-the-art measures for conceptual data models.

Keywords: Conceptual data models, software metrics, structural complexity, measures validation.

1. Introduction

Data modeling is the first step in database design, providing the link between the user's needs and the software solution that meets them. The choice of an appropriate representation of data is one of the most crucial tasks in the entire systems development process. Although the data modeling phase represents only a small proportion of the total systems development effort, its impact on the final result is probably greater than any other phase [1]. The data model is a major determinant of system development costs and quality. Additionally, as experience has proved, problems in the artifacts produced in the initial stages of system development propagate to the artefacts produced in later stages, where they are much more costly to identify and correct [2]. Therefore, the quality of data models must be evaluated, and the effort expended on improving it is likely to pay off many times over in later phases.

However, there are no generally accepted guidelines for evaluating the quality of data models, and little agreement even among experts as to what makes a "good" data model [3]. In general as Krogstie *et al* [4] remarked "most literature provides only bread and butter lists of useful properties without giving a systematic structure for evaluating them". Moreover these lists are mostly unstructured, use imprecise definitions, often overlap, and properties of models are often confused with language method properties [5]. Quality properties are not generally enough to ensure quality in practice, because different people will have different interpretations of the same concept. It is necessary to have quantitative and objective measures to reduce subjectivity and bias in the evaluation process.

Recently, some more rigorous frameworks have been proposed which attempt to address quality in data modeling in a much more systematic way [3–7] but most of them lack the quantitative assessment of data model quality.

Software engineers have been putting forward huge quantities of metrics for software products, processes and resources [8, 9]. Unfortunately, almost all the metrics are focused on programs, disregarding data models [10]. This corroborates the fact that compared to software engineering quality the concept of data model quality is poorly understood [11].

The main interest of this article is to provide a state-of-the-art measures for conceptual data models. We will present some proposals of metrics for data models proposed by Gray *et al* [12], Kesh [13], Moody [14], Genero *et al* [15] and Piattini *et al* [16]. We will focus on measures for entity relationship diagrams (ERD) metrics because ERD [17] is still the dominant method of data modeling [18]. In fact, most data modelers currently use some variant of the ERD [19].

This article is organized in the following way: in Sec. 2, we present different steps that are advisable to follow in the process of metric definition. In Sec. 3, we present five proposals of conceptual data model measures [12–16] checking if each one accomplish the steps suggested in Sec. 2. In Sec. 3, we present a summary and comparison of each metric proposal presented in Sec. 3. Finally, in Sec. 4, we summarize the article and present future trends in the area of measures for conceptual modeling.

2. Metrics Definition and Validation Process

For assuring that the metrics for data models (and also for other artifact produced along the IS life cycle) are valid metrics it is necessary to define them in a methodological way. Therefore the goal of this section is to highlight the different issues that must be taken into account in the process of metric definition and validation. Figure 1 shows three general steps that it is advisable to follow in the

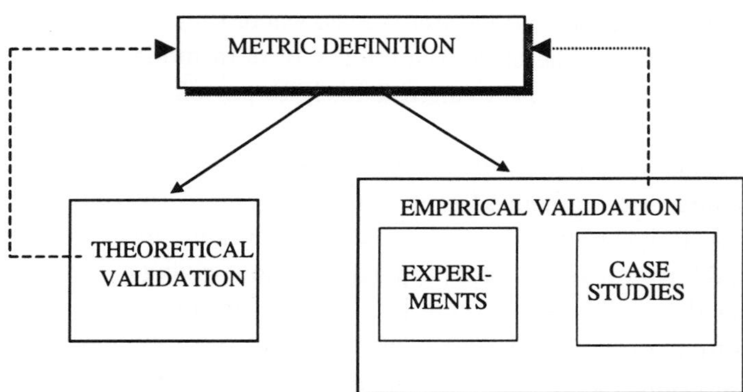

Fig. 1. Steps for metric definition.

process of metric definition and validation [23], and they will be explained in the following subsections.

This process is iterative, and each step can feed the others, which lead us to accept, improve, change or discard the proposed metrics.

2.1. *Metric definition*

The first step is the proposal of metrics with clear goals, i.e., a goal-oriented definition of metrics. The Goal/Question/Metric (GQM) paradigm [20, 21] provides a framework for deriving measures from measurement goals. In GQM each metric is deduced using a top-down approach covering three levels: at conceptual level goals are defined, at operational level questions are defined, and at the quantitative level metrics are derived. Using the GQM approach results in a set of metrics whose utility is clearly justified. As an improvement of GQM, [22] proposes a goal-oriented measurement model life cycle (MMLC), that is a more structured approach that for each phase identify the main activities with their inputs and outputs, and defines some templates deriving some of these activities. The MMLC focuses on the management activities pointed to generate, refine, and achieve the organizational goals.

Basically either GQM or the MMLC emphasize that the measurement goal should be clearly connected with an industrial goal, so the measurement program responds to a software organization's needs. The following is an example of a GQM goal:

> Analyze ERD for the purpose of *evaluating maintainability* from the viewpoint of the *database designer* or information system designer in *software development companies/departments.* The goal is therefore defined in terms of the entities shown in Fig. 2.

Moreover we can distinguish two kind of metrics: closed-ended metrics or open-ended metrics [23]. A closed-ended metric is one where measurements can only fall within a particular range. The ratio of some part to its corresponding whole is of

Object of study:	ERD
Purpose:	Evaluating
Quality focus:	Maintainability
Viewpoint:	Database designer/IS designer
Environment:	Software development companies/departments

Fig. 2. One example of goal definition.

this type. Its range can only be from zero to one. An example of a closed-ended metric is the number of all relationships in the ERD that are M:N, divided by the total number of relationships in the ERD. The open-ended metrics are those where at least one end of its range is not absolutely fixed. An example of an open-ended metric is the number of entities in an ERD.

Another aspect to take into account is that metrics can be defined at different "data model scopes": metrics for single different elements of the data model (e.g. number of attributes of an entity, number of attributes of a relationship, etc) or metrics for the model as a whole (e.g. number of entities in a model, number of relationships in a model, etc).

Data models metrics can be objective or subjective [24] i.e., they can be calculated using an objective method (such as counting the number of entities) or a subjective one (typically scores given by users or stakeholders). In general, subjective measures are believed to be of lower of quality that objective ones.

2.2. *Theoretical validation*

The main goal of theoretical validation is to check if the intuitive or formal idea of the attribute being measured is reflected in the measurement. This is done by analyzing the theoretical requisites which must be satisfied when measuring. Basically, it is based on the analysis of the properties of the attribute that we wish to measure.

Even though several attempts have been made to establish how to carry out theoretical validation in software measurement, there is not yet a standard, accepted way of theoretically validating a measure. As Van den Berg and Van den Broek [25] said, a standard on theoretical validation issues in software measurement is urgently required.

Work on validation theory has followed two paths which are complementary.

(1) Measurement theory-based approaches [26–28]: to check for a specific measure if the empirical relations between the elements of the real world established by the attribute being measured, are respected when measuring the attributes. Measurement theory gives clear definitions of terminology, a sound basis of software measures, criteria for experimentation, conditions for validation of software measures, foundations of prediction models, empirical properties of software measures, and criteria for measurement scales in the opinion of the measurement theory proponents. However, most research in the software measurement area does not address measurement scales. Much of it argues that scales are not so important. These arguments do not take into account that empirical properties of software measures are hidden behind scales. Units are also closely connected to measurement scales. The discussion of scale types is important for statistical operations. Because many empirical and numerical conditions are not covered by acertain

scale type, the consideration of the empirical and numerical conditions is necessary and very important, too.

(2) Property-based approaches [29–31]. Aim to formalize the empirical properties that a generic attribute of software or a system (e.g. the complexity or size) must satisfy in order for it to be used in the analysis of any measurement proposed for that attribute.

2.3. *Empirical validation*

As in other aspects of Software Engineering, proposing techniques and metrics is not enough; it is also necessary to perform an empirical validation of them to assure their utility in practice. Empirical validation is critical to the success of software measurement [9, 32–34]. Therefore, the goal of this step is to prove the practical utility of the proposed metrics. Although there are various ways of performing this step, basically we can divide the empirical validation into experimentation and case studies. Experimentation is usually made using controlled experiments and the case studies usually work with real data. Both of them are necessary, controlled experiments for having a first approach and case studies for making the results stronger. Replication of experiments is necessary because it is difficult to understand the applicability of isolated results from one study and, thus, to assess the true contribution to the field [34].

3. Metric Proposals

As we commented in the introduction, we focus mainly on metrics for ERD, because in the database design field is still the most dominant method of modeling [18]. Other metrics, which can be used for data models, can be found in Lethbridge [23] (which focus on knowledge models) and in Genero *et al* [35] (where a survey of OO models metrics can be found).

For each proposal, we use the metric definition and we analyze the following issues:

- Goal pursued.
- Metric scope.
- If the metrics are close or open ended.
- If the metrics are objective or subjective.
- If the metrics were theoretically validated.
- If the metrics were empirically validated.

3.1. *Gray et al's metric proposal* [12]

Gray *et al* [12] have proposed some objectives and open ended metrics to evaluate the quality of an ERD. The goal of these metrics is to provide designers of quantitative support for helping them to compare design alternatives and help them to take better decisions. Gray *et al* [12] suggested to use this measure for determining the effort required to implement a design, but they did not show how. Also, these metrics could help to identify design problems from the database design and optimize it, and if necessary improve the design.

• **ER metric.** The complexity of an ERD is an objective and open ended metric defined as:

$$E = \sum_{i=1}^{n} (E_i)^c$$

where

$$1 < c$$

$$n = \text{number of entities.}$$

The complexity of an entity "i" is:

$$E_i = D_i{}^* F_i$$

where

$$D_i = \text{data architecture complexity}$$

$$F_i = \text{functional complexity.}$$

The data architecture complexity for entity "i"is:

$$D_i = R_i{}^*(a^* FDA_i + b^* NFDA_i)$$

where

$$0 < a <= b$$

$$R_i = \text{number of relationships}$$

$$FDA_i = \text{number of functionally dependent attributes}$$

$$NFDA_i = \text{number of non-functionally dependent attributes.}$$

The values for coefficients a, b and c are likely to be highly dependent on each ERD, so they must be valued accordingly to each particular situation. The functional complexity, F_i, is assumed to be 1 for each entity.

• **Area metric.** Given two ERD the area metric M, is defined as:

$$M = \frac{Ae \times Ee^{+} Re^{\times} Ae^{+} Re^{\times} Ee}{A3 \times E3^{+} R3^{\times} A3^{+} R3^{\times} E3}$$

... where the numerator is calculated regarding the attributes, the entities and the relationships of an ERD.

And the denominator regarding the same ERD in its corresponding Third Normal Form.

$$A = \text{number of attributes}$$
$$E = \text{number of entities}$$
$$R = \text{number of relationships.}$$

This metric can be used in two ways:

(1) Comparing alternative designs for the same system: the value of $A \times E + R \times A + R \times E$ can be computed for each design and the values directly compared.
(2) Comparing designs for different systems: the ratios for a design and its corresponding design in Third Formal Norm are compared. That is if $M = D/N$ where D is $A \times E + R \times A + R \times E$ for a design and N is $A \times E + R \times A + R \times E$ for its corresponding in Third Formal Norm.

These measures were not theoretically validated and there are no empirical evidence of the utility of these metrics.

3.2. *Kesh's metric proposal* [13]

Kesh [13] develops a method for assessing the quality of an ERD. This author considers that data model quality is determined by both ontological and behavioural components. This method can be summarized in three steps:

(1) Calculate scores for the individual ontological components, both structure components (which refer to the relationship between elements that make up the model) and content components (which refer to the attribute of the entities). Structure components are suitability (o_1), soundness (o_2), consistency (o_3) and conciseness (o_4). Content components are completeness (o_5), cohesiveness (o_6) and validity (o_7).
(2) Combine the scores for relevant ontological components for each behavioural component: usability (from the user's point of view) (s_1), usability (from the designer's point of view) (s_2), maintainability (s_3), accuracy (s_4) and performance (s_5).
(3) Combine the scores for behavioural components to calculate the score of model quality.

Thus, the overall score for data model quality can be calculated as:

$$Q = w_1 \cdot s_1 + w_2 \cdot s_2 + w_3 \cdot s_3 + w_4 \cdot s_4 + w_5 \cdot s_5$$

where w_1, w_2, w_3, w_4, w_5 are the weights of the behavioural factors, and s_1, s_2, s_3, s_4, s_5 are the scores for the behavioural factors The value of the weights can be determined either by the importance of the factor to the organization or by some general agreement upon values. The scores s_1, s_2, s_3, s_4, s_5 are based on the combination of values of the ontological factors:

$$s_1 = (o_1 + o_3 + o_4 + o_5)/4$$

$$s_2 = (o_2 + o_3 + o_5 + o_6 + o_7)/5$$

$$s_3 = (o_2 + o_4 + o_6)/3$$

$$s_4 = (o_3 + o_5)/2$$

$$s_5 = (o_4 + o_5)/2$$

where $o_1 \cdots o_7$ are the ontological factors.

Ontological factors are, in their turn, based on user's scores between 1 and 5, or more complex formulas, as it is shown below:

- $\mathbf{o}_1$ (suitability score): the users should be asked whether they find the ERD suitable or not, rating it between 1 to 5.
- $\mathbf{o}_2$ (soundness score): similarly to o_1, o_2 can be estimated from a technical group not directly involved with the project.
- $\mathbf{o}_3$ (consistency score): can be calculated by deducting a certain amount f points for each inconsistency, in the following way:

  $$\mathbf{o}_3 = M - D_1$$

  where M = Maximum possible points (here 5 points) and D_1 is based on the ratio R = (number of inconsistencies/number of implications). The number of implications is given by $4n_1$, where n_1 is the number of relationships in the diagram because two implications area posible for each entity in a relationship.
- $\mathbf{o}_4$ (conciseness score): if n is the number of entities in an ERD, the minimum number of relationships needed will be $(n-1)$. Any ERD with $(n-1)$ relationships should get a perfect score of M (5 in this case). The worst possible situation is when every entity is connected to every other entity. The number of relationships in this case is $C\binom{n}{2}$. In this case, o_4 is zero. In an ERD with n_1 connections o_4 can therefore be calculated as

  $$\mathbf{o}_4 = M\left(\left(C\binom{n}{2} - n_1\right) \Big/ C\binom{n}{2} - (n-1)\right).$$

- $\mathbf{o}_5$ (completeness of content): to make sure that an ERD is complete, it has to be verified against the list of queries and reports to be generated by the database. The deduction for missing data for any query or report from M should be decided by the organization, depending on the importance of the query or the report.

- $\mathbf{o}_6$ (cohesiveness of content): is a measure of the cohesiveness of each entity. For each entity the cohesiveness is the size of the primary identifier. If the primary identifier is composed of only one attribute then the attributes have the possible highest cohesiveness and the score should be M. If the primary identifier has to use all attributes of the entity then it has no cohesiveness and $o_{6i} = 0$, where I denotes the number of that entity. If n_e is the number of attributes in the entity and n_p the number of attributes that make up the primary identifier, then:

$$\mathbf{o}_{6i} = M((n_e - n_p)/(n_e - 1))y\,\mathbf{o}_6 = \Sigma o_{6i}/n\,.$$

- $\mathbf{o}_7$ (validity of content): is calculated by assigning M is all attributes for all the entities are considered valid. If all attributes are considered invalid (i.e., none of them are placed in the right entities) then a score of zero should be assigned. If n_i are the total of invalid entities then:

$$\mathbf{o}_7 = M(1 - n_i/\Sigma n_e)\,.$$

If the scores on o_1 through o_7 fall below the organizational requirements the ERD has to be modified before proceeding to calculate the quality score.

Because of the nature of the metrics it requires the designers to interact with the users to get the measurements, thereby increasing the feedback from the users and the managers.

Kesh [13] suggested that the determination of an ERD quality is subjective, the value that he proposed of Q is an indicator of the ERD quality rather than a precise estimate.

The causal relationships between ontological and behavioural factors in an ERD has to be empirically validated and modified according the empirical data.

These measures were not theoretically validated.

After a real world application of the model, Kesh [13] concluded that his model provided a useful framework for analyzing and making revisions to the ERD. But he did not explain how his proposal really function in practice and he also suggested that both the model and the methodology should be applied to large-scale ERD.

3.3. *Moody's metric proposal* [14]

Moody [14] has defined a comprehensive set of metrics (see Table 1) for evaluating the quality of an ERD. Some of them are objective metrics (e.g. the number of entities within the ERD) while others are the result of the subjective scoring of the stakeholders (e.g. the ability of users to interpret the model correctly).

Goal: Assess different factors that influence ERD quality.

These metrics were neither theoretically nor empirically validated. Moody [14] suggested the necessity of their empirical validation but proposed that task as future work.

Table 1. Metrics to evaluate the quality factors [14].

Quality Factors	Metrics
Completeness	Number of items in the data model that do not correspond to user requirements Number of user requirements, which are not represented in the data model Number of items in the data model that correspond to user requirements but are inaccurately defined Number of inconsistencies with the process model.
Integrity	Number of business rules, which are not enforced by the data model Number of integrity constraints included in the data model that do not accurately correspond to business policies.
Flexibility	Number of elements in the model which are subject to change in the future Estimated cost of changes Strategic importance of changes.
Understandability	User rating of understandability of model Ability of users to interpret the model correctly Application developer rating of understandability.
Correctness	Number of violations to data modeling conventions Number of normal form violations Number of instances of redundancy within the model.
Simplicity	Number of entities Number of entities and relationships The weighted sum of constructs ($aN^E + bN^R + cN^A$), where N^E is the number of entities, N^R is the number of relationships, and N^A is the number of attributes.
Integration	Number of conflicts with the Corporate Data Model Number of conflicts with existing systems Rating by representatives of all business areas as to whether the data has been defined in a way which meets corporate needs rather than requirements of the application being developed.
Implementability	Technical risk rating Schedule risk rating Development cost estimate Number of physical level elements included in the data model.

3.4. *Genero et al's metric proposal* [15]

The idea of these authors focus on measuring the ERD maintainability. As an external quality attribute, maintainability can only be measured when the product is finished or nearly finished, so the idea is to define measures for ERD structural complexity (an internal attribute) and based on them to predict ERD maintainability, which influences the maintainability of the database which is finally implemented.

From a system theory point of view, a system is called complex if it is composed of many (different types of elements), with many (different types of) (dynamically changing) relationships between them [36]. The complexity of an ERD could be highly influenced by the different elements that compose it, such as entities, attributes, relationships, generalizations, etc. Hence it is not advisable to define a general measure for its complexity [37]. Following this reasoning Genero *et al* [15] have proposed a set of measures for measuring ERD structural complexity, following the notion of complexity of Henderson-Sellers [38]. These metrics allow database designers:

(1) a quantitative comparison of design alternatives, and therefore and objective selection among several ERD alternatives with equivalent semantic content; and
(2) a prediction of external quality characteristics, like maintainability in the initial phases of the IS life cycle and a better resource allocation based on these predictions.

These metrics are open ended and could be applied at diagram level. They are classified into the following categories:

Entity Metrics

- **NE metric:** Is the total the number of entities within the ERD.

Attribute Metrics

- **NA metric:** Is the total number of attributes that exist within the ERD, taking into account both entity and relationship attributes. In this number, we include simple attributes, composite attributes and also multivalued attributes, each of which take the value 1.
- **DA metric:** An ERD is minimal when every aspect of the requirements appears once in the diagram, i.e., an ERD is minimal if it does not have any redundancies. One of the sources of redundancies in the ERD is the existence of derived attributes. An attribute is derived when its value can be calculated or deduced from the values of other attributes. The Derived Attributes metric as the number of derived attributes existing in the ERD.
- **CA metric:** Is the total number of composite attributes within an ERD.
- **MVA metric:** Is total number of multivalued attributes within the ERD.

Relationship Metrics

- **NR metric:** Is the total number of relationships within the ERD, taking into account only common relationships.
- **M:NR metric:** Is the total number of M:N relationships within the ERD.
- **1:NR metric:** Is the total number of 1:N relationships (including also 1:1 relationships) within the ERD..
- **N-AryR metric:** Is the total number of N-ary relationships (not binary) within the ERD.
- **BinaryR metric:** Is the total number of binary relationships within the ERD.
- **NIS_AR metric:** Is the total number of relationships IS_A (generalization/specialization) that exist within the ERD. In this case, we consider one relationship for each child-parent pair within the IS_A relationship.
- **RefR metric:** Is the total number of reflexive relationships that exist within the ERD.
- **RR metric:** Another source of redundancy in an ERD is the existence of redundant relationships. We define the Redundant Relationship metric as the number of relationships that are redundant in the ERD.

These metrics were theoretically validated following the property-based approach proposed by Briand *et al* [30] in [39] and following the measurement theory-based framework proposed by Zuse [26] in [15].

Genero *et al* have carried out empirical validation of these metrics by means:

- A case study. In [40], it was demonstrated by means of a case study that some of the proposed metrics are heavily correlated with the time spent on the different phases of the development of the application programs that manage the data represented in the ERD.
- A controlled experiment. In [41], a controlled experiment was carried out with the aim of building a prediction model for the ERD maintainability based on the values of the proposed measures. For building the prediction model, we used an extension of the original Knowledge Discovery in Databases (KDD): the Fuzzy Prototypical Knowledge Discovery (FPKD) [42], that consist of the search for fuzzy prototypes that characterize the maintainability of an ERD. These prototypes lay the foundation of the prediction model that will lead us to predict ERD maintainability.

Further empirical validation, including the replication of that experiment and taken data with "real project" is required to draw on the final remarks.

3.5. *Piattini et al's metric proposal* [16]

Piattini *et al* [16] have proposed a set of objectives, close ended metric to evaluate the structural complexity of an ERD, with the goal of building a prediction model for the maintainability of an ERD.

- **RvsE metric:** Measures the relation that exists between the number of relationships and the number of entities in an ERD model.

$$RvsE = \left(\frac{N^R}{N^R + N^E}\right)^2$$

N^R is the number of relationships in the ERD. N^E is the number of entities in the ERD. $N^R + N^E > 0$.

In the number of relationship (N^R), the IS_A relationships is considered, taking into account one relationship for each pair child-parent within the IS_A relationship.

- **DA metric:** Is the number of derived attributes that exist within the ERD model, divided by the maximum number of derived attributes that may exist in an ERD (all attributes in the ERD model except one).

$$DA = \frac{N^{DA}}{N^A - 1}$$

N^{DA} is the number of derived attributes in the ERD. N^A is the number of attributes in the ERD. $N^A > 1$.

In the number of attributes in the ERD (N^A), simple attributes is included, composite attributes and also multivalued attributes, each of which take the value 1.

- **CA metric:** Assesses the number of composite attributes, compared with the number of attributes in an ERD.

$$CA = \frac{N^{CA}}{N^A}$$

N^{CA} is the number of composite attributes in the ERD. N^A is the number of attributes in the ERD. $N^A > 0$.

In the number of attributes in the ERD (N^A), simple attributes is included, composite attributes and also multivalued attributes, each of which take the value 1.

- **RR metric:** Is the number of relationships that are redundant in an ERD, divided by the number of relationships in the ERD minus one.

$$RR = \frac{N^{RR}}{N^R - 1}$$

N^{RR} is the number of redundant relationships in the ERD. N^R is the number of relationships in the ERD. $N^R > 1$.

In the number of relationship (N^R), the IS_A relationships is considered, taking into account one relationship for each pair child-parent within the IS_A relationship.

- **M:NRel metric:** Measures the number of $M : N$ relationships compared with the number of relationships in an ERD model.

$$M : N \operatorname{Re} l = \frac{N^{M:NR}}{N^R}$$

$N^{M:NR}$ is the number of $M : N$ relationships in the ERD. N^R is the number of relationships in the ERD. $N^R > 0$.

In the number of relationship (N^R), the IS_A relationships is considered, taking into account one relationship for each pair child-parent within the IS_A relationship.

- **IS_ARel metric:** Assesses the complexity of generalization/specialization hierarchies (IS_A) in one ERD. This metric combines two factors in order to measure the complexity of the inheritance hierarchy. The first factor is the fraction of entities that are leaves of the inheritance hierarchy. This measure, called FLeaf, is calculated thus:

$$F\text{Leaf} = \frac{N^{\text{Leaf}}}{N^E}$$

N^{Leaf} is the number of leaves in one generalization/specialization hierarchy. N^E is the number of entities in each generalization/specialization hierarchy. $N^E > 0$.

On its own, FLeaf has the undesirable property that, for a very shallow hierarchy (e.g. just two or three levels) with a high branching factor, it gives a measurement that is unreasonably high, from a subjective standpoint To correct this problem with Fleaf, an additional factor is used in the calculation of IS_ARel metric: the average number of direct and indirect supertype per non-root entity, ALLSup (the root entity is not counted since it cannot have parents).

IS_ARel metric is calculated using the following formula:

$$\text{Is\_A Re}\, l = F\text{Leaf} - \frac{F\text{Leaf}}{\text{ALLSup}}$$

This metric assesses the complexity of each IS_A hierarchy. The overall IS_ARel complexity is the average of all the IS_ARel complexities in the ERD.

These metrics were not theoretically validated.

Related to empirical validation, Genero *et al* [43] have carried out empirical validation of these metrics by means of a controlled experiment in order to ascertain the relationships that exist between the proposed metrics and maintainability sub-characteristics (understandability, legibility, simplicity, analyzability, modifiability, stability, and testability), and also to obtain a prediction model for ERD maintainability based on the metric values.

Further empirical validation is required to extract final conclusions, specially with data taken from "real projects", for example real data about maintenance effort.

4. Summary of the Different Proposals

Table 2 summarizes the most important characteristics of the main conceptual data model metrics proposals existing in the literature, which we present in Sec. 3. The first column of the table refers to the main source of the metrics. In the second one, the focus of the metrics is presented (usually complexity). The third column refers to the scope of the metrics: data model as a whole or single element of the data model. Next column shows if the metrics are calculated by an objective method or a subjective one (typically scores given by users or stakeholders). The fifth column reflects whether metrics are open or closed ended. And the last two columns reflect whether there are published studies in which either the theoretical or the empirical validation of the metrics have been carried out.

Seeing Table 2, we can conclude that the work about measures for conceptual data models is scarce. Most of the proposed metrics lack of theoretical and empirical validation and they have not been defined following any methodological way such as GQM [20, 21] or MMLC [22]. Only Genero *et al*'s proposal [15] partially follow most of the recommendations done in Sec. 2 about how to define valid metrics. Nevertheless, further validation is required to consider it as a final proposal.

The measurement of conceptual data models is an area that is not consolidated yet. Further research is needed about validation either theoretical or empirical. This can contribute to the definition of valid metrics, which can be useful for database

Table 2. Conceptual data model metrics.

Authors	Focus	Scope	Objective/ Subjective	Open/Closed Ended	Theoretical validation	Empirical validation
Gray *et al* [12]	Complexity	Conceptual Data Model	Objective	Open-ended	NO	NO
Kesh [13]	Ontological and behavioural	Conceptual data model	Objective and Subjective	Open-ended	NO	NO
Moody *et al* [6]	Several quality factors	Conceptual data model	Objective and Subjective	Open-ended	NO	NO
Genero *et al* [15]	Complexity	Conceptual data model	Objective	Open-ended	YES	Partial
Piattini *et al* [16]	Complexity	Data model	Objective	Closed ended	NO	Partial

designers to take better decisions in their design tasks, which is the most important goal that must pursue any measurement proposal if it pretends to be useful [44].

5. Conclusions

The importance of data models in software development and their influence in the final Information System quality and cost, emphasize the importance of data model quality. Data model quality must be addressed by rigorous and quantitative methods and techniques. As Moody remarks, for information modeling to progress from a "craft" to an engineering discipline, formal quality criteria and metrics need to be explicitly defined [14]. We focused on conceptual data models, because it is the first artifact produced in the database life cycle and its quality heavily influence the database finally implemented.

Nowadays, more research is needed into the aspects of software measurement in general, both from a theoretical and from a practical point of view. In our opinion, even more efforts are needed in defining and validating data model metrics. These metrics can be used to flag outlying models for special attention, and to help data designers in their tasks.

In this chapter some recent proposals in this sense have been summarized. The metrics proposed so far need to be validated in more cases and experiments, but could be used by practitioners as a starting point.

More research is also needed in data modeling process quality, as most of the works carried out so far have focused on data model product quality.

As we have already pointed out, the great diffusion of OO techniques for data modeling introduced also new elements that must be taken into account, such as aggregation or other kind of relationships, for which practically no measures exist. Therefore, the future work of measures for conceptual data models deal with OO models. Regarding OO models, it is also necessary to define metrics not only for measuring static diagrams like class diagrams [35], but also metrics for dynamic diagrams, such as state diagrams and activity diagrams.

References

1. G. C. Simsion, *Data Modeling Essentials* (Van Nostrand Reinhold, 1994).
2. B. Boehm, *Software Engineering Economics* (Prentice-Hall, 1981).
3. L. Moody and G. Shanks, "What makes a good data model? Evaluating the quality of entity relationships models", *Proceedings of the 13th International Conference on Conceptual Modeling (ER'94)*, Manchester, England (December 1994) 94–111.
4. J. Krogstie, O. I. Lindland and G. Sindre, "Towards a deeper understanding of quality in requirements engineering", *Proceedings of the 7th International Conference on Advanced Information Systems Engineering (CAISE)*, Jyvaskyla, Finland (June 1995) 82–95.
5. O. Lindland, G. Sindre and A. Solvberg, "Understanding quality in conceptual modeling", *IEEE Software* **11**, no. 2 (March 1994) 42–49.
6. L. Moody, G. Shanks and P. Darke, "Improving the quality of entity relationship models — Experience in research and practice", *Proceedings of the Seventeenth*

International Conference on Conceptual Modeling (*ER'98*), Singapore (November 1998) 255–276.

7. R. Schuette and T. Rotthowe, "The guidelines of modeling — An approach to enhance the quality in information models", *Proceedings of the Seventeenth International Conference on Conceptual Modeling* (*ER'98*), Singapore (November 1998) 240–254.
8. A. Melton (ed.), *Software Measurement* (International Thomson Computer Press, London, 1996).
9. N. Fenton and S. L. Pfleeger, *Software Metrics: A Rigorous Approach*, 2nd ed. (Chapman & Hall, London, 1997).
10. H. M. Sneed and O. Foshag, "Measuring legacy database structures", *Proceedings of the European Software Measurement Conference FESMA'98*, eds. Hooft and Peeters, Coombes (1998) 199–210.
11. P. Assenova and P. Johanneson, "Improving quality in conceptual modeling by the use of schema transformations", *Proceedings of the 15th International Conference of Conceptual Modeling* (*ER'96*), Cotbus, Germany (1996) 277–291.
12. R. Gray, B. Carey, N. McGlynn and A. Pengelly, "Design metrics for database systems", *BT Technology Journal* **9**, no. 4] (1991) 69–79.
13. S. Kesh, "Evaluating the quality of entity relationship models", *Information and Software Technology* **37**, no. 12 (1995) 681–689.
14. L. Moody, "Metrics for evaluating the quality of entity relationship models", *Proceedings of the Seventeenth International Conference on Conceptual Modeling* (*ER'98*), Singapore (November 1998) 213–225.
15. M. Genero, M. Piattini, C. Calero and M. Serrano, "Measures to get better quality databases", *ICEIS 2000*, Stafford (July 2000) 49–55.
16. M. Piattini, M. Genero, C. Calero, M. Polo and F. Ruiz, "Database quality", *Advanced Database Technology and Design*, Chap. 14, eds. M. Piattini and O. Díaz, Artech House (2000) 485–509.
17. P. Chen, "The entity-relationship model: Toward a unified view of data", *ACM Transactions on Database Systems* **1**, no. 1 (1976) 9–37.
18. R. Muller, *Database Design for Smarties. Using UML for Data Modeling* (Morgan Kaufmann, San Francisco, 1999).
19. T. Teorey, *Database Modeling and Design*, 3rd ed. (Morgan Kaufmann, San Francisco, 1999).
20. V. Basili and D. Weiss, "A methodology for collecting valid software engineering data", *IEEE Transactions on Software Engineering* **10** (1984) 728–738.
21. V. Basili and H. Rombach, "The TAME project: Towards improvement-oriented software environments", *IEEE Transactions on Software Engineering* **14** (1988) 758–773.
22. G. Cantone and P. Donzelli, "Production and maintenance of goal-oriented software measurement models", *Journal of Software Engineering and Knowledge Engineering* (World Scientific Publishing Co. Pte. Ltd., 2001) (to appear).
23. T. Lethbridge, "Metrics for concept-oriented knowledge bases", *International Journal of Software Engineering and Knowledge Engineering* **8**, no. 2 (1998) 161–188.
24. S. Morasca, "Software measurements", *Handbook of Software Engineering and Knowledge Engineering*, Vol. 1 (World Scientific Publishing Co. Pte. Ltd., 2001).
25. Van Den Berg and Van Den Broek, "Axiomatic validation in the software metric development process", *Software Measurement*, Chap. 10, ed. A. Melton (Thomson Computer Press, 1996).
26. H. Zuse, "A framework of software measurement", Walter de Gruyter (Berlin, 1998).

27. A. Melton, D. Gustafson, M. Bieman and L. Baker, "A mathematical perspective for software measures research", *IEE Software Engineering Journal* **5**, no. 5 (1990) 246–254.
28. G. Poels and G. Dedene, "Distance-based software measurement: Necessary and sufficient properties for software measures", *Information and Software Technology* **42**, no. 1 (2000) 35–46.
29. E. Weyuker, "Evaluating software complexity measures", *IEEE Transactions on Software Engineering* **14**, no. 9 (1988) 1357–1365.
30. L. Briand, S. Morasca and V. Basili, "Property-based software engineering measurement", *IEEE Transactions on Software Engineering* **22**, no. 6 (1996) 68–86.
31. S. Morasca and L. Briand, "Towards a theoretical framework for measuring software attributes", *Proceeding of the Fourth International Software Metrics Symposium* (1997) 119–126.
32. B. Kitchenham, S. Pflegger and N. Fenton, "Towards a framework for software measurement validation", *IEEE Transactions of Software Engineering* **21**, no. 12 (1995) 929–943.
33. N. F. Schneidewind, "Software metrics for quality control", *Proceedings of the Fourth International Software Metrics Symposium*, IEEE Computer Society Technical Council on Software Engineering (1997) 127–136.
34. V. R. Basili, F. Schull and F. Lanubile, "Building knowledge through families of experiments", *IEEE Transactions on Software Engineering* **25**, no. 4 (1999) 456–473.
35. M. Genero, M. Piattini and C. Calero, "Early measures for UML class diagrams", *L'Objet* **6**, no. 4 (Hermes Science Publications, 2000) 489–515.
36. G. Poels and G. Dedene, "Measures for assessing dynamic complexity aspect of object-oriented conceptual schemes", *Proceedings of the 19th International Conference on Conceptual Modeling* (*ER'2000*), Salt Lake City (October 2000) 499–512.
37. N. Fenton, "Software measurement: A necessary scientific basis", *IEEE Transactions on Software Engineering* **20**, no. 3 (1994) 199–206.
38. B. Henderson-Sellers, *Object-Oriented Metrics — Measures of Complexity* (Prentice-Hall, Upper Saddle River, NJ, 1996).
39. M. Genero, M. Piattini and C. Calero, "Formalization of metrics for conceptual data models", *UKAIS'2000*, Cardiff, April 26–28, 2000 (McGraw Hill International (UK) Limited, 2000) 99–100.
40. M. Genero, M. Piattini and C. Calero, "An approach to evaluate the complexity of conceptual database models", *2nd European Software Measurement Conference — FESMA-AEMES 2000*, Madrid (2000).
41. M. Genero, J. Olivas, M. Piattini and F. Romero, "Knowledge discovery for predicting entity relationship diagram maintainability", *SEKE'2001*, Argentina (2001) (to appear).
42. J. A. Olivas and F. P. Romero, "Fuzzy prototypical knowledge discovery. Application to forest fire prediction", *SEKE'2000*, Knowledge Systems Institute, Chicago, Ill. USA (2000) 47–54.
43. M. Genero, L. Jiménez and M. Piattini, "Measuring the quality of entity relationship diagrams", *Proceedings of the 19th International Conference on Conceptual Modeling* (*ER'2000*), Salt Lake City, USA (October 2000) 513–522.
44. N. Fenton and M. Neil, "Software metrics: A roadmap. Future of software engineering", ed. A. Finkelstein, ACM (2000) 359–370.

HOW MANY TESTS ARE ENOUGH?

TIM MENZIES
Department of Electrical & Computer Engineering,
University of British Columbia, 2356 Main Mall,
Vancouver, B.C., Canada V6T 1Z4
E-mail: tim@menzies.com

BOJAN CUKIC
NASA/WVU Software Research Laboratory,
Department of Computer Science and Electrical Engineering West Virginia University,
Morgantown, WV 26506-6109, USA
E-mail: cukic@csee.wvu.edu

1. Introduction

How many tests will be required to test software? At first glance, we might think that an impossibly large number of tests are required. A system containing V variables with S assignments may require one test for each combination of assignments, i.e.,

$$\#\text{tests} = N = S^V . \tag{1}$$

It is simple to show that this is an impossibly large number of tests. Consider one sample of fielded expert systems in which knowledge bases were found to contain between 55 and 510 "literals" [49]. Literals offer two assignments for each proposition: true or false; i.e., $S = 2$ and V is half the number of literals. Assuming:

- it takes one minute to consider each test result (which is a gross underestimate);
- the effective working year is 225 six hour days;

then a test of those sampled systems would take between 29 years and 10^{70} years (a time longer than the age of this universe).

The goal of this chapter is to offer an optimistic alternative to the pessimism of Eq. (1). After a review of the mathematics of testing, this chapter will conclude that in many cases, effective testing may need far fewer tests than Eq. (1). Various testing regimes will be discussed:

Black box methods (*BB*): In *BB* testing, input sets can be quickly built using automatic random selection of data. For nominal *BB* testing, these inputs are drawn from an operational profile describing the normal environment of a system [47]. For off-nominal BB testing, these inputs can come from within and without the operational profile. The discussion will focus on two special types of BB testing:

- If developers only require an approximate assessment of a system, then **approximate testing** can suffice.
- Depending on the goal of the testing, we can use **sampling theory** to explore less than S^V states of a program.
- Various **stopping rules** can be applied to control the time spent for testing.

White box methods (WB): In WB partition testing, analysts reflect over the internals of a program to invent test inputs that exercise K different *partitions* of a program. Each partition represents one class of behavior of the system.

Formal methods (FM): In FM testing, after the program or specification is understood, analysts must write its representation. This formal representation contains the essential features of the specification. It is a formal model, i.e., all its constructs have a precise semantics which can be revealed by automatic methods. Let x denote the level of rigor and F^xM denote a formal method with level-of-rigor x. At least four different styles of FM can be found in the literature:

- $F^{-1}M$ refers to very lightweight formal methods.
- F^0M refers to manual formal methods that rely heavily on mathematical representations.
- F^1M are the most common type of formal methods in use today. In F^1M testing, programs are written using conventional methods, then automatic formal methods are used to debug and revise the program.
- F^2M refers to full life cycle formal methods in which code is generated automatically from large libraries of formally proved components.

Before beginning, it is important to note that there are many methods of testing software other than those listed above (e.g. see the excellent discussions in [21, 35]). This chapter focuses on the methods listed above since we can precisely characterize some of their properties mathematically.

2. BB = Black Box Methods

BB methods are characterized by random inputs or inputs collected from the environment. BB tests are cheap to generate since analysts need not reflect over the internal complexities of their systems. When designing BB tests, test engineers make little or no use of the internal details of a system. Two broad classes of BB methods are *approximate testing* and *sampling*. Test engineers often adjust the

Text	N Tests	Text	N Tests
[28]	4..5	[8]	≈ 6
[6]	5..10	[17]	8..10
[56]	10	[10]	< 13
[42]	40	[50]	50
[4]	200		

Fig. 1. Number of tests proposed by different authors. Extended from a survey by [10].

effort associated with testing using *stopping rules.* Approximate testing, sampling, and stopping rules are discussed below.

Over half this chapter discusses BB since, surprisingly, it turns out that the random dice of BB testing are an excellent cost-effective method of *detecting errors.* Random BB tests are essential for analyzing system reliability since it is good practice to test outside of the situations defined by the analysts [26, p. 670]. Randomized selection of test inputs may uncover errors that could be missed if testing is biased by the incorrect assumptions of the analysts [32].

Lest this chapter over emphasises BB, it is important to stress now that BB techniques are blind to the internal structure of a program. Once an error is *detected* using BB, then other methods such as WB or FM are required to *localize* the source of that error.

2.1. *Approximate testing*

Our experience in the Australian and American software industry is that the final version of a software system is often fielded after only a handful of tests (dozens to hundreds). A literature review strongly suggests that this experience is not atypical. For example, much of the expert systems literature proposes evaluations based on very few tests, as indicated by Fig. 1. An exception can be found in [3], where it is proposed at least one test be conducted for every five rules and that "having more test cases than rules would be best".

Such small test sets can only ever be an *approximate test* of a system. For the rest of this section, we explore the case for approximate testing. We will find that in the majority of cases, approximate testing will suffice. However, a mathematical model of approximate testing suggests that approximate testing will fail at in at least 25% of cases. Hence, subsequent sections will try to improve on approximate testing.

Approximate testing assumes that:

(1) A system can be sampled via a small number of inputs.
(2) This small set of inputs might not be chosen with much care.

If our software contains pathways tangled like spaghetti, then these two assumption are clearly inappropriate. However, if software pathways are simple, then a few tests will adequately probe a system and approximate testing is an adequate strategy.

To see when approximate testing might work, consider the following example containing 15 binary variables $a, b, \ldots, n, o$. Equation (1) tells us that this system needs $2^{15} = 32{,}768$ tests. However, suppose that system has only one input and one output and pathways look like this:

$$\begin{array}{c} a \rightarrow b \rightarrow c \rightarrow d \rightarrow e \\ \text{input} \rightarrow f \rightarrow g \rightarrow h \rightarrow i \rightarrow j \quad \rightarrow \text{output} \\ k \rightarrow l \rightarrow m \rightarrow n \rightarrow o\,. \end{array}$$

Clearly, no tests are required for the top and bottom pathway since they are isolated from system inputs and outputs. Further, only a single test is required to cover the only pathway that connects inputs to outputs. If the paths in most programs look like this example, then software contains

(1) A *small number of simple i/o pathways* from inputs to outputs.
(2) *Large unreachable regions.*

If so, then any input, selected at random, that can propagate through to any output will test a significant portion of the usable parts of the system. Hence:

- A small number of such inputs would hence be sufficient to test a system.
- We can ignore Eq. (1) and endorse approximate testing.

2.1.1. *Empirical support for approximate testing*

There is much empirical evidence from the literature that real-world software comprises mostly simple i/o paths and large unreachable regions:

- Bieman & Schultz [5] studied how many sets of inputs are required to exercise all *du-pathways* in a system. A du-path is a link from where a variable is *defined* to where it is *used.* Figure 2 shows their experimental results. At least for the system they studied, in the overwhelming majority of their modules, very few inputs exercised all the du-pathways.

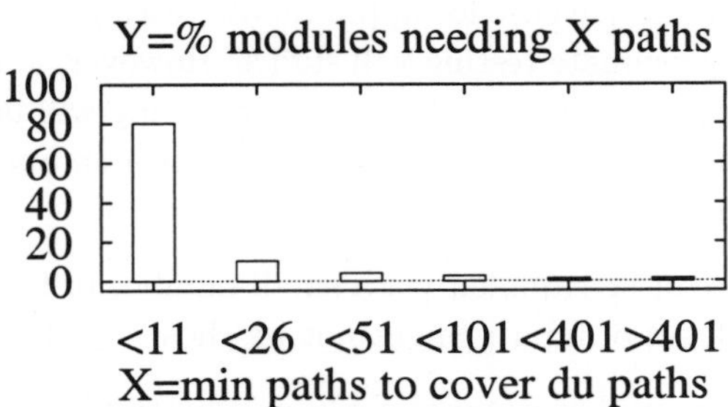

Fig. 2. An analysis of hundreds of modules in a software system. 83% of the modules could be fully explored using less than ten tests. From [5].

- Harrold *et al* [29] studied how control-flow diagrams grow as program size grows. A worst-case control-flow graph is one where every program statement links to every other statement; i.e., the edges in graph grow with the square of the number of statements. However, for over 4000 Fortran routines and 3147 "C" functions, the control flow graph grows linearly with the number of statements. That is, at least in the systems seen in that study, the program pathways form single-parent trees and not complicated tangles.
- Colomb [14] compared the inputs presented to a medical expert system with its internal structure. Based on the number variables V and their states S, an analysis like Eq. (1) made Colomb note that that system should have $S^V = 10^{14}$ internal states. However, after one year's operation, the inputs to that expert system only exercised 4000 states, i.e., in practice, this system only needed to handle a tiny fraction of the possible states ($4000 \ll 10^{14}$).
- Avritzer *et al* [2] studied the 857 different inputs seen in 355 days operation of an expert system. Massive overlap existed between these input sets. On average, the overlap between two randomly selected inputs was 52.9%. Further, a simple algorithm found that 26 carefully selected inputs covered 99% of the other inputs while 53 carefully selected inputs covered 99.9% of the other inputs.
- Horgan and Mathur [32] noted that testing often exhibits a *saturation* effect, i.e., most program paths get exercised early with little further improvement as testing continues. Saturation is consistent with programs containing large portions with simple shapes that are easily reached and other large portions that are so twisted in shape, that they will never be reachable. They report studies with the Unix report-generation language AWK [1]) and the word processor TEX [34]. Both AWK and TEX have been tested extensively for many years by their authors, with the assistance of a vast international user group. Elaborate test suites exist for those systems (e.g. [34]). Even after elaborate testing, large portions of TEX and AWK were not covered (see Fig. 3).

	% Coverage			
Program	Block	Decision	p-use	c-use
TEX	85	72	53	48
AWK	70	59	48	55

Fig. 3. Coverage reported by [32, p. 544]. "Block"= program blocks. "Decision"= program conditionals. "*P*-use"= pathways between where a variable is assigned and where it is used in a conditional. "*C*-use"= pathways between where a variable is assigned and where it is used, but not in a conditional.

2.1.2. *Theoretical support for approximate testing*

If these case studies represented the general case, then we should have great confidence in the utility of approximate testing. The average shape of software can be inferred from the odds of reaching any part of the system from random input. If the odds are high, then the pathways to that part must be simple. To infer these odds, Menzies & Cukic [39] assumed that software had been transformed into a possibly cyclic directed graph containing and-nodes and or-nodes (e.g. Fig. 4 would be converted to Fig. 5). A simplified description of their analysis is presented here. For reasons of space, that simple description ignores certain details presented in

```
procedure relax {
    if   tired=="no" AND weekend then {gotoMall; gotoParty;}
}
function weekend {
    return day=="saturday" OR day=="sunday"
}
procedure gotoMall {
    if   day=="sunday" then doThis
}
procedure gotoParty {
    atParty="yes"
     if    time>2am then   atParty="no";  gotoHome} else gotoParty;
}
procedure gotoHome {
    doThat
}
```

Fig. 4. A sample of procedural code.

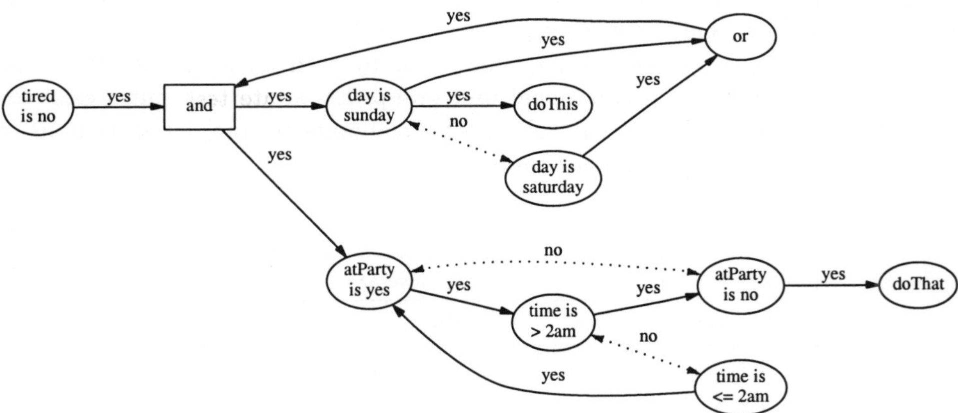

Fig. 5. Conversion of the procedural code in Fig. 4 to a graph containing no-edges (between incompatible nodes), and-nodes (which model conjunction), yes-edges (which model valid inferences), and or-nodes (which model disjunctions). And-nodes are shown as rectangles and or-nodes are shown as ellipses.

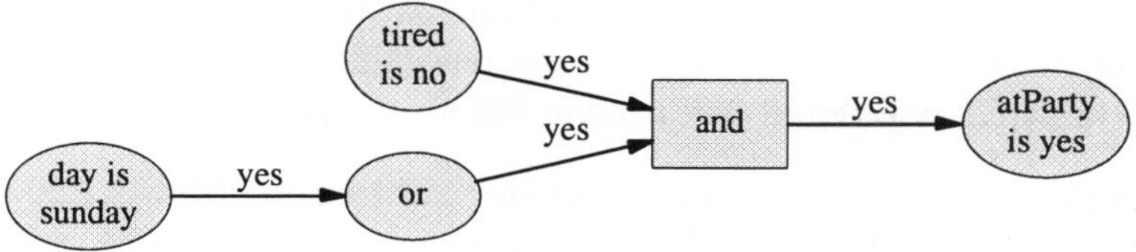

Fig. 6. A program pathway extracted from Fig. 5 that leads to "atParty=yes". And-nodes are shown as rectangles and or-nodes are shown as ellipses.

the full description of the model [41] such as random variables, and testing for loops/contradictions.

To compute the odds of reaching some part of a program graph, we need tools. Our first tool is the standard *sampling-with-replacement* expression of Eq. (2).

$$y = 1 - ((1 - x_j)^N) . \tag{2}$$

To derive this expression, recall that an event with probability x does not happen after N trials with probability $(1 - x)^N$. Hence, at probability y, the event will happen with the probability shown in Eq. (2). This equation assumes test independence, i.e., the effects of performing one test do not affect the others.

Our second tool is an average case analysis of the *reachability* of programs. Assume that "*in*" number of inputs have been presented to a graph containing V nodes. From these inputs, we grow a tree of pathways down to some random node within the graph (e.g. see the shaded tree in Fig. 6). The odds of reaching a node straight away from the inputs is $x_0 = \frac{in}{V}$. The probability of reaching an and-node with *andp* parents is the probability of reaching all its parents, i.e., $x_{and} = x_i^{andp}$ where x_i is the probability we computed in the prior step of the simulation (and x_0 being the base case). The probability of reaching an or-node with *orp* parents is the probability of not missing any of its parents, i.e., $x_{or} = 1 - (1 - x_i)^{orp}$ [via Eq. (2)]. If the ratio of and-nodes in a network is *andf*, then the ratio of or-nodes in the same network is $1 - andf$. The odds of reaching some random node x_j is the weighted sum of the probabilities of reaching and-nodes or or-nodes, i.e., $x_j = andf * x_{and} + orf * x_{or}$. We can convert x_j to the number of tests N required to be 99% sure of find a fault with probability x_j by rearranging Eq. (2) to:

$$N = \frac{\log(1 - 0.99)}{\log(1 - x_j)} . \tag{3}$$

After 150,000 simulations of this model, the number of random inputs required to be 99% sure of reaching a node were usually either surprisingly small or impractically large:

- In 55% of the runs, less than 100 random tests had a 99% chance of reaching any node. This result is consistent with numerous simple i/o pathways.

- In 20% of the runs, the number of random tests required to be 99% sure of reaching any node was between one million and 10^{14}. This result is consistent with large unreachable regions.

In the remaining 25% of cases, systems needed between 10,000 and 1,000,000 random tests to be probed adequately. In these remaining cases, a few approximate tests would be inadequate to probe a system.

The good news from this simulation is that for most systems ($55+25 = 75\%$), a small number of tests will yield as much information as an impossibly large number of tests. For these systems:

- There is no point conducting lengthy and expensive testing since a limited testing regime will yield as much information as an elaborate testing procedure.
- Approximate testing is an adequate test regime.

The bad news from this simulation is twofold. Firstly, the Menzies & Cukic model is an average-case analysis of the recommended effort associated with testing. By definition, such an average case analysis says little about extreme cases of high criticality.

Hence, our analysis must be used with care if applied to safety-critical software. Secondly, according to this model, approximate testing is inadequate in at least 25% of the space of systems explored by Menzies & Cukic. Hence, for those 25% of systems and for safety-critical systems, we need alternatives to approximate testing.

2.2. *Sampling*

One alternative to approximate testing is statistical sampling. Statistical sampling theory provides methods for assessing systems using far fewer tests than proposed by Eq. 1. This section will discuss two examples of sampling. The first example will use *t-tests* and the second example will use the *sampling-with-replacement* equation.

The advantage of these sampling techniques is that unlike Eq. (1), sampling techniques are not effected by the size of the system. The number of tests recommended by Eq. (1) grows exponentially as the system size grows. However, the number of tests recommended by (e.g. Eq. (3) (see below) only effected by required reliability.

The disadvantage of these sampling techniques was stated above. Once an error has been detected using cheap BB techniques, then other methods such as WB or FM may be required to localize and fix the error.

2.2.1. *Sampling using t-tests*

Using statistical t-tests, a surprisingly number of tests can certify even complex systems. This method will be presented by example.

A mere 40 tests was required to assess an expert system that controlled a complex chemical plant (125 kilometers of highly inter-connected piping) [42, 40]. The goal of that assessment was to test that the expert system was at least as good as human operators in running the plant. In that design, the expert system and the human operators took turns to run the plant. At the end of a statistically significant number of trials, the mean performance were compared using a t-test. Let m and n be the number of trials of expert system and the human experts respectively. Each trial generates a performance score (time till unusual operations): $X_1 \cdots X_m$ with mean μ_x for the humans; and performance scores $Y_1 \cdots Y_n$ with mean μ_y for the expert system. We need to find a Z value as follows:

$$Z = \frac{\mu_x - \mu_y}{\sqrt{\frac{S_x^2}{m} + \frac{S_y^2}{n}}} \quad \text{where} \quad S_x^2 = \frac{\Sigma(x_i - \mu_x)^2}{m-1} \quad \text{and} \quad S_y^2 = \frac{\Sigma(y_i - \mu_y)^2}{n-1}.$$

Let a be the degrees of freedom. If $n = m = 20$, the $a = n + m - 2 = 38$. We reject the hypothesis that expert system is worse than the human (i.e., $\mu_x < \mu_y$) with 95% confidence if Z is less than ($-t_{38,0.95} = -1.645$).

2.2.2. *Sampling with replacement*

Sampling-with-replacement, in which the recommended number of tests is computed from Eq. (3), can be used for software assessment. In this approach, it is assumed that systems need only be tested to some pre-specified level of reliability; e.g. a probability of failure on demand of 10^{-4}. Further, it is assumed that tests are selected at random and a single test does not effect the results of the other tests. Given these assumptions, then we can use the sampling-with-replacement expression of Eq. (3) to assess the cost-benefit curve of random testing. Consider a search for a moderately low-frequency event such as one-in-a-thousand. For this system, $x_j = 0.001$ and Eq. (3) tell us that 4603 randomly selected tests are required to be 99% certain that we will reveal that event. To compute other tests sizes using sampling-with-replacement, see Fig. 7.

2.3. *Stopping rules*

The discussion so far has assumed that the number of tests is somehow pre-specified and fixed. In practice, test engineers often use *stopping rules* to adjust the time spent in testing. Three such stopping rules are *reliability certification testing* and *Bayesian stopping rules*, and *fault-based testing.*

2.3.1. *Reliability certification testing*

Certification tests using reliability demonstration charts have been introduced by Musa, Iannino and Okumoto [46]. They are based on sequential sampling theory, which is very efficient in the sense of giving the result (reliability certification) at the earliest possible time, i.e., smallest possible number of tests.

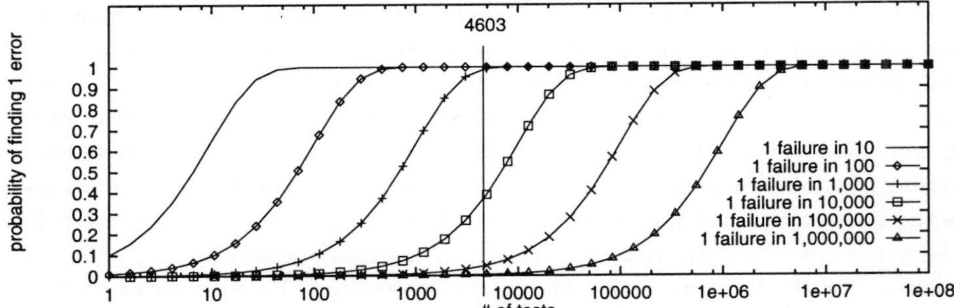

Fig. 7. Chance of finding an error $= 1 - (1 - failure\ rate)^{tests}$. Theoretically, 4603 tests are required to achieve a 99% chance of detecting moderately infrequent bugs; i.e., those which occur at a frequency of 1 in a thousand cases [27].

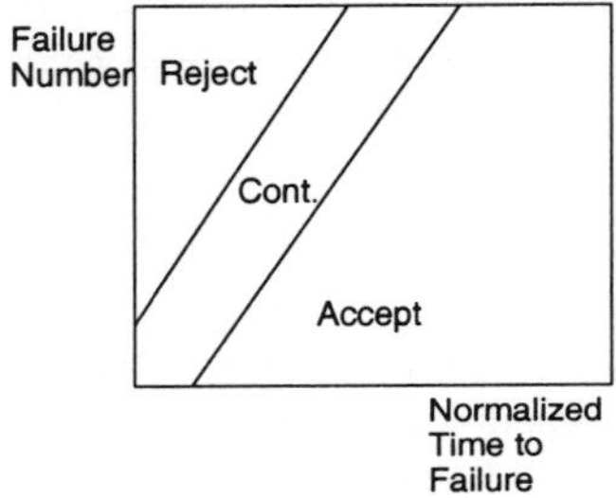

Fig. 8. The reliability demonstration chart.

A *reliability demonstration chart* is shown in Fig. 8. There are three regions on the chart: reject, test and accept. A failure is plotted to the chart when it occurs during random testing in which tests are selected according to the *operational profile* (an operational profile is a statement of what input values are expected at runtime). The vertical axis on the chart denotes the failure number, while the horizontal axis denotes normalized occurrence time (for example, occurrence time multiplied by the failure intensity objective). Depending on where the failure is plotted with respect to the graph regions, testing is stopped (with the program either accepted or rejected) or continued.

The number of tests required for reliability certification test in this technique depends on the position of the lines between reject, continue and accept regions. Their exact position will depend on

- The discrimination ratio, or the error in estimating failure intensity one is willing to accept.
- The consumer level of risk, or the probability one is willing to accept by falsely saying the failure intensity objective has been met when it is not.
- The supplier level risk, or the probability one is willing to accept by falsely saying the failure intensity objective has not been met when it is.

When risk levels and/or the discrimination ratio decrease, the continue region becomes larger. This situation requires more testing before reaching either accept or reject region.

This method is a practical version of a stopping rule, based on the required software reliability. It has seen its application in telecommunications industry. For details of how to set appropriate levels of risks and discrimination ratio, interested readers are encouraged to look for statistical details in [47].

2.3.2. *Bayesian stopping rules*

When safety critical systems are tested, the usual goal is to achieve certain level of confidence that the predefined level of reliability has been achieved. Recall that Eq. (2) said that 4603 successful tests are needed to have 99% confidence that the probability of failure is indeed less than or equal to 10^{-3}. However, this model does not address the question of what happens when failures occur *during* those 4603 tests. Suppose a failure is detected at test 3500. A common sense approach would require fixing the fault that caused the failure and the repetition of reliability certification, i.e., in this specific case, running all 4603 tests again. However, since failure occurrences in random testing are random events, debugging may not be necessary. In other words, program may actually be exhibiting the required reliability, even though it had failed.

The problem is how many additional tests need to be executed successfully following one or more failures, to be able to certify requested reliability without debugging.

Littlewood and Wright [36] proposed one solution, based on Bayesian statistics:

(1) At the start of the certification test, compute n_1, the number of failure free executions for the certification test to succeed and stop. This figure might come from Eq. (2).
(2) Execute the test cases. If all n_1 executions succeed, stop testing and software reliability can be certified at the required level. Otherwise, a failure is observed at execution s_1 and testing stops.
(3) In the light of evidence of one failure in s_1 executions, a number of further failure free executions, n_2, where $n_2 > n_1$, is determined.
(4) Test executions proceed and either n_2 executions succeed (and reliability certified), of a failure is observed on demand $s_1 + s_2$. In the later case, steps 3 and 4 keep being repeated.

Note that if the program does not have the required reliability, testing may continue forever. In a sense, this technique is similar to Musa's reliability certification charts, but the reasoning that leads to accept or continue testing decisions is different.

Stopping rules proposed by Littlewood *et al* [37] are based on Bayesian statistics. Assume that target reliability level for a program is 10^{-3}, denoted by p_0. Testing begins with an ignorance prior probability of failure Θ, meaning that Θ is equally likely to assume any value between 0 and 1. As successful tests are executed, followed by observed failures, the prior information changes to reflect these observations. These observations are incorporated in a *Beta distribution* with appropriate values for its two parameters. Whenever a failure occurs, in addition to an update to prior distribution of failure probability, the additional number of successful tests that indicate *a posterior* distribution confirming the target failure probability, p_0, is computed. Readers interested in understanding the details of this approach are encouraged to read [16, 36, 37].

2.3.3. *Fault-based testing*

Software fault injection is the process of physically injecting a fault into the program. *Fault seeding* is a statistical fault injection method used to estimate the number of faults remaining in the program after the testing has been performed [44]. Let M denote the known number of injected faults, k the total number of faults detected through testing, and m the number of injected faults detected by testing ($m \leq k$ and $m \leq M$). Under the assumption that both injected and inherent faults are equally likely to be detected, an estimate of the number of inherent faults N is

$$N = \frac{M}{m}(k - m)\,.$$

Stopping rules depend on the type of the program under test. Typical rules require that between 80% and 100% of the injected faults are detected by black box testing.

Mutation analysis is a technique similar to fault seeding [18]. Multiple copies of the program are made, and in each copy, one or more faults are injected using one of the mutant operators. Mutant program copies are tested with input data sets. The goal of mutation analysis is to determine which data set is able to detect the changes. Mutation analysis inspired Jeff Voas and his colleagues to estimate the conditional probability that, given a fault in the program location, the data state becomes infected and results in incorrect outputs. Systematic generation and injection of faults into different program locations, combined with measurements of the above mentioned probability, is called *sensitivity analysis* [55]. Further, Voas declares that in order to achieve *testable software*, one needs to perform sensitivity analysis and go back to the specification and design phase and change the insensitive program locations, that is, those which are responsible for not propagating (injected) faults into failures. Alternatively, instead of redesign, more testing effort can be directed towards program segments with lower testability. No stopping rules have been defined for sensitivity analysis testing.

Nowadays it is generally agreed that fault based testing does not provide an insight into how good the code is *per se*. It rather answers "what if" scenarios by simulating human factor errors and environment failures. When safety is of concern, fault-based methods can be a useful complement to reliability assessment but cannot replace it. The main drawback of fault-based testing for the reliability assessment is the questionable (oversimplified) representativeness of injected faults.

3. *WB* = White Box Testing

WB partition testing is a testing regime where, unlike *BB*, analysts have information about where they should look to repair a failed test. In *WB* testing, analysts reflect over the internals of a program to invent test inputs that exercise K different *partitions* within a program. Partitions divide up the program's behavior into *equivalence classes.* Each class represents one interesting behavior of the system. For example, one equivalence class might relate to an incorrect password being offered at a login prompt. *BB* testing might test that prompt again and again with hundred of combinations of different character strings. The same test developed using *WB* methods might require only two tests: one for a correct login password and one for an incorrect password.

Since *WB* tests let us examine the internals of a program, they can be used to define stopping rules for a test regime. An often used criteria is *coverage*; i.e., stop testing a system when we have *covered* all parts of it. Various coverage criteria have been defined such as

- Exercise all lines in the program at least once.
- Check that all conditionals have been used at least once.
- For every conditional branch, ensure that both branches have been exercised.
- Ensure that all pathways between where a variable is set and where it is used are covered. This coverage criteria has been further divided according to how the variable is used, e.g., used in a conditional, used outside of a conditional.

For example, the Modified Condition Decision Coverage (MC/DC) criterion is very frequently by software testers in the aviation industry [51] for software based airborne systems. In this specific environment, a 100% coverage is required.

One of the benefits of *WB* should be that analysts can use their expertise into the process of finding errors. A common pre-experimental intuition is that this expertise greatly increases the chances that *WB* will find more errors than *BB*. However this turns out not to be the usual case for three reasons: *incomplete coverage*, *partition creation* and *detection effectiveness* (discussed below). In general, *WB* is not better than *BB* at *detecting errors.* However, the real win with *WB* is that it is much better than *BB* at *locating errors* once they have been detected.

3.1. *Incomplete coverage*

Coverage-based *WB* testing can be an inadequate testing strategy. Fenton [22, p. 302] reports that even when we try to explore the entire space of a program, the average reachable "objects" (paths, linearly independent paths, edges, statements) is only 40% at most. Some evidence for Fenton's claim was seen in Fig. 3, even in mature, well-tested systems in frequent use, coverage may be far less than 100%.

Demanding full coverage can be prohibitively expensive. While MC/DC is less demanding than full branch condition coverage, it presents a huge cost overhead for large avionics systems. Boeing estimates that 40% of the software development costs for the 777 were spent on testing. Hence, testing to this standard has become a major cost driver in the development of new aircraft.[a]

Also, even if full coverage is achieved, coverage only comments on the structure of the code, and hence may not uncover problems associated with missing or incorrect requirements. Nor can coverage-based WB uncover systemic problems to do with the interaction between components. Other techniques such as BB are required to find these systemic problems.

3.2. *Problems with partition creation*

Creating the K partitions used in WB testing is a non-trivial task. An analyst must mentally consider how all inputs would flow into a system and past the program conditionals. If the program flows are pushed deep into the system, then the analyst will have a hard task ensuring that the flows are internally consistent. Automatic tools could be used to build the possible flows through a program.

Such automatic tools would face two problems. Firstly, they would have to execute over accurate representations of a system. Such a representation could come from either the specification documents or the actual system. If the specification is used, then experience strongly suggests that it will contain numerous inaccuracies that could confuse our automatic tools. If the actual system is used, then a call graph would have to be extracted from the code. Generating a correct call graph is problematic. For example, Murphy *et al* caution that in languages that support pointer to arbitrary constructs, then the problem is fundamentally intractable [45]. Different call graph generators tame this computational problem via a variety of heuristic design decisions. These heuristics alter the call graphs generated. For example, Murphy *et al* report significant differences in the graphs produced by different call graph generators [45].

The other problem with automatic partitioning is that it can be very slow. Gabow *et al* [24] showed that building pathways across programs with contradictions is *NP-complete* for all but the simplest software models (a software model is very simple if it is very small, or it is a simple tree, or it has a dependency networks with out-degree ≤ 1). No fast and complete algorithm for NP-complete tasks has been discovered, despite decades of research.

[a]The total development cost for the B777 was $5 billion. Approximately half of this was software development; hence roughly a billion dollars were spent on software testing.

3.3. *Detection effectiveness*

The other problem with WB is *detection effectiveness.* The chances of detecting an error with WB probing is nearly the same as with BB [27]. This is a counter-intuitive result but it is simple to demonstrate. Let us assume that our K partitions each have a different probability x_k of detecting an error. Clearly, the chances of finding all the errors in all the partitions after N_k tests in each partition is

$$1 - \left(\prod_{k=1}^{K} (1 - x_k)^{N_k} \right) \tag{4}$$

WB can be compared to BB if we compare Eq. (4) with the probability of finding an error with probability x_j after N random black box tests, i.e., Eq. (2). To make the comparison meaningful, we should insist that the total number of tests performed is the same, i.e., $N = \sum_{k=1}^{K} N_K$. [27] performs a lengthy comparison of the ratio of Eq. (4) to Eq. (2) using various relationships between x_k and x_j. In the overwhelming majority of their studies, this ratio was nearly always very close to unity, i.e., WB was not much better than BB at detecting errors.

This bizarre and surprising result has been duplicated many times (see the literature reviews in [26, 27]). In only two cases it has been refuted:

- In the special case where all inputs are equally likely, then it can be shown that WB using K partitions can be up to K times better than BB at finding errors [26]. However, given the high cost of creating the K partitions, a factor of K improvement in the utility of WB is not overly impressive.
- Suppose a programmer repeatedly comments out half the remaining code until an error disappears. In effect, this programmer is performing a binary-chop partitioning strategy to create a partition with an increased chance of holding the error. In this case, x_k would increase to a value much larger than x_j and WB becomes a viable testing regime. That is, while WB may be not much better than BB for *detecting* errors, it is superior for *localizing* errors once they have been detected [27].

4. FM = Formal Methods

The picture emerging here is that WB augments BB methods. We saw above that BB methods can be surprisingly useful at detecting errors, but may give little assistance in solving the detected errors. On the other hand, the costs of WB may not be justified given its relatively weak error detection properties (compared to BB). Nevertheless, WB is better than BB at localizing the source of an error.

Extending the picture, we say that FM testing augments WB and BB methods. FM combines a powerful first-order query mechanism for detecting errors and a method for finding the cause of the error. Theoretically, far fewer FM tests are required than with BB and WB, since a single FM first-order query is equivalent to many WB or BB test inputs [38]. Further, mature and highly optimized tools exist for FM testing.

As we shall see below, the benefits of FM come at considerable cost. Often only small critical sections of systems can be tested using FM. In [38], the authors argue that FM should be viewed as one method in a spectrum of testing regimes. Since formal methods can only be applied to a small part of a system, FM should be proceeded by cheaper forms of testing such as BB and WB to identify the important parts of a system.

4.1. *About FM*

In FM, we write a system *twice.*[b] Once a program or specification is understood, we write its again in a high-level formal representation. This representation contains the essential features of the specification. The representation is formal in the sense that all its constructs have a precise semantics which can be revealed by automatic *model checkers* such as SPIN [30].

A formal model has two parts: a *systems model* and a *properties model.* The systems model describes how the program can change the values of variables while the properties model describes global invariants that must be maintained when the system executes. Often, a temporal logic is used to express the properties model. Temporal logic is classical logic augmented with some temporal operators such as

$$\begin{aligned} \Box X &: \quad \text{always } X \text{ is true} \\ \Diamond X &: \quad \text{eventually } X \text{ is true} \\ \bigcirc X &: \quad X \text{ is true at the next time point} \\ X \bigcup Y &: \quad X \text{ is true until } Y \text{ is true}. \end{aligned}$$

For example, the simple pseudo-English requirement "the brake should always be applied between seeing the danger and the car stopping" might be written as the following properties model in temporal logic:

$$\Box((\text{danger} = \text{seen} \wedge !(\text{car} = \text{stop}) \ \wedge \Diamond\ (\text{car} = \text{stop})) \\ \rightarrow (\text{brake} = \text{on}\ \cup\ (\text{car} = \text{stop}))) .$$

Modern model checkers search the systems model for a method of proving the negation of the properties model. If successful, then these model checkers can return a *counter-example* that describes exactly how the systems model can fail. Analysts find these counter-examples very useful in tracing out the causes and fixed for a bug.

4.2. *The costs of FM*

The three costs of FM are the *writing cost*, the *running cost*, and the *rewriting costs.* The writing cost has two components. Firstly, there is a short supply of analysts skilled in creating temporal logic models. Secondly, even when analysts

[b]Exception: see F^2M, discussed below.

with the right skills are available, the writing process is time-consuming. In recent years, much progress has been made in reducing this writing cost. For example:

- In the KAOS system [54], analysts write a properties model by incrementally augmenting object-oriented scenario diagrams with temporal logic statements. Potentially, this research reduces the costs of formal requirements analysis by integrating the writing of the properties model into the rest of the system development.
- Dwyer *et al* [19, 20] have identified *temporal logic patterns* within the temporal logic formulae seen in many real-world properties models. For each pattern, they have defined an expansion from the intuitive pseudo-English form of the pattern to a formal temporal logic formulae. In this way, analysts are shielded from the complexity of formal logics.

Another significant cost of FM is the *running cost* of model checking. A rigorous analysis of formal properties implies a full-scale search through the systems model, i.e., Eq. (1). This space can be too large to explore, even on today's fast machines. Much of the research into FM focuses on how to reduce this running cost of model checking. Various techniques have been explored:

Abstraction or partial ordering: Only use the part of the space required for a particular proof. Implementations exploiting this technique can restrain how the space is traversed [25, 43], or constructed in the first place, e.g. [23, 52].

Clustering: Divide the systems model into sub-systems which can be reasoned about separately [11, 13, 48, 57].

Meta-knowledge: Avoid studying the entire space. Instead, only study succinct meta-knowledge of the space. One example used an eigenvector analysis of the long-term properties of the systems model under study [33].

Exploiting symmetry: Prove properties in some part of the systems model, then reuse those proofs if ever those parts are found elsewhere in the systems model [12].

Semantic minimization: Replace the space with some smaller, equivalent space [31] or ordered binary decision diagrams [7]. For example, the BANDERA system [15] reduces both the systems modeling cost and the execution cost via automatically extracting (slicing) the minimum portions of a JAVA program's bytecodes which are relevant to particular properties models.

While the above tools have all proved useful in their test domains, they may not be universally applicable:

- Certain optimizations require expensive pre-processing, such as [33].
- Exploiting symmetry is only useful if the system under study is highly symmetric.

- Clustering generally fails for tightly connected models.
- Splicing systems like BANDERA are very language specific. BANDERA only works on implemented JAVA systems and not for (e.g.) specification documents.

Due to the high running costs, a common cycle is to:

(1) Write a formal model.
(2) Try to run it.
(3) Realize that it is too large to check formally.
(4) Try to shrink the model it by rewriting it at some higher level of abstraction.

That is, apart from the *writing cost* and the *running cost*, the other cost of FM is the *rewriting cost.*

In summary, often only small descriptions of systems can be formally tested. Anecdotally, we know of one case where the invariants from 30 JAVA classes takes 1GB of main memory to check formally, even using a state-of-the-art automatic model checker. Testing larger systems may not be testable using FM since such larger systems would require exponentially more memory than 1GB. Consequently, in the general case, classic formal methods does not reduce the effort of testing a system. However, for the the kernel of mission-critical or safety-critical systems, the large cost of FM is often justified.

4.3. *Styles of formal methods*

The previous section described traditional FM. We denote this traditional style F^1M and distinguish it from other styles such as $F^{-1}M$ or *lightweight formal methods*; F^0M or *manual formal methods*; and F^2M or *full life cycle formal methods.* The index x in F^xM denotes the level of rigor and effort required to apply that style of formal methods testing.

One example of lightweight formal methods ($F^{-1}M$) is the work of Schnieder *et al* [52]. In this lightweight approach, a model checker was used to describe a system. However, only partial descriptions of the systems and properties models were constructed. Despite their incomplete nature, Schneider *et al* found that such partial models could still detect significant systems errors.

Leveson's work on software fault trees (SFT) [35] is an example of an ultra-lightweight formal method. SFTs have a fully formal semantics. Yet they are lightweight to construct since they are typically very small. For example, the SFT for an if-then-else statement has only a few entries since if-then-else is a simple construct. Leveson *et al* heuristically applied a library of SFTs to procedural code. They argue that SFTs found as many errors in less time than a traditional F^1M analysis. Note that this result endorses *either* the utility of $F^{-1}M$ *or* our above argument that approximate testing is often an adequate testing regime.

Manual formal methods (F^0M) implies the manual construction and manipulation of intricate mathematical descriptions of a systems model written in (e.g.) the Z notation. Due to the manual nature of F^0M, it can only be applied by highly skilled analysts to very small descriptions of programs.

F^1M was discussed in the previous section. F^1M can be criticized for applying too late in the software life cycle. Such critics rhetorically ask

> "Why debug an incorrect system into correctness? Would it not be better to build demonstrably correct systems in the first place?"

Advocates of this *write-it-right* F^2M approach build systems from libraries of components. Automatic refinement methods specialize and combine members of the component library into an executable [9, 53]. Knowledge about the particular application being constructed is used to constrain and inform the refinement process.

The dream of F^2M is that systems will never need testing since there were generated from components that have been formally proved correct using an automatic refinement method that has also been proved correct. The reality of F^2M is that the technology currently available for automatic generation is not perfect. While refining a single component may maintain the correctness of that component, when components combine it is not clear that correctness can be guaranteed. Also, the cost of building and maintaining the library of formally proved components is non-trivial. Extensive and elaborate mathematical annotations must be added to each component in order to support proving it's correctness and combining it with other components. An open question for F^2M research is "will the benefits of F^2M be out-weighted by the cost of developing the component library?".

5. Summary

We have explored how many tests it takes to certify software. Tests have been characterized as samples of the space of possible pathways within a program. Such pathways clump together variables and any probe into that clump will yield information about the entire clump. Hence, the required number of tests need not be exponential on program size.

A system can be tested approximately when a few randomly selected probes finds most of the clumps. This does not happen when the internal pathways are too complex to condense into a small number of clumps. Based on a simulation of reaching nodes in an and-or graph, it was argued above that such overly-complex paths occur at least 25% of the time. Hence, approximate testing cannot be endorsed for safety critical and mission critical systems.

To improve on approximate testing, we then exploring sampling. Given a known required level of reliability, then Eq. (2) can return the number of required random tests. For even moderate levels of reliability (e.g. find all faults with a frequency of one-in-a-thousand), then thousands of tests may be required [Eq. (2) says that at $x_j = 10^{-3}$, 4603 random tests are required to be 99% certain of finding the fault].

When sampling, test engineers often use feedback from the test results to control when to stop testing. Three stopping criteria discussed here were reliability certification testing, Bayesian stopping rules, and fault-based testing.

An alternative to random black box probing of a system is white box partitioning. White box testing allows an analyst to use knowledge of internal program structure to define test cases and stopping criteria based on system coverage. However, there any several drawbacks with white box testing including incomplete or expensive coverage, the cost of creating accurate partitions, and the comparative effectiveness of white box testing. Compared to random black box probing, white box testing is no better than *detecting errors* but is superior at *localizing errors.*

Formal methods can find errors with far fewer tests than white box or black box methods. Further, when an error is detected, formal method model checkers can return a counter-example showing exactly what must be changed to prevent the error. However, the benefits of formal methods come at considerable cost including the cost of writing the formal model (analysts skilled in formal analysis are in short supply), running the formal model (which, in the worst case, has to run through an exponential number of states in the program), and then rewriting the model if we need to reduce its size and associated runtime cost. Much research has been devoted to reducing these costs but, for the moment, formal methods can only be successfully applied to small descriptions of systems. Hence, it is good practice to precede formal methods with other, cheaper and less complete testing regimes, in order to focus the analysis on relevant portions.

This chapter reviewed different styles of formal methods. It is an open question if these different styles will change the way we use formal methods in the future. For example, full life cycle formal methods could remove the bugs before we insert them into our systems. However, this approach come at considerable cost. Lightweight formal methods are another exciting alternative style of formal methods. However, it is possible that "lightweight formal methods" are really just a synonym for "approximate testing", i.e., any testing regime (lightweight formal methods or random black box testing) will quickly reveal many bugs.

Acknowledgments

Helen Burgess provided invaluable editorial advice for this article.

References

1. A. V. Aho, B. W. Kernigham and P. J. Wienberger, *The AWK Programming Language* (Addison-Wesley, 1988).
2. A. Avritzer, J. P. Ros and E. J. Weyuker, "Reliability of rule-based systems", *IEEE Software* (September 1996) 76–82.
3. A. T. Bahill, K. Bharathan and R. F. Curlee, "How the testing techniques for a decision support systems changed over nine years", *IEEE Transactions on Systems, Man, and Cybernetics* **25**, no. 12 (December 1995) 1535–1542.

4. G. Betta, M. D'Apuzzo and A. Pietrosanto, "A knowledge-based approach to instrument fault detection and isolation", *IEEE Transactions of Instrumentation and Measurement* **44**, no. 6 (December 1995) 1109–1016.
5. J. M. Bieman and J. L. Schultz, "An empirical evaluation (and specification) of the all-du-paths testing criterion", *Software Engineering Journal* **7**, no. 1 (1992) 43–51.
6. D. G. Bobrow, S. Mittal and M. J. Stefik, "Expert systems: Perils and promise", *Communications of the ACM* **29** (1986) 880–894.
7. R. E. Bryant, "Symbolic Boolean manipulation with ordered binary decision diagrams", *ACM Computing Surveys* **24**, no. 3 (September 1992).
8. B. Buchanan, D. Barstow, R. Bechtel, J. Bennet, W. Clancey, C. Kulikowski, T. M. Mitchell and D. A. Waterman, "chapter constructing an expert system", *Building Expert Systems*, eds. F. Hayes-Roth, D. Waterman and D. Lenat (Addison-Wesley, 1983) 127–168.
9. W. Buntime, "Will domain-specific code synthesis become a silver bullet?", *IEEE Intelligent Systems* (March/April 1998) 9–15.
10. J. P. Caraca-Valente, L. Gonzalez, J. L. Morant and J. Pozas, "Knowledge-based systems validation: When to stop running test cases", *International Journal of Human-Computer Studies* (2000) (to appear).
11. D. J. Clancy and B. K. Kuipers, "Model decomposition and simulation: A component based qualitative simulation algorithm", *AAAI'97* (1997).
12. E. M. Clark and T. Filkorn, "Exploiting symmetry in temporal logic model checking", *Fifth International Conference on Computer Aided Verification* (Springer-Verlag, 1993).
13. P. Clark and T. Ng, "The CN2 induction algorithm", *Machine Learning* **3** (1989) 261–283.
14. R. M. Colomb, "Representation of propositional expert systems as partial functions", Artificial Intelligence (to appear) (1999). Available from *http://www.csee.uq.edu.au/~colomb/PartialFunctions.html*
15. J. Corbett, M. B. Dwyer, J. Hatcliff, S. Laubach, C. S. Pasarenu, Robby and H. Zheng, "Bandera: Extracting finite-state models from Java source code", *Proceedings of ICSE (2000)*, Limerick, Ireland (2000) 439–448.
16. B. Cukic and D. Chakrawarthy, "Bayesian framework for reliability assurance of a deployed safety critical system", *Proceedings of the 5th International Symposium on High Assurance Systems Engineering*, Albuquerque, NM (November 2000).
17. P. Davies, "Planning and expert systems", *ECAI '94* (1994).
18. R. DeMillo, R. Lipton and F. Sayad, "Hints on test data selection: Help for the practising programmer", *IEEE Computer* **11**, no. 4 (April 1987) 34–41.
19. M. B. Dwyer, G. S. Avrunin and J. C. Corbett, "A system specification of patterns", *http://www.cis.ksu.edu/santos/spec-patterns/* (1997).
20. M. B. Dwyer, G. S. Avrunin and J. C. Corbett, "Patterns in property specifications for finite-state verification", *ICSE98: Proceedings of the 21st International Conference on Software Engineering (ICSE'98)* (May 1998).
21. N. S. Eickelmann and D. J. Richardson, "An evaluation of software test environment architectures", *Proccesings, International Conference on Software Engineering* (1996) 353–364.
22. N. E. Fenton and S. L. Pfleeger, *Software Metrics: A Rigorous and Practical Approach* (International Thompson Press, 1997).
23. M. Fujita, "Model checking: Its basics and reality", *Asia and South Pacific — Design Automation Conference* (1998).

24. H. N. Gabow, S. N. Maheshwari and L. Osterweil, "On two problems in the generation of program test paths", *IEEE Transactions on Software Engineering* **SE-2** (1976) 227–231.
25. P. Godefroid, "On the costs and benefits of using partial-order methods for the verificiation of concurrent systems", *The 1996 DIMACS Workshop on Partial Order Methods in Verificaition* (July 24–26, 1996) 289–303 (invited papers).
26. W. J. Gutjhar, "Partition vs random testing: The influence of uncertainty", *IEEE Transactions on Software Engineering* **25**, no. 5 (September/October 1999) 661–674.
27. D. Hamlet and R. Taylor, "Partition testing does not inspire confidence", *IEEE Transactions on Software Engineering* **16**, no. 12 (December 1990) 1402–1411.
28. D. Harmon and D. King, *Expert Systems: Artificial Intelligence in Business* (John Wiley & Sons, 1983).
29. M. J. Harrold, J. A. Jones and G. Rothermel, "Empirical studies of control dependence graph size for C programs", *Empirical Software Engineering* **3** (1998) 203–211.
30. G. J. Holzmann, "The model checker SPIN", *IEEE Transactions on Software Engineering* **23**, no. 5 (May 1997) 279–295.
31. G. J. Holzmann and A. Puri, "A minimized automaton representation of reachable states" (1999).
32. J. Horgan and A. Mathur, "Software testing and reliability", ed. M. R. Lyu, *The Handbook of Software Reliability Engineering* (McGraw-Hill, 1996) 531–565.
33. Y. Ishida, "Using global properties for qualitative reasoning: A qualitative system theory", *Proceedings of IJCAI* (1989) 1174–1179.
34. D. E. Knuth, "A torture test for TEX", Technical Report STAN-CS-84-1027, Department of Computer Science, Stanford University (1984).
35. N. Leveson, *Safeware System Safety and Computers* (Addison-Wesley, 1995).
36. B. Littlewood and D. Wright, "Stopping rules for the operational testing of safety critical software", *Proceedings of the 25th Conference on Fault Tolerant Computing* (*FTCS'95*), Pasadena, CA (July 1995).
37. B. Littlewood and D. Wright, "Some conservative stopping rules for the operational testing of safety-critical software", *IEEE Transactions on Software Engineering* **23**, no. 11 (November 1997) 673–683.
38. M. Lowrey, M. Boyd and D. Kulkarni, "Towards a theory for integration of mathematical verification and empirical testing", *Proceedings of ASE'98 — Automated Software Engineering* (1998) 322–331.
39. T. Menzies and B. Cukic, "When to test less", *IEEE Software* **17**, no. 5 (2000) 107–112. Available from *http://tim.menzies.com/pdf/00iesoft.pdf*
40. T. Menzies, "Critical success metrics: Evaluation at the business-level", *International Journal of Human-Computer Studies, Special Issue on Evaluation of KE Techniques* **51**, no. 4 (October 1999) 783–799. Available from *http://tim.menzies.com/pdf/99csm.pdf*
41. T. Menzies, B. Cukic, H. Singh and J. Powell, "Testing nondeterminate systems", *ISSRE* (*2000*) (2000). Available from *http://tim.menzies.com/pdf/00issre.pdf*
42. T. J. Menzies, "Evaluation issues with critical success metrics", *Banff KA'98 Workshop* (1998). Available from *http://tim.menzies.com/pdf/97langevl.pdf*
43. T. J. Menzies and P. Compton, "Applications of abduction: Hypothesis testing of neuroendocrinological qualitative compartmental models", *Artificial Intelligence in Medicine* **10** (1997) 145–175. Available from *http://tim.menzies.com/pdf/96aim.pdf*
44. H. Mills, *Software Productivity* (Little, Brown, 1983).

45. G. C. Murphy, D. Notkin and E. S. C. Lan, "An empirical study of static call graph extractors", Technical Report TR95-8-01, Department of Computer Science and Engineering, University of Washington (1995).
46. J. Musa, A. Iannino and K. Okumoto, *Software Reliability: Measurement, Prediction, Application* (McGraw Hill, 1987).
47. J. Musa, *Software Reliability Engineered Testing* (McGraw-Hill, 1998).
48. K. M. Olender and L. J. Osterweil, "Interprocedural static analysis of sequencing constraints", *TOSEM* **1**, no. 2 (1992) 21–52.
49. A. D. Preece and R. Shinghal, "Verifying knowledge bases by anomaly detection: An experience report", *ECAI'92* (1992).
50. C. L. Ramsey and V. R. Basili, "An evaluation for expert systems for software engineering management", *IEEE Transactions on Software Engineering* **15** (1989) 747–759.
51. INC RTCA, RTCA DO178B: Software Considerations in Airborned Systems and Equipment Consideration (December 1, 1992).
52. F. Schneider, S. M. Easterbrook, J. R. Callahan, G. J. Holzmann, W. K. Reinholtz, A. Ko and M. Shahabuddin, "Validating requirements for fault tolerant systems using model checking", *3rd IEEE International Conference on Requirements Engineering* (1998).
53. D. R. Smith, "KIDS: A semi-automated program development system", *IEEE Transactions on Software Engineering (SE)* **16**, no. 9 (September 1990).
54. A. Van Lamsweerde and L. Willemet, "Inferring declarative requirements specifications from operational scenarios", *IEEE Transactions on Software Engineering, Special Issue on Scenario Management* (November 1998).
55. J. M. Voas and K. W. Miller, "Software testability: The new verification", *IEEE Software* (May 1995) 17–28.
56. V. L. Yu, L. M. Fagan, S. M. Wraith, W. J. Clancey, A. C. Scott, J. F. Hanigan, R. L. Blum, B. G. Buchanan and S. N. Cohen, "Antimicrobial selection by a computer: A blinded evaluation by infectious disease experts", *Journal of American Medical Association* **242** (1979) 1279–1282.
57. Z. Zhang, "An approach to hierarchy model checking via evaluating CTL hierarchically", *Fourth Asian Test Symposium* (1995).

VERIFICATION AND VALIDATION

ALFS T. BERZTISS

University of Pittsburgh, Department of Computer Science,
Pittsburgh PA 15260, USA

SYSLAB, University of Stockholm, Sweden

E-mail: alpha@cs.pitt.edu

This chapter complements the chapters on technical reviews and software reliability engineering in Vol. 1 of the handbook. It is primarily concerned with the verification of code by means of testing, but an example of an informal proof of a program is also given. A practitioner's view of testing is taken throughout, including an overview of how testing is done at Microsoft.

Keywords: Coverage criteria, performance test, program proof, risk, system test, testing.

1. Introduction

Products have to conform to their requirements, and a large part of the development budget for a product goes into ensuring that this is the case. This is a particularly important concern for software and knowledge engineers. Not only does the intangible nature of software present its own particular problems, but the prevalence of embedded software in other products, ranging from household electronics to aircraft, makes the dependability of its hosts largely dependent on that of the embedded software. The branch of software engineering that addresses software dependability is known as V&V, short for Verification and Validation. Borrowing Barry Boehm's formulation, validation ensures that we are building the right product, verification ensures that we are building the product in the right way. See [1] for a collection of definitions of V&V; a list of V&V tasks and issues is to be found in [2]. In Sec. 2, we introduce definitions of a number of terms that relate to V&V. However, in order to give structure to our survey, we need to arrive at working definitions of validation and of verification themselves, in the realization that there is no clear boundary between the two. This we now proceed to do.

In the early days of computing the standard approach was to write a program, and in the end determine whether the program corresponds to the client's requirements. Validation was supposed to be this final check of compliance with requirements. Such an approach can work quite well for small stand-alone programs, but for complex software systems it has been necessary to institute a disciplined approach that makes validation an integral part of early stages of software development, and ensures that verification takes place between all successive stages of software development.

Both parts of V&V address software quality, which covers a much wider range of concerns than just functional correctness. The additional concerns include usability, protection of users from their errors, portability, maintainability, and accuracy of results. In all of this, the purpose of validation is primarily to detect conceptual misunderstandings. We take the view that validation includes all the activities taken during software development to ensure that the client's expectations are being met, and that it is also a final check that an implementation satisfies its nonfunctional requirements. Verification is to detect errors made in the development process by ensuring that all representations of a software product — requirements, design, and code — are mutually consistent.

Validation is closely linked to requirements engineering. Very often a client's actual expectations for a software product are not fully expressed in a requirements document. Validation is to make sure that the unstated requirements are satisfied as well, or, to be more precise, that the requirements document is appropriately expanded. This cannot, of course, be achieved unless there is close interaction between the requirements engineering team and client representatives, who must cover all classes of the actual future users of the system. Validation, then, is very much a responsibility of the requirements engineering team. See [3] on requirements engineering in general; see [4] on the management of inconsistencies, which is a specialized aspect of V&V.

Validation of functionality is achieved by inspections, tests, and proofs. Inspections will not be discussed here — this topic is covered by [5]. The other types of validation are discussed in Sec. 3. As regards non-functional requirements, validation has to be by testing. In the case of usability and maintainability this may take the form of benchmarking, to be covered in Sec. 4. In the case of performance, tests have to be carried out in the actual operational environment. The problems associated with this mode of validation are looked at in Sec. 5. Reliability tests are similar to performance tests. It is next to impossible to build a large software system that is entirely free of faults. A realistic approach is to set a reliability requirement expressed as a probability that the system will not fail, and to test with data that correspond to expected usage patterns until this reliability level is reached. This topic will not be pursued here because it is addressed in [6].

Verification is by inspections, proofs, and tests. In the early stages of software development the easiest way to verify that different representations, e.g. design and specification, are consistent is by inspections. As noted earlier, this topic will not be dealt with here — see [5]. Proofs can establish that a program is consistent with its specification. Such proofs are the subject of Sec. 6.

The main focus of this chapter is the verification of software implementations by means of testing. Section 7 deals with types of tests and the limitations to testing. In Sec. 8, we consider testing according to coverage criteria, and Sec. 9 is an examination of partition testing. Integration tests and full system tests are covered in Sec. 10. In Sec. 11, we discuss criteria for when to stop testing, and the risks associated with inadequate testing. Section 12 deals with testability, and Sec. 13

with regression testing. In Sec. 14, we discuss the testing process as implemented at a large software company. Section 15 gives additional bibliographic pointers.

2. Some Definitions

The lack of a standard terminology makes it necessary to define a number of the terms we are using in this chapter. A *requirement* is a statement that is in principle *testable*; a *specification* is a statement that is in principle *provable.* If a statement is testable, then it can be experimentally shown that a program does or does not satisfy the statement; if a statement is provable, then it can be established by a formal logical proof or an informal argument that a program does or does not satisfy the statement. Specifications form a subset of requirements.

For example, the statement "the program satisfies the output predicate $P(x)$" is provable, the statement "the program has an average response time of 100 msec" is testable, but the statement "the program has a good response time" is too vague to be either. The qualifier "in principle" relates to both theoretical and practical problems. Thus, in general it is undecidable whether a program will stop. Moreover, even in decidable cases the proof of a program may be too difficult to find. Also, the statement "the average time between program failures is at least 8 years with 95% confidence" is testable in principle, but not in practice.

A *failure* is an observed deviation of a software system from its requirements. A *fault* is a software defect that can cause a failure, but it is possible that it will never do so during the lifetime of the system. An *error* is an action by a software developer that results in the introduction of a fault into a software system. A *problem* is a difficulty in the use or understanding of a software system, e.g. the inability to detect the fault responsible for a failure.

A software system is robust if it is fault- or failure-tolerant. A system is *fault-tolerant* if the effect of a fault is masked, i.e., if exercising of a fault does not result in failure — this can be achieved by running several different programs with the same functionality in parallel. A system is *failure-tolerant* if the consequences of failures are small. A system is *fail-safe* if failure does not create a safety hazard, and it is *fail-soft* if failure results in no more than graceful degradation of the system. In establishing these properties we have to consider not only the software system, but also the hardware on which the software operates, the communication networks to which it relates, and interfaces to its users.

3. Validation by Tests or Proofs

Validation by testing is applicable only in special circumstances, such as when the implementation is an executable specification, as can be the case with functional or logic programs, or when the implementation has been derived from the specification by correctness-preserving transformations. In other cases an implementation may be shown to be consistent with its specification by means of a proof. If under either of these approaches functionality failures of a validated program still occur, then they must be due to faults in the specification, or, less likely, the proof has been incorrectly applied or a transformation has been used that does not preserve correctness.

Validation by proof can be applied to formal specifications in order to demonstrate that they have correctly captured client expectations. This is done by showing that the software system corresponding to the specifications will have certain required properties. The most favorable attitude to formal specifications and their validation can be found in the UK, where formal methods are mandated by the government for some safety-critical applications. There is evidence that proofs of Z-specifications are more effective at discovering faults than unit testing — the ratio of effort expended to faults found in one particular project was approximately ten times higher for unit tests than for proofs of specifications [7]. However, we do not know whether, assuming the same development effort, ultimate reliability obtained without formal specification would have been lower or higher.

An example of a transformational approach is given in [8]. A railway control system is first defined as an abstract specification. This specification is validated and then refined into code.

Model checking is the use of tools to show that a system design satisfies a given set of properties [9]. A failure occurs when the system does not have a required property, and a tool then indicates the inputs that result in the failure. A problem with model checking is that the number of model states grows explosively. However, with a modern computer it is possible to deal with systems of more than 300,000 states quite easily [10].

4. Validation by Benchmarking

A benchmarking approach applies particularly well to the testing of usability and maintainability. The basis for this approach is a benchmark task that is to be performed as part of the acceptance testing of a system. The task is selected by an independent consultant.

To indicate the flavor of this approach, consider maintainability. After the requirements for a system have been formulated, the independent consultant changes the requirements somewhat. For example, the original requirements for an elevator system may require that a dispatcher module selects the elevator that is to stop at a particular floor to pick up passengers, and puts this floor on the agenda of this elevator. In the changed requirements, this floor goes on the agenda of every elevator, to be taken from the agendas of the other elevators after an elevator has stopped at this floor. After the system has been implemented, the consultant hands the modified requirements to the development team. The maintainability requirement is satisfied if the modification is carried out within a given time limit. It is not even necessary to wait for an implementation: the length of time it takes to carry out the change in a design can give a good indication of the maintainability of the system.

Usability tests require an implementation. Here the benchmark test is made up of a number of tasks that a group of users have to perform [11]. The tasks should cover as much of the functionality of the system as possible. After a learning period, the users perform the tasks. To test retention, the same procedure is repeated at a later time. In both cases the average time to perform the tasks, and the average number of errors made in the performance of the tasks are noted, and the usability test is passed if they are within acceptable limits.

5. Performance Testing

The determination that a software systems meets its performance requirements has to be by analytical estimation or by observation of the system in actual operation. It should be noted that performance tests carried out on a prototype can be misleading — responsiveness of the actual system may differ significantly from that of the prototype. Since responsiveness depends on design decisions made in early stages of the software process, very expensive design changes have to be made if responsiveness is found inadequate during the testing of an implementation. Some of the design issues that relate to performance are surveyed in [12, 13]. The use of a set of benchmarks (the SPEC benchmark set) for determining the performance of different computing platforms is covered in [13].

Fortunately, the likelihood that performance will be a problem is becoming increasingly remote. Performance used to be determined to a large extent by the demands put on the CPU of a shared mainframe, and the time it took to retrieve data from memory devices without random access. Today, for an application that requires rapid responses, the computer in use is likely to be dedicated to this application, and all memory is likely to be random access. Network communication has become the biggest concern, but the speed with which a credit card transaction at your local supermarket is being authorized shows that even this is no longer much of a problem. In any case, performance problems are highly specialized, addressed by communications engineers and designers of operating systems.

6. Program Proofs

Program proofs can be logical or mathematical. In a logical proof use is made of an inference system, and every step of the proof has to be justified by the application of a rule of inference. This means that the requirements for the program to be proven have to be expressed as a formal specification. One such inference system was developed by Hoare [15]: every statement type in Hoare's language has an axiom or a rule of inference associated with it. In stepping through a program, the objective is to use the rule associated with a statement to convert an input assertion into an output assertion. The initial input assertion defines valid input parameters; the final output assertion is a postcondition, i.e., formal specification of the program. A similar set of rules for a somewhat different language was developed by Dijkstra — the best exposition of Dijkstra's approach is to be found in [16].

However, formal program proofs are not being used much in practice, except on relatively small components of mission-critical software. Hoare himself has stated: "Formal methods and proof play no greater role in large-scale programming than they do in any other branch of modern engineering" [17].

Mathematical proofs are another matter. They are an integral part of the Cleanroom methodology [18]. Actually, under Cleanroom, the proofs are still rather formal, but they are not being written down. The author has given examples of mathematical proofs in [19]. Purists object to such proofs on the legitimate grounds that the proofs can be erroneous. The two most common errors that can be made is the disregard of some special cases, and the assumption of something as true that is in fact false, but, if one is aware of these traps, the use of mathematical proofs can be a cost-effective substitute for the very expensive logical proofs.

We shall give an example of one such proof, taken from [19]. The program is to format a text that consists of "significant" characters, and the break characters blank (BK) and newline (NL), in such a way that the output contains exactly the same words as the input, and in the same order, separated by breaks. The output is to contain no leading or trailing breaks, and no two consecutive breaks. The output

Table 1. A text formatter.

```
index:= 0;
linelength:= 0;
repeat
getword(string) < word, length >;
if length > 0 then begin
  if length > MAXPOS then begin (* special case *)
     outstring[1] := BK;
     index := 1;
  end
  else begin
     if index > 0 then begin (*insertion of break *)
        index := index + 1
        if linelength + 1 + length ≤ MAXPOS then begin
           outstring[index] := BK;
           linelength := linelength + 1 + length
        end
        else begin
           outstring[index] := NL;
           linelength := length
        end
     end
     else
        linelength := length
     for i := 1 to length do begin (* transfer of word *)
           index := index + 1
           outstring[index] := word[i]
     end
  end
end
until length=0 or length>MAXPOS
```

line length is to be MAXPOS, and if the input contains a word longer than this, the entire output is to consist of just the one BK character. As many words as possible are to be accommodated in each output line. The program in a Pascal-like language is shown as Table 1. The differences from conventional Pascal are slight, except that use is made of the generator *getword*, which returns, on each call, the next word of the input and its length, or zero if there are no more words in the input (or the input is empty to begin with).

An informal demonstration of the correctness of the program of Table 1 starts with a determination of what is to be proven. The hardest part is to achieve completeness of the statements to be proven. Here we have:

(a) An empty input results in empty output.
(b) When the length of a word exceeds MAXPOS, the output is a single BK.
(c) If no input word is longer than MAXPOS, every word is transferred to the output exactly once.
(d) There are no leading or trailing breaks in the output.
(e) The breaks are properly placed in the output.
(f) The program terminates properly.

We now prove these statements. (a) If the input is empty, the first call to *getword* sets *length* equal to zero, the processing section of the major loop is not entered, and exit from the loop takes place with the length of the output (namely *index*) still zero, as required. (b) The processing section of the loop begins with a test on the length of a word, and every word is tested until the exit from the loop takes place. If the length of a word exceeds MAXPOS, the first character of the output becomes a blank, the length of the output is set to 1, and exit from the loop takes place, again as required. (c) Every iteration of the loop results in a call to *getword*, and unless the length of the word delivered by *getword* is zero or greater than MAXPOS, all the characters of the word are transferred to *outstring* in contiguous locations. Since the transfer is followed at once by another call to *getword*, a word cannot be transferred more than once. (d) After a word with length between 1 and MAXPOS has been delivered, an appropriate break character is inserted *before* the word. This ensures that there will be no trailing break. The section that inserts breaks is bypassed when $index = 0$, which means that no leading break is inserted. (e) The section that inserts breaks is entered with *index* still indicating the position of the last character of the previous word in *outstring*. The incrementation of *index* before anything else will result in the proper placement of the break. The quantity $linelength + 1 + length$ is made up of the length of the line already assembled, the length of the current word, and allowance for the break that is to come between the two. If this quantity does not exceed MAXPOS, the break is BK, and we continue in the current line; otherwise it is NL, and since the current word then starts a new line, the length of this word is the new value of *linelength*. Consider what happens when $linelength + 1 + length =$ MAXPOS. Then a blank is inserted before the current word, and, although we could insert NL after this word, we postpone the insertion until after the next call to *getword*. If the call returns a "word" of zero length, nothing needs to be done. Otherwise the NL will be inserted between the old and the new words. (f) Abnormal termination has already been considered under (a) and (b). In the normal case the last word of the input is transferred to the output, the next call to *getword* results in *length* = 0, and exit from the loop takes place with *index* referring to the last character of the last word of the output text.

7. Testing: Classes, Types, and Limitations

Testing requires test plans, one for each class of testing. While the system requirements are being defined, an acceptance test plan is drawn up. While the requirements are refined into a design, an integration test plan is produced. While the design is further refined into unit definitions and code of individual units, a unit test plan is generated. The ANSI/IEEE Standard 829–1983 defines a test plan as "A document describing the scope, approach, resources, and schedule of intended testing activities. It identifies test items, the features to be tested, the testing tasks, who will do each task, and any risks requiring contingency planning." Chapter 12 of [20] deals with test plans and test documentation.

Under documentation, our view is that each test case is to be described by at least the input data, the expected result (if available), and the actual result obtained. This information is to be preserved because, after system modification, the modified system has to undergo regression testing, and selection of test cases for regression testing is helped by availability of such information.

In addition, a tool can save the path traced with each test input. Such information has two uses. First, if identical paths are followed in several test cases, only one of the cases needs to be saved. Second, only those test cases need be used in regression testing for which the paths go through sections that have been modified. Current-day technology makes possible the preservation of large amounts of test data. Also, if a test case results in failure, details regarding the failure and its resolution should be preserved. These details become part of a process data base, and allow more accurate estimates of project cost to be made for future projects.

The concept of *revealing subdomains* [21] gives a theoretical basis for a discussion of testing. The concept is simple: partition the input domain into components $D_1, D_2, \ldots, D_k$ in such a way that if a program fails for one input belonging to D_i, then the program will fail for all inputs in D_i. The $D_1, D_2, \ldots, D_k$ are revealing subdomains. Unfortunately we do know how to construct such a partition. Nevertheless, it provides an ideal to which we can try to approximate.

In practice an input domain is divided into subsets, and elements are selected from each subset as test cases. There are two approaches. One is called *black box* or *representative.* Black box testing methods are based on operational profiles, as discussed in [6], or on equivalence partitioning, which we consider in Sec. 9. The other, called *white box* or *directed*, and considered in Sec. 8, takes the structure of a program into consideration. Black box testing cannot detect dead code, i.e., code that cannot be reached under any input. Black box testing can easily miss serious faults, as shown by an example, which, though unrealistic, illustrates how a nonterminating loop can be missed:

> **if** $x = 6.2943$ **then**
>   **while** true **do** $x := x$
> **else** ...

The two approaches are sometimes combined [22–24]. This is essential for mission-critical systems. Such a system may contain an exception handler that we hope will never be exercised. However, should the exception arise, the exception handler must be totally reliable. Under strict usage-profile-based testing the exception handler would not get tested at all.

Testing is subject to several limitations. First, as a consequence of the Turing machine halting problem, it is difficult to establish that a program is free of nonterminating loops. Second, even in a loopless program, because of the non-existence of a general algorithm for solving two non-linear inequalities, it may not be possible to find an input that ensures that a particular path through the program is taken. Third, it may not be possible to tell whether a result is correct. This is the test oracle problem. The whole point of many programs is to arrive at results that cannot be obtained in any other way. Hence, there is really no way of testing such a program, and a result will be accepted as long as it "looks reasonable". Fortunately the verification of a result is sometimes much easier than its computation, as with NP-complete problems, e.g. the computation of Hamiltonian paths in digraphs is difficult, but checking that a path is Hamiltonian can be done in linear time. A brief introduction to test oracles can be found in [25]; [26] is a recent source of references to work on test oracles.

8. Testing Under Coverage Criteria

There has to be a measure of how complete we want testing to be, and how close we are to this goal. A common criterion is that 100% of a particular type of coverage is to be achieved. This may mean that every statement in a program is to be executed, or that at all decision points every branch out of the decision point is to be taken, or that for every definition of a variable a path is to be traversed to every use of that definition of the variable. These examples show that coverage criteria can be based on the program space alone (every statement executed), on control flow (every branch taken), or on data links (every definition-use linked).

We are particularly interested in statement coverage (S), and in some types of control-based coverage. Under branch coverage (B), every branch out of a decision point is to be taken at least once. Under condition coverage (C), if a condition is defined as a boolean expression of the form D BoolOp E, then D and E must each be evaluated to result in both true and false. Under multiple condition coverage (MC), still in terms of D BoolOp E, all four truth value combinations for D and

E must arise. Under path coverage (P), every path from entry to exit must be traversed. Figure 1 shows how these five types of coverage are related. Thus, by achieving MC, we also achieve BC, C, B, and S, but not P.

Let us use Fig. 2 to illustrate the coverage criteria. For statement coverage we need to have two test cases. One such test case is to make both $D \wedge E$ and $F \vee G$ true, the other is to make both of them false. With this set we achieve also branch coverage. Other sets that achieve S are possible. For example, a set in which one test case makes both D and E true and both F and G false, and the other makes both D and E false and both F and G true achieves S, and it also achieves BC, and hence B and C.

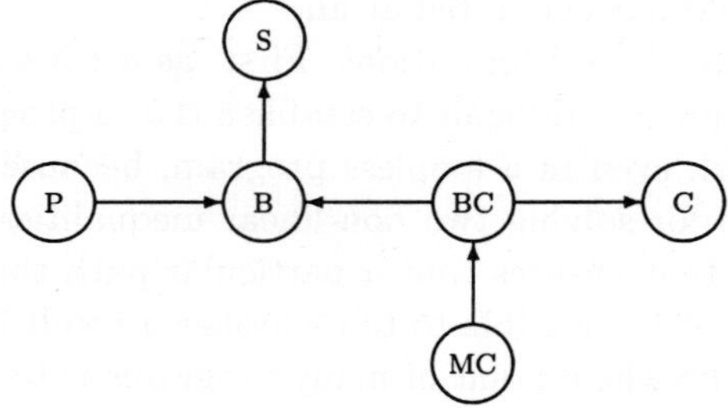

Fig. 1. Dependencies of some coverage criteria.

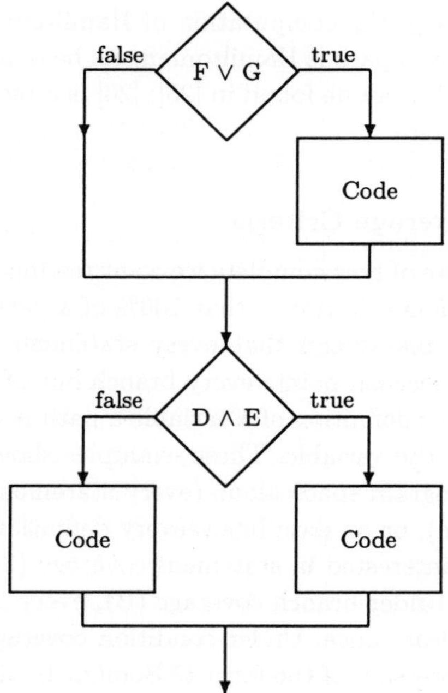

Fig. 2. Flowgraph of a simple program.

Table 2. Tests for MC and P.

	Multiple-condition Coverage				Path Coverage			
	Set 1	Set 2	Set 3	Set 4	Set 1	Set 2	Set 3	Set 4
D	T	T	F	F	T	T	F	F
E	T	F	T	F	T	T	F	F
F	T	T	F	F	T	F	T	F
G	T	F	T	F	T	F	T	F

For MC we need four test cases: first the four truth-value combinations for (D, E) are to be obtained, and then we hope to obtain the four combinations for (F, G) as well with the same data. Path coverage also needs four cases, but for our example none of the sets of four cases that give MC can give P as well. We need a different set of four test cases. Table 2 shows what D, E, F, and G have to evaluate to in each of the four test cases for MC and for P.

We now consider a few problems that arise with coverage-based testing. One relates to infeasible paths. Consider the code for sorting three items:

```
if A < B then
   exchange(A, B);
if B < C then
   exchange(B, C);
if A < B then
   exchange(A, B);
```

There should be $2 \times 2 \times 2 = 8$ paths, but there are only six permutations of three items. Hence two of the hypothetical paths cannot be taken, whatever the input. They are called infeasible. A minor matter relates to multiple condition coverage. If the D and E in, say, $D \wedge E$ are complex expressions, we want both D and E to be evaluated, but an efficient compiler will stop any further evaluation if the first expression evaluates to false.

The main problem is finding the right inputs. Tools have been designed to improve input selection for branch coverage. A tool described in [27] uses three different heuristics and measures the coverage level obtained. Code instrumentation for the measurement of coverage levels is relatively straightforward.

But full 100% coverage under any criterion is an ideal that is next to impossible to achieve, except in the testing of small units. Although testers may believe that they have achieved statement coverage at the 90% level, actual coverage may be only in the 50–60% range [28]. Even with full 100% coverage under unit testing the outlook is not bright because of the need to provide a test harness. It consists of drivers and stubs. Drivers provide the code unit with inputs, and this is not particularly problematic, but stubs simulate code units that are to be invoked by the code unit to be tested. The simulation can be unrealistic and misleading.

In Sec. 3, we noted that proofs had been found to be more effective than unit testing. The design of drivers and stubs, and regression testing of the code after fault removal can make unit testing expensive. The total omission of unit testing from the Cleanroom methodology [18] is therefore understandable.

Theoretical investigations have set up dependency structures of coverage criteria that greatly extend our Fig. 1. One such structure contains 22 coverage criteria, with path coverage the strongest and statement coverage the weakest [29]. Full path coverage cannot be achieved in the presence of loops because there is a different path for each number of iterations of a loop. This suggest that a criterion weaker than path coverage, but stronger than mere statement coverage should be selected.

One such is the all-uses criterion. It requires for each definition V_i^d of every variable V_i that at least one path be exercised from where V_i^d was defined to every statement in which V_i^d is used. The stronger du-paths criterion requires that all such paths be exercised. Since even 100% statement coverage is difficult to achieve, all such criteria are primarily of theoretical interest. Of course, if the paths between definition and uses are short, one can arbitrarily inject a value at V_i^d, and see to it that the paths to the uses of this variable are exercised, but the injected value need not be in the range that would arise with legitimate inputs to the system, and could thus give a misleading sense of security.

9. Equivalence Partition Testing

Under equivalence partition testing the input and the output are partitioned into equivalence classes, and test cases are selected in such a way that each class is covered. This approach was popularized by Myers [30]. For our example we take a calendar program that is to return the day of the week for each date between 1801/01/01 and 2100/12/31. We partition the input by month, getting 12 equivalence classes. The years are partitioned into leap years and years that are not leap years — of special interest are the years 2000 (a leap year) and 1900 (not a leap year). The output is partitioned on days of the week, giving seven classes. A test case may cover more than one class, e.g. with 2000/09/14 we cover a leap year, the month of September, and Thursday.

However, each invalid input class has to be covered by a separate test case because the program should respond differently to the different invalid input classes, e.g. generate different error messages. Examples of invalid inputs: day of the month outside range, day of the month outside range for this month (with February a special case), input month outside range, input year outside range. Moreover, because of different conventions for writing dates, the output should make users aware of possible errors that would go undetected. Because in writing 2001/05/10 the user can mean either May 10 or October 5, our program should spell out "May 10, 2001 is a Thursday."

Of particular interest are boundary values, such as the valid 1801/01/01 and 2100/12/31, and the invalid 1800/12/31 and 2101/01/01. Boundary values are determined by the domain for which a program is being developed. Examples of boundary values for several applications are given in Chap. 7 of [20].

For another set of boundary values, and instances of what Myers calls "error guessing", consider the sorting of an array of n elements, where $n \leq k$. We should run tests with $n = 0, 1, 2$ and with $n = k, k + 1$. We should also consider cases in which the input is already sorted, and the special instance in which all input values are identical.

Operational profiles, which are important in statistics-based software reliability engineering, lead to a partitioning of the input domain. The methods used to achieve the partitioning need not be restricted to testing aimed at reaching a particular reliability level, but can be used with applications like our calendar problem as well. The methods of reliability engineering can be applied only when there is a sufficiently large number of failures to be analyzed — for the calendar problem the number of failures is likely to be too small. As the test cases based on a partition are being executed, track can be kept of the degree of coverage achieved under a particular coverage criterion. This, too, is a quantitative measure, although not as informative as a reliability value. The construction of operational profiles is reviewed in [31].

10. Testing of a Full System

System tests can be approached in two ways. One is to integrate a component into a system as soon as it becomes available. An extreme case is the incremental approach exemplified by the "daily build" at Microsoft (see Sec. 14). At the other extreme, we have the Cleanroom approach under which no testing is done until the system is complete — actually there is some incremental testing, but the increments are very large, two or three for an entire system [32]. Incremental testing requires a test harness, which raises the problems we referred to in Sec. 8.

The complete system is subject to test in acceptance testing, but the developers must carry out full system tests in advance of this to avoid non-acceptance of the system. Such tests can be grouped into a number of distinct categories.

Full system functional test. Here the entire system is tested as a single unit. All black box tests that aim at achieving a quantitative reliability level (see [6]) belong to this category. White box tests on a full system should achieve a given level of coverage under the chosen coverage criterion.

Usability test. Although primarily concerned with the level of satisfaction of prospective users, and this is largely determined by the user interface, usability has a broader significance. In particular, a help system has to be checked against the system as implemented. Also, are users sufficiently protected from errors that they might make? Designers of products that have to be assembled try to design components in such a way that there is just one possible assembly sequence. Users of a software product should be prevented from setting up incorrect interaction sequences.

Security test. Security is a specialized area, and the security test, if needed, is to be designed by security experts.

Robustness test. The requirements for a system may state that it be robust, i.e., that it exhibit one or more of the robustness properties defined in Sec. 2. In particular, smooth recovery from failure is important. Thus, in case the system fails, is recovery easy? Are recovery procedures well documented? Does the system inform the user of its actions while it goes through the recovery process?

Stress test. The purpose of this test is to ensure that the system can cope with peak loads, such as everybody in a large organization wanting to look at e-mail at 09:05. It should also check that the system continues to function in some way when documented limits are exceeded — an air traffic control system designed for 75 aircraft should not collapse when the 76th plane enters the air space it controls.

Volume test. The volume test is to show that the system can operate at documented system limits over an extended time period. A few questions to be considered: Are overflows of data files allowed for? Can the operating system provide the needed support? Is there an intolerable performance degradation at system limits?

Configuration test. This test is needed when the system is to be implemented on several different platforms or is configured from reusable components. A system may work perfectly in the development environment, but may show strange behavior when ported to the site at which it will be used. If the system contains COTS (Commercial Off The Shelf) software or reuses components from a reuse library, the interfaces to the imported components have to be given special attention.

Documentation test. This test is to answer the following questions: Is the documentation complete? Is it reliable? Is it readable? This applies to both user manuals and maintenance manuals.

Maintainability test. This has to be based on a benchmark, as discussed in Sec. 4.

Compatibility test. When a new version of a system is being introduced, say of a document preparation system, the new version should cope with all inputs that were accepted by the old system, and it should produce exactly the same outputs for these inputs as the old system.

11. When Should Testing Stop

Testing of a software system usually stops in the morning of the day on which the system has to be delivered, or when the money runs out. An alternative to such an approach is to set a reliability value to be achieved, and testing does not stop before this reliability has been reached (see [6]). In terms of coverage-based testing, this is to continue until an acceptable level of coverage has been reached. Unfortunately only a few organizations have collected enough process data to allow them to make reasonably accurate predictions of how much effort will be needed to reach the required reliability or coverage level. The higher an organization is on the level ladder of the Capability Maturity Model of the Software Engineering Institute [33], the easier it is for the organization to approach testing with meaningful quantitative criteria.

Although an economic model for picking the appropriate reliability value at which to stop testing has been developed [34], the utility of such a model for predicting testing costs is questionable. It has to be realized that reliability estimates extrapolate past experience into the future, and extrapolation is always problematic. At the end of a test process the extrapolation is not very far into the future, and we can set acceptable confidence limits on a reliability estimate. Not so in the early estimation of testing costs. Since the extrapolation extends far into the future, the confidence range for the estimate is so broad that little faith can be put in the estimate. Therefore the decision of when to stop testing cannot be made *a priori*, but only after sizable amounts of failure data have been obtained.

The whole point of extensive testing is to reduce risks, but the nature of risk is sometimes misunderstood. We need to explore some myths.

The greatest risk is threat to human life. This is so in principle, but cost and convenience are also important. Otherwise automobiles would have been banned by consumer protection agencies. It has been estimated that the direct cost of the famous AT&T nine-hour breakdown was 60–70 million dollars [38]. Human life is rarely given this high a valuation in legal settlements. However, as pointed out in [39], a cost-benefit ratio, if made public, is not to outrage most members of the public. It is therefore important not to become cynical in a discussion on how to reduce testing costs.

Software failures are more likely than hardware failures. This myth arises from the observation that multiple copies of a hardware component can reduce failures, while common-cause failures limit the effectiveness of n-version software for improving reliability. Actually hardware failures may be more likely [40], but fault localization and removal is usually not as easy in software.

Software failures do not lead to court cases. Although product liability cases are not yet as common as for other classes of products, Chap. 14 of [20] shows that defective software can have serious legal consequences.

Software without faults cannot be produced. This certainly applies to large-scale systems based on read-write memory. But the software embedded in consumer products is of surprisingly high quality. Today, a television set can easily contain 500 Kbytes of ROM [41], and the set keeps working until the hardware wears out.

In critical situations human overrides should be standard. Some would find this reassuring, but I put greater trust in software than in human operators. This is due to testing: human operators are not "tested" to the same extent as a well-tested software system. Second, in many critical situations human reaction time is too slow to avert disaster.

The end conclusion is this. The decision of when to stop testing can be made objective by basing it on some explicit measure, but the selection of this measure is subjective. The selection has to be based on the risks involved, what weight is given to different consequences of a software failure, and what the budget permits.

12. Testability

In Sec. 9, we looked at a program for computing the day of week from a date. Effectiveness of black-box testing depends to some extent on the algorithm that a program implements. For instance, a feasible approach for the calendar problem would be to set up a table that stores the day of week for February 29 of each leap year, and to work forward or backward from one of these key dates to get the required result. Black-box testing would not be appropriate here — one wrong entry in the table would give wrong results for all dates covering four years, and we could easily miss picking a date in this period of time.

The ANSI/IEEE Standard 610.12 — 1990 defines testability as "(1) the degree to which a system or component facilitates the establishment of test criteria and the performance of tests to determine whether those criteria have been met, and (2) the degree to which a requirement is stated in terms that permit establishment of test criteria and performance of tests to determine whether those criteria have been met". This is a qualitative definition, and the table-based calendar algorithm has low testability in terms of this definition.

Voas and Miller [42] suggest a quantitative definition: the *testability* of a program P is the probability that if the program is faulty, then P will fail under the next test. Testability analysis does not reveal faults, but it can suggest places where faults can hide from testers. The analysis is based on the following observation: a fault at textual location L in program P results in failure if and only if an input results in L being reached (Execution condition), the data state that results from execution is in error (Infection condition), and infection results in an observable incorrect output or non-termination of a loop (Propagation condition).

The *sensitivity* of location L is the product of three quantities: the execution probability for L, the minimum infection probability at L, and the minimum propagation probability for L. A tool finds the probabilities. Execution probability is the ratio of test cases that lead to execution of L to the total number of test cases. For infection analysis a series of syntactic mutations are performed on L, and each mutant is executed with random inputs. If the data state of a mutant program differs from that of a program considered to be correct (called the "gold program"), infection has occurred. This supplies infection probabilities for all mutants. To get propagation probabilities, the tool changes the data state at L, and continues executing the changed and unchanged programs. Propagation has occurred if outputs from the two programs differ. Different propagation probabilities are obtained by perturbing different variables at L. Under this approach the testability of a large system is likely to be zero, but sensitivity measured at a location in a module can give an estimate of the testability of that module.

Both infection and propagation probabilities depend on perturbations of the software. Syntactic perturbation of code is known as *mutation testing*, which is not really a testing technique, but a means of estimating the effectiveness of test data for causing failures. Section 2.2.4 of [43] is a good introduction to mutation testing.

Briefly, one starts with a gold program and introduces faults of a specific type into this program by means of simple syntactic changes. These programs are mutants. Tests are performed on the mutants, and a mutant that fails under a test is said to be killed by the test. Some mutants are functionally equivalent to the gold program, and hence cannot be killed. A mutation score is the percentage of nonequivalent mutants killed by a test set. A mutation-adequate test set has a mutation score of 100%. The objective is to design mutation-adequate test sets.

Howden and Huang [44] introduce *detectability*, which is the probability that a V&V method will discover a fault in a software artifact if faults are present. Detectability is similar to testability, but while testability relates to programs, detectability relates to V&V methods. It can therefore be applied not just to code, but also to requirements and design.

Suppose a method M with detectability D is applied to program P, and no faults are detected. The risk of falsely concluding that P is free of faults is at most $(1 - D)$, and the *trustability* of P is at least $T = 1 - (1 - D)$. When N test cases are selected at random from the valid input space, the trustability becomes

$$T = 1 - (1 - D)^N .$$

In general, suppose methods $M_1, \ldots, M_r$ are applied to program P. Let D_{ij} be the detectability of method M_i for fault class $F_j, j \in 1 \cdots s$, and q_j be the probability that a fault of class F_j occurs in P. Then, with respect to all faults, P has trustability of at least

$$T = 1 - \max_{j=1}^{s} \left(\min_{i=1}^{r} q_j \left(1 - D_{ij}\right) \right) .$$

Howden and Huang describe various methods for estimating the q_j and D_{ij}, including testability analysis.

13. Regression Testing

Regression testing is to demonstrate that code has not been adversely affected by fault removal and other maintenance activities. It has to deal with two problems. First, regression testers should be able to tell which of the existing test cases are now relevant. Second, they have to write new test cases. Regression testing has been much neglected — in the 800+ pages of the *Handbook of Software Reliability Engineering* there are, as far as I can tell, just 28 lines of text that deal with this topic. A good source of references is [45].

We cannot deal with regression testing in detail here. However, we can list the different classes of program changes that have to be followed by regression testing afterwards. (a) Changes may be caused by fault removal as part of pre-release testing. We noted earlier that regression testing associated with such changes may increase the cost of unit testing. (b) Changes may be caused by removal of faults detected during field use — such faults are removed by interim patches, and are batched before a new release. (c) The addition of new functionality and code changes with no functionality change, e.g. to improve performance, can introduce serious faults at the interfaces of the new and the old components. (d) Functionality can also be reduced in a new release, e.g. by removal of functions that have seen little or no use in the field.

We noted earlier that traces of the paths followed through a program for different test cases can indicate which of the existing test cases are to be used in regression testing — the use of coverage data without going quite this far is studied in [46]. What also matters is how effective different test cases are for uncovering faults — see [47] for a study of the prioritization of test cases in regression testing.

14. Testing at Microsoft

Microsoft, a major software company, is atypical in that it puts extraordinary emphasis on testing and follows a principle of continuous testing while a product is being developed. In other companies only 10–15% of project staff are testers; at Microsoft there is a tester for each developer — according to [48], which is our primary source of information for the material in this section, in 1995 there were 1850 developer and 1850 testers. Continuous testing is necessary because Microsoft products may continue to evolve while they are being developed. At Microsoft, testers and developers have equal status, and they interact very closely. This is in keeping with the broader Microsoft principle of avoiding excessive compartmentalization. Thus, everyone in the company is to be aware of both business and technical considerations [49].

All development and testing activities are driven by the principle of *daily build.* Since testing cannot really be separated from development under this approach, let us outline the stages of the combined development/test process.

(1) Check out private copies of source code from a master version of the product and implement changes in these private copies.
(2) Build a "private release" of the product overnight, and test this private release. As noted, there are equal numbers of developers and testers, and testers often work side by side with developers, allowing test cases to be written as the code evolves.
(3) Synchronize code changes by file comparison of private release to current master release (in late afternoon, when no more changes to master version are allowed).
(4) Merge code changes: private releases are updated by reference to current master.
(5) Build a private release of this updated version overnight, and test it next morning.
(6) Execute a highly automated "quick test". Development is based on a product macro language that promotes reuse and, what concerns us here, promotes test automation.
(7) Check in the private copies into a new master version.

(8) Generate daily build — this is a new internal product release that is subjected to a series of automated tests under the control of a "build master".

Some very effective testing techniques have been developed at Microsoft. Here we can list just a few. Code is instrumented: developers include features in the code that can be switched on and off as required. Besides the ongoing tests that are performed in parallel with the writing of code, once a week the daily build is released to a testing group. Managers use data collected in these tests to check how well a project is progressing. Because of the continuing evolution of Microsoft products there are no formal technical reviews, but managers will review code written by new staff.

Usability is tested in a specialized laboratory staffed (in 1995) by around 30 specialists who observe the way representative users interact with a product. Other specialists set up and execute stress and volume tests. Internal use of a product begins as early as possible. For example, an operating system may be used in the further development of itself. Before general release, products may undergo beta tests that last for up to a year. For Windows NT 3.0 there were 75,000 beta testers.

15. Some Bibliographic Pointers

Software engineering has matured to such extent that much of the literature published a number of years ago still has relevance. Ould and Unwin have edited a survey of testing by members of the British Computer Society Working Group on Testing [50]. Much can still be learned from this 124-page monograph. Of particular interest is the presentation of testing from the points of view of managers, users, designers, and programmers. The book also emphasizes that test plans are to be tested as well. Beizer [25] presents an extensive taxonomy of faults and gives relative frequencies of the faults. Although the relative frequencies may change with changes in software development practice, the taxonomy itself will not change as rapidly. A huge list of various types of errors and faults occupies 74 pages in [20]. V&V activities have to be given much attention when an organization wants to advance in the level scheme of the Capability Maturity Model of the Software Engineering Institute. Relevant key process areas are Software Quality Assurance (Level 2), Software Product Engineering (Level 3), and Software Quality Management (Level 4) — see [33] for details.

For current developments the proceedings of the ACM SIGSOFT International Symposia on Software Testing and Analysis (ISSTA) are a good source of information. Some of the evolving areas are specification-based test case selection, model checking, regression testing, and the testing of special types of software, such as database applications, programs written in languages with exception handlers and in object-oriented languages, and tool support for the various tasks that define V&V. Internet searches will give the most up-to-date information.

References

1. T. Hoppe and P. Meseguer, "VVT terminology: A proposal", *IEEE Expert* **8**, no. 3 (June 1993) 48–55.
2. D. R. Wallace and R. U. Fujii, "Software verification and validation: An overview", *IEEE Software* **6**, no. 3 (May 1989) 10–17.
3. A. T. Berztiss, "Requirements engineering", *This Handbook*, Vol. 1.
4. G. Spanoudakis and A. Zisman, "Inconsistency management in software engineering: Survey and open research issues", *This Handbook*, Vol. 1.
5. A. T. Berztiss, "Technical reviews", *This Handbook*, Vol. 1.
6. A. T. Berztiss, "Software reliability engineering", *This Handbook*, Vol. 1.
7. S. King, J. Hammond, R, Chapman and A. Pryor, "Is proof more effective than testing?" *IEEE Transactions on Software Engineering* **26** (2000) 675–686.
8. A. E. Haxthausen and J. Peleska, "Formal development and verification of a distributed railway control system", *IEEE Transactions on Software Engineering* **26** (2000) 687–701.
9. E. M. Clarke, O. Grumberg and D. A. Peled, *Model Checking* (MIT Press, 1999).
10. W. Wang, Z. Hidvégi, A. D. Bailey and A. B. Whinston, "E-commerce design and assurance using model checking", *Computer* **33**, no. 3 (October 2000) 48–53.
11. B. M. E. de Waal and G. H. van der Heiden, "The evaluation of user-friendliness in the design process of user interfaces", *Human Factors in Information Systems Analysis and Design* (Elsevier, 1990) 93–103.
12. E. J. Weyuker and F. I. Vokolos, "Experience with performance testing of software systems: Issues, an approach, and case study", *IEEE Transactions on Software Engineering* **26** (2000) 1147–1156.
13. B. A. Nixon, "Management of performance requirements for information systems", *IEEE Transactions on Software Engineering* **26** (2000) 1122–1146.
14. R. Eigenmann (ed.), *Performance Evaluation and Benchmarking with Realistic Applications* (MIT Press, 2001).
15. C. A. R. Hoare, "An axiomatic basis of computer programming", *Communications of the ACM* **12** (1969) 576–580, 583.
16. D. Gries, *The Science of Programming* (Springer-Verlag, 1981).
17. C. A. R. Hoare, "The role of formal techniques: Past, current and future or how did software get so reliable without proof?" *Proceedings of the 18th International Conference on Software Engineering* (1996) 233–234.
18. H. D. Mills, "Zero defect software: Cleanroom engineering", *Advances in Computers* **36** (1993) 1–41.
19. A. Berztiss, *Programming with Generators: An Introduction* (Ellis Horwood, 1990).
20. C. Kaner, J. Falk and H. Q. Nguyen, *Testing Computer Software*, 2nd ed. (International Thomson Computer Press, 1993).
21. E. J. Weyuker and T. J. Ostrand, "Theories of program testing and the application of revealing subdomains", *IEEE Transactions on Software Engineering* **SE-6** (1980) 236–245.
22. W. E. Howden and Y. Huang, "Software trustability analysis", *ACM Transactions on Software Engineering Methodology* **4** (1995) 36–64.
23. J. H. R. May and A. D. Lunn, "A model of code sharing for estimating software failure on demand probabilities", *IEEE Transactions on Software Engineering* **21** (1995) 747–753.
24. B. Mitchell and S. J. Zeil, "A reliability model combining representative and directed testing", *Proceedings of the 18th International Conference on Software Engineering* (1996) 506–514.

25. B. Beizer, *Software Testing Techniques*, 2nd ed. (Van Nostrand Reinhold, 1990).
26. A. M. Memon, M. E. Pollack and M. L. Soffa, "Automated test oracles for GUIs", *Proceedings of the ACM SIGSOFT Eighth International Symposium on Foundations Software Engineering* [published as *Software Engineering Notes* **25**, no. 6 (November 2000)] 30–39.
27. K. H. Chang, J. H. Cross, W. H. Carlisle and S.-S. Liao, "A performance evaluation of heuristics-based test case generation methods for software branch coverage", *International Journal of Software Engineering and Knowledge Engineering* **6** (1996) 585–608.
28. P. Piwowarski, M. Ohba and J. Caruso, "Coverage measurement experience during function test", *Proceedings of the 15th International Conference on Software Engineering* (1993) 287–301.
29. H. Zhu, "A formal analysis of the subsume relation between software test adequacy criteria", *IEEE Transactions on Software Engineering* **22** (1996) 248–255.
30. G. J. Myers, *The Art of Software Testing* (Wiley, 1979).
31. J. Musa, G. Fuoco, N. Irving, D. Kropfl and B. Juhlin, "The operational profile", ed. M. R. Lyu, *Handbook of Software Reliability Engineering* (McGraw-Hill, 1996) 167–216.
32. M. Dyer, *The Cleanroom Approach to Quality Software Development* (Wiley, 1992).
33. M. C. Paulk *et al*, *The Capability Maturity Model: Guidelines for Improving the Software Process* (Addison-Wesley, 1995).
34. W. Ehrlich, B. Prasanna, J. Stampfel and J. Wu, "Determining the cost of a stop-test decision", *IEEE Software* **10**, no. 2 (March 1993) 33–42.
35. K. W. Miller, L. J. Morell, R. E. Noonan, S. K. Park, D. M. Nicol, B. W. Murrill and J. M. Voas, "Estimating the probability of failure when testing reveals no failures", *IEEE Transactions on Software Engineering* **18** (1992) 33–42.
36. R. W. Butler and G. B. Finelli, "The infeasibility of experimental quantification of life-critical software reliability", *IEEE Transactions on Software Engineering* **19** (1993) 3–12.
37. A. P. Nikora and M. R. Lyu, "Software reliability measurement experience", ed. M. R. Lyu, *Handbook of Software Reliability Engineering* (McGraw-Hill, 1996) 255–301.
38. T. C. K. Chou, "Beyond fault tolerance", *Computer* **30**, no. 4 (April 1997) 47–49.
39. W. R. Collins, K. W. Miller, B. J. Spielman and P. Wherry, "How good is good enough? An ethical analysis of software construction and use", *Communications of the ACM* **37**, no. 1 (January 1994) 81–91.
40. D. R. Kuhn, "Sources of failure in the public switched telephone network", *Computer* **30**, no. 4 (April 1997) 31–36.
41. J. Rooijmans, H. Aerts and M. van Genuchten, "Software quality in consumer electronics products", *IEEE Software* **13**, no. 1 (January 1996) 55–64.
42. J. Voas and K. Miller, "Software testability: The new verification", *IEEE Software* **12**, no. 3 (May 1995) 17–28.
43. R. A. DeMillo, W. M. McCracken, R. J. Martin and J. F. Passafiume, *Software Testing and Evaluation* (Benjamin/Cummings, 1987).
44. W. E. Howden and Y. Huang, "Software trustability analysis", *ACM Transactions on Software Engineering Methodology* **4** (1995) 36–64.
45. G. Rothermel and M. J. Harrold, "A safe, efficient regression test selection", *IEEE Transactions on Software Engineering* **23** (1997) 173–210.
46. D. S. Rosenblum and E. J. Weyuker, "Using coverage information to predict the cost-effectiveness of regression testing strategies", *IEEE Transactions on Software Engineering* **23** (1997) 146–156.

47. S. Elbaum, A. G. Malishevsky and G. Rothermel, "Prioritizing test cases for regression testing", *Proceedings of the ACM SIGSOFT 2000 International Symposium on Software Testing and Analysis* [published as *Software Engineering Notes* **25**, no. 5 (September 2000)] 102–112.
48. M. A. Cusumano and R. W. Selby, *Microsoft Secrets* (Free Press, 1995).
49. R. E. Stross, *The Microsoft Way* (Addison-Wesley, 1996).
50. M. A. Ould and C. Unwin (eds.), *Testing in Software Development* (Cambridge UP, 1986).

UNCERTAINTY MANAGEMENT

ALFS T. BERZTISS
University of Pittsburgh, Department of Computer Science,
Pittsburgh PA, 15260, USA
SYSLAB, University of Stockholm, Sweden
E-mail: alpha@cs.pitt.edu

The purpose of this fairly nontechnical introduction to uncertainty management is to identify various forms of uncertainty, and to survey methods for managing some of these uncertainties. Our emphasis is on topics that may not be familiar to software engineers or, to a lesser extent, to knowledge engineers. These topics include Bayesian estimation, fuzziness, time Petri nets, rough sets, belief and evidence, and possibility theory. Uncertainty management has been studied in the contexts of information systems and of artificial intelligence. We attempt to present a balanced view of the contributions from both areas.

Keywords: Belief, fuzziness, possibility, probability, rough set, time Petri net, uncertainty.

1. Introduction

Most decisions in life have to be made under uncertainty. This applies also to decisions made by software systems. But uncertainty can be managed, that is, it can be allowed for in a systematic and disciplined way. The purpose of this chapter is to survey approaches to the management of uncertainty. Section 2 is a catalog of different types of uncertainty. Section 3 is a brief survey of basic discrete probability and stochastic inference, including Bayesian inference. Fuzzy sets are introduced in Sec. 4, and fuzzy logic in Sec. 5. In Sec. 6, we outline the operation of a fuzzy control system, including defuzzification.

Time Petri nets allow the introduction of uncertainty into the time aspects of real-time processes. An application of time Petri nets is discussed in Sec. 7. Similarity gives rise to a particular type of uncertainty — given a set of objects that are to be grouped into different classes, what criteria should be used to put a particular object into one of the classes? The theory of rough sets, which is looked at in Sec. 8, is one way of dealing with this problem. Section 9 is concerned with belief, and Sec. 10 with possibility theory. In the interests of readability, we have avoided sprinkling the text with references, putting nearly all bibliographic pointers into Sec. 11.

2. Types of Uncertainty

In [1], which is probably the best reference on various aspects of uncertainty, uncertainty issues are partitioned into those that deal with fuzziness and those that deal with ambiguity. Fuzziness is taken to deal with lack of distinctions. Ambiguity problems are further partitioned into discord problems and nonspecificity. Discord is a disagreement when a choice between different alternatives is possible; nonspecificity relates to situations in which some such possible alternatives are not taken into account. In [2], we set up a finer classification scheme, which we present here in a somewhat expanded form. For quite a few of the uncertainty types there is no definite procedure for dealing with them, but awareness of their existence will at least cause us to make allowances for them.

Inconsistency. This arises when conflicting solutions to a problem are being advanced, notably in dietary recommendations and in economics. For example, both lowering and raising taxes may be suggested as a cure for reducing budget deficits. Software requirements can state that costs are to be low, and reliability is to be high — satisfaction of one of these objectives normally means that the other cannot be satisfied.

Permanent exceptions. Emus and penguins are exceptions to "All birds fly". This problem is easily solved by a more refined classification of the entities under consideration.

Temporary exceptions. Suppose that all vice-presidents are to have offices on a particular floor of the head office buiding. If Ms. Smith has been made a vice-president, but has not yet made a move to this floor, we have a temporary exception.

Limited validity. Although Jack may not own a car, there are times when he "has" a car, borrowed from his parents. It is not clear to what extent one "owns" a heavily mortgaged house.

Multiple options. People often have several addresses, used for different purposes. There may be different options on how to fly from place A to place B — cost or convenience may decide which of them is selected.

Nondeterminism. If a software system interacts with its environment the behavior of the system is not fully predictable from knowledge of its initial state.

Obscurity. A general trend in data may be obscured by temporal variations, e.g. monthly income of a ski resort.

Fuzziness. We designate Mr. Smith as tall, but tallness is not a well-defined property. We interpret a property as fuzzy if a precise measurement of this property can be obtained in principle. Examples of fuzzy terms: cold, old, loud.

Vagueness. In [1], vagueness is considered a sub-category of fuzziness. We consider vagueness to be distinct from fuzziness. In contrast to fuzzy terms, we call those terms vague for which no measurement process can exist. In "People feel uncomfortable when it is hot" the term "hot" is fuzzy, but "uncomfortable" is vague — we have no dependable way of measuring discomfort. Part of the research on uncertainty should be aimed at reducing vagueness by developing new measurement processes.

Faults. An electrical utility meter breaks down. In some circumstances it would help to know when this happened.

Either/or uncertainty. If this meter registers the same value over a period of time, it may be broken, but not necessarily. The rumor "Company X will show a loss this quarter" may be true or false, but we do not know which.

Cause/effect uncertainty. An effect is observed that could be due to different causes, singly or jointly. This is quite common in medical diagnosis. Analysis methods based on fault trees and Bayesian networks have been developed to deal with such situations.

No knowledge as negation. In logic programming, if the fact X is not in its knowledge base, not(X) is assumed true. For example, if the knowledge base does not contain "Mr. Khachaturian is married", and this cannot be derived from, say, "The husband of Mrs. Khachaturian is Mr. Khachaturian", the answer to the query "Is Mr. Khachaturian married?" will be "no".

Null values. This problem has been extensively studied by the data base community. It has two aspects. One is representational: when a value is missing, how should this be indicated? A missing value may exist, but be unknown (John's age), not exist at all (temperature data for a given place and date because no reading was taken), or be inapplicable (the name of the spouse of an unmarried person). Different null-markers may be used to differentiate between these three types of null values, but at times there may be uncertainty as to which marker is appropriate. The other aspect relates to query answering. If the data base does not contain data needed to respond to a query, an approximate answer may be given. Here the uncertainty relates to similarity: how are we to determine what approximate answer is appropriate?

Interpretation uncertainty. At one time the author worked in an insurance office where three different interpretations of "age" were in effect, namely age last birthday, age nearest birthday, and age next birthday. In the US, a weather forecast may state that tomorrow there is a 60% chance of precipitation. What exactly does this mean?

Rounding. This is interpretation uncertainty as it applies to numerical data. Is USD 5,000,000 an exact amount or is it a rounded estimate? As the purchase price for a mansion it is probably exact; as damage estimate due to flooding it is likely to be a rounded figure.

Noisy data. An experimentally determined value is nearly always uncertain to some degree, e.g. the speed of light. Also, data may become polluted during transmission, requiring the use of error-detecting codes.

Computational round-off. As an illustration, if one keeps adding up floating-point representations of the number 1, at some point the sum no longer changes. Different results are obtained depending on whether a series is added from the small values first or the large values first.

Computational result uncertainty. This can take two forms. First, the program is correct, but the result it gives need not be the required solution. The aim of nonlinear optimization is to find the maximum of an objective function. A two-variable function $f(x, y)$ can be pictured as a three-dimensional hilly terrain. Hill climbing methods will find the top of a hill, i.e., a solution, but there is no guarantee that this is the highest hill. The problem becomes more and more difficult as the number of variables goes up. Under the second form we have no way of telling whether a program is correct. The whole point of many programs is to arrive at results that cannot be obtained in any other way. Hence there is really no way of testing such a program, and a result will be accepted as long as it "looks reasonable".

Partial knowledge. Six prisoners escape. Their names are known. We also know that they have split into two groups. However, we may not know who is in each group, or even the size of each group.

Trends. An upward trend has been observed in global temperatures. Is this due to chance or is there an underlying reason for it?

Context-dependence. Many terms cannot be fully understood unless the context is known in which they arise. For example, a warm day near the Arctic Circle is likely to be cooler than a cool day near the Equator. Since the concepts "warm" and "cold" are fuzzy, the example shows that care must be taken in the interpretation of fuzzy terms. Although we take the boiling point of water to be 100°C, at high elevations it is actually lower.

3. Probabilistic Concepts

Probability theory was the earliest attempt to deal with uncertainty in a disciplined quantitative manner. Here we can do no more than give a very brief review of basic discrete probability. In particular, we introduce Bayesian estimation, which is being applied extensively in artificial intelligence to deal with uncertainty.

Consider an experiment that can have k possible outcomes or events a_1, $a_2, \ldots, a_k$. This experiment is performed n times, and the counts of observed outcomes are $n_1, n_2, \ldots, n_k$. Then $p(a_i) = n_i/n$ is the observed probability of outcome a_i. We have

$$\sum_{i=1}^{k} p(a_i) = \sum_{i=1}^{k} n_i/n = \frac{1}{n}\sum_{i=1}^{k} n_i = 1\,.$$

The probability of the disjunction of outcomes $a_1, a_2, \ldots, a_t$ is the sum of their respective probabilities; the probability of the conjunction of the outcomes is the product of their probabilities:

$$\sum_{i=1}^{t} p(a_i)\,; \qquad \prod_{i=1}^{t} p(a_i)\,.$$

Thus the probability of the throw of a die resulting in a 3 or a 6 is $1/6 + 1/6 = 1/3$, and the probability of the first throw of a die resulting in a 3 and the second throw in a 6 is $1/6 \times 1/6 = 1/36$.

Conditional probability determines the probability of an event, say A, given that another event, say B, has occurred:

$$P(A|B) = \frac{P(A \cap B)}{P(B)} .$$

Example: In unit testing of 100 code units 20 were found to have syntax errors, 10 to have semantic errors, and 6 to have both. If we select a unit that we know to have a syntax error, then the probability that it also has a semantic error is $0.06/0.20 = 0.30$.

The joint probability distribution of random variables X and Y is

$$f(x, y) = P(X = x, Y = y)$$

i.e., $f(x, y)$ is the probability that both x and y occur at the same time. From this we obtain marginal distributions:

$$g(x) = \sum_y f(x, y) , \quad h(y) = \sum_x f(x, y) .$$

Marginal distributions arise in Bayesian estimation.

Consider a 10×10 grid, in which 20 white and 10 black balls are randomly distributed as shown in Fig. 1. Now select a random sample of 50 of the 100 squares, marked with crosses in the the diagram on the right side of Fig. 1. These squares contain 13 white and 4 black balls, although, based on the distribution, we expect to get 10 and 5 balls, respectively. Instead of probabilities 0.20 and 0.10, we get experimental estimates 0.26 and 0.08. This suggests that we also need measures for the confidence we can put on the estimates, e.g. the ranges in which the true numbers of the balls are expected to lie with a probability of 0.95, say. All that we can say with absolute certainty is that the true number of balls lies between 17 and 67, and the upper limit is known only because the number of squares is 100 (there is a non-zero probability that every one of the 50 unexamined squares contains a ball).

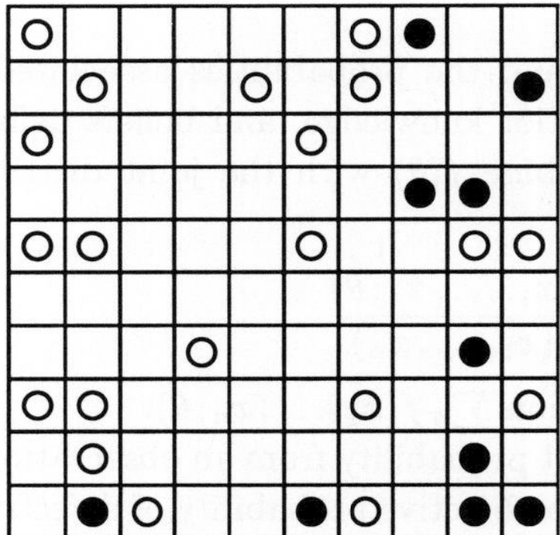
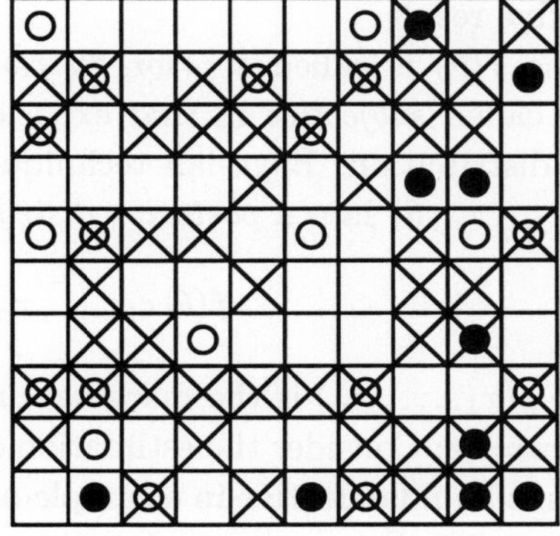

Fig. 1. An experiment in estimation.

From experimental observations we can obtain an estimator of a parameter, and a measure of the degree of confidence in this parameter. For example,

$$P(-0.26 < z < 0.26) = 0.95$$

means that 95% of the time in repeated experiments z will have a value within $(-0.26, 0.26)$. The main applications in computing relate to the measurement of software reliability and communication delays.

In most cases probabilities are established by experiments (observations). For example, to determine the frequency of left-handed people in the population, count them in a sample. This is the accepted scientific approach since Galileo. The probabilities obtained in this manner are called *objective* or *empirical.*

Subjectivists or Bayesians want to support estimates also with prior knowledge, and beliefs and values. For example, if you know that at the time of counting there is a convention of left-handed people in your city, this knowledge can be used to adjust the observed probability. This is fine, but sometimes a subjectivist may introduce beliefs in the analysis when this is not justified — in complex situations experiments have been known to give counterintuitive results. Bayesian estimation can be very useful, but care has to be taken when and how it is used.

Let us find an estimate of a parameter θ for the population defined by the function $f(x, \theta)$. To make this more concrete, consider Bernoulli trials, i.e., trials that can result in success with probability p and failure with probability $(1 - p)$. The binomial distribution applies, and it gives the probability of x successes in n trials as

$$b(x; n, p) = \binom{n}{x} p^x (1-p)^{n-x} .$$

In terms of this distribution, if we observe x successes in n trials, the θ is

$$\hat{p} = x/n .$$

Now suppose that we have additional information regarding θ, e.g. that we have a probability distribution $f(\theta)$ for it. This information allows us to improve the objective result.

The $f(\theta)$ is called a *prior distribution*, and the probabilities associated with it are called *subjective* in that experience, prior knowledge, and beliefs define the prior distribution. Bayesian techniques combine $f(\theta)$ with the joint distribution $f(x_1, \ldots, x_n; \theta)$ into a *posterior distribution*

$$f(\theta | x_1, \ldots, x_n) = \frac{f(x_1, \ldots, x_n; \theta)}{g(x_1, \ldots, x_n)}$$

where $g(x_1, \ldots, x_n)$ is the marginal distribution $\sum_\theta f(x_1, \ldots, x_n; \theta)$.

Example: Consider the estimation of defect probability from an observation that 1 item is found defective in a sample of 2. The objective probability of defectiveness is $1/2 = 0.5$. But suppose that the manufacturer tells us that the probability of finding 1 defective in 10 items is 0.6, and that of finding 2 defectives in 10 is

0.4, i.e., that $f(p) = 0.6$ when $p = 0.1$, and $f(p) = 0.4$ when $p = 0.2$. This is *a prior* distribution, subjective in the sense that it depends on how ready we are to believe the manufacturer. Let x be the number of defectives in the sample. Then the probability distribution for the sample is

$$f(x|p) = b(x; n, p) = \binom{2}{x} p^x (1-p)^{2-x} .$$

From this, the probabilities of a random sample of 2 yielding 1 defective are

$$f(1|0.1) = b(1; 2, 0.1) = \binom{2}{1} (0.1)(0.9) = 0.18$$

$$f(1|0.2) = b(1; 2, 0.2) = \binom{2}{1} (0.2)(0.8) = 0.32 .$$

But $f(x,p) = f(x|p)f(p)$, so that $f(1,0.1) = 0.108$ and $f(1,0.2) = 0.128$, and hence $g(1) = 0.108 + 0.128 = 0.236$. The posterior distribution for the proportion of defectives p when $x = 1$ is $f(1,p)/g(1)$, so that $f(0.1|x = 1) = 0.458$ and $f(0.2|x = 1) = 0.542$. Thus the Bayesian estimate of p is $(0.1)(0.458) + (0.2)(0.542)$ $= 0.154$, quite different from the objective estimate of 0.5.

4. Fuzzy Sets

If we can tell whether or not an element of a universal set U belongs to a set A, this set can be defined by its *characteristic function*:

$$f_A : U \to \{0, 1\}$$

such that $f_A(a) = 1$ if $a \in A$, $f_A(a) = 0$ if $a \notin A$. A set that has a characteristic function is *crisp*. This concept can be generalized by defining a *membership function*:

$$\mu_A : U \to [0, 1]$$

where $\mu_A(a)$ expresses a degree of membership of a in A, or the strength of a belief that a belongs to A. Such a set A is *fuzzy*. Fuzziness finds application in contexts where a strict demarcation between attribute values is inappropriate — we cannot select a particular value and say that it is cool when the temperature is below this value, and warm when it is above it; the transition from cool to warm is gradual. This observation led Zadeh to develop the theory of fuzzy sets.

Characteristic functions can be given a probabilistic interpretation. Thus, if we have a set of integers $A = \{n | 1 \leq n \leq 10\}$, then for all $1 \leq i \leq 10$, we have $f_A(i) = 1$, but also, for all $1 \leq i \leq 10$, the probability $P(i \in A)$ is 1. This suggests that the $\mu_A(a)$ can also be interpreted as probabilities, giving rise to a view that probability theory is all that is needed. However, fuzzy sets have been found very useful in practice, so that theoretical arguments relating to their necessity are of academic interest alone. In what follows we shall use an alternative notation, writing $A(x)$ for μ_A, and $A(a)$ for $\mu_A(a)$.

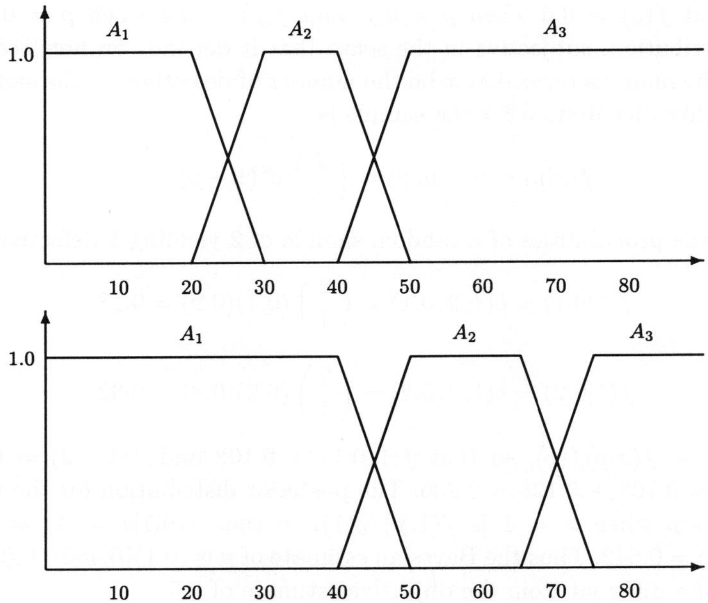

Fig. 2. Membership functions relating to age.

Figure 2 shows plots of membership functions A_1, A_2, A_3, which stand, respectively, for "young", "middle aged", and "old". There are two sets of plots, illustrating one problem we face with fuzzy concepts — they are often given very subjective interpretations. The upper diagram relates to how a 15-year old would define the membership functions; the lower diagram shows the interpretation given by a 70-year old.

Some definitions. A fuzzy set A is *normal* if $\exists a : A(a) = 1$. The *height* of A is $\max_a A(a)$. Set A is a *subset* of set B, $(A \subset B)$, if $\forall a \in U : B(a) \geq A(a)$. *Support* of A: $Supp(A) = \{a | A(a) > 0\}$; *core* of A: $Core(A) = \{a | A(a) = 1\}$. To illustrate these terms, define $U = \{a, b, c, d, e\}$, and fuzzy sets based on U:

$$A = \{1/a,\ 0.3/b,\ 0.2/c,\ 0.8/d,\ 0/e\}$$

$$B = \{0.6/a,\ 0.9/b,\ 0.1/c,\ 0.3/d,\ 0.2/e\}$$

$$C = \{1/a,\ 0.4/b,\ 0.2/c,\ 0.9/d,\ 0.2/e\}$$

where the value x in x/y is the degree of membership of y in its fuzzy set. Fuzzy sets A and C are normal (with height 1); the height of B is 0.9; $Supp(B) = Supp(C) = U$; $Supp(A) = \{a, b, c, d\}$. $Core(A) = Core(C) = \{a\}$; $Core(B) = \emptyset$; $A \subset C$.

Matters get very complicated when we turn to the fuzzy versions of set operations. There are several versions of intersections (called t-norms) and unions (called t-conorms). Much of the really extensive literature on fuzzy sets is concerned with selecting the appropriate t-norm and t-conorm for a particular application. The

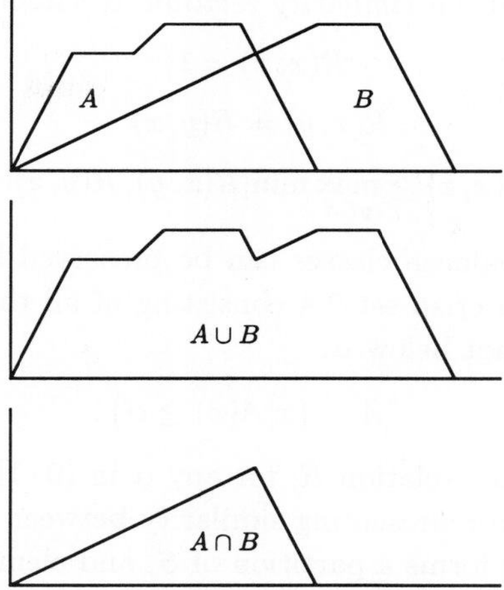

Fig. 3. Standard fuzzy set union and intersection.

three *standard* fuzzy set operations are defined as follows:

$$\bar{A}(a) = 1 - A(a)$$

$$(A \cap B)(a) = \min[A(a), B(a)]$$

$$(A \cup B)(a) = \max[A(a), B(a)]\,.$$

Figure 3 shows fuzzy sets A and B, represented by their membership functions, and their standard union and intersection.

Relations on fuzzy sets allow us to deal with similarity in a natural manner. An equivalence relation splits up a set into equivalence classes, e.g. "x is the same age as y" partitions a population according to age. In order for relation R on set S to be an equivalence relation, the relation has satisfy the following conditions for all $x, y, z \in S$:

$$\text{reflexivity} : R(x, x) = \text{true}$$

$$\text{symmetry} : R(x, y) = R(y, x)$$

$$\text{transitivity} : R(x, y) \wedge R(y, z) \rightarrow R(x, z)\,.$$

A similarity relation groups together similar entities, so we expect it to resemble the equivalence relation. However, transitivity does not hold, as, for example, "x and y have similar salaries" shows — salary x may be similar to salary $x + \delta x$, salary $x + \delta x$ similar to $x + 2\delta x$, $x + 2\delta x$ similar to $x + 3\delta x$, and so forth, but salaries x and, say, $x + 5\delta x$ need no longer be regarded as similar.

So similarity differs from equivalence with respect to transitivity. Transitivity now has to be fuzzy, and by making it fuzzy we obtain the fuzzy equivalence relation, which is commonly called the *similarity relation.* It satisfies, for all $x, y, z \in S$:

$$R(x,x) = 1$$

$$R(x,y) = R(y,x)$$

$$R(x,z) \geq \max_{y \in S} \min[R(x,y), R(y,z)]\,.$$

The concept of equivalence classes can be preserved by the use of α-cuts. An α-cut of fuzzy set A is a crisp set ${}^{\alpha}A$ consisting of all those elements of A whose membership grades are not below α:

$${}^{\alpha}A = \{x | A(x) \geq \alpha\}\,.$$

Applying this to the fuzzy relation R, for any α in (0, 1], the α-cut ${}^{\alpha}R$ creates a crisp equivalence relation representing similarity between its elements to degree α. Each such α-equivalence forms a partition of S, and elements x and y of S belong to the same block of this partition if $R(x,y) \geq \alpha$. If $\alpha_2 > \alpha_1$, then the partition induced by α_2 is a refinement of the partition induced by α_1, or is the same as this partition.

Example: Let the membership function for a fuzzy relation R on $\{a, b, \ldots, h\}$ be as shown in Fig. 4. Then the partition corresponding to $\alpha = 0.4$ has the blocks $\{a, e, f, g\}$, $\{b, c, h\}$, $\{d\}$; the partition corresponding to $\alpha = 0.7$ has the blocks $\{a, e, f\}$, $\{g\}$, $\{b, h\}$, $\{c\}$, $\{d\}$; the partition corresponding to $\alpha = 1.0$ has the blocks $\{a\}$, $\{e, f\}$, $\{g\}$, $\{b\}$, $\{h\}$, $\{c\}$, $\{d\}$.

Similarity creates uncertainty problems. The most serious is the question of what features determine the similarity of objects. For example, given three objects, characterized by the features of color, weight, cost, and the number of legs, where the characterization of object A is <white, 6 Kg, USD 75, 4>, that of B is <white,

	a	b	c	d	e	f	g	h
a	1.0	0	0	0	0.9	0.9	0.5	0
b	0	1.0	0.4	0	0	0	0	0.8
c	0	0.4	1.0	0	0	0	0	0.4
d	0	0	0	1.0	0	0	0	0
e	0.9	0	0	0	1.0	1.0	0.5	0
f	0.9	0	0	0	1.0	1.0	0.5	0
g	0.5	0	0	0	0.5	0.5	1.0	0
h	0	0.8	0.4	0	0	0	0	1.0

Fig. 4. Membership grades for a fuzzy relation.

7 Kg, USD 80, 4>, and that of C is <brown, 15 Kg, USD 400, 0>, we would assume A to have greater similarity to B than to C. We would probably think differently on learning that A and C are both chairs, but that B is a dog.

5. Fuzzy Logic

Here we shall merely sketch some of the approaches to the fuzzification of some concepts of classical logic, particularly with regard to implication. A fuzzy proposition is defined in terms of a universal set U, and a fuzzy set F based on U that represents some fuzzy predicate, such as "tall", "expensive", "high". Element u of U belongs to F with a membership grade $F(u)$. For example, with regard to a line of clothing we could have a membership function of "expensive" that is zero for prices below USD 50, rises linearly to 1 for prices between USD 50 and USD 300, and is constant at 1 beyond USD 300. Then the membership grade for an item that costs USD 150 is 0.4, and for an item that costs USD 225 it is 0.7. We take this membership grade to be the degree of the truth of the proposition "item x is expensive". The degree of truth of a proposition is thus a value in [0, 1]. Fuzzy union and intersection, as illustrated by Fig. 3, are defined in terms of the max and min functions, and so are the disjunction and conjunction of fuzzy propositions. We get

$$A(p \vee q) = \max(A(p), A(q))\,; \qquad A(p \wedge q) = \min(A(p), A(q))\,.$$

Definitions of fuzzy existential and universal quantifiers follow from this: the max or min operation extends over the entire fuzzy set to which the quantifier is applied. In addition there are specifically fuzzy quantifiers, which may be *absolute* or *relative.* Absolute quantifiers are semi-quantitative, e.g. about 10, much more than 100, at least about 0.5; relative quantifiers are defined on [0,1] — they are qualitative, e.g. almost all, about half, most.

Implication in the classical sense is a mapping from a pair of truth values to a truth value. Representing T and F by 1 and 0, we have:

$$\Im : \{0,1\} \times \{0,1\} \to \{0,1\}\,.$$

Classical implication can be expressed in numerous different equivalent forms, such as

$$\Im(p,q) = \bar{p} \vee q$$

$$\Im(p,q) = \bar{p} \vee (p \wedge q)$$

$$\Im(p,q) = (\bar{p} \wedge \bar{q}) \vee q\,.$$

The corresponding fuzzy implication function maps from the fuzzy truth values of propositions p and q to the truth value of "if p then q":

$$\Im : [0,1] \times [0,1] \to [0,1]\,.$$

Letting $\mathcal{U}$, $\mathcal{I}$, and $\mathcal{C}$ stand for fuzzy union, intersection, and complement, respectively, we get three fuzzy expressions corresponding to the three expressions above:

$$\Im(p,q) = \mathcal{U}(\mathcal{C}(p),q)$$

$$\Im(p,q) = \mathcal{U}(\mathcal{C}(p),\mathcal{I}(p,q))$$

$$\Im(p,q) = \mathcal{U}(\mathcal{I}(\mathcal{C}(p),\mathcal{C}(q)),q)\,.$$

The problem is that the fuzzy expressions are no longer equivalent. Moreover, if we use different interpretations of the fuzzy operations, each of our expressions results in several non-equivalent implications. For example, there are four well-known expressions corresponding to $\mathcal{U}(\mathcal{C}(p),q)$ alone.

6. Fuzzy Control Systems

Fuzzy control systems have proven themselves to be very useful in practice. For example, the Sendai subway control system in Japan has been operational since 1986, and its performance has exceeded that of manual operation. The construction of a fuzzy application has four steps.

- The first step is a determination of whether a fuzzy system is appropriate for the application. It is if system knowledge can be expressed as a set of heuristic qualitative rules. If, in the conventional sense, a system has to be defined by a complicated mathematical model, a fuzzy system may be simpler.
- Inputs and outputs are identified, as well as their ranges. The characteristics of measuring devices determine input ranges; the output range is determined by the control actions that are to be performed.
- Membership functions for all input and output parameters are determined, and a rule base is constructed. The rule base defines the control action to be taken for every combination of the inputs. Design of realistic membership functions and control rules is perhaps the hardest task. Usually the task is carried out iteratively.
- The system is validated: a determination is made for various sample inputs that the outputs are within their required ranges. Since it cannot be established analytically that a fuzzy system is stable, extensive testing is required (for the Sendai subway system there were 300,000 simulation tests and 3,000 riderless subway runs).

The operation of a fuzzy system consists of measurement of input parameters, their fuzzification, determination of the appropriate control rule or rules, and the selection of a control action by a process of defuzzification. For a steam turbine the appropriate inputs are the current temperature and pressure of the steam. These values lead to the selection of appropriate fuzzy sets for the input. These fuzzy

	Weak	Low	Normal	High	Strong
D	H	N	L	W	W
C	H	H	N	L	W
B	S	H	N	N	L
A	S	S	H	H	N

Fig. 5. A fuzzy rule base for a control system.

sets and the rule base determine a response in the form of a fuzzy set or sets, and defuzzification derives from this output a control action, which for the steam turbine is a throttle setting.

We have chosen an example in which there are two inputs, but the specific nature of these inputs is left undefined. One input, as shown in the upper left diagram of Fig. 6, is represented by a single fuzzy membership function. The domain of these input values is split into four distinct non-overlapping regions, A, B, C, and D, so that this input is not really fuzzy in the strict sense. The other input, as shown in the lower left diagram, is represented by five overlapping membership functions. We thus have 4×5 possible input classes, and Fig. 5 shows what control action is to be taken for each such class. This is a fuzzy rule base. The control actions are fuzzy, and are denoted S(trong), H(igh), N(ormal), L(ow), and W(eak). For our example, we assume that the first input falls into range B, and corresponds to a membership grade of 0.6. The other input is assumed to correspond to both Low (membership 0.2) and Normal (membership 0.8). Hence two control actions are relevant, H and N. Their membership functions are as shown in the upper right diagram of Fig. 6. Now, when two membership grades are combined, their minimum is taken. Hence, for the B and Low input the combined value is 0.6, and for B and Normal it is 0.2.

These values are used to cut off the top portions of the two membership functions of the fuzzy control variable. The result is the shape shown as the lower right diagram of Fig. 6. The horizontal axis represents the values of the control variable, e.g. the setting of a fuel valve, or the amount of pressure that is to be applied to the brakes of a vehicle.

In our graph the values of the control variable extend from 15.5 to 23.0. Defuzzification is the process of selecting a single value in this range. For control applications the most popular is the centroid method. It selects a value such that a line extended upward from this value on the horizontal axis splits the composite truncated membership function graph into two equal areas. The value 18.46 does so in our case. Other approaches are possible, e.g. chosing the midpoint of (15.5, 23.0), namely 19.25. The choice makes little difference as long as the system remains stable.

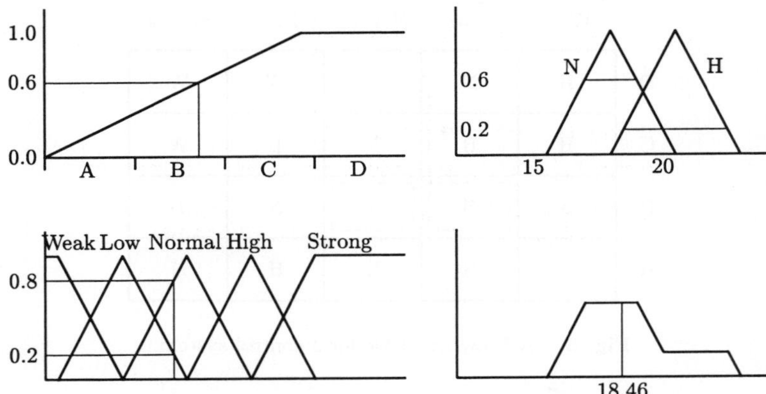

Fig. 6. Defuzzification.

7. Time Petri Nets

For this section, we assume some familiarity with basic concepts of Petri nets. To refresh memory, define a Petri net as the tuple $N = \langle P, T, F, m\rangle$, where

P is a set of places,
T is a set of transitions,
$F \subseteq (P \times T) \cup (T \times P)$ is a flow relation,
m: $P \to N^{+} \cup \{0\}$ is an initial marking that assigns $m(p) \geq 0$ to each place.

A transition t is enabled, i.e., it can fire if every place p_a, such that $\langle p_a, t\rangle \in F$, contains at least one token. The result of the firing is the loss of a token from each such place p_a and a gain of a token at each place p_b such that $\langle t, p_b\rangle \in F$. Petri nets can model non-determinacy: suppose place p contains a token, $\langle p, t_a\rangle$ and $\langle p, t_b\rangle$ belong to F, and both t_a and t_b are enabled; then either t_a or t_b can fire, and there is nothing in Petri net theory that determines which of the two is to fire or when the firing is to take place.

In time Petri nets the non-determinacy with respect to time is partially removed. A time Petri net is the tuple $N_t = \langle P, T, F, m, q\rangle$, where P, T, F, m are as before, and $q : T \to (\tau \times \tau)$ defines a time interval within which an enabled transition is to fire. The mapping q provides each transition with a pair of times (u, v). If the transition becomes enabled at time t, then it must fire within the time interval $(t + u, t + v)$, unless it has become disabled before time $t + v$ due to the firing of some other transition.

Figure 7 illustrates the use of time Petri nets to model uncertainty that may arise with real-time processes. Suppose we have a processing task that is to take between α and β time units, i.e., there is some uncertainty as to the length of time the task needs. The period $\delta = \beta - \alpha$ represents the valid time interval during

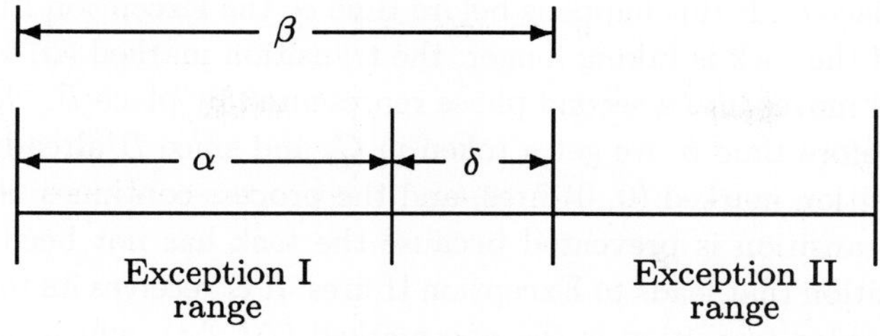

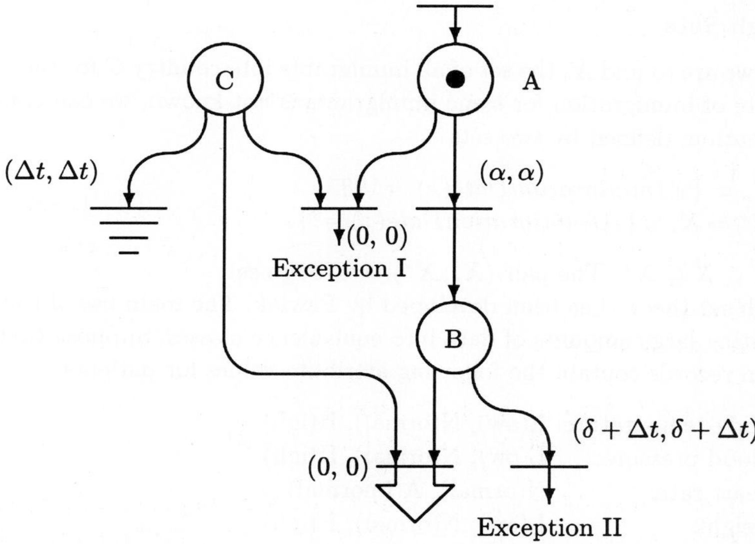

Fig. 7. Time Petri net for a real-time task.

which the task may take place. If it begins too early, Exception I arises; if it takes too long, Exception II goes into effect. The situation is illustrated by the upper diagram of Fig. 7.

In most processes early completion of a task is no problem. An example of where it is a problem arises with package routing. A bar code reader determines the destination of a package, and the package is sent toward a gate that is to open to receive the package. If the package arrives too early, the gate is not yet open; if too late, the gate has closed. In either case it shoots past a closed gate. In setting the times for which the gate is to open, allowance has to be made for some uncertainty in the time the package needs to reach the gate, but if the gate stays open for too long, packages will enter that are not destined for this gate.

In terms of Fig. 7, the task begins when a token arrives in place A, and we take this moment to be time zero. The completion of the task is signaled by the insertion of a token in place C. If this happens before time α, the Exception I transition fires immediately. If the task is taking longer, the transition marked (α, α) fires at time α, and the task moves into a second phase represented by place B. Now, if the task is completed before time β, we get a token in C, and since B already has a token, the lower transition marked (0, 0) fires, and the process continues normally. If the firing of this transition is prevented because the task has not been completed in time, the transition that leads to Exception II fires. If C receives its token after time β, the only enabled transition is the one marked $(\Delta t, \Delta t)$, which merely removes the token from C by "earthing" it.

8. Rough Sets

Suppose we are to find X, the set of all immigrants into country C for the year 1985. If the date of immigration for some immigrants is not known, we can construct an approximation, defined by two sets

$$X_* = \{x | ImmigrationDate(x) = 1985\}$$
$$X^* = X_* \cup \{x | ImmigrationDate(x) = ?\}.$$

Then $X_* \subseteq X \subseteq X^*$. The pair (X_*, X^*) is a rough set.

Rough set theory has been developed by Pawlak. The main use of rough sets is in separating large amounts of data into equivalence classes. Suppose that hospital admission records contain the following attribute values for patients:

body temperature:	L(ow), N(ormal), H(igh)
blood pressure:	L(ow), N(ormal), H(igh)
heart rate:	N(ormal), A(bnormal)
weight:	L(ow), N(ormal), H(igh)
insurance:	Y(es), N(o).

The patients can be grouped into $3 \times 3 \times 2 \times 3 \times 2 = 108$ classes. The patients in a particular class are said to be *indiscernible*. Each class is an *elementary set* in rough set terminology. Let us look at the records of eight patients.

	BT	BP	HR	Wt	Ins
p1	N	H	A	H	Y
p2	H	H	A	H	N
p3	H	N	N	N	Y
p4	H	L	N	L	Y
p5	N	L	A	L	Y
p6	H	H	A	H	N
p7	H	H	N	L	N
p8	L	L	A	L	Y

The attributes, separately and in combination, generate various elementary sets. Thus blood pressure generates {p1, p2, p6, p7}, {p3}, and {p4, p5, p8}, which correspond to H, N, and L, respectively; weight generates {p1, p2, p6}, {p3}, and {p4, p5, p7, p8}; and blood pressure and weight in combination generate {p1, p2, p6}, {p3}, {p4, p5, p8}, {p7}, which correspond to HH, NN, LL, and HL, respectively.

Suppose now that analysis of very many patient records shows that some combinations of BP and Wt can determine whether or not a patient has insurance.

BP	H	H	H	N	N	N	L	L	L
Wt	H	N	L	H	N	L	H	N	L
Ins	Y/N	Y	N	Y/N	Y	Y	Y/N	Y	Y

Patients in the HN, NN, NL, LN, and LL groups all have insurance, patients in the HL group do not, and about the rest we cannot tell. Hence, if we were asked which of our eight patients have insurance, and we only had the blood pressure and weight data to go by, we could say that p3, p4, p5, p8 definitely have it, but that we are not sure about p1, p2, and p6 (p7 definitely does not have it). The set of patients with insurance has thus the lower approximation {p3, p4, p5, p8}, and the upper approximation {p1, p2, p3, p4, p5, p6, p8}, which together define a rough set.

To put our discussion on a formal basis, introduce U, the universe of discourse, i.e., the set of all entities of interest for a particular application, A, the set of attributes that apply to elements of U, and $B \subseteq A$, the attributes under particular consideration. Define the indiscernability relation R_B:

$$R_B(x, y) \text{ if and only if } a(x) = a(y) \text{ for all } a \in B\,.$$

Let U/R_B (or simply U/B) be the partition induced on U by R_B. The blocks of U/B are B-elementary sets. Denote by $B(x)$ the block of U/B that contains element x. Every subset X of U has its B-lower and B-upper approximations:

$$B_*(X) = \{x \in U | B(x) \subseteq X\}$$

$$B^*(X) = \{x \in U | B(x) \cap X \neq \emptyset\}\,.$$

Thus, $B_*(X)$ is the union of all B-elementary sets that are contained in X, and $B^*(X)$ is the union of all B-elementary sets that overlap X. Sometimes $B_*(X)$ and $B^*(X)$ are written as $\underline{B}$ and $\bar{B}$, respectively. The accuracy of the approximation of set X with respect to B, written $\alpha_B(X)$, is the ratio $|B_*(X)|/|B^*(X)|$. Clearly $\alpha_B(X)$ lies between 0 and 1. The B-boundary of X is the set

$$BN_B = B^*(X) - B_*(X)\,.$$

Rough sets can be defined in terms of the *rough membership function*:

$$\mu_X^B(x) = \frac{|X \cup B(x)|}{|B(x)|}.$$

Since we do not know $|X|$, this function is of no direct use, but it makes some concepts clearer. We have

$$B_*(X) = \{x \in U | \mu_X^B(x) = 1\}$$
$$B^*(X) = \{x \in U | \mu_X^B(x) > 0\}$$
$$BN_B(X) = \{x \in U | 0 < \mu_X^B(x) \leq 1\}.$$

Also,

$$\mu_{X \cup Y}^B(x) \geq \max(\mu_X^B(x), \mu_Y^B(x))$$
$$\mu_{X \cap Y}^B(x) \leq \min(\mu_X^B(x), \mu_Y^B(x)).$$

Recall that the corresponding relationships for fuzzy memberships are equalities. This shows that fuzzy sets are a specialization of rough sets, but there is a difference between the two. Under fuzzy set theory we can regard, say, the blood pressure of a patient as both low and normal, but with different membership values. Under rough set theory the blood pressure is either low or normal, but the cardinalities of the sets of patients with low and normal blood pressure are uncertain. Whereas fuzzy sets are well suited for control systems, rough sets work well for classification.

Rough sets appear to be particularly well suited for data mining, which is the detection of significant relationships in data, particularly in data warehouses. This requires the identification of dependencies between attributes. A set of attributes D depends totally on a set of attributes C, denoted $C \Rightarrow D$, if values of attributes of D are uniquely determined by values of attributes of C. We call C the condition attributes, and D the decision attributes. More common is partial dependency, denoted $C \overset{\gamma}{\Rightarrow} D$, The parameter $\gamma(C, D)$, which takes values between 0 and 1, indicates the strength of the dependency:

$$\gamma(C, D) = \sum_{X \in U/D} \frac{|C_*(X)|}{|U|}$$

where U/D is the partition of U induced by D.

To illustrate dependencies we take a population of six people. The attributes are income (INC), with values {Low, Medium, High}, home ownership (HO), ownership of a PC (PC), and ownership of a mobile phone (MOB). We shall consider the first three to be condition attributes, and the last to be a decision attribute.

	INC	HO	PC	MOB
p1	Low	Yes	No	No
p2	Medium	No	Yes	Yes
p3	Medium	Yes	No	Yes
p4	High	Yes	Yes	Yes
p5	High	Yes	No	Yes
p6	Medium	No	Yes	No

The dependence of D = MOB on C = {INC, HO, PC} is not total — the condition attributes are the same for p2 and p6, but p2 does have a mobile while p6 does not. Hence $\gamma(C, D) = (1+1+1+1)/6 = 4/6$. But we also get $\gamma(C, D) = 4/6$ with C = {INC, HO} and with C = {INC, PC}. This shows that either of the attributes HO or PC is redundant, but not both. We have γ(INC, MOB) = 3/6, but γ(HO, MOB) = γ(PC, MOB) = 0.

A set of conditions $C'(C' \subset C)$ is a *D-reduct* of C if C' is a minimal subset of C such that

$$\gamma(C, D) = \gamma(C', D).$$

The intersection of all D-reducts is called a D-core. Here we have D-reducts {INC, PC} and {INC, HO}, so that the D-core is {INC}. A core contains the most important attributes for an application in that removal of a core-attribute reduces the classification power.

9. Belief and Evidence

Suppose we assign probability 0.6 to the proposition that the manager of the Internet company Hype.com is competent and trustworthy, and the manager states that in the last business quarter Hype.com lost only USD 20,000,000. Under the belief-function approach a belief of 0.6 is assigned to the manager's statement. This is an indirect approach: a confidence measure for one statement results in a confidence measure for another statement.

Now look at this from another angle: we gave a 0.4 probability that the manager is incompetent or not to be trusted. Should we say that the loss figure is to be disbelieved at a 0.4 level? Not necessarily. We may, for example, set this belief level at 0.2 — in common speech this is expressed as "giving the benefit of doubt" (also, the positive belief can be less than 0.6). A belief cannot be put above the corresponding probability, but it can be lower. This has led to the use of gambling terminology in some discussions of belief and evidence: the 0.6 belief is interpreted as an offer to give 6:10 odds on it, and the 0.2 belief as an offer of 2:10 odds. Using the symbol *Bel* to denote belief, $Bel(p \wedge \bar{p}) = 1$ for any proposition p. But in our example $Bel(p) = 0.6$ and $Bel(\bar{p}) = 0.2$, so that in general $Bel(p) + Bel(\bar{p}) \leq 1$.

In terms of sets, given a finite universal set U, the belief function Bel is a mapping from the power set of U to the unit interval,

$$Bel : \mathcal{P}(U) \to [0,1]$$

with properties

$$Bel(\emptyset) = 0\,, \quad Bel(U) = 1$$
$$Bel(A) + Bel(\bar{A}) \leq 1\,.$$

For a set $A \subset U$, $Bel(A)$ is the degree of belief (based on available evidence) that an element of U belongs to A.

Plausibility Pl is the dual of Bel:

$$Pl(A) = 1 - Bel(\bar{A})\,, \quad Bel(A) = 1 - Pl(\bar{A})$$
$$Pl(\emptyset) = 0\,, \quad Pl(U) = 1$$
$$Pl(A) + Pl(\bar{A}) \geq 1\,.$$

Introduce a basic probability assignment,

$$m : \mathcal{P}(U) \to [0,1]$$

such that $m(\emptyset) = 0$ and

$$\sum_{A \in \mathcal{P}(U)} m(A) = 1\,.$$

For each subset A of U, $m(A)$ represents the proportion to which available evidence supports the claim that a particular element of the universe belongs to A. If $|U| = 8$, then $|\mathcal{P}(U)| = 256$, which means that the average value of m is 0.004. However, for most subsets of U we can expect the value to be zero, so that the non-zero values will not be very low. Consider the sets A, B, C, and D shown in Fig. 8, where D is also the universal set. Although here the powerset has 16 elements, not all are distinct. For example, $AB = A$, where we are adopting a convention under which AB stands for $A \cup B$. Then the only sets of interest are A, B, C, D, AC, and BC.

We have

$$Bel(A) = \sum_{B|B \subseteq A} m(B)\,, \quad Pl(A) = \sum_{B|A \cap B \neq \emptyset} m(B)\,.$$

Explanation: $m(A)$ measures the degree of belief or evidence that an element of U belongs to set A and only to set A; $Bel(A)$ represents the belief that the element belongs to A as well as to subsets of A; $Pl(A)$ represents the belief that it belongs to A, to any of its subsets, and also to subsets that overlap A (hence $Pl(A) \geq Bel(A)$). With respect to Fig. 8,

$$Bel(A) = m(A) + m(B)$$

$$Pl(A) = m(A) + m(B) + m(C) + m(D) + m(AC)\,.$$

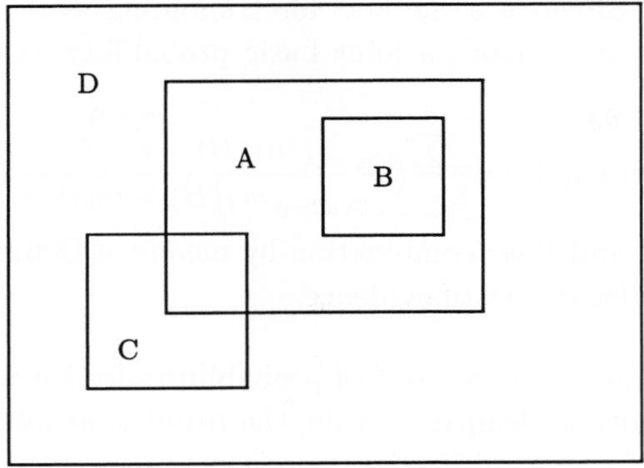

Fig. 8. A universal set with subsets.

A set A with $m(A) > 0$ is a *focal element* of m. It is a subset of U on which the available element focuses. The set of pairs $\{\langle A, m\rangle | m(A) > 0\}$ is a *body of evidence.*

Example 1: Let the universe consist of all possible cost estimates of a project, bounded by say USD 30,000 and 100,000. Define three sets on these costs:

$$30,000 \leq A < 50,000$$

$$50,000 \leq B < 70,000$$

$$70,000 \leq C < 100,000\,.$$

We construct a body of evidence, where the belief in particular cost estimates is based on past experience:

A	B	C	AB	AC	BC	ABC
0.05	0.20	0.15	0.15	0	0.35	0.10

Example 2: We take the universe to consist of three causes, a, b, c. An observed phenomenon (symptom) may be due to a single cause (a disease), or two causes in combination, or all causes. Here we assume the body of evidence to be as follows:

a	b	c	ab	ac	bc	abc
0.30	0.15	0.20	0.10	0.15	0.05	0.05

Let us return to Example 1. Suppose that another expert arrives at a different body of evidence:

A	B	C	AB	AC	BC	ABC
0.05	0.15	0.15	0.20	0	0.30	0.15

Evidence theory provides a method for combining evidence. Given evidence from two (independent) sources, a joint basic probability assignment is given by Dempster's rule:

$$m_{1,2}(A) = \frac{\sum_{B\cap C=A} m_1(B)\times m_2(C)}{1-\sum_{B\cup C=\emptyset} m_1(B)\times m_2(C)}\,.$$

Use of the m-values, and their combination by means of Dempster's rule is known as the Dempster-Shafer theory of evidence.

Example 3: If we combine the two sets of probabilities for the software cost estimation problem by means of Dempster's rule, the result is as follows:

	A	B	C	AB	AC	BC	ABC
m_1	0.05	0.20	0.15	0.15	0	0.35	0.10
m_2	0.05	0.15	0.15	0.20	0	0.30	0.15
$m_{1,2}$	0.039	0.440	0.190	0.087	0	0.226	0.018

Let us now look at how some of the values were arrived at. First we compute the denominator in Dempster's rule, which acts as normalizer to ensure that the $m_{1,2}$-values add up to 1. Denote it by K. Then we show how the values for $m_{1,2}(B)$ and $m_{1,2}(AB)$ were arrived at.

$$\begin{aligned} K &= 1-[m_1(A)m_2(B)+m_1(A)m_2(C)+m_1(A)m_2(BC)\\ &\quad +m_1(B)m_2(A)+m_1(B)m_2(C)+m_1(B)m_2(AC)\\ &\quad +m_1(C)m_2(A)+m_1(C)m_2(B)+m_1(C)m_2(AB)\\ &\quad +m_1(AB)m_2(C)+m_1(AC)m_2(B)+m_1(BC)m_2(A)]\\ &= 1-(0.0075+0.0075+\cdots+0.0175)=0.8300\,.\\ m_{1,2}(B) &= [m_1(B)m_2(B)+m_1(B)m_2(AB)+m_1(B)m_2(BC)\\ &\quad +m_1(B)m_2(ABC)+m_1(AB)m_2(B)+m_1(AB)m_2(BC)\\ &\quad +m_1(BC)m_2(B)+m_1(BC)m_2(AB)+m_1(ABC)m_2(B)]/K\\ &= (0.0300+0.0400+\cdots+0.0150)/0.8300=0.440\,.\\ m_{1,2}(AB) &= [m_1(AB)m_2(AB)+m_1(AB)m_2(ABC)+m_1ABC)m_2(AB)]/K\\ &= (0.0300+0.0225+0.0200)/0.8300=0.087\,. \end{aligned}$$

10. Possibility Theory

Zadeh has been concerned with linguistic values, which leads to the concept of "computing with words". The basis for this are possibility distributions. Consider V, a variable defined on a set X. This set can consist of numbers, but also of colors, employees, etc. Instead of allowing V to take just single values, we shall also allow fuzzy subsets of X as its values. Then we can state not only that "*John's age* is 25", but also that "*John's age* is *young*". In the latter case the variable *John's age* has assumed a linguistic value and *young* is represented by a fuzzy subset of X. In terms of a predicate *Age* we have that *Age*(*John*, 25) is true or false, but *Age*(*John*, *young*) does not work out so well. We can be fairly sure that John is not over 50, and all values up to 20 are certainly possible, but the middle range is uncertain. To measure such uncertainties, Zadeh introduced the concept of *possibility*.

In probability theory we have probability distribution functions

$$p : X \to [0,1], \text{ with } \sum_{x \in X} p(x) = 1 .$$

For a subset A of X, the probability measure for this set is

$$Prob(A) = \sum_{x \in A} p(x) .$$

Possibility distribution functions are the counterpart of this. For each $x \in X$, the possibility of x being a value of V (*John's age* in our example) in terms of the linguistic variable A (represented by a fuzzy subset of A), is written $\pi(x)$ — some authors use $r(x)$. Then

$$\pi : X \to [0,1], \text{ with } \max_{x \in X} \pi(x) = 1$$

such that $\pi(x) = A(x)$, where $A(x)$ is the membership grade of x in A, a fuzzy subset of X. The counterpart of $Prob(A)$ is $Poss(A)$, with the possibility measure for set A given by

$$Poss(A) = \max_{x \in A} \pi(x) .$$

Necessity is a measure related to possibility:

$$Nec(A) = 1 - Poss(\bar{A}) .$$

We can assume that the possibility distribution for John being young is 1.0 up to age 20, and that it then drops linearly to reach 0 at age 50. For any age up to 100, say, and any given person, if we have no additional knowledge, the possibility that this is the person's age is 1.0. Probability theory in a case like this assumes every age to be equally probable, so, given that the age has to be in [0, 100], all probabilities are 0.01.

In probability theory ignorance is interpreted as complete randomness, which implies a uniform distribution. But there is nothing that says that a uniform distribution is appropriate. In possibility theory one merely states that all values are equally possible, which does not imply that they are equally probable. Possibility statements are weaker than probability statements, and this is how it should be — it allows possibility theory to deal with states of knowledge that range from total ignorance to total information in a natural and simple manner.

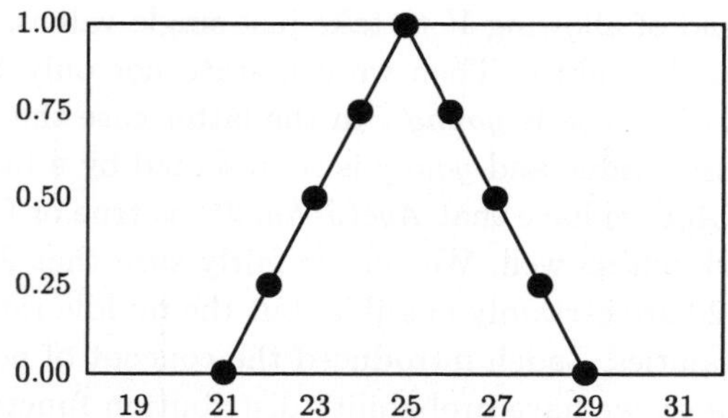

Fig. 9. A possibility distribution.

Possibilities may be linked to bodies of evidence $\langle A, m\rangle$. For this we have to use α-cut, which were introduced in Sec. 5. For fuzzy set A,

$$\alpha_1 \preceq \alpha_2 \rightarrow {}^{\alpha_1}A \supseteq {}^{\alpha_2}A\,.$$

Example: Let V be the set of ages, and consider the statement "V is about 25". The concept "about 25" is represented by fuzzy set T. The possibility distribution π with respect to "about 25" has the same values as the membership function T. We show it as Fig. 9.

We have the following significant α-cuts:

$$\begin{aligned}
\alpha = 1.00: &\quad A_1 = \{25\}\\
\alpha = 0.75: &\quad A_2 = \{24, 25, 26\}\\
\alpha = 0.50: &\quad A_3 = \{23, 24, 25, 26, 27\}\\
\alpha = 0.25: &\quad A_4 = \{22, 23, 24, 25, 26, 27, 28\}\\
\alpha = 0.00: &\quad A_5 = \{21, 22, 23, 24, 25, 26, 27, 28, 29\}\,.
\end{aligned}$$

These α-cuts correspond to focal elements, i.e., they are sets $A \in \mathcal{P}(V)$ such that $m(A) > 0$. It can be shown that for values $\pi_1, \pi_2, \ldots, \pi_n$,

$$\pi_i = \sum_{k=i}^{n} m_k$$

from which

$$\pi_{i-1} = \sum_{k=i-1}^{n} m_k$$

giving $m_i = \pi_i - \pi_{i+1}$, with $\pi_{n+1} = 0$ by convention.

Then, for our example, as expected,

$$\begin{aligned}
m(A_1 &= 1.00 - 0.75 = 0.25\\
m(A_2 &= 0.75 - 0.50 = 0.25\\
m(A_3 &= 0.50 - 0.25 = 0.25\\
m(A_4 &= 0.25 - 0.25 = 0.25\,.
\end{aligned}$$

11. Bibliographic Notes

In the introduction, we referred to the book by Klir and Yuan [1] as possibly the best reference on uncertainty. This encyclopaedic survey goes well beyond just fuzziness, and a literature search can start with its 1731 references, which are classified into categories. Dyreson [3] has generated a bibliography of uncertainty management for information systems. A collection of readings edited by Shafer and Pearl [4] deals with nearly all aspects of uncertainty in the context of AI reasoning systems. However, some of the papers may be somewhat advanced for a non-specialist. Measures of uncertainty in expert systems are considered in [5]. A survey by Klir [6] can also be recommended, and so can the survey by Parsons [7] on imperfect information in data and knowledge bases. The Parsons survey has 172 references, and an earlier survey by Ng and Adamson [8] has 75.

The literature on probability is, of course, overwhelming. For software and knowledge engineers the best choice may be a text addressed to engineers and scientists. Such texts have a high degree of rigor without getting into topics of merely theoretical interest. Walpole and Myers [9] is a good choice. The book by Allen [10] is addressed specifically to computer scientists, but its examples are somewhat dated for this Internet age. A collection of papers [11] provides examples of application of the Bayesian approach. The Bayesian approach has been used in a study of empirical software engineering cost models [12].

An outgrowth of the Bayesian method is the study of Bayesian networks [13]. Here the description of a system is separated into a qualitative and a quantitative component. The qualitative component represents relationships between variables or events by means of arcs of a graph; the quantitative component associates conditional probabilities with the arcs. The guest editors' introduction to a special section of the *IEEE Transactions on Knowledge and Data Engineering* [14] lists 43 references, most of which are recent; the special section contains four articles. An earlier survey provides 166 references [15]. Although often our aim in studying relationships is to discover cause-effect patterns, a relationship does not have to be a causal relationship. This aspect of uncertainty is studied in great detail in [16] (the book contains 379 references).

There are very many books on fuzzy sets and their extensions. Five are listed here, where my criterion for listing these books is that I have them. As noted earlier, [1] is the main reference. A book by Cox [17] takes a very practical approach, and the collection edited by Marks [18] contains papers, many of which are experience reports, from various IEEE conferences that took place in 1992 and 1993. Yager and Filev [19] give additional examples. The Terano *et al* book [20] complements the others in that it describes some successfully implemented fuzzy systems in Japan, where the earliest practical applications of fuzziness were made — of particular interest is the data on the Sendai Subway system. Two applications of fuzzy control in automobile design are discussed in [21, 22]. Defuzzification is very important in such work. Runkler [23] presents some of the more important defuzzification methods and investigates their properties. Three examples are used. Zadeh [24] discusses the notion that fuzzy logic is computing with words. Yen [25] brings new insights to fuzzy logic. For a symposium on fuzzy logic see the August 1994 issue of *IEEE Expert* — the symposium discussion was based on a paper by Elkan [26], which is a formal presentation of some misgivings about fuzzy logic. Mathematicians will find [27] informative.

Similarity, which we considered as a type of fuzzy relationship, has been defined as indistinguishability under an appropriate resolution [28]. Although the title of the paper does not suggest this, similarity is studied very thoroughly in [29]. A particular aspect of similarity arises with identification. Since no two signatures by the same person are the same, the recognition of a signature depends on how similar it is to a reference signature. It is nearly as important to prevent rejection of a true signature as to accept a falsification. Because of the difficulty of achieving this, the use of biometric features has become popular, particularly identification based on unique characteristics of the human iris [30]. A major application of similarity arises in the retrieval of reusable software components — see [31–33] on this. Similarity plays also an important role in case-based reasoning [34].

On Petri nets in general, the books by Peterson [35] and Reisig [36] give excellent introduction. Although published a while back, they are still current as regards the needs of practitioners. The topic of time Petri nets is covered thoroughly in [37]. Fuzzy Petri nets have been used for the representation of knowledge [38].

The literature on rough sets is not easy to read in that the most active researchers in this area make use of rather advanced mathematics, but [39] is a fairly accessible introduction. The major source of information on rough sets and their application is [40, 41]; [40] contains an excellent tutorial by Pawlak. For another example of the application of rough sets, see [42].

A very important uncertainty problem relates to the quality of data. There are two issues. First, the data in a data base are to be dependable, i.e., they are to model an up-to-date aspect of the world. Second, improper decisions are to be prevented when data in support of real-time decisions come from various sources of variable dependability. The second issue can be expressed as follows: given a set of evidence $\{E_j\}$, which consists of reported facts or measurements, and for each, a measure W_j of the data quality, i.e., a measure of its accuracy or of confidence in its source, decide among an exhaustive set of mutually exclusive hypotheses $\{H_i\}$. Dillard [43] considers several decision methods for selecting the appropriate hypothesis, including Dempster's rule, but in a simplified form. For a later investigation of the effect of data quality on decision making see [44]. In [45], the Dempster-Shafer theory is combined with fuzzy inferencing. The Dempster-Shafer theory is the basis for Yager's work on multicriteria decisions [46].

Management of inconsistency in software development is a major concern of software engineers. Because this topic has been recently surveyed by Spanoudakis and Zisman [47], we have not discussed it here. We merely draw attention to the distinction made by Robinson and Pawlowski [48] between inconsistencies, which are technical, and conflicts, which have a social basis. Awareness of this distinction can be useful in the management of uncertainties in other areas as well.

The management of uncertainty has been extensively studied in the context of information systems. The main topics have been uncertainty in general [49, 50], null values in data bases [51–53], avoidance of null responses to queries [54–56], vague and fuzzy queries [57–60], and the association of probabilities with attributes [61, 62]. The plausibility concept has been used in data base design [63].

References

1. G. J. Klir and B. Yuan, *Fuzzy Sets and Fuzzy Logic* (Prentice Hall PTR, 1995).
2. A. T. Berztiss, "Software methodologies for decision support", *Information & Management* **18** (1990) 221–229.
3. C. E. Dyreson, "A bibliography on uncertainty management in information systems", eds. A. Motro and P. Smets, *Uncertainty Management in Information Systems* (Kluwer, 1997) 413–458.
4. G. Shafer and J. Pearl (eds.), *Readings in Uncertain Reasoning* (Morgan Kaufmann, 1990).
5. P. Walley, "Measures of uncertainty in expert systems", *Artificial Intelligence* **83** (1996) 1–58.
6. G. J. Klir, "Developments in uncertainty-based information", *Advances in Computers* **36** (1993) 255–332.
7. S. Parsons, "Current approaches to handling imperfect information in data and knowledge bases", *IEEE Transactions on Knowledge and Data Engineering* **8** (1996) 353–372.
8. K.-C. Ng and B. Abramson, "Uncertainty management in expert systems", *IEEE Expert* **5**, no. 2 (April 1990) 29–48.
9. R. E. Walpole and R. H. Myers, *Probability and Statistics for Engineers and Scientists*, 4th ed. (Macmillan, 1989).
10. A. O. Allen, *Probability, Statistics, and Queueing Theory with Computer Science Applications* (Academic Press, 1978).
11. S. French and J. Q. Smith (eds.), *The Practice of Bayesian Analysis* (Arnold with Wiley, 1997).
12. S. Chulani, B. Boehm and B. Steece, "Bayesian analysis of empirical software engineering cost models", *IEEE Transactions on Software Engineering* **25** (1999) 573–583.
13. J. Pearl, *Probabilistic Reasoning in Intelligent Systems: Networks of Plausible Inference* (Morgan Kaufmann, 1988).
14. M. J. Druzdzel and L. C. v. d. Gaag, "Building probabilistic networks: 'Where do the numbers come from?' ", *IEEE Transactions on Knowledge and Data Engineering* **12** (2000) 481–486.
15. W. Buntine, "A guide to the literature on learning probabilistic networks from data", *IEEE Transactions on Knowledge and Data Engineering* **8** (1996) 195–210.
16. J. Pearl, *Causality: Models, Reasoning, and Inference* (Cambridge University Press, 2000).
17. E. Cox, *The Fuzzy Systems Handbook* (Academic Press, 1994).
18. R. J. Marks (ed.), *Fuzzy Logic Technology and Applications* (IEEE, 1994).
19. R. R. Yager and D. P. Filev, *Essential Fuzzy Modeling and Control* (Wiley, 1994).
20. T. Terano, K. Asai and M. Sugeno, *Applied Fuzzy Systems* (Academic Press, 1994) (Japanese edition in 1989).

21. R. Müller and G. Nöcker, "Intelligent cruise control with fuzzy logic", in [17], pp. 74–80.
22. G. F. Maurer, "A fuzzy logic controller for an ABS braking system", *IEEE Transactions on Fuzzy Systems* **3** (1995) 381–388.
23. T. A. Runkler, "Selection of appropriate defuzzification methods using application specific properties", *IEEE Transactions on Fuzzy Systems* **5** (1997) 72–79.
24. L. A. Zadeh, "Fuzzy logic = computing with words", *IEEE Transactions on Fuzzy Systems* **4** (1996) 103–111.
25. J. Yen, "Fuzzy logic — A modern perspective", *IEEE Transactions on Knowledge and Data Engineering* **11** (1999) 153–165.
26. C. Elkan, "The paradoxical success of fuzzy logic", *IEEE Expert* **9**, no. 4 (August 1994) 3–8.
27. E. Turunen, *Mathematics Behind Fuzzy Logic* (Physica-Verlag, 1999).
28. K. Georgatos, "Resolution spaces: A topological approach to similarity", *Proceedings of the 11th International Workshop on Database and Expert Systems Applications* (IEEE CS Press, 2000) 553–557.
29. S. Castano, G. Martella and P. Samarati, "Analysis, comparison, and design of role-based security specifications", *Data & Knowledge Engineering* **21** (1997) 31–55.
30. M. Negin *et al*, "An iris biometric system for public and personal use", *Computer* **33**, no. 2 (February 2000) 70–75.
31. E. Ostertag, J. Hendler, R. P. Diaz and C. Braun, "Computing similarity in a reuse library system: An AI-based approach", *ACM Transactions on Software Engineering Methodology* **1** (1992) 205–228.
32. M. G. Fugini and S. Faustle, "Retrieval of reusable components in a development information system", *Proceedings of the 3rd International Conference on Software Reusability* (1994) 89–98.
33. D. Merkl, A. M. Tjoa and G. Kappel, "Learning the semantic similarity of reusable software components", *Proceedings of the 3rd International Conference on Software Reusability* (1994) 33–41.
34. K.-D. Althoff, "Case based reasoning" (this volume).
35. J. L. Peterson, *Petri Net Theory and the Modeling of Systems* (Prentice-Hall, 1981).
36. W. Reisig, *Petri Nets — An Introduction* (Springer-Verlag, 1985).
37. D. Berthomieu and M. Diaz, "Modeling and verification of time dependent systems using time Petri nets", *IEEE Transactions on Software Engineering* **17** (1991) 259–273.
38. S.-M. Chen, J.-S. Ke and J.-F. Chang, "Knowledge representation using fuzzy Petri nets", *IEEE Transactions on Knowledge and Data Engineering* **2** (1990) 311–319 (correspondence on this paper: *ibid* **7** (1995) 190–192).
39. Z. Pawlak, J. Grzymala-Busse, R. Slowinski and W. Ziarko, "Rough sets", *Communications of the ACM* **38**, no. 11 (November 1995), 88–95.
40. L. Polkowski and A. Skowron (eds.), *Rough Sets in Knowledge Discovery 1: Methodology and Applications* (Physica-Verlag, 1998).
41. L. Polkowski and A. Skowron (eds.), *Rough Sets in Knowledge Discovery 2: Applications, Case Studies and Software Systems* (Physica-Verlag, 1998).
42. C.-C. Chan, "Incremental learning of production rules from examples under uncertainty: A rough set approach", *International Journal of Software Engineering and Knowledge Engineering* **1** (1991) 439–461.
43. R. A. Dillard, "Using data quality measures in decision-making algorithms", *IEEE Expert* **7**, no. 6 (December 1992) 63–72.
44. I. N. Chengalur-Smith, D. P. Ballou and H. L. Pazer, "The impact of data quality information on decision making: An exploratory analysis", *IEEE Transactions on Knowledge and Data Engineering* **11** (1999) 853–864.

45. C. Romer and A. Kandel, "Applicability analysis of fuzzy inference by means of generalized Dempster-Shafer theory", *IEEE Transactions on Fuzzy Systems* **3** (1995) 448–453.
46. R. R. Yager, "Hierarchical aggregation functions generated from belief structures", *IEEE Transactions on Fuzzy Systems* **8** (2000) 481–490.
47. G. Spanoudakis and A. Zisman, "Inconsistency management in software engineering: Survey and open research issues", *This Handbook*, Vol. 1.
48. W. Robinson and S. Pawlowski, "Managing requirements inconsistency with development goal monitors", *IEEE Transactions on Software Engineering* **25** (1999) 816–835.
49. J. M. Morrissey, "Imprecise information and uncertainty in information systems", *ACM Transactions on Information Systems* **8** (1990) 159–180.
50. A. Yazici, B. P. Buckles and F. E. Petry, "Handling complex and uncertain information in the ExIFO and NF^2 data models", *IEEE Transactions on Fuzzy Systems* **7** (1999) 659–676.
51. K.-C. Liu and R. Sunderraman, "Indefinite and maybe information in relational databases", *ACM Transactions on Database Systems* **15** (1990) 1–39.
52. K.-C. Liu and R. Sunderraman, "A generalized relational model for indefinite and maybe information", *IEEE Transactions on Knowledge and Data Engineering* **3** (1991) 65–77.
53. Q. Kong and G. Chen, "On deductive databases with incomplete information", *ACM Transactions on Information Systems* **13** (1995) 354–369.
54. T. Ichikawa and M. Hirakawa, "ARES: A relational database with the capability of performing flexible interpretation of queries", *IEEE Transactions on Software Engineering* **SE-12** (1986) 624–634.
55. M. Kao, N. Cercone and W.-S. Luk, "Providing quality responses with natural language interfaces: The null value problem", *IEEE Transactions on Software Engineering* **14** (1988) 959–984.
56. A. Motro, "FLEX: A tolerant and cooperative user interface to databases", *IEEE Transactions on Knowledge and Data Engineering* **2** (1990) 231–246.
57. A. T. Berztiss, "Imprecise queries and the quality of conceptual models", *Information Modelling and Knowledge Bases V* (IOS Press, 1994) 174–185.
58. P. Bosc and O. Pivert, "SQLf: A relational database language for fuzzy querying", *IEEE Transactions on Fuzzy Systems* **3** (1995) 1–17.
59. A. T. Berztiss, "Domain analysis and queries in context", *Proceedings of the 5th International Conference on Application of Natural Languages in Information Systems* (2001, to be published in the Springer Lecture Notes in Computer Science series).
60. G. S. Loo and K.-H. Lee, "An interface to databases for flexible query answering: A fuzzy-set approach", *Proceedings of the 10th International Conference on Database and Expert Systems Applications* (*Lecture Notes in Computer Science 1873*) (Springer, 2000) 654–663.
61. D. Barbara, H. Garcia-Molina and D. Porter, "The management of probabilistic data", *IEEE Transactions on Knowledge and Data Engineering* **4** (1992) 487–502.
62. L. Lakshmanan, N. Leone, R. Ross and V. Subrahmanian, "ProbView: A flexible probabilistic database system", *ACM Transactions on Database Systems* **22** (1997) 419–469.
63. M. Altus, "Meta-modeling in conceptual data base design using a plausibility function", *Information Modelling and Knowledge Bases VIII* (IOS Press, 1997) 113–128.

SOFTWARE PROJECT MANAGEMENT

VLADAN DEVEDZIC

Department of Information System,
FON - School of Business Administration,
University of Belgrade, POB 52, Jove Ilica 154,
11000 Belgrade, Yugoslavia
E-mail: devedzic@galeb.etf.bg.ac.yu

In order to organize and manage a software development project successfully, one must combine specific knowledge, skills, efforts, experience, capabilities, and even intuition. They are all necessary in order to be able answer questions such as: What artifacts to manage and control during software development? How to organize the development team? What are the indicators and measures of the product's quality? How to employ a certain set of development practices? How to transition a software development organization to a new modeling and/or development paradigm? How to create and maintain a good relationship with the customers and end-users? What remedial actions to take when something goes wrong in the course of the project? What are the heuristics that can help managers in conducting the software development process?

The manager of a software development project should answer the above questions in the context of the project itself. However, there is a vast amount of knowledge the manager should possess that transcends the boundaries of any specific project.

The purpose of this chapter is to provide an extended overview of many important issues around which such knowledge should be structured. The introductory section merely introduces the issues and the context within which the other sections discuss them. Each of the remaining sections covers one of the issues in more detail. The idea has been to provide a balanced coverage of the issues from both the manager's and the developer's perspectives.

Keywords: Software development process, management practices, metrics, organizational aspects, standards.

1. Introduction

Software development is a complex process involving such activities as domain analysis, requirements specification, communication with the customers and end-users, designing and producing different artifacts, adopting new paradigms and technologies, evaluating and testing software products, installing and maintaining the application at the end-user's site, providing customer support, organizing end-user's training, envisioning potential upgrades and negotiating about them with the customers, and many more.

In order to keep everything under control, eliminate delays, always stay within the budget, and prevent project runaways, i.e., situations in which cost and time exceed what was planned, software project managers must exercise control and guidance over the development team throughout the project's lifecycle [1]. In doing

Fig. 1. Some important issues of software project management.

so, they apply a number of tools of both economic and managerial nature. The first category of tools includes budgeting, periodic budget monitoring, user charge-back mechanism, continuous cost/benefit analysis, and budget deviation analysis. The managerial toolbox includes both long-range and short-term planning, schedule monitoring, feasibility analysis, software quality assurance, organizing project steering committees, and the like.

All of these activities and tools help manage a number of important issues in the process of software development. Figure 1 illustrates some of the issues, but definitely not all of them. The issues shown in Fig. 1 have been selected for an extended overview in the remainder of this chapter based on the following criteria:

- their priority in the concerns of most software project managers, according to the managers themselves — this is evident from the case studies, interviews, and reports of many software project managers and consultants in software industry worldwide (see, for example, [12, 20], and [49]);
- the frequency of their appearing as topics in the relevant, industry-oriented software engineering journals and magazines, such as *IEEE Computer*, *IEEE Software, and Communications of the ACM*, during the last decade; and
- their importance as identified by relevant committees, associations, and consortia of software developers (see, for example, [26]).

The chapter does not address the economic aspects of software project management, such as budgeting, negotiating, outsourcing, and contracts. The goal is to consider some of the important managerial issues specific to *software* development, not those that appear in other kinds of development projects as well.

2. Software Development Process

One of the primary duties of the manager of a software development project is to ensure that all of the project activities follow a certain predefined *process*, i.e., that the activities are organized as a series of actions conducing to a desirable end [33]. The activities are usually organized in distinct *phases*, and the process specifies what artifacts should be developed and delivered in each phase. For a software development team, conforming to a certain process means complying with an appropriate *order* of actions or operations. For the project manager, the process provides means for control and guidance of the individual team members and the team as a whole, as it offers criteria for tracing and evaluation of the project's deliverables and activities.

Software development process encompasses many different tasks, such as domain analysis and development planning, requirements specification, software design, implementation and testing, as well as software maintenance. Hence it is no surprise at all that a number of software development processes exist. Generally, processes vary with the project's goals (such as time to market, minimum cost, higher quality and customer satisfaction), available resources (e.g. the company's size, the number, knowledge, and experience of people — both engineers and support personnel — and hardware resources), and application domain.

However, every software developer and manager should note that processes are *very* important. It is absolutely necessary to follow a certain predefined process in software development. It helps developers understand, evaluate, control, learn, communicate, improve, predict, and certify their work. Since processes vary with the project's size, goals, and resources, as well as the level at which they are applied (e.g. the organization level, the team level, or the individual level), it is always important to define, measure, analyze, assess, compare, document, and change different processes.

There are several well-known examples of software development processes. Each process relies on a certain *model* of software development. The first well-established and well-documented software development process has followed the *waterfall model*. One of its variants is shown in Fig. 2. The model assumes that the process of software development proceeds through several phases in a more-or-less linear manner. The phases indicated in Fig. 2 are supposed to be relatively independent. There is not much feedback and returning to previous phases other than the one directly preceding the phase in focus. In other words, once a certain phase is finished it is considered closed, and the work proceeds with the next phase. Many developers have criticized the waterfall model for its rigidity in that sense, and for its failure to comply with the reality of ever-changing requirements and technology. However, the waterfall model is at least partially present in most of the other models as well, simply because of its natural order of phases in software development.

There have been many attempts to overcome the limitations of the waterfall model. Two common points in all such attempts are introduction of *iterations*

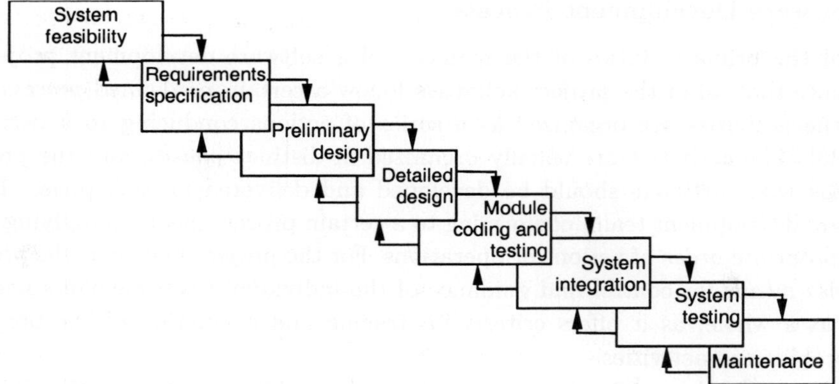

Fig. 2. The waterfall model of software development (based on [5]).

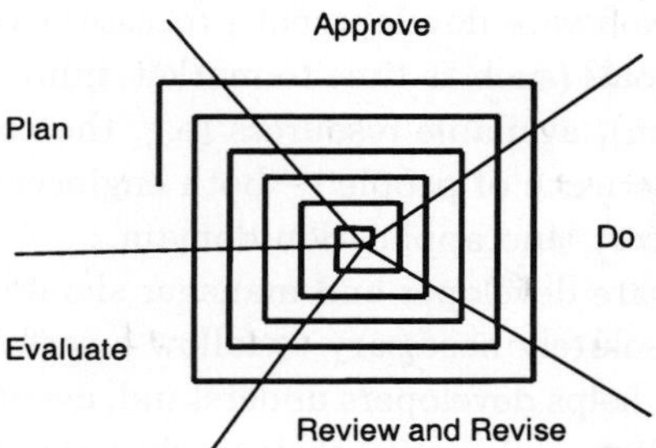

Fig. 3. The spiral model of software development (after [9] and [41]).

in software development activities and *incremental* development. Iterative and incremental software development means going through the same activities more than once, throughout the product's lifecycle, each time producing new deliverables and/or improving the old ones. The main advantage of working in that way is that each individual developer works on a small "work packet" at any given moment, which is much easier to control.

A classical example of iterative and incremental models is the *spiral model* [9], sketched in Fig. 3. In the spiral model, there are five core tasks: planning and design (largely corresponding to the classical analysis phase), approval (requirements specification), realization (design and implementation), revision (testing and modification), and evaluation (integration and system-level testing). The process iterates through these tasks, getting closer and closer to the end by adding increments (e.g. new functions, new design, new modules, new or improved testing procedures, new or improved parts of the user interface, new integration and testing certificates, and so on) to the product in each iteration. The spiral model underlies many processes, such as DBWA (Design By Walking Around) [50], and PADRE (Plan-Approve-Do-Review-Evaluate) [41]. The DBWA process combines the spiral model with multiple design views, flexible structuring of development teams, and dynamic changes in modes of working (e.g. working individually, working in pairs, or working in small teams), in order to improve the process efficiency and parallelism. The PADRE process uses the spiral model at multiple levels — the project level, the phase level, and the individual software module level — thus creating the "spiral in a spiral in a spiral" effect.

The *JNIDS model* (*Joint National Intelligence Development Staff*) [5] is similar to the spiral model in that it is also iterative and incremental. There are, however, six tasks in the JNIDS model: requirements analysis, team orchestration (i.e., the team-building stages, "forming, storming, norming, and performing"), design, coding, integration, and system implementation (delivery and maintenance). The model prescribes to iterate through all six tasks in every phase of software development. There are five phases (requirements identification, prototype development, the breadth of system functionality, system functionality refinement, and transition). They differ in the amount of time and effort they dedicate to each specific task. The first phase focuses most on requirements analysis, the second one focuses most on team orchestration, and so on. The last phase is concentrated most on integration and maintenance. Hence on the time axis the shift of the focus of attention in different phases generates a waterfall-like shape if the six tasks are put on the ordinal axis. However, an important difference between the classical waterfall and JNIDS models is that in the JNIDS model developers conduct their activities through *all* tasks in *each* phase.

The *Unified Process* for object-oriented software development [24] (Fig. 4), has recently become very popular. It is also iterative and incremental, just like the spiral and JNIDS models. All of its iterations go through five core workflows (tasks) shown in Fig. 4, and are grouped in four phases — inception (resulting in a global vision of the software product), elaboration (detailed analysis and design of the baseline architecture), construction (building the system's initial capability), and transition (product release). Just like in the JNIDS model, Fig. 4 shows "fuzzified" traces of the waterfall model in the Unified Process. The process is architecture-centric, meaning that its main deliverable is an executable architecture (the system), described by a set of models generated during the system development (use-case model, analysis model, design model, deployment model, implementation model, and test model). The models are represented using the standard UML diagrams [13]. The Unified Process is also use-case oriented, which means that generic scenarios of how the user or external applications use the system or its subsystems bind all the workflows and drive the iterations.

Being iterative, the Unified Process reduces additional development costs generated by unexpected situations (usually just a single iteration of work is lost). Iterating through all core workflows in every iteration, the process is compliant with the reality of ever changing and incomplete user requirements. The Unified Process is also risk-driven — it enforces examining areas of highest risk in every phase and every iteration, as well as doing the most critical tasks first. Hence it minimizes the

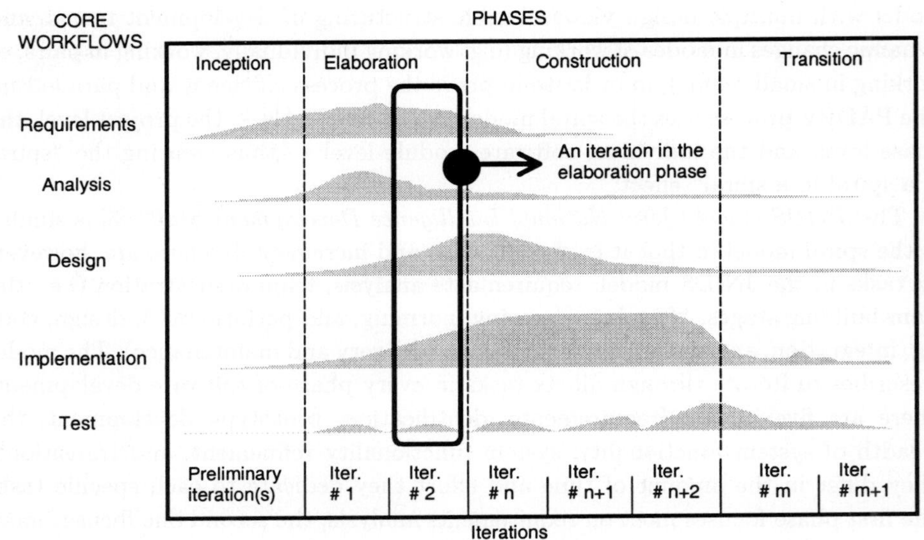

Fig. 4. Core workflows, phases, and iterations in the Unified Process of object-oriented software development (after [24]).

risk of project runaways. Managers can easily adapt the Unified Process to different application types, project sizes, development teams, and levels of competence.

Because of the importance of the Unified Process for software project management today, comments on some other issues from the Unified Process perspective are included in the following chapters.

3. Requirements Engineering

Requirements engineering is the discipline of gathering, analyzing, and formally specifying the user's needs, in order to use them as analysis components when developing a software system [18, 44]. Requirements *must* be oriented towards the user's real needs, not towards the development team and the project managers.

Almost all software development processes one way or another stress requirements analysis and specification as one of their core workflows. The reasons are simple. It is necessary to manage requirements as well as possible because a small change to requirements can profoundly affect the project's cost and schedule, since their definition underlies all design and implementation [40]. Unfortunately, in most practical projects it is not possible to freeze the requirements at the beginning of the project and not to change them. Requirements develop over time, and their development is a learning process, rather than a gathering one. The intended result of this process is a structured but evolving set of agreed, well understood, and carefully documented requirements [25]. This implies the need for requirements *traceability*, i.e., the ability to describe and follow the life of a requirement, in both a forward and backward direction, ideally through the whole system's life cycle.

The importance of constantly involving the users in the process of requirements analysis and specifications cannot be overemphasized. Only the users know their domain properly, and for that reason they should certainly participate in defining the system's functions, designing them, and evaluating their implementation and testing. The users should also participate in creating, verifying, and updating the requirements specification document for the project. The users should share with the developers the responsibility for the requirements' completeness and consistency. It is the project managers' duty to establish and maintain good relations with the users throughout the development process, as well as to consult them whenever the project gets stuck due to the development team's lack of domain understanding.

It is essential to make as explicit as possible all the requirements that reflect the user's work and the tasks that the software system under development is supposed to automate. Any situation in which users can find themselves when doing their job is the context that must be taken into account through requirements engineering. It is equally important not to concentrate on a single user's task, but to cover communication between users when the task requires collaboration.

There is a wide spectrum of techniques for requirements engineering. Whatever technique is applied, it is always desirable to involve the user to increase the correctness of the requirements specification. Some of the techniques are:

- structured interviews and questionnaires that the user fills in (inquiry-based requirements gathering);
- diagram-based requirements analysis (using multiple diagrams to sketch relevant parts of the user's work process and describe the requirements graphically);
- using metaphors of the user's work process (e.g. the office metaphor, or the agent/agency metaphor);
- scenario analysis (scenario is a typical sequence of activities characterizing the user's work process, hence it reflects what the user will do with the system and helps define the test procedures);
- using special-purpose software tools for requirements gathering (some of them can be simulation-based);
- requirements completeness and consistency checks (some of them can be automated, others must be performed manually);
- using special-purpose requirements-specification languages in order to describe requirements more formally and hence provide more automated requirements tracing;
- prototype system development, in order to make the requirements clear and to establish better mutual understanding with the users; and
- analyzing videotaped user's work process.

When managing software development according to the Unified Process, requirements are captured mostly through the use cases and use-case diagrams.

A use case can be described as a specific way of using the system from a user's (actor's) perspective [13]. Use-case diagrams graphically depict system behavior (use cases), i.e., a high level view of how the system is used as viewed from an outsider's (actor's) perspective [24].

4. Software Architecture

Software architecture encompasses specification and design of the application's global structure, leaving the details aside [42]. It is related to the general software organization in terms of its *components* and *connectors*. Components are things like modules, compilation units, objects, and files. Connectors define interactions among components through procedure calls, parameters of initialization, instructions for the linker, and so on.

Defining the architecture of a software system involves the choice of *architectural style*. Each architectural style defines a family of software systems organized in a similar way, the corresponding vocabulary of components and connectors, constraints in using the components and connectors in building the system according to that style, and the way the overall system behavior depends on the behavior of its components. Examples of software architectural styles include layered architectures, pipeline architecture, object-oriented architecture, event-based architecture, repository-based architecture, component-based systems (CBS) architectures, process-control architectures, real-time architectures, and various heterogeneous and Internet-based architectures.

As soon as the initial set of requirements is gathered, the project manager should direct the chief architect and some other engineers to define the initial software architecture of the system to be developed. Software architecture definition does not get sealed after the project begins. On the contrary, it is an evolving activity that continues through all the phases of the product's lifecycle. It interweaves with requirements specification, domain analysis, study of possibilities for reuse, and even design.

The Unified Process of software development treats the problem of software architecture definition and evolution as its central activity [24]. Software architecture is described by different views of the system being built, and these views are in turn represented by different UML models and diagrams.

One of the ultimate goals of the Unified Process is to produce and continuously evolve the system's *executable* architecture. Even in the project's early phases a limited version of the executable architecture must be developed and demonstrated. At the project's closure, it is important for the system architecture to support all of the use-cases specified through requirements engineering. However, in the early phases the architects should capture just a rough outline of the architecture. It is not viable to base that outline on all of the use cases. For that reason, architects first select the general architectural style in a use-case-independent way, and then refine it taking into account only a small subset of all the use-cases for the system.

That small subset usually contains no more than 5–10% of the whole set, but all the use-cases in the subset represent the key functions of the system under development. As the use cases are further specified and they mature, more of the architecture is discovered, and more details are introduced. This process continues until the architecture stabilizes.

Selecting an architectural style and evolving the software architecture is far from being simple, because it involves many issues other than just the system's overall structure. Project managers must be aware of such issues. The issues include the platform the system is to run on (e.g. the hardware architecture, operating system, database management system, and network protocols), global control structures, data communication, synchronization, and access protocols, reusable building blocks available, deployment considerations, legacy systems, the choice among multiple design alternatives, assignment of functions to modules and subsystems, the system's functionality, scalability, reliability, and usability, its comprehension and resilience to changes, and also its esthetical considerations.

For that reason, the architecture of a software system is considered a product in its own right, along with the main software product to be delivered to the customers. It is the development team that benefits most from the software architecture as a product.

5. Organizational Aspects

Software project management always involves various organizational aspects, such as creating and staffing development teams, assigning roles to the team members, modalities of software development, leadership considerations, interpersonal communication at work, staff training and embracing new technologies, organization's culture, social and ethical issues, and so on [3, 4, 12, 16]. Organizational aspects of software development are crucial for all successful projects. They are neither about hardware nor about software — they are about "peopleware", i.e., about using, coordinating, and managing human resources in an organization effectively. In the context of fast-paced and extremely fluid dynamics of software industry, the key to success or failure of software project is the way it is organized and managed.

The foundation of all organizational aspects in software development are the general principles shown in Fig. 5, as suggested in [16]. Experience shows that the four principles in the corners of the square in Fig. 5 constitute the roots of most software organizations' cultures, hence it is important for project managers to fully understand their meanings and importance. The principles are not mutually exclusive, and they all have advantages and disadvantages. Adopting any one of them in a new software organization does not guarantee success and does not necessarily result in projects' failure.

The principle of *hierarchy* implies a strict pyramid of leadership, roles, duties, and tasks in the organization, with strict adherence to the organization's internal rules. Drifting away from the predefined overall course of the organization is

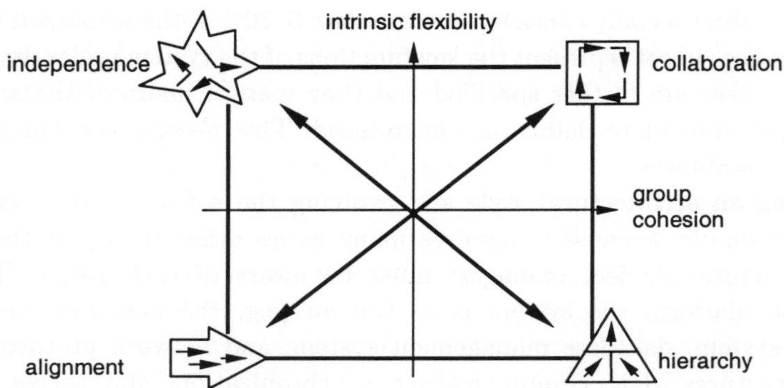

Fig. 5. General principles of software organizations (after [16]).

interpreted as a lack of loyality that may lead to the organization's instability, and is not tolerated.

On the opposite end of the same "dimension" is the principle of *independence*. It relies on the individuals' initiative and individuality in doing their jobs, directing their work, and to an extent even in decision making. Organizations that adopt this principle are usually open to innovation and changes, new technologies, and creative autonomy of their members.

Collaboration is the principle of intensive teamwork, in which invention is combined with stability, and individuality with collective interests through open discussion about all the problems that come along as the project advances. Roles and tasks are assigned flexibly, and there is a high degree of adaptivity among the team members due to the intensive information exchange between them.

Finally, the principle of *alignment* suggests referring each individual in an organization to the organization's common vision of collective goals and adopted technology. Each individual is expected to support the adopted uniform approach to software development and comply with the work of others in the organization.

Of course, there are many points in between the two extremes along each dimension; hence most software organizations can be actually represented as points somewhere in the square of Fig. 5. It is also important to note in Fig. 5 how the cohesion of the development team increases with the hierarchy and collaboration principles, as well as how the flexibility of the organization increases with independence and collaboration principles.

The four principles can affect a number of decisions in improving a software organization, development processes, and project management. For example, creating the development team for a software development project, staffing it, assigning roles to the team members, as well as selecting the project leader(s) can all vary to a notable extent depending on the organization's dominant principle. If the principle of hierarchy is the dominant one, well-suited team members are those that prefer precisely defined tasks, roles, and guidance, and the team leader should be a person of high authority who sets precise criteria and expects results. Under the principle of independence, a free-style, informal, charismatic leader is much more likely to create and lead the team successfully. The team members in that case should be independent individuals, who don't need guidance, and are always ready for initiative and open to changes. Similar suggestions exist for applying the principles of collaboration and alignment.

Put in other words, it is an appropriate *professional culture* that a software development organization must grow in order to be able to manage all of its organizational aspects successfully, both on the long-term and day-to-day bases [3]. A culture is established in an organization when its software engineers internalize the organization's professional values and common processes. Engineers should define these common processes from the practices they trust. Developers adopt and adhere to a professional discipline that orients them to add, modify, improve, or improvise such practices in order to achieve project objectives. Once people in the organization have internalized common practices, they transmit the culture through their behaviors, artifacts, and mentoring of others. An organization that lacks repeatable management or development practices does not have a professional culture. It is the responsibility of the organization's executives to enforce the above common principles or core beliefs that will help create, staff, orient and support development teams in practical projects.

There are efforts devoted to the institutionalization of repeatable common practices in software development organizations. Software Engineering Institute's *Capability Maturity Model* (*CMM*) [36, 45] is the most widely known among such efforts. CMM provides a reference for determining the maturity level of an organization's software processes and deals with the establishment of management structures that are to facilitate the development of the required professional culture. According to CMM, an organization can be at any one of five predefined maturity levels, in terms of its commitment to systematically perform the specific set of key practices that have been defined for a given level. At Level 1, the organization is typically chaotic and unmanaged, does not practice any uniform approach to the process of software development, budgets are always overrun, the products are unstable, and never meet the user's expectations. At Level 2, processes in the organization are controlled and maintained in detail, hence are repeatable. At Level 3, the organization contains a coherent, integrated set of well-defined software engineering and management processes, characterized by readiness criteria, completion criteria, inputs, outputs, and verification mechanisms. At Level 4, the organization formulates and strictly applies explicit assessment and feedback mechanisms, and uses them to measure efficiency and effectiveness in software development. Finally, the highest point in evolution is Level 5, at which the organization is capable of using the outcome data from its own processes for further self-improvement.

Some of the practices an organization may follow when establishing its professional discipline and culture are the following ([1, 3, 4, 12, 20, 21, 27] and [49]):

- flexible rotation of key roles and tasks (e.g. system design, integration, testing, code inspection) in the project team;
- maintaining a catalogue that specifies all key roles and responsibilities;
- the role of the project leader(s) is focused mostly on project management and system design, and much less on coding and testing;
- the project leader should have a small board of project advisors who set the project goals, prepare status reports on intermediate stages of development, care about resource management, monitor the project dynamics and stability, and suggest how to better staff the project;
- decision making should be based on consensus among the team members whenever possible; failing to allow for that may cause lacking of the sense of contribution to the project ultimate goal among those team members whose voice is "never heard";
- project manager's awareness of the "staffing profile" corresponding to the development process being applied is very important; for example, in object-oriented development processes it is necessary to have a chief architect throughout the development project; however, the number and efforts of system analysts and application engineers necessary to complete the tasks is rather small in the early phases, and increases significantly in the later phases of the project;
- planning transition to another development process or another technology should include an appropriate training of the development team members, mentoring and guidance among the team members in embracing the new technology, careful selection of new programming languages and tools, and strategic decisions related to software reuse;
- effective interpersonal communication is essential to a project's success, hence facilitating communication between team members should be a top priority for the project manager; this may include careful pairing of staff members and assigning a mediating duty to some other members according to their experience and technical background; and
- every software project manager should pay adequate attention to a number of ethical issues that always affect the project's success, the development team, and the team's relations to the customers; such issues include acting in the customer's and public interest, maintaining integrity and independence in professional judgement, adhering constantly to the highest professional standards possible, ensuring lifelong learning and supporting colleagues, and so on.

6. Management Strategies and Techniques

Software development is an extremely dynamic and fluid business, and it is difficult to plan everything at the beginning of a project. Therefore, efficient management of software projects must be based on some explicit, strategic goals and organization's interests. There are a number of useful lines to follow in that sense. Some of them are [3, 23]:

- balancing the need for structure and process control in software development with the need for flexibility, informality, and more effective communication processes;
- establishing software measurement programs and enforcing accountability for completion of software development milestones;
- *making management objectives and product vision clear to the development team members* (this is very importnt in practice, because far too often developers are in total ignorance of the broader strategy of a company, and the tactical decisions made by management to advance this strategy seem to them arbitrary and even hostile);
- identifying the most critical issues of the project and stressing the need to allocate most development resources, time, and efforts to such issues;
- organizing more visible and formal management processes for reviewing and approving potential product enhancements;
- emphasizing management approaches that facilitate flexibility and creativity within clearly defined boundaries;
- keeping-up with technological developments by enforcing life-long learning, training, courses, and seminars;
- developing more globally focused, culturally sensitive management capabilities;
- involving end-users in the development process in order to constantly provide advice on using the product in the real world, thus eliminating the customer-developer gap; and
- promoting orientation towards strategic business partnerships.

There is also a large number of managerial techniques that help monitor software product development on the day-to-day basis and make tactical decisions relevant to the development process [1, 3, 23, 41]:

- maintaining *progress charts* that show the percentage of completion for each module, at any given moment of product development;
- keeping track of all relevant facts about the product (e.g. previous versions, delivery dates, current version), the development process (the problems encountered, resulting delays, and the reasons why they have occurred), and discarded design alternatives in the *external group memory* (it is usually a special-purpose project-management software, or a site on the organization's server or Intranet, and sometimes even a site on the Internet); the external group memory can also serve as a board for discussion on all the relevant ideas that arise in the course of the project;
- estimating time and effort needed for each designer to complete a short-term task, e.g. an iteration in an iterative development process; for that

purpose, each designer may be required to initially fill-up and constantly update a *planning sheet* that contains both the designer's original estimates and actual measures (in days) of how long does it take to complete each activity for the task (activities may include analysis, design, coding, testing, and so on);

- emphasizing progress review mechanisms across the development effort;
- applying mechanisms of recognizing, rewarding, and leveraging extraordinary efforts and/or hyperproductivity, as an avenue to promote and retain key technological leaders;
- adapting the software development process to the characteristics of the product being developed;
- increasing parallelism in product development by reducing linear, sequential activities, encouraging relevant communication and social interactions among the team members, and changing the work modes when necessary;
- insisting on creating multiple design views, such as structural, functional, object-oriented, event-based, and data-flow; although sometimes redundant, multiple design views help cover design from multiple perspectives and make it more complete and more efficient; and
- enforcing the feedback mechanism in the development process, in order to detect inconsistencies in design as early as possible and reduce the costs of fixing them.

7. Risk Assessment

In order to prevent project runaways, meet deadlines, stay within the project's budget, and simultaneously maintain the product's high quality standards, it is essential to timely identify and periodically evaluate certain critical factors. Such factors include [1, 10, 29, 30]:

- estimating the project's size in the early phases — the project's size affects how the deadlines will be set up, and is positively correlated with monetary expense and risk;
- setting up the deadlines realistically — as a result, the necessary time to establish the rhythm of the project, prevent delays, and enter a steady state in which the effort is equally distributed from the beginning of the project, without putting an extra workload to the team members at the end of the project phases;
- collecting and studying reports on other similar projects — this provides the possibility of learning from the other projects' and other teams' experiences; in that sense, a process data base is essential for an organization that wants to go higher than Level 2 on the CMM level ladder; engineering management depends on measurements, and their proper use, and this data base is to be regarded as an organizational asset, and it is to be properly managed;

- top management commitment — if top management does not play a strong, active role in the project from initiation through implementation, then all other risks and issues may be impossible to address in a timely manner;
- failure to gain user commitment — when the users are actively involved in the requirements determination process, it creates a sense of ownership, thereby minimizing the risk that the end-user expectations will not be met and that the system will be rejected;
- timeliness of additional user requirements — it is essential to have the users involved in the development process from the beginning to the end; however, it is highly preferable to have the requirements frozen at a certain point in development;
- familiarity with technology — the higher the organization's experience with application languages, technology databases, hardware, and operating systems, the lower the risk in the project;
- insufficient/inappropriate staffing — the risk of failing to provide adequate staffing throughout the project can be mitigated by using disciplined development processes and methodologies to break the project down into manageable chunks, and developing contingency plans; and
- the degree of structure in the project's outputs — it is negatively correlated with the risk in the project.

In the context of the Unified Process of software development, it is adopted that one can never fully eliminate risks; at best, one can manage them [12, 24]. For that reason, the Unified Process stresses the need to drive software development as an architecture-centric activity. Architecture-centric approach forces the risk factors to emerge early in the development process and make the process simultaneously risk-driven — when the risk factors are identified early, managers can take steps to mitigate them. Experienced software project managers recommend to maintain a running list of project's top ten risk factors and use that list to drive each release [12].

8. Software Metrics

Measurement is a key factor for managing and improving software development. The purpose of the measurement process in software projects is to define and operate a context-specific set of metrics, and to describe the required guidelines and procedures for data collection and analysis [32]. Software measurement generates quantitative descriptions of key processes and products, enabling us to understand behavior and result [37]. Such descriptions can indicate the effort needed to complete the project, the product's quality, estimated schedules and time-to-market, rework effort, estimated project costs, and distribution of resources and costs by project phases. Software measurement makes possible to compare the project a development team is currently working on, to similar projects in terms of budget, costs, productivity, quality, staffing, development processes, and technology used.

In order to operate a metrics program during a software development project, the project manager must enforce continuous measurement of relevant factors. These factors depend on the overall management goals of the measurement process. In that sense, one can differentiate between the following kinds of software metrics [2, 11, 15, 19, 28, 31, 32, 47]:

- *Metrics for project size and team productivity*: typical and most widely used representatives of this kind of metrics are *source lines of code* (*SLOC*) and *function points*; the SLOC metric can be converted relatively accurately and easily into the number of programer-months needed to complete the project; function points are dimensionless numbers that indicate the application's functionality from the user's perspective, and can also be easily converted into the effort needed to complete the project or one of its parts.
- *Metrics for schedules*: these include the number of tasks completed on time, the number of tasks not completed on time, the number of tasks with changed schedules, and the number of postponed tasks.
- *Metrics for requirements specification*: the number of requests for change (RFC) in specification, the number of new requirements, and the RFC diagram (showing the dynamics of RFC over time).
- *Metrics for software testing*: these metrics are used to track the percentage of SLOC covered by the testing process; increasing that percentage reduces the number of errors to be discovered by the users and increases the product's quality.
- *Metrics for software quality*: they typically show the fault density (the number of errors per 1 KSLOC) and fault arrival and closing rates; as a rule of thumb, the product's quality is satisfactory if the fault density is lower than 0.25.
- *Metrics for project risk*: they measure confidence in the product's ready-to-deployment date (typically an S-shaped curve over time).

The most widely used metrics models include COCOMO [11], which is based on measuring SLOC, function points analysis [2, 19, 28, 47], GQM (Goal-Question-Metrics, based on systematic translation of the company's goals into the measurement process goals, and refinement by defining the concrete measurements to perform in order to support the goals) [32], and Chidamber–Kemerer's metrics suite for object-oriented software projects (specifying metrics for the number of methods per class, depth of inheritance tree, number of children, etc) [15].

9. Productivity

Generally, productivity is an output divided by the effort required to produce that output. In software development, the output is a completed software development project. In order to consider a software company's productivity, it is necessary to somehow translate that output into a meaningful measurement. Ideally, software project managers should base output measurement on a combination of a project's size, functionality, and quality [34]. However, such a measurement doesn't yet exist.

On the other hand, various databases of software projects from different business sectors are available nowadays. They make possible to select some projects that closely resemble specific projects in a software development organization, and use the selected projects as a reference for measuring the productivity of the organization's completed projects or estimating the productivity of the organization's new projects.

Alternatively, a company can compare their software development productivity to that of similar projects analytically, i.e., by using some empirical benchmarking equations. Such equations typically take the values of some key productivity factors and use them to calculate productivity in function points per hour. The values are discrete (1 — very low, 2 — low, 3 — average, 4 — high, 5 — very high). The key productivity factors include customer participation, staff availability, the use of standards in software development, the use of tools, requirements volatility, the application's logical complexity, staff's experience with the tools, and so on. There are also dozens of factors other than the key ones that also influence productivity. Here are two examples of productivity-calculation (benchmarking) equations [34]:

$$\begin{aligned}\text{Productivity [fp/hr]} &= 0.1072 \times \\ &\quad (\textit{number of different languages used})^{-0.4627} \times \\ &\quad (\textit{staffavailability})^{0.6651} \\ \text{Productivity [fp/hr]} &= 0.2127 \times \\ &\quad (\textit{sum of inquiries})^{0.1493} \times \\ &\quad (\textit{customer participation})^{-0.3950} .\end{aligned}$$

It is important to stress that the equations like these two depend on the customer's business sector (e.g. banking, insurance, manufacturing, wholesale-and-retail, and public administration). The first equation from above is used to calculate productivity in developing software for wholesale-and-retail business, while the second one corresponds to software development for the public administration sector. The numbers and the kinds of variables (factors) in equations are different for different business sectors.

Statistical analysis shows that software development productivitys variance with respect to some significant variables (considered individually) is different. For example, the productivity variance across companies is rather high — 45%, w.r.t. different operating system it is 19%, and w.r.t. different DBMS tools and hardware platforms it is 13%. Significant variables are different for different business sectors, each individual variable's effect on productivity is either positive or negative, and each variable accounts for a certain percentage in total productivity variance. For example, requirements volatility is a significant variable in most business sectors; its effect on productivity is always negative, and it accounts for 10% to 19% of total productivity variance across different business sectors.

Apart from using equations such as the two above for benchmarking purposes, software project managers can use them to determine the likely impact on productivity of changes in a key factor.

10. Software Testing

In spite of the fact that in every software development project the product undergoes testing, delivered software always contains residual defects. Software testing is a difficult, time-consuming process. It requires specific skills from software testers, skills that only partially overlap with those of software developers. Apart from mastering coding, testers must also possess a great deal of knowledge of formal languages, graph theory and algorithms [26, 48].

Typically, software testing proceeds in four phases [48]:

- modeling the software's environment;
- selecting test scenarios;
- running and evaluating test scenarios; and
- measuring testing progress.

In the first phase, the tester's task is to simulate the interaction between the application and its environment, be it the user or the other applications, taking into account all possible inputs and outputs that can cross the application's boundaries. The hardest part here is the fact that in many cases the interactions can go through numerous different file formats, communication protocols, GUIs, and file systems. The other hard part is the unpredictability of the user's actions — the software under test must account for that.

Since the number of possible test scenarios is usually extremely large, testers should select those scenarios that cover all code statements and all significant representatives of external events. Before running the selected scenarios, it is necessary to convert them into executable form (often as code) in order to simulate typical interactions between the system and the external world. Applying test scenarios manually is labor-intensive and error-prone. For that reason, testers try to automate the test scenarios as much as possible. In many environments, automated application of inputs through code that simulates users is possible, and tools are available to help.

Measuring testing progress is difficult, simply because it is not just counting the numbers of bugs found. As stated in the section on software metrics, specific metrics for software testing are used to measure the *coverage* of the tests applied (in terms of running all lines of the source code, forcing all the internal data to be initialized and used, applying all test scenarios, exploring all the inputs, and checking for functional completeness). Note also that software reliability engineering can greatly help — the *Cleanroom methodology* developed at IBM [35] has been particularly useful in improving software quality and providing a quantitative measure for the quality of a software product at its release. The Cleanroom approach provides for the transition of process technology to the project staff and integrates several proven software-engineering practices into one methodology [46]. The testing strategy of the Cleanroom methodology can be best described as random sample based on usage model that predicts field reliability, rather than a futile attempt for coverage and little insight on field reliability.

If the Unified Process is used to manage software development, software testing is performed in every iteration [24]. Test scenarios are defined from use cases, and comprise both functionality and performance testing. The advantage of this incremental and iterative approach to software testing is that in each iteration the testers test just some of the application. Moreover, the tests performed in early phases usually discover such bugs and faults that would cause more severe instability in the project's rhythm if they were discovered in later phases. In every iteration, tests also check whether the current iteration has jeopardized some of the previously built and tested architecture. If the project's size is large, it is impractical to manually run all the test cases, so the use of automated testing tools is recommended. Project managers should adopt the practice of enforcing thorough testing in every iteration, and not allowing the next iteration to begin before all the tests planned in the current iteration are completed. The entire project is considered completed only when all the UML models *and* all the tests are completed and delivered.

11. Software Quality Assurance

The goals of software quality assurance (SQA) are monitoring the software and its development process, ensuring compliance with standards and procedures, and ensuring that product, process, and standards defects are visible to management [26].

Quality is the operational behavior of a product required by its users [8]. It comprises a set of product characteristics, both external and internal. External quality characteristics are related to how the product works in its environment (e.g. usability and reliability). Internal quality characteristics reflect how the product is developed (characteristics such as structural complexity, size, test coverage, and fault rates). Important factors affecting product's quality characteristics are process maturity level of the company that has developed the software product, its development environment (such as the design methodology and CASE tools used), and the development team's skill and experience.

It is desirable for a software development organization to plan and control product quality *during* development. Projects managers cannot allow the luxury of going back and adding quality — by the time a quality problem is detected, it is probably too late to fix it [39]. For that reason, it is necessary to establish procedures and expectations for high levels of quality before any other development begins. Also, hiring developers proven to develop high-quality code, staffing the project accordingly, and enforcing peer-level code reviews and external reviews must be top priority of every software project management.

Planning and controlling software product quality during development requires [8]:

- establishing targets for the external quality characteristics;
- pursuing those targets during development by defining and monitoring targets for internal quality characteristics — this can be done using conventional software measures of size, fault rates, change rates, structure, test coverage, and so on, taken early in product development;
- establishing relationships between internal and external quality characteristics, using experience from similar past software development projects; and
- identifying and setting targets for internal quality characteristics.

In practice, all this can be done by first defining a *quality model* (in terms of measurable quality characteristics; it can be an international standard like ISO 9126, or a company-specific model), and then applying a *quality process.* Quality process includes quality specification (establishing the software product's quality requirements), planning (deciding on a suitable development process and setting target values for measurable internal quality characteristics), control (monitoring progress throughout development using internal software measures associated with deliverables and activities related to each major review point in development), and evaluation (measuring the actual values of the external quality characteristics and comparing each actual value with its target value). Maintaining and using a database of past projects helps perform each step in the process more successfully.

12. Software Configuration Management

The configuration of a software system is the function and/or physical characteristics of hardware, firmware, software or a combination thereof as set forth in technical documentation and achieved in a product [14]. It can also be thought of as a collection of specific versions of hardware, firmware, or software items combined according to specific build procedures to accomplish a particular purpose [26].

Software configuration management (SCM) comprises a set of technical, managerial, and administrative activities related to identifying the configuration of a software system at distinct points in time for the purpose of systematically controlling changes to the configuration, recording and reporting change processing and implementation status, verifying compliance with specified requirements, and maintaining the integrity and traceability of the configuration throughout the system life cycle [6]. Responsibilities of each software project manager related to SCM include enforcing the practice of SCM activities for the project, distributing the activities to the relevant individuals, and managing and administrating the results of these activities.

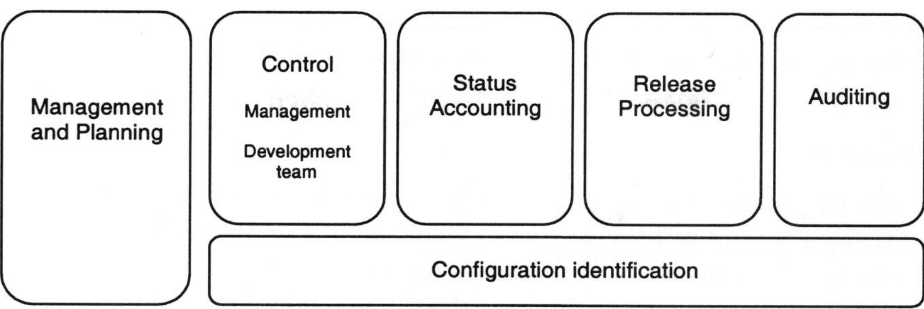

Fig. 6. Software configuration management activities (after [26]).

Figure 6 illustrates the activities encompassed by SCM. Since SCM is a supporting lifecycle process to software product development and maintenance, a successful SCM implementation requires careful management and planning. These are typically performed by the project manager or another designated individual, who does it in close relation with SQA activities. Management and planning activities cover all the other sets of activities shown in Fig. 6, establish all the relevant SCM policies, and result in recording/updating the Software Configuration Management Plan (SCMP) for the project. The SCMP is typically subject to SQA review and audit.

Configuration identification activities provide the basis for other SCM activities. These activities enumerate the configuration items to be controlled (such as plans, specifications, source and executable code, code libraries, data and data dictionaries, testing materials, software tools, and documentation for installation, maintenance, operations and software use), establish identification schemes for the items and their versions, and establish the tools and techniques to be used in acquiring and managing controlled items.

SCM control activities involve both managers and developers. Managers make decisions on whether some changes in configuration should be made or not, and authorize the changes. Developers perform change activities (code management) in a coordinated manner. Status reports are generated that account for each change in the configuration, and can be of use to various parties in the project, including managers, developers, testers, SQA team members, and maintenance engineers. The information obtained by status accounting can also serve as a basis for various measurements, such as the number of change requests per software configuration item and the average time needed to implement a change request. Release processing activities support customers and the maintenance team. They are related to identification, packaging and delivery of the elements of a product (such as the software, its documentation, release notes, and configuration data), as well as product version management (versions for different platforms or versions with varying capabilities). The software configuration auditing activity determines the extent to which an item satisfies the required functional and physical characteristics. Its ultimate goal is to evaluate the conformance of software products and processes to applicable regulations, standards, guidelines, plans, and procedures [26].

13. Standards

There are two major aspects of the term "standards" in software development. One of them is that of using widely accepted standards under the assumption that they embody "the common body of knowledge and accepted state of industry best practice" [43]. Such standards include universally recognized control frameworks for software process control and improvement. Some examples include ISO 9000, ISO 12207, TickIt, and CMM. They provide a basis for defining systematic activities, roles, and tasks that can be carried out in software development, independent of individual projects, companies, or designers. Furthermore, they make possible to understand and manage all of the diverse forms of software activity from the standpoint of a single framework. Software project managers should understand and apply these standards and frameworks as points of reference in software development, in order to ensure that quality is being designed and built into the products.

The ISO 9000 series of standards provide a generic model for the Quality Management System (QMS) of a supplier organization that is involved in design and development activities. It specifies the requirements against which the organization's QMS can be formally assessed. ISO 9000's issue of particular interest for software industry is ISO 9000-3 Guideline for the Application of ISO 9001 to the Development, Supply and Maintenance of Software.

The ISO 12207 standard covers the entire lifecycle of software, from inception through extinction. It details processes for acquiring and supplying software products and services.

TickIt is the standard related to ISO 9000-3. Its purpose is to fill in the gaps and clarify the relationship between ISO 9000-3 and ordinary software development operations. It does this by adding additional documentation and audit requirements to the ISO 9000-3 Guidelines, and by providing direction needed to implement ISO 9000-3 compliant quality system.

Software Engineering Institute's Capability Maturity Model (CMM), described in the *Organizational aspects* section does not have a formal status; hence it is called a model, or a framework, rather than a standard. It is used as a reference to establish the maturity level of an organization's software processes.

The other aspect of the term "standards" in software development is that of deploying organizational standards across the life of a project [38]. In large organizations, having many software development teams, some standardization of methods across teams is important. For example, an organization may prescribe standard (consistent) processes, roles, schedules, and reusability policies across teams and projects. It can lead to many benefits, including better planning, more predictable outcomes, increased staffing flexibility (decreased sensitivity to employee turnover), and reuse of experience.

In that sense, the most important standards are those used for the roles and processes in a development team. There are many such informal standards. Some of them are developed internally by a company for its sole use; other standards are developed and marketed by for-profit companies as products. A good example is the Microsoft Solutions Framework (MSF), which is used in a number of software development organizations. It revolves around a team with a process. The roles it prescribes are product management (focusing on customer satisfaction), program management (on-time delivery), development, testing, user education, and logistics planning (smooth rollout and migration). Each role may be played by a number of different people. The process model describes the project in terms of phases, milestones, activities, and deliverables. It also shows how they are related to the team model, and what practices and principles drive the product development (versioned releases, scheduling for an uncertain future, managing trade-offs, managing risk, maintaining a fixed ship-date mindset, breaking large projects into manageable parts, performing daily builds, and using bottom-up estimating). The process model also defines what documents each role is expected to deliver at precise points in the iterative process. MSF provides detailed document templates.

14. Best Practices

Not every practice of software development can be standardized, yet many of them have proved to be useful in a number of projects and organizations. Most of such practices come from experience, and it is extremely beneficial for every project that the project manager and the members of the development team are knowledgeable of as many such practices as possible. The following examples illustrate the idea of using such practices in software project management:

- Communication problems arising when a distributed team is developing software must be handled with special care. A kick-off meeting must be held face-to-face, and all the developers, partners, and contractors must attend. All product deliverables must be clearly defined in the very beginning. After this the communication between team members is mostly electronic. Time zones differences are not necessarily a problem — on the contrary, they may turn out to be an advantage, since by the time one group of developers comes to work in the morning, the testers may have already sent them the test results from the other side of the Globe! Some overlap in working hours is, however, desirable. Establishing *availability standards* (when and how the team members will be available for communication, how quickly they respond to emails, and so on) facilitates electronic communication in software development done by distributed teams [22].
- Top-down approach to software analysis and design should be enforced in software development projects when the application domain is numerically intensive, such as signal processing, pattern recognition, and

real-time control. The reason is that in such applications the data are not predictable enough, and developers are usually not familiar enough with the data. For example, if object-oriented design is used in developing such an application, then more general classes (located close to the top of the inheritance tree) should be designed first, and design of their children classes should come next. Contrary to that practice, developing a business-oriented application (an information system) suggests bottom-up approach. Developers of such applications usually know their data well, and it is quite natural to start the projects from modeling data to be stored in databases [20]. As for the top-down approach to analysis and design, note also that it may inhibit reuse. It may be more economical to look at what reuse and COTS (components-of-the-shelf) software components are available, and select a design based on them. Such a system may not fully meet a client's needs, but the client may be happy to accept it on the basis of its greatly lower cost.

- Productivity of a newly assembled development team should be calibrated in a pilot project. A small pilot project gives project manager the possibility of gaining a rough model of performance for every team member and for the team as a whole before the real work on a large application begins. Put simply, the work on a pilot project can give a multiplier factor m, so that if a certain team member estimates to take n weeks to do something, in reality he/she will need m times n weeks. This is important for schedule planning for the larger project. How trustworthy and realistic is the multiplier factor acquired that way depends to a large extent on whether the application domains of the pilot project and the larger application are the same or not and whether the team member(s) is (are) familiar with the domain(s) or not [12].

15. Discussion and Conclusions

Software project management issues described in this chapter represent the core of project manager's toolbox for leading the project to its successful completion. It is important to note that there are many more interesting topics and practices of software project management, other than those covered here. Due to the enormous expansion of IT, such practices continue to grow.

Again, if a certain issue specific to software development is not addressed in the chapter it doesn't mean that it is not important — it is just because it didn't satisfy some or all of the selection criteria stated in the end of the Introduction. For example, an important issue for every software project manager is contingency planning. It relates to the effect of strikes by personnel, fire, flooding, earthquakes, each of which can have a rather specific effect on the software process — copies of work products are to be kept off site, and be easily accessible. However, contingency planning doesn't get that much space in the relevant software engineering journals and magazines, or in the publications of the relevant committees associations.

Another such important issue is that of how the business reengineering efforts (reorganization of an entire enterprise) have, or should have, affected the management of software projects [17]. Recent results in that sense include reengineering of software enterprises in order to introduce CMM [7]. These efforts aim at reengineering of a software enterprise based on introducing some important principles into the organization, in terms of very general statements of what engineers do (e.g. software development follows a plan in accordance with requirements, requirements are ranked according to cost-effectiveness and are implemented incrementally, standards are used in development, design includes fault- and failure-tolerance, and so on). The principles are consistent with the capabilities that CMM recognizes as supportive of and important in the development of high quality software.

However, it is important to stress that even if all of the important practices and issues could be briefly covered here, software project management in reality requires a more detailed insight into the practices themselves and many case studies, as well as a lot of experience, judgment, and intuition. Experienced managers always take the issues and practices reported in the open literature just as rough guidelines and adapt them to the context of their current project. This suggests an important general rule of thumb: best practices of software project management are always those that can be applied to the system being built, the technology the developers use, and the organization that develops the system.

16. Software Project Management Topics on the Web

There are many software project management resources on the Web. The short list of URLs shown below has been composed according to the following criteria:

- the number of useful links following from that URL;
- how comprehensive the site is;
- how interesting the URL is for software project managers; and
- how interesting the URL is for practitioners and researchers.
- Software Engineering Institute (SEI):
  http://www.sei.cmu.edu
  This is one of the best starting points for all software engineering topics, including software project management. It includes a number of links to relevant on-line literature, conferences, and other resources.
- The International Conference on Software Engineering (ICSE):
  http://www.ul.ie/ icse2000
  ICSE is the largest software engineering conference. The topics cover all aspects of software engineering, including software project management. The program attracts both practitioners and researchers.
- The Unified Process:
  http://www.rational.com/products/rup/index.jtmpl

The Rational Software Corporation site contains various resources related to UML and Unified Process.

- Extreme Programming:
  http://www.extremeprogramming.org/
  eXtreme programming is a methodology designed to address the specific needs of small-team software development, facing vague and changing requirements.
- Requirements Engineering:
  http://www.cs.ucl.ac.uk/research/renoir/
  This is the site of Renoir, The European Union Requirements Engineering Network of Excellence.
- Software Metrics:
  http://www.udmercy.edu/academic/business/metrics.htm
  A number of links and resources related to software metrics.
- Productivity:
  http://www.sttf.fi/html/exppro.html
  Experience Pro, a tool incorporating the Experience database of software projects comprising data collected from companies operating in different business sectors. The data can be used for preliminary project planning, including cost estimation, reuse analysis, software-process-capability analysis, risk analysis, and productivity benchmarking.
- Software Testing:
  http://www.io.com/~wazmo/qa
  An annotated list of links to some of the Web's best testing information.
- Organization's Internal Standards:
  http://www.microsoft.com/msf/
  Microsoft Solutions Framework (MSF) that prescribes software development process model, principles, practices and roles to deploy consistently across development teams in a company.

References

1. N. Ahituv, M. Zviran and C. Glezer, "Top management toolbox for managing corporate IT", *Communications of the ACM* **42** (April 1999) 93–99.
2. A. J. Albrecht and J. E. Gaffney, "Software function, source lines of code, and development effort prediction: A software science validation", *IEEE Transactions on Software Engineering* **9** (1983) 639–648.
3. T. Athey, "Leadership challenges for the future", *IEEE Software* **15** (May/June 1998) 72–77.
4. K. Beck, *Extreme Programming Explained: Embrace Change* (Addison-Wesley, Reading, 2000).
5. M. De Bellis and C. Haapala, "User-centric software engineering", *IEEE Expert* **10** (February 1995) 34–41.
6. E. H. Bersoff, "Elements of software configuration management", eds. M. Dorfman and R. H. Thayer, *Software Engineering* (IEEE Computer Society Press, Los Alamitos, 1997) 345–356.

7. A. Berztiss, *Software Methods for Business Reengineering* (Springer, New York, 1996).
8. J. Boegh, S. Depanfilis, B. Kitchenham and A. Pasquini, "A method for software quality planning, control, and evaluation", *IEEE Software* **16** (March/April 1999) 69–77.
9. B. Boehm, "A spiral model of software development and enhencement", *IEEE Computer* **21** (May 1988) 61–72.
10. B. W. Boehm, "Software risk management: Principles and practices", *IEEE Software* **8** (January 1991) 32–41.
11. B. W. Boehm *et al*, "Cost models for future life cycle processes: COCOMO 2.0", *Annals of Software Engineering* **1** (November 1995) 1–24.
12. G. Booch, *Object Solutions — Managing the Object-Oriented Software Project* (Addison-Wesley, 1996).
13. G. Booch, J. Rumbaugh and I. Jacobson, *Unified Modelling Language User's Guide* (Addison-Wesley, 1999).
14. F. J. Buckley, *Implementing Configuration Management: Hardware, Software, and Firmware*, 2nd ed. (IEEE Computer Society Press, 1996).
15. S. R. Chidamber and C. F. Kemerer, "A metrics suite for object-oriented design", *IEEE Transactions on Software Engineering* **20** (1994) 476–493.
16. L. L. Constantine, "Work organization: Paradigms for project management and organization", *Communications of the ACM* **36** (October 1993) 35–43.
17. T. H. Davenport, *Process Innovation: Reengineering Work Through Information Technology* (Harvard Business School Press, 1993).
18. A. M. Davis and P. Hsia, "Giving voice to requirements engineering", *IEEE Software* **11** (March 1994) 12–17.
19. P. Deveaux, "Counting function points", ed. J. Keyes, *Software Engineering Productivity Handbook* (McGraw-Hill, 1993) 191–227.
20. M. E. Fayad and M. Cline, "Managing object-oriented software development", *IEEE Computer* **29** (September 1996) 26–32.
21. P. L. Ferdinandi, "Facilitating communication", *IEEE Software* **15** (September/October 1998) 92–96.
22. M. Haywood, "Working in virtual teams: A tale of two projects and many cities", *IEEE IT Professional* **2** (March/April 2000) 58–60.
23. K. Holtzblatt and H. Beyer, "Making customer-centered design work for teams", *Communications of the ACM* **36** (October 1993) 92–104.
24. I. Jacobson, G. Booch and J. Rumbaugh, *The Unified Software Development Process* (Addison-Wesley, 1999).
25. M. Jarke, "Requirements tracing", *Communications of the ACM* **41** (December 1998) 32–35.
26. Joint IEEE/CS-ACM Committee, *Guide to the Software Engineering Body of Knowledge — SWEBOK. http://www.swebok.org/* (December 2000).
27. Joint IEEE/CS-ACM Committee, *Software Engineering Code of Ethics. www.acm.org/serving/se/code.htm* (December 2000).
28. C. Jones, *Applied Software Measurement* (McGraw-Hill, 1991).
29. C. Jones, "Our worst current development practices", *IEEE Software* **12** (March 1996) 102–104.
30. M. Keil, P. E. Cule, K. Lyytinen and R. C. Schmidt, "A framework for identifying software project risks", *Communications of the ACM* **41** (November 1998) 76–83.
31. P. Kulik, "A practical approach to software metrics", *IEEE IT Professional* **2** (January/February 2000) 38–42.

32. L. Lavazza, "Providing automated support for the GQM measurement process", *IEEE Software* **17** (May/June 2000) 56–62.
33. M. Lindvall and I. Rus, "Process diversity in software development", *IEEE Software* **17** (July/August 2000) 14–18.
34. K. D. Maxwell and P. Forselius, "Benchmarking software development productivity", *IEEE Software* **17** (January/February 2000) 80–88.
35. H. D. Mills, M. Dyer and R. C. Linger, "Cleanroom software engineering", *IEEE Software* **4** (September 1987) 19–24.
36. M. C. Paulk *et al*, *The Capability Maturity Model: Guidelines for Improving the Software Process* (Addison-Wesley, 1995).
37. S. L. Pfleeger, R. Jefferey, B. Curtis and B. Kitchenham, "Status report on software measurement", *IEEE Software* **14** (March/April 1997) 33–43.
38. R. Rada and J. Craparo, "Standardizing software projects", *Communications of the ACM* **43** (December 2000) 21–25.
39. J. S. Reel, "Critical success factors in software projects", *IEEE Software* **16** (May/June 1999) 18–23.
40. D. J. Reifer, "Requirements management: The search for Nirvana", *IEEE Software* **17** (May/June 2000) 45–47.
41. M. Rettig and G. Simons, "A project planning and development process for small teams", *Communications of the ACM* **36** (October 1993) 45–55.
42. M. Shaw and D. Garlan, *Software Architecture: Perspectives on an Emerging Discipline* (Prentice Hall, Englewood Cliffs, 1996).
43. D. Shoemaker and V. Jovanovic, *Engineering a Better Software Organization* (Quest Publishing House, 1999).
44. J. Siddiqi, "Challenging universal truths of requirements engineering", *IEEE Software* **11** (March 1994) 18–20.
45. Software Engineering Institute's CMMI Product Development Team, *CMMI–SM for Systems Engineering/Software Engineering, Version 1.02, Continuous Representation* (CMU/SEI–2000–TR–019).
http://www.sei.cmu.edu/pub/documents/00.reports/pdf/00tr019.pdf (2000).
46. S. W. Sherer, A. Kouchakdjian and P. G. Arnold, "Experience using cleanroom software engineering", *IEEE Software* **13** (May 1996) 69–76.
47. S. A. Whitmire, "Applying function points to object-oriented software models", ed. J. Keyes, *Software Engineering Productivity Handbook* (McGraw-Hill, 1993) 229–244.
48. J. A. Whittaker, "What is software testing? And why is it so hard?", *IEEE Software* **17** (January/February 2000) 70–79.
49. S. Woodward, "Evolutionary project management", *IEEE Computer* **32** (October 1999) 49–57.
50. R. A. Zahniser, "Design by walking around", *Communications of the ACM* **36** (October 1993) 115–123.

REVERSE ENGINEERING

WILLIAM C. CHU*

Department of Computer Science and Information Engineering,
Tunghai University, Taichung, Taiwan
E-mail: chu@csie.thu.edu.tw

CHIH-WEI LU, CHIH-HUNG CHANG and YEH-CHING CHUNG

Department of Information Engineering, Feng Chia University, Taichung, Taiwan

XIAODONG LIU

School of Computing, Napier University, Edinburgh, Scotland

HONGJI YANG

Department of Computer Science, De Montfort University, Leicester, England

Software systems have become business-critical for many companies. These systems are usually large and complex. Some have evolved over decades and therefore are known as legacy systems. These legacy systems need to be maintained and evolved due to many factors, including error correction, requirements change, business rules change, structural re-organization, etc. A fundamental problem in maintaining and evolving legacy systems is to understand the subject system. *Reverse engineering* is the process of analyzing a subject system (a) to identify the system's components and their interrelationships and (b) to create representations of the system in another form or at a higher level of abstraction. In this chapter, we will discuss the problems, process, technologies, tools and future directions of reverse engineering.

Keywords: Legacy systems, software maintenance, software evolution, domain model, knowledge-based analysis, software process.

1. Introduction

Software systems have become business-critical for many companies. Companies now rely more on the services provided by software, and any failure of these services would have a serious consequence on the daily operation of the business. These systems are usually large and complex, and they have evolved over decades. They are known as *legacy systems* [73]. These legacy systems need to be maintained and evolved due to many factors, including error correction, requirements change, business rules change, structural re-organization, etc. A fundamental problem in maintaining and evolving legacy systems is to understand the subject system [53].

*Correspondence author.

However, most of the legacy systems are not well documented. As these old systems evolve, there is a need for the corresponding documentation and an understanding of the original design so that modifications to the software can be made properly.

Reverse engineering is the process of analyzing a subject system to identify the system's components and their interrelationships, and to create representations of the system in another form or at a higher level of abstraction [17]. Reverse engineering involves the identification or recovery of program requirements and/or design specifications that can aid in understanding and modifying the program. The main objective is to discover the underlying features of a system, including requirements, specifications, design and implementation. In other words, it is primarily intended to recover and record high-level information about the system, including:

- system structure: its components and their interrelationships, as expressed by their interfaces;
- functionality: what operations are performed on what components;
- dynamic behavior: system understanding about how input is transformed to output;
- rationale: design involves decision making between a number of alternatives at each design step; and
- construction: modules, documentation, test suites, etc.

Several purposes for undertaking reverse engineering are listed in [9]. These purposes can be classified into the *quality issues*, such as the simplification of complex software, improving the quality of software which contains errors, the removal of side effects from software, etc; the *management issues*, such as enforcing a programming standard, facilitating better software maintenance management techniques, etc; and the *technical issues*, such as allowing major changes in software to be implemented, discovering and recording the design of the system, and discovering and representing the underlying business model implicit in the software, etc.

Without the proper tools' support, the cost of reverse engineering software systems is very high. Reverse engineering tools provide mechanisms for data extraction, model creation, visualization, and annotation to assist programmers to understand a software system.

In this chapter, we will survey the technologies and tools related to the research of reverse engineering. The rest of this chapter is organized as follows. Section 2 lists the characteristics and problems of reverse engineering. Section 3 gives an overview of the reverse engineering process. Section 4 discusses the related technologies and tools, together with future research areas. Finally, Sec. 5 briefly summarizes our main points.

2. Characteristics/Problems

Reverse engineering is the"reverse progression" implementation of *forward engineering.* In order to understand the activities of reverse engineering, we should

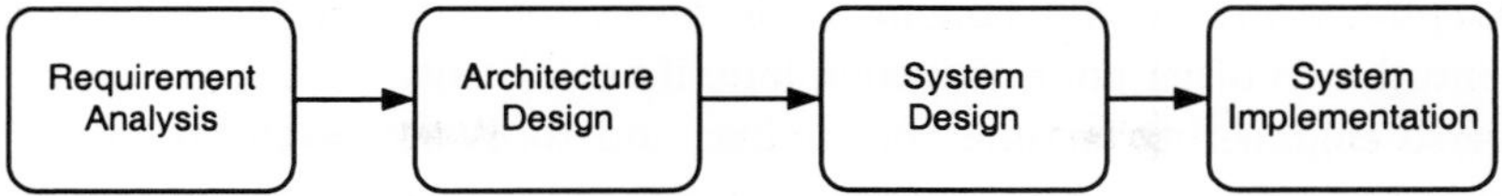

Fig. 1. The waterfall model of forward engineering.

first understand forward engineering. Figure 1 shows the phases of the "waterfall" model, for forward engineering, which is a typical process used to the construction of legacy systems. Generally in forward engineering, a program is composed through the process of requirement analysis, architecture design, system design, and system implementation. During the process of system development, design information that is not fully supported by a specific programming language is lost. The primary difficulty in maintenance and evolution of legacy systems is to recover the lost information [53].

Whereas forward engineering ends with a product, reverse engineering starts with the product — in this case, software such as legacy systems, which cannot be discard due to cost, time, or risk facts and which keep evolving to accommodate the changing functional or environmental requirements. In this evolving process, the critical roles of reverse engineering could be summarized as follows:

System Understanding: The extracted design information spans from system architecture to specification, and to logic design.

Basis for Maintenance and Redevelopment: The extracted design, specification, and architecture can then be used as the starting point for system improvement, including redesign, respecification, rearchitecture and redevelopment.

Reuse of Components: Reuse can happen at various abstraction forms, including design pattern, system architecture, specification, logical/physical design, and code pieces. Reverse engineering is an effective means of both identification and recovery of the reuse components.

The obvious starting point for reverse engineering is to comprehend code. In opposition to the process of development and refinement, reverse engineering tries to trace back the route and discover the original data that was lost during the implementation. However, due to the innate character and limitation of a specific programming language, general reverse engineering and program understanding approaches are often delimited by (1) considering only a fixed set of predefined views, or (2) considering either purely static or purely dynamic views of the application [64].

In addition to source code, documentation of systems, when it exists, is another source that can provide essential design information. For textual documentation analysis, studies in natural language understanding are needed [21]. Recently, visualization notations and display, e.g. class diagram in UML, are encouraged for document representation while developing a system using more modern technology like OO philosophy or OO language. However, for most of the legacy systems, documentation is often poor or incomplete, if not absent.

Reverse engineering is time consuming, and tools are essential to continuous changes in the software system and the personnel involved in its maintenance [29]. Several things make reverse engineering of legacy systems very difficult. These include inconsistent programming style, lack of staff who know the obsolete languages, inadequate or out-of-date documentation, system structure corruption, inaccurate or incomplete data, etc. The principle factors that affect the cost of reverse engineering include the quality of the software to be reverse engineered, the availability of tool support, the required extent of data conversion, and the availability of expert staff [73]. However, reverse engineering allows us to identify a system's components and create higher-level representations of the system. We can see this better by describing the process used in reverse engineering.

3. Reverse Engineering Process

In this section, we will introduce the process of reverse engineering and the activities of each phase of the process. The process can be divided into four phases: *Context Parsing*, *Component Analyzing*, *Design Recovering and Design Reconstructing* (Fig. 2).

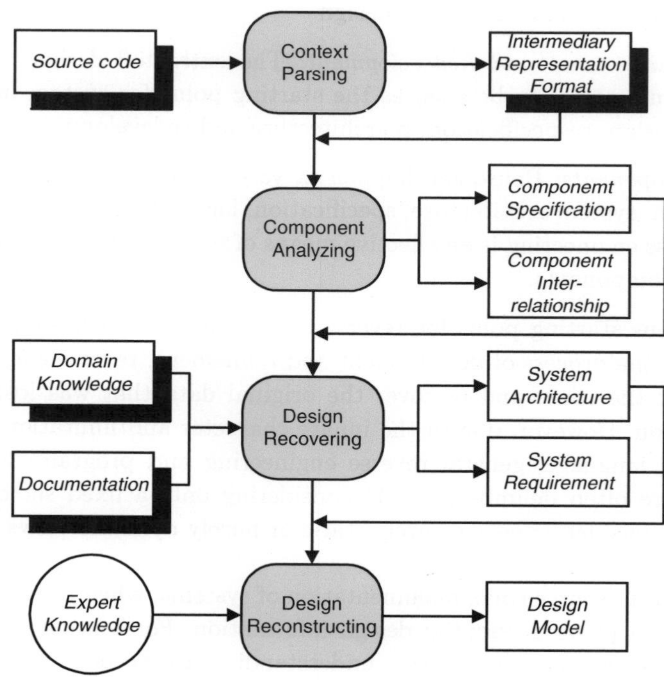

Fig. 2. Reverse engineering process.

- **Context Parsing Phase** — Context parsing, the first phase, analyses the source code and extracts syntactic and semantic program information. Techniques used in compilers such as token parsing and syntax analysis can be adopted here. In this phase, the parser generally parses source code and then transforms the code into a more structured representation as an intermediate form, e.g. the Abstract Syntax Tree (AST), which can be accepted as input of the next phase for systematic analysis. We use the term "*intermediary*" to indicate the intermediate representation that is transformed from source code.
- **Component Analyzing Phase** — The component analyzing phase takes the structure of the intermediate programs from the last phase to reveal the components' artifacts. The artifacts include structure chart, variables' attributes, functions' information, program slices, call graphs, data flow, definition-use graphs, and control dependencies. Many early researchers have provided approaches and tools [37, 61, 68] to successfully obtain data-flow diagrams, control-flow diagrams, and other related information during this stage. However, other high-level information — namely design knowledge embedded in source code — is not easy to discover. The reason is that the information has been refined during implementation. Most reverse engineering technologies provide systematic tools or methodologies to support this phase [1, 56, 61, 75]. But the latter phases of the process are mainly accomplished by manual efforts.
- **Design Recovering Phase** — One of the main barriers to building automatic tools for extracting design and domain knowledge from programs is the implicit knowledge information scattering around the code. In short, extracting original requirements and/or design knowledge from source code is always a very hard problem. Traditionally, this is tackled by domain experts. The cost is high and it takes a long time. Currently, with techniques that combine both structural and knowledge representation, analyzers can infer some high-level information successfully from the results of the last phase, according to some predefined rules of domain knowledge prepared by experts in advance, in certain domains [30, 49].

  Knowledge-based concept assignment and domain knowledge recovery, branches of research work under the software reverse engineering umbrella, seek to obtain a high-level view of source code [64]. The roles of recovered domain knowledge are two-fold: firstly, this recovered knowledge facilitates a quick understanding of the background of the application where software documentation is either lost or inconsistent [51]; secondly, it can be modified or reused to develop new applications by deploying off-the-shelf software components or up-to-date techniques.
- **Design Reconstructing Phase** — To accomplish the task completely, the process of reverse engineering includes a fourth phase, the design model reconstruction phase. In this phase, system models and design

specifications gained from the last phase can be further examined and integrated to reconstruct a precise view of the design model. The design model offers not only functionality and system behavior, but also the correct architecture that could be distorted in the original implementation. With a well-structured design model, effective software maintenance and software redevelopment can proceed [18].

Most research work carried out to date more or less follows this process.

4. Techniques and Tools

In this next section, we will introduce some of the techniques and tools used to carry out the reverse engineering process. The themes in Sec. 4.1 present a scenario of the current research and techniques in reverse engineering. In Sec. 4.2, selected application tools are introduced to show the achievements so far. At the end of this section, Table 2 summarizes the relations between the applications and the existing techniques for reverse engineering. Section 4.3 indicates possible future research areas, which can result in new techniques and tools in reverse engineering.

4.1. *Existing research and techniques*

This section presents a classification of the current research in reverse engineering. The research in each catagory normally involves one or more of the reverse engineering phases depicted in Sec. 3. Table 1 illustrates the linkage between the research issues and the involved phases.

- **Program Understanding** — Program understanding aims to facilitate the comprehension of a computing system by code examination. Information useful for comprehension is extracted and then presented in a style that complies with human cognition rules. Besides the computer science part, program understanding also includes the cognitive science of human mental processes in understanding programs. Program understanding can be achieved in a formal or an *ad hoc* manner. Program understanding is comparable with design recovery, because both of them start at the source code level [53].
- **Specification Recovery** — Specification recovery aims to extract a description of the functional and non-functional requirements of the examined system [53]. The description is made in terms of application domains [9, 17, 21, 71]. From the process point of view, specification recovery should be conducted in a bottom-up manner, because the only reliable information of the legacy software system is its source code. To support this bottom-up process, methods and tools are useful which generate abstract models from the source code, for example, the formal description model in suitable formal languages. The technique of software

Table 1. Research issues and their involvement in reverse engineering phases.

	Program Understanding	Specification Recovery	Design Recovery	Architecture Recovery	Business Rules Extraction	Cognitive Processes in Human Program Understanding	Intermediate Representation of Source Code	Discovery of Reusable Component	Knowledge-based Analysis
Context Parsing Phase	√	√	√	√			√		√
Component Analyzing Phase	√	√	√	√		√	√	√	√
Design Recovering Phase	√	√	√	√	√	√		√	√
Design Reconstructing Phase	√	√		√	√	√		√	√

visualization can be applied to give a more intuitive view of the systems, for example, to visualize program behavior or to animate the generated models. This is because the source code, as the underlying system representation, has an operational nature. From the specification structure point of view, the resulting specification recovery, i.e., the description model, should be top-down structured. This is to comply with the basic cognitive rules for a human to recognize complicated systems.

Some research issues in specification recovery include the following: (1) domain analysis and domain models, where research endeavors to recover system specification with the assistance of domain knowledge [12, 17, 28, 41, 71], (2) software visualization, where software can be animated to the maintainer to help him/her understand the program [4, 19, 21, 28], and (3) requirement tracing, where software maintainers often have to trace requirements in old code in order to find out in which part a specific functionality was implemented [3, 71].

- **Design Recovery** — The objective of this research area is to get a design description out of the source code [20, 24, 25]. There are two strategies to achieve this [39, 40, 41, 49, 67, 70, 77]. One is the fundamental method. The tools present the source code in such a way that a maintainer can conduct abstraction. In this method, the computer only retrieves information that is entirely included in the source code. The other is the knowledge-based method, where the tools aim to make the abstraction automatically or semi-automatically. They are analyzing the source code by using information from a knowledge base.

  Here, we summarize the most popular approaches in design recovery. (1) *Code Views* — Code views are representations of source code which cover the same information as a part of or the whole code but in a manner that accelerates the comprehension process. Examples are: call graphs, data flow, definition-use graphs, or control dependencies [26, 74]. (2) *Reformatting and Markup Languages* — Reformatting is the functional equivalent transformation of source code which changes only the structure to improve readability. Markup languages are languages for annotations of source code simply to improve the source code's appearance with the means of bold-faced key words, slanted comments, etc [27]. (3) *Hypertext* — Hypertext based methods and tools can be used to help browse the source code [60]. (4) *Source Code Analysis with Program Transformation and Abstraction Rules* — Concrete transformation and abstraction rules and inference algorithms are defined according to concrete source code language. By these rules and certain forms of knowledge in a database, source code can be transformed and abstracted into a higher level of abstraction [2, 4, 15, 16]. (5) *Data-Centered Program Understanding* — Data-centered methods focus on data and data relationships whereas control-centered methods focus on the control structure of a program, such as call graphs, control flow graphs and paths [43]. (6) *Program Slicing* — This technique attempts to decompose a large program into functionally self-contained slices. A program slice is a fragment of a program in which some statements not necessary for understanding a certain property of the program are omitted [7, 34].

- **Architecture Recovery** — The goal of this research area is to extract the system architecture from the legacy source code and available documentation, since such architecture provides an overview of the whole system. The growing popularity of component-based and distributed systems requires more advanced techniques for architecture recovery. Graphic representation is often used in this domain. Examples in this area include those in Carnegie Mellon University and Imperial College [42, 44, 45, 48, 82].
- **Business Rules Extraction** — Researchers in this theme hold the view that legacy systems have the most valuable asset embedded in them, that is, the business rules for the organization. Extracting and then reusing/enhancing these rules are critical to the evolution of computing systems. An example is the project conducted in Cardiff University trying to recover the useful business rules in the legacy system of British Telecom Ltd [69].
- **Cognitive Processes in Human Program Understanding** — This research issue focuses on the process in which a human reader understands source code. By cooperating with computer technology, the study of human cognitive processes can improve reverse engineering by making the approach and tools more supportive to human understanding [66, 72].
- **Intermediate Representation of Source Code** — Intermediate representations are used to improve the efficiency of the re-engineering of large systems. Source code is preprocessed and then the program information is stored in an intermediate representation. Queries on this intermediate representation will be faster than querying the source code directly [22]. There are two main topics in this research direction. (1) *Data and knowledge-based representation* is used to store and retrieve source code information. Relevant artificial intelligence technologies can be used to facilitate and optimize the process of reverse engineering [12, 31, 33, 55, 58, 59]. (2) *Graph based representation* is used to represent source code information [19, 46, 52], which can present a more intuitive overview.
- **Discovery of Reusable Components** — Identifying existing reusable components or, even further, extracting reusable components from legacy systems has been addressed by some researchers [10, 13, 15]. Research issues include (1) the criteria for evaluating the quality of reusable components, (2) the process to identify potential reusable components, and (3) how to extract a precise and comprehensive description of the discovered components.

- **Knowledge-based Analysis** — As the demand for software re-engineering is increasing dramatically, there is a growing realization that the design of effective software re-engineering tools must be smart enough so that frequently used domain knowledge can be recovered automatically from source code. This leads to the trend for and the need of knowledge-based analysis for reverse engineering.

  Numerous interesting topics have been addressed through researchers making efforts to recover domain knowledge from code. Some proposed domain knowledge representations include *plan* [1,4,5], *semantic/connectionist network* [8], and *tree/outline/hierarchy* [1,5]. Other approaches are to develop reasoning techniques, e.g. *classic reasoning* [1,5,38,47,76] and *inductive reasoning* [23]. New *control strategies* were also introduced for efficiency, e.g. bottom-up [8,38,49], top-down [8], dynamic programming/hybrid search [47] and flexible/multi-purpose application [79]. Recently, we also see some efforts to tackle the uncertainty issues inherent in the domain knowledge recovery process from code [50].

  Others related subjects are: knowledge space management [1]; program space management [38]; domain knowledge recovery assessment environment, e.g. MACS [30] and Menoda [54]; and embedding domain knowledge recovery into other tasks, e.g. transformation [32,78].

4.2. *Some existing tools*

The following tools were selected to reflect the typical applications of the existing reverse engineering techniques.

- **VIFOR** — VIFOR [61] is a tool for maintenance of large FORTRAN programs. It contains a database that stores information on all non-local declarations of the programs. VIFOR displays these views in browsers, which are specialized windows displaying the views graphically.
- **LOGISCOPE** — LOGISCOPE [68] analyzes a wide variety of languages to produce graphic aids and complexity metrics that can drastically reduce both time and error in program understanding.
- **SEELA** — SEELA [37] is a reverse engineering tool that supports the maintenance and documentation of structured programs. It features a top-down program display that increases the readability of structured programs and includes a structure editor, browser, printer, and source code documentation generator. SEELA works with Ada, Cobol, C. Pascal, PL/M and FORTRAN code. SEELA was designed to bridge the gap between the project's design description and the source code, instead of requiring a separate program-design-language (PDL) description.
- **Rigi** — Rigi [56] is a system for understanding large information spaces such as software programs, documentation, and the World Wide Web. This is done through a reverse engineering approach that models the

system by extracting artifacts from the information space, organizing them into higher level abstractions, and presenting the model graphically. The Rigi tool incorporates automatic clustering, but also allows user-defined grouping of the source model. It allows for hierarchically embedded views of different relations and presents a sophisticated user interface for manipulating these.

- **ManSART** — ManSART [14] is a software architecture recovery system for reverse engineering large-scale legacy systems. It semi-automatically recovers software structure and functionality abstractions working primarily from source. It interprets and integrates the results of localized, language-specific source analyses in the context of large-size systems written in multiple languages.
- **Shimba** — Shimba [75], a prototype reverse engineering environment, has been built to support the understanding of Java software. Shimba uses Rigi and SCED to analyze, visualize, and explore the static and dynamic aspects, respectively, of the subject system. The static software artifacts and their dependencies are extracted from Java byte code and viewed as directed graphs using the Rigi reverse engineering environment. The static dependency graphs of a subject system can be annotated with attributes, such as software quality measures, and then be analyzed and visualized using scripts through the end-user programmable interface. Shimba has recently been extended with the Chidamber and Kemerer suite of object-oriented metrics. The metrics measure properties of the classes, the inheritance hierarchy, and the interaction among classes of a subject system. Since Shimba is primarily intended for the analysis and exploration of Java software, the metrics have been tailored to measure properties of software components written in Java. These metrics can be applied in the context of understanding software systems using a reverse engineering environment. The static dependency graphs of the system under investigation show the measurements obtained by applying the object-oriented metrics to selected software components. Shimba provides tools to examine these measurements, to find software artifacts that have values that are in a given range, and to detect correlations among different measurements. The object-oriented analysis of the subject Java system can be investigated further by exporting the data to a spreadsheet.
- **Reasoning5 CBMS and Reasoning SDK** — Reasoning5 [62] is a Code-Based Management System (CBMS) runtime support for analysis and transformation software. It represents source code as an Abstract Syntax Tree, and then you can use the Reasoning Software Developer Kit to automate analysis and transformation of source code.
- **Maintainer's Assistant (MA) and Reengineering Assistant (RA)** — REFORM project developed a tool named the Maintainer's Assistant to assist the human maintainer handling assembler and S in a way that

is easy to use [6, 80]. One of the most important successes of Maintainer's Assistant is that it is based on a wide spectrum language whose syntax and semantics are formally defined. Maintainer's Assistant focuses on transformation rather than abstraction. Thus, it's limited in how to use multi-leveled abstractions and relevant abstraction rules to reach a good system reengineering, especially reverse engineering. The Wide Spectrum Language in Maintainer's Assistant is sequential and non-timed, which also limits its application domains. The Reengineering Assistant project [50, 81] proposes that extracting formal specifications semantically consistent with the original legacy system will facilitate further redesign and forward engineering. A formal approach to reverse engineering is proposed within a unified reengineering framework. The approach is based on a wide spectrum language, namely RWSL. Abstraction is the key technology to achieve successful specification extraction. The notion of abstraction is classified and precisely defined. Abstraction rules are developed with soundness proved. A supporting tool has been built to speed and scale up the approach.

- **AUTOSPEC** — The tool AUTOSPEC [15, 16, 35, 36] involves an approach to abstracting formal specifications from program code with weakest precondition *wp* and strongest postcondition *sp* predicate transformer. The difference between the *wp* and *sp* approaches is in the ability to directly apply a predicate transformer to a program (i.e., *sp*) vs using a predicate transformer as a guideline for constructing formal specifications (i.e., *wp*). In [36], the approach is extended to combine the use of informal methods, such as structured analysis, with formal techniques (*sp*) to reverse engineer imperative programs in *C*.
- **RevEngE** — The objective of the RevEngE program understanding project [42, 65] is to develop an integrated environment offering tools for subsystem identification and discovery to support reverse engineering processes, using a common software repository. In particular, the project addresses issues in the areas of software analysis technology, algorithms to extract system abstractions, integration technology applicable to CASE, user-interface technology to model, browse, and search large collections of software artifacts and reverse engineering process models interactively.
- **PURE** — The purpose of the Program Understanding and Reengineering (PURE) project [11, 57] is to develop technologies to analyze software systems or sub-systems, either at a fine-grained level (control and data dependencies) or at a more coarse-grained level (systems' high-level structure and behavior, i.e., software architecture), aiming at evaluating system characteristics, supporting user-assisted migration or restructuring, and more generally increasing software artifacts' quality.

Code analysis activity is focused on supporting program understanding, maintenance, and quality evaluation and assurance. The main effort is in the area of inter-procedural analysis among which data dependence, control dependence, slicing, pointers and arrays are analyzed. An intermediate language representation permits independence from the source programming language, given a front-end that translates the code in the intermediate language. Results can be saved in textual form, or a user interaction with the analyses is supported by a customized version of the text editor EMACS.

Analysis of source code at the architectural level is motivated by the fact that the first activity performed by maintenance programmers when approaching the task of understanding a system is often trying to discover its high-level structure, that is, identifying its subsystems and their relations: in short, the software architecture of the system. The software architecture goals are to identify architectural patterns and styles for distributed and object-oriented systems, to develop technologies to identify components and relations according to the defined patterns, to evaluate the quality of extracted design, and to support sound architecture recovery and migration across different architectural styles.

Table 2 illustrates the connection of the tools and the related technologies of reverse engineering.

4.3. *Future research areas*

There are still studies to be carried out in order to make reverse engineering techniques more practical. Possible research areas are:

- **Universal Intermediary** — Most reverse engineering assistant tools emphasize partial phases of the reverse engineering process, and they usually generate related results through diagrams of their own. Although some representations are widely used, e.g. the Abstract Syntax Tree (AST), there are still no common standards accepted yet. A universal intermediary is needed, and then comprehensive tools/environments can be achieved. XML (eXtensible Markup Language) [83] may be one of the candidates for such an intermediary.

  XML has the features of extensibility, structural description, and validation. The initial purpose of XML was to provide a standard format with representability and interchangeability on WWW documents. XML lets a user define his individual document format and present the information of the document through standardization [65], which can be adopted as a solution to the similar problem of individuality among programs.
- **Dynamic Analysis** — Most reverse engineering tools usually analyze program static properties instead of program dynamic behaviors that only show up at runtime. However, dynamic behavior analysis is also important. The increasing number of web-based and object-oriented applications

Table 2. Tools and the related technologies relationship.

	Program Understanding	Specification Recovery	Design Recovery	Architecture Recovery	Business Rules Extraction	Cognitive Processes in Human Program Understanding	Intermediate Representation of Source Code	Discovery of Reusable Component	Knowledge-based Analysis
VIFOR	√						√		
LOGISCOPE	√						√		
SEELA	√	√	√			√	√		
Rigi	√	√	√			√	√	√	
ManSART	√			√			√		
Shimba	√					√	√	√	
Reasoning5	√						√		
MA	√	√	√			√	√		√
RA	√	√	√			√	√	√	√
AUTOSPEC	√	√	√				√	√	√
RevEngE	√	√	√	√			√		
PURE	√	√	√	√	√	√	√	√	

makes dynamic analysis an issue of increasing importance. Some research is proposed in this regard, e.g. Richner and Ducasse [64] and Narat [58] had touched on this issue by analyzing subjects in Smalltalk. More general and integrated work is needed in this area.

- **New Software Technologies** — Many modern software technologies have recently been put forward to solve software development problems, like component-based development and system integration, design patterns and distributed object systems. Research aiming at reverse engineering such kinds of applications is still rare. Reverse engineering of such applications may have novel focuses, for example, more emphasis on the recovery of system architecture, and the construction of standard component description.
- **Web Applications** — Web applications are more and more popular as the Internet expands rapidly. Without doubt web applications will grow as the major target for the next-generation of reverse engineering. Web-based applications connect each of its sub-segments with hyperlinks. This nature of heterogeneity and disparateness dramatically increases the difficulty of the analysis and understanding to web applications. [63] proposed a prototype working in this direction.

5. Conclusion

Legacy systems play an essential role in industry. As business rules and environments change, it is easy to perceive the contrast between taking risks to replacing the legacy system with a new design or evolving the legacy system to meet new requirements. To start software maintenance and evolution, it is essential to understand the target system. Reverse engineering is the prerequisite operation for software maintenance and software re-engineering. Especially for the considerable number of poorly documented legacy systems in industry, reverse engineering clears the way for the extension of the use and value of systems and diminishes cost by avoiding unnecessary misunderstanding.

Responding to this realistic demand, many reverse engineering researchers already are trying to piece the vague information of a system into a clear picture. However, most of this work offers only partial assistance within the process of reverse engineering. Several gaps still need to be bridged to complete the task. Firstly, the inconsistency among various intermediaries of reverse engineering places a barrier for further integration. Secondly, dynamic information analysis has been seldom addressed by the reverse engineering tools.

In addition to textual analysis, formal methods and knowledge inference have been used as key techniques to find solutions. Even greater progress can be expected in the future; for example, design pattern extraction will be explored as a very high-level system description and reuse feature. Reusable component identification and extraction will keep being a hot issue. Moreover, the emersion of some modern software technologies increases the complexity of system understanding. For example, web-based applications may grow as the next foreseeable target for reverse engineering. Future researchers will need to make more effort to grasp this new-generation software trend. In short, though technology of reverse engineering has developed at a fast pace and solved many problems, many areas and problems still need to be addressed.

References

1. S. Abd-El-Hafiz and V. R. Basili, "Documenting programs using a library of tree structured plans", *Proceedings of the International Conference on Software Maintenance* (IEEE Computer Society Press, 1993) 152–161.
2. F. D. Anger, R. V. Rodriguez and M. Young, "Combining static and dynamic analysis of concurrent programs", *Proceedings of the International Conference on Software Maintenance* (IEEE Computer Society Press, 1995) 89–98.
3. P. Antonini, P. Benedusi, G. Cantone and A. Cimitile, "Maintenance and reverse engineering: Low-level design documents production and improvement", *Proceedings of the Conference on Software Maintenance* (IEEE Computer Society Press, 1987) 91–100.
4. R. Bachman, *A CASE for Reverse Engineering* (Cahners Publishing Company, July 1988) (Reprinted from DATAMATION).
5. F. Balmas, "Toward a framework for conceptual and formal outlines of programs", *Proceedings of the Fourth Working Conference on Reverse Engineering* (IEEE Computer Society, 1997) 226–235.
6. K. Bennett, T. Bull and H. Yang, "A transformation system for maintenance-turning theory into practice", *Proceedings of the International Conference on Software Maintenance* (IEEE Computer Society Press, 1992) 146–155.
7. V. Berzins, *Software Merging and Slicing* (IEEE Computer Society Press, 1995), ISBN 0-8186-6792-3.
8. T. J. Biggerstaff, B. G. Mitbander and D. Webster, "The concept assignment problem in program understanding", *Proceedings of the 15th International Conference on Software Engineering* (IEEE Computer Society Press, 1993) 482–498.
9. A. J. Brown, "Specifications and reverse engineering", *Journal of Software Maintenance: Research and Practice* **5**, no. 3 (1993) 147–153.
10. E. Burd and M. Munro, "A method for the identification of reusable units through the reengineering of legacy code", *Journal of Systems and Software* **44**, no. 2 (1998) 121–134.
11. E. Buss, *et al*, "Investigating reverse engineering technologies for the CAS program understanding project", *IBM Systems Journal* **33**, no. 3 (1994) 477–500.
12. G. Canfora, A. Cimitile and U. De Carlini, "A logic based approach to reverse engineering tools production", *Proceedings of the International Conference on Software Maintenance* (IEEE Computer Society Press, 1991) 83–91.
13. G. Canfora, A. De Lucia and M. Munro, "An integrated environment for reuse reengineering C code", *The Journal of Systems and Software* **42**, no. 2 (1998) 153–164.
14. M. P. Chase, S. M. Christey, D. R. Harris and A. S. Yeh, "Managing recovered function and structure of legacy software components", *Proceedings of the 5th Working Conference on Reverse Engineering* (IEEE Computer Society Press, 1998) 79–88.
15. B. Cheng, "Applying formal methods in automated software development", *Journal of Computer and Software Engineering* **2** (February 1994) 137–164.

16. B. Cheng and J. Jeng, "Reusing analogous components", *IEEE Transactions on Knowledge and Data Engineering* **9**, no. 2 (March–April 1997) 341–349.
17. E. J. Chikofsky and J. H. Cross, II ,"Reverse engineering and design recovery: A taxonomy", *IEEE Software* **7**, no. 1 (January 1990) 13–17.
18. W. C. Chu, C. W. Lu, C. H. Chang and Y. C. Chung, "Pattern-based software re-engineering", *Handbook of Software Engineering and Knowledge Engineering*, Vol. 1 (World Scientific Publishing, 2001).
19. A. Cimitile and U. De Carlini, "Reverse engineering: Algorithms for program graph production", *Software Practice and Experience* **21**, no. 5 (1991) 519–537.
20. B. Claybrook, "A specification method for specifying data and procedural abstractions", *IEEE Transactions on Software Engineering* **8**, no. 5 (September 1982) 449–459.
21. G. Clayton, S. Rugaber and L. Wills, "On the knowledge required to understand a program", *Proceedings of the 5th Working Conference on Reverse Engineering* (IEEE Computer Society Press, 1998) 69–78.
22. R. Clayton and S. Rugaber, "The representation problem in reverse engineering", *Proceedings of the First Working Conference on Reverse Engineering* (IEEE Computer Society Press, May 1993) 8–16.
23. W. Cohen, "Inductive specification recovery: Understanding software by learning from example behaviors", *Automated Software Engineering* **2**, no. 2 (Kluwer Academic Publishers, June 1995) 107–129.
24. A. Colbrook, C. Smythe and A. Darlison, "Data abstraction in a software re-engineering reference model", *Proceedings of the International Conference on Software Maintenance* (IEEE Computer Society Press, 1990) 2–11.
25. A. Colbrook and C. Smythe, "The retrospective introduction of abstraction into software", *Proceedings of the International Conference on Software Maintenance* (IEEE Computer Society Press, 1989) 166–173.
26. J. R. Cordy, N. L. Eliot and M. G. Robertson, "Turingtool: A user interface to aid in the software maintenance task", *IEEE Transactions on Software Engineering* **16**, no. 3 (March 1990) 294–301.
27. D. D. Cowan, D. M. Germàn, C. J. P. Lucena and A. von Staa, "Enhancing code for readability and comprehension using SGML", *Proceedings of the International Conference on Software Maintenance* (IEEE Computer Society Press, 1994) 181–190.
28. J. Cross, E. Chikofsky and C. May, "Reverse engineering", *Advances in Computers* **35** (1992) 199–254.
29. H. Dayani-Fard and I. Jurisica, "Reverse engineering by mining dynamic repositories", *Proceedings of the 5th Working Conference on Reverse Engineering* (IEEE Computer Society Press, 1998) 174–182.
30. C. Desclaux and M. Ribault, "Macs: Maintenance assistance capability for software maintenance", *Proceedings of the International Conference on Software Maintenance* (IEEE Computer Society Press, 1991) 2–12.
31. S. Dietrich and F. Calliss, "The application of deductive databases to inter-module code analysis", *Proceedings of the International Conference on Software Maintenance* (IEEE Computer Society Press, 1991) 120–128.
32. A. Engberts, W. Kozaczynski and J. Q. Ning, "Concept recognition-based program transformation", *Proceedings of the International Conference on Software Maintenance* (1991) 73–82.
33. W. B. Frakes and T. P. Pole, "An empirical study of representation methods for reusable software components", *IEEE Transactions on Software Engineering* **20**, no. 8 (1994) 617–630.

34. K. B. Gallagher and J. R. Lyle, "Using program slicing in software maintenance", *IEEE Transactions on Software Engineering* **17**, no. 8 (August 1991) 751–761.
35. G. C. Gannod and B. H. C. Cheng, "Strongest post-condition semantics as a basis for reverse engineering", *Journal of Automated Software Engineering* **3**, no. 1–2 (July 1996) 139–164.
36. G. C. Gannod and B. H. C. Cheng, "Using informal and formal techniques for the reverse engineering of C programs", *Proceedings of the Third Working Conference on Reverse Engineering* (IEEE Computer Society Press, 1996) 249–258.
37. J. Harband, "SEELA: Maintenance and documenting by reverse-engineering", *Proceedings of the International Conference on Software Maintenance* (IEEE Computer Society Press, 1990) 146.
38. J. Hartman, "Understanding natural programs using proper decomposition", *Proceedings of the 13th International Conference on Software Engineering* (IEEE Computer Society Press, 1991) 62–73.
39. P. A. Hausler, M. G. Pleszkoch, R. C. Linger and A. R. Hevner, "Using function abstraction to understand program behavior", *IEEE Software* **7**, no. 1 (January 1990) 55–63.
40. L. J. Holtzblatt, R. L. Piazza, H. B. Reubenstein, S. N. Roberts and D. R. Harris, "Design recovery for distributed systems", *IEEE Transactions on Software Engineering* **23**, no. 7 (July 1997) 461–472.
41. W. E. Howden and S. Pak, "Problem domain, structural and logical abstractions in reverse engineering", *Proceedings of the International Conference on Software Maintenance* (IEEE Computer Society Press, 1992) 214–224.
42. D. Jerding and S. Rugaber, "Using visualization for architectural localization and extraction", *Proceedings of the Fourth Working Conference on Reverse Engineering* (IEEE Computer Society Press, 1997) 56–65.
43. J. K. Joiner, W. T. Tsai, X. P. Chen, S. Subramanian, J. Sun and H. Gandamaneni, "Data-centered program understanding", *Proceedings of the International Conference on Software Maintenance* (IEEE Computer Society Press, 1994) 272–281.
44. R. Kasman and S. J. C. Oeere, "Playing detective: Reconstructing software architecture from available evidence", *Automated Software Engineering: An International Journal* **6**, no. 2 (Kluwer Academic Publishers, April 1999) 107–138.
45. R. Kazman, S. G. Woods and S. J. Carriere, "Requirements for integrating software architecture and reengineering models: CORUM II", *Proceedings of the Working Conference on Reverse Engineering* (IEEE Computer Society Press, 1998) 154–163.
46. D. A. Kinloch and M. Munro, "Understanding C programs using the combined C graph representation", *Proceedings of the International Conference on Software Maintenance* (IEEE Computer Society Press, 1994) 172–180.
47. K. Kontogiannis, R. DiMori, M. Bernstein and E. Merlo, "Localization of Design Concepts in Legacy Systems", *Proceedings of the International Conference on Software Maintenance* (IEEE Computer Society Press, 1994) 414–423.
48. R. Krikhaar, A. Postma, A. Sellink, M. Stroucken and C. Verhoef, "A two-phase process for software architecture improvement", *Proceedings of the International Conference on Software Maintenance* (IEEE Computer Society, 1999) 371–380.
49. P. J. Layzell, M. J. Freeman and P. Benedusi, "Improving reverse engineering through the use of multiple knowledge sources", *Journal of Software Maintenance: Research and Practice* **7**, no. 4 (July/August 1995) 279–299.
50. Y. Li, H. Yang and W. C. Chu, "A concept-oriented belief revision approach to domain knowledge recovery from source code", *Journal of Software Maintenance and Evolution: Research and Practice* **13**, no. 1 (January/February 2001) 31–52.

51. K. Liu, A. Alderson and Z. Qureshi, "Requirements recovery from legacy systems by analysing and modelling behaviour", *Proceedings of International Conference on Software Maintenance* (IEEE Computer Society Press, 1999) 3–12.
52. P. E. Livadas and P. K. Roy, "Program dependence analysis", *Proceedings of the International Conference on Software Maintenance* (IEEE Computer Society Press, 1992) 356–365.
53. A. V. Mayrhauser and A. M. Vans, "Program understanding: Models and experiments", *Advances in Computer* **40** (August 1995) 1–38.
54. N. C. Mendonca and J. Kramer, "A quality-based analysis of architecture recovery environments", *Proceedings of the 1st Euromicro Conference on Software Maintenance and Reengineering* (IEEE Computer Society Press, 1997) 54–59.
55. A. Mili, R. Mili and R. Mittermeir, "Storing and retrieving software components: A refinement based system", *Proceedings of the 16th International Conference on Software Engineering* (IEEE Computer Society Press, 1994) 91–100.
56. H. A. Müller, *Rigi User's Manual Version 5.4.4*, Department of Computer Science, University of Victoria (1998). Also on URL *http://www.rigi.csc.uvic.ca/*
57. J. Mylopoulos, *et al*, "Towards an integrated toolset for program understanding", *Proceedings of the 1994 IBM CAS Conference (CASCON'94)* (1994) 19–31.
58. V. Narat, "Using a relational database for software maintenance: A case study", *Proceedings of the International Conference on Software Maintenance* (IEEE Computer Society Press, 1993) 244–251.
59. S. Paul and A. Prakash, "Querying source code using an algebraic query language", *Proceedings of the International Conference on Software Maintenance* (IEEE Computer Society Press, 1994) 127–136.
60. V. Rajlich, "Incremental redocumentation with hypertext", *Proceedings of the First Euromicro Conference on Software Maintenance and Reengineering* (1997) 68–72.
61. V. Rajlich and N. Damaskinos, "Algorithm for graphic layout in VIFOR", *Proceedings of the International Conference on Software Maintenance* (IEEE Computer Society Press, 1990) 142–145.
62. Reasoning5 CBMS, Reasoning, Systems Inc. On URL *http://www.reasoning.com/* (2000).
63. F. Ricca and P. Tonella, "Web site analysis: Structure and evolution", *Proceedings of the International Conference on Software Maintenance* (IEEE Computer Society Press, 2000) 76–87.
64. T. Richner and S. Ducasse, "Recovering high-level views of object-oriented applications from static and dynamic information", *Proceedings of International Conference on Software Maintenance* (IEEE Computer Society Press, 1999) 13–22.
65. J. Rosenberg, J. Lennox and H. Schulzrinne, "Programming internet telephony services", *IEEE Internet Computing* **3**, no. 3 (May/June 1999) 63–72.
66. S. Rugaber, S. B. Ornburn and R. J. Leblanc Jr, "Recognizing design decisions in programs", *IEEE Software* **7**, no. 1 (January 1990) 46–54.
67. K. Sere and M. Wald'en, "Reverse engineering distributed algorithms", *Journal of Software Maintenance: Research and Practice* **8**, no. 2 (1996) 117–144.
68. M. A. Servello, "LOGISCOPE and the software maintenance crisis", *Proceedings of the International Conference on Software Maintenance* (IEEE Computer Society Press, 1990) 104.
69. J. Shao and C. Pound, "Extracting business rules from information systems", *BT Technology Journal* **17**, no. 4 (1999) 179–186, ISSN 1358–3948, **17**, no. 4 (1999) 179–186.

70. M. Sitaraman, B. W. Weide and W. F. Ogden, "On the practical need for abstraction relations to verify abstract data type representations", *IEEE Transactions on Software Engineering* **23**, no. 3 (March 1997) 157–170.
71. H. M. Sneed and G. Jandrasics, "Inverse transformation of software from code to specification", *Proceedings of the International Conference on Software Maintenance* (IEEE Computer Society, 1988) 102–109.
72. E. Soloway and K. Ehrlich, "Empirical studies of programming knowledge", *IEEE Transactions on Software Engineering* **SE-10**, no. 5 (September 1984) 595–609.
73. I. Sommerville, *Software Engineering, 5th ed.* (Addison-Wesley Publishing Co. Inc., Wokingham, England, 1995) 700–712.
74. M.-A. D. Storey and H. A. Muller, "Manipulating and documenting software structures using SHriMP views", *Proceedings of the International Conference on Software Maintenance* (IEEE Computer Society Press, 1995) 275–285.
75. T. Systä, P. Yu and H. Müller, "Analyzing Java software by combining metrics and program visualization", *Proceedings of the 4th European Conference on Software Maintenance and Reengineering* (IEEE Computer Society, 2000) 199–208. Also on URL *http://www.cs.tut.fi/~tsysta/*
76. *The Extensible Markup Language* (*XML*), The World Wide Web Consortium, on URL *http://www.w3.org/XML* (2001).
77. P. Tonella, R. Fiutem, G. Antoniol and E. Merlo, "Augmenting pattern-based architectural recovery with flow analysis: Mosaic — A case study", *Proceedings of the 3rd Working Conference on Reverse Engineering* (IEEE Computer Society, 1996) 198–207.
78. M. Ward, "Abstracting a specification from code", *Software Maintenance: Research and Practice* **5**, no. 2 (June 1993) 101–122.
79. R. C. Waters, "Program translation via abstraction and reimplementation", *IEEE Transactions on Software Engineering* **14**, no. 8 (August 1988) 1207–1228.
80. L. M. Wills, "Flexible control for program recognition", *Proceedings of the 1st Working Conference on Reverse Engineering* (IEEE Computer Society Press, 1993) 134–143.
81. H. Yang and K. H. Bennett, "Acquisition of ERA models from data intensive code", *Proceedings of the International Conference on Software Maintenance* (IEEE Computer Society, 1995) 116–123.
82. H. Yang, X. Liu and H. Zedan, "Tackling the abstraction problem for reverse engineering in a system re-engineering approach", *Proceedings of International Conference on Software Maintenance* (IEEE Computer Society Press, 1998) 284–293.
83. A. S. Yeh, D. R. Harris and M. P. Chase, "Manipulating recovered software architecture views", *Proceedings of the 19th International Conference on Software Engineering* (1997) 184–194.

SYNCHRONIZING INTERACTIVE WEB DOCUMENTS WITH FD-JAVA CONSTRAINTS

ANTONINA DATTOLO

Dipartimento di Matematica ed Applicazioni,
Università di Napoli "Federico II", via Cinthia, 80126 Napoli, Italy
E-mail: antos@unisa.it

VINCENZO LOIA

Dipartimento di Matematica ed Informatica,
Università di Salerno, via S. Allende, 84081 Baronissi, Salerno, Italy
E-mail: loia@unisa.it

MICHEL QUAGGETTO

LPTL-CNRS Universitè Pierre & Marie Curie,
Place Jussieu — 75252 Paris Cedex 05, France
E-mail: quaggetto@lptl.jussieu.fr

Interactive Electronic Technical Manuals (IETMs) are deliverable products for which the new technologies of interactive electronic data presentations are used to access any part of the technical manual-descriptive text, to provide multimedia description of maintenance and troubleshooting procedures, or illustrations. The design of IETMs on the Web must face non-trivial problems, in particular the flexibility and the reactivity of the digital manual bounded to the behavior of the media. This paper presents an extension of object-oriented programming towards the constraint-based approach, showing how it has been used to handle spatial as well as temporal layout in order to assure continuous and synchronized visualization. The computational target is Java extended towards finite domain (FD) constraint programming. Embedding FD constraints within an object-oriented language such as Java makes it possible to use advanced software solutions for Web-based complex media manipulations.

Keywords: Constraint programming in software engineering, object-oriented in software engineering, interactive applications on the web, Java implementation, IETM.

1. Introduction

In many interactive computer applications, it is often desirable to support the specification and manipulation of relationships between objects. Imagine that we have drawn two rectangles and a straight line, as shown in Fig. 1(a). The rectangles have the same dimensions. Then, we want the line to be connected to the middle points of the right edge of the first rectangle and the left edge of the second rectangle. Numerous programs can perform this simple operation, generating the result shown in Fig. 1(b). However, when either the line or one of the rectangles is changed, the relationship may not hold any longer. This is the situation shown

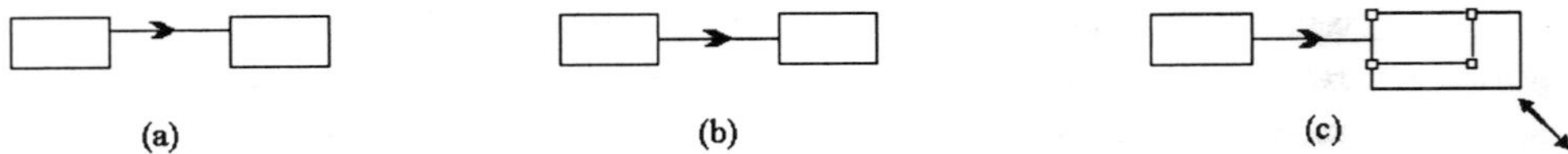

Fig. 1. (a) Two rectangles and a straight line. (b) They are horizontally centered. (c) Dragging the corner of a rectangle.

in Fig. 1(c), in which a dragging operation on a rectangle has been applied. To make the rectangles and the line being horizontally centered again, the centering operation needs to be repeated.

Some programs support the specification of relationships, keeping automatically the relationship for us.

A relationship that is specified explicitly between objects and is satisfied automatically by a program is called a *constraint* [1]. Constraints can express spatial, temporal or algebraic relationships. In the example of Fig. 1, we have imposed a spatial constraint.

In interactive applications, constraints must typically satisfied continuously in response to user-initiated operations. The most common application areas of constraint-based techniques are:

(1) Drawing programs [2]; spatial constraints can be simply described as algebraic relations.
(2) User interface construction [3]; graphical widgets need to be set up on the screen and connected by constraints.
(3) Simulation programs [4]; simulations of physical laws need application of spatial and temporal constraints.
(4) Theorem proving [5]. The proof of theorems requires the handling of temporal constraints.

Constraint-programming languages are an important paradigm useful for representing and solving constraint satisfaction problems (CSPs). This paper focuses the discussion on the constraint technology as an effective technology for constructing complex graphical user interfaces (GUIs). Because of the spectacular growth of the World Wide Web (shortly WWW or WEB), the recent interests of constraint programming have been attracted by the study of direct manipulation techniques of Web graphical objects. Java takes an important role in these activities thanks to its role for Internet programming. The essence of this paper is to describe an extension of the object-oriented model of Java towards finite domain (FD) constraint programming and to show how this extension has been used to handle spatial as well as temporal layout in order to assure continuous and synchronized Web visualization. To better experiment the benefits of this approach we apply the resulting Java programming model to the design of Interactive Electronic Technical Manuals (IETMs). An IETM is characterized by the presence of new technologies for interactive electronic data presentations in order to better allow the user to access any part of a digital technical manual.

The paper is organized as follows. Section 2 explains the motivation of this paper by correlating the problem of media synchronization with the current Web technologies. From this discussion we give prominence to a Java extension towards FD constraint programming. In Sec. 3, we illustrate a general Web-oriented architecture designed for IETMs. Section 4 underlines the interest in merging the object-oriented paradigm with constraint-based resolution. In Sec. 5, we deepen on the basic primitives that allow Java programmers to adopt a FD constraint programming style. To discuss the utility of these primitives in Sec. 6, we illustrate the use of FD Java constraints in the design of Web-based IETMs. In particular, we report how the constraints play a key role in the management of multimedia presentations of technical information. Concluding remarks close the paper.

2. Motivations

IETMs are deliverable products for which the new technologies of interactive electronic data presentations are used to access any part of the technical manual's descriptive text, to provide multimedia description of maintenance and troubleshooting procedures, or illustrations. Recent strong interest in developing IETMs around Web technologies is due to the immediate value added by the opportunity of sharing information [6]. The rich integration of multiple media increases the effectiveness of the IETMs when the system adapts the contents and display specifications to both the user profile and the system state.

Synchronizing multimedia on the Web is a difficult task. Currently three very recent technologies address this problem, SMIL (Synchronized Multimedia Integration Language) [7], ASF (Advanced Streaming Format) [8] and HTML+Time [9].

(1) SMIL [7] can be considered as an Extensible Markup Language (XML) [10] based application. SMIL is a language able to schedule multimedia presentations where audio, video, text and graphics are combined in real-time. All the different media elements are referenced from the SMIL file, similar to the way an HTML [11] page references its images, applets, and other elements. As opposite to other formats (AVI or MPEG), in SMIL presentations the text is external to the presentation, increasing accessibility and making easier the work of other applications (for example Web search engines). SMIL is very attractive because it is a text-based language, allowing to create code on-the-fly using a database.

(2) ASF (Advanced Streaming Format) [8], is a rich o-o programming language, as opposite to a plain text-based markup language like SMIL. Proposed by Microsoft as proprietary format, ASF intends to replace the popular AVI (Audio Video Interleave) format, improving the support of local playback (CD-ROM, DVD), HTTP playback, and media server streaming. Its main goals regard storage and transmission.

(3) HTML+Time (Timed Interactive Multimedia Extensions) [9], has been submitted to W3C by the joint team Microsoft, Compaq and

Macromedia. Its goal is to extend SMIL to the browser, without the need for any media server. In fact, HTML+Time extends HTML by adding a set of time-based attributes to its existing tag set. This approach should resolve one of the main drawbacks of SMIL, that is the fact that SMIL elements work in their own environment. By applying time attributes to an arbitrary HTML element, HTML+Time allows these same attributes to provide a powerful and simple means of describing the integration of the media element itself with other multimedia elements in the presentation. HTML+Time, being an extension to HTML 4.0, is based on plain text (as well as SMIL), and thus does not provide internal programming languages facilities, as opposite to ASF. While SMIL supports legacy browsers, HTML+Time needs the support of next generation browsers for interpretation.

The problem of media synchronization may be faced in its completeness by considering more abstract aspects related with graphical object management. The idea of performing an automatic design of graphical layout and visualization via constraint processing has been widely acknowledged by the research community [12]. First milestones appeared in the 60's with Sketchpad [13] and with the first widget [14].

At the programming level, the major difficulty is the conflict between two ways of constructing programs: object-oriented programming and constraint programming. Only recently, the synergy of Java [15] and constraint-based techniques [16] has revealed an interesting appeal especially for Web-based applications. In this regard, at least two different approaches can be distinguished, namely "linking" and "embedding".

(1) The first approach consists of *linking* Java with an external constraint programming language: in this case, Java plays the role of an interface between the constraint engine embedded in an external system and the Web documents. P*i*LL*o*W (Programming in Logic Languages on the Web) [17] is an example of a possible high-level bridge between logic programming applications and the Web.

    In later parts of this paper, we show a Java constraints programming model usable in a client-server architecture. This allows the programmer to design more flexible constraint-based applications distinguishing the control activities runnable on the server from those runnable on the client. Since this approach does not rely on external application, there is no need of linking additional systems to manage constraint solving [18], as opposite of [19] and [20].

(2) The second approach consists of *embedding* constraints in Java itself [4]. Java is then responsible for executing the constraint reasoning. As it is the case for any programming language, it is possible either to implement

a constraint-based library customized for specific applications or to extend Java with new instructions enabling constraint reasoning. In the work discussed in [21], a Web author as well a Web viewer can perform runtime constraint solving. An experimentation about the constraint approach to design complex graphical interfaces using Java can be found in [22], where constraints are used to specify the desired spatial layout of Web pages.

In later parts of this paper we show that it is possible to extend Java by embedding into it a general FD-level control flow concentrated in a small number of Java classes, without conceiving new constraint solver techniques. This approach allows the user to easily master the FD control mechanism, and stimulates further extension or specialization of the constraint solving mechanism according with more specific requirements.

To better introduce the reader to the issues related to constraint programming on the Web, this work presents an extension of Java towards constraint programming over finite domains (FD). The extension allows the declarative specification of constraints for the automatic display of contents over the Web. The proposal intends to be as general and flexible as possible, so that whatever the Constraint Satisfaction Problem (CSP) is, the programmer may keep the Java programming paradigm.

The design of the Java extensions has been accomplished to provide for:

— a declarative specification of Web contents by using basic and simple constructs,
— an easy integration in the Java o-o model [23], and
— an efficient execution (details about the constraint satisfaction issues as well as the implementation choices are not discussed in this paper since they are presented elsewhere [22]).

3. A Web-based Architecture for IETMs

The primary goal of an IETM architecture is to enable the acquisition and deployment of sharable and interoperable technical data in a network of distributed data sources and users. In this way, important benefits of IETMs can be obtained:

- User friendliness. An IETM allows the user to jump in any direction though the technical data, to move between different levels of detail and between completely different topics or external applications and databases.
- Frame rather than page oriented presentation increases familiarity and improves the presentation of technical documentation by reducing the overall cost of maintenance and training.
- Shifting from paper-based to electronic-based documentation improves productivity and reduces costs of printing, storage and distribution [24].

- The availability of a structured data model (i.e., the database of the product components), used as information source to create the visual representation (i.e., the manuals) enables a faster updating of the digital material.
- Portability/Interoperability (multiple volumes of documentation/ technical manuals on a single computer and interactive on-line training capabilities).

An example of IETM can be found in [25], in which the experimentation has been focused on building solution to manage electronic information about locomotive components, permitting maximal interoperability of technical information that, according with the user's needs is composed and proposed as:

- training session;
- decision Support System for troubleshooting diagnosis;
- information repository; and
- hypermedia documentation.

The discussed IETM architecture is composed of three basic layers:

(1) An authoring platform to effectively create and manage IETMs.
(2) An infrastructure that provides the technology to distribute, manage and present these IETMs.
(3) A system that allows an end-user to perform his job benefiting from sophisticated human-computer interaction, such as multimedia facilities.

The authoring system is based on different software components that help the designer in the specification of the architecture. Our design approach follows previous experiences dedicated to the design of open hypermedia authoring architectures (see [26]). The software components that perform the constraint flow management are enclosed in the "Constraint Interaction Technique Libraries" (CITL). These provide a wide range of interaction techniques, driven by FD constraint resolution, to manage menus, graphical sliders, on-screen light button, etc. The role of the constraints is determinant: the relations among the graphical objects are maintained by the constraints, no matter how the objects are manipulated.

CITL are based on a kernel constituted by a collection of primitive constraints (beside, under, over, equal, right-of, left-of, inside, and so on). Using this kernel it is possible to create more complex geometric constraints designed for graphical objects, such as rectangles, circles, text, trees, graphs, etc. The architecture runs in a distributed way, in an intranet environment. To support the server-centric choice we used the *Servlet* [27] approach. In fact, Java Servlets are powerful tools to improve efficiency and flexibility in the development of the server-side of Web applications. The major gain in its use is essentially due to avoiding the length overhead of loading CGI or Perl interpreters for each incoming request: the servlet code together with the JVM (Java Virtual Machine) [28] remain resident in the Web

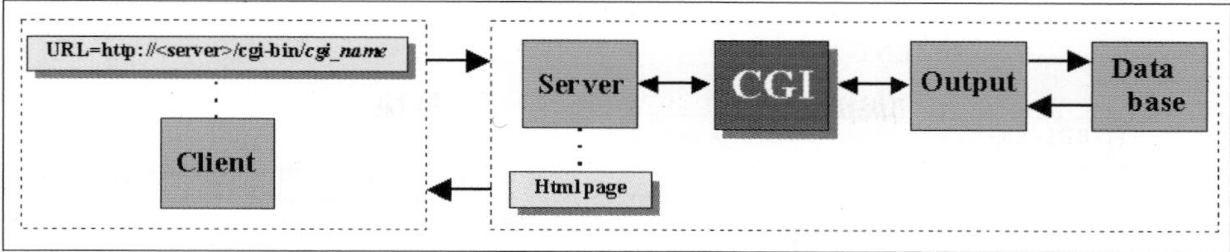

Fig. 2. CGI behavior.

server. Another important enhancement is the information hiding accomplished by the Java Servlet API on the underlying complexity of the Web server so to make easier the development of server centric systems. Furthermore, being Servlets written in Java itself, it possible to guarantee high level of portability and security, at least at the same level for client-side applets.

In order to better clarify the difference between the CGI and Servlet techniques we give in the next two figures (Figs. 2 and 3) an illustration of their basic functionality. The behavior of CGI is described in Fig. 2.

CGI is an acronym that stands for Common Gateway Interface. This interface provides a bridge between the browser and the server where the document resides in order to communicate and pass information back and forth. Web pages are created "on the fly" based on information from buttons, checkboxes, text input and so on. Normally when a Web browser looks up a URL the following actions take place:

(1) The client contacts the HTTP server with the URL.
(2) The HTTP server looks at the filename requested by the client and then sends that file back.
(3) The client displays the file in the appropriate format.

The CGI approach enables to set up the HTTP server so that whenever a file in a certain directory is requested, that file is not sent back but it is executed as a program. Whatever that program outputs, this is sent back to display. The programs are called *CGI scripts.* Primarily, this is done through the <FORM> tag. This attribute points to the location of a CGI script that will run on the server when the form is submitted to it. For a user with an account on an address "http://<server>", the action for a script might look like:

ACTION= "http://<server>/cgi-bin/cgi_name"

The server interprets the indication in the URL of the virtual directory */cgi-bin* as a request to execute the program. The program is executed, and at the end of the operations returns to the server an HTML [11] document that may be composed *on-the-fly* if it has not already been created. This document is sent to the client.

The behavior of a Servlet is described in Fig. 3. Java servlets are more efficient, easier to use, more powerful, more portable, and cheaper than traditional CGI and other alternative CGI-like technologies. The request originated from the client side

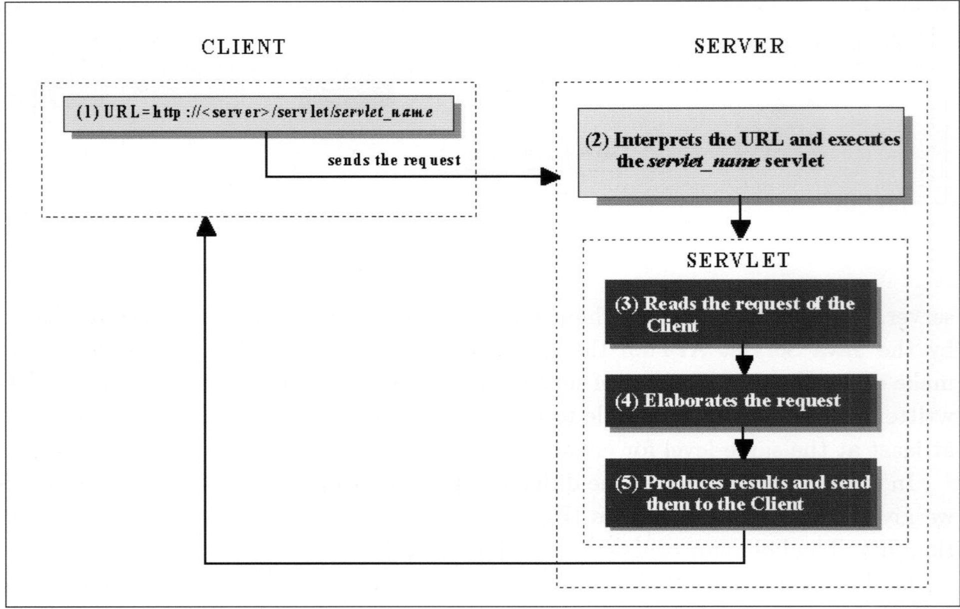

Fig. 3. Servlet behavior.

is received by the server that executed the Servlet <servlet_name>. Once that the servlet has terminated its execution, the result is returned to the client-side.

With Java Servlets, Web developers can create fast and efficient server-side applications in Java instead of using CGI and Perl. In fact, CGI was proposed in the early days of the Web where the typical situation was: a Web server receives a CGI request, it needs to start a completely different program, to allow the program to run, to allow the program to close down, and then to return the resulting text to the Web browser. If the page is requested several times, the overall effect is too expensive.

Servlets are persistent, platform independent, and incorporate all sorts of advanced features including security, easy database access, and much easier integration with Java applets.

The most important differences (and benefits) of Servlet use with respect to CGI-based approaches can be so listed:

- *Platform Independence.* Servlets can run on any platform without recompilation or rewriting.
- *Performance.* Servlets only need to be loaded once.
- *Extensibility.* Java is a robust, well-designed and fully o-o language.
- *Portability.* Servlets are actually a subset of the Java Server API: this means that they are able to run everything from Web Servers to Network Computers.

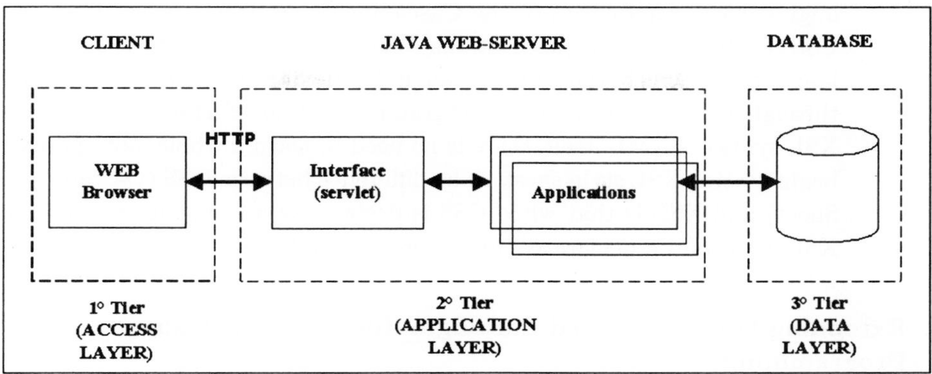

Fig. 4. The IETM architecture for the Web.

In Fig. 4, a top level representation of the architecture of an IETM for the Web is provided.

The platform is designed as a multi-tier architecture and it is organized in three layers:

- The *Access Layer* is used to build flexible interfaces based on open standards (XSL [29], XML [10]) through common web development environments.
- The *Application Layer* contains applications for specific tasks and operations. Application developers have access to the services and data through Java Servlets.
- The *Data Layer* allows access into legacy applications or data sources.

XML and XSL are open standards recommended by W3C (Word Wide Web Consortium); their impact is not only on the access layer, but especially on the data layer. A brief discussion that explains their role follows.

- XML (Extensible Markup Language) [10] is a set of tags and declarations, as HTML is. In contrast with HTML, rather than being concerned with formatting information on a page, XML focuses on providing information about the data itself and how it relates to other data. XML differs from HTML in three major aspects:
  - Information providers can define new tag and attribute names at will.
  - Document structures can be nested at any level of complexity.
  - Any XML document can contain an optional description of its grammar for use by applications, that need to perform structural validation.
- XSL (Extensible Style Language) [29] represents an attempt to create a more dynamic and powerful notation for defining document style, and to

augment the capabilities of the Cascading Style Sheets work (CSS1 and CSS2) [30] already in place at the W3C. XSL is a standard style-sheet language in which the author can indicate how to display XML data through a simple declarative programming style. Furthermore, because XSL syntax is XML itself, there is no need to learn a whole new syntax to begin writing XSL style-sheets. The difference between CSS (Cascade Style Sheet) and XSL is that while CSS is declarative and not user-extensible, XSL is primarily declarative and user-extensible.

4. Extending Object-oriented Paradigm Towards Constraint Programming

O-o programming [31] is a powerful and common model to support software design and specifically to construct interactive programs, thanks to its support for abstraction and modularity.

In o-o programming a system is modeled in terms of self-contained objects, whose internal structure is hidden from other objects. It is not possible to access directly the main internal structure of an object. Instead, each object in the system provides an interface i.e., a set of operations by which one can operate on the object. Objects co-operate each other to determine the dynamical behavior of the entire system. This kind of cooperation can conceptually be viewed as sending messages between objects.

The modeling of an o-o system requires a local view on the object in order to achieve well-defined behavior of the objects and make the code reusable [31]. O-o concepts are suitable for modeling reactive systems. In o-o programming, objects may change their state. Objects can be created dynamically at run-time. These notions together with message sending are useful for implementing correct response to external events such as those initiated from end-users.

There are almost two dozen of major o-o programming languages in use today, but the leading commercial o-o languages are far fewer in number:

- C++ [32] offers an easier transition via C, but it requires an o-o design approach in order to make proper use of this technology.
- Smalltalk [33] offers a pure o-o environment, with more rapid development time and greater flexibility and power.
- Java [15] is a mixture of C++ and Smalltalk. It is designed as a portable language that can run on any web-enabled computer; it is becoming the standard Internet and Intranet programming language.

The "constraint approach" to human-interface design is a trend that has reported an increasing interest because it is a natural way to declare and specify relationships to be respected among graphical objects.

The study of CSPs was initiated by Montanari [16], when he used them as a way of describing certain combinatorial problems arising in image-processing; it was quickly realized that the same general model was applicable to a much wider class of problems. The general problem has since been intensively studied, both theoretically and experimentally. The references [34, 35, 36] and [37] address general issues on this topic.

Formally, a CSP $\boldsymbol{P}$ is specified by a tuple

$$\boldsymbol{P} = (X, D, R_1(S_1), \ldots, R_n(S_n))$$

where

X is a finite set of variables
D is a finite set of values (the domain of $\boldsymbol{P}$)
Each pair $R_i(S_i)$ is a constraint.

A *solution* for $\boldsymbol{P}$ is an assignment of values from D to each of the variables in X, which satisfies all the constraints simultaneously.

Thus, problems modeled by means of constraint satisfaction [34] are represented by a finite set of variables, a set of finite domains associated with the variables, and a set of relations (or constraints) that limit the values that the variables can take. The main idea behind a CSP resolution is to assign only a value to each variable if the value is compatible with all the constraints [36].

A large body of methodologies exists for efficiently solving CSPs [37, 38] and [39]. However, three approaches are the most used [38]:

(1) *Generate-and-Test.* In this paradigm, each possible combination of the variables is systematically generated and then tested to see if it satisfies all the constraints. The first combination that satisfies all the constraints is the solution.
(2) *Backtracking.* In this method, variables are instantiated sequentially. If a partial instantiation violates any of the constraints, backtracking is performed to the most recently instantiated variable that still has alternatives available. Although this method is more efficient than the generate-and-test, its runtime complexity for most nontrivial problems is still exponential, due to thrashing [40]. The simplest cause is referred to as *node inconsistency* [41]. The constraint method illustrated in later parts of this paper follows the backtracking technique, even if we avoid some performances drawbacks thanks to a specific implementation strategy that minimizes the memory allocation [22].
(3) *Consistency Driven.* This algorithm uses information from the constraints to reduce the search space as early in the search as it is possible.

A wide variety of problems can be viewed as CSPs: the N-queens problem [36], the frequency assignment problem [42], many classical combinatorial problems [37], the crossword puzzles [34].

Several programming languages use constraint satisfaction techniques to solve constraints that have been declared by the programmer. The advantage is the one typical of declarative languages with respect to procedural ones, i.e., cognitive simplicity. The challenge is to have an associated effectiveness and efficiency of the run time processes.

In constraint programming, a system is modeled as a graph of constraints and objects. The constraints form the edges whereas the objects form the nodes in the graph. The constraints are used in CSPs to determine consistent state of the objects. Since the objects are related to each other through the constraints, changes on the objects and on the constraints normally have global effects on the entire system. Traditional constraint satisfaction algorithms usually operate on plain data-structures with all the variables directly visible. This is different from o-o programming where variables are hidden inside objects and cannot be directly accessed. In addition, traditional constraint satisfaction algorithms are applied in a way such that they take the entire set of variables. Small changes in the system are difficult to deal with using such algorithms. Thus constraint programming does not directly supports the description of reactive systems.

5. Finite Domain Programming and its Basic Constructs

A common idea behind a general constraint-based application is to design the solver as a black box that verifies the consistency of a set of constraints over a particular domain of interest. This choice determines a weakness in the flexibility and operational expressiveness of the system due to the rigid coupling of the constraint solving and a fixed set of predefined constraints.

An alternative approach, namely glass-box (intuitively: transparent), was introduced by [43] for constraints over Finite Domains (FD).

A Finite Domain is essentially a set of possible values (symbols, numbers) of finite cardinality. The constraints are expressed in the form of arithmetic relations, such as equations, disequations, inequations, and in the form of symbolic relations. The reasoning framework derives from the propagation and consistency techniques originating in CSP reported, for instance, in [16, 36, 41].

The glass-box framework is based on a single primitive constraint, `X` in `r`, that really embeds the propagation mechanism for constraint solving over FD.

As complex FD constraints (equations, inequations or disequations) are compiled into a set of `X` in `r` primitives, the constraint solving mode is expressed in a high-level model, making the language expressive enough to introduce new user-defined constraints without a penalty in execution or development time. Table 1 presents in a simplified mode the syntax of the primitive constraint `X` in `r`, showing the expressive power of this simple primitive.

Briefly, in `X` in `r`, `X` is a FD variable and `r` is a range of the form `t..t'` where `t` or `t'` is either an integer, a constant (including the greatest value `infinity`) or, more interestingly an indexical term such as min(Y) or max(Z).The main idea is

Table 1. Syntax of the primitive constraint X in r.

c ::=	X in r [when delay]	(Constraint)
r ::=	t .. t	(interval range)
	dom(X)	(indexical domain)
	r : r	(union)
	r & r	(intersection)
	- r	(complementation)
	r + t	(pointwise addition)
t ::=	n	(integer value)
	∞	(greatest value)
	min(X)	(indexical min)
	max(X)	(indexical max)
	t + t	(addition)
	t * t	(multiplication)
	t / t	(division)
delay ::=	x	(variable)
	X delay	(list of variables)

to translate higher-level user constraints into X in r expressions. As example, the constraint x = y + C can be translated obtaining:

$$\mathtt{x = y + c} \Rightarrow \mathtt{in(X,\ min(Y) + C,\ max(Y) + C);} \tag{1}$$

or, equivalently,

$$\mathtt{x = y + c} \Rightarrow \mathtt{in(Y,\ min(X) - C,\ max(X) - C);} \tag{2}$$

Analogously, the constraint x>y can be translated into:

$$\mathtt{x > y} \Rightarrow \mathtt{in(X,\ min(Y) + 1,\ infinity);} \tag{3}$$

or, equivalently,

$$\mathtt{x > y} \Rightarrow \mathtt{in(Y,\ 0,\ max(X) - 1);} \tag{4}$$

A constraint X in t t′ corresponding to the statement in(X, t, t′), will be activated whenever a variable occurring in its range has its value changed. So, the constraint expressed by (3) X in min(Y)+1..infinity will be activated each time Y sees its domain modified.

The basic solving activity is performed by the tell operation consisting in removing impossible values of X, that do not belong to r.

Here we discuss this last aspect by proposing the implementation of the primitive X in r. For any variable X related to a constraint X in r we create an object belonging to the class FD_var. We give in Fig. 5 the Java implementation of this class.

As the reader can note, the class FD_var is characterized by two slots, Min and Max in which we store respectively the minimal and maximal values of the current domain of X.

```
class FD_var{
public int Min=0,Max= infinity;
 ...
   public FD_var(int NewMin,int NewMax) {
      Max=NewMax;
      Min=NewMin;
 }
   public void tell(int L,int U) throws Backtrack {
      int OldMin=Min,OldMax=Max,modified=0;
       if (L> Min) modified=1; else L=Min;
       if (U< Max) modified=1; else U=Max;
      if (modified==1) {
         if (L > U) throw new Backtrack();
             else try {
             Max=U;Min=L;
             if (ListDependance.isEmpty()) {
                 Constraint.resolve();
               } else {
                 solve(ListDependance);
               }
           } finally {
             Max=OldMax; Min=OldMin;
           }
      }
} }
```

Fig. 5. The implementation of the class FD_var.

When a `X` in `r` constraint uses an indexical term on another variable `Y`, the variable `X` must be checked each time the domain `Y` is updated. In this case, for any constraint `X in r` indexing `Y`, the constraint `X in r` is added to the list `ListDependance` related to the variable `Y`, so that the constraints `X in r` inside `ListDependance` can be verified (the command `solve(ListDependance)`).

The condition `L > U` in the method `tell` represents the failure of the constraint as the order on the extremes is not respected (minimum overcomes maximum). In this case, the fail is performed by executing the exception `Backtrack()`. The control returns to the state of the computation where it is possible to apply an alternative.

5.1. *The class* in

The definition of in class is made of two parts:

- the relationships among the constrained variables; and
- the resolution of the constraints that reduces the domains of the constrained variables.

The primitive `X in r` is based on the definition of two abstract methods `solve` and `dispose` defined in the `class in` (see Fig. 6): `solve` specifies the resolution mechanism of the constraint, whereas `dispose` determines the removal of the resources when a constraint is eliminated.

```
class in{
    FD_var X;
    public void dispose()  {}
    Public void solve() throws Backtrack {}
 ...
}
```

Fig. 6. The class in.

```
class C1 extends in {
   FD_var Y;
   int C;
   C1 (FD_var X1,FD_var Y1,int C1) {
     X=X1;Y=Y1;C=C1;
     Y.AddListDependance(this);
  }
  public void dispose() {
    Y.DelListDependance(this);
    }
    public void solve() throws Backtrack {
    X.tell(Y.Min+C,Y.Max+C);
  }
}
```

Fig. 7. Example related to in class: the constraint C1.

```
class Constraint {
 ...
 static public void resolve ()  throws Backtrack {
  ...
 }
   public void dispose() {}
 public void solve() throws Backtrack {}
  }
```

Fig. 8. The class constraint.

For instance, the code related to the constraint `x = y + c` in the form (1) is shown in Fig. 7.

5.2. *The class* Constraint

The search of a solution is basically accomplished by the method **resolve** supported by the class **Constraint** (see Fig. 8). Two phases can be distinguished in the application of this method: the first one, called *propagation*, eliminates the values that do not satisfy the current solution by reducing the size of the domains, whereas the second phase, *enumeration*, sets values to variables not yet instantiated. This operation is executed whenever a fail triggers the search of an alternative solution.

Figure 9 shows the code related to the constraint $x = y + c$; it is based on the constraints C1 (given in Fig. 7) and C2 defined to treat the condition (2),

```
class equal extends Constraint {
  in XC1,XC2;
  public equal(FD_var X,FD_var Y,int  C) {
    XC1 = new C0(X,Y,C);
    XC2 = new C1(X,Y,C);
  }
 public void dispose () {
   XC1.dispose();XC2.dispose();
  }
  public void solve ()  throws Backtrack {
    and_solve(XC1,XC2);
  }
}
```

Fig. 9. The class equal.

and_solve($\mathbf{e_1}, \mathbf{e_2}, \ldots$) is a control mechanism provided by the class **Constraint**. This method specifies that all the constraint $\mathbf{e_i}$ must be solved. **or_solve**($\mathbf{e_1}, \mathbf{e_2}, \ldots$) is used when at least one constraint $\mathbf{e_i}$ must be satisfied.

6. FD Constraints for Spatial and Temporal Layouts

Now we can give Fig. 10 the complete representation of the Web-level IETM.

As the reader can note, the platform is designed as a multi-tier architecture where the Web document is built "on the fly", considering as basic format the XML standard, even though it is possible to produce documentation according to other specifications. An important role is played by the middle tier (Application Layer), composed of different applications skilled to perform specific tasks, as already mentioned in Fig. 3. In particular, we underline:

- The "skeleton Interpreter", designed to recognize specific duties during the parsing of the intermediate document format (for instance SQL query) in order to call external procedures.
- The Decision Support System (DSS) module. This application performs automatic troubleshooting with a considerable gain in maintenance procedures.
- Constraint Solver. This is essentially a library of Java classes based on the FD primitives described in this paper and on other more complex constraints implemented in an incrementally, o-o way.
- Java Beans Solver is the module skilled to apply temporal control mechanism on the media, as discussed later.

In general, the possibility of designing continuous multimedia presentation on the Web is based on the existence of two components: a format for authoring synchronized multimedia documents and a support for the transmission of the document over the network. In the following, we focus our attention on the first component, and we show how it can be addressed by using FD constraints.

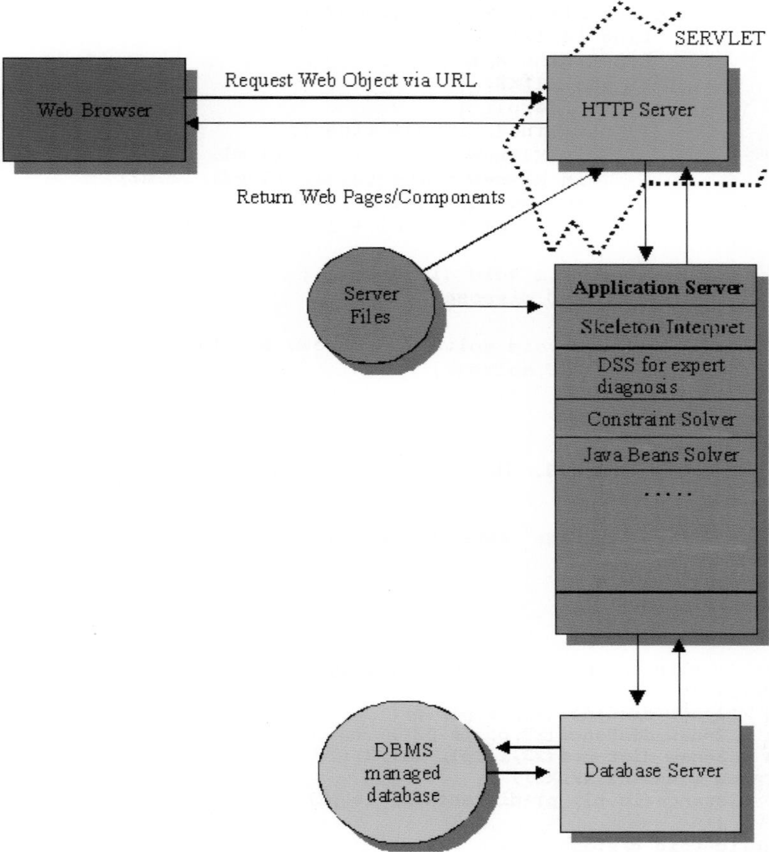

Fig. 10. Representation of a Web-level IETM.

6.1. *FD constraints for spatial layout*

By utilizing the primitive constraint `X in r` it is possible to account for constraints useful to describe the spatial behavior of graphical objects. The primitive constraints are essentially polynomial equations. Some examples follow:

- A ***point P*** has as its components the coordinates $\{P.x, P.y, P.z\}$ (considering a 3D layout).
- A ***line L*** in 2D has as its components $L.m1, L.m2$ and $L.b$, where $L.m1$ is the unit vector, $L.m2$ is normal to L and $L.b$ is the distance from the origin to L. The value of $L.b$ can be either positive or negative: a positive value means that the line is on the same side of the origin as $L.m1$ and $L.m2$, a negative values means that the line is on the opposite side of the origin $(L.m1, L.m2)$. Thus, in order to force two lines $L1$ and $L2$ in R^2 to be perpendicular, we define the following class (Fig. 11).

```
class LPerp extends Constraint{
 Line l1,l2;
 Constraint XC;
 FD_var X1,X2;
public LPerp() {
 l1=new Line();l2=new Line();
      in X1=new multequal(X1,l1.m1, l2.m1);
      in X2=new multequal(X2,l1.m2, l2.m2);
      XC=new equal(X1,X2,0);
      // l1.m1 * l2.m1 + l1.m2 * l2.m2 = 0
 }
    public void dispose () {
      XC.dispose();
  }
 public void solve ()  throws Backtrack {
      XC.solve();
  }
}
```

Fig. 11. How to define lines as perpendicular.

```
class PointOnLineSegm  extends Constraint{
Point p;
LineSeg ls;
Constraint XC;
FD_var X1,X2,X3;

public PointOnLineSegm(Point X,LineSeg Y) {
p=X;ls=Y;
In XI1=new distance(X1,ls.p1, p);
In XI2=new distance(X2,p, ls.p2);
In XI3=new distance(X3,ls.p1, ls.p2);
XC=new equal(X1,X2,X3);
// distance(ls.p1, p)+distance(p, ls.p2) = distance (ls.p1, ls.p2);
      }
public void dispose () {
XC.dispose();
    }
public void solve ()  throws Backtrack {
XC.solve();
   }}
```

Fig. 12. A point P lies on a line segment.

The constraint belongs to the class of non linear arithmetic constraints ($\mathbf{x}^*\mathbf{y} = \mathbf{z}$ multequal).

- ***Line segment S*** is given by its endpoints $S.p1$ and $S.p2$. To guarantee that a point P lies on a line segment Ls it is enough that the length of the segment is the sum of the distance from P to each of the endpoints (Fig. 12).

Through an incremental software design of constraint primitives it is possible to implement complex constraint-based interfaces.

Figure 13 shows an authoring module of IETM in which the user can select, edit and update the single parts of components.

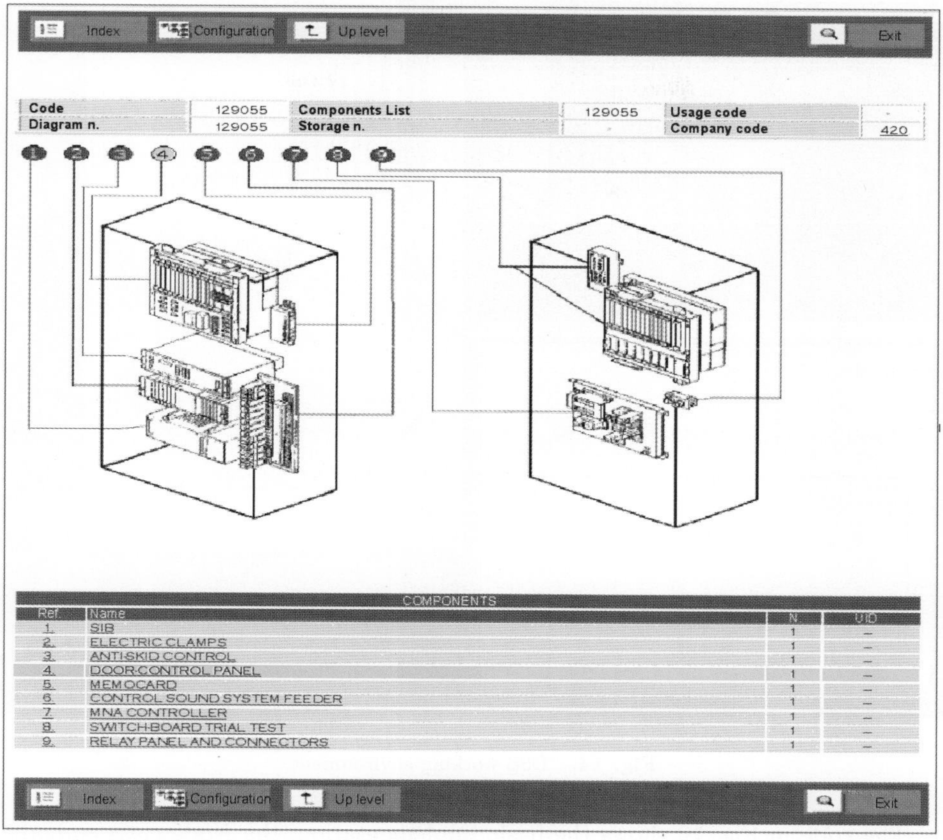

Fig. 13. Geometric spatial constraints.

A geometric constraint is automatically kept by the system: for each internal component the line that links the identifier number (see the circular nodes on the top level of the panel) with the external side of the referred item is always perpendicular to it.

Figure 14 shows the screen during a working session. The right top side window displays the layout of the railway station. The layout shows some sensible components; clicking on these object the system visualizes the bottom left side sub-window that provides different information, such as on-line documentation, repair activity, and so on.

In our example, the operator selects diagnostic support. This task is graphically supported by the decision tree shown in the right side of Fig. 14. The graphical arrangement of the tree is carried out by the client using data received from the server. This arrangement is done using FD-constraints that rule the graphical position of the nodes. Figure 15 shows the relationships used to generate a tree through FD-constraints.

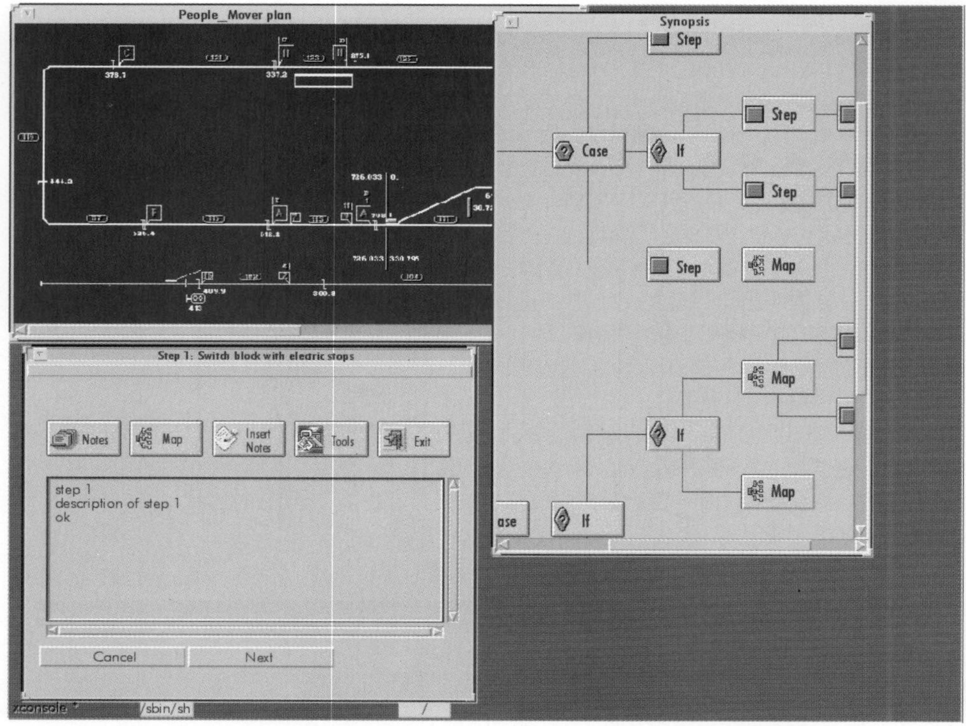

Fig. 14. DSS working environment.

The code in Fig. 16 shows the basic implementation; the Node class embodies two slots, namely `X` and `Y`, that belong to the class `FD_var`.

The father node must be located above the children nodes, in a central position. Let n be the father and s_i the children of n, with $0 \leq i \leq n$. The constraints that rule the position of the father are:

$$\mathtt{n.x} + \mathtt{w} = \mathtt{s_i.x} \Leftrightarrow \mathtt{beside(s_i.x,\ n.x,\ w)}$$

$$\mathtt{n.y} = (\mathtt{s_n.y} + \mathtt{s_0.y})/2 \Leftrightarrow \mathtt{center(n.y,\ s_n.y,\ s_0.y)}$$

The rule to locate the children among themselves is:

$$\mathtt{s_i.x} = \mathtt{s_{i+1}.x} \Leftrightarrow \mathtt{equal(s_i.x,\ s_{i+1}.x)}$$

$$\mathtt{ymax(s_i)} + \mathtt{h} = \mathtt{ymin(s_{i+1})} \Leftrightarrow \mathtt{under(ymax(s_i),\ ymin(s_{i+1}),h)}$$

The children nodes are vertically drawn thanks to the "father" constraints, whereas the "children" constraints handles the positioning of the node $\mathtt{s_{i+1}}$ so that the corresponding sub-trees of $\mathtt{s_{i+1}}$ and $\mathtt{s_i}$ do not overlap. Considering the sub-tree with root $\mathtt{s_1}$ in Fig. 15, then $\mathtt{ymax(s_1)}$ and $\mathtt{ymin(s_1)}$ provide correspondingly the `FD_var Y` of v_2 and the `FD_var Y` of the node p_0 (the minimum `Y` of any sub-tree).

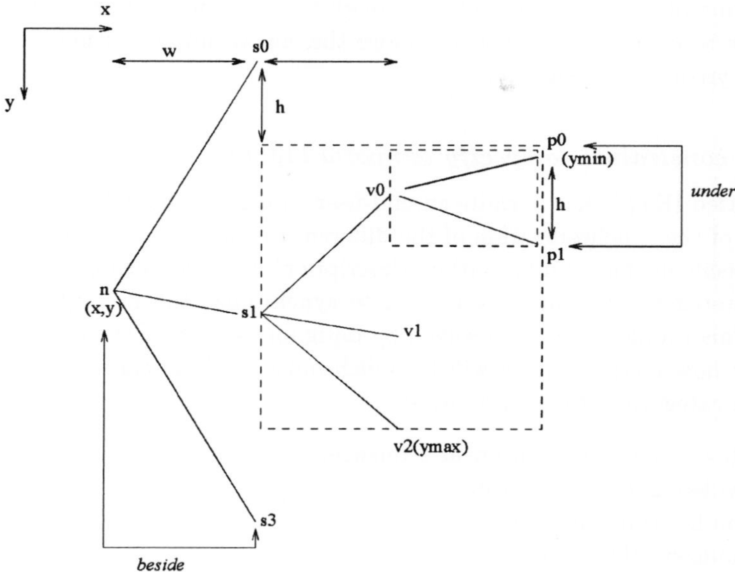

Fig. 15. Relationships to maintain in order to generate a tree with FD constraints.

```
   package graph;
   class Node {
    FD_var X,Y;
    ...
   }
class Tree {
     public Tree(Node r) {
       make_tree(r,r.subnodes());
       Constraint.resolve();
       }

void make_subnodes(Node si,ListNodes l)  {
  if (l.null())
  else {
       sj = l.car();
       new equal(si.x,sj.x, 0);
       if (si.subnodes().null()) {
           new  equal(si.y,sj.ymin(),h);
           make_subnode(sj,l.cdr());
           } else  {
                   new equal(si.ymax(),sj.ymin(),h );
                   make_tree(si,si.subnodes());
                   make_subnode(sj,l.cdr());
                   }
       }
   }

void make_tree(Node n, ListeNodes l) {
     new center(n.y,n.ymax(),n.ymin());
     make_subnode(l.car(),l.cdr());
     }
 ....
   }
```

Fig. 16. Java constraints for a tree.

The drawing of the tree is executed through the preorder tree visit; in this way it is possible to compute in advance (before the constraint resolution) the variables `ymax` and `ymin` of each sub-tree.

6.2. *FD constraints to specify temporal layout*

A Web-based IETM that permits an end-user to perform his job effectively should take care of the synchronization of the different media.

For specific technical information (description of mission-critical tasks, as repair and maintenance procedures) the need to synchronize the presentation becomes crucial. This problem has been solved by designing specific FD classes that enable to specify how media objects will be synchronized. These classes can handle the four basic categories of media objects:

- text : 2D objects in linear sequence;
- video: 2D layout + time;
- audio: time only; and
- images: 2D layout.

A media object is characterized by a start-time (ST), end-time (ET), and duration-time (DT).

FD constraints are useful tools to provide a declarative scheme specifying synchronization properties for media objects.

For instance, let `x`, `y` and `z` be three media objects.

- `x.start` gives the ST of `x` (the value is a date format (hh.mm.ss), ex. 14:23:04).
- `x.end` gives the ET of `x` (the value is a date format (hh.mm.ss), ex. 09:51:59).
- `x.dur` gives the DT of `x` (the value is a time format (mm.ss), ex. 02.38).

Thus, the statement `x.start = min(y.end,z.end)` specifies that media `x` can start only after the conclusion of the presentation either of the media `y` or the media `z`. In the same way `x.end = z.end` forces the two media to complete their presentation at the same time.

The implementation technique used to realize the synchronization framework is based on JavaBeans properties. JavaBeans [44] is the platform-neutral, component architecture for Java. JavaBeans allows developers to create software modules by putting together reusable components called "beans" that can later be composed together by a third party to create Java applications. Beans interact each other through properties that specify how objects, in our case graphical objects, are manipulated. Let us briefly focus on the beans properties.

Properties are aspects of a Bean's semblance and behavior that are modifiable at design time. More precisely, a property is a named attribute of a bean that is handled by getter and/or setter methods on the bean. The properties are introduced as "design patterns", i.e., specific rules when naming getter and setter method names. Sun provides the BeanBox approach as basic tool to support both the design-time mode (the beans are dropped into the BeanBox where the user can personalize) and a run-time mode, where all configuration details are hidden.

The BeanBox is a simple but powerful mechanism to define interaction schemes between objects, but we aim to improve the communication mechanism that manages the properties between the objects. In fact, once bounded a property, if the user decides to change it, any object that is registered as a listener for that property is notified: the listeners may accept or veto the changing, but in any case binding two properties A to B, specifies that changes in the values A are propagated to B, but not vice versa. Thus beans properties act as constraints to rule relationships between graphical components and how components should respond to external events. The beans constraint solver is then responsible for solving these constraint relationships, but its ability is restricted to straight-forwarding constraints, not in back-forwarding properties. We aim to solve this drawback by extending the beans properties towards bi-directional interaction between media thanks to the FD constraint model.

- The synchronization engine is provided thanks to three new classes added to JavaBean.
- `media_I` to handle a flow of images diffusion.
- `media_S` to treat the sound.
- `media_T` to manage text display.

In Fig. 17, we give basic issues of the implementation choices taken to implement the above classes.

The fields `Startequal`, `Startsup`, `Startinf`, `Endequal`, `Endsup` and `Endinf` belong to the type `Properties`. These slots are useful to define the constraints to apply at the starting (ending) of the media. These slots will contain a symbolic or textual value that specifies the synchronization activity of the media (`media_name.start` identifies a media `media_name` and a constraint on the triggering of the media via the method `setStartequal`).

The resolution of the temporal layout constraint takes place in different phases of systems. During the authoring phase, the designer provides the constraints by declaring the synchronization relationships. The constraint engine then solves the constraints by returning the set of correct values; this is used by the designer to specify the media object behavior assigning the obtained values to the slots start, duration, date. Hence the system is verified and once balanced it can be versioned.

At run time, the constraints that maintain constrained variables are executed whenever a constrained variable must be verified: this allows a transparent control mechanism that guarantees the agreement of the synchronization rules among the media objects.

Figure 18 shows a snapshot of a system developed to assist technical operators in maintenance procedures.

```
class FDVTIME extends FD_var { ... }
public class media extends Applet implements Runnable {
private String Startequal ="";
private String Startsup ="";
private String Startinf ="";
private String Endequal ="";
private String Endsup ="";
private String Endinf ="";
private FDVTIME start= new FDVTIME();
private FDVTIME end= new FDVTIME();
private FDVTIME dur= new FDVTIME();

static Hashtable ListMedia = new Hashtable();
public media() {
ListMedia.put(this.getName(),this);
// all the object MEDIA are usable
    }
public String getStartequal() {
return Startequal;
    }

// we can treat ObjectName , ObjectName.start,
// ObjectName.end , ObjectName.dur
public void setStartequal(String x) {
Startequal = x;
if (isSpecialKey(x)) {
this.start=getValueKey(x)
} else  {
media V=ListMedia.get(getMediaName(x));
char A=getMediaExtension(x);
int C=getMediaConstant(x);
switch (A) {
           case 's' :  new equal(this.start,V.start, C);  break ;
          // X.start= Y.start + C
            case 'e' :  new equal(this.start,V.end, C);    break ;
          // X.start= Y.end + C
           case 'd' :  new equal(this.start,V.dur, C);    break ;
         // X.start= Y.dur + C
           default :   new equal(this.start,V.start, 0);  break ;
        // X.start= Y.start
           }
        }
    }
    ...
}

public class media_I extends media {
...
  }
```

Fig. 17. JavaBeans extension towards temporal media synchronization.

The left side panel depicts the steps of the maintenance procedure. The right side is used to show a video. The behavior of the video has to be synchronized with an audio accompanying the presentation.

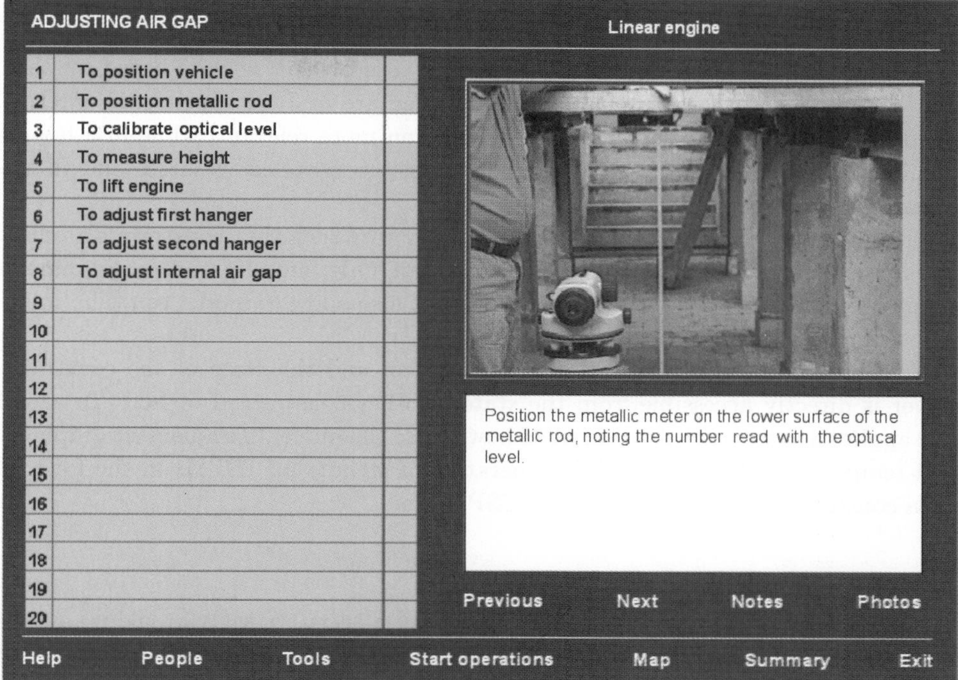

Fig. 18. Temporal constraints.

7. Concluding Remarks

Integrating multimedia objects into a Web synchronized multimedia presentation is a difficult task.

The case study discussed in this work is very different from the previous technologies. It is different from SMIL and HTML+Time, since we do not need to define new standards based on XML or HTML. Considering ASF, the model discussed here is not proprietary, since it is completely based on an extension of Java towards FD-constraint programming.

As a testimony for the expressiveness of constraint-based languages in real application, currently different research groups are active on the liaison between Java and FD constraint programming.

In most of the related works on Java, constraints and the Web, reported in the literature, we notice that the "real" solver is implemented outside Java, often in Prolog. Within such an architecture, the Java program is converted into a program executable on this solver, and the obtained solution is returned back to the Java program, to be used for a GUI (Graphical User Interface). Constraints are used to specify the desired layout of Web documents, as also the behavior of embedded applets.

Hybrid architectures are always conceptually harder to be used correctly, because they require the programmer to be familiar with different models of the underlying abstract machine. This is also the case of CSP solvers based on Java and Prolog. When the constraints to be satisfied are in Java applets, the interdependencies between the solver and Java are even more relevant, while in a hybrid architecture the user has a limited access to the constrained variables and to the solver.

Therefore, we believe that a software architecture such that constraints are first class citizens of the programming language not only simplify the programmer's cognitive load in the design of applications, but also allow to model run time interdependencies in a natural way.

In this paper any FD constraint is an object and the state of the constraint solver is directly accessible from the state of other constrained objects. In a real size application we have also described how to use the model to implement graphical and temporal dependencies in the generation of layouts for IETMs in the form of Java constraints associated to a Java CSP solver.

Acknowledgments

This work has largely benefited by a research collaboration with Ansaldo Trasporti, R & D Naples, Italy (*www.ansaldo.it*) in the frame of the national MURST project "Studio di convertitori innovativi per trazione elettrica: modelli, compatibilità, ambienti di sviluppo ed architetture multimediali secondo standard CALS". This work has been partially supported by the European Social Fund of European Communities.

The authors wish to thank the anonymous referees for their helpful comments on an earlier version of this paper.

References

1. J. Li, "Object-oriented constraint programming for interactive application", PhD Thesis, Department of Numerical Analysis and Computing Science, Royal Institute of Technology (1995), *http://www.nada.kth.se/~li/thesis.html*
2. M. Gleicher, "Integrating constraints and direct manipulation", *Proceedings of the 1992 Symposium on Interactive 3D Graphics* (1992) 171–174.
3. P. S. Barth, "An object-oriented approach to graphical interfaces", *Transactions on Graphics* **5**, no. 2 (1986) 142–172.
4. A. Borning, R. Lin and K. Marriot, "Constraint for the web", *Proceedings of the ACM Multimedia* (November 8–14, 1997).
5. R. Hirsch, "Tractable approximations for temporal constraint handling", *Artificial Intelligence* **116**, nos. 1–2 (January 2000) 287–295.
6. E. L. Jorgensen, "Proposed web-based architecture for the interoperability of naval aviation IETMs", Technical Report CDNSWC-TSSD-98-055, Naval Surface Warfare Center, Maryland, USA (March 1988).
7. Synchronized Multimedia Integration Language, W3C Working Draft (February 2, 1998).

8. ASF — White Paper from Microsoft, *http://www.microsoft.com/asf/whitepr/asfwp.htm*
9. HTML+Time W3C Note *http://wwww.w3.org/TR/1998/NOTE-HTMLplusTIME-19980918*
10. XML (Extensible Markup Language), *http://www.w3.org/XML*
11. HTML — Hypertext Markup Language — *http://www.w3.org/Markup/*
12. W. Hower and W. H. Graf, "Research in constraint-based layout", Visualization, CAD, and Related Topics: A Bibliographical Survey. *Proceedings of the International Workshop on Constraints for Graphics and Visualization*, Cassis, France (September 18, 1995).
13. I. E. Sutherland, "Sketchpad: A man-machine graphical communication system", *AFIPS Spring Joint Computer Conference* (1963).
14. W. M. Newman, "A system for interactive graphical programming", *AFIPS Spring Joint Computer Conference* (1968).
15. K. Arnold, J. Gosling and D. Holmes, *The Java Programming Language*, The Java Series (Addison-Wesley, 2000).
16. U. Montanari, "Networks of constraints: Fundamental properties and applications to picture processing", *Information Science* **7**, no. 2 (1974) 95–132.
17. D. Cabeza, M. Hermenegildo and S. Varma, PilloW/CIAO Library for INTERNET/WWW Programming using Computational Logic Systems, *Workshop on Constraint Reasoning on the Internet*, Schloss Hagenberg, Austria (November 1, 1997).
18. N. F. Zhou, S. Kaneko and K. Yamauchi, "DJ: A Java-based constraint language and system", *Proceedings of the Annual JSSST Conference* (1998).
19. M. Lawal, D. R. Gilbert and A. A. Letichevsky, "A web based course scheduler in constraint logic programming", *Workshop on Constraint Reasoning on the Internet*, Schloss Hagenberg, Austria (November 1, 1997).
20. R. Gilbert, I. Eidhammer and I. Jonasses, "StructWeb: Biosequence structure searching on the Web using clp(FD)", *Workshop on Constraint Reasoning on the Internet*, Schloss Hagenberg, Austria (November 1, 1997).
21. M. Torrens, R. Weigel and B. Faltings, "Java constraint library: Bringing constraint technology on the Internet using the Java language", *Proceedings of the Workshop on Constraint Reasoning on the Internet*, Scloss Hagenberg, Austria (November 1, 1997).
22. V. Loia and M. Quaggetto, "Embed finite domain constraint programming into Java and some web-based applications", *Software-Practice and Experiences* **29**, no. 4 (1999) 311–339.
23. J. Gosling, B. Joy and G. Steele, *The Java Language Specification*, The Java Series (Addison-Wesley, 1996).
24. R. G. Powell, "Estimating CALS benefits — A practical approach to a vexing problem", *Proceedings of CALS'92 Conference and Exposition*, Washington DC (June 1992).
25. A. Borrelli, P. Sposito, R. Esposito, M. Mele, A. Ruggieri, N. Cali, S. Mattera and V. Loia, "Maintenance in railways: an integrated environment of maintenance support", *Proceedings of World Congress on Railway Research (1997)* **D**, Florence, Italy (November 16–19, 1997) 295–303.
26. A. Dattolo and V. Loia, "Distributed information and control in a concurrent hypermedia-oriented system", *International Journal of Software Engineering and Knowledge Engineering* **10**, no. 3 (June 2000) 345–369.
27. P. I. Chang, "Inside the Java web server: An overview of Java web server 1.0", Java Servlets, and the JavaServer Architecture, *http://java.sun.com/features/1997/aug/jws1.html*

28. F. Yellin and T. Lindholm, *The Java Virtual Machine Specification*, The Java Series (Addison-Wesley, 1999).
29. XLS — A Proposal for XLS — *http://www.w3.org/TR/NOTE-XLS.html*
30. H. W. Lie and B. Bos, *Cascading Style Sheets: Designing for the Web* (Addison-Wesley, 1997).
31. Jacobson, *Object-Oriented Software Engineering: User Case Driven Approach* (Addison-Wesley, 1992).
32. B. Stroustrup, *C++ Programming Language*, 3rd edn. (Addison-Wesley, 1998).
33. A. Goldberg, *Smalltalk-80. The Language* (Addison-Wesley, 1989).
34. K. Macworth, "Constraint satisfaction", ed. S. C. Shapiro, *Encyclopedia of Artificial Intelligence* **1** (Wiley Interscience, 1992) 285–293.
35. S. Ruttkay, "Constraint satisfaction: A survey", *CWI Quarterly* **11**, no. 2–3 (1998) 163–214, *http://www.cwi.nl/~miente/Ruttkay/CWIQ-Ruttkay-981005.html*
36. E. Tsang, *Foundation of Constraint Satisfaction* (Academic Press, London, 1993).
37. J. Pearson and P. Jeavons, "A survey of tractable constraint satisfaction problems", Technical Report CSD-TR-97-15 (July 1997), *http://web.comlab.ox.ac.uk/oucl/research/areas/constraints/publications/pubs-ps/survey.ps*
38. V. Kumar, "Algorithms for constraint satisfaction problems: A survey", *AI Magazine* **13**, no. 1 (1992) 32–44.
39. M. Torrens, Solving CSPs, *http://liawww.epfl.ch/~torrens/Project/project/node13.html*
40. J. Gaschnig, "Performance measurement and analysis of certain search algorithms", PhD Thesis Dissertation, Department of Computer Science, Carnege Mellon University (1979).
41. K. Macworth, "Consistency in networks of relations", *Artificial Intelligence* **8**, no. 1 (1977) 99–118.
42. N. Dunkin and S. Allen, "Frequency assignment problems: Representations and solutions", TR CSD-TR-97-14, Department of Computer Science, Royal Holloway, University of London, Egham, Surrey, UK (1997).
43. P. Van Hentenryck, *Constraint Satisfaction in Logic Programming* (MIT Press, 1989).
44. JavaBeans: The Only Component Architecture for Java, *http://www.javasoft.com/beans/*

VERSIONS OF PROGRAM INTEGRATION

TAHAR KHAMMACI
University of Nantes, Institut de Recherche en Informatique de Nantes,
2, Rue de la Houssinière, B.P. 92208, F-44300, Nantes, France
E-mail: khammaci@irin.univ-nantes.fr

ZINE. E. BOURAS
University of Annaba, Department of Computer Science,
P.O. Box 12, DZ-23000, Annaba, Algeria
E-mail: bourasz@yahoo.com

Versions of program integration is an important task in software development and software maintenance. It concerns the merging process necessary when a source file diverges into multiple versions. Given a program *Base* and variants A and B, the goal of program integration is to determine whether the modifications interfere, and if they do not, to create an integrated program that includes both sets of changes as well as the portions of the *Base* program preserved in both variants A and B.

Keywords: Software engineering, configuration management, program integration, versions, software merging, programming languages.

1. Introduction

Versions of program integration is a subarea of software configuration management (SCM). SCM was born out of the 1968 NATO conference and it is an evolution of traditional configuration management. SCM is the discipline of controlling changes to software products and assisting developers in performing coordinated changes to software products. SCM is based on version management like that offered by SCCS [32], RCS [34] and others. The importance of SCM has been widely recognized, as reflected in particular in the Capability Maturity Model (CMM) developed by the Software Engineering Institute [26]. Fundamental SCM concepts are product structure, versioning infrastructure, configuration management, fully versioned DBMS, transaction, workspace, process management and versioning hypermedia [1, 4, 11, 14, 15, 20, 24, 37].

A survey about version models for software configuration management can be found in [10]. This survey provides a classification of different versioning paradigms and defines and relates fundamental concepts such as revisions, variants, configurations, and changes. Also, it provides an overview of systems that have significant impact on the development of the SCM discipline. More recently, a survey about software configuration management in software and hypermedia engineering is presented in [3]. This survey introduces readers to SCM in software and hypermedia engineering, presents general concepts, principles and techniques, and discusses the new challenges proposed by World Wide Web (WWW), which can be seen as a complex distributed hypermedia system and as a software development environment.

About the terminology of SCM, Bendix *et al* [3] defines a version as one specific instance of a configuration item and variants as an alternative versions of a configuration item. Conradi *et al* [10] defines a version model as the items to be versioned, the common properties shared by all versions of an item, and the deltas, that is, the differences between them.

The use of software configuration management in software engineering has several advantages like maintaining consistency between interdependent components, reconstructuring previously recorded software configurations, building derived objets from their sources, identifying of product components and their versions, controlling changes, auditing and review. According to [3], the advantages deriving from the versioning hypermedia are: exploratory authoring, distributed and collaborative authoring, long transactions and referential integrity of links. In other respects, in his survey, Conradi [10] proposes to classify program integration as an intensional versioning; that is, construction of versions based on rules describing consistent combinations. Therefore, program integration tools are semantic merging tools because they take into account the semantic of programs.

This chapter focuses on versions of program integration subarea of the software configuration management area. Versions of program integration is the task of analyzing a program *Base* and two or more variants, together with a correspondance between the program's components, in order to determine whether the changes made to create the variants from *Base* are compatible. If the changes are compatible, combining the variants to form a single, integrated program; otherwise identifying the source of the interference. The goal of versions of program integration is [15]: given a program *Base* and two program variants, *A* and *B*, each created by modifying separate copies of *Base*, the goal of program integration is the merging of *A* and *B* while preserving the changed behavior of *A* with respect to *Base* and the changed behavior of *B* with respect to *Base* and the unchanged behavior common to all three.

There are a number of works on the integration program area [6]: integrating functions [5], logic programs [23], specifications [12], program without procedure calls [15, 36] and program with procedure calls [7, 9]. These works are related to different problems: the integration that treats the *program extensions* [5, 12, 23] and the integration that addresses the *program modifications* problem [7, 9, 15, 36].

Binkley [7] identifies three situations where the need of program integration can arise:

- When a system is "customized" by a user and simultaneously upgraded by a maintainer, and the user desires a customized, upgraded version.
- When a system is being developed by multiple programmers who may simultaneously work with separate copies of the source files.

- When several versions of a program exist and the same enhancement or bug-fix is to be made to all of them.

Therefore, versions of program integration is a fastidious task if we want to make it by hand. Thus, we need a tool for assisting this task. Current program integration tools are text-based or semantic-based tools. Text-based tools like the *diff* 3 utility [27] is the first tool that implements an operation for merging files as strings of text. Semantic-based tools like the Horwitz-Prins-Reps (HPR) tool [15], its improvement, the Yang-Horwitz-Reps (YHR) tool [36], its direct extension [17] and its generalization [7] incorporate notion of semantics-preserving transformations. These tools use *program dependence graphs*, *system dependence graphs* and *program slicing* operations to produce an integrated program. Another semantic-based tool, named ATLACY (Automated Tool for evoLving legACY code), uses *relational expressions* and *program role* to generate an integrated program from a program *Base* and two variants [9, 21].

Specific applications for program integration to programming in the large are: propagation changes through related versions, separating consecutive program modifications and optimistic concurrency control [15].

The remainder of the chapter is organized as follows: Section 2 gives the problems addressed by program integration that are program extensions and program modifications. Section 3 introduces some basic concepts and notions used by most program integration algorithms: *program dependence graphs* (PDG), *system dependence graphs* (SDG), *program slicing*, *relational expressions* and *program role*. As most works are related to integrating program modifications, Sec. 4 contains an overview of program integration modifications techniques that are text-based or semantics-based. Section 5 summarizes the main conclusions of this survey and Sec. 6 provides resources for further reading.

2. Addressed Problems

Versions of program integration addresses two different problems that are *program extensions* [5, 12, 23] and *program modifications* [7, 9, 15, 36]. The distinction between the two problems is as follows: a program extension extends the domain of a partial function without altering any of the initially defined values, while a modification redefines values that were defined initially [5].

2.1. *Integration of program extensions*

Berzins [5] proposes in his work on integrating functions to merge variants A and B without regard to *Base*. The function that results from the merge preserves the (entire) behavior of both; thus, variants A and B cannot be merged if they conflict at any point where both are defined. In the work of Lakhotia *et al* [23] on integrating logic programs, 1-1 join operation is a two-way merge and there is no notion of interference. The authors do not treat the characterization of the semantic properties of the merged program. Finally, in Feather's work [12], specifications do not take

Base program into account, but although the integration process preserves syntactic modifications, it does not guarantee any semantics properties of the integrated specification.

2.2. *Integration of program modifications*

Works addressed to the integration of *program modifications* combine various independent enhancements of some versions of a software system into a new system that includes the semantics of both the enhancements and the old system.

The first program integration *modifications* is the work of Horwitz, Prins, and Reps [15]. These authors have proposed a program integration algorithm named, the HPR algorithm, that provides guarantees about how the execution behavior of the integated program relates to the behaviors of the *Base* program and the A, B variants. It supposes that there is a correspondance among components of *Base*, A and B. This algorithm takes as input a program *Base* and two variants *A*, *B*, and determines that the changes made to *Base* to produce *A* and *B* may interfere or it produces a new program *P* that integrates the two variants *A* and *B* with respect to program *Base*.

The HPR algorithm has been improved by Yang, Horwitz, and Reps [36] to be capable of accomodating semantics-preserving transformations as well as incorporating into the merged program the syntactic and semantic changes introduced into the variant programs. Also, the HPR algorithm has been directly extended [17] and generalized to handle programs that consist of multiple and possibly mutually recursives procedures [7].

Another work on *integrating program modifications* has been made by Bouras, Khammaci, and Ghoul [9]. In this work, a program with multiple procedures is represented formally using *relational expressions* and *program role*. The integration process consists of classifying roles on specific sets, merging results in order to produce a role system of the new version and generating from this the source code of a new version if there is no interference.

3. Program Integration Basic Concepts

Changes in the behaviour of a given program are detected and preserved in the integrated program by using dependence graphs and program slicing operations [7, 15, 17, 36] or *relational expressions* and *program role* [9, 21]. Programs that are concerned by these works are written in a restricted language that has only assignment statements, conditional statements, while loops, output statements and call statements.

3.1. *Program dependence graphs, system dependence graphs and program slicing*

To find the components of a program that represent a potentially changed behavior, the HPR algorithm [15], its improvement [36], its direct extension [17] and its

An Example Program
[1] Program
[2] P:=3.14
[3] rad:3
[4] if DEBUG = 1 then rad:=4 fi
[5] area:=P*(rad*rad)
[6] circ:=2*P*rad
[7] write(area)
[8] write (circ)
[9] End

Fig. 1. An example of monolithic program.

generalization [7] use *program dependence graphs* (PDG), *system dependence graphs* (SDG) and *program slicing* operations on these graphs. A survey about program slicing techniques can be found in [35] and their application on extracting precise *chops* in [22].

3.1.1. *The program dependence graph*

Instructions in a program, are linked by *data and control flow dependencies* [2, 7]. Two instructions have a *data dependencies* if they cannot be executed simultaneously because of a data conflict. *Data dependencies* can be flow dependencies, iteration dependencies, output dependencies or anti-dependencies. There are a *control dependencies* between two instructions e_1 and e_2, when e_1 specifies whether e_2 will be executed [2, 7]. For a *monolithic program*, without procedures, dependencies are represented by a directed graph named *Program Dependence Graph* (PDG) [13].

In this type of graphs, the vertex represents the instructions, and the edges their *data and control dependencies.* The root of PDG is a particular vertex called *Entry* representing the program title. Figure 2 shows the PDG for the example program.

3.1.2. *System dependence graphs*

For a *multi-procedure program*, there are two other dependence forms: *call dependencies* and *summary dependencies.* The first modelizes call statement and parameter passing. The second dependence form represents the execution effect of the input effective parameters on the output effective parameters, by abstracting the called procedure [7]. In this kind of program, dependencies are represented by a *System Dependence Graph* (SDG) [16, 25]. It is composed of a set of PDG linked by connecting edges which depict *call and summary dependencies* [7, 31]. A *call dependence* is represented either by an edge linking a call vertex to an entry vertex, or by edges linking actual vertex to formal vertex. There is an actual-in vertex (respectively

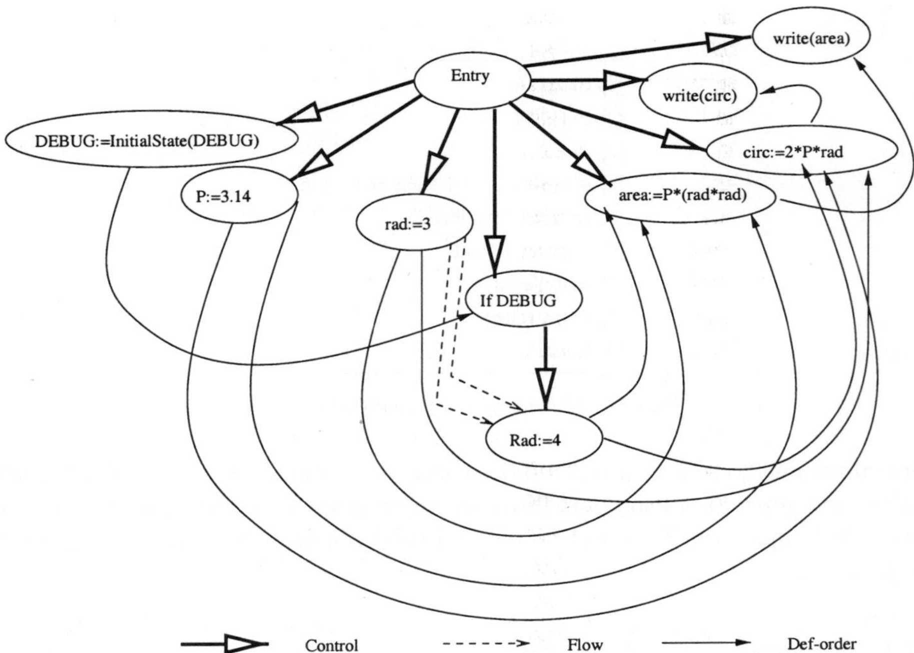

Fig. 2. The Program Dependence Graph (PDG) for the example program of Fig. 1.

actual-out vertex) for each actual-in parameter (respectively actual-out vertex). There is a formal-in vertex (respectively formal-out vertex) for each formal-in parameter (respectively formal-out vertex). Global variables are in general treated as "extra" actual parameters. The *summary edges* are represented by edges linking actual-in vertices to actual-out vertices. Their construction consists in identifying a path between actual-in and actual-out and avoid *unrealizable paths.*

3.1.3. *Program slicing*

The *slice* of a program with respect to program point p and variable x consists of all statements and predicates of the program that might affect the values of x at point p [16]. It has been introduced by Weiser [38] as a powerful method for automatically decomposing a program by analyzing its control and data flow.

A *program slice* is a minimum fragment for which the execution behavior is identical to the initial program behavior with respect to a given point [30, 38]. Program execution behavior with respect to a given point is defined as the set of all variable values generated by the program execution in this point [38]. In Weiser's terminology, a *slicing criterion* of a program P is a pair $\langle p, x\rangle$ where p is a program point and x is a subset of variables in P. In other words, a *program slice* is a program with an execution behavior identical to the one of the initial program with respect to a given criterion, but may have a reduced size.

Draw Source Code

```
[1] Program Draw
[2] Area:Real
[3] P:Real
[4] Rad:Real
[5] Circ:Real
[6] Debug:Integer
[7] Begin
[8] P:=3.1416
[9] Rad:=3
[10] Read (Debug)
[11] if (Debug = 1)then
[12] Rad:=4
[13] eif
[14] Prod(P,Rad,Rad,Area)
[15] Write(Area)
[16] Prod(2,P,Rad,Circ)
[17] Write(Circ)
[18] end
[19] Proc Prod(X,Y,Z,U: Real)
[20] T:Real
[21] begin
[22] Read (T)
[23] if T = 0 then
[24] U:= X*Y*Z
[25] else
[26] U:= X*Y*Z/T
[27] eif
[28] end
```

Fig. 3. An example of multi-procedure program.

Weiser [38] has introduced *backward slice.* A *backward slice* with respect to a program variable x and a given point p is composed of all instructions and predicates from which depends the computation of the value of x at point p. Binkley *et al* [7] have proposed *forward slice.* A *forward slice* with respect to a variable x and point p is composed by all the instructions and predicates which may depend on the value of x at point p. In other words, *forward slice* is the dual of *backward slice.*

Slices are automatically extracted by a traversal of a graph which represents explicitly program data and control flows [13, 16, 30]. For instance, Fig. 4 shows a *backward slice* and *forward slice* of Draw Program described in Fig. 3, with respectively criterion $\langle 15, \mathit{Area}\rangle$ and $\langle 8, P\rangle$.

Suppose that the maintainer wants to know for instance which instructions have an effect on the printed value by the instruction "[15] *Write*(*Area*)". The *backward slice* on criterion $\langle [15], \mathit{Area}\rangle$ allows the automatic extraction of these instructions (Fig. 4(a)). Likewise, if the comprehender wants to know the effect of any modification of the variable P in instruction "[8] P := 3.1416" on the rest of the program, *forward slice* with criterion $\langle [8], P\rangle$ identifies all the instructions which may be affected by this modification (Fig. 4(b)).

Depending on the nature of the program, intraprocedural slicing is a PDG traversal and interprocedural slicing is an identification of paths in the SDG.

3.2. *Relational expressions and program role*

To integrate versions of a program, another method adopts a formal specification modelling in term of *relational expressions* [33]. Thus, an imperative program is represented formally by internal form that explicit flow dependencies. From

(a). Backward Slice $C_r = \langle 15, Area \rangle$	(b). Forward Slice $C_r = \langle 8, P \rangle$
[1] Program Draw	
[2] Area:Real	
[3] P:Real	
[4] Rad:Real	
[6] Debug: Integer	
[7] Begin	
[8] P:=3.1416	**[8] P:=3.1416**
[9] Rad:=3	
[10] Read (Debug)	
[11] if Debug = 1 then	
[12] Rad:=4	
[13] eif	
[14] Prod(P,Rad,Rad,Area)	[14] Prod(P,Rad,Rad,Area)
[15] Write(Area)	[15] Write(Area)
	[16] Prod(2,P,Rad,Circ)
	[17] Write(Circ)
	[18] end
[19] Proc Prod(X,Y,Z,U: Real)	[19] Proc Prod(X,Y,Z,U: Real)
[20] T:Real	
[21] begin	[21] begin
[22] Read (T)	
[23] if T = 0 then	
[24] U:= X*Y*Z	[24] U:= X*Y*Z
[25] else	
[26] U:= X*Y*Z/T	[26] U:= X*Y*Z/T
[27] eif	
[28] End	[28] End

Fig. 4. The results reported by backward and forward slices for the Draw program of Fig. 3.

this internal form, a program is decomposed automatically into roles and their system.

3.2.1. *Relational expressions*

A program is represented formally by an internal form that makes dependencies explicit [9, 21]. Thus, a program is defined by a set of triplets, named *System Internal Form* (*SIF*), that represents explicitly dependencies between elementary actions. This triplet is noted as:

$$\langle Ac, Sem, As \rangle$$

It means that target actions Ac and source actions As have a dependence relationship according to the constraint Sem [2, 21].

(1) Ac and As actions: Elementary actions Ac and As are formally defined by the cartesian product:

$$Var \times Act \times IdDep,$$

where

Var can be a program, control, call variable or a formal parameter.
Act can be a definition, control or reference action.
IdDep is a unique identifier corresponding to an instruction site, an effective parameter or to a formal parameter.

(2) Sem dependence: Sem is defined by the triplet:

$$\langle Cdt, Exp, Ctr\rangle,$$

where

Cdt is a condition which must be true to execute actions Ac, it expresses the control constraint.
Exp is an expression to evaluate actions Ac, it expresses the data constraint.
Ctr is a dependence relationship. It can be a flow dependence FD, control dependence CD, flow and control dependence FCD, formal parameter flow FPF, effective parameter flow EPF.

The internal form of a given program consists of modeling data and control structures. Data structures are composed of variables and control structures are composed of procedure declarations. Every program is seen as a set of triplets. Beeing formal, this modeling allows automatic *program role* decomposition.

3.2.2. *Program role and role system*

From the SIF, an algorithm automatically decomposes the program into roles and role system. A role represents the behaviour by which a variable or a procedure is involved in the program. It is composed by all the instructions which define or modify a variable. Program role concept allows us to raise the abstraction levels of reasoning and it is not dependent on the number of instructions but rather on the number of different variables and procedures in a program. A *program role* is composed of its name, its type (control or information role), its behaviour (a list of statements that define and modify the role) and an interface (interactions with other roles). It has the structure as in Fig. 5. Figure 6 shows the schema of Rad *program role* extracted from the example program of Fig. 1.

A *role system* is composed by a set or roles operating in an environment according to a set of relationships between them. This *role system* represents the logical structure of program. It has a schema composed by its name, a set of *roles* and a

```
Role Name;
      Type : information or control;
      Statements : List of statements;
      Interface :
                 In : List of roles
                 Out : List of roles
End Role
```

Fig. 5. General schema of program role concept.

```
Role Rad;
      Type : information;
      Statements :
      [4] Rad : Real;
      [9] Rad : 3;
      [12] Rad : 4;
      Interface :
                 In : Draw
                 Out : Area, Circ
End Role
```

Fig. 6. Schema of Rad program role extracted from the example program of Fig. 3.

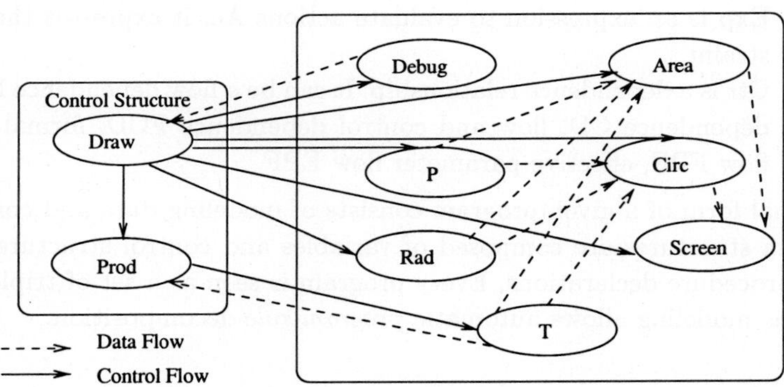

Fig. 7. Role System Graph corresponding to the example program of Fig. 3.

set of relationships between roles. A program P is defined by:

$$P = \{R, A, S, D\}$$

where

R is a set of roles in the system. R = {Ri/Ri = InformationRole ∨ Ri = ControlRole}.

A is a set of role actions. A = {Declare, Assign, Read, Write, Enter, Call, If, While, In, Out}.

S is a set of types of dependencies between actions. S = {FD, CD, FCD, EPF, FPF}.

D is a set of dependence relationships between roles actions. D = {Di/Di = $\langle Ac, Sem, As\rangle$ ∧ As, Ac ∈ A ∧ Sem ∈ S}.

Sets A and S are predefined for every program whereas sets R and D are specific to every program.

Roles and their interactions are represented explicitly by an oriented graph named *Role System Graph* (RSG) which represents the *global level.* In the RSG graph, a node depicts a *role name* and arcs the dependencies between *roles.* Figure 7 shows the RSG graph of the example program of Fig. 1.

In addition, the actions on the same *role* and their dependencies are represented explicitly by an oriented graph, named *Role Action Graph* (RAG) which symbolizes the *local level.* In this graph, a node symbolizes a *role action* and an arc a dependence relationship between *role actions.*

Extraction of *role system* consists of identifying the pairs $\langle X, Y \rangle$ which means that the role X depends on the role Y [21].

4. Program Integration Techniques

Versions of program integration can be grouped into two families: text-based and semantics-based techniques.

4.1. *Text-based integration technique*

Text-based integration technique, such as the one used by the UNIX *diff*3 utility [27], reconciles divergent lines of development. This technique has the advantage of being applicable to merging documents, data files, and other text objects as well as to merging programs. The problem with such technique is that it implements an operation for merging files as strings of text. This technique is necessarily of limited utility for integrating programs because the manner in which two programs are merged is unsafe. One has no guarantee about how the execution behavior of the merged program relates to the behaviors of the *Base* program and its variants.

Example: Figs. 8 and 9 show an example of text-based integration. Figure 8 presents three programs Base, A, and B. Figure 9(a) shows the incorporation in variant B of changes between the base program and variant A and Fig. 9(b) shows the incorporation in variant A of changes between the base program and variant B.

(a). Base Program	(b). Variant A	(c). Variant B
[1] If P then x:=0 fi	[1] If S then w:=4 fi	[1] If Q then x:=1 fi
[2] If Q then x:=1 fi	[2] If R then w:=3 fi	[2] If P then x:=0 fi
[3] y:=x	[3] z:=w	[3] y:=x
[4] If R then w:=3 fi	[4] If P then x:=0 fi	[4] If R then w:=3 fi
[5] If S then w:=4 fi	[5] If Q then x:=1 fi	[5] If S then w:=4 fi
[6] z:=w	[6] y:=x	[6] z:=w
[7] end	[7] end	[7] end

Fig. 8. An example of text-based integration, programs Base, A, and B.

(a). (Base, A), B	(b). (Base, B), A
[1] If Q then x:=1 fi	[1] If S then w:=4 fi
[2] If P then x:=0 fi	[2] If R then w:=3 fi
[3] y:=x	[3] z:=w
	[4] If P then x:=0 fi
	[5] If Q then x:=1 fi
	[6] y:=x
[7] end	[7] end

Fig. 9. The results of integrating programs Base, A, and B from Fig. 8.

In Fig. 9(a), the result program is unacceptable as the integration of Base, variants A and B whereas in Fig. 9(b), the result program is exactly the same as the one given as variant A and it does not account for the differences in behavior between Base et variant B; thus, it can hardly be considered an acceptable integration of Base, A, and B.

4.2. *Semantics-based integration technique*

Semantics-based integration technique makes use of knowledge of the programming language to determine the behavioral changes, in the test for interference, and in the method for combining non-interfering variants. Thus, this technique provides guarantees about how the execution behavior of the merged program relates to the behaviors of the base program and its variants.

4.2.1. *Integrating program without procedure calls*

The first program integration algorithm — called the HPR algorithm — was formulated by Horwitz, Prins, and Reps [15]. It is the first algorithm for semantics-based program integration. The HPR algorithm provides the first theoretical foundation for building a semantics-based program integration tool. Changes in behavior rather than changes in text are detected, and are preserved in the integrated program.

The HPR algorithm consists of the following steps:

(1) *Determining changed and preserved slices.* The PDGs G_{Base}, G_A, and G_B are constructed. Correspondences between "related" vertices of these graphs are assumed to be available. Sets of the affected points of G_A and G_B w.r.t G_{Base} are determined; these consist of vertices in G_A (G_B) which have a different slices in G_{Base}.

(2) *Forming the merged graph.* A merged PDG G_M is constructed from G_A, G_B, and the sets of affected points determined in step 1.

(3) *Testing for interference.* Using G_A, G_B, G_M and the sets of affected points computed in step 1, the algorithm determines whether or not the behaviors

of A and B are preserved in G_M. There are two possible ways in which the graph G_M can fail to represent a satisfactory integrated program. There are referred to as "Type I interference" and "Type II interference". Type I interference criterion is based on a comparison of slices of the variant graphs and with those of G_M. If the *slices*, according to the changed entities in a given variant are different in variant graphs and G_M then we get "Type I interference". "Type II interference" appears in the attempted reconstitution of merged program from G_M. It is possible that there is no such program because the merged graph G_M can be an unfeasible program dependence graph. If neither kind of interference occurs, program M is constructed from G_M. Otherwise, the change in A and B cannot be integrated.

Example: Fig. 10 shows four programs: Base (Fig. 10(a)), A (Fig. 10(b)), B (Fig. 10(c)) and Integrated Program (Fig. 10(d)). Program A has a supplementary instruction to compute diam. Program B, includes changes of P := 3.1416 instead of P := 3.14 and the name radius instead of rad. Integrated program is the result of integrating programs Base, A and B.

A semantic justification for the HPR algorithm is presented in [28] and an alternative formulation of this algorithm, based on Brouwerian algebras is presented in [29]. The algebraic laws that hold in such algebras are used to restate the algorithm and to prove properties such as associativity of consecutive integrations. The HPR algorithm has been improved by Yang, Horwitz and Reps [36] to extract what is changed in each of the variants by using limited slices rather than full slices. The YHR algorithm is capable of accomodating semantics preserving transformations.

(a). Base Program	(b). Variant A	(c). Variant B	(d). Integrated Program
Prog Base	Prog A	Prog B	Prog NewVers
P:=3.14	P:=3.14	P:=3.1416	P:=3.1416
rad:=3	rad:=3	radius:=3	radius:=3
If Debug then	If Debug then	If Debug then	If Debug then
rad:=4 fi	rad:=4 fi	radius:=4 fi	radius:=4 fi
area:=P*(rad*rad)	diam:=2*P	area:=P*(radius*radius)	diam:=2*P
circ:=2*P*rad	area:=P*(rad*rad)	circ:=2*P*radius	area:=P*(radius*radius)
Write(area)	circ:=2*P*rad	Write(area)	circ:=2*P*radius
Write(circ)	Write (diam)	Write(circ)	Write(diam)
End	Write (area)	End	Write(area)
	Write (circ)		Write(circ)
	End		End

Fig. 10. An example of semantics-based program integration, programs Base, A, B and integrated program.

4.2.2. *Integrating program with procedure calls*

The HPR algorithm has been directly extended to take into account programs with procedures calls [17]. The multi-procedure integration algorithm that results from the extension of HPR, makes use of *System Dependence Graph* (SDG) and interprocedural program slicing. As in the the HPR algorithm, the multi-procedure integration algorithm involves three steps: in the step 1, it identifies *slices* that represent changed behavior and *slices* that represent preserved behaviors, in the step 2, it combines these *slices* to form the merged *system dependence graph*, and in the step 3, it tests for interference. However, each intraprocedural slicing operation is reinterpreted as an interprocedural slicing operation that is a *System Dependence Graph* (*SDG*) operation. The algorithm obtained is unsatisfactory because it fails (i.e., reports interference) on many examples for which, intuitively, integration should succeed.

Example: Fig. 11 shows four programs: Base (Fig. 11(a)), A (Fig. 11(b)), B (Fig. 11(c)) and Integrated Program (Fig. 11(d)). Program A includes one modification, a:=3 instead of a:=1. Program B, includes changes of b:=4 instead of b:=2. The proposed integrated program is the intuitive result of integrating programs Base, A and B. For this example, the direct extension algorithm reports interference whereas the integration should succeed. Because the backward slices b(S_{Base},{x:=x+1}), b(S_A,{x:=x+1}), and b(S_B,{x:=x+1}) are pairwise unequal, the statement "x:=x+1" is an affected point in both variants; therefore the slices b(S_A,{x:=x+1}) and b(S_B,{x:=x+1}) are both included in the merged SDG S_M. However, because both slices are included in S_M, there are both "corrupted" in S_M; that is, although b(S_A,{x:=x+1}), and b(S_B,{x:=x+1}) are sub-graph of S_M, neither b(S_A,{x:=x+1}) nor b(S_B,{x:=x+1}). Consequently, graph S_M is found to have "Type I interference", and the integration algorithm reports interference.

(a). Base Program	(b). Variant A	(c). Variant B	(d). Proposed Integrated Program
Proc main	Proc A	Proc B	Proc main
a:=1	a:=3	a:=1	a:=3
b:=2	b:=2	b:=4	b:=4
call Incr(a)	call Incr(a)	call Incr(a)	call Incr(a)
call Incr(b)	call Incr(b)	call Incr(b)	call Incr(b)
Write(a)	Write(a)	Write(a)	Write(a)
Write(b)	Write(b)	Write(b)	Write(b)
End	End	End	End
Proc Incr(x)	Proc Incr(x)	Proc Incr(x)	Proc Incr(x)
x:=x+1	x:=x+1	x:=x+1	x:=x+1
end	end	end	end

Fig. 11. An example of program integration with procedure calls using the HPR algorithm direct extension.

The extension of the HPR algorithm needs to be revised to characterize better the goals of multi-procedure integration. In particular, the integration algorithm should capture the notion of changed execution behavior at a finer level of granularity. Thus, the HPR algorithm has been generalized to handle programs that consist of multiple (and possibly mutually resursive) procedures [7]. The key issue of the HPR algorithm generalization is how to take into account different calling contexts when determining what has changed in the variants A and B. The solution proposed involves identifying two types of components: the components affected regardless of how the procedure is called and the components affected by a change or new calling context. The generalized HPR algorithm makes use of *System Dependence Graph* (*SDG*) and interprocedural program slicing to identify these components, as well as components in *Base*, A and B with the same behavior.

Another algorithm for integrating multi-procedure programs has been proposed by Bouras, Khammaci and Ghoul [9]. This algorithm makes use of *relational expressions* to formally representing a *Base* program and its variants A and B, and *program role* in order to modeling the behaviour by which a variable or a procedure intervenes in the *Base* program and its variants. *Program roles* are extracted, compared and merged in order to produce a new version of the program. Changes can be caused by a local change according to a given *role* (intra-role) of by a global change between *roles* (inter-roles). Changes may be semantic in nature or not. Semantic changes may lead to unforeseen interference that leads to failure of the integration process. This algorithm involves five steps:

(1) Step 1: It carries out lexical, syntactic and semantic analysis of a source code program, gives a table of variable definitions, references and call points and elaborates program in the internal form (SIF) and instrumented source code.
(2) Step 2: It extracts *program roles* and *role system* information of every program (*Base* and *variants A, B*) and displays to the user the list of involved *program roles* and *role system.*
(3) Step 3: It deterrences four sets of *program roles* that are Unaltered Roles, Changed Named Roles, Changed Behaviours Roles, Changed Names and Behaviours Roles, and, four sets of relationships that are Unaltered Dependencies, Source Dependencies Changed, Target Dependencies Changed, Source and Target Dependencies Changed.
(4) Step 4: It chooses the *program roles* and the *role system* corresponding to the new version if there is no interference.
(5) Step 5: It reconstitutes the source code of the new version.

Example: Fig. 12 shows three programs: Base (Fig. 12(a)), A (Fig. 12(b)), B (Fig. 12(c)). Program A includes a supplementary instructions to calculate diam. Program B includes a change of instructions (PI := 3.1416 instead of PI := 3.14) and a change of name (radius instead of rad). Figure 13 shows the result of Step 2 of the algorithm.

(a). Base Program	(b). Variant A	(c). Variant B
program Base	program A	program B
var area:real	var area:real	var area:real
Pi:real	Pi:real	Pi:real
radius:real	radius:real	circ:real
Circ:real	Circ:real	Circ:real
debug:integer	debug:integer	debug:integer
Proc prod(x,y,z:real;var	diam:Real	Proc prod(x,y,z:real;var
u:real)		u:real)
var t:real	var t:real	var t:real
begin read(t)	begin	begin read(t)
if (T=0.0) then u:=x*y*x	read(t)	if (T=0.0) then u:=x*y*z
else u:=x*y*z/t	if (T=0.0) then u:=x*y*x	else u:=x*y*z/t
end	else u:=x*y*z/t	end
begin Pi:=3.14	end	begin
Radius:=3.0	begin	Pi:=3.1416
read (debug)	Pi:=3.14	Rad:=3.0
if (debug = 1) then	Radius:=3.0	read(debug)
Radius:=4.0		
prod(Pi,Radius,Radius,	Diam:=2.0*Pi	if (debug=1) then Rad:=4.0
Area)		
write(Area)	read(debug)	prod(Pi,Rad,Rad,Area)
Prod(2.0,Pi,Radius,Circ)	if (debug=1) then Radius:=4.0	write(Area)
write(circ)	prod(Pi,Radius,Radius,Area)	Prod (2.0,Pi,Rad,Circ)
end	write(Area)	write(circ)
	Prod(1.0,Diam,Radius,Circ)	end
	write(circ)	
	end	

Fig. 12. An example of program integration with procedure calls using program role concept.

Program	Roles
Base	Base, Debug, Prod, Area, PI, radius, Circ, T, Screen
A	A, Prod, Debug, Area, PI, radius, Circ, T, Screen, Diam
B	B, Prod, Debug, Area, PI, rad, Circ, T, Screen

Fig. 13. The result of the role decomposition step from Fig. 12.

The integration algorithm is based on intra-role and inter-role comparisons. Intra-role changes concern the change of name or behavior of a given role, without modification of its interface. It is then necessary to sort roles according to types of changes to identify semantic changes. By using role systems and roles worked out in the first, four sets of roles are distinguished: UR, CRN, CRB, CRNB.

UR (Unaltered Roles) contains unaltered roles in all programs. In this case the resulting role is the role of Base. In the example of Fig. 12, we have in this set: Screen, Area, Circ, Debug, Prod and T. CRN (Changed Role Names) concerns the set of roles having changed names but the same behavior. Informally, roles of CRN are the roles having only syntactic changes of their names in one or several variants. In the example of Fig. 12, Base (changed in A and B) and Radius (Rad in variant A) belong to this set. The resulting role has as name a concatenation of variant name roles. CRB (Changed Role Behaviors) concerns roles having changed behaviors but keep the same name. Informally, roles of CRB are the roles having semantic changes in one or several instructions in variants. In the example of Fig. 12, role PI has the same name in all programs. The change of PI:=3.14 by PI:=3.1416 induces that this role belongs to CRB. If role behavior has changed in a variant then this role will be the resulting role. Otherwise we have interference. Informally, CRNB (Changed Role Names and Behaviors) roles have semantic and syntactic changes in variants. CRNB represents the deleted roles from Base or the inserted roles in variants. In this case, if role belongs only to Base then it is interpreted by its elimination during the integration. Then it will be eliminated in the new version. If it belongs only to variants, it is interpreted by its insertion in one or several variants then in the new version. When we have an interference, the process produces failure.

Inter-roles changes concern global dependencies between roles. To identify the global changes four sets of relation are distinguished: UD, SDC, TDC, STDC.

UD (Unaltered Dependencies) concerns dependencies having identical source and target roles. In this case, we insert dependencies of Base in the *role system* of new version. SDC (Source Dependencies Change) is the set of dependencies where targets are the same and sources are different. TDC (Target Dependencies Change) is the set of relations where sources are the same and targets are different. STDC

```
NewVersion.pas
program Base_A_B ;
var area: real; radius: real; debug: integer; Diam :real; Circ :real ; Pi :real ;
procedure prod( x :real; y :real; z :real; var u: real) ;
var t : real ;
begin
read( t ) ; if ( t = 0.0 ) then u := x * y * z ;
else u := x * y * z / t ;
end ;

begin
radius := 3.0 ; read( debug ) ; Pi := 3.1416 ; Diam := 2.0 * Pi ;
if ( debug = 1 ) then radius := 4.0 ;
prod ( Pi, radius, radius, area ) ; write( area ) ;
prod ( 1.0, Diam, radius, Circ ) ; write( Circ ) ;
end.
```

Fig. 14. The result of integrated programs Base, A, and B from Fig. 12.

(Source and Target Dependencies changed) concerns the set of relations where the source and targets are different. For every element of SDC, TDC or STDC the resulting relations are dependencies of variants.

After the identification of intra-role and inter-role changes, the source code of the resulting program is generated from *role system* and *roles* selected previously. The order of instructions is done according to the constraint Sem that is composed by a triplet ⟨Cdt, Exp, Ctr⟩ (defined in Sec. 3.2). According to the control constraint Cdt and the data constraint expression Exp we can order the internal form of the program and write its source code. Figure 14 shows the source code of the new version for the programs of Fig. 12.

5. Conclusion

SCM as the discipline of organizing, controlling and managing evolving software systems. Over the past twenty years, SCM has been largely investigated and it has become an indispensable support for the development and authoring of software products. This chapter focuses on versions of program integration that is a sub-area of software configuration management. We have presented versions of program integration techniques that can be found in the present literature. Program integration is the task of analyzing a *Base* program and some versions (*A* and *B* for example) of this program in order to determine the set of program components of the new version that represent syntactic and semantic changes.

Program integration addresses two problems: program extensions and program modifications. Versions of program integration methods use *program dependence graphs*, *system dependence graphs*, *program slicing*, *relational expressions* and *program role*. Program integration modification techniques are text-based or semantics-based. The problem with the text-based technique is that it implements an operation for merging files as strings of text. This technique is necessarily of limited utility for integrating programs because the manner in which two programs are merged is unsafe. One has no guarantee about how the execution behavior of the merged program relates to the behaviors of the *Base* program and its variants. Semantic-based techniques provide such garantees, one must use information about the languages' semantics in the identification of behavioral changes, in the test for interference, and in the the method for combining non-interfering variants. Using program slicing techniques to program integration has the advantages of simplicity, safety and efficiency [6]. However, the facts that we cannot obtain abstraction levels and that there are as many slices as instructions in a given program make this approach inadequate to program integration [8]. *Program role* allows us to get abstraction levels, it is not due to the number of instruction but rather to the number of different variables and procedures of programs. From the program decomposition, the integration process consists in classifying *program roles* on specific sets, merging results in order to produce *role system* of new version and generating from this, the source code of a new version.

Finally, the HPR algorithm, its improvement, its direct extension and its generalization have been implemented in a prototype system, called the Wisconsin Program Integration System. This system is written in C and SSL (the specification language of the Synthesizer Generator) and runs under UNIX on a variety of workstations. The algorithm which use *program role* have been implemented in a prototype called ATLACY. This tool is written in a Visual C++ environment.

6. Resources

There is no journals or conferences completely dedicated to versions of program integration. Therefore, as versions of program integration is a software configuration management sub-area, the International Symposium on Software Configuration Management (SCM) is the major annual venue on this theme. The SCM-10 is an ICSE workshop and will be held in Toronto, Canada, May, 2001. Other conferences that address the theme of software configuration management are: *The International Conference on Software Engineering* (*ICSE*), *The European Software Engineering Conference* (*ESEC*) and *The ACM SIGSOFT Symposium on the Foundations of Software Engineering.*

The Information and Sofware Technology Journal (Elsevier Science) has published a Special Issue on Program Slicing in December 1998. This special issue was forwarded by M. Weiser. Other journals that edit articles on program integration are: *The ACM Transactions on Software Engineering and Methodology*, *The ACM Transactions on Programming Languages and Systems*, *The ACM Computing Surveys, The IEEE Transactions on Sofware Engineering and Software-Practice and Experience*, published by John Wiley & Sons.

Pointers for further readings on software configuration management can be found in *http://www.cmtoday.com/yp/configurationmanagement.html* and an attempt of unification of terminology have been proposed in *http://www.stsc.hill.af.mil/crosstalk/1995/jan/terms.asp.* Other pointers can be found in the IEEE standard [18] and [19]. The main project on versions of program integration is the Wisconsin Program Integration Project at the University of Wisconsin-Madison (*http://www.cs.wisc.edu/wpis/html*).

References

1. N. Belkhatir and J. Estublier, "Experience with a data base of programs", *Proceedings of the ACM SIGSOFT/SIGPLAN Software Engineering Symposium on Practical Software Development Environments*, Palo Alto, CA, USA, ACM SIGPLAN Notices **22**, no. 1 (1986) 84–91.
2. M. S. Bendelloul, Z. E. Bouras, S. Ghoul and T. Khammaci, "Program understanding assistance: A model and a fragmentation algorithm", *Software Engineering Review*, no. 45 (1997) 13–23 (in French).
3. L. Bendix, A. Dattalo and F. Vitali, "Software configuration management in software engineering and hypermedia engineering: A survey", *Handbook of Software Engineering and Knowledge Engineering* **1**, (World Scientific Publishing Company, Singapore, 2001) Vol. 1: Fundamentals, ISBN: 981-02-4973-X.

4. Y. Bernard, M. Lacroix, P. Lavency and M. Vanhoedenaghe, "Configuration management in an open environment", *Proceedings of the First European Software Engineering Conference* Strasbourg, France, *Lecture Notes in Computer Scienc 289* (Springer-Verlag, 1987) 35–43.
5. V. Berzins, "On merging software extensions", *Acta Informatica* **23** (1986) 607–619.
6. V. Berzins, *Software Merging and Slicing* (IEEE Computer Society Press, Los Alamitos, 1995).
7. D. Binkley, S. Horwitz and T. Reps, "Program integration for languages with procedure calls", *ACM Transactions on Software Engineering and Methodology* **4**, no. 1 (1995) 3–35.
8. Z. E. Bouras, T. Khammaci and S. Ghoul, "Role system to software maintenance", *Proceedings of the 4th African Conference on Research in Computer Science*, Dakar, Senegal (1998) 145–156 (in French).
9. Z. E. Bouras, T. Khammaci and S. Ghoul, "A new approach for program integration", *SAC Journal* **25** (2000) 3–11.
10. R. Conradi and B. Westfechtel, "Version models for software configuration management", *ACM Computing Surveys*, **30**, no. 2 (1998) 232–282.
11. K. Dittrich, W. Gotthard and P. C. Lockeman, "DAMOKLES — A database system for software system engineering", *Proceedings of the International Workshop on Advanced Programming Environment*, Trondheim, Norway (1986) 353–371.
12. M. S. Feather, "Detecting interference when merging specification evolutions", Information Sciences Institute, University of South California, Marina Del Rey, CA (1989).
13. J. Ferrante, K. Ottenstein and J. Warren, "The program dependence graph and its use in optimization", *ACM Transactions on Programming Languages and Systems* **9**, no. 3 (1987) 319–349.
14. T. Haque and J. Montes, "A configuration management system and more (on Alcatel's PMCS)", *Proceedings of the ACM Workshop on Software Version and Configuration Control*, Grassau, Germany (1988) 217–227.
15. S. Horwitz, J. Prins and T. Reps, "Integration non-interfering versions of programs", *ACM Transaction on Programming Languages and Systems* **11**, no. 3 (1989) 345–387.
16. S. Horwitz, T. Reps and D. Binkley, "Interprocedural slicing using dependence graphs", *ACM Transaction on Programming Languages and Systems* **12**, no. 1 (1990) 26–60.
17. S. Horwitz and T. Reps, "The use of program dependence graphs in software engineering", *Proceedings of the 14th ACM International Conference on Software Engineering*, Melbourne, Australia (1992) 392–411.
18. IEEE, *Standard for Software Configuration Management Plans: ANSI/IEEE Std 828-1983*, IEEE, New York (1983).
19. IEEE, *Guide to Software Configuration Management Plans: ANSI/IEEE Std 1042-1987*, IEEE, New York (1987).
20. G. E. Kaiser, "Modeling configurations as transactions", *Proceedings of the Second International Workshop on Software Configuration Management*, Princeton, USA (1989) 129–132.
21. T. Khammaci, Z. E. Bouras and M. S. Bendelloul, "Program understanding assistance: A role-based decomposition", *Proceedings of the 12th International Conference on Software Engineering and Knowledge Engineering* (*SEKE'2000*), Chicago, IL, USA (2000) 294–301.

22. T. Khammaci, Z. E. Bouras and S. Ghoul, "Program slicing: Precise chops extraction approaches", *Handbook of Software Engineering and Knowledge Engineering* **1** (World Scientific Publishing Company, Singapore 2001) Vol. 1: Fundamentals, ISBN: 981-02-4973-X.
23. A. Lakhotia and L. Sterling, "Composing recursive logic programs with clausal join", *New Generation Computing* **6**, no. 2 (1988) 211–225.
24. D. B. Leblang and R. P. Chase Jr, "Computer-aided software engineering in a distributed workstation environment", *Proceedings of the ACM SIGSOFT/SIGPLAN Software Environment Symposium on Practical Software Development Environment*, Pittsburg, USA, ACM SIGPLAN Notices **19**, no. 5 (1984) 104–112.
25. K. J. Ottenstein and L. M. Ottenstein, "The program dependence graph in a software development environment", *Proceedings of the ACM SIGSOFT/SIGPLAN Software Engineering Symposium on Pratical Software Development Environments*, Pittsburg, PA, USA (1984) 177–184, and *Sofware Engineering Notes* **9**, no. 3.
26. M. C. Paulk, C. V. Weber, B. Curtis and M. B. Chrissis, *The Capability Maturity Model-Guidelines for Improving the Software Process* (Addison-Wesley, Reading, MA, USA, 1997).
27. T. Reps and T. Teiltelbaum, *The Synthesizer Generator: A System for Constructing Language-based Editors* (Springer Verlag, New-York, USA, 1988).
28. T. Reps and W. Yang, "The semantics of program slicing and program integration", *Proceedings of the Colloquium on Current Issues in Programming Languages, Lecture Notes in Computer Science 352* (Springer Verlag, 1989) 60–74.
29. T. Reps, "Algebraic properties of program integration", *Science of Computer Programming* **17** (1991) 139–215.
30. T. Reps, S. Horwitz, M. Sagiv and G. Rosay, "Speeding up slicing", *ACM SIGSOFT Software Engineering Notes* **19**, no. 5 (1994) 11–20.
31. T. Reps and G. Rosay, "Precise interprocedural chopping", *ACM SIGSOFT Software Engineering Notes* **20**, no. 4 (1995) 41–52.
32. M. J. Rochkind, "The source code control system", *IEEE Transaction on Software Engineering* **1**, no. 4 (1975) 364–370.
33. J. M. Spivey, *Understanding Z: A Specification Language and its Formal Semantics*, (Cambridge University Press, UK, 1988).
34. W. F. Tichy, "RCS — A system for version control", *Software Practice and Experience* **15**, no. 7 (1985) 637–654.
35. F. Tip, "A survey of program slicing techniques", *Journal of Programming Languages* **3**, no. 5 (1995) 121–189.
36. W. Yang, S. Horwitz and T. Reps, "A program integration algorithm that accomodates semantic-preserving transformations", *ACM Transaction on Software Engineering and Methodology* **1**, no. 3 (1992) 310–354.
37. F. Vitali, "Versioning hypermedia", *ACM Computing Surveys*, **31** (1999) Issue 4es.
38. M. Weiser, "Program slicing", *IEEE Transactions on Software Engineering* **10**, no. 4 (1984) 352–357.

A SURVEY OF SOFTWARE INSPECTION TECHNOLOGIES

OLIVER LAITENBERGER
Fraunhofer Institute for Experimental Software Engineering (IESE), Sauerwiesen 6, D-67661 Kaiserslautern, Germany
E-mail: Oliver.Laitenberger@iese.fhg.de

Software inspection is a proven method that enables the detection and removal of defects in software artifacts as soon as these artifacts are created. It usually involves activities in which a team of qualified personnel determines whether the created artifact is of sufficient quality. Detected quality deficiencies are subsequently corrected. In this way, an inspection cannot only contribute towards software quality improvement, but also lead to significant budget and time benefits. These advantages have already been demonstrated in many software development projects and organizations.

After Fagan's seminal paper presented in 1976, the body of work in software inspection has greatly increased and matured. This survey is to provide an overview of the large body of contributions in the form of incremental improvements and/or new methodologies that have been proposed to leverage and amplify the benefits of inspections within software development and even maintenance projects. To structure this large volume of work, it introduces, as a first step, the core concepts and relationships that together embody the field of software inspection. In a second step, the survey discusses the inspection-related work in the context of the presented taxonomy.

The survey is beneficial for researchers as well as practitioners. Researchers can use the presented survey taxonomy to evaluate existing work in this field and identify new research areas. Practitioners, on the other hand, get information on the reported benefits of inspections. Moreover, they find an explanation of the various methodological variations and get guidance on how to instantiate the various taxonomy dimensions for the purpose of tailoring and performing inspections in their software projects.

Keywords: Software quality, defect costs, software inspection, reading techniques.

1. Introduction

It has been more than 20 years since Michael Fagan described the inspection approach in the software domain [40].[a] Since then many others, such as Gilb and Graham [47], have fine-tuned the inspection method to make it an even more cost-effective instrument for tackling quality deficiencies and defect costs. In fact, it has been claimed that inspection technologies can lead to the detection and correction of anywhere between 50% and 90% of the defects [47]. Moreover, early defect detection and removal improve the predictability of software projects and

[a] In this survey, we consider inspection to be an approach that involve a well-defined and disciplined process in which qualified personnel analyze a software product using a reading technique for the purpose of detecting defects. We acknowledge that others may define the term "software inspection" differently.

help project managers stay within schedule, since problems are unveiled throughout the early development phases. Most of the stated benefits of inspections have already been demonstrated in many projects and organizations. However, most of the published inspection work has not been integrated into a broader context, that is, into a coherent body of knowledge, hence making the work difficult to reconcile and evaluate for software practitioners. To provide a systematic and encompassing view of the research and practice in software inspection, this survey portrays the current state of the art and practice as published in available software inspection publications.

The survey consists of two main parts. The first includes a taxonomy of the core concepts and relationships that together embody the software inspection field. This taxonomy is organized around four primary dimensions — technical, economics, organizational, and tools — with which we attempt to characterize the nature of software inspection. While these primary dimensions are most relevant for the major areas of software development, we elicited from the literature particular sub-dimensions that are principal for the work in the software inspection area. The second part describes the various contributions and integrates them into the taxonomy, taking into account their specific particularities. This can make it much easier for researchers and practitioners to get an overview of relevant inspection work including its empirical validation. Researchers and practitioners can profit from this survey in different ways. Researchers can use the presented taxonomy to characterize new work in the inspection-related field and identify fruitful areas for future research. Practitioners, on the other hand, find information about inspection-related benefits. This information may pave the road for the use of the inspection method in projects. Moreover, they find a road-map in the form of a taxonomy that helps them focus quickly on the best suited inspection approach adapted to their particular environment.

1.1. *Integration of software inspection in the development context*

One prevalent reason for the use of inspection technology in software projects is the inevitability of defects. Even with the best development technologies in place, defects cannot be completely avoided. This stems from the fact that software development is a human-based activity, and, thus, prone to defects. A defect can be characterized as any product anomaly, that is, any deviation from the required quality properties that needs to be tracked and resolved.

To be most effective, software inspections need to be fully integrated into the software development process from a technical as well as from a management point of view. Figure 1 presents an example using a simplified version of the Vorgehensmodell (V-Model) [19]. The products are sufficiently generic, and are found in one form or another in most, if not all, development process models.

The V-model is not a process model *per se*, but rather a product model since it does not define the sequence of development steps that must be followed to create

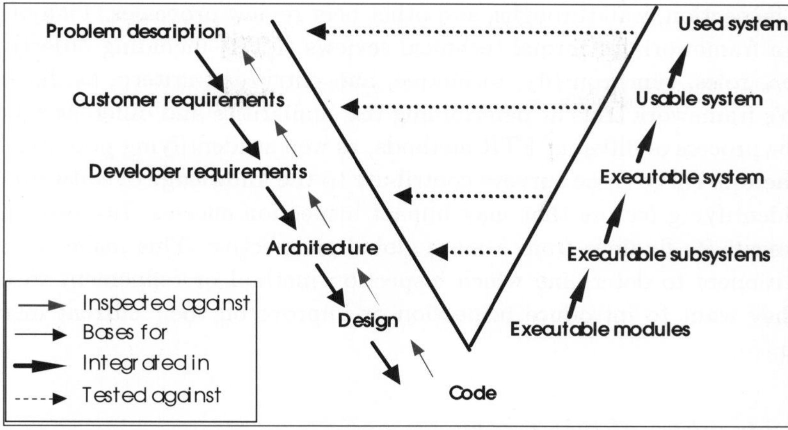

Fig. 1. A generic software development model.

the generic software development products. Hence, it is applicable with all process models for which products are developed in sequence, in parallel, or incrementally. The point is that the logical relationship between development products should be maintained and a software inspection can be triggered and scheduled as soon as a development product or parts of it are created. A typical example is a piece of code that is checked against the design document. This survey elaborates upon the question of how to set up and run inspections to achieve the stated goals, i.e., to achieve a certain level of effectiveness from a technical, economic, organizational, and tool perspective.

1.2. *Related work*

Findings about inspections have not been easy to reconcile and consolidate due to the sheer volume of work already published. Hence, it is not surprising that the available surveys [70, 83, 106, 127, 135] only cover the most relevant published research in their reviews.

Broadly speaking, existing surveys can be summarized as follows. Kim *et al* [70] present a framework for software development technical reviews including software inspection, Freedman and Weinberg's technical review [131], and Yourdon's walkthrough [140]. They segment the framework according to aims and benefits of reviews, human elements, review process, review outputs, and other matters. Macdonald *et al* [83] describe the scope of support for the currently available inspection process and review tools. Porter *et al* [106] focus their attention on the organizational attributes of the software inspection process, such as the team size or the number of sessions, to understand how these attributes influence the costs and benefits of software inspection. Wheeler *et al* [135] discuss the software inspection process as a particular type of peer review process and elaborate the differences between software inspection, walkthroughs, and other peer review processes. Tjahjono [127] presents a framework for formal technical reviews (FTR) including objective, collaboration, roles, synchronicity, technique, and entry/exit-criteria as dimensions. Tjahjono's framework aims at determining the similarities and differences between the review process of different FTR methods, as well as identifying potential review success factors. All of these surveys contribute to the knowledge of software inspection by identifying factors that may impact inspection success. However, none of them presents its findings from a more global perspective. This makes it difficult for practitioners to determine which inspection method or refinement to choose, should they want to introduce inspection or improve on their current inspection approach.

1.3. *Organization of this survey*

We organized this survey as follows. Section 2 presents the study methodology including our approach to identify and select the relevant software inspection literature. Section 3 describes the core concepts and relationships that together define the notion of software inspection in the form of a taxonomy. Section 4 discusses the most important literature sources in the context of the presented taxonomy. Section 5 concludes.

2. Study Methodology

2.1. *Survey motivation and principles*

Literature surveys have long played a central role in the accumulation of scientific knowledge. As science is a cumulative endeavor, any one theory or finding is suspect because of the large array of validity threats that must be ruled out. Moreover, all too often new techniques and methods are proposed and introduced, without building on the extensive body of knowledge that is incorporated in the ones already available. These problems can be somewhat alleviated by establishing the current facts using the mechanism of literature surveys. The facts are the dependable relationships among the various concepts that occur despite any biases that may be present in particular studies because of the implicit theories behind the investigators' choice of observations, measures, and instruments. Hence, a literature survey makes the implicit theories explicit by identifying their commonalities and differences, often from a specific angle when the body of knowledge has become very rich. In some cases, a literature survey may even be an impetus for the unification of existing theories to induce a new, more general theory that can be empirically tested afterwards.

To achieve these goals, a survey must fulfill several principles: First, it must be well-contained, that is, encapsulate its work within a clearly defined scope where the benefits of doing so can be well-understood and accepted. Second, a survey must provide profound breadth and depth regarding the literature relevant to its defined scope. Finally, it must present a unified vocabulary reconciling the most important terms in a field.

The first principle is the hardest to fulfill and illustrates the fact that there cannot be one single method for developing a survey since it is so tightly coupled with the notion of scope. The scope is, in fact, what defines the gist of a survey and hence, depending on the particular interest of the authors, a survey can be geared in different directions. This is clearly illustrated by the different directions taken by the five surveys we mentioned above. Each used a particular scope and rationale for its motivation.

To fulfill the second and third survey principles, finding and selecting the relevant literature is of utmost importance. We attempted to collect any publication fitting our definition of inspection, which captures, we believe, the essence of other definitions. However, no single method for locating relevant literature is perfect [28]. Hence, we utilized a combination of methods to locate articles and papers on our subject.

2.2. *Sampling approach*

We conducted searches of the following two inspection libraries: Bill Brykczynski's collection of inspection literature [21, 136] and the Formal Technical Review Library [59]. To be sure not to miss a paper recently published, we performed three additional steps in search of inspection articles: first, we employed a keyword search in the INSPECT database of the OCLC [97] and the library of the Association of Computing Machinery [3] using the keyword "software inspection". Second, we manually searched the following journals published 1990 and 1998: *IEEE Transactions on Software Engineering*, *IEEE Software*, *Journal of Systems and Software*, *Communications of the ACM*, and *ACM Software Engineering Notes*. Finally, we looked at the reference sections of books dealing with software inspection [47, 124] and some conference proceedings. Table 1 shows the results of our literature search.

Table 1. Summary of search results.

Source	Number of Articles
Literature in [136]	147
FTR-Library	204
OCLC Database	55
ACM Database	21
IEEE Transactions on Software Engineering	12
IEEE Software	9
Journal of Systems and Software	8
Communications of the ACM	4
ACM Software Engineering Notes	3
Other	17

The reader must keep in mind that some articles are cross-referenced among several libraries. We made the results of our literature search available on-line [44].

Considering the very large number of published articles available, it was impossible to give full attention to every article within this survey, although we carefully considered each and every one of them. We excluded articles based on the following rules: (a) the article is an opinion paper and, therefore, does not represent tangible inspection experiences, (b) it takes considerable effort (money or time) to get an article, (c) one or several authors published several papers about similar work in journals and conference proceedings — in this case, we considered the most relevant journal publication, (d) an article does only provide a weak research or practical contribution, although we acknowledge the subjectivity of this criteria. However, we avoided the dangers of ignoring papers because they do not fit neatly into our taxonomy. When in doubt, we included them. Overall, we included a total of 120 articles and reports about software inspection in this survey.

Although we consider the selected sample of papers as representative of the work in the inspection area, we are aware that the published papers are only a biased sample of inspection work actually carried out in reality. There are two principal reasons for this, which we can only be aware of, without any hope of overcoming them:

- The "File drawer problem" — unpublished as well as unretrievable null results stored away by unknown researchers [114]. When inspections are unsuccessfully applied, they are most often not reported in the literature. In all the articles we reviewed, there is only one, which shows that inspection did not have the expected benefits [122]. Yet, we believe that there might be more unsuccessful inspection trials.
- The successful use of inspection might also be only sporadically reported, since that may reveal defect information unpalatable to companies engaged in competitive industries [1].

3. A Taxonomy for Inspection Approaches

Based on the selected literature, we derived a taxonomy to articulate the core concepts and relationships of software inspection. This taxonomy is organized around four primary dimensions — technical, economic, organizational, and tools. With them, we characterized the nature of software inspection. For each primary dimension, we used a selection criterion in the form of a concrete goal to elicit from the relevant literature. Yet, though necessary, these four primary dimensions are not unique. They are relevant to the major areas of software development. Hence, we elicited from the literature particular sub-dimensions that we saw as fundamental to the nature and application of software inspection.

Figure 2 shows the elicited dimensions and sub-dimensions.

We briefly describe below each dimension and its associated primary goals. The major goal of the technical dimension is to characterize the different inspection

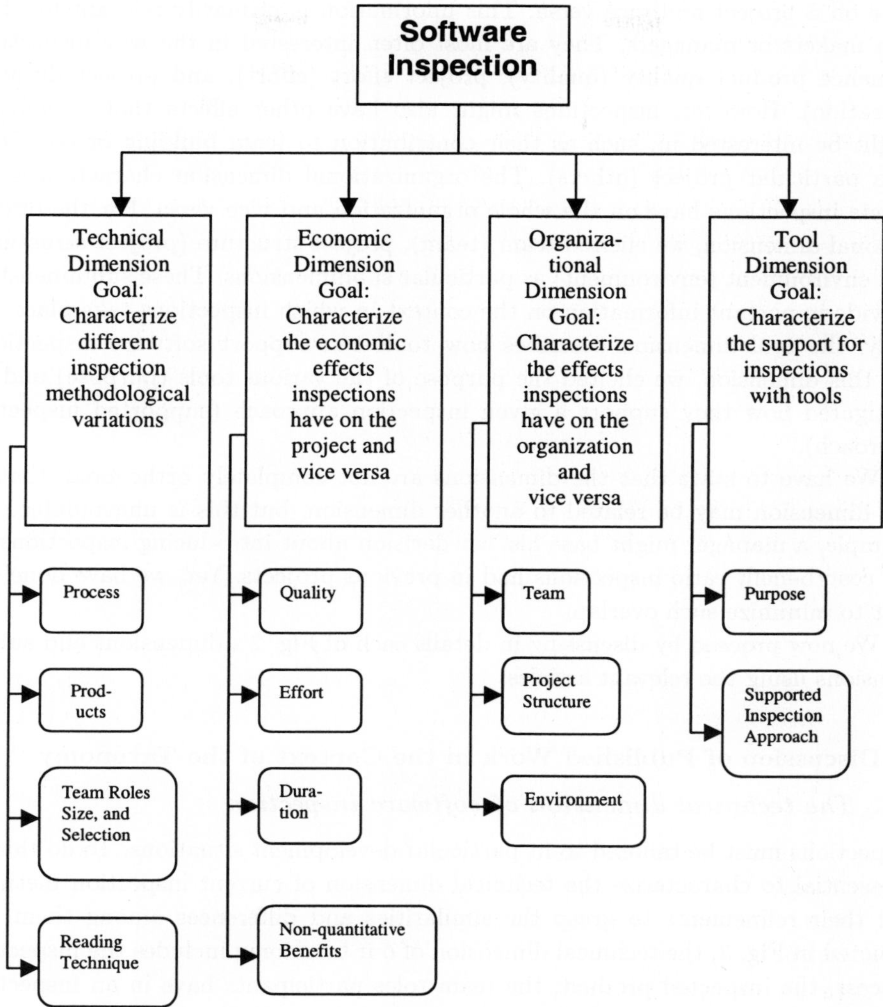

Fig. 2. Dimensions and subdimensions of the identified taxonomy.

methods so as to identify similarities and differences among them. For this, each inspection approach needs to be characterized in more detail according to the activities performed (process), the inspected software product (product), the different team roles as well as overall optimal size and selection (team roles, size, and selection), and the technique applied to detect defects in the software product (reading technique).[b] The dimension provides information on the effects that inspections

[b]Reading techniques formulate approaches that provide assistance for the inspectors. They help focus them on the important information in the document to be verified and some activities for performing the verification.

have on a project and vice versa. This information is primarily relevant for decision makers or managers. They are most often interested in the way inspections influence product quality (quality), project effort (effort), and project duration (duration). However, inspections might also have other effects that a manager might be interested in, such as their contribution to team building or education in a particular project (others). The organizational dimension characterizes the effects inspections have on the whole organization and vice versa. For the organizational dimension, we elicited team (team), project structure (project structure), and environment (environment) as particular subdimensions. These subdimensions provide important information on the context in which inspections take place. Finally, the tool dimension describes how tools can support software inspections. For this dimension, we elicited the purpose of the various tools (purpose) and investigated how they support a given inspection approach (supported inspection approach).

We have to state that the dimensions are not completely orthogonal, that is, one dimension may be related to another dimension, but this is unavoidable. For example, a manager might base his/her decision about introducing inspections on the cost/benefit ratio inspections had in previous projects. Yet, we have done our best to minimize such overlap.

We now proceed by discussing in details each of Fig. 2's dimensions and subdimensions using the relevant articles.

4. Discussion of Published Work in the Context of the Taxonomy

4.1. *The technical dimension of software inspection*

Inspections must be tailored to fit particular development situations. To do this, it is essential to characterize the technical dimension of current inspection methods and their refinements to grasp the similarities and differences among them. As depicted in Fig. 3, the technical dimension of our taxonomy includes the inspection process, the inspected product, the team roles participants have in an inspection as well as the team size, and the reading technique as subdimensions. Each of the subdimensions is discussed in more detail in this section. In total, we have identified 64 references relevant to this dimension.

4.1.1. *Process*

To explain the various similarities and differences among the inspection methods, a reference model for software inspection processes is needed. To define such a reference model, we adhered to the purpose of the various activities within an inspection rather than their organization. This allows us to provide an unbiased examination of the different approaches. We identified six major process phases: Planning, Overview, Defect Detection, Defect Collection, Defect Correction, and Follow-up. These phases can be found in many inspection methods or their refinements.

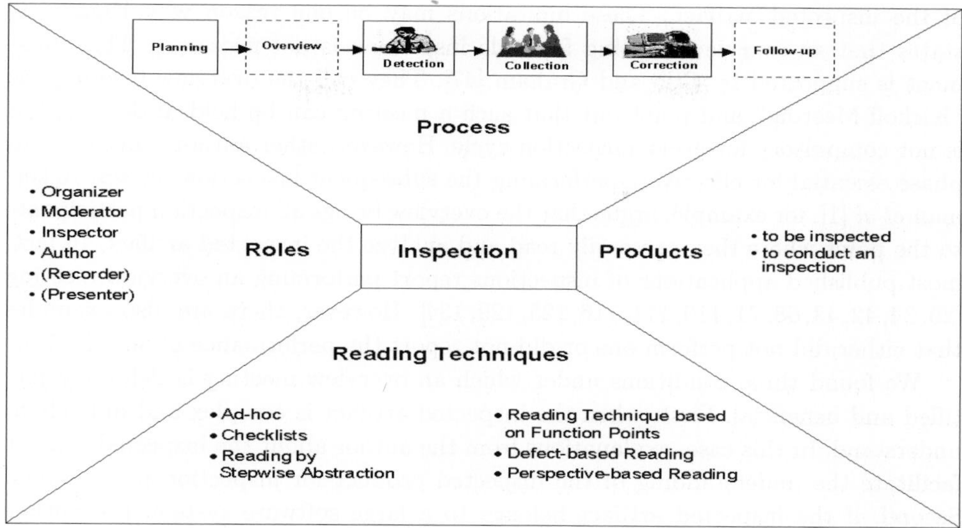

Fig. 3. The technical dimension of software inspection.

However, the question of how each phase is organized and performed often distinguishes one method from another.

4.1.2. *Planning*

The objective of the planning phase is to organize a particular inspection when materials to be inspected pass entry criteria, such as when source code successfully compiles without syntax errors. This phase includes the selection of inspection participants, their assignment to roles, the scheduling of the inspection meeting, and the partitioning and distribution of the inspection material. In most literature, this phase is not described in much detail, except in [1, 40, 47, 124]. However, we consider planning important to mention as a separate phase because there must be a person within a project or organization who is responsible for planning all inspection activities, even if such an individual plays numerous roles.

4.1.3. *Overview*

The overview phase consists of a first meeting in which the author explains the inspected product to other inspection participants. The main goal of the overview phase is to make the inspected product more lucid and, therefore, easier to understand and inspect for participants. Such a first meeting can be particularly valuable for the inspection of early artifacts, such as requirements or design documents, but also for complex source code. However, this meeting consumes effort and increases the duration of an inspection. Moreover, it may focus the attention of inspectors on particular issues, which prohibits an independent assessment of the inspected artifact. These limitations may be one reason why Fagan [40] states that an overview meeting for code inspection is not necessary. This statement is supported by Gilb and Graham [47]. They call the overview meeting the "Kickoff Meeting" and point out that such a meeting can be held, if desired, but is not compulsory for every inspection cycle. However, other authors consider this phase essential for effectively performing the subsequent inspection phases. Ackerman *et al* [1], for example, argue that the overview brings all inspection participants to the point where they can easily read and analyze the inspected artifact. In fact, most published applications of inspections report performing an overview meeting [29, 34, 42, 43, 68, 71, 110, 111, 116, 125, 129, 134]. However, there are also examples that either did not perform one or did not report the performance of one [13, 73].

We found three conditions under which an overview meeting is definitely justified and beneficial. First, when the inspected artifact is complex and difficult to understand. In this case, explanations from the author about the inspected artifact facilitate the understanding of the inspected product for inspection participants. Second, if the inspected artifact belongs to a large software system, the author may want to explain the relationship between the inspected artifact and the whole software system to other participants. Third, new team members participate in the inspection. Since they are inexperienced, explanations from the author put them in a position to inspect the artifact. In all three cases, explanations by the author may help other participants perform more effective inspection and save time in later inspection phases.

4.1.4. *Defect detection*

The defect detection phase can be considered the core of an inspection. The main goal of the defect detection phase is to scrutinize a software artifact to identify defects. How to organize this phase is still debated in the literature. More specifically, the issue is whether defect detection is more an individual activity and hence should be performed individually, or whether defect detection is a group activity and should therefore be conducted as part of a group meeting, that is, an inspection meeting. Fagan [40] reports that a group meeting provides a synergy effect, that is, most of the defects are detected because inspection participants meet and scrutinize the inspection artifact together. He makes the implicit assumption that interaction contributes something to an inspection that is more than the mere combination of individual results. Fagan refers to this effect as the "phantom" inspector. However, others found little synergy in an inspection meeting. The most cited reference for this position is a paper by L. Votta [130]. His position is empirically supported in [117].

In many cases, authors distinguish between a "preparation" phase of an inspection, which is performed individually, and a "meeting" phase of an inspection, which is performed within a group [1, 40, 46, 56, 124]. However, it often remains unclear whether the preparation phase is performed with the goal detecting defects or just understanding the inspected artifact to detect defects later on in a meeting phase. For example, Ackerman *et al* [1] state that a preparation phase lets the inspectors thoroughly understand the inspected artifact. They do not explicitly state that the goal of the preparation phase is defect detection. Bisant and Lyle [9] consider individual preparation as the vehicle for education. Other examples mention that the inspected artifact should be individually studied in detail throughout a preparation phase, but do not explicitly state education as a goal *per se* [25, 34, 42, 79].

Since the literature on software inspection does not provide a definite answer on which alternative to choose, we looked at some literature from the psychology of small group behavior [33, 80, 121]. Psychologists found that an answer to the question whether individuals or groups are more effective, depends upon the past experience of the persons involved, the kind of task they are attempting to complete, the process that is being investigated, and the measure of effectiveness. Since at least some of these parameters vary in the context of a software inspection, we recommend that the defect detection activity be organized as both individual and group activity with a strong emphasis on the former. Individual defect detection with the explicit goal to look for defects that should be resolved before the document is approved ensures that inspectors are well prepared for all following inspection steps. This may require extra effort on the inspectors' behalf since each of them has to understand and scrutinize the inspected document on an individual basis. However, the effort is justified because, if a group meeting is performed later on, each inspector can play an active role rather than hiding himself or herself in the group and, thus, make a significant contribution to the overall success of an inspection.

Knight and Myers [72, 73] suggested the Phased Inspection Method. The main idea behind Phased Inspections is for each inspection phase to be divided into several mini-inspections or phases. Mini-inspections are conducted by one or more inspectors and are aimed at detecting defects of one particular class or type. This is the most important difference to "conventional" inspections, which check for many classes or types of defects in a single examination. If there is more than one inspector, they will meet just to reconcile their defect list. The phases are done in sequence, that is, inspection does not progress to the next phase until rework has been completed on the previous phase.

Although Knight and Myers state that phased inspections are intended to be used on any work product, they only present some empirical evidence of the effectiveness of this approach for the code inspections. However, Porter *et al* argue based on the results of their experiments [108], that multiple session inspections, that is, mini-inspections, with repair in between are not more effective for defect detection but are more costly than conventional inspections. This may be one explanation why we did not find extensive use of the phased inspection approach in practice.

There has been noticeable growth in research on how individual defect detection takes place and can be supported with adequate techniques [5, 6, 109]. We tackle this issue later in more detail when we discuss reading techniques to support defect detection.

4.1.5. *Defect collection*

In most published inspection processes, more than one person participates in an inspection and scrutinizes a software artifact for defects. Hence, the defects detected by each inspection participant must be collected and documented. Furthermore, a decision must be made whether a purported defect is really a defect. These are the main objectives of the defect collection phase. A further objective may be to decide whether the inspected artifact needs to be reinspected. The defect collection phase is most often performed in a group meeting. There, the decision as to whether or not a defect is really a defect is often a group decision. The same holds for the decision as to whether to perform a reinspection. This decision is often based on a subjective estimation of the defect content. A recent study revealed that this estimate can be quite accurate [39]. To make the reinspection decision more objective, some authors suggest to apply statistical models, such as capture-recapture models, for estimating the remaining number of defects in the software product after inspection [2, 22, 38, 115, 137]. If the estimate exceeds a certain threshold, the software product needs to be reinspected. However, recent studies [14, 15] showed that statistical estimators are not very accurate for inspections with less than four inspection participants. Further research is necessary to validate this finding. In addition to statistical estimation models, graphical defect content estimation approaches are currently being investigated [138].

Since a group meeting is effort consuming and increases the development schedule, some authors suggest that such a meeting for inspections be abandoned. Instead, they offer the following alternatives [130]: managed meetings, depositions, and correspondence. Managed meetings are well-structured meetings with a limited number of participants. A deposition is a three-person meeting in which the author, a moderator, and an inspector collect the inspectors' findings and comments. Correspondence includes forms of communication where the inspections and author never actually meet (e.g. by using electronic mail). Some researchers have elaborated on these alternatives [63]. Sauer *et al* [118], for example, provide some theoretical underpinning for depositions. They suggest that the most experienced inspectors collect the defects and decide upon whether these are real or not.

In general, research does not seem to provide a conclusive answer to the question of whether inspection meetings pay off. We recommend that practitioners start with the "traditional" meeting-based approach and try later on whether non-meeting based approaches provide equivalent benefits. Regarding the benefits of group meetings, they also provide more intangible benefits such as dissemination of product information, development experiences, or enhancement of team spirit as reported in [30, 43]. Although difficult to measure, these benefits must be taken into account when a particular inspection approach is evaluated in addition to the number of defects it helps detect and remove.

On the other hand, these meetings are not problem-solving sessions. Neither personal conflicts among people or departments nor radically alternate solutions — complete rewrite or redesign — of the inspected artifact should be discussed there.

4.1.6. *Defect correction*

Throughout the defect correction phase, the author reworks and resolves defects found [40] or rationalizes their existence [122]. For this he or she edits the material and deals with each reported defect. There is only little discussion in the literature about this activity [47, 124].

4.1.7. *Follow-up*

The objective of the follow-up phase is to check whether the author has resolved all defects. For this, one of the inspection participants verifies the defect resolution. Doolan reports that the moderator checks that the author has taken some remedial action for each defect detected [34]. However, others do not report a follow-up phase [95, 116, 122]. They either did not perform one or did not consider it important. Furthermore, many consider the follow-up phase optional like the overview phase.

4.1.8. *Products*

The product dimension refers to the type of product that is usually inspected. The term product refers not only to the final delivered software system, but also to any documentation produced in the context of a software development project. Barry Boehm [12] stated that one of the most prevalent and costly mistakes made in software projects today is deferring the activity of detecting and correcting software problems until late in the project. This statement supports the use of software inspection for early life-cycle documents. However, a look at the literature reveals that in most cases inspection was applied to code documents. Figure 4 depicts how inspection was applied to various software products

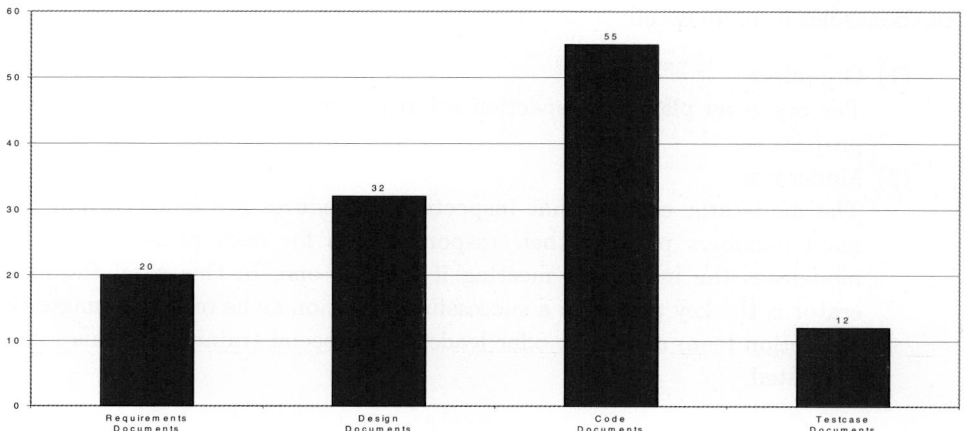

Fig. 4. Number of references for the inspection of various software development products.

phasewise.[c] We found 20, 32, 55 and 12 papers that talk about the inspection of requirements, design, code, and testcase documents, respectively. These numbers demonstrate that the use of inspection is biased towards code documents. Although code inspection improves the code quality and provides savings, the savings are higher for early life-cycle artifacts as shown in a recent study [16], which integrates published inspection results into a coherent cost/benefit-model. The results of the study reveal that the introduction of code inspection saves 39% of defect costs compared to testing alone. The introduction of design inspection saves 44% of defect costs compared to testing alone. These findings motivate the use of inspections especially throughout the early development phases.

The product dimension is also influenced by the development approach. Software inspections have been primarily used with products resulting from conventional structured development processes. Object-oriented products, particularly of the graphical form, have so far not been adequately addressed by inspection methods. Although some work in the area of object-oriented inspections exists [35, 128], there is a general lack of research regarding how the key features of the object-oriented paradigm impact software inspections.

4.1.9. *Team roles, size, and selection*

4.1.9.1. Team roles

Three important questions practitioners usually have about roles in software inspections are (1) what roles are involved in an inspection, (2) how many people are assigned to each role, and (3) how should people be selected for each roles. For the first question, a number of specific roles are assigned to inspection participants. Hence, each inspection participant has a clear and specific responsibility. The roles and their responsibilities are described in [1, 40, 116]. There is not much disagreement regarding the definition of inspection roles. In the following, we describe each of these roles in more detail:

(1) Organizer
The organizer plans all inspection activities within a project or even across projects.

(2) Moderator
The moderator ensures that inspection procedures are followed and that team members perform their responsibilities for each phase. He or she moderates the inspection meeting if there is one. In this case, the moderator is the key person in a successful inspection as he or she manages the inspection team and must offer leadership. Special training for this role is suggested.

[c]We should note that some articles describe software inspection for several products. This explains why we only included 119 articles in this diagram.

(3) Inspector
Inspectors are responsible for detecting defects in the target software product. Usually all team members can be assumed to be inspectors, regardless of their other roles in the inspection team.

(4) Reader/Presenter
If an inspection meeting is performed, the reader will present the inspected products at an appropriate pace and lead the team through the material in a complete and logical fashion. The material should be paraphrased at a suitable rate for detailed examination. Paraphrasing means that the reader should explain and interpret the material rather than reading it literally.

(5) Author
The author has developed the inspected product and is responsible for the correction of defects during rework. During an inspection meeting, he or she addresses specific questions the reader is not able to answer. The author must not serve as moderator, reader, or recorder.

(6) Recorder
The recorder is responsible for logging all defects in an inspection defect list during the inspection meeting.

(7) Collector
The collector collects the defects found by the inspectors if there is no inspection meeting.

4.1.9.2. Team size

To answer the second question, that is, how to assign resources to these roles in an optimal manner, the reported numbers in the literature are not uniform. Fagan recommends to keep the inspection team small, that is, four people [40] and Bisant and Lyle [9] have found performance advantages in an experiment with two persons: one inspector and the author, who can also be regarded as an inspector. Kusumoto *et al* recently investigated the two-person approach in an educational environment [75]. Weller presents some data from a field study using three to four inspectors [133]. Madachy presents data showing that the optimal size is between three and five people [87]. Bourgeois corroborates these results in a different study [13]. Porter *et al*'s experimental results suggest that reducing the number of inspectors from 4 to 2 may significantly reduce effort without increasing inspection interval or reducing effectiveness [107].

Martin *et al* proposed the N-fold inspection method [68, 89, 119]. This inspection method is based on the hypothesis that a single inspection team can find only a fraction of the defects in a software product and that multiple teams will not significantly duplicate each others efforts. In an N-fold inspection, N teams each carry out parallel independent inspections of the same software artifact. In a sense, N-fold inspection scales up some ideas of scenario-based reading techniques, which are applied in the conventional inspection approach on an individual level, to a team level. The inspection participants of each independent inspection follow the various inspection steps of a conventional inspection as outlined previously, that is, individual defect detection with an *ad hoc* reading technique and defect collection in a meeting. The N-Fold inspection approach ends with a final step in which the results of each inspection team are merged into one defect list. It has been hypothesized that N different teams will detect more defects than a single large inspection team. In fact, there is already empirical evidence confirming this hypothesis [129]. However, if N independent teams inspect one particular document, inspection cost will be high. This limits this inspection approach to the inspection of early life-cycle artifacts for which very high quality really does matter, such as the aircraft industry, or safety critical systems [129].

We assume that there is no definite answer to the optimal number of inspectors and team size. An answer rather depends on the type of product and the environment in which an inspection is performed and the costs associated with defect detection and correction in later development phases. However, in absence of a clear answer, we recommend starting with one team that consists of three to four people: one author, one or two inspectors, and one moderator (also playing the role of the presenter and scribe. After a few inspections, the benefits of adding an additional inspector or an additional team can be empirically evaluated. The evaluation involves an examination whether an additional person or team helps detect more defects, i.e., leads to an increase in inspection effectiveness and defect coverage. Of course, one must also address the question whether the effort for the extra person or team really pays off.

4.1.9.3. Team selection

The final question is how to select members of an inspection team. Primary candidates for the role of inspectors are personnel involved in product development [41]. Outside inspectors may be brought in when they have a particular expertise that would add to the inspection [96]. Inspectors should have good experience and knowledge[d] [10, 41, 124]. However, the selection of inspectors according to experience and knowledge has two major implications. First, inspection results heavily depend upon human factors. This often limits the pool of relevant inspectors to a few developers working on similar or interfacing products [1]. Second, personnel with little experience are not chosen as inspectors although they may learn and, thus, profit a lot from inspection. Defect detection, that is, reading techniques, which we discuss later on in more detail, may alleviate these problems.

It is sometimes recommended that managers should neither participate nor attend an inspection [68, 96]. This stems from the fact that inspections should be used to assess the quality of the software product, not the quality of the people who create the product [41]. Using inspection data to evaluate people may result in less

[d]In most cases, the kind of experience and knowledge is not well-defined in the articles.

than honest and thorough inspections, since inspectors may be reluctant to identify defects if finding them results in a poor performance evaluation for a colleague.

4.1.9.4. Reading technique

Recent empirical studies demonstrate that defect detection is more an individual than a group activity as assumed by many inspection methods and refinements [103, 130]. Moreover, these empirical studies show that a particular organization of the inspection process does not explain most of the variation in inspection results. Rather, one expects that inspection results depend on inspection participants themselves [108] and their strategies for understanding the inspected artifact [113]. Therefore, supporting inspection participants, that is, inspectors, with particular techniques that help them detect defects in software products, may increase the effectiveness of an inspection team most. We refer to such techniques as reading techniques.

A reading technique can be defined as a series of steps or procedures whose purpose is to guide an inspector in acquiring a deep understanding of the inspected software product. The comprehension of inspected software products is a prerequisite for detecting subtle and/or complex defects, those often causing the most problems if detected in later life-cycle phases. In a sense, a reading technique can be regarded as a mechanism or strategy for the individual inspector to detect defects in the inspected product. Of course, whether inspectors take advantage of this mechanism or strategy is up to them. At least, it is intended that inspectors use the available reading techniques since this makes the result of the defect detection activity less dependent on human factors, such as experience.

Even though reading is one of the key activities for individual defect detection [6], few documented reading techniques are currently available to support the activity. We found that *ad hoc* reading and checklist-based reading are the most popular reading techniques used today for defect detection in inspection [40, 47].

Ad hoc reading, by nature, offers very little reading support at all since a software product is simply given to inspectors without any direction or guidelines on how to proceed through it and what to look for. However, *ad hoc* does not mean that inspection participants do not scrutinize the inspected product systematically. The word "*ad hoc*" only refers to the fact that no technical support is given to them for the problem of how to detect defects in a software artifact. In this case, defect detection fully depends on the skill, the knowledge, and the experience of an inspector. Training sessions in program comprehension as presented in [113] may help subjects develop some of these capabilities to alleviate the lack of reading support. Although an *ad hoc* reading approach was only mentioned a few times in the literature [34, 122], we found many articles in which little was mentioned about how an inspector should proceed in order to detect defects. Hence, we assumed that in most of these cases no particular reading technique was provided because otherwise it would have been stated.

Checklists offer stronger, boilerplate support in the form of questions inspectors are to answer while reading the document. These questions concern quality aspects of the document. Checklists are advocated in more than 25 articles. See, for example, [1, 40, 41, 54, 126], and Gilb and Grahams' manuscript [47]. Although reading support in the form of a list of questions is better than none (such as *ad hoc*), checklist-based reading has several weaknesses. First, the questions are often general and not sufficiently tailored to a particular development environment. A prominent example is the following question: "Is the inspected artifact correct?" Although this checklist question provides a general framework for an inspector on what to check, it does not tell him or her in a precise manner how to ensure this quality attribute. In this way, the checklist provides little support for an inspector to understand the inspected artifact. But this can be vital to detect major application logic defects. Second, concrete instructions on how to use a checklist are often missing, that is, it is often unclear when and based on what information an inspector is to answer a particular checklist question. This weakness becomes apparent when looking at the example presented above. In fact, several strategies are actually feasible to address all the questions in a checklist. The following approach characterizes the one end of the spectrum: the inspector takes a single question, goes through the whole artifact, answers the question, and takes the next question. The other end is defined by the following procedure: the inspector reads the document. Afterwards he or she answers the questions of the checklist. It is quite unclear which approach inspectors follow when using a checklist and how they achieved their results in terms of defects detected. The final weakness of a checklist is the fact that checklist questions are often limited to the detection of defects that belong to particular defect types. Since the defect types are based on past defect information [24], inspectors may not focus on defect types not previously detected and, therefore, may miss whole classes of defects.

To address some of the presented difficulties, one can develop a checklist according to the following principles:

- The length of a checklist should not exceed one page.
- The checklist question should be phrased as precise as possible.
- The checklist should be structured so that the quality attribute is clear to the inspector and the question give hints on how to assure the quality attribute.

In some cases the length of a checklist may exceed one page. In these cases, it may be possible to make inspectors responsible for different parts of the checklist. Although these actions can be taken, a checklist still provides very little guidance for inspectors on how to perform the various checks. This weakness led to the development of more procedural reading techniques.

Techniques providing more structured and precise reading instructions include both a reading technique denoted "Reading by Stepwise Abstraction" for code documents advocated by the Cleanroom community [36, 37, 81], as well as a technique suggested by Parnas *et al* called Active Design Review [98, 99] for the inspection of design documents.

The technique "Reading by Stepwise Abstraction" was described in the context of the Verification-based Inspection approach [37]. This is an inspection variation used in conjunction with the Cleanroom software development method. Although this method requires the author(s) to perform various inspections of work products, the inspection process itself is not well described in the literature. We found that it consists of at least one step, in which individual inspectors examine the work product using "Reading by Stepwise Abstraction". This technique requires an inspector to read a sequence of statements in the code and to abstract the functions these statements compute. An inspector repeats this procedure until the final function of the inspected code artifact has been abstracted and can be compared to the specification. This reading technique is limited to code artifact, though it provides a more formal approach for inspectors to check the functional correctness [37]. We found little information on the inspection process after the individual defect detection step. However, the Cleanroom approach is one of the few development approaches in which defect detection and inspection activities are tightly integrated in and coupled with development activities. The Cleanroom approach and its integrated inspection approach have been applied to several development projects [6, 31, 36].

Parnas and Weiss suggest an inspection method denoted as Active Design Reviews (ADR) for inspecting design documents [98, 99]. The authors believe that in conventional design inspections, inspectors are given too much information to examine, and that they must participate in large meetings, which only allow for limited interaction between inspectors and author. To tackle theses issues inspectors are chosen based on their specific level of expertise skills and assigned to ensure thorough coverage of design documents. Only two roles are defined within the ADR process. An inspector has the expected responsibility of finding defects, while the designer is the author of the design being scrutinized. There is no indication of who is responsible for setting up and coordinating the review. The ADR process consists of three steps. It begins with an overview step, where the designer presents an overview of the design and meeting times are set. The next step is the defect detection step for which the author provides questionnaires to guide the inspectors. The questions are designed such that they can only be answered by careful study of the design document, that is, inspectors have to elaborate the answer instead of stating yes/no. Some of the questions reinforce an active inspection role by making assertions about design decisions. For example, he or she may be asked to write a program segment to implement a particular design in a low-level design document being inspected. The final step is defect collection, which is performed in inspection meetings. However, each inspection meeting is broken up into several smaller, specialized meetings, each of which concentrates on one quality property of the artifact. An example is checking consistency between assumptions and functions, that is, determining whether assumptions are consistent and detailed enough to ensure that functions can be correctly implemented and used.

Active Design Review is an important inspection variation because ADR inspectors are guided by a series of questions posed by the author(s) of the design in order to encourage a thorough defect detection step. Thus, inspectors get reading support when scrutinizing a design document. Although little empirical evidence shows the effectiveness of this approach, other researchers based their inspection variations upon these ideas [23, 72].

A more recent development in the area of reading techniques for individual defect detection in software inspection is Scenario-based reading [6]. The essence of the Scenario-based reading idea is the use of the notion of scenarios that provide custom guidance for inspectors on how to detect defects. A scenario may be a set of questions or a more detailed description for an inspector on how to perform the document review. Principally, a scenario limits the attention of an inspector to the detection of particular defects as defined by the custom guidance. Since each inspector may use a different scenario, and each scenario focuses on different defect types, it is expected that the inspection team, together, becomes more effective. Hence, it is clear that the effectiveness of a scenario-based reading technique depends on the content and design of the scenarios. So far, researchers have suggested three different approaches for developing scenarios and, therefore, three different scenario-based reading techniques: Defect-based Reading [109] for inspecting requirements documents, a scenario-based reading technique based on function points for inspecting requirements documents [23], and Perspective-based Reading for inspecting requirements documents [5] or code documents [76].

The main idea behind Defect-based Reading is for different inspectors to focus on different defect classes while scrutinizing a requirements document [93, 105, 109, 117]. For each defect class, there is a scenario consisting of a set of questions an inspector has to answer while reading. Answering the questions helps an inspector primarily detect defects of that particular class. The defect-based reading technique has been validated in a controlled experiment with students as subjects. The major finding was that inspectors applying Defect-based Reading detect more defects than inspectors applying either *ad hoc* or checklist-based reading.

Cheng and Jeffery have chosen a slightly different approach to define scenarios for defect detection in requirements documents [23]. This approach is based on Function Point Analysis (FPA). FPA defines a software system in terms of its inputs, files, inquiries, and outputs. The scenarios, that is, the Function Point Scenarios, are developed around these items. A Function Point Scenario consists of questions and directs the focus of an inspector to a specific function-point item within the inspected requirements document. The researchers carried out an experiment to investigate the effectiveness of this approach compared to an *ad hoc* approach. The experimental results show that, on average, inspectors following the *ad hoc* approach found more defects than inspectors following the function-point scenarios.

However, experience seemed to be a confounding factor that biased the results of the experiment.

The main idea behind the perspective-based reading technique is that a software product should be inspected from the perspective of different stakeholders [5, 18, 76, 77]. The rationale is that there is no single monolithic definition of software quality, and little general agreement about how to define any of the key quality properties, such as correctness, maintainability, or testability. Therefore, inspectors of an inspection team have to check software quality as well as the software quality factors of a software artifact from different perspectives. The perspectives mainly depend upon the roles people have within the software development or maintenance process. For each perspective, either one or multiple scenarios are defined, consisting of repeatable activities an inspector has to perform, and questions an inspector has to answer. The activities are typical for the role within the software development or maintenance process, and help an inspector increase his or her understanding of the software product from the particular perspective. For example, designing test cases is a typical activity performed by a tester. Therefore, an inspector reading from the perspective of a tester may have to think about designing test cases to gain an understanding of the software product from the tester's point of view. Once understanding is achieved, questions about an activity or questions about the result of an activity can help an inspector identify defects.

Reading a document from different perspectives is not a completely new idea. It was seeded in early articles on software inspection, but never worked out in detail. Fagan [40] reports that a piece of code should be inspected by the real tester. Fowler [42] suggests that each inspection participant should take a particular point of view when examining the work product. Graden *et al* [49] state that each inspector must denote the perspective (customer, requirements, design, test, maintenance) by which they have evaluated the deliverable. So far, the perspective-based reading technique has been applied to inspecting requirements documents [5], object-oriented design models [77], and code documents [76].

General prescriptions about which reading technique to use in which circumstances can rarely be given. However, in order to compare them, we set up the following criteria: Application Context, Usability, Repeatability, Adaptability, Coverage, Training, and Validation. The criteria are to provide answers to the following questions:

- Application Context: To which software products can a reading technique be applied and to which software products has a reading technique already been applied?
- Usability: Does a reading technique provide prescriptive guidelines on how to scrutinize a software product for defects?
- Repeatability: Are the results of an inspector's work repeatable, that is, are the results such as the detected defects, independent of the person looking for defects?

- Adaptability: Is a reading technique adaptable to particular aspects, e.g. notation of the document, or typical defect profiles in an environment?
- Coverage: Are all required quality properties of the software product, such as correctness or completeness, verified in an inspection?
- Training Required: Does the reading technique require some training on the inspectors' behalf?
- Validation: How was the reading technique validated, that is, how broadly has it been applied so far?

Table 2 characterizes each reading technique according to these criteria. We use question marks in cases for which no clear answer can be provided.

Table 2. Characterization of reading techniques.

Reading Technique	Characteristics						
	Application Context	Usability	Repeat-ability	Adapt-ability	Coverage	Training Required	Validation
Ad hoc	All Products	No	No	No	No	No	Industrial Practice
Checklists	All Products	No	No	Yes	Case Dependent	No	Industrial Practice
Reading by Stepwise Abstraction	All Products Allowing Abstraction, Functional Code	Yes	Yes	No	High for Correctness Defects	Yes	Applied primarily in Cleanroom Projects
Active Design Reviews	Design, Design	Yes	Yes	Yes	?	?	Initial Case Study
Defect-based Reading	All Products, Require-ments	Yes	Case Dependent	Yes	High	Yes	Experi-mental Validation
Reading Based on Function Points	All Products, Require-ments	Yes	Case Dependent	Yes	?	Yes	Experi-mental Validation
Perspective-based Reading	All Products, Require-ments, Design, Code	Yes	Yes	Yes	High	Yes	Experi-mental Validation and Initial Industrial Use

4.2. *The economic dimension of software inspection*

One of the most important criteria for choosing a particular inspection approach is the effort a particular inspection method or refinement consumes. Effort is an issue in which project managers are mainly interested. Hence, we refer to this dimension as the managerial dimension. To make a sound evaluation, that is, to determine whether it is worth spending effort on inspection, one must also consider how inspections affect the quality of the software product as well as the cost and the duration of the project in which they are applied. We discuss a sample of 24 articles in the context of these three subdimensions.

In the context of a software development project, the investigation of inspection benefits is usually done in a separate analysis phase after one or several inspections have been performed. The analysis phase, therefore, does not directly belong to the inspection process. It rather represents a kind of characterization or improvement process in addition to inspections.

4.2.1. *Quality*

Some authors state that inspections can reduce the number of defects reaching testing by ten times [45]. However, these statements are often based on personal opinion rather than on collected inspection data. Hence, we focus our discussion about quality on examples of published inspection data taken from the literature. We emphasize that many of the data reported in the literature are not presented in a manner that allows straightforward comparison and analysis as pointed out by [16]. Table 3 summarizes the results of our analysis. It demonstrates the current trend that inspections help detect defects and, thus, improve the quality of the inspected documents. We need to emphasize that a direct comparison of inspection results between environments should not be done, e.g. one company is not "better" than another one just because the defect detection effectiveness is higher.

Fagan [40] presents data from a development project at Aetna Life and Casualty. Two programmers have written an application program of eight modules (4439 non-commentary source statements) in Cobol. Design and code inspections were introduced into the development process. After 6 months of actual usage, 46 defects had been detected during development and usage of the program. Fagan reports that 38 defects had been detected by design and code inspections together, yielding a defect detection effectiveness for inspections of 82%. In this case, the defect detection effectiveness was defined as the ratio of defects found and the total number of defects in the inspected software product. The remaining 8 defects had been found during unit test and preparation for acceptance test. In another article, Fagan [41] publishes data from a project at IBM Respond, United Kingdom. Seven programers developed a program of 6271 LOC in PL/1. Over the life cycle of the product, 93% of all defects were detected by inspections. He also mentions two projects of the Standard Bank of South Africa (143 KLOC) and American Express (13 KLOC of

Table 3. Summary of inspection results with respect to quality.

Reference	Environment	Result
Fagan [40, 41]	Aetna Life Casuality	38 defects from 46 detected
	IBM Respond, United Kingdom	93% of all defects were detected by inspections
	Standard Bank of South Africa	Over 50% of all defects detected by inspection
Weller [132]	Bull HN Information Systems	70% of all defect detected by inspection
Grady and Van Slack [51]	Hewlett-Packard	60%–70% of all defects detected by inspection
Shirey [122]		60%–70% of all defects detected by inspection
Barnard and Price [4]	AT&T Bell Laboratories	30%–75% of all defects detected by inspection
McGibbon [92]	Cardiac Pacemakers Inc	70% to 90% of all defects detected by inspection
Collofello and Woodfield [26]	Large real time software project	Defect detection effectiveness is 54% for design inspection, 64% for code inspection, and 38% for testing
Kitchenham *et al.* [71]	ICL	57.7% of all defects found by code inspection
Franz and Shih [43]	Hewlett Packard	19% of all defects found by inspection
A. Gately [46]	Raytheon Systems Company	The average number of defects found by inspection is 18.2.
Conradi *et al.* [27]	Ericsson	The average number of defects found by inspection is 3.41.

system code), each with a defect detection effectiveness for inspections of over 50% without using trained inspection moderators.

Weller [132] presents data from a project at Bull HN Information Systems, which replaced inefficient C code for a control microprocessor with Forth. After system tests had been completed, code inspection effectiveness was around 70%. Grady and van Slack [51] report on experiences from achieving widespread inspection use at HP. In one of the company's divisions, inspections (focusing on code) typically found 60% to 70% of the defects. Shirey [122] states that defect detection effectiveness of inspections is typically reported to range from 60% to 70%. Barnard and Price [4] cite several references and report a defect detection effectiveness for code inspections varying from 30% to 75%. In their environment at AT&T Bell

Laboratories, the authors achieved a defect detection effectiveness for code inspections of more than 70%. McGibbon [92] presents data from Cardiac Pacemakers Inc where inspections are used to improve the quality of life-critical software. They observed that inspections removed 70% to 90% of all faults detected during development. Collofello and Woodfield [26] evaluated reliability — assurance techniques in a case study — a large real-time software project that consisted of about 700,000 lines of code developed by over 400 developers. The respective defect detection effectiveness is reported to be 54% for design inspections, 64% for code inspections, and 38% for testing. More recently, Raz and Yaung [110] presented the results of an analysis of defect escape data from design inspection in two maintenance releases of a large software product. They found that the less effective inspections were those with the largest time investment, the likelihood of defect escapes being clearly affected by the way in which the time was invested and by the size of the work product inspected. Kitchenham *et al.* [71] report on experience at ICL, where 57.7% of defects were found by software inspections. The total proportion of development effort devoted to inspections was only 6%. Gilb and Graham [47] include experience data from various sources in their discussion of the benefits and costs of inspections. IBM Rochester Labs publish values of 60% for source code inspections, 80% for inspections of pseudocode, and 88% for inspections of module and interface specifications. Grady [50] performs a cost/benefit analysis for different techniques, among them design and code inspections. He states that the average percentage of defects found for design inspections is 55%, and 60% for code inspections. Franz and Shih [43] present data from code inspection of a sales and inventory tracking systems project at HP. This was a batch system written in COBOL. Their data indicate that inspections had 19% effectiveness for defects that could also be found during testing. Myers [95] performed an experiment to compare program testing to code walkthroughs and inspections. This research is based on work performed earlier by Hetzel [53]. The subjects were 59 highly experienced data processing professionals testing and inspecting a PL/I program. Myers [95] reports an average effectiveness value of 38% for inspections. This controlled experiment was replicated several times [7, 66, 139] with similar results. A. Gately [46] presents some results from the Raytheon Systems Company. In this study, historical review data from a large real-time embedded system were analyzed. She found an average number of defects of 18.2 defects. Conradi *et al.* [27] present some review results from Ericsson. They studied two projects in which reviews and testing were used. The data comes from a site that passed CMM level 2 certification and aims for level 3 in the year 2000. They report an avarage number of defects of 3.41.

4.2.2. *Effort*

It is necessary for a project manager to have a precise understanding of the effort associated with inspections. Since inspection is a human-based activity, inspection costs are determined by human effort. The most important question addressed in

Table 4. Summary of inspection results with respect to effort.

Reference	Environment	Result
Kaner [68]	Jet Propulsion Laboratory	Ratio of the cost of fixing defects during inspection to fixing them during formal testing range from 1:10 to 1:34
Remus [112]	IBM Santa Teresa Lab	Ratio of the cost of fixing defects during inspection to fixing them during formal testing is 1:20
Kan [67]	IBM Rochester Lab	Ratio of the cost of fixing defects during inspection to fixing them during formal testing is 1:13
Ackerman *et al.* [1]	Different Projects	0.58–5 hours per defect found (lower than in testing)
Weller [133]	Bull HN Information Systems	1.43 hours per defect in inspection and 6 hours in testing
Collofello and Woodfield [26]	Large real time software project	7.5 hours per defect for design inspection, 6.3 hours per defect for code inspection, and 11.6 hours per defect for testing
Franz and Shih [43]	Hewlett Packard	1 hour per defect for inspection and 6 hours per defect for testing
Kelly *et al.* [69]	Jet Propulsion Laboratory	1.75 hours per defect of design inspection, 1.46 hours per defect for code inspection, 17 hours per defect for testing
Kitchenham *et al.* [71]	ICL	1.58 hours per defect in design inspection
Gilb and Graham [47]	Applicon	0.9 hours to find and fix a major defect
Bourgeois [13]	Lockheed Martin Western Development Labs	1.3 hours per defect found and 1.4-1.8 hour per defect found and fixed

literature is whether an inspection effort is worth making when compared to the effort for other defect detection activities, such as testing. Most of the literature present solid data supporting the claim that the costs for detecting and removing defects during inspections is much lower than detecting and removing the same defects in later phases. Table 4 summarizes the results of our analysis.

The Jet Propulsion Laboratory (JPL) found the ratio of the cost of fixing defects during inspections to fixing them during formal testing ranged from 1:10 to 1:34 [68], at the IBM Santa Teresa Lab the ratio was 1:20 [112], and at the IBM Rochester Lab it was 1:13 [67].

We must say that authors often relate the costs to either the size of the inspected product or the number of defects found. Ackerman *et al* [1] present data on different projects as a sample of values from the literature and from private reports:

- The development group for a small warehouse-inventory system used inspections on detailed design and code. For detailed design, they reported 3.6 hours of individual preparation per thousand lines, 3.6 hours of meeting time per thousand lines, 1.0 hours per defect found, and 4.8 hours per major defect found (major defects are those that will affect execution). For source code, the results were 7.9 hours of preparation per thousand lines, 4.4 hours of meetings per thousand lines, and 1.2 hours per defect found.
- A major government-systems developer reported the following results from inspection of more than 562,000 lines of detailed design and 249,000 lines of source code: for detailed design, 5.76 hours of individual preparation per thousand lines, 4.54 hours of meetings per thousand lines, and 0.58 hours per defect found. For code, 4.91 hours of individual preparation per thousand lines, 3.32 hours of meetings per thousand lines, and 0.67 hours per defect found.
- Two quality engineers from a major government-systems contractor reported 3 to 5 staff-hours per major defect detected by inspections, showing a surprising consistency over different applications and programming languages.
- A banking computer-services firm found that it took 4.5 hours to eliminate a defect by unit testing compared to 2.2 hours by inspection (these were probably source code inspections).
- An operating-system development organization for a large mainframe manufacturer reported that the average effort involved in finding a design defect by inspections is 1.4 staff-hours compared to 8.5 staff-hours of effort to find a defect by testing.

Weller [133] reports data from a project that performed a conversion of C code to Fortran for several timing-critical routines. While testing the rewritten code, it took 6 hours per failure. It was known from a pilot project in the organization that they had been finding defects in inspections at a cost of 1.43 hours per defect. Thus, the team stopped testing and inspected the rewritten code, detecting defects at a cost of less than 1 hour per defect.

Collofello and Woodfield [26] estimate some factors for which they had insufficient data. They performed a survey among many of the 400 members of a large real-time software project who were asked to estimate the effort needed to detect and correct a defect for different techniques. The results were 7.5 hours for a design error, 6.3 hours for a code error, both detected by inspections, 11.6 hours for an error found during testing, and 13.5 hours for an error discovered in the field.

Franz and Shihs data [43] indicate that the average effort per defect for code inspections was 1 hour and for testing 6 hours. In presenting the results of analyzing inspections data at JPL, Kelly *et al* [69] report that it takes up to 17 hours to fix defects during formal testing, based on a project at JPL. They also report approximately 1.75 hours to find and fix defects during design inspections, and approximately 1.46 hours during code inspections.

There are also examples that present findings from applying inspections only as a quality assurance activity. Kitchenham *et al* [71], for instance, report on experience at ICL where the cost of finding a defect in design inspections was 1.58 hours.

Gilb and Graham [47] include experience data from various sources in their discussion of the benefits and costs of inspections. A senior software engineer describes how software inspections started at Applicon. In the first year, 9 code inspections and 39 document inspections (documents other than code) were conducted and an average effort of 0.8 hours was spent to find and fix a major problem. After the second year, a total of 63 code inspections and 100 document inspections had been conducted and the average effort to find and fix a major problem was 0.9 hours.

Bourgeois [13] reports experience from a large maintenance program within Lockheed Martin Western Development Labs where software inspections replaced structured walkthroughs in a number of projects. The analyzed program was staffed by more than 75 engineers who maintain and enhance over 2 million lines of code. The average effort for 23 software inspections (6 participants) was 1.3 staff-hours per defect found and 2.7 staff-hours per defect found and fixed. Bourgeois also presents data from Jet Propulsion Laboratory, which is used as an industry standard. There, the average effort for 171 software inspections (5 inspection participants) was 1.1 staff-hours per defect found and 1.4 to 1.8 staff-hours per defect found and fixed.

Because inspection is a human-intensive activity and, therefore, effort consuming, managers are often critical or even reluctant to use them the first time. Part of the problem is the perception that software inspections cost more than they are worth. However, available quantitative evidence as presented above indicates that inspections have had significant positive impact on the quality of the developed software and that inspections are more cost-effective than other defect detection activities, such as testing. Furthermore, it is important to keep in mind that besides quality improvement and cost savings realized by finding and fixing defects before they reach the customer, other benefits are often associated with performing inspections. These benefits, such as learning, are often difficult to measure, but they also have an impact on quality, productivity, and the success of a software development project.

4.2.3. *Duration*

Inspections do not only consume effort, but they also have an impact on the product's development cycle time. Inspection activities are scheduled in a way in which all people involved can participate and fulfill their roles. Thus, the interval for the completion of all activities will range from at least a few days up to a few weeks. During this period, other work that relies on the inspected software product may be delayed. Hence, duration might be a crucial aspect for a project manager if time to market is a critical issue during development. However, only few articles present information on the global inspection duration.

Votta discusses the effects of time loss due to scheduling contention. He reports that inspection meetings account for 10% of the development interval [130]. Due to the delays, he advises substituting inspection meetings with other forms of defect collection.

4.3. *The organizational dimension of software inspection*

Fowler [42] states that the introduction of inspection is more than giving individuals the set of skills on how to perform inspections. It also introduces a new process within an organization. Hence, it affects the whole organization, that is, the team, the project structure, and the environment. We identified 6 references relevant to this dimension.

4.3.1. *Team*

An important factor regarding software inspection is the human factor. A software inspection is driven by its participants, i.e. the members of a project team. Hence, the success or failure of software inspection as a tool for quality improvement and cost reduction heavily depends on human factors. If team members are unwilling to perform inspections, all efforts will be deemed to fail. Franz and Shih [43] point out that attitude about defects is the key to effective inspections. Once the inevitability of defects is accepted, team members often welcome inspections as a defect detection method. To overcome objections, Russell reports on an advertising campaign to persuade project teams that inspections really do work [116]. An advice we often found in the literature was to exclude management from an inspection [43, 68]. This is suggested to avoid any misconception that inspection results are used for personnel evaluation. Furthermore, training is deemed essential [1, 42]. Training allows project members to build their own opinion on how inspections work and how crucial defect data are within an environment for triggering further empirically justified process improvements.

4.3.2. *Project structure*

Inspection *per se* is a human-based activity. Especially when meetings are performed, authors are confronted with the defects they created. This can easily result in personal conflicts, particularly in project environments with a strict hierarchy. Hence, one must consider the project structure to anticipate the conflict potential among participants. Depending on this potential for conflict, one must decide whether an inspection moderator belongs to the development team or must come from an independent department. This is vital in cases in which inspection is applied between sub-groups of one project. Personal conflicts within an inspection result in demotivation for performing inspection at all.

4.3.3. *Environment*

Introducing inspections is a technology transfer initiative. Hence, issues revolve around the need to deal with a software development organization, not just in terms of its workers but also in terms of its culture, management, budget, quality, and productivity goals. All these aspects can be subsumed in the subdimension environment of an organization. Fowler [42] states that preparing the organization for using inspections dovetails with adapting the inspections to the local technical issues. Furthermore, the new process must be carefully designed to serve in the organization's environment and culture. Based on their inspection experiences at Hewlett-Packard, Grady and Van Slack [51] suggest a four stage process for inspection technology transfer: experimental stage, initial guideline stage, widespread belief and adoption stage, and standardization stage. The experimental stage comprises the first inspection activities within an organization, and is often limited to a particular project of an organization. Based on the experiences in this project, first guidelines can be developed. This is the starting point for the initial guideline stage. In this stage, the inspection approach is defined in more detail and training material is created. The widespread belief and adoption stage takes advantage of the available experiences and training material to adopt inspection to several projects. Finally, the standardization stage helps build an infrastructure structure strong enough to achieve and hold inspection competence. This approach follows a typical new technology transfer model.

4.4. *The tool dimension of software inspection*

Currently, few tools supporting inspections are available. Some of them were developed by researchers to investigate software (often source code) inspection and none of the academic tools has reached commercial status yet. There may be some commercial tools available that we were not aware of, since they have not been discussed in the inspection literature. We analyzed, discussed, and classified the following ten inspection tools: (1) PAE (Program Assurance Environment) [8], which can be seen as an extended debugger and represents an exception in the list of tools. (2) InspecQ [73] concentrates on the support of the Phased Inspection process model developed by Knight and Meyers. (3) ICICLE [20] supports the defect detection phase as well as the defect collection phase in a face-to-face meeting. (4) Scrutiny [48] and (5) CSI [90], support synchronous, distributed meetings to enable the inspection process for geographically separated development teams. (6) CSRS [62] (7) InspectA [73], (8) Hypercode [101], and (9) AISA [102] removes the conventional defect collection phase and replace it with a public discussion phase were participants vote on defect-annotations. (10) ASSIST [83] uses its own process modeling language and executes any desired inspection process model. All tools provide more or less comfortable document handling facilities for browsing documents on-line.

To compare the various tools, we developed Table 5 according to the various phases of the inspection process. For the defect detection phase we added

Table 5. Overview of inspection tools.

	PAE	ICICLE	Scrutiny	CSRS	InspecQ	ASSISST	CSI/ CAIS	In- spectA	Hyper- Code	AISA
References										
Planning Support	–	–	–	X	X	X	–	X	X	–
Defect Detection Support	X	X	X	X	X	X	X	X	X	X
Automated Defect Detection	X	X	–	–	X	–	–	–	–	–
Annotation Support	–	X	X	X	X	X	X	X	X	X
Document Handling Support	C- Code	C- code	Code	Code/ Text	C- Code Ada	Code	Code	Code	Code/ Text	Code/ Text/ Graph
Reading Technique	Check- list	Check- list	–	Check- list	Check- list	–	Check- list	Check- list	–	–
Defect Collection Support	–	X	X	X	–	X	X	X	X	X
(Synch/ Asynch)/ (Local/ Distributed)	-/- -/-	S/- L/-	S/- L/D	-/A -/D	-/- -/-	S/A l/D	S/A L/D	-/A -/D	S/A -/D	-/A -/D
Defect Correction Support	–	–	–	–	–	–	–	(X)	(X)	X
Inspection Process	–	–	–	X	X	X	–	X	X	X
Control possible										
Process Measurement Support	–	X	X	X	–	X	X	X	X	X
Defect Statistics	–	X	X	X	–	X	X	X	X	X
Supported Infra- structure	Unix	Unix/ X- Windows	ConvB	Ergret	?	LAN	Suite	E-Mail	WWW	WWW

a row to characterize the capability of a tool to automate the defect detection process (e.g. with rule sets). For the defect collection phase, we added a row to determine whether a tool supports defect collection in a synchronous (i.e., same time), asynchronous (i.e., different time), local (i.e., same place), or distributed (i.e., different place) manner. We focused on whether a tool provides facilities to control and measure the inspection process, and on the infrastructure on which the tool is running (a cross "X" indicates support and a minus "–" no support). Of course, for source code products various compilers are available that can perform type and syntactical checking. This may remove some burden from inspectors. Furthermore, support tools, such as Lint for C, may help detect further classes of defects. However, the use of these tools is limited to particular development situations and may only lighten the inspection burden.

We must admit that the question of how to support inspections with tools is addressed by many researchers and companies. Hence, we might have missed some tool that may be beneficial for an inspection.

5. Conclusions

This paper presented a survey of work in the area of software inspection. The survey introduced a detailed description of the core concepts and relationships that together define the field of software inspection technologies.

This type of survey is beneficial to researchers and practitioners for various reasons. First, it provides a roadmap in the form of a taxonomy that allows for the identification of available inspection methods and experience. Hence, this survey helps identify the ingredients of the best-suited inspection approach for a particular situation through the combination of the various dimensions. Second, the work helps structure the large amount of published inspection work. This structure presents the gist of the inspection work so far performed and helps researchers and practitioners characterize the nature of new work in the inspection field. In a sense, this structure also helps define a common vocabulary that depicts the software inspection area. Third, the survey presents an overview of the current state of research as well as an analysis of today's knowledge in the software inspection field.

We have to state that each survey has its limitations because it can only be a snapshot of the work that is currently in progress. Furthermore, a survey usually represents only a fraction of articles that are available on a subject. However, in this case we analyzed more than four hundred references. We are therefore convinced that this survey represents a good snapshot of the inspection-related work.

Acknowledgment

I am grateful to Jean-Marc DeBaud who participated in an earlier version of this survey as well as the anonymous reviewers for their comments on this chapter.

References

1. A. F. Ackerman, L. S. Buchwald and F. H. Lewsky, "Software inspections: An effective verification process", *IEEE Software* **6**, no. 3 (1989) 31–36.
2. M. P. Ardissone, M. Spolverini and M. Valentini, "Statistical decision support method for in-process inspections", *Proceedings of the 4th International Conference on Achieving Quality In Software* (1998) 135–143.
3. Association of Computing Machinery, 1998, The ACM Digital Library, *http://www.acm.org/dl/*
4. J. Barnard and A. Price, "Managing code inspection information", *IEEE Software* **11**, no. 2 (1994) 59–69.
5. V. Basili, S. Green, O. Laitenberger, F. Lanubile, F. Shull, S. Sorumgard and M. Zelkowitz, "The empirical investigation of perspective-based reading", *Journal of Empirical Software Engineering* **2**, no. 1 (1996) 133–164.
6. V. R. Basili, "Evolving and packaging reading technologies", *Journal of Systems and Software* **38**, no. 1 (1997).
7. V. R. Basili and R. W. Selby, "Comparing the effectiveness of software testing techniques", *IEEE Transactions on Software Engineering* **13**, no. 12 (1987) 1278–1296.
8. F. Belli and R. Crisan, "Towards automation of checklist-based code-reviews", *Proceedings of the 8th International Symposium on Software Reliability Engineering*, 1996.
9. D. B. Bisant and J. R. Lyle, "A two-person inspection method to improve programming productivity", *IEEE Transactions on Software Engineering* **15**, no. 10 (1989) 1294–1304.
10. F. W. Blakely and M. E. Boles, "A case study of code inspections", *Hewlett-Packard Journal* **42**, no. 4 (1991) 58–63.
11. H. M. Blalock, *Theory Construction* (Prentice Hall, Englewood Cliffs, 1979).
12. B. W. Boehm, *Software Engineering Economics, Advances in Computing Science and Technology* (Prentice Hall, 1981).
13. K. V. Bourgeois, "Process insights from a large-scale software inspections data analysis", Cross Talk, *The Journal of Defense Software Engineering* (1996) 17–23.
14. L. Briand, K. El Emam, B. Freimut and O. Laitenberger, "Quantitative evaluation of capture-recapture models to control software inspections", *Proceedings of the 9th International Symposium on Software Reliability Engineering* (1997).
15. L. Briand, K. El Emam, B. Freimut and O. Laitenberger, "A comprehensive evaluation of capture-recapture models for estimating software defect content", *IEEE Transactions on Software Engineering* **26**, no. 6 (2000).
16. L. Briand, K. E. Emam, T. Fussbroich and O. Laitenberger, "Using simulation to build inspection efficiency benchmarks for development projects", *Proceedings of the 20th International Conference on Software Engineering* (1998) 340–349.
17. L. C. Briand, C. M. Differding and H. D. Rombach, "Practical guidelines for measurement-based process improvement", *Software Process* **2**, no. 4 (1996) 253–280.
18. L. C. Briand, B. G. Freimut, B. Klein, O. Laitenberger and G. Ruhe, "Quality assurance technologies for the EURO conversion — Industrial experience at Allianz Life Assurance", *2nd International Software Quality Week Europe*, Brussels, Belgium (1998).
19. A.-P. Bröhl and W. Dröschel, Das V-Modell, Oldenbourg (1995).
20. L. Brothers, V. Sembugamoorthy and M. Muller, "ICICLE: Groupware for code inspection", *Proceedings of the ACM Conference on Computer Supported Cooperative Work* (1990) 169–181.

21. B. Brykczynski and D. A. Wheeler, "An annotated bibliography on software inspections", *ACM SIGSOFT Software Engineering Notes* **18**, no. 1 (1993) 81–88.
22. K. Cai, "On estimating the number of defects remaining in software", *Journal of Systems and Software* **40** (1998) 93–114.
23. B. Cheng and R. Jeffrey, "Comparing inspection strategies for software requirements specifications", *Proceedings of the 1996 Australian Software Engineering Conference* (1996) 203–211.
24. Y. Chernak, "A statistical approach to the inspection checklist formal synthesis and improvement", *IEEE Transactions on Software Engineering* **22**, no. 12 (1996) 866–874.
25. D. A. Christenson, H. T. Steel and A. J. Lamperez, "Statistical quality control applied to code inspections", *IEEE Journal Selected Areas in Communication* **8**, no. 2 (1990) 196–200.
26. J. S. Collofello and S. N. Woodfield, "Evaluating the effectiveness of reliability-assurance techniques", *Journal of Systems and Software* **9** (1989) 191–195.
27. R. Conradi, A. S. Marjara and B. Skatevik, "Empirical studies of inspection and test data", *Proceedings of the First Conference on Product-Focused Process Improvement*, Oulo, Finland (1999).
28. H. M. Cooper, "Scientific guidelines for conducting integrative research reviews", *Review of Educational Research* **52**, no. 2 (1982) 291–302.
29. T. D. Crossman, "A method of controlling quality of applications software", *South African Computer Journal* **5** (1991) 70–74.
30. P. D'Astous and P. N. Robillard, "Characterizing implicit information during peer review meetings", *Proceedings of the 22nd International Conference on Software Engineering*, Limerick (2000).
31. M. Deck, "Cleanroom software engineering to reduce software cost", Technical Report, Cleanroom Software Engineering Associates, 6894 Flagstaff Rd. Boulder, CO 80302 (1994).
32. T. DeMarco, *Controlling Software Projects* (Yourdon Press, NY, 1982).
33. A. Dennis and J. Valacich, "Computer brainstorms: More heads are better than one", *Journal of Applied Social Psychology* **78**, no. 4 (1993) 531–537.
34. E. P. Doolan, "Experience with Fagan's inspection method", *Software-Practice and Experience* **22**, no. 3 (1992) 173–182.
35. A. Dunsmore, M. Roper and M. Wood, "Object-oriented inspection in the face of delocalisation", *Proceedings of the 22nd International Conference on Software Engineering*, Limerick (2000).
36. M. Dyer, *The Cleanroom Approach to Quality Software Development* John Wiley and Sons, Inc (1992a).
37. M. Dyer, "Verification-based inspection", *Proceedings of the 26th Annual Hawaii International Conference on System Sciences* (1992b) 418–427.
38. S. G. Eick, C. R. Loader, M. D. Long, L. G. Votta and S. VanderWiel, "Estimating software fault content before coding", *Proceedings of the 14th International Conference on Software Engineering* (1992) 59–65.
39. K. El Emam, O. Laitenberger and H. Harbich, "The application of subjective effectiveness to controlling software inspections", *Journal of Systems and Software* **54**, no. 2 (2000).
40. M. E. Fagan, "Design and code inspections to reduce errors in program development", *IBM Systems Journal* **15**, no. 3 (1976) 182–211.
41. M. E. Fagan, "Advances in software inspections", *IEEE Transactions on Software Engineering* **12**, no. 7 (1986) 744–751.

42. P. J. Fowler, "In-process inspections of workproducts at AT&T", *AT&T Technical Journal* **65**, no. 2 (1986) 102–112.
43. L. A. Franz and J. C. Shih, "Estimating the value of inspections and early testing for software projects", CS-TR- 6, *Hewlett-Packard Journal* (1994).
44. Fraunhofer Institute for Experimental Software Engineering, "An inspection bibliography", *http://www.iese.fhg.de/Inspections* (1998).
45. D. P. Freedman and G. M. Weinberg, *Handbook of Walkthroughs, Inspections, and Technical Reviews*, 3rd ed. (Dorset House Publishing, New York, 1990).
46. A. A. Gately, "Design and code inspection metrics", *International Conference on Software Management and Applications of Software Measurement*, San Jose, CA (1999).
47. T. Gilb and D. Graham, *Software Inspection* (Addison-Wesley Publishing Company, 1993).
48. J. Gintell, M. Houde and R. McKenney, "Lessons learned by building and using scrutiny, A collaborative software inspection system", *Proceedings of the 7th International Workshop on Computer-Aided Software Engineering* (1995) 350–357.
49. M. E. Graden, P. S. Horsley and T. C. Pingel, "The effects of software inspections on a major telecommunications-project", *AT&T Technical Journal* **65**, no. 3 (1986) 32–40.
50. R. B. Grady, "Successfully applying software metrics", *IEEE Computer* **27**, no. 9 (1994) 18–25.
51. R. B. Grady and T. Van Slack, "Key lessons in achieving widespread inspection use", *IEEE Software* **11**, no. 4 (1994) 46–57.
52. L. Hatton, "Does OO sync with how we think?", *IEEE Software* **15**, no. 3 (1998) 46–54.
53. W. C. Hetzel, "An experimental analysis of program verification methods", PhD Thesis, University of North Carolina at Chapel Hill, Department of Computer Science (1976).
54. W. H. Humphrey, *A Discipline for Software Engineering* (Addison-Wesley, 1995).
55. International Software Engineering Research Network (1998). Bibliography of the International Software Engineering Research Network, *http://www.iese.fhg.de/ISERN/pub/isern_biblio_tech.html*
56. J. Iisakka and I. Tervonen, "Painless improvements to the review process", *Software Quality Journal* **7** (1998) 11–20.
57. A. Jackson and D. Hoffman, "Inspecting module interface specifications", *Software Testing, Verification and Reliability* **4**, no. 2 (1994) 101–117.
58. P. Jalote and M. Haragopal, "Overcoming the NAH syndrome for inspection deployment", *Proceedings of the Twentieth International Conference on Software Engineering* (1998) 371–378.
59. P. Johnson, "The WWW formal technical review archive", *http://zero.ics.hawaii.edu/johnson/FTR* (1998a).
60. P. M. Johnson, "Reengineering inspection", *Communications of the ACM* **41**, no. 2 (1998b) 49–52.
61. P. M. Johnson and D. Tjahjono, "Improving software quality through computer supported collaborative review", *Proceedings of the 19th International Conference on Software Engineering* (1993) 61–76.
62. P. M. Johnson and D. Tjahjono, *Assessing Software Review Meetings: A Controlled Experimental Study Using CSRS* (ACM Press, 1997) 118–127.
63. P. M. Johnson and D. Tjahjono, "Does every inspection really need a meeting", *Journal of Empirical Software Engineering* **3**, no. 1 (1998) 9–35.

64. C. Jones, "Gaps in the object-oriented paradigm", *IEEE Computer* **27**, no. 6 (1994) 90–91.
65. C. Jones, "Software defect-removal efficiency", *IEEE Computer* **29**, no. 4 (1996) 94–95.
66. E. Kamsties and C. M. Lott, "An empirical evaluation of three defect-detection techniques", eds. W. Schäfer and P. Botella, *Proceedings of the 5th European Software Engineering Conference, Lecture Notes in Computer Science 989* (Springer-Verlag, 1993) 362–383.
67. S. H. Kan, *Metrics and Models in Software Quality Engineering* (Addison-Wesley Publishing Company, 1995).
68. C. Kaner, "The performance of the N-fold requirement inspection method", *Requirements Engineering Journal* **2**, no. 2 (1998) 114–116.
69. J. C. Kelly, J. S. Sherif and J. Hops, "An analysis of defect densities found during software inspections", *Journal of Systems and Software* **17** (1992) 111–117.
70. L. P. W. Kim, C. Sauer and R. Jeffery, "A framework for software development technical reviews", *Software Quality and Productivity: Theory, Practice, Education and Training* (1995).
71. B. Kitchenham, A. Kitchenham and J. Fellows, "The effects of inspections on software quality and productivity", Technical Report 1, *ICL Technical Journal* (1986).
72. J. C. Knight and E. A. Myers, "Phased inspections and their implementation", *ACM SIGSOFT Software Engineering Notes* **16**, no. 3 (1991) 29–35.
73. J. C. Knight and E. A. Myers, "An improved inspection technique", *Communications of the ACM* **36**, no. 11 (1993) 51–61.
74. S. Kusumoto, "Quantitative evaluation of software reviews and testing processes", PhD Thesis, Faculty of the Engineering Science of Osake University (1993).
75. S. Kusumoto, A. Chimura, T. Kikuno, K. Matsumoto and Y. Mohri, "A promising approach to two-person software review in an educational environment", *Journal of Systems and Software* no. 40 (1998) 115–123.
76. O. Laitenberger and J.-M. DeBaud, "Perspective-based reading of code documents at Robert Bosch GmbH", *Information and Software Technology* **39** (1997) 781–791.
77. O. Laitenberger, "Cost-effective detection of software defects with perspective-based inspection", PhD Thesis, University of Kaiserslautern, ISBN 3-8167-5583-6 (2000).
78. L. P. W. Land, C. Sauer and R. Jeffery, "Validating the defect detection performance advantage of group designs for software reviews: Report of a laboratory experiment using program code", *Proceedings of the 6th European Software Engineering Conference*, eds. M. Jazayeri and H. Schauer, *Lecture Notes in Computer Science 1301* (1997) 294–309.
79. S. Letovsky, J. Pinto, R. Lampert and E. Soloway, "A cognitive analysis of a code inspection", *Empirical Studies of Programming* (1987) 231–247.
80. J. M. Levine and R. L. Moreland, "Progress in small group research", *Annual Review of Psychology* **41** (1990) 585–634.
81. R. C. Linger, H. D. Mills and B. I. Witt, *Structured Programming: Theory and Practice* (Addison-Wesley Publishing Company, 1979).
82. F. Macdonald, Assist v1.1 User Manual Technical Report RR-96-199 [EFoCS-22-96], Empirical Foundations of Computer Science (EFoCS), University of Strathclyde, UK (1997).
83. F. Macdonald and J. Miller, "Modelling Software Inspection Methods for the Application of Tool Support", Technical Report RR-95-196 [EFoCS-16-95], Empirical Foundations of Computer Science (EFoCS), University of Strathclyde, UK (1995).

84. F. Macdonald, J. Miller, A. Brooks, M. Roper and M. Wood, "Applying inspection to object-oriented software", *Software Testing, Verification and Reliability* **6** (1996b) 61–82.
85. F. Macdonald, J. Miller, A. Brooks, M. Roper and M. Wood, "Automating the software inspection process", *Automated Software Engineering* **3** (1996a) 193–218.
86. J. M. MacLeod, "Implementing and sustaining a software inspection program in an R&D environment", *Hewlett-Packard Journal* (1993).
87. R. Madachy, L. Little and S. Fan, "Analysis of a successful inspection program", *Proceedings of the 18th Annual NASA Software Engineering Laboratory Workshop* (1993) 176–198.
88. J. J. Marciniak, "Reviews and audits", ed. J. J. Marciniak, *Encyclopedia of Software Engineering* **2** (John Wiley and Sons, 1994) 1084–1090.
89. J. Martin and W. T. Tsai, "N-fold inspection: A requirements analysis technique", *Communications of the ACM* **33**, no. 2 (1990) 225–232.
90. V. Mashayekhi, J. M. Drake, W. T. Tsai and J. Riedl, "Distributed, collaborative software inspection", *IEEE Software* **10** (1993) 66–75.
91. T. J. McCabe, "A complexity measure", *IEEE Transactions on Software Engineering* **2**, no. 4 (1976) 308–320.
92. T. McGibbon, "A business case for software process improvement", Technical Report F30602-92-C-0158, Data and Analysis Center for Software (DACS), *URL: http://www.dacs.com/techs/roi.soar/soar.html* (1996).
93. J. Miller, M. Wood and M. Roper, "Further experiences with scenarios and checklists", *Journal of Empirical Software Engineering* **3**, no. 3 (1998) 37–64.
94. P. Murphy and J. Miller, "A process for asynchronous software inspection", *Proceedings of the 8th International Workshop on Software Technology and Engineering Practice* (1997) 96–104.
95. G. J. Myers, "A controlled experiment in program testing and code walkthroughs/inspections", *Communications of the ACM* **21**, no. 9 (1978) 760–768.
96. National Aeronautics and Space Administration, 1993, Software Formal Inspection Guidebook. Technical Report NASA-GB-A302, National Aeronautics and Space Administration, *http://satc.gsfc.nasa.gov/fi/fipage.html*
97. OCLC, 1998, Online Computer Library Center, *http://www.oclc.org/oclc/menu/home1.html*
98. D. L. Parnas, "Active design reviews: Principles and practice", *Journal of Systems and Software* **7** (1987) 259–265.
99. D. L. Parnas and D. Weiss, "Active design reviews: Principles and practices", *Proceedings of the 8th International Conference on Software Engineering* (1985) 132–136, Also available as NRL Report 8927, November 18, 1985.
100. E. J. Pedhazur, *Multiple Regression in Behavioral Research*, 2nd ed. (Hartcourt Brace College Publishers, 1982).
101. J. Perpich, D. Perry, A. Porter, L. Votta and M. Wade, "Anywhere, anytime code inspections: Using the web to remove inspection bottlenecks in large-scale software development", *Proceedings of the 19th International Conference on Software Engineering* (1997) 14–21.
102. D. E. Perry, A. Porter, L. G. Votta and M. W. Wade, "Evaluating workflow and process automation in wide-area software development", ed. C. Montangero, *Proceedings of the 5th European Workshop on Software Process Technology, Lecture Notes in Computer Science 1149* (Springer-Verlag, Berlin, Heidelberg, 1996) 188–193.

103. A. A. Porter and P. M. Johnson, "Assessing software review meetings: Results of a comparative analysis of two experimental studies", *IEEE Transactions on Software Engineering* **23**, no. 3 (1997) 129–144.
104. A. A. Porter, H. Siy, A. Mockus and L. Votta, "Understanding the sources of variation in software inspections", *ACM Transactions on Software Engineering and Methodology* **7**, no. 1 (1998) 41–79.
105. A. A. Porter and L. Votta, "Comparing detection methods for software requirements inspection: A replication using professional subjects", *Journal of Empirical Software Engineering* **3**, no. 4 (1998) 355–378.
106. A. A. Porter, H. Siy and L. G. Votta, "A review of software inspections", Technical Report CS-TR-3552, UMIACS-TR-95-104, Department of Computer Science, University of Maryland, College Park, Maryland 20742 (1995a).
107. A. A. Porter, H. P. Siy, C. A. Toman and L. G. Votta, "An experiment to assess the cost-benefits of code inspections in large scale software development", *IEEE Transactions on Software Engineering* **23**, no. 6 (1997) 329–346.
108. A. A. Porter and L. G. Votta, "What makes inspections work?", *IEEE Software* (1997) 99–102.
109. A. A. Porter, L. G. Votta and V. R. Basili, "Comparing detection methods for software requirements inspections: A replicated experiment", *IEEE Transactions on Software Engineering* **21**, no. 6 (1995b) 563–575.
110. T. Raz and A. T. Yaung, "Factors affecting design inspection effectiveness in software development", *Information and Software Technology* **39** (1997) 297–305.
111. J. T. Reeve, "Applying the Fagan inspection technique", *Quality Forum* **17**, no. 1 (1991) 40–47.
112. H. Remus, "Integrated software validation in the view of inspections/reviews", *Software Validation* (1984) 57–65.
113. S. Rifkin and L. Deimel, "Applying program comprehension techniques to improve software inspection", *Proceedings of the 19th Annual NASA Software Engineering Laboratory Workshop*, NASA (1994).
114. R. Rosenthal, "The 'file drawer problem' and tolerance for null results", *Psychological Bulletin* **86**, no. 3 (1979) 638–641.
115. P. Runeson and C. Wohlin, "An experimental evaluation of an experience-based capture-recapture method in software code inspections", *Journal of Empirical Software Engineering* **3**, no. 4 (1998) 381–406.
116. G. W. Russell, "Experience with inspection in ultralarge-scale developments", *IEEE Software* **8**, no. 1 (1991) 25–31.
117. K. Sandahl, O. Blomkvist, J. Karlsson, C. Krysander, M. Lindvall and N. Ohlsson, "An extended replication of an experiment for assessing methods for software requirements inspection", **3**, no. 4 (1998) 327–354.
118. C. Sauer, R. Jeffery, L. Lau and P. Yetton, "The effectiveness of software development technical reviews: A behaviorally motivated program of research", *IEEE Transactions on Software Engineering* **26**, no. 1 (2000).
119. G. M. Schneider, J. Martin and W. T. Tsai, "An experimental study of fault detection in user requirements documents", *ACM Transactions on Software Engineering and Methodology* **1**, no. 2 (1992) 188–204.
120. C. B. Seaman and V. R. Basili, "Communication and organization: An empirical study of discussion in inspection meetings", *IEEE Transactions on Software Engineering* **24**, no. 6 (1998) 559–572.
121. M. E. Shaw, *Group Dynamics: The Psychology of Small Group Behaviour* (McGraw Hill Inc, 1976).

122. G. C. Shirey, "How inspections fail", *Proceedings of the 9th International Conference on Testing Computer Software* (1992) 151–159.
123. M. Stein, J. Riedl, S. Harner and V. Mashayekhi, "A case study of distributed, asynchronous software inspection", *Proceedings of the 19th International Conference on Software Engineering* (IEEE Computer Society Press, 1997) 107–117.
124. S. H. Strauss and R. G. Ebenau, *Software Inspection Process* McGraw Hill Systems Design and Implementation Series (1993).
125. F. N. Svendsen, "Experience with inspection in the maintenance of software", *Proceedings of the 2nd European Conference on Software Quality Assurance* (1992).
126. I. Tervonen, "Support for quality-based design and inspection", *IEEE Software* **13**, no. 1 (1996) 44–54.
127. D. Tjahjono, "Exploring the effectiveness of formal technical review factor with CSRS, a collaborative software review system", PhD Thesis, Department of Information and Computer Science, University of Hawaii (1996).
128. G. Travassos, F. Shull, M. Fredericks and V. R. Basili, "Detecting defects in object oriented designs: Using reading techniques to increase software quality", *Conference on Object-oriented Programming Systems, Languages and Applications (OOPSLA)* (1999).
129. L. L. Tripp, W. F. Stuck and B. K. Pflug, "The application of multiple team inspections on a safety-critical software standard", *Proceedings of the 4th Software Engineering Standards Application Workshop* (IEEE Computer Society Press, 1991) 106–111.
130. L. G. Votta, "Does every inspection need a meeting?", *ACM Software Engineering Notes* **18**, no. 5 (1993) 107–114.
131. G. M. Weinberg and D. P. Freedman, "Reviews, walkthroughs, and inspections", *IEEE Transactions on Software Engineering* **12**, no. 1 (1984) 68–72.
132. E. F. Weller, "Experiences with inspections at Bull HN information system", *Proceedings of the 4th Annual Software Quality Workshop*, 1992).
133. E. F. Weller, "Lessons from three years of inspection data", *IEEE Software* **10**, no. 5 (1993) 38–45.
134. G. Wenneson, "Quality assurance software inspections at NASA Ames: Metrics for feedback and modification", *Proceedings of the 10th Annual Software Engineering Workshop* (1985).
135. D. A. Wheeler, B. Brykczinski and R. N. Meeson, *Software Inspection — An Industrial Best Practice* (IEEE Computer Society Press, 1996).
136. D. A. Wheeler, B. Brykczynski and R. N. M. Jr, "Software peer reviews", ed. R. H. Thayer, Software Engineering Project Management, *IEEE Computer Society* (1997).
137. S. A. V. Wiel and L. G. Votta, "Assessing software designs using capture-recapture methods", *IEEE Transactions on Software Engineering* **19**, no. 11 (1993) 1045–1054.
138. C. Wohlin and P. Runeson, "Defect content estimations from review data", *Proceedings of the 20th International Conference on Software Engineering* (1998) 400–409.
139. M. Wood, M. Roper, A. Brooks and J. Miller, "Comparing and combining software defect detection techniques: A replicated empirical study", *Proceedings of the 6th European Software Engineering Conference, Lecture Notes in Computer Science 1301*, eds. M. Jazayeri and H. Schauer (1997) 262–277.
140. E. Yourdon, *Structured Walkthroughs*, 4th ed. (Prentice Hall, New York, 1989).
141. E. Yourdon, *Death March Projects* (Prentice Hall, 1997).

SE/KE REUSE RESEARCH: COMMON THEMES AND EMPIRICAL RESULTS

TIM MENZIES

Department of Electrical & Computer Engineering,
University of British Columbia, 2356 Main Mall, Vancouver, B.C., V6T 1Z4, Canada
http://tim.menzies.com; E-mail: tim@menzies.com

Despite the difference in tools and application domains, software engineers and knowledge engineers are exploring the same technique. In this *reuse-based* approach, components developed previously, are abstracted, then adapted for use in the current application. Knowledge engineers and software engineers may call their abstracted components different things (e.g. "ontologies" or "patterns") but the modeling intent is the same. While much research and practical effort has been applied to reuse-based development, the empirical evidence that it is a cost-effective methodology is not, as yet, convincing.

Keywords: Reuse, patterns, ontologies, problem solving methods, empirical results, costs, benefits.

1. Introduction

In the reuse approach to software construction, design is taken to be the re-shuffling of components developed previously, then abstracted into a reusable form. The idea of reusing old design work when doing new design work dates back at least to 1964 with Alexander's work on architecture [2, 3]. Contemporary expressions of this reuse approach include:

- Object-oriented design *patterns* [12, 48].
- Knowledge engineering research into *ontologies* [30, 34, 64].
- Knowledge engineering research into *problem solving methods* (PSMs) [14, 16, 50, 55].

Reusing patterns/ontologies/PSMs offers many advantages to designers. For example, suppose an analyst is reusing the financial knowledge shown in Fig. 1. Supposing our analyst is reviewing a design for some point-of-sale system. Note that the background knowledge includes a "subsequent transaction" term. When browsing this knowledge, the analyst might be reminded to ask the question "are the sold items ever returned to the store?". That is, browsing reusable knowledge can assist in auditing and improving the current version of a system description.

The rest of this article focuses on what is common between reuse in software engineering *and* knowledge engineering research and practice. In that union of work, we find a common notion of reusing abstractions (which are called patterns or

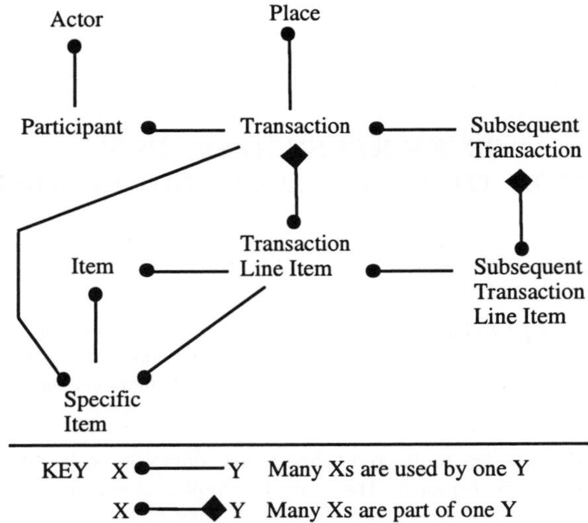

Fig. 1. Part of Coad *et al*'s [18] definition of a financial transaction.

ontologies, depending on which field you are in). Regardless of the name, the basics are the same. Section 2 discusses the benefits of reuse and Sec. 3 gives examples of reuse from the software engineering and knowledge engineering literature. Section 4 discusses the reality of the practice of reuse. Reuse of ontologies/patterns/PSMs comes at a cost. While reuse-based analysis can be exciting, it is an *economic issue* if reuse-based development is the best way to develop software. As we shall see, it is an open issue if the costs of reuse outweigh its benefits.

Since the focus of this article is narrow (on patterns/ontologies/PSMs), much of (e.g.) the standard software engineering literature is not discussed here. The interested reader is referred to [7, 8, 32, 36, 37, 40, 52].

2. Reuse: The Benefits

There are many potential benefits of reuse. Some of these benefits include the *communications* benefit; the *interoperability* benefit; the *browsing* and *searching* benefit; the *systems engineering* benefit; and the *guidance* benefit.

2.1. *The communications benefit*

Any communication task is simplified by a shared lexicon. Such a lexicon can be developed by reusing and generalizing terms seen in prior applications. Generalized lexicons are called different things in different domains. Knowledge engineers typically call them *ontologies* while software engineers call them *patterns*.

Ontologies/patterns can be used to systematically view and share a specific topic/problem. For example, ontologies provide a unified framework within an organization that reduces the terminological confusion [63] arising from different contexts and viewpoints for a particular domain.

Attempting to reuse knowledge is a useful teaching tool. For example, reusing knowledge can simplify a student's task when (e.g.) reading textbooks. Also, studying reusable abstractions are useful when tutoring software or knowledge engineering [48]. Such abstractions serve as a useful final initiation ritual for a novice designer. When they "get" abstractions, we know that the students are capable of comparing and contrasting a wide range of systems.

2.2. *The interoperability benefit*

Interoperability among systems with different modeling methods, paradigms, languages and software tools can be achieved with ontologies that act as an interlingua [38]. Without reusable abstractions, every pair of systems may require a different interface. With reusable abstractions, a set of systems can be mapped into one common abstract form. The economic benefits of this common form are clear. Without it, connecting N systems means building $(N^2 - N)/2$ interfaces (one for every pair of systems). With the common format, N systems can be interfaced via N interfaces (one between every system and the common abstract form). The interface definition language (IDL) of the CORBA distributed object system and XML are an examples of this kind of approach.

2.3. *The browsing/searching benefit*

The reusable knowledge within an ontology can assist an intelligent search engine while processing a query. For example, if a query returns no results, then the ontology could be used to automatically generalize the query to find the nearest partial matches.

2.4. *The systems engineering benefit*

If ontologies are the generalized *nouns* of a domain, problem solving methods (PSMs) are the generalized *verbs* from a domain. Such generalized verbs capture the important abstractions within a domain. Often the processing of a domain falls into cliched patterns of behavior. In knowledge engineering, these behavioral patterns are called PSMs.

Reusing ontologies and problem solving methods can simplify system development. Several examples are listed below from the knowledge engineering domain. More detailed examples from software engineering and knowledge engineering are offered later in this chapter:

- Kalfoglou executes the constraints found in existing ontologies to check new systems. Such pre-existing constraints, are a powerful tool for checking knowledge when other oracles are absent [33].

- One commercial company used the ontology associated with Motta's PSM design tools to formalize the regulations applicable to the design of the truck cabin [51]. This formalization, associated with a constraint analyzer, cut the design of the geometric layout of the cabin from 4 months to 1 day(!!).
- In the SPARK/ BURN/ FIREFIGHTER system, an intelligent PSM librarian was used to build nine KBS applications. Development times changed from one to 17 days (using the librarian) to a range of 63 to 250 days (without using the librarian) [44].
- The SALT editor used for the VT elevator configuration system restricted its knowledge editors to only those terms relevant for the propose-and-revise PSM used in VT [42, 43]. $^{2130}/_{3062} \approx 70\%$ of VT's rules could be auto-generated by SALT.
- RIME was an intelligent editor for simplifying the maintenance of DEC's XCON automatic computer configuration system. Bachant and McDermott [6] found that if a rule editor could access the ontology of the PSMs within XCON, then very large rules could be quickly built from very small specifications.

2.5. *The guidance benefit*

While we may use little of an ontology or a pattern or a PSM, it may still be useful as a "pointer tool". That is, the ontology/pattern/PSM could be used as a structuring tool for exploring a new domain. Roughly speaking, reusing abstracted forms of old knowledge is pointing the way saying "these kinds of things are important, even if these particular things are not". In this approach, developers kick-start the development with an ontology/pattern/PSM.

3. Examples of Reuse

To get a feel for the power of reuse-based design, the discussion now samples reuse work from the software engineering and knowledge engineering literature.

3.1. *Reuse in software engineering*

The work on object-oriented *patterns* is a good exemplar of reuse research in software engineering. Researchers in this area include the "gang-of-four" (GOF) [28]; the "gang-of-five"(GOV) [12]; Fowler [25]; Shaw and Garlan [57]; and Coad *et al* [18].

Consider the class hierarchy browser of Fig. 2. When a class name is selected in the upper-left list box, the methods of that class are displayed in the upper-right list box. If one of these methods is selected, then the source code for that method is displayed in the bottom text pane.

Now compare this class hierarchy browser with the disk browser shown in Fig. 3. When a directory name is selected in the upper-left list box, the files in that

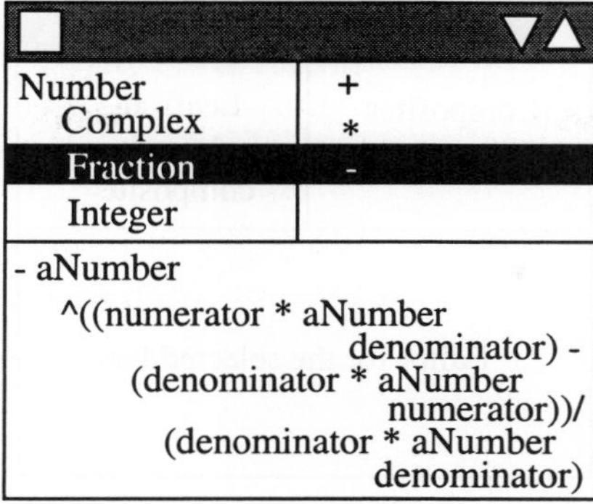

Fig. 2. A class hierarchy browser.

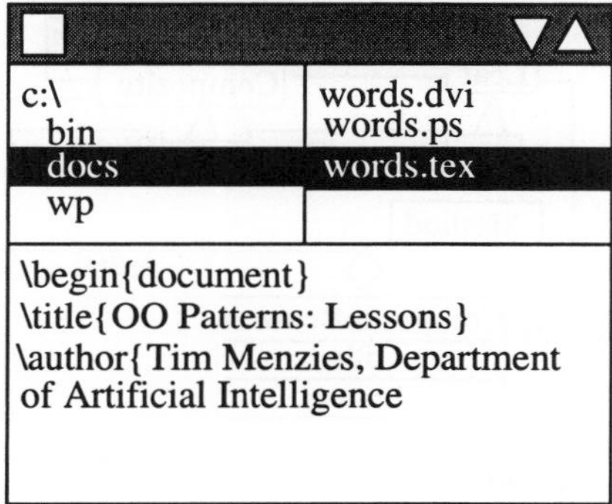

Fig. 3. A disk browser.

directory are displayed in the upper-right list box. If one of these files is selected, then the contents of that file are displayed in the bottom text pane.

Clearly, there is some similarity in the two browsers. Containers (classes or directories) are shown top-left. The things in the containers that are not themselves containers (methods and files) are shown top-right. The contents of these non-container things are shown in the bottom pane.

If we rename containers *composites* and the non-containers *leaves* then we can design one *composite browser* class that handles both class hierarchies and directory trees (see Fig. 4). That is, our disk browser and class hierarchy browser are both presentations of nested composites.

Figure 5 shows the inner structure of the composite browser. Composites contain either other composites or leaves. Leaves compile the contents of lower text-pane. Once this structure is in place, all that is required to convert a disk browser to a class hierarchy browser is to:

- Change the title of the window for "Disk Browser" to "Class Hierarchy Browser".

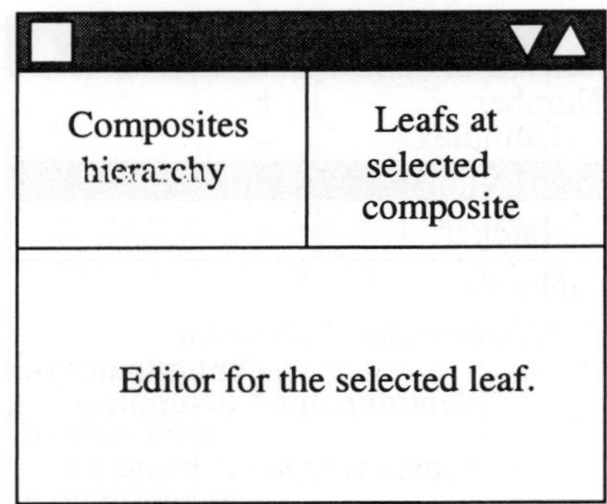

Fig. 4. A composite browser.

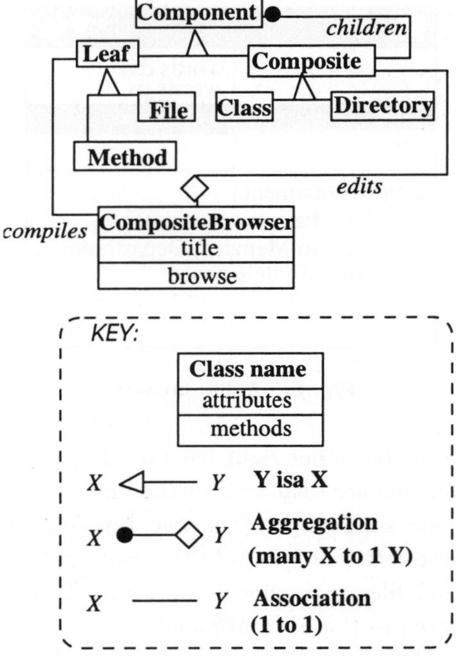

Fig. 5. Object model for the composite browser.

- Define `Class` beneath `Composite` and `Method` beneath `Leaf`.
- Implement the different `compiles` methods in `Method`. `Compiling` file contents implies transferring text to primary storage. `Compiling` method contents implies parsing the source code, etc.

We have just isolated a "pattern": a fragment of a high-level conceptual model which may be useful in many applications. The above design can be used to (i) brows a disk; (ii) browse a class hierarchy; or, more generally, browse any 1-to-many nested aggregation (e.g. players in teams, persons in companies, stock on shelves). This composite pattern is one of the 23 OO reuse design patterns listed by GOF. The above example suggests the power of such OO reuse patterns. Seemingly different problems can be resolved to a single design. OO reuse patterns could become a repository for experience which can benefit new designers. OO reuse patterns could also serve to unify the terminology of OO design, allowing experience from one application to migrate into another area.

Patterns have been documented in many formats. The GOV prefer the format: *context*, *problem*, *solution* [12]. The context describes a design situation. The problem describes the set of forces that repeatedly occur in that situation while the solution describes a configuration to balance those forces. This solution contains a description of the *static components* and the *runtime behavior*. In OO patterns: (i) the static components are described using class hierarchies and their relationships; and (ii) the runtime behaviors are described using some variant on collaboration diagrams [10]. The GOV argue that this format of a pattern is compatible with numerous other patterns researchers (p. 11 of [12]).

Patterns can be at different layers of abstraction. The GOV describe three layers of pattern abstraction:

(1) Low-level language-dependent *idiom* patterns.
(2) Middle-layer language independent *design* patterns describing a programmer's key mechanisms (e.g. the GOF patterns).
(3) Top-level *architectural patterns* that spread across the entire application [57]. Examples of architectural patterns are *layered* architectures (e.g. the three tiered database-model-dialog systems found commonly in standard management information system-style applications); pipe-and-filter (e.g. the dominant paradigm in UNIX shell scripts); or blackboards (an expert systems technique).

Patterns can be pitched at different audiences. For example, the GOV and GOF patterns are intended for programmers or implementation-aware analysts. Fowler describes *analysis patterns'*; i.e., high-level conceptual patterns which are used to communicate a design to the user community. Fowler was involved in the development of a large medical system. Analysis patterns were used to discuss the design of the system with doctors and nurses. Some patterns found in that medical system (Chap. 3 of [25]) were also useful in a corporate finance applications (Chap. 4 of [25]).

3.2. *Reuse in knowledge engineering*

OO patterns typically describe data structures that may repeat in many domains. Another kind of patterns are the behavioral patterns cataloged by knowledge engineers as problem solving methods (PSMs). The connection of patterns to PSMs is discussed elsewhere [48].

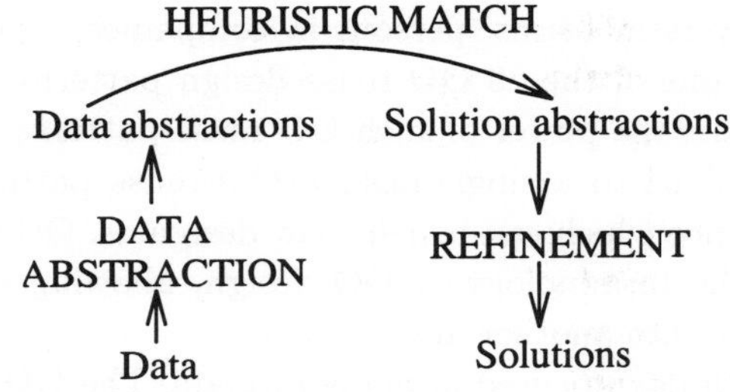

Fig. 6. Heuristic classification.

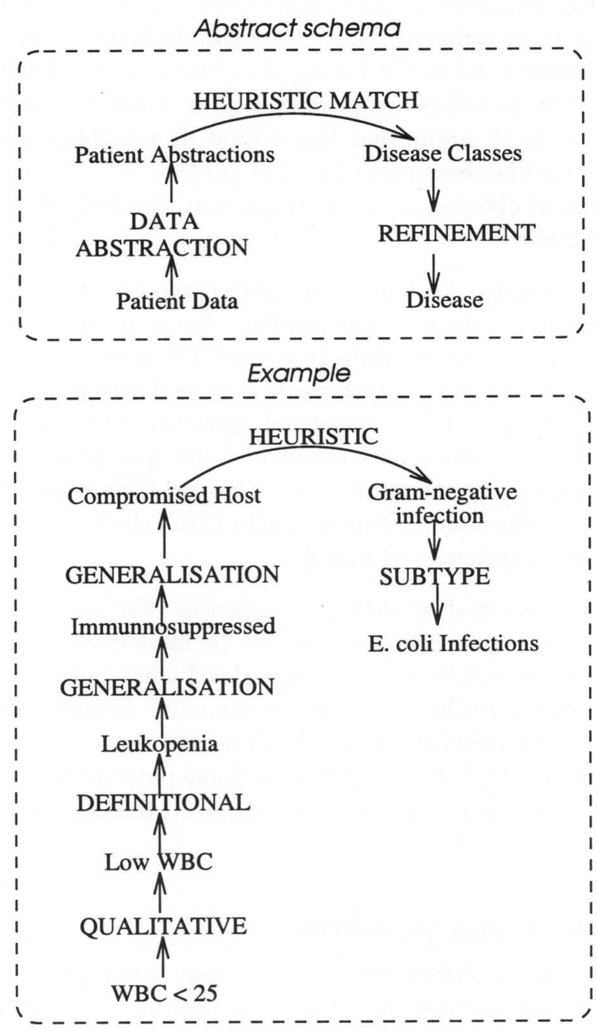

Fig. 7. MYCIN.

The goal of PSM modeling is to identify abstract reusable inference skeletons that appear in many expert systems; e.g. diagnosis, classification, monitoring, etc. Examples of this approach were listed above when discussing the systems engineering benefit of reuse. Other examples include generic tasks [15]; configurable role-limiting methods [29, 61]; model construction operators [17]; CommonKADS [55, 65]; the PROTEGE family of systems [24]; components of expertise [60]; MIKE [5]; and TINA [9].

The archetypal PSM is *heuristic classification*, first described by Clancey [16]. To find this PSM, Clancey reverse-engineered 10 expert systems written in a variety of tools and languages. He found that all these systems shared the same abstract inference skeletons, which he called *heuristic classification* (shown in Fig. 6).

For example, Fig. 7 shows Clancey's analysis of the MYCIN [11, 67] inference structure (abstract schema at top, followed by an example). MYCIN was a backward-chaining rule-based system that prescribed antibiotics. MYCIN worked by building an abstract model of the patient from the patient's data. This is then matched across to a hierarchy of disease classes. The final diagnosis is produced by following the class diseases hierarchy downwards, looking for the most specific disease that is relevant to this patient. Note the similarity with Fig. 6.

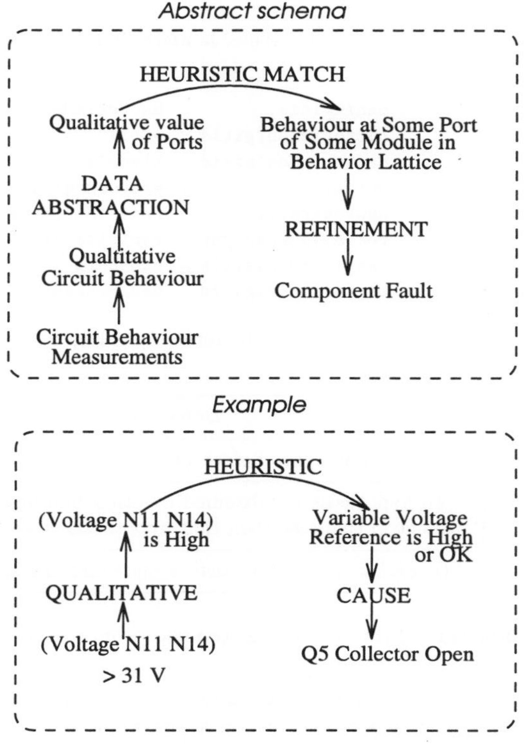

Fig. 8. SOPHIE III.

Figure 8 shows Clancey's analysis of another system, written in LISP which diagnoses an electronic circuit in terms of the component that is causing faulty behavior. The abstract schema is shown on top, and an example is shown underneath. Note the similarity with Figs. 6 and 7.

After the *Heuristic Classification* paper, Clancey refined his inference skeletons. In *Model Construction Operators* [17], Clancey argued that rules like Fig. 9 contain domain-specific terminology (see Fig. 10) as well as reusable inference strategies (see Fig. 11). If these are removed from the rule, then not only have we isolated the true business knowledge in the rule (see Fig. 12), but we also have found inference knowledge we can reuse elsewhere. Clancey's preferred architecture for expert systems is (i) a library of pre-defined problems solving strategies such as Fig. 11; and (ii) a separate knowledge base containing the special domain heuristics like Fig. 12.

```
if   the infection in meningitis                       and
     the type of infection in bacterial                and
     the patient has undergone surgery                 and
     the patient has undergone neurosurgery            and
     the neurosurgery-time was less than 2~months ago and
     the patient received a ventricular-urethral-shunt
then infection = e.coli (.8) or klebsiella (.75)
```

Fig. 9. A domain rule with hidden reusable nference fragments. From [17].

```
subtype(                meningitis,          bacteriaMenigitis       ).
subtype(                bacteriaMenigitis,   eColi                   ).
subtype(                bacteriaMenigitis,   klebsiella              ).
subsumes(               surgery,             neurosurgery            ).
subsumes(               neurosurgery,        recentNeurosurgery      ).
subsumes(               recentNeurosurgery,  ventricularUrethralShunt).
causalEvidence(         bacteriaMenigitis,   exposure                ).
circumstantialEvidence( bacteriaMenigitis,   neurosurgery            ).
```

Fig. 10. Domain-specific terms from Fig. 9.

Strategy	*Description*
exploreAndRefine	Explore super-types before sub-types.
findOut	If an hypothesis is subsumed by other findings which are not present in this case then that hypothesis is wrong.
testHypothesis	Test causal connections before mere circumstantial evidence.

Fig. 11. Problem solving strategies from Fig. 9.

```
if   the patient received a ventricular-urethral-shunt
then infection = e.coli (.8) or klebsiella (.75)
```

Fig. 12. The business knowledge of Fig. 9.

Inspired by Clancey's work, subsequent researchers sought other abstract inference skeletons. Tansley and Hayball [62] list over two dozen reusable inference skeletons including systematic diagnosis (localization and causal tracing), mixed mode diagnosis, verification, correlation, assessment, monitoring, simple classification, heuristic classification, systematic refinement, prediction, prediction of behavior and values, design (hierarchical and incremental), configuration(simple and incremental) planning, and scheduling. These skeletons are recorded using the KADS notation of Fig. 13 in which rectangles are data structures and ovals are functions. Given a `complaint`, the KADS abstract pattern for *diagnosis* is that a `system model` is `decomposed` into `hypothetical` candidate faulty components. A `norm` value is collected from the `system model`. An observation for that candidate is requested from the `observables` (stored internally as a `finding`). The candidate hypothesis is declared to be the diagnosis based on the `difference` between the `norm` value and the `finding`.

Note that Figs. 6 or 13 do not imply a particular execution order of their functions. Conceptually each function can be driven forwards or backwards to connect inputs to outputs or visa versa. The heuristic classification pattern of Fig. 6 could be driven from data to solutions to perform diagnosis; i.e., given the `data`, execute forwards `data-abstraction` then `heuristic match`, then `refinement`.

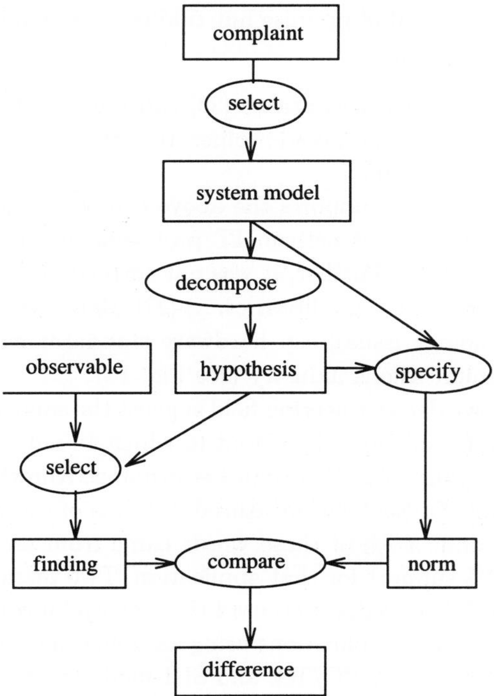

Fig. 13. KADS: diagnosis.

Alternatively, it could be driven from solutions to data to perform intelligent data collection; i.e., given `solutions`, execute backwards `refinement`, then `heuristic match`, then `data abstraction`. In this backwards reasoning, the generated `data` items become requests back to the environment in order to rule out certain possibilities. KADS explicitly models this procedural ordering of the function calls in a separate *task layer* diagram. For more on KADS-style development, see [50].

4. Problems with Reuse

Having discussed the *potential* uses of reuse, it is appropriate to next discuss the *reality* of reuse. Not all the benefits listed above have been achieved in practice. Even enthusiastic proponents of reuse note a puzzling lack of widespread reuse. For example:

> I do not think we have yet succeeded in software reuse. In the State of the Practice, I do not see a lot being applied. Yes, OO class frameworks, Java, Visual Basic, etc have facilitated the code reuse, but less is done, in general, at the higher level such as in the design and requirements phases of a project. In the State of the Art, I have not perceived any incremental progress although many issues have been addressed [31].
>
> Reuse continues to be a problem whose potential remains elusive. Each new solution remains full of promise but riddled with what look like insurmountable problems [53].

Even reuse enthusiasts such as Frakes [26] caution that there exist significant practical problems with the widespread proliferation of reuse libraries; e.g. problems with searching the reuse library.

A review of the literature supports the above claims. Frakes and Fox surveyed 100s of European and North American IT professionals to conclude that reuse levels were low (20% or less). Further, it was not correlated to technology (e.g. use of COBOL, C++, case tools, reuse libraries...) [27]. Reuse seemed to be correlated to non-software technology issues; e.g. hardware standards enabled high levels of reuse in the telecommunications industry (see Fig. 14).

Studies in the knowledge engineering field suggest the same pattern of low-levels of reuse. Cohen *et al* documented the extent to which an ontology *supported* application development within DARPA's High Performance Knowledge Based Systems (HPKB) initiative [19]. *Support* was measured in terms of the words that appeared in some new application: if $^2/_3$ of those words came from an ontology, then that ontology offered a 67% support for that application. Two teams were involved: one at SRI and one from Teknowledge who used the Cycorp knowledge base (hereafter CYC/Tek). The teams built applications using an upper ontology (UO) released by Cycorp. Along with the UO, CYC/Tek and SRI made their own local extensions. Both teams built and debugged their ontology using a set of sample questions (SQ) issued by the HPKB evaluation team. At a pre-announced date, 110 test questions

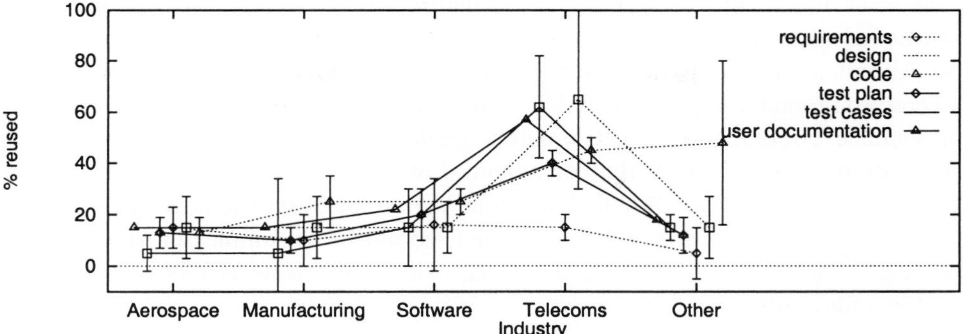

Fig. 14. 95% confidence intervals for reuse levels in different industries.

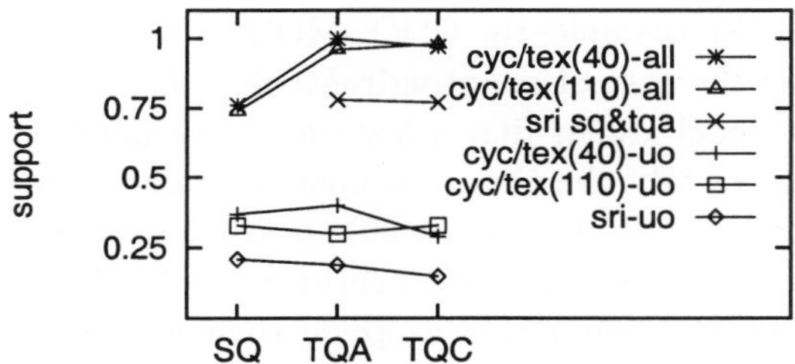

Fig. 15. Reuse of ontologies.

(TQA) were issued and the applications were scored. After a brief respite, a scope change was announced, followed (several days later) by test questions for the new scope (TQC). The SRI system analyzed by Cohen *et al* could only handle 40 of the 110 questions so the CYC/Tek results are divided into CYC/Tek(110) and CYC/Tek(40) where the latter is the subset of the CYC/Tek system relevant to the questions that SRI could handle. The results are shown in Fig. 15. Note that the local ontological extensions supported new applications 3–4 times more than the UO terms; as the scope change (TQA-TQC) the UO offered less and less support; and CYC/Tek's reuse of the UO was greater than that of SRI. These results suggested that the recent words you added yourself to an ontology offer more support than words added previously by other authors. That is, while developers might reuse their own work, they seem less likely to reuse the work of others.

So, despite the *potential* benefits of reuse, there are clearly problems with the *practice* of reuse. These problems include the *structuring* problem, the *productivity* problem, and the *stability* problem.

4.1. *The structuring problem*

Structuring the reusable knowledge is an open issue. Althoff argues that it is hard to build reusable knowledge without considerable experience with the domain.

The level of abstraction at which we formalize our reusable knowledge should be learned via extensive experience with that particular term [4]. Note that, according to Althoff, it is not necessarily true that reusable knowledge should always be expressed in some computer-readable form. Sometimes, simply rendering it on paper will suffice. For example, object-oriented "guidance patterns" serve to direct novice analysts to a set of issues that experienced analysts have found insightful. Such patterns include CHECKS [23], Caterpillar's Fate [35], and the strategies of Coad *et al* [18]. This type of reusable knowledge need not be as complex or as structured as (e.g.) Figs 1, 5, 6, or 13. A simple checklist comprising tick-boxes to yes-no answers may suffice.

4.2. *The productivity problem*

Another major problem is that reuse is not necessarily a more productive method of building systems. For example, the COCOMO-II software cost estimation model offers an estimate of the cost of adapting reusable sub-routines for a new project [1, p. 21]. [1] That model argues that a learning curve must be traversed before a module can be adapted. By the time you know enough to change a little of that module, you may as well have re-written 60% of it from scratch; see Fig. 16.

As another example, consider the Corbridge *et al* [22] study. In that study, international KA experts used PSMs to guide their analysis of a transcript of a patient talking to a doctor [22]. One group used a diagnosis PSM matured over many years; another used an abstract model invented very quickly (the "straw man"); and the rest used no model at all. The results are shown in Fig. 17. The "mature model" group performed as well as the "straw man" group. Further, the "no model" group out-performed the groups using the reuse models.

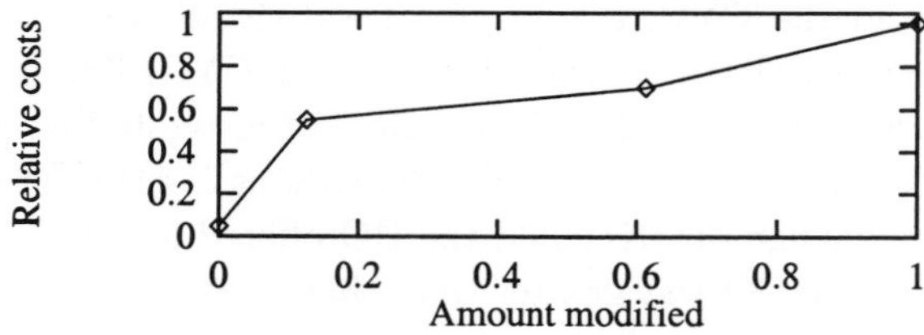

Fig. 16. COCOMO-II, the cost of reuse with X% changes.

Reuse Model	% disorders identified	% knowledge fragments identified
Straw man: invented very quickly	50	28
Mature model: decades of work	55	34
No model	75	41

Fig. 17. Productivity using different models.

	ft/min				
Capacity (lbs)	200	250	300	350	400
2000	√	√	×	√	√
2500	×	×	√	√	√
3000	×	√	√	√	√
3500	√	×	×	×	×
4000	×	×	×	×	×

Fig. 18. PSMs succeeding (√) or failing (×) to configure an elevator.

Further, note that successful reuse can actually *decrease* overall productivity. Consider a reuse library containing a bug. That error would be injected into every application that uses that library. For example, in the Sisyphus-II experiments, various research groups re-implemented part of the VT elevator configuration system [42]. All the groups implemented a PSM with the same error [68]. The Sisyphus-II propose-and-revise PSM was a local greedy search. Local hill-climbing may ignore solutions which are initially unpromising, but lead later on to better solutions. In one experiment, this local greedy search algorithm failed to configure 13/25 elevator configurations: see Fig. 18. Only one of the Sisyphus-II groups reported this error. Apparently, the rest trusted their reusable PSM so much, that they did not perform detailed validation studies. If other developers are as complacent about their reuse libraries, then reuse could decrease overall software productivity since they will spend more time chasing bugs introduced via reuse.

When discussing above the *Systems Engineering Benefit*, various studies were presented that seem to refute the thesis of this section. If reuse complicates productivity measures so much, why is it that Motta *et al* can say that example of truck cabin design, the time to develop the layout dropped from 4 months to 1 day? It is hard to assess such anecdotal evidence without more precise metrics collection [45, 46]. For example, when Motta's colleagues reduced their design time from 4 months to 1 day, how much of that reduction was due to the PSM framework and how much to the constraint analyzer used in that domain? Elsewhere [49], I have criticized overly-enthusiastic reports of reuse that lack detailed measures.[a] For example, proponents of reuse rarely track the on-going costs of maintaining with those components [47] (exception: [39]). Most reuse reports do not clearly distinguish between *verbatim reuse* and *reuse with some tinkering.* Recalling Fig. 16, such tinkering to customize a reusable component can significantly increase the cost and decrease the benefits of using reusable components.

[a]One of the few reuse reports that includes quality measures is [39]. However, that report refers to intra-institutional reuse, not widespread inter-institutional reuse.

A. Originally

```
  RULE(22310.01) IF  (bhthy or
      utsh_bhft4 or
      vhthy) and not on_t4
            and not surgery
            and (antithyroid or
                 hyperthyroid)
THEN DIAGNOSIS("...thyrotoxicosis")
```

B. Same rule, 3 years later

```
  RULE(22310.01) IF  ((((T3 is missing)
        or (T3 is low and
            T3_BORD is low))
        and TSH is missing
        and vhthy
        and not (query_t4 or on_t4 or
                 or surgery or tumour
                 or antithyroid
                 or hypothyroid
                 or hyperthyroid))
      or ((((utsh_bhft4 or
            (Hythe and T4 is missing
             and TSH is missing))
           and (antithyroid or
                hyperthyroid))
          or  utsh_bhft4
          or  ((Hythe or borthy)
               and T3 is missing
               and (TSH is undetect
                    or TSH is low)))
          and not on_t4 and not
              (tumour or surgery)))
     and (TT4 isnt low or T4U isnt low)
THEN DIAGNOSIS("...thyrotoxicosis")
```

Fig. 19. A rule maintained for 3 years.

4.3. *The stability problem*

If a reuse library is *unstable*, then it will be continually rewritten. The cost of extensive rewrites can negate the economic benefits of reuse.

Knowledge is often unstable and this instability can produce dramatic changes to knowledge. For example, half of XCON's thousands of rules were changed every year [59]. To some extent, this might be due to its changing operational requirements (XCON configured computers for DEC and DEC keeps releasing new computers). However, even in supposedly stable domains, knowledge keeps being patched. Garvin ES-1 [20] offered interpretations of biochemical results. Over its lifetime, the biochemical assay hardware remained constant and, presumably, humans did not evolve significantly. Yet KB maintenance was on-going. The kind of (dramatic) changes seen within that KB are shown in Fig. 19. The change in KB size of Gavrin ES-1 is shown in Fig. 20. Note that the rate of change within this system was linear; i.e., even in a stable domain, knowledge kept changing.[b]

What could cause instability in knowledge? One explanation is that consensus expert knowledge is hard to find. Hence, any attempt to record such a consensus implies a constant "pursuit and patch" of feuding ideas. There is some evidence

[b]Technically, the Garvin ES-1 size changes are also consistent with a logarithmic curve. However, a visual inspection of the plot strongly suggests a linear fit.

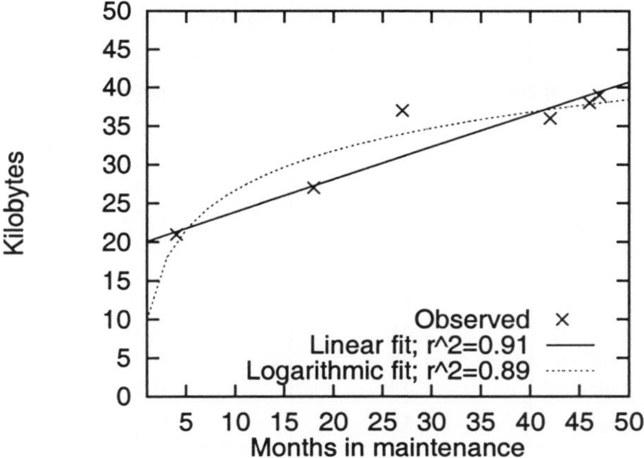

Fig. 20. KB changes in Garvin ES-1.

Expert	% understands	% agrees
E_1	62.5	81.2
E_2	77.8	94.4
E_3	85.7	78.6

Fig. 21. Self-agreement, 12 weeks later.

Expertpairs	% understands	% agrees
E_1,E_2	62.5	33.3
E_2,E_1	61.1	26.7
E_1,E_3	31.2	8.3
E_3,E_1	42.9	33.3
E_2,E_3	44.4	20.0
E_3,E_2	71.4	33.3

Fig. 22. Inter-expert agreement.

that experts disagree, even with themselves. Shaw used a terminology checking tool called repertory grids to compare the meaning of terms used by three geology experts on a common problem [58]. Two experiments were performed. In the calibrating experiment, experts reviewed their own knowledge, 12 weeks after they created it. This first experiment gives baseline expected agreement figures for a repertory grid analysis (see Fig. 21). In the second experiment, inter-expert agreement was analyzed (see Fig. 22). Note (e.g.) E_1,E_3: the results were much lower than in the calibration experiment suggesting that these experts held very different views about a supposedly standard problem in their field.

domain	Change in tree size	Change in classification error of the learned tree
demon	0.97	0.51
wave	1.91	0.95
diff	1.46	0.69
othello	1.68	0.8
heart	1.61	0.65
sleep	1.73	0.91
hyper	1.74	0.83
hypo	1.45	0.85
binding	1.51	0.82
replace	1.38	0.8
euthy	1.33	0.61
mean	1.52	0.77

Fig. 23. Impact of learning a decision tree from N or $2N$ examples.

Another reason for instability of knowledge is that new experience always gives new insights which significantly change old knowledge. This may be true for both human experts and automatic machine learners:

- Shalin *et al* [56] tried to find "accepted practice"; i.e., reused knowledge within expert communities. They found that experts do modify their behavior according to community standards of "accepted practice". However, it is only novices who slavishly re-apply that accepted practice. Experts adapt accepted practice when they apply it. That is, experts:
  - Partially match current problem to libraries of accepted practice.
  - Implement an acceptance test for their adaptation.
  - Modify the accepted practice library if acceptance failure.
- Catlett [13] used C4.5 [54] to learn decision trees for 11 problems using either all the $N = 3000..5000$ training cases or half the cases (randomly selected). The change in tree size and error rates are shown in Fig. 23. In all but one case (demon, first row), more experience meant significantly less errors, but larger theories.

The problem of knowledge instability has been seen in PSM libraries. Elsewhere [48], I have analyzed eight different supposedly reusable models of diagnosis (four from the PSM community, four from elsewhere). While some of these views on diagnosis share some common features, they reflect fundamentally divergent views on how to perform diagnosis. I therefore believe that, at least in the case of diagnosis, the consensus view has yet to stabilize and may not do so in the near future. More generally, I'm not sure that a consensus view on any of the PSMs has been reached, despite decades of research. There are significant differences between the list of PSM primitives offered by Clancey [17], KADS [66], and SBF. Also, the number and nature of the inference knowledge is not fixed. Often when a domain is analyzed, a new PSM is induced [41].

5. Discussion

The quest for appropriate reusable knowledge is fundamental to the western scientific tradition. Compton traces this quest back to the ancient Greeks:

> The reductionist assumption that one should be able to dig deep enough to find primitive concepts and the relationships between them on which knowledge is built finds its origins in Plato's concept of archetypes. That is, that there exist (literally) archetypes for all the things in the world and the concepts we use. Proposals such as (reuse) are essentially statements of belief that if the archetypes and relevant logical relationships can be found and manipulated intelligent thought can be reproduced [21, p. 280].

This chapter has offered numerous examples of reuse, and discussed the potential benefits and associated costs of reuse. In summary, reuse offers designers and educates a communications benefit, an interoperability benefit, and a browsing and search benefit. Reuse can *potentially* offer a systems engineering benefit and a guidance benefit. However, the review of the literature presented here suggests that it is at least an open issue if these last two potential benefits have been realized.

References

1. C. Abts, B. Clark, S. Devnani-Chulani, E. Horowitz, R. Madachy, D. Reifer, R. Selby and B. Steece, "COCOMO II model definition manual", Technical Report, Center for Software Engineering, USC, 1998, *http://sunset.usc.edu/COCOMOII/cocomox.html#downloads*
2. C. Alexander, *Notes on Synthesis of Form* (Harvard University Press, 1964).
3. C. Alexander, S. Ishikawa, S. Silverstein, I. Jacobsen, I. Fiksdahl-King and S. Angel, *A Pattern Language* (Oxford University Press, 1977).
4. K.-D. Althoff, M. Nick and C. Tautz, "Improving organizational memories through user feedback", ed. F. Bomarius, *Proceedings of the Workshop on Learning Software Organizations* (*LSO*) (*in conjunction with the 11th International Conference on Software Engineering and Knowledge Engineering, SEKE'99*), Kaiserslauten, Germany (June 1999) 27–44.
5. J. Angele, D. Fensel and R. Studer, "Domain and task modelling in MIKE", ed. A. Sutcliffe *et al*, *Domain Knowledge for Interactive System Design* (Chapman & Hall, 1996).
6. J. Bachant and J. McDermott, "R1 revisited: Four years in the trenches", *AI Magazine* (Fall, 1984) 21–32.
7. V. R. Basili and H. D. Rombach, "Support for comprehensive reuse", *Software Engineering Journal* (September 1991) 303–316.
8. P. G. Bassett, *Framing Software Reuse* (Yourdon Press, 1997).
9. R. Benjamins, "Problem-solving methods for diagnosis and their role in knowledge acquisition", *International Journal of Expert Systems: Research and Applications* **8**, no. 2 (1995) 93–120.

10. G. Booch, I. Jacobsen and J. Rumabugh, *The Unified Modeling Language User Guide* (Addison Wesley, 1999).
11. B. G. Buchanan and E. H. Shortliffe, *Rule-Based Expert Systems: The MYCIN Experiments of the Stanford Heuristic Programming Project* (Addison-Wesley, 1984).
12. F. Buschmann, R. Meunier, H. Rohnert, P. Sommerlad and M. Stal, *A System of Patterns: Pattern-Oriented Software Architecture* (John Wiley & Sons, 1996).
13. J. Catlett, "Inductive learning from subsets or disposal of excess training data considered harmful", *Australian Workshop on Knowledge Acqusition for Knowledge-Based Systems, Pokolbin* (1991) 53–67.
14. B. Chandrasekaran, "Towards a taxonomy of problem solving types", *AI Magazine* (Winter/Spring 1983) 9–17.
15. B. Chandrasekaran, T. R. Johnson and J. W. Smith, "Task structure analysis for knowledge modeling", *Communications of the ACM* **35**, no. 9 (1992) 124–137.
16. W. Clancey, "Heuristic classification", *Artificial Intelligence* **27** (1985) 289–350.
17. W. J. Clancey, "Model construction operators", *Artificial Intelligence* **53** (1992) 1–115.
18. P. Coad, D. North and M. Mayfield, *Object Models: Strategies, Patterns and Applications* (Prentice Hall, 1997).
19. P. Cohen, V. Chaudhri, A. Pease and R. Schrag, "Does prior knowledge facilitate the development of knowledge-based systems"? *AAAI'99* (1999).
20. P. Compton, K. Horn, J. R. Quinlan and L. Lazarus, "Maintaining an expert system", ed. J. R. Quinlan, *Applications of Expert Systems* (Addison Wesley, 1989) 366–385.
21. P. Compton, B. Kang, P. Preston and M. Mulholland, "Knowledge acquisition without analysis", *European Knowledge Acquisition Workshop* (1993).
22. C. Corbridge, N. P. Major and N. R. Shadbolt, "Models exposed: An empirical study", *Proceedings of the 9th AAAI-Sponsored Banff Knowledge Acquisition for Knowledge Based Systems* (1995).
23. W. Cunningham, "The CHECKS pattern language of information integrity", eds. J. Coplien and D. Schmidt, *Pattern Languages of Program Design* (Addison-Wesley, 1995). Also avialable at *http://c2.com/ppr/checks.html*
24. H. Eriksson, Y. Shahar, S. W. Tu, A. R. Puerta and M. A. Musen, "Task modeling with reusable problem-solving methods", *Artificial Intelligence* **79**, no. 2 (1995) 293–326.
25. M. Fowler, *Analysis Patterns: Reusable Object Models* (Addison Wesley, 1997).
26. W. B. Frakes, "Domain engineering education", *Proceedings of WISR9: The 9th Annual Workshop on Institutionalizing Software Reuse* (1999). Available from *http://www/umcs.maine.edu/~ftp/wisr/wisr9/final-papers/Frakes.html*
27. W. B. Frakes and C. J. Fox, "Sixteen questions about software reuse", *Communications of the ACM* **38**, no. 6 (June 1995) 75–87.
28. E. Gamma, R. Helm, R. Johnson and J. Vlissides, *Design Patterns: Elements of Reusable Object-Oriented Software* (Addison-Wesley, 1995).
29. Y. Gil and E. Melz, "Explicit representations of problem-solving strategies to support knowledge acquisition", *Proceedings AAAI' 96* (1996).
30. T. R. Gruber, "A translation approach to portable ontology specifications", *Knowledge Acquisition* **5**, no. 2 (1993) 199–220.
31. E. Guerrieri, "Reuse success — when and how"?, *Proceedings of WISR9: The 9th Annual Workshop on Institutionalizing Software Reuse*, 1999. Available from *http://www/umcs.maine.edu/~ftp/wisr/wisr9/final-papers/Guerrieri.html*

32. A. Mili, H. Mili and F. Mili, "Reusing software: Issues and research directions", *IEEE Transactions of Software Engineering* **21**, no. 6 (June 1995) 528–562. Available from *http://citeseer.nj.nec.com/mili95reusing.html*
33. Y. Kalfoglou and D. Robertson, "A case study in applying ontologies to augment and reason about the correctness of specifications", *Proceedings of the 11th International Conference on Software Engineering and Knowledge Engineering (SEKE'99)*, Kaiserslauten, Germany (June 1999) 64–71.
34. Y. Kalgoglou, "Ontologies in software design", ed. S. K. Chung, *Handbook of Software and Knowledge Engineering, Vol. 1* (2001).
35. N. Kerth, "Caterpillar's fate: A pattern language for transformation from analysis to design", eds. J. Coplien and D. Schmidt, *Pattern Languages of Program Design* (Addison-Wesley, 1995). Also available from *http://c2.com/ppr/catsfate.html*
36. C. W. Krueger, "Software reuse", *ACM Computing Surveys* **24**, no. 2 (1992) 131–183.
37. J. Leach, *Software Reuse: Methods, Models and Costs* (McGraw-Hill, 1997).
38. J. Lee, M. Gruninger, Y. Jin, T. Malone, A. Tate, G. Yost and other members of the PIF working group, "The PIF process interchange format and framework", *Knowledge Engineering Review* **13**, no. 1 (February 1998) 91–120.
39. W. Lim, "Effects of reuse on quality, productivity and economics", *IEEE Software* (1994) 23–30.
40. W. C. Lim, *Managing Software Reuse* (Prentice Hall, 1995).
41. M. Linster and M. Musen, "Use of KADS to create a conceptual model of the ONCOCIN task", *Knowledge Acquisition* **4**, no. 1 (1992) 55–88.
42. S. Marcus and J. McDermott, "SALT: A knowledge acquisition language for propose-and-revise systems", *Artificial Intelligence* **39**, no. 1 (1989) 1–37.
43. S. Marcus, J. Stout and J. McDermott, "VT: An expert elevator designer that uses knowledge-based backtracking", *AI Magazine* (Winter 1987) 41–58.
44. D. Marques, G. Dallemagne, G. Kliner, J. McDermott and D. Tung, "Easy programming: Empowering people to build their own applications", *IEEE Expert* (June 1992) 16–29.
45. T. Menzies, "hQkb — The High Quality Knowledge Base Initiative (Sisyphus V: Learning Design Assessment Knowledge)", *The 12th Workshop on Knowledge Acquisition, Modeling and Management, (KAW'99), Voyager Inn, Banff, Alberta, Canada October 16–22, 1999* (1999). Available from *http://tim.menzies.com/pdf/99hqkb.pdf*
46. T. Menzies, K. D. Althoff, Y. Kalfoglou and E. Motta, "Issues with meta-knowledge", *International Journal of Software Engineering and Knowledge Engineering* **10**, no. 4 (August 2000). Available from *http://tim.menzies.com/pdf/00sekej.pdf*
47. T. Menzies, B. Cukic, H. Singh and J. Powell, "Testing nondeterminate systems", *ISSRE 2000* (2000). Available from *http://tim.menzies.com/pdf/00issre.pdf*
48. T. J. Menzies, "OO patterns: Lessons from expert systems", *Software Practice and Experience* **27**, no. 12 (December 1997) 1457–1478. Available from *http://tim.menzies.com/pdf/97patern.pdf*
49. T. J. Menzies, "Towards situated knowledge acquisition", *International Journal of Human-Computer Studies* **49** (1998) 867–893. Available from *http://tim.menzies. com/pdf/98ijhcs.pdf*
50. E. Motta, "The knowledge modelling paradigm in knowledge engineering", ed. S. K. Chung, *Handbook of Software and Knowledge Engineering, Vol. 1* (2001).
51. E. Motta and Z. Zdrahal, "A library of problem-solving components based on the intergration of the search paradigm with task and method ontologies", *International Journal of Human Computer Studies* **49** (1998) 437–470.

52. P. A. V. Hall, *Software Reuse and Reverse Engineering in Practice* (Chapman & Hall, 1992).
53. D. E. Perry, "Some holes in the emperor's reused clothes", *Proceedings of WISR9: The 9th Annual Workshop on Institutionalizing Software Reuse* (1999). Available from *http://www/umcs.maine.edu/~ftp/wisr/wisr9/final-papers/Perry.html*
54. R. Quinlan, "Induction of decision trees", *Machine Learning* **1** (1986) 81–106.
55. A. TH. Schreiber, B. Wielinga, J. M. Akkermans, W. Van De Velde and R. de Hoog, "CommonKADS. A comprehensive methodology for KBS development", *IEEE Expert* **9**, no. 6 (1994) 28–37.
56. V. L. Shalin, N. D. Geddes, D. Bertram, M. A. Szczepkowski and D. Dubois, "Expertise in dynamic, physical task domains", eds. P. J. Feltovich, K. M. Ford and R. R. Hoffman, *Expertise in Context*, Chap. 9 (MIT Press, 1997) 195–217.
57. M. Shaw and D. Garlan, *Software Architecture: Perspectives on an Emerging Discipline* (Prentice Hall, 1996).
58. M. L. G. Shaw, "Validation in a knowledge acquisition system with multiple experts", *Proceedings of the International Conference on Fifth Generation Computer Systems* (1988) 1259–1266.
59. E. Soloway, J. Bachant and K. Jensen, "Assessing the maintainability of XCON-in-RIME: Coping with the problems of a VERY large rule-base", *AAAI'87* (1987) 824–829.
60. L. Steels, "Components of expertise", *AI Magazine* **11**, no. 2 (1990) 29–49.
61. B. Swartout and Y. Gill, "Flexible knowledge acquisition through explicit representation of knowledge roles", *1996 AAAI Spring Symposium on Acquisition, Learning and Demonstration: Automating Tasks for Users* (1996).
62. D. S. W. Tansley and C. C. Hayball, *Knowledge-Based Systems Analysis and Design* (Prentice-Hall, 1993).
63. M. Uschold, M. King, S. Moralee and Y. Zorgios, "The enterprise ontology", *The Knowledge Engineering Review* **13**, no. 1 (February 1998).
64. G. Van Heust, A. Th. Schreiber and B. J. Wielinga, "Using explicit ontologies in KBS development", *International Journal of Human Computer Studies* **45** (1997) 183–292.
65. B. J. Wielinga, A. T. Schreiber and J. A. Breuker, "KADS: A modeling approach to knowledge engineering", *Knowledge Acquisition* **4**, no. 1 (1992) 1–62.
66. B. J. Wielinga, A. T. Schreiber and J. A. Breuker, "KADS: A modeling approach to knowledge engineering", *Knowledge Acquisition* **4**, no. 1 (1992) 1–162.
67. V. L. Yu, L. M. Fagan, S. M. Wraith, W. J. Clancey, A. C. Scott, J. F. Hanigan, R. L. Blum, B. G. Buchanan and S. N. Cohen, "Antimicrobial selection by a computer: A blinded evaluation by infectious disease experts", *Journal of American Medical Association* **242** (1979) 1279–1282.
68. Z. Zdrahal and E. Motta, "Improving competence by intergrating case-based reasoning and heuristic search", *10th Banff Knowledge Acquisition for Knowledge-Based Systems Workshop, Banff, Canada, November 9–14 (1996)*.

SUPPORTING SOFTWARE PROCESSES USING KNOWLEDGE MANAGEMENT

RALF KNEUPER
Transport-, Informatik- und Logistik-Consulting (TLC) GmbH,
Kleyerstrasse 27, 60326 Frankfurt/M, Germany
Email: ralf.kneuper@gmx.de
URL: http://www.kneuper.de

In this paper, we describe how software processes can be supported using knowledge management, concentrating on the creative manual tasks performed by developers. The main support needed by developers is the availability of the knowledge about the development processes relevant to their task. As a result, software process modeling can be considered as a knowledge management task.

The paper provides an overview of the knowledge needed by developers. It then reviews various approaches to knowledge representation including artificial intelligence, structured plain text, and software process modeling approaches, to identify representation schemes suitable for software processes. Finally, the paper looks at the management aspects of software process knowledge.

Keywords: Software process, software process modeling, knowledge management, knowledge representation, XML.

1. Introduction

1.1. *Software processes*

Software processes are all the processes that are used to create software, including analysis, programming, configuration management, etc. Based on [49], we distinguish various kinds of software processes (see Fig. 1).

Software processes can be explicitly defined, or implicit processes that are used without thinking much about the process as such.

Reasons for defining (modeling) software processes are [24, p. 5][53]:

- defined processes put structure into software development;
- good software processes support developers in their work. Using the software process, developers know which step to take next, and they have templates for the results to be produced. As a result, they can concentrate their creativity on solving technical problems, rather than re-inventing the wheel, and solving problems that are caused by unclear cooperation with their colleagues;
- they form a basis for improvement and learning, including process monitoring and process simulation as well as process validation and verification;

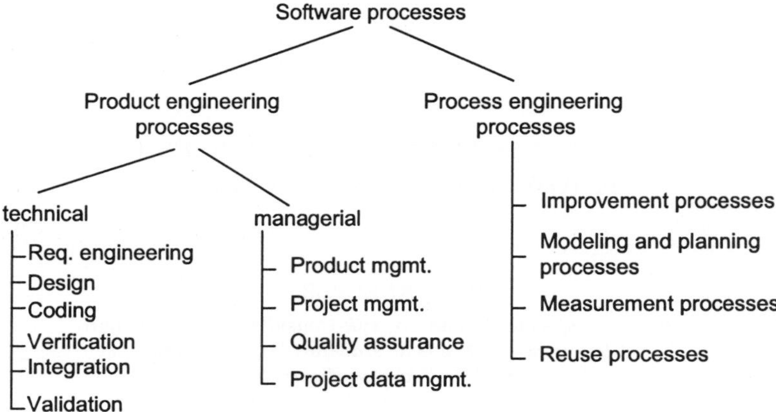

Fig. 1. Software processes (based on [49]).

- they make development more predictable. This is particularly important from the management perspective, since it helps to estimate correctly the time and cost needed for developing a system, and the resulting product quality; and
- computer-supported software processes additionally allow process enforcement, automation, and guidance.

Examples of defined software process models are the (Rational) Unified Process (RUP, see [38]) or the German V-Model (see [52, 56]), which both define fairly complete software process models including the various phases as well as supporting activities such as project management and quality assurance. On a rather coarse-grained level, there are various process models (also called phase models or life-cycle models) such as the waterfall model [51] or the spiral model [13] (see [15] for an overview of the different life-cycle models).

These models define the top level of a process model hierarchy (see Fig. 2). An organization typically does not use such a standard process model "as-is", but tailors it to its own special needs, assigning roles to departments, adding information about tools to be used for some process steps, adding specific or leaving out irrelevant steps. From this organizational process model an individual project then derives its project plan, again leaving out irrelevant steps (e.g. all steps that concern the creation of a database if the application does not include a database) and adding (project-) specific steps (e.g. create some artifact only required by this customer), and also iterating steps as appropriate (e.g. repeating the step "describe dialogue" four times since there are four dialogues in the application). Finally, of course, a project plan must include information about effort planned for the individual tasks, milestones, etc.

This does not imply that all three levels must always be present. Many organizations define their process model directly, without recourse to any standard model.

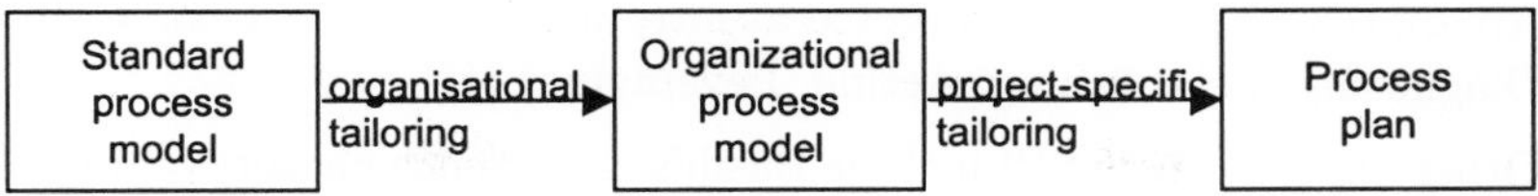

Fig. 2. Process model hierarchy.

Occasionally, a project plan is derived directly from some standard model, for example because the customer demands the use of this model. Many project plans are not based on any process model at all — this is quite common but falls outside the scope of this paper. And (last and least) some projects are run without any project plan at all.

Current issues in software processes research are (cf. [24, Sec. 1.8]).

Process formalisms and process modeling languages focused on creating notations to describe software processes, usually to be "read" by various tools used for:

- analysis, such as consistency checking ("Is every artifact that is used by an activity created by an earlier activity?" "Is every defined role assigned at least one task?") or for improvement "Which of these two ways of achieving a certain result is more efficient?"); and
- process support, such as tailoring a general process to a specific project, or process workflow support.

Process-centred environments called *process-sensitive software engineering environment* (PSEE) by [24], go one step further, integrating the various development tools into one environment under the control of some form of process engine, e.g. if a developer is assigned the task to create an entity/relationship model and starts this task, the appropriate editor for entity/relationship models is started up automatically.

Software process improvement (SPI) is concerned with ways to define concrete process models for an organization, to introduce them into the day-to-day work of the organization (which tends to be much more difficult than creating the model in the first place), and finally to continuously improve and adapt these models.

In contrast to the previous two items, SPI has little technical contents but focuses on soft factors such as management, organizational change, psychology, etc.

Probably the best known approach to SPI is the Capability Maturity Model (CMM) [18, 52, 53] (*http://www.sei.cmu.edu/cmm/cmm.html*), which defines five maturity levels and thus provides an improvement path for organizations developing software. SPICE [50] is based on similar ideas and working on an ISO standard 15504 [35] for assessing the maturity of software developing organizations.

An approach specifically targeted at introducing CMM is IDEAL (Initiating, Diagnosing, Establishing, Acting, Leveraging) [41].

Other approaches to SPI include Basili's Experience Factory and the Quality Improvement Paradigm [7–9] as well as approaches from quality management in general, not specific to software, such as ISO 9000 (with its software-specific interpretation, ISO 9000-3), Kaizen, and Total Quality Management.

Definition of software process, finally, is concerned with creating concrete software process models, either as a general standard, such as the German V-Modell, as a *de facto* standard such as the (Rational) Unified Process, or as an internal, company-specific process model (see e.g. [6, 43]). ISO 12207 [34] provides a lot of input on the contents of such a process model.

A good overview of the topic of software processes and the research questions involved, covering mainly process formalisms, process modeling languages, and process-centred environments, is given by [24, 49], the current state of the art can be found in *The Proceedings of the European Workshop on Software Process Technology Series* (*EWSPT*, e.g. [21, 27]) and *The International Conference on the Software Process Series* (*ICSP*).

More information on SPI can e.g. be found in [49], or, with a strong CMM bias, on the SEI web pages (*http://www.sei.cmu.edu*), or The Proceedings of the Annual SEPG (Software Engineering Process Group) and European SEPG conferences.

Another way to view software processes is that they are a form of knowledge. Managing software processes is a special case of knowledge management. The current paper follows this view to identify what can be learned from knowledge management for the support of software processes.

The remainder of this introduction will analyze how much support software process technology can give (see Sec. 1.2), and then define the basic concepts of *knowledge* (see Sec. 1.3) and *knowledge management* (see Sec. 1.4).

After that, in Sec. 2, we discuss the knowledge that is needed in the special case of software processes. Sec. 3 describes some approaches to knowledge representation and looks at their suitability for the kind of knowledge considered here. Since dealing with software process knowledge is a management task even more than a technical problem, Sec. 4 looks at the management aspects of process knowledge and their implications on software process technology. Finally, in Sec. 5, we draw some conclusions.

1.2. *Technology to support software processes*

Software development consists of a number of different kinds of tasks including

- creative tasks;
- administrative tasks; and
- communication tasks.

A common feature of these tasks is that they require a fairly large amount of knowledge.

Software process technology should therefore emphasize support for human developers in their task.

The obvious question now is what software process support human developers need for software development. The suggestion of this paper is that the main support needed is to provide *knowledge* to the developers, e.g. in the form of descriptions of tasks and artifacts (results) (cf. Sec. 2.2), or, more advanced, in the form of advice and guidance. Phrased differently, software process support should be considered as a *knowledge management* task [23].

Knowledge *management* is quite a different concept from knowledge *representation* as a topic of Artificial Intelligence, even though there is some overlap. Knowledge management is a management task mainly dealing with humans, while knowledge representation is concerned with formal representation of knowledge typically used for certain algorithms (such as reasoning and planning).

This is very different from the current paradigm in software process technology which concentrates on the attempt to automate software processes [49], as suggested in particular by Osterweil [46]. The basic assumption behind this approach is, obviously, that software development contains large tasks that are sufficiently simple to be formalized, or, put differently, it restricts attention to such tasks (compare [57]). This emphasis on automation and formalization results in a number of requirements that are important for the industrial use of software process support but are not satisfied by many software process support tools (see [36]).

The difference between the two paradigms (software process support as automation of software processes or as support for human knowledge workers) is not just of academic or scientific interest but has practical implications since software process models, like all models, are a form of reality construction. They are not neutral descriptions but have a purpose or bias. As a result, they help to create a mental model of software processes, be it as creative, mental processes or as a mechanizable, menial task. Such a mental model (or paradigm, see [39, Postscript Chap. 4]) influences the way we see the world and interpret the external stimuli. This is one of the reasons why it is important to have a paradigm that leads in a useful direction. Conradi *et al* in [20] argue similarly that automation in this context is of limited value. About software process research, they say:

> "Quite often, we want to provide automatic support to activities that simply do not need to be supported 'that far'. For instance, while it is certainly useful to clearly describe the steps in a design method, it is purposeless to formally model it to support its detailed enactment (e.g. by indicating which steps in the method have to be carried out and in which order). Developers will never accept a tool that operates at that level of detail. Moreover, it would be useless. You can use a design method effectively only if you 'know' it so deeply that it is part of your mental habit, and not

just because 'someone else' mandates what you are supposed to do at any time". [20, pp. 102f]

Quality management approaches such as CMM and ISO 9000 also move towards putting more structure into the software development process. However, this is not to be confused with automation of the processes — these approaches are mainly concerned with defining the manual processes, describing the steps to be performed (such as reviews) and the responsibility for these steps.

Coming back to the question of support of software processes using knowledge management: necessary tasks in the use of software processes that could be supported by knowledge management are

- define processes (knowledge elicitation and representation);
- introduce processes into the day-to-day work of the developers — just defining the processes and making the definition available is rarely enough;
- apply or live a process;
- improve and adapt the processes since they will never be perfect, and the environment keeps changing (new technology, better qualified developers, etc); and
- tailor and instantiate the processes to turn them into a project plan.

Since the tasks in this list are processes that work on the software processes, they are also called meta-processes. These meta-processes need to be closely coordinated with the software processes themselves since the meta-process can lead to a change of the process, possibly while the process is running (e.g. a process improvement that is introduced during the lifetime of a project, see [48]).

1.3. *What is knowledge?*

Following Davenport and Prusak, we distinguish the concepts of data, information and knowledge. The following definitions are based on [23, pp. 2–6]:

Data are a set of discrete, objective facts. A typical example of data in software process modeling is "an entity-relationship diagram consists of boxes representing entities and lines between the boxes, representing relationships between entities".

Information is data that "makes a difference" to the receiver. Put differently, information is data with added value, e.g. by putting it into context, by mathematical or statistical analysis, or by summarizing it in a more concise form. In software process modeling, examples for information are "developing a software system consists of the following tasks .... In task X_1, the artifact Y is produced and used as input for task X_2".

Knowledge "is a fluid mix of framed experience, values, contextual information, and expert insight that provides a framework for evaluating and incorporating new experiences and information" [23, p. 5]. Knowledge can be considered as information with added value, such as the relationship between different pieces of information, or the implications of that information on decisions and actions. Examples of knowledge in software process modeling are "Step A is not needed for Java applications developed for customer C". "If you have experienced developers, it is better to do step A before step B, while inexperienced developers have to do it the other way round". "Artifact Y is very important for complex applications but superfluous for simple applications". Part of the difficulty of applying such knowledge is that it depends on judgements about the current situation (Is developer D experienced? The answer to this question depends both on the developer and the tasks at hand — a developer may be an experienced Cobol programmer but know nothing about Java.)

Other authors, especially in the AI community, e.g. [26], define the term "knowledge" much wider, including what we called information. This leads to different answers to the question whether in software process modeling, we are dealing with *knowledge* or whether it really is *information* (or even data). According to the definition used here, a software process model itself does not contain knowledge but (at best) information. The challenge now is to present the model in such a form that the users (developers) are able to turn this information into knowledge — they have to "understand" the model. This implies providing sufficient information about context and implications, but also representing the model in a way such that it is easy to understand.

The same statement actually applies to any form of knowledge representation, whether in the form of a knowledge base, text book, process model, or other. The very act of representing knowledge turns it into data or information. Providing more such information about context and implications does not necessarily help to make this transition to knowledge; on the contrary, too much information can lead to information overload and the information turns into data since users can no longer cope with it.

1.4. *Knowledge management*

Knowledge management is the management discipline that is concerned with creating, preserving and applying the knowledge that is available within an organization. Typically, this is done using techniques such as training, process modeling, experience (data) bases, and networking of experts. For a very practical, hands-on report on applying knowledge management at a software house see e.g. [17]. For a large collection of references on knowledge management see e.g. *http://www.bcs-sges.org/kmreport/bibliography.htm*

As stated above, knowledge *management* is quite a different concept from knowledge *representation* as a topic of Artificial Intelligence, even though there is some overlap. Knowledge management is a management task mainly dealing with humans, while knowledge representation is concerned with formal representation of knowledge typically used for certain algorithms (such as reasoning and planning).

Hansen, Nohria and Tierney [28] distinguish two different approaches to knowledge management based on the importance they put on formalization:

The codification strategy puts the main emphasis on making tacit knowledge of the organization explicit, e.g. in a process model.

The personalization strategy concentrates on support for person-to-person knowledge transfer, leaving knowledge tacit but making it available by communication between people. A typical technique here is to describe *who* knows about a certain topic, rather than describing the topic itself in sufficient detail for someone else to read and apply it.

The main focus of the current article is on software process modeling and therefore on the codification strategy. Depending on context and the task at hand, either strategy can be useful.

However, it is important to keep in mind that knowledge essentially is human-based. If people (such as developers) need knowledge to solve a problem, they usually tend to ask their colleagues rather than search a database. The challenge for software process technology is to make the tools sufficiently useful for developers to prefer to use the tools rather than asking their colleagues.

For common tasks, this is a (within limits) achievable goal because it is more efficient to describe a common task once and use the description many times afterwards. For uncommon or very difficult tasks, this is not true and it makes more sense to direct the developer to an expert in the field under consideration. Therefore, software process models should not only provide information about the processes themselves but also about the experts to ask when going beyond the limits of the defined process.

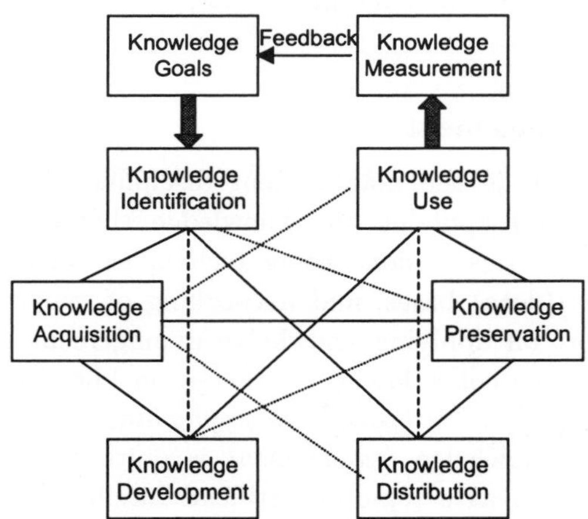

Fig. 3. Building blocks of knowledge management [47].

Probst [47] has defined a structure for knowledge management, called the "building blocks" of knowledge management (see Fig. 3).

In the special case of software processes, these building blocks essentially repeat, in a more structured way, the process support tasks mentioned in Sec. 1.2 above. We will look at them in more detail in Sec. 4.

2. Knowledge Needed

In this section, we describe the knowledge needed to support software processes in more detail.

Before we can do so, we need to define *who* needs the knowledge we are talking about. First of all, this includes the developers themselves and their project leaders, but also supporting personnel such as technical writers who write the user documentation, quality assurance personnel, etc. Furthermore, for customer-specific software (as opposed to off-the-shelf software) the customer of the software developed will often require knowledge about the processes used before signing a contract, and during a project to be able to provide or sign-off input such as requirements or domain knowledge. Similarly, management needs knowledge about the processes used in order to judge and optimize their effectiveness.

The knowledge needed includes an overview of the processes used (Sec. 2.1, descriptions of the tasks to be performed and the artifacts to be produced (Sec. 2.2), the development method used (Sec. 2.3), knowledge about best practices and lessons learned (Sec. 2.4), and other knowledge needed for software development (Sec. 2.5).

2.1. *Overview of processes used*

First of all, everyone involved needs an overview of the software processes used. This describes the type of life cycle used (waterfall, V-shaped, incremental, spiral, ...) as well as the phases in the life cycle together with their main goals, activities and results.

While for some groups, such as the customer, this may be all the knowledge needed about the software process, most users will need the overview to identify where their own piece of work fits in, which interfaces to other people or groups they have in the development process, to set priorities in case of conflict, etc.

2.2. *Description of tasks and artifacts*

This is the core part of software process support and includes templates for the various artifacts (such as a project plan or an entity-relationship model) to be developed as well as descriptions of the steps to be performed for a task, plus their pre- and post-conditions, and checklists to ensure completeness of the tasks.

Pre- and Post-conditions: Pre-conditions of a task are conditions that have to be satisfied at the beginning of the task, typically the previous existence of a certain artifact or the previous performance of a certain other task. For example, before programming of a component is started, the specification of the component should be complete.

Post-conditions, on the other hand, are conditions that are guaranteed to be satisfied at the end of a task, such as the existence of a certain artifact created by the task. Another typical usage of pre- and post-conditions concerns the status of an artifact. For example, the pre-condition of a review typically requires the existence of the result to be reviewed in status "draft" or similar. The post-condition states that the contents of the artifact has not changed, but that the artifact now has the status "accepted" or "rejected".

These dependencies between different tasks are one of the main difficulties in tailoring a process model to a specific context, since if one adds or deletes a task, all pre- and post-conditions of other tasks still have to be satisfied.

Knowledge about pre- and post-conditions is used in planning a project (pre- and post-conditions impose a partial order on the tasks to be performed, or even imply that a certain task needs to be added in order to satisfy the pre-condition of a later task) as well as in performing a given task, since the post-condition succinctly describes what is to be achieved by the task ("create artifact X"; "promote artifact Y from status 'draft' to status 'released')".

Finding a suitable sequence of tasks such that the pre-conditions of all tasks are guaranteed to be satisfied by post-conditions of earlier tasks is a typical example of a planning problem in AI [26, 30].

Description of steps and artifacts: The description of the steps to be performed and the artifacts produced is the central part of software process support for developers. This description typically includes the methods(s) used, any sub-steps, and templates for the artifacts produced.

Usage of these descriptions of steps and artifacts can vary a lot between developers: let's say they have a certain task, such as the specification of a dialogue with given functionality. Then depending on their experience, developers may follow the process described step by step, or they just get the template for the artifact needed and fill in the blanks. One of the problems in the latter case is, of course, to ensure that the developer at least gets the current version of the template and does not reuse an older one. A necessary, but not sufficient, condition for this is to make it very easy to get the template from the standard repository.

Other developers may just want to review the main steps to remind themselves of the general process, e.g. because they have not performed this particular task for some time, while yet others just need the details of one particular step. Software process technology has to support all these different uses and therefore present the relevant knowledge on different levels of detail.

2.3. *Development method used*

For the development method used, essentially the same applies as for the tasks and artifacts described above, since a development method can be described as a collection of tasks and artifacts. The main difference is the different level of abstraction: a method tends to be more high-level (when to perform a certain step?), while the description of a single task or artifact tends to contain a lot more detail.

2.4. *Best practices and lessons learned*

Best practices and lessons learned involve knowledge about approaches, techniques, etc that have proven useful in other contexts and might therefore be helpful for the developer to know about, even though it has not (yet) been expressed as a general process. Best practices can come from within the own organization or from the outside, i.e., practices that are used in other companies.

Knowledge about best practices and lessons learned is typically presented in the form of case studies, since it has not been or cannot be made fully explicit or sufficiently general to be included in the defined software processes. See [44, p. 55f] or [45] for some examples of knowledge bases containing lessons learned and best practices.

Reference [45] also describes a number of difficulties with best-practice knowledge bases:

- Where do you find knowledge about best practices? This is often not publicly available but has to be searched out.
- Best practices are constantly changing. Even if you have well-documented, useful best practices today, the same practices might be completely inadequate tomorrow, due to technology changes or market changes (e.g. time-to-market or quality level of the product is no longer acceptable).
- An active approach is needed; it is not sufficient to just gather knowledge about best practices, but best practices have to be created in the first place.

All these difficulties apply to all process model knowledge bases, not just to those containing best practices.

2.5. *General software engineering knowledge*

The following knowledge is also needed for software development but not usually considered part of software process models. The main difference between the knowledge listed here and the knowledge contained in a software process model is that the process model describes or prescribes the steps performed and the results created. The knowledge listed here helps the developers but does not state what they have to do.

In [42, p. 292] list the following relevant software engineering knowledge:

- domain knowledge,
- requirements knowledge,
- design knowledge,
- implementation knowledge,
- programming knowledge,
- quality factors,
- design rationale (see the Chapter on Rationale Management by Dutoit and Paech in this Handbook),
- historical knowledge.

Other knowledge needed includes

- development and target environment, tools: this is an aspect that is quite important for developers, although it is not really part of the software process as such. During their development tasks, developers need reference material on issues such as the programming language and the compiler, the DBMS used, middleware and operating system (for development and target environment), etc. This reference material has to be integrated into the development environment so that for any development process step, the necessary reference information is immediately available;
- measurement data: in order to continually improve the software processes, measurement data about properties such as software size and cost, productivity, number of defects found, etc must be stored and made available;
- developer skills;
- support information and typical problems; and
- market data (mainly, but not only, needed for creating off-the-shelf software products, as opposed to customer-specific software).

This kind of knowledge has to be handled by knowledge management [17] but will not be considered in this context since it is not really part of the software process itself.

2.6. *Administrative information*

In addition to the knowledge listed above, some administrative information needs to be stored with the process knowledge, such as author or owner of a process, release date, version, scope or area of applicability, etc. In this context, we will ignore such administrative information.

3. Knowledge Representation for Software Process Support

In the following, we will analyze some approaches to knowledge representation and their usability for the kind of knowledge described above. Based on an analysis of the requirements on such a knowledge representation notation in Sec. 3.1, we will look at AI approaches to knowledge representation (Sec. 3.2), software process modeling notations (Sec. 3.3), business process modeling notations (Sec. 3.4), and various forms of structured plain text (Sec. 3.5). In the summary (Sec. 3.6), a short comparison between the different approaches is given.

One should note that strictly speaking, we are not really talking about *knowledge* representation since, as described above, only people can have knowledge, not machines. If knowledge is represented in some form of knowledge repository, it turns into data or, at best, information. To turn these data back into knowledge requires a human who is able to interpret the data and make sense of it. However, following standard usage we will still talk about knowledge representation.

Many knowledge representation notations were created for use by automated reasoning and inference engines and not really designed to support humans in their work. Not surprisingly, they often turn out to be unsuitable for this task, partly because they do not support free text, explaining e.g. the steps to be performed to create a certain results.

3.1. *Requirements on knowledge representation*

Finlay and Dix [26, Chap. 1.4] suggest the following characteristics to assess knowledge representation schemes. Note that these criteria were originally intended for judging knowledge representation notations in artificial intelligence, to be used for automated deduction and similar algorithms, and are therefore less well-suited for judging notations for knowledge representation for human users. The definitions have therefore been slightly adapted for our purposes.

Expressiveness: A representation notation must be able to represent the various types of knowledge we wish to represent, on the appropriate levels of granularity.

The types of knowledge we want to represent in order to support software processes have been described in the previous section. One of the difficulties lies in the necessary combination of well-structured knowledge, such as "activity A takes artifact X_1 as input and produces X_2 as output", with ill-structured knowledge such as "to create a class model, it is usually best to start by ...". As a result, a notation that is used to represent knowledge for human users must allow ill-structured descriptions, i.e., free text.

Effectiveness: For structured knowledge, effectiveness implies that a representation scheme must provide a means for inferring new knowledge from old. Since in our case the emphasis is on making knowledge available to the human user rather than an inference engine, effectiveness means that users can find and use the knowledge needed for their work. This implies that appropriate search and selection mechanisms must be available, see below.

One way to make a knowledge representation notation more effective is the possibility to provide different views on the knowledge represented, e.g. for different groups of users (developer, manager, customer, automated tool, etc) or for different kinds of projects (structured or object-oriented development, large or small project, high-risk or low-risk, etc).

Efficiency: In our case, efficiency means that the user must be able to find the knowledge needed within a reasonably short time frame, and be able to find and use it with acceptable effort.

Generally speaking, any measures that make a representation more effective by making it easier to find and use the knowledge represented, also make the representation more efficient. For example, good search and selection algorithms or the possibility to provide different views help to increase efficiency as well as effectiveness.

An exception to this rule would be a measure that reduced user effort and time to find and use the knowledge, but that increased computer effort and time so much that the overall effort and time increased, e.g. due to particularly long searches.

Explicitness: A representation scheme must be able to provide an explanation of its inferences.

While for inferred (structured) knowledge this can be taken literally, ill-structured knowledge is considered explicit if for any knowledge found, a more detailed description of this knowledge is available. Put differently, a representation notation is considered explicit if it allows different levels of detail or abstraction.

Example: a project leader has found in the process model that in order to create a project plan, he needs to analyze, among (many) other tasks, the risks involved in the project. The process model will now (upon request) show what needs to be done for a risk analysis, covering technical risks, financial risks, etc. The project leader might now "drill down" to find out more about typical financial risks and how to handle them.

In [36], the author listed a number of requirements on software process technology, some of which are relevant in the current context as well. These are requirements that have a focus on the industrial use of a process model.

Accessibility: The representation must be accessible from different technical environments, and publication must be possible both in electronic and in paper format. This is less a requirement on the knowledge representation notation as such, but on the tool used to present the knowledge.

Modifiability: The representation must support easy modifications of the process described, to support continuous improvement and adaptation to a changing environment (cf. Sec. 1.2 on meta-processes). Among other things, this implies that some kind of consistency checking must be available, to prevent modifications from introducing inconsistencies.

Understandability: The representation must be easy to understand for developers. Their main objective is to understand the processes described and perform them. If developers have to think about the representation rather than the represented process, they will tend to ignore the defined process.

This requirement re-enforces the argument made above that knowledge representation notations for use by humans need to allow knowledge represented by free text, to make the more formal or structured knowledge easier to understand.

Search and Selection Mechanisms. When describing software processes, one quickly runs into the problem that developers cannot find the description of a certain task when they need it. To overcome this problem, searching and selection must be provided as part of the software process support used. Typical mechanisms for this purpose are

- keyword search and full-text search;
- different views based on various criteria such as role or project phase;
- tailoring/only showing relevant detail;
- intelligent agents [44, p. 59];
- visualization models [44, p. 60], such as Perspecta (*http://www.perspecta.com*) and InXight (*http://www.inxight.com*); and
- Ellmer *et al* [25] describe a search strategy specifically suited for a process library, based on neural networks (self-organizing maps).

3.2. *Artificial intelligence approaches to knowledge representation*

Standard approaches in artificial intelligence to representing knowledge are predicate calculus, production rules, semantic networks, frames, and scripts [26]. A newer approach to structuring knowledge and finding it again once it has been captured in a knowledge base is the use of ontologies [45].

Analysis of these approaches quickly shows that all of them are quite suitable for structured knowledge to be used for automated reasoning, but do not support the representation of knowledge for use by human readers. In particular, they do not allow free text, and are therefore not sufficiently expressive for our purposes. On the other hand, dealing with pre- and post-conditions of tasks is clearly a strong point of AI notations.

Similarly, they tend to be fairly effective and efficient for structured knowledge (since they were designed for that purpose) but less effective and quite inefficient for human users, looking for ill-structured knowledge. Even for structured knowledge, however, they are not ideal since they cannot easily handle the different kinds of entities used in software process modeling, such as tasks, artifacts, roles, etc.

The explicitness of software process models in AI notation depends on the detailed approach and the tools used — no general answer can be given. Accessibility is typically low since the notation is supported by a single tool.

Modification of described processes is possible but not easy since it is difficult to understand the consequences of the modifications. More generally, it is difficult to understand a process model and its interactions if the model is described using AI notations. However, this is eased by the fact that these notations allow experimentation and asking questions about the model, such as "what are the possible steps (i.e., applicable rules) once I have created artifact X?".

3.3. *Software process modeling approaches*

The following discussion is based on [24, 49, 55] which all contain an overview of software process modeling languages and approaches.

Software process modeling languages such as Appl/A [54], MSL (Marvel Strategy Language) [6, 12], and TEMPO [10, 11] are all very formal languages, used for automatically enacting or checking the processes, but not to be used by human users for their development tasks. Although SLANG [5] and Statemate [29, 33] are graphical representations of the software processes, they do not score much better regarding understandability. Only MVP-L (multi-view process modeling language) [16, 49] puts more emphasis on the human user and is therefore somewhat easier to understand — but still far from the kind of process model one would like to give to developers to tell them how they ought to perform a certain process.

These software process modeling languages are, to some extent, based upon ideas from AI knowledge representation, and therefore share many of their advantages and disadvantages. For example, they both are similarly effective and efficient for structured knowledge, and similarly ineffective and inefficient for unstructured knowledge.

However, concepts such as tasks, artifacts and roles are fundamental to software process modeling languages and therefore well supported, improving the expressiveness for structured knowledge.

Explicitness of software process models as well as the ease with which they can be modified depend on the actual modeling language used.

3.4. *Business process modeling approaches*

Since software processes are a special case of business processes, techniques for business process modeling can also be applied to software processes. Typically, business processes are modeled using some graphical, easy-to-understand representations such as flowcharts or Petri nets [1], or use cases and other UML notation [40], with attributes such as roles, effort, etc included as hypertext. (See [19, p. 50] for further references.)

This approach can also be applied for software processes, although many of the attributes, such as the duration of a process step, often cannot usefully be filled in since software processes have less structure than typical business processes. As a result, many of the standard process analysis techniques cannot be applied.

When applying this approach to software processes in order to support developers, one has to make sure that lengthy free text explanations are possible — many tools only allow a few lines of explanation.

Since business process modeling languages are usually more geared towards analysis and simulation of the processes modeled, there is little support for the people actually performing the process, such as making software process knowledge available to them.

Since analysis and simulation is typically performed by a small number of people (the *Process Engineer* or the *Software Engineering Process Group*), there is little emphasis in the tools on making the model available within a heterogeneous environment, although sometimes a Web interface is provided.

Business process models tend to be quite explicit in that there are different levels of the model, with atomic tasks on one level being further broken down on the level below.

Modification of a business process model is quite easy, with various checks available to ensure that no inconsistency is introduced.

3.5. *Structured plain text*

Structured plain text is the approach to representing software process models that is used most often in practice, see for example the German V-Modell [56] or the (*Rational*) *Unified Process*, which additionally includes links to supporting tools, see [38] and *http://www.rational.com*

Other common formats for representing software process models are HTML and document databases such as Lotus Notes. In particular, these formats score fairly high in accessibility, since they do not need special tools but use tools that many developers will have on their desk anyway, such as a browser.

XML: A fairly recent approach to structure text is the use of the *Extensible Markup Language* XML [14]. XML was heavily influenced by SGML and HTML, allowing for more complex markup than HTML with individual tags, but at the same time being considerably less difficult to handle than SGML (see *http://www.w3.org/XML/*, *http://www.xml.com* and `http://www.oasis-open.org` for more information about XML).

XML allows different views on the same data, such as different levels (beginner, advanced, check list, detailed reference), for different user types (developers, automated tools), or for different project types (small or large projects; customer-specific or off-the-shelf software).

To some extent, it is possible, using XML, to combine software process modeling approaches with additional descriptions in natural language that can be given to developers to help them perform their tasks. A pre-processor

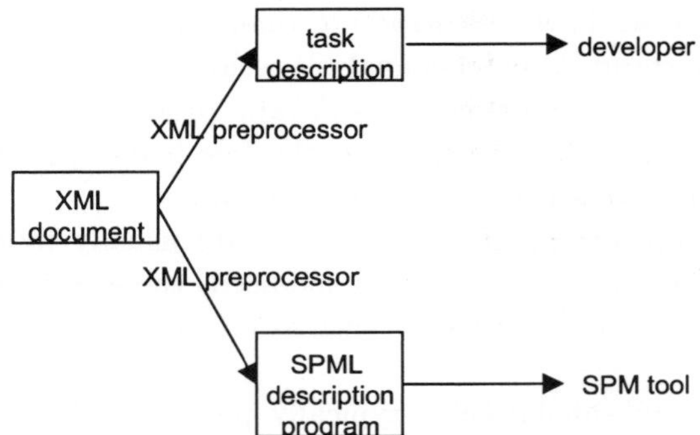

Fig. 4. Combining software process modeling languages (SPML)/tools with developer support using XML.

then has to remove these descriptions before the process model can be handled by the relevant enactment or analysis tools. Alternatively, the preprocessor removes the tool-specific parts to get a description of the software processes to be read and used by developers (Fig. 4). Some work in this direction is currently underway at the Fraunhofer Institute for Experimental Software Engineering (IESE) in Kaiserslautern.

Process patterns were first introduced by Coplien [22] and described more extensively by Ambler [2, 3, 4] (see also *http://www.ambysoft.com/processPatternsPage.html* for more resources on process patterns).

Each process pattern describes one problem in software development processes and suggests a solution to it. "A pattern is a general solution to a common problem or issue, one from which a specific solution may be derived" [2, p. 3].

Such a process pattern is described using the following structure:

- Problem.
- Context.
- Forces.
- Solution.
- Resulting context.
- Design rationale (this item is included by Coplien but not by Ambler).

Ambler distinguishes process patterns at different levels of detail, namely task, stage and phase process patterns. Together, these process patterns can be used to describe a full process model. On the other hand, individual patterns are particularly suited to describing best practices.

Process patterns are easy to understand and modify, but there is no support ensuring that the model is still consistent.

Since process patterns define a structure for the definition of software processes but no technical format, an arbitrary (hyper-) text format can be used; as a result, it

```
<?xml version="1.0" standalone="yes"?>
<processpattern>
<name>Form Follows Function</name>
<alias>Aggregate Roles into Activities</alias>
<problem>A project lacks well-defined roles.</problem>
<context>You know the key atomic process
activities.</context>
<forces>Activities are too small, and ...</forces>
<solution>Group closely related activities
...</solution>
<resultingcontext>A partial definition of roles for a
project. ...</resultingcontext>
<designrationale>The quality of this pattern needs to
be reviewed. ...</designrationale>
</processpattern>
```

Fig. 5. Example process pattern (from [22, Chap. 5]) using (simple) XML.

is easy to provide access to the process definition from whatever environment is needed.

As an approach to software process modeling, process patterns are quite different from XML (or Document Management Systems, see below), since they are concerned with the *logical* structure of process descriptions, while XML is concerned with their *physical* or technical structure. As a result, it is quite natural to combine process pattern with XML, where process patterns provide the chapter structure for process descriptions, and XML provides the syntax to denote the chapters and their contents, plus hypertext links as needed. A very simple example of a process pattern represented using XML is given in Fig. 5.

One of the strong points of XML is that it is easily accessible in a heterogeneous environment, including paper printout. Modification of XML documents is also easy, with some consistency checking possible (depending on the DTD and the tools used). Understanding an XML document itself, including the tags, is possible but not easy. However, one would not usually want to read the XML document itself, but only its presentation as defined by a style sheet. Assuming an appropriate style sheet, the presentation becomes easy to read.

Quality patterns are quite similar to process patterns, but specific to solving quality-related problems and documenting quality-related experience. They were developed by Houdek *et al* [31, 32] and use a more elaborate pattern structure than process patterns (see Fig. 6). However, there is no obvious reason why this pattern structure should be specific to quality-related experience and not be used for process patterns in general.

Document management systems: Software process models described as plain text can naturally be structured as a collection of documents. An obvious choice for storing such documents are document management systems (DMS)

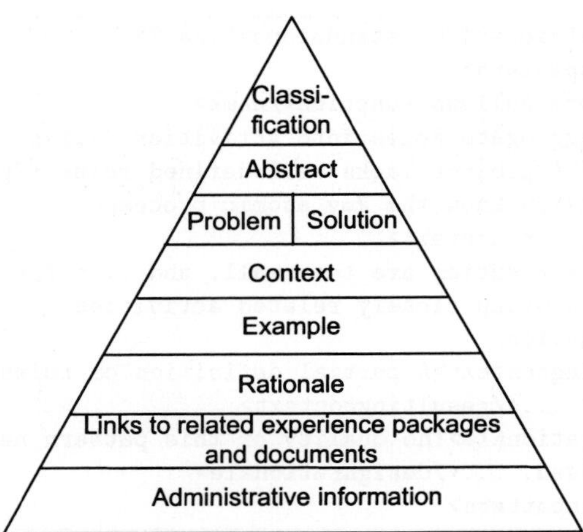

Fig. 6. Structure of a quality pattern [31].

which support storage, retrieval and versioning of documents. A typical tool used here is Lotus Notes, although its support for versioning of documents is rather weak. Lotus Notes, like some other document management systems, additionally has groupware capabilities that can be used for discussions and feedback mechanisms on the process model.

DMS support representation of both structured and unstructured knowledge and are therefore quite expressive. However, retrieval of represented knowledge is usually only supported by search and selection algorithms, while inference of new knowledge from existing (structured) knowledge is not available.

A strong point of DMS is the administration of links between different knowledge items, making it easy to provide more detail as needed (explicitness).

Access to the knowledge represented using a DMS is only via this DMS, but most providers of DMS make an effort to provide versions that run on different platforms and can be used in an heterogeneous environment.

Modification of the knowledge represented in a DMS is easy, but it is also easy to introduce inconsistencies. Some of these inconsistencies can be found by the DMS (depending on the tool used), such as links leading nowhere, but inconsistencies within the texts cannot be found.

3.6. *Summary*

Table 1 gives an overview of the requirements on software process representation notations as described in Sec. 3.1, and how the notations listed in Sec. 3.2 to Sec. 3.5 satisfy these requirements.

Table 1. Satisfaction of requirements on knowledge representation (+ fully satisfied; 0 partly satisfied; – not satisfied).

	AI Approaches	Software Process Modeling	Business Process Modeling	Structured Plain Text XML	Structured Plain Text Process Patterns	Structured Plain Text DMS
Expressiveness:						
structured k.	0	+	+	+	–	0
unstructured k.	–	–	0/–	+	+	+
Effectiveness:						
structured k.	+	+	0	+	–	–
unstructured k.	–	–	–	+	+	+
Efficiency:						
structured k.	+	+	0	+	–	–
unstructured k.	–	–	–	+	0	+
Explicitness	+/0/–	+/0/–	0/–	+	0	+
Accessibility	–	–	+	+	+	0
Modifiability	0	+/0/–	0/–	+/0	0	0
Understandability	–	–	+	+	+	+

For the requirements described here, the structured plain text approaches clearly seem most suitable, which was to be expected due to the requirement that the representation scheme must allow free text for the description of tasks etc.

In particular, XML looks promising as the way forward, since it supports the combined representation of free text and structured elements as needed for the automation of individual tasks. The challenge now lies in creating a document type definition (DTD) for process models that includes both aspects adequately. However, this is not an easy task since it amounts to defining a common meta-model for software process models in XML notation.

When talking about a *combined* representation, we really require that it is *one* integrated representation dealing with both aspects. Splitting the representation into two separate parts, containing a formal process model on the one hand and a human-readable description on the other, as suggested e.g. by [25], will lead to consistency problems, just like design documents hardly ever describe the design of the current implementation of a software system.

4. Managing Process Knowledge

As the term knowledge *management* suggests, handling knowledge is above all a management task rather than a technical problem of representing knowledge (even though some papers in this area, typically written by computer scientists, do give that impression). In this section, we will therefore look at the management aspects of process knowledge, in particular knowledge about software processes, and their implications on software process technology.

Well-known frameworks for the management of software process knowledge are the Experience Factory [7–9] and the Capability Maturity Model CMM [53], in particular the key process areas *Organizational Process Focus* (OPF) and *Organizational Process Definition* (OPD).

Additionally, most of the classic work [23] by Davenport and Prusak on knowledge management applies to the specific case of software process knowledge as well.

In the following, we will follow the structure defined by Probst (see Fig. 3).

4.1. *Knowledge goals*

The main goal of knowledge management as described in the current article is to support developers in performing the software development processes, i.e., in developing software. This operational goal supports the strategic goal of getting faster, cheaper, and producing software of higher quality.

4.2. *Knowledge identification*

The relevant knowledge is listed in Sec. 2.

4.3. *Knowledge acquisition*

In order to represent knowledge in a process model, it must be provided by those who know, such as developers. To some extent, it can also be provided by a software process engineer, a member of the software engineering process group or similar, or even bought in from outside by using some standard model, but all these approaches are very limited if the process model is actually to be *used* by developers and not just put on the shelf.

To make developers put their development tasks aside and share their knowledge with others by helping to define the software process model, the organization must ensure that developers consider this as beneficial for themselves. In [23, Chap. 2], Davenport and Prusak describe three "currencies" or potential benefits that can convince employees to share their knowledge:

Reciprocity: "If I help to define the software processes, others will provide knowledge for the process model that I can use". To ensure this, the organization has to ensure that many qualified people contribute to the process model, not just a few people who do all the work and gain comparatively little benefit. Alternatively, the organization might provide explicit benefits such as time (not having to do other work while describing software processes) or even bonus payments or little extras such as a bottle of champagne.

Repute: Being known as the "champion" or "guru" for a certain topic. For software process technology, this implies that one should make clearly visible who contributed to a process model.

Altruism: This does happen, but one cannot really plan on it for creating a process model.

If, on the other hand, providing knowledge for the process model is perceived as "keeping developers from doing real work", it just won't happen.

4.4. *Knowledge development*

> "Knowledge development consists of all the management activities intended to produce new internal or external knowledge on both the individual and the collective level". [47, p. 24]

Typical activities to develop software process knowledge include

Process improvement to refine and improve the knowledge about software processes.

Packaging and representing knowledge once it has been created, turning implicit into explicit knowledge that is much better understood and ready for distribution.

Training for those who define the processes, such as seminars in process modeling or attending conferences.

Training users such as developers in the defined processes, on the other hand, is part of knowledge distribution since it helps to spread the existing knowledge without creating any new knowledge.

4.5. *Knowledge distribution*

Based on the representation of the knowledge described above, it has to be distributed to those who need it. Although in principle, such distribution can be on paper, this approach usually leads to write-only descriptions that is not used (shelf-ware). If one wants the knowledge to be not just distributed but to arrive in the people's heads, knowledge distribution must use channels such as

Direct communication, using the various forms of training, such as standard taught seminars, training-on-the-job (assuming that it is performed as genuine training and not as a nice label on no training at all) or one-to-one coaching sessions. This in effect comes down to using the *personalization strategy* described by Hansen *et al* (see Sec. 1.4).

Electronic distribution, making the description of the software processes available in an electronic format as described in Sec. 3 (applying *Hansen's codification strategy*).

4.6. *Knowledge preservation*

Knowledge preservation deals with the fact that knowledge tends to disappear if nothing is done about it (knowledge entropy), because people forget or leave the company, or knowledge gets outdated.

To prevent such loss of knowledge, an adequate process for the preservation of the process (a meta-process) must be installed, for example as a continuous improvement process consisting of many small changes, or by defining releases of the process definitions on a longer time-frame.

4.7. *Knowledge use*

Use of software process knowledge consists of developing and maintaining software, applying the knowledge contained in the defined development processes. Even if knowledge is developed and distributed, however, this is no guarantee that the knowledge will be used. To achieve this, developers need to be trained in the use of the defined processes, the processes need to be defined in a way such that the developers see an advantage for themselves using them, and finally quality assurance needs to check the use of the defined processes.

Although use of software process knowledge by an individual user is possible, this does not really gain a lot. To achieve its full benefit, the whole team needs to use and apply the knowledge and all work to the same processes.

4.8. *Knowledge measurement*

Knowledge measurement is concerned with the evaluation and measurement of organizational knowledge. This measurement should be based on the goals that the organization wants to achieve with their knowledge management activities, in our case the support of developers in their task, and the faster, cheaper production of software of higher quality (cf. Sec. 4.1).

Example: one software house uses the following measurements to evaluate its organizational knowledge (this work is as yet unpublished):

Number of improvement suggestions per month for the defined processes. Since no process definition is perfect, this is a good indicator of how intensively the knowledge contained in the process definitions is used and accepted.

Number of read accesses to the individual parts of the process description. This is an indicator of which knowledge is used most and provides the most benefit.

At the same time, this is a good example of the possible problems with such measurements, since surprisingly, one of the documents accessed most often is out of date, as could already be seen from the title of the document. No good explanation of this effect was found.

Number of deviations from the standard processes as identified by quality assurance reviews. This is a good indicator of the usefulness of the documented knowledge as seen by its users, as well as the effectiveness of the introduction of this knowledge.

5. Conclusions

As has been described in this paper, software process modeling for practical use can be viewed as a (knowledge) management task, not only a technical one. This has a number of implications for software process technology, such as

- emphasis on making software process models easy to use and accessible;
- combination/integration of user-centred description and formal model. XML looks like a promising language for achieving this;
- make visible who contributed what to a software process model;
- software process knowledge should be presented on different levels of detail (checklist, detailed description, etc); and
- expressiveness, effectiveness, efficiency, explicitness, accessibility, modifiability, and understandability as described in Sec. 3.1.

There is already some work in the direction suggested here, see for example several papers at the SEKE'99 conference [37] under the heading of the *Learning Software Organization* (see also the Chapter by Ruhe in this Handbook). Furthermore, most or even all the process models in widespread practical use, outside research institutions, follow the route suggested here and concentrate on support for the manual development tasks, typically by describing (in structured plain text) the tasks and artifacts and providing artifact templates. See e.g. the German V-Modell, the (Rational) Unified Process, internal, company-specific process model such as [43], the processes published on *http://sepo.spawar.navy.mil/docs.html* and on the Software Engineering Information Repository (SEIR) (*http://seir.sei.cmu.edu/*).

However, a lot of work still needs to be done before the results are satisfying for practical use. Currently, one can have either the benefits of the work done on software process technology (automated enactment of some process steps, consistency and other automated checks), or the kind of support for development tasks performed by humans as described in this paper. Hopefully, future work will be able to combine both.

References

1. W. van der Aalst, J. Desel and A. Oberweis (eds.), *Business Process Management, Models, Techniques, and Empirical Studies*, *Lecture Notes in Computer Science 1806* (Springer, 2000).
2. S. W. Ambler, "An introduction to process patterns", White Paper, AmbySoft Inc (1998). Version of June 27, 1998. Online available at *http://www.ambysoft.com/processPatterns.pdf*
3. S. W. Ambler, *Process Patterns: Building Large-Scale Systems Using Object Technology* (SIGS Books/Cambridge University Press, July 1998).
4. S. W. Ambler, *More Process Patterns: Delivering Large-Scale Systems Using Object Technology* (SIGS Books/Cambridge University Press, September 1998).
5. S. C. Bandinelli, A. Fuggetta and S. Grigolli, "Process modeling in-the-large with SLANG", *Proceedings of the Second International Conference on the Software Process*, ed. L. Osterweil (IEEE Computer Society Press, February 1993) 75–83.

6. N. S. Barghouti, D. S. Rosenblum, D. G. Belanger and C. Alliegro, "Two case studies in modeling real, corporate processes", *Software Process — Improvement and Practice* (August 1995) 17–32.
7. V. R. Basili, "The experience factory and its relationship to other improvement paradigms in software engineering — ESEC'93" *Lecture Notes in Computer Science 717* (Springer, Heidelberg, 1993) 68–83.
8. V. R. Basili, G. Caldiera and H. D. Rombach, "Experience factory in encyclopedia of software engineering", Vol. 1, ed. J. Marciniak (Wiley, 1994) 469–476.
9. V. R. Basili, F. Shull and F. Lanubile, "Building knowledge through families of experiment", *IEEE Transactions on Software Engineering* (August 1999) 456–473.
10. N. Belkhatir, J. Estublier and W. L. Melo, "Software process model and work space control in the Adele system", *Proceedings of the Second International Conference on the Software Process*, ed. L. Osterweil (IEEE Computer Society Press, February 1993) 2–11.
11. N. Belkhatir and W.L. Melo, "Supporting software maintenance processes in TEMPO", *Proceedings of the Conference on Software Maintenance* (IEEE Computer Society Press, September 1993).
12. I. Ben-Shaul and G. Kaiser, *A Paradigm for Decentralized Process Modeling* (Kluwer, Boston 1995).
13. B. W. Boehm, "A spiral model of software development and enhancement", *IEEE Computer* **21**, no. 5 (May 1988) 61–72.
14. N. Bradley, *The XML Companion* (Addison-Wesley, 1998).
15. G. Bremer, Genealogie von Entwicklungsschemata in Vorgehensmodelle für die betriebliche Anwendungsentwicklung, eds., R. Kneuper, G. Müller-Luschnat and A. Oberweis (B. G. Teubner, Leipzig, 1998) 76–94 (in German).
16. A. Bröckers, C. M. Lott, H. D. Rombach and M. Verlage, "MVP language report", Technical Report 229/92, Department of Computer Science, University of Kaiserslautern, Germany (1992).
17. P. Brössler, "Knowledge management at a software house", A Progress Report in *Proceeding of the Workshop on Learning Software Organizations*, June 16, 1999, Kaiserslautern, Germany, ed. Frank Bomarius (1999) 77–83.
18. K. Caputo, *CMM Implementation Guide. Choreographing Software Process Improvement* (Addison-Wesley, 1998).
19. Y-H. Chen-Burger, D. Robertson and J. Stader, "Formal support for an informal business modelling method", *International Journal of Software Engineering and Knowledge Engineering* **10**, no. 1 (February 2000) 49–68.
20. R. Conradi, A. Fuggetta and M. L. Jaccheri, "Six theses on software process research in software process technology", *6th European Workshop* (*EWSPT'98*), Weybridge, UK, ed. V. Gruhn, *Lecture Notes in Computer Science* (Springer, Heidelberg, 1998) 100–104.
21. R. Conradi (ed.), "Software process technology", *7th European Workshop* (*EWSPT 2000*), Kaprun, Austria, *Lecture Notes in Computer Science 1780* (Springer, 2000).
22. J. O. Coplien, "A generative development-process pattern language", eds. J. O. Coplien and D. C. Schmidt, *Pattern Languages of Program Design* (Addison-Wesley, 1995). Presented at PLoP/94, Monticello, Il., (August 1994). Online available at *http://www.bell-labs.com/people/cope/Patterns/Process/index.html*
23. T. H. Davenport and L. Prusak, *Working Knowledge. How Organizations Manage What They Know* (Harvard Business School Press, Boston, 1998).

24. J.-C. Derniame, B. A. Kaba and D. Wastell (eds.), *Software Process: Principles, Methodology and Technology*, *Lecture Notes in Computer Science 1500* (Springer, Heidelberg, 1999).
25. E. Ellmer, D. Merkl, G. Quirchmayr and A. M. Tjoa, "Process model reuse to promote organizational learning in software development", *Proceedings of the 20th Annual International Computer Software and Applications Conference* (*COMPSAC'96*), Seoul, South Korea, August 1996 (IEEE CS Press, 1996) 21–26.
26. J. Finlay and A. Dix, *Artificial Intelligence* (UCL Press, University College London, 1996).
27. V. Gruhn (ed.), "Software Process Technology", *6th European Workshop* (*EWSPT'98*), Weybridge, UK, *Lecture Notes in Computer Science 1487* (Springer, 1998).
28. M. T. Hansen, N. Nohria and T. Tierney, "What's your strategy for managing knowledge", *Harvard Business Review* (March 1999) 106–116.
29. D. Harel, H. Lachover, A. Naamad, A. Pnueli, M. Politi, R. Sherman, A. Shtull-Trauring and M. Trakhtenbrot, "Statemate: A working environment for the development of complex reactive systems", *IEEE Transactions on Software Engineering* (April 1990).
30. J. Hertzberg, *Planen. Einführung in die Planerstellungsmethoden der Künstlichen Intelligenz.* Reihe Informatik, Band 65. BI Wissenschaftsverlag, (1989) (in German).
31. F. Houdek and C. Bunse, "Transferring experience: A practical approach and its application on software inspections", *Proceedings of the Workshop on Learning Software Organizations*, June 16, 1999, Kaiserslautern, Germany, ed. F. Bomarius (1999) 59–68.
32. F. Houdek and H. Kempter, "Quality patterns — An approach to packaging software engineering experience", *Proceedings of the ACM Symposium on Software Reusability SSR'97* (1997) 81–88.
33. W. S. Humphrey and M. Kellner, "Software process modeling: Principles of entity process models", *Proceedings of the Eleventh International Conference on Software Engineering* (May 1989) 331–342.
34. ISO/IEC, Information technology — Software life cycle processes ISO/IEC 12207 (1995).
35. ISO/IEC, Software Process Improvement and Capability dEtermination Standard ISO/IEC 15504 (1995).
36. R. Kneuper, "Requirements on software process technology from the viewpoint of commercial software development: Recommendations for research directions in software process technology", *6th European Workshop* (*EWSPT'98*), Weybridge, UK, ed. V. Gruhn, *Lecture Notes in Computer Science 1487* (Springer, Heidelberg, 1998) 111–115.
37. Knowledge Systems Institute, *Proceedings of the 11th International Conference on Software Engineering and Knowledge Engineering* (*SEKE'99*) (1999). Online available at *http://www.ksi.edu/publication.html*
38. P. Kruchten, *The Rational Unified Process — An Introduction* (Addison Wesley, Longman, 1999).
39. T. S. Kuhn, *The Structure of Scientific Revolutions*, 2nd ed. (The University of Chicago Press, 1970).
40. C. Marshall, *Enterprise Modeling with UML. Designing Successful Software Through Business Analysis* (Addison-Wesley, 1999).
41. B. McFeely, "Ideal: A user's guide for software process improvement", Technical Report CMU/SEI-96-HB-001, Software Engineering Institute, Carnegie-Mellon University (1996). Online available at *http://www.sei.cmu.edu*

42. J. Mylopoulos, A. Borgida and E. Yu, "Representing software engineering knowledge", *Automated Software Engineering* **4** (1997) 291–317.
43. J. Noack and B. Schienmann, "Introducing OO development in a large banking organization", *IEEE Software* (May 1999) 71–81.
44. D. E. O'Leary, "Enterprise knowledge management", *IEEE Computer* (March 1998) 54–61.
45. D. E. O'Leary, "Using AI in knowledge management: Knowledge bases and ontologies", *IEEE Intelligent Systems* (May/June 1998), 34–39.
46. L. Osterweil, "Software processes are software too", *Proceedings of the 9th International Conference on Software Engineering* (*ICSE9*) (1987) 2–13.
47. G. J. B. Probst, "Practical knowledge management: A model that works", *Prism*, ed. A. D. Little (2nd quarter 1998), 17–29, Online available at *http://know.unige.ch/Prismartikel.pdf*
48. I. Robertson, "An implementable meta-process", *Proceedings, Second World Congress on Integrated Design and Process Technology*, eds. M. M. Tanik, F. B. Bastani, D. Gibson and P. J. Fielding, Society for Design and Process Science (1996).
49. H. D. Rombach and M. Verlage, "Directions in software process research", *Advances in Computers* **41** (1995) 1–63.
50. T. Rout, "SPICE: A framework for software process assessment", *Software Process — Improvement and Practice* **1**, no. 1 (1995).
51. W. Royce, "Why software costs so much", *IEEE Software* **10**, no. 3 (May 1993) 90–91.
52. V. Schuppan and W. Rußwurm, "A CMM-based evaluation of the V-Model 97 in software process technology", *7th European Workshop* (*EWSPT 2000*), Kaprun, Austria, ed. R. Conradi, *Lecture Notes in Computer Science 1780* (Springer, Heidelberg, 2000) 69–83. Online available at *http://www.inf.ethz.ch/ schuppan/paperewspt.pdf.zip*
53. Software Engineering Institute, Carnegie Mellon University, *The Capability Maturity Model. Guidelines for Improving the Software Process*, The SEI Series in Software Engineering (Addison Wesley Longman, 1994).
54. R. N. Taylor, F. C. Belz, L. A. Clarke, L. Osterweil, R. W. Selby, J. C. Wileden, A. L. Wolf and M. Young, "Foundations for the Arcadia environment architecture", *Proceedings of the Third ACM SIGSOFT/SIGPLAN Symposium on Practical Software Development Environments*, Published as ACM SIGSOFT Software Engineering Notes, ed. P. Henderson (November 1988) 1–13.
55. M. Verlage, Modellierungssprachen für Vorgehensmodelle in Vorgehensmodelle für die betriebliche Anwendungsentwicklung, eds. R. Kneuper, G. Müller-Luschnat and A. Oberweis, B. G. Teubner, Leipzig (1998) 76–94 (in German).
56. V-Model, "Development standard for IT-systems of the Federal Republic of Germany, lifecycle process model". Online available at *http://www.v-modell.iabg.de/*
57. J. Weizenbaum, *Computer Power and Human Reason. From Judgment to Calculation* (Freeman, 1978).

KNOWLEDGE ELICITATION: THE STATE OF THE ART

TIM MENZIES
Department of Electrical & Computer Engineering,
University of British Columbia, 2356 Main Mall,
Vancouver, B.C., Canada V6T 1Z4
E-mail: tim@menzies.com

1. Introduction

Defining a discpline is always good practice. However, the generally accepted definition of *knowledge acquisition* (KA) may be too narrow to support an evaluation of the state of the art [66]. This chapter will extend the standard definition of KA to find evaluation data within that broader definition.

The majority of the community, including Shadbolt *et al* [103], defines KA as follows:

- KA is usually the process of mapping expert statements into conceptual models.
- KA usually tries to reuse older conceptual models to guide the development of new models.
- KA is usually an early life cycle activity that precedes much of the implementation details.

(While exceptions do exist,[a] these three points characterize of the majority of the work seen in the Japanese, North American, European, and Pacific region KA workshops.[b])

Despite several major international collaborative projects (the Sisyphus experiments [59, 99, 103]), little has been been concluded about the relative merits of different KA techniques. Shadbolt *et al* comment pessimistically that ...

> ... none of the Sisyphus experiments have yielded much evaluation information [103].

Shadbolt's pessimism is unfounded, but only if researchers look beyond standard KA literature. It is true that comparative statements about KA techniques are few and far between in the standard KA literature [66]. However, by looking

[a]Such as the "Australian KA club"; e.g. [13,24,27–29,37,54,55,58,69,71–73,75,77,79,94,95,115].
[b]For proceedings of these workshops, see *http://ksi.cpsc.ucalgary.ca/KAW/*.

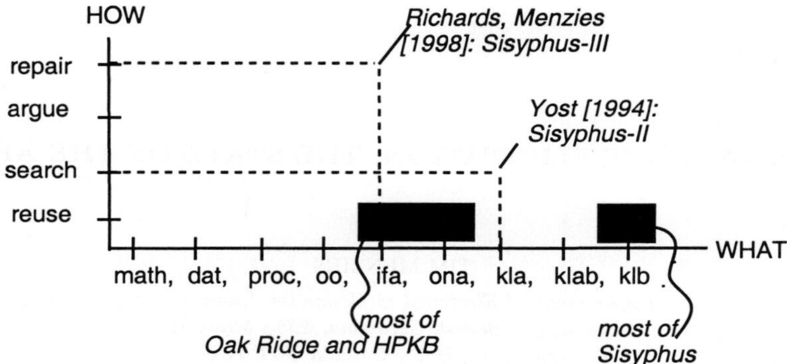

Fig. 1. A The *how* and *what* of contemporary knowledge engineering. Shown on this plot are various studies discussed in this chapter that explore part of this space. For an explanation of the terms used on the x-axis and y-axis, see the text.

further afield, this chapter will make several comparative statements about different techniques.

Figure 1 is an attempt to KA in a broader context. This broader context can be called the *knowledge elicitation* (KEL) space. The KEL space of Fig. 1 has two dimensions. The *how* dimension refers to how the elicitation process is organized. For example, if the developers make extensive use of a library of components, then *how = reuse*. The *what* dimension refers to the primary modeling construct used by the analysts. For example, if after talking to experts analysts write down object-oriented (OO) class diagrams, then *what=OO.*

The dimensions of Fig. 1 are not continuous and, truth to tell, are somehwat subjective. Nevertheless, I have found that Fig. 1 to offer insights into what has been done, and what has been ignored, in KA research. For example, the black boxes shown on the KEL space of Fig. 1 mark areas that have been extensively studied in the literature. Note that much of Fig. 1 is not black, i.e., much of the space is unexplored.

Why explore outside of the narrow range of current work? One reason is that it is easier to distinguish differences between objects that are held far apart. The KEL space includes more techniques that found in the standard KA literature. Within this broader space, we can find an answer to (e.g.) Shadbolt's pessimism since within this broader space, data points exist that let us assess contemporary KA and knowledge engineering techniques.

This chapter will conclude that there are many open issues in contemporary KEL that require more investigation and evaluation. Numerous texts describe effective methods for the evaluation of software in general [39] and AI software in particular [23]. For pointers to resources and examples of KEL evaluations, see [66]. Evaluating KEL techniques is not as hard as many researchers fear. For example, cost-effective methods of studying complex systems are discussed in [65, 73].

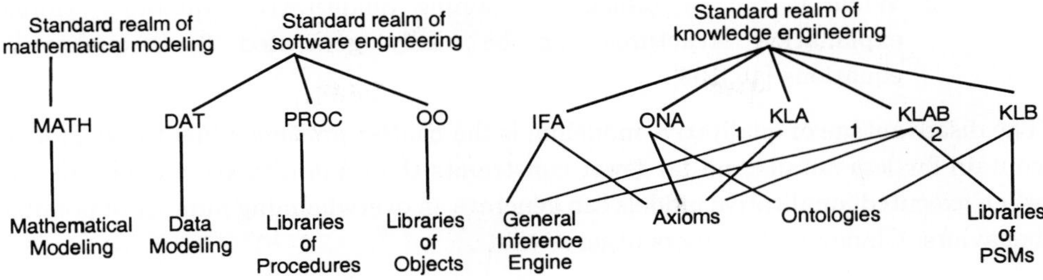

Fig. 2. *What* is written down as "knowledge". "1" denotes that the single inference engine is customizable; e.g. the knowledge engineer can provide operator selection rules to customize the problem space traversal [57]. "2" denotes that *PSMs* (defined in Sec. 2.7) in *KLAB* (defined in Sec. 2.8) are used only in an initial analysis stage.

2. What is the Form of the Elicited Knowledge?

This exploration of the KEL space begins with a definition of the *what* axis of Fig. 1. This axis shows what analysts write down when they record knowledge. Numerous notations exist such as the ones shown in Fig. 2. In that figure, the top-level division shows who used which notation. For example, MATH is a technique used in the *realm of mathematical modelers* while OO is a technique often used in the *realm of software engineers.* Seperate to these two realms is the *realm of knowledge engineers* who often use techniques not seen in standard software engineering or mathematical modeling (e.g. rule-based languages — called IFA in Fig. 2). For example, most of contemporary KEL research focuses on IFA, ONA, and KLB.

The rest of this section defined and discussed the middle layer in Fig. 2.

2.1. *What = MATH: mathematical representations*

Impressive and intuitive visual programming environments exist that allow end-users to model complex systems, then execute them using some mathematical equation solver [45, 50]. One advantage of the MATHs-based approach is that certain quality factors (stability, observability, controllability) can be rigorously determined [51].

An interesting variant on standard quantitative MATHematical modeling is qualitative modeling. Qualitative reasoning is the study of equations of physicals systems whose numeric values are replaced by one of three qualitative states: *UP*, *DOWN* or *STEADY* [52]. Qualitative models have at least two advantages over quantitative models and one major disadvantage. The advantages are:

1. Because they contain less details, qualitative modeling can be performed cheaply and early in a product's life cycle [117]. For example it is faster to elicit the qualitative knowledge that (e.g.) `a encourages b` than the quantitative knowledge that $b = 2.4\pi^{1.01*a}$.

2. While it can be difficult explaining quantitative equations, simple explanation structures can be easily generated from qualitative equations [45, 105].

The disadvantage of qualitative modeling is the *chatter problem.* Qualitative models contain far less details and far fewer constraints than quantitative models. Hence, when executed, qualitative models can generate an overwhelming number of possible behaviors. Clancy and Kuipers observe that ...

> Intractable branching due to irrelevant distinctions is one of the major factors hindering the application of qualitative reasoning techniques to large real-world problems [20].

One method for taming chatter is the DecSIM simulator in which the user divides the theory into several partitions [20]. These partitions are then simulated as separate units. While DecSIM has been able to offer richer simulations than standard qualitative reasoners, DecSIM's authors comment that "DecSIM cannot guarantee a tractable simulation for any model".

Another method for taming chatter is to impose modeling restrictions that dodge the branching problem. Three such restrictions are *avoiding unreachable models*, a *restricted simulation policy* and the use of *saturation languages*:

- In a *reachable* model, goals can be quickly found before chatter overwhelms the simulation. Detectors for reachable models expressed as directed graphs are discussed by Menzies and Cukic [67]. While these detectors can find chatter-prone models, they offer little help in stopping a model chattering.
- In a *saturation language*, if some property can't be reached after a very limited simulation, it is certain that it cannot be reached after a much longer simulation [76]. That is, any model written in a saturation language is also a *reachable model* (defined above). The disadvantage of these saturating languages (e.g. *iedge* [75, 114]) is that only very simple concepts can be expressed. However, the advantage of such saturation languages is that they can be searched using nearly linear time algorithms [63]. Hence, very large models can be processed. Further, despite their language restrictions, they are adequate to represent a wide range of interesting models such as propositional logical models, early life cycle software requirements [63], and qualitative medical knowledge about internal human physiology [78].
- A qualitative simulator can execute faster with less chatter if it restricts itself to only those behaviors that lead to pre-specified goals. This *restricted simulation policy* has been used to find previously undetected faults in theories published in international refereed medical journals [37, 68, 78]. Note that such a restricted simulation policy is not required for a model written in a saturation language.

2.2. *What = DAT: representations from data modeling*

Data modeling researchers assume that knowledge will be expressed in something like the entity-relationship models used by database designers. Theoretically, there is nothing stopping data modeling workers from developing knowledge based systems (KBS) [110]. However, in practice, conventional database manipulation languages are much stronger on IO functions and disc storage than intricate RAM-based manipulation of data. Nevertheless, the relational model offers impressive support for structuring knowledge such that it can be better maintained [33].

2.3. *What = PROC or OO: procedural or object-oriented or functional representations*

A popular method of expressing knowledge is in some procedural/functional (PROC) or object-oriented (OO) form. PROC and OO researchers reject the declarative representations used in the other approaches. In the 70's, this was a large research area. Proponents of *frame* representations (e.g. [81, 118]) argued that part of human expertise was "know-how" and these recipes of "how" to solve a problem were best modeled as (e.g.) Lisp procedures attached to frame slots. The debate continued after the 70s [7, 88] but the complexity of reasoning about procedures (e.g. [36]) drove most researchers to declarative characterizations of their frame-based knowledge (e.g. [9]). While some pure PROC/OO kept the faith (e.g. [7, 10]), pure PROC/OO KEL researchers are rare these days.

OO has become a very popular modeling paradigm in the commercial world [8]. OO languages are useful for many task; e.g. JAVA is a natural language for concurrent web-based applications. However, OO class hierarchies can *confuse* rather than *clarify* software maintenance. Hatton [48] reports one study over a six year period with a ≈50,000 LOC parser written and maintained in C++ and C. The programmers on this team were experienced in both language and used mature software processes (CMM-level 2^+). The average time chasing bugs in the C++ parser was much greater than in the C version (see Fig. 3). Hatton acknowledges that his results cannot distinguish between the effects of object-oriented hierarchies and the particulars of the implementation environments. However, he notes that

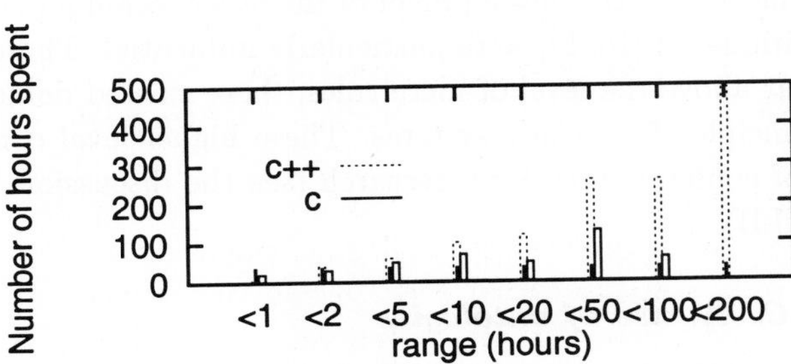

Fig. 3. Maintenance times: *OO > procedural*. From [48].

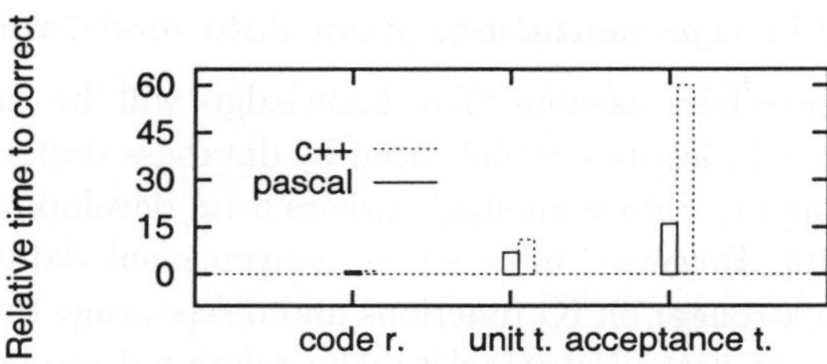

Fig. 4. Testing times: *OO > procedural*. "Code r"= time spent on code reviews. "Unit t."= time spent on unit testing. "Acceptance t"= time spent on acceptance testing. From [49].

analogous results have been reported elsewhere [49]; i.e., a C++ system was much slower to change later in the life cycle than an equivalent procedural system (see Fig. 4).

Hatton's explanation for these empirical results casts doubt on the utility of inheritance as a modeling construct. His argument is that the increased maintenance times of C++ are not due to the idiosyncrasies of the language. Rather, these problems arise from the distributed nature of properties in an inheritance hierarchy. Debugging such a hierarchy requires tracing up and down a hierarchy. During that trace, to understand some method in class X, the programmer must also *keep in mind* what is known about how class X effects a method in class Y. Hatton's argument is this *keeping in mind* process is slow and difficult for people since it requires reading and writing to long-term memory (something humans do very slowly and very poorly).

2.4. *What = IFA*: *inference over axioms*

In the IFA approach, there are domain facts and, usually, no explicit generalization of those facts. IFA typically commits to a single inference procedure. Examples of these inference engines include Prolog [56], OPS5 [42], SOAR [57, 97], PSCM [120], GSAT [101], ISAMP [32], ...

Crudely expressed, in the IFA approach, knowledge engineering is just a matter of stuffing axioms into an inference engine and letting the inference engine work it all out. IFA was how knowledge engineering was performed in the 70's. Drawbacks with IFA motivated the development of the other techniques described in this chapter. The critiques of [15, 17] were particularly influential. These writers argued convincingly that above the level of mere rules, there existed domain-independent organization principles for expert systems. These higher-level constructs are the focus of much of contemporary KEL research (see the discussion below on ONA, KLA, KLAB, KLB).

2.5. *What = ONA*: *use of ontologies*

ONA is short for "ONtologies + Axioms". Axioms are some logical assertion describing facts or rules in a domain. Ontologies model common domain terminology.

This terminology might include the data structures required by a problem solving method (PSM — discussed below). Using a good ontology, it is argued, can guide developers in the construction of new systems.

An active focus in ONA is the creation of ontologies. Ontologies may never execute — rather they may be an analysis tool for a domain. An example of ONA work might be software engineers who develop architectures or design patterns, but do not execute these abstractions directly (e.g. [44]).

Ontologies are a large area of active research. For more details on this work, see [53].

2.6. *What = KLA*: *Newell's knowledge-level*

KLA modeling adopts Newell's *knowledge-level* insight [86, 87]. According to Newell, intelligence may be modeled at the knowledge level as a search for appropriate operators that convert some current state to a goal state. Domain-specific knowledge is used to select the operators according to *the principle of rationality*; i.e., an intelligent agent will select an operator which its knowledge tells it will lead to the achievement of some of its goals.

KLA makes a strong commitment to a single inference procedure, which can be customized. This inference procedure features predominantly when modeling a system; e.g. [57, 80, 120]. For example, a KLA analyst would record the different states a system can take, the choices at each state, and the rationality operators that select how to move from this state towards the goal state.

2.7. *What = KLB*: *other knowledge-level modeling approaches*

KLB modeling assumes that new applications are built by reusing old problem solving methods (PSMs) and ontologies. A sample PSM is shown in Fig. 5. KLB modeling proceeds by first selecting a PSM, then collecting domain specific information relating to the data types in the selected PSM. For example, using this PSM, an analyst would be guided to ask "what are the `norm` values for the `observables`?".

KLB uses either libraries of PSMs [116] or explores a single PSM within such a library [60]. KLB makes extensive use of ontologies. At runtime, KLB may use a general inference engine to execute their systems (e.g. older versions of PROTEGE-II [35] compiled down to CLIPS [85]) but this inference engine does not feature in the design discussions.

Numerous libraries of PSM have been collected; e.g. SPARK/ BURN/ FIRE-FIGHTER [61]; generic tasks [16]; configurable role-limiting methods [46, 108]; model construction operators [19]; CommonKADS [100, 116]; the PROTEGE family of systems [35]; components of expertise [106]; MIKE [4]; and TINA [6].

There is a large research community working on KLB and this chapter is too short to discuss all that work. Another chapter in this handbook is especially devoted to KLB [83]. Note that the KLB community calls its activities "knowledge-level modeling" even though significant differences exist between KLB-style

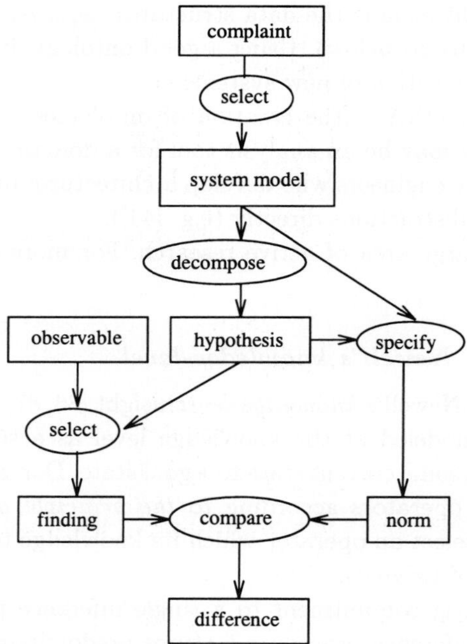

Fig. 5. A problem solving method (PSM) for diagnosis; ovals=functions, rectangles = data types.

knowledge level modeling and Newell-style KLA knowledge level modeling:

- Newell-style knowledge-level modeling is based on customizing a single search engine.
- The PSM/ontology community is based on the reuse of libraries of PSMs and ontologies.

2.8. *What = KLAB*

KLAB is a hybrid KLA/KLB approach in which PSMs are used to structure the analysis discussions, but then converted by the knowledge engineer at design time to KLA [16].

3. How is Knowledge Elicited?

Having described the *what* of the KEL space, it is now time to study the vertical *how* axis of Fig. 1. Moran and Carroll [82, p. 3] argue that four broad paradigms of *how* may be found in the literature. These four paradigms are described below.

3.1. *How = reuse*

How = reuse dates back at least to 1964 with Alexander's work on architecture [2, 3]. Design is taken to be the re-shuffling of components developed previously,

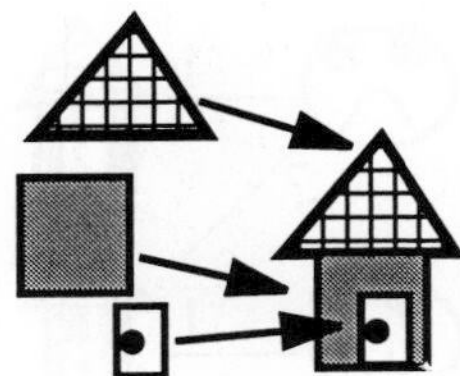

Fig. 6. An example of *how* = *reuse*. A house is built using parts found when the last house was built.

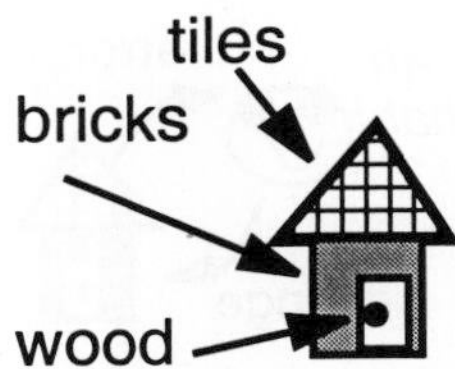

Fig. 7. An example of *how* = *search*. A house is built via a search of the space of what is known of bricks, tiles, and wood.

then abstracted into a reusable form. For example, in Fig. 6, a new house is built by reflecting over models developed when older houses were built.

Contemporary expressions of this approach include object-oriented design patterns [11, 70], and the knowledge engineering research into ontologies [47, 113] and problem solving methods (PSMs) [15, 17, 100]. Our reading of the literature is that this approach is the dominant paradigm in contemporary knowledge and software engineering.

KLB and ONT assume *how* = *reuse*. The fundamental premise of the KLB and ONT research is that conceptual models abstracted from old domains are power tools when reused in new domains.

3.2. *How* = *search*

The paradigm of construction-as-search dates back at least to 1969 with Simon's work on artificial intelligence [104]. According to Simon, design is the traversal of a space of possibilities, looking for pathways to goals. For example, to build a house, we might search through a space of constraints describing the relationship between building parts (see Fig. 7).

Contemporary expressions of this approach includes most of the AI search literature [90]. KLA assumes *how* = *search*, often using the SOAR toolkit [86, 87] with or without the PSCM extension [120].

3.3. *How* = *argue*

This paradigm dates back to at least 1972 with Ritell's work on *wicked problems* [96]. Wicked problems have many features, the most important being

Fig. 8. An example of *how* = *argue*. Let each stakeholder design their preferred house separately. The merits of the different houses can then be assessed.

Fig. 9. An example of *how* = *repair*. Build a house, find out that the living room gets too hot in summer, plant fruit trees for shade, make and sell the jam from the fruit.

that no objective measure of success exists. Designing solutions for wicked problems cannot aim to produce some perfectly correct answer since no such definition of *correct* exists. Hence, this approach to design tries to support effective debates by a community over a range of possible answers. For example, when building a house using *how* = *argue*, different stakeholders first elaborate their own version of the final product. The different versions are then explored and assessed (see Fig. 8).

Contemporary expressions of this approach includes the requirements engineering (RE) community. Requirements engineering is usually complicated by the incompleteness of the specification being developed: while a specification should be consistent, requirements are often very inconsistent. RE researchers such as [34], [40] and [89] argue that we should routinely expect specifications to reflect different and inconsistent viewpoints. Note that this paradigm requires more than one expert to be part of the knowledge acquisition process.

3.4. *How* = *repair*

This paradigm dates back to at least 1983 with Schon's work on the *reflective practitioner* [98]. In this approach, design mostly happens when some concrete artifact *talks back* to the designer — typically by failing in some important situation. That is, *how* = *repair* is less concerned with the creation of some initial artifact than the on-going re-interpretation and adjustment of that artifact. So, when building a house using *how* = *repair*, version $i + 1$ of the house is created using the lessons learnt from building version i.

Contemporary expressions of this approach include the situated cognition community [18, 74, 107], certain approaches to design rationale [12, 41], and knowledge engineering techniques that focus on maintenance rather than initial design. For example, in the *ripple-down-rules* (RDR) repair-based system, knowledge is organized into a *patch tree.* If a rule is found to be faulty, some patch logic is added on an *unless* link beneath the rule. The patch is itself a rule and so may be patched recursively. Whenever a new patch (rule) is added to an RDR system, the case which prompted the patch is included in the rule. These *cornerstone cases* are used below when fixing an RDR system. At runtime, the final conclusion is the conclusion of the last satisfied rule. If that conclusion is faulty, then the fault is localized to the last satisfied rule. For more details on ripple-down-rules, see [25, 26, 30, 43, 84, 92, 93].

4. Evaluations

The above discussion outlined what KEL researchers have been *doing.* However, Cohen warns:

> Researchers are very good at describing what they are *doing*, but not what they are *learning.* [23]

Hence, we need now to review what we have *learnt* after all that *doing.* The sequel looks for systems that use different combinations *how*'s and *what*'s. Some of those systems come from the Sisyphus work. By comparing these systems, we can at least identify the open issues in contemporary KEL.

4.1. *Need more than "just" rules?*

In the section *what* = *IFA*, it was commented that numerous researchers developed KLA, KLB and ONT approaches based on difficulties with IFA. It is an open issue whether the methods developed since IFA are more productive than old-fashioned IFA:

- In the Oak Ridge study, various researchers tried to build applications for the same problem. Most of the groups at Oak Ridge used IFA-based techniques and produced working prototypes. However, the group using an OO-based tool (RLL) did not produce a working system since most of their time was spent configuring the extensive representational options within their tool [5].
- In the Sisyphus-III initiative [103], Richards and Menzies [95] used an IFA RDR approach to produce a working system for lunar rock classification (RDR was introduced above in the section *what* = *repair*). In the same time frame, various reuse-based teams produced no working system since they were still debugging their upper-level ontologies.

The comparatively better performance of RDR for lunar rock classification in Sisyphus-III suggests the possibility that *how* = *repair* may be more productive than than *how* = *reuse* when building a system. Another data point supporting that possibility comes from DARPA's High Performance Knowledge Base initiative (HPKB) [14, 21, 22, 91]:

- The goal of HPKB was to increase the rate at which a KEL tool can collect axioms. Various teams participated in HPKB including many that used *how* = *reuse* methods. In HPKB year one, the George Mason team generated the most new axioms added per day (787 binary predicates) using DISCIPLE: an incremental knowledge acquisition tool [109]. DISCIPLE includes elaborate repair tools. Inside DISCIPLE are machine learning tools that abstract the supplied knowledge. The abstracted rules are then proposed to the user in order to generate rules which makes them more generally applicable. DISCIPLE requires meta-knowledge to execute, but the system builds and updates that meta-knowledge as it runs.

4.2. *Need more than "just" search?*

The distinction between KLA/KLB is the amount of effort devoted to *pre-modeling* the search procedure:

- Reuse of large libraries of problem solving methods or ontologies is not stressed in KLA. In KLA, there is a single hard-wired search procedure with customizable operators.
- In KLB, elaborate libraries of problem solving methods are used. These libraries contain declarative descriptions of procedures used to perform common tasks such as diagnosis (e.g. Fig. 5). These libraries are constantly being improved in order to simplify and improve the construction of new applications.

The Sisyphus-II initiative gives us one data point with which to compare KLA and KLB [99]:

- Yost [119] used a KLA tool (PSCMs) to solve an elevator configuration problem. The other participants in the Sisyphus-II study made extensive use of KLB [99]. Yost's reported development times were much less than any of the other teams. It is possible that Yost's extra experience with the domain gave him an advantage (Yost had analyzed the domain extensively prior to system construction). On the other hand, it is also possible that search-based approaches are more productive than reuse-based approaches.

The more elaborate the pre-modeling, the harder it is for a newcomer to use and understand the library of reusable components. This effect has been well studied in the SE literature:

- The COCOMO-II software cost estimation model offers an estimate of the cost of adapting reusable sub-routines for a new project [1, p. 21]. A

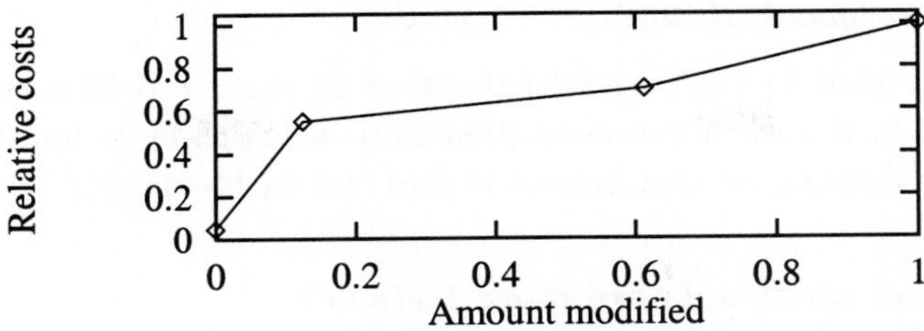

Fig. 10. COCOMO-II, the cost of reuse with $X\%$ changes. Y-axis shows the relative cost of changing vs rebuilding from scratch. Data from thousands of NASA software modules [1, p. 21].

learning curve must be traversed before a module can be adapted. By the time you know enough to change a little of that module, you may as well have re-written 60% of it from scratch; see Fig. 10.

A similar effect may well exist when reusing knowledge-based components:

- Cohen *et al* [21] studied how much ontologies supported the development of HPKB applications. The specific and recent terms added to an ontology offer more support than generic terms added previously by other authors. The former scored a constant 60% rate of reuse in contrast with the poor 22% rate of reuse scored by the broad ontologies. These results cast some doubt on the verbatim reuse benefits of generic ontologies but Cohen *et al* are quick to add that the generic terms may help designers to better structure their systems. However, they offer no empirical evidence to support this possibility.
- In another study, international KA experts used some background knowledge to guide their analysis of a transcript of a patient talking to a doctor [31]. One group could use a supposedly reusable model of diagnosis which had been matured over many years by many researchers. Other groups used either a reuse model of diagnosis invented very quickly (the "straw man") or no reuse model at all. The results are shown in Fig. 11. The "mature model" group performed as well as the "straw man" group. Further, the "no model" group out-performed the groups using the models!

Reuse Model	% Disorders Identified	% Knowledge Fragments Identified
Straw man: invented very quickly	50	28
Mature model: decades of work	55	34
No model	75	41

Fig. 11. Productivity using different models.

4.3. *ISA is a "good" thing?*

The ontologies used in ONT and KLB are often expressed in a type hierarchy. Recalling Fig. 3, if such a representation is to be read by a human, it will be fundamentally difficult for that human to find and fix flaws.

4.4. *High-level constructs are more testable?*

There are many claims that the high-level constructs of KLB's are easier to test e.g. [38, 102, 111, 112]. However, none of this work has yet to devise an experimental evaluation of their claims that *KLB = better testing*. Note that if any of these higher-level constructs are expressed as inheritance hierarchies, then recalling the last section, these hierarchies will be *harder* to manually debug than flatter representations.

While humans *may* be able to read and critique small models, automatic support is required to test models that grow beyond a trivial size. One method for such automatic testing is to search for pathways from known inputs to desired goals or faults. If any faults can be reached or if some goals can't be reached, the system can be faulted. In the case of nondeterministic AI systems, this search could get lost in all the nondeterministic options.

Menzies and Compton [68, 78] have shown that this nondeterministic testing problem can be mapped to the chatter problem. That is, the methods discussed above that solve the chatter problem can also address the problem of automatically testing nondeterministic systems. Recall that all these solutions to the chatter problem discussed above (in the section *what = MATH*) required restrictions on the types of models built, or the language used for the models, or how a model is exercised. Such restrictions are not acceptable to the KLB community. One of the premises of that community is that intelligence can be analyzed using knowledge *content* rather than knowledge *form*; i.e., it is irrelevant if it is expressed in rules or frames or *C* code or inheritance hierarchies or directed graphs or saturation languages. While form *may* be irrelevant for initial knowledge acquisition, it is *vital* when assessing the testability of an artifact.

5. Discussion

This chapter has briefly surveyed a range of techniques used in contemporary KEL (for more details, see [62]). One limitation with this survey is that it dealt only with *mostly manual* knowledge elicitation methods that have a *large human-in-the-loop component*. Methods for mostly automatic knowledge elicitation are discussed elsewhere [62–64].

The survey can be used in one of two ways. Firstly, it could be used as a simple road map describing contemporary methods. Secondly, the case studies in the last section might motivate the reader to explore the open issues in KEL. Clearly, the case studies are too few to make general conclusions about the utility of different

KEL techniques. However, the case studies at the very least suggest that we should be more active in critically assessing different KEL options.

Acknowledgments

Helen Burgess provided invaluable editorial advice for this article.

References

1. C. Abts, B. Clark, S. Devnani-Chulani, E. Horowitz, R. Madachy, D. Reifer, R. Selby and B. Steece, "COCOMO II model definition manual", Technical Report, Center for Software Engineering, USC,, 1998, *http://sunset.usc.edu/COCOMOII/cocomox.html #downloads*
2. C. Alexander, *Notes on Synthesis of Form* (Harvard University Press, 1964).
3. C. Alexander, S. Ishikawa, S. Silverstein, I. Jacobsen, I. Fiksdahl-King and S. Angel, *A Pattern Language* (Oxford University Press, 1977).
4. J. Angele, D. Fensel and R. Studer, "Domain and task modelling in mike", ed., A. Sutcliffe *et al*, *Domain Knowledge for Interactive System Design* (Chapman & Hall, 1996).
5. D. R. Barstow, N. Aiello, R. O. Duda, L. D. Erman, C. L. Forgy, D. Gorlin, R. D. Greiner, D. B. Lenat, P. E. London, J. McDermott, H. Penny Nii, P. Politakis, R. Reboh, S. Rosenchein, A. C. Scott, W. van Melle and S. M. Weiss, "Languages and tools for knowledge engineering", eds. F. Hayes-Roth, D. A. Waterman and D. B. Lenat, *Building Expert Systems*, Chap. 9 (Addison-Wesley, 1983) 283–345.
6. R. Benjamins, "Problem-solving methods for diagnosis and their role in knowledge acquisition", *International Journal of Expert Systems: Research and Applications* **8**, no. 2 (1995) 93–120.
7. L. Birnbaum, "Rigor Mortis: A response to Nilsson's logic and artificial intelligence", *Artificial Intelligence* **47** (1991) 57–77.
8. G. Booch, I. Jacobsen and J. Rumbaugh, *Version 1.0 of the Unified Modeling Language* (Rational, 1997), *http://www.rational.com/ot/uml/1.0/index.html*
9. R. J. Brachman, V. P. Gilbert and H. J. Levesque, "An essential hybrid reasoning system: Knowledge and symbol level accounts of krypton", eds. J. Mylopoulos and M. L. Brodie, *Readings in Artificial Intelligence and Databases* (Morgan Kaufmann, 1989) 293–300.
10. R. A. Brooks, "Intelligence without representation", *Artificial Intelligence* **47** (1991) 139–159.
11. F. Buschmann, R. Meunier, H. Rohnert, P. Sommerlad and M. Stal, *A System of Patterns: Pattern-Oriented Software Architecture* (John Wiley & Sons, 1996).
12. G. Casady, "Rationale in practice: templates for capturing and applying design expertise", eds. T. P. Moran and J. M. Carroll, *Design Rationale: Concepts, Techniques, and Use* (Lawerence Erlbaum Associates, 1996) 351–372.
13. J. Catlett, "Inductive learning from subsets or disposal of excess training data considered harmful", *Australian Workshop on Knowledge Acqusition for Knowledge-Based Systems, Pokolbin* (1991) 53–67.
14. M. Ceruti, C. Anken, A. Lin and S. Rubin, "Applications of high-performance knowledge-based technology", *Proceedings of IEEE Systems Man and Cybernetics* (2000). Available from *http://reliant.teknowledge.com/HPKB/Publications/ceruti.ps*
15. B. Chandrasekaran, "Towards a taxonomy of problem solving types", *AI Magazine* (Winter/Spring, 1983) 9–17.

16. B. Chandrasekaran, T. R. Johnson and J. W. Smith "Task structure analysis for knowledge modeling", *Communications of the ACM* **35**, no. 9 (1992) 124–137.
17. W. Clancey, "Heuristic classification", *Artificial Intelligence* **27** (1985) 289–350.
18. W. Clancey, "The knowledge level reinterpreted: Modeling how systems interact", *Machine Learning* **4**, no. 3–4 (1989) 285–293.
19. W. J. Clancey, "Model construction operators", *Artificial Intelligence* **53** (1992) 1–115.
20. D. J. Clancy and B. K. Kuipers, "Model decomposition and simulation: A component based qualitative simulation algorithm", *AAAI'97* (1997).
21. P. Cohen, V. Chaudhri, A. Pease and R. Schrag, "Does prior knowledge facilitate the development of knowledge-based systems?" *AAAI'99* (1999).
22. P. Cohen, R. Schrag, E. Jones, A. Pease, A. Lin, B. Starr, D. Gunning and M. Burke, "The darpa high-performance knowledge bases project", *AI Magazine* **19**, no. 4 (Winter, 1998) 25–49.
23. P. R. Cohen, *Empirical Methods for Artificial Intelligence* (MIT Press, 1995).
24. P. Compton, G. Edwards, B. Kang, L. Lazarus, R. Malor, T. Menzies, P. Preston, A. Srinivasan and C. Sammut, "Ripple down rules: Possibilities and limitations", *6th Banff AAAI Knowledge Acquisition for Knowledge Based Systems* (1991).
25. P. Compton, G. Edwards, A. Srinivasan, P. Malor, P. Preston, B. Kang and L. Lazarus, "Ripple-down-rules: Turning knowledge acquisition into knowledge maintenance", *Artificial Intelligence in Medicine* **4** (1992) 47–59.
26. P. Compton, K. Horn, J. R. Quinlan and L. Lazarus, "Maintaining an expert system", ed. J. R. Quinlan, *Applications of Expert Systems* (Addison Wesley, 1989) 366–385.
27. P. Compton, B. Kang, P. Preston and M. Mulholland, "Knowledge acquisition without analysis", *European Knowledge Acquisition Workshop* (1993).
28. P. Compton, P. Preston and B. Kang, "The use of simulated experts in evaluating knowledge acquisition" (1995).
29. P. Compton, Z. Ramadan, P. Preston, T. Le-Gia, V. Chellen, M. Mulholland, D. B. Hibbert, P. R. Haddad and B. Kang, "A trade-off between domain knowledge and problem-solving method power", *Banff Workshop on Knowledge Acquisition* (1998). Available from *http://ksi.cpsc.ucalgary.ca/KAW/KAW98/compton*
30. P. J. Compton and R. Jansen, "A philosophical basis for knowledge acquisition", *Knowledge Acquisition* **2** (1990) 241–257.
31. C. Corbridge, N. P. Major and N. R. Shadbolt, "Models exposed: An empirical study", *Proceedings of the 9th AAAI-Sponsored Banff Knowledge Acquisition for Knowledge Based Systems* (1995).
32. J. Crawford and A. Baker, "Experimental results on the application of satisfiability algorithms to scheduling problems", *AAAI'94* (1994).
33. J. Debenham, *Knowledge Engineering: Unifying Knowledge Base and Database Design* (Springer-Verlag, 1998).
34. S. Easterbrook, *Elicitation of Requirements from Multiple Perspectives*, PhD Thesis, Imperial College of Science Technology and Medicine, University of London (1991). Available from *http://research.ivv.nasa.gov/~steve/papers/index.html*
35. H. Eriksson, Y. Shahar, S. W. Tu, A. R. Puerta and M. A. Musen, "Task modeling with reusable problem-solving methods", *Artificial Intelligence* **79**, no. 2 (1995) 293–326.
36. D. W. Etherington and R. Reiter, "On inheritance hierarchies with exceptions", *AAAI'83* (1983) 104–108.

37. B. Feldman, P. Compton and G. Smythe, "Hypothesis testing: An appropriate task for knowledge-based systems", *4th AAAI-Sponsored Knowledge Acquisition for Knowledge-based Systems Workshop* (Banff, Canada, 1989).
38. D. Fensel and A. Schoenegge, "Hunting for assumptions as developing method for problem-solving methods", *Workshop on Problem-Solving Methods for Knowledge-based Systems, IJCAI'97* (August 23, 1997).
39. N E Fenton, *Software Metrics* (Chapman and Hall, London, 1991).
40. A. Finkelstein, D. Gabbay, A. Hunter, J. Kramer and B. Nuseibeh, "Inconsistency handling in multi-perspective specification", *IEEE Transactions on Software Engineering* **20**, no. 8 (1994) 569–578.
41. G. Fischer, A. C. Lemke, R. McCall and A. I. Morch, "Making argumentation serve design", eds. T. P. Moran and J. M. Carroll, *Design Rationale: Concepts, Techniques, and Use* (Lawerence Erlbaum Associates, 1996) 267–293.
42. C. L. Forgy, "RETE: A fast algorithm for the many pattern/many object pattern match problem", *Artificial Intelligence* **19** (1982) 17–37.
43. B. R. Gaines and P. Compton, "Induction of ripple down rules", *Proceedings, Australian AI'92* (World Scientific, 1992) 349–354.
44. E. Gamma, R. Helm, R. Johnson and J. Vlissides, *Design Patterns: Elements of Reusable Object-Oriented Software* (Addison-Wesley, 1995).
45. O. Patrice, Gautier and T. R. Gruber, Generating explanations of device behavior using compositional modeling and causal ordering, *AAAI'93* (1993) 264–270.
46. Y. Gil and E. Melz, "Explicit representations of problem-soving strategies to support knowledge acquisition", *Proceedings AAAI'96* (1996).
47. T. R. Gruber, "A translation approach to portable ontology specifications", *Knowledge Acquisition* **5**, no. 2 (1993) 199–220.
48. L. Hatton, "Does oo sync with how we think?" *IEEE Software* (May/June 1998) 46–54.
49. W. Humphrey, *A Discipline for Software Engineering* (McGraw Hill, 1995).
50. High Performance Software Inc. ithink 3.0.5 (1994).
51. Y. Ishida, "Using global properties for qualitative reasoning: A qualitative system theory", *Proceedings of IJCAI'89* (1989) 1174–1179.
52. Y. Iwasaki, "Qualitative physics", eds. P. R. Cohen, A. Barr and E. A. Feigenbaum, *The Handbook of Artificial Intelligence* **4** (Addison Wesley, 1989) 323–413.
53. Y. Kalgoglou, "Ontologies in software design", ed. S. K. Chang, *Handbook of Software and Knowledge Engineering, Vol. 1* (2001).
54. B. H. Kang and P. Compton, "A maintenance approach to case based reasoning", eds. M. Keane, J. P. Haton and M. Manago, *Advances in Case-Based Reasoning, Selected Papers from Second European Workshop, EWCBR'94, Lecture Notes in Artificial Intelligence 984* (Springer 1995) 226–239.
55. B. H. Kang, P. Compton and P. Preston, "Multiple classification ripple down rules: Evaluation and possibilities", *Proceedings of the 9th Banff Workshop on Knowledge Acquisition* (1995).
56. R. A. Kowalski, "The early years of logic programming", *Communications of the ACM* **31**, no. 1 (January 1988) 38–43.
57. J. E. Laird and A. Newell, "A universal weak method: Summary of results", *IJCAI'83* (1983) 771–773.
58. M. Lee, P. Compton and B. Jansen, "Modelling with context-dependant causality", *Proceedings of the Second Japan Knowledge Acquisition for Knowledge-Based Systems Workshop* (Kobe, Japan, 1992) 357–370.

59. M. Linster and M. Musen, "Use of KADS to create a conceptual model of the ONCOCIN task", *Knowledge Acquisition* **4**, no. 1 (1992) 55–88.
60. S. Marcus and J. McDermott, "SALT: A knowledge acquisition language for propose-and-revise systems", *Artificial Intelligence* **39**, no. 1 (1989) 1–37.
61. D. Marques, G. Dallemagne, G. Kliner, J. McDermott and D. Tung, "Easy programming: Empowering people to build their own applications", *IEEE Expert* (June 1992) 16–29.
62. T. Menzies, Knowledge maintenance: The state of the art. *The Knowledge Engineering Review* **14**, no. 1 (1999) 1–46. Available from *http://tim.menzies.com/pdf/97kmall.pdf*
63. T. Menzies, "Practical machine learning for software engineering and knowledge engineering", *Handbook of Software Engineering and Knowledge Engineering* (2001). Available from *http://tim.menzies.com/pdf/00ml.pdf*
64. T. Menzies and E. Sinsel, "Practical large scale what-if queries: Case studies with software risk assessment", *Proceedings ASE 2000* (2000). Available from *http://tim.menzies.com/pdf/00ase.pdf*
65. T. Menzies, E. Sinsel and T. Kurtz, "Learning to reduce risks with cocomo-ii", *Workshop on Intelligent Software Engineering, an ICSE 2000 Workshop, and NASA/WVU Software Research Lab* Fairmont, WV, Technical Report # NASA-IVV-99-027, 1999 (2000). Available from *http://tim.menzies.com/pdf/00wise.pdf*
66. T. Menzies and F. van Harmelen, "Editorial: Evaluating knowledge engineering techniques", *International Journal of Human-Computer Studies, Special Issue on Evaluation of Knowledge Engineering Techniques* **51**, no. 4 (October 1999) 717–727. Available from *http://tim.menzies.com/pdf/99ekeed.pdf*
67. T. Menzies, B. Cukic, H. Singh and J. Powell, "Testing nondeterminate systems", *ISSRE 2000* (2000). Available from *http://tim.menzies.com/pdf/00issre.pdf*
68. T. J. Menzies, *Principles for Generalised Testing of Knowledge Bases*, PhD Thesis, University of New South Wales (1995). Available from *http://tim.menzies.com/ pdf/95thesis.pdf*
69. T. J. Menzies, "Assessing responses to situated congition", *Proceedings of the 10th Knowledge Acquisition Workshop for Knowledge-Based Systems* (Banff, Canada, 1996). Available from *http://tim.menzies.com/pdf/96sitcog.pdf*
70. T. J. Menzies, "OO patterns: Lessons from expert systems", *Software Practice and Experience* **27**, no. 12 (December 1997) 1457–1478. Available from *http://tim.menzies.com/pdf/97patern.pdf*
71. T. J. Menzies, "Evaluation issues for problem solving methods", *Banff Knowledge Acquisition workshop, 1998* (1998). Available from *http://tim.menzies.com/pdf/97eval.pdf*
72. T. J. Menzies, "Evaluation issues for problem visual programming languages", *1998 Banff KA Workshop* (1998). Available from *http://tim.menzies.com/pdf/97evalvp.pdf*
73. T. J. Menzies, "Evaluation issues with critical success metrics", *Banff KA'1998 Workshop* (1998). Available from *http://tim.menzies.com/pdf/97langevl.pdf*
74. T. J. Menzies, "Towards situated knowledge acquisition", *International Journal of Human-Computer Studies* **49** (1998) 867–893. Available from *http://tim.menzies.com/pdf/98ijhcs.pdf*
75. T. J. Menzies, R. F. Cohen and S. Waugh, "Evaluating conceptual qualitative modeling languages", *Banff KAW'1998 Workshop* (1998). Available from *http://tim.menzies.com/pdf/97modlan.pdf*

76. T. J. Menzies, R. F. Cohen, S. Waugh and S. Goss, "Applications of abduction: Testing very long qualitative simulations", *IEEE Transactions of Data and Knowledge Engineering* (to appear) (2001). Available from *http://tim.menzies.com/pdf/97iedge.pdf*
77. T. J. Menzies and P. Compton, "Knowledge acquisition for performance systems; or: When can "tests" replace "tasks"?", *Proceedings of the 8th AAAI-Sponsored Banff Knowledge Acquisition for Knowledge-Based Systems Workshop* (Banff, Canada, 1994), *http://tim.menzies.com/pdf/banff94.pdf*
78. T. J. Menzies and P. Compton, "Applications of abduction: Hypothesis testing of neuroendocrinological qualitative compartmental models", *Artificial Intelligence in Medicine* **10** (1997) 145–175. Available from *http://tim.menzies.com/pdf/96aim.pdf*
79. T. J. Menzies and S. Goss, "Vague models and their implications for the kbs design cycle", *Proceedings PKAW'1996: Pacific Knowledge Acquisition Workshop and Monash University*, Department of Software Development Technical Report TR96-15 (1996). Available from *http://tim.menzies.com/pdf/96abmod.pdf*
80. T. J. Menzies and A. Mahidadia, "Ripple-down rationality: A framework for maintaining psms", *Workshop on Problem-Solving Methods for Knowledge-based Systems, IJCAI'97* (August 23, 1997). Available from *http://tim.menzies.com/pdf/97rdra.pdf*
81. M. Minsky, "A framework for representing knowledge", *The Psychology of Computer Vision* (1975).
82. T. P. Moran and J. M. Carroll, *Design Rationale: Concepts, Techniques, and Use* (Lawerence Erlbaum Associates, 1996).
83. E. Motta, "The knowledge modelling paradigm in knowledge engineering", ed. S. K. Chang, *Handbook of Software and Knowledge Engineering, Vol. 1* (2001).
84. M. Mulholland, P. Preston, B. Hibbert and P. Compton, "An expert system for ion chromatography developed using machine learning and knowledge in context", *Proceedings of the Sixth International Conference on Industrial and Engineering Applications of Artificial Intelligence and Expert Systems*, Edinburgh (1996).
85. NASA, CLIPS Reference Manual, Software Technology Branch, Lyndon B. Johnson Space Center (1991).
86. A. Newell, "The knowledge level", *Artificial Intelligence* **18** (1982) 87–127.
87. A. Newell, "Reflections on the knowledge level", *Artificial Intelligence* **59** (Feburary 1993) 31–38.
88. N. J. Nilsson, "Logic and artificial intelligence", *Artificial Intelligence* **47** (1991) 31–56.
89. B. Nuseibeh, "To be *and* not to be: On managing inconsistency in software development", *Proceedings of the 8th International Workshop on Software Specification and Design* (*IWSSD'8*) (IEEE CS Press, 1997) 164–169.
90. J. Pearl and R. E. Korf, "Search techniques", *Ann. Rev. Comput. Sci. 1987* **2** (1987) 451–467.
91. A. Pease, V. Chaudhri, F. Lehmann and A. Farquhar, "Practical knowledge representation and the darpa high performance knowledge bases project", *Proceedings of KR-2000* (2000). Available from *http://reliant.teknowledge.com/HPKB/Publications/KR-195.ps*
92. P. Preston, G. Edwards and P. Compton, "A 1600 rule expert system without knowledge engineers", ed. J. Leibowitz, *Second World Congress on Expert Systems* (1993).
93. D. Richards and P. Compton, "Combining formal concept analysis and ripple down rules to support the reuse of knowledge", *Proceedings of 1997 Conference on Software Engineering and Knowledge Engineering* (*SEKE'97*) Madrid (1997).

94. D. Richards and T. J. Menzies, "Extending knowledge engineering to requirements engineering from multiple perspectives", eds. T. J. Menzies, D. Richards and P. Compton, *Third Australian Knowledge Acquisition Workshop* (Perth, 1997). Available from *http://tim.menzies.com/pdf/97akawre.pdf*
95. D. Richards and T. J. Menzies, "Extending the Sisyphus III experiment from a knowledge engineering task to a requirements engineering task", *Banff Workshop on Knowledge Acquisition* (1998). Available from *http://tim.menzies.com/pdf/98kawre.pdf*
96. H. W. J. Rittel, "Second generation design methods", *Design Methods Group 5th Anniversary Report: DMG Occasional Paper, 1, 5–10.* (1972) Also in N. Cross (ed.), Developments in design methodology (Wiley & Sons, 1984) 317–327.
97. P. S. Rosenbloom, J. E. Laird and A. Newell, *The SOAR Papers* (The MIT Press, 1993).
98. D. A. Schon, *The Reflective Practioner* (Harper Collins/Basic Books, 1983).
99. A. Th. Schreiber and W. P. Birmingham, The sisyphus-vt initiative, *International Journal of Human-Computer Studies* **44**, no. 3–4 (March/April 1996).
100. A. TH. Schreiber, B. Wielinga, J. M. Akkermans, W. Van De Velde and R. de Hoog, "Commonkads: A comprehensive methodology for kbs development", *IEEE Expert* **9**, no. 6 (1994) 28–37.
101. B. Selman, H. Levesque and D. Mitchell, "A new method for solving hard satisfiability problems", *AAAI'92* (1992) 440–446.
102. N. Shadbolt and K. O'Hara, "Model-based expert systems and the explanations of expertise", eds. P. J. Feltovich, K. M. Ford and R. R. Hoffman, *Expertise in Context*, Chap. 13 (MIT Press, 1997) 315–337.
103. N. Shadbolt, K. O'Hara and L. Crow, "The experimental evaluation of knowledge acquisition techniques and methods: History, problems and new directions", *International Journal of Human-Computer Studies* (2000) (to appear).
104. H. Simon, *The Science of the Artificial* (MIT Press, 1969).
105. H. A. Simon, "On the definition of the causal relationship", *Journal Philosphy* **49** (1952) 517–528.
106. L. Steels, "Components of expertise", *AI Magazine* **11**, no. 2 (1990) 29–49.
107. L. Suchman, "Response to vera and simon's situated action: A symbolic interpretation", *Cognitive Science* **17** (1993) 71–75.
108. B. Swartout and Y. Gill, "Flexible knowledge acquisition through explicit representation of knowledge roles", *1996 AAAI Spring Symposium on Acquisition, Learning, and Demonstration: Automating Tasks for Users* (1996).
109. G. Tecuci, *Building Intelligent Agents: An Apprenticeship Multistrategy Learning Theory, Methodology, Tool and Case Studies* (Academic Press, 1998).
110. J. D. Ullman, *Principles of Database and Knowledge-base Systems* (Computer Science Press, 1988).
111. F. Van Harmelen and M. Aben, "Structure-preserving specification languages for knowledge-based systems", *International Journal of Human-Computer Studies* **44** (1996) 187–212.
112. F. Van Harmelen and A. T. Teije, "Validation and verification of conceptual models of diagnosis", *European Symposium on the Validation and Verification of Knowledge Based Systems*, Leuven, Belgium (1997).
113. G. Van Heust, A. Th. Schreiber and B. J. Wielinga, "Using explicit ontologies in kbs development", *International Journal of Human Computer Studies* **45** (1997) 183–292.

114. S. Waugh, T. J. Menzies and S. Goss, "Evaluating a qualitative reasoner", ed. Abdul Sattar, *Advanced Topics in Artificial Intelligence: 10th Australian Joint Conference on AI* (Springer-Verlag, 1997), *http://www.cse.unsw.edu.au/~timm/pub/docs*

115. G. I. Webb and J. Wells, "Experimental evaluation of integrating machine learning with knowledge acquisition through direct interaction with domain experts", *Proceedings PKAW '96: Pacific Knowledge Acquisition Workshop* (1996).

116. B. J. Wielinga, A. T. Schreiber and J. A. Breuker, "KADS: A modeling approach to knowledge engineering" *Knowledge Acquisition*, **4**, no. 1 (1992) 1–162.

117. B. C. Williams and J. DeKleer, "Qualitative reasoning about physical systems: A return to roots", *Artificial Intelligence* **51** (1991) 1–9.

118. T. Winograd, "Frame representations and the declarative/procedural controversy", *Readings in Knowledge Representation* (Morgan Kaufman, 1975) 185–210. Also available, eds. R. J. Brachmann and H. J. Levesque, *Readings in Knowledge Representation* (Morgan Kaufmann, Palo Alto, 1985).

119. G. Yost, "Implementing the Sisyphus-93 task using SOAR/TAQL", eds. B. R. Gaines and M. Musen, *Proceedings of the 8th AAAI-Sponsored Banff Knowledge Acquisition for Knowledge-Based Systems Workshop* **46**, no. 2 (1994) 21–46.

120. G. R. Yost and A. Newell, "A problem space approach to expert system specification", *IJCAI'89* (1989) 621–627.

NONMONOTONIC REASONING AND CONSISTENCY MANAGEMENT IN SOFTWARE ENGINEERING

KEN SATOH

National Institute of Informatics, 2-1-2 Hitotsubashi, Chiyoda-Ku, Tokyo, 101-8430, Japan
E-mail: ksatoh@db-ei.eng.hokudai.ac.jp

Consistency management is very important activity in software engineering since it relates with adaptation of change of environments or requirements. This consistency management is closely related with nonmonotonic reasoning systems in AI since nonmonotonic reasoning is a formalization of avoiding inconsistency.

In this chapter, we survey existing nonmonotonic reasoning systems (McCarthy's Circumscription and Reider's Default Logic) and discuss a usage of nonmonotonic reasoning systems for consistency management of software engineering.

Keywords: Nonmonotonic reasoning, consistency management, circumscription, default logic, exceptional handling, reconfiguration.

1. Introduction

In this chapter, we survey existing nonmonotonic reasoning systems and discuss a usage of nonmonotonic reasoning systems for consistency management of software engineering.

Lientz and Swanson [8] categorized maintenance activity as follows:

- changes in the software environment;
- new user requirements;
- fixing errors;
- preventing problems in the future;

and show that 75% of the activity is the first two types and 21% of the activity is the third type. This means that maintenance process mainly consists of adaptation of change of environments and requirements. If these changes are predictable, we can incorporate these changes in advance, but this kind of prediction is actually difficult as [2] mentioned.

> *If changes can be anticipated at design time, they can be built in by some form of parameterization. The fundamental problem, supported by 40 years of had experience, is that many changes actually required are those that the original designers cannot even conceive of*

From AI perspective, it is essentially difficult since the problem is related with the Qualification Problem [16] in AI. The Qualification problem is to give a set of conditions which properly defines a given concept or which gives a necessary and sufficient conditions for a successful action. However, since there are always unknown exceptions in a real world, it is essentially impossible to write up such conditions. In the above software maintenance problem, this means that we cannot foresee all changes and there will be unexpected changes. To solve the problem in AI, we introduce *nonmonotonic reasoning* so that if there are exceptions, we just minimize them and let ourselves be ready for normal situations. These researches closely relate with belief revision in AI since managing of inconsistency is a major concern of belief revision. Especially, belief revision researchers study "minimal belief revision" [7] which corresponds with minimal revised specification in the presence of inconsistency in software engineering. Actually, there is a close connection between belief revision and nonmonotonic reasoning [14] and therefore, in this chapter, we focus on nonmonotonic reasoning systems.

In software engineering, there are growing interests in consistency management of software [1, 3, 4]. A survey of these approaches can be found in [18]. This is because computer environments are rapidly changing and also software products are produced by many designers and programmers through the Internet so that inconsistency is often inevitable. Reference [3] handles the first systematic work on exception handling of integrity constraints in database specification and he proposes an isolation of such an exception from integrity constraints. Reference [1] proposes a recovery of isolation when the exception is resolved for temporary violation of integrity constraints. Reference [4] uses non-collapsible "quasi-classical logic" even in the existence of inconsistency and formalizes consistency management between multiple specifications defined by several users.

The original motivation of nonmonotonic reasoning systems is to formalize commonsense reasoning under incomplete information. If there is no decisive information, human uses commonsense to make a decision. We cannot formalize it in a classical logic since classical logic is monotonic in the sense that the derived results increase as more information is added, while commonsense reasoning is *nonmonotonic.* It sometimes produces false conclusions, and when a result is found to be false, then the result is removed. Therefore, we must formalize it in a different way.

Along this idea, several formalisms of nonmonotonic reasoning are provided [15, 17, 19]. We divide these systems into two categories; one is consistency-based nonmonotonic reasoning system and the other is minimal-model-based nonmonotonic reasoning system.

Consistency-based systems are based on the idea that if we can assume commonsense consistently, we assume the commonsense. These systems include Default Logic [19] and Autoepistemic Logic [17].

Minimal-model-based systems are based on the idea that there is an order over possible worlds and we assume that we are in the most plausible worlds which are compatible with the current knowledge. These systems include circumscription [15].

These systems are applicable to manage consistency in software specification and there are actually several researches directly applying nonmonotonic reasoning to software engineering [20–24]. References [21] and [24] use default rules as a specification and if contradiction occurs in specification, some of the default rules are retracted to maintain consistency. Recently, [20, 23, 24] propose a method of using *abduction* to maintain consistency.

In the subsequent sections, we discuss these two systems and show some applications in consistency management in software engineering.

2. Consistency-based Nonmonotonic Reasoning

Consistency-based nonmonotonic reasoning comes from an idea that if we can assume some knowledge without any inconsistency, then we assume that knowledge. For example, if we have a train in a time-table, and there is no information that the train is delayed, then we assume that the train is on time. If there is information that the train is delayed, then it lead to contradiction if we assume that the train is on time and so, we cannot assume such commonsense. There are two major logics based on this idea. One is called Default Logic [19] and the other is Autoepistemic Logic [17]. In Default Logic, we can define inference rules which use consistency of assumptions. On the other hand, in Autoepistemic Logic, we introduce a modal belief operator which can be used to express consistency. In the following, we focus on Default Logic.

Default Logic [19] introduces new inference rules called *default* into the first-order logic. For example, a piece of commonsense "A train in a time-table normally departs on time" can be defined in the following defaults:

$$\frac{Timetable(train, time) : Depart(train, time)}{Depart(train, time)}$$

where $Timetable(train, time)$ means that the timetable says that *train* departs at *time* and $Depart(train, time)$ means that *train* actually departs at *time*. The meaning of this default is that if $Timetable(train, time)$ is derived and it is consistent to assume $Depart(train, time)$ then $Depart(train, time)$ is derived. By this default, if there is no information that the train is delayed, then we can derive $Depart(train, time)$. On the other hand, if we have information that the train is delayed, that is, $\neg Depart(train, time)$ is derived, then we no longer use the above default.

The precise definition of default is the following [19].

Definition 2.1. Let $\mathbf{x}$ be a tuple of free variables and $\alpha(\mathbf{x}), \beta_1(\mathbf{x}), \ldots, \beta_m(\mathbf{x}), w(\mathbf{x})$ be a first-order formula which contains $\mathbf{x}$ as free variables. Then, a *default* is an inference rule of the form:

$$\frac{\alpha(\mathbf{x}) : \beta_1(\mathbf{x}), \ldots, \beta_m(\mathbf{x})}{w(\mathbf{x})}.$$

A default without free variables is called *closed default.*

We call $\alpha(\mathbf{x})$ *prerequisite*, $\beta_1(\mathbf{x}), \ldots, \beta_m(\mathbf{x})$ *justifications* and $w(\mathbf{x})$ *consequence* respectively.

Definition 2.2. Let D be a set of defaults and W be a set of axioms. A *default theory* is a pair (D, W). If D is a set of closed defaults then (D, W) is called *closed default theory*.

The definition of extension E from a closed default theory is defined as follows.[a]

Let D be a set of closed defaults. We define $CON(D)$ as a set of consequences of each default in D. And let E' and E be a set of formulas. We define $UD(D, E', E)$ as the following set of usable defaults in D with respect to E' and E:

$$\left\{ \frac{\alpha : \beta_1, \ldots, \beta_m}{w} \in D | \alpha \in E' \text{ and for every } \beta_i, \neg\beta_i \notin E \right\}.$$

Definition 2.3. An extension of (D, W) is E if E is equivalent to the smallest set of formulas E' such that $E' = Th(CON(UD(D, E', E)) \cup W)$ where $Th(X)$ is a set of tautological consequences of X.

Note that this definition is a fixed-point definition and so, we must solve the equation to know an extension. So, we must first give E and then check that it satisfies the above condition.

However, we can give a method of producing an extension based on a semantics of default logic [6] as follows.

A non-deterministic procedure of computing extensions

Step 0: $E_0 = Th(W)$, $i := 0$.
Step 1: **select** $\delta_i \in UD(D, E_i, E_i)$ such that the consequence of δ_i is not in E_i. If there is no such δ_i, **output** E_i else **go to** Step 2.
Step 2: $E_{i+1} = Th(E_i \cup \{w_i\})$ where w_i is the consequence of the default δ_i. If there is some $\delta_k (k = 0, \ldots, i)$ such that $\delta_k \notin UD(D, E_{i+1}, E_{i+1})$ then **fail** else $i := i + 1$ and **go to** Step 1.

If we can check all selections of defaults, then we can obtain all extensions of (D, W) from the above method. However, this method is not computable in general for the first-order default theory since it needs consistency check which is not computable in general for the first-order logic.

Consider the following default theory (D, W_1).

$$D = \left\{ \frac{Timetable(train, time) : Depart(train, time)}{Depart(train, time)} \right\}$$

$$W_1 = \{Timetable(T, 12:40)\}.$$

[a]If a default contains free variables, then it is regarded as a set of closed defaults such that free variables are replaced by every ground term in the considered language.

$Timetable(T, 12:40)$ expresses that the timetable says that the train T departs at 12:40. Then, we use the above procedure to obtain an extension of (D, W_1).

(0) $E_0 = Th(W_1)$.
(1) Since $Timetable(T, 12:40) \in E_0$ and $\neg Depart(T, 12:40) \notin E_0$,

$$\delta_0 = \frac{Timetable(T, 12:40) : Depart(T, 12:40)}{Depart(T, 12:40)}$$

is in $UD(D, E_0, E_0)$ and

$$E_1 = Th(E_0 \cup \{Depart(T, 12:40)\})\,.$$

(2) Since there is no default δ in $UD(D, E_1, E_1)$ other than δ_0, E_1 becomes a extension of (D, W_1).

Therefore, we can conclude that the train T departs on 12:40. However, this conclusion is not derived if contradictory information is added.

For example, if we add $\neg Depart(T, 12:40)$ to W_1 and get $W_2 = W_1 \cup \{\neg Depart(T, 12:40)\}$, then, the default used in the above can no longer be used.

(0) $E_0 = Th(W_2)$.
(1) Since there is no default δ for $UD(D, E_0, E_0)$, E_0 becomes an extension of (D, W_2).

Therefore, the previous conclusion is retracted.

Besides nonmonotonicity, Default Logic has the following distinct characteristics from monotonic logics.

(1) There might be multiple extensions. For example, consider the following (D, W) where $D = \{\frac{:\neg P}{Q}, \frac{:\neg Q}{P}\}$ and $W = \{\}$. Then, there are two extensions, $Th(\{Q\})$ and $Th(\{P\})$.
(2) There might be no extensions. For example, consider the following (D, W) where $D = \{\frac{:\neg P}{P}\}$ and $W = \{\}$.

There is a class of default theories which always have an extension. This class is called *normal default theory* which consists of defaults (called *normal defaults*) of the form:

$$\frac{\alpha(\mathbf{x}) : w(\mathbf{x})}{w(\mathbf{x})}\,.$$

3. Minimal-model-based Nonmonotonic Reasoning

Minimal-model-based nonmonotonic reasoning comes from an idea that we assume the most plausible worlds among possible worlds with respect to an plausible order. For example, if we have a train in a timetable, then we have two possible worlds in one of which the train departs on time and in the other of which the train does not depart on time. We introduce the order that the former is more plausible than the latter and assume that we are in the former world. If we know that the train is delayed, then the former world is no longer possible and so, we no longer assume that we are in the former world.

There is a major formalism of nonmonotonic reasoning based on this idea called *circumscription* [15]. Circumscription restricts objects which have a property P to only objects which are currently known to have the property P and assumes other objects do not have the property P.

Circumscription adds to original axiom set a second-order formula which expresses that there is no other object satisfying P other than those objects which are already known to satisfy P.

Definition 3.4. Let $A(P)$ be an axiom set which includes P. Then, circumscription w.r.t P is defined as follows.

$$Circum(A; P) \stackrel{\text{def}}{=} A(P) \wedge \neg\exists p(A(p) \wedge p < P)$$

where $A(p)$ is a formula obtained by replacing every occurrence of P in $A(P)$ by a predicate variable P and $p < P$ is an abbreviation of the following formula:

$$\forall x(p(x) \supset P(x)) \wedge \neg\forall x(P(x) \supset p(x)) .$$

An intuitive meaning of the definition is the following. We regard $A(P)$ as constraint about P. p also satisfies the same constraint if $A(p)$ is true. $p < P$ expresses that the extension of p is smaller than that of P. Therefore, $A(p) \wedge p < P$ means that p satisfies the constraint $A(p)$ and has smaller extension than P. Therefore, the whole definition:

$$A(P) \wedge \neg\exists p(A(p) \wedge p < P)$$

means that there is no extension of p which has smaller extension than P which satisfies the same constraint as that of P. In other words, P is the minimal extension which satisfies $A(P)$. We say that P *is minimized by circumscription.*

In circumscription, parametric predicates have an important role to perform commonsense reasoning. They can be varied to any extension in order to make minimized predicates as small as possible.

Definition 3.5. Let $A(P, Z)$ be an axiom set which includes P and Z. Then, *circumscription* w.r.t P with a parameter Z is defined as follows.

$$Circum(A; P; Z) \stackrel{\text{def}}{=} A(P, Z) \wedge \neg\exists p\exists z(A(p, z) \wedge p < P) .$$

An intuitive meaning of this formula is that there is no p and z which satisfies $A(p, z)$ and p has a smaller extension that P. In other words, even if we vary z to any predicate to make p as small as possible, we cannot make p smaller than P.

We can also extend the above definition so that we can minimize a tuple of predicates with a tuple of parameters. In that case, $p < P$ becomes:

$$\bigwedge_{i=1}^{n} \forall x(p(x) \supset P(x)) \wedge \neg \bigwedge_{i=1}^{n} \forall x(P(x) \supset p(x))$$

where $P = \langle P_1, \ldots, P_n \rangle$. We call this version of circumscription *parallel circumscription.*

If we use parallel circumscription to formalize the commonsense "A train in a time-table normally departs on time" as follows. We firstly introduce *abnormal predicate Ab* to express abnormal situations where the commonsense cannot be applicable and represent the commonsense as follows.

$$\forall train \forall time((Timetable(train, time) \land \neg Ab(train, time)) \supset Depart(train, time))\,.$$

Then, we minimize *Ab* to minimize abnormal situations with parameters *Timetable* and *Depart*. The usage of circumscription is to maximize situations by minimizing abnormal situations.

Suppose we know that timetable says that the train T departs at 12:40. Then, $A(Ab, Timetable, Depart)$ becomes a conjunction of $Timetable(T, 12:40)$ and the above formula about the commonsense of trains. Therefore, the circumscription of minimizing *Ab* becomes the following formula:

$$A(Ab, Timetable, Depart) \land \neg\exists ab \exists t \exists d(A(ab, t, d) \land ab < Ab)\,.$$

This formula is equivalent to the following formula:

$$\begin{aligned}
&A(Ab, Timetable, Depart) \land \\
&\forall ab \forall t \forall d((A(ab, t, d) \land \forall tr \forall ti(ab(tr, ti) \supset Ab(tr, ti))) \supset \\
&\quad \forall tr \forall ti(Ab(tr, ti) \equiv ab(tr, ti)))\,.
\end{aligned}$$

This formula means that if we find a tuple of predicate (ab, t, d) which satisfies $A(ab, t, d)$ and $\forall tr \forall ti(ab(tr, ti) \supset Ab(tr, ti))$ under the constraint $A(Ab, Timetable,$ $Depart)$, then *ab* is actually equivalent to *Ab*. Let us consider the following tuple of predicates:

(1) $ab = \lambda tr \lambda ti \mathbf{F}$
(2) $t = \lambda tr \lambda ti((tr = T) \land (ti = 12:40))$
(3) $d = \lambda tr \lambda ti((tr = T) \land (ti = 12:40))$

Then, $A(ab, t, d)$ becomes:

$$\begin{aligned}
&(T = T) \land (12:40 = 12:40) \land \\
&\forall tr \forall ti(((tr = T) \land (ti = 12:40) \land \neg\mathbf{F}) \supset ((tr = T) \land (ti = 12:40)))
\end{aligned}$$

which is tautology.

Moreover, $\forall tr \forall ti(ab(tr, ti) \supset Ab(tr, ti))$ becomes $\forall tr \forall ti(\mathbf{F} \supset Ab(tr, ti))$. Therefore, it also becomes tautology.

Thus, the definition of *ab*, that is, $\lambda tr \lambda ti \mathbf{F}$ is equivalent to *Ab*. This means that there is no abnormal situation. Then $A(Ab, Timetable, Departure)$ becomes:

$$\begin{aligned}
&Timetable(T, 12:40) \land \forall train \forall time(Timetable(train, time) \\
&\quad \supset Depart(train, time))\,.
\end{aligned}$$

And so, we can conclude $Depart(T, 12:40)$, that is, the train T departs at 12:40 on time.

Suppose that we happen to know that $\neg Depart(T, 12:40)$.
Then $A(Ab, Timetable, Departure)$ becomes:

$$Timetable(T, 12:40) \wedge \neg Depart(T, 12:40) \wedge$$
$$\forall train \forall time((Timetable(train, time) \wedge Ab(train, time)) \supset$$
$$Depart(train, time))\,.$$

Let us consider the following tuple of predicates:

(1) $ab = \lambda tr \lambda ti((tr = T) \wedge (ti = 12:40))$
(2) $t = \lambda tr \lambda ti((tr = T) \wedge (ti = 12:40))$
(3) $d = \lambda tr \lambda ti \mathbf{F}$

Then, $A(ab, t, d)$ becomes the following:

$$(T = T) \wedge (12:40 = 12:40) \wedge \neg \mathbf{F} \wedge$$
$$\forall tr \forall ti(((tr = T) \wedge (ti = 12:40) \wedge \neg((tr = T) \wedge (ti = 12:40))) \supset$$
$$((tr = T) \wedge (ti = 12:40)))$$

which is tautology.

Moreover, $\forall tr \forall ti(ab(tr, ti) \supset Ab(tr, ti))$ becomes:

$$\forall tr \forall ti(((tr = T) \wedge (ti = 12:40)) \supset Ab(tr, ti))$$

which is equivalent to $Ab(T, 12:40)$ which is true under
$A(Ab, Timetable,$
$Departure)$.

Thus, the definition of ab, that is, $\lambda tr \lambda ti((tr = T) \wedge (ti = 12:40))$ is equivalent to Ab. This means that there is an abnormal situation where the train T does not depart at 12:40. Then $A(Ab, Timetable, Departure)$ becomes:

$$Timetable(T, 12:40) \wedge \neg Depart(T, 12:40) \wedge$$
$$\forall train \forall time($$
$$(Timetable(train, time) \wedge \neg((train = T) \wedge (time = 12:40))) \supset$$
$$Depart(train, time))\,.$$

So, in this case we can no longer conclude $Depart(T, 12:40)$.

In circumscription, we have a model theory based on minimal models. Let us consider a circumscription of minimizing P with a parameter Z. We introduce an order $\leq^{P;Z}$ over interpretations I_1 and I_2 as follows.

$I_1 \leq^{P;Z} I_2$ if and only if

(1) I_1 and I_2 have the same domain D.
(2) I_1 and I_2 has the same interpretation except for P and Z.
(3) $(P)^{I_1} \subseteq (P)^{I_2}$ where $(P)^I$ is an interpretation of P in I.

The third condition expresses that I_1 does not have more elements which satisfy P than I_2. We also define $I_1 <^{P;Z} I_2$ as $I_1 \leq^{P;Z} I_2$ and $I_2 \not\leq^{P;Z} I_1$.

Definition 3.6. An interpretation I is a minimal model for A with respect to a minimized predicate P and a parameter Z if and only if I is a model of A such that there is no model of A, I' such that $I' <^{P;Z} I$.

Note that the order is based on set inclusion of interpretation of minimized predicates.

The following is relationship between formula of circumscription and minimal model.

Theorem 3.1. (Lifschitz [10])
An interpretation I is a model of $Circum(A; P; Z)$ if and only if M is minimal in the class of models of A with respect to $\leq^{P;Z}$.

This means that if we can derive something from $Circum(A; P; Z)$, then it is true in all minimal models of A. However, the converse is not always true since it is not computable in general to infer every formula which is true in all minimal models for an axiom set. Also, if there are no minimal models for some A, then circumscription $Circum(A; P; Z)$ leads to contradiction. Lifschitz [11] investigates some conditions of axiom set by which we can guarantee existence of minimal models.

McCarthy introduces a new form of circumscription called *prioritized circumscription* [16] to formalize prioritization between commonsense rules. Prioritized circumscription gives a priority of minimizing predicates. If there are conflicts between predicates in minimization, we firstly minimize predicates with higher priority and then minimize other weaker predicates.

Definition 3.7. Let $A(P_1, P_2, \ldots, P_k, Z)$ be an axiom set which includes $P_1, P_2, \ldots, P_k$ and Z. Then, *prioritized circumscription* w.r.t $P_1 > P_2 > \cdots > P_k$ with a parameter Z is defined as follows.

$$Circum(A; P_1 > P_2 > \ldots P_k; Z) \stackrel{\text{def}}{=}$$

$$A(P_1, P_2, \ldots, P_k, , Z) \wedge$$

$$\neg \exists p_1 \exists p_2 \ldots \exists p_k \exists z (A(p_1, p_2, \ldots, p_k, z) \wedge \langle p_1, \ldots, p_k \rangle \prec \langle P_1, \ldots, P_k \rangle)$$

where $\langle p_1, \ldots, p_k \rangle \prec \langle P_1, \ldots, P_k \rangle$ is an abbreviation of the following formula:

$$\bigwedge_{i=1}^{k} \left(\left(\bigwedge_{j=1}^{i-1} \forall x (p_j(x) \equiv P_j(x)) \right) \supset (\forall x (p_i(x) \supset P_i(x))) \right) \wedge$$

$$\neg \bigwedge_{i=1}^{k} \left(\left(\bigwedge_{j=1}^{i-1} \forall x (P_j(x) \equiv p_j(x)) \right) \supset (\forall x (P_i(x) \supset p_i(x))) \right).$$

Let us apply prioritized circumscription to the above inheritance system. We minimize Ab_{nfb} firstly and then minimize Ab_{fa}.

$$A(\text{ANIMAL}, \text{BIRD}, \text{FLY}, Ab_{nfb}, Ab_{fa}) \wedge$$
$$\neg\exists a \exists b \exists f \exists ab_{nfb} \exists ab_{fa}(A(a, b, f, ab_{nfb}, ab_{fa}) \wedge (\langle ab_{nfb}, ab_{fa}\rangle \prec \langle Ab_{nfb}, Ab_{fa}\rangle))$$

where $\langle ab_{nfb}, ab_{fa}\rangle \prec \langle Ab_{nfb}, Ab_{fa}\rangle$ is an abbreviation of the following formula:

$$(ab_{nfb} \supset Ab_{nfb}) \wedge ((ab_{nfb} \equiv Ab_{nfb}) \supset (ab_{fa} \supset Ab_{fa})) \wedge$$
$$\neg((Ab_{nfb} \supset ab_{nfb}) \wedge ((Ab_{nfb} \equiv ab_{nfb}) \supset (Ab_{fa} \supset ab_{fa}))).$$

This priority means that the rule for flying birds is stronger than the rule for non-flying animals. We firstly minimize Ab_{nfb}, that is, try to make Ab_{nfb} to be false. Then, since from A, FLY must be true, Ab_{fa} is true. This results fit our intention.

4. Applications of Nonmonotonic Reasoning to Consistency Management in Software Engineering

In this section, we discuss applications of nonmonotonic reasoning to consistency management.

4.1. *Exceptional handling*

Consider the following example of logical representation of a database and constraints which is inspired by the example in [3, p. 590].

Example 4.1. Integrity Constraints:
IC_1 : if f is a father, then his age should be more than 14.

$$(\forall e, f/Person)(\forall a/Years)$$
$$(Father(f, e) \wedge Age(f, a) \supset (a > 14))\wedge$$

IC_2 : if f is a father, then his age should be greater than his child's age.

$$(\forall e, f/Person)(\forall a, a_1, a_2/Years)$$
$$(Father(f, e) \wedge Age(f, a_1) \wedge Age(e, a_2) \supset (a_1 > a_2)).$$

Database Fact:
CharlieSr is a father of Charlie.

$$Father(CharlieSr, Charlie).$$

For simplicity, we only consider $F(S,C)$ for *Father* predicate, and only consider $A(S,14)$ and $A(C,16)$ for *Age* predicate.[b] Then, a database state which is consistent with IC_1 and IC_2 and the fact "$F(S,C)$" is either of the following:

$$S_1 = \{F(S,C), \neg A(S,14), \neg A(C,16)\}$$
$$S_2 = \{F(S,C), \neg A(S,14), A(C,16)\}.$$

Consider an addition of the following fact meaning that S is 14 years old:

$$A(S,14).$$

Then, we give up having the first integrity constraint to incorporate with the above addition since facts reflect real world.

Then, the database state which is consistent with the above fact $A(S,14)$ and the previous fact $F(S,C)$ is either of the following:

$$S_3 = \{F(S,C), A(S,14), \neg A(C,16)\}$$
$$S_4 = \{F(S,C),, A(S,14), A(C,16)\}.$$

Then, violation of integrity constraints in a new database are as follows:

New database states	violated ICs
S_3	IC_1
S_4	IC_1, IC_2

To make use of integrity constraints as much as possible even in the presence of inconsistency, Borgida proposes a change of one condition of the violated integrity constraint [3]. His idea is to change a part of applicability of the violated integrity constraint in order to restore consistency. This means that instead of considering the change of extension of all the predicates, we have to consider the change of applicability of violated integrity constraints.

Therefore, according to Brogida's idea, we should change the database state as S_3.

This idea can be related with the definition of Formula Circumscription [16] of minimizing negation of deletable formulas [22]. Formula Circumscription can be regarded as a formalization of above change where the new added knowledge corresponds with axioms in Formula Circumscription and the negation of deletable formulas correspond with minimized formulas in Formula Circumscription.

[b]We write "F" for "Father", "A" for "Age" predicates and "S" for "CharlieSr" and "C" for "Charlie".

Then, we can get the following as the syntactic definition of the new model consistent with the new information.

$$
\begin{aligned}
&New(\Psi, \Phi) = \\
&\quad K(\Psi) \wedge \alpha(\Psi) \wedge \\
&\quad\quad \neg\exists\Psi'(K(\Psi') \wedge \alpha(\Psi') \wedge \\
&\quad\quad\quad \bigwedge_{i=1}^{m} \forall \mathbf{x}((\phi_i(\Psi, \mathbf{x}) \supset \phi_i(\Psi', \mathbf{x})) \wedge \\
&\quad\quad\quad \neg \bigwedge_{i=1}^{m} \forall \mathbf{x}(\phi_i(\Psi', \mathbf{x}) \supset \phi_i(\Psi, \mathbf{x}))))
\end{aligned}
$$

where

(1) Ψ is a tuple of predicates $\langle p_1, \ldots, p_n \rangle$ used in the axioms.
(2) Φ is a tuple of formulas, $\langle \phi_1(\Psi, \mathbf{x}), \ldots, \phi_m(\Psi, \mathbf{x}) \rangle$ where $\mathbf{x}$ is a tuple of free variables in $\phi_1, \ldots, \phi_m$.
(3) $New(\Psi, \Phi)$ is a formula which corresponds with all the new revised models.
(4) $K(\Psi), \alpha(\Psi)$ are consistent first-order formulas which contain a tuple of predicates Ψ.

Example 4.2. Consider Example 4.1. In this example, $\Psi = \langle A, F \rangle$ $\Phi = \langle IC_1, IC_2 \rangle$.

Let UNA be unique name axioms such as $S \neq C$ and DCA be domain closure axioms which express that the domain only consists of S and C and 14 and 16. Then, $K(\Psi) = F(S, C) \wedge \wedge UNA \wedge DCA$ and $\alpha(\Psi) = A(S, 14)$. Then, $New(\Psi, \Phi)$ becomes[c]:

$$
\begin{aligned}
&New(\Psi, \Phi) = \\
&\quad F(S, C) \wedge A(S, 14) \wedge UNA \wedge DCA \wedge \\
&\quad \neg\exists f \exists a(f(S, C) \wedge a(S, 14) \wedge \\
&\quad\quad ((F(S, C) \wedge A(S, 14) \supset \mathbf{F}) \supset \\
&\quad\quad\quad (f(S, C) \wedge a(S, 14) \supset \mathbf{F})) \wedge \\
&\quad\quad ((F(S, C) \wedge A(S, 14) \wedge A(C, 16) \supset \mathbf{F}) \supset \\
&\quad\quad\quad (f(S, C) \wedge a(S, 14) \wedge a(C, 16) \supset \mathbf{F})) \wedge \\
&\quad\quad \neg(((f(S, C) \wedge a(S, 14) \supset \mathbf{F}) \supset \\
&\quad\quad\quad (F(S, C) \wedge A(S, 14) \supset \mathbf{F})) \wedge \\
&\quad\quad ((f(S, C) \wedge a(S, 14) \wedge a(C, 16) \supset \mathbf{F}) \supset \\
&\quad\quad\quad (F(S, C) \wedge A(S, 14) \wedge A(C, 16) \supset \mathbf{F})))) \,.
\end{aligned}
$$

[c]We reduce IC_1 and IC_2 to formulas without $<$ condition.

Since $F(S,C)$ must be true (so be $f(S,C)$) and $A(S,14)$ must be true (so be $a(S,14)$), this is equivalent to:

$$\begin{aligned} F(S,C) \wedge A(S,14) \wedge UNA \wedge DCA \wedge \\ \neg\exists f \exists a (f(S,C) \wedge a(S,14) \wedge \\ (a(C,16) \supset A(C,16)) \wedge \\ \neg(A(C,16) \supset a(C,16)))\,. \end{aligned}$$

This implies $F(S,C) \wedge A(S,14) \wedge \neg A(C,16)$ which is equivalent to the result of Example 4.1.

This can be also formalized by Default Logic. Instead of minimizing the exception of integrity constraints, we use integrity constraints as default rules.

4.2. *Module reconfiguration*

Suppose that the following are defined for the configuration of the software module.

- Specification of necessary function. The function which should be fulfilled is represented as integrity constraint.
- Coherence between modules. When a specific combination of modules interferes to the coherence of the system, the prohibition of the combination of these modules is specified as integrity constraint.
- Relation between functions and modules. The function that a certain module fulfills is represented as a clause in the persistent part of a logical specification.
- Current module configuration. The module is represented as a unit clause in a temporary part of the specification.
- Module group which can be added. The module which can be added is represented as a unit clause which can be added.

There are various sources of contradiction in the above setting. Adding a module may cause a contradiction if the combination of the added module and the existing module violates integrity constraints. Deleting a module may cause a contradiction if required function is not satisfied. Adding a requirement may cause a contradiction if it is not satisfied already by the current configuration. We have to maintain consistency by changing the configuration.

This change can be formalized by Default Logic. The relations between modules and functions are represented as logical implications, and we introduce new predicates which express deletion (called deletion predicates) or addition (called addition predicates) of modules and the current configuration are regarded as formulas with the negation of deletion predicates and addible modules are represented as formulas with addition predicates. And we add defaults which express predicates for the deletions of the modules are false by default.

Consider the following example. There are r_1, r_2, and r_3 as functions, and r_1 is assumed to be a function which should be fulfilled. It is assumed that there are m_1, m_2, and m_3 as modules, and m_1 is being currently installed, and that the combination of m_1 and m_2 causes the system error. Moreover, the relations between the module and the function shown below are provided.
Integrity Constraints:

$$\frac{:\neg r_1}{\mathbf{F}}$$

$$\frac{m_1 \wedge m_2 :}{\mathbf{F}}$$

Relations between Modules and Functions:

$$m_1 \supset r_1 .$$

$$m_1 \supset r_2 .$$

$$m_2 \supset r_1 .$$

$$m_2 \supset r_3 .$$

$$m_3 \supset r_2 .$$

$$m_3 \supset r_3 .$$

The Current Module Configuration:

$$\neg del_{\phi_1} \supset m_1$$

Addible Modules:

$$add_{\phi_2} \supset m_2$$

$$add_{\phi_3} \supset m_3$$

We also add defaults concerning with $del_{\phi_1}, add_{\phi_2}, add_{\phi_3}$ as follows:

$$\frac{:\neg del_{\phi_1}}{\neg del_{\phi_1}} \quad \frac{:\neg add_{\phi_2}}{\neg add_{\phi_2}} \quad \frac{: add_{\phi_2}}{add_{\phi_2}} \quad \frac{:\neg add_{\phi_3}}{\neg add_{\phi_3}} \quad \frac{: add_{\phi_3}}{add_{\phi_3}} .$$

Note that for the default rules for addition express that either add_{ϕ_i} or $\neg add_{\phi_i}$ will be assumed.

Moreover, we add closed world assumptions about modules and requirements.

$$\frac{:\neg r_i}{\neg r_i} \quad \frac{:\neg m_i}{\neg m_i} .$$

Suppose that we need a specification to achieve r_3 as well as r_1. Then, $\frac{:\neg r_3}{\mathbf{F}}$ is added to the above default theory.

If we choose extensions with minimal set of atoms with deletion and addition predicates, this gives minimal revision of configuration where only necessary deletion and addition of corresponding modules are achieved.

In this case, there are two such extensions one of which includes add_{ϕ_3} and the other of which includes del_{ϕ_1} and add_{ϕ_2}. These extensions represent two configurations; a configuration which adds m_3 and a configuration which adds m_2 and deletes m_1.

5. Conclusion

In this chapter, we survey nonmonotonic reasoning formalisms and show applications of nonmonotonic reasoning to managing consistency of software specification. The research is just starting and there remain much to be done. Some of these are the following.

- We need to decrease computational complexity either by introducing syntactical restriction of software specification or introducing some heuristics.
- We sometimes need to introduce priority over changes of specifications. When contradiction occurs and there are many ways to restore consistency, we had better have some criterion to choose the most preferable revised specification. We need to formalize this. A solution is proposed by [21] using epistemic entrenchment.
- We need to evaluate nonmonotonic reasoning formalisms by applying these formalisms to large and practical software engineering problems.

References

1. R. Balzer, "Tolerating inconsistency," *Proceedings of ICSE'13* (1991) 158–165.
2. K. H. Bennett and V. T. Rajlich, "Sotware maintenance and evolution: A road map," *The Future of Software Engineering*, ICSE-22 (2000) 75–78.
3. A. Borgida, "Language features for flexible handling of exceptions in information systems," *ACM Transactions on Database Systems* **10** (1985) 565–603.
4. A. C. W. Finkelstein, D. Gabbay, A. Hunter, J. Kramer and B. Nuseibeh, "Inconsistency handling in multiperspective specifications," *IEEE Transactions on Software Engineering* **20** (1994) 569–578.
5. D. W. Etherington, "Formalizing nonmonotonic reasoning systems," *Artificial Intelligence* **31** (1987) 495–498.
6. D. W. Etherington, "A semantics for default logic," *Proceedings of IJCAI'87* (1987) 495–498.
7. H. Katsuno and A. O. Mendelzon, "Propositional knowledge base revision and minimal change," *Artificial Intelligence* **52** (1991) 263–294.
8. B. P. Lientz and E. B. Swanson, *Software Maintenance Management* (Addison Wesley, 1980).
9. V. Lifschitz, "Some results on circumscription," *Proceedings of Nonmonotonic Reasoning Workshop* (1984) 151–164.
10. V. Lifschitz, "Computing circumscription," *Proceedings of IJCAI'85* (1985) 121–127.
11. V. Lifschitz, "On the satisfiability of circumscription," *Artificial Intelligence* **28** (1986) 17–27.
12. V. Lifschitz, "Pointwise circumscription: Preliminary report," *Proceedings of AAAI'86* (1986) 406–410.

13. V. Lifschitz, "On the declarative semantics of logic programs with negation," ed. J. Minker, *Foundations of Deductive Database and Logic Programming* (Morgan Kaufmann, 1987) 177–192.
14. D. Makinson and P. Gärdenfors, "Relations between the logic of theory change and nonmonotonic logic," eds. A. Fuhrmann and M. Morreau, *The Logic of Theory Change, Lecture Notes in Artificial Intelligence 465* (1991) 185–205.
15. J. McCarthy, "Circumscription — A form of non-monotonic reasoning," *Artificial Intelligence* **13** (1980) 27–29.
16. J. McCarthy, "Applications of circumscription to formalizing common-sense knowledge," *Artificial Intelligence* **28** (1986) 89–116.
17. R. C. Moore, "Semantical considerations on nonmonotonic logic," *Artificial Intelligence* **25** (1985) 75–94.
18. B. Nuseibeh, "To be and not to be: On managing inconsistency in software development," *Proceedings of the 8th IEEE International Workshop on Software Specification and Design (IWSSD'8)* (1996) 164–169.
19. R. Reiter, "A logic for default reasoning," *Artificial Intelligence* **13** (1980) 81–132.
20. A. Russo, R. Miller, B. Nuseibeh and J. Kramer, "An abductive approach for handling inconsistencies in SCR specifications," *Proceedings of the ICSE-2000 Workshop on Intelligent Software Engineering*, Limerick, Ireland (2000) 80–89.
21. M. Ryan, "Default in specification" *IEEE Proceedings of International Symposium on Requirements Engineering* (1993).
22. K. Satoh, "Computing minimal revised logic program by abduction," *Proceedings of the International Workshop on the Principles of Software Evolution, IWPSE'98*, Kyoto, Japan (1998) 177–182.
23. K. Satoh, "Consistency management in software engineering by abduction," *Proceedings of the ICSE-2000 Workshop on Intelligent Software Engineering*, Limerick, Ireland (2000) 90–99.
24. D. Zowghi and R. Offen, "A Logical framework for modeling and reasoning about the evolution of requirements", *IEEE Proceedings of the 3rd International Symposium on Requirements Engineering* (1997).

SOFTWARE PATTERNS

VLADAN DEVEDZIC

Department of Information Systems, FON - School of Business Administration, University of Belgrade, POB 52, Jove Ilica 154, 11000 Belgrade, Yugoslavia

Software patterns are attempts to describe successful solutions to common software problems [26]. Software patterns reflect common conceptual structures of these solutions, and can be applied over and over again when analyzing, designing, and producing applications in a particular context.

The purpose of this chapter is to gradually introduce the concept of software patterns and describe most frequently used classes of patterns. Key ideas are first presented by describing some practical needs and experiences of software designers. Then a commonly used classification of software patterns is shown, followed by an informal example that illustrates the presence of patterns in different fields of software engineering and knowledge engineering. The introductory part of the chapter closes with a brief history of software patterns.

The central part begins with a discussion of how the information and the knowledge of patterns are organized in practice and how designers should use that information/knowledge. Then the chapter dedicates one entire section to each one of the frequently used classes of patterns. Within any such a section, the objectives and the scope of the corresponding class of patterns are stated, and an example pattern is described in detail. The remainder of the chapter discusses the concept of pattern languages and some important research issues.

Keywords: Design patterns, analysis patterns, architectural patterns, organizational patterns, process patterns, pattern languages.

1. Introduction

Patterns are important because they help us to understand how people perceive the world [17]. It is valuable to base a computer system's analysis, organization, and design on this perception. In their own way, patterns represent knowledge and experience that underlies many redesign and reengineering efforts of developers that have struggled to achieve greater reuse and flexibility in their software.

1.1. *The key ideas of software patterns*

Software patterns contain useful models, their design rationale, and the assumptions and constraints of using the models. They facilitate reuse and sharing of the models and design knowledge by allowing software engineers to adapt the models to fit a specific problem.

It is extremely important to understand that developers *do not invent* software patterns. Rather, they *discover* patterns from experience in building practical systems. Upon discovery, they describe and document the patterns. Each pattern description states explicitly the general problem to which the pattern is applicable, the prescribed solution, assumptions and constraints of using the pattern in practice, and often some other information about the pattern, such as the motivation and driving forces for using the pattern, discussion of the pattern's advantages and disadvantages, and references to some known examples of using that pattern in practical applications. Once the pattern description is made public, other developers can apply it in their projects and use effectively the knowledge and experience it contains.

It is also of primary importance for developers to understand that using software patterns does not require knowledge of specific programming tricks or languages. Patterns only require a little extra effort in order to understand the recurring nature of solutions to specific problems, recognize instances of such problems in building specific software systems, and find a suitable way to apply already known solutions. The pay-off is definitely much larger that the extra effort: increased flexibility, modularity, and reuse of software, reduced development time, and efficient, elegant, and effective design solutions.

1.2. *Classes of software patterns*

Patterns exist in several phases of software development. The software patterns community has first discovered, described and classified a number of *design patterns.* They name, abstract, and identify the key aspects of common design structures that are useful in creating reusable object-oriented design [18]. Design patterns identify the participating classes and objects, as well as their roles, collaborations, and distribution of responsibilities in recurring, stereotypical problems of object-oriented design. They are relatively low-level abstractions, in the sense that they are concerned with classes, their instances, and relationships that must be eventually implemented as programs.

Note, however, that there are also lower-level patterns than design patterns. Novice practitioners in the world of software patterns will easily get used to the idea of software patterns starting from *idioms*, which are the patterns of source code levels [8, 18]. They express generally accepted conventions of certain programming languages or cultures, thus representing reuse in the small. For example, returning an integer value as the indicator of success/failure of some function is quite common in C/C++ programming. Some other examples of idioms include naming conventions, the use of exceptions, and the style of writing and documenting class interfaces. Such idioms represent commonly accepted programming style inside the culture.

More recent developments have also identified many patterns that transcend programming and go beyond software design *per se* [11]. *Analysis patterns* are reusable object models resulting from the activities of object-oriented analysis applied to common business problems [17]. They contain a lot of domain knowledge and experience, yet can be used in almost all kinds of business software.

Patterns for software architectures are concerned with an overall structure of a software system or subsystem that is appropriate to the problem domain and clarify designer's intentions about the organization of the system or subsystem [27]. Software architecture patterns are based on selected types of components and connectors (the generalized constituent elements of all software architectures), together with a control structure that governs execution.

Another frequently used class of software patterns is that of *organizational and process patterns* [3, 9, 12, 32]. These patterns apply to software development processes and organizational pragmatics, i.e., to software developers and users, relationships between them, and relationships between people and software [11].

There are many other classes of software patterns as well, although they are narrower in focus than the classes mentioned above. See the Web pages listed at the end of the chapter for a good insight into the full span of software patterns.

1.3. *An example*

The following example illustrates the existence and use of patterns at the level of software design. It shows how two specific design problems from different domains of software engineering and knowledge engineering abstract to a generalized design problem that can be solved successfully using a design pattern.

Suppose the designer of an intelligent software system wants to develop an explanation generator that can generate explanations for different users. In general, current level of understanding the system's domain is different for different users at any given moment. In intelligent software systems, that fact is reflected in the user model of each user. Novice users should get more general and easy explanations, while the system should generate more complex and detailed explanations to more advanced users. The problem is that the number of possible explanations of the same topic or process is open-ended. It should be anticipated that during the system maintenance another set of knowledge levels could be introduced in order to describe the user model more accurately. The explanation generator should not be modified each time another set of knowledge levels is introduced. On the contrary, it should be easy to add a new knowledge level easily.

The designer of the format converter in a document-processing system would face an analogous problem. A document in a certain reference format should be converted to many other different formats, and it should be easy to extend the converter when it has to support another new format.

The solution for the explanation generator problem is shown in Fig. 1. The solution for the format converter problem is quite similar. The general solution is shown in Fig. 2, and is well known in the patterns community as the *Builder* pattern [18]. The notation of Unified Modeling Language (UML) [6] is used in both figures to illustrate classes of objects and their relationships.

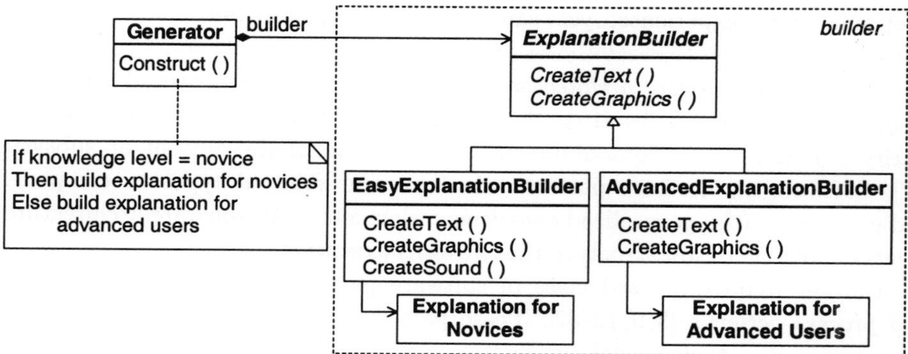

Fig. 1. Design of an explanation generator using the *Builder* pattern.

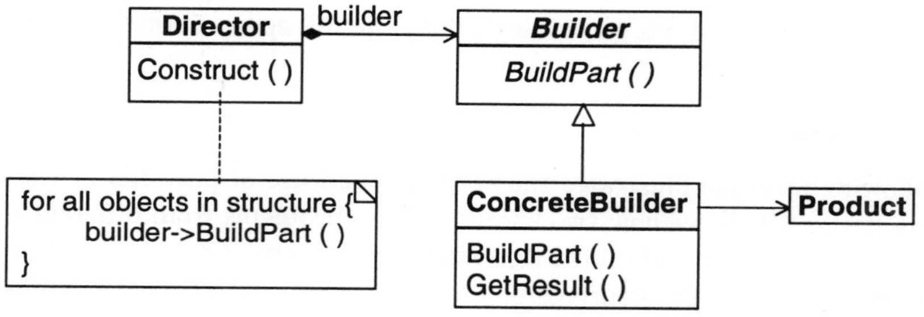

Fig. 2. The *Builder* pattern (after [18]).

In Fig. 1, the explanation generator can be configured with an Explanation-Builder, an object that converts a specific knowledge level from the user model to an appropriate type of explanation. Whenever the user requires an explanation, the explanation generator passes the request to the ExplanationBuilder object according to the user's knowledge level. Specialized explanation builders, like EasyExplanationBuilder or AdvancedExplanationBuilder, are responsible for carrying out the request. Note that their concrete implementations of the functions like CreateText and CreateGraphics provide polymorphism in generating explanations.

Generally, in both the explanation generator and format converter problems the algorithm for creating a complex object should be independent of the parts that make up the object and how they are assembled. Also, different representations are needed for the object that's constructed. Using the solution from Fig. 2 (the *Builder* pattern) provides both these features in the two problems considered here, as well as in all the similar problems. Since that solution is a fairly general one, it requires some minor adaptation in all specific cases. The abstract class Builder (e.g. ExplanationBuilder in Fig. 2) provides the interface for creating parts of the Product object (e.g. text and graphics of the explanation). Each ConcreteBuilder implements that interface. The designer configures the Director object (explanation generator) with the desired Builder object (types of explanation, according to the user's knowledge level). Director notifies the Builder each time a part of the product should be built. The Builder handles the requests from the Director and adds parts to the Product.

The point is that there are *many* patterns like the one in Fig. 2 that provide general solutions to common problems in software development. Familiarity with such patterns helps developers do their job more efficiently.

1.4. *History of software patterns*

Software patterns have evolved from several initiatives. In the late 80's and early 90's, object-oriented software development community has come across the idea of applying patterns in architectural design, proposed by Christopher Alexander [2]. It has become clear that similar approach could be used in software design as well. A number of software designers and researchers have started exploring that approach. As the first major result of these efforts, the classical "Gang of Four" book has appeared in the mid-90's [18]. It has covered a number of patterns discovered in object-oriented software design, and is actually still the best-known catalogue of design patterns to date.

Later efforts have shown that patterns exist in other activities of software development, e.g. in object-oriented analysis [17], in defining software architectures [27], as well as in organizing the entire development process [12]. Many researchers have also noticed that *collections* of inter-related patterns make sense as well. It has led to the development of many *pattern languages* [11, 13]. Recently, patterns and pattern languages are used even in creating software documentation [21], as well as in modeling variability in families of software products [20].

2. Patterns in Practice

Prespecified families of pattern-based solutions to common software engineering problems are available from *pattern catalogues*. Catalogues provide selected and readily usable descriptions of specific patterns. In practice, using patterns from the catalogues also requires some degree of customization and adaptation to the specific project. Developers can browse patterns in the catalogues in search of ideas for already existing solutions to many problems that are common in software engineering. Catalogues are well organized, so browsing them essentially means scanning the relevant patterns' sections that describe the pattern's purpose and how the pattern interrelates with other patterns.

2.1. *Describing patterns*

Individual patterns are described in catalogues using *templates* that provide uniform and consistent representation style. There is, however, no single format of such

- the pattern's ***name*** and ***classification***;
- the pattern's ***rationale*** and ***intent*** - what particular design issue or problem does it address;
- ***alternative name(s)*** of the pattern (if any);
- ***motivation*** - a scenario that illustrates a design problem and how the class and object structures in the pattern solve the problem;
- ***applicability*** - typical situations in which the pattern can be applied;
- ***structure*** - usually a class diagram depicting relations between the classes in the pattern;
- ***participants*** - the classes and/or objects participating in the pattern and their responsibilities;
- ***collaborations*** - how the patterns collaborate to carry out their responsibilities;
- ***consequences*** - what are the results and trade-offs of using the pattern;
- ***implementation*** - pitfalls, hints, techniques, and other issues to be aware of;
- ***sample code*** - illustrations of how the pattern might be implemented;
- ***known uses*** - examples of the pattern found in real systems (at least two examples);
- ***related patterns*** - what other design patterns are related to the one considered.

Fig. 3. A template for describing design patterns (after [18]).

- ***problem*** - the problem that the pattern addresses;
- ***context*** - the context where the pattern is useful;
- ***forces*** - the forces that drive the process of forming a solution;
- ***solution*** - the solution that resolves the forces;
- ***related patterns*** - what other patterns are related to the one considered.

Fig. 4. A more general template for describing software patterns (after [11, 17]).

templates. Typically, there are several different templates for each class of software patterns mentioned above, but there is also the most frequently used one within each class of patterns. For example, many people from the design patterns community use the format proposed in [18]. The format has the sections shown in Fig. 3.

On the other hand, catalogues of analysis, organizational and process patterns often follow some form the template shown in Fig. 4 [11, 17]. In that template, specifying the solution often involves showing a *diagram*. Most of these "parts" of a pattern are usually shown in the form of simple statements. Along with the pointers to related patterns, sometimes the pattern's *variants* are also described, and a *discussion* of the pattern's usefulness and limitations is provided.

2.2. *Using patterns*

Within the catalogues, patterns are classified so that it is possible to talk about families of related patterns. Moreover, many catalogues show *graphically* how other patterns from the same catalogue relate to the one being described, thus further refining the corresponding class of patterns. The classification helps designers find their way around the catalogues and also find the candidate patterns to be used in solving specific design problems. For example, within the class of design patterns there are *creational patterns* (concerned with the process of object creation), *structural patterns* (dealing with the composition of classes or objects), *behavioral patterns* (characterizing the way in which classes or objects interact and distribute responsibility), etc.

Using patterns in practice has several aspects. First, the designer of a specific system must know (or learn) what roles patterns play in developing an application of that type. For example, design patterns help solve design problems and increase reusability in different ways for different types of systems (e.g. for application programs, toolkits, and frameworks). Second, the designer should use pattern catalogues in order to select the appropriate pattern to solve a specific problem. This means considering:

- what family of patterns is related to that problem;
- in what way patterns from that family solve problems;
- what are their contexts;
- what are the consequences of using them;
- how they are interrelated;
- what kind of reuse could be supported; and
- in the reuse sense, what aspects of the particular design is variable.

Finally, once the right pattern is selected, its description should be read thoroughly, paying particular attention to the sections describing its context, structure, and limitations. Then the pattern should be adapted to the particular application domain and software engineering problem.

3. Design Patterns

Design patterns were the first class of software patterns that has been discovered and that has attracted software developers. They still remain the most widely used kind of software patterns in practical developments.

3.1. *Objectives and scope*

Design patterns are "simple and elegant solutions to specific problems in object-oriented software design" [18]. They capture static and dynamic structure of these solutions in a consistent and easily applied form. They contain knowledge and experience that underlies many redesign and recoding efforts of developers that have struggled to achieve greater reuse and flexibility in their software. Design patterns show generalized, domain-independent solutions of stereotypical problems that can be used many times without ever doing it the same way twice. Examples of such problems include representation of part-whole hierarchies, dynamic attachment of additional responsibilities to an object, accessing the elements of an aggregate object sequentially without exposing its underlying representation, and many more.

Software designers have discovered dozens of design patterns so far (see the URLs at the end of the chapter, as well as [Gamma *et al*, 1994], [19], and [22]). It is possible to use design patterns in object-oriented software development in any application domain by adapting the general design solutions that they prescribe to the problems in specific application domains.

3.2. *Examples*

The pattern description format used in this section follows the one from Fig. 3. However, due to space limitations, some sections from that template are omitted.

As the first example, consider the *Builder* pattern [18, 19] already described informally in the Introductory section. It has no alternative names.

Classification and intent. Builder is a creational design pattern. Its intent is to help separate the construction of a complex object from its representation. Such a separation makes it possible to create different representations by the same construction process.

Motivation. For a scenario that illustrates a design problem and how the class and object structures in the pattern solve the problem, see the example in the Introductory section.

Applicability. The *Builder* pattern is useful when an object must be constructed using different representations at different object instances and when the process of creating the object should be independent of the object's parts and the way they are assembled.

Structure, participants and collaborations. See Fig. 2, and the text that explains it.

Consequences. Using the *Builder* pattern lets designers vary the Product's internal representation (e.g. the contents of the explanation in Fig. 1). The pattern provides isolation of the code for representation from the code for construction. Construction of the Product is a step-by-step process, and is under the Director's control.

Implementation. The Builder class interface must be general enough to allow the construction of products for all kinds of concrete builders. Building the product step-by-step usually means appending results of construction requests to the product.

Known uses. Some examples of using the *Builder* pattern in knowledge engineering include different generators, such as explanation generator, exercise generator and hint generator [14]. Parsers in various compilers are also designed using the *Builder* pattern.

Related patterns. Builder goes together well with the *Composite* pattern (see below), and is similar to the *Abstract Factory* pattern (see, for example, [19] for details of *Abstract Factory*). In fact, the Products that *Builder* constructs are often *Composites.*

The second example is the *Composite* pattern [18, 19, 22]. It has no alternative names.

Classification and intent. Composite is a structural design pattern. Its intent is to compose objects into tree structures to represent part-whole hierarchies. It lets clients treat individual objects and compositions of objects uniformly.

Motivation. Lesson presentation planner of an educational system for individualized learning may decide to build an agenda of the topics to be presented during the lesson. Complex topics can be divided into simple elements, like concepts, text, graphics, and the like, or into a sequence of subtopics (simpler topics). Each subtopic in turn can be further subdivided into a lower level sequence of simple elements and other subtopics, producing an agenda like in the following example:

```
1.  Topic 1
        Text
        Graphics
        Concept A
        1.1.  Subtopic 1.1
        1.2.  Subtopic 1.2
              Text
              Concept B
              1.2.1.  Subtopic 1.2.1
              1.2.2.  Subtopic 1.2.2
2.  Topic 2
...
```

A simple implementation could define classes for simple elements, such as text and graphics, plus additional classes for subtopics as containers of simple elements. But in that case, the code using these classes would have to treat simple and container objects differently, which would be inefficient from the design point of view. Instead of that, the *Composite* pattern shows how to use recursive composition so that clients don't have to make this distinction. Moreover, using *Composite* makes it easier to achieve any desired depth of subtopics nesting.

Structure. The key to the *Composite* pattern is an abstract class that represents *both* primitive elements (concepts, text, and graphics) and their containers (subtopics). Figure 5 shows the general structure of the *Composite* pattern using the UML notation.

Participants and collaborations. The abstract class Component in Fig. 5 corresponds to the contents to be presented during the lesson in the example of lesson

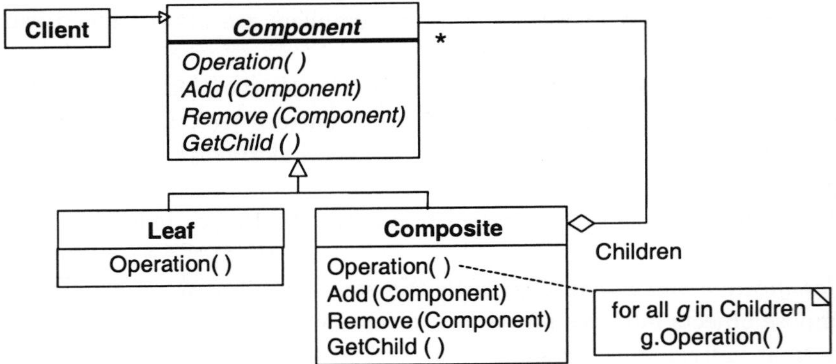

Fig. 5. Structure of the *Composite* pattern (after [18]).

presentation planner. It is responsible for providing a common interface to all objects in the composition, both simple (concepts, text, and graphics) and complex (topics and subtopics). The Add and Remove functions in Fig. 5 are examples of functions from such a common interface. It also defines the interface for accessing the child components of a complex object (a topic or a subtopic), e.g. the functions Operation and GetChild. The concrete classes Leaf (corresponding to simple contents of a lesson in the example) and Composite (corresponding to topics and subtopics) are derived from Component. The Leaf class represents leaf objects in the composition and has no children. It defines behavior for primitive objects in the composition. The Composite class implements child-related functions from the Component interface, stores child components, and defines behavior for components having children. A client object (e.g. the lesson presentation planner) interacts with any object in the composition through the common interface provided by the Component class. The client's requests are handled directly by Leaf recipients, and are usually forwarded to child components by Composite recipients.

Applicability. Typical situations in which the *Composite* pattern can be applied in software design include representing part-whole hierarchies of objects (such as composing topics, lessons, and curricula), and those when it should be possible to treat all objects in the composite structure uniformly by a client (such as a lesson presentation planner).

Consequences. Using the *Composite* pattern lets designers define hierarchies consisting of both primitive and composite entities, makes the client simple, also makes it easier to add new kinds of components, but can make the design overly general because it is hard to restrict the components in such a design.

Implementation. There are many things to consider when implementing the *Composite* pattern. Due to space limitations, only one of them will be mentioned here. It is related to child to parent references in a composite structure. Maintaining such references can make the design much more efficient, since it simplifies traversal and management of the composite structure. For example, having appropriate references from graphics objects to topics of a lesson is essential, especially when a graphics object can be presented during more than one topic presentation.

Known uses. Using the *Composite* pattern in designing several kinds of planners as parts of knowledge-based systems is described in [14]. Almost every user interface toolkit uses *Composite* for representing complex screen objects containing text, graphics, images, and other elements. Generally, *Composite* is used very often in object-oriented design.

Related patterns. *Composite* is often used with the patterns called *Chain of Responsibility*, *Iterator*, and *Decorator* (see [18, 19], and [22] for details of these patterns).

4. Analysis Patterns

These patterns describe the models of business processes that result repeatedly from the analysis phase of software development. Unlike design patterns, analysis patterns don't reflect actual software implementations. They convey conceptual structures of business processes [17]. However, one unusual feature of this class of patterns is that they are hard to classify into traditional vertical domains, such as finance, manufacturing, health care, and so on — they are often useful in more than one vertical domain.

4.1. *Objectives and scope*

Software analysis is not just listing requirements in use-cases — it involves creating a model of the domain as well. However, after creating a number of models, analysts often find that many aspects of a particular project revisit problems they have seen before [17]. Ideas they have used in the context of a previous project happen to be useful in the actual one, so the analysts can improve them and adapt them to new demands. Analysis patterns are groups of concepts and their relationships that represent such ideas, i.e., common constructions in business modeling. An analysis pattern may be relevant only to a single domain, but it may span several domains as well. For example, many models from health-care domain are also applicable to financial analysis. Hence, an abstract form of these models actually defines some analysis patterns.

To represent the structure of analysis patterns, people also use graphical notation as in the case of design patterns. There are also catalogues of analysis patterns. However, analysts generally don't use a strict template form for describing this kind of software patterns. They only vaguely follow the format shown in Fig. 4, but descriptions of analysis pattern look more like discussions of specific characteristics of business models, one or more pages in length. They often use several examples from specific business models to enhance the pattern presentation.

4.2. *Examples*

Analysis patterns are grouped into a number of groups, but again — each pattern from a certain group can be useful outside its group and outside the domain in which it was originally discovered. Some groups of analysis patterns are as follows:

- Accountability.
- Observations and Measurements.
- Observations for Corporate Finance.
- Referring to Objects.
- Inventory and Accounting.
- Planning.
- Trading.
- Application Facades.
- ....

The two examples of analysis patterns presented here come from [17].

The *Party* pattern is the basic pattern in the Accountability group. It is based on the generalization principle of object-oriented analysis. Party is the first more general concept from which specific concepts like person, company, organization, and the like can be derived directly to form the corresponding hierarchy. Hence, this pattern applies to modeling all hierarchical organizations.

For example, consider the problem of modeling the address book. Typical attributes of each person-related entry in any address book are the person's address, phone number, and email address. Likewise, the same attributes feature company-related entries in the address book as well. This could be modeled as in Fig. 6, but such a model would contain unnecessary duplications.

Using generalization, the analyst can introduce the Party class to encompass the Person and Company classes. This leads to the model in Fig. 7, which is much simpler and easier to maintain than the one from Fig. 6. The duplication is eliminated by "pulling up" the common attributes from more specific classes to the general one. The general analysis principle underlying the *Party* pattern is that in cases when identical attributes or identical behavior feature several object types (classes), these specific types should be combined into a general one and use inheritance to model the relationship between the general and specific types.

The *Party* pattern is related to several other patterns from the Accountability group (e.g. patterns like Organization hierarchies, Organization structure, Accountability, Accountability knowledge level, and Party type generalizations). As a matter

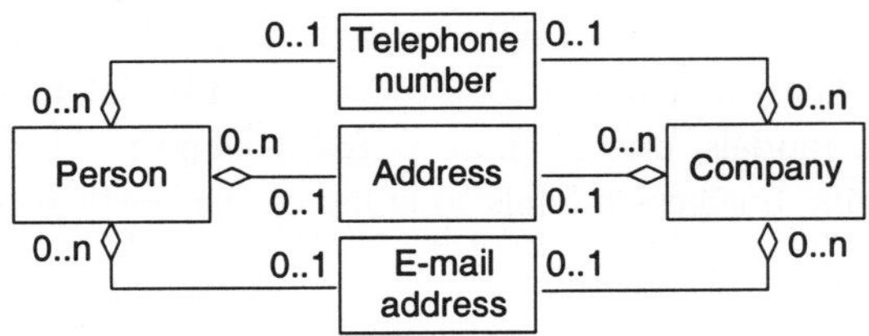

Fig. 6. Initial model of an address book.

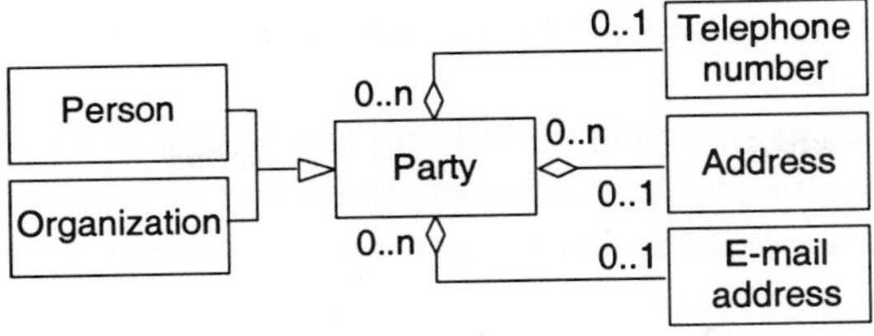

Fig. 7. The model of an address book using the *Party* pattern.

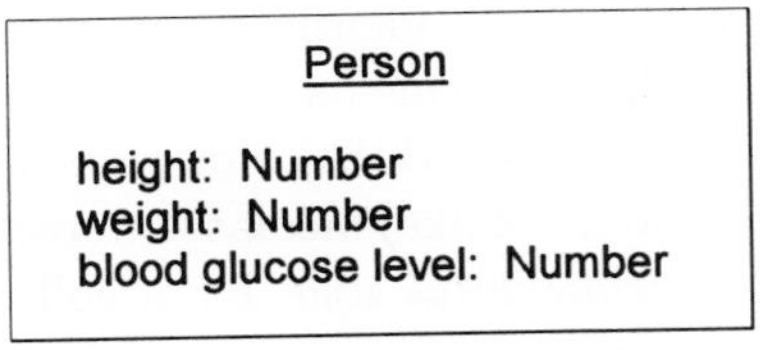

Person

height: Number
weight: Number
blood glucose level: Number

Fig. 8. Measurements as number attributes.

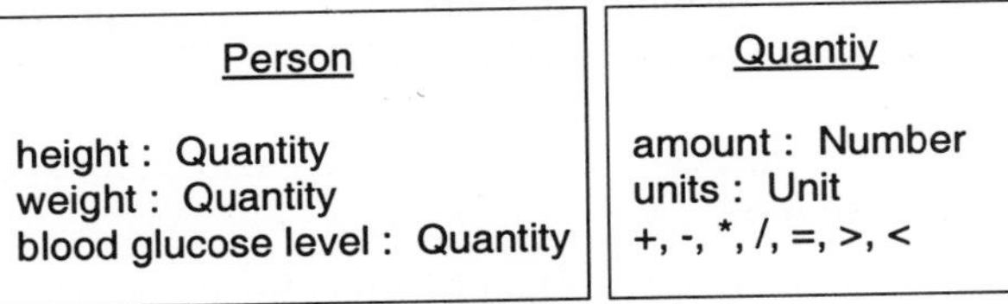

Fig. 9. Measurements as quantity attributes.

of fact, *Party* participates as a part of more complex patterns in its group. The same holds for some other analysis patterns as well.

The *Quantity* pattern belongs to the Observations and Measurements group. Many software systems record and update various kinds of measurements. The simplest way to do it is to record the measurements as numbers. It is shown in the example in Fig. 8. But there is a problem with this approach: what does it mean, for example, to say that a person's *height* is 5, or 155? It is the measurement unit that is missing here. It is possible to use attributes with more descriptive names, such as *height_in_cm*, but the representation remains awkward.

The *Quantity* pattern suggests a much better solution: introduce Quantity, a special-purpose type for representing measurements, which combines numbers, units, and operations. The modified Person type might look as in Fig. 9. With this modification, it becomes easy to specify that someone's weight is 80 kg. Over time, using various forms of the Quantity type becomes as frequent as using built-in types like integer or double.

A typical example of using the *Quantity* pattern is currency conversion in financial applications. Here the monetary values are represented as Quantities and use currencies as their units. Currency conversions can be specified as operations in the Quantity class.

The general analysis principle underlying the *Quantity* pattern is that in cases when identical behavior features different attributes of a data type (a class) and that behavior can be useful in other data types (classes) as well, the attributes should be combined into a unified fundamental data type (class).

5. Architectural Patterns (Patterns for Software Architectures)

Software systems are composed from identifiable *components* and *connectors* of various distinct types [27]. The components (e.g. compilation units or data files) interact in identifiable, distinct ways, and the connectors (e.g. table entries, dynamic data structures, system calls, and the like) mediate interactions among components. It is possible to define an *architectural style* for a collection of related systems. The style determines a coherent vocabulary of components and connectors (such as pipes, filters, clients, servers, parsers, databases, etc) and rules for their composition. It structures the design space for a family of related systems and reduces costs of implementation through reusable infrastructure. Styles provide guidance and analysis for building a broad class of architectures in a specific domain.

5.1. *Objectives and scope*

Patterns for software architectures can be identified by abstracting from the details of architectural styles. The main objective of this abstraction is to make the informal pattern clear, thus laying ground for subsequent formalization. In fact, these patterns impose an overall structure for a software system or subsystem that is appropriate to the problem domain and clarify the designer's intentions about the organization of the system or subsystem. They also provide information about the structure and help establish and maintain internal consistency, as well as perform appropriate style-specific analyses and checks.

Examples of patterns for software architectures include pipeline, layered architecture, data abstraction, repository, and many more.

Some of these patterns govern the overall architectural style that organizes the components [27]. Other architectural patterns identify an abstraction for component interaction, i.e., kinds of interactions among the components. In practice, designers shape up the system's initial overall design using one or more of these patterns — they may decide to elaborate a component of one pattern using some other pattern. For example, in a layered system some layers may be elaborated as pipelines and others as data abstractions. By continuing such an elaboration progressively and repeatedly, architectural issues eventually get resolved.

A typical template for describing architectural patterns is shown in Fig. 10. The fields of the template can be filled only with simple statements, or can contain longer descriptions.

- ***problem*** - the problem that the pattern addresses, i.e. the characteristics of the application requirements that lead the designer to select this pattern;
- ***context*** - the context where the pattem is useful, as well as the constraints in using it;
- ***solution*** - the system model captured by the pattern (the intuition about how the pattern's elements are integrated), together with the components, connectors, and control structure that make up the pattern;
- ***diagram*** - a figure showing the pattern's structure, components, and connectors;
- ***significant variants*** - major variants of the basic pattern;
- ***examples*** - references to examples that apply this pattern.

Fig. 10. A template for describing architectural patterns (after [27]).

5.2. *Examples*

The examples in this section are presented after [27].

The first example is the *Pipeline* pattern. It is a useful architectural choice for systems that perform a series of computations incrementally on a data stream.

Problem. A series of computations should be performed on ordered data. Sometimes these computations can proceed simultaneously.

Context. It is possible to decompose the problem into a set of transformations, each one processing an input data stream and generating an output data stream. A separate process performs each transformation. Each process takes its input data stream from one or more other processes and delivers its output stream to one or more other processes.

Solution. The system model of this pattern is data flow between the components (processes) called the *filters*. The components incrementally map data streams to data streams, thus making the data streams connectors of the architecture and data flow its control structure.

Diagram. See Fig. 11.

Significant variants. "Pure" filters, with local processing and little state. Alternatively, loops can be present in the topology, such as in Fig. 11. If a particular filter requires the entire input data stream before it can start its processing, then loops can significantly slow down the entire system.

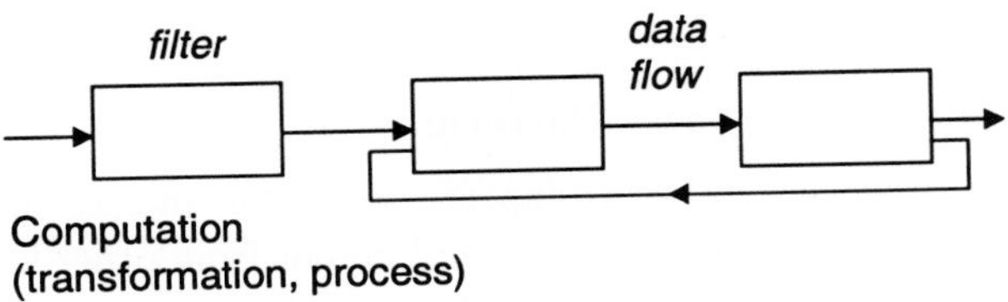

Fig. 11. The *Pipeline* architectural pattern (after [27]).

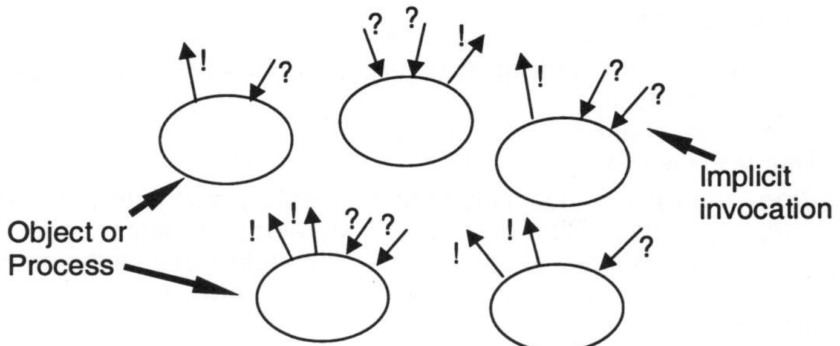

Fig. 12. The *Implicit Invocation* (*Event-Based*) architectural pattern (after [27]).

Examples. Unix programmers often use this pattern for prototyping, due to Unix' natural pipeline style of processing. Compiler designers also often use *Pipeline* to represent a series of translators.

The second example is the *Implicit Invocation* (*Event-Based*) pattern. It is suitable for systems that include a number of loosely coupled components, each of which carries out some operations that may (or may not) trigger other operations.

Problem. Architectural design of so-called "reactive systems", containing components that signal significant events without knowing the recipients. Other components that are interested in the events react by invoking some processes automatically upon receiving the signals.

Context. Reactive systems usually require an event handler. It registers components' interest in receiving events and notifies them when the events arise.

Solution. The system model of this pattern is a collection of independent reactive processes. The components are processes that signal significant events. The connectors are automatic invocations of other processes upon the appropriate events. The control structure is event-based and decentralized, since individual processes are not aware of the recipients of the signals they rise.

Diagram. See Fig. 12.

Significant variants. There are no significant variants of the pattern itself, but the level of sophistication of the event handler can vary a lot. Its reasoning about the correctness of the system depends on the components, the kinds of events, and the collective effect of processing the events.

Examples. Event processing in user interfaces, in operating systems, and in telecommunications.

6. Organizational and Process Patterns

Organizational and process patterns capture successful management practices of software development [3, 11]. They are much different from other kinds of patterns. They cover general development problems that all software organizations must face, hence they actually *support* software design, not *address* it directly [11].

6.1. *Objectives and scope*

Organizational patterns are about software-development organizations and about people who work in such organizations. Some organizational patterns can be used to shape a new organization and its development processes [12]. Others can be applied to evolution of existing organizations. Organizational patterns capture suitable management techniques and organizational structures in software development, thus affecting the ability of people to do their work. It should be noted that organizational patterns are usually drawn from case studies of organizations with high productivity and from common sense. It is hard to prescribe a suitable and simultaneously simple metrics for evaluating such patterns. For that reason, the value of organizational patterns is always judged empirically by managers of successful development organizations.

Templates for organizational patterns vary from quite informal descriptions to strictly structured ones, depending on the pattern's nature [9,11]. An example of structured template for organizational patterns is shown in Fig. 13.

Process patterns relate to the strategies that software professionals employ to solve problems that recur across organizations [3]. Each process pattern describes a collection of general techniques, actions, and/or tasks for developing object-oriented software. Figure 14 shows a typical template. An important feature of process

- ***problem*** - the problem that the pattern addresses in building, managing, or evolving a software-development organization;
- ***context*** - the context where the pattern is useful (e.g., the goals of building a new organization, the product's characteristics, typical roles in the development team, and the like);
- ***forces*** - the motivation and driving forces for using the pattern;
- ***solution*** - the organizational/managerial technique or practice captured by the pattern;
- ***resulting context*** - discussion of how applying the pattern changes or improves the organizational pragmatics;
- ***rationale*** - examples of organizations and situations where the pattern has been successfully used.

Fig. 13. A template for describing organizational patterns (after [12]).

- ***forces*** - the problem that the pattern addresses in the software development process and the driving forces for resolving the problem using that pattern;
- ***context*** - the initial context and entry conditions;
- ***solution*** - the techniques, actions, and/or tasks (activities) to be used to solve the problem, usually supported by a suitable diagram;
- ***resulting context*** - discussion of how applying the pattern changes or improves the software development process and possibly of what exit conditions must be met for the solution to be complete.

Fig. 14. A template for describing process patterns (after [3]).

patterns is that they suggest *what* to do, but not details of *how* to do something. Hence process patterns are reusable building blocks from which an organization can develop a tailored software process that meets its exact needs. There are three types of process patterns:

- *Task Process Patterns*: they are process patterns of the narrowest scope; these process patterns specify detailed steps to perform a specific task, such as technical review, component reuse, or software configuration management.
- *Stage Process Patterns*: these patterns prescribe the steps of a single project stage, such as requirements analysis, modeling, programming, and the like; not surprisingly, such patterns are often composed of several task process patterns.
- *Phase Process Patterns*: patterns of this type depict interactions among several stage process patterns and a single project phase, such as the inception, elaboration and construction phases.

Most organizational and process patterns support iterative and incremental software design. They have started to appear in mid-90's as a reflection of the fact that software development processes used in software organizations have gradually moved away from the traditional, linear "waterfall" model towards iterative and incremental development practices. Researchers have noticed many recurring practices in highly productive and successful organizations, and it is exactly such practices that form the skeleton of these kinds of patterns.

Also, most organizational and process patterns never come as individual patterns. They usually go together as groups of related patterns, i.e., as pattern languages (see the next section).

6.2. *Examples*

The first example is the organizational pattern called *Domain Expertise in Roles*, and it is defined within James Coplien's generative development-process pattern language [12].

Problem. How to match staff (people in the organization) to roles?

Context. Key atomic process roles and a characterization of the Developer role are known.

Forces. All the roles must be staffed with qualified individuals, but the more expertise is spread across roles the more complicated the communication between the people in the organization.

Solution. Hire experienced domain experts. Any given actor may fill several roles. Domain training is more important than process training.

Resulting context. The roles can be carried out more successfully and are more autonomous.

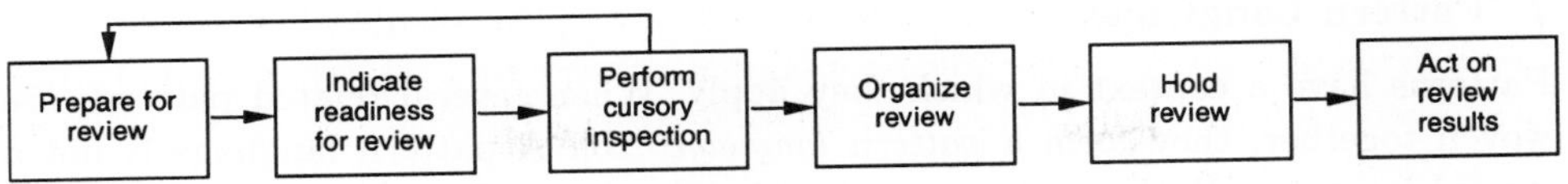

Fig. 15. The *Technical Review* process pattern (after [3]).

Rationale. In practice, many successful organizations hire deeply specialized experts. Experience shows that the roles of System Engineer and System Tester are often poorly staffed and should be paid special attention.

As the second example, consider the *Technical Review* task process pattern [3]. It addresses the problem of reviewing deliverables created during software development in order to meet the user's needs and ensure quality standards.

Forces. It is necessary to organize, conduct and follow through the review of one or more deliverables, such as models, prototypes, documents, or source code. Each deliverable should be validated for quality before building further on it. Defects in deliverables should be detected early, in order to decrease the costs of fixing them. The work of an individual developer must be communicated to the other team members, and one way to do it is to have the other team members review the work of that developer.

Context. The deliverables and the team are ready for the review process.

Solution. Figure 15 prescribes how to do the review process successfully. The team first prepares the items to be presented to the reviewers and then inform the review manager (usually the software quality assurance manager) that the items are ready for review. Then the review manager does a short, cursory overview of the work that has been done in order to ensure that the work to be reviewed is good enough to deserve gathering the review team. The next step is to plan, schedule, and organize the whole process, meaning to invite the proper people and hand out the necessary materials ahead of the review sessions. During the review process, it is necessary for the developers that have actually done the work to attend and explain/clarify details of their work. It is important to review everything thoroughly; hence the review process can take from several hours to several days depending on the number and complexity of deliverables to be reviewed. In the end, the review team produces a document that describes strengths and weaknesses of the deliverables. The development team should analyze the document and act properly in order to eliminate the weaknesses detected and explained in the document.

Resulting context. Managers are ensured that the development team has produced deliverables that satisfy the organization's quality standards. The developers have a better understanding of what is missing, what is unclear, and what must be improved in their work. Both team members and the reviewers usually learn or at least get initiated to new techniques during the review process.

7. Pattern Languages

Patterns have a context in which they apply. When several related patterns are woven together, they form a *pattern language* [26]. A pattern language is not a formal language. Rather it is a structured collection of interrelated patterns that provides vocabulary for talking about a particular problem.

7.1. *Objectives and scope*

By providing specific design and development vocabularies pattern languages help software developers communicate better. They cover particular domains and disciplines, such as concurrency, distribution, organizational design, business and electronic commerce, human interface design and many more [11]. Pattern languages help developers communicate architectural knowledge, help analysts avoid pitfalls and traps that other people have learned painfully by their own experience, and help designers learn a new design paradigm or architectural style [26].

It is important to note the difference between pattern catalogues and pattern languages. In pattern catalogues, individual patterns represent relatively independent solutions to common software design and development problems. In pattern languages, groups of related patterns are *integrated* on the grounds of experience in using individual patterns from catalogues — patterns in the same group often go together in different practical problems and are all suitable for particular areas of software design.

The number of patterns in the existing pattern languages varies from about half a dozen to several dozens, depending on the problem the language addresses.

In some pattern languages patterns are structured. Structures of pattern languages can take different forms, such as networks or trees. For example, in the G++ pattern language for design of large software control system [1], all the patterns are structured in a tree. A part of that tree is shown in Fig. 16. The nodes

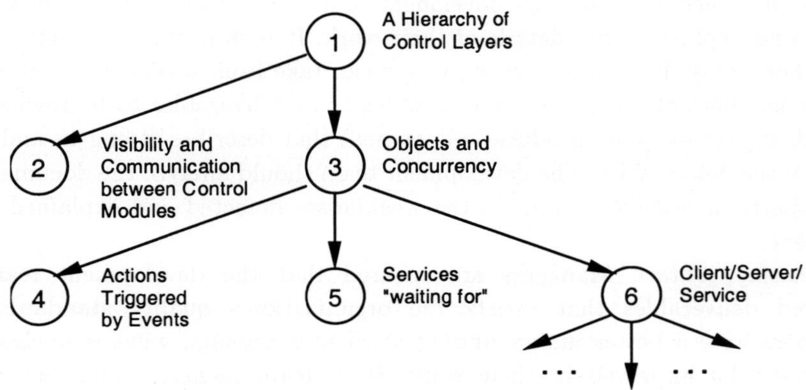

Fig. 16. A part of the G++ pattern language (after [1]).

of the tree represent individual patterns, i.e., design decision points, while the arcs represent the temporal sequence of decisions.

7.2. *Examples*

The first example is the G++ pattern language, Fig. 16. Since it addresses design of large software control system, its 11 patterns cover issues such as the organization of control modules in a hierarchy, the visibility requirements between the control modules, concurrency and distribution. For the sake of brevity, only the names and related problems of three selected patterns from the language are listed here. Interested readers should refer to [1] for a complete coverage of G++.

Pattern 1: A Hierarchy of Control Layers — it is necessary to arrange individual control modules in multiple layers and create the communication hierarchy between them.

Pattern 2: Visibility and Communication between Control Modules — these mechanisms must be established for both imperative and reactive communication.

Pattern 3: Objects and Concurrency — it is desirable to adopt the correct model for representing concurrency at different granularities.

The second example is the RAPPeL — a Requirements-Analysis-Process Pattern Language for object-oriented development [32]. It provides a direction and rationale for analysts, developers, and managers in requirements engineering for business applications. More than 100 patterns have been discovered in that area and integrated in RAPPeL, but the language is still under development. Some of the patterns are as follows.

Pattern 1: Building the Right Things — it is necessary to properly and thoroughly capture, communicate, understand, and validate the customer's real needs in order to create the requirements specification for the system that will "do the right things".

Pattern 9: Customer Rapport — how to build and establish a good relationship with a customer?

Pattern 20: Problem Domain Analysis — it is important to determine and define the essential nature of the problem domain in which the system is to be built?

Pattern 24: Finding and Defining the Domain Objects — how to best determine the objects in the problem domain and define their roles and responsibilities?

Pattern 50: User Interface Requirements — what is the best way and time to determine the requirements for the user interface?

8. Research Issues

Although software patterns have first and foremost attracted people from the world of industrial software development, many researchers from the broad field of software engineering have been involved in patterns from the very beginning. Research on software patterns is nowadays best presented on the dedicated pages on the Web, as well as on annual PLoP conferences (Pattern Languages of Programs) held from 1994.

From the PLoP conferences and the relevant Web pages it is easy to see that recent research efforts and trends in software patterns span across many areas. The following avenues are just a brief selection from such areas.

- *Risk Management Patterns.* These patterns capture strategies of project management by risk reduction [10]. The idea is to transfer the knowledge of successful project leaders to new project leaders by describing the successful risk management practices in a consistent, common format.
- *Patterns for component-based software.* Many projects today use a component-based approach to software development [31]. The main issues in component-based development are language and platform interoperability and separation of interface from implementation. Existing and newly constructed components are used on clients and servers to build flexible, reusable solutions on different platforms with different frameworks. Interested researchers from the software patterns community are trying to capture some of the recurring themes and best practices in component-based development that lead to winning software projects.
- *Patterns of social forces affecting software development.* Social forces of software development, such as skill mix, movement of people, and team structuring, do introduce some amount of bias in design decisions [9]. For example, a designer may make some decisions based on some privately evolved set of principles, and other designers have no way to judge what depends on such principles and what doesn't. The usual form of presenting software patterns hides that bias. The idea behind the patterns of this kind is to consistently document the interactions of social issues and software architecture. For example, these patterns stress such principles as creating interfaces around predicted points of variation, separating subsystems by staff skill requirements, ensuring there is an owner for each deliverable, and so on.
- *Domain-specific patterns.* Such patterns resemble analysis patterns to an extent, because they describe common solutions to typical problems of domain analysis. However, unlike analysis patterns they are strictly specific to a vertical domain. Each vertical domain has its own concepts, relations, structure, and organization, in addition to more general principles common to some other domains and that are captured by analysis patterns. In some cases, domain-specific patterns are possible to express (at least partially) using the knowledge of other classes of patterns. An example of such domain-specific patterns in the domain of education is presented in [14, 15].
- *Software patterns and knowledge engineering.* In knowledge engineering, an *ontology* represents the basic structure or armature around which

a knowledge base can be built [30]. It is well known that ontologies are "specifications of conceptualizations", they provide vocabulary of a problem domain, they also clarify the structure of knowledge, and they enable knowledge sharing. In other words, ontologies generally provide upper-level guidance and analysis for building sharable knowledge bases. Software patterns and ontologies are *not* the same concepts, but they have much in common. For example, design patterns also represent a kind of specifications, since they represent design solutions. They also provide some abstract, common, and general, though small vocabulary of specific design stereotypes. By clearly showing the intent, motivation, applicability, structure, participants and their collaborations, as well as consequences of applying them, design patterns also clarify parts of design knowledge and experience. Finally, design patterns are one way of sharing design knowledge and experience. For more comprehensive recent research on the relation between software patterns and ontologies, see [14].

- *Anti Patterns.* Anti patterns can be considered as an extension of design patterns. They provide the patterns of bad solutions and suggest refactoring techniques to improve the situations [7]. An anti-pattern is either a pattern that tells how to go from a problem to a bad solution, or a pattern that tells how to go from a bad solution to a good solution. A good anti pattern also shows why the bad solution looks attractive (e.g. it actually works in some narrow context), why it turns out to be bad, and what positive patterns are applicable in its stead. As an example, consider the *Design By Committee* anti pattern. It says that if no one single person in the team can be influential enough to present a design for a system and get it approved, to get the design done, a big committee of designers is assembled to solve the problem. They battle it out amongst themselves and finally take whatever comes out in the end. The result is a mish-mash of features in which everybody gets their share put in, since there was no unifying vision. Another example is the *Analysis Paralysis* pattern. It refers to the situations where a team of analysts gets stuck in building the application model forever. Other team members, such as designers and developers, have no work to do before the analysts deliver and are given busy work or some training. It happens almost always when the management insists on completing all analysis before beginning design, or when the project lacks clear goals. The common cures for this paralysis are keeping the models small, developing prototypes and making testing drive analysis, and minimizing the number of "analysts" to a single architect, turning everybody else into a developer.

Other notably attractive research topics include patterns for configuration and change management, business process reengineering, software testing, refactoring, and organization diagnostics.

9. Important Practical Issues

There are reports from actual development projects where software patterns have been applied. Such reports are very useful for researchers as well as practitioners, because they include advantages and disadvantages of the patterns in addition to experiential findings. They also present ways to avoid common traps and pitfalls of applying design patterns in practical software development processes. Many such reports can be found on the Web, starting from sites like Cetus Links (see the next section). Some others are available in published literature. For example, Kent Beck and his colleagues have described their experiences and lessons learned from applying patterns in a number of different industrial settings, including Hewitt Associates, Orient Overseas Container Limited, AT&T, Motorola, BNR, Siemens, and IBM [5]. Enumerating their lessons learned here should give novice practitioners an idea of what does it really mean to work with patterns in real-world projects:

- patterns serve as a good team communication medium;
- patterns are extracted from working design;
- patterns capture the essential parts of a design in a compact form;
- patterns can be used to record and encourage the reuse of "best practices";
- patterns are not necessarily object-oriented;
- the use of pattern mentors in an organization can speed the acceptance of patterns; and
- good patterns are difficult and time-consuming to write.

Another example is shown in [25]. The author describes how design patterns have been used in several projects in the domain of communication software, in order to enable widespread reuse of communication software architectures, developer expertise, and object-oriented framework components. The projects included the Motorola Iridium global personal communications system, a family of network monitoring applications for Ericsson telecommunication switches, and a system for transporting multimegabyte medical images over high-speed ATM networks.

It is also important for practitioners to know that there are efforts related to formally modeling software patterns. For example, the meta-pattern of W. Pree is considered as formally modeling design patterns to categorize a family of the patterns [24]. In a similar endeavor, J. Soukup has developed a special class, called the Pattern class, that encapsulates all the behavior and logic of individual patterns [28]. The Pattern class makes possible to clearly decouple application classes from patterns. Laudar *et al* have discussed modeling design patterns from the viewpoints of role, type and class, and representing these models visually [23]. There is also some work related to the formalization of filling hot spots of design patterns by using UML parametrization facility (e.g. see [19] and [29]).

Recent popularity of autonomous agents and agent-oriented software engineering has led to the discovery of specific *agent design patterns*, that capture good solutions to common problems in agent design. For example, Aridor and Lange report on several design patterns they have found in mobile agent applications [4].

There are some CASE tools where design patterns are embedded and/or which have the functions to manage design patterns. Apart from some earlier examples (e.g. [16]), a popular modern product suite of such tools includes Together Solo, Together Enterprise, Together Control Center from TogetherSoft (www.togethersoft.com).

10. Summary

The software patterns movement has emerged in the object-oriented community, from the studies of software reuse and from observations that ordinary, recurring solutions to typical software design and development projects should be given priority over using the latest technology. However, the movement has soon transcended the object-oriented community and spread all over the software development world, leading to the rapid development of patterns as an important software engineering problem-solving discipline per se and to the specific patterns community and culture. The goal of the pattern community is to build a body of literature and other resources to support software design and development in general. There is less focus on technology than on a culture to document and support sound design.

The roots of the discipline of software patterns stem from many disciplines, including literate programming, but most notably from Alexander's work on urban planning and building architecture [2]. The landmark work that has determined the real beginning of the patterns movement in software engineering has been the famous *Gang of Four* book on object-oriented design patterns [18]. Although the majority of the software community is still using patterns largely for software design, from the times of the *Gang of Four* book patterns have been used for domains as diverse as software analysis, development organization and process, exposition and teaching, software architecture, component-based software development, and many more. The discipline continues to grow and to attract more and more people to the community.

Software Patterns on the Web

There are many software patterns resources on the Web. The short list of URLs shown below has been composed according to the following criteria:

- the number of useful links following from that URL;
- how comprehensive the site is; and
- how interesting the URL is for researchers.

As for the first two criteria, the first four URLs below provide the best starting points. The other sites listed satisfy all three criteria but are focused on specific classes of software patterns and pattern languages.

- Cetus Links:
  http://www.objenv.com/cetus/oo_patterns.html
- Patterns Home Page 1:
  http://hillside.net/patterns/patterns.html
- Patterns Home Page 2:
  http://st-www.cs.uiuc.edu/users/patterns/patterns.html
- Patterns Archive:
  http://www.DistributedObjects.com/portfolio/archives/patterns/index.html
- Design Patterns Home Page:
  http://st-www.cs.uiuc.edu/users/patterns/patterns.html
- Analysis Patterns:
  http://www.aw.com/cseng/titles/0-201-89542-0/apsupp/index.htm
  http://www.martinfowler.com/
  http://www.martinfowler.com/ap2/index.html
- Organizational Patterns:
  http://www.bell-labs.com/cgi-user/OrgPatterns/OrgPatterns?ProjectIndex
- The Process Patterns Resource Page:
  http://www.ambysoft.com/processPatternsPage.html
- Design Patterns and Pattern Languages:
  http://siesta.cs.wustl.edu/~schmidt/patterns.html
- Jim Coplien's Process Pattern Language:
  http://www.bell-labs.com/people/cope/Patterns/Process/index.html

References

1. A. Aarsten, D. Brugali and G. Menga, "Designing concurrent and distributed control systems", *Communications of the ACM* **39** (October 1996) 50–58.
2. C. Alexander, S. Ishikawa, M. Silverstein, M. Jacobson, I. Fiksdahl-King and S. Angel, *A Pattern Language* (Oxford University Press, New York, 1977).
3. S. Ambler, *Process Patterns: Building Large-Scale Systems Using Object Technology* (Cambridge University Press, Cambridge, MA, July 1998).
4. Y. Aridor and D. B. Lange, "Agent design patterns: Elements of agent application design", *Proceedings of Autonomous Agents '98*, Minneapolis, MN (1998) 108–115.
5. K. Beck, J. O. Coplien, R. Crocker, L. Dominick, G. Meszaros, F. Paulisch and J. Vlissides, "Industrial experience with design patterns", *Proceedings of 18th International Conference on Software Engineering*, Berlin, Germany (February 1996) 103–114.
6. G. Booch, J. Rumbaugh and I. Jacobson, *Unified Modelling Language User's Guide* (Addison-Wesley, Reading, 1999).
7. W. J. Brown, R. C. Malveau, Brown, H. W. McCormick, III and T. J. Mowbray, *AntiPatterns: Refactoring Software, Architectures, and Projects in Crisis* (John Wiley & Sons, New York, 1998).
8. F. Buschmann, R. Meunier, H. Rohnert, P. Sommerlad and M. Stal, *Pattern-Oriented Software Architecture — A System of Patterns* (John Wiley & Sons, New York, 1996).

9. A. Cockburn, "The interaction of social issues and software architecture", *Communications of the ACM* **39** (October 1996) 40–46.
10. A. Cockburn (ed.), *Surviving Object-Oriented Projects* (Addison-Wesley, Reading, 1998).
11. J. Coplien and D. Schmidt (eds.), *Pattern Languages of Program Design* (Addison-Wesley, Reading, 1995).
12. J. Coplien, "A generative development-process pattern language", eds. J. Coplien and D. Schmidt, *Pattern Languages of Program Design* (Addison-Wesley, Reading, 1995).
13. J. Coplien, J. Vlissides and N. Kerth (eds.), *Pattern Languages of Program Design — Vol. 2* (Addison-Wesley, Reading, 1996).
14. V. Devedzic, "Ontologies: Borrowing from software patterns", *ACM Intelligence Magazine* **10** (Fall, 1999) 14–24.
15. V. Devedzic, "Intelligent tutoring systems — Using design patterns", *International Journal of Knowledge-Based Intelligent Engineering Systems* **4** (January 2000) 25–32.
16. G. Florijn, M. Meijers, P. van Winsen, "Tool support for object-oriented patterns", eds. M. Aksit and S. Matsuoka, *Proceedings of ECOOP'97*, Jyväskylä, Finland, 1997, *Lecture Notes in Computer Science* **1241** (Springer Verlag, Berlin, 1997) 134–143.
17. M. Fowler, *Analysis Patterns: Reusable Object Models* (Addison-Wesley, Reading, 1997).
18. E. Gamma, R. Helm, R. Johnson and J. Vlissides, *Design Patterns: Elements of Reusable Object-Oriented Software* (Addison-Wesley, Reading, 1995).
19. M. Grand, *Patterns in Java — A Catalog of Reusable Design Patterns Illustrated with UML* (John Wiley & Sons, New York, 1998).
20. B. Keepence and M. Mannion, "Using patterns to model variability in product families", *IEEE Software* **16** (July/August, 1999) 102–108.
21. J. Kotula, "Using patterns to create component documentation", *IEEE Software* **15** (March/April 1998) 84–92.
22. C. Larman, *Applying UML and Patterns — An Introduction to Object-Oriented Analysis and Design* (Prentice-Hall, Upper Saddle River, 1998).
23. A. Laudar *et al*, "Precise visual specification of design patterns", *Lecture Notes in Computer Science* **1445** (Springer-Verlag, Berlin, 1998) 114–134.
24. W. Pree, *Design Patterns for Object-Oriented Software Development* (Addison-Wesley, Reading, 1994).
25. D. Schmidt, "Using design patterns to develop reusable object-oriented communication software", *Communications of the ACM* **38** (October 1995) 65–74.
26. D. Schmidt, M. Fayad and R. E. Johnson, "Software patterns", *Communications of the ACM* **39** (October 1996) 37–39.
27. M. Shaw, "Patterns for software architectures", eds. J. Coplien and D. Schmidt, *Pattern Languages of Program Design* (Addison-Wesley, Reading, 1995) 453–462.
28. J. Soukup, "Implementing patterns", eds. J. Coplien and D. Schmidt, *Pattern Languages of Program Design* (Addison-Wesley, Reading, 1995) 395–412.
29. G. Sunye *et al*, "Design patterns application in UML", *Lecture Notes in Computer Science* **1850** (Springer-Verlag, Berlin, 2000) 44–62.
30. W. Swartout and A. Tate, "Ontologies", Guest Editors' Introduction, *IEEE Intelligent Systems* **14**, Special Issue on Ontologies (January/February 1999) 18–19.
31. C. Szyperski, *Component Software: Beyond Object-Oriented Programming* (Addison-Wesley, Reading, 1998).
32. B. Whitenack, "RAPPeL: A requirements-analysis-process pattern language for object-oriented development", eds. J. Coplien and D. Schmidt, *Pattern Languages of Program Design* (Addison-Wesley, Reading, 1995) 259–292.

APPLICATION OF KNOWLEDGE-BASED SYSTEMS FOR SUPERVISION AND CONTROL OF MACHINING PROCESSES

RODOLFO E. HABER*,†, A. ALIQUE and S. ROS

Instituto de Automática Industrial (CSIC), Ctra.de Campo Real, Km. 0.200, la Poveda, Arganda del Rey, Madrid, 28500, Spain

**School of Computer Science and Engineering, Universidad Autónoma de Madrid, Ciudad Universitaria de Cantoblanco Ctra. de Colmenar Viejo, km. 15. 28049 — Madrid, Spain*

†*E-mail: Rodolfo.Haber@ii.uam.es*

R. H. HABER

Departamento de Control Automático, Universidad de Oriente, Santiago de Cuba, Cuba

E-mail: rhaber@iai.csic.es

One of the ways of attaining higher productivity and profitability in machining processes is to enhance process supervision and control systems. Because of the nonlinear behavior and complexity of machining processes, researchers have used knowledge-based techniques to improve the performance of such systems. Their main reason for using this approach is that a suitable process model is indispensable for both automatic supervision and control, yet traditional approaches frequently fail to yield appropriate models of complex (nonlinear, time-varying, ill-defined) processes, such as machining certainly is, while knowledge-based methods provide novel tools for dealing with process complexity. One of the most powerful of these tools is fuzzy logic, which was the authors' chosen design approach. An overview is given of the main aspects of fuzzy logic and its application to modeling and control by means of the so-called Fuzzy Logic Device (FLD). Available methods suitable for process supervision are also reviewed, including pattern recognition and so-called intelligent supervision. Emphasis is placed on modeling by means of fuzzy clustering techniques. The machining process is typified with a systemic (input/output) approach, as is necessary for modeling and control purposes. Finally the authors' experience with successful applications of fuzzy logic to the modeling (fuzzy clustering) and control (fuzzy hierarchical control) of the machining process, implemented in a machining center, is presented. These thoroughly assessed real-world implementations corroborate the potential of knowledge-based techniques.

Keywords: Knowledge-based systems, fuzzy control, fuzzy modeling, machining process, hierarchical fuzzy control, hierarchical fuzzy supervision.

1. Introduction

Today's manufacturing industry is characterized by an increase in the demand for just-in-time production and global manufacturing. Manufacturing has more demanding productivity and profitability requirements that can be satisfied only if production systems are highly automated and extremely flexible [57]. One of the main activities the manufacturing industry has to deal with is machining, a process that includes operations that range from roughing to finishing. There are a number of angles from which to view the optimization of the machining process, angles where minimum production cost, maximum productivity and maximum profit are significant factors.

There are also various different ways of implementing machining process optimization. The implementation on which we will focus here attains optimal goals via automatic supervision and control of the machining process. The spectrum of available "conventional" methods (so named to distinguish them from knowledge-based and intelligent methods) for designing supervision and control systems is very wide. Certainly for a long time traditional (conventional) supervision and control schemes such as Proportional-Integral-Derivative single control loops were used in machine tool electromechanical processes, yielding very limited profits.

In the incessant pursuit of better performance, newer approaches have been also tested such as Model Reference Adaptive Control (MRAC) [5], which incorporates an on-line estimation scheme to tune controller parameters for time-varying process dynamics. Another recently applied method is Robust Control based on the Quantitative Feedback Theory (QFT) [89]. The results of these tests, however, have not lived up to expectations, because all these approaches, like all conventional approaches, have the indispensable design requisite of an accurate (traditional) process model, i.e., differential equations, transfer functions, state equations among others. Unfortunately accurate models of this sort are not attainable at present for machining process.

The work reported in this chapter represents the present status of a rapidly emerging area that has been under detailed investigation at IAI-CSIC[a] since 1975. In 1981, a group of IAI researchers led the Institute into the area by participating in the project on the first Computer Numerical Control (CNC) manufactured in Spain [3]. The group's scientific objectives evolved, eventually producing a general methodology for the design and implementation of intelligent control and supervisory systems for complex electromechanical plants.

In the early 90's, important strides were made toward real-time evaluation of machining parameters and integration of the information gathered from multisensorial systems [29]. Work later intensified, focusing mainly on modern modeling and control strategies, combining the use of knowledge engineering and artificial intelligence techniques such as Fuzzy Logic (FL) and Artificial Neural Networks (ANN). In 1993, a fuzzy control system based on a simple look-up table and a new hierarchical control scheme was successfully tested by the IAI group [30], as were other noteworthy contributions to the field of the analysis of self-excited vibrations and the application of a novel strategy for modeling complex processes on the basis of fuzzy clustering techniques [90]. A milling machine tool was used as a test bed

[a]Institute of Industrial Automation, Spanish Council for Scientific Research.

for evaluating the efficacy of the corresponding algorithms under field conditions [31, 32].

The achievements revealed that improved performance and process optimization could be attained using knowledge-based systems [33]. In fact such achievements encouraged further work in this field, leading in later years to outstanding results in the design and implementation of real-time fuzzy control systems with different self-tuning strategies, as well as the stability analysis of those control systems [34]. The authors have also released important findings on the integration of fuzzy supervision and hierarchical control to optimize the machining process [83]. Nowadays the research effort is concentrated on designing new hierarchical intelligent modeling strategies and exploring new ways of achieving better modeling results [35].

It has become quite clear by now that the design requirements for control and modeling systems for complex processes cannot be fulfilled by classical approaches alone. New methods must be investigated and used that can take advantage of human experience, methods that have learning capabilities and can deal with imprecision and uncertainty. Perhaps software engineering and knowledge engineering should overlap in a unified approach to designing and implementing knowledge-based control and supervision systems. If so, the approaches herein described should have enormous potential as a methodology of great practical relevance.

Let us look at the machining process. The machining process involves physical phenomena that are very difficult to describe accurately using traditional mathematical models because of the essence of the process itself; this is the main reason why there are no such models available. This being so, knowledge-based process supervision and hierarchical control can provide an alternative way of optimizing machine tool performance [86, 111]. Indeed, the complexity and uncertainty of processes like the milling process are what make what is known as *intelligent systems technology* a feasible option to classic formal description.

Fuzzy Logic (FL) is one such intelligent technique, and it has proven useful in control and industrial engineering as a very practical optimizing tool. The growing number of successful industrial applications of fuzzy logic worldwide really provides the best credentials the technique could hope for [40, 56]. FL can be used to build process models on the basis of the expertise of experienced human operators. Also, through FL supervisory and control systems can be invested with the verbally expressed experience of a trained operator. Through FL we can plug human knowledge, expressed in qualitative terms, into models and control systems to provide us with an alternative mathematical formalism for computation, human reasoning, and the integration of qualitative and quantitative information. The goal of this paper therefore is to give an overview of the application of knowledge-based systems to machining process supervision and hierarchical control.

In Sec. 1, we provide a tutorial introduction to fuzzy logic and decision-making. Next, we summarize some fundamental concepts and definitions involved in what is called the Fuzzy Logic Device (FLD). After that we explain the design parameters, the operating principles and the relationships among hierarchy, supervision and control. In Sec. 2, we provide an overview of intelligent supervision, focusing on the fuzzy c-means (FCM) technique and how it can be applied to process modeling, aiming at model-based process fault detection. In Sec. 3, we present a brief study of the machining process, explaining why it is considered a complex process and setting up the milling process as a case study. In Sec. 4, we apply the FCM criterion for modeling, showing the results obtained when applied to the milling process. In Sec. 5, we design and apply a fuzzy logic controller to optimize the milling process. We explain the design procedure, implementation and the corresponding experimental results. Finally we give some concluding remarks.

2. Fuzzy Logic and Control

Nowadays the so-called intelligent techniques for designing supervisory and control systems offer appropriate solutions, even in the presence of uncertainty and high complexity of physical processes. One of the pioneer intelligent methods is Fuzzy Logic, which gave us a new and powerful tool for dealing with these problems in situations where there is essential inaccuracy in models, information, objectives, constraints and control actions [115].

When a paper's subject matter is based on a relatively recent scientific contribution, as is our paper based on Fuzzy Logic, it is a very sound practice to introduce at least some brief historic antecedents. A historic review of fuzzy logic and its applications to control and modeling, however, goes beyond the scope of this paper. A thorough recount of leading personalities (names such as Lofti Zadeh, Ebrahim Mamdani and Michio Sugeno), important groups and "schools", milestones and all the hundreds of excellent practical applications would be so broad as to exceed by far the space permitted to a single paper. The applications of fuzzy logic invade many fields [18, 97], including the automatic train operation system [114], elevator control [27], automobile transmission control [38], video camcorders [47], DC locomotives [96], steam generator control [46], and air conditioners [104], etc. For a good survey of the rich history that has been written in the thirty plus years since Zadeh gave birth to Fuzzy Logic, we recommend that the interested reader see [81].

2.1. *Linguistic variables*

One of the most important concepts in fuzzy logic is the linguistic variable [117]. In the classical viewpoint we only deal with conventional variables, and it is necessary for us to understand how variables have to be transformed before they can be handled by fuzzy systems.

The linguistic variable is characterized by a quintuple $(\chi, T_e, (\chi), D, G, M)$ in which χ represents the name of the variable, $T_e(\chi)$ the set of linguistic values (attributes, adjectives) of χ, D is the universe of discourse, G is the syntactic rule to generate χ names, and M the semantic rule to associate each value with its meaning. Therefore the variable χ can be transformed (mapped) into a "linguistic variable χ", and vice-versa.

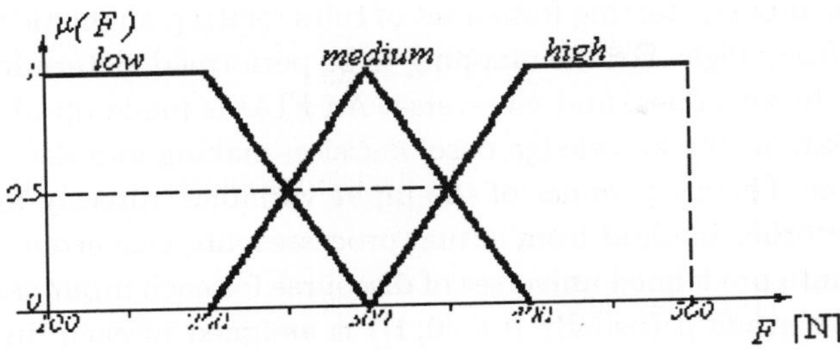

Fig. 1. Linguistic variable cutting force.

For example, if *cutting force* is interpreted as a linguistic variable (see Fig. 1), then T_e is the set of linguistic attributes defined for the cutting force. The fuzzy partition in the universe of discourse will be performed according to those attributes (*low*, *medium*, *high*, *very high*, etc). For example:

$$T_e(\textit{cutting force}) = \{\textit{low}, \textit{ medium}, \textit{ high}, \ldots\}$$

$$D(\textit{cutting force}) = [0, 500]\,.$$

In this case, use of the syntactic rule is not necessary because the attributes follow a natural order. However, in other cases attribute location needs to be arranged, e.g.:

$$T_e(\textit{cutting force}) = \{\textit{fairly high}, \textit{ excessively high}, \textit{ very high}, \ldots\}\,.$$

Then the syntactic rule could be: $G: \ldots$, "*very high*" at the upper end of D, and after that "*excessively high*" and "*fairly high*", respectively. The semantic rule M, for instance, allows us to interpret in our example that the cutting force is classified completely (100%) as "*high*" above about 400 N, the value at which membership in this set declines linearly down to zero at 300 N.

$$M_{HIGH} = \begin{cases} \mu_{HIGH} = 1, & F \geq 400 \text{ N} \\ \mu_{HIGH} = \dfrac{F}{100} - 3, & 300 \text{ N} \leq F \leq 400 \text{ N} \\ \mu_{HIGH} = 0, & F \leq 300 \text{ N}\,. \end{cases}$$

2.2. *Fuzzy Logic Device (FLD)*

Zadeh's conclusions suggested using a fuzzy rule-based (human reasoning-based) approach to the analysis of complex systems and provided a decision-making procedure together with a mathematical tool [118]. In general, fuzzy systems are knowledge-based systems that can be built up from expert operator criteria and can be considered universal approximators where input/output mapping is deterministic, time invariant and nonlinear [59, 66].

Let us look at the definition of a fuzzy logic device (FLD). The FLD is a general concept, in which a deterministic output (crisp values) is the result of the mapping of deterministic inputs, starting from a set of rules relating linguistic variables to one another using fuzzy logic. For the mapping to be performed, deterministic values are converted into fuzzy values, and vice-versa. An FLD is made up of four functional blocks: fuzzification, the knowledge base, decision-making and defuzzification.

Fuzzification: The crisp values of the input variables, directly measured or obtained by some other method from actual processes, are converted into qualitative values that fit into predefined universes of discourse for each input variable. A membership value or grade μ (usually $\mu \in [0,1]$) is assigned to each linguistic term of the inputs by means of membership functions.

Knowledge base: The knowledge base contains all knowledge about the system; in a way it represents the "process model". It includes the database and the rule structure. In the database, membership functions are defined in numerical terms. In the rule structure, goals and control strategies are expressed in the form of linguistic rules.

Decision-making: Outputs inferred from actual input are generated in the decision-making stage. Fuzzy implications are used, attempting to emulate human decision-making. The rule base provides the grounds for the inference. Some authors do not make any conceptual distinction between "knowledge base" and "decision-making", but have only one block named "control rules application" [75]. The application of control rules embodies both theoretical categories, since "rule activation" generates some given fuzzy output based on a fuzzified input. Some criterion (e.g. minimum, maximum, bounded product) is then applied and considered as the truth-value for the rule conclusion.

Defuzzification: Crisp output values are obtained in this stage, as a sort of compromise among different fuzzy values. This function is required whenever a numerical value (or a set of numerical values) is needed as an FLD response to a concrete real-world problem. Different methods can be used to obtain final crisp values for the output, as will be shown later on.

The classic configuration universally accepted as representing the four functional blocks described above is shown in Fig. 2. It is important to understand that these blocks have a functional meaning, so it is not necessary to separate them algorithmically or physically, as might be concluded from the diagram.

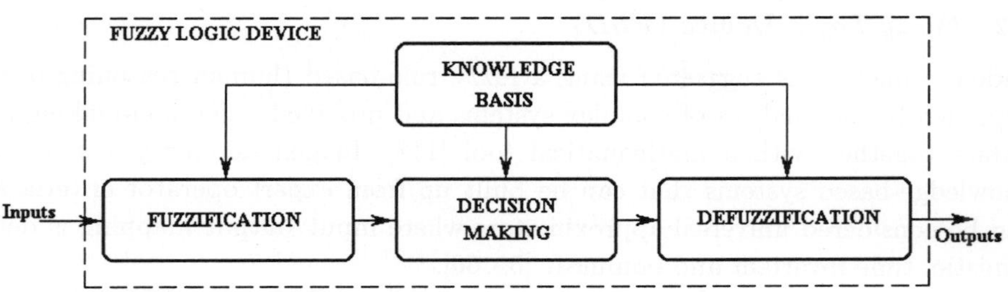

Fig. 2. Block diagram of a fuzzy logic device.

The FLD must be particularized as an automatic controller, a model, etc. depending on the origin and destination of the input/output variables (conventional, deterministic). For instance, a Fuzzy Logic Controller (FLC) would have the state variables or the output variables of the controlled process at its input, and the action or control variables at its output. A Fuzzy Model (FM) would have the same input and output variables as the modeled process. Of course an FLD can also be designated as a fuzzy decision-making device, because the outputs represent decisions made in response to a given situation at the input.

2.3. *Static characteristic. Design parameters of an FLD*

Regarding its input-output mapping, FLD's have severely nonlinear input/output characteristics. The static characteristic of a typical two-input (x_1, x_2), one-output (y) FLD is shown in Fig. 3. The shape of the surface (in general a hypersurface) depends on the knowledge base.

There are many parameters involved in designing an FLD, and they determine the shape of this nonlinear hypersurface. The need to define linguistic variables by means of the FLD's input/output variables causes there to be a high number of parameters (design parameters) with usable information about the fuzzy partitions. The definition of operations in the decision-making procedure provides additional design data. So, there is enormous flexibility in the design stages, but the drawback is that these parameters have to be properly tuned. The main FLD design parameters are illustrated in Fig. 4. Only a few of them will be discussed in this section; the others will be addressed in the next section using a typical example.

One of the most significant steps is the selection of input/output variables (this topic will be addressed fully in Sec. 2.1). After the variables have been selected, the membership functions must be chosen and the fuzzy partition of universes of discourse must be done. A membership function allocates fuzzy membership values ($\mu(\chi) \in [0, 1]$) to the crisp values of the input variable. The most popular shapes

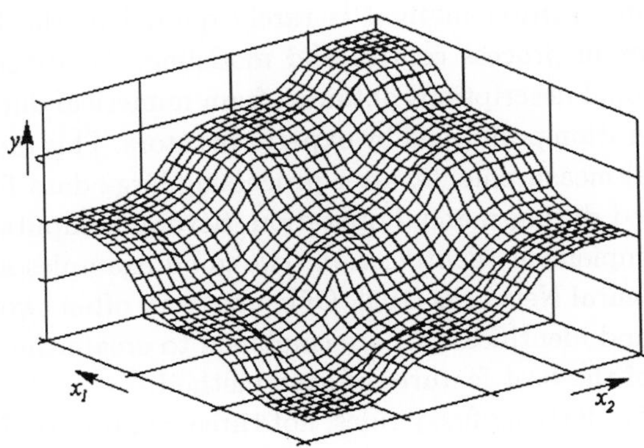

Fig. 3. Static characteristic of a two-input/one-output FLD.

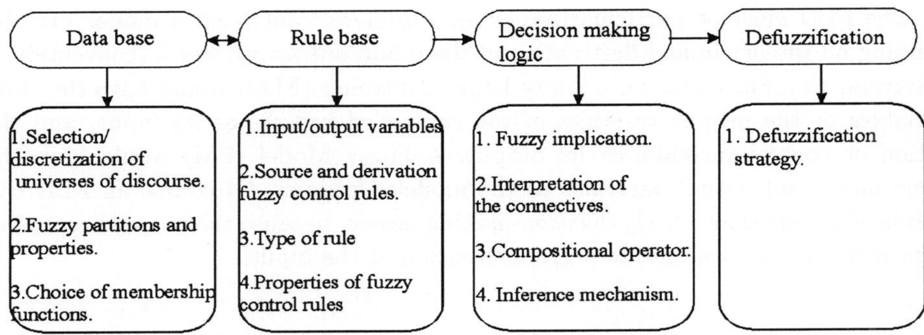

Fig. 4. Main FLD design parameters.

of membership functions are triangular and trapezoidal, although Gaussian and sigmoidal functions are also employed, depending on the application field.

The fuzzy partition of input/output spaces is what determines the "granularity" of the control or model obtainable with an FLD. A heuristic procedure is usually applied to find the optimal fuzzy partition, although some algorithms based on neural networks and genetic algorithms are currently available for this purpose as well [9, 44]. Another design issue is the completion of certain properties (e.g. the completeness property that must be incorporated into data and rule bases). The reader can find more details in [23].

The main step in FLD design is undoubtedly the derivation of fuzzy control rules. Tong [105] classified the ways for creating rules as *verbalization*, *fuzzification* and *identification.* The first method, the *verbalization* technique, assumes that the rule basis is formulated from verbal process descriptions obtained from skilled operators and technologists [51, 73]. *Fuzzification* (not to be confused with the fuzzification stage of the FLD) provides fuzzy decisional models drawn from ordinary (classical) mathematical expressions and using Zadeh's Extension Principle. Usually in processes as complex as those at hand here such mathematical expressions are not available, so fuzzification method is rarely quoted in the literature devoted to FLD applications in process control and modeling. *Identification* involves the generation of relational descriptions obtained from numerical data gathered during manual process operation performed by expert operators. This method provides the objectivity of actual measurements, after processing large data files containing the information gathered during manual operation. Several computational procedures can be applied to implement *identification*; two good examples are Fuzzy Clustering and Artificial Neural Networks [102]. Of course very often two or more methods (e.g. verbalization and identification) are combined to create the rule base in order to take advantage of the best features of each method.

Four strategies for deriving fuzzy rules, not three, are reported in [64]. The third and fourth strategies involve the utilization of fuzzy or neural network models to generate a set of fuzzy control rules and the use of learning to create the set of fuzzy rules, respectively. For instance, using the fuzzy model we can generate a set of fuzzy control rules for attaining optimal performance of a dynamic system [26]. In contrast, the fourth strategy focuses on human or automatic learning, which entails the ability to create fuzzy control rules and to modify them based on experience or self-organizing algorithms [85, 95]. The learning procedures themselves can also be based on fuzzy relational equations [82], neural methods [43, 84, 109], template-based methods [107] and clustering [49].

2.4. *Principles of FLD. An individual case of a Fuzzy Logic Controller (FLC)*

The FLC is based on human reasoning and the human strategy for dealing with process complexity (i.e., the decision-making model of the expert operator). The knowledge base of an approximate reasoning-based controller contains a collection of linguistic control rules that are stated using linguistic variables. For simplicity's sake, two classical inputs, i.e., error (e) and the change in error (ce), and one output, the control action (u), are considered in the following example of an FLD. This FLD is therefore really a *fuzzy logic controller* (FLC).

Each rule represents the fuzzy control action $[u]$ for each combination of fuzzy inputs $[e, ce]$. This is considered a linguistic model, and its rules may be expressed as follows:

$$\begin{aligned}
&\vdots\\
&R_i : [e] is [\mathrm{E}_i] AND [ce] is [\mathrm{CE}_j] \cdots THEN [u] is [\mathrm{U}_{ij}]; \ldots\\
&ALSO\\
&R_{i+1} : [e] is [\mathrm{E}_{i+1}] AND [ce] is [\mathrm{CE}_{j+1}] \cdots THEN [u] is [\mathrm{U}_{i+1j+1\ldots}]; \ldots\\
&ALSO\\
&\vdots
\end{aligned} \qquad (1)$$

where $\lfloor \mathrm{E}_i, \mathrm{CE}_j \rfloor$, $i = 1, \ldots, n$; $j = 1, \ldots, m$ are fuzzy sets for e and ce, with their respective membership functions $\lfloor \mu_{\mathrm{E}_i}(e), \mu_{\mathrm{CE}_j}(ce) \rfloor$ and universes of discourse $[D_{\mathrm{E}}, D_{\mathrm{CE}}]$. u is the output variable with a corresponding fuzzy set U_{ij}. The whole rule base is formed by $m \times n$ rules.

In order to explain the decision-making procedure of an FLC, let us take a rough overview of the sentence connectives "*and*" and "*also*" and the compositional rule of inference. The implication function is represented by a fuzzy relationship:

$$\mu_{R_i}(e, ce, u) \triangleq \mu_{(\mathrm{E}_i \text{ and } \mathrm{CE}_{ji} \to \mathrm{U}_{ij})}(e, ce) = [\mu_{\mathrm{E}_i}(e) \text{ and } \mu_{\mathrm{CE}_j}(ce)] \to \mu_{\mathrm{U}_{ij}}(u) \qquad (2)$$

where $[\mathrm{E}_i, \mathrm{CE}_j]$ is a fuzzy set $e \times ce$ in $D_{\mathrm{E}} \times D_{\mathrm{CE}}$ and $e \in D_{\mathrm{E}}$, $ce \in D_{\mathrm{CE}}$, $u \in D_{\mathrm{U}}$.

Generally speaking, the so-called triangular norms (t-norms) are associated with fuzzy implication, whereas the so-called triangular co-norms (s-norms) are used in fuzzy conjunction and disjunction. Typical t-norms are the intersection (minimum) and the algebraic product. Two common s-norms are union (maximum) and bounded sum. The reader can find more details on these topics in [65].

For instance, using the Mamdani definition of implication $R_i = (\mathrm{E}_i \cap \mathrm{CE}_j) \times \mathrm{U}_{ij}$:

$$\begin{gathered} \mu_{R_i}(e, ce, u) = \mathrm{T}\left(\mu_{\mathrm{E}_i}(e), \mu_{\mathrm{CE}_j}(ce), \mu_{\mathrm{U}_{ij}}(u)\right) \\ e \in D_{\mathrm{E}}, ce \in D_{\mathrm{CE}}, u \in D_{\mathrm{U}} \end{gathered} \tag{3}$$

where T is a t-norm for the *and* operator.

Once the fuzzy implication has been defined, a t-norm or s-norm must be used to interpret the connective also. In other words, it is necessary to calculate from the yielded expression $R = \bigcup_{i=1}^{m \times n} R_i$:

$$\begin{gathered} \mu_R(e, ce, u) = S(\mu_{R_1}(e, ce, u), \ldots, \mu_{R_{m \times n}}(e, ce, u)) \\ e \in D_{\mathrm{E}}, ce \in D_{\mathrm{CE}}, u \in D_{\mathrm{U}} \end{gathered} \tag{4}$$

where S is an s-norm for the *else* operator.

The choice of given t-norm and s-norm determines the compositional rule of inference. Consequently, a number of possible compositional operators are described in the literature [120]. In FLC applications the "Sup-Min" [116] and "Sup-Product" [48] compositional operators (Sup-Star, Sup-*) are the most popular. Both operators use the *maximum* (union) as the s-norm for calculating μ_R (the maximum among the membership grades $\mu_{R_i}, \ldots, \mu_{R_{m \times n}}$). The difference between them lies in the t-norm for calculating μ_{R_i}, $i = 1, \ldots, m \times n$. The Sup-Min operator uses the *minimum* (intersection), i.e., minimum among the membership grades of e, ce and u corresponding to the ith rule, while Sup-Product uses the product, i.e., algebraic product of the membership grades of e, ce and u corresponding to the ith rule. However, when the ultimate purpose at issue is modeling, others operators could be used, such as the sup-bounded-product and the sup-drastic-product [77]. Through the expression $\mathrm{U} = (\mathrm{E} \cap \mathrm{CE}) \circ \mathrm{R}$, we can obtain

$$\mu_{\mathrm{U}}(u) = \sup_{\forall e, ce} T(\mu_{\mathrm{E}}(e), \mu_{\mathrm{CE}}(ce), \mu_R(e, ce, u)), \forall u\,. \tag{5}$$

Considering some specific inputs $[e \quad ce] = \lfloor e^* \quad ce^* \rfloor$:

$$\mu_{\mathrm{U}}(u) = S_{i=1}^{m \times n}(T(\mu_{\mathrm{E}_i}(e^*), \mu_{\mathrm{CE}_j}(ce^*), \mu_{\mathrm{U}_{ij}}(u)))\,. \tag{6}$$

Rules can be additionally weighted using weighting (strength) factors. If we define the strength of the rule R_i as $\alpha_i = T(\mu_{\mathrm{E}_i}(e^*), \mu_{\mathrm{CE}_j}(ce^*))$, then the strength of each rule reflected on its consequence is calculated by $\mu_{\mathrm{U}}(u) = S_{\forall ij}(\alpha_i, \mu_{\mathrm{U}_{ij}}(u)), \forall u$.

Let us consider, for instance, the sup-product operation

$$\begin{gathered} \mu_{\mathrm{U}_{ij}}(u) = \alpha_i \cdot \mu_{\mathrm{U}_{ij}}(u) \\ \mu_{\mathrm{U}}(u) = \underset{\forall ij}{\mathrm{S}}\,(\mu_{\mathrm{U}_{ij}}(u)), \forall u \end{gathered} \tag{7}$$

and taking the maximum:

$$\mu_{\mathrm{U}}(u) = \max_{\forall ij}(\mu_{\mathrm{U}_{ij}}(u)) \,. \tag{8}$$

Finally, to produce a crisp control action, some *defuzzification procedure* must be applied to the fuzzy set $\mu_{\mathrm{U}}(u)$. Drawn from the compositional rule of inference (e.g. Sup-Min), the decision-making procedure generates the possibilistic distribution μ_R vs u (or a set of distributions for multiple input/multiple output systems), from which the crisp value $u = u^*$ should be extracted. There are basically three traditional defuzzification methods: the maximum, mean of maximum (MOM) and center of area (COA).

In the maximum criterion, a crisp output is chosen as the point on the output universe of discourse for which the overall fuzzy set achieves the maximum value the first time, as u increases.

$$u^* = \min\left(\arg \sup_{U \in \mathrm{U}}(\mu_{\mathrm{U}}(u))\right) . \tag{9}$$

The MOM method generates the crisp output as a mean value of all elements of the universe of discourse having the maximal membership grades. Considering a discrete universe

$$u^* = \frac{1}{m}\sum_{u_i \in \mathrm{U}} u_i \tag{10}$$

where U is the set of elements (values) in u that attain the maximum value of $\mu_{\mathrm{U}}(u)$, and m is the cardinality of U.

The COA yields better results, because it takes more useful information into account.

$$u^* = \frac{\int_{\mathrm{U}} u \cdot \mu_{\mathrm{U}}(u)\mathrm{d}u}{\int_{\mathrm{U}} \mu_{\mathrm{U}}(u)\mathrm{d}u} \,. \tag{11}$$

Assuming a discrete universe, we have for the COA:

$$u^* = \frac{\sum_i \mu_{\mathrm{U}}(u_i) \cdot u_i}{\sum_i \mu_{\mathrm{U}}(u_i)} \,. \tag{12}$$

More details on defuzzification techniques can be found in [112].

2.5. *Hierarchy in a supervision and control scheme*

There are several types of systems that use an FLD as their main system component, and therefore many schemes for modeling and control systems are available. Indeed, the right choice of FLD architecture contributes to the fulfillment of the system's objectives. Wang and Tyan [108] give a classification of the most useful schemes for fuzzy logic-based modeling and fuzzy control:

FLD for input selection (type 1) [119],
FLD for feedback error/output control (type 2) [54],

FLD for controlling the parameters of dynamic systems (type 3) [58],
FLD for choosing the best compensator (type 4) [53, 78],
FLD derived from a multiple performance index (type 5) [114],
FLD as a mathematical model for unknown or complex system dynamics (type 6) [113],
Hierarchical FLD (type 7) [69].

We must select the appropriate control and modeling schemes for accomplishing our goal. In this chapter, we will focus on hierarchical fuzzy control schemes. Hierarchical control aims at achieving better system performance even in the case of unexpected changes in system parameters, i.e., when accurate process models are unavailable. If the process model is not thoroughly known and so the premises of the control design method (e.g. adaptive control method) are violated, the only way to improve the control system's behavior is to set up control strategies at a supervisory (higher) level. Heuristic knowledge or other well-suited artificial intelligence-based methods (e.g. neural networks and evolutionary algorithms) can be used for this purpose [28, 60, 71].

In the field of fuzzy logic, hierarchical control and supervision have been widely studied as a possible solution for optimizing complex systems [80]. A variety of schemes can be implemented in order to profit from the advantages of this architecture, and the applications run all the way from fault-tolerant aircraft control problems to servo systems supervision [61, 67].

Hierarchical fuzzy control allows any available data from the low-level control system to be used at a higher level to characterize the system's current behavior. Moreover, hierarchical fuzzy control can be used to integrate extra information (in addition to that concerning the usual control-loop variables such as output, error, etc) into the control decision-making process, and even to incorporate certain human user or operator inputs [98]. In many cases, a hierarchical approach is an advantageous option for process optimization, instead of sophisticated design and implementation of high-performance low-level controllers, because the hierarchical approach can compensate for factors that are not taken into account in the design of low-level controllers [10].

Thanks to the very essence of its structure, a hierarchical structure can ensure flexibility and compatibility with other controllers that have already been installed. It has other strong points as well, such as the relatively low cost of investments in improving automation scheme performance, the possibility of exploiting already-installed low-level regulation systems, and the relatively low cost of measurement systems (very few additional sensors are required), which make hierarchical fuzzy control a wise choice from the economic and practical viewpoints.

One of the simplest hierarchical schemes is depicted in Fig. 5. The design procedure for the case where only a single performance goal must be fulfilled can be summarized as follows: first, a representative controlled variable of the process under study (y') must be selected. Hierarchical control is carried out by modifying

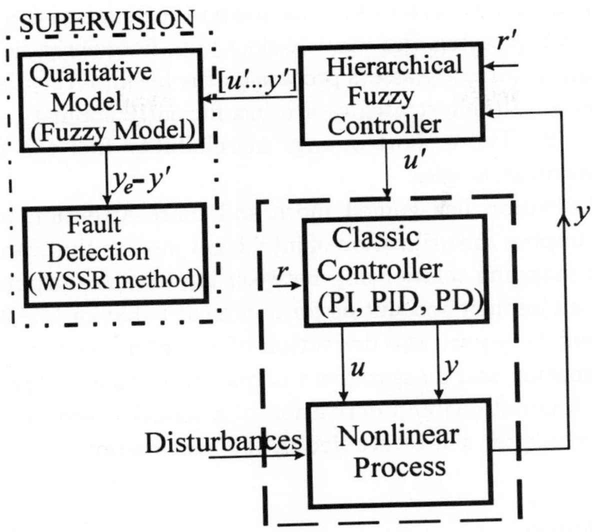

Fig. 5. Diagram of a hierarchical fuzzy control and supervisory system for a nonlinear process.

the reference values (set points) given by the user (e.g. operator) (u'). This way the process can be optimized. The procedure for applying this scheme to milling process supervision and control will be described later on.

Remark 1. Whenever hierarchical levels are going to be applied, goals and tasks must be broken down into levels of resolution. In a hierarchically structured intelligent system architecture, control bandwidth, perceptual resolution of spatial and temporal patterns and models decrease about an order of magnitude with each step upward in the hierarchy [2].

3. Intelligent Supervision

Now let us look at intelligent process supervision. One way to deal with process supervision is to use a process model, estimate process parameters, and then undertake some action. The widespread introduction of supervision and coordination levels into classical control schemes is designed to monitor controller performance and perform actions if errors are detected in operation [7, 68, 79].

The basic tasks that can be accomplished at the supervision level are monitoring of estimated parameters, detection of the matching degree (process model), decision-making, and closed-loop process monitoring. Important tasks such as the starting process, the selection of the best control algorithm, and the procedure for deciding controller parameters are performed at the coordination level. Consequently, supervision should look at changes in process behavior whose origins may be traceable to variations in the process's static parameters (gains) or dynamic parameters (time constants).

In the case of industrial processes, the purpose of supervision is to alert the operator to what is happening and what to do. Quite frequently, however, classical supervisory systems incorrectly assess process status because they lack the relevant information or because their strategies are insufficiently sophisticated to account for certain events [8]. These shortcomings in reliability fuel the development of intelligent supervision strategies.

Intelligent supervision has gained more and more attention in recent years, largely because it implies the utilization of intelligent models that can better approximate the correct mapping relationship between inputs and outputs of a dynamic system, including an implicit accounting for nonlinear behavior [4, 62, 103]. Furthermore, physical models require the derivation of complex mathematical equations involving the estimation and measurement of quantities that are presently difficult to ascertain. The foundations and derivation of a model based on fuzzy logic and cluster analysis techniques will be studied in the next sections.

3.1. *Fuzzy modeling*

A model may be considered to be a depiction of the physical properties of an object or process, so if we have a model of the process, we actually have a tool for planning, recognition and depiction of the information involved in the process. Moreover with a model we can infer properties from the process that can be used to understand, predict and control the process itself.

There are two ways of dealing with process modeling. The first approach is known as the "white box", and it is based on the assumption that the process can be fully described by mathematical equations (e.g. differential equations) representing the corresponding physical laws [72]. The second approach is based on the idea that the process is completely unknown and there is no *a priori* knowledge of the model structure to reflect the process's physical behavior. The unknown model parameters are estimated using experimental data to obtain an input/output relationship. An appropriate "black box" structure can be used as a function approximator. The main advantage of the "black box" approach when using accurately measured data is that it is possible to develop a model without requiring physical process knowledge [100]. The drawbacks of this method lie in the structure of the model, which is unable to offer any physical meaning. In practice the best way is to combine the two approaches, if possible, so that the more thoroughly-known parts can be modeled using physical knowledge and the less-known ones can be approximated through the "black box" approach. This is what is known as the "gray box" approach [17].

Sometimes the process is extremely complex and fraught with uncertainty, and its behavior is practically impossible to describe exactly. In that case an approach based on artificial intelligence techniques like fuzzy logic is the right way to address the problem. A fuzzy model can be viewed as a mathematical representation of the characteristics of a process by means of fuzzy logic statements.

The simplest and easiest way to obtain a fuzzy model is to create its knowledge base using verbalization techniques. Frequently, however, a complete verbal description of how a complex process behaves is quite difficult to obtain. In such situations verbalization can be complemented by an identification procedure of some sort. So then, an initial fuzzy model can be built from measured input/output ("black box") data by applying pattern recognition techniques. By the same techniques, we can gather engineering knowledge about the process (e.g. the approximate order of the system) and finally incorporate expert operator criteria, expressed in qualitative and imprecise fashion but confirmed by practical experience.

Pattern classification and recognition, as a novel but already mature scientific area, has at its disposal a wide stock of methods, approaches and procedures, the foremost among them being Bayesian and maximum likelihood approaches [11, 19], nonparametric techniques, stochastic and nonmetric methods [25], artificial neural networks [16, 37, 39, 42] and clustering analysis [92]. The reader can find details on some of the above-mentioned and other pattern recognition methods in [87, 94]. The usefulness of fuzzy set theory in pattern recognition and cluster analysis was also recognized in the mid-60's [91], and the literature dealing with pattern recognition and fuzzy clustering is now quite extensive [12, 14]. Fuzzy pattern recognition ranges from fuzzy image processing to control and modeling applications [15]. Another relatively common approach is fuzzy equivalence relation-based hierarchical clustering [56].

The aforementioned scientific results and practical applications have proven the relevance of fuzzy set theory to cluster analysis [13]. Because our specific interest lies in fuzzy clustering techniques, and for the sake of easier understanding, we will try to clarify what clustering means. Let us consider that we have a data set resulting from the observation of some physical process (e.g. real time measurement). Cluster analysis technique provides data grouping by means of the identification of an integer $c(2 < c < n)$ and the partitioning of the data space into subsets (i.e., clusters). A basic principle in cluster analysis is that members of a cluster should be more "similar" to one another than they are to the members of other clusters. Clustering therefore seeks associations among the subsets of a sample. The same associations may be plausibly expected to exist in the process from which the data were drawn. Indeed, thanks to fuzzy set theory, it is possible to assign one object to as many classes (clusters) as necessary.

3.2. *Fuzzy c-Means (FCM) criterion*

The main problem with clustering is how to decide the most appropriate number of clusters (c) in the data space and, of course, the criterion of classification. There are many possible functional methods for finding c-optimal partitions on the basis of different clustering criteria. The FCM criterion is based on a measure of dissimilarity (J_w), which penalizes the distance from a given data point to the center of each cluster, weighted by the membership value of that same point to that cluster.

$$J_w = \sum_{i=1}^{n} \sum_{j=1}^{c} (\mu_{ij})^m \|z_j - v_i\|^2 \tag{13}$$

where n is the number of data to be clustered, c is the number of clusters, μ_{ij} is the membership grade of jth value to the ith cluster, $(\delta_{ij})^2 = \|z_j - v_i\|^2 = (z_j - v_i)^T(z_j - v_i)$ represent the distance from the jth data to the center of the ith cluster, and m is a suitable weighting exponent $m \in [1, \infty)$.

The method provides an iterative algorithm that can achieve the c-optimal partition. The algorithm starts with a data set that is to be classified in a number of fuzzy clusters. Each fuzzy cluster is characterized by a set value, which shows the membership grade of every datum to each cluster. In order to find the c-optimal partition, i.e., the optimal partition corresponding to c clusters, the membership grades and the center of the fuzzy cluster have to be calculated iteratively until the minimum of the given objective function (J_w) is reached. In general, J_w is minimized when the clusters (c) are near those points that have a higher estimated possibility of being in cluster (i). Because Eq. (13) rarely has analytic solutions, the cluster centers and points are estimated iteratively until a small positive threshold (γ), serving as a stopping criterion, is reached.

A fuzzy model can be then obtained using a description language based on fuzzy logic statements. The model can be expressed by IF$\cdots$THEN rules as:

$$R_i : \text{IF } x_1 \text{ is } A_1^i \text{ and } x_2 \text{ is } A_2^i \text{ and } \cdots \text{ and } x_n \text{ is } A_n^i \text{ THEN } y \text{ is } B^i$$

where x_j, $j = 1 \cdots n$ are input variables, y is the output variable, A_j^i is the fuzzy set of the jth input linguistic variable participating in the ith rule, and B^i is the fuzzy set of the output linguistic variable involved in the ith rule.

Once the rule base is complete, the same mathematical procedures as described above for FLD can be used for the inference (e.g. Sup-Product, Sup-Min) and for defuzzification (e.g. COA, see Eq. 11). The algorithm herein described is based on [101] with some minor modifications. It could be summarized as follows:

Starting from an input/output data file, fuzzy clustering is applied to the output space, and then the algorithm projects the resultant clusters into the input space. The number of clusters determines the number of rules, except when more than one fuzzy partition corresponds to the same output cluster. Optimal clustering is achieved using a criterion based on the optimal center of clusters and the optimal membership values assigned for partitions computed applying the FCM method. The criterion for obtaining the optimum value of $c(O_V(c))$ seeks not only the minimal distances among clustered data and the center of their own cluster, but also the maximal distance among centers of clusters (v_i):

$$O_v(c) = \sum_{i=1}^{n} \sum_{j=1}^{c} (\mu_{ij})^m (\|z_j - v_i\|^2 - \|v_i - \bar{z}\|^2)\,. \tag{14}$$

Once the optimal number of clusters and the projections on the basis of $A_1(x_1^i) = A_1(x_2^i) = \cdots = B(y^i)$ have been found, the next step is to compute the membership functions for both output and input variables. In this case, trapezoidal membership functions were chosen, and their parameters must be adjusted by means of an iterative algorithm described in [1].

Remark 2. The procedure is repeated $l = 1, 2 \ldots$ times until $\|Y^{(l)} - Y^{(l-1)}\| < \gamma$, where $Y = \lfloor \mu_{ij} \rfloor$. A common value for the stopping criterion is $\gamma = \{0.01 \div 0.001\}$. The error norm usually chosen for the stopping criterion is $\max_{ij}(|\mu_{ij}^{(l)} - \mu_{ij}^{(l-1)}|)$.

Remark 3. The values of c and m are very important for successful calculation because of their influence on $Y = \lfloor \mu_{ij} \rfloor$. As $m \to \infty$ the partition becomes "fuzzier" ($\mu_{ij} = 1/c$). A typical value is $m = 2$.

3.3. *Fault detection*

Fault detection is very closely related to supervision and process optimization. On the other hand, fault detection methods are frequently based on human knowledge. For instance, a deep study has revealed that the *simple and time-fixed limits* are elementary strategies that require *a priori* knowledge about transient and size limits of the signals [45]. Nevertheless, false alarms can occur using such elementary strategies, mainly when automatic supervision systems incorrectly assess process status. Incorrect functioning like this may occur when the fault detection procedure is too simple to account for certain events, and part of the essential information is wasted. Another fault detection method is the so-called *part signature.* The way this method works is that some suitable signal generated by the process is recorded under normal working conditions, and its limits are calculated on the basis of the signature. However, most of the systems that use this strategy only permit upper bounds to be set [99]. Of all the methods available for industrial processes, model-based fault detection can be considered the most popular approach [41]. The essence of this method is the comparison of actual process behavior with the behavior of a process reference model. However, as explained above, the availability of a "good" process model is severely limited when the process is nonlinear and complex.

Models identified through fuzzy clustering allow us to use system residuals to detect and isolate failures [106], taking advantage of nonlinear models, which fully describe process dynamics. Here is a simple explanation of the weighted sum squared residuals (WSSR) method for detecting failures. The WSSR method is based on the residual sequence ($e_M(k)$):

$$e_M(k) = y'(k) - y_e(k) \tag{15}$$

where $y'(k)$ is the process's actual output, $y_e(k)$ is the predicted (model) output, and k is the discrete time.

Under normal operating conditions, the process is considered a zero-mean white-noise process with a covariance matrix $R(k)$. The deviation of a certain variable η is used to detect the failure on the basis of some threshold (ε) computed empirically and the length of the chosen time window $[k - N - 1 : k]$.

$$\eta = \sum_{j=k-N+1}^{k} e_M{}^{\mathrm{T}}(k) \cdot R(k) \cdot e_M(k) \begin{cases} > \varepsilon \Rightarrow \text{fault} \\ \leq \varepsilon \Rightarrow \text{no fault}\,. \end{cases} \tag{16}$$

Problems with WSSR method accuracy may arise if system residuals do not identically equal zero during normal operation. This can be solved by further post-processing (e.g. low-pass filtering) of the residuals. Another fault detection strategy called the generalized likelihood ratio (GLR) technique is explained in [110].

4. The Machining Process

Machine tools equipped with a CNC are a harmonious blend of manufacturing and computing techniques. However, the automatic execution of complicated operations at high speed together with the increased demand for operator security have obliged CNC's to extend their functions to include monitoring and protection of motors, drivers, peripheral devices and cutting tools as well as providing optimizing functions for cutting speeds. A panoramic view of a typical machining center together with other measurement devices is given in Fig. 6.

The machining process, also known as the metal removal process, is widely used in manufacturing. It consists of four basic types of operations: turning, drilling, milling, and grinding, performed by different machine tools. One of the most complex of those four operations is the milling process [55, 93]. The reasons the milling process was selected as a case study in machining process research are the process's intrinsic non-linear characteristics and the relatively poor performance of on-line

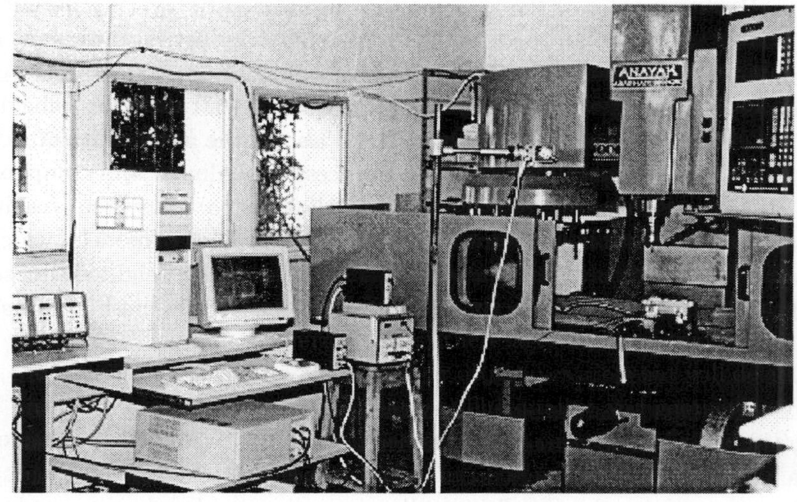

Fig. 6. Overall view of a typical machining center.

control and monitoring systems for the milling process, in comparison with turning and drilling processes [22, 36, 70, 76]. For instance, some studies reveal that monitoring systems have been applied (mostly to the turning and drilling processes) with 50%, 28% and 22% success at detecting tool breakage, tool wear and collision, respectively [20]. The characteristics of the milling process motivated us to focus our attention on optimizing the milling process on the basis of *intelligent systems technology*, as detailed later on.

Let us perform a system analysis of the milling process for optimizing overall machine tool performance. This is a typical electromechanical system. The electrical portion of the system includes DC and AC rotational motors, amplifiers, sensors and other components. The mechanical portion includes the rigid structure and the body with its different shafts, gears and reducer.

Usually, when machining is performed, operators mainly focus on checking limit values, operation sequences, machine tool and peripheral failures, chip geometry, chatter appearance and cutting tool condition (wear or breakage). The behavior of the cutting tool is a telling factor in manufacturing processes. Attention therefore generally focuses on tool condition monitoring (wear and breakage), and corrective action is taken to adjust cutting conditions and speeds in real time and to replace tools.

On the other hand, the basis for every control and supervisory system is the safe, accurate acquisition of sensor signals. From the industrial viewpoint, sensors should meet a series of requirements ensuring (in addition to adequate accuracy, sensitivity, cost, etc) robustness, reliability, and non-intrusive behavior under normal working conditions. Different measurement principles may be used in the machining process, such as force, power, torque, acoustic emission, acceleration, velocity, speed and camera/laser. However almost all the sensors for those principles fail to meet the metal-shaping industry's needs. Two classical examples are the *dynamometric platform*, which normally exhibits high accuracy and sensitivity but has many restrictions concerning cost, wiring, reliability and susceptibility to machine strokes, and the *current sensor*, which exhibits limited accuracy and requires a tedious calibration procedure. Hence, the selection of a given sensor is always the result of a trade-off among the various candidates.

In the world of machining, cutting force is considered to be the variable that best describes the cutting process. The information gleaned from the force pattern can be used to evaluate the quality and geometric profile of the cutting surface. In addition, oscillatory responses and peaks in the cutting force pattern may be the result of overloading, which would indicate a process irregularity and an increased danger of tool breakage or workpiece damage, so cutting force monitoring is frequently used to detect tool wear and breakage. On the other hand, cutting force regulation (e.g. mean cutting force control) is closely related to improvements in the metal removal rate (MRR) and overall optimization of machining processes. Cutting force can be directly and accurately measured by dynamometers or indirectly measured, e.g. inferred, from spindle-drive current consumption [6]. Because current sensors are economical, easy to install devices requiring no significant wiring and providing a fast time response, they are good for industrial applications [52].

4.1. *System characterization*

In terms of control system design and modeling, the most important aspects are the variables, parameters and typical measures of performance that we use to characterize the system so that it will help us see the process like a "black box". In other words, our first step was to select the input/output variables, disturbances, parameters, constraints, and performance indices. This is not a trivial task; selection plays a decisive role in the future results at other stages of design.

Among the enormous quantity of variables and parameters involved in the machine tool and the machining process, the most relevant factors in terms of automation tasks must be selected. After carrying a preliminary study, we selected:

- The spatial position of the cutting tool, considering the Cartesian coordinate axes $(x, y, z)[mm]$.
- Spindle speed $(s)[rpm]$.
- Relative feed speed between tool and worktable (f, feed rate) $[mm/min]$.
- Cutting power invested in removing metal chips from the workpiece $(P_c)[kW]$.
- Cutting force exerted during the removal of metal chips (F, cutting force) $[N]$.
- Radial depth of cut (a, cutting depth) $[mm]$.
- Diameter of the cutting tool $(d)[mm]$.

The laws of physics, of course, establish formal relationships among these variables. Other variables are also available in terms of measuring, but their relative suitability depends on the tasks to be performed in the design.

There are other properties and physical phenomena that influence the milling process, sometimes randomly. For instance, there are differences in tool condition (wear, breakage) and tool geometry, variations in workpiece "machinability" (e.g. material composition), machine structure (rigidity and rating), nonlinear vibration (e.g. chatter), and many restrictions on the sensors responsible for measurements (cost, wiring, sensitivity, linearity, precision, reliability and machine strokes).

In order to evaluate system performance, we need to select certain suitable performance indices. In the milling process, there are basically two operations — roughing and finishing. The differences in their objectives are what will decide which performance index is useful in each operation. The quality and geometric profile of the cutting surface is paramount in finishing operations, whereas the quantity of metal removed from the workpiece is the main issue in roughing operations.

This research work dealt essentially with roughing, so the main index was the metal removal rate (MRR). The MRR represents the instantaneous productivity of

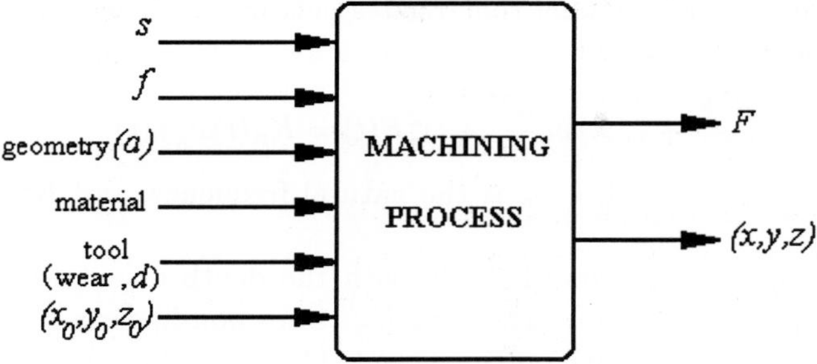

Fig. 7. Machining process using the black box approach.

milling [mm^3/min]. After some simplifications, an empirical expression for calculating the MRR was obtained [21]:

$$\mathrm{MRR} = 3,4865 \times 10^{-6} \cdot d \cdot s \cdot F\,. \tag{17}$$

This means that, machining with a selected tool and a given spindle speed, the resulting MRR is directly related to the cutting force, so a high MRR can be seen as equivalent to a high cutting force.

Now, the knowledge about the process for the purpose of control system design can be simplified by looking at the plant as a black box with its input/output variables, parameters, constraints and objectives, as shown in Fig. 7.

Considering the intended use of this model, inputs may be subdivided into input (action) variables such as s and f, and disturbances such as workpiece properties (hardness, "machinability", etc). Other spurious disturbances, such as variation in the power supply, part wear, and so on, are also included. The type of cutting tool (diameter, number of teeth, material, etc) and depth of cut (a) are considered process parameters. The output variables are the cutting force (F), which is related to the constraint given by the available power at the spindle motor, and the spatial position of the cutting tool. Another constraint is given by the prevention of vibration from self-excited oscillations (chatter). The type of machining at issue (here it is roughing) determines the system objectives as well as the performance index (MRR).

4.2. *Mathematical model from the classical viewpoint*

As stated above, the characteristics of the machining process severely limit the use of classical mathematical tools for modeling [24]. Even so, a classical mathematical model could provide a characterization of the dynamic behavior of the milling process that could help investigate and analyze machine tool performance and limitations.

The dynamics of the milling process (cutting force response to changes in feed rate) can be approximately modeled using at least a second-order differential equation. A second-order model that relates cutting force (F) to feed rate (f) is reported in the literature [63]

$$\frac{d^2F}{dt^2} + 2\xi(t)\omega_n\frac{dF}{dt} + \omega_n^2F(t) = K_n(t)\omega_n^2f(t) \tag{18}$$

where ξ is the damping ratio, ω_n is the natural frequency, and K_n is the process gain.

The damping ratio ξ grows linearly with the depth of cut (a) and decreases slightly with spindle speed (s). The gain K_n varies non-linearly with the depth of cut and decreases slightly with cutting speed. The natural frequency ω_n also varies depending on cutting parameters.

So far various different models have been obtained using second-order differential equations [88]. Such models are only valid over a narrow spectrum, and they cannot trespass certain limits in representing the above-mentioned process complexity and uncertainty; this, again, is the reason for our decision to use a knowledge-based approach to machining process supervision and control.

5. Fuzzy Modeling and Its Application to the Milling Process

We will now address the creation of a fuzzy model of the machine tool cutting process by applying the FCM algorithms we have described in Sec. 3.2. This model should be excited at the input with the cutting parameters and should offer relevant information about process status at the output. The input variables we selected for this model were the cutting condition vector (see Eq. 19) under fixed conditions of cutting tool diameter and workpiece hardness, which can be taken as constants during a given operation. The output variable we selected was cutting force.

$$\begin{aligned} \boldsymbol{x}^T &= [x_1 \quad x_2 \quad x_3] = [f \quad s \quad a] \\ y &= F\,. \end{aligned} \tag{19}$$

The test bed was a 5.8-kW, 4-axis milling machine, the ANAK-MATIC-2000-CNC, equipped with a Fagor Automation 8025 CNC, which was interfaced with a personal computer over a 9600-baud RS-232 communications link. To measure cutting force, we used a dynamometer (Kistler 9257B), which is a piezoelectric transducer for measuring forces in three components along the machine tool axes F_x, F_y and F_z. The signals were captured by means of an acquisition card connected to a personal computer and stored in data files for further processing (see Fig. 8).

Using these data files, the procedure to apply the algorithm described in Sec. 3.2 is straightforward. The threshold (ε) (see Eq. 16) must be computed empirically on the basis of parameters such as workpiece material, tool diameter, and cutting condition vector, and selected according to the "best" model. A general software tool running on a suitable platform (Windows 9X) that allows FCM criterion from input/output data files to be applied (C++) was successfully developed.

A library containing a collection of models, created according to the respective machining parameters (i.e., workpiece hardness, tool characteristics and cutting

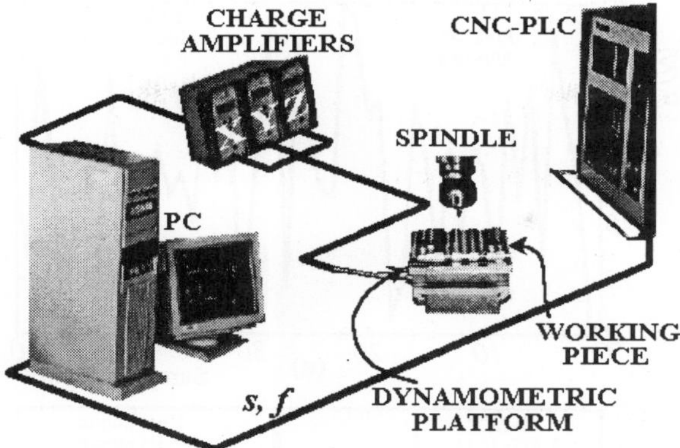

Fig. 8. Diagram of the experimental platform.

conditions) was built so that the right model could be activated for the specific machining operation. Different data sets were employed for obtaining and validating the resulting model. Validation was based on what are known as the performance index (PI) and the relative performance index (RPI), calculated as

$$PI = \sum_{i=1}^{n} \frac{(y_i - \hat{y}_i)^2}{n} \tag{20}$$

$$RPI = \sum_{i=1}^{n} \frac{|y_i - \hat{y}_i|}{n \cdot y_i} \cdot 100 \tag{21}$$

where n is the data number, y_i is the actual output, and $\hat{y}_i$ is the estimated output.

For a given typical example, the resulting number of clusters was four, and the model was composed of four rules. Figure 9 shows the resulting values of PI and RPI as well as the plots of actual model output for two cases: (a) a model obtained with one set of data and validated with the same set, and (b) a model obtained with one set of data and validated with another entirely different set (cross validation). As can be inferred from the plots, the resulting model of the milling machine cutting process exhibits a very good outcome. PI and RPI figures for the different data sets are very encouraging. This result confirms that the technique is very powerful and allows us to deal with uncertainty and incomplete knowledge.

6. FLC and Its Application to the Milling Process

In this section, we will describe how fuzzy logic control can be applied to the machining process. The scenario is the same as shown in Sec. 4.1. Therefore, the input/output characteristic is similar to the one illustrated in Fig. 7. Figure 10 shows the diagram representing the milling process.

The next step is to define the control scheme. The essence of our procedure was to keep the basic control system structure fixed, with the aim of developing

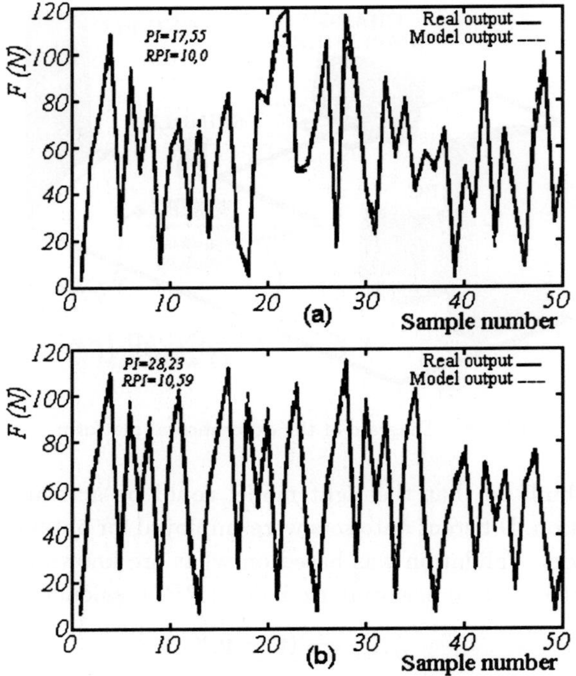

Fig. 9. Actual and estimated output for cases (a) and (b).

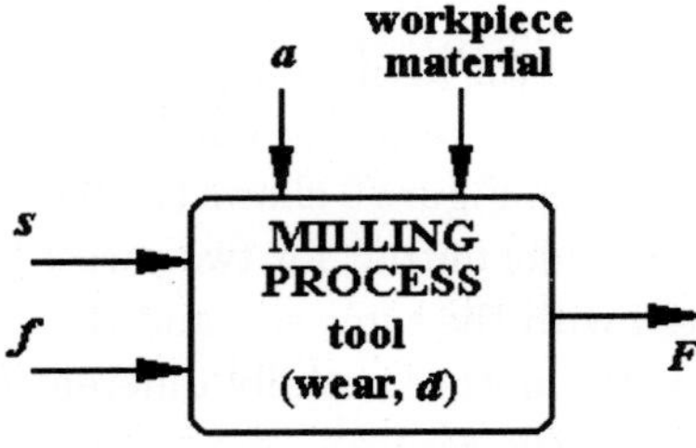

Fig. 10. Diagram representing the milling process.

a non-intrusive additional device. The corresponding hierarchical control system diagram is shown in Fig. 11.

The two lower blocks together with their interconnection represent the low-level control system. The spatial-position control loop of the cutting tool $\underline{x} = [x \quad y \quad z]^T$ and the velocity control loop for feed rate and spindle speed are included. The set point values for these variables ($\underline{x}^*$ and f^*) are represented by the external feedback (from the meta-system).

The objective for this hierarchical fuzzy control system is to manipulate the machine tool's cutting conditions, with some further possibilities in addition to those

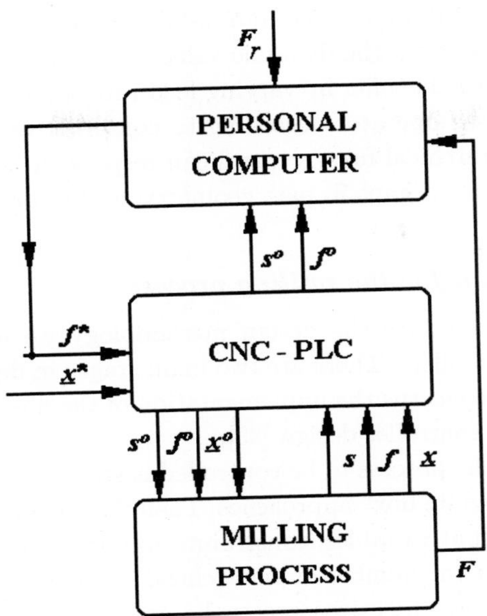

Fig. 11. Control scheme.

provided by the CNC-PLC alone. Optimization can be achieved, because the CNC-PLC allows a multi-level control architecture. This means that while servocontrol loops and the interpolator are at the lower levels, we can put the fuzzy controller (as well as other compensation or monitoring programs) at a higher level of the control hierarchy. As was explained in Sec. 2.5, in a case like this, hierarchical control is advantageous, because allows to perform tasks such as tool condition monitoring and machine failure detection, productivity enhancement through a higher MRR, and compensation for factors (e.g. position errors) not considered in the low-level servo design. Furthermore, there is another very important feature: all these achievements are made at a relatively low cost and without essential modifications of the standard hardware, nor any disturbance to the normal operation of low-level control loops, the interpolator and/or any other component of the machine tool.

We added a personal computer to the control scheme in order to measure the cutting force F and to perform the generation of f^* values. In this new context, while the CNC-PLC guides the sequence of tool positions and/or the path of the tool during machining, the hierarchical fuzzy controller determines the proper feed rate (f). Other measurement devices such as sensors and an acquisition card (A/D device, filters etc) were installed.

The set point of the cutting force (F_r) is fixed manually so that the MRR reaches the maximum allowable value under the rest of the technological constraints. This kind of system belongs to the category of supervisory systems because of the automatic generation of set points to be applied at the lower control level [99]. The variables $\underline{x}^o$, S^o and f^o represent the internal references for the CNC-PLC control loops, which may differ from the dynamic values generated by the computer for f.

We can obtain many benefits by varying feed rate, which under normal cutting conditions is set by the operator according to conservative criteria. By adjusting this variable, the hierarchical fuzzy control can respond to variations in workpiece hardness, depth of cut, air gaps in part geometry, and so on.

6.1. *Fuzzy algorithm for the milling process*

In this section, we introduce the design methodology we followed for designing hierarchical fuzzy controllers. There are two main stages in designing a hierarchical fuzzy controller. One concerns the implementation of the hierarchical level, and the second involves fuzzy controller design [33].

In the first stage, the process to be controlled is studied, attempting to combine the "black box" and "white box" approaches. Then the most meaningful variables of the process, input/output variables, constraints and objectives, as described above, are selected. After that the number of hierarchical levels may be chosen, depending on how many tasks and objectives are to be solved and fulfilled. Likewise, the connection between the process and the hierarchical level has to be established.

In the second stage, we address the issue of designing the fuzzy controller, bearing in mind that here, as in any control system design, we have to run a stability analysis. The reader can find more details about strategies for checking the stability of control systems of the type herein introduced in the literature [50].

Our fuzzy controller follows rather classic lines. The actual core of the controller performs on-line actions to control the feed rate (speed rate could also be included). The three basic tasks known as fuzzification, decision-making and defuzzification were implemented on-line. The main design steps for this controller and their corresponding implementation were:

Defining input and output variables, fuzzy partitioning, and building the membership functions.

The input variables included in the error vector $\boldsymbol{e}$ are the cutting force error (ΔF in Newtons) and the change in cutting force error ($\Delta^2 F$ in Newtons). Error and change in error are two variables commonly used in fuzzy control. The manipulated (action) variable we selected is the feed rate increment (Δf in percentage of the initial value programmed into the CNC), whereas the spindle speed is considered constant and preset by the operator:

$$\boldsymbol{e}^T = \lfloor K_E \cdot \Delta F \quad K_{CE} \cdot \Delta^2 F \rfloor; \; u = [GC \cdot \Delta f] \tag{22}$$

where K_E, K_{CE} and GC are scaling factors for inputs (error and change in error) and output (change in feed rate), respectively.

The fuzzy partition of universes of discourse and the creation of the rule base were drawn from the criteria of skilled operators, although we did have to apply a "cut and trial" procedure as well. Figure 12 shows the initial fuzzy partition

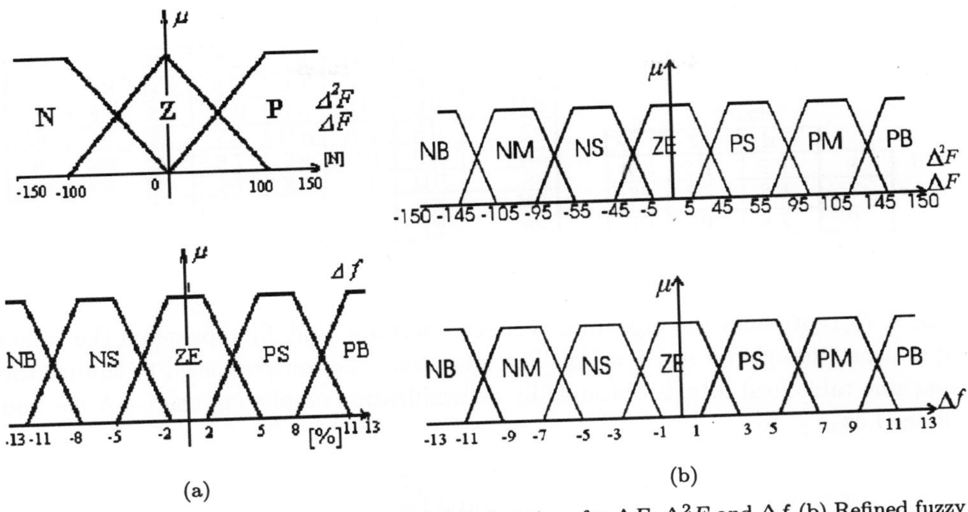

Fig. 12. (a) Initial partitions and membership functions for ΔF, $\Delta^2 F$ and Δf (b) Refined fuzzy partitions and membership functions.

obtained (see Fig. 12(a)) and a refined partition for enhancing the "granularity" of the controller characteristic (see Fig. 12(b)).

Constructing the rule base and generating crisp output.

We will consider a set of rules consisting of linguistic statements that link each antecedent with its respective consequent, having, for instance, the following syntax:

$$\text{IF } \Delta F \text{ is positive AND } \Delta^2 F \text{ is positive THEN } \Delta f \text{ is Positive Big}\,.$$

During normal manual operation, the operator selects a constant feed rate for the whole machining path, corresponding to the points of the workpiece that produce maximum cutting force (conservative criterion). An efficient operator, however, should adjust the feed rate in real time according to the cutting parameters to improve the MRR. By relating operator experience with a suitable variable whose dynamic behavior represents the status of the process (i.e., cutting force), we can establish the control rules. So, on the basis of keeping a constant cutting force, when the force increases (e.g. due to increased depth of cut), the feed rate should be reduced. On the other hand, when the force decreases due, for instance, to air gaps in the part, the feed rate should be increased to maximize MRR. A matrix arrangement of the rule basis is shown in Table 1.

The controller output is inferred by means of the compositional rule (see Sec. 2.4). The Sup-Product compositional operator was selected for the compositional rule of inference. Applying the T_2 norm (product), developing the implication, and applying S_1 s-norm (maximum) we obtained

$$\mu(\Delta F, \Delta^2 F, \Delta f) = \mathop{S_1^{m\times n}}_{i=1} [T_2[\mu_{\Delta F_i}(\Delta F), \mu_{\Delta^2 F_i}(\Delta^2 F), \mu_{\Delta f_i}(\Delta f)]] \tag{23}$$

Table 1. Rule bases of FLC: (a) 9 rules, (b) 49 rules.

Δ^2F ⇓ \ ⇒ ΔF	N	Z	P
N	NB	NS	ZE
Z	NS	ZE	PS
P	ZE	PS	PB

(a)

$\Delta F \backslash \Delta^2 F$	NB	NM	NS	ZE	PS	PM	PB
NB	NB	NB	NB	NB	NM	NS	ZE
NM	NB	NB	NB	NM	NS	ZE	PS
NS	NB	NB	NM	NS	ZE	PS	PM
ZE	NB	NM	NS	ZE	PS	PM	PB
PS	NM	NS	ZE	PS	PM	PB	PB
PM	NS	ZE	PS	PM	PB	PB	PB
PB	ZE	PS	PM	PB	PB	PB	PB

(b)

where T_2 represents the algebraic product operation and S_1 represents the union operation (max), $m \times n = 9$ or 49. The crisp controller output, used to change the machine table feed rate, is obtained by defuzzification employing the COA method defined as

$$\Delta f = \frac{\sum_i \mu_R(\Delta fi) \cdot \Delta fi}{\sum_i \mu_R(\Delta fi)} \tag{24}$$

where Δf is the crisp value of Δfi for a given crisp input $(\Delta Fi, \Delta^2 Fi)$, and $\mu_R(\Delta f_i)$ is the membership function (output possibility distribution) corresponding to the fuzzy union.

The output scaling factor (GC) multiplied by the crisp control action (generated at each sampling instant) defines the final actions that will be applied to the CNC set points:

$$\Delta f^*(\mathrm{k}) = GC\ \Delta f(\mathrm{k})\,. \tag{25}$$

The strategy used to compute f determines what type of fuzzy regulator is to be used. In this case it is a PI-wise regulator:

$$f^*(k) = f(k-1) + \Delta f^*(k)\,. \tag{26}$$

The control scheme was implemented on the basis of these definitions. We developed the real-time control and monitoring system in C/C++ programming language on a Pentium PC. Feed rate values (f) were generated on-line by the controller and fed in with the cutting force set point (F_r) and measured value (F). A current sensor was used for measuring the cutting force, according to the advantages mentioned in Sec. 3. The relationship between the current consumed at the spindle axis motor and the cutting force was fair enough to make a real industrial implementation of our control system feasible. The actual cutting force values were estimated from a calibration library that was previously obtained.

In order to cover situations typical of the milling process, we performed two types of experiments, taking into account that the resulting force in machining operations might exhibit oscillations due to cutter run-out, part machinability and load disturbance.

In order to have a basis of comparison; a linear controller was selected as alternative to the fuzzy controller. Due to the limited disposability of linear models of the machining process (indispensable in any traditional linear design), the linear controller's parameters were estimated from the best linear approximation of the fuzzy controller following [74]. Considering an equilibrium point $(\Delta F, \Delta^2 F, \Delta f) = (0, 0, 0)$, the parameters of the linear controller were obtained after minimizing the following function

$$\sum_{i=1}^{n} \beta_i^2 = \sum_{i=1}^{n} (-\lambda_{\Delta F} \cdot \Delta F - \lambda_{\Delta^2 F} \cdot \Delta^2 F + \Delta f_i)^2 \tag{27}$$

where T_S is the sampling period, K is the proportional constant, T_i is the integral constant, and $\lambda_{\Delta^2 F} = K, \lambda_{\Delta F} = K \cdot T_S / T_i$. As a result we obtained a PI regulator with saturation:

$$\begin{aligned} \Delta f_{PI} &= K \Delta^2 F + \frac{K \cdot T}{T_i} \Delta F \\ &= 0.076[\Delta^2 F + \Delta F] \,. \end{aligned} \tag{28}$$

6.2. *Evaluation and experimental results*

A DURAL aluminum alloy workpiece was used for the experimental field tests. The radial depth of cut was kept constant during each test. Machining was supposed to be done in one direction only. New (unworn) milling cutters were used in these experiments. A two-fluted milling tool 25 mm in diameter was chosen. For this tool and the cutting conditions, we set our reference value at about 450 N. As nominal values for the main cutting conditions we selected 800 rpm for the spindle speed and 100 mm/min for the feed rate.

For this first run, a very irregular depth-of-cut profile was chosen intentionally, with six step-shaped disturbances in the depth of cut, designed to emulate load disturbances as shown in Fig. 13.

Next we performed a comparison of the results attained with different rule bases (illustrated in Table 1) and two popular compositional rules of inference,

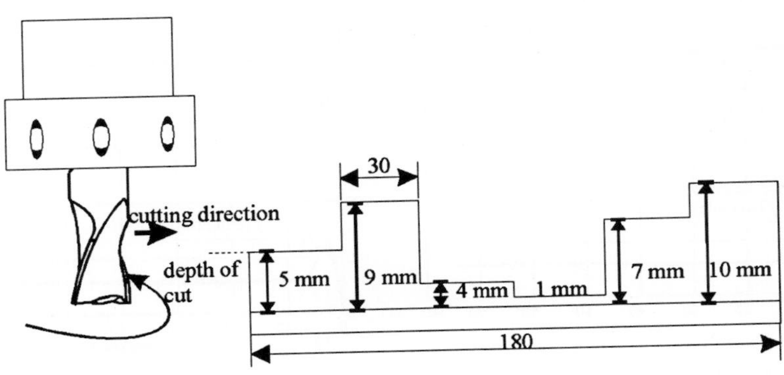

Fig. 13. Highly irregular six-stepped profile used for the first run.

"Sup-Product" and "Sup-Min". In this experimental stage, one step-shaped disturbance in the depth of cut was used, because that is the most frequent cut of all and it is considered enough for test objectives.

Accuracy (average absolute error (AAE) and mean square error (MSE)), peak time (Tp), overshoot (M_{pt}), and oscillations in the transient response could serve as suitable figures for assessing the control system's behavior. The transient response was also studied in detail, because undesirable oscillations could be harmful to both surface quality and tool. Moreover, M_{pt} should be tracked as a warning of dangerous situations and proximity to the control loop's instability.

The results of the first run when applying a PI hierarchical controller (see Eq. 28) and a hierarchical fuzzy controller are illustrated in Fig. 14. When the

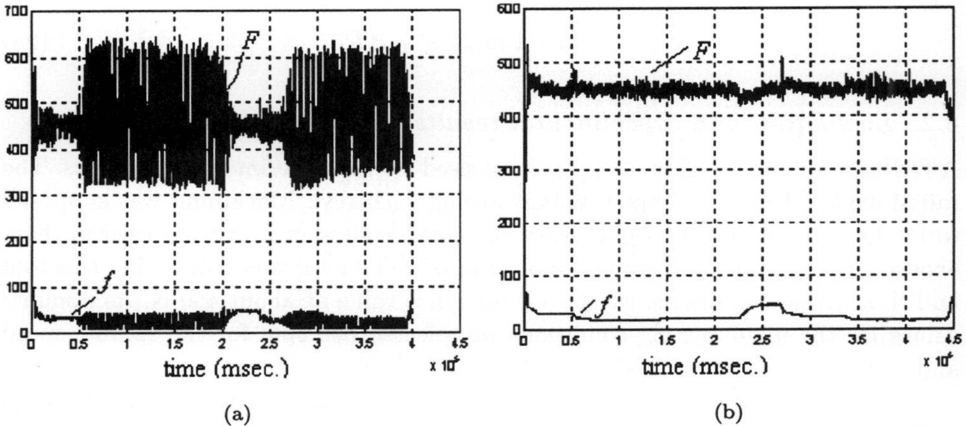

Fig. 14. Cutting force control using (a) hierarchical linear controller (b) hierarchical fuzzy controller.

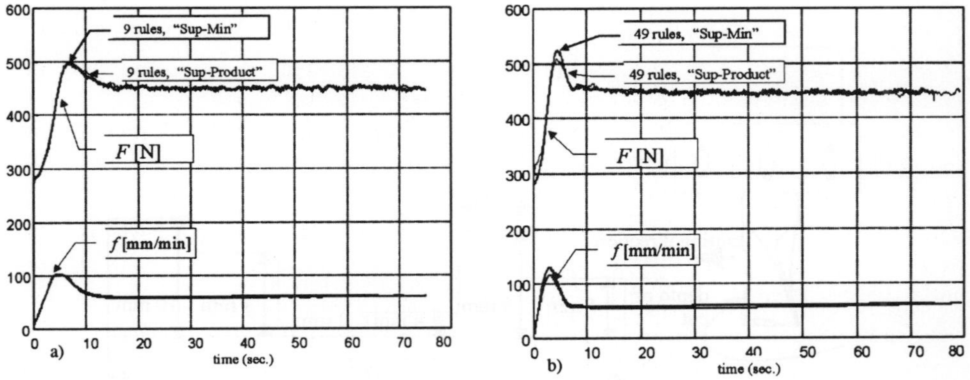

Fig. 15. Step responses of a hierarchical fuzzy control system using 9 and 49 rules and "Sup-Min" and "Sup-Product" rules of inference.

Table 2. Performance indices of the different operators and rule bases implemented.

# Rules	Sup-*	$AAE(\%)$	$MSE(\%)$	$M_{pt}(\%)$	Tp (sec)
9	Product	2.8	7.3	10.9	7
9	Minimum	2.6	7.2	10.4	7
49	Product	2.1	5.1	13.3	4.5
49	Minimum	2.2	6.1	16.4	4.5

linear controller was used, the closed-loop response became unstable. The figure clearly shows that the fuzzy controller yields better results than linear control loops. Dynamically, the time response was quite satisfactory, not only because of the cutting force vs time pattern, but also the workpiece surface. The MRR was increased too.

The step responses of different hierarchical fuzzy controllers are depicted in Fig. 15. The results of applying a 9-rule rule base (see Table 1(a)) are shown in Fig. 15(a). There is no great difference in performance between the two compositional rules of inference we analyzed. The transient response is adequate, corroborating the robustness of fuzzy controllers. Cutting force behavior under a rule base of 49 rules was very similar. All error-based performance indices and peak times were lower than the figures obtained for 9 rules, while the overshoots were higher. The performance index figures are summarized in Table 2.

7. Final Comments

Rather than drawing conclusions, we would like to make some final comments to underline certain aspects of this work that could be interesting. In this paper, we introduce the design and implementation of a knowledge-based system for process supervision and control and its application to the machining process. Fuzzy logic-based approaches (Fuzzy Logic Controllers and Fuzzy Models) are used effectively to deal with the lack of precise, reliable sensors, process complexity and time-varying processes. Furthermore, because the machining process still depends on available skill and operator knowledge despite computer numerical control capabilities, fuzzy logic-based strategies have proven to be a good choice.

From the theoretical standpoint, this work offers a survey of fuzzy logic control and modeling, explaining how a fuzzy model and a hierarchical fuzzy controller can be easily designed, implemented and obtained. The experimental results show the excellent behavior of fuzzy models and the advantages of a fuzzy controller over a linear controller. We can draw other important conclusions as well from the use of different rule bases and compositional rules of inference. There were no significant differences between the results of applying "Sup-Min" and "Sup-Product" compositional operators. On the other hand, a tradeoff among accuracy, transient response and time requirements for computing control actions must be considered when selecting rule bases of different sizes.

The illustrative examples, that were introduced in order to uphold the validity of the theoretical approaches examined along the paper, have been brought from the results attained by the authors. All work, from hypothesis to implementation and experimentation, including design and analysis, was done following classical patterns of intelligent automation: verbalization, the "black box" approach, and process knowledge engineering.

Although we never ignored the conceptual aspects, our focus at all times lay on the practical implementation of our work. We wanted (and fortunately also succeeded) to produce results that would work, not just under experimental conditions, but with enough universality to make the design viable for introduction in the machine tool sector of industry.

References

1. E. Aguero, C. Rodriguez, J. R. Alique and S. Ros, "Fuzzy model of cutting process on a milling machine", *Intelligent Systems Engineering* **3**, no. 4 (1994) 236–244.
2. J. S. Albus, "Outline for a theory of intelligence", *IEEE Transactions on System, Man and Cybernetics* **21**, no. 3 (1991) 473–508.
3. J. R. Alique, "Numerical control", Marcombo, Madrid, 1981 (in Spanish).
4. A. Alique and R. E. Haber *et al*, "A neural network-based model for the prediction of cutting force in milling process: A progress study on a real case", *Proceedings of 15th IEEE Intelligent Symposium on Intelligent Control* (2000) 121–125.
5. Y. Altintas, F. Sassani and F. Ordubadl, "Design and analysis of adaptive controllers for milling process", *Transaction of CSME* **14**, no. 1 (1990) 17–25.
6. Y. Altintas, "Prediction of cutting forces and tool breakage in milling from feed drive current measurements", *ASME Journal of Engineering Industry* **11** (1992) 386–392.
7. A. Angsana and K. M. Passino, "Distributed fuzzy control of flexible manufacturing systems", *IEEE Transaction on Control Systems Technology* **2**, no. 4 (1994) 423–435.
8. K. Åström and T. Hagglung, "PID Controllers: Theory, design and tuning", *Instrument Society of America*, 2nd ed. (1995) 298–304.
9. G. Babu and M. Murty, "Clustering with evolution strategies", *Pattern Recognition* **27**, no. 2 (1994) 321–329.
10. H. R. Berenji, Y.-Y. Chen, C.-C. Lee, J.-S Yang and S. Murugesan, "A hierarchical approach to designing approximate reasoning-based controllers for dynamic physical systems", *Uncertainty in Artificial Intelligence*, eds. P. P. Bonissone, M. Henrion, L. N. Canal and J. F. Lemmer, **6** (Elsevier, 1991) 331–343.
11. J. M. Bernardo and A. F. M. Smith *Bayesian Theory* (Wiley, New York, 1996).
12. J. C. Bezdek, "Cluster validity with fuzzy sets", *Journal of Cybernetics* **3**, no. 3 (1974) 58–73.
13. J. C. Bezdek, *A Convergence Theorem for the Fuzzy Isodata Clustering Algorithms, Fuzzy Model for Pattern Recognition*, eds. J. C. Bezdek and S. K. Pal (IEEE Press, New York, 1992) 130–137.
14. J. C. Bezdek, "A new review of probabilistic, fuzzy and neural models for pattern recognition", *Journal of Intelligent and Fuzzy Systems* **1**, no. 1 (1993) 1–25.
15. J. C. Bezdek and S. Pal, *Fuzzy Models for Pattern Recognition* (IEEE Press, New York, 1992).
16. C. M. Bishop, *Neural Networks for Pattern Recognition* (Oxford University Press, Oxford, UK, 1995).

17. T. Bohlin, "A case study of Grey box modeling", *Automatica* **30**, no. 2 (1994) 307–318.
18. P. P. Bonnisone *et al*, "Industrial applications of fuzzy logic at general electric", *Proceedings of IEEE* **83**, no. 3 (1995) 450–465
19. D. Braverman, "Learning filters for optimum pattern recognition", *IRE Transaction on Information Theory* **8** (1962) 280–285.
20. G. Byrne, D. Dornfeld, I. Inasaki, G. Ketteler, W. König and R. Teti, "Tool condition monitoring (TCM) — The status of research and industrial application", *Annals of the CIRP* **44**, no. 2 (1995) 541–567.
21. M. D. Santos, C. R. Peres, S. Ros, J. R. Alique and A. Alique, "End milling process stress monitoring by current sensor", *Canadian Society of Mechanical Engineering* (1996) 6–9.
22. R. X. Du, M. A. Elbestawi and S. Li, "Tool condition monitoring in turning using fuzzy sets theory", *International Journal of Machine Tools Manufacturing* **32**, no. 6 (1992) 781–796.
23. D. Dubois and H. Prade, *Fuzzy Sets and Systems: Theory and Applications* (Academic Press, 1980).
24. D. Dubois, "An application of fuzzy arithmetic to the optimization of industrial machining processes", *Mathematical Modeling* **9**, no. 6 (1987) 461–475.
25. R. O. Duda, P. E. Hart and D. G. Stork, *Pattern Classification*, 2nd ed. (Wiley, New York, 2001).
26. D. Filev, "Fuzzy modeling of complex systems", *International Journal of Approximate Reasoning* **4** (1991) 281–290.
27. F. Fujitec, "Flex-8800 series elevator group control system", Fujitec Co., Ltd., Osaka, Japan (1988).
28. P. P. Groumpos and C. D. Stylios, "Modelling supervisory control systems using fuzzy cognitive maps", *Chaos, Solitons and Fractals* **11**, no. 1 (2000) 329–336.
29. D. Guinea, L. J. Barrios, A. Ruiz and F. Betancourt, "Multisensor information integration", *Sensors Review* (July 1990) 133–136.
30. R. H. Haber, C. R. Peres, A. Alique, J. R. Alique and S. Ros, "Two approaches for a fuzzy supervisory control system of a vertical milling machine", *Sixth IFSA World Congress I* (1995) 397–401.
31. R. Haber, C. Peres, J. R. Alique and S. Ros, "Fuzzy supervisory control of end milling process", *Information Sciences* **89** (1996) 95–106.
32. R. E. Haber, R. Haber, C. R. Peres, A. Alique and S. Ros, "Optimal tuning of hierarchical fuzzy controller applied to vertical milling machine", *VII IFSA World Congress III* (1997) 354–360.
33. R. E. Haber and C. R. Peres, *et al*, "Towards intelligent machining: Hierarchical fuzzy control for end milling process", *IEEE Transactions on Control Systems Technology* **6**, no. 2 (1998) 188–199.
34. R. E. Haber and R. H. Haber *et al*, "Hierarchical fuzzy control of milling process with a self tuning algorithm", *Proceedings of the 15th IEEE Intelligent Symposium on Intelligent Control* (2000) 115–120.
35. R. E. Haber, R. H. Haber, C. R. Peres, A. Alique and S. Ros, "Model of the milling process on the basis of cutting force: A neural network approach", *Advances in Neural Networks and Applications*, ed. N. Mastorakis, Artificial Intelligence Series, (World Scientific and Engineering Society Press, 2001) 378–384.
36. M. M. Hanna, A. Buck and R. Smith, "Fuzzy Petri nets with neural networks to model products quality from a CNC-milling machining centre", *IEEE Transactions on Systems, Man and Cybernetics, (Systems and Humans)* Part A **26**, no. 5 (1996) 638–645.

37. M. H. Hassoun, *Fundamentals of Artificial Neural Networks* (MIT Press, Cambridge, MA, 1995).
38. K. Hayashi *et al*, "Neuro-fuzzy transmission control for automotive with variable loads", *IEEE Transaction on Control Systems Technology* **3**, no. 1 (1995) 49–53.
39. S. Haykin, *Neural Networks: A Comprehensive Foundation* 2nd edn. (IEEE Press, New York, March 1999).
40. K. Hirota and M. Sugeno, "Industrial applications of fuzzy technology in the world", *Advances in Fuzzy Systems Applications and Theory 2* (World Scientific, Singapore, 1995).
41. R. Isermann, "Process fault detection based modelling and estimation methods — A survey", *Automatica* **20**, no. 4 (1984) 387–404.
42. A. K. Jain, J. Mao and K. Moidin, "Artificial neural networks: A tutorial", *Computer* **29**, no. 3 (1996) 31–44.
43. J. S. Jang, "ANFIS: Adaptive-network-based fuzzy inference system", *IEEE Transaction on System, Man and Cybernetics* **23**, no. 3 (1993) 665–685.
44. J-.S. Jang, *Neuro-Fuzzy and Soft-Computing: A Computational Approach to Learning and Machine Intelligence* (Prentice Hall, 1996).
45. K. Jemielniak, "Commercial tool condition monitoring systems", *V International Conference on Monitoring and Automatic Supervision in Manufacturing*, Poland (August 20–21, 1998) 59–70.
46. C.-H. Jung and K.-C. Kwon, "A fuzzy controller with a real-time tuning algorithm and its application to a steam generator water level control", *Control and Cybernetics* **27**, no. 4 (1998) 545–564
47. K. Kaneda and H. Honma, "Fuzzy — AF video camera" (Cannon Videokid E08), *Journal of Japan Society of Fuzzy Theory and Systems* **3** (1991) 43–47.
48. A. Kaufmann and M. M. Gupta, *Introduction to Fuzzy Arithmetic: Theory and Applications* (Van Nostrand Reinhold, New York, 1985).
49. J. M. Keller, M. R. Gray and J. A. Givens, "A fuzzy *k*-nearest neighbor algorithm", *IEEE Transaction on System, Man and Cybernetics* **15**, no. 4 (1985) 580–585.
50. R. Kelly, R. H. Haber, R. E. Haber and F. Reyes, "Lyapunov stable control of robot manipulator: A fuzzy self-tuning procedure", *International Journal of Intelligent Automation and Soft Computing* **5**, no. 4 (1999) 313–326.
51. W. J. M. Kickert and H. R. Van Nauta Lemke, "Application of a fuzzy controller in a warm water plant", *Automatica* **12**, no. 4 (1976) 301–308.
52. T. Kim and P. Kim, "Adaptive cutting force control for a machining center by using indirect cutting force measurements", *International Journal of Machine Tools Manufacturing* **36**, no. 8 (1996) 925–937.
53. S. W. Kim, E. T. Kim and M. Park, "A new adaptive fuzzy controller using the parallel structure of fuzzy controller and its application", *Fuzzy Sets and Systems* **81** (1996) 205–226.
54. P. J. King and E. H. Mamdani, "The application of fuzzy control systems to industrial processes", *Automatica* **13** (1977) 235–242.
55. R. J. King, *Handbook of High Speed Machining Technology* (McGraw Hill, New York, 1985).
56. G. Klir and B. Yuan, *Fuzzy Sets and Fuzzy Logic: Theory and Applications* (Prentice Hall, 1995).
57. Y. Koren, "Control of machine tools", *Journal of Manufacturing Science and Engineering* **119** (1997) 749–755.
58. B. Kosko, *Neural Networks and Fuzzy Systems* (Prentice Hall, Englewood Cliffs, NJ, 1991).

59. B. Kosko, "Fuzzy systems as universal approximators", *IEEE Transactions on Computers* **43** (1994) 1329–1333
60. S.-Y. Kung, J. Taur and S.-H. Lin, "Synergistic modeling and applications of hierarchical fuzzy neural networks", *Proceedings of the IEEE* **87**, no. 9 (1999) 1550–1574.
61. W. A. Kwong, K. M. Passino, E. G. Laukonen and S. Yurkovich, "Expert supervision of fuzzy learning systems for fault tolerant aircraft control", *Proceedings of the IEEE* **83**, no. 3 (1995) 466–483.
62. E. G. Laukonen, K. M. Passino, V. Krishnaswami, G.-C. Luh and G. Rizzoni, "Fault detection and isolation for an experimental internal combustion engine via fuzzy identification", *IEEE Transactions on Control Systems Technology* **3**, no. 3 (1995) 347–355.
63. L. K. Lauderbaugh and A. G. Ulsoy, "Model reference adaptive force control in milling", *ASME Journal Engineering of Industry* **111** (1989) 13–21.
64. C. C. Lee, "Fuzzy logic in control systems: Fuzzy logic controller — Part I", *IEEE Transaction on System, Man and Cybernetics* **20**, no. 2 (1990) 404–418.
65. C. C. Lee, "Fuzzy logic in control systems: Fuzzy logic controller — Part II", *IEEE Transaction on Systems, Man and Cybernetics* **20**, no. 2 (1990) 419–435.
66. F. L. Lewis and K. Liu, "Towards a paradigm for fuzzy logic control", *Automatica* **32**, no. 2 (1995) 167–181.
67. Y. Li and C. Lau, "Development of fuzzy algorithms for servo systems", *IEEE Control System Magazine* **9**, no. 2 (1989) 65–72.
68. P. U. Lima and G. N. Saridis, "Intelligent controllers as hierarchical stochastic automata", *IEEE Transaction on Systems, Man and Cybernetics* **29**, no. 2 (1999) 151–163.
69. C. Lin, F.-L. Jeng, C.-S. Lee and R. Raghavan, "Hierarchical fuzzy logic water-level control in advanced boiling water reactors", *Nuclear Technology* **118**, no. 3 (1997) 254–263.
70. L.-C Lin and G.-Y. Lee, "Hierarchical fuzzy control for C-axis of CNC turning centers using genetic algorithms", *Journal of Intelligent and Robotic Systems: Theory and Applications* **25**, no. 3 (1999) 255–275.
71. D. A. Linkens and H. O. Nyongesa, "A hierarchical multivariable fuzzy controller for learning with genetic algorithms", *International Journal of Control* **63**, no. 5 (1996) 865–883.
72. L. Ljung, *System Identification: Theory for the User*, 2nd edn. (Prentice Hall, January 1999).
73. E. H. Mamdani and S. Assilian, "An experiment in linguistic synthesis with a fuzzy logic controller", *International Journal Man-machine Studies* **7**, no. 1 (1975) 1–13.
74. F. Matía, A. Jiménez, R. Galán and F. Sanz, "Fuzzy controllers: Lifting the linear-nonlinear frontier", *Fuzzy Sets and Systems* **52**, no. 2 (1992) 113–128.
75. F. Matía and A. Jiménez, "On optimal implementation of fuzzy controllers", *International Journal of Intelligent Control Systems* **1**, no. 3 (1996) 407–415.
76. L. Ming, Y. Xiaohong and Y. Shuzi, "Tool wear length estimation with a self-learning fuzzy inference algorithm in finish milling", *International Journal of Advanced Manufacturing Technology* **15**, no. 8 (1999) 537–545.
77. M. Mizumoto, "Note on the arithmetic rule by Zadeh for fuzzy conditional inference", *Cybernetic Systems* **12** (1981) 247–306.
78. K. Narendra, J. Balakrishnan and K. Ciliz, "Adaptation and learning using multiple models, switching and tuning, control systems magazine", **15**, no. 3 (1995) 37–51.
79. Y. Nemoto, "A plant supervision and control network", *Mitsubishi Electric Advance* **82** (1998) 10–12.

80. A. Ollero and A. J. García-Cerezo, "Direct digital control, auto-tuning and supervision using fuzzy logic", *Fuzzy Sets and Systems* **30** (1989) 135–153.
81. K. M. Passino and S. Yurkovich, *Fuzzy Control* (Addison Wesley, 1998) 391–405.
82. W. Pedrycz, "Identification in fuzzy systems", *IEEE Transaction on System, Man and Cybernetics* **14** (1984) 361–366.
83. C. R Peres, R. Haber, R. E. Haber, A. Alique and S. Ros, "Fuzzy model and hierarchical fuzzy control integration", *Computers in Industry* **39**, no. 3 (1999) 199–207.
84. M. L. Presti, R. Poluzzi and A. M. Zanaboni, "Synthesis of fuzzy controllers through neural networks", *Fuzzy Sets and Systems* **71** (1995) 47–70.
85. T. J. Prozcyk and E. H. Mamdani, "A linguistic self-organizing process controller", *Automatica* **15** (1979) 15–30.
86. G. V. Raju and J. Zhou, "Adaptive hierarchical fuzzy controller", *IEEE Transaction on System, Man and Cybernetics* **23**, no. 4 (1993) 973–980.
87. B. D. Ripley, *Pattern Recognition and Neural Networks* (Cambridge University Press, Cambridge, UK, 1996).
88. S. J. Rober and Y. C. Shin, "Control of cutting force for milling processes using an extended model reference adaptive control scheme", *Journal of Manufacturing Science and Engineering* **118** (1996) 339–347.
89. S. J. Rober, Y. C. Shin and O. D. I. Nwokah, "A digital robust controller for cutting force control in the end milling process", *Journal of Dynamic Systems, Measurement and Control, Transaction of the ASME* **119** (1997) 146–152.
90. C. Rodríguez, R. Haber, J. R. Alique and E. Agüero, "Modeling of machine-tool cutting process applying fuzzy logic and clustering analysis", *Proceedings of the II European Congress on Intelligent Techniques and Soft Computing, EUFIT'94*, Aachen Germany **II** (1994) 1071–1075.
91. E. H. Ruspini, "A new approach to clustering", *Information and Control* **15**, no. 1 (1969) 22–32.
92. E. Ruspini, "Numerical methods for clustering", *Information Science* **2** (1970) 319–350.
93. H. Schulz, Hochgeschwindigkeits-bearbeitung (High Speed Machining) (Carl Hansen Verlag Munchen Wien, Munich, 1999) (in German).
94. J. Schurmann, *Pattern Classification: A Unified View of Statistical and Neural Approaches* (Wiley, New York, 1996).
95. S. Shao, "Fuzzy self-organising controller and its application for dynamic processes", *Fuzzy Sets and Systems* **26** (1988) 151–164.
96. I. S. Shaw, W. Mors and J. D. Van Wyk, "Embedded fuzzy controller for a DC locomotive", *Transaction of IEE* (1996) 65–76.
97. I. S. Shaw, "New trends in control engineering", *III Brazilian Symposium of Intelligent Automation, UFES*, Vitoria, Brazil (3-5 September 1997) 1–17.
98. C. W. de Silva, "Considerations of hierarchical fuzzy control", *Theoretical Aspects of Fuzzy Control*, eds. H. T. Nguyen, M. Sugeno, R. Tong and R. R. Yager (Wiley, New York, 1995) 183–234.
99. B. Sohlberg, *Supervision and Control for Industrial Processes, Advances in Industrial Control* (Springer, Berlin, 1997).
100. J. Sjoberg, Q. Zhang, L. Ljung, A. Benveniste, B. Deylon, P. Glorennec, H. Hjalmarson and A. Juditsky, "Nonlinear black-box modeling in system identification: A unified overview", *Automatica* **31**, no. 12 (1995) 1725–1750.
101. M. Sugeno and T. Yasukawa, "A fuzzy logic based approach to qualitative modeling", *IEEE Transaction on Fuzzy Systems* **1**, no. 1 (1993) 7–31.

102. M. Sugeno and K. Murakami, "An experimental study on fuzzy parking control using a model car", *Industrial Applications of Fuzzy Control*, ed. M. Sugeno (Amsterdam, North Holland, 1985) 125–138.
103. T. Takagi and M. Sugeno, "Fuzzy identification of systems and its applications to modelling and control", *IEEE Transaction on System, Man and Cybernetics* **15**, no. 1 (1985) 116–132.
104. T. Tobi and T. Hanafusa, "A practical application of fuzzy control for an air-conditioning system", *International Journal of Approximate Reasoning* **5** (1991) 331–348.
105. R. M. Tong, *The Construction and Evaluation of Fuzzy Models, Advances in Fuzzy Set Theory and Applications* eds. M. M. Gupta, R. K. Ragade and R. R. Yager (North-Holland, 1979) 559–575.
106. S. Tzafestas and K. Watanabe, "Modern approaches to system sensor fault detection and diagnosis", *Journal A* **31**, no. 4 (1990) 42–57.
107. L.-X. Wang and J. M. Mendel, "Generating fuzzy rules by learning from examples", *IEEE Transaction on System, Man and Cybernetics* **22**, no. 6 (1992) 1414–1427.
108. P. P. Wang and C. Y. Tyan, "Fuzzy dynamic system and fuzzy linguistic controller classification", *Automatica* **30**, no. 11 (1994) 1769–1774.
109. B. Widrow and M. A. Lehr, "Adaptive neural networks and their applications", *International Journal of Intelligent Systems* **8** (1993) 453–508.
110. A. S. Willsky, "A survey of design methods for failure detection in dynamic systems", *Automatica* **12** (1976) 601–611.
111. R. R. Yager, "On a hierarchical structure for fuzzy modeling and control", *IEEE Transaction on Systems, Man and Cybernetics* **23**, no. 4 (1993) 1189–1197.
112. R. Yager and D. Filev, *Essentials of Fuzzy Modeling and Control* (John Wiley & Sons, New York, 1994) 313–354.
113. O. Yagishita, O. Itoh and M. Sugeno, "Application of fuzzy reasoning to the water purification process", *Industrial Applications of Fuzzy Control*, ed. M. Sugeno (Elsevier, 1985) 19–38.
114. S. Yasunobu and S. Miyamoto, "Automatic train operation system by predictive fuzzy control", *Industrial Applications of Fuzzy Control Editor*, ed. M. Sugeno (1985) 1–18.
115. L. A. Zadeh, "Fuzzy sets", *Information and Control* **8** (1965) 338–353.
116. L. A. Zadeh, "Fuzzy algorithm", *Information and Control* **12** (1968) 3–13.
117. L. A. Zadeh, "The concept of a linguistic variable and its application to approximate reasoning", Part 1, *Information Science* **8** (1975) 199–249.
118. L. A. Zadeh, "Outline of a new approach to the analysis complex systems and decision processes", *IEEE Transaction Systems, Man and Cybernetics* **3** (1973) 28–44.
119. L. A. Zadeh, "Fuzzy logic", *IEEE Computer* **4** (1988) 83–93.
120. H.-J. Zimmermann, *Fuzzy Sets Theory and Its Application*, 3rd edn. (Kluwer, Boston, 1996).

NEW PARADIGM FOR DEVELOPING EVOLUTIONARY SOFTWARE TO SUPPORT E-BUSINESS

ATHULA GINIGE

Head, School of Computing and Information Technology,
College of Science, Technology and Environment,
University of Western Sydney,
Locked Bag 1797, Penrith South DC NSW 1797, Australia
E-mail: a.ginige@uws.edu.au

In today's global economy for businesses to be competitive they need to support their business process with appropriate Information and Communication Technologies. Having realized this, few years' ago large organizations started implementing Enterprise Resource Planning (ERP) solutions. These solutions are very expensive and also need large teams to implement and train their users. This prevented small to medium size (Enterprises SME) adapting these solutions. Further the effectiveness of this big-bang approach has now become questionable.

We have been working with a large number of SMEs in Western Sydney Region assisting them to enhance their business processes by using information and communication technologies. Through this work we have established that e-Transformation is a process. It cannot be done as an one off project. When organizations undergo e-Transformation, the organization structure and business process need to evolve to make optimum use of new technologies available for storing, accessing and processing of information. Similarly software applications that facilitate storing, accessing and processing of information needs to evolve to meet the organizational needs.

Current software development paradigms require developer and user to arrive at an agreed set of specifications at the start of a software development project. Thus these development paradigms are not suitable if we have to develop software that has to evolve with the evolution of an organization.

After carrying out an in depth analysis of how organizations undergo E Transformation process based on the interaction among business processes, technology and people we have now developed a component based approach to developing software that can evolve with the organization. To support this paradigm shift now we are in the process of developing a set of web based tools.

Keywords: E-Transformation, Software Development Paradigms, Evolutionary Software, e-Business, Component based architecture, Business Process Re-engineering, Software Development Methodologies.

1. Introduction

The way we can store, access, process and share information has changed considerably in the last few years due to advances in information and communication technologies. This is having a major impact on businesses in terms of business strategies, how they market products, service their customers and the way they conduct their business processes.

Many large organizations are spending considerable amounts of money on IT to aid their business processes, in order to be competitive in the emerging global economy. Either they develop in-house solutions or purchase Enterprise Resource Planning (ERP) applications developed by a third party [1]. The aim of these packages is to integrate information-based processes within and across functional areas in an organization. The high cost of developing an in-house solution or buying a third party solution has limited this approach to very large enterprises. Further, in mid-1999, we saw articles such as "ERP R.I.P." [2], "E.R.P. Staying Out of Trouble" [3] appearing, indicating that the ERP market is reaching a saturation point.

In the last few years, we have been working with business organizations in the Western Sydney region of Australia assisting them to undergo a process of e-transformation. The Western Sydney region has over 72,000 business organizations. Over 80% of these are Small to Medium Enterprises (SME). These organizations do not have the financial strength of a large organization to make a large one-time commitment of funds to implement an ERP solution. Nor do they have the ability to release a group of people from their day-to-day activities to be trained in using the new IT solution and, in turn, train others. Further these organizations are not in a position to fully specify the software solution that they need to make their business processes more efficient and effective.

When developing software using traditional approaches, the very first step is to convert the user requirements into a complete specification. We put a lot of emphasis in getting this specification right. When we develop software using a traditional approach, we know that if we have to change the specifications at a later date it is going to be expensive. The business organizations are not static. They are evolving. Thus their need to store, access, share and process information is also changing. This is marking it hard for a business organization to fully specify the software requirement to integrate their information-based processes.

All this makes it impossible to successfully use traditional approaches to software development when developing e-Business applications for the SME sector.

2. E-Transformation

In order to assist these organizations to integrate information-based business processes, we had to develop a new approach to developing the underlying software. The first step was to understand the e-transformation process a typical bricks and mortar company will undergo. When working with these companies we found that the business processes they use can be divided into internal and external processes based on whether the people that use these processes are entirely within the organization or some are external to the organization such as customers and suppliers. We then developed a way of mapping the evolution of these processes when these become gradually IT enabled [4]. This mapping is shown in Fig. 1.

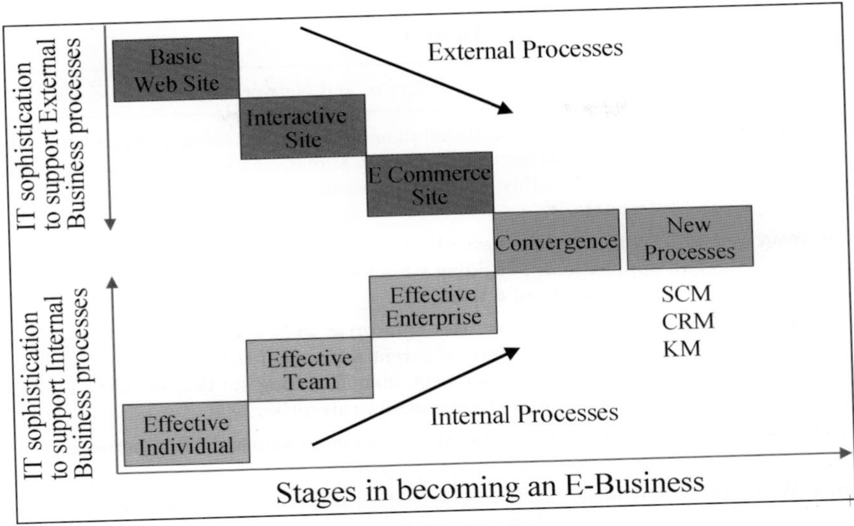

Fig. 1. Roadmap to become an e-Business.

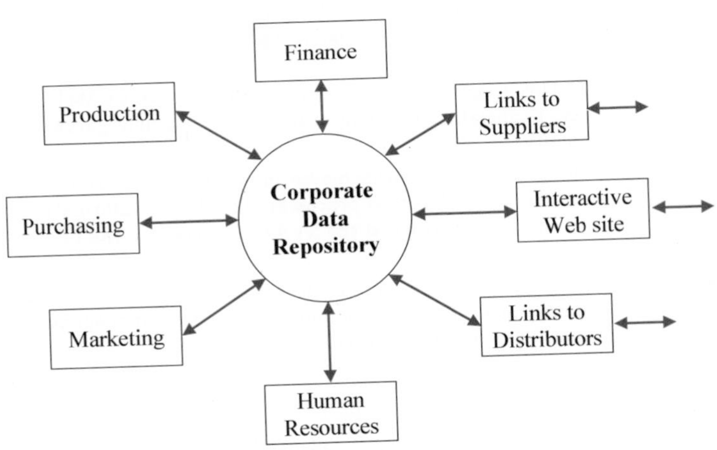

Fig. 2. Flow of information in an organization that has reached the convergence stage.

An important thing about this diagrammatic representation was that each stage in this diagram corresponds to having specific hardware, software and networking capabilities within the organization as shown in Table 1.

A very important milestone of the e-transformation process is the state of convergence. At this state, most of the information that is used by the organization is in digital form and is available for all appropriate people to use and process. To achieve this state, it is essential to have a very well thought out e-transformation process. Often what happens is organizations implement specific solutions using

Table 1.

Stage	Hardware, Software and Networking Infrastructure
Effective Individual	Individuals with stand-alone computers having productivity software such as accounting packages spreadsheets, word processors etc installed. Possibly dial-up connection to the Internet for individual e-mail accounts.
Effective Team	Computers are networked. People can work in teams using networked applications. Providing e-mail and Intranet capabilities can enhance the productivity of a team.
Effective Organization	Organization now uses enterprise wide applications — a single application that supports different sections of the organization such as purchasing, sales, accounting, manufacturing etc thus enabling information integration and sharing across enterprise.
Basic Web Site	Organization having its own domain name and "Brouherware" type web site hosted with an ISP.
Interactive Web Site	Organizations having web sites that provide two way flow of information. From these Web sites users should be able to get immediate responses to structured queries such as a quotation for a particular product configuration the user has selected. Also, another feature would be to provide personalised information to frequent visitors. These types of Web sites can be hosted with an ISP, although are better hosted on site. This requires a Web server and a high speed dedicated connection to the Internet.
E-Commerce Site	At this stage the organization should have secure Web servers to facilitate financial transactions or a link to a payment gateway to obtain this facility.
Convergence	Organization has now achieved integration of information that needs to support all its business processes. The flow of information of an organization that has reached the level of convergence can be viewed as shown in Fig. 2.
New Processes	Such organizations can now develop new processes, such as supply chain management (SCM), customer relationship management (CRM) and knowledge management (KM).

different applications and it becomes impossible to share data across these different applications. If data such as a list of employees and their details has to be duplicated, then it is not possible to achieve the state of convergence. When an organization has to keep multiple working copies of the same data it becomes very difficult, if not impossible, to keep all copies up to date and consistent.

We also have developed an overall framework that SMEs can use [4] for e-business transformation. This is shown in Fig. 3. E-Transformation is not a one-off activity; rather it is a continuous, evolutionary process. Each iteration would e-enable some part of its business processes. If this is to be successful, it is important to consider how to optimize the business process through Business Process Re-engineering and how to train the workforce through appropriate change management activities in addition to IT enabling the business process.

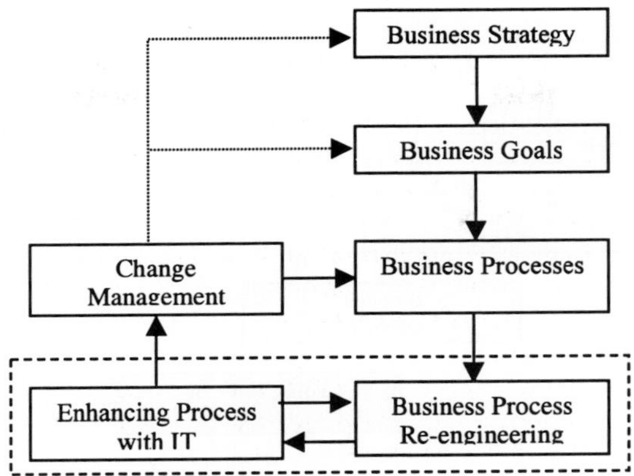

Fig. 3. A process for e-business transformation.

3. Current Software Development Paradigms

From the above discussion, it is clear that a business cannot transform into an e-Business in a single cycle. This transformation cannot be done as a project. It is a process that will happen over many years. When an organization undergoes an e-transformation, IT infrastructure becomes an integral part of that organization and it also needs to change and evolve with the organization.

It is useful to review some of the major software development paradigms to see whether these can be adapted to meet the above requirement — developing software for an evolving organization. Developing large software applications is a complex task. To successfully carry out this task, like any other complex task, we need to divide it into to manageable sub-tasks and arrange these sub-tasks along a time line paying attention to what needs to be completed before another sub-task can begin.

Still a widely used software development paradigm is the waterfall method first proposed by Royce in 1970 [7]. In the initial paradigm the task of developing a complex software application was divided into a set of sub-tasks consisting of Requirements Analysis, Design, Coding and Testing. These sub-tasks were arranged along a time line like water falling from top to the bottom without any feedback from lower phases to phases that were completed earlier. This paradigm helped many early developers to manage the complexity of their software development task.

Soon the developers found that when working on a detailed activity often it becomes necessary to change some design decisions that were taken in the previous phases. Thus there needs to be some feedback mechanism from lower level activities in the waterfall model to higher level activities. Further, depending on the complexity of the software application that needs to be developed the four basic development phases mentioned above can be expanded into few additional phases shown in Fig. 4.

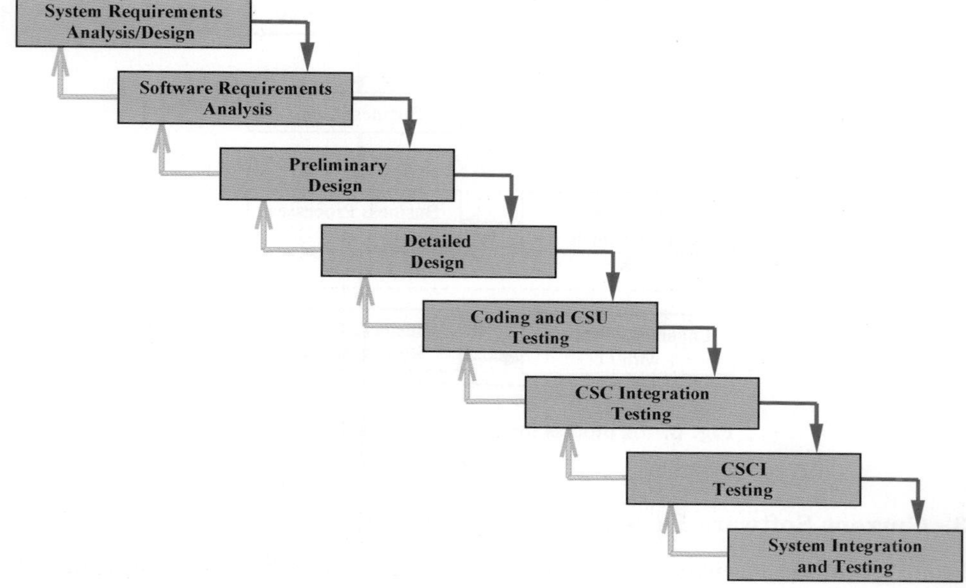

Fig. 4. Refined waterfall model with feedback.

The developers soon discovered further difficulties with this model when using to develop large complex software applications. This model requires capturing all of user requirements at the requirements analysis phases. Once the development process is into the design and implementation phases if there is a change in requirements or an omission while capturing requirements were detected, correcting this can be very expensive. The rule of thumb is if cost of making a correction or a change while at requirement analysis phase is 1 unit, then in the design phase, it will be 10 units, coding phase is 100 units and after deployment it is 1000 units.

Another major draw back of this development approach when using to develop large complex software applications is the long time lag from the start of the project until users see the product. In this model after user requirements have been captured there is very little interaction with the users until the software application is developed. Thus, any omissions in capturing user requirements or errors resulting in what user actually wants and what the developer thought user wants etc, will not get detected until the application is fully developed. As mentioned earlier, trying to correct these after software application has been developed can be very costly. Further, during the time it took to develop the software application the user requirements can change, making the software application that was developed unsuitable for the purpose.

To address these shortcomings in the Waterfall model, people started to come up with various other models. Among these a widely accepted approach was the "Spiral Model" that was proposed by Boehm [8]. This model allows the software

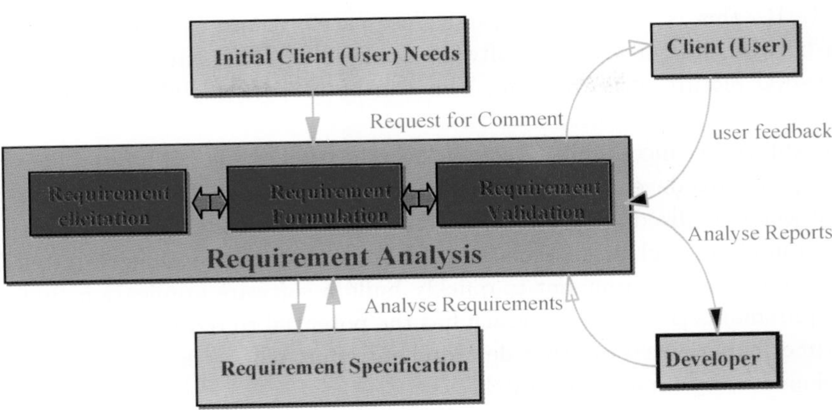

Fig. 5. Requirements analysis and specification phase.

applications to be developed in an incremental manner. It uses a cyclic approach to develop increasingly detailed elaborations of a software systems definition, culminating in incremental releases of the system's operational capability. As users can review each release of the application and provide feedback, this approach increases the user interaction with developers during the development phase, thus reduce the risks associated with the project. The original approach has now been further refined into a new model called "WinWin spiral model" [9].

An important aspect of these development approaches was the need to accurately capture user requirements, as this was one of the critical success factors in almost every project. Thus people developed fairly detailed approaches to capture and verify user requirements before proceeding to the design phase. One such approach is shown in Fig. 5.

As software applications grew in scope and complexity early, approaches to software development broke down. This lead to phenomena known as the "Software crisis" [16] with many applications failing to meet the user requirements or not being able to complete within time and budget.

Thus, with software applications becoming more and more complex, people were forced to develop better ways to conceptualize, design, and implement these applications. Next, we saw software applications being conceptualize as set of interacting objects. This formed the basis for the emergence of few different object oriented analysis and design approaches [10–12]. These approaches were later combined to create the Unified Modelling Language (UML) [13].

As mentioned earlier, one of the major challenges in developing a software application is that of building the right system — one that meets users' needs at a reasonable cost. This is made difficult because developers with their own jargon have to communicate with users, who have their own, more arcane jargon. How to achieve good communication, along with good understanding of the users world is a very challenging problem.

In UML, this is addressed through "use case". A use case is a typical interaction between a user and the software application. The sum of all use cases is the external picture of the system. This can be used to explain what the system does [14].

The ability to conceptualize a software application as a set of interacting objects also led people to develop component based approaches to develop these systems. Each object is realized as one or more reusable components. Idea here is to have standard modules such as an accounting package that can be plugged into a Component Execution Environment to quickly build a software application that meets user requirements [15]. This approach has the potential to reduce the long development times experienced in other development approaches where most of the code is developed every time from scratch.

4. Need for a New Paradigm for Software Development

One central theme in all of the above development approaches is the need to capture user requirements and develop an agreed set of specifications. In the Water fall model, people tried to do this up front. When it was realized that it is very difficult if not impossible to fully capture user requirements at the start of a development project, iterative approaches such as Spiral model were developed. Also it became necessary to improve the techniques used to capture user requirements. UML addressed this trough "use case". Today, when developing any large software application, considerable amount of time and resources are allocated to capturing user requirements by developers.

Now we need to develop software applications to support information flow within and external to evolving organizations. Because of the very nature of evolution, it is impossible for an organization to fully specify what type of functions and features are required in these applications now and in the future. Thus, any software development methodology that requires "developing an agreed set of specifications" up front is not suitable to develop the underlying software needed to integrate information-based processes within and across functional areas in a SME. We need a new software development paradigm and an application architecture that will enable software to evolve with the organization.

Armour, in his article "The case for a new business model: Is software a product or a medium?" argues that software can be viewed as a medium which can be used to store knowledge [5]. If we take this view then what we need is a software framework that can be set-up in an organization which is capable of capturing and storing the organization's knowledge and information and provide appropriate access to the relevant people. Such a framework should have the following main features.

- Should be able to add new functions and change existing functions while the system is operational. There should be no need to re-compile and install the software every time a change is made to an existing function or a new function is added.

- Should be able to add and change fields in databases or data structures in data repositories while system is operational.
- Should have a user management and authentication system. Liked to this there should be facilities to manage who have access to what functions and information in the system.
- Though technically not essential, we also found having a distributed data repository and functions on multiple servers improves the access efficiency and also the confidence among users.

In addition to the above-mentioned essential operational requirements, the system should also have tools to support the evolutionary process of the organization. Thus non-IT professionals (people who know the business processes best) should be able to create new functions or modify existing functions and to change data structure in data repositories to support evolving business process via a suitable interface such as visual programming interface. This type of tool built into a system will enable people that know about business processes to store their knowledge in terms of work flow, business logic and data elements into a framework in a quick and easy way. This business knowledge can then be used by others to carry out business processes in that organization.

The essential paradigm shift in this approach is rather than developing more and more sophisticated approaches to capture user requirements by IT professionals and then implementing the software system, user is empowered to specify what the user wants using a set of software tools. These should include various steps in a business process, business logic associated with each step, what information needs to flow among different steps, which users should have access to different steps etc. This specification is then converted into a necessary code. At the early stages, this conversion can be done by IT professionals, but gradually this needs to be automated. Once automated, the business user through few iterations can arrive at appropriate software application to support a business process. If there is a change to the business process the user should be able to modify the software application to reflect this change using the same set of software tools. This will form the basis to create evolutionary software applications.

5. Architecture and Technologies for Evolutionary Software Applications

Before we can implement a concept such as above, we need to have appropriate technologies to support the implementation of this concept. The Web provided us with client server architecture and a simple protocol — HTTP: Hypertext Transfer protocol, to manage the flow of information between a client (the Web browser) and a Web Server [17, 18]. The wide adaptation of this protocol made it into a standard now being managed by the World Wide Web consortium (www.w3c.org). Current Web servers can now extend the basic 2-tier architecture of the original World Wide Web to N tier architecture using CGI (Common Gateway Interface)

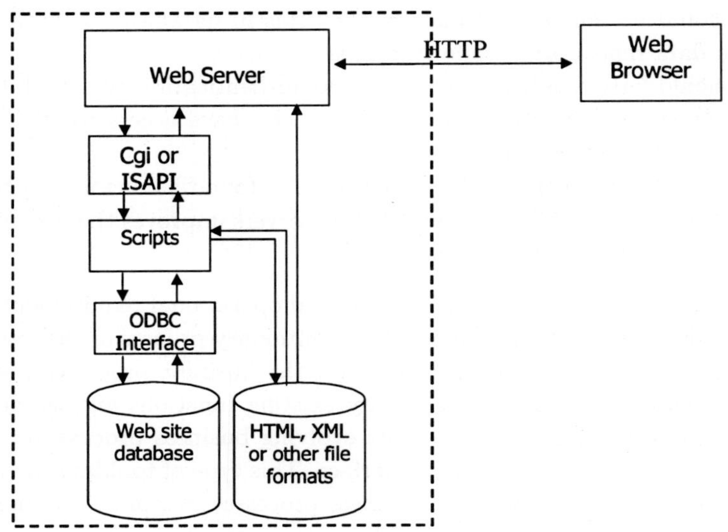

Fig. 6. Basic architecture of a 4 tier Web server.

Table 2. Means of fulfilling the requirements.

Requirement	Means of Fulfillment
Uniform look and feel across all the Web pages that can easily be changed	Creation of Web pages using templates
Consistency of information that may appear in different places or pages	Storing information in a single place (in a database or as an XML file) — without duplication of information in different places or databases — and retrieving the required information for presentation where and when needed.
Ease of information update and maintenance	Provision of a back-end system to edit information in a data repository. It could have Web interface for easy access from anywhere.
Ability to easily add new Web pages	Dynamic generation of navigational links, rather than predetermined static navigational links.
Ability to easily add new functions	Dynamic generation of program code and providing necessary links for authorized users to access the new function.
Decentralized system administration	Provision of a multi-user login system to access back-end systems and using a "user administration system" that can assign specific functions and data sets to content managers and other developers/administrators.
Mechanisms for quality control and assessing the relevance of information	Include metadata for Web pages. Also use a Web robot for gathering salient information, process the information gathered and take appropriate action(s) for ensuring quality or relevance of information presented.

or API (Application Programming Interface) facilities available in these servers as shown in Fig. 6.

When developing evolutionary software, we need to build into the original embryonic shell features such as the ability to update and maintain information contained in the application, ability to add new information pages (change the structure) and ability to add new functions users can perform. Table 2 summaries some of the important requirements when developing a software application that can evolve and how these requirements can be fulfilled.

6. C-BEADS: Component Based E-Application Deployment Shell

We have now developed a Web based embryonic shell to which various web based e-business applications can be plugged in. This we call C-BEADS: Component Based e-Application Deployment Shell.

Most of the inflexibility associated with current ERP solutions have been identified to monolithic architecture of these systems [1]. Component-based architecture is one way to overcome this problem. The idea of components has evolved from object-oriented systems modelling. Components hide their internal complexity, communicate through clearly defined interfaces, and are both configurable and extensible. One can plug in components to an appropriate framework to obtain different information processing functions.

The architecture that we selected for the framework was very similar to the architecture which Shaw [6] has classified as "Repository Architectural Pattern". According to Shaw, this architecture is suitable for applications in which central issue is establishing, augmenting and maintaining a complex body of information. Typically, the information must be manipulated in a wide variety of ways. Often long-term persistence may also be required.

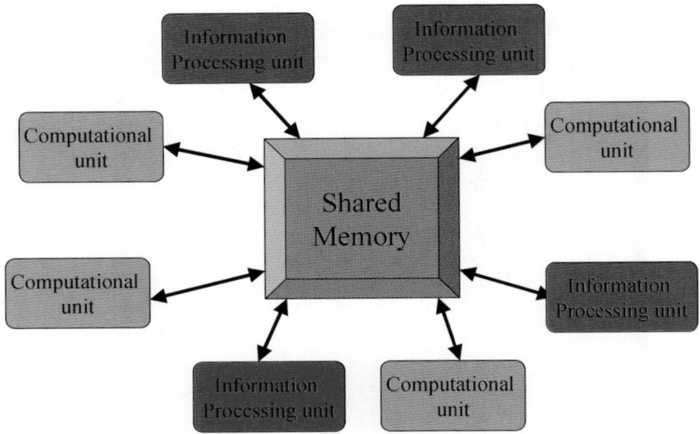

Fig. 7. The repository architectural pattern.

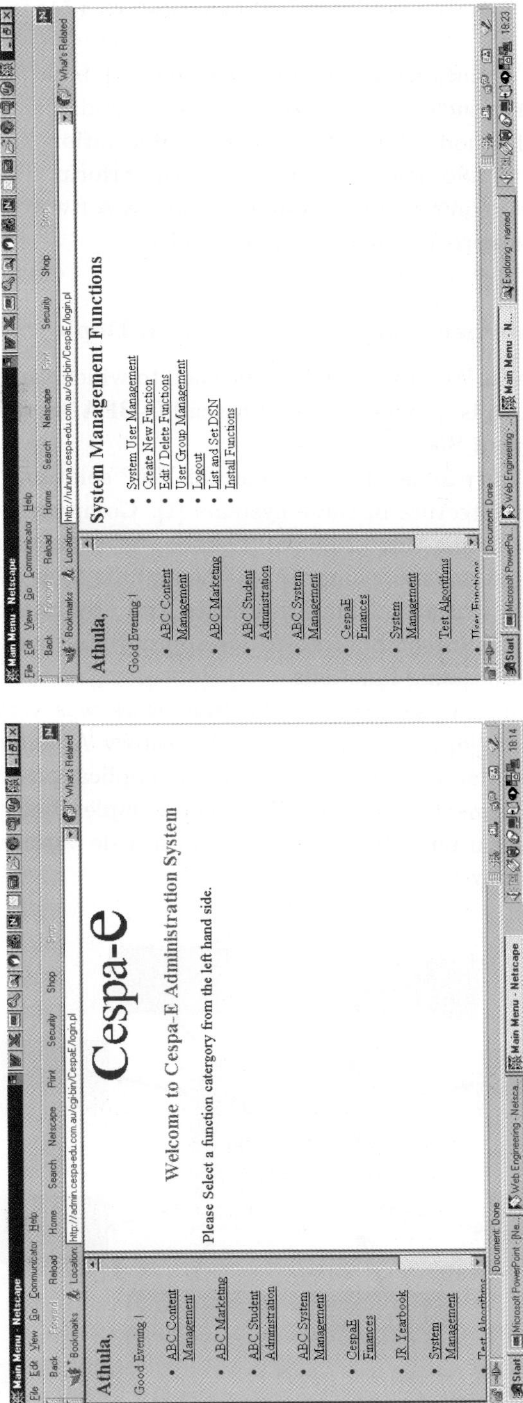

Fig. 8. Screen dumps of an application based on C-BEADS.

The components of this architectural pattern are single logical memory along with many processes to carry out computations or add, edit or delete information elements in the data repository. These processes interact with memory by direct data access or procedure calls as shown in Fig. 7.

When you compare this architecture with the flow of information in an organization that has reached the convergence stage as shown in Fig. 3, one can see this architecture pattern is ideally suited to support e-Business applications.

One very significant point to note in C-BEADS architecture is that there are some processes, which interact with data repository to change the structure of the data repository itself. This requires that all processes not to be reliant on a specific structure of the data repository, as it is essential for an organization to change what data it needs to capture and store as it evolves.

Figure 8 shows two screen dumps of an application based on C-BEADS.

How to mange user access to functions and data repositories is something that is well understood. The challenging aspect of C-BEADS is to provide the ability to add and change functions and data structures in data repositories while the system is in use. Within "System Management Functions" there is a function to create new functions. This is shown in the second screen dump. Using this function, an authorized user can create a new function template. In this version of C-BEADS, the detailed code related to business logic and information flow needs to be manually coded.

The current implementation supports the physical data repository to be distributed among multiple servers, but is treated as a single logical entity. There are user management functions to add and delete users and the ability to create user groups. The access to different business functions is assigned to users by making them members of various user groups.

Using this base architecture next, we are aiming to build various tools with appropriate visual interfaces for non-IT professionals to add and change functions and data structures to support the evolving business processes.

7. Conclusions

The next phase would be to develop tools to model the business processes using a visual programming language and automate the generation of code and necessary data elements in the repository. A survey of various approaches for business process modeling is being conducted at the moment.

As part of our research program to investigate how typical bricks and mortar SMEs can transform into e-Business we have established that these organizations have to gradually IT enable their internal and external business processes and reach a state of convergence. At the state of convergence all information that is important for its day-to-day operation and decision making is available in digital format. This information can be accessed and processed by all relevant people, internal and external to the organization and the organization has a proper information management framework in place. This requires a holistic approach to e-transformation rather than a piecemeal approach.

A successful e-transformation process not only deals with IT-enabling of business processes but also includes Business Process Re-engineering and Change Management. It is an iterative process that can take many years. As part of the e-transformation process it is necessary to develop software that can integrate information-based processes within and external to the organization. The required software cannot be developed using a project based software development approach as requirements are evolving with the organization and cannot be frozen at a given point in time.

We approached this problem by developing a software framework that is capable of capturing the corporate knowledge in terms of business processes and data required for day-to-day operations. This software framework is based on component architecture that will enable different functions to be plugged-in when required. It also has functions that allow users to make changes to the structure of the data repository.

We have established the technical feasibility of implementing this architecture. We believe this paradigm shift, which enables us to treat software as a medium to capture knowledge, will assist in successfully IT-enabling business processes used by SMEs.

References

1. K. Kumar and J. Hillegersberg, "ERP experience and evolution", *Communications of the ACM* **43**, no. 4 (April 2000).
2. "ERP R.I.P.", *The Economics* (June 26, 1999).
3. T. Stern, "ERP's fight for life", *www. informationweek.com* (April 12, 1999).
4. A. Ginige, S. Murugesan and P. Kazanis, "A road map for successfully transforming SMEs into e-Businesses", *Cutter IT Journal* **14**, no. 5 (May 2001).
5. P. G. Armour, "The case for a new business model: Is software a product or a medium", *Communications of the ACM* **43**, no. 8 (August 2000).
6. M. Shaw and D. Garlan, *Software Architecture — Perspective on an Emerging Discipline* (Prentice-Hall, 1996).
7. W. W. Royce, "Managing the development of large software systems: Concepts and techniques", *Proc.* WESCON, 1970.
8. B. Boehm, "A sprial model for software development and enhancement", *IEEE Computer* (May 1988).
9. B. Boehm and A. Egyed, *et al.*, "Using the Win Win sprial model: Case", *IEEE Computer* (July 1998).
10. G. Booch, *Object Oriented Analysis and Design with Applications* (Addison-Wesley, 1994).
11. I. Jacobson and M. Christerson, *et al.*, *Object Oriented Software Engineering: A Use Case Driven Approach* (Addison-Wesley 1992).
12. J. Rumbaugh and M. Blaha, *et al.*, *Object Oriented Modelling and Design* (Prentice Hall, 1991).
13. J. Rumbaugh, I. Jacobson and G. Booch, *The Unified Modelling Language Reference Manual* (Addison-Wesley, 1999).

14. M. Fowler and K. Scott, *UML Distilled* (Addison-Wesley, 1997).
15. P. Allen, *Realizing e-Business with Components* (Addison-Wesley, 2001).
16. W. Gibbs, "Software's chronic crisis", *Scientific American* **271**, no. 3 (1994).
17. S. Murugesan and Y. Deshpande (eds.), *Web Engineering*, Lecture Notes in Computer Science — Hot Topics, *Lecture Notes in Computer Science 2016*, Springer-Verlag, Heidelberg, Germany (2001), *http://www.springer.de/comp/lncs/hottopic.html*
18. WebE (Web Engineering) Home, *http://aeims.uws.edu.au/WebEhome/*

A SURVEY OF SYSTEM-LEVEL DESIGN NOTATIONS FOR EMBEDDED SYSTEMS

J. L. DÍAZ-HERRERA

School of Computing and Software Engineering,
Southern Polytechnic State University,
1100 South Marietta Parkway, Marietta, GA 30060-2896
E-mail: jdiaz@spsu.edu

There are many specific languages in use today for various aspects of embedded systems specification, design, and synthesis. The move to a single system-level notation to address the multiple-paradigm, multiple-analyses problem of embedded systems design is discussed. We survey efforts currently underway to deal with the need to reduce the semantic gap between system-level specifications and IP (Intellectual Property) implementation decisions; we specifically describe in detail the languages SpecC, SDL, SystemC, and Rosetta. We also present proposed extensions to UML that implement isomorphic mappings to some of these system-level notations.

Keywords: Embedded systems specification languages, system-level notations, SpecC, SystemC, SDL, Rosetta, UML extensions.

1. Introduction

Plummeting hardware costs are leading to rapid growth in new application areas, and especially in the embedded systems arena. The embedded system market, and more specifically systems-on-a-chip (SoC), is expected to reach more than $26.5 billion in 2003 [1]. Due to this greatly increased demand, there is an ever more important need for effective implementation in hardware and software to drastically reduce time to market. The implementation must also meet the requirements and constraints efficiently to lower cost. Hence, the right architectural choices must be made at the outset, as early in the design process as possible.

Embedded system applications range from small scale devices such as smart phones, personal digital assistants (PDAs), set-top boxes, to large enterprise servers and network computers, radar systems, automotive, avionics, etc. These systems are characterized by some unique factors. They are in close contact with their environment; they must meet stringent requirements of time, power and weight constraints; and they are expected to have higher levels of dependability (this includes attributes such as reliability, robustness, fault-tolerance, availability, etc). In today's post-PC era, embedded systems are increasingly more software-driven, as more and more of the functionality is placed in software. Ideally, this functionality should be portable over a variety of platforms such as PDA, PCS phone, PCs, telecom switches, automotive devices, home networks, etc. But, since these applications are highly device dependent, they require that routine functionality be custom-written, often repeatedly from scratch, each time a new system is built for the hardware being controlled.

Designing embedded electronics products involves a diversity of creative professionals including systems, hardware, and software engineers involved in conceptualization, creation, implementation, testing, and manufacturing of the product. This process requires many steps and iterations as explained below; historically, each of these steps has had its own specialized notations and tools.

More recently, we are witnessing a strong movement to create "new" *system-level design notations addressing both structural and behavioral specification of both hardware and software components, and their intercommunication mechanisms verifiable early in the design process* [2]. It is likely that one or more of these notations will make a major impact on the embedded systems market. It would be therefore important for software engineers in particular, since a lot of the system functionality is being placed on software, to be familiar with these languages.

The purpose of this chapter is thus to present a survey of system-level design notations. In Sec. 2, we briefly present background aspects of the design problem. We then, in Sec. 3, provide a summary of each of the principal system-level notations being put forward today to address many of these issues. These are the groups working on SpecC [3, 4], SDL [5], SystemC [6], and Rosetta [7]. We conclude with a comparative summary and a brief discussion on ongoing research proposing extensions to UML [8] to cater for embedded systems requirements as described by these notations.

2. Embedded Systems Specification and Design

A simplified view of the embedded systems development process is shown in the flow chart on Fig. 1. In this figure, we highlight the major steps in going from a set of needs to a product/solution that involves both computer hardware and software. The first three steps are part of systems engineering, an area that deals with high-level structures — such as the overall system architecture, and the tradeoffs of partitioning functionality into hardware or software. Co-design then follows, where hardware and software engineers are concerned with implementation details and the integration of hardware and software. These steps are usually performed in parallel.

Hardware development provides the computer system architecture and the physical devices. The hardware design has responsibilities for providing general-purpose processing and storage elements, and physical interfacing to the controlled system/environment. Software development includes application and system software. Thus, the "form factor" (area, power, weight, etc) depends on the hardware, whereas correct and timely functionality depend mostly on the embedded software. Dependability is a function of both hardware and software, and of their interaction. The Hw/Sw integration is a complex task, and includes operating systems, device drives, APIs and the software interfacing the hardware.

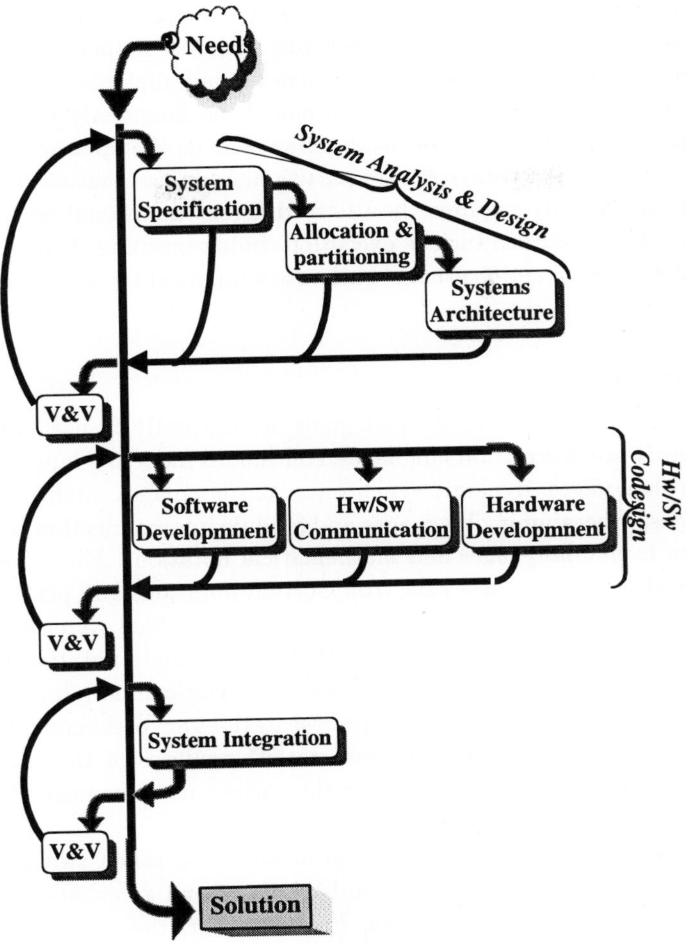

Fig. 1. Integrated embedded systems design process.

Real-time embedded software design is further constrained, as compared to conventional software, by the domain requirements for interaction with the physical world. Unlike other information processing systems, real-time embedded software, in most instances, must "embody" the laws of physics to control its environment and it is thus hampered by the complexities of the dynamics of the real world.

Developing embedded systems can be seen as a continuum of successive elaboration of models, representing different viewpoints at varying degrees of abstraction. There has been a proliferation of "specialized" modeling techniques to tackle the complexity of embedded systems design and development. A fundamental problem facing embedded system design is the *inability of representing ALL the design information in an appropriate "standard" modeling notation*, one that is suitable for analysis at various levels of abstraction and that can present the design from various view points. For example, system functionality is specified at the highest level of abstraction, without regard for behavior being implemented in hardware or software, and yet it needs to be subject to model checking analyses to demonstrate certain important properties. The next refinement of the specification model includes decisions on hardware/software partitioning and allocation of architectural elements. This typically requires the use of different notational concepts. Successive refinements add details such as execution timing profiling (benchmarking) and communication timing and synthesis, each also supported by specific notations and tools.

2.1. *Design notations*

Many different notations with distinct goals are currently in use, ranging from a variety of hardware description languages, continuous modeling languages, protocol specification languages, dynamic synchronization languages, architecture description languages, programming languages and module interconnection languages, and a plethora of formal languages and mathematical notations. For a fairly complete list see [9], and for a good survey see [10]. Current notations and practices by themselves are not entirely satisfactory for all aspects of embedded systems development.

A major issue has been the selection of the appropriate notation that cover as many of these steps as possible and/or provide a semantic underlying "language" for all these models. Many aspects of these representations are orthogonal to each other, which makes it difficult to perform "integrated" analyses of the various models, especially since different tools supporting the various notations usually suffer from the lack of interoperability among them.

Previous attempts to address these problems have taken two avenues, a *co-simulation approach* based on a common backplane, and a *compositional approach* based on a single, "integrated" model. In the former, the various analysis tools corresponding to the different notations are cognizant of the semantics of an underlying common backplane (see Fig. 2(a)). The basis for the second, compositional approach is the translation of all different notations to a single "integrated" notation with its own analysis tool (see Fig. 2(b)). An important question is whether semantic analyses can be made from the unification or integration of these models.

There are two fundamental aspects to this problem, different views/levels of abstraction, and system level validation.

2.1.1. *Different views and levels of abstraction*

Components for both hardware and software blocks are typically specified from two viewpoints, namely structural (physical) and behavioral (logical). In addition, there are several levels of abstraction when specifying requirements for embedded systems; these go from the high-level system concept down to the register-transfer logic (RTL) level.

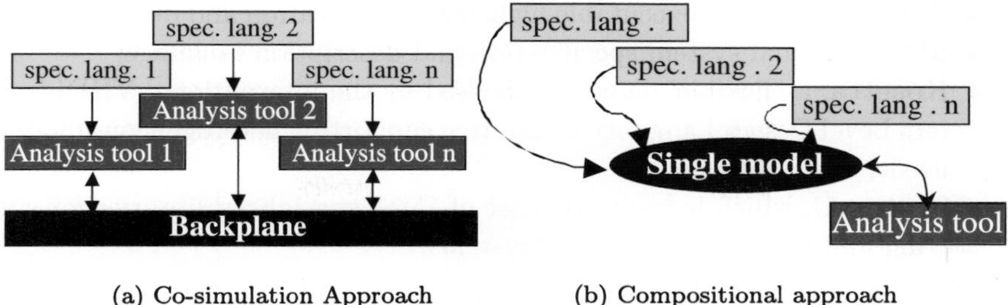

(a) Co-simulation Approach (b) Compositional approach

Fig. 2. Multiple-notation analysis approaches.

A critical aspect of any specification notation is the ability to define "truly reusable" components from specification to silicon with the understanding of their need for adaptation when reused. For this, we must be able to capture the component/system information in a consistent and "standard" form, in such a way that engineers other than the original designers can integrate components.

Specific modeling and design aspects include architectural design and optimization analysis; system test design and analysis; object (Hw/Sw) design and analysis; component (Hw/Sw) implementation and testing, etc.

2.1.2. *System-level validation*

The focus here is to develop an executable specification capable of expressing concurrency and other critical aspects in the system being described such as timely communication and synchronization.

Furthermore, components/systems must not be specified with design information tightly coupled, e.g. for a specific technology. Specifications must be "portable" and independent of specific simulators, capable of being verified in different environments (or chips). To aid in the validation and verification processes, specification languages must be either formal or executable (or both).

Specific issues that need addressing for system-level validation include behavior of mixed signals computations (analog, digital, wireless), real-time related behavior, size, weight, area, and power (SWAP) constraints, hardware/software interfaces, system integration and co-simulation, etc.

3. System-level Notations

Currently, several competing efforts are underway to deal with the system-level design problem. The overall goal is to provide a broad-spectrum integrating notation, addressing the multiple-language, multiple-analyses problem of embedded systems design by combining levels of abstraction (vertical integration), and heterogeneous conceptual models (horizontal integration). In what follows we present a summary of each of the most prominent proposed system-level notations. We describe four system-level notations being subject of intense study lately. The notations are

- **SpecC**, a C-based executable high-level specification and design language;
- **SDL**, a formal system specification and description language;
- **Rosetta**, a "flexible" language devised by the international VHDL's System Level Design Language committee supporting heterogeneous modeling needs; and
- **SystemC**, which is basically a set of C++ specialized libraries for specifying and designing embedded systems.

The description of these notations will follow primarily a syntactic-based approach followed by a brief description of the notation's semantics in terms of its executable model. We describe each notation's basic concepts in terms of its facilities for

(1) *Architectural design and analysis* — the notation's principal features for describing behavior (functional or logical specification) and structure (physical specification).
(2) *System test design and analysis* — the notation's execution semantics; specification of synchronization, exception handling and timing constraints.
(3) *Component (Hw/Sw) design and analysis* — algorithmic specification; concurrency.
(4) *Component (Hw/Sw) implementation and testing* — the use of the notation in the design and implementation phases.
(5) *System-level validation* — includes aspects of the behavior of mixed signals; real-time related behavior; size, weight, area, and power (SWAP) constraints; hardware/software interfaces; and system integration and co-simulation.

These concepts collectively represent important aspects of embedded systems modeling and design specification, as well as of system-level validation presented in the previous section.

3.1. *SpecC*

The SpecC language evolved around 1997 from the integration of system-level concepts (from the more graphical notation known as SpecCharts [11]) with the C programming language. Consequently, SpecC is not an object-oriented language since many of the typical object-oriented features are not present such as inheritance, polymorphism, etc, although the notion of "behavioral types" is used, and it is meant to be more of the concept of abstract data types than classes.

3.1.1. *Architectural design and analysis: SpecC basic concepts*

Fundamentally, SpecC specifies a system through the concepts of *behaviors* that interact via *channels* through *ports* and *interfaces.* There is a clear separation between

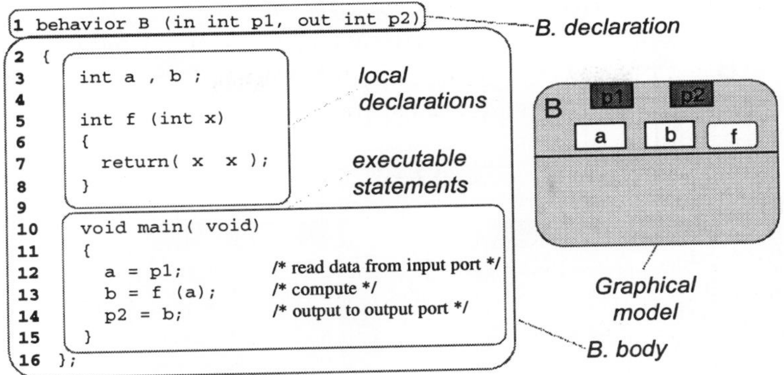

Fig. 3. Behavior structure in SpecC, in both text and graphical form.

computation and communication whereby behaviors model computation, and communication is modeled by using shared variables and/or channels. Specifications can be shown both graphically or textually (see Fig. 3).

A **behavior** declaration consists of an optional number of ports and interfaces. Through its ports, a behavior can communicate with other behaviors. A behavior's body consists of an optional set of behavior instantiations, local variables and methods, and a mandatory **main** method. All methods in a behavior are private, except the **main** method. The **main** method of a behavior is called whenever an instantiated behavior is executed. The completion of the **main** method determines the completion of the execution of the corresponding behavior.

The concept of **Interfaces** is also critical in SpecC. Interfaces are used to connect behaviors with channels in a way that both, behaviors and channels are easily interchangeable with compatible counterparts ("plug-and-play"). An interface is like a "class" (or more like a type) that consists of a set of method declarations. A behavior with a port of interface type can call the communication methods declared in that interface. The channel or behavior that implements an interface supplies method implementations for the method declarations found in the interface. Thus, for each interface, multiple channels can provide an implementation of the declared communication methods.

A hierarchical network of interconnected behaviors describes the functionality of a system (see Fig. 4). Designs are specified in a hierarchical manner using top-down decomposition. A behavior is called a composite behavior if it contains instantiations of other behaviors. Otherwise, it is called a leaf behavior; leaf behaviors specify basic algorithms.

3.1.2. *System test design and analysis*

SpecC is an executable specification language. The system being specified is "simulated" under a model whose semantics have well defined timing and synchronization

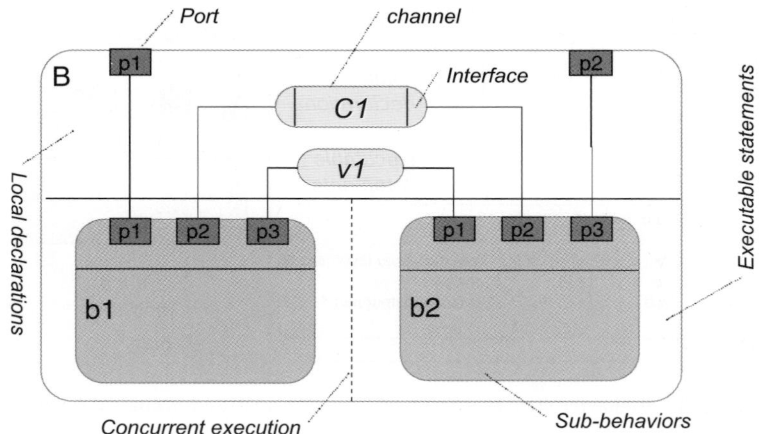

Fig. 4. Behaviors, channels, and shared variables connected via ports.

constructs, as well as facilities for handling asynchronous events (such as interrupts and exceptions). These are discussed next.

Every SpecC specification starts with the execution of the **main** method of the **Main** behavior. The latter is a composite behavior containing the test-bench for a design as well as the instantiation of the behavior(s) of the actual design specification. SpecC specifications are submitted to the various tools for compilation and subsequent execution (simulation).

In SpecC, the **time** type represents simulation time. This is an implementation dependent integral type used only with the **waitfor** statement and with the **do-timing** construct. The **waitfor** statement species delay of execution time. Whenever the simulator reaches such statement, the execution of the current behavior is suspended. As soon as the number of time units specified in the argument increases the simulation time, the execution of the current behavior resumes. The **do-timing** construct can be used to specify timing constraints in terms of ranges (minimum and maximum times). In the construct, the do block defines labeled statements which must be executed according to the constraints specified in the timing block.

There are three statements in SpecC to support synchronization between concurrent executing behaviors: **wait**, **notify** and **notifyone**. Each of these statements takes a list of *events* as its argument. The **wait** statement suspends the current behavior from execution until one of the specified events is notified by another behavior. The execution of the waiting behavior is then resumed. The **notify** statement triggers all specified events so that all behaviors waiting on one of those events can continue their execution. The **notifyone** statement acts similar as the **notify** statement but notifies exactly one behavior from all behaviors waiting on the specified events.

The **try-trap-interrupt** construct deals with two types of exception handling: abortion (or trap) and interrupt. With **try**, a behavior is made sensitive to the events listed with the trap and interrupt declarations. Whenever such an event occurs while executing the **try** behavior its execution is immediately suspended. For an **interrupt** event, the specified interrupt handler is executed and after its completion the execution of the **try** behavior is resumed. For a **trap** event, the suspended execution is aborted and the trap handler takes over the execution.

3.1.3. *Component (Hw/Sw) design and analysis: SpecC functional specification*

SpecC specification of functionality at the leaf behavior (object) level corresponds to the specification of algorithmic execution. A behavior's main method may contain specifications of sequential or and concurrent execution. **Sequential** execution of statements and behaviors is the same as in standard C. The sequential control flow can be programmed using the standard C constructs. See Fig. 5(a).

Concurrent execution of behaviors can be specified with the **par** statement. Every statement in the compound statement block following the **par** keyword forms a new thread of control and is executed in parallel. (See Fig. 5(b).) The execution of the **par** statement completes when each thread of control has finished its execution. Concurrent threads of control are not really executed in parallel; apparent concurrency is simulated as part of the simulation run-time system. **Pipelined** execution, specified by the **pipe** statement similarly to the **par** construct, is a special form of concurrent execution. All statements in the compound statement block after the **pipe** keyword form a new thread of control. They are executed in a pipelined fashion (in parallel but obey the specification order). The **pipe** statement never finishes through normal execution. In the example above (see Fig. 5(c)), the behaviors a, b and c form a pipeline of behaviors. In the first iteration, only "a" is executed. When "a" finishes execution, the second iteration starts, and behaviors "a" and "b" are executed in parallel. In the third iteration, after "a" and "b" have completed, "c" is executed in parallel with "a" and "b." This last iteration is repeated forever.

In order to support buffered communication in pipelines, the piped storage class is used for connecting pipeline stages. A piped storage variable can be thought of as

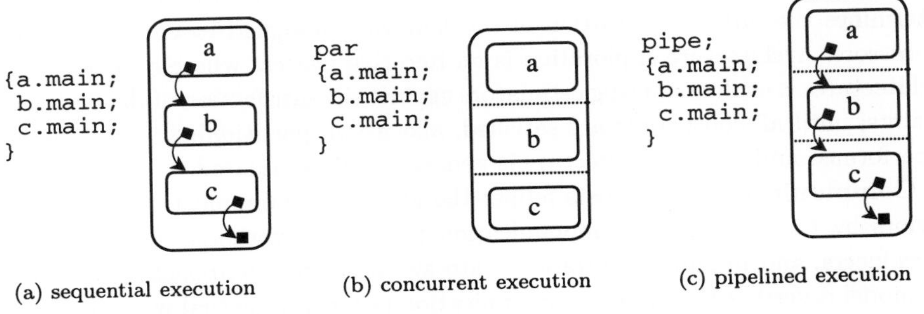

(a) sequential execution (b) concurrent execution (c) pipelined execution

Fig. 5. SpecC execution modes.

a variable with two storage places. Write access always writes to the first storage, read access reads from the second storage. The contents of the first storage are shifted to the second storage whenever a new iteration starts in the **pipe** statement.

Similarly, **Finite State Machine** (FSM) execution is a special form of sequential execution, one that allows explicit specification of state transitions. The **fsm** construct species a list of state transitions where the states are actually instantiated behaviors. A state transition is a triple {`current_state`, `condition`, `next_state`}. The `current_state` and the `next_state` take the form of labels and denote behavior instances. The `condition` is an expression that has to be evaluated as true for the transition to become valid.

The execution of a **fsm** construct starts with the execution of the first behavior that is listed in the transition list. Once the behavior has finished, its state transition determines the next behavior to be executed. The conditions of the transitions are evaluated in the order they are specified and as soon as one condition is true the specified next behavior is started. If none of the conditions is true the next behavior defaults to the next behavior listed (similar to a case statement without break). A break statement terminates the execution of the **fsm** construct.

3.1.4. *Component (Hw/Sw) implementation and testing*

The SpecC initial specification model describes the system functionality and constraints, without any reference to implementation details. SpecC currently supports the partitioning, allocation, and synthesis of behavior graphically only, with a manual identification of what goes into the hardware (as ASICs) and what goes into software (running on a general-purpose computer).

The synthesis flow is broken into two major activities: architecture exploration and communication synthesis. **Architecture exploration**, which through a series of well-defined steps gradually refines the specification into a selected target architecture, includes the steps of allocation, partitioning, and scheduling. *Allocation* determines the number and types of the system components, such as general-purpose or custom processors, memories, and busses. Next, *partitioning* distributes the behaviors that comprise the system functionality amongst the allocated processing elements, assigns variables to memories and channels to busses. *Scheduling* determines the order of execution of the behaviors assigned to either the various processors. Architecture exploration is an iterative process whereby several target architectures is evaluated using estimators against the satisfaction of the design constraints; until all constraints are satisfied, allocation, partitioning, and scheduling is performed and a new architecture is generated and evaluated.

Communication synthesis refines the abstract communications between behaviors by the insertion of communication protocols, synthesis of interfaces and transducers, and in-lining of protocols into synthesizable components. The resulting model describes the system communication in terms of actual wires and timing relationships as described by bus protocols. The result of the synthesis flow is handed off to the back-end tools which include compilers and a high-level synthesis tools. The software part consisting of C code and the hardware part of behavioral C (VHDL) code for high-level synthesis. After software compilation and hardware synthesis, a final implementation model is generated, representing a clock-cycle accurate description of the whole system ready for manufacturing.

3.1.5. *System-level validation in SpecC*

After each refinement step in the synthesis flow, the corresponding SpecC graphical model is updated with the design decisions made. This results in the possibility, in the validation flow that is orthogonal to the synthesis flow, to perform simulation, analysis, and estimation. For example, the design model is statically analyzed to estimate certain quality metrics such as performance, cost, and power consumption. The results are back annotated into the model for simulation and further synthesis.

The simulation provides data for validation of design correctness in terms of functionality, performance, and other constraints; this can continuously be done during the various design stages. For example, at the specification stage, the simulation can verify the functional correctness, whereas after architecture exploration, the simulation model will verify the performance of behaviors on different processing elements (PEs). After communication synthesis we can verify the communication and synchronization between processing elements.

3.1.6. *SpecC future developments*

Several Japanese and some US and European system companies (more than 30 at the time of writing) have joined the SpecC high-level description language consortium [12]. Toshiba proposed SpecC as a standard open language in 2000, and conversations are underway to find ways to link the effort to other very similar C-based languages, such as SystemC (see below). Proponents claim that SpecC is at a higher level for describing embedded systems.

3.2. *SDL*

The Specification and Description Language (SDL), originally devised in 1968 for telecommunications products to handle control switching systems, in conjunction with the accompanying Message Sequence Chart (MSC) [13], allow the specification to implementation of discrete, reactive real-time systems. The first, small, SDL ITU (International Telecommunication Union) standard was produced in 1976, and it has been updated every four years. All ITU standards (called Recommendations — they recommend norms to national bodies) are the result of collaborative work.

The current standard, SDL-2000, simply SDL from now on, has support for object modeling and implementation. The standard for SDL is Z.100, which gives a definition of SDL in a precise and concise way, and therefore is a language reference manual. The Z.109 document defines SDL as a UML profile giving the mapping of UML concepts (see Sec. 4.1), whereas Z.120 is similar to Z.100, but for MSC.

3.2.1. *Architectural design and analysis*: *SDL basic concepts*

SDL-2000 incorporates the object-oriented notions of packages, classes, inheritance, associations, etc. all based on UML. It also incorporates typical embedded systems concepts such as channels, interfaces, and signals, and introduces the concept of agents (active system components). Although graphical presentation is one of the key features of SDL, there is also a Textual representation known as SDL/PR — Phrase Representation. The accompanying MSC notation is basically equivalent to UML's sequence diagrams.

SDL provides structuring concepts that facilitate the specification of large and complex systems. These constructs allow the breaking of the system specification down into manageable units that may be handled and understood independently. Decomposition may be performed in a number of steps resulting in a hierarchical structure of units defining the system at different levels.

The most fundamental concepts of SDL are those of a *system*, *block*, *process*, and *services*. **Block** agents provide structure. A **system** is the outermost block. A system diagram comprises, among other entities, a set of blocks and channels. Blocks are connected with each other and with the (system) environment by channels. *Channels* are unidirectional/bidirectional communication devices. Figure 6(a) illustrates the tope level description (system diagram) and a block description. A block can be refined into either a set of processes or a set of (sub)blocks.

Processes specify leaf behaviors of a block — unless the process itself is decomposed into services. See Fig. 6(b) for an example of a process diagram. *Signal routes* allow the intercommunication between processes or between a process and its block interface (boundary). **Services** have their behavior specified as state machines. State machines provide a unified model that allows mixing on one diagram the concepts for blocks, processes, and services.

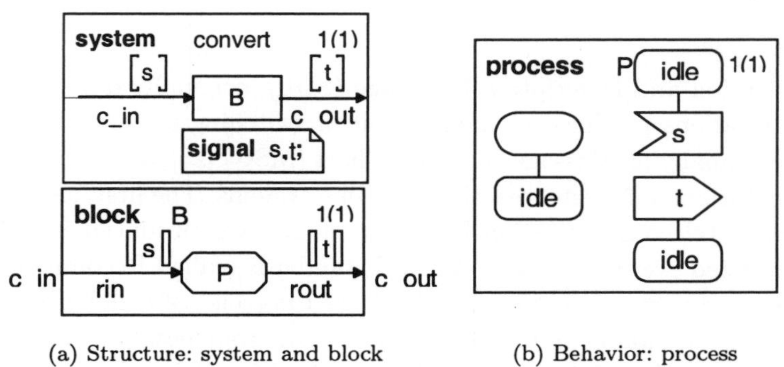

(a) Structure: system and block (b) Behavior: process

Fig. 6. SDL fundamental specification elements.

A complete system is structured as a tree of referenced diagrams with the system diagram as the root. The processes and communication paths provide interfaces to/from the processes. Variables defined in a block (or system) are contained within the block's (or system's) process agent, which is implicit if one is not defined explicitly. This means that agents within a system are blocks and processes that are interpreted concurrently with each other and with the possible state machine of the system.

Systems, blocks, and processes can be types and hence there could be several instances of the same entity. A type defines properties that instances of the type have, and that can be inherited by other types. There can also be aggregations of other types. Associations and inheritance can show the relationship between type symbols.

In order for a type definition to be used in different systems it has to be defined as part of a *package*. Definitions as parts of a package define types, signal lists, remote specifications, and synonyms. Definitions within a package are made visible to another scope unit by a package use clause (a concept borrowed from the Ada programming language[a]).

3.2.2. *System test design and analysis*

A SDL specification defines system behavior in a stimulus/response fashion, assuming that both stimuli and responses are discrete and carry information. In particular, a system specification is seen as the sequence of responses to any given sequence of stimuli. The system specification model is based on the concept of communicating extended finite state machines.

Systems specified in SDL behave according to the stimuli exchanged with the external world. This external world is called the *environment*. A complete SDL system is a set of communicating process agents. Several instances of the same agent set may exist at the same time and be interpreted asynchronously and in parallel or alternating with each other and with instances of other agent sets in the system. There is one or more agent instances in the environment, and therefore stimuli flowing from the environment towards the system have associated identities of these agent instances.

An SDL-specification has the combined semantics of the system agent (if one is given) with the packages. If no system agent is specified, the specification simply provides a set of definitions for use in other specifications. When the system is executed (simulated) there is one instance of the "system agent", and one or more instances of other agents (additional blocks and processes inside the system diagram). This is a dynamic structure since the number of instances can change during the execution of the system, as agents are created, and agents stop

[a]The Ada programming language has been used as a system-definition language; there are also hardware definition languages based on Ada. Due to space constraints, we do not discuss this further here.

themselves. Inter-process communication is based on point-to-point asynchronous message exchanges.

The definition of time in SDL is a little vague. It supports two concepts, that of directly accessing the time, and the use of timers (triggers). Two data types specify object to handle time, namely *time* (an instance in time) and *duration* (a period of time). The **now** construct returns the current time. A timer instance is an object, which can be active or inactive. When an inactive timer is set, a Time value is associated with the timer. Provided there is no reset or other setting of this timer before the system time reaches this Time value, a signal with the same name as the timer is put in the input port of the agent. A timer is active from the moment of setting up to the moment of consumption of the timer signal.

3.2.3. *Component (Hw/Sw) design and analysis: SDL functional specification*

Process agents, "autonomous reactive classes", represent all the behavior in SDL. Each process is a state machine. The simplest processes (with no data variables) are finite state machines. It is the data within process agents and passed by signals which provides the SDL system with its behavior. Data has no existence in SDL without process agents.

Communication in SDL takes place by *channels* between agents. However, channels can be given explicitly and are derived implicitly from the stimuli that agents handle and generate. Channels convey the stimuli passed between the agents of the system as signals (for example a remote procedure can be considered as an exchange of signals). A channel can be considered as one or two independent unidirectional paths between two agents or between an agent and its environment. A channel may also connect the state machine (composite state) of an agent with the environment and with contained agents. A channel definition represents a transportation path for signals (including the implicit signals implied by remote procedures and remote variables).

A *gate* is similar to a channel but it gives a connection point on an agent or agent-type and defines a set of stimuli that are handled, and the stimuli that are generated. Such definitions result in implicit channels.

A list of other features in SDL-2000 that support programming and integration with other approaches is:

- Interfaces, class symbols as references, and associations.
- Composite states.
- A unified agent concept for blocks, processes and services, that allows mixing on one diagram.
- New data model, including object data and direct support of ASN.1.
- Interfaces as PID sorts.

- Type based creation of processes. A system type definition is a top-level agent type definition. Also, someone familiar with data in a language such as C++ or Java should find data types in SDL-2000 easy to understand.
- Textual algorithms, allowing them to be placed concisely on SDL/PR diagrams and supporting a loop construct. Methods and operators are defined as algorithms.
- Nested packages; (ODL and CORBA support).
- Exceptions and exception handling — including timeouts on remote procedures.

3.2.4. *Component (Hw/Sw) implementation and testing*

The SDL + methodology focuses on the analysis and design phases, what they call draft design and formalization. There is no specific support for partitioning, allocation, and behavior and communication syntheses.

Furthermore, SDL is a specification technique, not a programming language, which abstracts away from implementation aspects. The standard does not specify details of how to implement the SDL semantics. More specifically, it does not specify how to implement the underlying communication between different SDL processes and the environment, nor concurrent process and time management.

3.2.5. *System-level validation in SDL*

SDL is also an executable specification language. Run-time synchronization and exception handling, time and timing behavior in SDL are discussed next.

The stimuli handled by an agent determine the interface that it offers. The stimuli generated by an agent determine the interface it requires. Every agent has an implicit interface with the same name as the agent covering each signal, remote procedure, remote variable, and any exception that it handles. An interface defines a set of stimuli handled by an agent. There can be different interfaces defining different subsets of all the stimuli handled by an agent. An interface can inherit properties from other interfaces. Typically, an interface offered by a block will inherit interfaces from agents within the block.

Concerning communication, SDL is based on the concept of Communicating Extended FSMs. Processes (CEFSM) communicate and cooperate by exchanging *signals* which may carry data (via parameters). Each process instance in an SDL system represents an independent asynchronous executing CEFSM. A process instance may start execution as soon as one of its trigger conditions holds, such as the expiration of a timeout, or certain state of a local variable. Transitions of a single process instance are executed sequentially. Triggers can be prioritized.

A system is separated from its environment by a system boundary and contains a set of agents. Communication between the system and the environment or between agents within the system can take place using signals, remote procedures, and remote variables. Within a system, these communication means are conveyed on explicit or implicit channels. The channels connect the contained agents to one another or to the system boundary.

An agent instance has a communicating extended finite state machine defined by its explicit or implicit state machine definition. Whenever the state machine is in a state, on input of a given signal, it will perform a certain sequence of actions, denoted as a transition. The completion of the transition results in the state machine of the agent instance waiting in another state, which is not necessarily different from the first one. Variable objects in other agents are accessed by an implicit exchange of signals between agents.

A signal instance is a flow of information between agents, and is an instantiation of a signal type defined by a signal definition. A signal instance can be sent by either the environment or an agent and is always directed to either an agent or the environment. A signal instance is created when an *Output-node* is interpreted and ceases to exist when an *Input-node* is interpreted. When a signal instance is sent, interpretation of the *Output-node* either implies that the signal is put directly in the input port of the destination agent, or that the signal is sent via a channel without delay. A remote procedure or remote variable on a channel is said to be outgoing from an importer and incoming to an exporter.

A remote procedure call by a requesting agent causes the requesting agent to wait until the server agent has interpreted the procedure. Signals sent to the requesting agent while it is waiting are saved. The server agent will interpret the requested procedure in the next state where save of the procedure is not specified, subject to the normal ordering of reception of signals.

A state represents a particular condition in which the state machine of an agent may consume a signal instance. If a signal instance is consumed, the associated transition is interpreted. A transition may also be interpreted as the result of a continuous signal or a spontaneous transition.

An exception instance transfers control to an exception handler. An exception instance is created implicitly by the underlying system or explicitly by a *Raise-node*; the exception instance ceases to exist if a Handle-node or Else-handle-node catches it. Creation of an exception instance breaks the normal flow of control within an agent, operation, or procedure. An unhandled exception propagates (dynamically) outwards to the caller and is treated as if it were created at the place of the invocation. A number of exception types are predefined within the package Predefined. It is also allowed for the specifier to create instances of these exception types explicitly.

3.2.6. *SDL future development*

"No major enhancements to SDL are planned for the future, and for the period 2000–2003 (at least) the ITU expert group have terms of reference to keep the language stable. Some studies are planned. The program in the short term has a revised formal definition of SDL, a revised CIF and methodology update by 2001.

There is an ongoing study of time and performance issues that could lead to changes to SDL, or some way of linking requirements such as time deadlines to SDL models. There needs to be a binding of MSC data to SDL, and there is a need to be able to define encoding of SDL data on interfaces".

3.3. *Rosetta*

The VHDL's international System Level Design Language committee, SLDL for short, is currently examining solutions and problems presented by a heterogeneous modeling language [14]. SLDL is a worldwide standards initiative that is actively developing an interoperable language environment for the specification and high-level design of microelectronics-based systems. SLDL is focused on addressing system-on-a-chip design constraints and behavior at architectural levels prior to HW-SW partitioning.

The Rosetta language under development "(named after the Rosetta stone, which contained text in three different alphabets and thus helped in understanding each one)" [15] proposes to raise the level of abstraction much higher than currently available RTL-based languages. Rosetta provides modeling support for different design domains using multiple-domain semantics and syntax appropriate for each. Each domain theory provides a semantic and representational framework for one or more design domains. Domain theories include data, computation, and communication models for describing systems *facets*. A facet is a model of a component or system that provides information specific to a domain of interest.

3.3.1. *Architectural design and analysis*: *SLDL basic concepts*

The basic unit of specification in Rosetta is termed a *facet*. Each facet defines a single aspect of a component or a system from a particular perspective. A facet is a parameterized construct used to encapsulate Rosetta definitions. Facets consist of four major parts: (i) a parameter list; (ii) a collection of declarations; (iii) a domain; and (iv) a collection of labeled terms. Facets form the basic semantic unit of any Rosetta specification and are used to define everything from basic unit specifications through components and systems, including system models, system components, architectures, libraries, and semantic domains.

Facets are defined using two mechanisms: (i) direct definition, and (ii) composition from other facets. Direct definition is achieved using a traditional syntax similar to a procedure in a conventional programming language or a theory in an algebraic specification language. The general formal for a facet definition is as follows:

```
facet <facet-label>(<parameters>) is
   <declarations>
begin <domain>
   < terms >
end <facet-label>;
```

Each facet defines a model. The interface defines means for customizing and communicating with the facet. The domain defines the modeling paradigm. Terms define facet properties using definitions from the domain. In the following example, the sort-req facet uses the state-based domain to define functional requirements for a simple sorting component. It defines sort requirements, precondition, postconditions, and invariants.

Facet sort-const defines sort power constraints. Finally, both sort-req and sort-const describe the facet *sort*.

```
facet sort-req(i::in sequence(T); o::out sequence(T)) is
begin state-based
  pre: true;
  post: permute(o',i) and ordered(o');
  inv: true;
end sort-req;

facet sort-const
  power::real;
begin constraints
  p1: power <= 5mW;
end sort-const

sort::facet = sort-req and sort-const
```

3.3.2. *System test design and analysis*

The modeling flow of Resetta is as follows: (1) Choose domains for component modeling, (2) Define component facets using domains, (3) Assemble facets into individual components, (4) Assemble components into systems using structural assembly techniques, and (5) Analyze components and systems using domain specific tools or domain integration tools.

Defining a set of facets and interactions between them specifies the functionality of a system/component.

3.3.3. *Component (Hw/Sw) design and analysis: SLDL functional specification*

Domains provide modeling abstractions for developing facets and components. For example, constraint modeling, discrete time modeling, continuous time modeling, finite state modeling and operational modeling are typical modeling domains.

A domain is a special purpose facet that defines a domain theory for facets. The syntax for a domain is defined as:

```
domain <name> (f::facet) is
  <declarations>;
```

```
begin <domain>
  <terms>
end <name>;
```

where <name> is the label naming the domain; <declarations> are items defined in the facet, <domain> is the domain facet extended by the new definition, and <terms> define that new domain facet. All domains are parameterized over a single facet variable that represents a placeholder for the facet including the domain theory.

As with facet definition, a domain definition extends the theory provided by its referenced domain. It is therefore possible to define a latticed of domains that inherit and specialize each other. The following figure shows one such specification lattice including pre-defined domain definitions.

The **state-based domain** provides a mechanism for specifying how a component or system changes state. It provides a basic type, S, for states and a state variable, s::S, which represents the current state. In addition, it provides a definition for next, a function that generates a new state from a given state. Thus, if s is the current state, then `next(s)` is the next state. The **finite-state** and **infinite-state domains** are simply extensions of the state-based domain where a set of possible states is known to be finite or infinite (and ordered), respectively. Using these domains is exactly the same as using the state-based domain with the additional restriction of assuring the existence of a state ordering and that next generates new states in order. The **discrete-time domain** is an extension of the infinite-state domain where the set of possible states is the set of natural numbers and the next state function is constrained to be the addition of a discrete value to the current state.

The **Continuous-time domain** provides a mechanism for defining temporal specifications using a maximally general notion of time specifications; continuous time specifications allow reference to any specific time. Time becomes real-valued. This differs from the discrete-time domain where time values were restricted to the natural numbers, a countable infinite set.

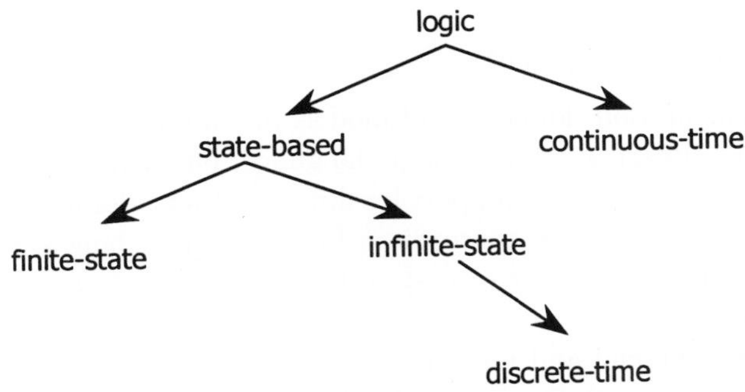

Fig. 7. SLDL pre-defined domains.

3.3.4. *Component (Hw/Sw) implementation and testing*

Rosetta similarly to SDL does not provide explicit support for the later design phases of partitioning, allocation, and synthesis.

3.3.5. *System-level validation in Rosetta*

In Rosetta, the time handling and timing behavior are expressed by selecting the right domain type for the facet. There are two kinds of domains where time values are used: discrete time domain and continuous time domain.

The discrete-time domain is a special case of the infinite-state domain where: (i) each state has an associated time value, and (ii) time values increased by a fixed amount. Specifically, in the discrete-time domain, time is a natural number denoted by t, and the discrete time quanta, denoted by delta, is a non-zero natural number.

The discrete-time domain is the workhorse of the state-based specification domain. It is exceptionally useful when defining digital systems of all types. Using certain expressions, it can provide a mechanism for constraining the value of variables in the next state and looking several discrete time units in the future, which are useful when defining delays in digital circuits.

Continuous time specifications provide a mechanism for defining temporal specifications using a maximally general notion of time. Unlike discrete time specifications, continuous time specifications allow reference to any specific time. Time becomes real-valued. The continuous-time facet provides a type T representing time that is real valued.

The function `next` is defined as `x'` for any variable `x`. The time derivative, or instantaneous change associated with `x` is defined as `deriv(x@t)` or simply `deriv(x)` by viewing x as a function of time. An nth order time derivative can be referenced by recursive application of `deriv`. For example, the second derivative is defined `deriv(deriv(x))`.

Combining these time values into a facet, one can specify a system's timing behavior and time handling.

3.3.6. *Rosetta future development*

Development of definition domains and models of computing and communication continues. SLDL's Rosetta is not a single language, but a variety of multi-faceted languages. It provides modeling support for different design domains using multiple-domain semantics and syntax appropriate for each, describing systems *facets.* A facet is a model of a component or system that provides information specific to a domain of interest.

A series of commercial and military examples will be prepared using Rosetta, culminating in a working SoC prepared by AverStar [16], the University of Kansas [17], and Texas Instruments.

3.4. *SystemC*

SystemC [18], a C++ modeling platform, was made available for free web download in September 1999, by leading EDA, IP, semiconductor, systems and embedded software companies, as part of an initiative known as the "Open SystemC Initiative" (OSCI) [19].

SystemC is not a new notation like SpecC, but a methodology backed by a collection of C++ class library to support embedded system design work [20]. More specifically, to specify, simulate and optimize system designs at higher levels of abstraction (including performance analysis as well as behavior correctness). It is also expected that SystemC will make it easier to create new and reuse old IP. The methodology and supporting environment will try to traverse the path to hardware/software implementations from high-level specification more efficiently.

The SystemC Class Library provides the necessary constructs to model system architecture including hardware timing, concurrency, and reactive behavior that are missing in standard C++. SystemC building blocks include multiple concurrent processes, communication mechanisms, and a rich variety of hardware data types. All the building blocks are C++ classes, and SystemC makes full use of the C++ language. SystemC consists of a set of header files describing the classes and a link library that contains the simulation kernel. Thus, any ANSI C++-compliant compiler can compile SystemC, together with the specification being developed. The SystemC library also contains the simulation kernel. The resulting executable specification serves as a simulator for the system described (similar to SpecC).

3.4.1. *Architectural design and analysis*: *SystemC basic concepts*

SystemC supports the description of the architecture of complex systems consisting of both hardware and software components.

Modules, a container class, are the basic building blocks in SystemC. This is a hierarchical entity used to define the system structure. A module can have other modules contained wherein. Modules have an exported interface. The SystemC macro SC_MODULE allows the declaration of modules. A module may contain other elements such as ports, logical signals, local data, processes, and constructors. These elements implement the functionality specified by the module.

Module ports allow modules to connect to other modules and to pass data to and from the processes of a module. SystemC supports single-direction and bi- directional ports. **Module Signals** represent communication "paths" between ports of lower level modules together. Signals represent physical wires and carry data, whereas ports determine the direction of data and implement a protocol. "Soft" signals support communication among software components. SystemC supports resolved and unresolved signals. Resolved signals can have more than one driver (a bus) while unresolved signals can have only one driver. SystemC supports a rich set of port and signal types for modeling at different levels of abstraction, from the functional to the RTL. **Communication protocols** define

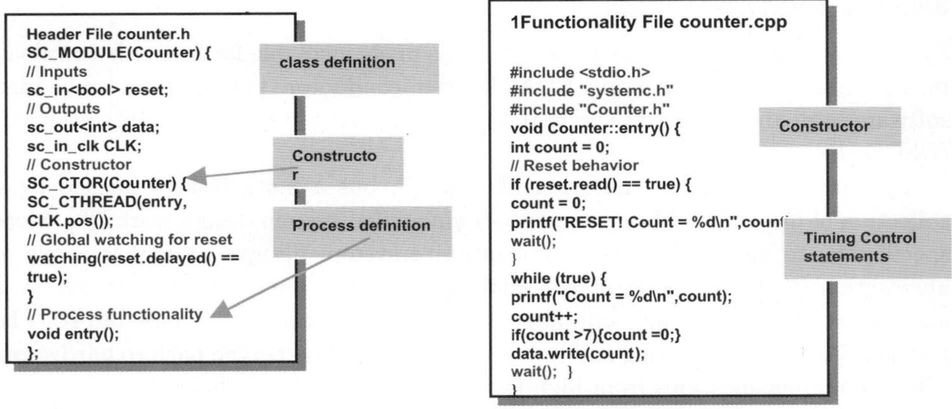

Fig. 8. Module declaration and instantiation.

the communication semantics of ports. This multi-level communication semantics enables the description of SoC and system I/O protocols with different levels of communication abstraction including data transaction, bus-cycle, and clock-cycle levels.

A **process** is the part of the module that actually implements behavior. Processes are like C++ methods and functions implementing specified functionality. Processes have the added semantics that they are registered with the SystemC kernel. SystemC provides different process abstractions to be used by hardware and software designers including method processes, thread processes, and clocked threaded processes. Signal value changes can cause events that are sent to processes.

The last module element is the **constructor**. As usual, the module constructor creates and initializes an instance of a module. Unlike the usual way to specify class constructors in C++, module constructors are specified by the macro SC_CTOR. The instance name of the module is passed as a parameter to the constructor. See Figure 8 for an illustration.

3.4.2. *Component (Hw/Sw) design and analysis: SystemC functional specification*

In SystemC, a complete system description consists of multiple concurrent processes. Using the SystemC library, a system can be specified at various levels of abstraction. At the highest level, only the functionality of the system may be modeled. For hardware implementation, models can be written either in a behavioral style or in a RTL style. The software part of a system can be naturally described as C or C++ algorithms.

Since SystemC is totally based on C++, it supports multiple design domain types at various abstraction levels, including arbitrary precision types. The fixed precision data types allow for fast simulation, the arbitrary precision types can be used for computations with large numbers, and the fixed-point data types can be used for DSP applications. SystemC supports both two-valued and four-valued data types. There are no size limitations for arbitrary precision SystemC types. There is also a corresponding set of overloaded operators and type conversion mechanisms.

The real work of the modules is performed in processes. Processes are functions that are identified to the SystemC kernel and called whenever these processes' signals are "sensitive to" change value. Processes have sensitivity lists, i.e., a list of signals that cause the process to be invoked whenever the value of a signal in this list change. Processes cause other processes to execute by assigning new values to signals in the sensitivity list of the other process.

A process contains a number of statements that implement the functionality of the process. These statements are executed sequentially until the end of the process occurs, or the process is suspended by one of the **wait** function calls. Some processes behave just like functions. Other processes are called only once at the beginning of the simulation; a process may be suspended waiting for a condition to be true. The condition can be a clock edge and/or a signal expression. Processes are not hierarchical, and no process can call another process directly.

Three types of SystemC processes are available, namely Methods, Threads, and Clocked Threads. A *method process* executes and returns control back to the simulation kernel. In the figure below, when input `xin` changes, method `extract_id` is invoked. Method `extract_id` will execute and assign a value to port `id`. When the method terminates, control is returned back to the SystemC scheduler. Method processes cannot be suspended or contain loops.

A *thread process* can be suspended and reactivated. It can contain **wait()** functions that suspend its execution until an event occurs on one of its signals

```
// rcv.h
#include "systemc.h"
#include "frame.h"

SC_MODULE(rcv) {
sc_in<frame_type> xin;
sc_out<int> id;
void extract_id();
SC_CTOR(rcv) {
SC_METHOD(extract_id);
sensitive(xin);}
};
```

```
// rcv.cc
#include "systemc.h"
#include "rcv.h"
#include "frame.h"

void rcv::extract_id() {
frame_type frame;
frame = xin;
if(frame.type == 1) {
id = frame.ida;
} else {
id = frame.idb;}
}
```

Fig. 9. Method execution.

from the process sensitive list. This event will reactivate the thread process from the statement the process was last suspended.

Clocked Thread Processes are a special case of a Thread Process, and are only triggered on one edge of one clock, which matches the way hardware is typically implemented with synthesis tools. Clocked threads can be used to create implicit state machines within design descriptions. An implicit state machine is one in which its states are not explicitly defined, but described as sets of statement with **wait()** calls between them.

3.4.3. *Component (Hw/Sw) implementation and testing*

The SystemC methodology starts with an initial model submitted to simulation whose results is feedback to the design model, and the cycle repeated. Eventually, once simulation results are satisfactory, the model is gradually refined adding necessary hardware and timing information to the system model and repeating the model-simulation cycle again.

SystemC follows the same direction than SpecC in separating communication from behavior, also with the ultimate goal of making it easier to embed an IP block into a SoC. Communication and behaviors are refined independently. New protocols can be added to a port or communication link without changing the interconnection between modules.

The SystemC design flow follows the traditional initial model, refinement, partitioning, implementation and testing, found in electronic systems design. The first two phases are part of the design exploration, and hence iterative. After partitioning hardware and software implementation follow in parallel. To explicitly support the design flow, SystemC define four model levels, each more refined and specific. The top-level model, at the *Untimed Functional (UTF) Level*, is an executable specification of the system functionality without defining its target architecture. The system is specified as functional modules (behavior) communicating over abstract channels. All modules execute in zero time during the simulation but in a defined order.

The first refinement of the initial model, at the *Timed Functional (TF) Level*, a run-time or duration is added to some functional modules. The next refinement, at the *Bus-Cycle Accurate (BCA) Level* processes are synchronized using a clock signal; thus transactions on a bus cycle are modeled accurately. Finally the last model refinement, at the *Cycle Accurate (CA) Level*, all behavior is clock-cycle accurate and synthesizable.

During the design exploration, performance modeling and analysis together with Hw/Sw partitioning are done at the functional level for simplicity and effectiveness. Hw modules are mapped to an implementation architecture, while Sw modules are mapped into tasks; inter-task communication and synchronization is implemented by the run-time software support system (typically a real-time operating system, RTOS).

3.4.4. *System-level validation in SystemC*

SystemC supports modeling at different levels of abstraction and top-down specification refinement. Interfaces between software and hardware and between hardware blocks can be easily described either at the Bos-cycle-accurate level or at the cycle-accurate level. Since SystemC specifications are actually C++ programs, these models can co-exist during system simulation. C/C++ and the SystemC classes can be used not only for the development of the system, but also for the testbench. Processes communicate with one another through signals, and explicit clocks can be used to order events and synchronize processes.

SystemC has the notion of clocks as special objects that generate timing signals. Clocks are the timekeepers of the system during simulation; they order events in time so that parallel events in hardware are properly modeled in the simulation. Multiple clocks, with arbitrary phase relationship, are supported. SystemC includes an ultra lightweight cycle-based simulation kernel that allows high-speed simulation. Typically clocks are created at the top level of the design in the testbench and passed down through the module hierarchy to the rest of the design. This allows areas of the design or the entire design to be synchronized by the same clock. SystemC also supports untimed models at different levels of abstraction, ranging from high level functional models to detailed clock cycle accurate RTL models. It supports iterative refinement of high level models into lower levels of abstraction, as described in the previous section.

SystemC provides mechanisms for modeling reactive behavior, waiting on clock edges, events, and signal transitions can synchronize processes. SystemC also supports watching for a certain event, regardless of the execution stage of the process (the most common example is the watching of a reset signal).

Another special feature of SystemC is the ability to **trace waveforms**. SystemC provides functions that help create a VCD (Value Change Dump), ASCII WIF (Waveform Intermediate Format), or ISDB (Integrated Signal Database) file that contains the values of variables and signals as they change during simulation. The SystemC kernel contains basic routines to dump waveforms to a file (VCD, WIF, and ISDB format), that can be viewed by typical waveform viewers. The waveforms defined in these files can be viewed using standard waveform viewers that support the VCD, WIF, or ISDB formats.

3.4.5. *SystemC future development*

SystemC is a C++ class library and a methodology that can be used to effectively create a cycle accurate model of software algorithms, hardware architecture, and interfaces of SoC (System On a Chip) and system level designs.

Early in 2000, there was a concerted approach between the two C-based camps, SpecC and SystemC, to at least consult with each other, if not an outright merger of the two efforts [21]. At the time of writing, SystemC seems to be gaining more acceptance and the momentum behind it seems undeniable [22, 23].

4. Summary and Conclusions

Systems on a Chip have become very large and complex made up of millions of lines of software, millions of transistors of digital hardware, tens of thousands of active analog components, and microwave and miniature mechanical components on a single silicon chip. Analysis by simulation is no longer feasible, and test-benches are expensive and time consuming. To address this complexity industry is focusing on higher-level notation and tools, whereby systems can be specified and verified at higher levels of functionality and tested by combining modular blocks (also known as intellectual property or IP cores). There is no question that the motivation to bridge the gap between system-level specification and design implementation is complexity.

In this chapter, we have surveyed four major efforts taking place today. **SpecC** is a new notation based on the C programming language. SpecC is a relatively small language, quite easy to learn. The power of SpecC is on its very high level constructs such as `par` and `pipe`, to specify concurrent execution, fsm for specifying finite state machines, and the notion of interchangeable interfaces. The corresponding graphical notation is also very useful.

SystemC is more focused on hardware design in C, by adding supporting C++ type class libraries. Several such libraries are becoming available, the problem now is that there is no general agreement on a standard form for these "extensions". The Open SystemC Initiative (OSCI) is in the process of forming an independent organization to look into the convergence of these proposed extensions. Furthermore, as we mentioned earlier, conversations are taking place between the OSCI and the SpecC high-level description language consortium for finding a way to link the two C-based efforts.

The original **SDL** is an international, mature standard in development since the late 60's. It also has an accompanying graphical notation. The current version SDL-2000 is actually a "new" language (a substantial number of new concepts and constructs were introduced), but one not based on any particular programming language; it is, however, much more complex than SpecC. It directly supports object-oriented concepts as defined by UML.

The **Rosetta** language is the result of the System Level Design Language (SLDL) project started by the EDA Industry Council, and whose members include major silicon vendors such as Intel, Motorola, and Texas Instruments. The goal of the project is to apply modern techniques of language design and formal methods to the complex SoC engineering problem. A preliminary design for a formal language that addresses these requirements (Rosetta) has been produced and is under evaluation by the EDA industry.

4.1. *Ongoing research*

Current work is focusing in four areas as follows: (1) refining and standardizing specification languages, (2) defining methodologies and support tools for the design

process, (3) looking at the use of purer object-oriented technology in terms of executable specification languages, specifically Java, and (4) modeling techniques and tools, e.g. UML. There is also a concomitant effort to standardize on at least a single set of concepts [24, 25].

An important question is which way industry is likely to go between adopting a language based on a more traditional and known notation like C, or defining a complete "new" technology [26]. Working against a C-based solution is the language's lack of high-level features for specifying concurrency and interprocess communication [27]. These are key issues for system modeling since these embedded systems are intrinsically parallel.

The VSIA [28, 29, 30] is "standardizing a definition for *interface-based design* at all levels of abstraction". At the system level this implies a common virtual component specification and unified taxonomy, and a well-defined separation of communication (external interface) and behavior (internal logic).

We are also witnessing attempts to use Java, or Java-based notations, for system level specification [31]. An interesting approach [32] presents two complementary views of objects, first as components (software or hardware) in a structural view, and second as connections between components which are themselves represented by methods in a behavioral view.

A number of UML extensions are being proposed to model real-time behavior; these include particularly Rose-RT [33], ARTiSAN [34], Rhapsody [35], and ObjectGeode [36]. In addition, there is a move to create isomorphic (and semantic homomorphisms) mappings between system-level notations and UML [37, 38].[b] Detailed reviews of these efforts are outside the scope of this chapter.

In terms of system-level notations, an isomorphic UML mapping has already been done for SDL [39]. The resulting specification was based for usage with Rational Rose-RT, which has the capability to execute the models and to generate automatically complete programs from such specifications.

Earlier in the Yamacraw project, we experienced with this idea and provided a UML mapping for a distributed, event-driven formalism, to show the viability of the approach [40]. We mapped ECho [41] to UML and made corresponding modifications of the Rational Rose-RT toolset to implement the mapping. ECho is an event delivery middleware system whose semantics and structure are similar to those of CORBA's event service specifications. We are currently working on a mapping of SpecC concepts into UML [42]; we have built a parser to go from the SpecC written notation to our UML mapping expressed in XMI [43]. Designers can thus specify models directly using SpecC modeling concepts depicted using UML formalisms and notations.

The overall idea is to be able to use a general modeling language, such as UML, and to define mappings to concepts from existing system-level notations supporting

[b] It is worth mentioning that UML itself is an attempt to unification of several orthogonal elements such as data (classes), behavior (states), and execution flow (actions).

various modeling techniques. This mapping works two ways, namely at the front-end analysts deal directly with UML models, and at the back-end designers are able to use their conventional analyses tools which are "seamlessly" connected via UML implementation technology such as XMI. This way, the semantic gap between system-level specifications and IP-level implementation decisions is reduced.

Acknowledgments

The author is grateful to his students of the embedded systems analysis and design class for their hard work, and specially to Ruhksana Alam, Hanmei Chen, and Hasrsha Padmanabha for their implementation efforts of some of the ideas presented.

References

1. S.-Y. Chiang, "Foundries and the dawn of an open IP era", *IEEE Computer* (April 2001) 43–46.
2. G. Moretti, "Get a handle on design languages" *EDN* (June 5, 2000) 60–72, *http://www.ednmag.com*
3. R. Dömer, J. Zhu and D. D. Gajski, *The SpecC Language Reference Manual*, Technical Report ICS-98-13, Department of Information and Computer Science, University of California, Irvine (March 1998).
4. D. Gajski *et al.*, *Spec C: Specification Language and Design Methodology* (Kluwer Academic Pub, 2000).
5. ITU-T Recommendations Z.100, Z.105, Z.107, Z.109 (11/99), *www.itu.ch* or *www.itu.int/itudoc/itu-t/approved/z/index.html*
6. SystemC Community, *http://www.systemc.org*
7. System Level Design Language Initiative, *http://www.inmet.com/SLDL/*
8. OMG Unified Modeling Language Specification, Version 1.3, 1st ed. (March 2000) *http://www.omg.org/*
9. V. Berman, *Candidate Systems Description Notations*, *http://www.inmet.com/SLDL/notations.html*
10. J. Mermet, "System on chip specification and design languages standardization", *Proceedings of Ada-Europe'99 Reliable Software Technologies*, eds. M. González-Harbour and J. A. de la Puente, *Lecture Notes in Computer Science 1622* (Springer-Verlag, 1999).
11. D. D. Gaski, F. Vahid, S. Narayan and J. Gong, *Specification and Design of Embedded Systems* (Prentice-Hall, 1994).
12. SpecC Consortium, *http://www.specc.org*
13. ITU-T Recommendations Z.120 (11/99), *www.itu.ch* or *www.itu.int/itudoc/itu-t/approved/z/index.html*
14. VHDL's International System Level Design Language Committee, *http://www.vsi.org/*
15. P. Alexander and D. Barton, "Rosetta provides support for system-level design", *EETimes.com*, (Special issues, 2000).
16. Titan System Corporation Avestar Group, *http://www.averstar.com/products/ SLDL.html*
17. Rosetta, *http://www.ittc.ukans.edu/Projects/rosetta/*

18. G. Arnout, "SystemC standard", *Asia and South Pacific Design Automation Conference* (2000) 573–577.
19. J. Gerlach and W. Rosenstiel, "System level design using the SystemC modeling platform", *http://www.systemc.org*
20. L. Semeria and A. Ghosh, "Methodology for hardware/software co-verification in C/C++", *Asia and South Pacific Design Automation Conference* (2000) 405–408.
21. A. Cataldo, "SpecC opens dialogue with SystemC camp", *Electronic Engineering Times* (March 27, 2000), *http://www.eetimes.com/*
22. R. Goering, "C level backs SystemC", *Electronic Engineering Times* (March 12, 2001) *http://www.eetimes.com/*
23. H.-J. Schlebusch, "SystemC based hardware synthesis becomes reality", *26th Euromicro Conference* **1** (2000) 434.
24. C. K. Lennard, P. Schaumont, G. de Jong, A. Haverinen and P. Hardee, "Standards for system-level design: Practical reality or solution in search of a question?", *Design, Automation and Test in Europe Conference* (2000) 576–583.
25. S. Y. Liao, "Towards a new standard for system-level design", *Eighth International Workshop on Hardware/Software Codesign* (2000) 2–6.
26. G. Prophet, "System-level design languages: to C or not to C?", *Electronic Design Notes* (October 14, 1999) 135–146, *http://www.ednmag.com*
27. L. Semeria and A. Ghosh, "Methodology for hardware/software co-verification in C/C++", *Asia and South Pacific Design Automation Conference* (2000) 405–408.
28. C. K. Lennard, "VSIA develops system-level modeling standards", *Electronic Engineering Times* (June 9, 2000), *http://www.eetimes.com*
29. System-Level Interface Behavioral Documentation Standard Version 1, *System-Level Design DWG (SLD 1 1.0)* — (Revision Date: March 24, 2000) *www.vsi.org*
30. VSIA System Level Design Model Taxonomy Document Version 1 (SLDTAX 1 1.0) *System Level Design DWG* (Released: January 1999).
31. J. Fleischmann, K. Buchenrieder and R. Kress, "Codesign of embedded systems based on Java and reconfigurable hardware components", *Design, Automation and Test in Europe Conference Proceedings* (1999) 768–769.
32. T. Kuhn, C. Schulz-Key and W. Rosenstiel, "Object oriented hardware specification with Java", *Workshop on Synthesis and System Integration of Mixed Technologies (SASIMI'2000)*, Kyoto, Japan (2000).
33. B. Selic and J. Rumbaugh, *Using UML for Modeling Complex Real-Time Systems* (ObjectTime Limited, 1998).
34. A. Moore and N. Cooling, *Real-Time Perspective — Overview* (Version 1.0), ARTiSAN Software (1998).
35. B. P. Douglass, *Doing Hard-Time: Developing Real-Time Systems with UML, Objects, Frameworks and Patterns* (Addison-Wesley Pub. Co., 1999).
36. P. LeBlanc and V. Encontre, *ObjectGeode: Method Guidelines* (Verilog SA, 1996).
37. S. Heyhoe, "UML, SDL ensure design compliance", *Electronic Engineering Times* (February 28, 2000) *http://www.eetimes.com*
38. R. Goering, "UML language eyes system-level design role", *Electronic Engineering Times* (September 29, 2000) *http://www.eetimes.com*
39. B. Selic and J. Raumbaugh, "Mapping SDL to UML", A Rational Software White Paper.
40. J. Sierra, "UML->ECho Mapping", MS Project Report, SPSU, Department of Computer Science (Spring 2000).
41. G. Eisenhauer, *The ECho Event Delivery System*, College of Computing, Georgia Institute of Technology (1999).

42. J. L. Díaz-Herrera, "An isomorphic mapping for SpecC in UML", Object-oriented Modeling of Embedded RT Systems, OMER-2, Germany (May 2001).
43. OMG XML Metadata Interchange (XMI) Specification, Version 1.0 (June 2000) *http://www.omg.org/*

AGENT-ORIENTED SOFTWARE CONSTRUCTION WITH UML

FEDERICO BERGENTI and AGOSTINO POGGI
Dipartimento di Ingegneria dell'Informazione,
Università degli Studi di Parma,
Parco Area delle Scienze 181A, 43100, Parma, Italy
E-mail: {bergenti,poggi}@ce.unipr.it

In the last years, an increasing number of computing systems are being realized by taking advantage of autonomous agents. Traditional software engineering methodologies are insufficient to be used in the development of such systems because of the particular characteristics of autonomous agents. Therefore, a lot of work has been done to extend traditional software engineering methodologies for agent systems and its result has been the definition of new methodologies of *agent-oriented software engineering*. This chapter introduces the basic concepts of agent-oriented software engineering showing the new artefacts that we introduced to analyze, design and implement multi-agent systems. In particular, we present a set of agent-oriented diagrams that support the modeling of: (i) the architecture of the multi-agent system, (ii) the ontology followed by agents and (iii) the interaction protocols used to coordinate agents. These artefacts are described, exploiting an UML-based notation that exploits stereotypes to provide agent-oriented semantics to class and collaboration diagrams.

Keywords: Software agents, agent-oriented software engineering, UML.

1. Introduction

The ever-increasing importance of the Web in everyday life is driving the need of software capable of coping with open and dynamic environments. More than other technologies, software agents seem to have the necessary characteristics to support the development of open and flexible software systems [22, 32, 44]. This is the reason why the research on agents and multi-agent systems has come to a new life in the recent years, leaving artificial intelligence laboratories to reach the realm of real-world software development. The creation of FIPA, the decision of OMG to raise the status of the Agent Working Group to special interest group and the agent-oriented software engineering workshop (AOSE) at ICSE are only indications of the importance that this technology is gaining. In particular, the creation of FIPA — the Foundation for Intelligent Physical Agents — in 1996 seems to be one of the major causes for the interest that nowadays industry is having for agent technologies. FIPA's mission is to promote "*technologies and interoperability specifications that facilitate the end-to-end inter-working of intelligent agent systems in modern commercial and industrial settings*" and its goal is "*to overcome the destructive competition between incoherent concurrent proprietary technologies in the marketplace*". Surprisingly, the community of agent technologies has not yet adopted an accepted definition for the word agent and many, and somehow opposite, definitions are available. In this paper, we do not take this debate into account and we restrict the agent abstraction only to express the characteristics that make agents ideal for the development of open and flexible software systems. This chapter introduces the fundamental concepts of agent-oriented software engineering taking the pragmatic approach of showing the new artefacts that the architect can exploit to model a system at the agent level of abstraction. The next section introduces software agents. Section 3 presents the main works on agent-oriented software engineering. Section 4 describes how UML diagrams can be used as basis for agent-oriented software engineering. Finally, Sec. 5 presents some conclusions.

2. Software Agents

We introduce our informal characterization of software agents emphasizing the features that we will exploit in the definition of the artefacts described in the following sections. The definition presented here is adapted from [44]: an agent is a software system that is (i) situated in some environment, (ii) capable of autonomous actions in order to meet its objectives and (iii) capable of communicating with other agents. This definition raises several points that should be discussed to show that agents can be naturally used in software engineering as a first-class abstraction. Such a discussion involves the unresolved debate on the differences between objects and agents, as it should be clear that they are somehow similar abstractions.

Agents are situated systems and the environment provides agents the essential information to work. This emphasizes that agents are intended to work with non-agentized entities and the importance of reification is weaken with respect to the object-oriented approach. In the object-oriented picture, everything must be reified, as objects are not intended to interact with the environment. Agents naturally interact with their environment and take advantage of this possibility to bring about their objectives.

The most important characteristic that we associate with agents is the ability to act in complete autonomy, i.e., agents have their own objectives and they are capable of acting to bring about them without any external coercion. This is sometimes summarized with the phrase: "*agents can say go*" [29], to emphasize that they are not requested to wait for an external command to act, but they can decide to act because they have an explicit goal to achieve. As a direct consequence of this characteristic, agents are allowed to refuse acting if they believe that the outcome of an action may prohibit them to achieve their goals, and we say that "*agents can say no*" [29].

Autonomy is probably the most important difference between agents and concurrent or active objects. An object is not explicitly associated with a goal and its role in the system is implicitly defined by when and how the other objects send messages to it. An agent is explicitly associated with a goal and its interaction with the environment and with the other agents are mainly directed to achieve this goal.

Another characteristic that we associate with agents is the so-called social ability, i.e., the possibility that agents have to communicate with other agents. Various communication models are available, but all these models mainly derive from *speech act theory* [39]. KQML (Knowledge Query Manipulation Language) is probably the most known agent communication language [12, 13]. KQML is a protocol for exchanging information and knowledge whose main feature is that all the information for understanding the content of the message is included in the communication itself.

FIPA ACL — Agent Communication Language — is a language for the communication between agents that is proposed by FIPA consortium [14]. The syntax of the FIPA ACL is very close to the syntax of KQML. However, despite syntactic similarity, there are fundamental differences between KQML and FIPA ACL, the most evident being the existence of a formal semantics for FIPA ACL which should eliminate any ambiguity and confusion from the usage of the language.

Each FIPA ACL message is structured in two parts: a communication part and a content part. The communication part carries content-independent information such as the identification of the sender and the receiver. On the contrary, the content part bares the meaning of the message and it is structured as a performative and a domain content. The performative is a domain-independent verb that specifies the meaning that the sender of the message wanted to associate with the domain content. FIPA specifies a set of performatives, such as inform, request and query, that agents can use to communicate. The domain content of the message is a sentence expressed in some language and following some ontology that actually bares the meaning of the message. FIPA does not prescribe any language for expressing domain contents and when an agent receives a message, it comes to know the language and the ontology used in the domain content exploiting the communication part of the message. The structure of a FIPA ACL message introduces some overhead because the data sent may be redundant in some cases. However, the advantage is that message processing is simpler and may be easily used for the interaction of heterogeneous agents.

FIPA communication model is not limited to isolated messages exchanged by agents, but it also allows messages to be grouped into interaction protocols. Interaction protocols are domain-independent courses of messages that can be instantiated in concrete conversations between agents. They are intended to abstract a common path of performatives from the set of possible conversations to ease the realization of agents. FIPA provides a set of general-purpose interaction protocols and it also provides guidelines for the realization of application-specific interaction protocols [14].

FIPA guarantees interoperability because the syntax and the semantic of FIPA ACL are standardized and communicating agents are supposed to share a common ontology and a common language for expressing domain contents. At the moment, only a few systems [3, 37] support the semantic of FIPA ACL, while many other support only the syntax of it [1, 2, 27, 33]. The latter systems rely on the common syntax of ACL and on the set of general-purpose interaction protocols to support interoperability. This kind of interoperability is not sufficient to support the realization of open and flexible systems and FIPA decided to address this problem explicitly devoting resources to provide a more feasible means to support service-level interoperability.

The characteristic autonomy and FIPA service-level interoperability justify the interest for agents in the realisation of complex and dynamic applications capable, for example, of managing the resources available on the Web. Autonomy is necessary when dealing with dynamic environments to allow software systems adapting to unpredictable situations. We cannot delegate to the developer the prediction of all possible courses of events that may occur in the Web. Inter-operability is a necessary condition for the implementation of open systems [16, 17, 31]. Every second new information and new services become available on the Web and users cannot wait for developers evolving their products to take advantage of these new resources.

3. Agent-oriented Software Engineering

The research on agent-oriented software engineering is based on the possibility to model a software system at the agent level of abstraction [4, 7, 20, 21, 26, 42, 46, 47]. This level of abstraction considers agents as atomic entities that communicate to implement the functionality of the system. Various initiatives [26, 47] are devoted to establish a methodology for an agent-oriented development process and this work shows a brief overview of the common ideas behind such methodologies to demonstrate how the introduction of the agent level of abstraction can change the software development cycle. In the following of the section, some of most interesting agent-oriented methodologies to develop multi-agent systems are described.

The AAII methodology for agent-oriented analysis and development [24] is based on object-oriented methodologies enhanced with some agent-based concepts. This methodology derives from a long experience in realizing multi-agent systems through the belief-desire-intention technology [34]. A multi-agent system is represented through both internal and external models. The external models mainly described the interactions between agents while the internal models is entirely dedicated to the description of the internal of the different agents in term of their beliefs, desires and intentions.

Cassiopeia methodology [9] is based on a bottom up development process. In particular, the methodology proposes three steps. The first step identifies the elementary behavious that are implied by the overall system task. The second step identifies the relationships between elementary behaviours. Finally, the third step identifies the "organizational behaviours" of the system representing the way in which agents form themselves into groups.

MAS-CommonKADS methodology [19] extends the models defined in Common KADS [38] adding technology from object-oriented methodologies and from protocol engineering for describing the agent protocols [36]. This methodology starts with a conceptualization phase from which defines a first description of the system from the user point of view. Then it uses a set of models for the analysis and design of the system through a risk-driven life cycle. The models used are: the agent model, describing the main features of agents, the task model, describing the tasks carried out by agents, the expertise model, describing the knowledge that agents need to carry out their tasks, the coordination model, describing interactions between agents, the organization model, describing the organization of the agent society, the communication model, describing the interaction between humans and agents, and, finally, the design model, that collects the previous models.

The Gaia methodology [47] tries to build a multi-agent system through a process of organizational design. This methodology borrows some terminology and notation from object-oriented analysis and design and, in particular, from FUSION [8]. The objective of the analysis stage is to capture the system organization as a collection of roles that stand in certain relationships to one another and that take part in a set of systematic interactions with other roles. There are not a mapping one-to-one between roles and individuals (agents), but often an individual can take on many roles. A role is defined by four attributes: responsibilities, permissions, activities and protocols. Responsibilities determine functionality and are the key role attributes. Permissions are the "right" associated with a role. Activities are computations associated with a role that an agent can take without interacting with other agents. Finally, protocols define the way that a role interact with other roles.

4. Using UML for Developing Agent Systems

Even if the agent level is the natural level of abstraction for describing a multi-agent system, the lack of accepted diagrammatic notations and design tools might prevent architects from exploiting its benefits. The research community of agent-oriented software engineering is currently addressing this problem investigating the possibility of extending UML [5] to support the basic agent-oriented concepts such as agent, ontology and interaction protocol. This research trend has led to various extensions of UML [10, 15, 28, 29], but such notations are not completely accepted because they are not yet supported by CASE tools. It is worth noting that one of the main goals of the AUML initiative [29] is to encourage CASE-tools vendors to support an agent-oriented notation in their products. In the remaining of this section we introduce the basic concepts of agent-oriented software engineering taking the pragmatic approach of showing the new artefacts that the architect can realize and introducing an UML-based notation to describe such artefacts. Our UML-based notation does not require extensions to the usual UML diagrams and any off-the-shelf CASE tool can support it. This approach has the advantage of allowing architects using our notation without either the need for agent-enabled CASE tools or, when the CASE tool support UML extensions (e.g. Rational Rose Case tool) the need for extending the CASE tool with new diagrams and for learning to use such kinds of diagrams.

4.1. *Agent-oriented analysis*

The analysis phase is intended to examine the domain of the problem to specify what the software system is intended to do. In general, this phase should be reasonably independent from the technology used to develop the system and the system itself should be seen as a black box interacting with its environment. This is the reason why talking about agent-oriented analysis may seem an oxymoron. Nevertheless, some kinds of agents, such as personal assistants or information agents, are directly in contact with the user and they provide pieces of functionality that must be considered during the analysis. Therefore, we introduce agent-oriented use cases to allow the architect specifying the interactions that some kinds of agent have with the user, with the environment and with the rest of the system. Even if they are modeled out of the black box bounding the system, such agents are part of the system under construction and they are analyzed separately only to take their special role in providing functionality into account. In order to represent agent-oriented use case diagrams, we introduce the stereotype *agent*, easing the implementation of tools managing such diagrams, and we treat agents as common actors. Figure 1 shows a simple agent-oriented use case diagram describing a system implementing a personal assistant capable of buying CDs on behalf of its user. We will discuss this example in more detail in the rest of this section, as we will use it to introduce other agent-oriented diagrams.

Another reason for introducing agent-oriented analysis is the importance of data modeling in the realization of multi-agent systems. Agents use ontologies to associate a meaning to messages and the most important ontology-description languages, such as Ontolingua [13], allow describing the domain of the problem in terms of entities and relations between entities. The kinds of artefacts produced during the modeling of an ontology are similar to the ones produced during the usual

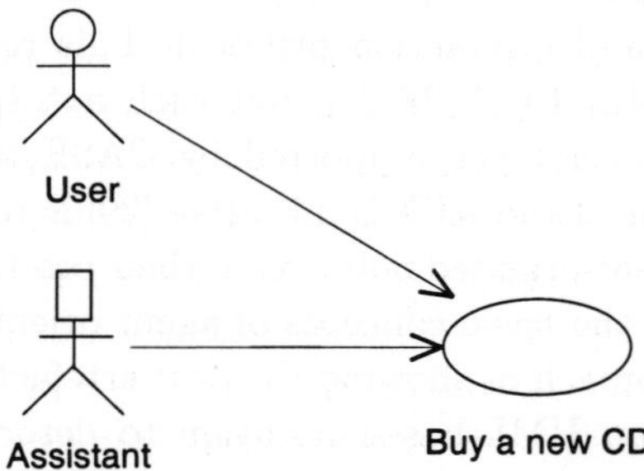

Fig. 1. Agent-oriented use case diagram of the CD shop example.

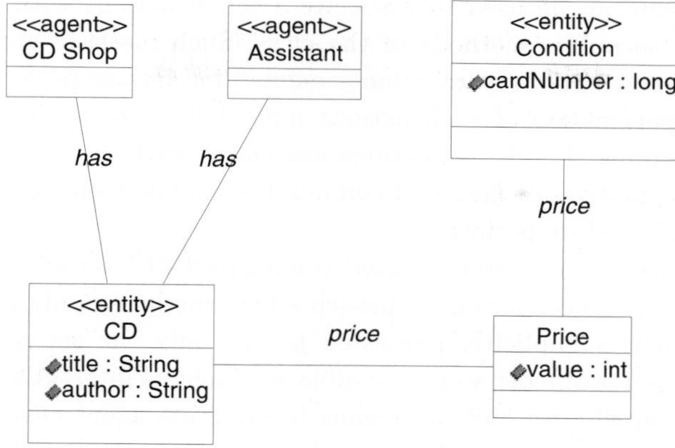

Fig. 2. Ontology diagram of the CD shop example.

data-modeling phase. This is due to the fact that ontologies are not engineered, to avoid constraining how agents can be realized, and therefore they are simply a description of the domain data. The similarity between data modeling and ontology modeling suggests using similar notations. We propose to use a variant of conceptual diagrams [25], that we call *ontology diagrams*, to model ontologies. An ontology diagram is a class diagram where classes model classes of entities defined in the ontology. We tag the classes in ontology diagrams, i.e., *entity classes*, with the stereotype *entity*. Entities are structured using public attributes. Ontology diagrams allow defining relations between classes and we use such relations to model the predicates provided by the ontology. Figure 2 shows the ontology of the CD shop example. This diagram comprises three classes of entities: CDs, prices and payment conditions. CDs are characterized by a title and by an author; prices are characterized by an integer value, while payment conditions comprise only a credit card number. The diagram shows also four predicates: two *has* predicates and two *price* predicates defined over different entity classes.

4.2. *Agent-oriented design*

Designing a multi-agent system at the agent level requires modeling the architecture of the multi-agent system and the interactions between agents. Such elements can be modeled using some UML class diagrams, we call *architecture diagrams* that identify the roles [23] that agents play in the system. Each role is associated with a class, that we call agent class, and we introduce the stereotype agent to tag such classes because they equals the ones used in agent-oriented use case diagrams. Associations between agent classes describe possible associations between agents playing different roles. Such associations are basically used to express acquaintance because it is common to promote flexibility in the multi-agent system avoiding the use of associations to spread responsibilities across agents.

An agent class can be used to associate a set of actions with a role. Actions are represented as public methods of the class. Such methods must be declared void because no concept of return value is defined for actions performed by agents. Moreover, the parameters of such actions must belong to entity classes defined in ontology diagrams. The list of actions associated with an agent class does not include the performatives of the agent communication language because we suppose to use FIPA ACL and its performatives.

Object protocols, the object-oriented counterpart of interaction protocols, are not included in UML because our approach allows modeling only known protocols and the developer is implicitly requested to use only the set of FIPA general-purpose interaction protocols, so the possible ways agents interact are "predefined". This is the reason why we have no means to annotate agent classes with the list of supported interaction protocols except for using comments. The motivation of this choice is simply to preserve interoperability. In fact, introducing application-specific interaction protocols may lead to the following problems. Even if we provide agents with a run-time description of a protocol, it is extremely difficult to implement an agent capable of taking such a description and learning how to use the protocol without any explicit help from the developer. Therefore, agents using application-specific protocols may not be able to run in open systems where third-party agents join and leave the system dynamically. Moreover, the semantics of the paths of a protocol must be coherent with the semantics of the employed performatives. This coherence is very difficult to achieve and only well-studied and accepted protocols can guarantee this property. If an application-specific interaction cannot be expressed as a combination of general-purpose protocols, we can use the notation introduced by Odell *et al* [28, 29] to create new interaction protocols from scratch.

Figure 3 shows the architecture diagram for the CD shop example. It shows two classes of agents: personal assistants and CD shop agents. Agents belonging to such classes support the FIPA contract net protocol [14, 41] the FIPA request protocol [14]. Moreover, CD shop agents can be requested to perform an action called *sell*. Such an action requires the identification of the personal assistant buying the CD, the description of the CD it wants to buy and its payment conditions.

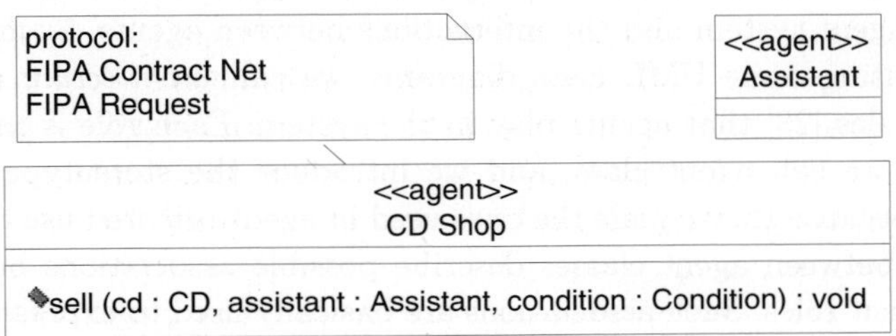

Fig. 3. Architecture diagram of the CD shop example.

4.3. *Agent-oriented implementation*

The need of an agent-oriented support to develop software was felt long before the introduction of agent-oriented software engineering with the definition of agent-oriented programming languages such as Agent0 [40] and Telescript [43]. Nowadays, the approach of agent-oriented languages is no longer adopted and the greater majority of agents are developed in Java taking advantage of one of the available agent platforms. Agent platforms are run-time environments that manage the lifecycle of agents and provide the necessary communication resources: means for sending and receiving messages, white and yellow pages services. Such communications reach either agents within the same platform or agents on different platforms transparently to the developer. This is a fundamental characteristic of agent platforms as it allows supporting open systems where agents join and leave dynamically. In addition, an agent platform can be physically distributed across a set of network nodes. The distribution and cooperation of agents residing on different platforms implies the conformance to a standard. At the moment, only FIPA is producing specifications for agent platforms and these specifications are the basis for the Java Specification Request JSR-000085 — Java Agent Services.

Agent platforms, such as Jade [1] and Fipa-Os [33], provide only a transport layer and some basic services, but they do not provide any support for autonomy. Moreover, they lack support for service-level interoperability because they do not take into account the semantics of the agent communication language. Therefore, another kind of development tool, called agent-development toolkit, was introduced to provide the developer with high-level abstraction from the BDI agent architecture [44]. These tools, such as dMars [11], Jack [6], AgentBuilder [35], Jam [18] and Zeus [27], provide a way for rapidly prototyping agents but they do not seem to produce sufficiently robust and efficient agents for their adoption in industrial-strength projects mainly because of their immaturity.

Recently, we implemented an agent-development toolkit called ParADE (Parma Development Environment) [3] to support autonomy and inter-operability over existing FIPA-compliant platforms. Even if ParADE could have been implemented over any existing agent platform, its current implementation works on top of Jade [1] to take advantage of its services. The goal driving the work on ParADE is providing the agent developer with a hybrid agent architecture capable of promoting interoperability and supporting autonomy exploiting the semantics of FIPA ACL. Such an architecture is basically goal-oriented but it also integrates reactive behaviours. This approach is chosen because goal-orientation is a fundamental key in supporting the semantics of FIPA ACL and we think that reactive agents are easier to design and to implement. Goal-oriented agents are inherently autonomous because they act to achieve their goals without requiring the developer to foresee all possible flows of events.

ParADE is composed of a set of development tools supporting the developer at the agent level and at the object level. The agent level allows describing agents in terms of their BDI-like characteristics such as beliefs, goals and social organization. At this level of abstraction, the developer can produce UML models as described in this paper to generate code for agents. This code relies on ParADE development library and on the services provided by the underlying agent platform. It is worth noting that ParADE does not integrate any CASE tool because the code generator works with XMI [30] files that any off-the-shelf CASE tool should be able to produce. The code generated from agent-level models is only a skeleton and the developer is requested to complete it at the object level integrating application-specific behaviours. Such behaviours are implemented by using the ParADE development library to access ParADE components such as the knowledge base and the planning engine. This two-level approach has the advantage of supporting the production of code from UML models at the agent level without taking implementation details into account. Moreover, it allows integrating legacy code and supporting application-specific optimizations at the object level.

5. Conclusions

Software engineering is founded on the possibility to model a system at different levels of abstraction. Agent-oriented software engineering introduces a new level, called agent level, to allow the software architect describing a system in terms of interacting agents. At this level of abstraction, an agent is considered as an atomic entity that communicates with other agents to implement the functionality of the system. This work introduces the basis of agent-oriented software engineering exploiting the pragmatic point of view of showing the new artefacts provided to the architect to model systems at the agent level. Such artefacts can be produced using an UML-based notation supported by any off-the-shelf CASE tool to allow architects adopting it without the need for agent-enabled CASE tools.

Three agent-oriented diagrams are introduced to model the basic elements characterizing the agent level of abstraction: the interactions between agents and the environment, the architecture of the multi-agent system and the ontology followed by agents. Agent-oriented use case diagrams are simple extensions of usual use case diagrams that allow introducing agents and modeling their interactions with the user, with the environment and with the rest of the system. Architecture diagrams allow modeling the architecture of the multi-agent system in terms of a set of agent classes connected through relations. Each class is characterized by the actions that an agent belonging to it can be requested to perform. The relations between classes may be used to express the network of acquaintance that an agent can build at runtime. Ontology diagrams allow defining a model of the environment composed of entities and relations. These relations can be used to specify the predicates that agents can use to communicate and therefore ontology diagrams can be used to model the domain-content of messages.

Acknowledgements

This work is partially supported by CSELT and by the European Commission through the contracts IST-1999-12217, CoMMA — Corporate Memory Management through Agents — and IST-1999-10211, LEAP — Lightweight Extensible Agent Platform.

References

1. F. Bellifemine, A. Poggi and G. Rimassa, "Developing multi-agent systems with JADE", *Proceedings of the Seventh International Workshop on Agent Theories, Architectures, and Languages* (*ATAL'2000*) (2000) 85–99.
2. F. Bergenti and A. Poggi, "A development environment for the realization of open and scalable multi-agent systems", *Proceedings of the Ninth European Workshop on Multi-Agent Systems,* (*MAAMAW'99*) (1999) 52–62.
3. F. Bergenti and A. Poggi, "A development toolkit to realise autonomous and interoperable agents", *Proceedings of the Fifth International Conference on Autonomous Agents* (*Agents'2001*) (2001) 632–639.
4. F. Bergenti and A. Poggi, "Exploiting UML in the design of multi-agent systems", *Proceedings ECOOP Workshop on Engineering Societies in the Agents' World 2000* (*ESAW'2000*) (2000) 96–103.
5. G. Booch, J. Rumbaugh and I. Jacobson, *Unified Modeling Language User's Guide* (Addison-Wesley, 1999).
6. P. Busetta, R. Rnnquist, A. Hodgson and A. Lucas, "JACK intelligent agents — Components for intelligent agents in Java", AgentLink News Letter (January 1999).
7. P. Ciancarini and M. J. Wooldridge, "Agent-oriented software engineering", *Lecture Notes in Computer Science* 1957 (Springer-Verlag, 2001).
8. D. Coleman, P. Arnold, S. Bodoff, C. Dollin, H. Gilchrist, F. Hayes and P. Jeremaes, *Object-Oriented Development: The FUSION Method* (Prentice Hall, 1994).
9. A. Collinot, A. Drogoul and P. Benhamou, "Agent oriented design of a soccer robot team", *Proceedings ICMAS'96* (1996) 41–47.
10. S. Cranefield and M. Purvis, "UML as an ontology modeling language", *Proceedings of the Workshop on Intelligent Information Integration, 16th International Joint Conference on Artificial Intelligence* (*IJCAI'99*) (1999).
11. M. d'Inverno, D. Kinny, M. Luck and M. Wooldridge, "A formal specification of dMARS", eds. M. P. Singh, A. S. Rao and M. Wooldridge, *Intelligent Agents IV, Lecture Notes in Artificial Intelligence 1365* (Springer-Verlag, 1998) 155–176.
12. T. Finin, J. Weber, G. Wiederhold, M. Genesereth, R. Fritzson, D. McKay, J. McGuire, P. Pelavin, S. Shapiro and C. Beck, "Specification of the KQML agent-communication language", Enterprise Integration Technologies, EIT TR 92-04, Palo Alto, CA (1992).
13. T. Finin, Y. Labrou and J. Mayfield, "KQML as an agent communication language", ed. M. J. Bradshaw, *Software Agents* (MIT Press, 1997).
14. FIPA, "FIPA 99 specification: Agent communication language, part 2", available at *http://www.fipa.org*
15. FIPA Technical Committee C, "Extending UML for the specification of agent interaction protocols", Response to the OMG Analysis and Design Task Force UML RTF 2.0 Request for Information (1999).
16. M. R. Genesereth and R. E. Fikes, "Knowledge interchange format — Version 3 — reference manual", Technical Report Logic-92-1, Stanford University (1992).

17. M. R. Genesereth, N. Singh and M. Syed, "A distributed and anonymous knowledge sharing approach to software interoperation", *International Journal of Cooperative Information Systems* **4**, no. 4 (1995) 339–367.
18. M. J. Huber, "JAM: A BDI-theoretic mobile agent architecture", *Proceedings of the Third International Conference on Autonomous Agents* (*Agent'99*) (1999) 236–243.
19. C. A. Iglesias, M. Garijo, J. C. A. González and J. R. Velasco, "Analysis and design of multiagent systems using MAS-CommonKADS", *Proceedings of the International Workshop on Agent Theories, Architectures, and Languages* (*ATAL'97*) (1997) 313–327.
20. C. A. Iglesias, M. Garijo and J. C. A. González, "Survey of agent-oriented methodologies", *Proceedings of the International Workshop on Agent Theories, Architectures, and Languages* (*ATAL'98*) (1998) 317–330.
21. N. R. Jennings, "On agent-based software engineering", *Artificial Intelligence* **117** (2000) 277–296.
22. N. R. Jennings and M. Wooldridge, "Agent oriented software engineering", ed. M. J. Bradshaw, *Handbook of Agent Technology* (MIT Press, 2000).
23. E. A. Kendall, "Agent roles and role models: New abstractions for multiagent system analysis and design", *Proceedings of the International Workshop on Intelligent Agents in Information and Process Management* (1998).
24. D. Kinny, A. S. Rao and M. P. Georgeff, "A methodology and modeling technique for systems of BDI agents", eds. W. Van De Velde and J. W. Perram, Agent Breaking Away, *Proceedings of the Seventh European Workshop on Modeling Autonomous Agents in a Multi-Agent World, Lecture Notes in Artificial Intelligence 1038* (Springer–Verlag, 1996) 56–71.
25. C. Larman, *Applying UML and Patterns* (Prentice Hall, 1997).
26. MESSAGE Consortium, "Deliverable 1: Initial methodology", deliverable of the EURESCOM Project P907-GI (2000).
27. H. S. Nwana, D. T. Ndumu and L. C. Lee, "ZEUS: An advanced toolkit for engineering distributed multi-agent systems", *Proceedings of PAAM'98* (1998) 377–391.
28. J. Odell and C. Bock, "Suggested UML extensions for agents", Response to the OMG Analysis and Design Task Force UML RTF 2.0 Request for Information (1999).
29. J. Odell, V. Parunak and B. Bauer, "Representing agent interaction protocols in UML", *Proceedings of Agents* (2000).
30. OMG, "XML metadata interchange — Version 1.1", available at *http://www.omg.org*
31. P. F. Patel-Schneider and B. Swartout, "Description-logic knowledge representation system specification", DARPA KSE Technical Report (1993).
32. R. S. Patil, R. E. Fikes, P. F. Patel-Scheneider, D. McKay, T. Finin, T. Gruber and R. Neches, "The DARPA knowledge sharing effort: Progress report", *Proceedings of the Third Conference on Principles of Knowledge Representation and Reasoning* (1992) 103–114.
33. S. Poslad, P. Buckle and R. Hadingham, "The FIPA-OS agent platform: Open source for open standards", available at *http://fipa-os.sourceforge.net*
34. A. S. Rao and M. P. Georgeff, "BDI agents: From theory to practice", *Proceedings of the First International Conference on Multi-Agent Systems* (1995) 312–319.
35. Reticular Systems, "AgentBuilder — An integrated toolkit for constructing intelligence software agents", available at *http://www.agentbuilder.com*
36. E. Rudolph, J. Grabowski and P. Graubmann, "Tutorial on message sequence charts (MSC)", *Proceedings of FORTE/PSTV'96 Conference* (1996).
37. M. D. Sadek, "Dialogue acts are rational plans", *Proceedings ESCA/ETRW Workshop on the Structure of Multimodal Dialogue* (1991) 1–29.

38. A. T. Schreiber, B. J. Wielinga, J. M. Akkermans and W. Van De Velde, "CommonKADS: A comprehensive methodology for KBS development", Deliverable DM1.2a KADS-II/M1/RR/UvA/70/1.1, University of Amsterdam (1994).
39. J. R. Searle, *Speech Acts: An Essay in the Philosophy of Language* (Cambridge University Press, Cambridge, 1969).
40. Y. Shoham, "An overview of agent-oriented programming", ed. J. M. Bradshow, *Software Agents* (AAAI Press, 1997).
41. R. Smith, "The contract net protocol: High-level communications and control in a distributed problems solver", *IEEE Transactions on Computers* **29**, no. 12 (1980) 1104–1113.
42. J. Treur, "Methodologies and software engineering for agent systems", available at *http://www.cs.vu.nl/~treur*
43. J. White, "Mobile agents", ed. J. M. Bradshow, *Software Agents* (AAAI Press, 1997).
44. M. Wooldridge, "Agent-based software engineering", *IEE Proceedings on Software Engineering* **144**, no. 1 (1997) 26–37.
45. M. Wooldridge, "Intelligent agents", ed. G. Weiss, *Multiagent Systems: A Modern Approach to Distributed Artificial Intelligence* (MIT Press, 1999).
46. M. Wooldridge and N. Jennings, "Software engineering with agents: Pitfalls and pratfalls", *IEEE Internet Computing* **3**, no. 3 (1999) 20–27.
47. M. Wooldridge, N. R. Jennings and D. Kinny, "The Gaia methodology for agent-oriented analysis and design", *Journal of Autonomous Agents and Multi-Agent Systems* **3**, no. 3 (2000) 285–312.

IMPROVING UML DESIGNS USING AUTOMATIC DESIGN PATTERN DETECTION

FEDERICO BERGENTI and AGOSTINO POGGI
Dipartimento di Ingegneria dell'Informazione, Università degli Studi di Parma, Parco Area delle Scienze 181A, 43100, Parma, Italy
E-mail: {*bergenti,poggi*}*@ce.unipr.it*

Design patterns are considered one of the most valuable tools to produce quality designs and a general-purpose technique to improve a design is to identify all pattern realizations and to apply well-known rules to improve them. This technique requires finding all pattern realizations used in a design and it is a rather tedious task. This paper shows the work in the literature on assistants for programmers and software architects and presents a system called *IDEA* (*Interactive DEsign Assistant*). IDEA is an interactive design assistant for software architects meant for automating the task of finding and improving the realizations of design patterns. Basically, IDEA is capable of automatically (i) finding the patterns employed in a UML diagram and (ii) producing critiques about these patterns. The core of IDEA is the module that automatically detects the pattern realizations found in the model that the architect is producing. When this module finds a pattern realization, a set of design rules are verified to test if the design could be improved. Any violation to these rules fires a critique that is proposed to the engineer as a possible design improvement. Currently, a prototypal implementation of IDEA is integrated with two popular CASE tools.

Keywords: Automatic design pattern detection, critique generation, design pattern, UML.

1. Introduction

The design of complex software systems has been shown a very difficult task [2] and support tools are always needed to produce quality designs. Design patterns are considered one of the most valuable tools the engineer can adopt in the design of complex systems. Moreover, from the early days of the research on this topic, patterns have been recognized as an important means to document existing designs [10]. Patterns are fundamental abstractions that an engineer can use to come to a better comprehension of a complex software design.

One of the simplest, yet more powerful, techniques to improve a design is to use patterns whenever possible and to follow some well-known rules to realize them. The application of this technique to an existing design is tedious because it requires finding all pattern realizations used in the design. This obliges analyzing the diagrams comprised in the design to identify possible pattern realizations and then applying pattern-specific rules to improve the found realizations. The automation of this task is a desirable feature for an assistant intended to improve the work of the software architect. This paper shows the work found in the literature about automated assistants for programmers and architects and introduces a novel system, called *IDEA* (*Interactive DEsign Assistant*), that addresses the problem of automating the refactoring of existing designs exploiting design patterns to propose critiques [6, 18].

2. Automated Assistants for Programmers and Software Architects

Automated assistants are considered a valuable tool in mature fields of engineering and almost all CAD systems for electronics and mechanics provide, at least, model checking capabilities. A number of automated assistants have been developed to help the engineer in most of the phases of the software lifecycle. These assistants can be roughly classified into *generative* systems and *critiquing* systems. Generative systems help the engineer producing new artifacts using generative techniques, i.e., techniques generating solution from general-purpose solution templates. Critiquing systems are meant to provide critiques on existing artifacts to improve their realization. They rely on analyzing existing artifacts and on suggesting improvement rules.

Design patterns can be used to describe a complex software system in terms of higher-level abstractions than classes, objects and messages. Nevertheless, only a few automated assistant currently employ patterns as basic abstractions for design and reverse engineering. This is due to the fact that patterns are a suitable language for humans, but a rather complex language for automated systems: they derive from a concrete design experience and they cannot be easily formalized, or cannot be formalized at all. The first characteristic implies that an engineer could find a design solution quite similar to a pattern without noticing the resemblance. The second characteristic suggests that only experience can drive the engineer in using patterns and general-purpose rules stating where to use a particular pattern are not generally available. These characteristics suggest that engineers can take benefit from an automated assistant capable of criticizing their design choices with respect to design patterns. Such an assistant could analyze a design model to:

- find automatically all pattern realizations in order to assign a role to the design elements;
- propose pattern-specific critiques directed to improve the design or to enforce design rules;
- suggest alternative realizations of the patterns emphasizing the achievable improvements;
- propose a pattern to solve a particular design problem, at least for those patterns having a formal application rule; and
- find recurrent design solutions that can be the base for new patterns.

Assistants could couple the listed processes with learning capabilities to model their behavior on the engineers design style.

Design patterns can be exploited both in generative and critiquing systems because they represent general-purpose solution that (i) generative systems can adapt to specific problems and (ii) critiquing systems can use to come to a better comprehension of the existing artifacts.

The most famous automated assistant for software engineering is the Programmer's Apprentice [15, 16] developed at the MIT Artificial Intelligence Laboratory by Rich and Waters. This system uses a knowledge base about software design and implementation to detect errors made by the programmer or to select implementation choices automatically. This knowledge base is expressed in terms of *clichès*, i.e., "*commonly used combinations of elements with familiar name*" [16]. The primary difference between a clichè and a design pattern is the level of abstraction. A clichè may represent an algorithm fragment or an abstract data type, but it does not say anything about the interaction between objects. This is the reason why clichès can be used to describe an object implementation but they cannot represent an object architecture. The low level of abstraction that characterizes clichès allows the Programmer's Apprentice to detect their occurrences in source codes and design models easily.

More recently, Argo/UML [19, 20], a CASE tool developed at the University of California by Robbins, Hilbert and Redmiles, integrates a CASE tool with an automated assistant. Argo/UML supports UML and provides the engineer with online critiques about the model under construction. These critiques range from simple naming conventions to suggestions about possible design improvements. Argo/UML selects the critiques searching particular structures in the current UML model. The selected critiques are then proposed to the engineer in a to-do list. Anyway, Argo/UML does not incorporate a knowledge base about design patterns because the structures it uses to fire the critiques are too fine-grained. As an example, it checks for classes without operations or informs the engineer to adopt names strictly related to the application domain, avoiding names such as adapter or proxy.

A tool capable of exploiting the information contained in a design model at the pattern level was proposed, but no longer supported, by Florijn, Meijers and van Winsen [4, 11]. This tool is capable of detecting all pattern realizations in an OMT model and to exploit this information to associate a set of roles to the classes composing the detected pattern realizations. The detection algorithm is based on *fragments*. These are typed design elements that can be composed to represent the elements of an OMT model. The pattern detection is performed matching graphs of fragments corresponding to pattern templates with the design model.

Design patterns and similar structures are widely used in reverse engineering tools to extract high-level knowledge from a source code. One of the most famous systems that try to do this is PAT (Program Analysis Tool) [8, 9] developed at the University of Illinois by Harandi and Ning. PAT is an analysis and debugging tool that detects *events*, that are abstract concepts contained in a code, and uses them to describe *plans* [8]. Plans are high-level views of a code that capture properties that can be used for documentation or re-engineering. Plans are lower-level concepts than design patterns because they are intended to work with source codes written in an imperative language. The extension of this approach to object-oriented languages and design patterns is proposed by many other systems [1, 3, 7, 11, 13, 17, 21, 22]. These systems are designed to work off-line and to process a source code to detect all pattern realizations. These systems help the generation of high-quality documentation directly in the code or in the first steps of the re-engineering process. Anyway, source code analysis can be applied too late in the development process to represent a valuable tool in the design phase.

IDEA (Interactive DEsign Assistant) is a critiquing system that we developed to work in direct interaction with the software architect to propose pattern-specific critiques. This task is performed detecting all pattern realizations in the UML design under construction and selecting suitable critiques intended to improve them. IDEA takes as input an UML design exported in XMI format and uses the class and collaboration diagrams in it to detect all pattern realizations. If the information needed to detect a pattern can be acquired from these diagrams, IDEA can detect it and we call it *detectable.* Some pattern fall out of this category because they are not completely defined in terms of classes, objects and interactions, and we call these patterns *undetectable.* This is the case, for example, of patterns such as the Façade or the Interpreter [5]. These patterns are characterized by their role in the whole design rather than by their structure and therefore their automatic detection would require an overall comprehension of the model. This comprehension requires a deep understanding of the diagrams comprised in the design and nowadays no system capable of performing this task is available.

When a pattern realization is found, IDEA checks pattern-specific rules to select a set of critiques directed to improve this realization. Each critique is statically associated with a high, medium or low importance that quantifies the relevance of the corresponding rule violation. These critiques are directed to improve the pattern realizations suggesting:

- names for classes, attributes and operations: for example, the name of a factory method in the Factory Method pattern should end with the suffix *Factory*;
- a scope for operations: for example, hook methods in the Template Method pattern should be declared protected to access them only through template methods;
- operations that are likely to be missing in a class, such as an operation to access the components of a composite object in the Composite pattern;
- operations that are likely to be dangerous for reusability, such as providing a direct access to the subject of a proxy object in the Proxy pattern; and
- techniques that can be used to solve design problems: for example, the Iterator pattern can be used to access the components of a composite object in the Composite pattern.

It is worth noting that these critiques are pattern-specific and they require a high-level understanding of the design than usual style rules [12, 14] do not require. Therefore pattern-unaware critiquing systems cannot provide such critiques.

IDEA is extensible and customizable and the engineer can provide new patterns and new rules to select and fire new critiques. At the moment, the architect can customize IDEA implementing Prolog rules that are directly integrated in the knowledge base of IDEA. The implementation of a graphic tool to describe such rules is planned for a future activity.

The help that IDEA can provide to the engineer is not limited to the proposal of rules concerning the patterns employed in a design. The automatic detection of the patterns in a model can represent a valuable tool to check the coherence between the concrete design and the actual engineer's intentions. A discrepancy between the result of this process and the engineer's intentions could raise the following consequences:

- if the engineer wanted to employ a pattern but this cannot be detected, probably the design is wrong or it can be improved; and
- the detection of a pattern where the engineer did not plan to use it may lead to a better comprehension and documentation of the design.

The following sessions describe IDEA in more detail and show the benefits that it can provide in the production of quality designs exploiting the so called GoF patterns, i.e., the patterns identified by Gamma, Helm, Johnson and Vlissides [5].

3. IDEA

IDEA pattern detection process provides the engineer with two lists, the *pattern list* and the *to-do list.* The pattern list is the list of all patterns that IDEA found in the UML model. Each pattern in the list is characterized by a name and by a list of participants. Each participant is associated with the role it plays in the pattern. The to-do list is the list of all selected critiques ordered by their importance. IDEA dynamically maintains these lists adding and removing items when necessary. Moreover, IDEA allows the engineer controlling the pattern detection directly through the pattern and to-do lists. If the engineer explicitly removes a pattern or a critique, IDEA does not propose it anymore until the corresponding structure in the model changes. Figure 1 shows the class diagram of a realization of the Composite pattern and a tabular view of the output of the pattern detection.

3.1. *Design-pattern detection algorithm*

The design-pattern detection algorithm is the core of IDEA because it allows gathering the information needed to provide useful critiques to the engineer. This algorithm is responsible for the analysis of the class and collaboration diagrams of the UML design model to acquire all available information. This process cannot

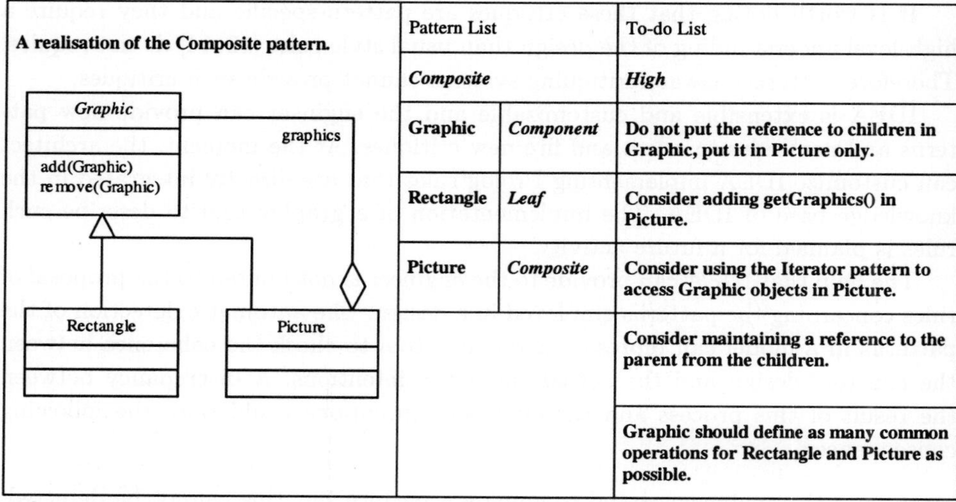

Fig. 1. Realization of the Composite pattern and some of the selected critiques.

be easily formalized because of the informal nature of patterns. Even if a design pattern is always presented with a reference solution, the simple detection of this solution in the UML model is not always satisfactory. For example, the Façade pattern solves the problem: "*Provide a unified interface to a set of interfaces in a subsystem. Façade defines a higher-level interface that makes the subsystem easier to use*" [5]. The proposed solution is a set of general guidelines that should be adopted to realize a Façade pattern, but it does not represent a template that can be used to detect all realizations of this pattern in a model. This is a consequence of the fact that the Façade pattern identifies a particular role of a class in a model, but this role can be expressed only in terms of an overall comprehension of the model. Similar problems are met when trying to detect patterns requiring a fine-grained understanding of the model. For example, the Singleton pattern solves the problem: "*Ensure a class only has one instance, and provide a global point of access to it*" [5]. The detection of a realization of the Singleton pattern requires finding a condition forcing the number of singleton objects to one. This condition cannot be easily expressed in a UML model, and it is often expressed only informally or it is not expressed at all. These problems prevent IDEA from detecting many of the design patterns found in the literature, anyway the number of detectable patterns and the number of related critiques suggest that IDEA can provide a valuable help to the engineer.

The pattern detection algorithm has a cascaded structure comprising four steps, as shown in Fig. 2. First, the class diagrams are exploited to detect groups of classes that may represent a pattern realization. Then, the collaboration diagrams are used to refine this detection matching the object interaction with pattern-specific object interactions. The third step consolidates the obtained results gathering the pattern

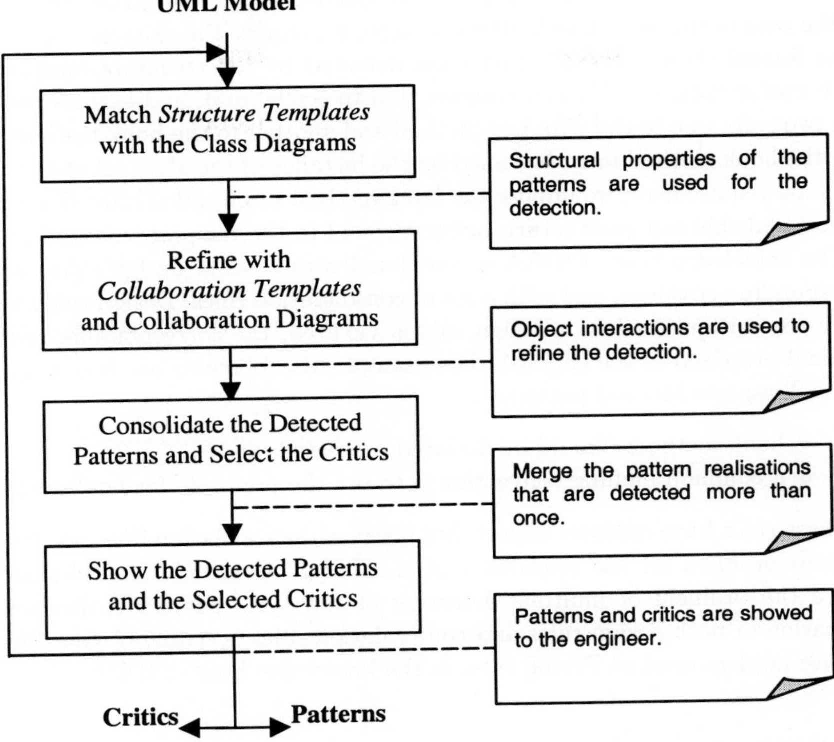

Fig. 2. Architecture of the pattern-detection algorithm.

realizations that are detected more than once, as the rules used for the detection can find a single pattern realization many times. This happens, for example, when a pattern comprises a base class with an unspecified number of derived classes. To keep the detection rules simple, the base class is requested to have only one derived class. This implies that IDEA detects as many pattern realizations as the number of derived classes actually used in the model. The purpose of the consolidation step is to gather these realizations into a single realization. The last step of the pattern-detection algorithm presents the obtained results to the engineer.

Each pattern in the knowledge base is described in terms of a *structure template* and a *collaboration template*. Both these types of template are internally described as Prolog rules. The structure template identifies pattern-specific constraints that a portion of a class diagram must satisfy to belong to a pattern realization. For example, the structure template of the Template Method pattern states that such a pattern is made by an abstract class that contains, at least, two different operations. The structure template is not enough to detect the realizations of a Template Method pattern because almost any class satisfies these constraints. We use the collaboration template to exploit pattern-specific constraints on the collaboration diagrams and to refine the detection performed through the structure template. For the case of the Template Method pattern, we require the existence of an object whose formal class is the abstract class detected by the structure template in a collaboration diagram. Then, we require that the collaboration diagrams contain at least two calls: one to the template method and another to the hook method. Moreover, the hook method must be called by the instance of the abstract class to itself. As a final requirement, we impose the hook method to be called after the template method and this call must return before the call to the template method returns.

The knowledge base of IDEA is completed with a set of design rules, with the corresponding critiques, and with a set of consolidation rules. Design rules are used to fire the critiques: when a design rule is violated, the corresponding critique is fired and proposed to the engineer. For example, the following are two design rules for the Template Method pattern:

- hook methods should be declared protected; and
- a common naming convention is to use the prefix *do* for hook methods.

These rules have medium importance because their violation does not represent a serious problem for the reusability of the design. Consolidation rules are used to face the problem of multiple detection of the same pattern realization. The application of both design rules and consolidation rules is straightforward because they are implemented as Prolog rules in the knowledge base of IDEA.

3.2. *System architecture*

IDEA is based on a modular design that has two main objectives: to allow its integration with existing CASE tools and to support various user interfaces. The first constraint is imposed by the desire to promote the use of IDEA and this can be achieved only supporting off-the-shelf CASE tools. At the moment, IDEA is integrated with two popular CASE tools: Rose from Rational and Argo/UML [20] from the University of California. The second constraint derives from the extreme importance that the user interface plays for automated assistants. IDEA proactively prompts the engineer with the results of its analysis and this must not be annoying. For this reason, IDEA supports various user interfaces that can be selected with a simple configuration tool.

The design of IDEA can be split into three major modules: the input module, the reasoning engine and the user-interface module. The input module is delegated to constantly retrieve the current UML model from the CASE tool. This process depends on the available CASE tool, but it is often sufficient to read the back-up copy of the model that the CASE tool constantly saves. Once retrieved, the class and collaboration diagrams are extracted from the model and they are transformed into a standard representation. To allow the engineer to directly interact with the pattern detection process, the input module supplies also a model-dependent knowledge base to the reasoning engine. This knowledge base is created by the input module to reflect the information that the user provides by means of the user interface. This information allows modifying the pattern detection process to suppress critiques or falsely detected patterns.

The reasoning engine is delegated to analyze the model retrieved by the input module with respect to the available knowledge base. This knowledge base comprises a model-dependent part provided by the engineer and a model-independent part used to detect the pattern realizations. The model-independent knowledge base is loaded at launch-time and can be completely customized by the engineer providing new Prolog rules. This part of the knowledge base contains the set of design rules with associated critiques and the set of detectable design patterns. The reasoning engine uses this knowledge base to produce the pattern list and the to-do list and then exploits the model-dependent knowledge base to filter these lists to remove the entries explicitly cancelled by the engineer.

The reasoning engine passes the produced lists to the user interface module to show them to the engineer. Currently, IDEA supports two user-interface modules, one for the integration with the Rational Rose and one for Argo/UML. The first uses Microsoft Agent to provide an anthropomorphic assistant similar to Microsoft Office assistants. The latter integrates the results and IDEA critiques with the critiquing engine provided by Argo/UML. Figure 3 shows an Argo/UML window containing a class diagram and a report window generated by IDEA. The report window contains two tables that provide information about all the realizations of the Abstract Factory pattern detected in the model. The first table shows the results obtained using only the structure templates, while the second shows the results obtained considering also the collaboration templates. The rows of these tables contain the roles defined in the pattern, while the columns, except for the first, enumerates the detected pattern realizations. In the example shown in Fig. 2, the report window contains the four roles defined in the Abstract Factory pattern and just one pattern realization.

IDEA is implemented completely in Java and it integrates a small Prolog interpreter written in Java. Anyway, user interfaces are most likely implemented using native code when the CASE tool is not platform independent. This is the reason why the integration with Rational Rose requires a tool we developed called *Observer* to allow IDEA interacting easily with the engineer. The integration with Argo/UML does not require such techniques because Argo/UML is distributed with full source code. Moreover, Argo/UML already provides the tools needed to implement an interactive critiquing system. IDEA is completely integrated with Argo/UML: it adds a menu to ask for services such as report windows and it also integrates the critiques about the design patterns directly in the critique folders.

4. Detecting GoF Patterns

The knowledge base of IDEA contains the rules for detecting a subset of the GoF patterns [5] and this section presents such rules. These rules are expressed

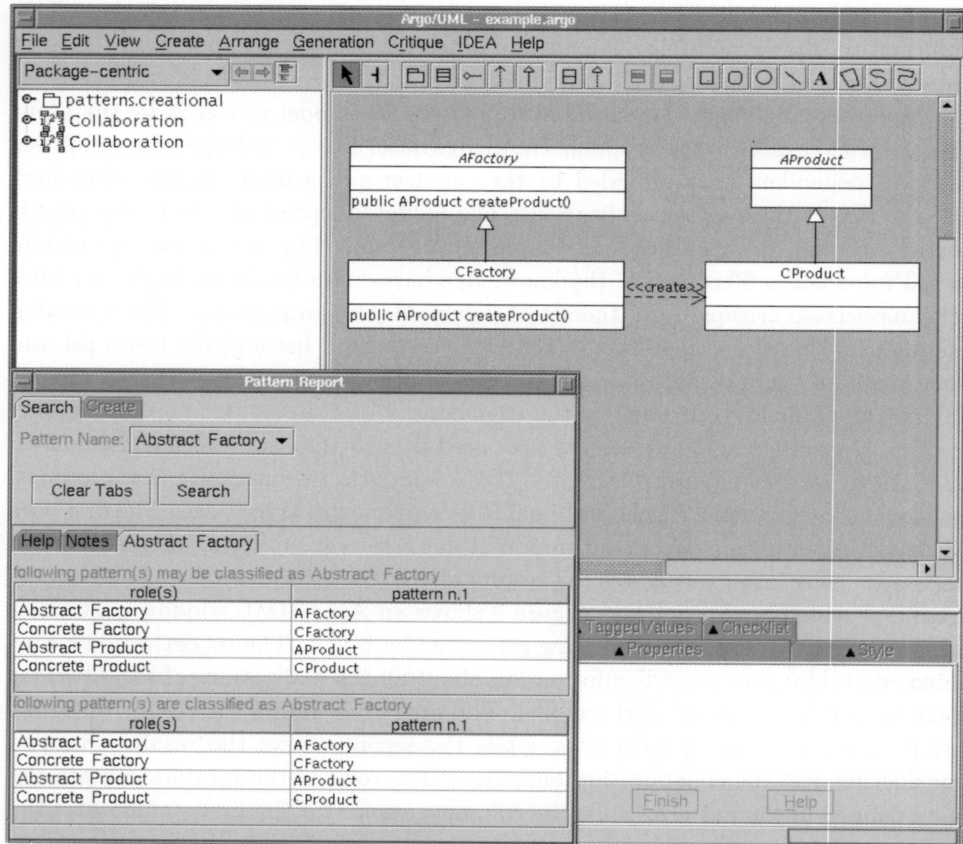

Fig. 3. Argo/UML with a report window generated by IDEA.

using a particular convention [4] suggested by an analysis of many patterns found in the literature. Patterns heavily rely on inheritance to realize reusable class architectures, anyway they never require the inheritance relations to be direct. For example, the Proxy pattern requires that the proxy class inherits from the subject class, but it does not forbid the engineer to add another class between these two classes. This added class inherits from the subject class and it is inherited by the proxy class. This degree of freedom is the reason why, in the rest of this section, the word inheritance does not refer to direct inheritance, but it refers to a possibly cascaded inheritance.

The Adapter pattern can be realized using two different structures, one is based on multiple inheritance while the other is based on single inheritance. These Adapter realizations can be detected using a structure template that selects triplets of classes: target, adapter and adaptee. In the Adapter realization based on single inheritance, the adapter inherits from the target and is associated with the adaptee.

On the contrary, the adapter realization based on multiple inheritance requires that the adapter inherits both from the target and from the adaptee. In both of these cases, the target must contain at least one abstract operation implemented by the adapter and the collaboration template requires the implementation of this operation to be partially delegated to the adaptee.

The detection of the Bridge pattern requires finding a triplet of classes: abstraction, implementor and concrete implementor. The concrete implementor inherits from the implementor and implements, at least, one of its abstract operations. The abstraction and the implementor are related by means of a one-to-one containment association. The collaboration template states that, at least, one of the operations in the abstraction must delegate its responsibilities to one abstract operation of the implementor.

The Composite pattern can be detected searching for all triplets of classes: component, composite and leaf. Composite and leaf inherit from the component class and each composite object contains a set of components with no restrictions on the cardinality of the containment. The complete detection of the Composite pattern is performed using also a collaboration template. The composite class must implement at least one abstract operation inherited from the component and this operation must delegate part of its responsibilities to the component objects.

The Decorator pattern is quite similar to the Composite pattern and it can be detected following similar rules. In the simplest case, the collaboration templates are identical, while the structure templates are slightly different. In fact, the Decorator pattern requires the containment association to be one-to-one. When the design contains more than one decorator class, the Decorator pattern is composed of four classes for the introduction of an abstract decorator class, but this modification does not change substantially the detection rules.

The Factory Method pattern involves four classes: the product, the concrete product, the creator and the concrete creator. The concrete product inherits from the product and the concrete creator inherits from the creator, but only the creator is abstract because it contains an abstract operation that is implemented in the concrete creator. This operation is the factory method and so it must return a product object. The first hint about the presence of a Factory Method pattern in a class diagram is the presence of a create association between the concrete product and the concrete creator that allows concrete creator objects to create concrete product objects. The collaboration template refines this detection choosing the creator operations that send a create message to a concrete product object.

The detection of the Abstract Factory pattern can be based on the detection of factory methods. In fact, one of the possibilities to implement an abstract factory is to create an abstract class containing a factory method for each product family. This suggests that an abstract factory can be detected searching for all abstract classes containing a factory method.

The Iterator pattern is composed of four classes: the aggregate, the concrete aggregate, the iterator and the concrete iterator. The aggregate and the iterator classes are abstract and they are implemented respectively by the concrete aggregate and the concrete iterator. The aggregate provides a factory method, implemented by the concrete aggregate, that can be used to produce iterator objects. The structure template can be completed with an association between the iterator and the aggregate or between their concrete counterparts. This association is directed from the iterator, or the concrete iterator, to the aggregate, or to the concrete aggregate. The collaboration template is particularly important for the detection of the Iterator pattern because the constraints imposed by the structure template are too weak. Such a template requires the iterator object to be used to navigate the corresponding aggregate object. This can be expressed stating that the iterator object must be used mainly within loops containing at least two calls to its operations. In fact, the iterator object is used, at least, for two purposes: to access the current element in the aggregate and to move to the next element in the traversal. Generally, the iterator object is also used for the termination condition of the loop, but this is not a necessary condition and it cannot be used to detect the pattern.

The Observer pattern requires the presence of four classes: the subject, the observer and their implementations, the concrete subject and the concrete observer. The subject is associated with a set of observers and the association allows, at least, reaching the observer from the subject. The concrete observer is associated with the concrete subject and this association is one-to-one and allows the concrete observer to access the concrete subject. This association can be substituted with an association, with the same properties, between the observer and the subject. The concrete observer must implement, at least, one of the abstract operations of the observer. The collaboration template exploits these operations to impose a characteristic object protocol. The protocol is initiated by a real subject object calling an abstract operation on all observer objects. Then, each observer object delegates a part of its responsibility to the subject object that initiated the protocol calling an abstract operation implemented by the concrete subject. A possible alternative is that some observer object decides to call directly a concrete subject object without using the indirection provided by the subject class.

The detection of a Prototype pattern requires finding two classes, the prototype and the concrete prototype, connected by an inheritance relation. The prototype must define an abstract clone operation and the concrete prototype must implement it. This operation can be identified easily in languages such as C++ or Java. In fact, the clone operation in C++ is the copy constructor, while in Java this operation is called `clone` and all classes have it because it is inherited from the class `Object`.

The Proxy pattern is composed by three classes: the subject, the real subject and the proxy. The real subject and the proxy are associated and both inherit from the subject. All public operations in the subject are abstract and the collaboration template requires them to be all implemented by both the proxy and the real subject. Moreover, each inherited operation in the proxy must be partially delegated to the real subject.

5. Conclusions

The use of design patterns is considered fundamental for the production of quality designs and a general-purpose technique to improve an existing design is to search for all pattern realizations to apply well-known rules to improve them. This technique involves finding all pattern realizations employed in a design and therefore it is a rather tedious task for the engineer. This paper presents the work found in the literature about automated assistants for the programmer and the software architect and introduces IDEA, a design assistant meant to provide online, pattern-oriented help to the architect. IDEA works with the architect in the production of an UML model providing critiques about the pattern realizations found in the model. IDEA analyses the model, finds all pattern realizations employed in it and then proposes critiques directed to improve these realizations.

The core of IDEA is the module that automatically detects the pattern realizations in the UML model. The engineer is not required to adopt a modified UML notation because IDEA knows a set of well-known patterns and exploits this knowledge to perform the detection autonomously. This process is implemented analyzing the class and collaboration diagrams comprised in the model to match them against pattern-specific structures. Class diagrams are used to identify groups of classes that can constitute a pattern realization. Collaboration diagrams refine this detection matching the object interactions with pattern-specific interactions. When IDEA finds a pattern realization, it verifies a set of design rules to test if this realization can be improved. Any rule violation fires a critique that is proposed to the software engineer as a possible improvement for the design. Currently, IDEA recognizes a subset of the GoF patterns and it is integrated with two popular CASE tools.

Acknowledgements

We would like to thank Massimiliano Gerardi for the implementation of some relevant parts of IDEA. This work is partially supported by "Progetto di Ricerca Applicata 5% del CNR — Multimedialità".

References

1. J. Bansiya, "Automating design-pattern identification", *Dr. Dobb's Journal* (1998).
2. F. P. Brooks, "No silver bullet: Essence and accidents of software engineering", *IEEE Computer* **20**, no. 4 (1987).
3. K. Brown, "Design reverse-engineering and automated design pattern detection in smallTalk", available at *http://www2.ncsu.edu/*
4. G. Florijn, M. Meijers and P. van Winsen, "Tool support for object-oriented patterns", *Proceedings of the European Conference on Object-Oriented Programming (ECOOP'97)* (1997).
5. E. Gamma, R. Helm, R. Johnson and J. Vlissides, *Design Patterns: Elements of Reusable Object-oriented Software* (Addison-Wesley, 1995).

6. A. Girgensohn, "End-user modifiability in knowledge-based design environments", PhD Thesis, University of Colorado (1992).
7. D. Gruijs, "A framework of concepts for representing object-oriented design and design patterns", Technical Report INF/SCR-97-28, Utrecht University (1997).
8. M. Harandi and J. Ning, "Knowledge-based program analysis", *IEEE Software* (January 1990).
9. M. Harandi and J. Ning, "PAT: A Knowledge-based program analysis tool", *Proceedings of the Working Conference on Reverse Engineering* (1988).
10. R. Johnson, "Documenting frameworks using patterns", *Proceedings of the Conference on Object-oriented Systems, Languages and Applications* (1992) 63–76.
11. M. Maijers, "Tool support for object-oriented design patterns", Technical Report INF/SCR96-28, Utrecht University (1996).
12. S. Mayers, *Effective C++: 50 Ways to Improve Your Programs and Designs* (Addison-Wesley, 1992).
13. Parasoft, "Programming effectively in C++", Available at *http://www.parasoft.com/*
14. R. S. Pressman, *Software Engineering: A Practitioner's Approach* (McGraw-Hill, 1992).
15. C. Rich and R. Waters, "The programmers apprentice: A research overview," *IEEE Computer* **21**, no. 11 (1988) 10–25.
16. C. Rich and R. Waters, *The Programmer's Apprentice* (Addison-Wesley, 1990).
17. C. Rich and C. Wills, "Recognizing a program's design: A graph-parsing approach", *IEEE Software* **7**, no. 1 (1990) 82–89.
18. J. E. Robbins, "Design critiquing systems", Available at *http://www.ics.uci.edu/*
19. J. E. Robbins and D. F. Redmiles, "Software architecture critics in the argo design environment", *Knowledge-based Systems* **11**, no. 1 (1998).
20. J. E. Robbins, D. M. Hilbert and D. F. Redmiles, "Argo: A design environment for evolving software architectures", *Proceedings of the 1997 International Conference on Software Engineering* (1997).
21. M. Sefika, A. Sane and R. H. Campbell, "Monitoring compliance of a software system with its high-level design model", *Proceedings of the International Conference on Software Engineering* (*ICSE'96*) (1996).
22. F. Shull, W. L. Melo and V. R. Basili, "An inductive method for discovering design patterns from object-oriented software systems", Technical Report UMIACS-TR-96-10, University of Maryland (1996).

INDEX